Philosophical Problems in the Law

DAVID M. ADAMS

California State Polytechnic
University, Pomona

Wadsworth Publishing Company
Belmont, California
A Division of Wadsworth, Inc.

PHILOSOPHY EDITOR: Kenneth King
EDITORIAL ASSISTANT: Cynthia Campbell
PRODUCTION EDITOR: Robin Lockwood, Bookman Productions
PRINT BUYER: Martha Branch
COPY EDITOR: Candace Demeduc
COVER: Donna Davis
COVER PHOTOGRAPH: © Bob Wickley/SuperStock, Inc.
SIGNING REPRESENTATIVE: Rita Kinsman
COMPOSITOR: TCSystems
PRINTER: Malloy Lithographing, Inc.

This book is printed on acid-free paper that meets Environmental Protection Agency standards for recycled paper.

1 2 3 4 5 6 7 8 9 10—96 95 94 93 92

Library of Congress Cataloging-in-Publication Data

Adams, David M., 1953-
   Philosophical problems in the law / David M. Adams.
      p.   cm.
   Includes bibliographical references.
   ISBN 0-534-16338-6
   1. Law—United States.   2. Law—Philosophy.
3. Law—United States—Interpretation and
construction.   I. Title.
   KF379.A3   1992
   349.73—dc20
   [347.3]   91-4131
                                                        CIP

Contents

Chapter V   Criminal Law   413

Chapter VI   Tort Law   537

Preface

Challenges and Aims

This text began in frustration. Teaching a course in the philosophy of law to undergraduates at a four-year college or university presents challenges philosophy instructors often do not face in their other courses. These challenges derive from two basic features of a course in the philosophy of law. First, although the course normally draws some philosophy majors, frequently the largest constituency consists of a diverse audience of prelaw students majoring in everything from business administration and criminal justice to history and English literature. For many students, this course is their first exposure to philosophy. Second, the primary source materials for the course—judicial opinions and commentaries upon these opinions—are written in a drab technical vocabulary for an audience of trained professionals. As such, the materials presuppose substantial specialized knowledge.

The instructor thus faces two challenges: (1) to teach students with varying ability levels and disciplinary backgrounds without presupposing too much sophistication either with philosophy or law and legal institutions, and (2) to motivate students, many of whom most likely are not philosophy majors, to care about the philosophical problems the law raises, to promote philosophical engagement with the law and legal texts. These challenges in turn generate two others: how to balance the exploration of contemporary issues and cases with an examination of broader philosophical problems and how to provide enough and the right kind of primary source material.

Philosophical Problems in the Law, both in content and organization addresses the foregoing challenges and implements their ensuing objectives: reaching a diverse audience and motivating philosophical puzzlement about the law.

Content

Designed for use in introductory-level courses in philosophy of law or jurisprudence, the selections in the text were chosen for both their overall accessibility and philosophical merit. Where more difficult philosophical or legal concepts or arguments are involved, they are first presented and explained in chapter introductions.

To motivate engagement with the material, abstract issues and problems (the nature of law, the methods of legal reasoning, the limits of freedom of expression, the purposes of criminal punishment) are situated, wherever possible, within a concrete context of controversial cases and emerging issues (the legality of "war-crimes" trials, the debate over interpreting the Constitution, flag-burning and political protest, the "subway vigilante," "scarlet-letter" punishments).

I have included issues and cases arising within several areas of the law; constitutional cases and controversies do, however, predominate. I believe that this is a defensible choice as constitutional doctrine and theory both mirror and illustrate numerous and large philosophical assumptions and debates and as a consequence often are more intrinsically captivating and at least marginally familiar to students.

Organization

The organization of both individual chapters and the entire text reflects the aim of making the material more readily "teachable." Instead of being structured around explicitly philosophical theories and debates (with which students are unlikely to be as familiar), the text is organized around general areas of law—constitutional, criminal, and civil—and within each area more specifically around particular issues and questions, for example, racist speech and free expression, liability for criminal attempts, the nature of "cruel and unusual" punishments, the legal enforcement of a duty to rescue.

Most chapters begin with an illustrative case or recent controversy; all chapters include both an introductory overview and two or more sets of Study Questions that provoke students to apply and extend knowledge and insights gained from the readings. Each chapter also contains several Cases for Further Reflection, usable as vehicles for classroom discussion or in connection with assigned written work. Additional suggested readings appear at the end of each chapter.

Two further learning aids are included: an *appendix*, offering a brief explanation of legal citations and published law reports, and a *glossary of legal terms*, for easy reference to frequently used legal terminology.

Alternative Paths

The text is arranged in six chapters, each chapter treating a general topic. Chapters I and II deal with the "traditional" jurisprudential problems of the nature of law and legal reasoning. Chapters III and IV explore issues of liberty and equality in a constitutional setting. Chapter V confronts philosophical problems reflected in the criminal law, and Chapter VI does the same for the law of tort.

Each chapter has been framed to make it as self-contained as possible, permitting the instructor to pursue alternative paths through the text. Some instructors may wish, for example, to begin with Chapter III, on freedom of expression, move through the chapters on criminal and tort law, and then return to the more heavily theoretical problems dealt with in Chapters I and II. This strategy enables students to encounter first a variety of more specific issues and read a number of judicial opinions, thus building up to an understanding of what is at stake in debates over the proper methods of legal reasoning or between naturalist and positivist theories of law. Alternatively, the order of Chapters I and II may be reversed, asking students first to explore what it means for judges and other legal actors to enforce "the law" (in this case, of the Constitution) and then broadening to an examination of the nature of law and legality itself, as embodied in the classical jurisprudential theories.

Contributors

The contributors represent a broad spectrum of scholars and practitioners, embracing the work of legal academics, political theorists, and members of the bench and bar, in addition to well-known philosophers. I have also included, alongside more traditional sources, writings representative of newer, emerging perspectives in legal theory, for example, feminist legal scholarship and critical legal studies.

Acknowledgments

Many people kindly contributed their ideas and time to help me with this book: Leslie Bender, Syracuse University; John Bogart, University of Southern California; Andrew Buchwalter, University of North Florida; Steve Burton, University of Iowa; Philip Devine, Providence College; Leslie Francis, University of Utah; Howard Gillman, University of Southern California; Tom Grey, Stanford Law School; Lynne Henderson, Indiana University; H. Hamner Hill, Southeast Missouri State University; Larry Houlgate, California Polytechnic State University; Paul Menzel, Pacific Lutheran University; Michael Meyer, Santa Clara University; Michele Moody-Adams, University of Rochester; Kathleen Dean Moore, Oregon State University; Ronald Moore, University of Washington; Laurie Shrage, California State Polytechnic University, Pomona; Larry Solum, Loyola Law School; William Starr, Marquette University; Dick Wasserstrom, University of California, Santa Cruz. Rita Kinsman at Wadsworth helped me find a willing publisher; Candace Demeduc copy edited with amazing thoroughness; and Robin Lockwood kept the whole project on schedule. And of course the unstoppable Ken King, whose determination proved invaluable. Thanks to all.

To Diane, Aubrey, and Aaron, for their commitment and love.

Biographical Note

David M. Adams is Assistant Professor and Chair of Philosophy at the California State Polytechnic University, Pomona. He is a graduate of the University of California at Berkeley and the University of Washington (Ph.D.) and holds a master's degree in law from Stanford University. His publications include articles in ethics, social philosophy, and legal theory.

Introduction

You may be puzzled by the title of this book. The idea that there could be philosophical problems in the law, in addition to the ordinary ones with which lawyers get paid to deal, does initially appear strange. Most of us, before we know much about it, regard the law as definite, clear, and unproblematic—at least where we agree with it. We imagine it to be written down in a collection of dusty books stored in a museum. We assume that the only problems raised by the law are those whose solution can be obtained with no more effort than is required to locate the correct dusty book and apply whatever rule it prescribes for the situation at hand.

This museum view of the law is a myth, albeit an extremely powerful one. As the materials in this book will demonstrate, the law, far from being fixed and static, is actually dynamic and changing, continually being rethought and reshaped. And it is when we probe only slightly beneath the changing surface that we confront a maze of extremely challenging questions. Nor should this be surprising. For despite its history and traditions, its technicalities and arcane terminology, the law remains, like all aspects of human endeavor, an effort to come to grips with some of the genuine perplexities of life and the world witihin which we find ourselves.

What are the principles and standards by which we should agree to live? Why are they valid? And how can we know? What do I owe to others? What care or concern must I show for them? What may I, as an individual living among many others, freely believe? Or say? Or do? Which sufferings should society's law strive to ameliorate? How may it do so? For which sufferings must I bear responsibility? And why is it I who must answer for them? What is the "rule of law"? Why is it good? And how can it be attained? Must law be just? Or can it be evil? And how would we know the difference?

Such questions possess a special urgency and significance for us all, and this in two ways. On the one hand, they probe deeply into the nature of the world we inhabit and the lives we live. They raise difficult questions about the fabric of concepts and ideas we use to make the world understandable to us: ideas like responsibility; freedom; authority;

knowledge; suffering; justice; good and evil. This is the stuff of philosophy: the attempt to reflect in a careful and sustained way upon the meaning of these ideas and concepts, and the questions they raise.

Yet these very questions are at the same time the stuff of the law. They are confronted almost at every turn—even if sometimes concealed behind technical jargon and everyday concerns—by those who make, interpret, and otherwise try to understand the principles and beliefs that together make up the fabric of law. And it is for this reason that the urgency of such questions is compounded; for a judge or lawmaker faced with situations whose solutions cannot but raise such problems may not simply set them aside for another day. Statutes must be interpreted, litigants heard, juries instructed, decisions made, and sentences pronounced. The law thus becomes a kind of living laboratory of philosophical investigation and experimentation, advancing theories, debating ideas, and defending solutions.

In this book, we will explore various ways in which law both provokes and seeks to respond to the many sources of philosophical puzzlement.

Chapter I

The Nature of Law

The rule of law is something with which we daily live, but which we rarely pause to try to understand. We know that we must pay our taxes, stop at red lights, and refrain from stealing other people's property. We know that if we are being threatened with a lawsuit we had better get a lawyer, and that if the suit is filed we may well wind up in court before a judge. We know that the judge's job is to apply something called "the law," as opposed to simply doing as he or she pleases, and we have a vague sense that this requirement is part of what it means to live in a society governed by the "rule of law," as opposed to the "rule of men." But what does living under the rule of law really mean? Why do we think it is better to live in a society in which there are statutes and judges than one in which these are absent?

Most of us are aware of the old theory that a regime of law is necessary in order to keep us in line, to prevent the "war of all against all" that some warn would immediately follow upon the breakdown of "law and order."

Is law then exclusively about power, control over others? If so, who (or what) holds that power? Those who "make" the law? If so, how is the rule of law different from the rule of men? When the Allied nations, at the conclusion of World War II, put on trial the highest-ranking officials of the German government, was this merely (as some critics contended) the arbitrary exercise of naked power, an organized act of revenge? Or was it an attempt to reassert the primacy of law? If, as many people believed, punishing the Nazi leaders was the morally right thing to do, does this fact itself mean that the Nuremberg trials were genuine *legal* proceedings? What is the relationship between that which is morally right and that which is the law? It is obvious to most people that not everything that is morally wrong is also "against the law"; and similarly, not everything that is illegal is "wrong" in a moral sense. Do legality and morality have any more than a coincidental connection? Can a system of immoral rules and principles be a *legal* system? These are the questions and issues explored in Chapter One.

The first section provides a concrete context within which to approach the foregoing questions about the nature of law and legality: the so-called Nuremberg trials, held at the close of World War II. Robert Jackson and Charles Wyzanski debate the nature of the "law" to which the Nazi leaders were subjected. The second section explores the two classical theories of law, legal positivism and natural law theory. H. L. A. Hart and Lon Fuller debate the merits and demerits of positivism as an account of the nature of law. Stanley Paulson reviews the attempts by many of the Nazi defendants at Nuremberg to appeal to positivism in their defense; and Martin Luther King, Jr., reveals how he sought to apply the traditional natural law position of thinkers like Aquinas and Augustine to the modern world.

The concluding section of this chapter examines three further views of the nature of law, each with roots in the twentieth century: American legal realism, represented here in the essay by Oliver Wendell Holmes; the interpretive theory of contemporary legal philosopher Ronald Dworkin; and the views associated with the critical legal studies movement, discussed by Andrew Altman.

A. What Is Law?

The Nuremberg Trial

In November 1983, a retired autoworker from the suburbs of Cleveland, Ohio, John Demjanjuk, was arrested by the FBI at the request of the government of the nation of Israel. Following several unsuccessful appeals, Demjanjuk was extradited to (surrendered to the authorities of) Israel. The Israelis claimed to possess overwhelming evidence that the inconspicuous-looking Demjanjuk was in reality the sadistic "Ivan the Terrible" of Treblinka, a Nazi officer during World War II, posted to one of Hitler's most infamous death camps; a man who eagerly sent thousands to their deaths in gas chambers.

For many, the *Demjanjuk* case raised memories of the horrors of the Nazi regime; and the controversy surrounding his trial in Israel recalled the debate sparked by similar trials held nearly forty years previously, at the German town of Nuremberg. The problems raised and questions posed by Nuremberg and similar trials provide an illuminating perspective from which to view the fundamental controversy over the nature of law.

At the conclusion of World War II, the Allied powers were faced with the problem of what to do with the senior officials of the Nazi government and with the highest-ranking officers in the Nazi military. It was decided, after some debate, that they should be brought to trial in the first in a series of international legal proceedings. Before the proceedings were over, several series of trials had been held in which German industrialists, judges, lawyers, and businessmen, in addition to military and political leaders, were tried. The first and most dramatic of these trials began in October 1945 and lasted until October of the following year. Twenty-two of the highest-ranking Nazi civilian and military leaders were tried; three were completely exonerated, seven received prison terms, and twelve were handed death sentences and executed.

The Trial of the Major War Criminals proceeded pursuant to an agreement signed by the Allied powers on August 8, 1945: the Treaty of London. This agreement created what became the Charter for the International Military Tribunal at Nuremberg. The Charter specified three categories of criminal activity, for violation of each of which at least several of the twenty-two defendants were charged:

> Crimes Against Peace: namely, planning, preparation, initiation or waging a war of aggression, or a war in violation of international treaties, agreements, or assurances, or participation in a Common Plan or Conspiracy for the accomplishment of the foregoing . . . ;
> War Crimes: namely, violations of the laws or customs of war. Such violations shall include . . . murder, ill-treatment or deportation to slave labor or for any other purpose of civilian population of or in

> occupied territory, murder or ill-treatment of prisoners of war . . . wanton destruction of cities, towns, or villages, or devastation not justified by military necessity . . . ;
> Crimes Against Humanity: namely, murder, extermination, enslavement, deportation, and other inhumane acts committed against any civilian population, before or during the war, or persecutions on political, racial, or religious grounds . . . whether or not in violation of domestic law of the country where perpetrated.[1]

Based on these definitions, the Allied prosecutors at the Tribunal indicted the Nazis on four counts: conspiracy to wage aggressive war; waging an aggressive war; commission of war crimes; and perpetration of crimes against humanity.

The evidence presented at the trial overwhelmingly implicated many of the defendants in acts of systematic and deliberate barbarism. It would not have been sufficient for their purposes, however, for the American, British, French, and Soviet prosecutors simply to have condemned the Nazis *morally*; for this was to be a *legal* proceeding, and the Nazis were therefore to be punished (if at all) for having violated the *law*, however much what they did (or instructed others to do) was regarded by everyone involved as grossly immoral. The Nazis were to be sent to prison—or to the hangman—for conduct which was *illegal*; and it is here that serious questions were raised, and continue to be raised, about the Nuremberg trials. These questions, which we will explore throughout this chapter, converge on a core philosophical issue: What was the status of the "law" under which the Nazi leaders were prosecuted? What was the *legal* basis for the categories of criminality and standards of individual liability endorsed by the Charter? Is the Charter itself valid "law"? If so, by virtue of what?

Controversies Regarding Nuremberg

Two opposing responses to these questions—two different conceptions of the trials themselves—are represented in our selections by Robert Jackson, chief American prosecutor of Nuremberg (then on leave from the United States Supreme Court), and Charles Wyzanski, a noted Massachusetts judge.

Wyzanski questions the legality of the Charter's basic provisions with the charge that the Charter created "new law" *ex post facto,* "after the fact." As Wyzanski implies, the Charter and the Tribunal were legal novelties in at least two ways: one party to the proceeding became prosecutor, judge, and jury; and the Charter sought to combine elements from both Anglo-American and Continental legal systems. This last proved especially difficult, as the two systems differ, both from the standpoint of legal procedure and as regards the content of the (substantive) law. In the English and American systems, as most of us are aware, trials proceed according to a strict division of function. Each of the opposing sides has the responsibility to make the best possible case it can for its position by uncovering all the facts it believes to be relevant and by noting all the pertinent legal issues and authorities bearing on the dispute. The role of the judge is essentially that of an umpire, reminding each side of what the proper procedures are and penalizing one or the other for violations of the rules. In many European courtrooms, however, this rigid division of labor is not observed; the effort to discover the truth and arrive at a just verdict is conducted in a more collaborative way, with the judge in particular playing a much more active and inquisitorial role than would be permitted in the United States or Britain.

The German defense attorneys at Nuremberg complained bitterly that they were hampered by the Tribunal's decision to rely for the most part upon the Anglo-American procedural system. They also complained that the accusation of participation in a "conspiracy" or "common plan" to start a war had no counterpart in, and was not recognized by, the law of Germany. Wyzanski raises a deeper problem: The Tribunal's "law" effectively permitted it to hold anyone who joined in the Nazi war effort personally liable for anything done by anyone else similarly engaged, and this, Wyzanski insists, was fundamentally unjust.

Behind Wyzanski's specific complaints lies a general concern with the conditions under which an action or decision can be said to be in accord with the rule of law. Wyzanski accuses the Allies of abrogating or negating a principle that is fundamental to the ideas of law and legality: *nullum crimen et nulla poena sine lege,* "[there can be] no crime and no penalty without a[n already existing] law." The Charter creates *ex post facto* law, making something punishable after it has been done. Such laws are forbidden by the United States Constitution; and Wyzanski seems to think that the Charter loses in a crucial way its status as "law" by including *ex post facto* provisions.

Wyzanski also questions the wisdom of trials such as those at Nuremberg. If, as seems likely, the Allies never intended that the Nazis go free, are they not reducing a legal proceeding to a propaganda device? This "debases justice" and suggests the same kind of hypocrisy of which the Allies accused the Hitler regime.

In his opening address before the Tribunal, Robert Jackson responds to the objections raised by Wyzanski. Waging an aggressive war was a crime in international law long before the start of World War II, Jackson claims, and the Germans knew this. Jackson notes several international treaties and agreements, signed by numerous nations in the early part of this century which, he claims, had the effect of outlawing aggressive warfare. Aggressive warfare was made illegal by these agreements and by international custom; moreover, Jackson adds, the nations of the world have a right to create new customs, to enter into new agreements and understandings that can then serve as a further platform for the development and growth of international law. We cannot allow the defendants to take refuge, Jackson argues, behind the hope that international law will continue to "lag so far behind the moral sense of mankind." To agree with the assertion that the Charter is not law because its core provisions are *ex post facto* would be foolish; for the claim is both empty and hypocritical. How could anyone be surprised to discover that genocide and torture are crimes? And how could those guilty of such atrocities have the gall to hide behind the principles of the moral and legal order that their actions sought so completely to repudiate?

Wyzanski believes that Jackson and the Tribunal have sacrificed the principle of *nullum crimen* on the altar of "higher justice." He suggests that international law, as it stood at the time the Nazis began the war, did not unequivocally make aggressive warfare a crime for which individual persons could be held liable. After all, no leading Western nation, in the period from the early 1920s to 1939, condemned any war as an illegal act of aggression. Yet, Wyzanski assumes, someone must have been an aggressor in the confrontations that took place during that time. Shocking and immoral as it was, Wyzanski concludes, the conduct of the Nazis was not for that reason also a contravention of law.

Endnote

1 See *Nazi Conspiracy and Aggression*, Vol. 1, Office of the United States Chief of Counsel for Prosecution of Axis Criminality (Washington, D.C.: U.S. Government Printing Office, 1946), pp. 5–12.

Opening Address for the United States, Nuremberg Trials

ROBERT H. JACKSON

May it please Your Honors,

The privilege of opening the first trial in history for crimes against the peace of the world imposes a grave responsibility. The wrongs which we seek to condemn and punish have been so calculated, so malignant and so devastating, that civilization cannot tolerate their being ignored because it cannot survive their being repeated. That four great nations, flushed with victory and stung with injury stay the hand of vengeance and voluntarily submit their captive enemies to the judgment of the law is one of the most significant tributes that Power ever has paid to Reason.

This tribunal, while it is novel and experimental, is not the product of abstract speculations nor is it created to vindicate legalistic theories. This inquest represents the practical effort of four of the most mighty of nations, with the support of seventeen more, to utilize International Law to meet the greatest menace of our times—aggressive war. The common sense of mankind demands that law shall not stop with the punishment of petty crimes by little people. It must also reach men who possess themselves of great power and make deliberate and concerted use of it to set in motion evils which leave no home in the world untouched. It is a cause of this magnitude that the United Nations will lay before Your Honors.

In the prisoners' dock sit twenty-odd broken men. Reproached by the humiliation of those they have led almost as bitterly as by the desolation of those they have attacked, their personal capacity for evil is forever past. It is hard now to perceive in these miserable men as captives the power by which as Nazi leaders they once dominated much of the world and terrified most of it. Merely as individuals, their fate is of little consequence to the world.

What makes this inquest significant is that those prisoners represent sinister influence that will lurk in the world long after their bodies have returned to dust. They are living symbols of racial hatreds, or terrorism and violence, and of the arrogance and cruelty of power. They are symbols of fierce nationalisms and militarism, of intrigue and war-making which have embroiled Europe generation after generation, crushing its manhood, destroying its homes, and impoverishing its life. They have so identified themselves with the philosophies they conceived and with the forces they directed that any tenderness to them is a victory and an encouragement to all the evils which are attached to their names. Civilization can afford no compromise with the social forces which would gain renewed strength if we deal ambiguously or indecisively with the men in whom those forces now precariously survive.

What these men stand for we will patiently and temperately disclose. We will give you undeniable proofs of incredible events. The catalogue of crimes will omit nothing that could be conceived by a pathological pride, cruelty, and lust for power. These men created in Germany, under the *Fuehrerprinzip*, a National Socialist despotism equalled only by the dynasties of the ancient East. They took from the German people all those dignities and freedoms that we hold natural and inalienable rights in every human being. The people were compensated by inflaming and gratifying hatreds toward those who were marked as "scape-goats." Against their opponents, including Jews, Catholics, and free labor the Nazis directed such a campaign of arrogance, brutality, and annihilation as the world has not witnessed since the pre-Christian ages. They excited the German ambition to be a "master race," which of course implies serfdom for others. They led their people on a mad gamble for domination. They diverted social energies and resources to the creation of what they thought to be an invincible war machine. They overran their neighbors. To sustain the "master race" in its [war-making], they enslaved millions of human beings and brought them into Germany, where these hapless creatures now wander as "displaced persons." At length bestiality and bad faith reached such excess that they aroused the sleeping strength of imperiled civilization. Its united efforts have ground the German war machine to fragments. But the struggle has left Europe a liberated yet prostrate land where a demoralized society struggles to survive. These are the fruits of the sinister forces that sit with these defendants in the prisoners' dock.

In justice to the nations and the men associated in this prosecution, I must remind you of certain difficulties which may leave their mark on this case. Never before in legal history has an effort been made to bring within the scope of a single litigation the developments of a decade, covering a whole Continent, and involving a score of nations, countless individuals, and innumerable events. Despite the magnitude of the task, the world has demanded immediate action. This demand has had to be met, though perhaps at the cost of finished craftsmanship. In my country, established courts, following familiar procedures, applying well thumbed precedents, and dealing with the legal consequences of local and limited events seldom commence a trial within a year of the event in litigation. Yet less than eight months ago today the courtroom in which you sit was an enemy fortress in the hands of German SS troops. Less than eight months ago nearly all our witnesses and documents were in enemy hands. The law had not been codified, no procedure had been established, no Tribunal was in existence, no usable courthouse stood here, none of the hundreds of tons of official German documents had been examined, no

prosecuting staff had been assembled, nearly all the present defendants were at large, and the four prosecuting powers had not yet joined in common cause to try them. I should be the last to deny that the case may well suffer from imcomplete researches and quite likely will not be the example of professional work which any of the prosecuting nations would normally wish to sponsor. It is, however, a completely adequate case to the judgment we shall ask you to render, and its full development we shall be obliged to leave to historians.

Before I discuss particulars of evidence, some general considerations which may affect the credit of this trial in the eyes of the world should be candidly faced. There is a dramatic disparity between the circumstances of the accusers and of the accused that might discredit our work if we should falter, in even minor matters, in being fair and temperate.

Unfortunately, the nature of these crimes is such that both prosecution and judgment must be by victor nations over vanquished foes. The worldwide scope of the aggressions carried out by these men has left but few real neutrals. Either the victors must judge the vanquished or we must leave the defeated to judge themselves. After the First World War, we learned the futility of the latter course. The former high station of these defendants, the notoriety of their acts, and the adaptability of their conduct to provoke retaliation make it hard to distinguish between the demand for a just and measured retribution, and the unthinking cry for vengeance which arises from the anguish of war. It is our task, so far as humanly possible, to draw the line between the two. We must never forget that the record on which we judge these defendants today is the record on which history will judge us tomorrow. To pass these defendants a poisoned chalice is to put it to our own lips as well. We must summon such detachment and intellectual integrity to our task that this trial will commend itself to posterity as fulfilling humanity's aspirations to do justice.

At the very outset, let us dispose of the contention that to put these men to trial is to do them an injustice entitling them to some special consideration. These defendants may be hard pressed but they are not ill used. Let us see what alternative they would have to being tried.

More than a majority of these prisoners surrendered to or were tracked down by forces of the

United States. Could they expect us to make American custody a shelter for our enemies against the just wrath of our Allies? Did we spend American lives to capture them only to save them from punishment? Under the principles of the Moscow Declaration, those suspected war criminals who are not to be tried internationally must be turned over to individual governments for trial at the scene of their outrages. Many less responsible and less culpable American-held prisoners have been and will be turned over to other United Nations for local trial. If these defendants should succeed, for any reason, in escaping the condemnation of this Tribunal, or if they obstruct or abort this trial, those who are American-held prisoners will be delivered up to our continental Allies. For these defendants, however, we have set up an International Tribunal and have undertaken the burden of participating in a complicated effort to give them fair and dispassionate hearings. That is the best known protection to any man with a defense worthy of being heard.

If these men are the first war leaders of a defeated nation to be prosecuted in the name of the law, they are also the first to be given a chance to plead for their lives in the name of the law. Realistically, the Charter of this Tribunal, which gives them a hearing, is also the source of their only hope. It may be that these men of troubled conscience, whose only wish is that the world forget them, do not regard a trial as a favor. But they do have a fair opportunity to defend themselves—a favor which these men, when in power, rarely extended to their fellow countrymen. Despite the fact that public opinion already condemns their acts, we agree that here they must be given a presumption of innocence, and we accept the burden of proving criminal acts and the responsibility of these defendants for their commission.

When I say that we do not ask for convictions unless we prove crime, I do not mean mere technical or incidental transgression of international conventions. We charge guilt on planned and intended conduct that involves moral as well as legal wrong. And we do not mean conduct that is a natural and human, even if illegal, cutting of corners, such as many of us might well have committed had we been in the defendants' positions. It is not because they yielded to the normal frailties of human beings that we accuse them. It is their abnormal and inhuman conduct which brings them to this bar.

We will not ask you to convict these men on the testimony of their foes. There is no count of the Indictment that cannot be proved by books and records. The Germans were always meticulous record keepers, and these defendants had their share of the Teutonic passion for thoroughness in putting things on paper. Nor were they without vanity. They arranged frequently to be photographed in action. We will show you their own films. You will see their own conduct and hear their own voices as these defendants reenact for you, from the screen, some of the events in the course of the conspiracy.

We would also make clear that we have no purpose to incriminate the whole German people. We know that the Nazi Party was not put in power by a majority of the German vote. We know it came to power by an evil alliance between the most extreme of the Nazi revolutionists, the most unrestrained of the German reactionaries, and the most aggressive of the German militarists. If the German populace had willingly accepted the Nazi program, no Stormtroopers would have been needed in the early days of the Party and there would have been no need for concentration camps or the Gestapo, both of which institutions were inaugurated as soon as the Nazis gained control of the German state. Only after these lawless innovations proved successful at home were they taken abroad.

The German people should know by now that the people of the United States hold them in no fear, and in no hate. It is true that the Germans have taught us the horrors of modern warfare, but the ruin that lies from the Rhine to the Danube shows that we, like our Allies, have not been dull pupils. If we are not awed by German fortitude and proficiency in war, and if we are not persuaded of their political maturity, we do respect their skill in the arts of peace, their technical competence, and the sober, industrious and self-disciplined character of the masses of the German people. In 1933, we saw the German people recovering prestige in the commercial, industrial and artistic world after the set-back of the last war. We beheld their progress neither with envy nor malice. The Nazi regime interrupted this advance. The recoil of the Nazi aggression has left Germany in ruins. The Nazi readiness to pledge the German work without hesitation and to break it without shame has fastened upon German diplomacy a reputation for duplicity that will handicap it for years. Nazi arrogance has made the boast of the "master race" a taunt that will be thrown at Germans the world over for generations. The Nazi nightmare has given the German name a new and sinister significance throughout the world which will retard Germany a century. The German, no less than the non-German world, has accounts to settle with these defendants.

The fact of the war and the course of the war, which is the central theme of our case, is history. From September 1st, 1939, when the German armies crossed the Polish frontiers, until September, 1942, when they met epic resistance at Stalingrad, German arms seemed invincible. Denmark and Norway, The Netherlands and France, Belgium and Luxembourg, the Balkans and Africa, Poland and the Baltic States, and parts of Russia, all had been overrun and conquered by swift, powerful, well-aimed blows. That attack upon the peace of the world is the crime against international society which brings into international cognizance crimes in its aid and preparation which otherwise might be only internal concerns. It was aggressive war, which the nations of the world had renounced. It was war in violation of treaties, by which the peace of the world was sought to be safeguarded.

This war did not just happen—it was planned and prepared for over a long period of time and with no small skill and cunning. The world has perhaps never seen such a concentration and stimulation of the energies of any people as that which enabled Germany twenty years after it was defeated, disarmed, and dismembered to come so near carrying out its plan to dominate Europe. Whatever else we may say of those who were the authors of this war, they did achieve a stupendous work in organization, and our first task is to examine the means by which these defendants and their fellow conspirators prepared and incited Germany to go to war.

In general, our case will disclose these defendants all uniting at some time with the Nazi Party in a plan which they well knew could be accomplished only by an outbreak of war in Europe. Their seizure of the German state, their subjugation of the German people, their terrorism and extermination of dissident elements, their planning and waging of war, their calculated and planned ruthlessness in the conduct of warfare, their deliberate and planned criminality toward conquered peoples, all these are ends for which they acted in concert; and all these are phases of the conspiracy, a conspiracy which reached one goal only to set out for another and more ambitious one. We shall also trace for you the intricate web of organizations which these men formed and utilized to accomplish these ends. We will show how the entire structure of offices and officials was dedicated to the criminal purposes and committed to use of the criminal methods planned by these defendants and their co-conspirators, many of whom war and suicide have put beyond reach.

It is my purpose to open the case, particularly under Count One of the Indictment, and to deal with the common plan or conspiracy to achieve ends possible only by resort to crimes against peace, war crimes, and crimes against humanity. My emphasis will not be on individual barbarities and perversions which may have occurred independently of any central plan. One of the dangers ever present is that this trial may be protracted by details of particular wrongs and that we will become lost in a "wilderness of single instances." Nor will I now dwell on the activity of individual defendants except as it may contribute to exposition of the common plan.

The case as presented by the United States will be concerned with the brains and authority back of all the crimes. These defendants were men of a station and rank which does not soil its own hands with blood. They were men who knew how to use lesser folk as tools. We want to reach the planners and designers, the inciters and leaders without whose evil architecture the world would not have been for so long scourged with the violence and lawlessness, and wracked with the agonies and convulsions of this terrible war.

. . .

Even the most warlike of peoples have recognized in the name of humanity some limitations on the savagery of warfare. Rules to that end have been embodied in international conventions to which Germany became a party. This code had prescribed certain restraints as to the treatment of belligerents. The enemy was entitled to surrender and to receive quarter and good treatment as a prisoner of war. We will show by German documents that these rights were denied, that prisoners of war were given brutal treatment and often murdered. This was particularly true in the case of captured airmen, often my countrymen.

. . .

Civilized usage and conventions to which Germany was a party had prescribed certain immunities for civilian populations unfortunate enough to dwell in lands overrun by hostile armies. The German occupation forces, controlled or commanded by men on trial before you, committed a long series of outrages against the inhabitants of occupied territory that would be incredible except for captured orders and the captured reports showing the fidelity with which these orders were executed.

. . .

The end of the war and capture of these prisoners presented the victorious Allies with the question whether there is any legal responsibility on high-ranking men for acts which I have described. Must such wrongs either be ignored or redressed in hot blood? Is there no standard in the law for a deliberate and reasoned judgment on such conduct?

The Charter of this Tribunal evidences a faith that the law is not only to govern the conduct of little men, but that even rulers are, as Lord Chief Justice Coke put it to King James, "under God and the law." The United States believed that the law long has afforded standards by which a juridical hearing could be conducted to make sure that we punish only the right men and for the right reasons. Following the instructions of the late President Roosevelt and the decision of the Yalta conference, President Truman directed representatives of the United States to formulate a proposed International Agreement, which was submitted during the San Francisco Conference to Foreign Ministers of the United Kingdom, the Soviet Union, and the Provisional Government of France. With many modifications, that proposal has become the Charter of this Tribunal.

But the Agreement which sets up the standards by which these prisoners are to be judged does not express the views of the signatory nations alone. Other nations with diverse but highly respected systems of jurisprudence also have signified adherence to it. These are Belgium, The Netherlands, Denmark, Norway, Czechoslovakia, Luxembourg, Poland, Greece, Yugoslavia, Ethiopia, Australia, Haiti, Honduras, Panama, New Zealand, Venezuela, and India. You judge, therefore, under an organic act which represents the wisdom, the sense of justice, and the will of twenty-one governments, representing an overwhelming majority of all civilized people.

The Charter by which this Tribunal has its being embodies certain legal concepts which are inseparable from its jurisdiction and which must govern its decision. These, as I have said, also are conditions attached to the grant of any hearing to defendants. The validity of the provisions of the Charter is conclusive upon us all whether we have accepted the duty of judging or of prosecuting under it, as well as upon the defendants, who can point to no other law which gives them a right to be heard at all. My able and experienced colleagues believe, as do I, that it will contribute to the expedition and clarity of this trial if I expound briefly the application of the legal philosophy of the Charter to the facts I have recited.

While this declaration of the law by the Charter is final, it may be contended that the prisoners on trial are entitled to have it applied to their conduct only most charitably if at all. It may be said that this is new law, not authoritatively declared at the time they did the acts it condemns, and that this declaration of the law has taken them by surprise.

I cannot, of course, deny that these men are surprised that this is the law; they really are surprised that there is any such thing as law. These defendants did not rely on any law at all. Their program ignored and defied all law. That this is so will appear from many acts and statements, of which I cite but a few. In the Fuehrer's speech to all military commanders on November 23, 1939, he reminded them that at the moment Germany had a pact with Russia, but declared, "Agreements are to be kept only as long as they serve a certain purpose." Later on in the same speech he announced, "A violation of the neutrality of Holland and Belgium will be of no importance" (*789–PS*). A Top Secret document, entitled "Warfare as a Problem of Organization," dispatched by the Chief of the High Command to all Commanders on April 19, 1938, declared that "the normal rules of war toward neutrals may be considered to apply on the basis whether operation of rules will create greater advantages or disadvantages for belligerents"(*L–211*). And from the files of the German Navy Staff, we have a "Memorandum on Intensified Naval War," dated October 15, 1939, which begins by stating a desire to comply with International Law. "However," it continues, "if decisive successes are expected from any measure considered as a war necessity, it must be carried through even if it is not in agreement with international law" (*UK–65*). International Law, natural law, German law, any law at all was to these men simply a propaganda device to be invoked when it helped and to be ignored when it would condemn what they wanted to do. That men may be protected in relying upon the law at the time they act is the reason we find laws of retrospective operation unjust. But these men cannot bring themselves within the reason of the rule which in some systems of jurisprudence prohibits *ex post facto* laws. They cannot show that they ever relied upon International Law in any state or paid it the slightest regard.

The Third Count of the Indictment is based on the definition of war crimes contained in the Charter. I have outlined to you the systematic course of conduct toward civilian populations and combat forces which violates international conventions to which Germany was a party. Of the criminal nature of these acts at least, the defendants had, as we shall show, clear knowledge. Accordingly, they took pains to conceal their violations. It will appear that the defendants Keitel and Jodl were informed by official legal advisors that the orders to brand Russian prisoners of war, to shackle British prisoners of war, and to execute commando prisoners were clear violations of International Law. Nevertheless, these orders were put into effect. The same is true of orders issued for the assassination of General Giraud and General Weygand, which failed to be executed only because of a ruse on the part of Admiral Canaris, who was himself later executed for his part in the plot to take Hitler's life on July 20, 1944 (*Affidavit A*).

The Fourth Count of the Indictment is based on crimes against humanity. Chief among these are mass killings of countless human beings in cold blood. Does it take these men by surprise that murder is treated as a crime?

The First and Second Counts of the Indictment add to these crimes the crime of plotting and waging wars of aggression and wars in violation of nine treaties to which Germany was a party. There was a time, in fact I think the time of the [F]irst World War, when it could not have been said that warinciting or war-making was a crime in law, however reprehensible in morals.

Of course, it was under the law of all civilized peoples a crime for one man with his bare knuckles to assault another. How did it come that multiplying this crime by a million, and adding fire arms to bare knuckles, made a legally innocent act? The doctrine was that one could not be regarded as criminal for committing the usual violent acts in the conduct of legitimate warfare. The age of imperialistic expansion during the Eighteenth and Nineteenth Centuries added the foul doctrine, contrary to the teachings of early Christian and International Law scholars such as Grotius, that all wars are to be regarded as legitimate wars. The sum of these two doctrines was to give [war-making] a complete immunity from accountability to law.

This was intolerable for an age that called itself civilized. Plain people, with their earthly common sense, revolted at such fictions and legalisms so contrary to ethical principles and demanded checks on war immunity. Statesmen and international lawyers at first cautiously responded by adopting rules of warfare designed to make the conduct of war more civilized. The effort was to set legal limits to the violence that could be done to civilian populations and to combatants as well.

The common sense of men after the First World War demanded, however, that the law's condemnation of war reach deeper, and that the law condemn not merely uncivilized ways of waging war, but also the waging in any way of uncivilized wars—wars of agression. The world's statesmen again went only as far as they were forced to go. Their efforts were timid and cautious and often less explicit than we might have hoped. But the 1920's did outlaw aggressive war.

The reestablishment of the principle that there are unjust wars and that unjust wars are illegal is traceable in many steps. One of the most significant is the Briand-Kellogg Pact of 1928, by which Germany, Italy, and Japan, in common with practically all the nations of the world, renounced war as an instrument of national policy, bound themselves to seek the settlement of disputes only by pacific means, and condemned recourse to war for the solution of international controversies. This pact altered the legal status of a war of aggression. As Mr. Stimson, the United States Secretary of State put it in 1932, such a war "is no longer to be the source and subject of rights. It is no longer to be the principle around which the duties, the conduct, and the rights of nations revolve. It is an illegal thing. . . . By that very act, we have made obsolete many legal precedents and have given the legal profession the task of reexamining many of its codes and treaties."

The Geneva Protocol of 1924 for the Pacific Settlement of International Disputes, signed by the representatives of forty-eight governments, declared that "a war of aggression constitutes . . . an international crime." The Eighth Assembly of the League of Nations in 1927, on unanimous resolution of the representatives of forty-eight member nations, including Germany, declared that a war of aggression constitutes an international crime. At the Sixth Pan-American Conference of 1928, the twenty-one American Republics unanimously adopted a resolution stating that "[a] war of aggression constitutes an international crime against the human species."

A failure of these Nazis to heed, or to understand the force and meaning of this evolution in the legal thought of the world is not a defense or a mitigation. If anything, it aggravates their offense and makes it the more mandatory that the law they have flouted be vindicated by juridical application to their lawless conduct. Indeed, by their own law—had they heeded any law—these principles were binding on these defendants. Article 4 of the Weimar Constitution provided that "The generally accepted rules of international law are to be considered as binding integral parts of the law of the German Reich" (*2050-PS*). Can there be any doubt that the outlawry of aggressive war was one of the "generally accepted rules of international law" in 1939?

Any resort to war—to any kind of a war—is a resort to means that are inherently criminal. War inevitably is a course of killings, assaults, deprivations of liberty, and destruction of property. An honestly defensive war is, of course, legal and saves those lawfully conducting it from criminality. But inherently criminal acts cannot be defended by showing that those who committed them were engaged in a war, when war itself is illegal. The very minimum legal consequence of the treaties making aggressive wars illegal is to strip those who incite or wage them of every defense the law ever gave, and to leave warmakers subject to judgment by the usually accepted principles of the law of crimes.

But if it be thought that the Charter, whose declarations concededly bind us all, does contain new law I still do not shrink from demanding its strict application by this Tribunal. The rule of law in the world, flouted by the lawlessness incited by these defendants, had to be restored at the cost to my country of over a million casualties, not to mention those of other nations. I cannot subscribe to the perverted reasoning that society may advance and strengthen the rule of law by the expenditure of morally innocent lives but that progress in the law may never be made at the price of morally guilty lives.

It is true, of course, that we have no judicial precedent for the Charter. But International Law is more than a scholarly collection of abstract and immutable principles. It is an outgrowth of treaties and agreements between nations and of accepted customs. Yet every custom has its origin in some single act, and every agreement has to be initiated by the action of some state. Unless we are prepared to abandon every principle of growth for International Law, we cannot deny that our own day has the right to institute customs and to conclude agreements that will themselves become sources of a newer and strengthened International Law. International Law is not capable of development by the normal processes of legislation for there is no continuing international legislative authority. Innovations and revisions in International Law are brought about by the action of governments designed to meet a change in circumstances. It grows, as did the Common Law, through decisions reached from time to time in adapting settled principles to new situations. The fact is that when the law evolves by the case method, as did the Common Law and as International Law must do if it is to advance at all, it advances at the expense of those who wrongly guessed the law and learned too late their error. The law, so far as International Law can be decreed, had been clearly pronounced when these acts took place. Hence, I am not disturbed by the lack of judicial precedent for the inquiry we propose to conduct.

. . .

Nuremberg: A Fair Trial?

CHARLES E. WYZANSKI, JR.

1

The Nuremberg War Trial has a strong claim to be considered the most significant as well as the most debatable event since the conclusion of hostilities. To those who support the trial it promises the first effective recognition of a world law for the punishment of malefactors who start wars or conduct them in bestial fashion. To the adverse critics the trial appears in many aspects a negation of principles which they regard as the heart of any system of justice under law.

This sharp division of opinion has not been fully aired largely because it relates to an issue of foreign policy upon which this nation has already acted and on which debate may seem useless or, worse, merely to impair this country's prestige and power abroad. Moreover, to the casual newspaper reader the long-range implications of the trial are not obvious. He sees most clearly that there are in the dock a score of widely known men who plainly deserve punishment. And he is pleased to note that four victorious nations, who have not been unanimous on all post-war questions, have, by a miracle of administrative skill, united in a proceeding that is overcoming the obstacles of varied languages, professional habits, and legal traditions. But the more profound observer is aware that the foundations of the Nuremberg trial may mark a watershed of modern law.

Before I come to the discussion of the legal and political questions involved, let me make it clear that nothing I may say about the Nuremberg trial should be construed as a suggestion that the individual Nuremberg defendants or others who have done grievous wrongs should be set at liberty. In my opinion there are valid reasons why several

thousand Germans, including many defendants at Nuremberg, should either by death or by imprisonment be permanently removed from civilized society. If prevention, deterrence, retribution, nay even vengeance are ever adequate motives for punitive action, then punitive action is justified against a substantial number of Germans. But the question is: Upon what theory may that action properly be taken?

The starting point is the indictment of October 18, 1945, charging some twenty individuals and various organizations, in four counts, with conspiracy, crimes against peace, war crimes, and crimes against humanity. Let me examine the offenses that are called in Count 3 of the indictment "war crimes," in the strict sense.

It is sometimes said that there is no international law of war crimes. But most jurists would agree that there is at least an abbreviated list of war crimes upon which the nations of the world have agreed. Thus in Articles 46 and 47 of the Hague Convention of 1907, the United States and many other countries accepted the rules that in an occupied territory of a hostile state "family honour and rights, the lives of persons, and private property, as well as religious conviction and practice, must be respected. Private property cannot be confiscated. Pillage is formally forbidden. And consistently the Supreme Court of the United States has recognized that rules of this character are part of our law. In short, there can be no doubt of the legal right of this nation prior to the signing of a peace treaty to use a military tribunal for the purpose of trying and punishing a German if, as Count 3 charges, in occupied territory he murdered a Polish civilian, or tortured a Czech, or raped a Frenchwoman, or robbed a Belgian. Moreover, there is no doubt of the military tribunal's parallel right to try and to punish a German if he has murdered, tortured, or maltreated a prisoner of war.

In connection with war crimes of this sort there is only one question of law worth discussing here: Is it a defense to a soldier or civilian defendant that he acted under the order of a superior?

From *The Atlantic Monthly*, Vol. 177 (April 1946), pp. 66–70. Reprinted with permission of *The Atlantic Monthly* and the Wyzanski Estate.

The defense of superior orders is, upon the authorities, an open question. Without going into details, it may be said that superior orders have never been recognized as a complete defense by German, Russian, or French law, and that they have not been so recognized by civilian courts in the United States or the British Commonwealth of Nations, but they tend to be taken as a complete excuse by Anglo-American military manuals. In this state of the authorities, if the International Military Tribunal in connection with a charge of a war crime refuses to recognize superior orders as a defense, it will not be making a retroactive determination or applying an *ex post facto* law. It will be merely settling an open question of law as every court frequently does.

The refusal to recognize the superior-order defense not only is not repugnant to the *ex post facto* principle, but is consonant with our ideas of justice. Basically, we cannot admit that military efficiency is the paramount consideration. And we cannot even admit that individual self-preservation is the highest value. This is not a new question. Just as it is settled that X is guilty of murder if, in order that he and Y, who are adrift on a raft, may not die of starvation, he kills their companion, Z; so a German soldier is guilty of murder if, in order that he may not be shot for disobedience and his wife tortured in a concentration camp, he shoots a Catholic priest. This is hard doctrine, but the law cannot recognize as an absolute excuse for a killing that the killer was acting under compulsion—for such a recognition not only would leave the structure of society at the mercy of criminals of sufficient ruthlessness, but also would place the cornerstone of justice on the quicksand of self-interest.

Of course, there always remains the fundamental separateness of the problem of guilt and the problem of treatment. And no one would expect a tribunal to mete out its severest penalty to a defendant who yielded to wrongdoing only out of fear of loss of his life or his family's.

2

In addition to "war crimes," the indictment, in Count 4, charges the defendants with "crimes against humanity." This count embraces the mur-

der, torture, and persecution of minority groups, such as Jews, inside Germany both before and after the outbreak of war. It is alleged in paragraph X of the indictment that these wrongs "constituted violations of international conventions, of internal penal laws, of the general principles of criminal law as derived from the criminal law of all civilized nations and were involved in and part of a systematic course of conduct."

I shall pass for the time being the last phrase just quoted, for that is merely a way of saying that the Nazis persecuted the minority German groups to harden the German will for aggression and to develop an issue that would divide other countries. In other words, the legal validity of that phrase rests upon the same considerations as the validity of the charge of "crimes against the peace."

I consider first the legal validity of the other phrases upon which is premised the charge that murdering, torturing, and persecuting German Jews and other non-Nazis from 1933 to 1939 as well as from 1939 to 1945 are crimes. And before I say anything of the legal question, let me make it abundantly clear that as a human being I regard these murders, tortures, and persecutions as being morally quite as repugnant and loathsome as the murders, tortures, and persecutions of the civilian and military personnel of American and Allied nations.

In paragraph X of the indictment, reference is first made to "international conventions." There is no citation of any particular international convention which in explicit words forbids a state or its inhabitants to murder its own citizens, in time either of war or of peace. I know of no such convention. And I, therefore, conclude that when the draftsman of the indictment used the phrase "international conventions" he was using the words loosely and almost analogously with the other phrase, "general principles of criminal law as derived from the criminal law of all civilized nations." He means to say that there exists, to cover the most atrocious conduct, a broad principle of universal international criminal law which is according to the law of most penal codes and public sentiment in most places, and for violations of which an offender may be tried by any new court that one or more of the world powers may create.

If that were the only basis for the trial and punishment of those who murdered or tortured German citizens, it would be a basis that would not satisfy most lawyers. It would resemble the universally condemned Nazi law of June 28, 1935, which provided: "Any person who commits an act which the law declares to be punishable or which is deserving of penalty according to the fundamental conceptions of the penal law and sound popular feeling, shall be punished." It would fly straight in the face of the most fundamental rules of criminal justice—that criminal laws shall not be *ex post facto* and that there shall be *nullum crimen et nulla poena sine lege*—no crime and no penalty without an antecedent law.

The feeling against a law evolved after the commission of an offense is deeply rooted. Demosthenes and Cicero knew the evil of retroactive laws: philosophers as diverse as Hobbes and Locke declared their hostility to it; and virtually every constitutional government has some prohibition of *ex post facto* legislation, often in the very words of Magna Carta, or Article I of the United States Constitution, or Article 8 of the French Declaration of Rights. The antagonism to *ex post facto* laws is not based on a lawyer's prejudice encased in a Latin maxim. It rests on the political truth that if a law can be created after an offense, then power is to that extent absolute and arbitrary. To allow retroactive legislation is to disparage the principle of constitutional limitation. It is to abandon what is usually regarded as one of the essential values at the core of our democratic faith.

But, fortunately, so far as concerns murders of German minorities, the indictment was not required to invent new law. The indictment specifically mentions "internal penal laws." And these laws are enough in view of the way the question would arise in a criminal proceeding.

Under universally accepted principles of law, an occupying belligerent power may and indeed often does establish its own tribunals to administer the domestic law of the occupied country for the inhabitants. Thus if Adolph killed Berthold before the American Army occupied Munich, it would be normal for the United States government to set up a military tribunal to try and to punish Adolph.

But suppose Adolph raised as a defense the contention that he was acting pursuant to orders from superiors which were the law of Germany. If that defense were raised, and if we assume (contrary to what some German jurists tell us) that in Germany there were on the statute books pertinent exculpatory laws, nonetheless under well-known principles of German law, going back to the Middle Ages and differing from current Anglo-American theories, the superior order could be disregarded

by a court applying German law, on the ground that it was so repugnant to "natural law" as to be void. That is, perhaps a German tribunal or one applying German law can disregard an obviously outrageous statute or executive order as offensive to natural law just as the Supreme Court of the United States can disregard a statute or executive order as offensive to the United States Constitution.

But further suppose that Adolph raised as a defense the point that the wrong was so old as to be barred by some statute of limitations. If there is such a statute in Germany, the limitation may be set aside without involving any violation of the *ex post facto* principle. As our own Supreme Court has pointed out, to set aside a statute of limitation is not to create a new offense.

3

I turn now to Count 2 of the indictment, which charges "crimes against peace." This is the count that has attracted greatest interest. It alleges that the defendants participated "in the planning, preparation, initiation and waging of wars of aggression, which were also wars in violation of international treaties, agreements and assurances."

This charge is attacked in many quarters on the ground it rests on *ex post facto* law. The reply has been that in the last generation there has accumulated a mounting body of international sentiment which indicates that wars of aggression are wrong and that a killing by a person acting on behalf of an aggressor power is not an excusable homicide. Reference is made not only to the Briand-Kellogg Pact of August 27, 1928, but to deliberations of the League of Nations in 1924 and subsequent years—all of which are said to show an increasing awareness of a new standard of conduct. Specific treaties outlawing wars of aggression are cited. And, having regard to the manner by which all early criminal law evolves and the manner by which international law grows, it is claimed that now it is unlawful to wage an aggressive war and it is criminal to aid in preparing for such a war, whether by political, military, financial, or industrial means.

One difficulty with that reply is that the body of growing custom to which reference is made is custom directed at sovereign states, not at individuals. There is no convention or treaty which places obligations explicitly upon an individual not to aid in waging an aggressive war. Thus, from the point of view of the individual, the charge of a "crime against peace" appears in one aspect like a retroactive law. At the time he acted, almost all informed jurists would have told him that individuals who engaged in aggressive war were not in the legal sense criminals.

Another difficulty is the possible bias of the Tribunal in connection with Count 2. Unlike the crimes in Counts 3 and 4, Count 2 charges a political crime. The crime which is asserted is tried not before a dispassionate neutral bench, but before the very persons alleged to be victims. There is not even one neutral sitting beside them.

And what is most serious is that there is doubt as to the sincerity of our belief that all wars of aggression are crimes. A question may be raised whether the United Nations are prepared to submit to scrutiny the attack of Russia on Poland, or on Finland, or the American encouragement to the Russians to break their treaty with Japan. Every one of these actions may have been proper, but we hardly admit that they are subject to international judgment.

These considerations make the second count of the Nuremberg indictment look to be of uncertain foundation and uncertain limits. To some the count may appear as nothing more than the ancient rule that the vanquished are at the mercy of the victor. To others it may appear as the mere declaration of an always latent doctrine that the leaders of a nation are subject to outside judgment as to their motives in waging war.

The other feature of the Nuremberg indictment is Count 1, charging a "conspiracy." Paragraph III of the indictment alleges that the "conspiracy embraced the commission of Crimes against Peace; . . . it came to embrace the commission of War Crimes . . . and Crimes against Humanity."

In international as well as in national law there may be for almost any crime what the older lawyers would have called principal offenders and accessories. If Adolph is determined to kill Sam, and talks the matter over with Berthold, Carl, and Dietrich, and Berthold agrees to borrow the money to buy a pistol, and Carl agrees to make a holster for the pistol, and all of them proceed as planned and then Adolph gives the pistol and holster to Dietrich, who goes out alone and actually shoots Sam without excuse, then, of course, Adolph, Berthold, Carl, and Dietrich are all guilty of murder. They should not be allowed to escape with the plea Macbeth offered for Banquo's murder, "Thou canst not say I did it."

If the conspiracy charge in Count 1 meant no more than that those are guilty who plan a murder and with knowledge finance and equip the murderer, no one would quarrel with the count. But it would appear that Count 1 means to establish some additional separate substantive offense of conspiracy. That is, it asserts that there is in international law a wrong which consists in acting together for an unlawful end, and that he who joins in that action is liable not only for what he planned, or participated in, or could reasonably have foreseen would happen, but is liable for what every one of his fellows did in the course of the conspiracy. Almost as broad a doctrine of conspiracy exists in municipal law.

But what is the basis for asserting so broad a substantive crime exists in international law? Where is the treaty, the custom, the academic learning on which it is based? Is this not a type of "crime" which was first described and defined either in London or in Nuremberg sometime in the year 1945?

Aside from the fact that the notion is new, is it not fundamentally unjust? The crime of conspiracy was originally developed by the Court of Star Chamber on the theory that any unlicensed joint action of private persons was a threat to the public, and so if the action was in any part unlawful it was all unlawful. The analogies of the municipal law of conspiracy therefore seem out of place in considering for international purposes the effect of joint political action. After all, in a government or other large social community there exists among the top officials, civilian and military, together with their financial and industrial collaborators, a kind of over-all working arrangement which may always be looked upon, if its invidious connotation be disregarded, as a "conspiracy." That is, government implies "breathing together." And is everyone who, knowing the purposes of the party in power, participates in government or joins with officials to be held for every act of the government?

To take a case which is perhaps not so obvious, is everyone who joins a political party, even one with some illegal purposes, to be held liable to the world for the action that every member takes, even if that action is not declared in the party platform and was not known to or consented to by the person charged as a wrongdoer? To put upon any individual such responsibility for action of the group seems literally to step back in history to a point before the prophet Ezekiel and to reject the more recent religious and democratic teachings that guilt is personal.

═══

4

Turning now from the legal basis of the indictment, I propose briefly to consider whether, quite apart from legal technicalities, the procedure of an international military tribunal on the Nuremberg pattern is a politically acceptable way of dealing with the offenders in the dock and those others whom we may legitimately feel should be punished.

The chief arguments usually given for this quasi-judicial trial are that it gives the culprits a chance to say anything that can be said on their behalf, that it gives both the world today and the world tomorrow a chance to see the justice of the Allied cause and the wickedness of the [Nazis] and that it sets a firm foundation for a future world order wherein individuals will know that if they embark on schemes of aggression or murder or torture or persecution they will be severely dealt with by the world.

The first argument has some merit. The defendants, after hearing and seeing the evidence against them, will have an opportunity without torture and with the aid of counsel to make statements on their own behalf. For us and for them this opportunity will make the proceeding more convincing. Yet the defendants will not have the right to make the type of presentation that at least English-speaking persons have thought the indispensable concomitant of a fair trial. No one expects that Ribbentrop will be allowed to summon Molotov to disprove the charge that in invading Poland Germany started an aggressive war. No one anticipates that the defense, if it has the evidence, will be given as long a time to present its evidence as the prosecution takes. And there is nothing more foreign to those proceedings than either the presumption that the defendants are innocent until proved guilty or the doctrine that any adverse public comment on the defendants before the verdict is prejudicial to their receiving a fair trial. The basic approach is that these men should not have a chance to go free. And that being so, they ought not to be tried in a court of law.

As to the second point, one objection is purely pragmatic. There is a reasonable doubt whether this kind of trial, despite the voluminous and accessible record it makes, persuades anyone. It brings out new evidence, but does it change men's minds? Most reporters say that the Germans are neither interested in nor persuaded by these proceedings, which they regard as partisan. They regard the proceedings not as marking a rebirth of law in Central Europe but as a political judgment on their former leaders. The same attitude may prevail in future because of the departure from accepted legal standards.

A more profound objection to the second point is that to regard a trial as a propaganda device is to debase justice. To be sure, most trials do and should incidentally educate the public. Yet any judge knows that if he, or counsel, or the parties regard a trial primarily as a public demonstration, or even as a general inquest, then there enter considerations which would otherwise be regarded as improper. In a political inquiry and even more in the spread of propaganda, the appeal is likely to be to the unreflecting thought and the deep-seated emotions of the crowd, untrammeled by any fixed standards. The objective is to create outside the courtroom a desired state of affairs. In a trial the appeal is to the disinterested judgment of reasonable men guided by established precepts. The objective is to make inside the courtroom a sound disposition of a pending case according to settled principles.

The argument that these trials set a firm foundation for a future world legal structure is perhaps debatable. The spectacle of individual liability for a world wrong may lead to future treaties and agreements specifying individual liability. If this were the outcome and if, for example, with respect to wars of aggression, war crimes, and use of atomic energy the nations should agree upon world rules establishing individual liability, then this would be a great gain. But it is by no means clear that this trial will further any such program.

At the moment, the world is most impressed by the undeniable dignity and efficiency of the proceedings and by the horrible events recited in the testimony. But, upon reflection, the informed public may be disturbed by the repudiation of widely accepted concepts of legal justice. It may see too great a resemblance between this proceeding and others which we ourselves have condemned. If in the end there is a generally accepted view that Nuremberg was an example of high politics masquerading as law, then the trial instead of promoting may retard the coming of the day of world law.

Quite apart from the effect of the Nuremberg trial upon the particular defendants involved, there is the disturbing effect of the trial upon domestic justice here and abroad. "We but teach bloody instructions, which, being taught, return to plague the inventor." Our acceptance of the notions of *ex post facto* law and group guilt blunt much of our criticism of Nazi law. Indeed our complaisance may mark the beginning of an age of reaction in constitutionalism in particular and of law in general. Have we forgotten that law is not power, but restraint on power?

If the Nuremberg trial of the leading Nazis should never have been undertaken, it does not follow that we should not have punished these men. It would have been consistent with our philosophy and our law to have disposed of such of the defendants as were in the ordinary sense murderers by individual, routine, undramatic military trials. This was the course proposed in the speeches of the Archbishop of York, Viscount Cecil, Lord Wright, and others in the great debate of March 20, 1945, in the House of Lords. In such trials the evidence and the legal issues would have a stark simplicity and the lesson would be inescapable.

For those who were not chargeable with ordinary crimes but only with political crimes such as planning an aggressive war, would it not have been better to proceed by an executive determination—that is, a proscription directed at certain named individuals? The form of the determination need not have been absolute on its face. It might have been a summary order reciting the offense and allowing the named persons to show cause why they should not be punished, thus giving them a chance to show any mistake of identification or gross mistake of fact.

There are precedents for such executive determination in the cases of Napoleon and of the Boxer rebels. Such a disposition would avoid the inevitably misleading characteristics of the present proceedings, such as a charge presented in the form of an "indictment," the participation of celebrated civil judges and the legal formalities of rulings on evidence and on law. It is these characteristics which may make the Nuremberg trial such a potential danger to law everywhere. Moreover, if

it were generally felt that we ought not to take a man's life without the form of a trial, then the executive determination could be limited to imprisonment. The example of Napoleon shows that our consciences would have no reason to be disturbed about the removal from society and the permanent detention of irresponsible men who are a threat to the peace of the world.

To be sure, such an executive determination is *ex post facto*. Indeed, it is a bill of attainder. To be sure, it is also an exhibition of power and not of restraint. But its very merit is its naked and unassumed character. It confesses itself to be not legal justice but political. The truthful facing of the character of our action would make it more certain that the case would not become a precedent in domestic law.

As Lord Digby said in 1641 regarding the Strafford bill of attainder, "There is in Parliament a double Power of Life and Death by Bill, a Judicial Power, and a legislative; the measure of the one, is what is legally just; of the other, what is Prudentially and Politickly fit for the good and preservation of the whole. But these two, under favour, are not to be confounded in Judgment: We must not piece up want of legality with matter of convenience, nor the defailance of prudential fitness with a pretence of Legal Justice."

This emphasis on procedural regularity is not legalistic or, as it is sometimes now said, conceptualistic. If there is one axiom that emerges clearly from the history of constitutionalism and from the study of any bill of rights or any charter of freedom, it is that procedural safeguards are the very substance of the liberties we cherish. Not only the specific guarantees with respect to criminal trials, but the general promise of "due process of law," have always been phrased and interpreted primarily in their procedural aspect. Indeed it hardly lies in the mouth of any supporter of the Nuremberg proceedings to disparage such procedural considerations; for may it not be said that the reason that the authors of those proceedings cast them in the form of a trial was to persuade the public that the customary safeguards and liberties were preserved?

It is against this deceptive appearance, big with evil consequences for law everywhere, that as a matter of civil courage all of us, judges as well as lawyers and laymen, however silent we ordinarily are, ought to speak out. It is for their silence on such matters that we justly criticize the Germans.

And it is the test of our sincere belief in justice under law never to allow it to be confused with what are merely our interest, our ingenuity, and our power.

Study Questions

1. What are the reasons behind the *nullum crimen* principle? What do they tell us about the nature of law and the difference between law and morality?

2. In his opening statement at Nuremberg, Jackson asks (rhetorically): "Does it take these men by surprise that murder is treated as a crime?" In what sense is Jackson using "crime" here? Could the force of his remark be trading on an equivocation between crime as a *moral* wrong and crime as a *legal* wrong?

3. Some of the Nazi defendants at Nuremberg raised the defense of obedience to superior orders: "I was ordered to kill the civilians." Assuming such orders were given by Hitler or his top aides, were such orders legal, given a natural law theory? Given a positivist theory?

B. *Classical Theories of Law*

Natural Law Versus Positivism

The history of legal philosophy is importantly shaped by the conflict between two opposing, general conceptions of law and legality. The first is called *natural law theory,* or simply *naturalism.* Naturalism holds that the phenomenon we call "law" can adequately be understood only in relation to a certain view about the nature of *moral* judgments and standards. What we recognize and venerate as law, according to naturalism, is both essentially connected to and grounded in a "natural moral order"—that is, principles and standards not simply made up by humans but rather part of an objective moral order present in the universe and accessible to human reason. Naturalism holds that human practices and institutions are to be measured against these "higher" standards, and where they fall short of the mark, specific human arrangements, whether statutes, executive orders, or constitutions, fail fully to have the character of law.

Positivism, by contrast, holds that the phenomenon of law is best understood as a system of orders, commands, or rules enforced by power. For the positivist, law is that which has been "posited," that is, made, enacted, or laid down in some prescribed fashion. It is as such purely human product; "artificial," rather than "natural." Moreover, for the positivist, a rule of law need have no connection with what is morally right or correct or true in order to qualify as law: there is no necessary connection between what law is and what it ought to be.

Legal Positivism

As H. L. A. Hart points out in this selection, positivism came into its own as a distinct and well-formulated legal theory in the late eighteenth and early nineteenth centuries in the writings of two British philosophers, Jeremy Bentham and John

Austin. Central to the legal theory of both was the conviction that law as it is is not necessarily law as it ought to be. It does not, they believed, follow from the fact that because a statute or an ordinance is valid law it is also morally good or right. A statute *could*, of course, coincide with what is right, but the fact of its being the "law" does not guarantee this. The morality and legality of a rule are in this way distinct and separate. This "separability thesis," as later positivists have come to call it, led both Bentham and Austin to distinguish sharply between the task of giving an accurate, descriptive account of what law is—"expository" or "analytical" jurisprudence—and the task of evaluating the law morally, stating what it *ought to be*—"censorial" or "normative" jurisprudence.

As Hart makes clear, in addition to their commitment to positivism, Bentham and Austin shared an allegiance to a general moral and political outlook known as *utilitarianism*. We will have occasion to encounter utilitarianism more later; for now it is enough to note its basic features. Utilitarianism is one among several ethical theories or views of moral life that regard the *consequences* of an act as the sole or exclusive factor to be weighed in determining whether the act is morally right or good. More specifically, utilitarians such as Bentham argue that an action is right or good only if it brings more overall happiness (or at least less unhappiness) into the world than any alternative course of action open to a person at a given time. Bentham appealed to this "Principle of Utility" frequently when it came to evaluating the law from a moral standpoint; and he often found the laws of the England of his time sadly lacking from the perspective of bringing about the greatest happiness.

The essay reprinted here is taken from the writings of a contemporary positivist, H. L. A. Hart. Hart's essay and especially his book *The Concept of Law* are widely regarded as central statements of modern positivism. While not all contemporary positivists agree with Hart, all acknowledge that he has largely set the terms in which the contemporary debate about positivism has taken place. Hart's aims in the selected essay are twofold: (1) to clarify the core positivistic commitment to the "separability" of law and morals; and (2) to defend the separability thesis against a variety of objections. Much of what Hart has to say is written against a background of familiarity with

the basic outlines of the theories of Bentham and especially Austin. It will therefore be useful to acquaint ourselves briefly with the outlines of Austin's account and with the deficiencies that Hart and others have noted in it.

What is law? According to Austin, law is a command issued by a sovereign. What is a command? It is a signification of desire, backed by a credible threat of punishment, a threat that can in all likelihood be carried out. Is anyone's command a law? No; only the command of the "sovereign" can be certified as law. Who (or what) is the sovereign? Austin makes no attempt to define the sovereign in terms of some normative or value-laden criterion, such as "he who has the right to rule" or "he who legitimately rules." Instead, Austin argues that the sovereign is that person or group of persons which is habitually obeyed by the bulk of a given population but which does not in fact habitually obey anyone else; the sovereign is the "unobeying obeyed." So, if some person, X, is habitually obeyed by the bulk of the population and yet does not in fact habitually obey anyone else, then that person is the sovereign. If X then expresses the desire that certain things be done (or not done) and makes a credible threat that failure to comply will be punished, X has issued a command and his or her command is law.

Austin's model is elegant in its simplicity; but it is open to seemingly decisive objections, as Hart and others have pointed out. The most fundamental of these objections has to do with the notions of command and sovereign. A command is a desire backed by a threat. Do all laws fit this model? Do all laws have sanctions? Austin's model makes some sense if the paradigm of law is, for example, criminal law. But what about other types of law? What about the law of contracts or of wills? What about American constitutional law? If I enter into a contract with you or write a will leaving you all my money, am I being commanded? By whom? And to do what? Austin tried to deal with these and similar cases by claiming that there *is*, after all, a sanction with which I am being threatened in these cases, what Austin called the "sanction of nullity": the sovereign will "punish" me by not giving effect to my will or my contract in the event that, for example, I don't fill them out properly. But this seems contrived. Isn't the situation better described by saying that the laws of wills and contracts *empower* me to do certain things (for example, sell my house) or bring about certain effects (for example, give all my property to my wife)? The aim here isn't to punish but to facilitate.

The laws of our own Constitution don't command us to continue their observance. If the citizens of what is now the United States were overwhelmingly to decide to repudiate the Constitution in its entirety next Friday at noon, would we all be punished for doing so? It seems not; but that fact does not incline us to say that the Constitution is not "law," at least in some sense. It merely shows that the Constitution is not law as a command (or series of commands) but rather is law as a structure or system of relative powers and competencies designed to facilitate or effect certain aims.

Austin's conception of sovereignty raises further difficulties. Do all legal systems necessarily have Austinian sovereigns? Consider again our own constitutional democracy. Do we have a sovereign? Who is it? To the extent that we can think in these terms at all, we view *ourselves* ("we the people") as those in charge. Austin it seems would have us then say that we (the people) in our constitution-enacting-and-maintaining role are sovereign over ourselves in our role as citizens. But does this preserve any of the simplicity of Austin's initial model? Furthermore, in our constitutional democracy we have grown accustomed to thinking of ours as a *limited* government. But can Austin's model make sense of limitations upon the power of sovereigns? To do so, Austin would have to argue that sovereigns, in their sovereign capacity, issue commands to themselves in their capacity as citizens. But then of course what distinguishes between these two aspects of sovereigns must be some notion of *official* capacity, and this idea cannot be spelled out in terms of Austin's theory.

To see why this last is so, consider the following problem. All those persons who presently serve as United States senators meet at a football field on a holiday and "vote" to make themselves each "king" of the states from which they come (forget about the problem of having two kings from each state). None of us would be prepared to say that this vote has made "law," since (we would explain) the senators were not acting in their "official" capacity. But Austin has no room for official capacity; his theory sees only these individuals, who are after all the same people (and people habitually obeyed, though not on this occasion) whether in or out of the Senate chamber.

Hart's Theory

In "Positivism and the Separation of Law and Morals," Oxford philosopher H. L. A. Hart notes that critics of positivism sometimes conflate the separability thesis—the claim that legality and morality are separate issues—with Austin's command theory of law, reasoning that since the latter is open to serious objections, so must be the former. Hart believes, however, that it is possible to adhere to the separability thesis (and to a utilitarian moral outlook) and still reject Austin's command model; and this is indeed Hart's position.

Hart considers several objections to the separation of law and morals so important to positivism. Some critics argue that law and morality cannot be separated for the reason that legal rules cannot always say how they are to be applied. For example, the general rule "No vehicles in the park" cannot be applied to the specific situation of my rocket-powered skateboard without the exercise of moral judgment: Should I be allowed to ride through the park on my skateboard? Any positivists who think differently, so these critics say, are guilty of the error of "formalism," the belief that all rules of law can be unambiguously and straightforwardly applied to any situation with complete logical certainty. Hart responds that this criticism relies on a false dilemma: we can, Hart believes, adhere to the separability thesis and yet not fall victim either to a direct appeal to moral values when interpreting a rule like "No vehicles in the park" nor to the silliness of formalism. Judges can resolve these "penumbral," or "fuzzy," cases by appeal to accepted social policies and purposes.

A further objection to the positivistic insistence that a rule can still be a rule of law even if it is immoral is made by those who have lived under evil legal regimes, like that in effect in Germany during the Nazi period. These critics complain that the positivist separation of law and morals can have (and has had) pernicious effects: by insisting that laws remain valid even if immoral, positivism has been easily exploited by corrupt "law-and-order" regimes eager to exact compliance with their regulations. Hart tries to argue that the proper response to these critics is not to reject the separability thesis but to recognize that though they may still be the law, some rules or regulations may simply be too morally outrageous to obey.

Hart does make one seeming concession to the natural law position. We do have, Hart admits, an obvious need for a system of legal protections and regulations with some minimal moral content. Legal rules prohibiting physical violence are necessary, for example, not because the presence of such values is entailed by the very idea of something's being the law, but simply given the contingent fact that human beings are vulnerable to physical harm and abuse. This, says Hart, is the core of good sense in the naturalist position; but it is an error to mistake the necessity for such laws for a truth about the nature of law as such.

Positivism and Nuremberg

Stanley Paulson's "Classical Legal Positivism at Nuremberg" explains the way in which the core of Austin's positivism—law as a command of the sovereign—was used by the Nazi defendants at Nuremberg. Armed with the classical positivist theory of law, many of the Nazi defendants sought to escape liability by urging on various grounds that, whatever else it was doing, the Tribunal could not be conducting a properly *legal* proceeding or enforcing the law, since there could be no law to enforce. Austin's conception of sovereignty implies that where A and B are sovereign powers no positive law can exist between them. There can be no "law" to which both Germany and the Allied governments were subjected, since this would (on Austin's model) require a "higher" power to which each of these governments paid habitual obedience. But then the governments in question could not be sovereigns in the first place. Paulson also tries to show how the command doctrine and the idea of absolute sovereignty were used to support a defense of compliance with superior orders.

Natural Law Theory

Naturalism has a rich and varied history, extending back to the ancient Greeks and Romans. One of the most elaborate and thorough expositions of the naturalist position was given by the thirteenth-century Catholic theologian, Thomas Aquinas.[1]

St. Thomas Aquinas

Aquinas argued that there are actually four types of law: eternal, divine, natural, and human. Eternal law represents God's overall plan for the universe. Divine law was for Aquinas the revealed word of God, the principles revealed by Scripture. Divine law is necessary, so Aquinas thought, because human beings have a supernatural destiny to which we must be guided, our native intellect being inadequate to reveal to us the nature of this destiny and how to secure it. Human law, by contrast with eternal and divine law, is created by us for the purpose of carrying out the requirements of the natural law.

What then is natural law? Aquinas argued that since all things are subject to divine providence and thus are "ruled and measured" by eternal law, all things "partake" in some way of eternal law. Aquinas believed that humans, as rational beings, occupy a special place in God's eternal plan, in that we can understand eternal law as it applies to us and can allow that understanding to guide our conduct. Eternal law as it applies to human conduct Aquinas calls "natural law."

What does natural law tell us to do? In answering this question, Aquinas invoked (as he often did) a distinction drawn by the Greek philosopher Aristotle. Aristotle had distinguished between two kinds of reason: speculative and practical. Speculative reason is that capacity we have as reasoning beings to apprehend or understand certain truths, such as the truths of mathematics and geometry. Practical reason is not concerned with these abstract matters but rather with human action. Practical reason tells us what things we should value, what goods we should seek in life, and how to obtain them. Aquinas and Aristotle held that, in both speculative and practical reason, certain principles are *per se nota*, known through themselves. These are self-evident propositions, requiring no proof (in the sense of being derivable from something else). As examples of self-evident principles of speculative reason, Aquinas included the principle of noncontradiction ("What is, is, and what is not, is not") and certain truths of mathematics and geometry. Turning to practical reason, Aquinas claimed that the first and most fundamental principle or "precept" of natural law is "Good is to be done and evil avoided." Other examples he

gives include "One should not kill one's father";
and "God's precepts are to be obeyed."

How does natural law relate to human law?
Aquinas maintained that human law is necessary
to implement and adapt the basic precepts of natural law, which are quite general, to the changing
needs and contexts of human societies. The basic
precepts are the same for everyone and do not
change; but the detailed conclusions drawn from
these basic precepts may differ from place to place
and time to time and human law reflects this fact.
"Goods held in trust for another should be returned" is, according to Aquinas, a requirement of
natural law, but it should not be followed when the
good is a gun and the person to whom it should be
returned is in a homicidal frenzy. Human law must
adjust the principles of natural law to specific situations. Moreover, since human communities need
many detailed regulations and ordinances simply
in order to function (for example, tax and traffic
laws), natural law requires that they be made,
though it does not of course dictate their particular
content (for example, natural law does not require
that we drive on the right; only that the community
establish some rule so as to meet the fundamental
requirement that health and safety be protected).

What about a situation in which human law
fails to conform to natural law? It is here that
Aquinas's naturalism has potentially far-reaching
consequences. For Aquinas insisted that human
enactments or measures that contravene natural
law are not laws "but a perversion of law"; they are
"acts of violence" and do not bind in conscience.
While it is still debated exactly what Aquinas
meant by such statements, these remarks have
seemed to many to imply that any human "laws"
at odds with natural law have no legal validity.
Even entire legal systems, Aquinas suggests, if
they are evil "perversions" of natural law (for example, the legal regime of the Nazis) may stand
invalidated on that ground.

Martin Luther King, Jr.'s "Letter from Birmingham Jail" illustrates one way in which
Aquinas's views on the relationship of natural to
human law can be translated into political action
and moral commitment. Writing from a jail cell in
Alabama in 1963, King responds to criticism of his
disobedience to the segregationist statutes of the
South by appealing to a "higher" law—the natural
law—and invokes the core naturalist claim that
these human enactments, these racist statutes,
have forfeited their status as "law" by virtue of
their obvious immorality.

Fuller and Fidelity to Law

This section concludes with an essay by the late
Harvard jurist Lon Fuller, a piece written as a response to the essay by Hart. While careful not
to endorse the classical natural law theory of
Aquinas, Fuller's critique of Hart's positivism
nonetheless bears a recognizable "naturalistic"
stamp in its insistence that "law" and "what is
morally right" are in an important sense inseparable.

Fuller is especially interested in the legal problems that arose in Germany after the Nazi period,
represented, for example, by the case of the
houswife-turned-informer. Hart, says Fuller, misunderstands these cases. Hart incorrectly assumes
that something deserving the name of "law" persisted throughout the Nazi reign and that it did so
in a way that makes meaningful the ideal of *fidelity
to law*. Fidelity to law, as Fuller understands it,
refers to the idea that a statute or an ordinance is
something deserving of loyalty and respect simply
by virtue of its being the law. Fuller maintains that
positivism cannot explain or make sense of the
ideal of fidelity to law and that positivism is therefore descriptively false or inaccurate.

Fuller concedes that a particular rule of law can
still be law even if it is immoral, but he denies that
such rules can remain law if they are part of an
entire legal system that is itself deeply evil and
unjust. Fuller defends the decision of the postwar
German courts in the "grudge-informer" cases on
the grounds that Nazi "law" was not law at all, as it
failed to comprise in any meaningful sense a legal
order. Fuller chronicles a number of features of Nazi
law and its operation with the aim of showing that,
for any system of *legal* rules to exist, certain minimum *moral* demands must be satisfied: impartial
enforcement, fair notice, promulgation, and so on.
Law has its own "internal morality." Law is not
mere order but good order. The positivist insistence on the separation of law and morality does
not illuminate the kind of problem raised by the
grudge-informer cases. As Fuller sees it, positivism
recommends that the German courts acknowledge

the validity of Nazi law and then refuse to apply it. But, Fuller responds, how can it further our understanding of fidelity to law to insist that a court should refuse to apply and enforce what it admits is valid law? Positivism, Fuller concludes, fails for the reason that it can give no coherent meaning to the moral obligation of loyalty to law.

Endnote

[1] See *Summa Theologica, The Basic Writings of Saint Thomas Aquinas*, Vol. 2, Anton C. Pegis (ed.) (New York: Random House, 1945), pp. 742ff.

Positivism and the Separation of Law and Morals

H. L. A. HART

In this article I shall discuss and attempt to defend a view which Mr. Justice Holmes, among others, held and for which he and they have been much criticized. But I wish first to say why I think that Holmes, whatever the vicissitudes of his American reputation may be, will always remain for Englishmen a heroic figure in jurisprudence. This will be so because he magically combined two qualities: one of them is imaginative power, which English legal thinking has often lacked; the other is clarity, which English legal thinking usually possesses. The English lawyer who turns to read Holmes is made to see that what he had taken to be settled and stable is really always on the move. To make this discovery with Holmes is to be with a guide whose words may leave you unconvinced, sometimes even repelled, but never mystified. Like our own Austin, with whom Holmes shared many ideals and thoughts, Holmes was sometimes clearly wrong; but again like Austin, when this was so he was always wrong clearly. This surely is a sovereign virtue in jurisprudence. Clarity I know is said not to be enough; this may be true, but there are still questions in jurisprudence where the issues are confused because they are discussed in a style which Holmes would have spurned for its

obscurity. Perhaps this is inevitable: jurisprudence trembles so uncertainly on the margin of many subjects that there will always be need for someone, in Bentham's phrase, "to pluck the mask of Mystery" from its face.[1] This is true, to a preeminent degree, of the subject of this article. Contemporary voices tell us we must recognize something obscured by the legal "positivists" whose day is now over: that there is a "point of intersection between law and morals,"[2] or that what *is* and what *ought* to be are somehow indissolubly fused or inseparable,[3] though the positivists denied it. What do these phrases mean? Or rather which of the many things that they *could* mean, *do* they mean? Which of them do "positivists" deny and why is it wrong to do so?

I

I shall present the subject as part of the history of an idea. At the close of the eighteenth century and the beginning of the nineteenth the most earnest thinkers in England about legal and social problems and the architects of great reforms were the great Utilitarians. Two of them, Bentham and Austin, constantly insisted on the need to distinguish, firmly and with the maximum of clarity, law as it is from law as it ought to be. This theme haunts their work, and they condemned the natural-law

From *Harvard Law Review*, Vol. 71 (1958), pp. 593–629. Copyright © 1958 by the Harvard Law Review Association. Reprinted with permission of the *Harvard Law Review*.

thinkers precisely because they had blurred this apparently simple but vital distinction. By contrast, at the present time in this country and to a lesser extent in England, this separation between law and morals is held to be superficial and wrong. Some critics have thought that it blinds men to the true nature of law and its roots in social life.[4] Others have thought it not only intellectually misleading but corrupting in practice, at its worst apt to weaken resistance to state tyranny or absolutism,[5] and at its best apt to bring law into disrespect. The nonpejorative name "Legal Positivism," like most terms which are used as missiles in intellectual battles, has come to stand for a baffling multitude of different sins. One of them is the sin, real or alleged, of insisting, as Austin and Bentham did, on the separation of law as it is and law as it ought to be.

How then has this reversal of the wheel come about? What are the theoretical errors in this distinction? Have the practical consequences of stressing the distinction as Bentham and Austin did been bad? Should we now reject it or keep it? In considering these questions we should recall the social philosophy which went along with the Utilitarians' insistence on this distinction. They stood firmly but on their own utilitarian ground for all the principles of liberalism in law and government. No one has ever combined, with such even-minded sanity as the Utilitarians, the passion for reform with respect for law together with a due recognition of the need to control the abuse of power even when power is in the hands of reformers. One by one in Bentham's works you can identify the elements of the *Rechtstaat* and all the principles for the defense of which the terminology of natural law has in our day been revived. Here are liberty of speech, and of press, the right of association,[6] the need that laws should be published and made widely known before they are enforced,[7] the need to control administrative agencies,[8] the insistence that there should be no criminal liability without fault,[9] and the importance of the principle of legality, *nulla poena sine lege*.[10] Some, I know, find the political and moral insight of the Utilitarians a very simple one, but we should not mistake this simplicity for superficiality nor forget how favorably their simplicities compare with the profundities of other thinkers. Take only one example: Bentham on slavery. He says the question at issue is not whether those who are held as slaves can reason, but simply whether they suffer.[11] Does this not compare well with the discus-

sion of the question in terms of whether or not there are some men whom Nature had fitted only to be the living instruments of others? We owe it to Bentham more than anyone else that we have stopped discussing this and similar questions of social policy in that form.

So Bentham and Austin were not dry analysts fiddling with verbal distinctions while cities burned, but were the vanguard of a movement which laboured with passionate intensity and much success to bring about a better society and better laws. Why then did they insist on the separation of law as it is and law as it ought to be? What did they mean? Let us first see what they said. Austin formulated the doctrine:

> The existence of law is one thing; its merit or demerit is another. Whether it be or be not is one enquiry; whether it be or be not conformable to an assumed standard, is a different enquiry. A law, which actually exists, is a law, though we happen to dislike it, or though it vary from the text, by which we regulate our approbation and disapprobation. This truth, when formally announced as an abstract proposition, is so simple and glaring that it seems idle to insist upon it. But simple and glaring as it is, when enunciated in abstract expressions the enumeration of the instances in which it has been forgotten would fill a volume.
>
> Sir William Blackstone, for example, says in his "Commentaries," that the laws of God are superior in obligation to all other laws; that no human laws should be suffered to contradict them; that human laws are of no validity if contrary to them; and that all valid laws derive their force from that Divine original.
>
> Now, he *may* mean that all human laws ought to conform to the Divine laws. If this be his meaning, I assent to it without hesitation. . . . Perhaps, again, he means that human lawgivers are themselves obliged by the Divine laws to fashion the laws which they impose by that ultimate standard, because if they do not, God will punish them. To this also I entirely assent. . . .
>
> But the meaning of this passage of Blackstone, if it has a meaning, seems rather to be this: that no human law which conflicts

with the Divine law is obligatory or binding; in other words, that no human law which conflicts with the Divine law *is a law*. . . .[12]

Austin's protest against blurring the distinction between what law is and what it ought to be is quite general: it is a mistake, whatever our standard of what ought to be, whatever "the text by which we regulate our approbation or disapprobation." His examples, however, are always a confusion between law as it is and law as morality would require it to be. For him, it must be remembered, the fundamental principles of morality were God's commands, to which utility was an "index": besides this there was the actual accepted morality of a social group or "positive" morality.

Bentham insisted on this distinction without characterizing morality by reference to God but only, of course, by reference to the principles of utility. Both thinkers' prime reason for this insistence was to enable men to see steadily the precise issues posed by the existence of morally bad laws, and to understand the specific character of the authority of a legal order. Bentham's general recipe for life under the government of laws was simple: it was *"to obey punctually; to censure freely."*[13] But Bentham was especially aware, as an anxious spectator of the French revolution, that his was not enough: the time might come in any society when the law's commands were so evil that the question of resistance had to be faced, and it was then essential that the issues at stake at this point should neither be oversimplified nor obscured.[14] Yet, this was precisely what the confusion between law and morals had done and Bentham found that the confusion had spread symmetrically in two different directions. On the one hand Bentham had in mind the anarchist who argues thus: "This ought not to be the law, therefore it is not and I am free not merely to censure but to disregard it." On the other hand he thought of the reactionary who argues: "This is the law, therefore it is what it ought to be," and thus stifles criticism at its birth. Both errors, Bentham thought, were to be found in Blackstone: there was his incautious statement that human laws were invalid if contrary to the law of God,[15] and "that spirit of obsequious *quietism* that seems constitutional in our Author" which "will scarce ever let him recognise a difference" between what is and what ought to be.[16] This indeed was for Bentham the occupational disease of lawyers: "[I]n the eyes of lawyers—not to speak of their dupes—that is to say, as yet, the generality of non-lawyers—the *is* and *ought to be* . . . were one and indivisible."[17] There are therefore two dangers between which insistence on this distinction will help us to steer: the danger that law and its authority may be dissolved in man's conceptions of what law ought to be and the danger that the existing law may supplant morality as a final test of conduct and so escape criticism.

In view of later criticisms it is also important to distinguish several thing that the Utilitarians did not mean by insisting on their separation of law and morals. They certainly accepted many of the things that might be called "the intersection of law and morals." First, they never denied that, as a matter of historical fact, the development of legal systems had been powerfully influenced by moral opinion, and, conversely, that moral standards had been profoundly influenced by law, so that the content of many legal rules mirrored moral rules or principles. It is not in fact always easy to trace this historical causal connection, but Bentham was certainly ready to admit its existence; so too Austin spoke of the "frequent coincidence"[18] of positive law and morality and attributed the confusion of what law is with what law ought to be to this very fact.

Secondly, neither Bentham nor his followers denied that by explicit legal provisions moral principles might at different points be brought into a legal system and form part of its rules, or that courts might be legally bound to decide in accordance with what they thought just or best. Bentham indeed recognized, as Austin did not, that even the supreme legislative power might be subjected to legal restraints by a constitution[19] and would not have denied that moral principles, like those of the fifth amendment, might form the content of such legal constitutional restraints. Austin differed in thinking that restraints on the supreme legislative power could not have the force of law, but would remain merely political or moral checks;[20] but of course he would have recognized that a statute, for example, might confer a delegated legislative power and restrict the area of its exercise by reference to moral principles.

What both Bentham and Austin were anxious to assert were the following two simple things: first, in the absence of an expressed constitutional or legal provision, it could not follow from the mere fact that a rule violated standards of morality that it was not a rule of law; and, conversely, it could not follow from the mere fact that a rule was morally desirable that it was a rule of law.

The history of this simple doctrine in the nineteenth century is too long and too intricate to trace here. Let me summarize it by saying that after it was propounded to the world by Austin it dominated English jurisprudence and constitutes part of the framework of most of those curiously English and perhaps unsatisfactory productions—the omnibus surveys of the whole field of jurisprudence. A succession of these were published after a full text of Austin's lectures finally appeared in 1863. In each of them the utilitarian separation of law and morals is treated as something that enables lawyers to attain a new clarity. Austin was said by one of his English successors, Amos, "to have delivered the law from the dead body of morality that still clung to it";[21] and even Maine, who was critical of Austin at many points, did not question this part of his doctrine. In the United States men like N. St. John Green,[22] Gray, and Holmes considered that insistence on this distinction had enabled the understanding of law as a means of social control to get off to a fruitful new start; they welcomed it both as self-evident and as illuminating—as a revealing tautology. This distinction is, of course, one of the main themes of Holmes' most famous essay "The Path of the Law,"[23] but the place it had in the estimation of these American writers is best seen in what Gray wrote at the turn of the century in *The Nature and Sources of the Law*. He said:

> The great gain in its fundamental conceptions which Jurisprudence made during the last century was the recognition of the truth that the Law of a State . . . is not an ideal, but something which actually exists. . . . [I]t is not that which ought to be, but that which is. To fix this definitely in the Jurisprudence of the Common Law, is the feat that Austin accomplished.[24]

II

So much for the doctrine in the heyday of its success. Let us turn now to some of the criticisms. Undoubtedly, when Bentham and Austin insisted on the distinction between law as it is and as it

ought to be, they had in mind *particular* laws the meanings of which were clear and so not in dispute, and they were concerned to argue that such laws, even if morally outrageous, were still laws. It is, however, necessary, in considering the criticisms which later developed, to consider more than those criticisms which were directed to this particular point if we are to get at the root of the dissatisfaction felt; we must also take account of the objection that, even if what the Utilitarians said on this particular point were true, their insistence on it, in a terminology suggesting a general cleavage between what is and ought to be law, obscured the fact that at other points there is an essential point of contact between the two. So in what follows I shall consider not only criticisms of the particular point which the Utilitarians had in mind but also the claim that an essential connection between law and morals emerges if we examine how laws, the meanings of which are in dispute, are interpreted and applied in concrete cases; and that this connection emerges again if we widen our point of view and ask, not whether every particular rule of law must satisfy a moral minimum in order to be a law, but whether a system of rules which altogether failed to do this could be a legal system.

There is, however, one major initial complexity by which criticism has been much confused. We must remember that the Utilitarians combined with their insistence on the separation of law and morals two other equally famous but distinct doctrines. One was the important truth that a purely analytical study of legal concepts, a study of the meaning of the distinctive vocabulary of the law, was as vital to our understanding of the nature of law as historical or sociological studies, though of course it could not supplant them. The other doctrine was the famous imperative theory of law—that law is essentially a command.

These three doctrines constitute the utilitarian tradition in jurisprudence; yet they are distinct doctrines. It is possible to endorse the separation between law and morals and to value analytical inquiries into the meaning of legal concepts and yet think it wrong to conceive of law as essentially a command. One source of great confusion in the criticism of the separation of law and morals was the belief that the falsity of any one of these three doctrines in the utilitarian tradition showed the other two to be false; what was worse was the failure to see that there were three quite separate doctrines in this tradition. The indiscriminate use of the label "positivism" to designate ambiguously each one of these three separate doctrines (together with some others which the Utilitarians never professed) has perhaps confused the issue more than any other single factor.[25] Some of the early American critics of the Austinian doctrine were, however, admirably clear on just this matter. Gray, for example, added at the end of the tribute to Austin, which I have already quoted, the words, "He may have been wrong in treating the Law of the State as being the command of the sovereign"[26] and he touched shrewdly on many points where the command theory is defective. But other critics have been less clearheaded and have thought that the inadequacies of the command theory which gradually came to light were sufficient to demonstrate the falsity of the separation of law and morals.

This was a mistake, but a natural one. To see how natural it was we must look a little more closely at the command idea. The famous theory that law is a command was a part of a wider and more ambitious claim. Austin said that the notion of a command was "the *key* to the sciences of jurisprudence and morals,"[27] and contemporary attempts to elucidate moral judgments in terms of "imperative" or "prescriptive" utterances echo this ambitious claim. But the command theory, viewed as an effort to identify even the quintessence of law, let alone the quintessence of morals, seems breathtaking in its simplicity and quite inadequate. There is much, even in the simplest legal system, that is distorted if presented as a command. Yet the Utilitarians thought that the essence of a legal system could be conveyed if the notion of a command were supplemented by that of a habit of obedience. The simple scheme was this: What is a command? It is simply an expression by one person of the desire that another person should do or abstain from some action, accompanied by a threat of punishment which is likely to follow disobedience. Commands are laws if two conditions are satisfied: first, they must be general; second, they must be commanded by what (as both Bentham and Austin claimed) exists in every political society whatever its constitutional form, namely, a person or a group of persons who are in receipt of habitual obedience from most of the society but pay no such obedience to others. These persons are its sovereign. Thus law is the command of the uncommanded commanders of society—the cre-

ation of the legally untrammelled will of the sovereign who is by definition outside the law.

It is easy to see that this account of a legal system is threadbare. One can also see why it might seem that its inadequacy is due to the omission of some essential connection with morality. The situation which the simple trilogy of command, sanction, and sovereign avails to describe, if you take these notions at all precisely, is like that of a gunman saying to his victim, "Give me your money or your life." The only difference is that in the case of a legal system the gunman says it to a large number of people who are accustomed to the racket and habitually surrender to it. Law surely is not the gunman situation writ large, and legal order is surely not to be thus simply identified with compulsion.

This scheme, despite the points of obvious analogy between a statute and a command, omits some of the most characteristic elements of law. Let me cite a few. It is wrong to think of a legislature (and a fortiori an electorate) with a changing membership, as a group of persons habitually obeyed: this simple idea is suited only to a monarch sufficiently long-lived for a "habit" to grow up. Even if we waive this point, nothing which legislators do makes law unless they comply with fundamental accepted rules specifying the essential lawmaking procedures. This is true even in a system having a simple unitary constitution like the British. These fundamental accepted rules specifying what the legislature must do to legislate are not commands habitually obeyed, nor can they be expressed as habits of obedience to persons. They lie at the root of a legal system, and what is most missing in the utilitarian scheme is an analysis of what it is for a social group and its officials to accept such rules. This notion, not that of a command as Austin claimed, is the "key to the science of jurisprudence," or at least one of the keys.

Again, Austin, in the case of a democracy, looked past the legislators to the electorate as "the sovereign" (or in England as part of it). He thought that in the United States the mass of the electors to the state and federal legislatures were the sovereign whose commands, given by their "agents" in the legislatures, were law. But on this footing the whole notion of the sovereign outside the law being "habitually obeyed" by the "bulk" of the population must go: for in this case the "bulk" obeys the bulk, that is, it obeys itself. Plainly the general acceptance of the authority of a lawmaking procedure, irrespective of the changing individuals who operate it from time to time, can be only distorted by an analysis in terms of mass habitual obedience to certain persons who are by definition outside the law, just as the cognate but much simpler phenomenon of the general social acceptance of a rule, say of taking off the hat when entering a church, would be distorted if represented as habitual obedience by the mass to specific persons.

Other critics dimly sensed a further and more important defect in the command theory, yet blurred the edge of an important criticism by assuming that the defect was due to the failure to insist upon some important connection between law and morals. This more radical defect is as follows. The picture that the command theory draws of life under law is essentially a simple relationship of the commander to the commanded, of superior to inferior, of top to bottom; the relationship is vertical between the commanders or authors of the law conceived of as essentially outside the law and those who are commanded and subject to the law. In this picture no place, or only an accidental or subordinate place, is afforded for a distinction between types of legal rules which are in fact radically different. Some laws require men to act in certain ways or to abstain from acting whether they wish to or not. The criminal law consists largely of rules of this sort: like commands they are simply "obeyed" or "disobeyed." But other legal rules are presented to society in quite different ways and have quite different functions. They provide facilities more or less elaborate for individuals to create structures of rights and duties for the conduct of life within the coercive framework of the law. Such are the rules enabling individuals to make contracts, wills, and trusts, and generally to mould their legal relations with others. Such rules, unlike the criminal law, are not factors designed to obstruct wishes and choices of an antisocial sort. On the contrary, these rules provide facilities for the realization of wishes and choices. They do not say (like commands) "do this whether you wish it or not," but rather "if you wish to do this, here is the way to do it." Under these rules we exercise powers, make claims, and assert rights. These phrases mark off characteristic features of laws that confer rights and powers; they are laws which are, so to speak, put at the disposition of individuals in a way in which the criminal law is not. Much ingenuity has gone into the task of "reducing" laws of this second sort to some complex variant of laws of the first sort. The effort to show that laws conferring rights are "really" only conditional stipulations of sanctions to be exacted from the person ultimately under a legal duty characterizes much of Kelsen's work.[28] Yet to urge this is really just to exhibit dogmatic determination to suppress one aspect of the legal system in order to maintain the theory that the stipulation of a sanction, like Austin's command, represents the quintessence of law. One might as well urge that the rules of baseball were "really" only complex conditional directions to the scorer and that this showed their real or "essential" nature.

One of the first jurists in England to break with the Austinian tradition, Salmond, complained that the analysis in terms of commands left the notion of a right unprovided with a place.[29] But he confused the point. He argued first, and correctly, that if laws are merely commands it is inexplicable that we should have come to speak of legal rights and powers as conferred or arising under them, but then wrongly concluded that the rules of a legal system must necessarily be connected with moral rules or principles of justice and that only on this footing could the phenomenon of legal rights be explained. Otherwise, Salmond thought, we would have to say that a mere "verbal coincidence" connects the concepts of legal and moral right. Similarly, continental critics of the Utilitarians, always alive to the complexity of the notion of a subjective right, insisted that the command theory gave it no place. Hägerström insisted that if laws were merely commands the notion of an individual's right was really inexplicable, for commands are, as he said, something which we either obey or we do not obey; they do not confer rights.[30] But he, too, concluded that moral, or, as he put it, common-sense, notions of justice must therefore be necessarily involved in the analysis of any legal structure elaborate enough to confer rights.[31]

Yet, surely these arguments are confused. Rules that confer rights, though distinct from commands, need not be moral rules or coincide with them. Rights, after all, exist under the rules of ceremonies, games, and in many other spheres regulated by rules which are irrelevant to the question of justice or what the law ought to be. Nor need rules which confer rights be just or morally good rules. The rights of a master over his slaves show us that. "Their merit or demerit," as Austin termed it, depends on how rights are distributed in society and over whom or what they are exercised.

These critics indeed revealed the inadequacy of the simple notions of command and habit for the analysis of law; at many points it is apparent that the social acceptance of a rule or standard of authority (even if it is motivated only by fear or superstition or rests on inertia) must be brought into the analysis and cannot itself be reduced to the two simple terms. Yet nothing in this showed the utilitarian insistence on the distinction between the existence of law and its "merits" to be wrong.

III

I now turn to a distinctively American criticism of the separation of the law that is from the law that ought to be. It emerged from the critical study of the judicial process with which American jurisprudence has been on the whole so beneficially occupied. The most skeptical of these critics—the loosely named "Realists" of the 1930's—perhaps too naïvely accepted the conceptual framework of the natural sciences as adequate for the characterization of law and for the analysis of rule-guided action of which a living system of law at least partly consists. But they opened men's eyes to what actually goes on when courts decide cases, and the contrast they drew between the actual facts of judicial decision and the traditional terminology for describing it as if it were a wholly logical operation was usually illuminating; for in spite of some exaggeration the "Realists" made us acutely conscious of one cardinal feature of human language and human thought, emphasis on which is vital not only for the understanding of law but in areas of philosophy far beyond the confines of jurisprudence. The insight of this school may be presented in the following example. A legal rule forbids you to take a vehicle into the public park. Plainly this forbids an automobile, but what about bicycles, roller skates, toy automobiles? What about airplanes? Are these, as we say, to be called "vehicles" for the purpose of the rule or not? If we are to communicate with each other at all, and if, as in the most elementary form of law, we are to express our intentions that a certain type of behavior be regulated by rules, then the general words we use—like "vehicle" in the case I consider—must have some standard instance in which no doubts are felt about its application. There must be a core of settled

meaning, but there will be, as well, a penumbra of debatable cases in which words are neither obviously applicable nor obviously ruled out. These cases will each have some features in common with the standard case; they will lack others or be accompanied by features not present in the standard case. Human invention and natural processes continually throw up such variants on the familiar, and if we are to say that these ranges of facts do or do not fall under existing rules, then the classifier must make a decision which is not dictated to him, for the facts and phenomena to which we fit our words and apply our rules are as it were *dumb*. The toy automobile cannot speak up and say, "I am a vehicle for the purpose of this legal rule," nor can the roller skates chorus, "We are not a vehicle." Fact situations do not await us neatly labeled, creased, and folded, nor is their legal classification written on them to be simply read off by the judge. Instead, in applying legal rules, someone must take the responsibility of deciding that words do or do not cover some case in hand with all the practical consequences involved in this decision.

We may call the problems which arise outside the hard core of standard instances or settled meaning "problems of the penumbra"; they are always with us whether in relation to such trivial things as the regulation of the use of the public park or in relation to the multidimensional generalities of a constitution. If a penumbra of uncertainty must surround all legal rules, then their application to specific cases in the penumbral area cannot be a matter of logical deduction, and so deductive reasoning, which for generations has been cherished as the very perfection of human reasoning, cannot serve as a model for what judges, or indeed anyone, should do in bringing particular cases under general rules. In this area men cannot live by deduction alone. And it follows that if legal arguments and legal decisions of penumbral questions are to be rational, their rationality must lie in something other than a logical relation to premises. So if it is rational or "sound" to argue and to decide that for the purposes of this rule an airplane is not a vehicle, this argument must be sound or rational without being logically conclusive. What is it then that makes such decisions correct or at least better than alternative decisions? Again, it seems true to say that the criterion which makes a decision sound in such cases is some concept of what the law ought to be; it is easy to slide from that into saying that it must be a moral judgment about what

Judges role

law ought to be. So here we touch upon a point of necessary "intersection between law and morals" which demonstrates the falsity or, at any rate, the misleading character of the Utilitarians' emphatic insistence on the separation of law as it is and ought to be. Surely, Bentham and Austin could only have written as they did because they misunderstood or neglected this aspect of the judicial process, because they ignored the problems of the penumbra.

The misconception of the judicial process which ignores the problems of the penumbra and which views the process as consisting preeminently in deductive reasoning is often stigmatized as the error of "formalism" or "literalism." My question now is, how and to what extent does the demonstration of this error show the utilitarian distinction to be wrong or misleading? Here there are many issues which have been confused, but I can only disentangle some. The charge of formalism has been leveled both at the "positivist" legal theorist and at the courts, but of course it must be a very different charge in each case. Leveled at the legal theorist, the charge means that he has made a theoretical mistake about the character of legal decision; he has thought of the reasoning involved as consisting in deduction from premises in which the judges' practical choices or decisions play no part. It would be easy to show that Austin was guiltless of this error; only an entire misconception of what analytical jurisprudence is and why he thought it important has led to the view that he, or any other analyst, believed that the law was a closed logical system in which judges deduced their decisions from premises.[32] On the contrary, he was very much alive to the character of language, to its vagueness or open character;[33] he thought that in the penumbral situation judges must necessarily legislate,[34] and, in accents that sometimes recall those of the late Judge Jerome Frank, he berated the common-law judges for legislating feebly and timidly and for blindly relying on real or fancied analogies with past cases instead of adapting their decisions to the growing needs of society as revealed by the moral standard of utility.[35] The villains of this piece, responsible for the conception of the judge as an automaton, are not the Utilitarian thinkers. The responsibility, if it is to be laid at the door of any theorist, is with thinkers like Blackstone and, at an earlier stage, Montesquieu. The root of this evil is preoccupation with the separation of powers and Blackstone's "childish fiction"

Conclusion

austin

(as Austin termed it) that judges only "find," never "make," law.

But we are concerned with "formalism" as a vice not of jurists but of judges. What precisely is it for a judge to commit this error, to be a "formalist," "automatic," a "slot machine"? Curiously enough the literature which is full of the denunciation of these vices never makes this clear in concrete terms; instead we have only descriptions which cannot mean what they appear to say: it is said that in the formalist error courts make an excessive use of logic, take a thing to "a dryly logical extreme,"[36] or make an excessive use of analytical methods. But just how in being a formalist does a judge make an excessive use of logic? It is clear that the essence of his error is to give some general term an interpretation which is blind to social values and consequences (or which is in some other way stupid or perhaps merely disliked by critics). But logic does not prescribe interpretation of terms; it dictates neither the stupid nor intelligent interpretation of any expression. Logic only tells you hypothetically that *if* you give a certain term a certain interpretation then a certain conclusion follows. Logic is silent on how to classify particulars—and this is the heart of a judicial decision. So this reference to logic and to logical extremes is a misnomer for something else, which must be this. A judge has to apply a rule to a concrete case—perhaps the rule that one may not take a stolen "vehicle" across state lines, and in this case an airplane has been taken.[37] He either does not see or pretends not to see that the general terms of this rule are susceptible of different interpretations and that he has a choice left open uncontrolled by linguistic conventions. He ignores, or is blind to, the fact that he is in the area of the penumbra and is not dealing with a standard case. Instead of choosing in the light of social aims, the judge fixes the meaning in a different way. He either takes the meaning that the word most obviously suggests in its ordinary nonlegal context to ordinary men, or one which the word has been given in some other legal context, or, still worse, he thinks of a standard case and then arbitrarily identifies certain features in it—for example, in the case of a vehicle, (1) normally used on land, (2) capable of carrying a human person, (3) capable of being self-propelled—and treats these three as always necessary and always sufficient conditions for the use in all contexts of the word "vehicle," irrespective of the social consequences of giving it this interpretation. This choice, not "logic," would force the judge to include a toy motor car (if electrically propelled) and to exclude bicycles and the airplane. In all this there is possibly great stupidity but no more "logic," and no less, than in cases in which the interpretation given to a general term and the consequent application of some general rule to a particular case is consciously controlled by some identified social aim.

Decisions made in a fashion as blind as this would scarcely deserve the name of decisions; we might as well toss a penny in applying a rule of law. But it is at least doubtful whether any judicial decisions (even in England) have been quite as automatic as this. Rather, either the interpretations stigmatized as automatic have resulted from the conviction that it is fairer in a criminal statute to take a meaning which would jump to the mind of the ordinary man at the cost even of defeating other values, and this itself is a social policy (though possibly a bad one); or much more frequently, what is stigmatized as "mechanical" and "automatic" is a determined choice made indeed in the light of a social aim but of a conservative social aim. Certainly many of the Supreme Court decisions at the turn of the century which have been so stigmatized[38] represent clear choices in the penumbral area to give effect to a policy of a conservative type. This is peculiarly true of Mr. Justice Peckham's opinions defining the spheres of police power and due process.[39]

But how does the wrongness of deciding cases in an automatic and mechanical way and the rightness of deciding cases by reference to social purposes show that the utilitarian insistence on the distinction between what the law is and what it ought to be is wrong? I take it that no one who wished to use these vices of formalism as proof that the distinction between what is and what ought to be is mistaken would deny that the decisions stigmatized as automatic are law; nor would he deny that the system in which such automatic decisions are made is a legal system. Surely he would say that they are law, but they are bad law, they ought not to be law. But this would be to use the distinction, not to refute it; and of course both Bentham and Austin used it to attack judges for failing to decide penumbral cases in accordance with the growing needs of society.

Clearly, if the demonstration of the errors of formalism is to show the utilitarian distinction to be wrong, the point must be drastically restated. The point must be not merely that a judicial decision to

be rational must be made in the light of some conception of what ought to be, but that the aims, the social policies and purposes to which judges should appeal if their decisions are to be rational, are themselves to be considered as part of the law in some suitably wide sense of "law" which is held to be more illuminating than that used by the Utilitarians. This restatement of the point would have the following consequence: instead of saying that the recurrence of penumbral questions shows us that legal rules are essentially incomplete, and that, when they fail to determine decisions, judges must legislate and so exercise a creative choice between alternatives, we shall say that the social policies which guide the judges' choice are in a sense there for them to discover; the judges are only "drawing out" of the rule what, if it is properly understood, is "latent" within it. To call this judicial legislation is to obscure some essential continuity between the clear cases of the rule's application and the penumbral decisions. I shall question later whether this way of talking is salutory, but I wish at this time to point out something obvious, but likely, if not stated, to tangle the issues. It does not follow that, because the opposite of a decision reached blindly in the formalist or literalist manner is a decision intelligently reached by reference to some conception of what ought to be, we have a junction of law and morals. We must, I think, beware of thinking in a too simple-minded fashion about the word "ought." This is not because there is no distinction to be made between law as it is and ought to be. Far from it. It is because the distinction should be between what is and what from many different points of view ought to be. The word "ought" merely reflects the presence of some standard of criticism; one of these standards is a moral standard but not all standards are moral. We say to our neighbour, "You ought not to lie," and that may certainly be a moral judgment, but we should remember that the baffled poisoner may say, "I ought to have given her a second dose." The point here is that intelligent decisions which we oppose to mechanical or formal decisions are not necessarily identical with decisions defensible on moral grounds. We may say of many a decision: "Yes, that is right; that is as it ought to be," and we may mean only that some accepted purpose or policy has been thereby advanced; we may not mean to endorse the moral propriety of the policy or the decision. So the contrast between the mechanical decision and the intelligent one can be reproduced inside a system dedicated to the pursuit of the most evil aims. It does not exist as a contrast to be found only in legal systems which, like our own, widely recognize principles of justice and moral claims of individuals.

An example may make this point plainer. With us the task of sentencing in criminal cases is the one that seems most obviously to demand from the judge the exercise of moral judgment. Here the factors to be weighed seem clearly to be moral factors: society must not be exposed to wanton attack; too much misery must not be inflicted on either the victim or his dependents; efforts must be made to enable him to lead a better life and regain a position in the society whose laws he has violated. To a judge striking the balance among these claims, with all the discretion and perplexities involved, his task seems as plain an example of the exercise of moral judgment as could be; and it seems to be the polar opposite of some mechanical application of a tariff of penalties fixing a sentence careless of the moral claims which in our system have to be weighed. So here intelligent and rational decision is guided however uncertainly by moral aims. But we have only to vary the example to see that this need not necessarily be so and surely, if it need not necessarily be so, the Utilitarian point remains unshaken. Under the Nazi regime men were sentenced by courts for criticism of the regime. Here the choice of sentence might be guided exclusively by consideration of what was needed to maintain the state's tyranny effectively. What sentence would both terrorize the public at large and keep the friends and family of the prisoner in suspense so that both hope and fear would cooperate as factors making for subservience? The prisoner of such a system would be regarded simply as an object to be used in pursuit of these aims. Yet, in contrast with a mechanical decision, decision on these grounds would be intelligent and purposive, and from one point of view the decision would be as it ought to be. Of course, I am not unaware that a whole philosophical tradition has sought to demonstrate the fact that we cannot correctly call decisions or behavior truly rational unless they are in conformity with moral aims and principles. But the example I have used seems to me to serve at least as a warning that we cannot use the errors of formalism as something which per se demonstrates the falsity of the utilitarian insistence on the distinction between law as it is and law as *morally* it ought to be.

We can now return to the main point. If it is true that the intelligent decision of penumbral questions is one made not mechanically but in the light of aims, purposes, and policies, though not necessarily in the light of anything we would call moral principles, is it wise to express this important fact by saying that the firm utilitarian distinction between what the law is and what it ought to be should be dropped? Perhaps the claim that it is wise cannot be theoretically refuted for it is, in effect, an *invitation* to revise our conception of what a legal rule is. We are invited to include in the "rule" the various aims and policies in the light of which its penumbral cases are decided on the ground that these aims have, because of their importance, as much right to be called law as the core of legal rules whose meaning is settled. But though an invitation cannot be refuted, it may be refused and I would proffer two reasons for refusing this invitation. First, everything we have learned about the judicial process can be expressed in other less mysterious ways. We can say laws are incurably incomplete and we must decide the penumbral cases rationally by reference to social aims. I think Holmes, who had such a vivid appreciation of the fact that "general propositions do not decide concrete cases," would have put it that way. Second, to insist on the utilitarian distinction is to emphasize that the hard core of settled meaning is law in some centrally important sense and that even if there are borderlines, there must first be lines. If this were not so the notion of rules controlling courts' decisions would be senseless as some of the "Realists"—in their most extreme moods, and, I think, on bad grounds—claimed.[40]

By contrast, to soften the distinction, to assert mysteriously that there is some fused identity between law as it is and as it ought to be, is to suggest that all legal questions are fundamentally like those of the penumbra. It is to assert that there is no central element of actual law to be seen in the core of central meaning which rules have, that there is nothing in the nature of a legal rule inconsistent with *all* questions being open to reconsideration in the light of social policy. Of course, it is good to be occupied with the penumbra. Its problems are rightly the daily diet of the law schools. But to be occupied with the penumbra is one thing, to be preoccupied with it another. And preoccupation with the penumbra is, if I may say so, as rich a source of confusion in the American legal tradition as formalism in the English. Of course we might abandon the notion that rules have authority; we might cease to attach force or even meaning to an argument that a case falls clearly within a rule and the scope of a precedent. We might call all such reasoning "automatic" or "mechanical," which is already the routine invective of the courts. But until we decide that this *is* what we want, we should not encourage it by obliterating the Utilitarian distinction.

IV

The third criticism of the separation of law and morals is of a very different character; it certainly is less an intellectual argument against the Utilitarian distinction than a passionate appeal supported not by detailed reasoning but by reminders of a terrible experience. For it consists of the testimony of those who have descended into Hell, and, like Ulysses or Dante, brought back a message for human beings. Only in this case the Hell was not beneath or beyond earth, but on it; it was a Hell created on earth by men for other men.

This appeal comes from those German thinkers who lived through the Nazi regime and reflected upon its evil manifestations in the legal system. One of these thinkers, Gustav Radbruch, had himself shared the "positivist" doctrine until the Nazi tyranny, but he was converted by this experience and so his appeal to other men to discard the doctrine of the separation of law and morals has the special poignancy of a recantation. What is important about this criticism is that it really does confront the particular point which Bentham and Austin had in mind in urging the separation of law as it is and as it ought to be. These German thinkers put their insistence on the need to join together what the Utilitarians separated just where this separation was of most importance in the eyes of the Utilitarians; for they were concerned with the problem posed by the existence of morally evil laws.

Before his conversion Radbruch held that resistance to law was a matter for the personal conscience, to be thought out by the individual as a moral problem, and the validity of a law could not be disproved by showing that its requirements were morally evil or even by showing that the effect of compliance with the law would be more evil than the effect of disobedience. Austin, it may be recalled, was emphatic in condemning those who

said that if human laws conflicted with the fundamental principles of morality then they cease to be laws, as talking "stark nonsense."

read in class

> The most pernicious laws, and therefore those which are most opposed to the will of God, have been and are continually enforced as laws by judicial tribunals. Suppose an act innocuous, or positively beneficial, be prohibited by the sovereign under the penalty of death; if I commit this act, I shall be tried and condemned, and if I object to the sentence, that it is contrary to the law of God . . . the court of justice will demonstrate the inconclusiveness of my reasoning by hanging me up, in pursuance of the law of which I have impugned the validity. An exception, demurrer, or plea, founded on the law of God was never heard in a Court of Justice, from the creation of the world down to the present moment.[41]

These are strong, indeed brutal words, but we must remember that they went along—in the case of Austin and, of course, Bentham—with the conviction that if laws reached a certain degree of iniquity then there would be a plain moral obligation to resist them and to withhold obedience. We shall see, when we consider the alternatives, that this simple presentation of the human dilemma which may arise has much to be said for it.

Radbruch, however, had concluded from the ease with which the Nazi regime had exploited subservience to mere law—or expressed, as he thought, in the "positivist" slogan "law as law" (*Gesetz als Gesetz*)—and from the failure of the German legal profession to protest against the enormities which they were required to perpetrate in the name of law, that "positivism" (meaning here the insistence on the separation of law as it is from law as it ought to be) had powerfully contributed to the horrors. His considered reflections led him to the doctrine that the fundamental principles of humanitarian morality were part of the very concept of *Recht* or Legality and that no positive enactment or statute, however clearly it was expressed and however clearly it conformed with the formal criteria of validity of a given legal system, could be valid if it contravened basic principles of morality. This doctrine can be appreciated fully only if the nuances imported by the German word *Recht* are grasped. But it is clear that the doctrine meant that every lawyer and judge should denounce statutes that transgressed the fundamental principles not as merely immoral or wrong but as having no legal character, and enactments which on this ground lack the quality of law should not be taken into account in working out the legal position of any given individual in particular circumstances. The striking recantation of his previous doctrine is unfortunately omitted from the translation of his works, but it should be read by all who wish to think afresh on the question of the interconnection of law and morals.[42]

It is impossible to read without sympathy Radbruch's passionate demand that the German legal conscience should be open to the demands of morality and his complaint that this has been too little the case in the German tradition. On the other hand there is an extraordinary naïveté in the view that insensitiveness to the demands of morality and subservience to state power in a people like the Germans should have arisen from the belief that law might be law though it failed to conform with the minimum requirements of morality. Rather this terrible history prompts inquiry into why emphasis on the slogan "law is law," and the distinction between law and morals, acquired a sinister character in Germany, but elsewhere, as with the Utilitarians themselves, went along with the most enlightened liberal attitudes. But something more disturbing than naïveté is latent in Radbruch's whole presentation of the issues to which the existence of morally iniquitous laws give rise. It is not, I think, uncharitable to say that we can see in his argument that he has only half digested the spiritual message of liberalism which he is seeking to convey to the legal profession. For everything that he says is really dependent upon an enormous overvaluation of the importance of the bare fact that a rule may be said to be a valid rule of law, as if this, once declared, was conclusive of the final moral question: "Ought this rule of law to be obeyed?" Surely the truly liberal answer to any sinister use of the slogan "law is law" or of the distinction between law and morals is, "Very well, but that does not conclude the question. Law is not morality; do not let it supplant morality."

However, we are not left to a mere academic discussion in order to evaluate the plea which Radbruch made for the revision of the distinction between law and morals. After the war Radbruch's conception of law as containing in itself the essential moral principle of humanitarianism was applied in practice by German courts in certain cases

in which local war criminals, spies, and informers under the Nazi regime were punished. The special importance of these cases is that the persons accused of these crimes claimed that what they had done was not illegal under the laws of the regime in force at the time these actions were performed. This plea was met with the reply that the laws upon which they relied were invalid as contravening the fundamental principles of morality. Let me cite briefly one of these cases.[43]

In 1944 a woman, wishing to be rid of her husband, denounced him to the authorities for insulting remarks he had made about Hitler while home on leave from the German army. The wife was under no legal duty to report his acts, though what he had said was apparently in violation of statutes making it illegal to make statements detrimental to the government of the Third Reich or to impair by any means the military defense of the German people. The husband was arrested and sentenced to death, apparently pursuant to these statutes, though he was not executed but was sent to the front. In 1949 the wife was prosecuted in a West German court for an offense which we would describe as illegally depriving a person of his freedom (*rechtswidrige Freiheitsberaubung*). This was punishable as a crime under the German Criminal Code of 1871 which had remained in force continuously since its enactment. The wife pleaded that her husband's imprisonment was pursuant to the Nazi statutes and hence that she had committed no crime. The court of appeal to which the case ultimately came held that the wife was guilty of procuring the deprivation of her husband's liberty by denouncing him to the German courts, even though he had been sentenced by a court for having violated a statute, since, to quote the words of the court, the statute "was contrary to the sound conscience and sense of justice of all decent human beings." This reasoning was followed in many cases which have been hailed as a triumph of the doctrines of natural law and as signaling the overthrow of positivism. The unqualified satisfaction with this result seems to me to be hysteria. Many of us might applaud the objective—that of punishing a woman for an outrageously immoral act—but this was secured only by declaring a statute established since 1934 not to have the force of law, and at least the wisdom of this course must be doubted. There were, of course, two other choices. One was to let the woman go unpunished; one can sympathize with and endorse the view that this might have been a bad thing to do. The other was to face the fact that if the woman were to be punished it must be pursuant to the introduction of a frankly retrospective law and with a full consciousness of what was sacrificed in securing her punishment in this way. Odious as retrospective criminal legislation and punishment may be, to have pursued it openly in this case would at least have had the merits of candour. It would have made plain that in punishing the woman a choice had to be made between two evils, that of leaving her unpunished and that of sacrificing a very precious principle of morality endorsed by most legal systems. Surely if we have learned anything from the history of morals it is that the thing to do with a moral quandary is not to hide it. Like nettles, the occasions when life forces us to choose between the lesser of two evils must be grasped with the consciousness that they are what they are. The vice of this use of the principle that, at certain limiting points, what is utterly immoral cannot be law or lawful is that it will serve to cloak the true nature of the problems with which we are faced and will encourage the romantic optimism that all the values we cherish ultimately will fit into a single system, that no one of them has to be sacrificed or compromised to accommodate another.

> "All Discord Harmony not understood
> All Partial Evil Universal Good"

This is surely untrue and there is an insincerity in any formulation of our problem which allows us to describe the treatment of the dilemma as if it were the disposition of the ordinary case.

It may seem perhaps to make too much of forms, even perhaps of words, to emphasize one way of disposing of this difficult case as compared with another which might have led, so far as the woman was concerned, to exactly the same result. Why should we dramatize the difference between them? We might punish the woman under a new retrospective law and declare overtly that we were doing something inconsistent with our principles as the lesser of two evils; or we might allow the case to pass as one in which we do not point out precisely where we sacrifice such a principle. But candour is not just one among many minor virtues of the administration of law, just as it is not merely a minor virtue of morality. For if we adopt Radbruch's view, and with him and the German courts make our protest against evil law in the form

of an assertion that certain rules cannot be law because of their moral iniquity, we confuse one of the most powerful, because it is the simplest, forms of moral criticism. If with the Utilitarians we speak plainly, we say that laws may be law but too evil to be obeyed. This is a moral condemnation which everyone can understand and it makes an immediate and obvious claim to moral attention. If, on the other hand, we formulate our objection as an assertion that these evil things are not law, here is an assertion which many people do not believe, and if they are disposed to consider it at all, it would seem to raise a whole host of philosophical issues before it can be accepted. So perhaps the most important single lesson to be learned from this form of the denial of the Utilitarian distinction is the one that the Utilitarians were most concerned to teach: when we have the ample resources of plain speech we must not present the moral criticism of institutions as propositions of a disputable philosophy.

V

I have endeavored to show that, in spite of all that has been learned and experienced since the Utilitarians wrote, and in spite of the defects of other parts of their doctrine, their protest against the confusion of what is and what ought to be law has a moral as well as an intellectual value. Yet it may well be said that, though this distinction is valid and important if applied to any particular law of a system, it is at least misleading if we attempt to apply it to "law," that is, to the notion of a legal system, and that if we insist, as I have, on the narrower truth (or truism), we obscure a wider (or deeper) truth. After all, it may be urged, we have learned that there are many things which are untrue of laws taken separately, but which are true and important in a legal system considered as a whole. For example, the connection between law and sanctions and between the existence of law and its "efficacy" must be understood in this more general way. It is surely not arguable (without some desperate extension of the word "sanction" or artificial narrowing of the word "law") that every law in a municipal legal system must have a sanction, yet it is at least plausible to argue that a legal system must, to be a legal system, provide sanctions for certain of its rules. So too, a rule of law may be said to exist though enforced or obeyed in only a minority of cases, but this could not be said of a legal system as a whole. Perhaps the differences with respect to laws taken separately and a legal system as a whole are also true of the connection between moral (or some other) conceptions of what law ought to be and law in this wider sense.

This line of argument, found (at least in embryo form) in Austin, where he draws attention to the fact that every developed legal system contains certain fundamental notions which are "necessary" and "bottomed in the common nature of man,"[44] is worth pursuing—up to a point—and I shall say briefly why and how far this is so.

We must avoid, if we can, the arid wastes of inappropriate definition, for, in relation to a concept as many-sided and vague as that of a legal system, disputes about the "essential" character, or necessity to the whole, of any single element soon begin to look like disputes about whether chess could be "chess" if played without pawns. There is a wish, which may be understandable, to cut straight through the question whether a legal system, to be a legal system, must measure up to some moral or other standard with simple statements of fact: for example, that no system which utterly failed in this respect has ever existed or could endure; that the normally fulfilled assumption that a legal system aims at some form of justice colours the whole way in which we interpret specific rules in particular cases, and if this normally fulfilled assumption were not fulfilled no one would have any reason to obey except fear (and probably not that) and still less, of course, any moral obligation to obey. The connection between law and moral standards and principles of justice is therefore as little arbitrary and as "necessary" as the connection between law and sanctions, and the pursuit of the question whether this necessity is logical (part of the "meaning" of law) or merely factual or causal can safely be left as an innocent pastime for philosophers.

Yet in two respects I should wish to go further (even though this involves the use of a philosophical fantasy) and show what could intelligibly be meant by the claim that certain provisions in a legal system are "necessary." The world in which we live, and we who live in it, may one day change in many different ways; and if this change were radical enough not only would certain statements of fact now true be false and vice versa, but whole ways of thinking and talking which constitute our present conceptual apparatus, through which we see the world and each other, would lapse. We have only to consider how the whole of our social, moral, and legal life, as we understand it now, depends on the contingent fact that though our bodies do change in shape, size, and other physical properties they do not do this so drastically nor with such quicksilver rapidity and irregularity that we cannot identify each other as the same persistent individual over considerable spans of time. Though this is but a contingent fact which may one day be different, on it at present rest huge structures of our thought and principles of action and social life. Similarly, consider the following possibility (not because it is more than a possibility but because it reveals why we think certain things necessary in a legal system and what we mean by this): suppose that men were to become invulnerable to attack by each other, were clad perhaps like giant land crabs with an impenetrable carapace, and could extract the food they needed from the air by some internal chemical process. In such circumstances (the details of which can be left to science fiction) rules forbidding the free use of violence and rules constituting the minimum form of property—with its rights and duties sufficient to enable food to grow and be retained until eaten—would not have the necessary nonarbitrary status which they have for us, constituted as we are in a would like ours. At present, and until such radical changes supervene, such rules are so fundamental that if a legal system did not have them there would be no point in having any other rules at all. Such rules overlap with basic moral principles vetoing murder, violence, and theft; and so we can add to the factual statement that all legal systems in fact coincide with morality at such vital points, the statement that this is, in this sense, necessarily so. And why not call it a "natural" necessity?

Of course even this much depends on the fact that in asking what content a legal system must have we take this question to be worth asking only if we who consider it cherish the humble aim of survival in close proximity to our fellows. Natural-law theory, however, in all its protean guises, attempts to push the argument much further and to assert that human beings are equally devoted to and united in their conception of aims (the pursuit of knowledge, justice to their fellow men) other than that of survival, and these dictate a further

[margin annotations: "necessary rules", "Natural necessity", "live in close proximate"]

necessary content to a legal system (over and above my humble minimum) without which it would be pointless. Of course we must be careful not to exaggerate the differences among human beings, but it seems to me that above this minimum the purposes men have for living in society are too conflicting and varying to make possible much extension of the argument that some fuller overlap of legal rules and moral standards is "necessary" in this sense.

Another aspect of the matter deserves attention. If we attach to a legal system the minimum meaning that it must consist of general rules— general both in the sense that they refer to courses of action, not single actions, and to multiplicities of men, not single individuals—this meaning connotes the principle of treating like cases alike, though the criteria of when cases are alike will be, so far, only the general elements specified in the rules. It is, however, true that *one* essential element of the concept of justice is the principle of treating like cases alike. This is justice in the administration of the law, not justice of the law. So there is, in the very notion of law consisting of general rules, something which prevents us from treating it as if morally it is utterly neutral, without any necessary contact with moral principles. Natural procedural justice consists therefore of those principles of objectivity and impartiality in the administration of the law which implement just this aspect of law and which are designed to ensure that rules are applied only to what are genuinely cases of the rule or at least to minimize the risks of inequalities in this sense.

These two reasons (or excuses) for talking of a certain overlap between legal and moral standards as necessary and natural, of course, should not satisfy anyone who is really disturbed by the Utilitarian or "positivist" insistence that law and morality are distinct. This is so because a legal system that satisfied these minimum requirements might apply, with the most pedantic impartiality as between the persons affected, laws which were hideously oppressive, and might deny to a vast rightless slave population the minimum benefits of protection from violence and theft. The stink of such societies is, after all, still in our nostrils and to argue that they have (or had) no legal system would only involve the repetition of the argument. Only if the rules failed to provide these essential benefits and protection for anyone—even for a slave-owning group—would the minimum be un-

satisfied and the system sink to the status of a set of meaningless taboos. Of course no one denied those benefits would have any reason to obey except fear and would have every moral reason to revolt.

VI

I should be less than candid if I did not, in conclusion, consider something which, I suspect, most troubles those who react strongly against "legal positivism." Emphasis on the distinction between law as it is and law as it ought to be may be taken to depend upon and to entail what are called "subjectivist" and "relativist" or "noncognitive" theories concerning the very nature of moral judgments, moral distinctions, or "values." Of course the Utilitarians themselves (as distinct from later positivists like Kelsen) did not countenance any such theories, however unsatisfactory their moral philosophy may appear to us now. Austin thought ultimate moral principles were the commands of God, known to us by revelation or through the "index" of utility, and Bentham thought they were verifiable propositions about utility. Nonetheless I think (though I cannot prove) that insistence upon the distinction between law as it is and ought to be has been, under the general head of "positivism," confused with a moral theory according to which statements of what is the case ("statements of fact") belong to a category or type radically different from statements of what ought to be ("value statements"). It may therefore be well to dispel this source of confusion.

There are many contemporary variants of this type of moral theory: according to some, judgments of what ought to be, or ought to be done, either are or include as essential elements expressions of "feeling," "emotion," or "attitudes" or "subjective preferences"; in others such judgments both express feelings or emotions or attitudes and enjoin others to share them. In other variants such judgments indicate that a particular case falls under a general principle or policy of action which the speaker has "chosen" or to which he is "committed" and which is itself not a recognition of what is the case but analogous to a general "imperative" or command addressed to all including the speaker himself. Common to all these variants is the insistence that judgments of what ought to be done, because they contain such "non-cognitive" elements, cannot be argued for or established by rational methods as statements of fact can be, and cannot be shown to follow from any statement of fact but only from other judgments of what ought to be done in conjunction with some statement of fact. We cannot, on such a theory, demonstrate, *e.g.*, that an action was wrong, ought not to have been done, merely by showing that it consisted of the deliberate infliction of pain solely for the gratification of the agent. We only show it to be wrong if we add to those verifiable "cognitive" statements of fact a general principle not itself verifiable or "cognitive" that the infliction of pain in such circumstances is wrong, ought not to be done. Together with this general distinction between statements of what is and what ought to be go sharp parallel distinctions between statements about means and statements of moral ends. We can rationally discover and debate what are appropriate means to given ends, but ends are not rationally discoverable or debatable; they are "fiats of the will," expressions of "emotions," "preferences," or "attitudes."

Against all such views (which are of course far subtler than this crude survey can convey) others urge that all these sharp distinctions between is and ought, fact and value, means and ends, cognitive and noncognitive, are wrong. In acknowledging ultimate ends or moral values we are recognizing something as much imposed upon us by the character of the world in which we live, as little a matter of choice, attitude, feeling, emotion as the truth of factual judgments about what is the case. The characteristic moral argument is not one in which the parties are reduced to expressing or kindling feelings or emotions or issuing exhortations or commands to each other but one by which parties come to acknowledge after closer examination and reflection that an initially disputed case falls within the ambit of a vaguely apprehended principle (itself no more "subjective," no more a "fiat of our will" than any other principle of classification) and this has as much title to be called "cognitive" or "rational" as any other initially disputed classification of particulars.

Let us now suppose that we accept this rejection of "noncognitive" theories of morality and this denial of the drastic distinction in type between statements of what is and what ought to be, and that moral judgments are as rationally defensible as any other kind of judgments. What would follow from this as to the nature of the connection between law as it is and law as it ought to be? Surely, from this alone, nothing. Laws, however morally iniquitous, would still (so far as this point is concerned) be laws. The only difference which the acceptance of this view of the nature of moral judgments would make would be that the moral iniquity of such laws would be something that could be demonstrated; it would surely follow merely from a statement of what the rule required to be done that the rule was morally wrong and so ought not to be law or conversely that it was morally desirable and ought to be law. But the demonstration of this would not show the rule not to be (or to be) law. Proof that the principles by which we evaluate or condemn laws are rationally discoverable, and not mere "fiats of the will," leaves untouched the fact that there are laws which may have any degree of iniquity or stupidity and still be laws. And conversely there are rules that have every moral qualification to be laws and yet are not laws.

Surely something further or more specific must be said if disproof of "noncognitivism" or kindred theories in ethics is to be relevant to the distinction between law as it is and law as it ought to be, and to lead to the abandonment at some point or some softening of this distinction. No one has done more than Professor Lon Fuller of the Harvard Law School in his various writings to make clear such a line of argument and I will end by criticising what I take to be its central point. It is a point which again emerges when we consider not those legal rules or parts of legal rules the meanings of which are clear and excite no debate but the interpretation of rules in concrete cases where doubts are initially felt and argument develops about their meaning. In no legal system is the scope of legal rules restricted to the range of concrete instances which were present or are believed to have been present in the minds of legislators; this indeed is one of the important differences between a legal rule and a command. Yet, when rules are recognized as applying to instances beyond any that legislators did or could have considered, their extension to such new cases often presents itself not as a deliberate choice or fiat on the part of those who so interpret the rule. It appears neither as a decision to give the rule a new or extended meaning nor as a guess as to what legislators, dead perhaps in the eighteenth century, would have said had they been alive in the twentieth century. Rather, the inclusion of the new case under the rule *decisions*

takes its place as a natural elaboration of the rule, as something implementing a "purpose" which it seems natural to attribute (in some sense) to the rule itself rather than to any particular person dead or alive. The Utilitarian description of such interpretative extension of old rules to new cases as judicial legislation fails to do justice to this phenomenon; it gives no hint of the differences between a deliberate fiat or decision to treat the new case in the same way as past cases and a recognition (in which there is little that is deliberate or even voluntary) that inclusion of the new case under the rule will implement or articulate a continuing and identical purpose, hitherto less specifically apprehended.

Perhaps many lawyers and judges will see in this language something that precisely fits their experience; others may think it a romantic gloss on facts better stated in the Utilitarian language of judicial "legislation" or in the modern American terminology of "creative choice."

To make the point clear Professor Fuller uses a nonlegal example from the philosopher Wittgenstein which is, I think, illuminating.

> Someone says to me: "Show the children a game." I teach them gaming with dice and the other says "I did not mean that sort of game." Must the exclusion of the game with dice have come before his mind when he gave me the order?[45]

Something important does seem to me to be touched on in this example. Perhaps there are the following (distinguishable) points. First, we normally do interpret not only what people are trying to do but what they say in the light of assumed common human objectives so that unless the contrary were expressly indicated we would not interpret an instruction to show a young child a game as a mandate to introduce him to gambling even though in other contexts the word "game" would be naturally so interpreted. Second, very often, the speaker whose words are thus interpreted might say: "Yes, that's what I mean [or "that's what I meant all along"] though I never thought of it until you put this particular case to me." Third, when we thus recognize, perhaps after argument or consultation with others, a particular case not specifically envisaged beforehand as falling within the ambit of some vaguely expressed instruction, we may find this experience falsified by description of it as a mere decision on our part so to treat the particular case, and that we can only describe this

faithfully as coming to realize and to articulate what we "really" want or our "true purpose"—phrases which Professor Fuller uses later in the same article.[46]

I am sure that many philosophical discussions of the character of moral argument would benefit from attention to cases of the sort instanced by Professor Fuller. Such attention would help to provide a corrective to the view that there is a sharp separation between "ends" and "means" and that in debating "ends" we can only work on each other nonrationally, and that rational argument is reserved for discussion of "means." But I think the relevance of his point to the issue whether it is correct or wise to insist on the distinction between law as it is and law as it ought to be is very small indeed. Its net effect is that in interpreting legal rules there are some cases which we find after reflection to be so natural an elaboration or articulation of the rule that to think of and refer to this as "legislation," "making law," or a "fiat" on our part would be misleading. So, the argument must be, it would be misleading to distinguish in such cases between what the rule is and what it ought to be—at least in some sense of ought. We think it ought to include the new case and come to see after reflection that it really does. But even if this way of presenting a recognizable experience as an example of a fusion between is and ought to be is admitted, two caveats must be borne in mind. The first is that "ought" in this case need have nothing to do with morals for the reasons explained already in section III: there may be just the same sense that a new case will implement and articulate the purpose of a rule in interpreting the rules of a game or some hideously immoral code of oppression whose immorality is appreciated by those called in to interpret it. They too can see what the "spirit" of the game they are playing requires in previously unenvisaged cases. More important is this: after all is said and done we must remember how rare in the law is the phenomenon held to justify this way of talking, how exceptional is this feeling that one way of deciding a case is imposed upon us as the only natural or rational elaboration of some rule. Surely it cannot be doubted that, for most cases of interpretation, the language of choice between alternatives, "judicial legislation" or even "fiat" (though not arbitrary fiat), better conveys the realities of the situation.

Within the framework of relatively well-settled law there jostle too many alternatives too nearly equal in attraction between which judge and

means + ends

lawyer must uncertainly pick their way to make appropriate here language which may well describe those experiences which we have in interpreting our own or others' principles of conduct, intention, or wishes, when we are not conscious of exercising a deliberate choice, but rather of recognising something awaiting recognition. To use in the description of the interpretation of laws the suggested terminology of a fusion or inability to separate what is law and ought to be will serve (like earlier stories that judges only find, never make, law) only to conceal the facts, that here is anywhere we live among uncertainties between which we have to choose, and that the existing law imposes only limits on our choice and not the choice itself.

Endnotes

[1] Bentham, *A Fragment on Government*, in 1 Works 221, 235 (Bowring ed. 1859) (preface, 41st para.).

[2] D'Entrèves, Natural Law 116 (2d ed. 1952).

[3] Fuller, The Law in Quest of Itself 12 (1940); Brecht, *The Myth of Is and Ought*, 54 Harv. L. Rev. 811 (1941); Fuller, *Human Purpose and Natural Law*, 53 J. Philos 697 (1953).

[4] See Friedmann, Legal Theory 154, 294–95 (3d ed. 1953). Friedmann also says of Austin that "by his sharp distinction between the science of legislation and the science of law," he "inaugurated an era of legal positivism and self-sufficiency which enabled the rising national State to assert its authority undisturbed by juristic doubts." *Id.* at 416. Yet, "the existence of a highly organised State which claimed sovereignty and unconditional obedience of the citizen" is said to be "the political condition which makes analytical positivism possible." *Id.* at 163. There is therefore some difficulty in determining which, in this account, is to be hen and which egg (analytical positivism or political condition). Apart from this, there seems to be little evidence that any national State rising in or after 1832 (when the *Province of Jurisprudence Determined* was first published) was enabled to assert its authority by Austin's work or "the era of legal positivism" which he "inaugurated."

[5] See Radbruch, *Die Erneuerung des Rechts*, 2 Die Wandlung 8 (Germany 1947); Radbruch, *Gesetzliches Unrecht und Übergesetzliches Recht*, 1 Süddeutsche Juristen-Zeitung 105 (Germany 1946) (reprinted in Radbruch, Rechtsphilosophie 347 (4th ed. 1950)). Radbruch's views are discussed at pp. 617–21 *infra*.

[6] Bentham, *A Fragment on Government*, in 1 Works 221, 230 (Bowring ed. 1859) (preface, 16th para.); Bentham,

Principles of Penal Law, in 1 Works 365, 574–75, 576–78 (Bowring ed. 1859) (pt. III, c. XXI, 8th para., 12th para.).

[7] Bentham, *Of Promulgation of the Laws*, in 1 Works 155 (Bowring ed. 1859); Bentham, *Principles of the Civil Code*, in 1 Works 297, 323 (Bowring ed. 1859) (pt. I, c. XVII, 2d para.); Bentham, *A Fragment on Government*, in 1 Works 221, 233 n.[*m*] (Bowring ed. 1859) (preface, 35th para.).

[8] Bentham, *Principles of Penal Law*, in 1 Works 365, 576 (Bowring ed. 1859) (pt. III, c. XXI, 10th para., 11th para.).

[9] Bentham, *Principles of Morals and Legislation*, in 1 Works 1, 84 (Bowring ed. 1859) (c. XIII).

[10] Bentham, *Anarchical Fallacies*, in 2 Works 489, 511–12 (Bowring ed. 1859) (art. VIII); Bentham, *Principles of Morals and Legislation*, in 1 Works 1, 144 (Bowring ed. 1859) (c. XIX, 11th para.).

[11] *Id.* at 142 n.§ (c. XIX, 4th para. n.§).

[12] Austin, The Province of Jurisprudence Determined 184–85 (Library of Ideas ed. 1954).

[13] Bentham, *A Fragment on Government*, in 1 Works 221, 230 (Bowring ed. 1859) (preface, 16th para.).

[14] See Bentham, *Principles of Legislation*, in The Theory of Legislation 1, 65 n.* (Ogden ed. 1931) (c. XII, 2d. para. n.*).

> Here we touch upon the most difficult of questions. If the law is not what it ought to be; if it openly combats the principle of utility; ought we to obey it? Ought we to violate it? Ought we to remain neuter between the law which commands an evil, and morality which forbids it?

See also Bentham, *A Fragment on Government*, in 1 Works 221, 287–88 (Bowring ed. 1859) (c. IV, 20th–25th paras.).

[15] 1 Blackstone, Commentaries *41. Bentham criticized "this dangerous maxim," saying "the natural tendency of such a doctrine is to impel a man, by the force of conscience, to rise up in arms against any law whatever that he happens not to like." Bentham, *A Fragment on Government*, in 1 Works 221, 287 (Bowring ed. 1859) (c. IV, 19th para.). See also Bentham, A Comment on the Commentaries 49 (1928) (c. III). For an expression of a fear lest anarchy result from such a doctrine, combined with a recognition that resistance may be justified on grounds of utility, see Austin, *op. cit. supra* note 12, at 186.

[16] Bentham, *A Fragment on Government*, in 1 Works 221, 294 (Bowring ed. 1859) (c. V, 10th para.).

[17] Bentham, *A Commentary on Humphreys' Real Property Code*, in 5 Works 389 (Bowring ed. 1843).

[18] Austin, *op. cit. supra* note 12, at 162.

[19] Bentham, *A Fragment on Government*, in 1 Works 221, 289–90 (Bowring ed. 1859) (c. IV, 33d–34th paras.).

[20] See Austin, *op. cit. supra* note 12, at 231.

[21] Amos, The Science of Law 4 (5th ed. 1881). See also Markby, Elements of Law 4–5 (5th ed. 1896):

> Austin, by establishing the distinction between positive law and morals, not only laid the foundation for a science of law, but cleared the conception of law . . . of a number of pernicious consequences to which . . . it had been supposed to lead. Positive laws, as Austin has shown, must be legally binding, and yet a law may be unjust. . . . He has admitted that law itself may be immoral, in which case it may be our moral duty to disobey it. . . .

Cf. Holland, Jurisprudence 1–20 (1880).

[22] See Green, Book Review, 6 Am. L. Rev. 57, 61 (1871) (reprinted in Green, Essays and Notes on the Law of Tort and Crime 31, 35 (1933)).

[23] 10 Harv. L. Rev. 457 (1897).

[24] Gray, The Nature and Sources of the Law 94 (1st ed. 1909) (§ 213).

[25] It may help to identify five (there may be more) meanings of "positivism" bandied about in contemporary jurisprudence:

(1) the contention that laws are commands of human beings, see pp. 602–06 *infra*,

(2) the contention that there is no necessary connection between law and morals or law as it is and ought to be, see pp. 594–600 *supra*,

(3) the contention that the analysis (or study of the meaning) of legal concepts is (a) worth pursuing and (b) to be distinguished from historical inquiries into the causes or origins of laws, from sociological inquiries into the relation of law and other social phenomena, and from the criticism or appraisal of law whether in terms of morals, social aims, "functions," or otherwise, see pp. 608–10 *infra*,

(4) the contention that a legal system is a "closed logical system" in which correct legal decisions can be deduced by logical means from predetermined legal rules without reference to social aims, policies, moral standards, see pp. 608–10 *infra*, and

(5) the contention that moral judgments cannot be established or defended, as statements of facts can, by rational argument, evidence, or proof ("noncognitivism" in ethics), see pp. 624–26 *infra*.

Bentham and Austin held the views described in (1), (2), and (3) but not those in (4) and (5). Opinion (4) is often ascribed to analytical jurists, see pp. 608–10 *infra*, but I know of no "analyst" who held this view.

[26] Gray, The Nature and Sources of the Law 94–95 (2d ed. 1921).

[27] Austin, *op. cit. supra* note 12, at 13.

[28] See, *e.g.*, Kelsen, General Theory of Law and State 58–61, 143–44 (1945). According to Kelsen, all laws, not only those conferring rights and powers, are reducible to such "primary norms" conditionally stipulating sanctions.

[29] Salmond, The First Principles of Jurisprudence 97–98 (1893). He protested against "the creed of what is termed the English school of jurisprudence," because it "attempted to deprive the idea of law of that ethical significance which is one of its most essential elements." *Id.* at 9, 10.

[30] Hägerström, Inquiries Into the Nature of Law and Morals 217 (Olivecrona ed. 1953): "[T]he whole theory of the subjective rights of private individuals . . . is incompatible with the imperative theory." See also *id.* at 221:

> The description of them [claims to legal protection] as rights is wholly derived from the idea that the law which is concerned with them is a true expression of rights and duties in the sense in which the popular notion of justice understands these terms.

[31] *Id.* at 218.

[32] This misunderstanding of analytical jurisprudence is to be found in, among others, Stone, The Province and Function of Law 141 (1950):

> In short, rejecting the implied assumption that all propositions of all parts of the law must be logically consistent with each other and proceed on a single set of definitions . . . he [Cardozo, J.,] denied that the law is actually what the analytical jurist, *for his limited purposes*, assumes it to be.

See also *id.* at 49, 52, 138, 140; Friedmann, Legal Theory 209 (3d ed. 1953). This misunderstanding seems to depend on the unexamined and false belief that analytical studies of the meaning of legal terms would be impossible or absurd if, to reach sound decisions in particular cases, more than a capacity for formal logical reasoning from unambiguous and clear predetermined premises is required.

[33] See the discussion of vagueness and uncertainty in law, in Austin, *op. cit. supra* note 12, at 202–05, 207, in which Austin recognized that, in consequence of this vagueness, often only "fallible tests" can be provided for determining whether particular cases fall under general expressions.

[34] See Austin, *op. cit. supra* note 12, at 191: "I cannot understand how any person who has considered the subject can suppose that society could possibly have gone on if judges had not legislated. . . ." As a corrective to the belief that the analytical jurist must take a "slot machine" or "mechanical" view of the judicial process it is worth noting the following observations made by Austin:

(1) Whenever law has to be applied, the " 'competition of opposite analogies' " may arise, for the case "may resemble in some of its points" cases to which the rule has been applied in the past and in other points "cases from which the application of the law has been withheld." 2 Austin, Lectures on Jurisprudence 633 (5th ed. 1885).

(2) Judges have commonly decided cases and so derived new rules by "building" on a variety of grounds including sometimes (in Austin's opinion too rarely) their views of what law ought to be. Most commonly they have derived law from preexisting law by "consequence founded on analogy," *i.e.,* they have made a new rule "in *consequence* of the existence of a similar rule applying to subjects which are *analogous.* . . ." 2 *id.* at 638–39.

(3) "[I]f every rule in a system of law were perfectly definite or precise," these difficulties incident to the application of law would not arise. "But the ideal completeness and correctness I now have imagined is not attainable in fact . . . though the system had been built and ordered with matchless solicitude and skill." 2 *id.* at 997–98. Of course he thought that much could and should be done by codification to eliminate uncertainty. See 2 *id.* at 662–81.

[35] 2 *id.* at 641:

> Nothing, indeed, can be more natural, than that legislators, direct or judicial (especially if they be narrow-minded, timid and unskillful), should lean as much as they can on the examples set by their predecessors.

See also 2 *id.* at 647:

> But it is much to be regretted that Judges of capacity, experience and weight, have not seized every opportunity of introducing a new rule (a rule beneficial for the future). . . . This is the reproach I should be inclined to make against Lord Eldon. . . . [T]he Judges of the Common Law Courts would not do what they ought to have done, namely to model their rules of law and of procedure to the growing exigencies of society, instead of stupidly and sulkily adhering to the old and barbarous usages.

[36] Hynes v. New York Cent. R.R., 231 N.Y. 229, 235, 131 N.E. 898, 900 (1921); see Pound, Interpretations of Legal History 123 (2d ed. 1930); Stone, *op. cit. supra* note 32, at 140–41.

[37] See McBoyle v. United States, 283 U.S. 25 (1931).

[38] See, *e.g.,* Pound, *Mechanical Jurisprudence,* 8 Colum. L. Rev. 605, 615–16 (1908).

[39] See, *e.g.,* Lochner v. New York, 198 U.S. 45 (1905). Justice Peckham's opinion that there were no reasonable grounds for interfering with the right of free contract by determining the hours of labour in the occupation of a baker may indeed be a wrongheaded piece of conservatism but there is nothing automatic or mechanical about it.

[40] One recantation of this extreme position is worth mention in the present context. In the first edition of *The Bramble Bush,* Professor Llewellyn committed himself wholeheartedly to the view that "what these officials do about disputes is, to my mind, the law itself" and that *"rules . . . are important so far as they help you . . . predict what judges will do. . . . That is all their importance, except as pretty playthings."* Llewellyn, The Bramble Bush 3, 5 (1st ed. 1930). In the second edition he said that these were "unhappy words when not more fully developed, and they are plainly at best a very partial statement of the whole truth. . . . [O]ne office of law is to control officials in some part, and to guide them even . . . where no thoroughgoing control is possible, or is desired. . . . [T]he words fail to take proper account . . . of the office of the institution of law as an instrument of conscious shaping. . . ." Llewellyn, The Bramble Bush 9 (2d ed. 1951).

[41] Austin, The Province of Jurisprudence Determined 185 (Library of Ideas ed. 1954).

[42] See Radbruch, *Gesetzliches Unrecht und Übergesetzliches Recht,* I Süddeutsche Juristen-Zeitung 105 (Germany 1946) (reprinted in Radbruch, Rechtsphilosophie 347 (4th ed. 1950)). I have used the translation of part of this essay and of Radbruch, *Die Erneuerung des Rechts,* 2 Die Wandlung 8 (Germany 1947), prepared by Professor Lon Fuller of the Harvard Law School as a mimeographed supplement to the readings in jurisprudence used in his course at Harvard.

[43] Judgment of July 27, 1949, Oberlandesgericht, Bamberg, 5 Süddeutsche Juristen-Zeitung 207 (Germany 1950), 64 Harv. L. Rev. 1005 (1951); see Friedmann, Legal Theory 457 (3d ed. 1953).

[44] Austin, *Uses of the Study of Jurisprudence,* in The Province of Jurisprudence Determined 365, 373, 367–69 (Library of Ideas ed. 1954).

[45] Fuller, *Human Purpose and Natural Law,* 53 J. Philos. 697, 700 (1956).

[46] *Id.* at 701, 702.

Classical Legal Positivism at Nuremberg

STANLEY PAULSON

I

[margin note: articles + argument]

Of the three principal criminal defenses raised at the Nuremberg Trials—the defenses of act of state, superior orders, and ex post facto law—two were expressly rejected in the Nuremberg Charter, and all three were rejected in the prosecution's arguments and later in the Tribunal's Judgment. To those skeptical of the legitimacy of the trials, the rejection of the defenses can be explained in terms of parochial political considerations ("Allied policy") but cannot be justified on either legal or philosophical grounds.

Is the skeptic's position on the rejection of the defenses warranted? I argue that it is not. The skeptic fails to take account of an underlying dispute between defense counsel on the one hand and the prosecution and Tribunal on the other—a dispute over the applicability of doctrines of classical legal positivism to the Nuremberg Trials that reflects radically different philosophical persuasions about the nature of law.[1] Specifically, drawing on material from the proceedings of the International Military Tribunal at Nuremberg,[2] I show that, as understood and presented by defense counsel, the defenses of act of state and superior orders presuppose the doctrine of absolute sovereignty, one of two fundamental doctrines of classical legal positivism. And I offer an interpretation of the defense of ex post facto law in terms of the other fundamental doctrine of classical legal positivism, the doctrine that laws are commands. Given my contention that there are noncontingent links between the doctrines of classical legal positivism and the Nuremberg criminal defenses, the Tribunal's grounds for rejecting the doctrines apply as well to its rejection of the defenses. Although my concern

[margin note: question these statements]

here is to show that the noncontingent links exist, I believe it could also be shown that the Tribunal was justified in rejecting classical legal positivism, a theory of law that precludes the very possibility of international law. To demonstrate the latter, however, would require a developed philosophy of international law, something well beyond the scope of this paper.

I begin by sketching the two fundamental doctrines of classical legal positivism as they are set out by the most historically influential proponent of that theory, John Austin. Then, after introducing the law of the Nuremberg Charter, I examine the defenses of act of state, superior orders, and most problematic, ex post facto law, as material from the proceedings of the International Military Tribunal bears on each.

II

Jean Bodin's *Six Books of the Commonwealth* (1576) is a convenient mark of the transition from a medieval world, which regarded law as prior to and more fundamental than the institutions of politics, to a modern world, which regards law as an instrument of the state. The "absolute and perpetual power" of Bodin's prince, "not bound by the laws of his predecessors, still less . . . by his own laws," is "the distinguishing mark of the sovereign," and in this respect the prince is a modern figure. But in another respect the prince remains medieval, for his power is "subject to the laws of God and of nature, and even to certain human laws common to all nations."[3]

John Austin's sovereign, on the other hand, is a thoroughly modern figure. In *The Province of Jurisprudence Determined* (1832), Austin distinguishes

From *Philosophy & Public Affairs*, Vol. 4 (1975), pp. 132–158. Copyright © 1975 Princeton University Press. Reprinted with permission of Princeton University Press.

austin's position

between "*natural* law" and "the aggregate of the rules, established by political superiors [that] is frequently styled *positive* law, or law existing *by position*," and he confines "the term *law*, as used simply and strictly," to positive law.[4] The ensuing theory, classical legal positivism, rests on two fundamental doctrines, the command doctrine and the doctrine of absolute sovereignty. The command doctrine is itself to be understood in terms of the components of the legal norm.

-intent
-expression
-power

Austin speaks of three such components: the commander's intention that a party act (or forbear from acting) in a particular way, the commander's expression of his intention to the party, and—central to the command doctrine—the commander's power to impose a sanction if the commanded party fails to comply with the directive.[5] The power to impose a sanction is not, however, to be understood as a property of the commander. A would-be commander may have power, without thereby having power over the party to whom he issues his directive—as in the case of a sovereign's "command" to a second sovereign. Rather, power is to be understood as a relation between commander and commanded, or more generally, between superior and inferior, a relation I speak of as the *power relation*.[6] Austin suggests the relation when he says: "the term *superiority* signifies *might*: the power of affecting others with evil or pain, and of forcing them, through fear of that evil, to fashion their conduct to one's wishes."[7]

power relation

The power relation requires inter alia that the commanding party be able to impose a sanction when there is a lack of compliance and that the commanded party be able to comply.[8] The inability either of the commanding party to impose a sanction or of the commanded party to comply is, for a particular directive, enough to defeat the claim that there exists a power relation of superior to inferior and, with it, the claim that the directive is a legal norm. I return to this requirement of the power relation in examining the ex post facto defense, below.

No power
No Claim

The other fundamental doctrine of classical legal positivism is that of absolute sovereignty. Austin understands sovereignty, in the language of the command doctrine, as an instance of the power relation of superior to inferior, with the critical qualification that the superior member of the power relation in this instance is not the inferior member in some other instance. What is perhaps the most distinctive feature of sovereignty in Aus-

tin is that it issues from a factual state of affairs. To underline this feature we may ask: Who has the right in a society to issue directives, to delegate authority, to be in a word the sovereign power? The answer of James Bryce is representative: "The person or body to whom in the last resort the law attributes this right is the logically supreme power, or Sovereign, in the State."[9] For Austin, however, the identity of the sovereign is not a question of legal right, but a question of who satisfies certain factual conditions. As he puts it in a well-known passage:

> The superiority which is styled sovereignty
> . . . is distinguished from other superiority
> . . . by the following marks or charac-
> ters:—1. The *bulk* of the given society are
> in a *habit* of obedience or submission to a
> *determinate* and *common* superior. . . . 2.
> That certain individual, or that certain body
> of individuals, is *not* in a habit of obedience
> to a determinate human superior.[10]

Austin's sovereign is above the law

The sharp contrast between Austin's view and that represented here by Bryce is in the end a difference between a sovereign power above the law and one subject to the law. Austin's sovereign, having unlimited legal power to enforce his commands, is himself "incapable of *legal* limitation."[11]

Several corollaries of the doctrine of absolute sovereignty are of special interest in connection with the defenses at Nuremberg. One corollary, pertaining to the act of state defense, is the notion of a positive legal right as a triadic relation, or a relation among duty-bearer, right-holder, and sovereign. As we will see, Austin uses this notion to demonstrate, by way of reductio ad absurdum arguments, that the sovereign cannot be either a duty-bearer or a right-holder. Another corollary, this one with an impact on the defense of superior orders, is the requirement of unconditional obedience. Given the sovereign's legally unlimited power, subjects cannot legally condition their obedience to the sovereign on, for example, moral grounds. As the legal positivist cliché has it, there is no necessary connection between positive law and morality.

important

Given the doctrines of command and absolute sovereignty, it is not surprising that classical legal positivism has no place for international law. In the course of distinguishing three classes of norms, Austin points up differences between international law and what he speaks of as positive law.[12] The

74 charges in Charter / Charter

first class of norms, positive law or law "strictly so called," stems from a determinate source that, in promulgating the law, manifests the power relation. An example is an ordinary legislative enactment. A second class, standing between positive law and international law, is law "properly so called." Like positive law, law "properly so called" stems from a determinate source, but it differs from positive law in that its promulgation does not reflect the power relation. An example here is a state's law directed not to its subjects but to a co-equal state. Finally, there is international law, a species of law "improperly so called." Austin refers to international law as the body of "laws which regard the conduct of sovereigns or supreme governments in their various relations to one another." As other species of law "improperly so called," he mentions *"the rules of honour"* and *"the law set by fashion."* Stemming from no determinate source, these norms are *"laws set* or *imposed by general opinion."*[13]

Criticism of austin

In speaking of classical legal positivism, I have in mind the philosophical theory developed from Austin's two doctrines. The theory has been widely—and correctly—criticized for failing to take account of sources of law that are independent of the state, in particular, indigenous sources; for failing to distinguish between de jure and de facto sovereignty; for failing to take account of functions of legal rules other than the "command" function; for failing to take account of legal obligations of the state; and for a variety of other defects.[14] Still, the theory persists as a conceptual picture of law, "accepted," as Ronald Dworkin puts it, "in one form or another by most working and academic lawyers who hold views on jurisprudence."[15] And the theory provided the rationale for the defenses raised at Nuremberg. Before turning to the defenses, let us look briefly at the law of the Nuremberg Charter.

III

Meeting in London in August of 1945, the Allied Powers concluded an Agreement for the Prosecution and Punishment of the Major War Criminals of the European Axis, in which they declared their intention to establish an International Military Tribunal for the trial of those war criminals "whose offenses have no particular geographical location."[16] The Charter of the Tribunal, annexed to the Agreement, granted jurisdiction over crimes against peace, war crimes, and crimes against humanity, and over conspiracy to commit these crimes, as they were defined in the Charter.[17] Article 6(a) of the Charter defined crimes against peace:

> CRIMES AGAINST PEACE: namely, planning, preparation, initiation or waging of a war of aggression, or a war in violation of international treaties, agreements or assurances, or participation in a Common Plan or Conspiracy for the accomplishment of any of the foregoing.

Article 6(b) defined war crimes:

> WAR CRIMES: namely, violations of the laws or customs of war. Such violations shall include, but not be limited to, murder, ill-treatment or deportation to slave labor or for any other purpose of civilian population of or in occupied territory, murder or ill-treatment of prisoners of war or persons on the seas, killing of hostages, plunder of public or private property, wanton destruction of cities, towns, or villages, or devastation not justified by military necessity.

Article 6(c), defining crimes against humanity, extended the application of the law of the Charter to certain acts committed against German nationals:

> CRIMES AGAINST HUMANITY: namely, murder, extermination, enslavement, deportation, and other inhumane acts committed against any civilian population, before or during the war, or persecutions on political, racial, or religious grounds in execution of or in connection with any crime within the jurisdiction of the Tribunal, whether or not in violation of domestic law of the country where perpetrated.

A statement dealing with conspiracy appeared in a paragraph following article 6(c) of the Charter:

> Leaders, organizers, instigators, and accomplices participating in the formulation or execution of a Common Plan or Conspiracy to commit any of the foregoing crimes are responsible for all acts performed by any persons in execution of such plan.[18]

Twenty-four high-ranking Nazi officials and a number of Nazi organizations were indicted on two or more of four counts, corresponding to the four types of offenses over which the Charter had granted jurisdiction.[19] The trial was in open session for nearly a year (14 November 1945 to 1 October 1946). After reviewing the enormous mass of evidence, the Tribunal in its Judgment concluded inter alia that "resort to a war of aggression is not merely illegal, but is criminal"; that the defendants' role in the "planning and preparation" of aggressive war was abundantly clear; that war crimes were committed "on a vast scale, never before seen in the history of war"; and that "inhumane acts charged in the Indictment, and committed after the beginning of the war, [that] did not constitute War Crimes . . . were all committed in execution of, or in connection with, the aggressive war, and therefore constituted Crimes against Humanity."[20] Of the twenty-two individual defendants actually tried, only three were acquitted on all counts: sentences imposed on the others ranged from ten years imprisonment to death.[21] Of the seven Nazi organizations tried, four were declared criminal.[22]

IV

The defense of act of state, providing for imputation to the state of an individual's act as an "act of state" and thereby precluding adjudication before a foreign or international forum, was expressly rejected in article 7 of the Nuremberg Charter:

> The official position of defendants, whether as Heads of State or responsible officials in Government departments, shall not be considered as freeing them from responsibility or mitigating punishment.[23]

Notwithstanding the Charter provision, counsel for the defense at a number of points raised the act of state defense and, with it, the doctrine of absolute sovereignty. How, exactly, is the defense related to absolute sovereignty?

Acts of state are "acts performed by individuals in their capacity as organs of the State and therefore acts imputed to the State."[24] Imputation of an individual's act to the state might be thought not only to shield the actor from a claim by an injured party but also to deprive the injured party of his claim altogether, for he cannot have, as a matter of positive law, any claim against a sovereign state. Or so it would be argued, as Austin's concept of a positive legal right as a triadic relation illustrates.[25] Assume, as members of Austin's triadic relation, a sovereign (*A*) who sets the positive law, an individual (*B*) on whom a right is conferred, and another (*C*) on whom a duty is imposed. By the method of reductio ad absurdum it can be demonstrated that *A*, the sovereign, cannot stand in either of the positions occupied by *B* and *C*. If, for example, *A* rather than *C* owed a duty to *B*, what would the result be? The supposition that *A* is a duty-bearer implies in Austin's scheme a "superior sovereign" setting the positive law from which *A*'s duty and *B*'s right emanate, contrary to the hypothesis that *A* is sovereign.[26] Similarly for the supposition that *A* is a right-holder.

One qualification to the act of state defense, as stated above, is essential. An individual performs "acts of state" in his capacity as an "organ of the state," but it is not enough that *he*, an official rather than a private individual, acts. The individual acts in an official capacity only if his acts are "performed at the government's command or with its authorization."[27] The requirement that the individual's acts be authorized by his government establishes a distinction, in the conduct of officials, between lawful (authorized) and unlawful (unauthorized) acts. Whether an official's act is lawful may be determined through citizens' claims against the official. And such claims are allowed by Austin's analysis of a legal right as a triadic relation.[28] If an official acts in excess of the powers of his office, he is personally liable; and the relation here between duty-bearer (the official) and the right-holder (the citizen) emanates from, and is enforced by, the third party to the relation, the sovereign. This way around the act of state defense, preserving the dogma of absolute sovereignty while at the same time avoiding a grant of license to officials, is well established in English domestic law.[29]

The situation is different in the international context, where to invoke the Austinian doctrine of absolute sovereignty and its corollary regarding positive legal rights is tantamount to raising the act of state defense. Suppose that sovereign state *A* brings a claim, either in its courts or before an international forum, against sovereign state *B* or against an individual for an act imputed to state *B* as an act of state. The claim implies a "superior sovereign," the third member of the legal relation, who sets the positive law from which *A*'s right and *B*'s duty emanate. But this is contrary to the hypothesis that *A* and *B* are themselves sovereign powers. The doctrine of sovereignty means inter alia that positive law always emanates from a superior power. Between *A* and *B*, which are equal powers, there can be no positive law.[30] It was this doctrine that counsel for the defense at Nuremberg invoked in the course of raising the act of state defense, and this doctrine that the prosecution and Tribunal rejected in denying that defense.

The arguments of Professor Hermann Jahrreiss, associate defense counsel,[31] are prominent here. In his statement concerning juridical aspects of the trial, Jahrreiss raised the act of state defense and, with it, the doctrine of absolute sovereignty.[32] He began by asking the Tribunal to suppose, contrary to fact, that there had existed in the 1930s not the ineffectual Kellogg-Briand Pact of 1928[33] but "a general and unambiguous [peace] pact . . . accepted and applied by the contracting parties in fundamental and factual agreement." Given this supposition, "Would the liability of individuals to punishment for the breach of such a treaty be founded in international law?" Jahrreiss answered that "not even the liability of the state to punishment, let alone that of individuals," would be so founded. For although a state could be said to have committed an offense against "international law," a violation, that is, of an obligation incurred by consent, the offending state would not be subject to punishment under international criminal law. And what is more, individuals could not be said to have committed any offense whatever under international law. Jahrreiss appealed directly to the doctrine of absolute sovereignty to support the immunity of individuals from prosecution by an international forum. The prosecution of individuals, he asserted, "cannot take place as long as the sovereignty of states is the organizational basic principle of interstate order."[34]

What does Jahrreiss'[s] appeal to the doctrine of absolute sovereignty amount to? He assumed that the acts of the defendants were within the scope of the powers delegated to them and could be imputed to the state as acts of state, thereby granting the individual defendants legal immunity. He then used this assumption in the international context, arguing that it would be contrary to the doctrine of absolute sovereignty to grant a for-

eign or international forum the power to hold an individual legally liable for acts imputed to the individual's state as acts of state. If liability under positive law could be imposed by a foreign or international forum, that would set limits on what is by definition unlimited, the legal power of the sovereign state. The upshot of the argument is clear. If an individual has no legal liability for a breach of the ideal peace pact of Jahrreiss's supposition, the same conclusion holds a fortiori for a breach of the existing Kellogg-Briand Pact.

Moreover, the doctrine of absolute sovereignty gave Jahrreiss a means of denying the applicability of nonpositivist criteria for the identification of law—consent, perhaps, or consonance with morality. For Jahrreiss to have allowed such criteria would have left open the possibility that a legal order other than the positive legal order, for example, international law, had the better claim to legitimacy and might therefore prevail over positive law in cases where norms from each order conflicted. The prosecution and Tribunal clearly rejected Jahrreiss'[s] presupposition of absolute sovereignty but were less clear on the matter of the applicability of nonpositivist criteria for the identification of law.

Sir Hartley Shawcross, chief prosecutor for the United Kingdom,[35] directly attacked the classical legal positivist doctrine of absolute sovereignty in his reply to Jahrreiss, arguing that the doctrine is incompatible with commonplace obligations of governments.[36] According to the classical legal positivist, only individuals have legal obligations, and only because the state has power to secure compliance by imposing sanctions. Shawcross argued that states also have legal obligations, but a state's obligations cannot be said to be conditioned on the state's power. Classical legal positivism, restricting as it does the scope of legal obligation to the extent of state power, must be rejected in any system of law that recognizes the legal validity of a state's obligations. As Shawcross put it, referring expressly to the classical legal positivist, "Legal purists may contend that nothing is law which is not imposed from above by a sovereign body having the power to compel obedience. That idea of the analytical jurists has never been applicable to International Law. If it had, the undoubted obligation of States in matters of contract and tort could not exist."[37]

In its Judgment, the Tribunal reaffirmed article 7 of the Charter and rejected the classical legal positivist doctrine of absolute sovereignty.

Speaking directly to article 7, the Tribunal contended that "the very essence of the Charter is that individuals have international duties which transcend the national obligations of obedience imposed by the individual state." Having rejected the doctrine of absolute sovereignty as it applied to acts of the defendants, the Tribunal likewise rejected the act of state defense as it applied to these same acts. As the Tribunal put it, "He who violates the laws of war cannot obtain immunity while acting in pursuance of the authority of the state if the state in authorizing action moves outside its competence under international law."[38]

The viability of the defense of act of state as understood and presented by defense counsel at Nuremberg presupposes the applicability of the doctrine of absolute sovereignty. A parallel presupposition is at work in connection with the defense of superior orders.

presuppose -
take for
granted

V

Superior
order
defence

The defense of superior orders, according to which the accused is not criminally liable for committing an act ordered by his superior, was rejected in article 8 of the Nuremberg Charter although allowed as a factor in mitigation of punishment. In the words of the Charter:

> The fact that the defendant acted pursuant to order of his Government or of a superior shall not free him from responsibility, but may be considered in mitigation of punishment if the Tribunal determines that justice so requires.[39]

The Charter's rejection of an unqualified defense of superior orders reflected the German Military Code[40] and also the newly revised law of war manuals of Great Britain and the United States.[41] Nevertheless, counsel for the defense at a number of points raised the defense of superior orders and, with it, the classical legal positivist doctrine of absolute sovereignty and its corollary, the requirement of unconditional obedience. In considering the relation of the defense to the doctrine of absolute sovereignty, it will be useful to begin with a fairly typical case, that of a foot soldier who is issued iniquitous orders.

Imagine that a soldier in the field has just been ordered by his commanding officer to kill prisoners of war and that the order reflects the will of the military command structure and the policies of the state. The soldier sees himself faced with a genuine moral dilemma posed by the consequences of obedience to the order on the one hand and disobedience on the other. If he obeys, the consequences for the prisoners are clear; and if he disobeys, he is virtually assured of prosecution before a court-martial for a serious violation of military law. The soldier, desiring both to preserve the prisoners' lives and to avoid prosecution, hopes to challenge successfully his commanding officer's order.

One challenge available to him speaks to the morality of the order. Can the soldier legally justify disobedience on grounds that the act in question is immoral? According to the doctrine of absolute sovereignty, he cannot; to contend otherwise is to allow a legal obligation to be overturned on extra-legal grounds—here, on moral grounds. As an expression of the sovereign, the commanding officer's order, coupled with legally unlimited power to enforce obedience, is sufficient to establish a legal obligation, and the obligation is unconditional. If the obligation can be overturned at all, it can be done only by successfully challenging it *qua* legal obligation. One challenge directed to the legal validity of the order is based on the incompatibility of the order with international law, specifically, with the law of war. Can the soldier legally justify disobedience on grounds that the order is contrary to the law of war? Again, according to the doctrine of absolute sovereignty, he cannot; to hold otherwise is to introduce just another "extra-legal" ground. Since the sovereign is incapable of legal limitation, there cannot be, as defense counsel Hans Laternser put it, "any question of a crime if the order requires action which is not directed against the authority of the State, but on the contrary is demanded by that authority."[42]

When associate defense counsel Jahrreiss raised the defense of superior orders, it was not, however, in the familiar context of a foot soldier's orders from his superior, but in the extraordinary context of the Nazi defendants, policy-makers in Hitler's Germany. That Jahrreiss presupposed the doctrine of absolute sovereignty is evident throughout his argument, and nowhere more so than in his reification of the absolute sovereign in the person of Hitler. Jahrreiss first addressed the moral and international legal challenges to orders

classical positive position

violation moral
+
war grounds

given by a superior, challenges we have looked at in connection with the foot soldier. Observing that orders "can always be measured . . . against the rules of international law, morality, and religion," Jahrreiss argued that to allow officials to use such rules to determine for themselves whether orders are lawful and to "decide accordingly whether to obey or refuse" would be to undermine the sovereignty of the state. Unilateral decisions made by officials on the legal validity of orders would in the end imperil the state's "supreme orders, which must be binding on the hierarchy if the authority of the state is to subsist at all." Having dismissed the moral and international legal standards, Jahrreiss asked whether an order could be measured "against the existing written and unwritten law of the state concerned." He addressed himself here specifically to challenges to orders defective in legal form. For example, could an official challenge the legal validity of an order if "the person giving the order has exceeded his competency or made a mistake in form"? Again resting his case on the doctrine of absolute sovereignty, Jahrreiss denied officials this right of challenge, maintaining that "there must under every government exist orders that are binding on the members of the hierarchy under all circumstances, and therefore represent law to the officials concerned, even though outsiders may find that they are defective as regards content or form. . . ."[43]

Jahrreiss'[s] primary interest, however, was in the legal status of the orders of Hitler himself.[44] These directives, decisions, instructions, and the like were defective if judged by traditional standards, the standards, for example, of the Weimar Constitution. But the so-called Enabling Act of 24 March 1933 swept away the old standards. The Act in effect authorized Hitler to change statutory and even constitutional law by decree, thereby giving legal credence to the abolition of the separation of powers in Germany.[45] The result, Jahrreiss argued, was a doctrine of absolute sovereignty personified in Hitler. "Now in a state in which the entire power to make final decisions is concentrated in the hands of a single individual, the orders of this one man are absolutely binding on the members of the hierarchy. This individual is their sovereign, their *legibus solutus*."[46] In offering this characterization of Hitler, Jahrreiss suggests that the Nazi defendants' duty of unconditional obedience to Hitler was not unlike that of the foot soldier's to his commanding officer.

Sir Hartley Shawcross, replying to Jahrreiss'[s] effort to raise the defense of superior orders, expressly rejected the classical legal positivist requirement of unconditional obedience, arguing that "no rule of international law . . . provides immunity for those who obey orders which—whether legal or not in the country where they are issued—are manifestly contrary to the very law of nature from which international law has grown" and are illegal by "every test of international law, of common conscience, [and] of elementary humanity." International law "must consider the legality of what is done by international and not by municipal tests."[47]

Robert H. Jackson, chief of counsel for the United States,[48] argued that the joint use of the defense of superior orders and the defense of act of state generates an absurdity.[49] If individual *A* is not legally responsible for an act because his superior, *B*, ordered him to perform that act, then according to the converse of the defense of superior orders, the doctrine of respondeat superior, *B* is responsible. Now suppose that *B* is head of state. He cannot invoke the defense of superior orders to free himself of responsibility, but he can impute his act to the state as an "act of state." "Those in lower ranks were protected against liability by the orders of their superiors. The superiors were protected because their orders were called acts of state."[50] As Jackson observed, "the combination of these two doctrines means that nobody is responsible."[51]

In its Judgment, the Tribunal reaffirmed article 8 of the Charter, holding its provisions to be "in conformity with the law of all nations." And the Tribunal dismissed the arguments of defense counsel.

> That a soldier was ordered to kill or torture in violation of the international law of war has never been recognized as a defense to such acts of brutality. . . . The true test, which is found in varying degrees in the criminal law of most nations, is not the existence of the order, but whether moral choice was in fact possible.[52]

The Tribunal's "test" conditions the availability of a defense on the possibility of a moral choice, but what was meant by "moral choice" is not obvious. The "choice" may be understood in genuinely moral terms, inviting serious reflection on the propriety of harming or killing innocent persons to avoid one's own punishment or death. On this interpretation, the soldier has a "moral choice" even when faced with death.[53] But "choice" may also be understood simply as ruling out a situation in which, as Brigadier General Telford Taylor expressed it, "opportunity for reflection, choice, and the exercise of responsibility is non-existent or limited."[54] Given either interpretation, what is significant is that the Tribunal based its test on this "choice." For the possibility of a choice to obey runs directly counter to the classical legal positivist requirement of unconditional obedience to state law and involves a rejection of the doctrine underlying that requirement, namely the doctrine of absolute sovereignty.

That the defense of superior orders presupposes sovereignty is not surprising, for the defense plays its primary role in military law, a body of law in which such concepts as authority and orders predominate. As one theorist puts it, a paradigm of "unconditional obedience to an external, norm-establishing authority" is "a military formation, where a host of people are subjected in their movements to a military order to which they all conform."[55] Unlike the superior orders defense, however, the defense of ex post facto law has no obvious connection to the doctrines of classical legal positivism.

VI

Defense counsel at Nuremberg frequently objected that the law of the Charter, in particular one or more of the classes of offenses cited in article 6, was void as ex post facto law. For example, Otto Stahmer, counsel for defendant Goering, protested the creation of "new material law by threatening punishment for crimes which, at the time of their perpetration, at least as far as individuals are concerned, did not carry any punishment."[56]

Speaking generally, to prohibit ex post facto law is to constrain legal officials and agencies from changing the law retroactively in a way that works to the disadvantage of defendants in criminal proceedings. What is known as the ex post facto defense, or the claim made on behalf of a criminal defendant that the prohibition of ex post facto law has been violated, takes a variety of specific forms, at least two of which were evident at Nuremberg. Stahmer's charge of ex post facto law, quoted

above, is an example of the form of the defense sometimes referred to as the rule *nulla poena sine lege,* according to which no person shall be punished for proscribed acts except pursuant to a preexisting statute that fixes a penalty for these acts. To apply the *nulla poena* rule at Nuremberg, it would be sufficient to show that the Charter's provisions made punishable a violation of an obligation that was not punishable at the time of the violation. The *nulla poena* rule raises questions not about the existence of a legal obligation, but only about the enactment of provisions for punishing violations of that obligation. Enactment of such provisions after the fact of violation, that is, post factum, is what the rule prohibits.

According to another form of the ex post facto defense, sometimes termed the rule *nullum crimen sine lege,* no person shall be held criminally liable for acts not expressly proscribed in a preexisting statute. To apply the *nullum crimen* rule at Nuremberg, it would be necessary to show that the Charter's provisions established new obligations that imposed liability retroactively. When defense counsel Stahmer argued that the offense described as conspiracy to wage aggressive war constituted a new obligation, because "conspiracy as used by the Prosecution is entirely unknown to German law," he was invoking the *nullum crimen* rule.[57]

The prohibition of ex post facto law, expressed here in the *nulla poena* and *nullum crimen* rules, is not derivable from the doctrines of classical legal positivism. Indeed, the ex post facto prohibition is generally understood by jurists as an application of the principle of "legality," "*Rechtsstaat*," or "the rule of law," a pervasive principle that embodies the moral ideals of law.[58] Thus understood, the prohibition is not consistent with, much less derivable from, the doctrines of classical legal positivism. While the prohibition marks a point at which law and state power may diverge, classical legal positivism regards law as an expression of state power. And while the prohibition imposes constraints on state power, classical legal positivism holds state power to be unlimited.

How then might defense counsel have invoked the ex post facto prohibition on classical legal positivist grounds? One possibility would have been to invoke it not as a moral constraint on the Tribunal's power to apply Nuremberg Charter law but rather as a logical limitation on that power. In fact, associate defense counsel Jahrreiss did provide part of an argument invoking the ex post facto prohibition on logical, rather than moral, grounds. By drawing on Jahrreiss and by supposing, contrary to fact, that the command doctrine is applicable to the trial (as defense counsel at some points argued), an argument invoking the ex post facto prohibition on logical grounds can be constructed.

Sketched here in terms of the Nuremberg Charter law on crimes against peace, the argument has three distinct parts. *First,* as Jahrreiss argued, at the time the defendants committed the acts for which they were later prosecuted, there were no applicable legal norms proscribing those acts. *Second,* although the Nuremberg Charter represents for the prosecution and Tribunal merely the addition of sanctions to previously existing legal norms, the Charter represents for the classical legal positivist the enactment of new law. *Third,* it is not possible—not possible logically—to apply Charter law to acts antedating the enactment of that law; that is to say, a present command can have no application to a past act. Let us consider each of the three parts of the argument more closely.

In the course of his statement on juridical aspects of the trial, associate defense counsel Jahrreiss argued that at the time the defendants conspired to wage and did wage aggressive war, there were no legal norms proscribing such acts; and that therefore the Charter's article 6(a) dealing with aggressive war—crimes against peace—ran afoul of the prohibition of ex post facto law. There was to be no doubt that the argument would proceed along positivist lines. As Jahrreiss noted, "I am dealing only with the problems of law as it is at present valid, not with the problems of such law as could or should be demanded in the name of ethics or of human progress."[59]

Jahrreiss contended that even if the international norms created by the conventions of the 1920s had enjoyed legal status initially, a point he was by no means willing to concede, by the mid-1930s they had lost all claim to such status.[60] The League of Nations Covenant, providing for the principle of collective responsibility of the members of the League,[61] and the Kellogg-Briand Pact (or Pact of Paris), outlawing war as an instrument of national policy, were dead letters by the mid-1930s. To support his contention, Jahrreiss surveyed the collapse of the system of collective security planned around the League Covenant and the Kellogg-Briand Pact, pointing to a lack of compliance with these conventions and to a lack of any

power to respond to "violations" with sanctions, in effect demonstrating that the power relation of the classical legal positivist's command doctrine was not operative. By the late 1930s, the collapse of collective security arrangements was evident to all, and England, Russia, and the United States said as much. Prime Minister Chamberlain, quoted by Jahrreiss, proclaimed in February of 1938 in the House of Commons that

> . . . the League as constituted today is unable to provide collective security for anybody . . . we must not delude ourselves, and, still more, we must not try to delude small weak nations into thinking that they will be protected by the League against aggression . . . when we know that nothing of the kind can be expected.[62]

Similarly, Russia's attitude toward German designs on Poland—affected not least of all by her desire to share in the spoils—was dictated entirely by "the old rules of power politics." In the German-Russian Frontier and Friendship Pact of 1939, which gave details of the Polish partition, "no mention is made of the Pact of Paris or the League of Nations Covenant." The collapse of the system of collective security, Jahrreiss continued, was also evident to the United States. Taking note in September of 1939 of the state of war in Europe, President Roosevelt insisted that the United States "conform with neutrality regulations in the strictest manner." But far from dealing the system of collective security arrangements a death blow, Jahrreiss argued that the United States declaration of neutrality merely acknowledged that "the system had already been dead for years."[63]

What did all of this mean for the ex post facto law question? In Jahrreiss'[s] view, at the time the defendants conspired to wage aggressive war, there were, for want of compliance and of the power to impose sanctions, no legal norms proscribing such activity. Nor, for the same reasons, were there legal norms proscribing the actual waging of aggressive war. The annexation of Austria, the dismemberment of Czechoslovakia, the destruction of Poland—these German conquests were not, therefore, in violation of international law. Or so Jahrreiss argued.

Given the first part of the argument, provided by Jahrreiss, it can be said that there was no law applicable to the defendants' acts at the time the acts were committed. From this it follows that the Charter, in proscribing aggressive war, enacted new law. To put it another way, the norms established by the conventions of the 1920s had, for want of sanctions, no legal status; the Charter, in attaching sanctions to these preexisting norms, thus marked the emergence of new law.

It is instructive here to compare with Jahrreiss'[s] position that of the prosecution, for whom the Charter merely added to preexisting legal obligations the power to impose sanctions. As United Kingdom chief prosecutor Shawcross put it, "The only innovation which this Charter has introduced is to provide machinery, long overdue, to carry out the existing law, and there is no substance in the complaint that the Charter is a piece of *post factum* legislation. . . ."[64] Shawcross contended that in the international field, "the existence of law has never been dependent on the existence of a correlated sanction external to the law itself."[65] Rejecting the classical legal positivist's characterization of law in terms of the power to impose sanctions and interpreting the preexisting norms as legal obligations, the prosecution granted only that the Charter might be in violation of the *nulla poena* rule. And, as it happened, this was an innocuous concession, for the prosecution (and the Tribunal) refused on both moral and international legal grounds to recognize the *nulla poena* rule.[66]

More generally, the contrast between the position of the prosecution and that of Jahrreiss is this: What for the prosecution was merely the addition of sanctions to preexisting law was for the positivist-minded defense counsel the enactment of new law. And what would have been for the prosecution merely a violation of the *nulla poena* rule (had the prosecution been disposed to recognize this rule), was for the positivist-minded defense counsel a violation of the *nullum crimen* rule.

Given the second part of the classical legal positivist argument invoking the ex post facto defense, the Charter's article 6(a) proscribing aggressive war can be said to represent new law, and in the Nuremberg proceedings this law was applied to a period of time prior to the law's enactment. It is this application of Charter law that violates the *nullum crimen* rule and prompts the classical legal positivist to raise an objection based not on morality but on logic. What purports to be an application of law to a time antedating the law's enactment is, the positivist argues, not even a possible application. As Austin puts it, "Obligation regards the future. An obligation to a past act, or an obligation to a past forbearance, is a contradiction in terms."[67]

The "contradiction" that Austin speaks of here may be demonstrated by appealing to the power relation, one component of the classical legal positivist's command doctrine, and specifically, to the requirement of the power relation that there be at least a possibility of compliance with the directive. (i) In the case of a directive to perform a past act, one lacks the ability to comply, thereby ruling out any possibility of compliance with the directive. (ii) But if there is no possibility of compliance, there exists no power relation between the directing and directed parties. (iii) Finally, if there exists no power relation, the directive in question is not a command, not a legal norm. The "contradiction" is thus generated by the supposition that the modality of command, understood by Austin as entailing the ability of the commanded party to perform, may have among its instances commands that ex hypothesi cannot be performed.

Although a legal agency cannot apply law to a period of time prior to enactment of the law, it may, notwithstanding this logical disability, have extra-legal power to impose penalties for acts committed prior to enactment of the law. Why is such power extra-legal? Because the legal power to impose penalties or sanctions is, for the classical legal positivist, noncontingently linked to the issuing of commands.[68] Where there is no command, as in the case of a directive to perform a past act, the subsequent imposition of a penalty cannot be for failing to comply with a command. But where the penalty is not a response to a "commanded" act or forbearance, it is not a response to any legally recognized act or forbearance. It is, in the classical legal positivist's view, extra-legal.

The Tribunal presented a view of the ex post facto question diametrically opposed to that sketched above. Briefly reviewing "the state of international law in 1939," the Tribunal argued, concerning crimes against peace, that the Kellogg-Briand Pact was binding on the sixty-three nations, "including Germany, Italy, and Japan," that had signed the pact. The pact was binding even though it "does not expressly enact that [aggressive] wars are crimes, or set up courts to try those who make such wars."[69] As authority for its position the Tribunal appealed to the parallel case of war crimes. The signatories of the Hague Convention of 1907,[70] which "prohibited resort to certain methods of waging war," were, the Tribunal observed, bound by the obligations expressed therein, even though the Convention nowhere designates as criminal certain methods of waging war or prescribes any sentence or makes "any mention . . . of a court [with jurisdiction] to try and punish offenders."[71]

Contending that international norms may be identified as legal norms apart from the power relation of the classical legal positivist's command doctrine, the Tribunal, like chief prosecuting counsel Shawcross, was not sympathetic to the view that the Charter's addition of sanctions to international norms marked the enactment of new law; and it was, therefore, unmoved by the contention of defense counsel that, in its application, the Charter was ex post facto law.

━━

VII

It has been my concern to show that noncontingent links exist between doctrines of classical legal positivism on the one hand and the Nuremberg criminal defenses on the other. The defenses of act of state and superior orders both presuppose the doctrine of absolute sovereignty, presuppositions illustrated, respectively, by Austin's analysis of positive legal rights as triadic relations and by the requirement of unconditional obedience. One feature of the command doctrine, the requirement of the power relation that the commanded party be able to comply, provides a basis for invoking the *nullum crimen* rule, one form of the defense of ex post facto law.

These noncontingent links are noteworthy, for they provide a means of replying to the skeptic, who explains the rejection of criminal defenses at Nuremberg in altogether parochial terms and denies that the rejection can be justified. Although the Tribunal's rejection of the defenses may appear arbitrary or capricious when the defenses are considered independently of their underlying classical legal positivist doctrines, the skeptic is challenged once it is shown, as the noncontingent links show, that the rejection of the defenses follows from the rejection of underlying classical legal positivist doctrines. Moreover, good reasons can be given, I believe, for the rejection of the underlying doctrines.

A complete reply to the skeptic would require a statement of these reasons. I have tried here to set the stage for such a statement; the elaboration of the reasons themselves would ultimately call for a philosophy of international law.

Endnotes

[1] Academic lawyers, however, have been aware of the underlying philosophical dispute. See A. L. Goodhart, "The Legality of the Nuremberg Trials," *Juridical Review* 58 (1946): 1–19; A. L. Goodhart, "Questions and Answers Concerning the Nuremberg Trials," *International Law Quarterly* 1 (1947): 525–531; Lord Wright, "Natural Law and International Law," *Interpretations of Modern Legal Philosophies*, ed. Paul Sayre (New York, 1947), pp. 794–807; Lord Wright, "War Crimes under International Law," *Law Quarterly Review* 62 (1946): 40–52; Quincy Wright, "Legal Positivism and the Nuremberg Judgment," *American Journal of International Law* 42 (1948): 405–414. In these papers there are attempts to defend the legitimacy of the Nuremberg Trials in terms of "Justice and its handmaid, Natural Law," as Lord Wright puts it. For discussion on related issues, see H. L. A. Hart, "Positivism and the Separation of Law and Morals," *Harvard Law Review* 71 (1958): 593, 615–621; and Lon L. Fuller, "Positivism and Fidelity to Law—A Reply to Professor Hart," *Harvard Law Review* 71 (1958): 630, 648–661.

I have profited from Quincy Wright's paper (above), and from Hans Kelsen's paper on "Collective and Individual Responsibility" (see fn. 24, below). Both papers are suggestive on the relationship of legal positivism to the act of state defense, one of my particular concerns.

[2] With incidental exceptions, all of the trial material I consider is from the November 1945–October 1946 proceedings of the International Military Tribunal at Nuremberg, reported in the first 22 volumes of *Trial of the Major War Criminals before the International Military Tribunal* (Nuremberg, 1947–1949), hereafter cited as *IMT*, with volume number preceding and page number(s) following. Additional material, which also supports the position I argue here, may be found in the October 1946–April 1949 proceedings of the United States Military Tribunal at Nuremberg, reported in the 15 volumes of *Trials of War Criminals before the Nuernberg Military Tribunals under Control Council Law No. 10* (Washington, 1949–1953), hereafter cited as *NMT*, with volume number preceding and page number(s) following.

[3] Jean Bodin, *Six Books of the Commonwealth*, trans. M. J. Tooley (Oxford, 1955), pp. 25, 28.

[4] John Austin, *The Province of Jurisprudence Determined*, ed. H. L. A. Hart (London, 1954), p. 11. First published in 1832, the *Province* consists of the first six lectures of what was published posthumously as the

Lectures on Jurisprudence (see fn.8, below). (Here, as in all of the material I quote, the emphasis is in the original.)

[5] Austin, *Province*, p. 17, and see pp. 13–14.

[6] In a forthcoming paper entitled "Two Models of Legal Commands," I consider in some detail the command doctrine and the role played therein by the power relation.

[7] Austin, *Province*, p. 24.

[8] Ibid., p. 14; John Austin, *Lectures on Jurisprudence*, 5th ed. (London, 1885), vol. 1, p. 453.

[9] James Bryce, *Studies in History and Jurisprudence* (New York, 1901), vol. 2, p. 505.

[10] Austin, *Province*, pp. 193–194.

[11] Ibid., p. 254.

[12] See generally ibid., pp. 118–157.

[13] Ibid., p. 140.

[14] See, respectively, Sir Henry Maine, *Lectures on the Early History of Institutions* (London, 1875), chaps. 12–13; Bryce, *Studies*, vol. 2, chap. 10; H. L. A. Hart, *The Concept of Law* (Oxford, 1961), chaps. 2–3; Roger Fisher, "Bringing Law to Bear on Governments," *Harvard Law Review* 74 (1961): 1130–1140; and generally, Hart, *The Concept of Law*, chaps. 2–4.

[15] Ronald M. Dworkin, "The Model of Rules," *University of Chicago Law Review* 35 (1967): 14, 17, reprinted under the title "Is Law a System of Rules?" in *Essays in Legal Philosophy*, ed. Robert S. Summers (Oxford, 1968), pp. 25, 28.

[16] London Agreement, 8 Aug. 1945, 1 *IMT* 8–9. The plan followed the Moscow Declaration of 30 Oct. 1943, *Department of State Bulletin* 9 (1943): 307, 310–311.

[17] The following quotations are from 1 *IMT* 11.

[18] This language, corresponding to the language of Count One in the Indictment (1 *IMT* 29), appears to apply to all three of the aforementioned classes of offenses. In its Judgment, however, the Tribunal held that the Charter's language on conspiracy did not itself establish "a new and separate crime" and that the corresponding count in the Indictment therefore applied only to crimes against peace, for which article 6(a) of the Charter established law dealing with a "Common Plan or Conspiracy." 1 *IMT* 226.

[19] See Indictment, 1 *IMT* 27–92.

[20] Judgment, 1 *IMT* 222, 224, 226, 254–255.

[21] See ibid., pp. 279–341; and Sentences, 1 *IMT* 365–367.

[22] See judgment, 1 *IMT* 255–279.

[23] 1 *IMT* 12.

[24] Hans Kelsen, "Collective and Individual Responsibility in International Law with Particular Regard to the Punishment of War Criminals," *California Law Review* 31 (1943): 530, 533. Associate defense counsel Jahrreiss cited Kelsen's paper as authority for the position that "in questions of breach of the peace, the liability of individuals to punishment does not exist according to general international law at present valid." 17 *IMT* 478. Kelsen, however, was not in sympathy with Jahrreiss'[s] defense. Anticipating the prosecution of Axis war criminals, Kelsen had argued that in their case the enactment of rules to establish individual criminal liability retroactively would be justified on moral grounds. See Kelsen, *Peace Through Law* (Chapel Hill, 1944), pp. 87–88, and "The Rule against *Ex Post Facto* Laws and the Prosecution of the Axis War Criminals," *Judge Advocate Journal* 2 (1945): 8–12, 46.

[25] See Austin, *Province*, p. 284.

[26] Ibid., p. 290.

[27] Kelsen, "Collective and Individual Responsibility," p. 539.

[28] See Austin, *Province*, pp. 265–266.

[29] See, e.g., Lord Cave, in Johnstone v. Pedlar, *Appeal Cases* 2 (1921): 262, 275: "When a wrong has been done by the King's officer to a British subject, the person wronged has no legal remedy against the Sovereign, for 'the King can do no wrong'; but he may sue the King's officer for the tortious act, and the latter cannot plead the authority of the Sovereign, for 'from the maxim that the King cannot do wrong it follows, as a necessary consequence, that the King cannot authorize wrong.' "

[30] See Austin, *Province*, p. 139.

[31] Professor of law at Cologne and associate defense counsel for defendant Jodl, Hermann Jahrreiss delivered a long statement on juridical aspects of the trial: it represents the most sustained effort by defense counsel to provide a philosophical basis for the defense position. See 17 *IMT* 458–494. For later reflections by Jahrreiss, see his testimony before the United States Military Tribunal at Nuremberg as an expert defense witness on German constitutional law, in 3 *NMT* 252–284. See also his "Die Fortentwicklung des Völkerrechts," *Jahrbuch für Internationales und Ausländisches Öffentliches Recht* 2 (1949): 654–666, reprinted in Jahrreiss, *Mensch und Staat* (Cologne, 1957), pp. 233–253.

[32] See generally 17 *IMT* 476–481.

[33] General Treaty for Renunciation of War as an Instrument of National Policy, 27 Aug. 1928, *League of Nations Treaty Series* 94 (1929): 57–64.

[34] 17 *IMT* 476, 477, 478.

[35] English barrister, attorney general, Labor member of Parliament, and chief prosecutor for the United Kingdom, Sir Hartley Shawcross was perhaps philosophically the most sophisticated counsel arguing before the International Military Tribunal. See his opening statement, 3 *IMT* 91–145, and closing statement, 19

IMT 433–529. For later reflections see his "International Law: A Statement of the British View of Its Role," *American Bar Association Journal* 33 (1947): 31–35, and "Robert H. Jackson's Contributions during the Nuremberg Trials," *Mr. Justice Jackson: Four Lectures in His Honor* (New York, 1969), pp. 87–136.

[36] See generally 19 *IMT* 458–465.

[37] Ibid., p. 463. (Here I draw the quotation from the British printing of the trial proceedings, *The Trial of German Major War Criminals* 19 [1949]: 426, since there is an error at this point in the *IMT* text of the proceedings.) See also 3 *IMT* 94.

[38] Judgment, 1 *IMT* 223.

[39] 1 *IMT* 12.

[40] § 47, *Militärstrafgesetzbuch.* Law of 10 Oct. 1940, *Reichsgesetzblatt*, Teil 1 (1940): 1347, 1351. Section 47 denied the unqualified defense to one who "went beyond the order as given" or acted knowing "that the superior's order referred to an act aimed at a civil or military felony or misdemeanor." Although defendant Jodl was reported to have said that he did not remember a single prosecution under section 47 "in his 30 years of service" (19 *IMT* 43, Exner, defense counsel), section 47 had been used in the past and had yielded a conviction in the well-known *Llandovery Castle* case—a 1921 German prosecution stemming from the First World War, in which two German submarine officers were charged with shooting at British lifeboats in violation of the laws of war. See "German War Trials: Judgment in the Case of Lieutenants Dithmar and Boldt," *American Journal of International Law* 16 (1922): 708–724.

[41] Until 1944, the British *Manual of the Laws and Usages of War on Land* and the U.S. *Rules of Land Warfare* both allowed the defense, the latter specifically providing that "Individuals of the armed forces will not be punished for these offenses [i.e., for violations of the laws of war] in case they are committed under the orders or sanction of their government or commanders." FM 27–10, 1 Oct. 1940 ed., para. 347. In 1944, both the British *Manual* and the U.S. *Rules* rejected the defense, the latter providing that "Individuals and organizations who violate the accepted laws and customs of war may be punished therefor. However, the fact that the acts complained of were done pursuant to order of a superior or government sanction may be taken into consideration in determining culpability, either by way of defense or in mitigation of punishment. The person giving such orders may also be punished." Para. 345.1 (change of 15 Nov. 1944). The British Ministry of Defence *Manual of Military Law*, 12th ed. (1972), Part I, para. 23, and Part III, para. 627, and the United States Department of the Army *Law of Land Warfare*, FM 27–10 (1956), para. 509(a), have both maintained this later position.

[42] 22 *IMT* 83.

[43] 17 *IMT* 484–485.

[44] See generally ibid., pp. 481–494.

[45] *Gesetz zur Behebung der Not von Volk und Reich* [Law for Eliminating the Distress of People and Reich]. Law of 24 Mar. 1933, *Reichsgesetzblatt*, Teil 1 (1933): 141. See art. 1 (in part): "Apart from the procedure provided in the Reich Constitution, laws of the Reich can also be decreed by the Reich Government"; and art. 2 (in part): "Laws decreed by the Reich Government may depart from the Reich Constitution as long as they do not have as their object the institutions of the Reich Parliament [*Reichstag*] and the Reich Council [*Reichsrat*] as such." See also Jahrreiss'[s] discussion of the so-called Enabling Act in his testimony as an expert defense witness, 3 *NMT* 252–284.

[46] 17 *IMT* 486.

[47] 19 *IMT* 465–466.

[48] Mr. Justice Jackson interrupted his tenure on the Supreme Court to represent the United States at the London Conference (see fn. 16, above) and to argue before the International Military Tribunal as chief of counsel of the United States prosecution. The "Report from Robert H. Jackson to the President," *Department of State Bulletin* 12 (1945): 1071–1078, is a projection of the prosecution's arguments. For Jackson's arguments at trial, see his well-known opening statement, 2 *IMT* 98–155, reprinted as Robert H. Jackson, *The Case against the Nazi War Criminals* (New York, 1946); and his closing statement, 19 *IMT* 397–432. For later reflections see Jackson, "Nürnberg in Retrospect," *Canadian Bar Review* 27 (1949): 761–781, reprinted in *American Bar Association Journal* 35 (1949): 813–816, 881–887.

[49] 2 *IMT* 149–150. See also 19 *IMT* 423–424; and "Report to the President," pp. 1073–1074.

[50] 2 *IMT* 150.

[51] "Report to the President," p. 1073.

[52] 1 *IMT* 224.

[53] See Morris Greenspan, *The Modern Law of Land Warfare* (Berkeley, 1959), p. 494.

[54] *The High Command Case* (United States v. Wilhelm von Leeb, et al.), 11 *NMT* 373. (Telford Taylor, an associate trial counsel for the United States prosecution at the International Military Trial, was chief of counsel for the prosecution at the later United States Military Trials.)

[55] E. B. Pashukanis, "The General Theory of Law and Marxism," *Soviet Legal Philosophy*, trans. H. W. Babb (Cambridge, Mass., 1951), p. 154, cited in Lon L. Fuller, *The Morality of Law*, 2nd ed. (New Haven, 1969), p. 113.

[56] 17 *IMT* 501.

[57] Ibid., pp. 508–509.

[58] For applications of the principle of legality to the prohibition of ex post facto law, see Fuller, *The Morality of Law*, pp. 41–44, 51–62; Jerome Hall, *General Principles of Criminal Law*, 2nd ed. (Indianapolis, 1960), chap. 2; John Rawls, *A Theory of Justice* (Cambridge, Mass., 1971), p. 238.

[59] 17 *IMT* 459.

[60] See ibid., pp. 467–469.

[61] See League of Nations Covenant, art. 16, para. 1.

[62] 17 *IMT* 465.

[63] Ibid., pp. 466, 467.

[64] 19 *IMT* 464.

[65] Ibid., p. 463.

[66] Shawcross'[s] statement here is representative: "There is all the difference between saying to a man, 'You will now be punished for what was not a crime at all at the time you committed it,' and in saying to him, 'You will now pay the penalty for conduct which was contrary to law and a crime when you executed it, although, owing to the imperfection of the international machinery, there was at that time no court competent to pronounce judgment against you.' It is that latter course which we adopt, and if that be retroactivity, we proclaim it to be most fully consistent with that higher justice which, in the practice of civilized states, has set a definite limit to the retroactive operation of laws." 3 *IMT* 106. See also 2 *IMT* 144 (Jackson); Judgment, 1 *IMT* 219–221; Judgment, *The Hostage Case* (United States v. Wilhelm List, et al.), 11 *NMT* 1239.

[67] Austin, *Lectures*, vol. 1, p. 444, and see pp. 485–486. See also Austin, *Province*, p. 20.

[68] See Austin, *Province*, pp. 14, 17–18.

[69] Judgment, 1 *IMT* 219, 220.

[70] Hague Convention No. IV Respecting the Laws and Customs of War on Land, 18 Oct. 1907, *U.S. Statutes at Large* 36 (1911): 2277–2309.

[71] Judgment, 1 *IMT* 220–221.

Letter from Birmingham Jail

MARTIN LUTHER KING, JR.

My dear Fellow Clergymen,

While confined here in the Birmingham city jail, I came across your recent statement calling our present activities "unwise and untimely." Seldom, if ever, do I pause to answer criticism of my work and ideas. If I sought to answer all of the criticisms that cross my desk, my secretaries would be engaged in little else in the course of the day, and I would have no time for constructive work. But since I feel that you are men of genuine good will and your criticisms are sincerely set forth, I would like to answer your statement in what I hope will be patient and reasonable terms.

I think I should give the reason for my being in Birmingham, since you have been influenced by the argument of "outsiders coming in." I have the honor of serving as president of the Southern Christian Leadership Conference, an organization operating in every southern state, with headquarters in Atlanta, Georgia. We have some eighty-five affiliate organizations all across the South—one being the Alabama Christian Movement for Human Rights. Whenever necessary and possible we share staff, educational and financial resources with our affiliates. Several months ago our local affiliate here in Birmingham invited us to be on call to engage in a nonviolent direct-action program if such were deemed necessary. We readily consented and when the hour came we lived up to our promises. So I am here, along with several members of my staff, because we were invited here. I am here because I have basic organizational ties here.

Beyond this, I am in Birmingham because injustice is here. Just as the eighth century prophets left their little villages and carried their "thus saith the Lord" far beyond the boundaries of their home-towns; and just as the Apostle Paul left his little village of Tarsus and carried the gospel of Jesus Christ to practically every hamlet and city of the Graeco-Roman world, I too am compelled to carry the gospel of freedom beyond my particular home-town. Like Paul, I must constantly respond to the Macedonian call for aid.

Moreover, I am cognizant of the interrelated-ness of all communities and states. I cannot sit idly by in Atlanta and not be concerned about what happens in Birmingham. Injustice anywhere is a threat to justice everywhere. We are caught in an inescapable network of mutuality, tied in a single garment of destiny. Whatever affects one directly affects all indirectly. Never again can we afford to live with the narrow, provincial "outside agitator" idea. Anyone who lives in the United States can never be considered an outsider anywhere in this country.

You deplore the demonstrations that are pres-ently taking place in Birmingham. But I am sorry that your statement did not express a similar con-cern for the conditions that brought the demon-strations into being. I am sure that each of you would want to go beyond the superficial social analyst who looks merely at effects, and does not grapple with underlying causes. I would not hesi-tate to say that it is unfortunate that so-called dem-onstrations are taking place in Birmingham at this time, but I would say in more emphatic terms that it is even more unfortunate that the white power structure of this city left the Negro community with no other alternative.

. . .

You may well ask, "Why direct action? Why sit-ins, marches, etc.? Isn't negotiation a better path?" You are exactly right in your call for negoti-ation. Indeed, this is the purpose of direct action. Nonviolent direct action seeks to create such a cri-sis and establish such creative tension that a com-munity that has constantly refused to negotiate is forced to confront the issue. It seeks so to drama-tize the issue that it can no longer be ignored. I just referred to the creation of tension as a part of the work of the nonviolent resister. This may sound rather shocking. But I must confess that I am not afraid of the word tension. I have earnestly worked

and preached against violent tension, but there is a type of constructive nonviolent tension that is nec-essary for growth. Just as Socrates felt that it was necessary to create a tension in the mind so that individuals could rise from the bondage of myths and half-truths to the unfettered realm of creative analysis and objective appraisal, we must see the need of having nonviolent gadflies to create the kind of tension in society that will help men to rise from the dark depths of prejudice and racism to the majestic heights of understanding and brother-hood. So the purpose of the direct action is to create a situation so crisis-packed that it will inevi-tably open the door to negotiation. We, therefore, concur with you in your call for negotiation. Too long has our beloved Southland been bogged down in the tragic attempt to live in monologue rather than dialogue.

. . .

We know through painful experience that freedom is never voluntarily given by the op-pressor; it must be demanded by the oppressed. Frankly, I have never yet engaged in a [direct-action] movement that was "well-timed," accord-ing to the timetable of those who have not suffered unduly from the disease of segregation. For years now I have heard the words "Wait!" It rings in the ear of every Negro with a piercing familiarity. This "Wait" has almost always meant "Never." It has been a tranquilizing thalidomide, relieving the emotional stress for a moment, only to give birth to an ill-formed infant of frustration. We must come to see with the distinguished jurist of yesterday that "justice too long delayed is justice denied." We have waited for more than 340 years for our constitutional and God-given rights. The nations of Asia and Africa are moving with jetlike speed to-ward the goal of political independence, and we still creep at horse and buggy pace toward the gaining of a cup of coffee at a lunch counter. I guess it is easy for those who have never felt the stinging darts of segregation to say, "Wait." But when you have seen vicious mobs lynch your mothers and fathers at will and drown your sisters and brothers at whim; when you have seen hate-filled po-licemen curse, kick, brutalize and even kill your black brothers and sisters with impunity; when you see the vast majority of your twenty million Negro brothers smothering in an airtight cage of poverty in the midst of an affluent society; when you suddenly find your tongue twisted and your speech stammering as you seek to explain to your six-year-old daughter why she can't go to the public amusement park that has just been advertised on television, and see tears welling up in her little eyes when she is told that Funtown is closed to colored children, and see the depressing clouds of inferiority begin to form in her little mental sky, and see her begin to distort her little personality by unconsciously developing a bitterness toward white people; when you have to concoct an answer for a five-year-old son asking in agonizing pathos: "Daddy, why do white people treat colored people so mean?"; when you take a cross-country drive and find it necessary to sleep night after night in the uncomfortable corners of your automobile because no motel will accept you; when you are humiliated day in and day out by nagging signs reading "white" and "colored"; when your first name becomes "nigger" and your middle name becomes "boy" (however old you are) and your last name becomes "John," and when your wife and mother are never given the respected title "Mrs."; when you are harried by day and haunted by night by the fact that you are a Negro, living constantly at tiptoe stance never quite knowing what to expect next, and plagued with inner fears and outer resentments; when you are forever fighting a degenerating sense of "nobodiness"; then you will understand why we find it difficult to wait. There comes a time when the cup of endurance runs over, and men are no longer willing to be plunged into an abyss of injustice where they experience the blackness of corroding despair. I hope, sirs, you can understand our legitimate and unavoidable impatience.

You express a great deal of anxiety over our willingness to break laws. This is certainly a legitimate concern. Since we so diligently urge people to obey the Supreme Court's decision of 1954 outlawing segregation in the public schools, it is rather strange and paradoxical to find us consciously breaking laws. One may well ask, "How can you advocate breaking some laws and obeying others?" The answer is found in the fact that there are two types of laws: there are *just* and there are *unjust* laws. I would agree with Saint Augustine that "An unjust law is no law at all."

Now what is the difference between the two? How does one determine when a law is just or unjust? A just law is a man-made code that squares with the moral law or the law of God. An unjust law is a code that is out of harmony with the moral law. To put it in the terms of Saint Thomas Aquinas, an unjust law is a human law that is not rooted in eternal and natural law. Any law that uplifts human personality is just. Any law that degrades human personality is unjust. All segregation statutes are unjust because segregation distorts the soul and damages the personality. It gives the segregator a false sense of superiority, and the segregated a false sense of inferiority. To use the words of Martin Buber, the great Jewish philosopher, segregation substitutes an "I-it" relationship for the "I-thou" relationship, and ends up relegating persons to the status of things. So segregation is not only politically, economically and sociologically unsound, but it is morally wrong and sinful. Paul Tillich has said that sin is separation. Isn't segregation an existential expression of man's tragic separation, an expression of his awful estrangement, his terrible sinfulness? So I can urge men to disobey segregation ordinances because they are morally wrong.

Let us turn to a more concrete example of just and unjust laws. An unjust law is a code that a majority inflicts on a minority that is not binding on itself. This is difference made legal. On the other hand a just law is a code that a majority compels a minority to follow that it is willing to follow itself. This is sameness made legal.

Let me give another explanation. An unjust law is a code inflicted upon a minority which that minority had no part in enacting or creating because they did not have the unhampered right to vote. Who can say that the legislature of Alabama which set up the segregation laws was democratically elected? Throughout the state of Alabama all types of conniving methods are used to prevent Negroes from becoming registered voters and there are some counties without a single Negro registered to vote despite the fact that the Negro constitutes a majority of the population. Can any law set up in such a state be considered democratically structured?

These are just a few examples of unjust and just laws. There are some instances when a law is just on its face and unjust in its application. For instance, I was arrested Friday on a change of parading without a permit. Now there is nothing wrong with an ordinance which requires a permit for a parade, but when the ordinance is used to preserve segregation and to deny citizens the First Amendment privilege of peaceful assembly and peaceful protest, then it becomes unjust.

I hope you can see the distinction I am trying

2. breaking vs Non-compliance

Anarchy

to point out. In no sense do I advocate evading or defying the law as the rabid segregationist would do. This would lead to anarchy. One who breaks an unjust law must do it *openly*, *lovingly* (not hatefully as the white mothers did in New Orleans when they were seen on television screaming "nigger, nigger, nigger"), and with a willingness to accept the penalty. I submit that an individual who breaks a law that conscience tells him is unjust, and willingly accepts the penalty by staying in jail to arouse the conscience of the community over its injustice, is in reality expressing the very highest respect for law.

Of course, there is nothing new about this kind of civil disobedience. It was seen sublimely in the refusal of Shadrach, Meshach and Abednego to obey the laws of Nebuchadnezzar because a higher moral law was involved. It was practiced superbly by the early Christians who were willing to face hungry lions and the excruciating pain of chopping blocks, before submitting to certain unjust laws of the Roman Empire. To a degree academic freedom is a reality today because Socrates practiced civil disobedience.

Accepting Positivism

We can never forget that everything Hitler did in Germany was "legal" and everything the Hungarian freedom fighters did in Hungary was "illegal." It was "illegal" to aid and comfort a Jew in Hitler's Germany. But I am sure that if I had lived in Germany during that time I would have aided and comforted my Jewish brothers even though it was illegal. If I lived in a Communist country today where certain principles dear to the Christian faith are suppressed, I believe I would openly advocate disobeying these anti-religious laws. I must make two honest confessions to you, my Christian and Jewish brothers. First, I must confess that over the last few years I have been gravely disappointed with the white moderate. I have almost reached the regrettable conclusion that the Negro's great stumbling block in the stride toward freedom is not the White Citizen's Counciler or the Ku Klux Klanner, but the white moderate who is more devoted to "order" than to justice; who prefers a negative peace which is the absence of tension to a positive peace which is the presence of justice; who constantly says, "I agree with you in the goal you seek, but I can't agree with your methods of direct action"; who paternalistically feels that he can set the timetable for another man's freedom; who lives by the myth of time and who constantly advised the Negro to wait until a "more convenient season." Shallow understanding from people of good will is

more frustrating than absolute misunderstanding from people of ill will. Lukewarm acceptance is much more bewildering than outright rejection.

I had hoped that the white moderate would understand that law and order exist for the purpose of establishing justice, and that when they fail to do this they become dangerously structured dams that block the flow of social progress. I had hoped that the white moderate would understand that the present tension of the South is merely a necessary phase of the transition from an obnoxious negative peace, where the Negro passively accepted his unjust plight, to a substance-filled positive peace, where all men will respect the dignity and worth of human personality. Actually, we who engage in nonviolent direct action are not the creators of tension. We merely bring to the surface the hidden tension that is already alive. We bring it out in the open where it can be seen and dealt with. Like a boil that can never be cured as long as it is covered up but must be opened with all its pus-flowing ugliness to the natural medicines of air and light, injustice must likewise be exposed, with all of the tension its exposing creates, to the light of human conscience and the air of national opinion before it can be cured.

In your statement you asserted that our actions, even though peaceful, must be condemned because they precipitate violence. But can this assertion be logically made? Isn't this like condemning the robbed man because his possession of money precipitated the evil act of robbery? Isn't this like condemning Socrates because his unswerving commitment to truth and his philosophical delvings precipitated the misguided popular mind to make him drink the hemlock? Isn't this like condemning Jesus because His unique God-consciousness and never-ceasing devotion to his will precipitated the evil act of crucifixion? We must come to see, as federal courts have consistently affirmed, that it is immoral to urge an individual to withdraw his efforts to gain his basic constitutional rights because the quest precipitates violence. Society must protect the robbed and punish the robber.

. . .

In spite of my shattered dreams of the past, I came to Birmingham with the hope that the white religious leadership of this community would see the justice of our cause, and with deep moral concern, serve as the channel through which our just grievances would get to the power structure. I had hoped that each of you would understand. But again I have been disappointed. I have heard numerous religious leaders of the South call upon their worshippers to comply with a desegregation decision because it is the *law,* but I have longed to hear white ministers say, "Follow this decree because integration is morally *right* and the Negro is your brother." In the midst of blatant injustices inflicted upon the Negro, I have watched white churches stand on the sideline and merely mouth pious irrelevancies and sanctimonious trivialities. In the midst of a mighty struggle to rid our nation of racial and economic injustice, I have heard so many ministers say, "Those are social issues with which the gospel has no real concern," and I have watched so many churches commit themselves to a completely otherworldly religion which made a strange distinction between body and soul, the sacred and the secular.

. . .

I must close now. But before closing I am impelled to mention one other point in your statement that troubled me profoundly. You warmly commended the Birmingham police force for keeping "order" and "preventing violence." I don't believe you would have so warmly commended the police force if you had seen its angry violent dogs literally biting six unarmed, nonviolent Negroes. I don't believe you would so quickly commend the policemen if you would observe their ugly and inhuman treatment of Negroes here in the city jail; if you would watch them push and curse old Negro women and young Negro girls; if you would see them slap and kick old Negro men and young boys; if you will observe them, as they did on two occasions, refuse to give us food because we wanted to sing our grace together. I'm sorry that I can't join you in your praise for the police department.

It is true that they have been rather disciplined in their public handling of the demonstrators. In this sense they have been rather publicly "nonviolent." But for what purpose? To preserve the evil system of segregation. Over the last few years I have consistently preached that nonviolence demands that the means we use must be as pure as the ends we seek. So I have tried to make it clear that it is wrong to use immoral means to attain moral ends. But now I must affirm that it is just as wrong, or even more so, to use moral means to preserve immoral ends. Maybe Mr. Connor and his policemen have been rather publicly nonviolent, as Chief Pritchett was in Albany, Georgia, but they have used the moral means of nonviolence to maintain the immoral end of flagrant racial injustice. T. S. Eliot has said that there is no greater treason than to do the right deed for the wrong reason.

Positivism and Fidelity to Law

LON FULLER

Professor Hart has made an enduring contribution to the literature of legal philosophy. I doubt if the issues he discusses will ever again assume quite the form they had before being touched

From *Harvard Law Review,* Vol. 71 (1958), pp. 630–672. Copyright © 1958 by the Harvard Law Review Association. Reprinted with permission of the *Harvard Law Review* and the Trustee for the Lon L. Fuller Trust.

by his analytical powers. His argument is no mere restatement of Bentham, Austin, Gray, and Holmes. Their views receive in his exposition a clarity and a new depth that are uniquely his own.

I must confess that when I first encountered the thoughts of Professor Hart's essay, his argument seemed to me to suffer from a deep inner contradiction. On the one hand, he rejects emphatically any confusion of "what is" with "what ought to be." He will tolerate no "merger" of law and conceptions of what law ought to be, but at the most an antiseptic "intersection." Intelligible communication on any subject, he seems to imply, becomes impossible if we leave it uncertain whether we are talking about "what is" or "what ought to be." Yet it was precisely this uncertainty about Professor Hart's own argument which made it difficult for me at first to follow the thread of his thought. At times he seemed to be saying that the distinction between law and morality is something that exists, and will continue to exist, however we may talk about it. It expresses a reality which, whether we like it or not, we must accept if we are to avoid talking nonsense. At other times, he seemed to be warning us that the reality of the distinction is itself in danger and that if we do not mend our ways of thinking and talking we may lose a "precious moral ideal," that of fidelity to law. It is not clear, in other words, whether in Professor Hart's own thinking the distinction between law and morality simply "is," or is something that "ought to be" and that we should join with him in helping to create and maintain.

These were the perplexities I had about Professor Hart's argument when I first encountered it. But on reflection I am sure any criticism of his essay as being self-contradictory would be both unfair and unprofitable. There is no reason why the argument for a strict separation of law and morality cannot be rested on the double ground that this separation serves both intellectual clarity and moral integrity. If there are certain difficulties in bringing these two lines of reasoning into proper relation to one another, these difficulties affect also the position of those who reject the views of Austin, Gray, and Holmes. For those of us who find the "positivist" position unacceptable do ourselves rest our argument on the double ground that its intellectual clarity is specious and that its effects are, or may be, harmful. On the one hand, we assert that Austin's definition of law, for example, violates the reality it purports to describe. Being false in fact, it cannot serve effectively what Kelsen calls "an interest of cognition." On the other hand, we assert that under some conditions the same conception of law may become dangerous, since in human affairs what men mistakenly accept as real tends, by the very act of their acceptance, to become real.

It is a cardinal virtue of Professor Hart's argument that for the first time it opens the way for a truly profitable exchange of views between those whose differences center on the distinction between law and morality. Hitherto there has been no real joinder of issue between the opposing camps. On the one side, we encounter a series of definitional fiats. A rule of law is—that is to say, it really and simply and always is—the command of a sovereign, a rule laid down by a judge, a prediction of the future incidence of state force, a pattern of official behavior, etc. When we ask what purpose these definitions serve, we receive the answer, "Why, no purpose, except to describe accurately the social reality that corresponds to the word 'law.'" When we reply, "But it doesn't look like that to me," the answer comes back, "Well, it does to me." There the matter has to rest.

This state of affairs has been most unsatisfactory for those of us who are convinced that "positivistic" theories have had a distorting effect on the aims of legal philosophy. Our dissatisfaction arose not merely from the impasse we confronted, but because this impasse seemed to us so unnecessary. All that was needed to surmount it was an acknowledgment on the other side that its definitions of "what law really is" are not mere images of some datum of experience, but direction posts for the application of human energies. Since this acknowledgement was not forthcoming, the impasse and its frustrations continued. There is indeed no frustration greater than to be confronted by a theory which purports merely to describe, when it not only plainly prescribes, but owes its special prescriptive powers precisely to the fact that it disclaims prescriptive intentions. Into this murky debate, some shafts of light did occasionally break through, as in Kelsen's casual admission, apparently never repeated, that his whole system might well rest on an emotional preference for the ideal of order over that of justice.[1] But I have to confess that in general the dispute that has been conducted during the last twenty years has not been very profitable.

Now, with Professor Hart's paper, the discussion takes a new and promising turn. It is now explicitly acknowledged on both sides that one of the chief issues is how we can best define and serve the ideal of fidelity to law. Law, as something deserving loyalty, must represent a human achievement: it cannot be a simple fiat of power or a repetitive pattern discernible in the behavior of state officials. The respect we owe to human laws must surely be something different from the respect we accord to the law of gravitation. If laws, even bad laws, have a claim to our respect, then law must represent some general direction of human effort that we can understand and describe, and that we can approve in principle even at the moment when it seems to us to miss its mark.

If, as I believe, it is a cardinal virtue of Professor Hart's argument that it brings into the dispute the issue of fidelity to law, its chief defect, if I may say so, lies in a failure to perceive and accept the implications that this enlargement of the frame of argument necessarily entails. This defect seems to me more or less to permeate the whole essay, but it comes most prominently to the fore in his discussion of Gustav Radbruch and the Nazi regime.[2] Without any inquiry into the actual workings of whatever remained of a legal system under the Nazis, Professor Hart assumes that something must have persisted that still deserved the name of law in a sense that would make meaningful the ideal of fidelity to law. Not that Professor Hart believes the Nazis' laws should have been obeyed. Rather he considers that a decision to disobey them presented not a mere question of prudence or courage, but a genuine moral dilemma in which the ideal of fidelity to law had to be sacrificed in favor of more fundamental goals. I should have thought it unwise to pass such a judgment without first inquiring with more particularity what "law" itself meant under the Nazi regime.

I shall present later my reasons for thinking that Professor Hart is profoundly mistaken in his estimate of the Nazi situation and that he gravely misinterprets the thought of Professor Radbruch. But first I shall turn to some preliminary definitional problems in which what I regard as the central defect in Professor Hart's thesis seems immediately apparent.

I. The Definition of Law

Throughout his essay Professor Hart aligns himself with a general position which he associates with the names of Bentham, Austin, Gray, and Holmes. He recognizes, of course, that the conceptions of these men as to "what law is" vary considerably,

but this diversity he apparently considers irrelevant in his defense of their general school of thought.

If the only issue were that of stipulating a meaning for the word "law" that would be conducive to intellectual clarity, there might be much justification for treating all of these men as working in the same direction. Austin, for example, defines law as the command of the highest legislative power, called the sovereign. For Gray, on the other hand, law consists in the rules laid down by judges. A statute is, for Gray, not a law, but only a source of law, which becomes law only after it has been interpreted and applied by a court. Now if our only object were to obtain that clarity which comes from making our definitions explicit and then adhering strictly to those definitions, one could argue plausibly that either conception of the meaning of "law" will do. Both conceptions appear to avoid a confusion of morals and law, and both writers let the reader know what meaning they propose to attribute to the word "law."

The matter assumes a very different aspect, however, if our interest lies in the ideal of fidelity to law, for then it may become a matter of capital importance what position is assigned to the judiciary in the general frame of government. Confirmation for this observation may be found in the slight rumbling of constitutional crisis to be heard in this country today. During the past year readers of newspapers have been writing to their editors urging solemnly, and even apparently with sincerity, that we should abolish the Supreme Court as a first step toward a restoration of the rule of law. It is unlikely that this remedy for our governmental ills derives from any deep study of Austin or Gray, but surely those who propose it could hardly be expected to view with indifference the divergent definitions of law offered by those two jurists. If it be said that it is a perversion of Gray's meaning to extract from his writings any moral for present controversies about the role of the Supreme Court, then it seems to me there is equal reason for treating what he wrote as irrelevant to the issue of fidelity to law generally.

Another difference of opinion among the writers defended by Professor Hart concerns Bentham and Austin and their views on constitutional limitations on the power of the sovereign. Bentham considered that a constitution might preclude the highest legislative power from issuing certain kinds of laws. For Austin, on the other hand, any legal limit on the highest lawmaking power was an absurdity and an impossibility. What guide to conscience would be offered by these two writers in a crisis that might some day arise out of the provision of our constitution to the effect that the amending power can never be used to deprive any state without its consent of its equal representation in the Senate?[3] Surely it is not only in the affairs of everyday life that we need clarity about the obligation of fidelity to law, but most particularly and urgently in times of trouble. If all the positivist school has to offer in such times is the observation that, however you may choose to define law, it is always something different from morals, its teachings are not of much use to us.

I suggest, then, that Professor Hart's thesis as it now stands is essentially incomplete and that before he can attain the goals he seeks he will have to concern himself more closely with a definition of law that will make meaningful the obligation of fidelity to law.

II. *The Definition of Morality*

It is characteristic of those sharing the point of view of Professor Hart that their primary concern is to preserve the integrity of the concept of law. Accordingly, they have generally sought a precise definition of law, but have not been at pains to state just what it is they mean to exclude by their definitions. They are like men building a wall for the defense of a village, who must know what it is they wish to protect, but who need not, and indeed cannot, know what invading forces those walls may have to turn back.

When Austin and Gray distinguish law from morality, the word "morality" stands indiscriminately for almost every conceivable standard by which human conduct may be judged that is not itself law. The inner voice of conscience, notions of right and wrong based on religious belief, common conceptions of decency and fair play, culturally conditioned prejudices—all of these are grouped together under the heading of "morality" and are excluded from the domain of law. For the most part Professor Hart follows in the tradition of his predecessors. When he speaks of morality he seems generally to have in mind all sorts of extralegal notions about "what ought to be," regardless of

their sources, pretensions, or intrinsic worth. This is particularly apparent in his treatment of the problem of interpretation, where uncodified notions of what ought to be are viewed as affecting only the penumbra of law, leaving its hard core untouched.

Toward the end of the essay, however, Professor Hart's argument takes a turn that seems to depart from the prevailing tenor of his thought. This consists in reminding us that there is such a thing as an immoral morality and that there are many standards of "what ought to be" that can hardly be called moral.[4] Let us grant, he says, that the judge may properly and inevitably legislate in the penumbra of a legal enactment, and that this legislation (in default of any other standard) must be guided by the judge's notions of what ought to be. Still, this would be true even in a society devoted to the most evil ends, where the judge would supply the insufficiencies of the statute with the iniquity that seemed to him most apt for the occasion. Let us also grant, says Professor Hart toward the end of his essay, that there is at times even something that looks like discovery in the judicial process, when a judge by restating a principle seems to bring more clearly to light what was really sought from the beginning. Again, he reminds us, this could happen in a society devoted to the highest refinements of sin, where the implicit demands of an evil rule might be a matter for discovery when the rule was applied to a situation not consciously considered when it was formulated.

I take it that this is to be a warning addressed to those who wish "to infuse more morality into the law." Professor Hart is reminding them that if their program is adopted the morality that actually gets infused may not be to their liking. If this is his point it is certainly a valid one, though one wishes it had been made more explicitly, for it raises much the most fundamental issue of his whole argument. Since the point is made obliquely, and I may have misinterpreted it, in commenting I shall have to content myself with a few summary observations and questions.

First, Professor Hart seems to assume that evil aims may have as much coherence and inner logic as good ones. I, for one, refuse to accept that assumption. I realize that I am here raising, or perhaps dodging, questions that lead into the most difficult problems of the epistemology of ethics. Even if I were competent to undertake an excursus in that direction, this is not the place for it. I shall have to rest on the assertion of a belief that may seem naïve, namely, that coherence and goodness have more affinity than coherence and evil. Accepting this belief, I also believe that when men are compelled to explain and justify their decisions, the effect will generally be to pull those decisions toward goodness, by whatever standards of ultimate goodness there are. Accepting these beliefs, I find a considerable incongruity in any conception that envisages a possible future in which the common law would "work itself pure from case to case" toward a more perfect realization of iniquity.

Second, if there is a serious danger in our society that a weakening of the partition between law and morality would permit an infusion of "immoral morality," the question remains, what is the most effective protection against this danger? I cannot myself believe it is to be found in the positivist position espoused by Austin, Gray, Holmes, and Hart. For those writers seem to me to falsify the problem into a specious simplicity which leaves untouched the difficult issues where real dangers lie.

Third, let us suppose a judge bent on realizing through his decisions an objective that most ordinary citizens would regard as mistaken or evil. Would such a judge be likely to suspend the letter of the statute by openly invoking a "higher law"? Or would he be more likely to take refuge behind the maxim that "law is law" and explain his decision in such a way that it would appear to be demanded by the law itself?

Fourth, neither Professor Hart nor I belong to anything that could be said in a significant sense to be a "minority group" in our respective countries. This has its advantages and disadvantages to one aspiring to a philosophic view of law and government. But suppose we were both transported to a country where our beliefs were anathemas, and where we, in turn, regarded the prevailing morality as thoroughly evil. No doubt in this situation we would have reason to fear that the law might be covertly manipulated to our disadvantage; I doubt if either of us would be apprehensive that its injunctions would be set aside by an appeal to a morality higher than law. If we felt that the law itself was our safest refuge, would it not be because even in the most perverted regimes there is a certain hesitancy about writing cruelties, intolerances, and inhumanities into law? And is it not clear that this hesitancy itself derives, not from a separation of law and morals, but precisely from an identification of law with those demands of morality that

are the most urgent and the most obviously justifiable, which no man need be ashamed to profess?

Fifth, over great areas where the judicial process functions, the danger of an infusion of immoral, or at least unwelcome, morality does not, I suggest, present a real issue. Here the danger is precisely the opposite. For example, in the field of commercial law the British courts in recent years have, if I may say so, fallen into a "law-is-law" formalism that constitutes a kind of belated counterrevolution against all that was accomplished by Mansfield.[5] The matter has reached a stage approaching crisis as commercial cases are increasingly being taken to arbitration. The chief reason for this development is that arbitrators are willing to take into account the needs of commerce and ordinary standards of commercial fairness. I realize that Professor Hart repudiates "formalism," but I shall try to show later why I think his theory necessarily leads in that direction.[6]

Sixth, in the thinking of many there is one question that predominates in any discussion of the relation of law and morals, to the point of coloring everything that is said or heard on the subject. I refer to the kind of question raised by the Pope's pronouncement concerning the duty of Catholic judges in divorce actions.[7] This pronouncement does indeed raise grave issues. But it does not present a problem of the relation between law, on the one hand, and, on the other, generally shared views of right conduct that have grown spontaneously through experience and discussion. The issue is rather that of a conflict between two pronouncements, both of which claim to be authoritative; if you will, it is one kind of law against another. When this kind of issue is taken as the key to the whole problem of law and morality, the discussion is so denatured and distorted that profitable exchange becomes impossible. In mentioning this last aspect of the dispute about "positivism," I do not mean to intimate that Professor Hart's own discussion is dominated by any *arrière-pensée*; I know it is not. At the same time I am quite sure that I have indicated accurately the issue that will be uppermost in the minds of many as they read this essay.

In resting content with these scant remarks, I do not want to seem to simplify the problem in a direction opposite to that taken by Professor Hart. The questions raised by "immoral morality" deserve a more careful exploration than either Professor Hart or I have offered in these pages.

III. *The Moral Foundations of a Legal Order*

Professor Hart emphatically rejects "the command theory of law," according to which law is simply a command backed by a force sufficient to make it effective. He observes that such a command can be given by a man with a loaded gun, and "law surely is not the gunman situation writ large."[8] There is no need to dwell here on the inadequacies of the command theory, since Professor Hart has already revealed its defects more clearly and succinctly than I could. His conclusion is that the foundation of a legal system is not coercive power, but certain "fundamental accepted rules specifying the essential lawmaking procedures."[9]

When I reached this point in his essay, I felt certain that Professor Hart was about to acknowledge an important qualification on his thesis. I confidently expected that he would go on to say something like this: I have insisted throughout on the importance of keeping sharp the distinction between law and morality. The question may now be raised, therefore, as to the nature of these fundamental rules that furnish the framework within which the making of law takes place. On the one hand, they seem to be rules, not of law, but of morality. They derive their efficacy from a general acceptance, which in turn rests ultimately on a perception that they are right and necessary. They can hardly be said to be law in the sense of an authoritative pronouncement, since their function is to state when a pronouncement is authoritative. On the other hand, in the daily functioning of the legal system they are often treated and applied much as ordinary rules of law are. Here, then, we must confess there is something that can be called a "merger" of law and morality, and to which the term "intersection" is scarcely appropriate.

Instead of pursuing some such course of thought, to my surprise I found Professor Hart leaving completely untouched the nature of the fundamental rules that make law itself possible, and turning his attention instead to what he considers a confusion of thought on the part of the critics of positivism. Leaving out of account his discussion of analytical jurisprudence, his argument runs something as follows: Two views are associated with the names of Bentham and Austin. One is the command theory of law, the other is an insistence on the separation of law and morality.

Critics of these writers came in time to perceive—"dimly" Professor Hart says—that the command theory is untenable. By a loose association of ideas they wrongly supposed that in advancing reasons for rejecting the command theory they had also refuted the view that law and morality must be sharply separated. This was a "natural mistake," but plainly a mistake just the same.

I do not think any mistake is committed in believing that Bentham and Austin's error in formulating improperly and too simply the problem of the relation of law and morals was part of a larger error that led to the command theory of law. I think the connection between these two errors can be made clear if we ask ourselves what would have happened to Austin's system of thought if he had abandoned the command theory.

One who reads Austin's Lectures V and VI[10] cannot help being impressed by the way he hangs doggedly to the command theory, in spite of the fact that every pull of his own keen mind was toward abandoning it. In the case of a sovereign monarch, law is what the monarch commands. But what shall we say of the "laws" of succession which tell who the "lawful" monarch is? It is of the essence of a command that it be addressed by a superior to an inferior, yet in the case of a "sovereign many," say, a parliament, the sovereign seems to command itself since a member of parliament may be convicted under a law he himself drafted and voted for. The sovereign must be unlimited in legal power, for who could adjudicate the legal bounds of a supreme lawmaking power? Yet a "sovereign many" must accept the limitation of rules before it can make law at all. Such a body can gain the power to issue commands only by acting in a corporate capacity"; this it can do only by proceeding "agreeably to the modes and forms" established and accepted for the making of law. Judges exercise a power delegated to them by the supreme lawmaking power, and are commissioned to carry out its "direct or circuitous commands." Yet in a federal system it is the courts which must resolve conflicts of competence between the federation and its components.

All of these problems Austin sees with varying degrees of explicitness, and he struggles mightily with them. Over and over again he teeters on the edge of an abandonment of the command theory in favor of what Professor Hart has described as a view that discerns the foundations of a legal order in "certain fundamental accepted rules specifying the essential lawmaking procedures." Yet he never takes the plunge. He does not take it because he had a sure insight that it would forfeit the black-and-white distinction between law and morality that was the whole object of his Lectures—indeed, one may say, the enduring object of a dedicated life. For if law is made possible by "fundamental accepted rules"—which for Austin must be rules, not of law, but of positive morality—what are we to say of the rules that the lawmaking power enacts to regulate its own lawmaking? We have election laws, laws allocating legislative representation to specific geographic areas, rules of parliamentary procedure, rules for the qualification of voters, and many other laws and rules of similar nature. These do not remain fixed, and all of them shape in varying degrees the lawmaking process. Yet how are we to distinguish between those basic rules that owe their validity to acceptance, and those which are properly rules of law, valid even when men generally consider them to be evil or ill-advised? In other words, how are we to define the words "fundamental" and "essential" in Professor Hart's own formulation: "certain fundamental accepted rules specifying the essential lawmaking procedure"?

The solution for this problem in Kelsen's theory is instructive. Kelsen does in fact take the plunge over which Austin hesitated too long. Kelsen realizes that before we can distinguish between what is law and what is not, there must be an acceptance of some basic procedure by which law is made. In any legal system there must be some fundamental rule that points unambiguously to the source from which laws must come in order to be laws. This rule Kelsen called "the basic norm." In his own words,

> The basic norm is not valid because it
> has been created in a certain way, but its
> validity is assumed by virtue of its content. It
> is valid, then, like a norm of natural law.
> . . . The idea of a pure positive law,
> like that of natural law, has its limita-
> tions.[11]

It will be noted that Kelsen speaks, not as Professor Hart does, of "fundamental rules" that regulate the making of law, but of a single rule or norm. Of course, there is no such single rule in any modern society. The notion of the basic norm is admittedly a symbol, not a fact. It is a symbol that embodies the positivist quest for some clear and unambiguous test of law, for some clean, sharp line that will divide the rules which owe their validity to

their source and those which owe their validity to acceptance and intrinsic appeal. The difficulties Austin avoided by sticking with the command theory, Kelsen avoids by a fiction which simplifies reality into a form that can be absorbed by positivism.

A full exploration of all the problems that result when we recognize that law becomes possible only by virtue of rules that are not law, would require drawing into consideration the effect of the presence or absence of a written constitution. Such a constitution in some ways simplifies the problems I have been discussing, and in some ways complicates them. In so far as a written constitution defines basic lawmaking procedure, it may remove the perplexities that arise when a parliament in effect defines itself. At the same time, a legislature operating under a written constitution may enact statutes that profoundly affect the lawmaking procedure and its predictable outcome. If these statutes are drafted with sufficient cunning, they may remain within the frame of the constitution and yet undermine the institutions it was intended to establish. If the "court-packing" proposal of the 'thirties does not illustrate this danger unequivocally, it at least suggests that the fear of it is not fanciful. No written constitution can be self-executing. To be effective it requires not merely the respectful deference we show for ordinary legal enactments, but that willing convergence of effort we give to moral principles in which we have an active belief. One may properly work to amend a constitution, but so long as it remains unamended one must work with it, not against it or around it. All this amounts to saying that to be effective a written constitution must be accepted, at least provisionally, not just as law, but as good law.

What have these considerations to do with the ideal of fidelity to law? I think they have a great deal to do with it, and that they reveal the essential incapacity of the positivistic view to serve that ideal effectively. For I believe that a realization of this ideal is something for which we must plan, and that is precisely what positivism refuses to do.

Let me illustrate what I mean by planning for a realization of the ideal of fidelity to law. Suppose we are drafting a written constitution for a country just emerging from a period of violence and disorder in which any thread of legal continuity with previous governments has been broken. Obviously such a constitution cannot lift itself unaided into legality; it cannot be law simply because it says

[handwritten: Strong words]

it is. We should keep in mind that the efficacy of our work will depend upon general acceptance and that to make this acceptance secure there must be a general belief that the constitution itself is necessary, right, and good. The provisions of the constitution should, therefore, be kept simple and understandable, not only in language, but also in purpose. Preambles and other explanations of what is being sought, which would be objectionable in an ordinary statute, may find an appropriate place in our constitution. We should think of our constitution as establishing a basic procedural framework for future governmental action in the enactment and administration of laws. Substantive limitations on the power of government should be kept to a minimum and should generally be confined to those for which a need can be generally appreciated. In so far as possible, substantive aims should be achieved procedurally, on the principle that if men are compelled to act in the right way, they will generally do the right things.

These considerations seem to have been widely ignored in the constitutions that have come into existence since World War II. Not uncommonly these constitutions incorporate a host of economic and political measures of the type one would ordinarily associate with statutory law. It is hardly likely that these measures have been written into the constitution because they represent aims that are generally shared. One suspects that the reason for their inclusion is precisely the opposite, namely, a fear that they would not be able to survive the vicissitudes of an ordinary exercise of parliamentary power. Thus, the divisions of opinion that are a normal accompaniment of lawmaking are written into the document that makes law itself possible. This is obviously a procedure that contains serious dangers for a future realization of the ideal of fidelity to law.

I have ventured these remarks on the making of constitutions not because I think they can claim any special profundity, but because I wished to illustrate what I mean by planning the conditions that will make it possible to realize the ideal of fidelity to law. Even within the limits of my modest purpose, what I have said may be clearly wrong. If so, it would not be for me to say whether I am also wrong clearly. I will, however, venture to assert that if I am wrong, I am wrong significantly. What disturbs me about the school of legal positivism is that it not only refuses to deal with problems of the sort I have just discussed, but bans them on principle from the province of legal philosophy. In its concern to assign the right labels to the things men do, this school seems to lose all interest in asking whether men are doing the right things.

IV. *The Morality of Law Itself*

[handwritten: order vs good order]

Most of the issues raised by Professor Hart's essay can be restated in terms of the distinction between order and good order. Law may be said to represent order *simpliciter*. Good order is law that corresponds to the demands of justice, or morality, or men's notions of what ought to be. This rephrasing of the issue is useful in bringing to light the ambitious nature of Professor Hart's undertaking, for surely we would all agree that it is no easy thing to distinguish order from good order. When it is said, for example, that law simply represents that public order which obtains under all governments—democratic, Fascist, or Communist[12]—the order intended is certainly not that of a morgue or cemetery. We must mean a functioning order, and such an order has to be at least good enough to be considered as functioning by some standard or other. A reminder that workable order usually requires some play in the joints, and therefore cannot be too orderly, is enough to suggest some of the complexities that would be involved in any attempt to draw a sharp distinction between order and good order.

For the time being, however, let us suppose we can in fact clearly separate the concept of order from that of good order. Even in this unreal and abstract form the notion of order itself contains what may be called a moral element. Let me illustrate this "morality of order" in its crudest and most elementary form. Let us suppose an absolute monarch, whose word is the only law known to his subjects. We may further suppose him to be utterly selfish and to seek in his relations with his subjects solely his own advantage. This monarch from time to time issues commands, promising rewards for compliance and threatening punishment for disobedience. He is, however, a dissolute and forgetful fellow, who never makes the slightest attempt to ascertain who have in fact followed his directions and who have not. As a result he habitually punishes loyalty and rewards disobedience. It is apparent that this monarch will never achieve even his own selfish aims until he is ready to accept that minimum self-restraint that will create a meaningful connection between his words and his actions.

Let us now suppose that our monarch undergoes a change of heart and begins to pay some attention to what he said yesterday when, today, he has occasion to distribute bounty or to order the chopping off of heads. Under the strain of this new responsibility, however, our monarch relaxes his attention in other directions and becomes hopelessly slothful in the phrasing of his commands. His orders become so ambiguous and are uttered in so inaudible a tone that his subjects never have any clear idea what he wants them to do. Here, again, it is apparent that if our monarch for his own selfish advantage wants to create in his realm anything like a system of law he will have to pull himself together and assume still another responsibility.

Law, considered merely as order, contains, then, its own implicit morality. This morality of order must be respected if we are to create anything that can be called law, even bad law. Law by itself is powerless to bring this morality into existence. Until our monarch is really ready to face the responsibilities of his position, it will do no good for him to issue still another futile command, this time self-addressed and threatening himself with punishment if he does not mend his ways.

There is a twofold sense in which it is true that law cannot be built on law. First of all, the authority to make law must be supported by moral attitudes that accord to it the competency it claims. Here we are dealing with a morality external to law, which makes law possible. But this alone is not enough. We may stipulate that in our monarchy the accepted "basic norm" designates the monarch himself as the only possible source of law. We still cannot have law until our monarch is ready to accept the internal morality of law itself.

In the life of a nation these external and internal moralities of law reciprocally influence one another; a deterioration of the one will almost inevitably produce a deterioration in the other. So closely related are they that when the anthropologist Lowie speaks of "the generally accepted ethical postulates underlying our . . . legal institutions as their ultimate sanction and guaranteeing their smooth functioning,"[13] he may be presumed to have both of them in mind.

What I have called "the internal morality of law" seems to be almost completely neglected by Professor Hart. He does make brief mention of

"justice in the administration of the law," which consists in the like treatment of like cases, by whatever elevated or perverted standards the word "like" may be defined.[14] But he quickly dismisses this aspect of law as having no special relevance to his main enterprise.

In this I believe he is profoundly mistaken. It is his neglect to analyze the demands of a morality of order that leads him throughout his essay to treat law as a datum projecting itself into human experience and not as an object of human striving. When we realize that order itself is something that must be worked for, it becomes apparent that the existence of a legal system, even a bad or evil legal system, is always a matter of degree. When we recognize this simple fact of everyday legal experience, it becomes impossible to dismiss the problems presented by the Nazi regime with a simple assertion: "Under the Nazis there was law, even if it was bad law." We have instead to inquire how much of a legal system survived the general debasement and perversion of all forms of social order that occurred under the Nazi rule, and what moral implications this mutilated system had for the conscientious citizen forced to live under it.

It is not necessary, however, to dwell on such moral upheavals as the Nazi regime to see how completely uncapable the positivistic philosophy is of serving the high moral ideal it professes, that of fidelity to law. Its default in serving this ideal actually becomes most apparent, I believe, in the everyday problems that confront those who are earnestly desirous of meeting the moral demands of a legal order, but who have responsible functions to discharge in the very order toward which loyalty is due.

Let us suppose the case of a trial judge who has had an extensive experience in commercial matters and before whom a great many commercial disputes are tried. As a subordinate in a judicial hierarchy, our judge has of course the duty to follow the law laid down by his supreme court. Our imaginary Scrutton has the misfortune, however, to live under a supreme court which he considers woefully ignorant of the ways and needs of commerce. To his mind, many of this court's decisions in the field of commercial law simply do not make sense. If a conscientious judge caught in this dilemma were to turn to the positivistic philosophy what succor could he expect? It will certainly do no good to remind him that he has an obligation of fidelity to law. He is aware of this already and painfully so, since it is the source of his predicament. Nor will it help to say that if he legislates, it must be "interstitially," or that his contributions must be "confined from molar to molecular motions."[15] This mode of statement may be congenial to those who like to think of law, not as a purposive thing, but as an expression of the dimensions and directions of state power. But I cannot believe that the essentially trite idea behind this advice can be lifted by literary eloquence to the point where it will offer any real help to our judge; for one thing, it may be impossible for him to know whether his supreme court would regard any particular contribution of his as being wide or narrow.

Nor is it likely that a distinction between core and penumbra would be helpful. The predicament of our judge may well derive, not from particular precedents, but from a mistaken conception of the nature of commerce which extends over many decisions and penetrates them in varying degrees. So far as his problem arises from the use of particular words, he may well find that the supreme court often uses the ordinary terms of commerce in senses foreign to actual business dealings. If he interprets those words as a business executive or accountant would, he may well reduce the precedents he is bound to apply to a logical shambles. On the other hand, he may find great difficulty in discerning the exact sense in which the supreme court used those words, since in his mind that sense is itself the product of a confusion.

Is it not clear that it is precisely positivism's insistence on a rigid separation of law as it is from law as it ought to be that renders the positivistic philosophy incapable of aiding our judge? Is it not also clear that our judge can never achieve a satisfactory resolution of his dilemma unless he views his duty of fidelity to law in a context which also embraces his responsibility for making law what it ought to be?

The case I have supposed may seem extreme, but the problem it suggests pervades our whole legal system. If the divergence of views between our judge and his supreme court were less drastic, it would be more difficult to present his predicament graphically, but the perplexity of his position might actually increase. Perplexities of this sort are a normal accompaniment of the discharge of any adjudicative function; they perhaps reach their most poignant intensity in the field of administrative law.

One can imagine a case—surely not likely in Professor Hart's country or mine—where a judge might hold profound moral convictions that were exactly the opposite of those held, with equal attachment, by his supreme court. He might also be convinced that the precedents he was bound to apply were the direct product of a morality he considered abhorrent. If such a judge did not find the solution for his dilemma in surrendering his office, he might well be driven to a wooden and literal application of precedents which he could not otherwise apply because he was incapable of understanding the philosophy that animated them. But I doubt that a judge in this situation would need the help of legal positivism to find these melancholy escapes from his predicament. Nor do I think that such a predicament is likely to arise within a nation where both law and good law are regarded as collaborative human achievements in need of constant renewal, and where lawyers are still at least as interested in asking "What is good law?" as they are in asking "What is law?"

V. *The Problem of Restoring Respect for Law and Justice After the Collapse of a Regime That Respected Neither*

After the collapse of the Nazi regime the German courts were faced with a truly frightful predicament. It was impossible for them to declare the whole dictatorship illegal or to treat as void every decision and legal enactment that had emanated from Hitler's government. Intolerable dislocations would have resulted from any such wholesale outlawing of all that occurred over a span of twelve years. On the other hand, it was equally impossible to carry forward into the new government the effects of every Nazi perversity that had been committed in the name of law; any such course would have tainted an indefinite future with the poisons of Nazism.

This predicament—which was, indeed, a pervasive one, affecting all branches of law—came to a dramatic head in a series of cases involving informers who had taken advantage of the Nazi terror to get rid of personal enemies or unwanted spouses. If all Nazi statutes and judicial decisions were indiscriminately "law," then these despicable

Internal morality of Law

creatures were guiltless, since they had turned their victims over to processes which the Nazis themselves knew by the name of law. Yet it was intolerable, especially for the surviving relatives and friends of the victims, that these people should go about unpunished, while the objects of their spite were dead, or were just being released after years of imprisonment, or, more painful still, simply remained unaccounted for.

The urgency of this situation does not by any means escape Professor Hart. Indeed, he is moved to recommend an expedient that is surely not lacking itself in a certain air of desperation. He suggests that a retroactive criminal statute would have been the least objectionable solution to the problem. This statute would have punished the informer, and branded him as a criminal, for an act which Professor Hart regards as having been perfectly legal when he committed it.[16]

On the other hand, Professor Hart condemns without qualification those judicial decisions in which the courts themselves undertook to declare void certain of the Nazi statutes under which the informer's victims had been convicted. One cannot help raising at this point the question whether the issue as presented by Professor Hart himself is truly that of fidelity to law. Surely it would be a necessary implication of a retroactive criminal statute against informers that, for purposes of that statute at least, the Nazi laws as applied to the informers or their victims were to be regarded as void. With this turn the question seems no longer to be whether what was once law can now be declared not to have been law, but rather who should do the dirty work, the courts or the legislature.

But, as Professor Hart himself suggests, the issues at stake are much too serious to risk losing them in a semantic tangle. Even if the whole question were one of words, we should remind ourselves that we are in an area where words have a powerful effect on human attitudes. I should like, therefore, to undertake a defense of the German courts, and to advance reasons why, in my opinion, their decisions do not represent the abandonment of legal principle that Professor Hart sees in them. In order to understand the background of those decisions we shall have to move a little closer within smelling distance of the witches' caldron than we have been brought so far by Professor Hart. We shall have also to consider an aspect of the problem ignored in his essay, namely, the degree to which the Nazis observed what I have called the inner morality of law itself.

Throughout his discussion Professor Hart seems to assume that the only difference between Nazi law and, say, English law is that the Nazis used their laws to achieve ends that are odious to an Englishman. This assumption is, I think, seriously mistaken, and Professor Hart's acceptance of it seems to me to render his discussion unresponsive to the problem it purports to address.

Throughout their period of control the Nazis took generous advantage of a device not wholly unknown to American legislatures, the retroactive statute curing past legal irregularities. The most dramatic use of the curative powers of such a statute occurred on July 3, 1934, after the "Roehm purge." When this intraparty shooting affair was over and more than seventy Nazis had been—one can hardly avoid saying—"rubbed out," Hitler returned to Berlin and procured from his cabinet a law ratifying and confirming the measures taken between June 30 and July 1, 1934, without mentioning the names of those who were now considered to have been lawfully executed.[17] Some time later Hitler declared that during the Roehm purge "the supreme court of the German people . . . consisted of myself,"[18] surely not an overstatement of the capacity in which he acted if one takes seriously the enactment conferring retroactive legality on "the measures taken."

Now in England and America it would never occur to anyone to say that "it is in the nature of law that it cannot be retroactive," although, of course, constitutional inhibitions may prohibit certain kinds of retroactivity. We would say it is normal for a law to operate prospectively, and that it may be arguable that it ought never operate otherwise, but there would be a certain occult unpersuasiveness in any assertion that retroactivity violates the very nature of law itself. Yet we have only to imagine a country in which *all* laws are retroactive in order to see that retroactivity presents a real problem for the internal morality of law. If we suppose an absolute monarch who allows his realm to exist in a constant state of anarchy, we would hardly say that he could create a regime of law simply by enacting a curative statute conferring legality on everything that had happened up to its date and by announcing an intention to enact similar statutes every six months in the future.

A general increase in the resort to statutes curative of past legal irregularities represents a deterioration in that form of legal morality without which law itself cannot exist. The threat of such statutes hangs over the whole legal system, and robs every law on the books of some of its significance. And surely a general threat of this sort is implied when a government is willing to use such a statute to transform into lawful execution what was simple murder when it happened.

During the Nazi regime there were repeated rumors of "secret laws." In the article criticized by Professor Hart, Radbruch mentions a report that the wholesale killings in concentration camps were made "lawful" by a secret enactment.[19] Now surely there can be no greater legal monstrosity than a secret statute. Would anyone seriously recommend that following the war the German courts should have searched for unpublished laws among the files left by Hitler's government so that citizens' rights could be determined by a reference to these laws?

The extent of the legislator's obligation to make his laws known to his subjects is, of course, a problem of legal morality that has been under active discussion at least since the Secession of the Plebs. There is probably no modern state that has not been plagued by this problem in one form or another. It is most likely to arise in modern societies with respect to unpublished administrative directions. Often these are regarded in quite good faith by those who issue them as affecting only matters of internal organization. But since the procedures followed by an administrative agency, even in its "internal" actions, may seriously affect the rights and interests of the citizen, these unpublished, or "secret," regulations are often a subject for complaint.

But as with retroactivity, what in most societies is kept under control by the tacit restraints of legal decency broke out in monstrous form under Hitler. Indeed, so loose was the whole Nazi morality of law that it is not easy to know just what should be regarded as an unpublished or secret law. Since unpublished instructions to those administering the law could destroy the letter of any published law by imposing on it an outrageous interpretation, there was a sense in which the meaning of every law was "secret." Even a verbal order from Hitler that a thousand prisoners in concentration camps be put to death was at once an administrative direction and a validation of everything done under it as being "lawful."

But the most important affronts to the morality of law by Hitler's government took no such subtle forms as those exemplified in the bizarre outcroppings I have just discussed. In the first place, when legal forms became inconvenient, it was always possible for the Nazis to bypass them entirely and "to act through the party in the streets." There was no one who dared bring them to account for whatever outrages might thus be committed. In the second place, the Nazi-dominated courts were always ready to disregard any statute, even those enacted by the Nazis themselves, if this suited their convenience or if they feared that a lawyer-like interpretation might incur displeasure "above."

This complete willingness of the Nazis to disregard even their own enactments was an important factor leading Radbruch to take the position he did in the articles so severely criticized by Professor Hart. I do not believe that any fair appraisal of the action of the postwar German courts is possible unless we take this factor into account, as Professor Hart fails completely to do.

These remarks may seem inconclusive in their generality and to rest more on assertion than evidentiary fact. Let us turn at once, then, to the actual case discussed by Professor Hart.[20]

In 1944 a German soldier paid a short visit to his wife while under travel orders on a reassignment. During the single day he was home, he conveyed privately to his wife something of his opinion of the Hitler government. He expressed disapproval of (*sich abfällig geäussert über*) Hitler and leading personalities of the Nazi party. He also said it was too bad Hitler had not met his end in the assassination attempt that had occurred on July 20th of that year. Shortly after his departure, his wife, who during his long absence on military duty "had turned to other men" and who wished to get rid of him, reported his remarks to the local leader of the Nazi party, observing that "a man who would say a thing like that does not deserve to live." The result was a trial of the husband by a military tribunal and a sentence of death. After a short period of imprisonment, instead of being executed, he was sent to the front again. After the collapse of the Nazi regime, the wife was brought to trial for having procured the imprisonment of her husband. Her defense rested on the ground that her husband's statements to her about Hitler and the Nazis constituted a crime under the laws then in force. Accordingly, when she informed on her husband she was simply bringing a criminal to justice.

This defense rested on two statutes, one passed in 1934, the other in 1938. Let us first consider the second of these enactments, which was part of a more comprehensive legislation creating a whole series of special wartime criminal offenses. I reproduce below a translation of the only pertinent section:

> The following persons are guilty of destroying the national power of resistance and shall be punished by death: Whoever publicly solicits or incites a refusal to fulfill the obligations of service in the armed forces of Germany, or in armed forces allied with Germany, or who otherwise publicly seeks to injure or destroy the will of the German people or an allied people to assert themselves stalwartly against their enemies.[21]

It is almost inconceivable that a court of present-day Germany would hold the husband's remarks to his wife, who was barred from military duty by her sex, to be a violation of the final catchall provision of this statute, particularly when it is recalled that the text reproduced above was part of a more comprehensive enactment dealing with such things as harboring deserters, escaping military duty by self-inflicted injuries, and the like. The question arises, then, as to the extent to which the interpretive principles applied by the courts of Hitler's government should be accepted in determining whether the husband's remarks were indeed unlawful.

This question becomes acute when we note that the act applies only to *public* acts or utterances, whereas the husband's remarks were in the privacy of his own home. Now it appears that the Nazi courts (and it should be noted we are dealing with a special military court) quite generally disregarded this limitation and extended the act to all utterances, private and public.[22] Is Professor Hart prepared to say that the legal meaning of this statute is to be determined in the light of this apparently uniform principle of judicial interpretation?

Let us turn now to the other statute upon which Professor Hart relies in assuming that the husband's utterance was unlawful. This is the act of 1934, the relevant portions of which are translated below:

> (1) Whoever publicly makes spiteful or provocative statements directed against, or statements which disclose a base disposition toward, the leading personalities of the nation or of the National Socialist German Workers' Party, or toward measures taken or institutions established by them, and of such a nature as to undermine the

people's confidence in their political leadership, shall be punished by imprisonment.
> (2) Malicious utterances not made in public shall be treated in the same manner as public utterances when the person making them realized or should have realized they would reach the public.
> (3) Prosecution for such utterances shall be only on the order of the National Minister of Justice; in case the utterance was directed against a leading personality of the National Socialist German Workers' Party, the Minister of Justice shall order prosecution only with the advice and consent of the Representative of the Leader.
> (4) The National Minister of Justice shall, with the advice and consent of the Representative of the Leader, determine who shall belong to the class of leading personalities for purposes of Section 1 above.[23]

Extended comment on this legislative monstrosity is scarcely called for, overlarded and undermined as it is by uncontrolled administrative discretion. We may note only: first, that it offers no justification whatever for the death penalty actually imposed on the husband, though never carried out; second, that if the wife's act in informing on her husband made his remarks "public," there is no such thing as a private utterance under this statute. I should like to ask the reader whether he can actually share Professor Hart's indignation that, in the perplexities of the postwar reconstruction, the German courts saw fit to declare this thing not a law. Can it be argued seriously that it would have been more beseeming to the judicial process if the postwar courts had undertaken a study of "the interpretative principles" in force during Hitler's rule and had then solemnly applied those "principles" to ascertain the meaning of this statute? On the other hand, would the courts really have been showing respect for Nazi law if they had construed the Nazi statutes by their own, quite different, standards of interpretation?

Professor Hart castigates the German courts and Radbruch, not so much for what they believed had to be done, but because they failed to see that they were confronted by a moral dilemma of a sort that would have been immediately apparent to Bentham and Austin. By the simple dodge of saying, "When a statute is sufficiently evil it ceases to be law," they ran away from the problem they should have faced.

This criticism is, I believe, without justification. So far as the courts are concerned, matters certainly would not have been helped if, instead of saying, "This is not law," they had said, "This is law but it is so evil we will refuse to apply it." Surely moral confusion reaches its height when a court refuses to apply something it admits to be law, and Professor Hart does not recommend any such "facing of the true issue" by the courts themselves. He would have preferred a retroactive statute. Curiously, this was also the preference of Radbruch.[24] But unlike Professor Hart, the German courts and Gustav Radbruch were living participants in a situation of drastic emergency. The informer problem was a pressing one, and if legal institutions were to be rehabilitated in Germany it would not do to allow the people to begin taking the law into their own hands, as might have occurred while the courts were waiting for a statute.

As for Gustav Radbruch, it is, I believe, wholly unjust to say that he did not know he was faced with a moral dilemma. His postwar writings repeatedly stress the antinomies confronted in the effort to rebuild decent and orderly government in Germany. As for the ideal of fidelity to law, I shall let Radbruch's own words state his position:

> We must not conceal from ourselves—
> especially not in the light of our experiences during the twelve-year dictatorship—
> what frightful dangers for the rule of law
> can be contained in the notion of "statutory lawlessness" and in refusing the quality of law to duly enacted statutes.[25]

The situation is not that legal positivism enables a man to know when he faces a difficult problem of choice, while Radbruch's beliefs deceive him into thinking there is no problem to face. The real issue dividing Professors Hart and Radbruch is: How shall we state the problem? What is the nature of the dilemma in which we are caught?

I hope I am not being unjust to Professor Hart when I say that I can find no way of describing the dilemma as he sees it but to use some such words as the following: On the one hand, we have an amoral datum called law, which has the peculiar quality of creating a moral duty to obey it. On the other hand, we have a moral duty to do what we think is right and decent. When we are confronted by a statute we believe to be thoroughly evil, we have to choose between those two duties.

If this is the positivist position, then I have no hesitancy in rejecting it. The "dilemma" it states has the verbal formulation of a problem, but the problem it states makes no sense. It is like saying I have to choose between giving food to a starving man and being mimsy with the borogoves. I do not think it is unfair to the positivistic philosophy to say that it never gives any coherent meaning to the moral obligation of fidelity to law. This obligation seems to be conceived as sui generis, wholly unrelated to any of the ordinary, extralegal ends of human life. The fundamental postulate of positivism—that law must be strictly severed from morality—seems to deny the possibility of any bridge between the obligation to obey law and other moral obligations. No mediating principle can measure their respective demands on conscience, for they exist in wholly separate worlds.

While I would not subscribe to all of Radbruch's postwar views—especially those relating to "higher law"—I think he saw, much more clearly than does Professor Hart, the true nature of the dilemma confronted by Germany in seeking to rebuild her shattered legal institutions. Germany had to restore both respect for law and respect for justice. Though neither of these could be restored without the other, painful antinomies were encountered in attempting to restore both at once, as Radbruch saw all too clearly. Essentially Radbruch saw the dilemma as that of meeting the demands of order, on the one hand, and those of good order, on the other. Of course no pat formula can be derived from this phrasing of the problem. But, unlike legal positivism, it does not present us with opposing demands that have no living contact with one another, that simply shout their contradictions across a vacuum. As we seek order, we can meaningfully remind ourselves that order itself will do us no good unless it is good for something. As we seek to make our order good, we can remind ourselves that justice itself is impossible without order, and that we must not lose order itself in the attempt to make it good.

VI. *The Moral Implications of Legal Positivism*

We now reach the question whether there is any ground for Gustav Radbruch's belief that a general acceptance of the positivistic philosophy in pre-Nazi Germany made smoother the route to dictatorship. Understandably, Professor Hart regards this as the most outrageous of all charges against positivism.

Here indeed we enter upon a hazardous area of controversy, where ugly words and ugly charges have become commonplace. During the last half century in this country no issue of legal philosophy has caused more spilling of ink and adrenalin than the assertion that there are "totalitarian" implications in the views of Oliver Wendell Holmes, Jr. Even the most cautiously phrased criticisms of that grand old figure from the age of Darwin, Huxley, and Haeckel seem to stir the reader's mind with the memory of past acerbities.[26] It does no good to suggest that perhaps Holmes did not perceive all the implications of his own philosophy, for this is merely to substitute one insult for another. Nor does it help much to recall the dictum of one of the closest companions of Holmes' youth —surely no imperceptive observer—that Holmes was "composed of at least two and a half different people rolled into one, and the way he keeps them together in one tight skin, without quarreling any more than they do, is remarkable."[27]

In venturing upon these roughest of all jurisprudential waters, one is not reassured to see even so moderate a man as Professor Hart indulging in some pretty broad strokes of the oar. Radbruch disclosed "an extraordinary naïveté" in assessing the temper of his own profession in Germany and in supposing that its adherence of positivism helped the Nazis to power.[28] His judgment on this and other matters shows that he had "only half digested the spiritual message of liberalism" he mistakenly thought he was conveying to his countrymen.[29] A state of "hysteria"[30] is revealed by those who see a wholesome reorientation of German legal thinking in such judicial decisions as were rendered in the informer cases.

Let us put aside at least the blunter tools of invective and address ourselves as calmly as we can to the question whether legal positivism, as practiced and preached in Germany, had, or could have had, any causal connection with Hitler's ascent to power. It should be recalled that in the seventy-five years before the Nazi regime the positivistic philosophy had achieved in Germany a standing such as it enjoyed in no other country. Austin praised a German scholar for bringing international law within the clarity-producing restraints of positivism.[31] Gray reported with pleasure that the "abler" German jurists of his time were "abjuring all *'nicht positivisches Recht,'* " and cited

Bergbohm as an example.[32] This is an illuminating example, for Bergbohm was a scholar whose ambition was to make German positivism live up to its own pretensions. He was distressed to encounter vestigial traces of natural-law thinking in writings claiming to be positivistic. In particular, he was disturbed by the frequent recurrence of such notions as that law owes its efficacy to a perceived moral need for order, or that it is in the nature of man that he requires a legal order, etc. Bergbohm announced a program, never realized, to drive from positivistic thinking these last miasmas from the swamp of natural law.[33] German jurists generally tended to regard the Anglo-American common law as a messy and unprincipled conglomerate of law and morals.[34] Positivism was the only theory of law that could claim to be "scientific" in an Age of Science. Dissenters from this view were characterized by positivists with that epithet modern man fears above all others: "naïve." The result was that it could be reported by 1927 that "to be found guilty of adherence to natural law theories is a kind of social disgrace."[35]

To this background we must add the observation that the Germans seem never to have achieved that curious ability possessed by the British, and to some extent by the Americans, of holding their logic on short leash. When a German defines law, he means his definition to be taken seriously. If a German writer had hit upon the slogan of American legal realism, "Law is simply the behavior patterns of judges and other state officials," he would not have regarded this as an interesting little conversation-starter. He would have believed it and acted on it.

German legal positivism not only banned from legal science any consideration of the moral ends of law, but it was also indifferent to what I have called the inner morality of law itself. The German lawyer was therefore peculiarly prepared to accept as "law" anything that called itself by that name, was printed at government expense, and seemed to come *"von oben herab."*

In the light of these considerations I cannot see either absurdity or perversity in the suggestion that the attitudes prevailing in the German legal profession were helpful to the Nazis. Hitler did not come to power by a violent revolution. He was Chancellor before he became the Leader. The exploitation of legal forms started cautiously and became bolder as power was consolidated. The first attacks on the established order were on ramparts which, if they were manned by anyone, were manned by lawyers and judges. These ramparts fell almost without a struggle.

Professor Hart and others have been understandably distressed by references to a "higher law" in some of the decisions concerning informers and in Radbruch's postwar writings. I suggest that if German jurisprudence had concerned itself more with the inner morality of law, it would not have been necessary to invoke any notion of this sort in declaring void the more outrageous Nazi statutes.

To me there is nothing shocking in saying that a dictatorship which clothes itself with a tinsel of legal form can so far depart from the morality of order, from the inner morality of law itself, that it ceases to be a legal system. When a system calling itself law is predicated upon a general disregard by judges of the terms of the laws they purport to enforce, when this system habitually cures its legal irregularities, even the grossest, by retroactive statutes, when it has only to resort to forays of terror in the streets, which no one dares challenge, in order to escape even those scant restraints imposed by the pretence of legality—when all these things have become true of a dictatorship, it is not hard for me, at least, to deny to it the name of law.

I believe that the invalidity of the statutes involved in the informer cases could have been grounded on considerations such as I have just outlined. But if you were raised with a generation that said "law is law" and meant it, you may feel the only way you can escape one law is to set another off against it, and this perforce must be a "higher law." Hence these notions of "higher law," which are a justifiable cause for alarm, may themselves be a belated fruit of German legal positivism.

It should be remarked at this point that it is chiefly in Roman Catholic writings that the theory of natural law is considered, not simply as a search for those principles that will enable men to live together successfully, but as a quest for something that can be called "a higher law." This identification of natural law with a law that is above human laws seemings in fact to be demanded by any doctrine that asserts the possibility of an authoritative pronouncement of the demands of natural law. In those areas affected by such pronouncements as have so far been issued, the conflict between Roman Catholic doctrine and opposing views seems to me to be a conflict between two forms of positivism. Fortunately, over most of the area with which lawyers are concerned, no such pronouncements

exist. In these areas I think those of us who are not adherents of its faith can be grateful to the Catholic Church for having kept alive the rationalistic tradition in ethics.

I do not assert that the solution I have suggested for the informer cases would not have entailed its own difficulties, particularly the familiar one of knowing where to stop. But I think it demonstrable that the most serious deterioration in legal morality under Hitler took place in branches of the law like those involved in the informer cases; no comparable deterioration was to be observed in the ordinary branches of private law. It was in those areas where the ends of law were most odious by ordinary standards of decency that the morality of law itself was most flagrantly disregarded. In other words, where one would have been most tempted to say, "This is so evil it cannot be a law," one could usually have said instead, "This thing is the product of a system so oblivious to the morality of law that it is not entitled to be called a law." I think there is something more than accident here, for the overlapping suggests that legal morality cannot live when it is severed from a striving toward justice and decency.

But as an actual solution for the informer cases, I, like Professors Hart and Radbruch, would have preferred a retroactive statute. My reason for this preference is not that this is the most nearly lawful way of making unlawful what was once law. Rather I would see such a statute as a way of symbolizing a sharp break with the past, as a means of isolating a kind of cleanup operation from the normal functioning of the judicial process. By this isolation it would become possible for the judiciary to return more rapidly to a condition in which the demands of legal morality could be given proper respect. In other words, it would make it possible to plan more effectively to regain for the ideal of fidelity to law its normal meaning.

VII. *The Problem of Interpretation: The Core and the Penumbra*

It is essential that we be just as clear as we can be about the meaning of Professor Hart's doctrine of "the core and the penumbra,"[36] because I believe the casual reader is likely to misinterpret what he has to say. Such a reader is apt to suppose that

Professor Hart is merely describing something that is a matter of everyday experience for the lawyer, namely, that in the interpretation of legal rules it is typically the case (though not universally so) that there are some situations which will seem to fall rather clearly within the rule, while others will be more doubtful. Professor Hart's thesis takes no such jejune form. His extended discussion of the core and the penumbra is not just a complicated way of recognizing that some cases are hard, while others are easy. Instead, on the basis of a theory about language meaning generally, he is proposing a theory of judicial interpretation which is, I believe, wholly novel. Certainly it has never been put forward in so uncompromising a form before.

As I understand Professor Hart's thesis (if we add some tacit assumptions implied by it, as well as some qualifications he would no doubt wish his readers to supply) a full statement would run something as follows: The task of interpretation is commonly that of determining the meaning of the individual words of a legal rule, like "vehicle" in a rule excluding vehicles from a park. More particularly, the task of interpretation is to determine the range of reference of such a word, or the aggregate of things to which it points. Communication is possible only because words have a "standard instance," or a "core of meaning" that remains relatively constant, whatever the context in which the word may appear. Except in unusual circumstances, it will always be proper to regard a word like "vehicle" as embracing its "standard instance," that is, that aggregate of things it would include in all ordinary contexts, within or without the law. This meaning the word will have in any legal rule, whatever its purpose. In applying the word to its "standard instance," no creative role is assumed by the judge. He is simply applying the law "as it is."

In addition to a constant core, however, words also have a penumbra of meaning which, unlike the core, will vary from context to context. When the object in question (say, a tricycle) falls within this penumbral area, the judge is forced to assume a more creative role. He must now undertake, for the first time, an interpretation of the rule in the light of its purpose or aim. Having in mind what was sought by the regulation concerning parks, ought it to be considered as barring tricycles? When questions of this sort are decided there is at least an "intersection" of "is" and "ought," since the judge, in deciding what the rule "is," does so in

the light of his notions of what "it ought to be" in order to carry out its purpose.

If I have properly interpreted Professor Hart's theory as it affects the "hard core," then I think it is quite untenable. The most obvious defect of his theory lies in its assumption that problems of interpretation typically turn on the meaning of individual words. Surely no judge applying a rule of the common law ever followed any such procedure as that described (and, I take it, prescribed) by Professor Hart; indeed, we do not normally even think of his problem as being one of "interpretation." Even in the case of statutes, we commonly have to assign meaning, not to a single word, but to a sentence, a paragraph, or a whole page or more of text. Surely a paragraph does not have a "standard instance" that remains constant whatever the context in which it appears. If a statute seems to have a kind of "core meaning" that we can apply without a too precise inquiry into its exact purpose, this is because we can see that, however one might formulate the precise objective of the statute, *this* case would still come within it.

Even in situations where our interpretive difficulties seem to head up in a single word, Professor Hart's analysis seems to me to give no real account of what does or should happen. In his illustration of the "vehicle," although he tells us this word has a core of meaning that in all contexts defines unequivocally a range of objects embraced by it, he never tells us what these objects might be. If the rule excluding vehicles from parks seems easy to apply in some cases, I submit this is because we can see clearly enough what the rule "is aiming at in general" so that we know there is no need to worry about the difference between Fords and Cadillacs. If in some cases we seem to be able to apply the rule without asking what its purpose is, this is not because we can treat a directive arrangement as if it had no purpose. It is rather because, for example, whether the rule be intended to preserve quiet in the park, or to save carefree strollers from injury, we know, "without thinking," that a noisy automobile must be excluded.

What would Professor Hart say if some local patriots wanted to mount on a pedestal in the park a truck used in World War II, while other citizens, regarding the proposed memorial as an eyesore, support their stand by the "no vehicle" rule? Does this truck, in perfect working order, fall within the core or the penumbra?

Professor Hart seems to assert that unless

words have "standard instances" that remain constant regardless of context, effective communication would break down and it would become impossible to construct a system of "rules which have authority."[37] If in every context words took on a unique meaning, peculiar to that context, the whole process of interpretation would become so uncertain and subjective that the ideal of a rule of law would lose its meaning. In other words, Professor Hart seems to be saying that unless we are prepared to accept his analysis of interpretation, we must surrender all hope of giving an effective meaning to the ideal of fidelity to law. This presents a very dark prospect indeed, if one believes, as I do, that we cannot accept his theory of interpretation. I do not take so gloomy a view of the future of the ideal of fidelity to law.

An illustration will help to test, not only Professor Hart's theory of the core and the penumbra, but its relevance to the ideal of fidelity to law as well. Let us suppose that in leafing through the statutes, we come upon the following enactment: "It shall be a misdemeanor, punishable by a fine of five dollars, to sleep in any railway station." We have no trouble in perceiving the general nature of the target toward which this statute is aimed. Indeed, we are likely at once to call to mind the picture of a disheveled tramp, spread out in an ungainly fashion on one of the benches of the station, keeping weary passengers on their feet and filling their ears with raucous and alcoholic snores. This vision may fairly be said to represent the "obvious instance" contemplated by the statute, though certainly it is far from being the "standard instance" of the physiological state called "sleep."

Now let us see how this example bears on the ideal of fidelity to law. Suppose I am a judge, and that two men are brought before me for violating this statute. The first is a passenger who was waiting at 3 A.M. for a delayed train. When he was arrested he was sitting upright in an orderly fashion, but was heard by the arresting officer to be gently snoring. The second is a man who had brought a blanket and pillow to the station and had obviously settled himself down for the night. He was arrested, however, before he had a chance to go to sleep. Which of these cases presents the "standard instance" of the word "sleep"? If I disregard that question, and decide to fine the second man and set free the first, have I violated a duty of fidelity to law? Have I violated that duty if I interpret the word "sleep" as used in this statute to mean something like "to spread oneself out on a bench or floor to spend the night, or as if to spend the night"?

Testing another aspect of Professor Hart's theory, is it really ever possible to interpret a word in a statute without knowing the aim of the statute? Suppose we encounter the following incomplete sentence: "All improvements must be promptly reported to . . . ." Professor Hart's theory seems to assert that even if we have only this fragment before us we can safely construe the word "improvement" to apply to its "standard instance," though we would have to know the rest of the sentence before we could deal intelligently with "problems of the penumbra." Yet surely in the truncated sentence I have quoted, the word "improvement" is almost as devoid of meaning as the symbol "X."

The word "improvement" will immediately take on meaning if we fill out the sentence with the words, "the head nurse," or, "the Town Planning Authority," though the two meanings that come to mind are radically dissimilar. It can hardly be said that these two meanings represent some kind of penumbral accretion to the word's "standard instance." And one wonders, parenthetically, how helpful the theory of the core and the penumbra would be in deciding whether, when the report is to be made to the planning authorities, the word "improvement" includes an unmortgageable monstrosity of a house that lowers the market value of the land on which it is built.

It will be instructive, I think, to consider the effect of other ways of filling out the sentence. Suppose we add to, "All improvements must be promptly reported to . . ." the words, "the Dean of the Graduate Division." Here we no longer seem, as we once did, to be groping in the dark; rather, we seem now to be reaching into an empty box. We achieve a little better orientation if the final clause reads, "to the Principal of the School," and we feel completely at ease if it becomes, "to the Chairman of the Committee on Relations with the Parents of Children in the Primary Division."

It should be noted that in deciding what the word "improvement" means in all these cases, we do not proceed simply by placing the word in some general context, such as hospital practice, town planning, or education. If this were so, the "improvement" in the last instance might just as well be that of the teacher as that of the pupil. Rather, we ask ourselves, What can this rule be for? What evil does it seek to avert? What good is it intended to promote? When it is "the head nurse" who receives the report, we are apt to find ourselves asking, "Is there, perhaps, a shortage of hospital space, so that patients who improve sufficiently are sent home or are assigned to a ward where they will receive less attention?" If "Principal" offers more orientation than "Dean of the Graduate Division," this must be because we know something about the differences between primary education and education on the postgraduate university level. We must have some minimum acquaintance with the ways in which these two educational enterprises are conducted, and with the problems encountered in both of them, before any distinction between "Principal" and "Dean of the Graduate Division" would affect our interpretation of "improvement." We must, in other words, be sufficiently capable of putting ourselves in the position of those who drafted the rule to know what they thought "ought to be." It is the light of this "ought" that we must decide what the rule "is."

Turning now to the phenomenon Professor Hart calls "preoccupation with the penumbra," we have to ask ourselves what is actually contributed to the process of interpretation by the common practice of supposing various "borderline" situations. Professor Hart seems to say, "Why, nothing at all, unless we are working with problems of the penumbra." If this is what he means, I find his view a puzzling one, for it still leaves unexplained why, under his theory, if one is dealing with a penumbral problem, it could be useful to think about other penumbral problems.

Throughout his whole discussion of interpretation, Professor Hart seems to assume that it is a kind of cataloguing procedure. A judge faced with a novel situation is like a library clerk who has to decide where to shelve a new book. There are easy cases: the *Bible* belongs under Religion, *The Wealth of Nations* under Economics, etc. Then there are hard cases, when the librarian has to exercise a kind of creative choice, as in deciding whether *Das Kapital* belongs under Politics or Economics, *Gulliver's Travels* under Fantasy or Philosophy. But whether the decision where to shelve is easy or hard, once it is made all the librarian has to do is to put the book away. And so it is with judges, Professor Hart seems to say, in all essential particulars. Surely the judicial process is something more than a cataloguing procedure. The judge does not dis-

charge his responsibility when he pins an apt diagnostic label on the case. He has to do something about it, to treat it, if you will. It is this larger responsibility which explains why interpretative problems almost never turn on a single word, and also why lawyers for generations have found the putting of imaginary borderline cases useful, not only "on the penumbra," but in order to know where the penumbra begins.

These points can be made clear, I believe, by drawing again on our example of the statutory fragment which reads, "All improvements must be promptly reported to. . . ." Whatever the concluding phrase may be, the judge has not solved his problems simply by deciding what kind of improvement is meant. Almost all of the words in the sentence may require interpretation, but most obviously this is so of "promptly" and "reported." What kind of "report" is contemplated: a written note, a call at the office, entry in a hospital record? How specific must it be? Will it be enough to say "a lot better," or "a big house with a bay window"?

Now it should be apparent to any lawyer that in interpreting words like "improvement," "prompt," and "report," no real help is obtained by asking how some extralegal "standard instance" would define these words. But, much more important, when these words are all parts of a single structure of thought, they are in interaction with one another during the process of interpretation. "What is an 'improvement'? Well, it must be something that can be made the subject of a report. So, for purposes of this statute 'improvement' really means 'reportable improvement.' What kind of 'report' must be made? Well, that depends upon the sort of 'improvement' about which information is desired and the reasons for desiring the information."

When we look beyond individual words to the statute as a whole, it becomes apparent how the putting of hypothetical cases assists the interpretative process generally. By pulling our minds first in one direction, then in another, these cases help us to understand the fabric of thought before us. This fabric is something we seek to discern, so that we may know truly what it is, but it is also something that we inevitably help to create as we strive (in accordance with our obligation of fidelity to law) to make the statute a coherent, workable whole.

I should have considered all these remarks much too trite to put down here if they did not seem to be demanded in an answer to the theory of interpretation proposed by Professor Hart, a theory by which he puts such store that he implies we cannot have fidelity to law in any meaningful sense unless we are prepared to accept it. Can it be possible that the positivistic philosophy demands that we abandon a view of interpretation which sees as its central concern, not words, but purpose and structure? If so, then the stakes in this battle of schools are indeed high.

I am puzzled by the novelty Professor Hart attributes to the lessons I once tried to draw from Wittgenstein's example about teaching a game to children.[38] I was simply trying to show the role reflection plays in deciding what ought to be done. I was trying to make such simple points as that decisions about what ought to be done are improved by reflection, by an exchange of views with others sharing the same problems, and by imagining various situations that might be presented. I was assuming that all of these innocent and familiar measures might serve to sharpen our perception of what we were trying to do, and that the product of the whole process might be, not merely a more apt choice of means for the end sought, but a clarification of the end itself. I had thought that a famous judge of the English bench had something like this in mind when he spoke of the common law as working "itself pure."[39] If this view of the judicial process is no longer entertained in the country of its origin, I can only say that, whatever the vicissitudes of Lord Mansfield's British reputation may be, he will always remain for us in this country a heroic figure of jurisprudence.

I have stressed here the deficiencies of Professor Hart's theory as that theory affects judicial interpretation. I believe, however, that its defects go deeper and result ultimately from a mistaken theory about the meaning of language generally. Professor Hart seems to subscribe to what may be called "the pointer theory of meaning,"[40] a theory which ignores or minimizes the effect on the meaning of words of the speaker's purpose and the structure of language. Characteristically, this school of thought embraces the notion of "common usage." The reason is, of course, that it is only with the aid of this notion that it can seem to attain the inert datum of meaning it seeks, a meaning isolated from the effects of purpose and structure.

It would not do to attempt here an extended excursus into linguistic theory. I shall have to content myself with remarking that the theory of meaning implied in Professor Hart's essay seems

to me to have been rejected by three men who stand at the very head of modern developments in logical analysis: Wittgenstein, Russell, and Whitehead. Wittgenstein's posthumous *Philosophical Investigations* constitutes a sort of running commentary on the way words shift and transform their meanings as they move from context to context. Russell repudiates the cult of "common usage," and asks what "instance" of the word "word" itself can be given that does not imply some specific intention in the use of it.[41] Whitehead explains the appeal that "the deceptive identity of the repeated word" has for modern philosophers; only by assuming some linguistic constant (such as the "core of meaning") can validity be claimed for procedures of logic which of necessity move the word from one context to another.[42]

VIII. *The Moral and Emotional Foundations of Positivism*

If we ignore the specific theories of law associated with the positivistic philosophy, I believe we can say that the dominant tone of positivism is set by a fear of a purposive interpretation of law and legal institutions, or at least by a fear that such an interpretation may be pushed too far. I think one can find confirmatory traces of this fear in all of those classified as "positivists" by Professor Hart, with the outstanding exception of Bentham, who is in all things a case apart and who was worlds removed from anything that could be called *ethical* positivism.

Now the belief that many of us hold, that this fear of purpose takes a morbid turn in positivism, should not mislead us into thinking that the fear is wholly without justification, or that it reflects no significant problem in the organization of society.

Fidelity to law *can* become impossible if we do not accept the broader responsibilities (themselves purposive, as all responsibilities are and must be) that go with a purposive interpretation of law. One can imagine a course of reasoning that might run as follows: This statute says absinthe shall not be sold. What is its purpose? To promote health. Now, as everyone knows, absinthe is a sound, wholesome, and beneficial beverage. Therefore, interpreting the statute in the light of its purpose, I construe it to direct a general sale and consumption of that most healthful of beverages, absinthe.

If the risk of this sort of thing is implicit in a purposive interpretation, what measures can we take to eliminate it, or to reduce it to bearable proportions? One is tempted to say, "Why, just use ordinary common sense." But this would be an evasion, and would amount to saying that although we know the answer, we cannot say what it is. To give a better answer, I fear I shall have to depart from those high standards of clarity Professor Hart so rightly prizes and so generally exemplifies. I shall have to say that the answer lies in the concept of *structure*. A statute or a rule of common law has, either explicitly, or by virtue of its relation with other rules, something that may be called a structural integrity. This is what we have in mind when we speak of "the intent of the statute," though we know it is men who have intentions and not words on paper. Within the limits of that structure, fidelity to law not only permits but demands a creative role from the judge, but beyond that structure it does not permit him to go. Of course, the structure of which I speak presents its own "problems of the penumbra." But the penumbra in this case surrounds something real, something that has a meaning and integrity of its own. It is not a purposeless collocation of words that gets its meaning on loan from lay usage.

It is one of the great virtues of Professor Hart's essay that it makes explicit positivism's concern for the ideal of fidelity to law. Yet I believe, though I cannot prove, that the basic reason why positivism fears a purposive interpretation is not that it may lead to anarchy, but that it may push us too far in the opposite direction. It sees in a purposive interpretation, carried too far, a threat to human freedom and human dignity.

Let me illustrate what I mean by supposing that I am a man without religious beliefs living in a community of ardent Protestant Christian faith. A statute in this community makes it unlawful for me to play golf on Sunday. I find this statute an annoyance and accept its restraints reluctantly. But the annoyance I feel is not greatly different from that I might experience if, though it were lawful to play on Sunday, a power failure prevented me from taking the streetcar I would normally use in reaching the course. In the vernacular, "it is just one of those things."

What a different complexion the whole matter assumes if a statute compels me to attend church,

or, worse still, to kneel and recite prayers! Here I may feel a direct affront to my integrity as a human being. Yet the purpose of both statutes may well be to increase church attendance. The difference may even seem to be that the first statute seeks its end slyly and by indirection, the second, honestly and openly. Yet surely this is a case in which indirection has its virtues and honesty its heavy price in human dignity.

Now I believe that positivism fears that a too explicit and uninhibited interpretation in terms of purpose may well push the first kind of statute in the direction of the second. If this is a basic concern underlying the positivistic philosophy, that philosophy is dealing with a real problem, however inept its response to the problem may seem to be. For this problem of the impressed purpose is a crucial one in our society. One thinks of the obligation to bargain "in good faith" imposed by the National Labor Relations Act.[43] One recalls the remark that to punish a criminal is less of an affront to his dignity than to reform and improve him. The statutory preamble comes to mind: the increasing use made of it, its legislative wisdom, the significance that should be accorded to it in judicial interpretation. The flag salute cases[44] will, of course, occur to everyone. I myself recall the splendid analysis by Professor von Hippel of the things that were fundamentally wrong about Nazism, and his conclusion that the grossest of all Nazi perversities was that of coercing acts, like the putting out of flags and saying, "Heil Hitler!" that have meaning only when done voluntarily, or, more accurately, have a meaning when coerced that is wholly parasitic on an association of them with past voluntary expressions.[45]

Questions of this sort are undoubtedly becoming more acute as the state assumes a more active role with respect to economic activity. No significant economic activity can be organized exclusively by "don'ts." By its nature economic production requires a co-operative effort. In the economic field there is a special reason, therefore, to fear that "This you may not do" will be transformed into "This you must do—but willingly." As we all know, the most tempting opportunity for effecting this transformation is presented by what is called in administrative practice "the prehearing conference," in which the negative threat of a statute's sanctions may be used by its administrators to induce what they regard, in all good conscience, as "the proper attitude."

I look forward to the day when legal philosophy can address itself earnestly to issues of this sort, and not simply exploit them to score points in favor of a position already taken. Professor Hart's essay seems to me to open the way for such a discussion, for it eliminates from the positivistic philosophy a pretense that has hitherto obscured every issue touched by it. I mean, of course, the pretense of the ethical neutrality of positivism. That is why I can say in all sincerity that, despite my almost paragraph-by-paragraph disagreement with the views expressed in this essay, I believe Professor Hart has made an enduring contribution to legal philosophy.

Endnotes

[1] Kelsen, *Die Idee des Naturrechtes,* 7 Zeitschrift für Offentliches Recht 221, 248 (Austria 1927).

[2] Hart, *Positivism and the Separation of Law and Morals,* 71 Harv. L. Rev. 593, 615–21 (1958).

[3] U.S. Const. art. V.

[4] Hart, *supra* note 2, at 624.

[5] For an outstanding example, see G. Scammell and Nephew, Ltd. v. Ouston, [1941] A.C. 251 (1940). I personally would be inclined to put the same head Victoria Laundry, Ltd. v. Newman Industries, Ltd., [1949] 2 K.B. 528 (C.A.).

[6] See Hart, *supra* note 2, at 608–12.

[7] See N.Y. Times, Nov. 8, 1949, p. 1, col 4 (late city ed.) (report of a speech made on November 7, 1949 to the Central Committee of the Union of Catholic Italian Lawyers).

[8] Hart, *supra* note 2, at 603.

[9] *Ibid.*

[10] I Austin, Lectures on Jurisprudence 167–341 (5th ed. 1885).

[11] Kelsen, General Theory of Law and State 401 (3d ed. 1949).

[12] *E.g.,* Friedmann, *The Planned State and the Rule of Law,* 22 Austr. L.J. 162, 207 (1948).

[13] Lowie, The Origin of the State 113 (1927).

[14] Hart, *supra* note 2, at 623–24.

[15] Southern Pac. Co. v. Jensen, 244 U.S. 205, 221 (1917) (Holmes, J., dissenting), paraphrasing Storti v. Commonwealth, 178 Mass. 549, 554. 60 N.E. 210, 211 (1901) (Holmes, C.J.), in which it was held that a statute providing for electrocution as a means of inflicting the punishment of death was not cruel or unusual punishment within the Massachusetts Declaration of Rights,

Mass. Const. pt. First, art. XXVI, simply because it accomplished its object by molecular, rather than molar, motions.

[16] See Hart, *supra* note 2, at 619–20.

[17] N.Y. Times, July 4, 1934, p. 3, col. 3 (late city ed.).

[18] See N.Y. Times, July 14, 1934, p. 5, col. 2 (late city ed.).

[19] Radbruch, *Die Erneuerung des Rechts,* 2 Die Wandlung 8, 9 (Germany 1947). A useful discussion of the Nazi practice with reference to the publicity given laws will be found in Giese, *Verkündung und Gesetzeskraft,* 76 Archiv Des Öffenlichen Rechts 464, 471–72 (Germany 1951). I rely on this article for the remarks that follow in the text.

[20] Judgment of July 27, 1949, Oberlandesgericht, Bamberg, 5 Süddeutsche Juristen-Zeitung 207 (Germany 1950), 64 Harv. L. Rev. 1005 (1951).

[21] The passage translated is § 5 of a statute creating a Kriegssonderstrafrecht. Law of Aug. 17, 1938, [1939] 2 Reichsgesetzblatt pt. 1, at 1456. The translation is mine.

[22] See 5 Süddeutsche Juristen-Zeitung 207, 210 (Germany 1950).

[23] The translated passage is article II of A Law Against Malicious Attacks on the State and the Party and for the Protection of the Party Uniform, Law of Dec. 20, 1934, [1934] 1 Reichsgesetzblatt 1269. The translation is mine.

[24] See Radbruch, *Die Erneuerung des Rechts,* 2 Die Wandlung 8, 10 (Germany 1947).

[25] Radbruch, *Gesetzliches Unrecht und Übergesetzliches Recht,* 1 Süddeutsche Juristen-Zeitung 105, 107 (Germany 1946) (reprinted in Radbruch, Rechtsphilosophie 347, 354 (4th ed. 1950)). The translation is mine.

[26] See, *e.g.,* Howe, *The Positivism of Mr. Justice Holmes,* 64 Harv. L. Rev. 529 (1951).

[27] See 1 Perry, The Thought and Character of William James 297 (1935) (quoting a letter written by William James in 1869).

[28] Hart, *supra* note 2, at 617–18.

[29] *Id.* at 618.

[30] *Id.* at 619.

[31] 1 Austin, Lectures on Jurisprudence 173 (5th ed. 1885) (Lecture V).

[32] Gray, The Nature and Sources of the Law 96 (2d ed. 1921).

[33] 1 Bergbohm, Jurisprudenz und Rechtsphilosophie 355–552 (1892).

[34] See, *e.g.,* Heller, *Die Krisis der Staatslehre,* 55 Archiv für Sozialwissenschaft und Sozialpólitik 289, 309 (Germany 1926).

[35] Voegelin, *Kelsen's Pure Theory of Law*, 42 Pol. Sci. Q. 268, 269 (1927).

[36] Hart, *supra* note 2, at 606–08.

[37] See *id.* at 607.

[38] Fuller, *Human Purpose and Natural Law*, 53 J. Philos. 697, 700 (1956).

[39] Omychund v. Barker, 1 Atk. 21, 33, 26 Eng. Rep. 15, 22–23 (Ch. 1744) (argument of Solicitor-General Murray, later Lord Mansfield):

> All occasions do not arise at once; . . . a statute very seldom can take in all cases, therefore the common law, *that works itself pure* by rules drawn from the fountain of justice, is for this reason superior to an act of parliament.

[40] I am speaking of the linguistic theory that seems to be implied in the essay under discussion here. In Professor Hart's brilliant inaugural address, *Definition and Theory in Jurisprudence*, 70 L.Q. Rev. 37 (1954), the most important point made is that terms like "rule," "right," and "legal person" cannot be defined by pointing to correspondent things or actions in the external world, but can only be understood in terms of the function performed by them in the larger system, just as one cannot understand the umpire's ruling, "Y're out!" without having at least a general familiarity with the rules of baseball. Even in the analysis presented in the inaugural address, however, Professor Hart seems to think that the dependence of meaning on function and context is a peculiarity of formal and explicit systems, like those of a game or a legal system. He seems not to recognize that what he has to say about explicit systems is also true of countless informal and overlapping systems that run through language as a whole. These implicit systematic or structural elements in language often enable us to understand at once the meaning of a word used in a wholly novel sense, as in the statement, "Experts regard the English Channel as the most difficult swim in the world." In the essay now being discussed, Professor Hart seems nowhere to recognize that a rule or statute has a structural or systematic quality that reflects itself in some measure into the meaning of every principal term in it.

[41] Russell, *The Cult of "Common Usage,"* in Portraits from Memory and Other Essays 166, 170–71 (1956).

[42] Whitehead, *Analysis of Meaning*, in Essays in Science and Philosophy 122, 127 (1947).

[43] § 8(d), added by 61 Stat. 142 (1947), 29 U.S.C. § 158(d) (1952); see NLRA §§ 8(a)(5), (b)(3), as amended, 61 Stat. 141 (1947), 29 U.S.C. §§ 158(a)(5), (b)(3) (1952).

[44] Minersville School Dist. v. Gobitis, 310 U.S. 586 (1940), *overruled*, West Virginia State Bd. of Educ. v. Barnette, 319 U.S. 624 (1943).

[45] Von Hippel, Die Nationalsozialistische Herrschafisordnung als War nung und Lehre 6–7 (1946).

Study Questions

1. In what ways does the positivist separation of law and morals help to clarify the kind of dilemma faced by the postwar German courts in the grudge-informer cases, as Hart claims?

2. In *The Province of Jurisprudence Determined*, Austin insists that "the existence of law is one thing; its merit or demerit is another. Whether it be or be not is one enquiry; whether it be or be not conformable to an assumed standard, is a different enquiry. A law, which actually exists, is a law, though we happen to dislike it, or though it vary from the text, by which we regulate our approbation or disapprobation." Does this statement reflect your understanding of "law"? Given this view, how could Austin explain or account for the idea that there is a moral obligation to obey the law? Does the claim that something is the "law" or is "lawful" carry with it any moral or normative connotation? Does the mere fact that something is the law supply a reason for compliance with it?

3. Martin Luther King, Jr. quotes Saint Augustine's famous remark that "an unjust law is no law at all." It has frequently been objected that this claim is plainly false, even absurd. How can something fail to be "law" simply because it is unjust or in some other way immoral? King himself, it is observed, was punished and put in jail for, as we would say, "breaking the law." Assuming we believe that King was in the right and the racially discriminatory statutes and practices of the South were unjust, does the fact that King wound up in jail prove that unjust laws nonetheless remain laws? Does that fact of itself refute Augustine? If not, why not?

4. What could Aquinas have meant when he claimed that human enactments that fail to square with natural law are "not law but perversions of law" that do not "bind in conscience"?

5. Fuller claims that a consistently and thoroughly evil legal *system* is an impossibility, since all legal systems must incorporate his "inner morality of law." Do you agree that such a legal system is impossible? How much actual moral content do they have? Could Fuller's principles be satisfied by a legal system that still contained much wickedness? Give examples.

C. Modern Theories of Law

American Legal Realism

The theories of law we have so far examined, positivism and naturalism, are undeniably abstract and seemingly far removed from those day-to-day activities of lawyers, judges, and police officers that most of us would at least initially identify as comprising the "law." During the first several decades of this century, a group of American legal scholars defended an approach to the study of law and legal systems quite unlike that found in Aquinas and Austin. These scholars, who later came to be called *legal realists*, wrote with the explicit aim of understanding the law in its daily operation by focusing on what judges and lawyers (and others) actually *do*, rather than what they, or theorists like Aquinas and Austin, *say* they do. The concern of the legal realists lay with the "law in action," not with the "law in books." In this section we encounter the views of two prominent theorists associated with the realist movement.

Holmes and the "Bad Man"

Oliver Wendell Holmes's career spanned a vast period in American history, from before the Civil War to the New Deal. Holmes was a teacher, writer, judge, and justice of the United States Supreme Court, and while he has always defied neat classification into one or another jurisprudential camp, his essay "The Path of the Law," reprinted here, became a classic statement of several key realist themes. To appreciate fully what Holmes has to say, we need to have a clearer sense of the context within which he and other realists wrote, and in particular a clearer understanding of the conception of law against which he and they were reacting.

The nineteenth century saw a tremendous growth and expansion of the traditional sciences, as well as the birth of new realms of scientific investigation, such as psychology and biology. The growing social and intellectual prestige of the sciences fueled the desire of legal scholars to make law a "scientific" discipline. In 1870, the new dean of Harvard Law School, Christopher Columbus Langdell, instituted a series of reforms in legal education with the aim of teaching law as a science. Prominent among these reforms was the introduction of the "case method" of legal study: the student was to confront and analyze the opinions written by judges deciding particular disputes in order to extract from them the fundamental principles of law. Behind Langdell's case method stood a conception of the nature of law that Langdell shared with other influential scholars and teachers, including James Barr Ames, Joseph Beale, and Samuel Williston. According to these men, law is a completely self-contained and thoroughly consistent and systematic body of principles and rules. Once a judge or student extracts the rule from the authoritative sources, he or she can logically deduce what conclusion that rule requires in any given case. In this way, every possible legal dispute has a uniquely correct solution that can be rigorously deduced from a coherent set of basic axioms. Law becomes a kind of social geometry.

No sooner was this vision articulated than realists like Holmes began to assail it. They attacked the formalism of the "law-as-science" theorists: "The life of the law has not been logic, it has been experience," as Holmes famously remarked. And the experience that is most relevant here is the experience and perspective of the "bad man," the cynic whose only concern is with the bottom line: How much can I get away with before bringing the power of the state down upon me? Holmes provides several examples of this bad-man perspective in "The Path of the Law" as, for example, in his theory of contract. A contract, says Holmes, is not a moral commitment that the law wants me to keep.

This is shown, for example, by the fact that I may be sued for breach of contract even though I intended to make no such commitment. A contract is merely what the bad man would take it to be: a choice to perform as promised or ignore the promise and pay the penalty. In a similar fashion, when I injure another through my negligent behavior, the law of tort requires that I pay damages to the person affected. From the perspective of the bad man such a penalty is no different from a tax: each is a negative consequence brought on by my conduct. To understand the law, then, is to be able to predict when and under what circumstances one's conduct will trigger society's response. By thus washing the law in "cynical acid," Holmes seeks to boil law down to its bare essentials.

The realists attacked the formalism of the Langdellian legal scholars in another way: by insisting that judges and courts deciding actual disputes do not reason in a logically rigorous fashion from general principles of legal doctrine to particular conclusions in specific situations. As Holmes notes, law and legal doctrine develop only slowly and as a result of judges' decisions; and this development is embedded in history and tradition in a way far deeper than the law-as-science people were willing to admit. Since law develops in this way, the realists claimed, it is futile to seek or expect much "logic" in it. The law is not a rigid body of fixed and unchanging rules but a shifting and flexible social institution, with sufficient play to accommodate the balancing of various and competing interests within a society.

Rationalization and Rule-Skepticism

Holmes and other realists had to admit, of course, that judges and lawyers often write and talk *as if* they were deciding a case, or arguing for a particular position, by deducing conclusions from "rules of law" in a straightforward fashion. But the statements made by judges in their opinions, many realists insisted, are frequently little more than rationalizations for decisions that they had already arrived at on grounds or for reasons other than that the "rules" required them to decide in a particular way. Realists like Jerome Frank argued that legal reasoning characteristically proceeds "backwards," beginning with an intuitive judgment or

"gut feeling" that a particular decision is correct or right and proceeding to a rationalization of that decision so cast in legal jargon that it appears to follow from the rules in a logical way.[1] (A few judges have even admitted publicly that this is indeed how they work. See the selection by Joseph Hutcheson in Chapter Two.)

Coupled with their theory of legal reasoning as rationalization stands the realist's *rule-skepticism*. "The law . . . consists of *decisions*, not of rules."[2] By denying that the law consists of rules, some realists pushed their doctrine of the flux and flexibility of the law to the limit. Frank, in particular, challenged the concept of *stare decisis* or the doctrine of precedent. This is the idea that a court's decision in one case can serve to guide the decision of future cases that are similar to the original one in relevant ways. (For more on the concept of "following precedent," see Chapter Two.) The realists repeatedly emphasized the indeterminacy or looseness of *stare decisis* by pointing out that a particular ruling in one case never binds a decision maker in any future case, because the future decision maker can always find some aspect of the later case that can serve as a ground for differentiating or "distinguishing" it from the prior one.

The bottom line for the realists was that law is a matter of *prediction*: "The prophecies of what the courts will do in fact, and nothing more pretentious are what I mean by the law";[3] "Law . . . as to any given situation is either (a) actual law, i.e., a specific past decision, as to that situation, or (b) probable law, i.e., a guess as to a specific future decision."[4] Accordingly, many realists advocated the study of judicial behavior, arguing that to understand law you must concentrate on the patterns of decisions revealed in actual cases as these are the most reliable guides to, and the most accurate basis for, prediction of what future courts will do.

Law as Interpretation

One of the most widely debated theories of law to have emerged in recent years has been defended and refined by Oxford legal philosopher Ronald Dworkin. Published in a number of essays and books, Dworkin's jurisprudence has undergone several changes, at least some of which will be briefly noted here.

Since Dworkin's own views emerged quite explicitly from his criticisms of certain aspects of Hart's positivism (see the previous section), it will be useful to review briefly these aspects of Hart's position, which were developed at great length in his book *The Concept of Law* (1961).

Positivism and Rules

In *The Concept of Law*, H. L. A. Hart attempted to give a fresh start to positivism by resolving the problems implicit in Austin's theory. Austin conceived of law and of a legal system on the model of a holdup by an armed robber: order backed by threats. Law is merely the "gunman situation writ large." Hart argued that this view confuses two quite different states of affairs: being *obliged* to give my money to the robber (to avoid being hurt) and being legally *obligated* to pay my taxes by April 15 (to avoid a penalty). Feeling obliged is just that—a feeling, a psychological state. But being under an obligation is a feature of life that is *social* and that essentially involves the idea of a social rule. Hart argued that a shared activity or practice cannot constitute a social rule unless the people whose rule it is manifest a certain attitude toward it: that they accept and use the rule to guide their conduct. In this sense, "Pay your taxes by April 15" is a social rule because most of us use it (however reluctantly) to guide our conduct and help us plan. "Give me your money or else" is, on the other hand, plainly not such a rule.

Hart summarized his own theory of law as the view that law is a system of rules, a union of *primary* and *secondary* rules. Primary rules are those social rules that concern themselves directly with the way we live and behave: "No one may drive faster than 55 mph" or "Pay your taxes by April 15" are just such rules. Secondary rules, on the other hand, are "secondary" in the sense that their subject matter is not human behavior but rather the primary rules themselves: "The traffic code is exclusively the jurisdiction of the state" and "Proposed changes in the tax code must be approved by Congress" are examples of secondary rules. In order for a body of rules to qualify as *legal* rules, according to Hart, there must be secondary rules to supplement the primary ones. Of particular interest here is Hart's notion of a *rule of recognition*. This is a secondary rule that specifies criteria for what counts as a primary rule. "Whatever the chief utters is law" or "Whatever the legislatures enact consistently with the Constitution is law" are examples of rules of recognition. "Pay your taxes by April 15" is a valid rule of law then, because it was created (enacted by a legislature) in the way specified by the ultimate rule of recognition of our legal system.

Much debate has accompanied what Hart says about the existence of rules of recognition. What does it mean for such rules to exist? To say that the rule of recognition exists cannot mean that it is valid because enacted in accordance with a procedure laid down in the rule of recognition; plainly, the rule cannot validate itself. The existence of the rule of recognition must be a matter of descriptive fact, it simply *is* the rule acknowledged by most legal actors within a given system.

Dworkin's Critique of Positivism

In an early essay,[5] Dworkin summarized what he took to be the essential commitments of Hart's positivism: (1) The law of a community consists of a body of rules identifiable as legal based on their "pedigree," how they came about. (2) If a given case is not covered by a "pedigreeable" rule, the court must exercise discretion by going beyond the law to reach a decision. (3) Since legal rights can only be specified by rules, in any case that is not covered by rules, the court's resolution of the case cannot involve enforcing anyone's *legal* rights.

One of Dworkin's primary jurisprudential concerns has been to develop and defend a theory of adjudication: an account of how courts can and ought to reason to a conclusion in those "hard" cases in which no settled rule applies. And it was this concern that animated Dworkin's critique of Hart's positivism. Dworkin's core insight was that when courts reason about hard cases, they appeal to standards other than positivistic rules: they appeal to *principles*. Unlike rules, principles have no discernable "pedigree" in Hart's sense. Principles function as a reason in favor of a particular decision, but do not compel a result in the way a rule does. Moreover, a principle like "No one should profit from his own wrongdoing," invoked in the famous *Riggs* case (reprinted at the end of this chapter), can remain a principle of our law despite the fact that it is not always followed. Finally, principles frequently give expression to underlying or background *rights* held by one of the parties to a dispute, and such rights frequently "trump" or take priority over other considerations.

Are principles part of the law? Or do they stand outside it? Hart's theory, says Dworkin, must treat principles as extralegal standards to which judges could appeal once the rules have run out, so that the court is then no longer bound by any standards set by the authority of law. Dworkin regards Hart's picture as both *descriptively* inaccurate and *normatively* (or from a moral point of view) unattractive. It is inaccurate since courts *do*, Dworkin thinks, invoke principles and background rights; it is morally unattractive since the model of the judge enjoying broad discretion once the genuine rules have run out suggests that he or she can and should ignore, or at least significantly downplay, the rights of litigants and focus instead on policy considerations, asking, for example, what decision will be best for society as a whole.

Dworkin's Theory of Law

In "Natural Law Revisited," reprinted here, Dworkin restates his theories of law and adjudication so as to show how the question "What is law?" depends for its solution on correct answers to moral questions. At the same time, Dworkin tries to situate his theory within the context of recent work by various legal scholars who compare literary texts and the approaches to interpreting and reasoning about them with legal texts and the processes of legal reasoning. A central controversy in both literary and legal theory has turned on the extent to which textual interpretation, whether it be of a novel or a constitution, is merely a "subjective" process in which the interpreter imposes whatever meaning he or she chooses. Is there any sense in which textual interpretation can be said to be "objective"? And what would that mean? Are there meaningful constraints upon interpretive activity? These questions take on particular significance in the law as they intersect with the common assumption that legal reasoning must be conceived as a special form of interpretive activity, distinct

from political decision making. Dworkin's discussion of these issues in our selection presents in outline the theory developed at much greater length in his recent book, *Law's Empire*.

Adjudication, according to Dworkin, is a form of interpretive activity. Judges are like contributors to a "chain novel": they must take the statutes, prior cases, and other legal materials before them and try to make sense of these in a way that allows them to continue to extend whatever "story" the materials tell in a definite direction. In *Law's Empire*, Dworkin argues that this conception of judicial interpretation follows from a more general view of what it means to *interpret* anything, be it a text, a work of art, or what have you. This general view says that in order for me to interpret a theatrical play, for example, I must seek to understand it "from the inside out," trying to grasp what it means to the "society" (actors, audience, critics) whose play it is.

Similarly, the interpretation of a social practice like law involves the attempt to understand it as a way of life created and sustained by its participants, people who see themselves as part of a larger community ("community of principle," "interpretive community") held together by a commitment to the rule of law. And this means, Dworkin believes, that interpretation cannot simply involve discovering the intent of the author of the play or the drafter of a statute. Instead, interpretation must be *constructive*. This means that interpreters must try to see the play or the law in its best light, as the coherent embodiment of some unifying theme or point. For judges trying to interpret a series of earlier precedents, this means that they must seek to state the best constructive interpretation of the legal doctrine of their community as it is expressed in those precedents. And this will require judges at some point to rely upon their own opinions and convictions as they attempt to find the best interpretation of the existing law.

Dworkin cautions us not to misunderstand this last point. Because interpretation is not a mechanical process, the interpreters' own opinions must inevitably shape their interpretation to some degree, but this does not mean that judges can, for example, simply do whatever they please when faced with a hard case. Part of understanding and interpreting the law of their community requires that judges respect values that are deeply rooted in their society. Values of fairness and democratic rule, for example, require that they must balance their own opinions against public opinion (as expressed, say, by the votes of representatives in Congress); and the value of due process requires judges to protect people's expectation by not allowing the judges' interpretations of the law to deviate radically or break too decisively with the past.

Judges, then, look for a "reading" or interpretation that will contribute to the legal "story" by portraying the law in its best light. But what if several, competing interpretations or readings of that past are possible? Here interpreters must measure and compare these readings along two dimensions. First, the dimension of "fit": How well and to what degree does a particular reading explain all the fundamental features of our law? And second, the dimension of value: How well does that reading present our law as something coherent and worthwhile? Whichever interpretation succeeds best on both of these scorecards becomes the interpretation judges must choose and enforce. Dworkin sums up his overall theory by calling it "law as integrity": The law is the product of that interpretation which most faithfully sums up the texts, principles, and values of a given community into a coherent and morally attractive whole.

While he does not object to the label "naturalism" to describe this view, Dworkin makes it clear that this is a naturalism of a very different sort from that defended by Aquinas or King. Dworkin's judges are not free to follow just any normative or moral principle, nor do the principles to which they do appeal derive their validity from a natural moral order. Dworkin's judges are permitted to recognize only those moral principles and values "present," either explicitly or implicitly, in the legal history and tradition of their community and to recognize them only for that reason, not because they have some independent moral or religious basis.

In our selection, Dworkin considers and rejects three views that seek to challenge law as integrity: skepticism, conventionalism, and instrumentalism. The skeptical threat turns on Dworkin's requirement that judges seek the best interpretation of the existing law. The philosophical skeptic denies that there is a "best" interpretation of anything, or that one interpretation of a statute or novel can be "better" than another. Conventionalists, who hold that the law of a community consists only of the explicit and unambiguous conventions and practices already established, at-

tack "law as integrity" as antidemocratic, since it seemingly allows judges to impose upon everyone the judges' own view of the "best" interpretation of the law. Dworkin responds by arguing that his view is no less democratic than theirs. Finally, Dworkin tries to show that instrumentalism, the view that judges should decide hard cases solely with a view to the future good of the community and without regard for consistency with past decisions, leads to intolerable consequences because it denies the existence of a network of rights and principles that every citizen has a right to have enforced.

Critical Legal Studies

Throughout this chapter we have been concerned with the questions "What does it mean to live under the 'rule of law' as opposed to the 'rule of men'?" "What is legality and how does it differ from morality?" We have so far examined several theories that try to provide answers by offering accounts of the nature of law and the value of legality. The final essay in this chapter discusses the views of an emerging school of legal theory, one that challenges the assumptions about the nature and importance of the rule of law held, so it is claimed, by many representatives of the familiar, established theories. This recent perspective is *critical legal studies*.

Many members of the critical legal studies (CLS) movement have challenged the very possibility of a society based upon the "rule of law." They perceive a deep inconsistency between the concept of the rule of law and the theory of political liberalism with which that concept has come to be associated. The work of one prominent critical legalist, Roberto Unger, can be used to illustrate the CLS position.[6]

The most familiar conception of the rule of law, Unger thinks, presupposes a society characterized by certain features: a pervasive belief in the "subjectivity" of values; a concomitant pluralism and diversity of moral, religious, and political viewpoints; and the conviction that the government must (given the foregoing facts) remain scrupulously neutral on questions dealing with the "best" way to live. The presence of these conditions, Unger believes, gives rise to two problems that the rule of law is supposed to solve: how to form and sustain a workable social order under conditions of deep moral and political disagreement (the "problem of order"); and how to do this in a way that won't amount simply to domination of one group through subjugation to the values of another (the "problem of freedom"). The attempt to solve these problems gives rise to the ideal of the rule of law, the view that the exercise of collective force should be regulated by general, clear, and authoritative norms that have been set out in advance and are made applicable to all.

Unger's fundamental objection to this "liberal legalism" is that the very conditions that give rise to the need for the rule of law also make it impossible. The rule of law requires government neutrality in both the enactment and the interpretation of law, neutrality in both legislation and adjudication. But statutes and ordinances invariably are colored by the value biases of those with sufficient political power to get them voted into law; and the interpretation of such laws, once established, inevitably relies on the subjective views and values of the interpreter (usually a judge). Since there can be no neutral process either for the enactment or for the interpretation of law, there is a paradox concealed in the very idea of legality.

CLS, *Realism, and Dworkin*

In his article, philosopher Andrew Altman discusses a different, though related, aspect of the work of CLS scholars such as Unger and Duncan Kennedy. This is the claim that much of the existing body of American legal doctrine is a "patchwork quilt" of competing and often inconsistent rules, concepts, moral principles, and political commitments. Altman's concern is to show that CLS can be understood as the jurisprudential successor to American legal realism by describing the ways in which CLS refines and develops the realist thesis of the "looseness" of legal rules.

Altman tries to identify the sense in which, for the realists, law is indeterminate, incapable of precise statement. Altman rejects the view of Hart that indeterminacy resides only *within* rules by virtue of their vague and "open-textured" terms (as in

Hart's example of the term vehicle in "No vehicle in the park"). Rather, the lesson of the realists is that indeterminacy exists *among* the rules since, for any given case, a number of competing precedents can be found, each suggesting a different rule.

Hart and many other legal philosophers, says Altman, have failed fully to appreciate the realist indeterminacy claim. Furthermore, they have failed to recognize the extent to which that claim poses a further difficulty for positivism, a difficulty that opponents of positivism like Dworkin could try to exploit. If the realists are correct, so Dworkin could argue, then choice among legal rules is subject to a debilitating uncertainty that cannot fail to undermine any semblance of a "system of rules" applicable to any given case. But this indeterminacy is not a problem if law consists of moral principles and ideals, in addition to the texts of statutes and constitutions, and if understanding what the law requires in a given case involves developing an interpretation of those materials that gives them their best moral justification within the "soundest" theory of law. The indeterminacy of rules is not a threat if principles and interpretation can supply what rules lack.

But can even Dworkin's theory combat indeterminacy? It is here that Altman turns our attention to CLS. Altman canvasses several arguments found in CLS literature, all of which conclude that the law is simply too riffled with inconsistencies and tensions to be capable of being given the kind of coherent and morally attractive reading or interpretation that Dworkin's theories of law and adjudication require.

Endnotes

[1] See Jerome Frank, *Law and the Modern Mind* (New York: Anchor Books/Doubleday, 1963).

[2] *Ibid.*, p. 50.

[3] Holmes, "The Path of the Law," *infra*.

[4] Frank, *Law and the Modern Mind*, pp. 50–51.

[5] "The Model of Rules," in Dworkin, *Taking Rights Seriously* (Cambridge, Mass.: Harvard University Press, 1977), pp. 14–45.

[6] The argument outlined here is developed by Unger in *Knowledge and Politics* (New York: Free Press, 1975), chap. 2.

The Path of the Law

OLIVER WENDELL HOLMES

When we study law we are not studying a mystery but a well-known profession. We are studying what we shall want in order to appear before judges, or to advise people in such a way as to keep them out of court. The reason why it is a profession, why people will pay lawyers to argue for them or to advise them, is that in societies like ours the command of the public force is intrusted to the judges in certain cases, and the whole power of the state will be put forth, if necessary, to carry out their judgments and decrees. People want to know under what circumstances and how far they will run the risk of coming against what is so much stronger than themselves, and hence it becomes a business to find out when this danger is to be feared. The object of our study, then, is prediction, the prediction of the incidence of the public force through the instrumentality of the courts.

The means of the study are a body of reports, of treatises, and of statutes, in this country and in England, extending back for six hundred years, and now increasing annually by hundreds. In these sibylline leaves are gathered the scattered prophecies of the past upon the cases in which the axe will fall. These are what properly have been called the oracles of the law. Far the most important and pretty nearly the whole meaning of every new effort of legal thought is to make these prophecies more precise, and to generalize them into a thoroughly connected system. The process is one, from a lawyer's statement of a case, eliminating as it does all the dramatic elements with which his client's story has clothed it, and retaining only the facts of legal import, up to the final analyses and abstract universals of theoretic jurisprudence. The reason why a lawyer does not mention that his client wore a white hat when he made a contract, while Mrs. Quickly would be sure to dwell upon it along with the parcel gilt goblet and the sea-coal fire, is that he foresees that the public force will act in the same way whatever his client had upon his head. It is to make the prophecies easier to be remembered and to be understood that the teachings of the decisions of the past are put into general

propositions and gathered into text-books, or that statutes are passed in a general form. The primary rights and duties with which jurisprudence busies itself again are nothing but prophecies. One of the many evil effects of the confusion between legal and moral ideas, about which I shall have something to say in a moment, is that theory is apt to get the cart before the horse, and to consider the right or the duty as something existing apart from and independent of the consequences of its breach, to which certain sanctions are added afterward. But, as I shall try to show, a legal duty so called is nothing but a prediction that if a man does or omits certain things he will be made to suffer in this or that way by judgment of the court; and so of a legal right.

The number of our predictions when generalized and reduced to a system is not unmanageably large. They present themselves as a finite body of dogma which may be mastered within a reasonable time. It is a great mistake to be frightened by the ever-increasing number of reports. The reports of a given jurisdiction in the course of a generation take up pretty much the whole body of the law, and restate it from the present point of view. We could reconstruct the corpus from them if all that went before were burned. The use of the earlier reports is mainly historical, a use about which I shall have something to say before I have finished.

I wish, if I can, to lay down some first principles for the study of this body of dogma or systematized prediction which we call the law, for men who want to use it as the instrument of their business to enable them to prophesy in their turn, and, as bearing upon the study, I wish to point out an ideal which as yet our law has not attained.

The first thing for a business-like understanding of the matter is to understand its limits, and therefore I think it desirable at once to point out and dispel a confusion between morality and law, which sometimes rises to the height of conscious theory, and more often and indeed constantly is making trouble in detail without reaching the point of consciousness. You can see very plainly that a bad man has as much reason as a good one for wishing to avoid an encounter with the public force, and therefore you can see the practical importance of the distinction between morality and law. A man who cares nothing for an ethical rule which is believed and practised by his neighbors is likely nevertheless to care a good deal to avoid being made to pay money, and will want to keep out of jail if he can.

I take it for granted that no hearer of mine will misinterpret what I have to say as the language of cynicism. The law is the witness and external deposit of our moral life. Its history is the history of the moral development of the race. The practice of it, in spite of popular jests, tends to make good citizens and good men. When I emphasize the difference between law and morals I do so with reference to a single end, that of learning and understanding the law. For that purpose you must definitely master its specific marks, and it is for that I ask you for the moment to imagine yourselves indifferent to other and greater things.

I do not say that there is not a wider point of view from which the distinction between law and morals becomes of secondary or no importance, as all mathematical distinctions vanish in presence of the infinite. But I do say that that distinction is of the first importance for the object which we are here to consider—a right study and mastery of the law as a business with well understood limits, a body of dogma enclosed within definite lines. I have just shown the practical reason for saying so. *If you want to know the law and nothing else, you must look at it as a bad man, who cares only for the material consequences which such knowledge enables him to predict,* not as a good one, who finds his reasons for conduct, whether inside the law or outside of it, in the vaguer sanctions of conscience. The theoretical importance of the distinction is no less, if you would reason on your subject aright. The law is full of phraseology drawn from morals, and by the mere force of language continually invites us to pass from one domain to the other without perceiving it, as we are sure to do unless we have the boundary constantly before our minds. The law talks about rights, and duties, and malice, and intent, and negligence, and so forth, and nothing is easier, or, I may say, more common in legal reasoning, than to take these words in their moral sense, at some stage of the argument, and so to drop into fallacy. For instance, when we speak of the rights of man in a moral sense, we mean to mark the limits of interference with individual freedom which we think are prescribed by conscience, or by our ideal, however reached. Yet it is certain that many laws have been enforced in the past, and it is likely that some are enforced now, which are condemned by the most enlightened opinion of the time, or which at all events pass the limit of interference as many consciences would draw it. Manifestly, therefore, nothing but confusion of thought can result from assuming that the rights of man in a moral sense are equally rights in the sense of the Constitution and the law. No doubt simple and extreme cases can be put of imaginable laws which the statute-making power would not dare to enact, even in the absence of written constitutional prohibitions, because the community would rise in rebellion and fight; and this gives some plausibility to the proposition that the law, if not a part of morality, is limited by it. But this limit of power is not coextensive with any system of morals. For the most part it falls far within the lines of any such system, and in some cases may extend beyond them, for reasons drawn from the habits of a particular people at a particular time. I once heard the late Professor Agassiz say that a German population would rise if you added two cents to the price of a glass of beer. A statute in such a case would be empty words, not because it was wrong, but because it could not be enforced. No one will deny that wrong statutes can be and are enforced, and we should not all agree as to which were the wrong ones.

The confusion with which I am dealing besets confessedly legal conceptions. Take the fundamental question, What constitutes the law? You will find some text writers telling you that it is something different from what is decided by the courts of Massachusetts or England, that it is a system of reason, that it is a deduction from principles of ethics or admitted axioms or what not, which may or may not coincide with the decisions. But if we take the view of our friend the bad man we shall find that he does not care two straws for the axioms or deductions, but that he does want to know what the Massachusetts or English courts are likely to do in fact. I am much of his mind. The prophecies of what the courts will do in fact, and nothing more pretentious, are what I mean by the law.

Take again a notion which as popularly understood is the widest conception which the law contains—the notion of legal duty, to which already I have referred. We fill the word with all the content which we draw from morals. But what

← contract

does it mean to a bad man? Mainly, and in the first place, a prophecy that if he does certain things he will be subjected to disagreeable consequences by way of imprisonment or compulsory payment of money. But from his point of view, what is the difference between being fined and being taxed a certain sum for doing a certain thing? That his point of view is the test of legal principles is shown by the many discussions which have arisen in the courts on the very question whether a given statutory liability is a penalty or a tax. On the answer to this question depends the decision whether conduct is legally wrong or right, and also whether a man is under compulsion or free. Leaving the criminal law on one side, what is the difference between the liability under the mill acts or statutes authorizing a taking by eminent domain and the liability for what we call a wrongful conversion of property where restoration is out of the question. In both cases the party taking another man's property has to pay its fair value as assessed by a jury, and no more. What significance is there in calling one taking right and another wrong from the point of view of the law? It does not matter, so far as the given consequence, the compulsory payment, is concerned, whether the act to which it is attached is described in terms of praise or in terms of blame, or whether the law purports to prohibit it or to allow it. If it matters at all, still speaking from the bad man's point of view, it must be because in one case and not in the other some further disadvantages, or at least some further consequences, are attached to the act by the law. The only other disadvantages thus attached to it which I ever have been able to think of are to be found in two somewhat insignificant legal doctrines, both of which might be abolished without disturbance. One is, that a contract to do a prohibited act is unlawful, and the other, that, if one of two or more joint wrongdoers has to pay all the damages, he cannot recover contribution from his fellows. And that I believe is all. You see how the vague circumference of the notion of duty shrinks and at the same time grows more precise when we wash it with cynical acid and expel everything except the object of our study, the operations of the law.

Nowhere is the confusion between legal and moral ideas more manifest than in the law of contract. Among other things, here again the so called primary rights and duties are invested with a mystic significance beyond what can be assigned and explained. The duty to keep a contract at common

law means a prediction that you must pay damages if you do not keep it—and nothing else. If you commit a tort, you are liable to pay a compensatory sum. If you commit a contract, you are liable to pay a compensatory sum unless the promised event comes to pass, and that is all the difference. But such a mode of looking at the matter stinks in the nostrils of those who think it advantageous to get as much ethics into the law as they can. It was good enough for Lord Coke, however, and here, as in many other cases, I am content to abide with him. In *Bromage v. Genning,*[1] a prohibition was sought in the King's Bench against a suit in the marches of Wales for the specific performance of a covenant to grant a lease, and Coke said that it would subvert the intention of the covenantor, since he intends it to be at his election either to lose the damages or to make the lease. Sergeant Harris for the plaintiff confessed that he moved the matter against his conscience, and a prohibition was granted. This goes further than we should go now, but it shows what I venture to say has been the common law point of view from the beginning, although Mr. Harriman, in his very able little book upon Contracts has been misled, as I humbly think, to a different conclusion.

I have spoken only of the common law, because there are some cases in which a logical justification can be found for speaking of civil liabilities as imposing duties in an intelligible sense. These are the relatively few in which equity will grant an injunction, and will enforce it by putting the defendant in prison or otherwise punishing him unless he complies with the order of the court. But I hardly think it advisable to shape general theory from the exception, and I think it would be better to cease troubling ourselves about primary rights and sanctions altogether, than to describe our prophecies concerning the liabilities commonly imposed by the law in those inappropriate terms.

I mentioned, as other examples of the use by the law of words drawn from morals, malice, intent, and negligence. It is enough to take malice as it is used in the law of civil liability for wrongs—what we lawyers call the law of torts—to show that it means something different in law from what it means in morals, and also to show how the difference has been obscured by giving to principles which have little or nothing to do with each other the same name. Three hundred years ago a parson preached a sermon and told a story out of Fox's *Book of Martyrs* of a man who had assisted at the torture of one of the saints, and afterward died, suffering compensatory inward torment. It happened that Fox was wrong. The man was alive and chanced to hear the sermon, and thereupon he sued the parson. Chief Justice Wray instructed the jury that the defendant was not liable, because the story was told innocently, without malice. He took malice in the moral sense, as importing a malevolent motive. But nowadays no one doubts that a man may be liable, without any malevolent motive at all, for false statements manifestly calculated to inflict temporal damage. In stating the case in pleading, we still should call the defendant's conduct malicious; but, in my opinion at least, the word means nothing about motives, or even about the defendant's attitude toward the future, but only signifies that the tendency of his conduct under the known circumstances was very plainly to cause the plaintiff temporal harm.[2]

In the law of contract the use of moral phraseology has led to equal confusion, as I have shown in part already, but only in part. Morals deal with the actual internal state of the individual's mind, what he actually intends. From the time of the Romans down to now, this mode of dealing has affected the language of the law as to contract, and the language used has reacted upon the thought. We talk about a contract as a meeting of the minds of the parties, and thence it is inferred in various cases that there is no contract because their minds have not met; that is, because they have intended different things or because one party has not known of the assent of the other. Yet nothing is more certain than that parties may be bound by a contract to things which neither of them intended, and when one does not know of the other's assent. Suppose a contract is executed in due form and in writing to deliver a lecture, mentioning no time. One of the parties thinks that the promise will be construed to mean at once, within a week. The other thinks that it means when he is ready. The court says that it means within a reasonable time. The parties are bound by the contract as it is interpreted by the court, yet neither of them meant what the court declares that they have said. In my opinion no one will understand the true theory of contract or be able even to discuss some fundamental questions intelligently until he has understood that all contracts are formal, that the making of a contract depends not on the agreement of two minds in one intention, but on the agreement of two sets of external signs—not on the parties' hav-

ing *meant* the same thing but on their having *said* the same thing. Furthermore, as the signs may be addressed to one sense or another—to sight or to hearing—on the nature of the sign will depend the moment when the contract is made. If the sign is tangible, for instance, a letter, the contract is made when the letter of acceptance is delivered. If it is necessary that the minds of the parties meet, there will be no contract until the acceptance can be read—none, for example, if the acceptance be snatched from the hand of the offerer by a third person.

This is not the time to work out a theory in detail, or to answer many obvious doubts and questions which are suggested by these general views. I know of none which are not easy to answer, but what I am trying to do now is only by a series of hints to throw some light on the narrow path of legal doctrine, and upon two pitfalls which, as it seems to me, lie perilously near to it. Of the first of these I have said enough. I hope that my illustrations have shown the danger, both to speculation and to practice, of confounding morality with law, and the trap which legal language lays for us on that side of our way. For my own part, I often doubt whether it would not be a gain if every word of moral significance could be banished from the law altogether, and other words adopted which should convey legal ideas uncolored by anything outside the law. We should lose the fossil records of a good deal of history and the majesty got from ethical associations, but by ridding ourselves of an unnecessary confusion we should gain very much in the clearness of our thought.

So much for the limits of the law. The next thing which I wish to consider is what are the forces which determine its content and its growth. You may assume, with Hobbes and Bentham and Austin, that all law emanates from the sovereign, even when the first human beings to enunciate it are the judges, or you may think that law is the voice of the Zeitgeist, or what you like. It is all one to my present purpose. Even if every decision required the sanction of an emperor with despotic power and a whimsical turn of mind, we should be interested none the less, still with a view to prediction, in discovering some order, some rational explanation, and some principle of growth for the rules which he laid down. In every system there are such explanations and principles to be found. It is with regard to them that a second fallacy comes in, which I think it important to expose.

The fallacy to which I refer is the notion that the only force at work in the development of the law is logic. In the broadest sense, indeed, that notion would be true. The postulate on which we think about the universe is that there is a fixed quantitative relation between every phenomenon and its antecedents and consequents. If there is such a thing as a phenomenon without these fixed quantitative relations, it is a miracle. It is outside the law of cause and effect, and as such transcends our power of thought, or at least is something to or from which we cannot reason. The condition of our thinking about the universe is that it is capable of being thought about rationally, or, in other words, that every part of it is effect and cause in the same sense in which those parts are with which we are most familiar. So in the broadest sense it is true that the law is a logical development, like everything else. The danger of which I speak is not the admission that the principles governing other phenomena also govern the law, but the notion that a given system, ours, for instance, can be worked out like mathematics from some general axioms of conduct. This is the natural error of the schools, but it is not confined to them. I once heard a very eminent judge say that he never let a decision go until he was absolutely sure that it was right. So judicial dissent often is blamed, as if it meant simply that one side or the other were not doing their sums right, and, if they would take more trouble, agreement inevitably would come.

This mode of thinking is entirely natural. The training of lawyers is a training in logic. The processes of analogy, discrimination, and deduction are those in which they are most at home. The language of judicial decision is mainly the language of logic. And the logical method and form flatter that longing for certainty and for repose which is in every human mind. But certainty generally is illusion, and repose is not the destiny of man. Behind the logical form lies a judgment as to the relative worth and importance of competing legislative grounds, often an inarticulate and unconscious judgment, it is true, and yet the very root and nerve of the whole proceeding. You can give any conclusion a logical form. You always can imply a condition in a contract. But why do you imply it? It is because of some belief as to the practice of the community or of a class, or because of some opinion as to policy, or, in short, because of some attitude of yours upon a matter not capable of exact quantitative measurement, and therefore not capable of founding exact logical conclusions. Such matters really are battle grounds where the means do not exist for determinations that shall be good for all time, and where the decision can do no more than embody the preference of a given body in a given time and place. We do not realize how large a part of our law is open to reconsideration upon a slight change in the habit of the public mind. No concrete proposition is self evident, no matter how ready we may be to accept it, not even Mr. Herbert Spencer's "Every man has a right to do what he wills, provided he interferes not with a like right on the part of his neighbors."

Why is a false and injurious statement privileged, if it is made honestly in giving information about a servant. It is because it has been thought more important that information should be given freely, than that a man should be protected from what under other circumstances would be an actionable wrong. Why is a man at liberty to set up a business which he knows will ruin his neighbor? It is because the public good is supposed to be best subserved by free competition. Obviously such judgments of relative importance may vary in different times and places. Why does a judge instruct a jury that an employer is not liable to an employee for an injury received in the course of his employment unless he is negligent, and why do the jury generally find for the plaintiff if the case is allowed to go to them? It is because the traditional policy of our law is to confine liability to cases where a prudent man might have foreseen the injury, or at least the danger, while the inclination of a very large part of the community is to make certain classes of persons insure the safety of those with whom they deal. Since the last words were written, I have seen the requirement of such insurance put forth as part of the programme of one of the best known labor organizations. There is a concealed, half conscious battle on the question of legislative policy, and if any one thinks that it can be settled deductively, or once for all, I only can say that I think he is theoretically wrong, and that I am certain that his conclusion will not be accepted in practice *semper ubique et ab omnibus.*

Indeed, I think that even now our theory upon this matter is open to reconsideration, although I am not prepared to say how I should decide if a reconsideration were proposed. Our law of torts comes from the old days of isolated, ungeneralized wrongs, assaults, slanders, and the like, where the damages might be taken to lie where they fell by legal judgment. But the torts with which our courts are kept busy to-day are mainly the incidents of certain well known businesses. They are injuries to person or property by railroads, factories, and the like. The liability for them is estimated, and sooner or later goes into the price paid by the public. The public really pays the damages, and the question of liability, if pressed far enough, is really the question how far it is desirable that the public should insure the safety of those whose work it uses. It might be said that in such cases the chance of a jury finding for the defendant is merely a chance, once in a while rather arbitrarily interrupting the regular course of recovery, most likely in the case of an unusually conscientious plaintiff, and therefore better done away with. On the other hand, the economic value even of a life to the community can be estimated, and no recovery, it may be said, ought to go beyond that amount. It is conceivable that some day in certain cases we may find ourselves imitating, on a higher plane, the tariff for life and limb which we see in the *Leges Barbarorum*.

I think that the judges themselves have failed adequately to recognize their duty of weighing considerations of social advantage. The duty is inevitable, and the result of the often proclaimed judicial aversion to deal with such considerations is simply to leave the very ground and foundation of judgments inarticulate, and often unconscious, as I have said. When socialism first began to be talked about, the comfortable classes of the community were a good deal frightened. I suspect that this fear has influenced judicial action both here and in England, yet it is certain that it is not a conscious factor in the decisions to which I refer. I think that something similar has led people who no longer hope to control the legislatures to look to the courts as expounders of the Constitutions, and that in some courts new principles have been discovered outside the bodies of those instruments, which may be generalized into acceptance of the economic doctrines which prevailed about fifty years ago, and a wholesale prohibition of what a tribunal of lawyers does not think about right. I cannot but believe that if the training of lawyers led them habitually to consider more definitely and explicitly the social advantage on which the rule they lay down must be justified, they sometimes would hesitate where now they are confident, and see that really they were taking sides upon debatable and often burning questions.

So much for the fallacy of logical form. Now let us consider the present condition of the law as a subject for study, and the ideal toward which it tends. We still are far from the point of view which I desire to see reached. No one has reached it or can reach it as yet. We are only at the beginning of a philosophical reaction, and of a reconsideration of the worth of doctrines which for the most part still are taken for granted without any deliberate, conscious, and systematic questioning of their grounds. The development of our law has gone on for nearly a thousand years, like the development of a plant, each generation taking the inevitable next step, mind, like matter, simply obeying a law of spontaneous growth. It is perfectly natural and right that it should have been so. Imitation is a necessity of human nature, as has been illustrated by a remarkable French writer, M. Tarde, in an admirable book, *Les Lois de l'Imitation*. Most of the things we do, we do for no better reason than that our fathers have done them or that our neighbors do them, and the same is true of a larger part than we suspect of what we think. The reason is a good one, because our short life gives us no time for a better, but it is not the best. It does not follow, because we all are compelled to take on faith at second hand most of the rules on which we base our action and our thought, that each of us may not try to set some corner of his world in the order of reason, or that all of us collectively should not aspire to carry reason as far as it will go throughout the whole domain. In regard to the law, it is true, no doubt, that an evolutionist will hesitate to affirm universal validity for his social ideals, or for the principles which he thinks should be embodied in legislation. He is content if he can prove them best for here and now. He may be ready to admit that he knows nothing about an absolute best in the cosmos, and even that he knows next to nothing about a permanent best for men. Still it is true that a body of law is more rational and more civilized when every rule it contains is referred articulately and definitely to an end which it subserves, and when the grounds for desiring that end are stated or are ready to be stated in words.

At present, in very many cases, if we want to know why a rule of law has taken its particular shape, and more or less if we want to know why it exists at all, we go to tradition. We follow it into the Year Books, and perhaps beyond them to the customs of the Salian Franks, and somewhere in the past, in the German forests, in the needs of Norman kings, in the assumptions of a dominant class, in the absence of generalized ideas, we find out the practical motive for what now best is justified by the mere fact of its acceptance and that men are accustomed to it. The rational study of law is still to a large extent of the study of history. History must be a part of the study, because without it we cannot know the precise scope of rules which it is our business to know. It is a part of the rational study, because it is the first step toward an enlightened scepticism, that is, [toward] a deliberate reconsideration of the worth of those rules. When you get the dragon out of his cave on to the plain and in the daylight, you can count his teeth and claws, and see just what is his strength. But to get him out is only the first step. The next is either to kill him, or to tame him and make him a useful animal. For the rational study of the law the black-letter man may be the man of the present, but the man of the future is the man of statistics and the master of economics. It is revolting to have no better reason for a rule of law than that so it was laid down in the time of Henry IV. It is still more revolting if the grounds upon which it was laid down have vanished long since, and the rule simply persists from blind imitation of the past. I am thinking of the technical rule as to trespass *ab initio*, as it is called, which I attempted to explain in a recent Massachusetts case.[3]

Let me take an illustration, which can be stated in a few words, to show how the social end which is aimed at by a rule of law is obscured and only partially attained in consequence of the fact that the rule owes its form to a gradual historical development, instead of being reshaped as a whole, with conscious articulate reference to the end in view. We think it desirable to prevent one man's property being misappropriated by another, and so we make larceny a crime. The evil is the same whether the misappropriation is made by a man into whose hands the owner has put the property, or by one who wrongfully takes it away. But primitive law in its weakness did not get much beyond an effort to prevent violence, and very naturally made a wrongful taking, a trespass, part of its definition of the crime. In modern times the judges enlarged the definition a little by holding that, if the wrong-doer gets possession by a trick or device, the crime is committed. This really was giving up the requirement of a trespass, and it would have been more logical, as well as truer to the present object of the law, to abandon the requirement altogether. That, however, would have seemed too bold, and was left to statute. Statutes were passed making embezzlement a crime. But the force of tradition caused the crime of embezzlement to be regarded as so far distinct from larceny that to this day, in some jurisdictions at least, a slip corner is kept open for thieves to contend, if indicted for larceny, that they should have been indicted for embezzlement, and if indicted for embezzlement, that they should have been indicted for larceny, and to escape on that ground.

Far more fundamental questions still await a better answer than that we do as our fathers have done. What have we better than a blind guess to show that the criminal law in its present form does more good than harm? I do not stop to refer to the effect which it has had in degrading prisoners and in plunging them further into crime, or to the question whether fine and imprisonment do not fall more heavily on a criminal's wife and children than on himself. I have in mind more far-reaching questions. Does punishment deter? Do we deal with criminals on proper principles? A modern school of Continental criminalists plumes itself on the formula, first suggested, it is said, by Gall, that we must consider the criminal rather than the crime. The formula does not carry us very far, but the inquiries which have been started look toward an answer of my questions based on science for the first time. If the typical criminal is a degenerate, bound to swindle or to murder by as deep seated an organic necessity as that which makes the rattlesnake bite, it is idle to talk of deterring him by the classical method of imprisonment. He must be got rid of; he cannot be improved, or frightened out of his structural reaction. If, on the other hand, crime, like normal human conduct, is mainly a matter of imitation, punishment fairly may be expected to help to keep it out of fashion. The study of criminals has been thought by some well known men of science to sustain the former hypothesis. The statistics of the relative increase of crime in crowded places like large cities, where example has the greatest chance to work, and in less populated parts, where the contagion spreads more slowly, have been used with great force in favor of the latter view. But there is weighty authority for the belief that, however this may be, "not the nature of the crime, but the dangerousness of the criminal, constitutes the only reasonable legal criterion to guide the inevitable social reaction against the criminal."[4]

The impediments to rational generalization, which I illustrated from the law of larceny, are shown in the other branches of the law, as well as in that of crime. Take the law of tort or civil liability for damages apart from contract and the like. Is there any general theory of such liability, or are the cases in which it exists simply to be enumerated, and to be explained each on its special ground, as is easy to believe from the fact that the right of action for a certain well known classes of wrongs like trespass or slander has its special history for each class? I think that there is a general theory to be discovered, although resting in tendency rather than established and accepted. I think that the law regards the infliction of temporal damage by a responsible person as actionable, if under the circumstances known to him the danger of his act is manifest according to common experience, or according to his own experience if it is more than common, except in cases where upon special grounds of policy the law refuses to protect the plaintiff or grants a privilege to the defendant.[5] I think that commonly malice, intent, and negligence mean only that the danger was manifest to a greater or less degree, under the circumstances known to the actor, although in some cases of privilege malice may mean an actual malevolent motive, and such a motive may take away a permission knowingly to inflict harm, which otherwise would be granted on this or that ground of dominant public good. But when I stated my view to a very eminent English judge the other day, he said: "You are discussing what the law ought to be; as the law is, you must show a right. A man is not liable for negligence unless he is subject to a duty." If our difference was more than a difference in words, or with regard to the proportion between the exceptions and the rule, then, in his opinion, liability for an act cannot be referred to the manifest tendency of the act to cause temporal damage in general as a sufficient explanation, but must be referred to the special nature of the damage, or must be derived from some special circumstances outside of the tendency of the act, for which no generalized explanation exists. I think that such a view is wrong, but it is familiar, and I dare say generally is accepted in England.

Everywhere the basis of principle is tradition, to such an extent that we even are in danger of making the rôle of history more important than it is. The other day Professor Ames wrote a learned article to show, among other things, that the common law did not recognize the defence of fraud in actions upon specialties, and the moral might seem

to be that the personal character of that defence is due to its equitable origin. But if, as I have said, all contracts are formal, the difference is not merely historical, but theoretic, between defects of form which prevent a contract from being made, and mistaken motives which manifestly could not be considered in any system that we should call rational except against one who was privy to those motives. It is not confined to specialties, but is of universal application. I ought to add that I do not suppose that Mr. Ames would disagree with what I suggest.

However, if we consider the law of contract, we find it full of history. The distinctions between debt, covenant, and assumpsit are merely historical. The classification of certain obligations to pay money, imposed by the law irrespective of any bargain as quasi contracts, is merely historical. The doctrine of consideration is merely historical. The effect given to a seal is to be explained by history alone. Consideration is a mere form. Is it a useful form? If so, why should it not be required in all contracts? A seal is a mere form, and is vanishing in the scroll and in enactments that a consideration must be given, seal or no seal. Why should any merely historical distinction be allowed to affect the rights and obligations of business men?

Since I wrote this discourse I have come on a very good example of the way in which tradition not only overrides rational policy, but overrides it after first having been misunderstood and having been given a new and broader scope than it had when it had a meaning. It is the settled law of England that a material alteration of a written contract by a party avoids it as against him. The doctrine is contrary to the general tendency of the law. We do not tell a jury that if a man ever has lied in one particular he is to be presumed to lie in all. Even if a man has tried to defraud, it seems no sufficient reason for preventing him from proving the truth. Objections of like nature in general go to the weight, not to the admissibility, of evidence. Moreover, this rule is irrespective of fraud, and is not confined to evidence. It is not merely that you cannot use the writing, but that the contract is at an end. What does this mean? The existence of a written contract depends on the fact that the offerer and offeree have interchanged their written expressions, not on the continued existence of those expressions. But in the case of a bond, the primitive notion was different. The contract was inseparable from the parchment. If a stranger destroyed it, or tore off the seal, or altered it, the obligee could not recover, however free from fault, because the defendant's contract, that is, the actual tangible bond which he had sealed, could not be produced in the form in which it bound him. About a hundred years ago Lord Kenyon undertook to use his reason on this tradition, as he sometimes did to the detriment of the law, and, not understanding it, said he could see no reason why what was true of a bond should not be true of other contracts. His decision happened to be right, as it concerned a promissory note, where again the common law regarded the contract as inseparable from the paper on which it was written, but the reasoning was general, and soon was extended to other written contracts, and various absurd and unreal grounds of policy were invented to account for the enlarged rule.

I trust that no one will understand me to be speaking with disrespect of the law, because I criticise it so freely. I venerate the law, and especially our system of law, as one of the vastest products of the human mind. No one knows better than I do the countless number of great intellects that have spent themselves in making some addition or improvement, the greatest of which is trifling when compared with the mighty whole. It has the final title to respect that it exists, that it is not a Hegelian dream, but a part of the lives of men. But one may criticise even what one reveres. Law is the business to which my life is devoted, and I should show less than devotion if I did not do what in me lies to improve it, and, when I perceive what seems to me the ideal of its future, if I hesitated to point it out and to press toward it with all my heart.

Perhaps I have said enough to show the part which the study of history necessarily plays in the intelligent study of the law as it is to-day. In the teaching of this school and at Cambridge it is in no danger of being undervalued. Mr. Bigelow here and Mr. Ames and Mr. Thayer there have made important contributions which will not be forgotten, and in England the recent history of early English law by Sir Frederick Pollock and Mr. Maitland has lent the subject an almost deceptive charm. We must beware of the pitfall of antiquarianism, and must remember that for our purposes our only interest in the past is for the light it throws upon the present. I look forward to a time when the part played by history in the explanation of dogma shall be very small, and instead of ingenious research we shall spend our energy on a study of the ends sought to be attained and the reasons for desiring them. As a step toward that ideal it seems to me that every lawyer ought to seek an understanding of economics. The present divorce between the schools of political economy and law seems to me an evidence of how much progress in philosophical study still remains to be made. In the present state of political economy, indeed, we come again upon history on a larger scale, but there we are called on to consider and weigh the ends of legislation, the means of attaining them, and the cost. We learn that for everything we have we give up something else, and we are taught to set the advantage we gain against the other advantage we lose, and to know what we are doing when we elect.

There is another study which sometimes is undervalued by the practical minded, for which I wish to say a good word, although I think a good deal of pretty poor stuff goes under that name. I mean the study of what is called jurisprudence. Jurisprudence, as I look at it, is simply law in its most generalized part. Every effort to reduce a case to a rule is an effort of jurisprudence, although the name as used in English is confined to the broadest rules and most fundamental conceptions. One mark of a great lawyer is that he sees the application of the broadest rules. There is a story of a Vermont justice of the peace before whom a suit was brought by one farmer against another for breaking a churn. The justice took time to consider, and then said that he had looked through the statutes and could find nothing about churns, and gave judgment for the defendant. The same state of mind is shown in all our common digests and text-books. Applications of rudimentary rules of contract or tort are tucked away under the head of Railroads or Telegraphs or go to swell treatises on historical subdivisions, such as Shipping or Equity, or are gathered under an arbitrary title which is thought likely to appeal to the practical mind, such as Mercantile Law. If a man goes into law it pays to be a master of it, and to be a master of it means to look straight through all the dramatic incidents and to discern the true basis for prophecy. Therefore, it is well to have an accurate notion of what you mean by law, by a right, by a duty, by malice, intent, and negligence, by ownership, by possession, and so forth. I have in my mind cases in which the highest courts seem to me to have floundered because they had no clear ideas on some of these themes. I have illustrated their importance already. If a further illustration is wished, it may be found by reading the Appendix to Sir James Stephen's *Criminal Law* on the subject of possession, and then turning to Pollock and Wright's enlightened book. Sir James Stephen is not the only writer whose attempts to analyze legal ideas have been confused by striving for a useless quintessence of all systems, instead of an accurate anatomy of one. The trouble with Austin was that he did not know enough English law. But still it is a practical advantage to master Austin, and his predecessors, Hobbes and Bentham, and his worthy successors, Holland and Pollock. Sir Frederick Pollock's recent little book is touched with the felicity which marks all his works, and is wholly free from the perverting influence of Roman models.

The advice of the elders to young men is very apt to be as unreal as a list of the hundred best books. At least in my day I had my share of such counsels, and high among the unrealities I place the recommendation to study the Roman law. I assume that such advice means more than collecting a few Latin maxims with which to ornament the discourse—the purpose for which Lord Coke recommended Bracton. If that is all that is wanted, the title *De Regulis Juris Antiqui* can be read in an hour. I assume that, if it is well to study the Roman Law, it is well to study it as a working system. That means mastering a set of technicalities more difficult and less understood than our own, and studying another course of history by which even more than our own the Roman law must be explained. If any one doubts me, let him read Keller's *Der Römische Civil Process und die Actionen,* a treatise on the praetor's edict, Muirhead's most interesting *Historical Introduction to the Private Law of Rome,* and, to give him the best chance, Sohm's admirable *Institutes.* No. The way to gain a liberal view of your subject is not to read something else, but to get to the bottom of the subject itself. The means of doing that are, in the first place, to follow the existing body of dogma into its highest generalizations by the help of jurisprudence; next, to discover from history how it has come to be what it is; and, finally, so far as you can, to consider the ends which the several rules seek to accomplish, the reasons why those ends are desired, what is given up to gain them, and whether they are worth the price.

We have too little theory in the law rather than too much, especially on this final branch of study. When I was speaking of history, I mentioned larceny as an example to show how the law suffered from not having embodied in a clear form a rule which will accomplish its manifest purpose. In that case the trouble was due to the survival of forms coming from a time when a more limited purpose was entertained. Let me now give an example to show the practical importance, for the decision of actual cases, of understanding the reasons of the law, by taking an example from the rules which, so far as I know, never have been explained or theorized about in any adequate way. I refer to statutes of limitation and the law of prescription. The end of such rules is obvious, but what is the justification for depriving a man of his rights, a pure evil as far as it goes, in consequence of the lapse of time? Sometimes the loss of evidence is referred to, but that is a secondary matter. Sometimes the desirability of peace, but why is peace more desirable after twenty years than before? It is increasingly likely to come without the aid of legislation. Sometimes it is said that, if a man neglects to enforce his rights, he cannot complain if, after a while, the law follows his example. Now if this is all that can be said about it, you probably will decide a case I am going to put, for the plaintiff; if you take the view which I shall suggest, you possibly will decide it for the defendant. A man is sued for trespass upon land, and justifies under a right of way. He proves that he has used the way openly and adversely for twenty years, but it turns out that the plaintiff had granted a license to a person whom he reasonably supposed to be the defendant's agent, although not so in fact, and therefore had assumed that the use of the way was permissive, in which case no right would be gained. Has the defendant gained a right or not? If his gaining it stands on the fault and neglect of the landowner in the ordinary sense, as seems commonly to be supposed, there has been no such neglect, and the right of way has not been acquired. But if I were the defendant's counsel, I should suggest that the foundation of the acquisition of rights by lapse of time is to be looked for in the position of the person who gains them, not in that of the loser. Sir Henry Maine has made it fashionable to connect the archaic notion of property with prescription. But the connection is further back than the first recorded history. It is in the nature of man's mind. A thing which you have enjoyed and used as your own for a long time, whether property or an opinion, takes root in your being and cannot be torn away without your resenting the act and trying to defend yourself, however you came by it. The law can ask no better justification than the deepest instincts of man. It is only by way of reply to the suggestion that you are disappointing the former owner, that you refer to his neglect having allowed the gradual dissociation between himself and what he claims, and the gradual association of it with another. If he knows that another is doing acts which on their face show that he is on the way toward establishing such an association, I should argue that in justice to that other he was bound at his peril to find out whether the other was acting under his permission, to see that he was warned, and if necessary, stopped.

I have been speaking about the study of the law, and I have said next to nothing of what commonly is talked about in that connection—textbooks and the case system, and all the machinery with which a student comes most immediately in contact. Nor shall I say anything about them. Theory is my subject, not practical details. The modes of teaching have been improved since my time, no doubt, but ability and industry will master the raw material with any mode. Theory is the most important part of the dogma of the law, as the architect is the most important man who takes part in the building of a house. The most important improvements of the last twenty-five years are improvements in theory. It is not to be feared as unpractical, for, to the competent, is simply means going to the bottom of the subject. For the incompetent, it sometimes is true, as has been said, that an interest in general ideas means an absence of particular knowledge. I remember in army days reading of a youth who, being examined for the lowest grade and being asked a question about squadron drill, answered that he never had considered the evolutions of less than ten thousand men. But the weak and foolish must be left to their folly. The danger is that the able and practical minded should look with indifference or distrust upon ideas the connection of which with their business is remote. I heard a story, the other day, of a man who had a valet to whom he paid high wages, subject to deduction for faults. One of his deductions was, "For lack of imagination, five dollars." The lack is not confined to valets. The object of ambition, power, generally presents itself nowadays in the form of money alone. Money is the most immediate form, and is a proper object of desire. "The fortune," said Rachel,

"is the measure of the intelligence." That is a good text to waken people out of a fool's paradise. But, as Hegel says,[6] "It is in the end not the appetite, but the opinion, which has to be satisfied." To an imagination of any scope the most far-reaching form of power is not money, it is the command of ideas. If you want great examples, read Mr. Leslie Stephen's *History of English Thought in the Eighteenth Century*, and see how a hundred years after his death the abstract speculations of Descartes had become a practical force controlling the conduct of men. Read the works of the great German jurists, and see how much more the world is governed to-day by Kant than by Bonaparte. We cannot all be Descartes or Kant, but we all want happiness. And happiness, I am sure from having known many successful men, cannot be won simply by being counsel for great corporations and having an income of fifty thousand dollars. An intellect great enough to win the prize needs other food besides success. The remoter and more general aspects of the law are those which give it universal interest. It is through them that you not only become a great master in your calling, but connect your subject with the universe and catch an echo of the infinite, a glimpse of its unfathomable process, a hint of the universal law.

Endnotes

[1] Roll. Rep. 368.

[2] See Hanson *v.* Globe Newspaper Co., 159 Mass. 293, 302.

[3] Commonwealth *v.* Rubin, 165 Mass. 453.

[4] Havelock Ellis, *The Criminal*, 41, citing Garofalo. See also Ferri, *Sociologie Criminelle, passim.* Compare Tarde, *La Philosophie Pénale.*

[5] An example of the law's refusing to protect the plaintiff is when he is interrupted by a stranger in the use of a valuable way, which he has travelled adversely for a week less than the period of prescription. A week later he will have gained a right, but now he is only a trespasser. Example of privilege I have given already. One of the best is competition in business.

[6] Phil. des Rechts, § 190.

"Natural" Law Revisited

RONALD A. DWORKIN

I. What Is Naturalism?

Everyone likes categories, and legal philosophers like them very much. So we spend a good deal of time, not all of it profitably, labeling ourselves and the theories of law we defend. One label, however, is particularly dreaded: no one wants to be called a natural lawyer. Natural law insists that what the law is depends in some way on what the law should be. This seems metaphysical or at least vaguely religious. In any case it seems plainly wrong. If some theory of law is shown to be a natural law theory, therefore, people can be excused if they do not attend to it much further.

In the past several years, I have tried to defend a theory about how judges should decide cases that some critics (though not all) say is a natural law theory and should be rejected for that reason. I have of course made the pious and familiar objection to this charge, that it is better to look at theories than labels. But since labels are so much a part of our common intellectual life it is almost as silly to flee as to hurl them. If the crude description of natural law I just gave is correct, that any theory which makes the content of law sometimes depend on the correct answer to some moral question is a natural law theory, then I am guilty of natural law. I am not now interested, I should add, in whether this crude characterization is historically correct, or whether it succeeds in distinguishing natural law from positivist theories of law. My present concern is rather this. Suppose this *is* natural law. What in the world is wrong with it?

A. Naturalism

I shall start by giving the picture of adjudication I want to defend a name, and it is a name which

From *University of Florida Law Review*, Vol. 34 (1982), pp. 165–188. Reprinted with permission of the *University of Florida Law Review*.

accepts the crude characterization. I shall call this picture naturalism. According to naturalism, judges should decide hard cases by interpreting the political structure of their community in the following, perhaps special way: by trying to find the best *justification* they can find, in principles of political morality, for the structure as a whole, from the most profound constitutional rules and arrangements to the details of, for example, the private law of tort or contract. Suppose the question arises for the first time, for example, whether and in what circumstances careless drivers are liable, not only for physical injuries to those whom they run down, but also for any emotional damage suffered by relatives of the victim who are watching. According to naturalism, judges should then ask the following questions of the history (including the contemporary history) of their political structure. Does the best possible justification of that history suppose a principle according to which people who are injured emotionally in this way have a right to recover damages in court? If so, what, more precisely, is that principle? Does it entail, for example, that only immediate relatives of the person physically injured have that right? Or only relatives on the scene of the accident, who might themselves have suffered physical damage?

Of course a judge who is faced with these questions in an actual case cannot undertake anything like a full justification of all parts of the constitutional arrangement, statutory system and judicial precedents that make up his "law." I had to invent a mythical judge, called Hercules, with superhuman powers in order even to contemplate what a full justification of the entire system would be like.[1] Real judges can attempt only what we might call a partial justification of the law. They can try to justify, under some set of principles, those parts of the legal background which seem to them immediately relevant, like, for example, the prior judicial decisions about recovery for various sorts of damage in automobile accidents. Nevertheless it is useful to describe this as a partial justification—as a part of what Hercules himself would do—in order to emphasize that, according to this picture, a judge should regard the law he mines and studies as embedded in a much larger system, so that it is always relevant for him to expand his investigation by asking whether the conclusions he reaches are consistent with what he would have discovered had his study been wider.

It is obvious why this theory of adjudication invites the charge of natural law. It makes each judge's decision about the burden of past law depend on his judgment about the best political justification of that law, and this is of course a matter of political morality. Before I consider whether this provides a fatal defect in the theory, however, I must try to show how the theory might work in practice. It may help to look beyond law to other enterprises in which participants extend a discipline into the future by re-examining its past. This process is in fact characteristic of the general activity we call interpretation, which has a large place in literary criticism, history, philosophy and many other activities. Indeed, the picture of adjudication I have just sketched draws on a sense of what interpretation is like in these various activities, and I shall try to explicate the picture through an analogy to literary interpretation.[2] I shall, however, pursue that analogy in a special context designed to minimize some of the evident differences between law and literature, and so make the comparison more illuminating.

B. The Chain Novel

Imagine, then, that a group of novelists is engaged for a particular project. They draw lots to determine the order of play. The lowest number writes the opening chapter of a novel, which he then sends to the next number who is given the following assignment. He must add a chapter to that novel, which he must write so as to make the novel being constructed the best novel it can be. When he completes his chapter, he then sends the two chapters to the next novelist, who has the same assignment, and so forth. Now every novelist but the first has the responsibility of interpreting what has gone before in the sense of interpretation I described for a naturalist judge. Each novelist must decide what the characters are "really" like; what motives in fact guide them; what the point or theme of the developing novel is; how far some literary device or figure consciously or unconsciously used can be said to contribute to these,

and therefore should be extended, refined, trimmed or dropped. He must decide all this in order to send the novel further in one direction rather than another. But all these decisions must be made, in accordance with the directions given, by asking which decisions make the continuing novel better as a novel.

Some novels have in fact been written in this way (including the soft-core pornographic novel NAKED CAME THE STRANGER) though for a debunking purpose, and certain parlor games, for rainy weekends in English country houses, have something of the same structure. But in this case the novelists are expected to take their responsibilities seriously, and to recognize the duty to create, so far as they can, a single unified novel rather than, for example, a series of independent short stories with characters bearing the same names. Perhaps this is an impossible assignment; perhaps the project is doomed to produce, not simply an impossibly bad novel, but no novel at all, because the best theory of art requires a single creator, or if more than one, that each have some control over the whole. (But what about legends and jokes? What about the Old Testament, or, on some theories, the ILLIAD?) I need not push that question further, because I am interested only in the fact that the assignment makes sense, that each of the novelists in the chain can have some sense of what he or she is asked to do, whatever misgivings each might have about the value or character of what will then be produced.

The crucial question each must face is this. What is the difference between continuing the novel in the best possible way, by writing plot and development that can be seen to flow from what has gone before, and starting a fresh novel with characters having the same names? Suppose you are a novelist well down the chain, and are handed several chapters which are, in fact, the first sections of the Dickens short novel, A CHRISTMAS CAROL. You consider these two interpretations of the central character: that Scrooge is irredeemably, inherently evil, and so an example of the degradation of which human nature is intrinsically capable, or that Scrooge is inherently good, but progressively corrupted by the false values and perverse demands of high capitalist society. The interpretation you adopt will obviously make an enormous difference in the way you continue the story. You aim, in accordance with your instructions, to make the continuing novel the best novel it can be; but you must nevertheless choose an interpretation that makes the novel a single work of art. So you will have to respect the text you have been given, and not choose an interpretation that you believe the text rules out. The picture that text gives of Scrooge's early life, for example, might be incompatible with the claim that he is inherently wicked. In that case you have no choice. If, on the other hand, the text is equally consistent with both interpretations, then you do have a choice. You will choose the interpretation that you believe makes the work more significant or otherwise better, and this will probably (though not inevitably) depend on whether you think people like Scrooge are in fact, in the real world, born bad or corrupted by capitalism.

Now consider a more complex case. Suppose the text does not absolutely rule out either interpretation, but is marginally less consistent with one, which is, however, the interpretation you would pick if they both fit equally well. Suppose you believe that the original sin interpretation (as we might call it) is much the more accurate depiction of human nature. But if you choose that interpretation you will have to regard certain incidents and attributions established in the text you were given as "mistakes." You must then ask yourself which interpretation makes the work of art better *on the whole*, recognizing, as you will, that a novel whose plot is inconsistent or otherwise lacks integrity is thereby flawed. You must ask whether the novel is still better as a novel, read as a study of original sin, even though it must now be regarded as containing some "mistakes" in plot, than it would be with fewer "mistakes" but a less revealing picture of human nature. You may never have reflected on that question before, but that is no reason why you may not do so now, and once you make up your mind you will believe that the correct interpretation of Scrooge's character is the interpretation that makes the novel better on the whole.

C. The Chain of Law

Naturalism is a theory of adjudication not of the interpretation of novels. But naturalism supposes that common law adjudication is a chain enterprise sharing many of the features of the story we invented. According to naturalism, a judge should decide fresh cases in the spirit of a novelist in the chain writing a fresh chapter. The judge must make creative decisions, but must try to make these decisions "going on as before" rather than by starting in a new direction as if writing on a clean slate. He must read through (or have some good idea through his legal training and experience) what other judges in the past have written, not simply to discover what these other judges have said, or their state of mind when they said it, but to reach an opinion about what they have collectively *done*, in the way that each of our novelists formed an opinion about the collective novel so far written. Of course, the best interpretation of past judicial decisions is the interpretation that shows these in the best light, not aesthetically but politically, as coming as close to the correct ideals of a just legal system as possible. Judges in the chain of law share with the chain novelists the imperative of interpretation, but they bring different standards of success—political rather than aesthetic—to bear on that enterprise.

The analogy shows, I hope, how far naturalism allows a judge's beliefs about the personal and political rights people have "naturally"—that is, apart from the law—to enter his judgments about what the law requires. It does not instruct him to regard these beliefs as the only test of law. A judge's background and moral convictions will influence his decisions about what legal rights people have under the law. But the brute facts of legal history will nevertheless limit the role these convictions can play in those decisions. The same distinction we found in literary interpretation, between interpretation and ideal, holds here as well. An Agatha Christie mystery thriller cannot be interpreted as a philosophical novel about the meaning of death even by someone who believes that a successful philosophical novel would be a greater literary achievement than a successful mystery. It cannot be interpreted that way because, if it is, too much of the book must be seen as accidental, and too little as integrated, in plot, style and trope, with its alleged genre or point. Interpreted that way it becomes a shambles and so a failure rather than a success at anything at all. In the same way, a judge cannot plausibly discover, in a long and unbroken string of prior judicial decisions in favor of the manufacturers of defective products, any principle establishing strong consumers' rights. For that discovery would not show the history of judicial practice in a better light; on the contrary it would show it as the history of cynicism and inconsistency, perhaps of incoherence. A naturalist judge must show the facts of history in the best light he can, and this means that he must not show that history as unprincipled chaos.

Of course this responsibility, for judges as well as novelists, may best be fulfilled by a dramatic reinterpretation that both unifies what has gone before and gives it new meaning or point. This explains why a naturalist decision, though it is in this way tied to the past, may yet seem radical. A naturalist judge might find, in some principle that has not yet been recognized in judicial argument, a brilliantly unifying account of past decisions that shows them in a better light than ever before. American legal education celebrates dozens of such events in our own history. In the most famous single common law decision in American jurisprudence, for example, Cardozo reinterpreted a variety of cases to find, in these cases, the principle on which the modern law of negligence was built.[3]

Nevertheless the constraint, that a judge must continue the past and not invent a better past, will often have the consequence that a naturalist judge cannot reach decisions that he would otherwise, given his own political theory, want to reach. A judge who, as a matter of political conviction, believes in consumers' rights may nevertheless have to concede that the law of his jurisdiction has rejected this idea. It is in one way misleading to say, however, that he will be then forced to make decisions *at variance with* his political convictions. The principle that judges should decide consistently with principle, and that law should be coherent, is part of his convictions, and it is this principle that makes the decision he otherwise opposes necessary.

D. Interpretation in Practice

In this section I shall try to show how a self-conscious naturalist judge might construct a working approach to adjudication, and the role his background moral and political convictions would play in that working approach. When we imagined you to be a novelist in the chain novel, several pages ago, we considered how you would continue the first few chapters of A CHRISTMAS CAROL. We distinguished two dimensions of a successful interpretation. An interpretation must "fit" the data it interprets, in order not to show the novel as sloppy or incoherent, and it must also show that data in its best light, as serving as well as can be some proper ambition of novels. Just now, in noticing how a naturalist judge who believed in consumers' rights

might nevertheless have to abandon the claim that consumers' rights are embedded in legal history, . . . the same distinction between these two dimensions was relied upon. A naturalist judge would be forced to reject a politically attractive interpretation, we supposed, simply because he did not believe it fit the record well enough. If fit is indeed an independent dimension of success in interpretation, then any judge's working approach would include some tacit conception of what "fit" is, and of how well a particular interpretation must fit the record of judicial and other legal decisions in order to count as acceptable.

This helps us to explain why two naturalist judges might reach different interpretations of past judicial decisions about accidents, for example. They might hold different conceptions of "fit" or "best fit," so that, for instance, one thinks that an interpretation provides an acceptable fit only if it is supported by the opinions of judges in prior cases, while the other thinks it is sufficient, to satisfy the dimension of fit, that an interpretation fit the actual decisions these judges reached even if it finds no echo in their opinions. This difference might be enough to explain, for example, why one judge could accept an "economic" interpretation of the accident cases—that the point of negligence law is to reduce the overall social costs of accidents—while another judge, who also found that interpretation politically congenial, would feel bound by his beliefs about the requirement of fit to reject it.

At some point, however, this explanation of differences between two judges' theories of the same body of law would become strained and artificial. Suppose Judge X believes, for example, that pedestrians ought to look out for themselves, and have no business walking in areas in which drivers are known normally to exceed the legal speed limit. He might rely on this opinion in deciding that "our law recognizes no general right to recover whenever someone is injured by a speeding driver while walking on a highway where most drivers speed." If Judge Y reaches a different judgment about what the law is, because he believes that pedestrians should be entitled to assume that people will obey the law even when there is good evidence that they will not, then it would strain language to explain this difference by saying that these judges disagree about the way or the degree in which an interpretation of the law must fit past decisions. We would do better to say that these judges interpret the law differently, in this instance, because they bring different background theories of political morality to their interpretations just as two art critics might disagree about the correct interpretation of impressionism because they bring different theories about the value of art to that exercise.

Any naturalist judge's working approach to interpretation will recognize this distinction between two "dimensions" of interpretations of the prior law, and so we might think of such a theory as falling into two parts. One part refines and develops the idea that an interpretation must fit the data it interprets. This part takes up positions on questions like the following. How many decisions (roughly) can an interpretation set aside as mistakes, and still count as an interpretation of the string of decisions that includes those "mistakes?" How far is an interpretation better if it is more consistent with later rather than earlier past decisions? How far and in what way must a good interpretation fit the opinions judges write as well as the decisions they make? How far must it take account of popular morality contemporary with the decisions it offers to interpret? A second part of any judge's tacit theory of interpretation, however, will be quite independent of these "formal" issues. It will contain the substantive ideals of political morality on which he relies in deciding whether any putative interpretation is to be preferred because it shows legal practice to be better as a matter of substantive justice. Of course, if any working approach to interpretation has these two parts, then it must also have principles that combine or adjudicate between them.

This account of the main structure of a working theory of interpretation has heuristic appeal. It provides judges, and others who interpret the law, with a model they might use in identifying the approach they have been using, and self-consciously to inspect and improve that model. A thoughtful judge might establish for himself, for example, a rough "threshold" of fit which any interpretation of data must meet in order to be "acceptable" on the dimension of fit, and then suppose that if more than one interpretation of some part of the law meets this threshold, the choice among these should be made, not through further and more precise comparisons between the two along that dimension, but by choosing the interpretation which is "substantively" better, that is, which better promotes the political ideals he thinks correct. Such a judge might say, for example, that since both the foreseeability and the area-of-physical-risk interpretaions rise above the

threshold of fit with the emotional damage cases I mentioned earlier, foreseeability is better *as an interpretation* because it better accords with the "natural" rights of people injured in accidents.

The practical advantages of adopting such a threshold of fit are plain enough. A working theory need specify that threshold in only a rough and impressionistic way. If two interpretations both satisfy the threshold, then, as I said, a judge who uses such a theory need make no further comparisons along that dimension in order to establish which of them in fact supplies the "better" fit, and he may therefore avoid many of the difficult and perhaps arbitrary decisions about better fit that a theory without this feature might require him to make. But there are nevertheless evident dangers in taking the device too seriously, as other than a rule-of-thumb practical approach. A judge might be tricked into thinking that these two dimensions of interpretations are in some way deeply competitive with one another, that they represent the influence of two different and sometimes contradictory ambitions of adjudication.

He will then worry about those inevitable cases in which it is unclear whether some substantively attractive interpretation does indeed meet the threshold of fit. He will think that in such cases he must define that threshold, not impressionistically, as calling for a "decent" fit, but precisely, perhaps everything will then turn on whether that interpretation in fact just meets or just fails the crucial test. This rigid attitude toward the heuristic distinction would miss the point that any plausible theory of interpretation, in law as in literature, will call for some cross influence between the level of fit at which the threshold is fixed and the substantive issues involved. If an interpretation of some string of cases is far superior "substantively" it may be given the benefit of a less stringent test of fit for that reason.

For once again the underlying issue is simply one of comparing two pictures of the judicial past to see which offers a more attractive picture, from the standpoint of political morality, overall. The distinction between the dimensions of fit and substance is a rough distinction in service of that issue. The idea of a threshold of fit, and therefore of a lexical ordering between the two dimensions, is simply a working hypothesis, valuable so far as the impressionistic characterization of fit on which it depends is adequate, but which must be abandoned in favor of a more sophisticated and piecemeal analysis when the occasion demands.

Of course the moment when more sophisticated analysis becomes necessary, because the impressionistic distinction of the working theory no longer serves, is a moment of difficulty calling for fresh political judgments that may be hard to make. Suppose a judge faces, for the first time, the possibility of overruling a narrow rule followed for some time in his jurisdiction. Suppose, for example, that the courts have consistently held, since the issue was first raised, that lawyers may not be sued in negligence. Our judge believes that this rule is wrong and unjust, and that it is inconsistent in principle with the general rule allowing actions in negligence against other professional people like doctors and accountants. Suppose he can nevertheless find some putative principle, in which others find though he does not, which would justify the distinction the law has drawn. Like the principle, for example, that lawyers owe obligations to the courts or to abstract justice, it would be unfair to impose on the many legal obligation of due care to their clients. He must ask whether the best interpretation of the past includes *that* principle in spite of the fact that he himself would reject it.

Neither answer to this question will seem wholly attractive to him. If he holds that the law does include this putative principle, then this argument would present the law, including the past decisions about suits against lawyers as coherent; but he would then expose what he would believe to be a flaw in the substantive law. He would be supposing that the law includes a principle he believes is wrong, and therefore has no place in a just and wise system. If he decides that the law does not include the putative principle, on the other hand, then he can properly regard this entire line of cases about actions against lawyers as mistakes, and ignore or overrule them; but he then exposes a flaw in the record of a different sort, namely that past judges have acted in an unprincipled way, and a demerit in his own decision, that it treats the lawyer who loses the present case differently from how judges have treated other lawyers in the past. He must ask which is, in the end, the greater of these flaws; which way of reading the record shows it, in the last analysis, in the better and which in the worse light.

It would be absurd to suppose that all the lawyers and judges of any common law community share some set of convictions from which a single answer to that question could be deduced. Or even that many lawyers or judges would have ready at hand some convictions of their own which

could supply an answer without further ado. But it is nevertheless possible for any judge to confront issues like these in a principled way, and this is what naturalism demands of him. He must accept that in deciding one way rather than another about the force of a line of precedents, for example, he is developing a working theory of legal interpretation in one rather than another direction, and this must seem to him the right direction as a matter of political principle, not simply an appealing direction for the moment because he likes the answer it recommends in the immediate case before him. Of course there is, in this counsel, much room for deception, including self-deception. But in most cases it will be possible for judges to recognize when they have submitted some issue to the discipline this description requires and also to recognize when some other judge has not.

Let me recapitulate. Interpretation is not a mechanical process. Nevertheless, judges can form working styles of interpretation, adequate for routine cases, and ready for refinement when cases are not routine. These working styles will include what I called formal features. They will set out, impressionistically, an account of fit, and may characterize a threshold of fit an interpretation must achieve in order to be eligible. But they will also contain a substantive part, formed from the judge's background political morality, or rather that part of his background morality which has become articulate in the course of his career. Sometimes this heuristic distinction between fit and substantive justice, as dimensions of a successful interpretation, will itself seem problematic, and a judge will be forced to elaborate that distinction by reflecting further on the full set of the substantive and procedural political rights of citizens a just legal system must respect and serve. In this way any truly hard case develops as well as engages a judge's style of adjudication.

2. Is It *Delusion*?

A. *Internal and External Scepticism*

I have been describing naturalism as a theory about how judges should decide cases. It is of course a further question whether American (or any other) judges actually do decide cases that way. I shall not pursue that further question now. Instead, I want to consider certain arguments that I expect will be

108

made against naturalism simply as a recommendation. In fact, many of the classical objections to "natural law" theories are objections to such theories as models for, rather than descriptions of, judicial practice. I shall begin with what might be called the sceptical attack.

I put my description of naturalism in what might be called a subjective mode. I described the question which, according to naturalism, judges should put to themselves and answer from their own convictions. Someone is bound to object that, although each judge can answer these questions for himself, different judges will give different answers, and no single answer can be said to be *objectively* right. "There are as many different 'best' interpretations as there are interpreters," he will say, "because no one can offer any argument in favor of one interpretation over another, except that it strikes him as the best, and it will strike some other interpreter as the worst. No doubt judges (as well as many other people) would deny this. They think their opinions can have some objective standing, that they can be either true or false. But this is delusion merely."

What response can naturalism, as I have described it, make to this sceptical challenge? We must begin by asking what kind of scepticism is in play. I have in mind a distinction which, once again, might be easier to state if we return to a literary analogy. Suppose we are studying Hamlet and the question is put by some critic whether, before the play begins, Hamlet and Ophelia have been lovers. This is a question of interpretation, and two critics who disagree might present arguments trying to show why the play is, all things considered, more valuable as a work of art on one or the other understanding about Hamlet and Ophelia. But plainly a third position is possible. Someone might argue that it makes no difference to the importance or value of the play which of these assumptions is made about the lovers, because the play's importance lies in a humanistic vision of life and fate, not in any detail of plot or character whose reading would be affected by either assumption. This third position argues that the right answer to this particular question of interpretation is only that there is no right answer; that there is no "best" interpretation of the sexual relationship between Hamlet and Ophelia, only "different" interpretations, because neither interpretation would make the play more or less valuable as a work of art. This might strike you (it does me) as

exactly the right position to take on this particular issue. It is, in a sense, a sceptical position, because it denies "truth" both to the proposition that Hamlet slept with Ophelia, and to the apparently contrary proposition that he did not. But if this is scepticism, it is what [we] might call *internal* scepticism. It does not challenge the idea that good arguments can in principle be found for one interpretation of Hamlet rather than another. On the contrary it *relies* on an interpretive argument—that the value of the play lies in a dimension that does not intersect the sexual question—in order to reach its "sceptical" position on that question.

Contrast the position of someone who says that no one interpretation of any work of art could ever succeed in showing it to be either really better or really worse, because there is not and cannot be any such thing as "value" in art at all. He means that there is something very wrong with the enterprise of interpretation (at least as I have described it) as a whole, not simply with particular issues or arguments within it. Of course he may have arguments for his position, or think he has; but these will not be arguments that, like the arguments of the internal sceptic, explicitly assume a positive theory of the value of art in general or of a particular work of art. They will be a priori, philosophical arguments attempting to show that the very idea of value in art is a deep mistake, that people who say they find a work of art "good" or "valuable" are not describing any objective property, but only expressing their own subjective reaction. This is *external* scepticism about art, and about interpretation in art.

B. The Threat of Scepticism

If a lawyer says that no one interpretation of a legal record can be "objectively" the correct interpretation, he might have external scepticism in mind. He might mean that if two judges disagree about the "correct" interpretation of the emotional damages cases, because they hold different theories of what a just law of negligence would be like, their disagreement is for that reason alone merely "subjective," and neither side can be "objectively" right. I cannot consider, in this essay, the various arguments that philosophers have offered for external scepticism about political morality. The best of these arguments rely on a general thesis of philosophy that might be called the "demonstrability hypothesis." This holds that no proposition can be true unless the means exist, at least in principle, to demonstrate its truth through arguments to everyone who understands the language and is rational. If the demonstrability hypothesis is correct, then external scepticism is right about a great many human enterprises and activities; perhaps about all of them, including the activities we call scientific. I know of no good reason to accept the demonstrability hypothesis (it is at least an embarrassment that this hypothesis cannot itself be demonstrated in the sense if requires) and I am not myself an external sceptic. But rather than pursue the question of the demonstrability hypothesis, I shall change the subject.

Suppose you are an external sceptic about justice and other aspects of political morality. What follows about the question of how judges should decide cases? About whether naturalism is better than other (more conservative or more radical) theories of adjudication? You might think it follows that you should take no further interest in these questions at all. If so, I have some sympathy with your view. After all, you believe, on what you take to be impressive philosophical grounds, that no way of deciding cases at law can really be thought to be any better than any other, and that no way of interpreting legal practice can be preferred to any other on rational grounds. The "correct" theory of what judges should do is only a matter of what judges feel like doing, or of what they believe will advance political causes to which they happen to be drawn. The "correct" interpretation of legal practice is only a matter of reading legal history so that it appeals to you, or so that you can use it in your own political interests. If you are convinced of these externally sceptical propositions, you might well do better to take up the interesting questions raised by certain sociologists of law—questions about the connection between judges' economic class and the decisions they are likely to reach, for example. Or to take up the study of strategies for working your will on judges if you ever come to argue before them, or on other judges if you ever join the bench yourself. Your external scepticism might well persuade you to take up these "practical" questions and set aside the "theoretical" questions you have come to see as meaningless.

But it is worth noticing that philosophers who say they are external sceptics rarely draw that sort of practical conclusion for themselves. Most of them seem to take a rather different line, which I do not myself fully understand, but which can, I think, fairly be represented as follows. External scepticism is not a position within an enterprise, but about an enterprise. It does not tell us to stop making the kinds of arguments we are disposed to make and accept and act on within morality or politics, but only to change our beliefs about what we are doing when we act this way. Imagine that some chessplayers thought that chess was an "objective" battle between forces of light and darkness, so that when black won good had triumphed in some metaphysical sense. External sceptics about chess would reject this view, and think that chess was entertainment merely; but they would not thereupon cease playing chess or play it any differently from their deluded fellow players. So external sceptics about political morality will still have opinions and make arguments about justice; they will simply understand, in their philosophical moments, that when they do this they are not discovering timeless and objective truths.

If you are an external sceptic who takes this attitude, you will have driven a wedge between your external scepticism and any judgments you might make about how judges should decide cases, in general, or about what the best justification is of some part of the law, in particular. You will have your own opinions about these matters, which you will express in arguments or, if you are an academic lawyer, in law review articles or, if you are a judge, in your decisions. You may well come to believe that the best interpretation of the emotional [damage] cases shows them to be grounded in the principle of foreseeability, for example. When you retreat to your philosophical study, you will have a particular view about the opinions you expressed or exhibited while you were "playing the game." You will believe that your opinions about the best justification of the emotional damage cases were "merely" subjective opinions (whatever that means) with no basis in any "objective" reality. But this does not itself provide any argument in favor of *other* opinions about the best interpretation. In particular, it does not provide any argument in favor of the *internally* sceptical opinion that no interpretation of the accident cases is best.

Of course your external scepticism leaves you free to take up that internally sceptical position if you believe you have good internal arguments for it. Suppose you are trying to decide whether the best interpretation of the emotional damage cases lies in the principle that people in the area of physical risk may recover for emotional damage, or the broader principle that anyone whose emotional damage was foreseeable may recover. After the most diligent search and reflection asking yourself exactly the questions naturalism poses, you may find that the case for neither of these interpretations seems to you any stronger than the case for the other. I think this is very unlikely, but that is beside the present point, which is only that it is possible. You would be internally sceptical, in this way, about any uniquely "correct" interpretation of this group of cases; but you would have supplied an affirmative argument, beginning in your naturalistic theory, for that internally sceptical conclusion. It would not have mattered whether you were an external sceptic, who nevertheless "played the game" as a naturalist, or an external "believer" who thought that naturalism was stitched into the fabric of the universe. You would have reached the same internally sceptical conclusion, on these assumed beliefs and facts, in either case.

What is, then, the threat that external scepticism poses to naturalism? It is potentially very threatening indeed, not only to naturalism, but to all its rival theories of adjudication as well. It may persuade you to try to have nothing to do with morality or legal theory at all, though I do not think you will succeed in giving up these immensely important human activities. If this very great threat fails (as it seems to have failed for almost all external sceptics) then no influence remains. For in whatever spirit you do enter any of these enterprises—however firmly your fingers may be crossed—the full range of positions within the enterprise is open to you on equal terms. If you end in some internally sceptical position of some sort, this will be because of the internal power of the arguments that drove you there, not because of your external sceptical credentials.

We must now consider another possibility. The sceptical attack upon naturalism may in fact consist, not in the external scepticism I have been discussing, but in some global form of internal scepticism. I just conceded the possibility that we might find reason for internal scepticism about the best interpretation of some particular body of law. Suppose we had reasons to be internally sceptical about the best interpretation of any and all parts of the law? It is hard to imagine the plausible arguments that would bring us to that conclusion, but not hard to imagine how someone with bizarre

views might be brought to it. Suppose one holds that all morality rests on God's will, and had just decided that there is no God. Or he believes that only spontaneous and unreflective decisions can have moral value, and that no judicial decision can either be spontaneous or encourage spontaneity. These would be arguments not rejecting the idea or sense of morality, as in the case of external scepticism, but employing what the author takes to be the best conception of morality in service of a wholesale internally sceptical position. If this position were in fact the right view to take up about political morality, then it would always be wrong to suppose that one interpretation of past judicial decisions was better than another, at least in cases when both passed the threshold test of fit. Naturalism would therefore be a silly theory to recommend to judges. So the threat of [internal] scepticism, it materializes, is in fact much greater than the threat of external scepticism. But (as the examples I chose may have suggested) I cannot think of any plausible arguments for global internal scepticism about political morality.

Of course, nothing in this short discussion disputes the claim, which is plainly true, that different judges hold different political moralities, and will therefore disagree about the best justification of the past. Or the claim, equally true, that there will be no way for any side in such disagreements to prove that it is right and its opponents wrong. The demonstrability thesis (as I said) argues from these undeniable facts to general external scepticism. But even if we reject that thesis, as I do, the bare fact of disagreement may be thought to support an independent challenge of naturalism, which does not depend on either external or internal scepticism. For it may be said that whether or not there is an objectively right answer to the question of justification, it is unfair that the answer of one judge be accepted as final when he has no way to prove, as against those who disagree, that his position is better. This is part of the argument from democracy to which we must now turn.

3. Is It *Undemocratic?*

So if we are to reject naturalism, in favor of some other positive theory of adjudication, this cannot be by virtue of any general appeal to external scepticism as a philosophical doctrine. We need arguments of substantive political morality showing why naturalism is unwise or unjust. In the remaining sections of the essay I shall consider certain arguments, that I have either heard or invented, to that effect. Of course arguments against naturalism must compare it, unfavorably, with some other theory, and arguments that might be effective in the context of one such comparison would be self-defeating in another.

I shall consider, first, the arguments that might be made against naturalism from the standpoint of what I believe is a more positivist theory of adjudication, though nothing turns on whether this theory is properly called positivism. Someone might propose, as an alternative to naturalism, that judges should decide cases in the following way. First, they should identify the persons or institutions which are authorized to make law by the social conventions of their community. Next, they should check the record of history to see whether any such persons or institutions have laid down a rule of law whose language unambiguously covers the case at hand. If so, they should decide that case by applying that rule. If not—if history shows that no rule has been laid down deciding the case either way—then they should create the best rule for the future, and apply it retrospectively. The rule they thus create would then become, for later judges, part of the record endorsed by convention, so that later judges facing the same issue could then find, in that decision, language settling the matter for them. We might call this theory of adjudication "conventionalism."

Some people are drawn to conventionalism, over naturalism, because they think the former is more democratic. It argues that people only have the rights, in court, that legislators and judges, whom convention recognizes to have legislative power, have already decided to give them. Naturalism, on the other hand, assigns judges the power to draw from judicial history rights that no official institution has ever sanctioned before, and to do so on no stronger argument than that the past is seen in a better light, according to the convictions of the judges, if these rights are presupposed. This seems the antithesis of what democracy requires.

But this argument mistakes the cases in which a conventionalist and a naturalist are likely to disagree. Conventionalist judges can dispose of cases at the first stage, by copying the decisions already made by elected officials, only in those cases in which some statute exactly in point unambiguously dictates a particular result. Any conscientious naturalist is very likely to make exactly the same decisions in those "simple" cases, so conventionalism cannot be more democratic because it decides these differently. The two styles of adjudication will normally recommend different decisions only when some fresh judicial judgment is required which goes beyond what the legislature has unarguably said, either because the statute in play is open to different interpretations, or because no particular statute is in play at all. But in these "hard" cases the difference between the two theories of adjudication cannot be that one defers to the legislature's judgment while the other challenges that judgment. Because, by hypothesis, there is no legislative judgment that can be treated in either of these ways. Conventionalism argues that the judge must, in these "hard" cases, choose the rule of decision which best promotes the good society as he conceives it. It is hardly more democratic for judges to rely on their own convictions about the best design of the future than to rely instead on their convictions about the best interpretation of the past.

So the argument from democracy in favor of conventionalism over naturalism seems to come to nothing. Be we should consider one possible counter-argument. I have been assuming that conventionalism and naturalism will designate the same cases as "easy," that is, as cases in which no fresh judgment is required by the judge. But perhaps a naturalist has more room than a conventionalist to deny that an apparently "easy" case really is. Consider the following example. Since naturalism encourages a judge to rely on his own convictions about which interpretation shows the past in the best light, it permits outrageous political convictions to generate outrageous judicial decisions. Suppose a naturalist judge believes that majority will is tyranny. He believes that our political institutions should be arranged so that statutes are enforced only when they have been enacted by a two-thirds vote. He acknowledges that he cannot apply this prinicple unless it provides an acceptable fit with past practice, but he sets the threshold of fit low enough, in perfect good faith, so as to be able conscientiously to claim that all counter-examples (all cases in which statutes passed by a bare majority have been enforced by the courts) are "mistakes."

This is no doubt possible. Nothing in the design of naturalism insures that a judge with silly or mad opinions will not be appointed; but nothing in the design of conventionalism insures that either;

and conventionalism will not prevent him from reaching preposterous decisions once appointed. A conventionalist judge needs a concept of convention. He must decide, for example, whether it is a convention of our society that the Constitution should be followed, and nothing in the structure of conventionalism can insure that a judge will in fact reach the correct answer to that question. No theory of adjudication can guarantee that only sensible decisions will be reached by judges who embrace that theory. We can protect ourselves from madness or gross stupidity only by independent procedures governing how judges are to be appointed, how their decisions may be appealed and reversed, and how they may be removed from office if this should appear necessary.

But it may now be said that naturalism would encourage anti-democratic decisions from judges who hold, not mad, but plausible and even attractive political convictions, and who deploy perfectly sensible theories about how much of the past an interpretation must fit. For naturalism leaves no doctrine or practice immune from re-examination. We may use an earlier example as an illustration. Suppose a firm line of cases has rejected the idea that clients may sue lawyers who are negligent. Conventionalism is then committed (so it might be said) to continuing that doctrine until it is reversed by legislation, which seems the democratic solution. But naturalism encourages judges to put this line of cases in a wider context, and ask whether the rule refusing recovery against negligent lawyers would not itself be rejected by the best justification of the rest of the law, which allows recovery for negligent injury of almost every other kind. So a naturalist might be led to overrule these cases, which a conventionalist would leave for the legislature to review.

Indeed there is nothing in the theory of naturalism, as I described it, which would prevent an intelligent and sensible naturalist from taking the same line with certain statutes. Suppose an old statute makes blasphemy a crime and, though it has not been enforced in centuries, it is suddenly revived by a public prosecutor anxious to make a splash. A naturalist judge might well develop a theory of obsolescence, even though this had never been recognized in the jurisdiction before. He might say that the best interpretation of judicial practice as a whole yields the following qualification to the rule that statutes are always to be enforced. "Old statutes quite at variance with the

spirit of the present time, which would not be enacted by the present legislature, and which have not been employed since ancient times, are unavailable as grounds of criminal prosecution." If prosecutors have not tried to revive old statutes in the fairly recent past, this qualification would be consistent with judicial practice, and it might plausibly be thought to show that practice in a better light, as both more rational and more closely tying what counts as valid legislation to the will of the people.

So both in the case of precedent and legislation a competent naturalist judge might find certain cases hard, and amenable to the command of imaginative reinterpretation, which a conventionalist must concede to be easy even when the obvious answer is unattractive. So perhaps naturalism would sometimes produce "novel" decisions by sensible judges that conventionalism would discourage. But is it right to say that naturalism is for this reason less "democratic." A minimally competent naturalist judge would begin his argument by recognizing, indeed, insisting, that our political system is a democracy; he would continue by arguing that democracy, properly understood, is best served by a coherent rather than an unprincipled private law of negligence, and by an institution of legislation that is sensitive rather than obdurate to changes in popular morality. So the disagreement between naturalism and conventionalism about which cases are really "easy" is not a disagreement between those who oppose and those who respect democracy; it is rather the more familiar disagreement about what democracy really is. When the disagreement is seen in this light, it is far from apparent that the naturalist has the worst of the argument. In the next section, I shall argue that naturalism respects, better than its rivals, a right that has seemed to many people crucial to the idea of democracy, which is the right each person has to be treated, by his government, as an equal.

4. Is It Crazy?

A. Instrumentalism

We must turn now to the arguments that might be made against naturalism, not from the standpoint of conventionalism, but from the different direction of a more radical theory I shall call instrumentalism. This theory encourages judges always to look to the future: to try to make the community as good and wise and just a community as it can be, with no essential regard to what it has been until now. Of course, instrumentalist judges will differ, among themselves, about the correct model of the good community. Some will define this in almost exclusively economic terms. They will think that a rich community is for that reason a good community. Others will take a more utilitarian line, and emphasize the importance of personal and political rights, and will therefore provide, in their account of the good society, that certain fundamental interests of individuals like liberty of conscience or a decent standard of living, be respected at the cost of general wealth or average happiness.

An instrumentalist judge will see himself or herself as an officer of government charged with contributing to the good society according to his or her conception of what that is. Of course, a sensible instrumentalist judge will acknowledge the importance of institutional factors as either an obstacle or opportunity in this enterprise. He will understand, in particular, that the rules he fashions must work together with the rules provided by other institutions and other officials, so that he is constrained by what we might call consistency in strategy. If the legislature and other judges have laid down rules in the past that he is powerless to overrule, for example, he must not create rules of his own which, operating alongside those established rules, would produce chaos. For that would make the community worse not better off through his efforts. But instrumentalism denies that judges should be constrained by the past in any less pragmatic way than that. It denies, in particular, that they should also seek consistency in principle, by making their decisions conform to the best interpretation, as the naturalist conceives this, of the past. Naturalism insists that the past should be allowed to cast a shadow over the future beyond the pragmatic requirements of strategy. Instrumentalism condemns this as irrational.

In order to bring out the difference between the two theories, consider this situation. You think that it would be best, all things considered, if no one were ever allowed to recover damages for emotional injury. You think this because you believe that actions for emotional damage involve the risk of fraud, and force insurance premiums higher than the optimum for economic efficiency. Of course you think, as part of this view, that no one has what we might call a moral right that the law provide damages for emotional injuries. If you thought anyone did have such a right, then you would think that the good society should recognize that right and enforce it by producing the appropriate legislation even at the cost of efficiency. But since you think people have no such moral right you think that society would be better off, on the whole, if it provided no legal right to such damages.

Now suppose you are an instrumentalist judge faced with a suit by a mother who suffered emotional injury when she heard, on the telephone, that her son had been run down by a careless driver. You find, when you search the books, that the other judges of your jurisdiction have consistently awarded recovery for emotional damages to relatives who actually saw physical damage to someone they loved. Of course you think that all these decisions are wrong. You would be tempted to overrule the whole line of decisions if you could, but suppose this is beyond your power. The line might include decisions of the highest court of the state, for example, and you might be sitting in a lower court. You will nevertheless grasp the opportunity to limit the damage these cases do to the community's welfare, according to your convictions, by declaring that only relatives who actually saw the injury may recover for emotional damage. This will create no practical contradictions, or inconsistency in strategy.

What objection could there be to this instrumentalist solution to the problem, assuming as you do, that it conduces to a better state of affairs, on the whole, than the opposite decision? A naturalist might be led by his naturalism to the opposite decision, even if he shared your assumptions about the best state of affairs. He would be unable to find any principled distinction between seeing and hearing about an accident, and he would be forced to concede that the best justification of the past recognizes a judicial right to recover for emotional damage if that damage was reasonably forseeable. Of course he might try to show (as the naturalist judge in the example I considered earlier was able to show about actions in negligence against lawyers) that allowing recovery for emotional damage was inconsistent with some broader line of cases. But suppose he could not show this, as indeed he is unlikely to be able to do. He would then be forced to decide the present case for the plaintiff mother, therefore compounding the damage to the future. What could be the possible sense or other merit in that? This is the basis of the instrumentalist charge: that insofar as naturalism requires different decisions from those an instrumentalist would reach, naturalism is crazy.

Naturalism seems to assume that in these circumstances it would be for some reason *unfair* to decide against her. But why? She has (by hypothesis) no moral right to a rule allowing her damages. On the contrary, the situation would be better if no one were ever required to pay damage for her sort of injury. The fact that our judicial process has made one mistake is no good argument for making that mistake more general. Of course, a naturalist cannot say that it would be unfair to decide against the mother because most judges in the past have behaved as naturalists. It would beg the present question to say that this provides a reason why a judicial decision that offends naturalism is unfair. For the question at issue is whether it is unfair to reach a decision which offends the best interpretation of the past. If we want to sustain naturalism as against instrumentalism, we must argue that the fact that a given principle figures in the best justification of legal practice as a whole provides a reason for extending that principle into the future, and we must not rely on that very claim in making our case for it. But how can we then argue the case? What can we say to the instrumentalist who claims, reasonably enough, that two mistakes are worse than one?

B. *The Political Order*

The naturalist might begin his reply by noticing that the dispute now in play is wider than simply a dispute about how judges should decide cases. Naturalism assumes and instrumentalism denies that the members of a community can have rights and duties against one another, and against the community as such, just by virtue of the political history of the community. That they can have rights and duties they would not have if that history had been different. But this is the idea familiar not only to lawyers but to our general political rhetoric. Politicians say that America is a democracy, and therefore that certain things ought and ought not to be done. Or that America respects the rule of law, and therefore that Congress should not enact certain laws.

We should give a name to the idea behind this rhetoric. Let us say that the set of political rights people have just by virtue of the political history of their community constitutes the "political order" of the community. Naturalism recognizes that communities have political orders, and offers an account of what a political order is. A community's political order is provided by the principles assumed in the best interpretation (in the sense we have been using) of its concrete political structures, practices and decisions. Naturalism supposes that people have a right to have this order enforced, in court, on demand. It is not true that every rule of law a legislature or court adopts is part of the political order, properly understood. The best interpretation of the order as a whole may show this particular rule inconsistent with the rest, and so a "mistake" that should be ignored in stating what the order really is. But if it is indeed part of the genuine political order, properly understood, that people suffering emotional injury are entitled to damages against the tortfeasor, then someone who has suffered such damage is for that reason entitled to a judicial order to that effect.

Of course naturalism is a theory about *judicial* rights, that is, about the rights people have to win [lawsuits]. It takes no position about how far the political order furnishes or constrains the rights people have to particular legislation in their favor, or their rights to revolt or otherwise to establish a very different political order. If the political order includes a constitution which, properly interpreted, disables the legislature from changing the present order in certain ways, then people do have judicial rights, under this order, that the courts not enforce legislation which contradicts these commands. But naturalism, as such, leaves the legislature otherwise free to improve the present order, both in detail and, if appropriate, radically. The idea, that people have an abstract judicial right to the enforcement of the present order, imposes a kind of conservatism on politics; but this is a conservatism imposed on adjudication alone.

Instrumentalism challenges not simply naturalism's conception of a political order, but the concept of a political order itself. It denies the fact that political history that has taken a certain form can ever be the ground of a genuine right or duty at least against a court. This is the upshot of the instrumentalist's thesis that there are no judicial rights by virtue of the judicial past. He believes that a judge is never obliged, by the nature of the past, to work against the best solution for the future. The instrumentalist argues that the idea that judges are constrained in this way is irrational. Of course he recognizes each society has a distinctive political past, and concedes that most people believe their rights and duties are, at least in some ways, a function of the past. But the instrumentalist holds that this opinion is silly.

Now what arguments does the naturalist have available in reply? We might begin by considering one familiar argument a naturalist might be tempted to make, though only to reject it. Someone might argue that judges should never attempt to change the political order because this would require them to make judgments of political morality which ought to be left to the peoples' elected representatives. So judges should accept the popular idea of a political order, and enforce that order as history presents it to them, for that reason. This is like the (bad) argument we supposed a conventionalist might make against naturalism; in any case it is not an argument a naturalist can make against instrumentalism because, according to naturalism, a judge must make decisions of political morality in order to decide what the political order, properly construed, really is. We labored that point in our description of how a naturalist judge would go about deciding which interpretation of the past was the best interpretation. There is, for the naturalist, a crucial distinction between interpreting and improving the political order of the community, but these are both activities which engage the judge's moral sense.

For much the same reason the naturalist cannot use another familiar argument often made in favor of judicial conservatism. It is sometimes said that judges do great damage to social efficiency when they surprise litigants by changing established rules of law. Once again this is an argument that a conventionalist might be tempted to employ against naturalism. But it is unavailable to naturalism because nothing insures that a naturalist judge's interpretation of the past will not prove surprising. A naturalist is charged with discovering and enforcing the best interpretation of his community's political structure and past decisions, but the interpretation he believes best may be (as we saw in the example of Cardozo's decision in *McPherson v. Buick*) interpretation that has occurred to no one else. In any case, the argument is a bad argument against instrumentalism for a different reason. This argument supposes that a novel decision, such as an instrumentalist might make, will

in fact be unwise, pragmatically, for the future. But if this is really so, then an instrumentalist is ready to take that into account in deciding which decision will be best for the future. We noticed that an instrumentalist will look to the past, not as a source of rights, but strategically, to discover whether his judgment will in fact have the beneficial effects on the future he supposes. If disregarding some established line of precedent will actually diminish efficiency, because it will discourage people from counting on established rules of law in planning their affairs, then this is exactly the kind of strategic consideration instrumentalism stands ready to acknowledge.

A naturalist must find his defense of naturalism—of his idea that the standing political order is a source of judicial rights—elsewhere. He must meet the instrumentalist's challenge directly, by showing why people can have genuine political rights just by virtue of the actual political history of their community, and why these rights hold with special force in litigation. Can we find such an argument for naturalism? We might begin by stipulating a general requirement of justice in government. Any government must treat its citizens as equals, as equally entitled to concern and respect. Of course this general requirement is very abstract. Different people—and different societies—will have different views of what it is to treat people as equals. But we can nevertheless speak of a general duty of government to treat its citizens this way, and derive from this two distinct and more concrete responsibilities. The first is the responsibility, in creating a political order, to respect whatever underlying moral and political rights citizens may have in the name of genuine equality. The second is the obligation to extend whatever political order it does create equally and consistently to everyone.

These obligations are distinct because they can be fulfilled or violated independently. A society may develop a conception of justice that we, as critics of that society, reject. In its pursuit of efficiency or other collective goals, it may violate rights we think people have as individuals, but it may nevertheless enforce that conception consistently and, in that sense, fairly, allowing to everyone the resources, opportunities, and protections each is entitled to have under the theory it has adopted. It may, on the other hand, put in place an admirable political order; it may adopt a general scheme of principles and institutions, which we, as critics, approve as exactly what justice requires; but it may nevertheless fail to enforce and scheme consistently, so that some people do not have the resources and opportunities the public order requires them to have.

Once we recognize both the fact and the independence of these two rights, we see how it is possible that a government might commit the following special form of injustice. It might deny to some people a right it has, but need not have, extended to others. But that is exactly what the instrumentalist judge I just imagined does in denying the mother her suit for emotional damages. In one sense the situation that follows his decision is an improvement over the situation that would have resulted had he decided for the mother. If he is right in thinking that allowing recovery for emotional damage is not required by morality, and that it is damaging to the economy, then there will be less "unnecessary" damage to economic efficiency. But the plaintiff mother in this case nevertheless has a complaint. Though she has no right to a legal regime under which people in her position recover damages, she does have a right that the legal regime in force be consistently applied to her. Otherwise society fails to give her justice according to its conception of what justice requires, and that is a failure to treat her with equal concern and respect. One of her political rights has been violated.

So the naturalist's approach to this case is correct, and the instrumentalist's wrong, because the former respects and the latter violates the plaintiff's right to be treated as an equal. This is enough to make out what I am presently most anxious to show: that instrumentalism is wrong in assuming that the political order cannot be an independent source of rights. Of course the case I supposed as an example made it easier to demonstrate that point; it is implausible to think that a negligent driver has a moral right *not* to have the law recognize emotional damages. So the defendant driver seemed to have no proper objection to a naturalist judge's decision in favor of the mother. We can easily imagine cases, however, in which even the best interpretation of the community's law would show that it failed to recognize a substantive right someone ought to have.

Suppose, for example, that someone sues for damages for invasion of privacy, but even the most sophisticated interpretation of the law of the community fails to reveal a principle sustaining any such right. Now the situation reveals a conflict (as we might put it) between the two rights that follow from the abstract right to justice. A naturalist judge, who denies the action, will have upheld the defendant's right to a consistent application of the public order, but failed to uphold the plaintiff's right to a better public order. Naturalism insists that the function of courts, at least in a political society meeting minimum standards of justice, is to address the former rather than the latter right. No doubt more argument is necessary (which I cannot supply here) to sustain that choice. Once the two rights are distinguished, however, and both recognized, that choice is not crazy. Naturalism is not, as the present objection supposed, irrational.

But what if the condition I just mentioned is not met? What if the best interpretation of the legal system (or some important part of it) shows it to be wicked? Suppose that the most sophisticated interpretation of our Constitution, at the time of the Fugitive Slave Acts, contained no principle in virtue of which slaves had a right to be free, so that even a naturalist judge would have had to recognize those unfortunate statutes as perfectly constitutional. An instrumentalist might well want to say that here, at least, instrumentalism would provide a better guide to decision, because it would advise the judge to ignore the constitutional structure, if he could get away with this, and find some way to thwart the Acts. But naturalism has the virtue, even in cases like this one, of bringing to the surface an issue of political morality that cannot be ignored.

Of course a constitutional structure that permits slavery is deeply defective. It violates people's first political right: the right to a public order that treats them as equals. The more difficult issue is this: is there any room, in this sorry picture, for the slaveholders' second right? Does the slaveholder whose slaves have escaped have any right, however weak, that the constitutional system be enforced on his behalf, as it is on behalf of the slaveowner who has managed to keep his slaves imprisoned at home? If you were a naturalist judge, you might think that he does. In that case you would have to decide the Fugitive Slave [c]ases for the slaveowners even though you despise them and deplore that constitution, and even though you privately work for a constitutional amendment or even for civil war. But you might also come to the opposite conclusion. You might think that no one can have any right, even a weak right, to the equal benefit of wicked laws. In that case you would decide against the slaveowners if you could, because the underlying reason for your concern with the past, which is people's abstract rights to institutional consistency, would have exhausted its power. It would not matter if you put your conclusion in the terminology of older natural law theories, and said that the Fugitive Slave Acts were not really law. Or if you used the language of modern positivism, and said that though they were law they were too evil to be enforced. For the important issue is not what you say but what you do, and, though naturalism does not in itself answer the difficult moral question I posed, it does tell you what consequences for your decision follow from the answer you give to that question.

C. The Two Ideals

Perhaps you will allow me a summary of this last part of my argument. Our political system admits of two ideals; it is imperfect in two ways. It stands in the shadow of an external ideal, which is the ideal of a perfectly just and effective system. This is the challenge it offers to legislation, and, beyond that, to the political will and sense of justice of the community which has the standing power to make it better, closer to the external ideal of what a political system should be. But unless it is a very bad political system it stands also in the shadow of a different, internal ideal, which is the ideal of itself made pure. This is the challenge it offers to adjudication: the challenge of making the standards that govern our collective lives articulate, coherent and effective. Naturalism insists on the difference between the two ideals, and makes that difference the nerve of the rule of law.

People will disagree about what the internal ideal of our order is like, perhaps just as much as they disagree about the external ideal our order should pursue. Indeed they will disagree about the former precisely because they disagree about the latter. So no one will have any guarantee that, if he should come to court, those who judge him accord-

ing to naturalism will reach the result that he himself thought was the best interpretation of our order when he acted. That is inevitable in any community which recognizes what is plainly true: that people have rights beyond the rights conventionalism recognizes, that is, that they have rights beyond the strict and narrow limits within which everyone agrees what these rights are. But naturalism at least takes the actual political order, properly interpreted, as the common standard, so that citizens are encouraged to put to themselves the same questions that officials who adjudicate their disputes will ask in judging them. No doubt this practice will cause surprise and disappointment, even despair. No doubt it will produce injustice. Its virtue is that it seems less vulnerable, in all these respects, than available alternatives for bringing the rule of principle to an imperfect world.

We can, as a community, strive towards these two ideals at the same time, though through different institutions and practice. We embrace the two ideals as an agenda for sustained and continuing debate. We have no hope—and indeed no wish— that the debate will end. We understand that the decision of political officials must be accepted, from time to time. But we insist that this is only because someone's decisions must be accepted and not because these decisions come guaranteed for accuracy. We know that the quality of the debate is itself, quite apart from any agreement it might produce, something that makes ourselves and our community better. This is the image we should have of politics and of our lives in politics. Our courts play a distinct, sovereign and indispensible role in this image. They are the forum of the second ideal.

Endnotes

[1] R. Dworkin, Taking Rights Seriously 105–130 (1977).
[2] R. Dworkin, Law and Interpretation, Critical Inquiry (1982).
[3] McPherson v. Buick, 217 N.Y. 382, 111 N.E. 1050 (N.Y. 1916).

Legal Realism, Critical Legal Studies, and Dworkin

ANDREW ALTMAN

I

In contemporary Anglo-American legal philosophy, little attention has been paid to the work in legal theory carried out in this country during the first half of the century. Indeed, it would be only a slight exaggeration to say that legal theory prior to the publication of H. L. A. Hart's classic, *The Concept of Law,* is generally treated as belonging to a kind of prehistorical legal philosophy.[1] Contemporary authors feel it unnecessary to grapple with the theories belonging to this prehistory, as it is widely viewed that such theories have been transcended by the work of Hart and those who followed in his wake.

Nowhere is this attitude toward the legal theories of the first half of the century more evident than in the contemporary treatment of American legal realism. Attention to the realist movement is, to say the least, scanty. Ronald Dworkin devotes approximately one page to the movement in the more than three hundred pages of *Taking Rights Seriously.*[2] Theodore Benditt is more generous in the space he devotes to discussing realism: two chapters of his *Law as Rule and Principle.* Yet, Benditt treats realism as little more than a historical relic.[3] To be sure, realism is regarded as having had its insights, but they are thought of as having been long ago recognized and absorbed into mainstream legal philosophy, while the deficiencies have been presumably identified and repudiated. Such is the dominant message about realism transmitted by most current work in legal philosophy.[4]

A principal part of the explanation for why most current legal philosophers seem to accept this message lies, I believe, in the apparently cogent critique of realism offered by Hart in *The Concept of Law.* Hart's theory absorbed many of the claims associated with the realist movement. At the same time, he repudiated what were called the "excesses" of realism by invoking a well worked out conception of law as a system of rules. Among those so-called excesses was the idea that the law was shot through with indeterminacy, so that in almost any dispute which reached the stage of litigation the law failed to dictate any specific outcome. Hart's theoretical strategy was to admit that there was a significant amount of indeterminacy in the law, but to argue that such indeterminacy necessarily occupied a peripheral zone in the work of the legal system. Hart thus domesticated the realist indeterminacy thesis. Subsequently, under the influence of Ronald Dworkin, mainstream legal philosophy became preoccupied with the issue of whether or not Hart had himself exaggerated the zone of legal indeterminacy. The more radical indeterminacy of the realist was consigned to the category of realist excesses which everyone now recognized and repudiated.

In this article, I shall begin by examining the realist indeterminacy thesis. Hart's criticisms of realism, I argue, do not come to grips with the most radical source of legal indeterminacy posited by realism. The same may be said for the extensive set of criticisms offered by Benditt. Dworkin's jurisprudence will then be analyzed as an effort to provide a superior response to realism than that offered by Hart. In assessing the Dworkinian approach, I shall be especially concerned to explore its relations to the only contemporary school of legal thought which has tried to utilize and expand upon the realist indeterminacy analysis, namely, the Critical Legal Studies movement (hereafter referred to as CLS). Although it will prove impossible to resolve the basic disagreements between Dworkin and CLS in the context of this article, I shall try to show that CLS does raise some very serious and unanswered questions about the soundness of Dworkinian jurisprudence and of mainstream legal philosophy in general.

From *Philosophy & Public Affairs,* Vol. 15 (1986), pp. 205–235. Copyright © 1986 Princeton University Press. Reprinted with permission of Princeton University Press.

II

One of the now familiar theses defended by Hart in *The Concept of Law* is that there are some cases in which the rules of a legal system do not clearly specify the correct legal outcome.[5] Hart claims that such cases arise because of the ineliminable open-texture of natural language: all general terms have a penumbral range in which it is unclear and irresolvably controversial as to whether the term applies to some particular. Yet, this penumbral range of extensional indeterminacy is necessarily much smaller than the core extension in which the term's application is clear and uncontroversial. For Hart, then, the indeterminacy of law is a peripheral phenomenon in a system of rules which, by and large, does provide specific outcomes to cases.

The realist analysis of indeterminacy sees it as both more pervasive and deeper than the indeterminacy Hart attributes to the legal order. For the realist, there is no way to confine indeterminacy to some peripheral region of the law. For my purposes here, I shall be concerned mainly with the realist analysis of common-law adjudication. It should not be forgotten, however, that the realists could and did extend their analysis to all types of adjudication found in our legal system, including those involving statutory and constitutional issues.[6]

The realist analysis of indeterminacy can be presented in two stages.[7] The first stage proceeded from the idea that there was always a cluster of rules relevant to the decision in any litigated case. Thus, deciding whether an uncle's promise to pay his nephew a handsome sum of money if he refrained from smoking, drinking, and playing pool was enforceable brought into play a number of rules, for example, rules regarding offer, acceptance, consideration, revocation, and so on.[8] The realists understood that the vagueness of any one of these rules could affect the outcome of the case. In any single case, then, there were multiple potential points of indeterminacy due to rule vagueness, not a single point as Hart's account sometimes seems to suggest.

The second stage of the realist analysis began with the rejection of a distinction central to the doctrine of precedent, namely, that between holding and dictum.[9] The holding in a case referred to the essential grounds of the decision and thus what subsequent judges were bound by. The dicta were everything in an opinion not essential to the decision, for example, comments about points of law not treated as the basis of the outcome. The realists argued that in its actual operation the common-law system treated the distinction as a vague and shifting one. Even when the judge writing an opinion characterized part of it as "the holding," judges writing subsequent opinions were not bound by the original judge's perception of what was essential for the decision. Subsequent judges were indeed bound by the decision itself, that is, by the finding for or against the plaintiff, and very rarely was the decision in a precedent labeled as mistaken. But this apparently strict obligation to follow precedent was highly misleading, according to the realists. For later judges had tremendous leeway in being able to redefine the holding and the dictum in the precedential cases. This leeway enabled judges, in effect, to rewrite the rules of law on which earlier cases had been decided. The upshot was that in almost any case which reached the stage of litigation, a judge could find opinions which read relevant precedents as stating one legal rule and other opinions which read the precedents as stating a contrary rule. The common-law judge thus faced an indeterminate legal situation in which he had to render a decision by choosing which of the competing rules was to govern the case. In other words, while the realists claimed that all cases implicated a cluster of rules, they also contended that in any cluster there were competing rules leading to opposing outcomes.[10]

It is this second form of indeterminacy which the realist saw as the deepest and most pervasive. Depending upon how a judge would read the holdings in the cases deemed to be precedents, she would extract different rules of law capable of generating conflicting outcomes in the case before her. In the common-law system, it was left undetermined as to which rules, of a number of incompatible rules, were to govern a case. This type of indeterminacy cuts a much deeper and wider path than the kind Hart was willing to acknowledge. For Hart, the cases afflicted with indeterminacy are the ones in which we know which rule applies but are uncertain over the outcome because the rule contains some vague general term. This second type of realist indeterminacy stems from the fact that the choice of which rules to apply in the first place is not dictated by the law and that competing rules will be available in almost any case which reaches the stage of litigation.

In discussing realism, Hart makes three concessions to realist indeterminacy claims, while at the same time coupling each claim with a major qualification designed to show that actual indeterminacy is far less radical than realism suggests. First, Hart concedes that "there is no single method of determining the rule for which a given authoritative precedent is an authority." But he quickly adds: "Notwithstanding this, in the vast majority of decided cases, there is very little doubt. The headnote is usually correct enough."[11] It is simply question begging, though, for Hart to assert that the headnote usually provides a sufficiently accurate statement of the correct rule. The realist point is that there is nothing that can be thought of as "the correct rule" for which a precedent stands, and so there is no standard against which one can say that a given rule is "correct enough." On the realist analysis, the headnote, or indeed a later opinion, states only one of any number of competing rules which may, with equal legitimacy, be said to constitute the holding of a case. Hart's assertions do nothing to show that this analysis is wrong; they merely presuppose that it is wrong.

Hart's second concession to realism is that "there is no authoritative or uniquely correct formulation of any rule to be extracted from cases." But then he adds that "there is often very general agreement, when the bearing of a precedent on a later case is in issue, that a given formulation is adequate."[12] Hart seems to be saying here that lawyers may disagree on the precise formulation of a rule but still agree on the correct outcome of a case and so be able to accept, for the purposes of the case, a formulation which, in the given instance, straddles the different versions of the rule. This claim may very well be accurate, but it fails to defeat the realist indeterminacy claims for two reasons. It assumes that the problem of being able to extract conflicting rules from the same line of precedents has been resolved, and, as I argued in connection with Hart's first pair of points, that assumption is question begging. Second, even if there is general agreement on the outcome of a case and on some rough statement of the governing rule (and this, of course, ignores the disagreement which will always be found between the attorneys for the litigants), it does not follow that they agree on the outcome because they agree (roughly) on the legal rule which is said to govern the case. In other words, it does not follow that the law determines the outcome. Agreement on the outcome and on the rough statement of the rule used to justify the outcome may both be the result of some more fundamental political value choice which is agreed upon. Indeed, this is exactly what the realist analysis would suggest by way of explaining broad agreement on outcomes and rules. Realism is not committed to denying broad agreement. It is simply committed to the view that the agreement cannot be explained by the determinacy of the law. Thus, Hart's invocation of agreement here does nothing to defeat the realist's indeterminacy thesis.

Hart's third concession to realism is that courts invariably engage in narrowing and widening the rules which precedents lay down. Yet he says that, despite this, the doctrine of precedent has produced "a body of rules of which a vast number, of both major and minor importance, are as determinate as any statutory rule."[13] The problem with this claim, though, is that it misses the crucial realist point regarding the availability of competing rules: let each legal rule be as precise as is humanly possible, the realists insist that the legal system contains competing rules which will be available for a judge to choose in almost any litigated case. The claims made by Hart in his effort to domesticate the realist notion of legal indeterminacy all systematically fail to deal with this crucial realist point.

Benditt's arguments against realism are similarly flawed: none of them directly attack the problem of competing rules.[14] Indeed, this is not surprising, since Benditt's entire account of realism is distorted by his insistence on interpreting realism as denying the existence of authoritative legal rules.[15] While such "rule nihilism" may be suggested in some of the remarks of some realists, the more influential members and allies of the movement were clear that it is precisely the existence of competing *authoritative* rules which creates the radical indeterminacy problem. Llewellyn, perhaps the principal spokesperson for realism during its heyday, characterizes the problem as due to the fact that there are opposing "authoritative premises" for any case.[16] And Dewey's highly influential piece, "Logical Method and Law," stresses the problem of choice among competing rules, rather than denying the existence of authoritative rules.[17] Realists were undoubtedly a very heterogeneous group, at least when measured by their ideas about law, and some of the criticisms made by Hart and Benditt against some realist claims are persuasive.[18] But the standard criticisms do not touch the realist thesis that there is a pervasive indeterminacy in the legal system owing to the existence of competing rules of law.

III

To this point, I have portrayed the realists as focusing upon the choice of competing legal rules which judges in common-law cases must make. This may seem to leave the realist open to one of the principal criticisms which Dworkinians have made of Hart: the law is more than just legal rules. It is also the ethical principles and ideals of which the rules are an (albeit imperfect) expression, and it is these principles and ideals which help to guide judges to a determinate outcome.[19] Indeed, the Dworkinian might try to use the realist indeterminacy analysis to his advantage: if the law were simply a collection of rules, as Hart thinks, it would be afflicted by exactly the kind of deep and pervasive indeterminacy which the realist posits. Yet, if the law were indeterminate to the degree suggested by the realist analysis, it would not be much more than a pious fraud: judges would be "legislating" not only in penumbral cases, but in all cases. Judges would always be creating law, in flagrant violation of their institutional duty to apply preexisting law. The Dworkinian may conclude that we face this choice: either include principles and ideals as part of the law in order to contain (and, perhaps, eliminate) the indeterminacy it would have were it simply a collection of rules or admit that common-law adjudication is a fraud. Although the latter choice is logically possible, assumptions shared by both Dworkin and his positivist critics make it an entirely implausible one from their point of view. The only plausible alternative may thus seem to be the acceptance of Dworkin's important idea that ethical principles be understood as part of the law even when they are not explicitly formulated in some authoritative legal text or clearly identifiable by the application of some noncontroversial, positivist rule for specifying authoritative legal norms in terms of their source. Thus, Dworkin argues that adjudication requires the invocation of principles which take judges "well past the point where it would be accurate to say that any 'test' of pedigree exists. . . ."[20] Moreover, such principles are, on Dworkin's view, binding on

judges and so we must realize that "legal obligation . . . [is] . . . imposed by a constellation of principles as well as by an established rule."[21] Indeed, it is this constellation of principles which must guide the judge to a determinate outcome when the relevant legal rules are in competition with one another. For instance, the principles could indicate to the judge the proper scope of application of each of the competing rules and thus resolve any apparent conflict by showing that just one of the rules was properly applicable in the case at hand.

Yet, which principles are legally binding? Dworkin's answer is that they are those which belong to the "soundest theory of the settled law."[22] The settled law consists of those legal rules and doctrines which would be accepted as authoritative by the consensus of the legal community. The soundest theory is the most defensible ethical and political theory which coheres with and justifies those legal rules and doctrines. The coherence does not have to be perfect, for Dworkin allows that the soundest theory may characterize some rules and legal outcomes as mistakes, but coherence with most of the settled law is demanded. In principle, the soundest theory is to encompass every area of law: every branch of the common law, all statutes, the whole body of administrative law, and the entire range of constitutional law. Of course, Dworkin recognizes that no merely human judge could ever formulate and defend such a theory. But his character, Hercules, is intended to show us that, in principle, such a theory could be formulated and defended by a sufficiently great intelligence.[23] Even though the fictional, judicial Hercules has powers far beyond those of mortal judges, Dworkin tells us that mortal judges are committed both to the logical possibility of such a character and to the task of trying to arrive at the outcome he would arrive at were he to be hearing their cases. Mortal judges thus can and do appeal to principles in reaching determinate outcomes, and, in doing so, they are giving force to preexisting legal obligations, and not simply making a political choice among competing legal rules.

It should be noted that the realists were not blind to seeing legal rules as expressions of ethical principles. Nonetheless, there are tremendous differences between the way in which a realist such as Thurman Arnold viewed these principles and the way in which Dworkin and his followers see them. Arnold was thoroughly cynical about the ethical ideals in terms of which the law was understood: they were high-sounding phrases which appealed to people's emotions and satisfied their need to think of the legal order as more than just some arbitrary and contingent setup. But they had no meaning other than this emotive one and could not be the subject of any rational discussion or defense.[24] Other realists, such as Felix Cohen, were not at all cynical and believed that ethical principles were amenable to rational discussion. Yet they did little to analyze carefully the ethical principles embedded in law or to examine the implications of the existence of such principles for the problem of indeterminacy.[25]

In this section, I have raised the possibility that Dworkin's jurisprudential project succeeds where Hart failed in defeating the radical realist indeterminacy thesis. However, it would be premature to make a judgment regarding the success of Dworkin's project in this respect, for scholars in the Critical Legal Studies movement have picked up and elaborated realist ideas in a way that seriously threatens the foundations of Dworkinian jurisprudence. It is to CLS that I shall turn presently. One important point should be made before I do that, however. For the most part, proponents of CLS and Dworkinians have ignored one another's positions. There are some passing references to CLS in some pieces by avowed Dworkinians, such as Charles Fried.[26] And there is some treatment of Dworkin in the CLS literature.[27] Yet, neither side seems to do anything more than make very superficial, highly polemical points against the other. The interchange of ideas between Dworkinians and CLSers is one which I have constructed with the deliberate aim of avoiding the superficial polemics which have thus far characterized the few occasions on which the one side has deigned in print to deal with the position of the other.

IV

CLS scholars accept the Dworkinian idea that legal rules are infused with ethical principles and ideals.[28] Moreover, they take such principles as seriously as Dworkinians in that they conceive of the articulation and examination of such principles to be one of the major tasks of legal theory.[29] Thus, Duncan Kennedy has analyzed the role in the form

and content of legal doctrine of what he characterizes as "individualist" and "altruist" ethical conceptions. And Roberto Unger has examined the normative principles which he takes to be embodied in the common law of contracts.[30] Yet, one of the main themes of CLS work is that the incorporation of ethical principles and ideals into the law cuts against Dworkinian efforts to rescue legal determinacy. The operative claim in CLS analysis is that the law is infused with irresolvably opposed principles and ideals. Kennedy writes that the opposing ethical conceptions which inform legal doctrine "reflect a deeper level of contradiction. At this deeper level, we are divided, among ourselves and also within ourselves, between irreconcilable visions of humanity and society, and between radically different aspirations for our common future."[31] While the realists stress competing rules, CLSers stress competing, and indeed irreconcilable, principles and ideals. Yet, the basic theme is the same: the judge must make a choice which is not dictated by the law. In the CLS analysis, the choice is one of several competing principles or ideals to be used in guiding her to a decision. Different choices lead to different outcomes. Thus, from the CLS perspective, the jurisprudential invocation of principles only serves to push back to another stage the point at which legal indeterminacy enters and judicial choice takes place.

The Dworkinian response would be to deny that legal indeterminacy follows from the fact that the law contains principles which pull in opposing directions. One of Dworkin's major points in his account of principles is that they have differing weights.[32] Thus, even if we have a case in which two competing principles appear applicable, for example, "A person should not be held liable unless she was at fault" versus "As between two innocents, the one who caused the harm should pay," Dworkin will argue that, in all likelihood, one of those principles will carry greater weight in the case at hand and it is that principle which determines the correct legal outcome. Dworkin does allow for the possibility that there may be a case in which the weights of all applicable principles are exactly equal, leaving the legal outcome truly indeterminate, but goes on to claim that such cases will be extremely rare in any developed legal system.

It must be noted here that Dworkin's conception of the soundest theory of the settled law assumes that there is some metalevel principle for determining the appropriate weights to be as-

weighing?

signed to the different principles which may be applicable in a given case. This assumption becomes clear once we see that Dworkin's conception of the soundest theory rejects intuitionism, according to which relative weights are intuited in each case without there being any higher order standard in virtue of which each principle has its particular weight. Dworkin's position is that there is a legal fact of the matter regarding the weight of a given principle in a given case, and this fact is determined by the weight that principle receives according to the standards of the soundest theory of the settled law. Moreover, this rejection of intuitionism is firmly rooted in a commitment to the rule of law ideal.[33] That ideal requires that legal decisions be the outcome of reasoning that can be reconstructed according to principles which can be articulated and understood. To use a term which has been popular among legal theorists, judicial decision must be "principled."[34] This means that the judge cannot simply appeal to his inarticulate sense that a particular principle is weightier than some competing principle in the case before him. He must believe that there is some higher order principle which makes the one weightier than the other, and he must at least try to figure out and articulate what that higher order principle is.

Now, one line of CLS attack against Dworkin is to argue that there is no discoverable metaprinciple for assigning weights. Duncan Kennedy suggests this line in discussing the possibility of using moral theory to justify legal doctrine. Kennedy admits that, in the context of the fact situation of a particular case, opposing principles do not necessarily carry the same weight: "we are able to distinguish particular fact situations in which one side is more plausible than the other. The difficulty, the mystery, is that there are no available metaprinciples to explain just what it is about these particular situations that make them ripe for resolution."[35] Actually, Kennedy's point should be put in a less sweeping way: no one has come up with such metaprinciples, and it is implausible to think that it can be done. When put in these terms, the CLS position becomes an essentially reactive one which awaits Dworkinian efforts and then reacts against them: Dworkinians put forth their rational/ethical reconstructions of the law (or some portion of it), complete with metaprinciples for assigning weights to principles, and then CLSers and others attempt to show that the reconstruction is inadequate and incoherent. The burden of production

thus seems to be on the Dworkinians. What have they produced?

The closest thing we have from them of a Dworkinian reconstruction of a portion of the settled law is Charles Fried's effort to reconstruct contract law on the basis of the principle that one ought to keep one's promises and related conceptions from a liberal individualist philosophy.[36] Yet, Fried sought to avoid the problem of developing metaprinciples by narrowly defining the body of law which he attempted to reconstruct. Thus, he did not attempt to incorporate collective bargaining law with its decidedly greater collectivist orientation than the common law of contracts, and he even banished to other fields of law doctrines which are standardly treated as part of the common law of contracts but which do not fit neatly with the individualist principles animating his reconstruction.[37] This is not to imply any assessment regarding the success or failure of Fried's effort to reconstruct his highly streamlined body of contract law. For now my point is the modest one that by gerrymandering doctrine, he attempted, in effect, to evade the difficulty of developing higher order standards to harmonize the competing principles which infuse the law of contracts, and so he simply delayed tackling one of the principal obstacles in the path of constructing the kind of theory which Dworkinian jurisprudence presumes we can and should build.

It is important to recognize here that I am not talking about the theory which Dworkin's Hercules would try to construct, one encompassing the entire body of the law. Rather, what is at issue is a theory for some connected but limited portion of the law, such as the law of contracts. Both CLS and I assume that Dworkinians are committed to the notion that such limited theories can be built by humans, not merely by gods. For if humans cannot construct even such modest theories, the problem of legal indeterminacy will be irresolvable from a human point of view, no matter what may be true from a divine point of view. If the rule of law is to be a guiding ideal for humans, and not just gods, then the problem of legal indeterminacy must be resolvable from a human point of view. Moreover, Dworkinian jurisprudence itself prohibits evasion of the problem of competing principles by so gerrymandering doctrine that one never has to harmonize such principles. Dworkin is clear that different parts of the law have to be understood in terms of each other, for example, a statute affecting tort liability will properly play a role in a judge's decision in a common-law tort action.[38] The judge cannot ignore the statute on the ground that it embodies principles in some tension with common-law principles and thus is difficult to reconcile with them. The judge is supposed to (try to) reconcile the tension and not avoid facing it.

CLS scholars would clearly go further than I have so far and reject as wrongheaded even the relatively modest project Fried has undertaken to reconstruct common-law contract doctrine from the promise principle. In addition, CLSers would judge as totally implausible the belief that any coherent Dworkinian theory, complete with meta-principles, can be developed for any significant portion of the settled law. Yet, the CLS claims in this regard are unpersuasive, given the argument that has been adduced in their behalf to this point. Even if it is admitted that there are difficulties in the way of constructing a Dworkinian theory for any significant portion of the settled law because such a portion will invariably embody principles in tension with one another, surely no argument has yet been given that makes it implausible to believe that such a theory can be constructed. Nonetheless, the points made so far do not by any means exhaust the potential CLS critique of Dworkinian jurisprudence. While CLS rhetoric often does make the invalid leap from the premise that there are competing principles which infuse settled doctrine to the conclusion that there must be pervasive legal indeterminacy, there are within CLS distinct and more powerful lines of reasoning against the viability of the Dworkinian project.

The additional lines of reasoning are premised on the idea that the settled law is the transitory and contingent outcome of ideological struggles among social factions in which conflicting conceptions of justice, goodness, and social and political life get compromised, truncated, vitiated, and adjusted.[39] The point here is not simply that there are competing principles embodied in settled doctrine, although that is a starting point for the statement of the problem. More fundamentally, the point is that these principles have their weight and scope of application in the settled law determined, not by some metalevel philosophical principle which imposes order and harmony, but by an ideological power struggle in which coherent theories become compromised and truncated as they fit themselves into the body of law. The settled law as a whole, and each field within it, represents the (temporary)

outcome of such an ideological conflict. This is, to be sure, a causal claim about the genesis of legal doctrines and principles, rather than a logical one regarding the lack of amenability of such doctrines and principles to rational reconstruction. But the CLS position can be interpreted as linking the logical claim to the causal one. The position is that it is implausible to believe that any system of norms generated by such a process of struggle and compromise will be capable of an ethically principled reconstruction. Unger summarizes the CLS view this way:

> . . . it would be strange if the results of a coherent, richly developed normative theory were to coincide with a major portion of any extended branch of law. The many conflicts of interest and vision that lawmaking involves, fought out by countless minds and wills working at cross purposes, would have to be the vehicle of an immanent moral rationality whose message could be articulated by a single cohesive theory. This daring and implausible sanctification of the actual is in fact undertaken by the dominant legal theories. . . .[40]

This idea that the law is a patchwork quilt, as it were, of irreconcilably opposed ideologies is tied to CLS's version of the repudiation of the distinction between law (adjudication) and politics. Sometimes CLS scholars suggest that the distinction unravels principally because of the fact that controversial normative and descriptive judgments are just as much an ineliminable part of adjudication as they are of politics. Yet, I think that there is a more important, though related, way in which the distinction is thought to unravel. The idea is this: all of those ideological controversies which play a significant part in the public debate of our political culture are replicated in the argument of judicial decision. In other words, the spectrum of ideological controversy in politics is reproduced in the law. Of course, CLS recognizes that in legal argument the controversies will often be masked or hidden by talk of the intent of the framers, the requirements of *stare decisis*, and so on. The point is that the same ideological debates which fragment political discourse are replicated in one form or another in legal argument. As a patchwork quilt of irreconcilable ideologies, the law is a mirror which faithfully reflects the fragmentation of our political culture. Such, at least, is a principal CLS theme.

How is it possible to parlay these CLS ideas regarding the patchwork-quilt character of doctrine and the unraveling of the law/politics distinction into a cogent argument against Dworkinian jurisprudence? I think there are two principal lines of argument. The first seeks to show that it makes no sense to think there is any soundest theory of the settled law. The second seeks to show that the Dworkinian theory fails on its own terms to provide a satisfactory account of the legitimacy of judicial decision making. Let us explore each of these lines of argument in turn.

V

One possible line of CLS argument is that legal doctrine is so internally inconsistent that it is implausible to believe that there is any single, coherent theory capable of justifying enough of it to satisfy the Dworkinian fit requirement. Consistently applying any of the theories embodied in some significant portion of the law across the entire body of doctrine would, the argument goes, involve such substantial doctrinal reconstruction that it would violate the Dworkinian mandate that any theory invoked to decide cases fit or cohere with the bulk of the settled law. Thus, ethically principled reconstruction of any substantial portion of doctrine is ruled out by the law's internal contradictions, such contradictions being symptomatic of the law's conception in ideological compromise and struggle and of its tendency to reflect the range of political conflict present in the culture. This means that there simply is no soundest theory of the settled law, and so the Dworkinian efforts to rescue legal determinacy by appealing to such a notion fail.

It may be helpful in clarifying this CLS argument to show how Dworkin's responses to more conventional criticisms of his jurisprudence completely fail to come to grips with the central claim of this argument. A typical conventional criticism will claim that legal indeterminacy survives the Dworkinian efforts to erase it because there are multiple, conflicting theories no one of which can be cogently established as providing an account of the settled law which is superior to that of any of the other theories. In other words, the concept of the soundest theory really has more than one refer-

ent, and they provide different answers to questions regarding who should win cases.[41]

Dworkin's response to this type of criticism is in two stages. First, he argues that, although there may be several theories which fit the settled law well enough when one is talking about the settled law of a simple, undeveloped legal system, the probability of that happening in a complex and developed system such as we have is very small. Second, he claims that even if there were several theories which fit well enough, that would not defeat his claims since the soundest theory would be the one from those several which is most defensible on the grounds of political and ethical philosophy. Thus, he concludes that two claims must be sustained in order to defeat his position: that there are multiple theories which fit the settled law well enough, and that political and ethical philosophy suffer from an indeterminacy (or an irremediable subjectivity) which makes it impossible to choose just one of those theories as the most defensible.[42]

However convincing this Dworkinian argument may be against conventional legal philosophers, it does not even begin to join the issue with CLS. For the CLS patchwork-quilt argument is not that there is legal indeterminacy due to the fact that there are several "soundest theories"; rather the argument is that there is indeterminacy because there are none. Or, more accurately, the argument is that there is indeterminacy because of what excludes the possibility of any soundest theory, namely, the internally incoherent character of legal doctrine. This argument makes it completely beside the point whether ethical and political philosophy is indeterminate or subjective. If doctrine is as internally contradictory as CLS claims, then Dworkinian jurisprudence fails to rescue legal determinacy even if there is a uniquely and objectively true ethical and political philosophy.

Dworkin's replies to conventional critics of his jurisprudence are essentially irrelevant here because these critics share Dworkin's assumption that doctrine is by and large coherent. More generally, the conventional critics share Dworkin's assumption that legal doctrine and argument are largely in good logical order, though they believe that indeterminacy has a somewhat broader toehold in the law than Dworkin is willing to admit. CLS dissents from these assumptions. In this respect the CLS position may be usefully analogized with Alasdair MacIntyre's diagnosis of the ethical thought of modern culture.[43] MacIntyre argues that such thought is internally incoherent. This state of incoherence is due to the fact that modern ethical thought amounts to an amalgam of fragments of irreconcilable ethical views. Conventional philosophers not only fail to perceive the utter incoherence of modern ethical thought, but operate on the assumption that it is largely in good order. For them the issue is the best way to systematize that thought, not whether it is so self-contradictory that systematization is impossible. The result is that the debates fought out among conventional ethical philosophers, such as Rawls and Nozick, do not join the issue with MacIntyre's position. He repudiates the assumptions which the conventional antagonists share. In a very similar way, the debate between Dworkin and his conventional critics fails to join the issue with CLS. They assume a doctrinal coherence which CLS repudiates, and so the conventional debate takes place in terms which are largely irrelevant to the CLS position.

Duncan Kennedy makes the CLS position on doctrinal incoherence plain in his description of a private law field which he takes to be representative of doctrine in general:

> In contract law, for example, there are *two* principles: there is a reliance, solidarity, joint enterprise concept, and there is a hands-off, arms length, expectancy-oriented, "no flexibility and no excuses" orientation. They can be developed very coherently, but only if one accepts that they are inconsistent. There are fifteen or twenty contract doctrines about which there is a conflict. . . . That is the structure of contract doctrine, and it's typical. Doctrine is not consistent or coherent. The outcomes of these conflicts form a patchwork, rather than following straight lines.[44]

Given the terms in which the CLS position has been stated, it is clear what the Dworkinian reply must be in order to join the issue: that doctrine is not as internally contradictory as CLS claims. The main argument would have to be that any internal inconsistencies in legal doctrine are merely marginal, capable of characterization as "mistakes" without any substantial rupture to the fabric of doctrine. This argument would be supplemented, I think, by one to the effect that CLS exaggerates the degree to which theory must fit the settled law in order to be said to fit well enough. To make out these arguments would not be at all easy. CLS

analyses have sought to exhibit the deep and pervasive incoherence of doctrine in such areas as constitutional law, labor law, contract law, administrative law, and criminal law, to name only a few.[45] Indeed, I think it is accurate to say that CLS has, through these analyses, made a much more thorough and stronger case for the incoherence of legal doctrine than MacIntyre has made for the incoherence of ethical thought. Meanwhile, Dworkinians have done little to respond to these CLS analyses. Moreover, Dworkin's most recent efforts to clarify the character of the fit test provide little ammunition against the CLS argument. Let us briefly examine those efforts in order to see why this is so.

Dworkin's recent writing indicates that the fit test is more sophisticated than some of his critics have taken it to be.[46] He tells us that the degree of fit is not just a matter of adding up the number of precedents and rules for which a given theory accounts. One must also take into consideration such factors as the trend of recent decisions. Two theories may account for the same number of precedents and rules, but, if one accounts for more of the recent decisions and the other for more of the older decisions, then the former has a better fit, according to Dworkin.

Dworkin does not indicate how much weight should be given to the capacity to account for recent trends. Nor does he explain why accounting for a trend in new decisions makes for a better fit than accounting for the pre-trend pattern of old ones. Moreover, he ignores the point that the question of what counts as significant trend and what counts as an insignificant blip or anomaly is not a theory-neutral one. What counts as a trend from the perspective of one theory may count as an anomaly to be ignored from the perspective of another. It does no good to be told here that the soundest theory of the law determines what is a trend and what is an anomaly, since the fit test is supposed to help us figure out which theory is the soundest one. But, more to the point for the doctrinal incoherence issue, the CLS contention is that the patchwork character of law is manifested within the body of recent decisions and not just between recent ones and old ones. There may be trends but there are countertrends as well. Some decisions may introduce or expand new lines of doctrine, but other recent decisions will continue the older lines. By characterizing the former as "trends" and giving their line of doctrine greater

trends vs/countertrends

weight, Dworkin is merely picking out one line of doctrine for favored status from among several conflicting lines. His aim does seem to be to reduce doctrinal dissonance, but he provides no argument for giving greater importance to trends than countertrends and so he does not succeed.

Even if Dworkin were able to provide some convincing argument for according greater importance to trends, it is not at all obvious that he would thereby solve the problem of doctrinal incoherence. His recent writing explicitly states that there is some threshold level of fit which any theory must satisfy in order to be the soundest theory of the law.[47] Presumably, this threshold would require a theory to account for most, but not all, of the doctrinal materials. However, CLS analyses suggest that doctrinal incoherence is so deep and pervasive that, even if one grants that accounting for certain doctrinal lines (the trends) gives somewhat better fit than accounting for others (the countertrends), any coherent theory will prove incompatible with such a broad range of doctrine as to make implausible the notion that it has satisfied the threshold. These analyses do not conclusively establish the point, but they do raise a strong prima facie case to which there has been only the most meager response by conventional legal philosophers of any stripe, Dworkinian or otherwise.

It seems to me, then, that the patchwork-quilt line of argument presents unmet and serious challenges to the viability of the Dworkinian jurisprudential project, as well as to other conventional legal philosophies. Even if this CLS argument is met by some cogent conventional response, however, there is an independent line of CLS argument against another key Dworkinian position. Let us now turn to that position.

VI

Hard cases

Dworkin is concerned to defend the legitimacy of judicial decision making that invokes controversial principles of ethical or political philosophy. The Dworkinian judge is licensed to reply on such principles because, as Dworkin well realizes, it is inevitable that a judge who, in a hard case, seeks to enunciate and invoke the principles embodied in the settled law will fail to find principles on which everyone can agree. If the judge is to guide her

decision by the principles she thinks are embodied in the law, then the reliance of adjudication on controversial principles is inescapable, at least for many cases. In this sense, Dworkin is willing to acknowledge that adjudication is "political."[48] Yet, he thinks that such an acknowledgment does nothing to impugn the legitimacy of the adjudication.

Dworkin's arguments in favor of the legitimacy of such admittedly "political adjudication" are not entirely clear. Let me suggest the following as the principal Dworkinian argument on this point. The invocation of controversial ethical or political principles in adjudication is constrained by the judicial duty to decide a hard case according to the dictates of the soundest theory of the settled law. Thus, the "political" reasoning and choice of the judge take place within much narrower confines than if she were a legislator deciding what sort of legislative enactment was best. As Dworkin says in his discussion of a judge deciding an abortion case, it is one thing for her to decide whether political philosophy dictates that government should acknowledge a right to an abortion, and it is quite another for her to decide whether the settled law of our legal/political system is best accounted for by a theory incorporating a conception of dignity which entails such a right.[49] The former decision is, of course, appropriate for a legislature, not a court. Yet, it is the latter decision, not the former, which the Dworkinian judge is under a duty to make, and it is a decision which is made within much narrower confines than the former. Thus, it is misguided to think that the kind of "political adjudication" endorsed by Dworkinian jurisprudence constitutes an illegitimately broad exercise of judicial power and is tantamount to judicial legislation. Such adjudication is inevitably controversial, but it is substantially constrained by the duty under which judges, but not legislators, act.

Dworkin on judge on abortion

Certain CLS claims regarding the law/politics distinction can be parlayed into an argument against this Dworkinian defense of the legitimacy of adjudication in hard cases. What makes this CLS argument particularly interesting for current purposes is that it does not hinge on the adequacy of the patchwork-quilt argument examined in the preceding section. Indeed, it can be construed as granting, *arguendo*, that there is a unique soundest theory of the law which does dictate the correct legal outcomes in hard cases. Let us set the stage for such a CLS argument.

In trying to undo the law/politics distinction, CLS claims that the spectrum of ideological controversy in the political arena is replicated in the legal forum. The claim means that all of the arguments and ideologies which are a significant part of political debate in our culture are to be found, in one form or another, in legal argument and doctrine. It is undoubtedly true that certain ideological viewpoints are foreclosed from the legal arena. Thus, the ideology of Islamic theocracy is to be found embodied nowhere in our legal doctrine. But such ideologies also play no significant role in the internal political debates of our polity.

It is also undeniable that the canons of legal argument place certain formal constraints on the ideological controversies which manifest themselves within judicial decision making. Judges cannot ignore the authoritative texts of the legal culture: the Constitution, statutes, case law, and so on. And legal argument is constrained by the need to phrase itself in terms of the framer's intent, *stare decisis*, and so on. Controversy in the political arena is not bound as strongly by such formal constraints, even though the language of legal opinion does often spill over into the political arena. CLS does not deny any of these distinctive, formal marks of legal argument. What they do claim is that beneath these legal forms one can find all of the significant ideological controversies of the political culture. The substance of the political debates is replicated in judicial argument, even if the form of the debates is distinctive. Legal form fails to screen out or significantly reduce the range of ideological conflict present within the general political culture.

CLS supports these contentions regarding the range of ideological conflict within legal doctrine and argument by analyses of doctrinal principles and the kinds of arguments found in judicial decisions. Consider again Kennedy's description of the structure of contract law. Doctrines from the "solidarity" side of contract law, for example, those of duress, unconscionability, and reasonable reliance, are taken to embody the principles of the political left: welfare-state liberals and, to some extent, left-wing egalitarians. Doctrines from the "individualist" side, such as those of consideration, the revocability of an offer until there is acceptance, and the demand that acceptance be a mirror image of the offer, are taken to embody the principles of the political right: free-marketeers and libertarians. The political middle is represented by attempts to mix the two sides of doctrine in varying pro-

portions (attempts which, in CLS eyes, are doomed to logical incoherence for reasons made clear in the patchwork-quilt argument). A hard case emerges when the two sides of doctrine collide in a single fact situation: there was no consideration, but there was reliance; or there was consideration, but it was quite disproportionate in value to what was received in exchange. The CLS view is that such cases implicate doctrinal materials and arguments representing the spectrum of conflicting political viewpoints.

The CLS claim that the range of ideological conflict in the political arena is replicated in legal doctrine and argument can be viewed in two ways. On the first, it is taken as reinforcing the patchwork-quilt argument against Dworkin. To the extent that one documents the claim, one lends support to the idea that doctrine is a patchwork quilt of inconsistent political ideologies of which no single, coherent political theory could ever capture very much. Take Kennedy's account of contract law. The CLS argument can be put this way: to the extent that we have no reason to believe that the political philosophy of a welfare-state liberal can be reconciled with that of a libertarian, we have no reason to think that the opposing doctrines of contract law can be logically reconciled with one another, for those doctrines are the legal embodiment of just those opposing political philosophies (or something close to them). The position is then generalized to cover all fields of law. This way of setting up the CLS argument is, at bottom, another effort to show that the law is too internally incoherent for there to be any soundest theory of it and thereby to discredit Dworkin's attempts to defend judicial legitimacy by invoking a judicial duty to decide according to the dictates of the soundest theory.

There is, however, another way to view the CLS claim about the range of ideological conflict embodied in legal doctrine. This alternate reading leads to a line of argument whose key contention is that, even if there were a Dworkinian soundest theory, it would impose no practical constraint on judges whose favored political ideology is in conflict with the one embodied in that theory. The theory would exert no effective pull or tug on the decisions of judges who fail to share its ideology. This is because judges who conscientiously attempt to carry out their Dworkinian duty to decide a hard case according to the soundest theory of the law will read their favored ideology into the settled and see it as the soundest theory. This would happen, the argument goes, because the authoritative legal materials, in replicating the ideological conflicts of the political arena, contain a sufficient number of doctrines, rules, and arguments representing any politically significant ideology that a judge who conscientiously consults the materials would find his favored ideology in some substantial portion of the settled law and conclude that it was the soundest theory of the law.

Of course, no one expects that the true soundest theory of law will have the power to persuade all conscientious judges of its status. However, the Dworkinian argument for the legitimacy of adjudication in hard cases does presuppose that the theory imposes some practical constraint on judicial decision making by exerting a kind of gravitational pull on those judges who recognize their abstract duty to decide according to the soundest theory but who are in fact in ideological disagreement with the principles of the true theory. (Keep in mind that this judicial duty is abstract in the sense that the statement of the duty contains no specification of the particular theory which is the soundest one, and so recognition of the duty, by itself, does nothing to insure that a judge's decisions will be pulled in any particular direction.) The pull of the true soundest theory doesn't have to be an irresistible one, but, for the Dworkinian legitimacy argument to work, it must be substantial enough to make a difference to the decisions of conscientious judges who in fact hold to an ideology which conflicts with the soundest theory. Many of the decisions of these judges would have to be different from what they would be if there were no soundest theory, and the difference has to be explainable in terms of the pull of the theory. If the soundest theory were to lack any such pull, then the constraint imposed by the duty to decide according to the soundest theory would be illusory, and the Dworkinian defense of judicial legitimacy would fall apart. The CLS argument is that the constraint is an illusion. Judges holding to virtually any ideology which is of significance in the American political arena will simply read their favored ideology into the settled law as its soundest theory. This can be and is done, even by the most conscientious judge, because each view on the political spectrum is embodied in some substantial portion of the authoritative materials.

It should be noted that the CLS view on this point is not the same as a view often expressed by mainstream critics of Dworkin and against which Dworkin has directed several arguments. That view consists of the idea that in a hard case, the law "runs out" and the judge makes her decision in a kind of legal vacuum. Dworkin has argued quite forcefully that this gives us a false picture of how judges should and characteristically do go about deciding hard cases.[50] It leads us to think that judges first consult the authoritative materials, find that there is no unambiguous answer there, and then proceed to forget the legal materials and decide by some wholly extralegal criterion. Dworkin counters with a picture of judges who search for the most cogent principles and theories which can be thought of as embodied in the relevant authoritative materials and who decide according to such principles and theories. This is, in Dworkin's eyes, the search for (the relevant portion of) the soundest theory of the settled law.

CLS can agree with Dworkin's important point that judges do not leave the authoritative materials behind when they make a decision in a case where those materials fail to dictate unambiguously an answer to the case. It can also agree with Dworkin that in such cases judges look for the most convincing principles and theories embodied in the materials.[51] The point of the present CLS argument is that, even though judges typically do decide in such Dworkinian fashion and even if there happens to be a soundest theory dictating the correct legal outcome, the existence of such a theory makes no practical difference because a judge will typically see her favored ideology as constituting that theory. The soundest theory is not some brooding omnipresence in the sky, but rather a brooding irrelevance in the sky (assuming it is anywhere at all).

There are two potential lines of response for the Dworkinian to this CLS argument. The first is to deny that the full spectrum of ideological controversy in politics is to be found in legal doctrine and decision and so to hold on to the idea that legal form, particularly the fit requirement, does screen out a significant range of political controversy. This line of response does not appear to me to be very promising. There are a host of CLS analyses of both private and public law, making quite persuasive its contention regarding the extent of ideological controversy within legal doctrine and argument.

A second line of response is to deny that the legitimacy of "political adjudication" in hard cases hinges on whether or not ideological controversy within the law is as wide as it is in the political arena. The idea is that Dworkin's defense of adjudication works, even if the law/politics distinction unravels in precisely the way CLS asserts. In fact, we can find in Dworkin's work two arguments which can be construed in this way. They concern the issue of whether courts have correctly held that there is a legal right to an abortion under our constitutional arrangements. Dworkin imagines the issue turning on the question of whether the concept of dignity implicit in our legal and political institutions implies the existence of such a right.[52] He then examines the suggestion that legislatures, which reflect the will and ideas of the ordinary person, rather than courts, are the most appropriate forum in which to find the answer to such a question. In other words, the suggestion is the positivist one that in hard cases courts should act as legislatures would.

Dworkin claims that there are two arguments against such a suggestion and, by implication, in favor of the judge deciding the issue by what she thinks the (soundest theory of the) law dictates, and not by what (she thinks) the legislature thinks it ought to be.[53] The first argument is that judges think more carefully about the meaning our institutions give to the idea of dignity when they decide cases than ordinary folks do when they cast their ballots (or politicians do when they vote on legislation). Judges are thus thought to have greater competence in handling such hard cases than legislatures do. The second argument is that a Dworkinian judge will legitimately refuse to defer to legislative judgment, even if she thinks that it does reflect the considered opinion of the ordinary person, when she thinks that the opinion is inconsistent with the soundest theory of the law. This is legitimate because such a judge believes that the law really does have a determinate answer to the hard case before her and that it is her duty to discover and announce it, whatever anyone else thinks. By doing so she is acting no differently from a positivist judge in an easy case, who would certainly refrain from a decision contrary to his legal judgment, no matter what the ordinary person/legislature may think.

Neither one of these arguments provides a convincing response to the CLS position. The first would justify the most far-reaching judicial usurpations on the grounds that judges have thought more carefully about the issue in question than did the electorate or their representatives. There is vir-

tually no legislative enactment or policy which is safe from such reasoning. The second argument clearly begs the whole question of whether the law is determinate in hard cases. The Dworkinian judge may believe that it is, but, if that belief is incorrect or even unjustified, it can hardly be claimed that her refusal to defer to legislative judgment in a hard case is analogous to the positivist judge's refusal to do so in an easy case. Yet, even granting the law's determinacy, Dworkin's argument presumes that the soundest theory of the law does impose some effective constraints on judicial decision making. For otherwise there will be no practical difference between a legal regime in which judges have no duty to decide hard cases according to the dictates of (the soundest theory of) the law but may decide such cases on the basis of their favored ideology, and one in which they do have such a duty. Dworkin's views commit him to the claim that there is not only a difference between the two regimes, but that the latter sort of regime alone can be legitimated in terms of the principles of liberal democracy.

Let me hasten to add that CLS does not accept an important assumption shared by both Dworkinians and their positivist critics, namely, that the exercise of judicial power, even in hard cases, is largely legitimate and that the issue is over how to account for that legitimacy. For CLSers, the legitimacy of the exercise of judicial power is not something that can be assumed but is deeply problematic. Thus, they are no more persuaded by the positivist's efforts to wrap judicial decision in the cloak of legislative legitimacy than they are by Dworkin's invocation of the duty to decide by the soundest theory of law. From the CLS perspective, the positivist injunction to decide according to the will of the legislature leaves as much room for judges to make their favored ideology the basis of decision as does the Dworkinian injunction to decide according to the soundest theory. My principal point here, though, concerns Dworkinian jurisprudence. Dworkinians must show that the soundest theory of law is not only a logical possibility, given the tensions existing within doctrine, but that it can exert an effective practical constraint on judges who hold conflicting ideological views. CLS's law/politics argument raises serious doubts about whether the theory, even conceding its existence, would exert any such constraint, and thus far Dworkinians have done little to assuage such doubts.

VII

In this article, I have not aimed at providing the last word on the points of contention between CLS and Dworkinian jurisprudence. I have tried to locate some of the more important issues within a frame that recognizes the influence of legal realism on contemporary legal thought. CLS has picked up and elaborated upon the realist contention that the law largely fails to determine the outcome in cases which are brought to litigation. Among the important advances of the CLS analysis over that of their realist forerunners are: the effort to take seriously and to analyze the conflicting ethical visions and principles which infuse legal doctrine; the painstaking attempts to display doctrinal inconsistencies and incoherencies; and the effort to show how debates in the political arena are replicated in unsuspected corners of private-law doctrine. I believe that these are substantial advances on the realist position and that they can be parlayed into powerful arguments which are thus far unmet by Dworkinians or indeed by conventional legal philosophers of any stripe. It is well past the time when legal philosophers can justifiably ignore the body of work associated with the Critical Legal Studies movement.

Endnotes

[1] H. L. A. Hart, *The Concept of Law* (Oxford: Oxford University Press, 1961).

[2] Ronald Dworkin, *Taking Rights Seriously* (Cambridge, MA: Harvard University Press, 1977), pp. 3–4; also see pp. 15–16.

[3] Theodore Benditt, *Law as Rule and Principle* (Stanford: Stanford University Press, 1978), chaps. 1–2. In his preface, Benditt says that his reason for such an extended treatment of realism is that "students find [it] interesting and persuasive." (p. vii.) It is difficult for me to interpret the remark as anything but a put-down of both realism and any contemporary theorists who find it both interesting and persuasive.

[4] A principal exception to the general failure to treat realism as having contemporary significance is R. S. Summers, *Instrumentalism and American Legal Theory* (Ithaca, NY: Cornell University Press, 1982). Also see the articles in the "Symposium on American Legal Theory," *Cornell Law Review* 66 (1981): 860. It is useful to think of the realist movement as constituted by six distinct themes. First, there is the instrumentalist theme, according to which law should be understood and evaluated as animated by social purposes and policies. This theme has been absorbed into much mainstream legal thinking. Second, there is the behaviorist theme, which reduces the meaning of legal concepts and doctrines to the particular actions of legal officials. Such a theory of meaning stands repudiated by virtually all contemporary theorists. (See footnote 18 below.) The third theme is that of legal indeterminacy, which is the focus of this article. Fourth, there is the anticonceptualist theme, according to which legal thinking should always take place at a very low level of abstraction and should never stray very far from the particular fact pattern presented by a case. (See footnote 28 below.) Fifth, there is the realist idea that private law concepts and doctrines ought to be reconceptualized so that they are understood as instruments of state imposed regulatory policies. This theme, which is clearly related to the instrumentalist one, has been a major influence on contemporary legal scholars working in the area of contract law. See Patrick Atiyah, *The Rise and Fall of Freedom of Contract* (Oxford: Oxford University Press, 1979), pp. 405–419, and Grant Gilmore, *The Death of Contract* (Columbus, Ohio: Ohio State University Press, 1974). Finally, there is the master theme of legal realism, that of the breakdown of any sharp distinction between law (adjudication) and politics. Each of the five previous themes can be understood as various ways in which the realists tried to unravel that distinction.

[5] Hart, *The Concept of Law*, pp. 119, 123–25.

[6] A provocative realist analysis of constitutional adjudication is found in George Braden, "The Search for Objectivity in Constitutional Law," *Yale Law Journal* 57 (1948): 571. The classic realist statement of the indeterminacy of statutory interpretation is found in Appendix C of Karl Llewellyn, *The Common Law Tradition* (Boston: Little, Brown, 1960), pp. 521–35. Also see his *The Bramble Bush* (New York: Oceana, 1960), pp. 88–90.

[7] On the indeterminacy of the common-law system, see Llewellyn, *The Bramble Bush*, pp. 61–77; also see the chapter, "The Leeways of Precedent," in *The Common Law Tradition*.

[8] The facts in this example are from *Hamer v. Sidway* 124 NY 538 (1891).

[9] For a general historical discussion of *stare decisis*, see Harold J. Berman and William R. Greiner, *The Nature and Functions of Law*, 4th ed. (Mineola, NY: Foundation Press, 1980), pp. 587–88. For a realist critique of the distinction between holding and dictum, see Felix Cohen, "The Ethical Basis of Legal Criticism," *Yale Law Journal* 41 (1931): 201.

[10] Llewellyn, "Some Realism About Realism," *Harvard Law Review* 44 (1931): 1222, 1252.

[11] Hart, *The Concept of Law*, p. 131.

[12] Ibid.

[13] Ibid., p. 132.

[14] Benditt, *Law as Rule and Principle,* pp. 25–42.

[15] Ibid., pp. 10–11, 22.

[16] Llewellyn, "Some Realism About Realism," p. 1252. Llewellyn takes fellow realist Jerome Frank to task for suggesting that rules and precedents lack authoritative status; see his contribution to *"Law and the Modern Mind:* A Symposium," *Columbia Law Review* 31 (1931): 82, 90.

[17] John Dewey, "Logical Method and Law," *Cornell Law Quarterly* 10 (1924): 17.

[18] For example, the criticism Hart and Benditt make of the theory of the meaning endorsed by realists is extremely persuasive. The theory is asserted in Felix Cohen, "Transcendental Nonsense and the Functional Approach," *Columbia Law Review* 35 (1935): 809. The seminal statement of the position is in Oliver Wendell Holmes, *The Path of the Law, Collected Papers* (New York: Harcourt, Brace, 1921), p. 173. For the criticisms, see Hart, *The Concept of Law,* pp. 39, 88; Benditt, *Law as Rule and Principle,* pp. 46–50.

[19] Dworkin, *Taking Rights Seriously,* pp. 25–26, 36, 44–45, 67–68, 71–80, 82–90, 96–97, 105ff.

[20] Ibid., p. 67.

[21] Ibid., p. 44.

[22] Ibid., pp. 67–68, 79, 283, and 340.

[23] Ibid., pp. 105ff.

[24] Thurman Arnold, "Law Enforcement: An Attempt at Social Dissection," *Yale Law Journal* 42 (1932); 1, 12–13, 23. *Symbols of Government* (New Haven: Yale University Press, 1935), pp. 71, 125, 248–49.

[25] Felix Cohen was the realist most concerned with ethical issues in the law. See almost any of his essays in Lucy K. Cohen, ed., *The Legal Conscience: Selected Papers of Felix S. Cohen* (New Haven: Yale University Press, 1960). There was, however, a considerable tension between Cohen's highly reductionist theory of the meaning of legal concepts, on the one hand, and his efforts to see the law as infused with cognitively meaningful ethical ideals, on the other. That kind of theory makes it very difficult to explain how ideals can impose any cognitively meaningful, normative constraints on the operation of the legal system and leads quite readily to Arnold's kind of cynical emotivism. For a closely related criticism of Cohen, see Martin Golding, "Realism and Functionalism in the Legal Thought of Felix S. Cohen," *Cornell Law Review* 66 (1981): 1032, 1054.

[26] Charles Fried, "The Laws of Change: The Cunning of Reason in Moral and Legal History," *Journal of Legal Studies* 9 (1980): 335, and *Contract as Promise* (Cambridge, MA: Harvard University Press, 1981), pp. 2–3, 90–91, and 149. It is interesting that Fried gives endorsement to Dworkin's jurisprudence even though his political commitments are decidedly less liberal than those of Dworkin. I characterize Fried as a Dworkinian on account of his endorsement of Dworkin's ideas that legal doctrine is animated by and derivable from moral principles, that judges are obligated to resolve cases in the light of such principles, that the law has a determinate answer for all cases which come before it, and that it is only because the law is animated by moral principles that it has determinate answers for such disputes. See *Contract as Promise,* pp. 67–69.

[27] See Elizabeth Mensch, "The History of Mainstream Legal Thought," in David Kairys, ed., *The Politics of Law* (New York: Pantheon, 1982), p. 19, and Peter Gabel, "Review of *Taking Rights Seriously,*" *Harvard Law Review* 91 (1977): 302. Mensch dismisses Dworkin's theory in six lines of a footnote, characterizing his contribution to jurisprudence as "vastly overrated." Gabel's treatment is more extended, and yet he never really joins the issue with Dworkin. He simply assumes that judges pervasively exercise political choice in a way that is inconsistent with Dworkin's theory. Instead of meeting Dworkin on his own terms, Gabel takes for granted the truth of an orthodox version of historical materialism and seeks to expose Dworkin's jurisprudence as just the latest in a series of theoretical efforts to justify capitalism.

It is important to realize that Critical Legal Studies embraces a substantial variety of conflicting theoretical approaches, many of them quite hostile to anything similar to orthodox Marxist theory. (See footnote 39 below.) In this article, I shall be able to touch upon only a few of the more important themes developed in the literature. Among the important themes which will be left untreated are the critique of social hierarchy and the rather vigorous "left-wing" egalitarianism which accompany many CLS writings. It is often pointed out, correctly I believe, that there is no necessary connection between CLS claims regarding legal indeterminacy and its egalitarian political vision. But this simply means that the one does not logically stand or fall with the other. There is, however, a kind of strategic connection: CLS's political vision requires that one see the current legal order as essentially illegitimate. CLS's claims regarding legal indeterminacy serve to delegitimate that order by undercutting that order's own conception of why it is legitimate. See Duncan Kennedy, "The Political Significance of the Structure of the Law School Curriculum," *Seton Hall Law Review* 14 (1983): 1, 14. For an extensive bibliography of CLS writings, see *Yale Law Journal* 94 (1984): 464.

[28] A seminal CLS text on this theme is Duncan Kennedy, "Form and Substance in Private Law Adjudication," *Harvard Law Review* 89 (1976): 1685. This text and other CLS writings exhibit an important difference with legal realism on the so-called issue of "conceptualism." Several realists argued that legal thinking

should take place at a very low level of abstraction. Abstractions, especially those purporting to represent ethical ideals, were rejected as useless or worse in the conduct of legal thinking. CLS scholars have not followed these realists on the point. It is true that some, such as Kennedy, have suggested that judicial decisions rest on an appreciation of the peculiar fact pattern of the case at bar, rather than any effort to see the result as following from highly abstract principles which transcend that fact pattern. This is because Kennedy believes that ascending to higher levels of abstraction does not add to the cogency of arguments made in terms of the case's particular fact pattern. Disagreements which arise at the lower levels of abstraction will, in his view, simply be replicated at the higher level. And yet much of Kennedy's work, as well as that of other CLS theorists, is premised on the assumption that very high level abstractions have tremendous heuristic value in thinking about the law. Kennedy's "Form and Substance in Private Law Adjudication" is an extended examination of two abstractions which he calls "individualism" and "altruism." The premise is that the abstractions, each representing a competing ideal for human social life, will help us better grasp the terrain of legal doctrine, even if it will not help us in the end make a clinching legal argument. Moreover, some CLS writers clearly believe that such systematic thinking can be of far more than heuristic importance and teach us something crucial about the historical development of legal doctrine and its connection to social transformation generally. See Morton Horwitz, "Review of G. Gilmore, *The Ages of American Law*," *Buffalo Law Review* 27 (1977): 47, and *The Transformation of American Law, 1780–1860* (Cambridge, MA: Harvard University Press, 1977).

29 There is some disagreement within CLS regarding the task of constructing a defensible ethical theory. Roberto Unger considers it desirable to undertake the task and thinks there is no good reason to believe that it will never succeed. His most recent steps in carrying out the task are in *Passion: An Essay on Personality* (New York: Free Press, 1984). Duncan Kennedy is skeptical about the value, and prospects for success, of any such ethical theorizing. See his *Legal Education and the Reproduction of Hierarchy* (Cambridge: Afar, 1983), pp. 82–83. It would be a mistake, however, to infer from this that Kennedy is an ethical subjectivist of some sort. See "Form and Substance in Private Law Adjudication," pp. 1771–72.

30 Kennedy, "Form and Substance in Private Law Adjudication"; Unger, "Critical Legal Studies Movement," *Harvard Law Review* 96 (1983): 561, 616–46. Also see Kennedy, "The Structure of Blackstone's Commentaries," *Buffalo Law Review* 28 (1978): 205. Morton Horwitz, *The Transformation of American Law: 1780–1860* (Cambridge, MA: Harvard University Press, 1977); and Mark Kelman, "Interpretive Construction in the Sub-

stantive Criminal Law," *Stanford Law Review* 33 (1981): 591.

31 Kennedy, "Form and Substance in Private Law Adjudication," p. 1685.

32 Dworkin, *Taking Rights Seriously*, p. 26.

33 Dworkin, "A Reply by Ronald Dworkin," in M. Cohen, ed., *Ronald Dworkin and Contemporary Jurisprudence* (Totowa, NJ: Rowman and Allanheld, 1984), pp. 278–79.

34 Articulating the dominant view of his time, and one which is still widely held, Herbert Wechsler wrote that "the main constituent of the judicial process is that it must be genuinely principled, resting on analyses and reasons quite transcending the immediate result that is achieved." "Toward Neutral Principles of Constitutional Law," *Harvard Law Review* 73 (1959): 1, 15. Dworkin is clearly a direct heir of this view, although I believe that his effort to draw a sharp distinction between principle and policy for the purpose of distinguishing the legal from the legislative process goes beyond what the main legal theorists of the 1950s would have endorsed. See *Taking Rights Seriously*, pp. 82–84 and contrast with Henry Hart and Albert Sacks, *The Legal Process* (tent. ed. 1958), pp. 158–71.

35 Kennedy, "Form and Substance in Private Law Adjudication," p. 1724.

36 Fried, *Contract as Promise*.

37 Among the best CLS analyses of labor law are Karl Klare, "Judicial Deradicalization of the Wagner Act and the Origins of Modern Legal Consciousness, pp. 1937–1941," *Minnesota Law Review* 62 (1978): 265, and "Critical Legal Theory and Labor Relations Law," in Kairys, ed., *The Politics of Law*, pp. 65–88. In *Contract as Promise*, Fried does not discuss labor law or collective bargaining at all, except to mention that they do not fit his model of obligations willed by the individual upon himself (p. 2). For Fried's discussion of the doctrines which he expels from contract law, see his remarks on unjust enrichment and reasonable reliance, pp. 23–26.

38 Dworkin, *Taking Rights Seriously*, pp. 119–20.

39 Unger, "The Critical Legal Studies Movement," p. 571. This line of CLS argument presumes the falsity of the thesis of orthodox Marxism that law is a superstructural phenomenon which merely reinforces the existing relations of production by giving expression to the ideology of the dominant economic class. Many CLS writers repudiate this Marxist position. They see law and ideology generally as much more complex than can be captured by notions such as "capitalist," and they see causation in social life as much more complex than theories regarding superstructure and base can suggest. See, for example, Kennedy, "The Structure of Blackstone's Commentaries," pp. 362–63, fn. 56, and Klare, "Critical Theory and Labor Relations

Law." For a CLS description of modern Western society as more complicated than that portrayed in the class analysis of orthodox Marxism, see Unger, *Knowledge and Politics* (New York: Free Press, 1975), pp. 151–85, and *Law in Modern Society* (New York: Free Press, 1976), pp. 66–76, 171.

[40] Unger, "The Critical Legal Studies Movement," p. 571.

[41] For such a conventional criticism of Dworkin, see Neil MacCormick, "Dworkin as Pre-Benthamite," in Cohen, ed., *Ronald Dworkin and Contemporary Jurisprudence*, pp. 184–85, 192.

[42] Dworkin, "No Right Answer?" *New York University Law Review* 53 (1978): 1, 31–33; also see "A Reply by Ronald Dworkin," in Cohen, ed., *Ronald Dworkin and Contemporary Jurisprudence*, pp. 278–79.

[43] Alasdair MacIntyre, *After Virtue* (Notre Dame, IN: University of Notre Dame Press, 1981), see esp. pp. 2–4, 227–37.

[44] Kennedy, "The Political Significance of the Structure of the Law School Curriculum," p. 15.

[45] See, e.g., Mark Tushnet, "Critical Legal Studies and Constitutional Law: An Essay in Deconstruction," *Stanford Law Review* 36 (1984): 623; Paul Brest, "State Action and Liberal Theory: A Casenote on *Flagg Brothers v. Brooks*," *University of Pennsylvania Law Review* 130 (1982); 130; Richard Parker, "The Past of Constitutional Theory—And Its Future," *Ohio State Law Journal* 42 (1981): 223; Karl Klare, "The Public/Private Distinction in Labor Law," *University of Pennsylvania Law Review* 130 (1982): 1358; Gerald Frug, "The Ideology of Bureaucracy in American Law," *Harvard Law Review* 97 (1984): 1276; Unger, "The Critical Legal Studies Movement," pp. 602–47, and Kelman, "Interpretive Construction in the Substantive Criminal Law."

[46] Dworkin, "A Reply by Ronald Dworkin," p. 272.

[47] Ibid.

[48] Dworkin, *Taking Rights Seriously*, p. 127.

[49] Ibid.

[50] Ibid., pp. 35–45, 81–130.

[51] CLS would naturally add that, to the extent that judges think that there is a soundest theory of the law, they are victims of legal false-consciousness.

[52] Dworkin, *Taking Rights Seriously*, pp. 127–29.

[53] Ibid., p. 129.

Study Questions

1. It has been suggested that the realist insistence on the almost complete indeterminacy of the law resulted from a distorted or skewed perspective, one explained by the so-called *selection hypothesis*: Those cases that reach the appellate court level, and upon which legal scholars (like the realists) tend to focus, are just those cases in which the law is uncertain and in which the opposing arguments are fairly equally balanced. The great bulk of the law, however, the argument continues, is far more stable and determinate than the realists would admit. Does this explanation undermine legal realism?

2. Does the realist indeterminacy thesis express a necessary feature of law or legality? Or is it simply a contingent claim about a specific legal system or legal culture, namely, our own?

3. Dworkin argues that the "law" as it applies to any given case is more than simply the positive rules, encompassing as it does all those principles and ideals that are part of the best or soundest overall justification or interpretation of the existing rules. Could there be such a "best" theory? And if so, could any of us come to know it?

4. Dworkin argues that the task of a court is always to search for the interpretation of the existing state of the law that depicts it in the best moral light. How would this procedure apply to a judge in Nazi Germany who rejects the Nazi laws as immoral?

5. Dworkin compares the task of a judge to that of a contributor to a chain novel, and he assumes that, as in the case of the novelist, the judge will be constrained or limited in his interpretation by the work of earlier judges, earlier contributors to the legal novel. Is Dworkin correct that interpretive activity is constrained in this way? What implications would the indeterminacy thesis of the realists have for Dworkin's theory of interpretation?

6. Does the rule-skepticism of the realists represent an abandonment of the idea of the rule of law? If so, does this count for or against realism?

7. What kind of legal neutrality does the rule of law really require? Is any legal system that endorses the rule of law thoroughly neutral on all questions of value? Think back to Fuller's discussion of the "inner morality" of law. What would a proponent of CLS say to Fuller's argument that the very idea of legality carries with it certain value commitments?

Cases for Further Reflection

Zabella v. Pakel
242 F. 2nd 452 (1957)[1]
United States Court of Appeals,
Seventh Circuit

This case nicely contrasts the competing claims of moral and legal obligation. Which theory of law is presupposed by the court's reasoning?

[On September 1, 1931, the defendant, Pakel, gave a promissory note to the plaintiff, Zabella, promising Zabella he would pay him $4,577 by the time one year had elapsed. Pakel did not pay the money. In 1937, Pakel declared bankruptcy, a legal status that normally limits the ability of creditors to collect outstanding debts. In September 1954, Zabella filed suit to collect on the note. Zabella claimed that in 1952 Pakel had made another, verbal promise to pay the old debt. Pakel argued that he was under no legal obligation to keep his promise, as both the statute of limitations and his bankruptcy precluded Zabella's suit. Zabella won a verdict in his favor; however, the district court entered a "judgment notwithstanding the verdict," setting aside Zabella's award. Zabella appealed.]

Duffy, Chief Judge. Defendant Pakel is President and Manager of the Chicago Savings and Loan Association. In the 1920s he was a contractor. For a time during that period, Zabella worked for him as a carpenter. From time to time defendant borrowed money from plaintiff. None of it was repaid, but defendant executed new notes for the amounts due plus interest. The note given on September 1, 1931 for $4,577.00 and which is the subject of this suit included amounts due on previous notes and was the last note received by plaintiff from defendant.

. . .

Defendant's discharge in bankruptcy would be a bar to recovery by suit on the note or the debt unless defendant made a new promise to pay same. The moral obligation which defendant had to pay his debts would be a sufficient consideration. . . . The situation as to a new promise to pay is different when considering the bar of the statute of limitations. Chap. 83, Ill. Rev. Stat. 1955 Sec. 17 reads as follows: "Actions on . . . promissory notes . . . or other evidences of indebtedness in writing, shall be commenced within ten years next after the cause of action accrued. . . ." Thus, any new promise to pay the note must be in writing. Plaintiff admits there was no written promise by defendant.

. . .

We hold the transactions in 1952 were not sufficient to show defendant made a part payment upon the note under circumstances from which a new promise to pay the balance could be inferred. Of course, the jury was justified in thinking that defendant who then was in a position of some affluence and was the Chief Executive Officer of the Chicago Savings and Loan Association should feel obligated to pay an honest debt to an old friend, employee and countryman. Nevertheless, we are obliged to follow the law of Illinois. The strongest version of any alleged promise of defendant in 1952 is contained in the testimony of the plaintiff as follows: "I asked him if he could pay me any money on that note, and he says, 'Not right now I can't.' He says he just working and has salary. If some extra he will have it and he will pay." The suggestion that payments would be made under certain vague conditions that might obtain in the future were not a sufficient basis for the jury's verdict favorable to the plaintiff. . . .

Judgment: Affirmed.

---

[1] See the appendix for an explanation of legal citations and the system of classifying and storing legal materials to which they refer.

Riggs et al. v. Palmer
22 N.E. 188 (1889)
Court of Appeals of New York

The confrontation between naturalism and positivism is well joined in this case. As you read through the case, consider these questions: Are the precedents cited by Earl convincing? What is the source of the authoritativeness of the "fundamental maxims" of "universal law" invoked by Earl to support the judgment that Elmer Palmer must not be allowed to collect under his grandfather's will?

Earl [Judge]. On the 13th day of August, 1880, Francis B. Palmer made his last will and testament, in which he gave small legacies to his two daughters, Mrs. Riggs and Mrs. Preston, the plaintiffs in this action, and the remainder of his estate to his grandson, the defendant Elmer E. Palmer, subject to the support of Susan Palmer, his mother, with a gift over to the two daughers, subject to the support of Mrs. Palmer in case Elmer should survive him and die under age, unmarried, and without any issue. The testator, at the date of his will, owned a farm, and considerable personal property. He was a widower, and thereafter, in March, 1882, he was married to Mrs. Bresee, with whom, before his marriage, he entered into an antenuptial contract, in which it was agreed that in lieu of dower and all other claims upon his estate in case she survived him she should have her support upon his farm during her life, and such support was expressly charged upon the farm. At the date of the will, and subsequently to the death of the testator, Elmer lived with him as a member of his family, and at his death was 16 years old. He knew of the provisions made in his favor in the will, and, that he might prevent his grandfather from revoking such provisions, which he had manifested some intention to do, and to obtain the speedy enjoyment and immediate possession of his property, he willfully murdered him by poisoning him. He now claims the property, and the sole question for our determination is, can he have it?

The defendants say that the testator is dead; that his will was made in due form, and has been admitted to probate; and that therefore it must have effect according to the letter of the law. It is quite true that statutes regulating the making, proof, and effects of wills and devolution of property if literally construed, and if their force and effect can in no way and under no circumstances be controlled or modified, give this property to the murderer. The purpose of those statutes was to enable testators to dispose of their estates to the objects of their bounty at death, and to carry into effect their final wishes legally expressed; and in considering and giving effect to them this purpose must be kept in view. It was the intention of the law-makers that the donees in a will should have the property given to them. But it never could have been their intention that a donee who murdered the testator to make the will operative should have any benefit under it. If such a case had been present in their minds, and it had been supposed necessary to make some provision of law to meet it, it cannot be doubted that they would have provided for it. It is a familiar canon of construction that a thing which is within the intention of the makers of a statute is as much within the statute as if it were within the letter; and a thing which is within the letter of the statute is not within the statute unless it be within the intention of the makers. The writers of laws do not always express their intention perfectly, but either exceed it or fall short of it, so that judges are to collect it from probable or rational conjectures only, and this is called "rational interpretation;" and Rutherford, in his Institutes, (page 420,) says: "Where we make use of rational interpretation, sometimes we restrain the meaning of the writer so as to take in less, and sometimes we extend or enlarge his meaning so as to take in more, than his words express." Such a construction ought to put upon a statute as will best answer the intention which the makers had in view. . . . [M]any cases are mentioned where it was held that matters embraced in the general words of statutes nevertheless were not within the statutes, because it could not have been the intention of the law-makers that they should be included. They were taken out of the statutes by an equitable construction; and it is said in Bacon: "By an equitable construction a case not within the letter of a statute is sometimes holden to be within the meaning, because it is within the mischief for which a remedy is provided. The reason for such construction is that the law-makers could not set down every case in express terms. In order to form a right judgment whether a case be within the equity of a statute, it is a good way to suppose the law-maker present, and that you have asked him this question. Did you intend to comprehend this case? Then you must give yourself such answer as you imagine he, being an upright and reasonable man, would have given. If this be that he did mean to comprehend it, you may safely hold the case to be within the equity of the statute; for while you do no more than he would have done, you do not act contrary to the statute, but in conformity thereto." In some cases the letter of a legislative act is restrained by an equitable construction; in others, it is enlarged; in others, the construction is contrary to the letter. The equitable construction which restrains the letter of a statute is defined by Aristotle as frequently quoted in this manner: *Æquitas est correctio legis generaliter latæ qua parte deficit.* If the [law-makers] could, as to this case, be consulted, would they say that they intended by their general language that the property of a testator or of an ancestor should pass to one who had taken his life for the express purpose of getting his property? In 1 Bl. Comm. 91, the learned author, speaking of the construction of statutes, says: "If there arise out of them collaterally any absurd consequences manifestly contradictory to common reason, they are with regard to those collateral consequences void. [. . .] Where some collateral matter arises out of the general words, and happens to be unreasonable, there the judges are in decency to conclude that this consequence was not foreseen by the parliament, and therefore they are at liberty to expound the statute by equity, and only *quoad hoc* disregard it;" and he gives as an illustration, if an act of parliament gives a man power to try all causes that arise within his manor of Dale, yet, if a cause should arise in which he himself is party, the act is construed not to extend to that, because it is unreasonable that any man should determine his own quarrel. There was a statute in Bologna that whoever drew blood in the streets should be severely punished, and yet it was held not to apply to the case of a barber who opened a vein in the street. It is commanded in the decalogue that no work shall be done on the Sabbath, and yet giving the command a rational interpretation founded upon its design the Infallible Judge held that it did not prohibit works of necessity, charity, or benevolence on that day.

What could be more unreasonable than to suppose that it was the legislative intention in the general laws passed for the orderly, peaceable, and just devolution of property that they should have operation in favor of one who murdered his ancestor that he might speedily come into the possession of his estate? Such an intention is inconceivable. We need not, therefore, be much troubled by the general language contained in the laws. Besides, all laws, as well as all contracts, may be controlled in their operation and effect by general, fundamental maxims of the common law. No one shall be permitted to profit by his own fraud, or to take advantge of his own wrong, or to found any claim upon his own iniquity, or to acquire property by his own crime. These maxims are dictated by public policy, have their foundation in universal law administered in all civilized countries, and have nowhere been superseded by statutes. They were applied in the decision of the case of Insurance Co. v. Armstrong, 117 U.S. 599, 6 Sup. Ct. Rep. 877. There it was held that the person who procured a policy upon the life of another, payable at his death, and then murdered the assured to make the policy payable, could not recover thereon. Mr. Justice FIELD, writing the opinion, said: "Independently of any proof of the motives of Hunter in obtaining the policy, and even assuming that they were just and proper, he forfeited all rights under it when, to secure its immediate payment, he murdered the assured. It would be a reproach to the jurisprudence of the country if one could recover insurance money payable on the death of a party whose life he had feloniously taken. As well might he recover insurance money upon a building he had wilfully fired." These maxims, without any statute giving them force or operation, frequently control the effect and nullify the language of wills. A will procured by fraud and deception, like any other instrument, may be decreed void, and set aside; and so a particular portion of a will may be excluded from probate, or held inoperative, if induced by the fraud or undue influence of the person in whose favor it is. Allen v. McPherson, 1 H. L. Cas. 191; Harrison's Appeal, 48 Conn. 202. So a will may contain provisions which are immoral, irreligious, or against public policy, and they will be held void.

Here there was no certainty that this murderer would survive the testator, or that the testator would not change his will, and there was no certainty that he would get his property if nature was allowed to take its course. He therefore murdered the testator expressly to vest himself with an estate. Under such circumstances, what law, human or divine, will allow him to take the estate and enjoy the fruits of his crime? The will spoke and became operative at the death of the testator. He caused that death, and thus by his crime made it speak and have operation. Shall it speak and operate in his favor? If he had met the testator, and taken his property by force, he would have had no title to it. Shall he acquire title by murdering him? If he had gone to the testator's house, and by force compelled him, or by fraud or undue influence had induced him, to will him his property, the law would not allow him to hold it. But can he give effect and operation to a will by murder, and yet take the property? To answer these questions in the affirmative it seems to me would be a reproach to the jurisprudence of our state, and an offense against public policy. Under the civil law, evolved from the general principles of natural law and justice by many generations of jurisconsults, philosophers, and statemen, one cannot take property by inheritance or will from an ancestor or benefactor whom he has murdered. . . . In the Civil Code of Lower Canada the provisions on the subject in the Code Napoleon have been substantially copied. But, so far as I can find, in no country where the common law prevails has it been deemed important to enact a law to provide for such a case. Our revisers and law-makers were familiar with the civil law, and they did not deem it important to incorporate into our statutes its provisions upon [this] subject. This is not a *casus omissus*. It was evidently supposed that the maxims of the common law were sufficient to regulate such a case, and that a specific enactment for that purpose was not needed. For the same reasons the defendant Palmer cannot take any of this property as heir. Just before the murder he was not an heir, and it was not certain that he ever would be. He might have died before his grandfather, or might have been disinherited by him. He made himself an heir by the murder, and he seeks to take property as the fruit of his crime. What has before been said as to him as legatee applies to him with equal force as an heir. He cannot vest himself with title by crime. My view of this case does not inflict upon Elmer any greater or other punishment for his crime than the law specifies. It takes from him no property, but simply holds that he shall not acquire property by his crime, and thus be rewarded for its commission.

Our attention is called to Owens v. Owens, 100 N.C. 240, 6 S.E. Rep. 794, as a case quite like this. There a wife had been convicted of being an accessory before the fact to the murder of her husband, and it was held that she was nevertheless entitled to dower. I am unwilling to assent to the doctrine of that case. The [statutes] provide dower for a wife who has the misfortune to survive her husband, and thus lose his support and protection. It is clear beyond their purpose to make provision for a wife who by her own crime makes herself a widow, and willfully and intentionally deprives herself of the support and protection of her husband. As she might have died before him, and "though" never have been his widow, she cannot by her crime vest herself with an estate. The principle which lies at the bottom of the maxim *volenti non fit injuria* should be applied to such a case, and a widow should not, for the purpose of acquiring, as such, property rights, be permitted to allege a widowhood which she has wickedly and intentionally created.

Gray, [Judge] (dissenting). The appellants' argument for a reversal of the judgment, which dismissed their complaint, is that the respondent unlawfully prevented a revocation of the existing will, or a new will from being made, by his crime; and that he terminated the enjoyment of the testator of his property, and effected his own succession to it, by the same crime. They say that to permit the respondent to take the property willed to him would be to permit him to take advantage of his own wrong. To sustain their position that the appellants' counsel has submitted an able and elaborate brief, and, if I believed that the decision of the question could be effected by considerations of an equitable nature, I should not hesitate to assent to views which commend themselves to the conscience. But the matter does not lie within the domain of conscience. We are bound by the rigid rules of law, which have been established by the legislature, and within the limits of which the determination of this question is confined. The question we are dealing with is whether a testamentary disposition can be altered, or a will revoked, after the testator's death, through an appeal to the courts, when the legislature has by its enactments prescribed exactly when and how wills may be made, altered, and revoked, and apparently, as it seems to me, when they have been fully complied with, has left no room for the exercise of an equitable jurisdiction by courts over such matters. Modern jurisprudence, in recognizing the right of the individual, under more or less restrictions, to dispose of his property after his death, subjects it to legislative control, both as to extent and as to mode of exercise. Complete freedom of testamentory disposition of one's property has not been and is not the universal rule, as we see from the provisions of the Napoleonic Code, from the systems of jurisprudence in countries which are modeled upon the Roman law, and from the statutes of many of our states. To the statutory restraints which are imposed upon the disposition of one's property by will are added strict and systematic statutory rules for the execution, alteration, and revocation of the will, which must be, at least substantially, if not exactly, followed to insure validity and performance. The reason for the establishment of such rules, we may naturally assume, consists in the purpose to create those safeguards about these grave and important acts which experience has demonstrated to be the wisest and surest. That freedom which is permitted to be exercised in the testamentary disposition of one's estate by the laws of the state is subject to its being exercised in conformity with the regulations of the statutes. The capacity and the power of the individual to dispose of his property after death, and the mode by which that power can be exercised, are matters of which the legislature has assumed the entire control, and has undertaken to regulate with comprehensive particularity. . . .

I cannot find any support for the argument that the respondent's succession to the property should be avoided because of his criminal act, when the laws are silent. Public policy does not demand it; for the demands of public policy are satisfied by the proper execution of the laws and the punishment of the crime. There has been no convention between the testator and his legatee. The appellants' argument practically amounts to this: that, as the legatee has been guilty of a crime, by the commission of which he is placed in a position to sooner receive the benefits of the testamentary provision, his rights to the property should be forfeited, and he should be divested of his estate. To allow their argument to prevail would involve the diversion by the court of the testator's estate into the hands of persons whom, possibly enough, for all we know, the testator might not have chosen or desired as its recipients. Practically the court is asked to make another will for the testator. The laws do not warrant this judicial action, and mere presumption would not be strong enough to sustain it. But, more than this, to concede the appellants' views would involve the imposition of an additional punishment or penalty upon the respondent. What power or warrant have the courts to add to the respondent's penalties by depriving him of property? The law has punished

him for his crime, and we may not say that it was an insufficient punishment. In the trial and punishment of the respondent the law has vindicated itself for the outrage which he committed, and further judicial utterance upon the subject of punishment or deprivation of rights is barred. We may not, in the language of the court in People v. Thornton, 25 Hun, 456, "enhance the pains, penalties, and forfeitures provided by law for the punishment of crime." The judgment should be affirmed, with costs.

The Antelope
23 U.S. (19 Wheat.) 66 (1825)
United States Supreme Court

An opinion by legendary Chief Justice John Marshall, this early case represents yet another clash between positive and natural law, set here in the context of the law of nations. Can you explain why, if both the (positive) statutes of the United States and the principles of the "law of nature" condemn the slave trade, Marshall nonetheless orders the return of the slaves to their "owners"? Why does Marshall hold that the positive law of nations "trumps" the positive law of the United States?

[In 1808 the Congress prohibited the importation of slaves into the United States. Subsequent federal laws punished persons who engaged in the slave trade, requiring that their ships be forfeited and that the Negroes be returned to Africa. The slave ship *Antelope,* carrying over two hundred African slaves, was intercepted off the coast of Florida by a United States vessel for suspected violation of the slave-trade laws. The governments of Spain and Portugal insisted that the ship and its cargo be released, maintaining that the Africans were the property of Spanish and Portuguese citizens. The U.S. government resisted and presented the Supreme Court with the question of whether the U.S. federal laws applied to forfeit slaves owned by foreign nationals.]

Marshall, Chief Justice.

In prosecuting this appeal, the United States assert no property in themselves. They appear in the character of guardians, or next friends, of these Africans, who are brought, without any act of their own, into the bosom of our country, insist on their right to freedom, and submit their claim to the laws of the land, and to the tribunals of the nation. The consuls of Spain and Portugal, respectively, demand these Africans as slaves, who have, in the regular cause of legitimate commerce, been acquired as property, by the subjects of their respective sovereigns, and claim their restitution under the laws of the United States.

In examining claims of this momentous importance—claims in which the sacred rights of liberty and of property come in conflict with each other—which have drawn from the bar a degree of talent and of eloquence, worthy of the questions that have been discussed, their court must not yield to feelings which might seduce it from the path of duty, and must obey the mandate of the law.

That the course of opinion on the slave-trade should be unsettled, ought to excite no surprise. The Christian and civilized nations of the world, with whom we have most intercourse, have all been engaged in it. However abhorrent this traffic may be to a mind whose original feelings are not blunted by familiarity with the practice, it has been sanctioned, in modern times, by the laws of all nations who possess distant colonies, each of whom has engaged in it as a common commercial business, which no other could rightfully interrupt. It has claimed all the sanction which could be derived from long usage and general acquiescence. That trade could not be considered as contrary to the law of nations which was authorized and protected by the laws of all commercial nations; the right to carry on which was claimed by each, and allowed by each.

The course of unexamined opinion, which was founded on this inveterate usage, received its first check in America; and, as soon as these states acquired the right of self-government, the traffic was forbidden by most of them. In the beginning of this century, several humane and enlightened individuals of Great Britain devoted themselves to the cause of the Africans; and by frequent appeals to the nation, in which the enormity of this commerce was unveiled and exposed to the public eye, the general sentiment was at length roused against it, and the feelings of justice and humanity, regaining their long-lost ascendency, prevailed so far in the British parliament, as to obtain an act for its abolition. The utmost efforts of the British government, as well as of that of the United States, have since been assiduously employed in its suppression. It has been denounced by both, in terms of great severity, and those concerned in it are sub-

jected to the heaviest penalties which law can inflict. In addition to these measures, operating on their own people, they have used all their influence to bring other nations into the same system, and to interdict this trade by the consent of all. Public sentiment has, in both countries, kept pace with the measures of government; and the opinion is extensively, if not universally, entertained, that this unnatural traffic ought to be suppressed. While its illegality is asserted by some governments, but not admitted by all; while the detestation in which it is held, is growing daily, and even those nations who tolerate it, in fact, almost disavow their own conduct, and rather connive at, than legalize, the acts of their subjects, it is not wonderful, that public feeling should march somewhat in advance of strict law, and that opposite opinions should be entertained on the precise cases in which our own laws may control and limit the practice of others. Indeed, we ought not to be surprised, if, in this novel series of cases, even courts of justice should, in some instances, have carried the principle of suppression further than a more deliberate consideration of the subject would justify. . . .

The question, whether the slave-trade is prohibited by the law of nations has been seriously propounded, and both the affirmative and negative of the proposition have been maintained with equal earnestness. That it is contrary to the law of nature, will scarcely be denied. That every man has a natural right to the fruits of his own labor, is generally admitted; and that no other person can rightfully deprive him of those fruits, and appropriate them against his will, seems to be the necessary result of this admission. But from the earliest times, war has existed, and war confers rights in which all have acquiesced. Among the most enlightened nations of antiquity, one of these was, that the victor might enslave the vanquished. This, which was the usage of all, could not be pronounced repugnant to the law of nations, which is certainly to be tried by the test of general usage. That which has received the assent of all, must be the law of all. Slavery, then, has its origin in force; but as the world has agreed, that it is a legitimate result of force, the state of things which is thus produced by general consent, cannot be pronounced unlawful.

Throughout Christendom, this harsh rule has been exploded, and war is no longer considered, as giving a right to enslave captives. But this triumph of humanity has not been universal. The parties to the modern law of nations do not propagate their principles by force, and Africa has not yet adopted them. Throughout the whole extent of that immense continent, so far as we know its history, it is still the law of nations, that prisoners are slaves. Can those who have themselves renounced this law, be permitted to participate in its effects, by purchasing the beings who are its victims? Whatever might be the answer of a moralist to this question, a jurist must search for its legal solution, in those principles of action which are sanctioned by the usages, the national acts, and the general assent, of that portion of the world of which he considers himself as a part, and to whose law the appeal is made. If we resort to this standard, as the test of international law, the question, as has already been observed, is decided in favor of the legality of the trade. Both Europe and America embarked in it; and for nearly two centuries, it was carried on, without opposition, and without censure. A jurist could not say, that a practice, thus supported, was illegal, and that those engaged in it might be punished, either personally or by deprivation of property. In this commerce thus sanctioned by universal assent, every nation had an equal right to engage. How is their right to be lost? Each may renounce it for its own people; but can this renunciation affect others?

No principle of general law is more universally acknowledged, than the perfect equality of nations. Russia and Geneva have equal rights. It results from this equality, that no one can rightfully impose a rule on another. Each legislates for itself, but its legislation can operate on itself alone. A right, then, which is vested in all, by the consent of all, can be divested only by consent; and this trade, in which all have participated, must remain lawful to those who cannot be induced to relinquish it. As no nation can prescribe a rule for others, none can make a law of nations; and this traffic remains lawful to those whose governments have not forbidden it. If it be consistent with the law of nations, it cannot in itself be piracy. It can be made so only by statute; and the obligation of the statute cannot transcend the legislative power of the state which may enact it.

If it be neither repugnant to the law of nations, nor piracy, it is almost superfluous to say, in this court, that the right of bringing in for adjudication, in time of peace, even where the vessel belongs to a nation which has prohibited the trade, cannot ex-

ist. The courts of no country execute the penal laws of another; and the course of the American government, on the subject of visitation and search, would decide any case in which that right had been exercised by an American cruiser, on the vessel of a foreign nation, not violating our municipal laws, against the captors. It follows, that a foreign vessel engaged in the African slave-trade, captured on the high seas, in time of peace, by an American cruiser, and brought in for adjudication, would be restored. . . .

The general question being disposed of, it remains to examine the circumstances of the particular case. [The Court denied the Portuguese claims, taking judicial notice of the fact that] Americans, and others who cannot use the flag of their own nations, carry on this criminal and inhuman traffic, under the flags of other countries. . . . [The real owner of the Africans claimed by Portugal] belongs to some other nation, and feels the necessity of concealment. [Because the Court was evenly divided over the legitimacy of the Spanish claim, it affirmed the lower court's decree, though it reduced the number of Africans to be restored to the Spanish owners.]

The Problem of the Grudge Informer
Lon Fuller

Fuller's imaginary case presents you with a difficult choice: What will you do as the newly elected Minister of Justice? As you read the recommendations of the various deputies, try to detect appeals to one or another of the theories about the nature of law covered in this chapter. Do any of the deputies come close to your solution?

By a narrow margin you have been elected Minister of Justice of your country, a nation of some twenty million inhabitants. At the outset of your term of office you are confronted by a serious problem that will be described below. But first the background of this problem must be presented.

From *The Morality of Law* (New Haven: Yale University Press, 1969), pp. 245–253. Reprinted with permission of Yale University Press.

For many decades your country enjoyed a peaceful, constitutional and democratic government. However, some time ago it came upon bad times. Normal relations were disrupted by a deepening economic depression and by an increasing antagonism among various factional groups, formed along economic, political, and religious lines. The proverbial man on horseback appeared in the form of the Headman of a political party or society that called itself the Purple Shirts.

In a national election attended by much disorder the Headman was elected President of the Republic and his party obtained a majority of the seats in the General Assembly. The success of the party at the polls was partly brought about by a campaign of reckless promises and ingenious falsifications, and partly by the physical intimidation of night-riding Purple Shirts who frightened many people away from the polls who would have voted against the party.

When the Purple Shirts arrived in power they took no steps to repeal the ancient Constitution or any of its provisions. They also left intact the Civil and Criminal Codes and the Code of Procedure. No official action was taken to dismiss any government official or remove any judge from the bench. Elections continued to be held at intervals and ballots were counted with apparent honesty. Nevertheless, the country lived under a reign of terror.

Judges who rendered decisions contrary to the wishes of the party were beaten and murdered. The accepted meaning of the Criminal Code was perverted to place political opponents in jail. Secret statutes were passed, the contents of which were known only to the upper levels of the party hierarchy. Retroactive statutes were enacted which made acts criminal that were legally innocent when committed. No attention was paid by the government to the restraints of the Constitution, of antecedent laws, or even of its own laws. All opposing political parties were disbanded. Thousands of political opponents were put to death, either methodically in prisons or in sporadic night forays of terror. A general amnesty was declared in favor of persons under sentence for acts "committed in defending the fatherland against subversion." Under this amnesty a general liberation of all prisoners who were members of the Purple Shirt party was effected. No one not a member of the party was released under the amnesty.

The Purple Shirts as a matter of deliberate policy preserved an element of flexibility in their oper-ations by acting at times through the apparatus of the state which they controlled. Choice between the two methods of proceeding was purely a matter of expediency. For example, when the inner circle of the party decided to ruin all the former Socialist-Republicans (whose party put up a last-ditch resistance to the new regime), a dispute arose as to the best way of confiscating their property. One faction, perhaps still influenced by pre-revolutionary conceptions, wanted to accomplish this by a statute declaring their goods forfeited for criminal acts. Another wanted to do it by compelling the owners to deed their property over at the point of a bayonet. This group argued against the proposed statute on the ground that it would attract unfavorable comment abroad. The Headman decided in favor of direct action through the party to be followed by a secret statute ratifying the party's action and confirming the titles obtained by threats of physical violence.

The Purple Shirts have now been overthrown and a democratic and constitutional government restored. Some difficult problems have, however, been left behind by the deposed regime. These you and your associates in the new government must find some way of solving. One of these problems is that of the "grudge informer."

During the Purple Shirt regime a great many people worked off grudges by reporting their enemies to the party or to the government authorities. The activities reported were such things as the private expression of views critical of the government, listening to foreign radio broadcasts, associating with known wreckers and hooligans, hoarding more than the permitted amount of dried eggs, failing to report a loss of identification papers within five days, etc. As things then stood with the administration of justice, any of these acts, if proved, could lead to a sentence of death. In some cases this sentence was authorized by "emergency" statutes; in others it was imposed without statutory warrant, though by judges duly appointed to their offices.

After the overthrow of the Purple Shirts, a strong public demand grew up that these grudge informers be punished. The interim government, which preceded that with which you are associated, temporized on this matter. Meanwhile it has become a burning issue and a decision concerning it can no longer be postponed. Accordingly, your first act as Minister of Justice has been to address yourself to it. You have asked your five Deputies to give thought to the matter and to bring their recommendations to conference. At the conference the five Deputies speak in turn as follows:

FIRST DEPUTY. "It is perfectly clear to me that we can do nothing about these so-called grudge informers. The acts they reported were unlawful according to the rules of the government then in actual control of the nation's affairs. The sentences imposed on their victims were rendered in accordance with principles of law then obtaining. These principles differed from those familiar to us in ways that we consider detestable. Nevertheless they were then the law of the land. One of the principal differences between that law and our own lies in the much wider discretion it accorded to the judge in criminal matters. This rule and its consequences are as much entitled to respect by us as the reform which the Purple Shirts introduced into the law of wills, whereby only two witnesses were required instead of three. It is immaterial that the rule granting the judge a more or less uncontrolled discretion in criminal cases was never formally enacted but was a matter of tacit acceptance. Exactly the same thing can be said of the opposite rule which we accept that restricts the judge's discretion narrowly. The difference between ourselves and the Purple Shirts is not that theirs was an unlawful government—a contradiction in terms—but lies rather in the field of ideology. No one has a greater abhorrence than I for Purple Shirtism. Yet the fundamental difference between our philosophy and theirs is that we permit and tolerate differences in viewpoint, while they attempted to impose their monolithic code on everyone. Our whole system of government assumes that law is a flexible thing, capable of expressing and effectuating many different aims. The cardinal point of our creed is that when an objective has been duly incorporated into a law or judicial decree it must be provisionally accepted even by those that hate it, who must await their chance at the polls, or in another litigation, to secure a legal recognition of their own aims. The Purple Shirts, on the other hand, simply disregarded laws that incorporated objectives of which they did not approve, not even considering it worth the effort involved to repeal them. If we now seek to unscramble the acts of the Purple Shirt regime, declaring this judgment invalid, that statute void, this sentence excessive, we shall be doing exactly the thing we most condemn in them. I recognize that it will take courage to carry through with the program I recommend and we shall have to resist strong pressures of public opinion. We shall also have to be prepared to prevent the people from taking the law into their own hands. In the long run, however, I believe the course I recommend is the only one that will insure the triumph of the conceptions of law and government in which we believe."

SECOND DEPUTY. "Curiously, I arrive at the same conclusion as my colleague, by an exactly opposite route. To me it seems absurd to call the Purple Shirt regime a lawful government. A legal system does not exist simply because policemen continue to patrol the streets and wear uniforms or because a constitution and code are left on the shelf unrepealed. A legal system presupposes laws that are known, or can be known, by those subject to them. It presupposes some uniformity of action and that like cases will be given like treatment. It presupposes the absence of some lawless power, like the Purple Shirt Party, standing above the government and able at any time to interfere with the administration of justice whenever it does not function according to the whims of that power. All of these presuppositions enter into the very conception of an order of law and have nothing to do with political and economic ideologies. In my opinion law in any ordinary sense of the word ceased to exist when the Purple Shirts came to power. During their regime we had, in effect, an interregnum in the rule of law. Instead of a government of laws we had a war of all against all conducted behind barred doors, in dark alleyways, in palace intrigues, and prison-yard conspiracies. The acts of these so-called grudge informers were just one phase of that war. For us to condemn these acts as criminal would involve as much incongruity as if we were to attempt to apply juristic conceptions to the struggle for existence that goes on in the jungle or beneath the surface of the sea. We must put this whole dark, lawless chapter of our history behind us like a bad dream. If we stir among its hatreds, we shall bring upon ourselves something of its evil spirit and risk infection from its miasmas. I therefore say with my colleague, let bygones be bygones. Let us do nothing about the so-called grudge informers. What they did do was neither lawful nor contrary to law, for they lived, not under a regime of law, but under one of anarchy and terror."

THIRD DEPUTY. "I have a profound suspicion of any kind of reasoning that proceeds by an 'either-or' alternative. I do not think we need to assume either, on the one hand, that in some manner the whole of the Purple Shirt regime was outside the realm of law, or, on the other, that all of its doings are entitled to full credence as the acts of a lawful government. My two colleagues have unwittingly delivered powerful arguments against these extreme assumptions by demonstrating that both of them lead to the same absurd conclusion, a conclusion that is ethically and politically impossible. If one reflects about the matter without emotion it becomes clear that we did not have during the Purple Shirt regime a 'war of all against all.' Under the surface much of what we call normal human life went on—marriages were contracted, goods were sold, wills were drafted and executed. This life was attended by the usual dislocations—automobile accidents, bankruptcies, unwitnessed wills, defamatory misprints in the newspapers. Much of this normal life and most of these equally normal dislocations of it were unaffected by the Purple Shirt ideology. The legal questions that arose in this area were handled by the courts much as they had been formerly and much as they are being handled today. It would invite an intolerable chaos if we were to declare everything that happened under the Purple Shirts to be without legal basis. On the other hand, we certainly cannot say that the murders committed in the streets by members of the party acting under orders from the Headman were lawful simply because the party had achieved control of the government and its chief had become President of the Republic. If we must condemn the criminal acts of the party and its members, it would seem absurd to uphold every act which happened to be canalized through the apparatus of the government that had become, in effect, the alter ego of the Purple Shirt Party. We must therefore, in this situation, as in most human affairs, discriminate. Where the Purple Shirt philosophy intruded itself and perverted the administration of justice from its normal aims and uses, there we must interfere. Among these perversions of justice I would count, for example, the case of a man who was in love with another man's wife and brought about the death of the husband by informing against him for a wholly trivial offense, that is, for not reporting a loss of his identification papers within five days. This informer was a murderer under the Criminal Code which was in effect

at the time of his act and which the Purple Shirts had not repealed. He encompassed the death of one who stood in the way of his illicit passions and utilized the courts for the realization of his murderous intent. He knew that the courts were themselves the pliant instruments of whatever policy the Purple Shirts might for the moment consider expedient. There are other cases that are equally clear. I admit that there are also some that are less clear. We shall be embarrassed, for example, by the cases of mere busybodies who reported to the authorities everything that looked suspect. Some of these persons acted not from desire to get rid of those they accused, but with a desire to curry favor with the party, to divert suspicions (perhaps ill-founded) raised against themselves, or through sheer officiousness. I don't know how these cases should be handled, and make no recommendation with regard to them. But the fact that these troublesome cases exist should not deter us from acting at once in the cases that are clear, of which there are far too many to permit us to disregard them."

FOURTH DEPUTY. "Like my colleague I too distrust 'either-or' reasoning, but I think we need to reflect more than he has about where we are headed. This proposal to pick and choose among the acts of the deposed regime is thoroughly objectionable. It is, in fact, Purple Shirtism itself, pure and simple. We like this law, so let us enforce it. We like this judgment, let it stand. This law we don't like, therefore it never was a law at all. This governmental act we disapprove, let it be deemed a nullity. If we proceed this way, we take toward the laws and acts of the Purple Shirt government precisely the unprincipled attitude they took toward the laws and acts of the government they supplanted. We shall have chaos, with every judge and every prosecuting attorney a law unto himself. Instead of ending the abuses of the Purple Shirt regime, my colleague's proposal would perpetuate them. There is only one way of dealing with this problem that is compatible with our philosophy of law and government and that is to deal with it by duly enacted law, I mean, by a special statute directed toward it. Let us study this whole problem of the grudge informer, get all the relevant facts, and draft a comprehensive law dealing with it. We shall not then be twisting old laws to purposes for which they were never intended. We shall furthermore provide penalties appropriate to the offense and not treat every informer as a murderer simply because the one he informed against was ultimately executed. I admit that we shall encounter some difficult problems of draftsmanship. Among other things, we shall have to assign a definite legal meaning to 'grudge' and that will not be easy. We should not be deterred by these difficulties, however, from adopting the only course that will lead us out of a condition of lawless, personal rule."

FIFTH DEPUTY. "I find a considerable irony in the last proposal. It speaks of putting a definite end to the abuses of the Purple Shirtism, yet it proposes to do this by resorting to one of the most hated devices of the Purple Shirt regime, the ex post facto criminal statute. My colleague dreads the conclusion that will result if we attempt without a statute to undo and redress 'wrong' acts of the departed order, while we uphold and enforce its 'right' acts. Yet he seems not to realize that his proposed statute is a wholly specious cure for this uncertainty. It is easy to make a plausible argument for an undrafted statute; we all agree it would be nice to have things down in black and white on paper. But just what would this statute provide? One of my colleagues speaks of someone who had failed for five days to report a loss of his identification papers. My colleague implies that the judicial sentence imposed for that offense, namely death, was so utterly disproportionate as to be clearly wrong. But we must remember that at that time the underground movement against the Purple Shirts was mounting in intensity and that the Purple Shirts were being harassed constantly by people with false identification papers. From their point of view

they had a real problem, and the only objection we can make to their solution of it (other than the fact that we didn't want them to solve it) was that they acted with somewhat more rigor than the occasion seemed to demand. How will my colleague deal with this case in his statute, and with all of its cousins and second cousins? Will he deny the existence of any need for law and order under the Purple Shirt regime? I will not go further into the difficulties involved in drafting this proposed statute, since they are evident enough to anyone who reflects. I shall instead turn to may own solution. It has been said on very respectable authority that the main purpose of the criminal law is to give an outlet to the human instinct for revenge. There are times, and I believe this is one of them, when we should allow that instinct to express itself directly without the intervention of forms of law. This matter of the grudge informers is already in process of straightening itself out. One reads almost every day that a former lackey of the Purple Shirt regime has met his just reward in some unguarded spot. The people are quietly handling this thing in their own way and if we leave them alone, and instruct our public prosecutors to do the same, there will soon be no problem left for us to solve. There will be some disorders, of course, and a few innocent heads will be broken. But our government and our legal system will not be involved in the affair and we shall not find ourselves hopelessly bogged down in an attempt to unscramble all the deeds and misdeeds of the Purple Shirts."

As Minister of Justice which of these recommendations would you adopt?

Suggestions for Further Reading

Adams, D. M., "Skepticism and the Apologetics of Law," *Canadian Journal of Law and Jurisprudence*, Vol. 3 (1990): 69–90.

Altman, A., *Critical Legal Studies: A Liberal Critique* (Princeton, N.J.: Princeton University Press, 1990).

Austin, J., *The Province of Jurisprudence Determined* (London: Weidenfeld & Nicolson, 1954).

Balkin, J. M., "Taking Ideology Seriously: Ronald Dworkin and the CLS Critique," *UMKC Law Review*, Vol. 55 (1987): 392–437.

Bentham, J., *Of Laws in General* (ed. H. L. A. Hart) (London: Althone Press, 1970).

Benton, W., and Grimm, G., *Nuremberg: German Views of the War Trials* (Dallas: Southern Methodist University Press, 1955).

Cohen, M. (Ed.), *Ronald Dworkin and Contemporary Jurisprudence* (Totowa, N.J.: Rowman & Allanheld, 1984).

Conot, R. E., *Justice at Nuremberg* (New York: Harper & Row, 1983).

D'Entreves, A. P., *Natural Law* (London: Hutchinson University Library, 1970).

Dworkin, R., *Taking Rights Seriously* (Cambridge, Mass.: Harvard University Press, 1977).

Dworkin, R., *A Matter of Principle* (Cambridge, Mass.: Harvard University Press, 1985).

Dworkin, R., *Law's Empire* (Cambridge, Mass.: Harvard University Press, 1986).

Essays on Critical Legal Studies (Cambridge, Mass.: Harvard Law Review Association, 1986).

Finnis, J., *Natural Law and Natural Rights* (Oxford: Clarendon Press, 1980).

Fogelson, S., "The Nuremberg Legacy: An Unfulfilled Promise," *Southern California Law Review*, Vol. 63 (1990): 833–905.

Frank, J., *Law and the Modern Mind* (Garden City, N.Y.: Doubleday, 1963).

Glueck, S., *The Nuremberg Trial and Aggressive War* (New York: Alfred A. Knopf, 1946).

Golding, M., *Philosophy of Law* (Englewood Cliffs, N.J.: Prentice-Hall, 1975).

Grey, T. C., "Langdell's Orthodoxy," *University of Pittsburgh Law Review*, Vol. 45 (1983): 1–53.

Hart, H. L. A., *The Concept of Law* (London: Oxford University Press, 1961).

Hart, H. L. A., *Essays of Jurisprudence and Philosophy* (Oxford: Clarendon Press, 1983).

Kelman, M., *A Guide to Critical Legal Studies* (Cambridge, Mass.: Harvard University Press, 1987).

Llewellyn, K., *The Bramble Bush* (New York: Columbia University Press, 1930).

Llewellyn, K., "Some Realism About Realism," in K. Llewellyn, *Jurisprudence: Realism in Theory and Practice* (Chicago: University of Chicago Press, 1962), pp. 41–76.

Lucey, F., "Natural Law and American Legal Realism," *Georgetown Law Journal*, Vol. 30 (1942): 493–511.

Lyons, D., *Ethics and the Rule of Law* (Cambridge: Cambridge University Press, 1984).

Meltzer, B., "A Note on Some Aspects of the Nuremberg Debate," *University of Chicago Law Review*, Vol. 14 (1947): 455–469.

Morgan, E. M., "Retributory Theater," *American University Journal of International Law and Policy*, Vol. 3 (1988): 1–64.

Murphy, J., and Coleman, J., *Philosophy of Law: An Introduction to Jurisprudence*, rev. ed. (Boulder, Colo.: Westview Press, 1970).

Pincoffs, E., *Philosophy of Law: A Brief Introduction* (Belmont, Calif.: Wadsworth, 1991).

Posner, R., *Law and Literature* (Cambridge, Mass.: Harvard University Press, 1988).

Posner, R., *The Problems of Jurisprudence* (Cambridge, Mass.: Harvard University Press; 1990).

Raz, J., *The Concept of a Legal System* (Oxford: Clarendon Press, 1970).

Simpson, A. W. B., *Cannibalism and the Common Law* (Chicago: University of Chicago Press, 1984).

Solum, L., "On the Indeterminacy Crisis: Critiquing Critical Dogma," *Chicago Law Review*, Vol. 54 (1987): 462–503.

Soper, P., "Making Sense of Modern Jurisprudence," *Creighton Law Review*, Vol. 22 (1988): 67–88.

Symposium on Critical Legal Studies, *Stanford Law Review*, Vol. 36 (1984): 1–674.

Unger, R., *Knowledge and Politics* (New York: Free Press, 1975).

Unger, R., *The Critical Legal Studies Movement* (Cambridge, Mass.: Harvard University Press, 1986).

West, R., "Jurisprudence and Gender," *University of Chicago Law Review*, Vol. 55 (1988): 1–72.

Chapter II

Legal Reasoning and Constitutional Interpretation

In the summer of 1987, President Ronald Reagan nominated Judge Robert Bork, then serving as a federal circuit court of appeals judge, to fill a vacancy on the United States Supreme Court. Judge Bork, an outspoken and articulate conservative, had written and spoken widely throughout his career on matters of constitutional law and social policy and had been especially critical of many controversial Supreme Court decisions dealing with civil rights, freedom of speech and religion, privacy, and affirmative action, among others.

Bork's nomination (and eventual rejection by the Senate) sparked a nationwide debate on the meaning of our law, how it is to be interpreted, and what the job of a judge should be. Had the Supreme Court of the 1950s and 1960s acted irresponsibly, as Bork alleged, by "reading into" the Constitution its own moral, social, and political agenda? Or had it simply enforced the "true" meaning of the Constitution? What is the difference between "reading things into" the Constitution and "finding" them there already? What does it mean to interpret a consitution or a statute responsibly? How does one reason from vague and open-ended language such as "due process" or "equal protection" to concrete decisions in particular cases, from general principles to specific results? In what way are judges' decisions guided by the law, rather than by their own opinions? These questions form the focus for Chapter Two.

The first section of this chapter introduces these concerns and issues with an exploration of one of the most divisive areas of constitutional jurisprudence, the "right of privacy." The *Griswold* and *Bowers* cases set a frame-work for the debate; the selections by Robert Bork and Mark Tushnet dispute the legitimacy and scope of constitutional privacy. Laurence Tribe addresses the larger question of how the Constitution is to be interpreted and understood.

The readings in the second section take a step back from the controversy over privacy to examine the basic tools and methods of legal reasoning. Steve Burton and Joseph Hutcheson discuss the roles of precedent and of reasoning by analogy and question the extent to which these methods steer judges toward a decision or are steered by them to whatever decision they like.

A. *Interpreting the Constitution:*
The Right of Privacy

Introduction

Throughout the Senate confirmation hearings for Judge Bork, and more recently during the hearings for Justice David Souter, the American public was treated to hours of testimony bristling with legal jargon and technicalities. *"Stare decisis,"* "the Ninth Amendment," and "the *Griswold* penumbra" sounded like a foreign language to most and seemed far removed from our everyday experience of and concerns about the law. Yet the issues regarding the nature and legitimacy of reasoning about the Constitution, of which these esoteric terms are a part, are not only familiar to most of us but are ones that can affect our lives significantly. This is nowhere more clearly the case than in the efforts of courts to apply the techniques of legal reasoning to the United States Constitution.

Perhaps the best way to grasp the issues around which this chapter turns is to begin with a brief recitation of a handful of rulings issued by the Supreme Court in the past few years. Among the more controversial holdings, then, are these (many of which we will encounter later in this text): a state that arrests and imprisons homosexuals for practicing sodomy in their bedrooms does not violate their constitutional rights; a law that requires "creationism" be taught in the public schools violates the First Amendment because it "establishes a religion"; a statutory rape law providing that only males are punishable for rape does not violate their right to "equal protection of the laws"; there is no constitutionally protected right to use the drug peyote as part of a religious ceremony; no state may execute a person who was under the age of sixteen at the time of the capital offense; no American citizens have a right of privacy in their garbage; neither Congress nor the states may prohibit the burning of the American flag as a form of political protest; irreversibly comatose persons who have not made clearly known their wishes regarding life-support have no constitutionally protected "right to die." This is of course but a small sampling of an increasingly long list of controversial decisions handed down by the courts each year, decisions touching freedom of speech and of the press, freedom of religion, racial and sexual equality, criminal liability and punishment, personal autonomy and privacy, and so on.

Accustomed as we are to hearing of these controversial rulings, the reaction they provoke in many of us is still the same: Who are the justices of the Supreme Court to lay down the law in a community that purports at least to be a democracy? In making these delicate and often disturbing decisions, many say, the Supreme Court and lower courts are going too far; they are overstepping their legitimate function, which is to "apply" the law, not to "make" it. (This sentiment was echoed in President Reagan's familiar call for judges who would "interpret" the Constitution and not "legislate" from the bench.") This common complaint about the courts and their controversial rulings actually disguises two fundamental questions about constitutional interpretation and judicial reasoning. First, in a democracy who should have the right to issue authoritative interpretations of the Constitution? Second, what is the proper method of understanding what the Constitution requires or permits or forbids? The first of these questions has come to be called the "counter-majoritarian difficulty": What justifies permitting a body, neither elected nor otherwise politically accountable in any significant way, to overrule the judgments of the people as expressed by their representatives? Why shouldn't interpreting the Constitution itself be a democratic process?

The second question, and the one with which we shall be concerned in this chapter, is equally daunting. The Constitution, on its face at least, makes absolutely no reference whatever to privacy, garbage, sodomy, creationism, peyote, statutory rape, flag burning, or the irreversibly comatose. It has been made to speak to these issues only through *acts of interpretation*. But what governs or controls or constrains these acts of interpreta-

tion? What tells us whether the interpretation has been done well or badly, correctly or incorrectly? Is there any standard of "correctness" here at all? Or are constitutional decisions simply choices dictated by the private moral and political convictions of the judge?

Griswold and the Right of Privacy

No area of constitutional adjudication has posed these questions about interpretation more acutely than the Supreme Court's "privacy" rulings, dealing primarily with abortion and sexual matters. How should the text of the Constitution and the Court's subsequent decisions be interpreted in regard to privacy and personal sexual autonomy? Is there any principled interpretive methodology that can settle such cases noncontroversially? Are any of the Court's privacy rulings legitimate? Two prominent privacy cases serve as our focus for these questions, *Griswold v. Connecticut* and *Bowers v. Hardwick*.

In 1961, Griswold, the director of the Planned Parenthood League of Connecticut, was arrested for violating a state statute forbidding the dissemination of contraceptive devices and information, even to married persons. Griswold contended that the statute violated the Constitution, and the Supreme Court agreed. Writing for the majority, Justice Douglas argued that the statute violates the general right of privacy granted by the Constitution to all citizens. Douglas was aware that "privacy" occurs nowhere in the text of the Constitution; nonetheless he found a right of privacy in the "penumbras," the faint shadows of several of the amendments to the Constitution. To establish this, Douglas relied partly upon precedent, the authority of prior cases. In the *Pierce* and *Meyer* cases from the 1920s, for example, it had been held that the First Amendment protects the rights of parents to send their children to private schools and to teach them a foreign language. In *NAACP v. Alabama*, the Court had protected the freedom to associate by preventing disclosure of an organization's membership list. The Third and Fourth Amendments protect a person's interest in the privacy and sanctity of the home; and the Fifth Amendment, Douglas continued, protects people against being forced to disclose things about themselves. Douglas believed that these textual require-ments and prior cases add up to a general right of privacy relating to matters of marriage, children, and family; the state of Connecticut must have a good reason for invading this zone of privacy. Douglas insisted that it did not. After all, if the purpose of the statute is to discourage illicit sexual relations (as the state claimed), why make even birth control counseling for married persons punishable?

At least two other arguments were given in *Griswold* to support the finding of a right of privacy in the Constitution. Justice Goldberg asserted one of these arguments by invoking the Ninth Amend-ment: "The enumeration in the Constitution, of certain rights, shall not be construed to deny or disparage others retained by the people." Gold-berg believed privacy to be one of the rights "re-tained by the people," and he contended that the Connecticut statute violated the "due process" clause of the Fourteenth Amendment, which protects (in Harlan's language) "values implicit in the concept of ordered liberty," rights that are "fundamental." One of these values or rights, Har-lan believed, is privacy in the home, and this in-cludes marital privacy. Finally, Justice Black, in dissent, admitted that he found the Connnecticut law offensive but that he could find no specific provision of the Constitution protecting a general right of privacy. The majority's arguments, he thought, are little better than a vehicle through which the justices rationalized their invalidation of a law they find personally offensive. This, Black insisted, is not their job.

A number of significant decisions extending the scope of the right of privacy followed in the wake of *Griswold*, striking down laws prohibiting interracial marriage, extending the right of privacy to include the possession of obscene materials in one's own home, reversing a conviction for public distribution of contraceptives to *unmarried* persons, and invalidating prohibitions on the sale of non-prescription contraceptives to persons under the age of sixteen.[1] By far the most controversial exten-sion of *Griswold*, however, came in 1973 in the case of *Roe v. Wade*, in which the Court struck down criminal abortion statutes that prohibited abortions except to save the life of the mother. Justice Black-mun's opinion for the Court applied the privacy right to the decision to abort: "The right of privacy, whether it be founded in the Fourteenth Amend-ment's concept of personal liberty and restrictions

upon state action, as we feel it is, or, as the District Court determined, in the Ninth Amendment's res-ervation of rights to the people, is broad enough to encompass a woman's decision whether or not to terminate her pregnancy."[2]

Bowers v. Hardwick, decided by the Supreme Court in 1986, raises deep questions about *Griswold* and its aftermath: What did *Griswold* really decide? Just what is the scope of the constitutional right of privacy?

Michael Hardwick had been cited for drinking in public; he missed his first court appearance, and a warrant for his arrest was issued. Hardwick sub-sequently paid his fine, but the warrant was not recalled. The officer charged with executing the warrant appeared at Hardwick's home and a guest admitted him. The officer then saw Hardwick, in his bedroom, engaged in oral sex with another man, an act which is a felony in Georgia. Hardwick was arrested for violating the sodomy statute and he challenged the law's constitutionality before the Supreme Court. Justice White, writing for the Court, framed the issue in this way: Does the Con-stitution confer a fundamental right to engage in homosexual sodomy? White answered no. Hard-wick's conduct is not protected, White maintained, by the rationale of the line of cases stretching from *Pierce* and *Meyer* through *Griswold* and *Roe*, for those cases dealt only with intimate matters per-taining to family, marriage, and procreation, none of which are at stake in homosexual sodomy. Nor is Hardwick's sexual conduct one of the "fundamen-tal values" or liberties "deeply rooted in our Nation's history and traditions," a point White supported by citing the long history of the crimina-lization of homosexual conduct. Nor can Hard-wick rely on privacy in the home, as not everything that occurs in the home is constitutionally pro-tected.

In his dissent, Justice Blackmun distinguished between two ideas or threads running throughout the privacy cases: privacy in certain decisions in-volving personal autonomy in intimate matters and privacy in certain locations, such as the home. Blackmun argued that both of these are implicated in *Bowers*. We protect choices regarding marriage, child bearing, and child rearing not because they are the only constitutionally important interests, but because each deals with the most fundamental ways in which individuals define themselves, with the lives that they must make for themselves. Plainly, Blackmun argued, sexual orientation and sexual conduct are crucial parts of one's self-definition. Furthermore, the incident here took place in Hardwick's bedroom, and there is a textual basis, Blackmun thought, for protecting privacy in the home, as earlier cases made clear.

The Limits of Privacy

The selections by Robert Bork and Mark Tushnet each set out various criticisms of the source, legitimacy, and scope of the constitutional right of privacy. Bork is concerned with what he (and others) see as the growing politicizing, or political involvement, of the courts: the pursuit by judges of a political agenda (usually liberal), which should be voted on by legislatures rather than inserted into the law by courts. Such "activism" threatens the legitimacy of the rule of law. Bork would have courts follow "the only thing that can be called law," namely, "the principles of the text, whether Constitution of statute, as generally understood at the time of enactment."[3] This is the premise of Bork's theory of constitutional interpretation, what he calls a jurisprudence of "original understanding."

Bork roundly criticizes Douglas's argument in *Griswold,* arguing that no number of specific constitutional freedoms, even including their "penumbras," add up to a distinct and general "right of privacy," a right that Douglas created and that, Bork alleges, hovers uncertainly over the only rights with a genuine constitutional basis. Bork repeatedly presses the question of what the right of privacy includes, given that it has no actual basis in the Constitution. He concludes that no major case in the Court's privacy jurisprudence has the support, by way of precedent, of anything in the constitutional text or in the holdings or of any of the earlier cases in the series. Each is a fresh act of judicial policy making, and this is nowhere more evident, Bork believes, than in Justice Blackmun's dissent in *Bowers.*

Elsewhere, Bork asserts that the privacy decisions, along with other "activist" holdings, violate three core requirements of permissible constitutional interpretation: that constitutional principles and rights be neutrally derived, defined, and applied.[4] Privacy is not neutrally derivable from the text but read into it by judges with a particular

moral bias. Nor has constitutional privacy been neutrally defined; indeed, its scope has not been defined at all. And at what level of generality should a right like that of privacy be understood and applied? Should it be viewed narrowly, following White in *Bowers*? Or should it be viewed expansively and at a higher level of generality or abstraction, as Blackmun urges? Since the right of privacy has not been neutrally derived from the Constitution to begin with, Bork reasons, it is no wonder that these questions have no answer.

Like Bork, critical legalist Mark Tushnet also criticizes the *Griswold* and *Roe* decisions, though for a different reason. Tushnet develops his criticisms of the privacy decisions as a way of illustrating a more general point: that the aspiration to make legal reasoning into a neutral process, so that judges cannot just do whatever they want, can never be realized. Tushnet considers and rejects two conceptions of the neutrality requirement: reliance on precedent and legal reasoning as a "craft" or "art." Each method fails for much the same reason. The fact that no given case announces its own holding, that none states once and for all the definitive "rule" for which it stands, means that consistency or coherence with past decisions can mean different things to different judges, forcing them to rely upon their own convictions rather than the neutral constraint of the law. Reliance upon the "craft of judging" as a way of placing fetters on judges is undermined by the fact that it consists of nothing more than a set of techniques for manipulating and adjusting fact and doctrine in a variety of ways. The "neutrality" of such an art thus disappears.

Reading the Constitution

How, Laurence Tribe asks, are we to read the Constitution? How are we to make sense of its language and make it speak to the controversies of the last part of the twentieth century? These questions of course raise others: How closely are we tied to what the framers themselves thought? Why should we be bound to their intentions at all? If the Constitution is to be a "living" force in our lives today, mustn't it change with the times? But how is that possible? Can the Constitution simply mean whatever any judge takes it to mean?

Tribe insists that, if the document is to be authoritative and supreme law, it cannot be infinitely maleable: it is not the case that it can be read in *any* way. Equally, however, Tribe is convinced that any responsible reader or interpreter of the Constitution cannot avoid allowing some element of his or her own views to enter into that reading. Tribe discusses several of the positions recently defended in this debate, for example, the appeal to "original intent." He argues that no one position is satisfying because almost all pull back to one or another of two extremes: reading the Constitution too finely, so that it becomes a collection of unrelated items strung together; or reading it too broadly, so that it becomes a seamless web of abstractions, inattentive to the ways in which the Constitution is a creature of our history, a sometimes inconsistent record of changes and compromises. Readers of the Constitution must recognize that the document is multidimensional and pluralistic and that the process of interpreting it must reflect this. They must be content with finding or locating adequate reasons to justify one or another constitutional decision, where adequacy is measured neither by slavish literalism nor through appeal to a comprehensive and unified theory of the Constitution.

Originalism

One theory of constitutional interpretation mentioned by Tribe has been defended by legal theorists like Robert Bork and by judges like Chief Justice William Rehnquist. This is what Bork refers to as a jurisprudence of "original understanding" or more simply "originalism." The basic idea behind originalism is fairly simple: The courts should always strive to interpret statutory and constitutional language by seeking to discover, resurrect, and apply the intent of the authors of the statute or of the Constitution. The search for authorial intent (which has its advocates elsewhere, for example, in literary theory), although requiring the gathering of historical evidence of various kinds, relies chiefly upon the language of the written text as the most important source of evidence regarding that intent.

Originalists defend their theory as a coherent and nonarbitrary interpretive methodology: The written text has an objective meaning that can be found, not made up. Bork insists that "there is a historical Constitution that was understood by those who enacted it to have a meaning of its own. The intended meaning has an existence independent of anything judges may say."[5] By deriving and applying this meaning, courts can settle problems that otherwise plague current constitutional decision making, for example, the difficulty of determining at what level of generality a constitutional principle or right is to be defined. Original understanding avoids the problem, Bork claims, by "finding the level of generality that interpretation of the words, structure, and history of the Constitution fairly supports."[6] Bork sums up the view this way: "What is the meaning of a rule . . . ? It is the meaning understood at the time of the law's enactment. . . . Law is a public act. Secret reservations and intentions count for nothing. All that counts is how the words used in the Constitution would have been understood at the time. The original understanding is thus manifested in the words used and in the secondary materials, such as debates at the conventions, public discussion, newspaper articles, dictionaries in use at the time, and the like."[7]

Originalism, as a interpretive methodology, raises a number of questions and has been subjected to a variety of criticisms. The theory says that we are to look for the original intent, the intent of the "authors" of the Constitution. But this hides a crucial problem. Who are the authors? The framers of the document, those who actually wrote it in Philadelphia? Or perhaps the adopters, those people in the various colonial conventions who voted to ratify the document? There are reasons for discounting either group. It is not clear why the intent of the framers, an elite group of wealthy property owners, unelected by anyone, should be privileged in this way, especially if one of the driving forces behind originalism is to square constitutional interpretation with democracy. On the other hand, people vote for things, including constitutions, with all manner of purposes and motives. What reason is there to think that the majority of New Yorkers who voted to ratify the Constitution expressed any uniform "intention" with regard to anything on which the Constitution speaks? These are the *epistemological* difficulties posed by originalism, that is, problems dealing with what we can know of the

intentions of the authors of a statute or a constitution. How can we know the intent of people who
lived so long ago? And even if we could unearth
their thoughts, might we not find that they neither
intended nor did not intend for (say) garbage to be
private or for "creationism" to be taught, that is,
that they simply never thought about the constitutionality of these matters at all?

Despite its failings, the originalist theory of
constitutional interpretation is, as Tribe notes, a
response to a serious difficulty: If we don't look to
the intent of the drafters or framers of a statute or a
constitution to give meaning to vague or open-
ended language, then what anchors a reading or an
interpretation to the text at all? Can we permit
judges or other constitutional interpreters to rely
solely and directly upon their own value judgments in their role as interpreters? Or to appeal to
the precepts of "natural law" or the principles of
"correct moral reasoning"? To invoke America's
"fundamental traditions"? To defer to public consensus or majoritarian sentiment? The basic difficulty with all these ways of reasoning within and
from the Constitution is, according to the originalist, the same in every case: None yields any real
constraint on the task of interpreting the Constitution since each can be employed or invoked to
support almost any decision. Our "traditions" are
many and various, the "correct" moral theory no-
toriously difficult to find, and the view of the majority often that which the contitutional language
(particularly in the Bill of Rights) seeks to protect us
against.

Endnotes

[1] See, respectively, *Loving v. Virginia* 388 U.S. 1 (1967);
Stanley v. Georgia 394 U.S. 577 (1969); *Eisenstadt v. Baird*
405 U.S. 438 (1972); and *Carey v. Population Services* 431
U.S. 678 (1977).

[2] 410 U.S. 153, 164–165.

[3] Bork, *The Tempting of America* (New York: Free Press,
1990), chap. 7.

[4] *Ibid.*, chap. 7.

[5] *Ibid.*, p. 176.

[6] *Ibid.*, p. 150.

[7] *Ibid.*, p. 144.

Bowers v. Hardwick
478 U.S. 186 (1986)
United States Supreme Court

Justice White delivered the opinion of the Court.

In August 1982, respondent Hardwick (hereafter respondent) was charged with violating the
Georgia statute criminalizing sodomy by committing that act with another adult male in the bedroom of respondent's home. After a preliminary
hearing, the District Attorney decided not to
present the matter to the grand jury unless further
evidence developed.

Respondent then brought suit in the Federal
District Court, challenging the constitutionality of
the statute insofar as it criminalized sodomy. He
asserted that he was a practicing homosexual, that
the Georgia sodomy statute, as administered by
the defendants, placed him in imminent danger of
arrest, and that the statute for several reasons violates the Federal Constitution. The District Court
granted the defendents' motion to dismiss for failure to state a claim. . . .

A divided panel of the Court of Appeals for the
Eleventh Circuit reversed.

. . .

. . . Relying on our decisions in *Griswold v.
Connecticut*, 381 U.S. 479 . . . (1965); *Eisenstadt v.
Baird*, 405 U.S. 438 . . . (1972); *Stanley v. Georgia*,
394 U.S. 557 . . . (1969); and *Roe v. Wade*, 410 U.S.
113 . . . (1973), the court went on to hold that the
Georgia statute violated respondent's fundamental
rights because his homosexual activity is a private
and intimate association that is beyond the reach of
state regulation by reason of the Ninth Amendment and the Due Process Clause of the Fourteenth
Amendment.

. . . We agree with petitioner that the Court of
Appeals erred, and hence reverse its judgment.

. . . This case does not require a judgment on
whether laws against sodomy between consenting
adults in general, or between homosexuals in particular, are wise or desirable. It raises no question
about the right or propriety of state legislative decisions to repeal their laws that criminalize homosexual sodomy, or of state-court decisions invalidating
those laws on state constitutional grounds. The
issue presented is whether the Federal Consti-

tution confers a fundamental right upon homosexuals to engage in sodomy and hence invalidates the laws of the many States that still make such conduct illegal and have done so for a very long time. The case also calls for some judgment about the limits of the Court's role in carrying out its constitutional mandate.

We first register our disagreement with the Court of Appeals and with respondent that the Court's prior cases have construed the Constitution to confer a right of privacy that extends to homosexual sodomy and for all intents and purposes have decided this case. The reach of this line of cases was sketched in *Carey v. Population Services International*, 431 U.S. 678, 685 . . . (1977). *Pierce v. Society of Sisters*, 268 U.S. 510 . . . (1925), and *Meyer v. Nebraska*, 262 U.S. 390 . . . (1923), were described as dealing with child rearing and education; *Prince v. Massachusetts*, 321 U.S. 158 . . . (1944), with family relationships; *Skinner v. Oklahoma ex rel. Williamson*, 316 U.S. 535 . . . (1942), with procreation; *Loving v. Virginia*, 388 U.S. 1 . . . (1967), with marriage; *Griswold v. Connecticut, supra*, and *Eisenstadt v. Baird, supra*, with contraception; and *Roe v. Wade*, 410 U.S. 113 . . . (1973), with abortion. The latter three cases were interpreted as construing the Due Process Clause of the Fourteenth Amendment to confer a fundamental individual right to decide whether or not to beget or bear a child. . . .

Accepting the decisions in these cases and the above description of them, we think it evident that none of the rights announced in those cases bears any resemblance to the claimed constitutional right of homosexuals to engage in acts of sodomy that is asserted in this case. No connection between family, marriage, or procreation on the one hand and homosexual activity on the other has been demonstrated, either by the Court of Appeals or by respondent. Moreover, any claim that these cases nevertheless stand for the proposition that any kind of private sexual conduct between consenting adults is constitutionally insulated from state proscription is unsupportable. Indeed, the Court's opinion in *Carey* twice asserted that the privacy right, which the *Griswold* line of cases found to be one of the protections provided by the Due Process Clause, did not reach so far. . . .

Precedent aside, however, respondent would have us announce, as the Court of Appeals did, a fundamental right to engage in homosexual sodomy. This we are quite unwilling to do. It is true

that despite the language of the Due Process Clauses of the Fifth and Fourteenth Amendments, which appears to focus only on the processes by which life, liberty, or property is taken, the cases are legion in which those Clauses have been interpreted to have substantive content, subsuming rights that to a great extent are immune from federal or state regulation or proscription. Among such cases are those recognizing rights that have little or no textual support in the constitutional language. *Meyer, Prince,* and *Pierce* fall in this category, as do the privacy cases from *Griswold* to *Carey*.

Striving to assure itself and the public that announcing rights not readily indentifiable in the Constitution's text involves much more than the imposition of the Justices' own choice of values on the States and the Federal Government, the Court has sought to identify the nature of the rights qualifying for heightened judicial protection. In *Palko v. Connecticut*, 302 U.S. 319 . . . (1937), it was said that this category includes those fundamental liberties that are "implicit in the concept of ordered liberty," such that "neither liberty nor justice would exist if [they] were sacrificed." A different description of fundamental liberties appeared in *Moore v. East Cleveland*, 431 U.S. 494, 503 . . . (1977) (opinion of Powell, J.), where they are characterized as those liberties that are "deeply rooted in this Nation's history and tradition." . . .

It is obvious to us that neither of these formulations would extend a fundamental right to homosexuals to engage in acts of consensual sodomy. Proscriptions against that conduct have ancient roots. . . . Sodomy was a criminal offense at common law and was forbidden by the laws of the original thirteen States when they ratified the Bill of Rights. In 1868, when the Fourteenth Amendment was ratified, all but 5 of the 37 States in the Union had criminal sodomy laws. In fact, until 1961, all 50 States outlawed sodomy, and today, 24 States and the District of Columbia continue to provide criminal penalties for sodomy performed in private and between consenting adults. . . . Against this background, to claim that a right to engage in such conduct is "deeply rooted in this Nation's history and tradition" or "implicit in the concept of ordered liberty" is, at best, facetious.

. . . Nor are we inclined to take a more expansive view of our authority to discover new fundamental rights imbedded in the Due Process Clause. The Court is most vulnerable and comes nearest to illegitimacy when it deals with judge-made constitutional law having little or no cognizable roots in the language or design of the Constitution. That this is so was painfully demonstrated by the face-off between the Executive and the Court in the 1930's, which resulted in the repudiation of much of the substantive gloss that the Court had placed on the Due Process Clauses of the Fifth and Fourteenth Amendments. There should be, therefore, great resistance to expand the substantive reach of those Clauses, particularly if it requires redefining the category of rights deemed to be fundamental. Otherwise, the Judiciary necessarily takes to itself further authority to govern the country without express constitutional authority. The claimed right pressed on us today falls far short of overcoming this resistance.

Respondent, however, asserts that the result should be different where the homosexual conduct occurs in the privacy of the home. He relies on *Stanley v. Georgia*, 394 U.S. 557 . . . (1969), where the Court held that the First Amendment prevents conviction for possessing and reading obscene material in the privacy of one's home: "If the First Amendment means anything, it means that a State has no business telling a man, sitting alone in his house, what books he may read or what films he may watch." . . .

Stanley did protect conduct that would not have been protected outside the home, and it partially prevented the enforcement of state obscenity laws; but the decision was firmly grounded in the First Amendment. The right pressed upon us here has no similar support in the text of the Constitution, and it does not qualify for recognition under the prevailing principles for construing the Fourteenth Amendment. Its limits are also difficult to discern. Plainly enough, otherwise illegal conduct is not always immunized whenever it occurs in the home. Victimless crimes, such as the possession and use of illegal drugs, do not escape the law where they are committed at home. *Stanley* itself recognized that its holding offered no protection for the possession in the home of drugs, firearms, or stolen goods. . . . And if respondent's submission is limited to the voluntary sexual conduct between consenting adults, it would be difficult, except by fiat, to limit the claimed right to homosexual conduct while leaving exposed to prosecution adultery, incest, and other sexual crimes even though they are committed in the home. We are unwilling to start down that road.

. . . Even if the conduct at issue here is not a fundamental right, respondent asserts that there must be a rational basis for the law and that there is none in this case other than the presumed belief of a majority of the electorate in Georgia that homosexual sodomy is immoral and unacceptable. This is said to be an inadequate rationale to support the law. The law, however, is constantly based on notions of morality, and if all laws representing essentially moral choices are to be invalidated under the Due Process Clause, the courts will be very busy indeed. Even respondent makes no such claim, but insists that majority sentiments about the morality of homosexuality should be declared inadequate. We do not agree, and are unpersuaded that the sodomy laws of some 25 States should be invalidated on this basis.

Accordingly, the judgment of the Court of Appeals is

Reversed.

. . .

Justice Blackmun, with whom Justice Brennan, Justice Marshall, and Justice Stevens join, dissenting.

This case is no more about "a fundamental right to engage in homosexual sodomy," as the Court purports to declare, than *Stanley v. Georgia* . . . was about a fundamental right to watch obscene movies, or *Katz v. United States*, 389 U.S. 347 . . . (1967), was about a fundamental right to place interstate bets from a telephone booth. Rather, this case is about "the most comprehensive of rights and the right most valued by civilized men," namely, "the right to be let alone." *Olmstead v. United States*, 277 U.S. 438, 478 . . . (1928) (Brandeis, [Justice], dissenting).

The statute at issue, Ga. Code Ann. § 16–6–2 (1984), denies individuals the right to decide for themselves whether to engage in particular forms of private, consensual sexual activity. The Court concludes that § 16–6–2 is valid essentially because "the laws of . . . many States . . . still make such conduct illegal and have done so for a very long time." . . . But the fact that the moral judgments expressed by statutes like § 16–6–2 may be " 'natural and familiar . . . ought not to conclude our judgment upon the question whether statutes embodying them conflict with the Constitution of the United states.' " *Roe v. Wade*, . . . (1973), quoting *Lochner v. New York*, 198 U.S. 45, 76. . . . (1905)

(Holmes, J., dissenting). Like Justice Holmes, I believe that "[i]t is revolting to have no better reason for a rule of law than that so it was laid down in the time of Henry IV. It is still more revolting if the grounds upon which it was laid down have vanished long since, and the rule simply persists from blind imitation of the past." Holmes, The Path of the Law, 10 Harv. L. Rev. 457, 469 (1897). I believe we must analyze Hardwick's claim in the light of the values that underlie the constitutional right to privacy. If that right means anything, it means that, before Georgia can prosecute its citizens for making choices about the most intimate aspects of their lives, it must do more than assert that the choice they have made is an ' "abominable crime not fit to be named among Christians.' " . . .

I

In its haste to reverse the Court of Appeals and hold that the Constitution does not "confe[r] a fundamental right upon homosexuals to engage in sodomy," . . . the Court relegates the actual statute being challenged to a footnote and ignores the procedural posture of the case before it. A fair reading of the statute and of the complaint clearly reveals that the majority has distorted the question this case presents.

First, the Court's almost obsessive focus on homosexual activity is particularly hard to justify in light of the broad language Georgia has used. Unlike the Court, the Georgia Legislature has not proceeded on the assumption that homosexuals are so different from other citizens that their lives may be controlled in a way that would not be tolerated if it limited the choices of those other citizens. . . . Rather, Georgia has provided that "[a] person commits the offense of sodomy when he performs or submits to any sexual act involving the sex organs of one person and the mouth or anus of another." . . . The sex or status of the persons who engage in the act is irrelevant as a matter of state law. In fact, to the extent I can discern a legislative purpose for Georgia's 1968 enactment of § 16–6–2, that purpose seems to have been to broaden the coverage of the law to reach heterosexual as well as homosexual activity. I therefore see no basis for the Court's decision to treat this case as an "as ap-

plied" challenge to § 16–6–2 . . . or for Georgia's attempt, both in its brief and at oral argument, to defend § 16–6–2 solely on the grounds that it prohibits homosexual activity. Michael Hardwick's standing may rest in significant part on Georgia's apparent willingness to enforce against homosexuals a law it seems not to have any desire to enforce against heterosexuals. . . . But his claim that § 16–6–2 involves an unconstitutional intrusion into his privacy and his right of intimate association does not depend in any way on his sexual orientation.

Second, I disagree with the Court's refusal to consider whether § 16–6–2 runs afoul of the Eighth or Ninth Amendments or the Equal Protection Clause of the Fourteenth Amendment. . . . Respondent's complaint expressly invoked the Ninth Amendment . . . and he relied heavily before this Court on *Griswold v. Connecticut* . . . (1965), which identifies that Amendment as one of the specific constitutional provisions giving "life and substance" to our understanding of privacy.

. . .

II

"Our cases long have recognized that the Constitution embodies a promise that a certain private sphere of individual liberty will be kept largely beyond the reach of government." *Thornburgh v. American College of Obstetricians & Gynecologists,* 476 U.S. 747, 772 . . . (1986). In construing the right to privacy, the Court has proceeded along two somewhat distinct, albeit complementary, lines. First, it has recognized a privacy interest with reference to certain *decisions* that are properly for the individual to make. . . . Second, it has recognized a privacy interest with reference to certain *places* without regard for the particular activities in which the individuals who occupy them are engaged. . . . The case before us implicates both the decisional and the spatial aspects of the right to privacy.

A

The Court concludes today that none of our prior cases dealing with various decisions that individ-

uals are entitled to make free of governmental interference "bears any resemblance to the claimed
constitutional right of homosexuals to engage in
acts of sodomy that is asserted in this case." . . .
While it is true that these cases may be characterized by their connection to protection of the family,
. . . the Court's conclusion that they extend no
further than this boundary ignores the warning in
Moore v. East Cleveland . . . (1977) (plurality opinion), against "clos[ing] our eyes to the basic reasons why certain rights associated with the family
have been accorded shelter under the Fourteenth
Amendment's Due Process Clause." We protect
those rights not because they contribute, in some
direct and material way, to the general public welfare, but because they form so central a part of an
individual's life. "[T]he concept of privacy embodies the 'moral fact that a person belongs to
himself and not others nor to society as a whole.'"
*Thornburgh v. American College of Obstetricians &
Gynecologists* . . . (Stevens, [Justice], concurring),
quoting Fried, Correspondence, 6 Phil. & Pub. Affairs 288–289 (1977). And so we protect the decision whether to marry precisely because marriage
"is an association that promotes a way of life, not
causes; a harmony in living, not political faiths; a
bilateral loyalty, not commercial or social projects."
Griswold. . . . We protect the decision whether to
have a child because parenthood alters so dramatically an individual's self-definition, not because of
demographic considerations or the Bible's command to be fruitful and multiply. . . . And we
protect the family because it contributes so powerfully to the happiness of individuals, not because
of a preference for stereotypical households. . . .
The Court recognized in *Roberts* . . . that the "ability independently to define one's identity that
is central to any concept of liberty" cannot truly
be exercised in a vacuum; we all depend on the
"emotional enrichment from close ties with
others." . . .

Only the most willful blindness could obscure
the fact that sexual intimacy is "a sensitive, key
relationship of human existence, central to family
life, community welfare, and the development of
human personality," *Paris Adult Theatre I v. Slaton*,
413 U.S. 49, 63 . . . (1973) . . . The fact that individuals define themselves in a significant way
through their intimate sexual relationships with
others suggests, in a Nation as diverse as ours, that
there may be many "right" ways of conducting

those relationships, and that much of the richness
of a relationship will come from the freedom an
individual has to *choose* the form and nature of
these intensely personal bonds.

. . .

In a variety of circumstances we have recognized that a necessary corollary of giving individuals freedom to choose how to conduct their lives is
acceptance of the fact that different individuals will
make different choices. For example, in holding
that the clearly important state interest in public
education should give way to a competing claim by
the Amish to the effect that extended formal
schooling threatened their way of life, the Court
declared: "There can be no assumption that today's majority is 'right' and the Amish and others
like them are 'wrong.' A way of life that is odd or
even erratic but interferes with no rights or interests of others is not to be condemned because it is
different." *Wisconsin v. Yoder*, 406 U.S. 205, 223–
224 . . . (1972). The Court claims that its decision
today merely refuses to recognize a fundamental
right to engage in homosexual sodomy; what the
Court really has refused to recognize is the fundamental interest all individuals have in controlling
the nature of their intimate associations with
others.

B

The behavior for which Hardwick faces prosecution occurred in his own home, a place to which
the Fourth Amendment attaches special significance. The court's treatment of this aspect of the
case is symptomatic of its overall refusal to consider the broad principles that have informed our
treatment of privacy in specific cases. Just as the
right to privacy is more than the mere aggregation
of a number of entitlements to engage in specific
behavior, so too, protecting the physical integrity
of the home is more than merely a means of protecting specific activities that often take place there.
Even when our understanding of the contours of
the right to privacy depends on "reference to a
'place,'" . . . "the essence of a Fourth Amendment violation is 'not the breaking of [a person's]
doors, and the rummaging of his drawers,' but
rather is 'the invasion of his indefeasible right of
personal security, personal liberty and private

property.' " *California v. Ciraolo,* 476 U.S. 207, 226 . . . (1986) (Powell, [Justice], dissenting), quoting *Boyd v. United States,* 116 U.S. 616, 630 . . . (1886).

The Court's interpretation of the pivotal case of *Stanley v. Georgia* . . . (1969) . . . is entirely unconvincing. *Stanley* held that Georgia's undoubted power to punish the public distribution of constitutionally unprotected, obscene material did not permit the State to punish the private possession of such material. According to the majority here, *Stanley* relied entirely on the First Amendment, and thus, it is claimed, sheds no light on cases not involving printed materials. . . . But that is not what *Stanley* said. Rather, the *Stanley* Court anchored its holding in the Fourth Amendment's special protection for the individual in his home:

' "The makers of our Constitution undertook to secure conditions favorable to the pursuit of happiness. They recognized the significance of man's spiritual nature, of his feelings and of his intellect. They knew that only a part of the pain, pleasure and satisfactions of life are to be found in material things. They sought to protect Americans in their beliefs, their thoughts, their emotions and their sensations.'

. . .

"These are the rights that appellant is asserting in the case before us. He is asserting the right to read or observe what he pleases—the right to satisfy his intellectual and emotional needs in the privacy of his own home." 394 U.S., at 564–565, 89 S.Ct., at 1248, quoting *Olmstead v. United States,* 277 U.S., at 478, . . . (Brandeis, J., dissenting).

The central place that *Stanley* gives Justice Brandeis'[s] dissent in *Olmstead,* a case raising *no* First Amendment claim, shows that *Stanley* rested as much on the Court's understanding of the Fourth Amendment as it did on the First. Indeed, in *Paris Adult Theatre I v. Slaton,* . . . the Court suggested that reliance on the Fourth Amendment not only supported the Court's outcome in *Stanley* but actually was *necessary* to it: "If obscene material unprotected by the First Amendment in itself carried with it a 'penumbra' of constitutionally protected privacy, this Court would not have found it necessary to decide *Stanley* on the narrow basis of the 'privacy of the home,' which was hardly more than a reaffirmation that 'a man's home is his castle.' " . . . . "The right of the people to be secure in

their . . . houses," expressly guaranteed by the Fourth Amendment, is perhaps the most "textual" of the various constitutional provisions that inform our understanding of the right to privacy, and thus I cannot agree with the Court's statement that "[t]he right pressed upon us here has no . . . support in the text of the Constitution." . . . Indeed, the right of an individual to conduct intimate relationships in the intimacy of his or her own home seems to me to be the heart of the Constitution's protection of privacy.

III

The Court's failure to comprehend the magnitude of the liberty interests at stake in this case leads it to slight the question whether petitioner, on behalf of the State, has justified Georgia's infringement on these interests. I believe that neither of the two general justifications for § 16–6–2 that petitioner has advanced warrants dismissing respondent's challenge for failure to state a claim.

First, petitioner asserts that the acts made criminal by the statute may have serious adverse consequences for "the general public health and welfare," such as spreading communicable diseases or fostering other criminal activity. Inasmuch as this case was dismissed by the District Court on the pleadings, it is not surprising that the record before us is barren of any evidence to support petitioner's claim.

. . .

. . . Nothing in the record before the Court provides any justification for finding the activity forbidden by § 16–6–2 to be physically dangerous, either to the persons engaged in it or to others.[1]

The core of petitioner's defense of § 16–6–2, however, is that respondent and others who engage in the conduct prohibited by § 16–6–2 interfere with Georgia's exercise of the ' "right of the Nation and of the States to maintain a decent society.' "

. . .

. . . Essentially, petitioner argues, and the Court agrees, that the fact that the acts described in

§ 16–6–2 "for hundreds of years, if not thousands, have been uniformly condemned as immoral" is a sufficient reason to permit a State to ban them today. . . .

I cannot agree that either the length of time a majority has held its convictions or the passions with which it defends them can withdraw legislation from this Court's scrutiny.

. . .

. . . As Justice Jackson wrote so eloquently for the Court in *West Virginia Board of Education v. Barnette,* 319 U.S. 624, 641–642 . . . (1943), "we apply the limitations of the Constitution with no fear that freedom to be intellectually and spiritually diverse or even contrary will disintegrate the social organization. . . . [F]reedom to differ is not limited to things that do not matter much. That would be a mere shadow of freedom. The test of its substance is the right to differ as to things that touch the heart of the existing order." . . . It is precisely because the issue raised by this case touches the heart of what makes individuals what they are that we should be especially sensitive to the rights of those whose choices upset the majority.

The assertion that "traditional Judeo-Christian values proscribe" the conduct involved . . . cannot provide an adequate justification for § 16–6–2.

. . .

. . . That certain, but by no means all, religious groups condemn the behavior at issue gives the State no license to impose their judgments on the entire citizenry. The legitimacy of secular legislation depends instead on whether the State can advance some justification for its law beyond its conformity to religious doctrine.

. . .

. . . Thus, far from buttressing his case, petitioner's invocation of Leviticus, Romans, St. Thomas Aquinas, and sodomy's heretical status during the Middle Ages undermines his suggestion that § 16–6–2 represents a legitimate use of secular coercive power. A State can no more punish private behavior because of religious intolerance than it can punish such behavior because of racial animus.

. . .

. . .

. . . No matter how uncomfortable a certain group may make the majority of this Court, we have held that "[m]ere public intolerance or animosity cannot constitutionally justify the deprivation of a person's physical liberty." *O'Connor v. Donaldson,* 422 U.S. 563, 575 . . . (1975).

Nor can § 16–6–2 be justified as a "morally neutral" exercise of Georgia's power to "protect the public environment." . . . Certainly, some private behavior can affect the fabric of society as a whole. Reasonable people may differ about whether particular sexual acts are moral or immoral, but "we have ample evidence for believing that people will not abandon morality, will not think any better of murder, cruelty and dishonesty, merely because some private sexual practice which they abominate is not punished by the law." H. L. A. Hart, Immorality and Treason, reprinted in The Law as Literature 220, 225 (L. Blom-Cooper ed. 1961). Petitioner and the Court fail to see the difference between laws that protect public sensibilities and those that enforce private morality. Statutes banning public sexual activity are entirely consistent with protecting the individual's liberty interest in decisions concerning sexual relations: the same recognition that those decisions are intensely private which justifies protecting them from governmental interference can justify protecting individuals from unwilling exposure to the sexual activities of others. But the mere fact that intimate behavior may be punished when it takes place in public cannot dictate how States can regulate intimate behavior that occurs in intimate places.

. . .

This case involves no real interference with the rights of others, for the mere knowledge that other individuals do not adhere to one's value system cannot be a legally cognizable interest . . . let alone an interest that can justify invading the houses, hearts, and minds of citizens who choose to live their lives differently.

━━

IV

It took but three years for the Court to see the error in its analysis in *Minersville School District v. Gobitis,*

310 U.S. 586 . . . (1940), and to recognize that the threat to national cohesion posed by a refusal to salute the flag was vastly outweighed by the threat to those same values posed by compelling such a salute. See *West Virginia Board of Education v. Barnette*, 310 U.S. 624 . . . (1943). I can only hope that here, too, the Court soon will reconsider its analysis and conclude that depriving individuals of the right to choose for themselves how to conduct their intimate relationships poses a far greater threat to the values most deeply rooted in our Nation's history than tolerance of nonconformity could ever do. Because I think the Court today betrays those values, I dissent.

Endnote

[1] Although I do not think it necessary to decide today issues that are not even remotely before us, it does seem to me that a court could find simple, analytically sound distinctions between certain private, consensual sexual conduct, on the one hand, and adultery and incest (the only two vaguely specific "sexual crimes" to which the majority points . . .), on the other. For example, marriage, in addition to its spiritual aspects, is a civil contract that entitles the contracting parties to a variety of governmentally provided benefits. A State might define the contractual commitment necessary to become eligible for these benefits to include a commitment of fidelity and then punish individuals for breaching that contract. Moreover, a State might conclude that adultery is likely to injure third persons, in particular, spouses and children of persons who engage in extramarital affairs. With respect to incest, a court might well agree with respondent that the nature of familial relationships renders true consent to incestuous activity sufficiently problematical that a blanket prohibition of such activity is warranted. . . . Notably, the Court makes no effort to explain why it has chosen to group private, consensual homosexual activity with adultery and incest rather than with private, consensual heterosexual activity by unmarried persons or, indeed, with oral or anal sex within marriage.

Griswold v. Connecticut
381 U.S. 479 (1965)
United States Supreme Court

Douglas, [Justice].

Appellant Griswold is Executive Director of the Planned Parenthood League of Connecticut.

Appellant Buxton is a licensed physician and a professor at the Yale Medical School who served as Medical Director for the League at its Center in New Haven—a center open and operating from November 1 to November 10, 1961, when appellants were arrested.

They gave information, instruction, and medical advice to *married persons* as to the means of preventing conception. They examined the wife and prescribed the best contaceptive device or material for her use. Fees were usually charged, although some couples were serviced free.

The statutes whose constitutionality is involved in this appeal are §§53-32 and 54-196 of the General Statutes of Connecticut (1958 rev.). The former provides: "Any person who uses any drug, medicinal article or instrument for the purpose of preventing conception shall be fined not less than fifty dollars or imprisoned not less than sixty days nor more than one year or be both fined and imprisoned."

Section 54-196 provides: "Any person who assists, abets, counsels, causes, hires or commands another to commit any offense may be prosecuted and punished as if he were the principal offender."

The appellants were found guilty as accessories and fined $100 each, against the claim that the accessory statute as so applied violated the Fourteenth Amendment. The Appellate Division of the Circuit Court affirmed. The Supreme Court of Errors affirmed that judgment. We noted probable jurisdiction. . . .

Coming to the merits, we are met with a wide range of questions that implicate the Due Process Clause of the Fourteenth Amendment. Overtones of some arguments suggest that Lochner v. New York should be our guide. But we decline that invitation. . . . We do not sit as a super-legislature to determine the wisdom, need, and propriety of laws that touch economic problems, business affairs, or social conditions. This law, however, operates directly on an intimate relation of husband and wife and their physician's role in one aspect of that relation.

The association of people is not mentioned in the Constitution nor in the Bill of Rights. The right to educate a child in a school of the parents' choice—whether public or private or parochial—is also not mentioned. Nor is the right to study any particular subject or any foreign language. Yet the First Amendment has been construed to include certain of those rights.

By Pierce v. Society of Sisters the right to educate one's children as one chooses is made applicable to the States by the force of the First and Fourteenth Amendments. By Meyer v. Nebraska the same dignity is given the right to study the German language in a private school. In other words, the State may not consistently with the spirit of the First Amendment, contract the spectrum of available knowledge. The right of freedom of speech and press includes not only the right to utter or to print, but the right to distribute, the right to receive, the right to read and freedom of inquiry, freedom of thought, and freedom to teach—indeed the freedom of the entire university community. Without those peripheral rights the specific rights would be less secure. And so we reaffirm the principle of the *Pierce* and the *Meyer* cases.

In NAACP v. Alabama, 357 U.S. 449 (1958), we protected the "freedom to associate and privacy in one's associations," noting that freedom of association was a peripheral First Amendment right. Disclosure of membership lists of a constitutionally valid association, we held, was invalid, "as entailing the likelihood of a substantial restraint upon the exercise by petitioner's members of their right to freedom of association." In other words, the First Amendment has a penumbra where privacy is protected from governmental intrusion. In like context, we have protected forms of "association" that are not political in the customary sense but pertain to the social, legal, and economic benefit of the members. NAACP v. Button 371 U.S. 415 (1963). In Schware v. Board of Bar Examiners, 353 U.S. 232 (1957), we held it not permissible to bar a lawyer from practice, because he had once been a member of the Communist Party. . . .

Those cases involved more than the "right of assembly"—a right that extends to all irrespective of their race or ideology. The right of "association," like the right of belief, is more than the right to attend a meeting; it includes the right to express one's attitudes or philosophies by membership in a group or by affiliation with it or by other lawful means. Association in that context is a form of expression of opinion; and while it is not expressly included in the First Amendment its existence is necessary in making the express guarantees fully meaningful.

The foregoing cases suggest that specific guarantees in the Bill of Rights have penumbras, formed by emanations from those guarantees that help give them life and substance. . . . Various guarantees create zones of privacy. The right of association contained in the penumbra of the First Amendment is one, as we have seen. The Third Amendment in its prohibition against the quartering of soldiers "in any house" in time of peace without the consent of the owner is another facet of that privacy. The Fourth Amendment explicitly affirms the "right of the people to be secure in their persons, houses, papers, and effects, against unreasonable searches and seizures." The Fifth Amendment in its Self-Incrimination Clause enables the citizen to create a zone of privacy which government may not force him to surrender to his detriment. The Ninth Amendment provides: "The enumeration in the Constitution, of certain rights, shall not be construed to deny or disparage others retained by the people."

The Fourth and Fifth Amendments were described in Boyd v. United States, 116 U.S. 616 (1886), as protection against all governmental invasions "of the sanctity of a man's home and the privacies of life." We recently referred . . . to the Fourth Amendment as creating a "right to privacy, no less important than any other right carefully and particularly reserved to the people." . . .

The present case, then, concerns a relationship lying within the zone of privacy created by several fundamental constitutional guarantees. And it concerns a law which, in forbidding the *use* of contraceptives rather than regulating their manufacture or sale, seeks to achieve its goals by means having a maximum destructive impact upon that relationship. Such a law cannot stand in light of the familiar principle, so often applied by this Court, that a "governmental purpose to control or prevent activities constitutionally subject to state regulation may not be achieved by means which sweep unnecessarily broadly and thereby invade the area of protected freedoms." . . . Would we allow the police to search the sacred precincts of marital bedrooms for telltale signs of the use of contraceptives? The very idea is repulsive to the notions of privacy surrounding the marriage relationship.

We deal with a right of privacy older than the Bill of Rights—older than our political parties, older than our school system. Marriage is a coming together for better or for worse, hopefully enduring, and intimate to the degree of being sacred. It is an association that promotes a way of life, not causes; a harmony in living, not political faiths; a bilateral loyalty, not commercial or social projects.

Yet it is an association for as noble a purpose as any involved in our prior decisions.

Reversed.

Goldberg, [Justice], joined by Warren, [Chief Justice], and Brennan, [Justice], concurring.

I agree with the Court that Connecticut's birth-control law unconstitutionally intrudes upon the right of marital privacy, and I join in its opinion and judgment. Although I have not accepted the view that "due process" as used in the Fourteenth Amendment incorporates all of the first eight Amendments, I do agree that the concept of liberty protects those personal rights that are fundamental, and is not confined to the specific terms of the Bill of Rights. My conclusion that the concept of liberty is not so restricted and that it embraces the right of marital privacy though that right is not mentioned explicitly in the Constitution is supported . . . by the language and history of the Ninth Amendment. . . .

The Ninth Amendment . . . was proffered to quiet expressed fears that a bill of specifically enumerated rights could not be sufficiently broad to cover all essential rights and that the specific mention of certain rights would be interpreted as a denial that others were protected. . . . [T]he Framers did not intend that the first eight amendments be construed to exhaust the basic and fundamental rights which the Constitution guaranteed to the people.

. . . To hold that a right so basic and fundamental and so deep-rooted in our society as the right of privacy in marriage may be infringed because that right is not guaranteed in so many words by the first eight amendments to the Constitution is to ignore the Ninth Amendment and to give it no effect whatsoever. . . .

I do not mean to imply that the Ninth Amendment is applied against the States by the Fourteenth. Nor do I mean to state that the Ninth Amendment constitutes an independent source of rights protected from infringement by either the States or the Federal Government. Rather the Ninth Amendment simply lends strong support to the view that the "liberty" protected by the Fifth and Fourteenth Amendments from infringement by the Federal Government or the States is not restricted to rights specifically mentioned in the first eight amendments. . . .

In determining which rights are fundamental, judges are not left at large to decide cases in light of their personal and private notions. Rather, they must look to the "traditions and [collective] conscience of our people" to determine whether a principle is "so rooted [there] . . . as to be ranked as fundamental." The inquiry is whether a right involved "is of such a character that it cannot be denied without violating those 'fundamental principles of liberty and justice which lie at the base of all our civil and political institutions.' "

The entire fabric of the Constitution and the purposes that clearly underlie its specific guarantees demonstrate that the rights to marital privacy and to marry and raise a family are of similar order and magnitude as the fundamental rights specifically protected.

Although the Constitution does not speak in so many words of the right of privacy in marriage, I cannot believe that it offers these fundamental rights no protection. The fact that no particular provision of the Constitution explicitly forbids the State from disrupting the traditional relation of the family—a relation as old and as fundamental as our entire civilization—surely does not show that the Government was meant to have the power to do so. . . .

The logic of the dissents would sanction federal or state legislation that seems to me even more plainly unconstitutional than the statute before us. Surely the Government, absent a showing of a compelling subordinating state interest, could not decree that all husbands and wives must be sterilized after two children have been born to them. Yet by their reasoning such an invasion of marital privacy would not be subject to constitutional challenge because, while it might be "silly," no provision of the Constitution specifically prevents the Government from curtailing the marital right to bear children and raise a family. . . .

In a long series of cases this Court has held that where fundamental personal liberties are involved, they may not be abridged by the States simply on a showing that a regulatory statute has some rational relationship to the effectuation of a proper state purpose. "Where there is a significant encroachment upon personal liberty, the State may prevail only upon showing a subordinating interest which is compelling." . . . The law must be shown "necessary, and not merely rationally related, to the accomplishment of a permissible state policy." . . .

Although the Connecticut birth-control law obviously encroaches upon a fundamental personal liberty, the State does not show that the law serves any "subordinating [state] interest which is compelling" or that it is "necessary . . . to the accomplishment of a permissible state policy." The State, at most, argues that there is some rational relation between this statute and what is admittedly a legitimate subject of state concern—the discouraging of extra-marital relations. Its says that preventing the use of birth-control devices by married persons helps prevent the indulgence by some in such extra-marital relations. The rationality of this justification is dubious, particularly in light of the admitted widespread availability to all persons in the State of Connecticut, unmarried as well as married, of birth-control devices for the prevention of disease, as distinguished from the prevention of conception. But, in any event, it is clear that the state interest in safeguarding marital fidelity can be served by a more discriminately tailored statute, which does not, like the present one, sweep unnecessarily broadly, reaching far beyond the evil sought to be dealt with and intruding upon the privacy of all married couples. . . . The State of Connecticut does have statutes, the constitutionality of which is beyond doubt, which prohibit adultery and fornication. These statutes demonstrate that means for achieving the same basic purpose of protecting marital fidelity are available to Connecticut without the need to "invade the area of protected freedoms." . . .

In sum, I believe that the right to privacy in the marital relation is fundamental and basic—a personal right "retained by the people" within the meaning of the Ninth Amendment. Connecticut cannot constitutionally abridge this fundamental right, which is protected by the Fourteenth Amendment from infringement by the States. I agree with the Court that petitioners' convictions must therefore be reversed.

. . .

Harlan, [Justice], concurring. . . .

In my view, the proper constitutional inquiry in this case is whether this Connecticut statute infringes the Due Process Clause of the Fourteenth Amendment because the enactment violates basic values "implicit in the concept of ordered liberty. . . ." For reasons state[d] at length in my dissenting opinion in *Poe v. Ullman* ([367 U.S. 487 (1961)], I believe that it does. While the relevant inquiry may be aided by resort to one or more of the provisions of the Bill of Rights, it is not dependent on them or any of their radiations. The Due Process Clause of the Fourteenth Amendment stands, in my opinion, on its own bottom.

. . .

White, [Justice], concurring. . . .

In my view, this Connecticut law as applied to married couples deprives them of "liberty" without due process of law, as that concept is used in the Fourteenth Amendment. I therefore concur in the judgment of the Court reversing these convictions under Connecticut's aiding and abetting statute. . . .

[T]his is not the first time this Court has had occasion to articulate that the liberty entitled to protection under the Fourteenth Amendment includes the right "to marry, establish a home and bring up children," . . . and "the liberty . . . to direct the upbringing and education of children," . . . and that these are among "the basic civil rights of man." . . . These decisions affirm that there is a "realm of family life which the state cannot enter" without substantial justification. . . . Surely the right invoked in this case, to be free of regulation of the intimacies of the marriage relationship, "come[s] to this Court with a momentum for respect lacking when appeal is made to liberties which derive merely from shifting economic arrangements." . . .

An examination of the justification offered, however, cannot be avoided by saying that the Connecticut anti-use statute invades a protected area of privacy and association or that it demeans the marriage relationship. The nature of the right invaded is pertinent, to be sure, for statutes regulating sensitive areas of liberty do, under the cases of this Court, require "strict scrutiny," Skinner v. Oklahoma, and "must be viewed in the light of less drastic means for achieving the same basic purpose." "Where there is a significant encroachment upon personal liberty, the State may prevail only upon showing a subordinating interest which is compelling." But such statutes, if reasonably necessary for the effectuation of a legitimate and substantial state interest, and not arbitrary or capricious in application, are not invalid under the Due Process Clause.

As I read the opinions of the Connecticut courts and the argument of Connecticut in this Court, the State claims but one justification for its anti-use statute. . . . [T]he statute is said to serve the State's policy against all forms of promiscuous or illicit sexual relationships, be they premarital or extramarital, concededly a permissible and legitimate legislative goal.

Without taking issue with the premise that the fear of conception operates as a deterrent to such relationships in addition to the criminal proscriptions Connecticut has against such conduct, I wholly fail to see how the ban on the use of contraceptives by married couples in any way reinforces the State's ban on illicit sexual relationships. Connecticut does not bar the importation or possession of contraceptive devices; they are not considered contraband material under state law, and their availability in that State is not seriously disputed. The only way Connecticut seeks to limit or control the availability of such devices is through its general aiding and abetting statute whose operation in this context has been quite obviously ineffective and whose most serious use has been against birth-control clinics rendering advice to married, rather than unmarried, persons. . . . Moreover, it would appear that the sale of contraceptives to prevent disease is plainly legal under Connecticut law.

In these circumstances one is rather hard pressed to explain how the ban on use by married persons in any way prevents use of such devices by persons engaging in illicit sexual relations and thereby contributes to the State's policy against such relationships. . . . At most the broad ban is of marginal utility to the declared objective. A statute limiting its prohibition on use to persons engaging in the prohibited relationship would serve the end posited by Connecticut in the same way, and with the same effectiveness, or ineffectiveness, as the broad anti-use statute under attack in this case. I find nothing in this record justifying the sweeping scope of this statute, with its telling effect on the freedoms of married persons, and therefore conclude that it deprives such persons of liberty without due process of law.

Black, [Justice], joined by Stewart, [Justice], dissenting. . . .

In order that there may be no room at all to doubt why I vote as I do, I feet constrained to add that the law is every bit as offensive to me as it is to my Brethren of the majority. . . . There is no single one of the graphic and eloquent strictures and criticisms fired at the policy of this Connecticut law

either by the Court's opinion or by those of my concurring Brethren to which I cannot subscribe—except their conclusion that the evil qualities they see in the law make it unconstitutional. . . .

The Court talks about a constitutional "right of privacy" as though there is some constitutional provision or provisions forbidding any law ever to be passed which might abridge the "privacy" of individuals. But there is not. There are, of course, guarantees in certain specific constitutional provisions which are designed in part to protect privacy at certain times and places with respect to certain activities. Such, for example, is the Fourth Amendment's guarantee against "unreasonable searches and seizures." But I think it belittles that Amendment to talk about it as though it protects nothing but "privacy." . . .

One of the most effective ways of diluting or expanding a constitutionally guaranteed right is to substitute for the crucial word or words of a constitutional guarantee another word or words, more or less flexible and more or less restricted in meaning. . . . "Privacy" is a broad, abstract and ambiguous concept which can easily be shrunken in meaning but which can also, on the other hand, easily be interpreted as a constitutional ban against many things other than searches and seizures. . . . For these reasons I get nowhere in this case by talk about a constitutional "right of privacy" as an emanation from one or more contitutional provisions. I like my privacy as well as the next one, but I am nevertheless compelled to admit that government has a right to invade it unless prohibited by some specific constitutional provision. . . .

I discuss the due process and Ninth Amendment arguments together because on analysis they turn out to be the same thing—merely using different words to claim for this Court and the federal judiciary power to invalidate any legislative act which the judges find irrational, unreasonable or offensive. . . .

Of the cases on which my Brothers White and Goldberg rely so heavily, undoubtedly the reasoning of two of them supports their result here—as would that of a number of others which they do not bother to name. . . . The two they do cite and quote from, Meyer v. Nebraska, and Pierce v. Society of Sisters, were both decided in opinions by Mr. Justice McReynolds which elaborated the same natural law due process philosophy found in Lochner v. New York, one of the cases on which he relied in *Meyer*, along with such other long-discredited decisions as, e.g., Adkins v. Children's Hospital. . . . Without expressing an opinion as to whether either of those cases reached a correct result in light of our later decisions applying the First Amendment to the States through the Fourteenth, I merely point out that the reasoning stated in *Meyer* and *Pierce* was the same natural law due process philosophy which many later opinions repudiated, and which I cannot accept. . . .

My Brother Goldberg has adopted the recent discovery that the Ninth Amendment as well as the Due Process Clause can be used by this Court as authority to strike down all state legislation which this court thinks violates "fundamental principles of liberty and justice," or is contrary to the "traditions and [collective] conscience of our people." He also states, without proof satisfactory to me, that in making decisions on this basis judges will not consider "their personal and private notions." One may ask how they can avoid considering them. Our Court certainly has no machinery with which to take a Gallup Poll. And the scientific miracles of this age have not yet produced a gadget which the Court can use to determine what traditions are

rooted in the "[collective] conscience of our people." Moreover, one would certainly have to look far beyond the language of the Ninth Amendment to find that the Framers vested in this Court any such awesome veto powers over lawmaking, either by the States or by the Congress. . . . That Amendment was passed not to broaden the powers of this Court or any other department of "the General Government," but, as every student of history knows, to assure the people that the Constitution in all its provisions was intended to limit the Federal Government to the powers granted expressly or by necessary implication. . . .

The Due Process Clause with an "arbitrary and capricious" or "shocking to the conscience" formula was liberally used by this Court to strike down economic legislation in the early decades of this century, threatening, many people thought, the tranquility and stability of the Nation. That formula, based on subjective considerations of "natural justice," is no less dangerous when used to enforce this Court's view about personal rights than those about economic rights. . . .

The Right of Privacy

ROBERT BORK

The 1965 decision in *Griswold* v. *Connecticut*[1] was insignificant in itself but momentous for the future of constitutional law. Connecticut had an ancient statute making it criminal to use contraceptives. The state also had a general accessory statute allowing the punishment of any person who aided another in committing an offense. On its face, the statute criminalizing the use of contraceptives made no distinction between married couples and

others. But the statute also had never been enforced against anyone who used contraceptives, married or not. There was, of course, no prospect that it ever would be enforced. If any Connecticut official had been mad enough to attempt enforcement, the law would at once have been removed from the books and the official from his office. Indeed, some Yale law professors had gotten the statute all the way to the Supreme Court a few years previously, and the Court had refused to decide it precisely because there was no showing that the law was ever enforced. The professors had some difficulty arranging a test case but finally managed to have two doctors who gave birth control information fined $100 apiece as accessories.

Such enforcement in the area as there was

From *The Tempting of America: The Political Seduction of the Law* (New York: Free Press, 1990), pp. 95–100. Copyright © 1990 by Robert H. Bork. Reprinted with permission of The Free Press, a Division of Macmillan, Inc.

consisted of the occasional application of the accessory statute against birth control clinics, usually clinics that advertised. The situation was similar to the enforcement of many antigambling laws. They may cover all forms of gambling on their faces, but they are in fact enforced only against commercial gambling. An official who began arresting the priest at the church bingo party or friends having their monthly poker game at home would have made a most unwise career decision and would be quite unlikely to get a conviction. There are a number of statutes like these in various state codes, such as the statutes flatly prohibiting sodomy and other "unnatural practices," which apply on their faces to all couples, married or unmarried, heterosexual or homosexual. The statutes are never enforced, but legislators, who would be aghast at any enforcement effort, nevertheless often refuse to repeal them.

There is a problem with laws like these. They are kept in the codebooks as precatory statements, affirmations of moral principle. It is quite arguable that this is an improper use of law, most particularly of criminal law, that statutes should not be on the books if no one intends to enforce them. It has been suggested that if anyone tried to enforce a law that had moldered in disuse for many years, the statute should be declared void by reason of desuetude or that the defendant should go free because the law had not provided fair warning.

But these were not the issues in *Griswold*. Indeed, getting off on such grounds was the last thing the defendants and their lawyers wanted. Since the lawyers had a difficult time getting the state even to fine two doctors as accessories, it seems obvious that the case was not arranged out of any fear of prosecution, and certainly not the prosecution of married couples. *Griswold* is more plausibly viewed as an attempt to enlist the Court on one side of one issue in a cultural struggle. Though the statute was originally enacted when the old Yankee culture dominated Connecticut politics, it was now quite popular with the Catholic hierarchy and with many lay Catholics whose religious values it paralleled. The case against the law was worked up by members of the Yale law school faculty and was supported by the Planned Parenthood Federation of America, Inc., the Catholic Council on Civil Liberties, and the American Civil Liberties Union. A ruling of unconstitutionality may have been sought as a statement that opposition to contraception is benighted and, therefore, a statement about whose cultural values are dominant. Be that as it may, the upshot was a new constitutional doctrine perfectly suited, and later used, to enlist the Court on the side of moral relativism in sexual matters.

Justice Douglas's majority opinion dealt with the case as if Connecticut had devoted itself to sexual fascism. "Would we allow the police to search the sacred precincts of marital bedrooms for telltale signs of the use of contraceptives? The very idea is repulsive to the notions of privacy surrounding the marriage relationship."[2] That was both true and entirely irrelevant to the case before the Court. Courts usually judge statutes by the way in which they are actually enforced, not by imagining horrible events that have never happened, never will happen, and could be stopped by courts if they ever seemed about to happen. Just as in *Skinner* he had treated a proposal to sterilize three-time felons as raising the specter of racial genocide, Douglas raised the stakes to the sky here by treating Connecticut as though it was threatening the institution of marriage. "We deal with a right of privacy older than the Bill of Rights—older than our political parties, older than our school system." The thought was incoherent. What the right of privacy's age in comparison with that of our political parties and school system had to do with anything was unclear, and where the "right" came from if not from the Bill of Rights it is impossible to understand. No court had ever invalidated a statute on the basis of the right Douglas described. That makes it all the more perplexing that Douglas in fact purported to derive the right of privacy not from some pre-existing right or law of nature, but from the Bill of Rights. It is important to understand Justice Douglas's argument both because the method, though without merit, continually recurs in constitutional adjudication and because the "right of privacy" has become a loose canon in the law. Douglas began by pointing out that "specific guarantees in the Bill of Rights have penumbras, formed by emanations from those guarantees that help give them life and substance." There is nothing exceptional about that thought, other than the language of penumbras and emanations. Courts often give protection to a constitutional freedom by creating a buffer zone, by prohibiting a government from doing something not in itself forbidden but likely to lead to an invasion of a right specified in the Constitution. Douglas cited *NAACP* v. *Alabama*,[3] in which the Supreme Court held that the state could not force the disclosure of the organization's membership lists since that would have a deterrent effect upon the members' first amendment rights of political and legal action. That may well have been part of the purpose of the statute. But for this anticipated effect upon guaranteed freedoms, there would be no constitutional objection to the required disclosure of membership. The right not to disclose had no life of its own independent of the rights specified in the first amendment.

Douglas named the buffer zone or "penumbra" of the first amendment a protection of "privacy," although, in *NAACP* v. *Alabama*, of course, confidentiality of membership was required not for the sake of individual privacy but to protect the public activities of politics and litigation. Douglas then asserted that other amendments create "zones of privacy." These were the first, third (soldiers not to be quartered in private homes), fourth (ban on unreasonable searches and seizures), and fifth (freedom from self-incrimination). There was no particularly good reason to use the word "privacy" for the freedoms cited, except for the fact that the opinion was building toward those "sacred precincts of marital bedrooms." The phrase "areas of freedom" would have been more accurate since the provisions cited protect both private and public behavior.

None of the amendments cited, and none of their buffer or penumbral zones, covered the case before the Court. The Connecticut statute was not invalid under any provision of the Bill of Rights, no matter how extended. Since the statute in question did not threaten any quaranteed freedom, it did not fall within any "emanation." *Griswold* v. *Connecticut* was, therefore, not like *NAACP* v. *Alabama*. Justice Douglas bypassed that seemingly insuperable difficulty by simply asserting that the various separate "zones of privacy" created by each separate provision of the Bill of Rights somehow created a general but wholly undefined "right of privacy" that is independent of and lies outside any right or "zone of privacy" to be found in the Constitution. Douglas did not explain how it was that the Framers created five or six specific rights that could, with considerable stretching, be called "privacy," and, though the Framers chose not to create more, the Court could nevertheless invent a general right of privacy that the Framers had, inexplicably, left out. It really does not matter to the decision what the Bill of Rights covers or does not cover.

Douglas closed the *Griswold* opinion with a burst of passionate oratory. "Marriage is a coming together for better or for worse, hopefully enduring, and intimate to the degree of being sacred. It is an association that promotes a way of life, not causes; a harmony in living, not political faiths; a bilateral loyalty, not commercial or social projects. Yet it is an association for as noble a purpose as any involved in our prior decisions."[4] It is almost a matter for regret that Connecticut had not threatened the institution of marriage, or even attempted to prevent anyone from using contraceptives, since that left some admirable sentiments, expressed with rhetorical fervor, dangling irrelevantly in midair. But the protection of marriage was not the point of *Griswold*. The creation of a new device for judicial power to remake the Constitution was the point.

The *Griswold* opinion, of course, began by denying that any such power was being assumed. "[W]e are met with a wide range of questions that implicate the Due Process Clause of the 14th Amendment. Overtones of some arguments suggest that [*Lochner* v. *New York*] should be our guide. But we decline that invitation. . . . We do not sit as a super-legislature to determine the wisdom, need, and propriety of laws that touch economic problems, business affairs, or social conditions."[5] *Griswold*, as an assumption of judicial power unrelated to the Constitution is, however, indistinguishable from *Lochner*. And the nature of that power, its lack of rationale or structure, ensured that it could not be confined.

The Court majority said there was now a right of privacy but did not even intimate an answer to the question, "Privacy to do what?" People often take addictive drugs in private, some men physically abuse their wives and children in private, executives conspire to fix prices in private, Mafiosi confer with their button men in private. If these sound bizarre, one professor at a prominent law school has suggested that the right of privacy may create a right to engage in prostitution. Moreover, as we shall see, the Court has extended the right of privacy to activities that can in no sense be said to be done in private. The truth is that "privacy" will turn out to protect those activities that enough Justices to form a majority think ought to be protected and not activities with which they have little sympathy.

If one called the zones of the separate rights of the Bill of Rights zones of "freedom," which would be more accurate, then, should one care to follow Douglas's logic, the zones would add up to a general right of freedom independent of any provision of the Constitution. A general right of freedom—a constitutional right to be free of regulation by law—is a manifest impossibility. Such a right would posit a state of nature, and its law would be that of the jungle. If the Court had created a general "right of freedom," we would know at once, therefore, that the new right would necessarily be applied selectively, and, if we were given no explanation of the scope of the new right, we would know that the "right" was nothing more than a warrant judges had created for themselves to do whatever they wished. That, as we shall see in the next chapter, is precisely what happened with the new, general, undefined, and unexplained "right of privacy."

Justice Black's dissent stated: "I like my privacy as well as the next one, but I am nevertheless compelled to admit that government has a right to invade it unless prohibited by some specific constitutional provision."[6] He found none. "The Court talks about a constitutional 'right of privacy' as though there is some constitutional provision or provisions forbidding any law ever to be passed which might abridge the 'privacy' of individuals. But there is not." He pointed out that there are "certain specific constitutional provisions which are designed in part to protect privacy at certain times and places with respect to certain activities." But there was no general right of the sort Douglas had created. Justice Stewart's dissent referred to the statute as "an uncommonly silly law" but noted that its asininity was not before the Court.[7] He could "find no such general right of privacy in the Bill of Rights, in any other part of the Constitution, or in any case ever before decided by this Court." He also observed that the "Court does not say how far the new constitutional right of privacy announced today extends." That was twenty-four years ago, and the Court still has not told us.

. . .

Endnotes

[1] 381 U.S. 479 (1965).

[2] Id. at 485–86.

[3] 357 U.S. 449 (1958).

[4] 381 U.S. at 486.

[5] Id. at 481–482.

[6] [*Id.*] at 507, 508, 510 (Black, [Justice], dissenting).

[7] [*Id.*] at 527, 530 n. 7 (Stewart, [Justice], dissenting).

The Indeterminacy of Privacy

MARK TUSHNET

The rule of law, according to the liberal conception, is meant to protect us against the exercise of arbitrary power. The theory of neutral principles asserts that a requirement of consistency, the core of the ideal of the rule of law, places sufficient bounds on judges to reduce the risk of arbitrariness to an acceptable level. The question is whether the concepts of neutrality and consistency can be developed in ways that are adequate for the task. This section examines two candidates for a definition of neutrality.[1] It argues that each fails to provide the kinds of contraints on judges that the liberal tradition requires: The limits they place on judges are either empty or dependent on a sociology of law that undermines the liberal tradition's assumptions about society.[2]

If neutrality is to serve as a meaningful guide, it must be understood not as a standard for the content of principles[3] but rather as a constraint on the process by which principles are selected, justified, and applied. Thus, the possible explications

From *Red, White, and Blue: A Critical Analysis of Constitutional Law* (Cambridge: Harvard University Press, 1988), pp. 46–57. Copyright © 1988 by the President and Fellows of Harvard College. Reprinted with permission of Harvard University Press.

of neutrality focus on the judicial process and the need for "neutral application." This focus transfers our attention from the principles themselves to the judges who purport to use them.

One preliminary difficulty should be noted. The demand for neutral application ultimately rests on the claim that without neutrality a decision "wholly lack[s] . . . legitimacy."[4] In this context legitimacy is a normative concept[5] [Herbert] Wechsler claimed that neutral principles are an essential component of the practice of judging in our society. Such an appeal to the essence of a social practice draws on a vision of how ideal courts act, a vision stimulated by reflection on the proper place of the courts in our social fabric. Legitimacy is a matter of concordance with the demands of this ideal. These demands, however, ultimately prove empty, for rather than constrain the proper role of courts the concept of neutrality presupposes a shared understanding and acceptance of any constraints.

What, then, are methodologically neutral principles? The best explication looks to the past. It would impose as a necessary condition for justification that a decision be consistent with the relevant precedents.[6] Michael Perry's discussion of the abortion funding cases exemplifies this approach. Perry, in the best recent application of the theory of neutral principles, attempts to identify the operative principle in *Roe v. Wade*, a highly abstract principle concerning the relation between governmental powers and constitutional protections, and to criticize the Court's later ruling in *Harris v. McRae* for inconsistency with that principle.

In 1973 the Supreme Court held in *Roe v. Wade* that state criminal statutes restricting the availability of abortions were unconstitutional.[7] Seven years later the Court upheld legislation that denied public funds for abortion to those otherwise qualified for public assistance in paying for medical care.[8] Perry contends that the abortion funding decision is "plainly wrong" because it "is inconsistent with the narrowest possible coherent reading of *Roe*." Perry extracts that reading as follows. The Court struck down the statutes in *Roe* because the pregnant woman's interest in terminating the pregnancy is greater than the government's interest in preventing the taking of the life of the fetus. According to Perry, this entails the conclusion that "*no* governmental action can be predicated on the view that . . . abortion is per se morally objectionable."[9] Perry's premise is that government is permitted to use a factor as a predicate for restrictive

legislation only if that factor is entitled to no constitutional protection.

Perry rejects as "deeply flawed" and "fundamentally confused" the position taken by the Court in the funding cases. . . .[10] This position is that *Roe* barred the government from criminalizing abortions only because criminal sanctions place an undue burden on the woman's interest in terminating the pregnancy; refusing to fund abortions does not similarly burden that interest. Perry claims that *Roe* is coherent only if it precludes the government from taking *any* action predicated on the view that abortion is wrong. To allow the government to take such action would force us to the "rather strange" position that the Constitution permits the government "to establish a legal principle" and simultaneously "protect[s] a person's interest in disregarding that principle once established."[11]

There is nothing strange, however, about the supposed paradox; whether we think the position is strange depends on how we define principles and interest. The applicable general principle might be that government can take all actions predicated on the moral view except insofar as they unduly burden some individual interest.[12] Alternatively, we might identify an *independent* moral principle for objecting to tax-funded abortions— for example, that governments may be responsive to the views of taxpayers who object, on moral grounds, to the use of their money to pay for abortions. The government would not be taking the view that abortion is wrong, and its actions would therefore not be inconsistent with what Perry describes as the minimum principle of *Roe*.

The argument just made can be generalized. At the moment a decision is announced we cannot identify the principle that it embodies. Each decision can be justified by many principles, and we learn what principle justified Case 1 only when a court in Case 2 tells us.[13] Behind the court's statement about Case 1 lies all the creativity to which the hermeneutic theory of historical understanding directed our attention. When *Roe* was decided we might have thought that it rested on Perry's principle, but the funding cases show us that we were "wrong" and that *Roe* "in fact" rested on one of the alternatives just spelled out. The theory of neutral principles thus loses almost all of its constraining force. We have only to compare Case 2, which is now decided, with Case 1 to see if a principle from Case 1 has been neutrally applied in Case 2. If the demand is merely that the opinion

Precedents can be made to apply [margin note]

in Case 2 deploy some reading of the earlier case from which the holding in Case 2 follows, the openness of the precedents means that the demand can always be satisfied. And if the demand is rather that the holding be derived from the principles actually articulated in the relevant precedents, differences between Case 2 and the precedents will inevitably demand a degree of reinterpretation of the old principles. New cases always present issues different from those settled by prior cases.[14] Thus, to decide a new case a judge must take some liberties with the old principles if they are to be applied at all. There is, however, no principled way to determine how many liberties can be taken; hence this reading of the theory likewise provides no meaningful constraints.

decision can both conform & depart from precedent [margin note]

The central problem here is that, given the difficulty of isolating a single principle for which a particular precedent stands, we lack any criteria for distinguishing between cases that depart from and those that conform to the principles of their precedents. In fact, any case can compellingly be placed in either category. Such a universal claim cannot be validated by example. But two examples of cases that simultaneously depart from and conform to their precedents can at least make the claim plausible.

The first is *Griswold v. Connecticut*, in which the Court held that a state could not constitutionally prohibit the dissemination of contraceptive information or devices to married people.[15] *Griswold* relied in part on *Pierce v. Society of Sisters*[16] and *Meyer v. Nebraska*.[17] *Pierce* held unconstitutional a requirement that children attend public rather than private schools; *Meyer* held that a state could not prohibit the teaching of foreign languages to young children. In *Griswold* the Court said that these cases relied on a contitutionally protected interest, conveniently labeled "privacy," that was identical to the interest in the contraceptive case.

In one view *Griswold* tortures these precedents. Both were old-fashioned substantive due process cases, which emphasized interference "with the calling of modern language teachers . . . and with the power of parents to control the education of their own." In this view the most one can fairly find in *Meyer* and *Pierce* is a principle about freedom in inquiry, rather narrower than a principle of privacy. Yet one can say with equal force that *Griswold* identifies for us the true privacy principle of *Meyer* and *Pierce*, in the way that the abortion funding cases identify the true principle of *Roe v. Wade*. Just as hermeneutic originalism empha-

sizes the creativity that is involved when judges impute to the framers a set of intentions, so the retrospective approach to neutral principles must recognize the extensive creativity exercised by a judge when he or she imputes to a precedent "the" principle that justifies both the precedent and the judge's present holding.

A second example is *Brandenburg v. Ohio*.[18] The state of Ohio had prosecuted a leader of the Ku Klux Klan for violating its crimial syndicalism statute, which prohibited advocating the propriety of violence as a means of political reform. The Court held that the conviction violated the first amendment, which, according to the decision, permits punishment of advocacy of illegal conduct only when "such advocacy is directed to inciting or producing imminent lawless action and is likely to incite or produce such action." Remarkably, the Court derived this test from *Dennis v. United States*, in which the Court upheld the convictions of leaders of the Communist Party for violating a federal sedition law.[19] This reading is, to say the least, an innovative interpretation of *Dennis*, which explicitly stated a different test—"the gravity of the 'evil,' discounted by its probability"—that left the decision largely to the jury.[20] A dispassionate observer would find it hard to reconcile the results in *Dennis* and *Brandenburg* without invoking the extralegal point that Cold War hysteria obviously affected the 1951 decision in *Dennis*. Again the requirement of retrospective neutrality may be satisfied if we interpret *Brandenburg's* use of *Dennis* as the creative reworking of precedents within authorized bounds.

The examples illustrate a general point. In a legal system with a relatively extensive body of precedent and well-developed techniques of legal reasoning, it will always be possible to show how today's decision is consistent with the relevant past ones, but, conversely, it will also always be possible to show how today's decision is inconsistent with the precedents. This symmetry, of course, drains "consistency" of any normative content.

The difficulties with neutral principles theory are on a par with the problems in understanding originalism that were noted earlier. Understanding the intentions of the framers requires a special kind of creative re-creation of the past; the creativity involved in such a re-creation dashes any hopes that originalism can effectively constrain judicial decisions, because many alternative re-creations of the framers' intentions on any given issue are always possible. In the same way, the result of the inquiry into neutral principles theory indicates that, although it is possible to discuss a given decision's consistency with previous precedents, requiring consistency of this kind similarly fails to constrain judges sufficiently and thereby fails to advance the underlying liberal project.

This critique points the way to a more refined version—what I will term the craft interpretation—of the neutral principles theorists' calls for consistency. The failings of this alternative bring out the underlying reasons why the demand for consistency cannot do the job expected of it.

Every decision reworks its precedents. A decision picks up some threads that received little emphasis before and stresses them. It deprecates what seemed important before by emphasizing the factual setting of the precedents. The techniques are well-known; indeed, learning them is at the core of legal education. But they are techniques. This recognition suggests that we attempt to define consistency as a matter of craft. When push comes to shove, adherents of neutral principles simply offer us lyrical descriptions of the sense of professionalism in lieu of sharper characterizations of the constraints on judges. For example, Charles Black attempts to resolve the question whether law can rely on neutral principles by depicting "the art of law" living between the two poles of subjective preference and objective validation in much the same way that "the art of music has its life somewhere between traffic noise and a tuning fork—more disciplined by far than the one, with an unfathomably complex inner discipline of its own, far richer than the other, with inexhaustible variety of resource."[21] The difficulty then is to specify the limits to craft. One limit may be that a judge cannot lie about the precedents, for example by grossly mischaracterizing the facts.[22] Black adds that "decision [must] be taken in knowledge of and with consideration of certainly known facts of public life."[23] Clearly these limits are not terribly restrictive.

If we cannot specify limits to craft, perhaps we could identify some decisions that are within and some that are outside the limits, in order to provide the basis for an inductive and intuitive generalization. The limits of craft, however, are so broad that in any interesting case any reasonably skilled lawyer can reach whatever result he or she wants.[24] The craft interpretation thus fails to constrain the results that a reasonably skilled judge can reach and leaves the judge free to enforce his or her personal values, as long as the opinions supporting those values are well written. Such an outcome is inconsistent with the requirements of the liberal tradition in that, once again, the demand for neutral principles fails in any appreciable way to limit the possibility of judicial tyranny.

The best example of this problem is *Roe v. Wade*. It seems to be generally agreed that, as a matter of simple craft, Justice Blackmun's opinion for the Court was dreadful.[25] The central issue before the Court was whether a pregnant woman has a constitutionally protected interest in terminating her pregnancy. When his opinion reached that issue, Justice Blackmun simply listed a number of cases in which "a right of personal privacy, or a guarantee of certain areas or zones of privacy," had been recognized. Then he said, "This right of privacy, whether it be founded in the 14th Amendment's concept of personal liberty . . . or . . . in the Ninth Amendment's reservation of rights to the people, is broad enough to encompass the woman's decision whether or not to terminate her pregnancy.[26] This may well fail to satisfy the current requirements of the craft.

The conclusion that we are to draw, however, is either uninteresting or irrelevant to constitutional theory. Insofar as *Roe* gives us evidence, we can conclude that Justice Blackmun is a terrible judge. The point of constitutional theory, though, would seem to be to keep judges in line. If the result in *Roe* can be defended by judges more skilled than Justice Blackmun, the requirements of craft would mean only that skillful judges can do things, and can survive professional criticism, that less skillful ones cannot. For example, John Hart Ely argues that although *Roe* is beyond acceptable limits, *Griswold* is within them (perhaps near the edge).[27] Justice Douglas'[s] opinion for the Court in *Griswold* identified a number of constitutional provisions that in his view explicitly protect one or another aspect of personal privacy. The opinion then noted that the Court had in the past protected interests closely related to those expressly protected. By arguing that those "penumbral" interests overlap in the area of marital use of contraceptives, Justice Douglas could hold the statute unconstitutional.

If *Griswold* is acceptable we need only repeat its method in *Roe*. Indeed, Justice Douglas followed just that course in a brilliant concurring opinion. Even if *Griswold* is rejected as well, skilled lawyers could rewrite *Roe* to defend its outcome.[28] There is in fact a cottage industry of constitutional law scholars who write revised opinions for controversial decisions.[29] Thus, even the craft version of neutrality in application collapses. Neutral principles, like other theories, are supposed to guarantee that judges do not do whatever they want. The craft version means that untalented judges will not be able to get away with whatever they want, but talented judges will be able to use the tools of the craft to do what they want. It is not easy to see what this theory has to recommend it, beyond its self-interested defense of elitist academic lawyers.

The other difficulty with the craft interpretation runs deeper. Craft limitations make sense only if we agree on what the craft is. But consider the craft of "writing novels." Its practice includes Trollope writing *The Eustace Diamonds,* Joyce writing *Finnegan's Wake,* and Mailer writing *The Executioner's Song.*[30] We might think of Justice Blackmun's opinion in *Roe* as an innovation akin to Joyce's or Mailer's. It is the totally unreasoned judicial opinion. To say that it does not look like Justice Powell's decision in some other case is like saying that a Cubist "portrait" does not portray its subject in the manner that a member of the academy would paint it. The observation is true but irrelevant to the enterprise in which the artist or judge was engaged and to our ultimate assessment of his or her product.

We can now survey our progress in the attempt to define "neutral principles." The proposed definitions left us with judges who can enforce their personal values unconstrained by the neutrality requirement. The craft interpretation may seem plausible because it appeals to an intuitive sense that the institution of judging involves people who are guided by and committed to general rules applied consistently. But the very notions of generality and consistency can be specified only by reference to an established institutional setting. We can know what we mean by "acting consistently" only if we understand the institution of judging in our society. Thus, if the theory of neutral principles proves unable to satisfy its demand for rule-guided judicial decision making in a way that can constrain or define the judicial institution, in the final analysis it is the institution—or our conception of it—that constrains the concept of rule guidedness.

Consider the following mutiple choice question: "Which pair of numbers comes next in the series 1, 3, 5, 7 . . . ? (*a*)9, 11; (*b*) 11, 13; (*c*) 25, 18."[31] It is easy to show that any of the answers is correct. The first is correct if the rule generating the series is "List the odd numbers"; the second is correct if the rule is "List the odd prime numbers"; and the third is correct if a more complex rule generates the series.[32] Thus, if asked to follow the underlying rule—the "principle" of the series—we can justify a tremendous range of divergent answers by constructing the rule so that it generates the answer we want. As the Legal Realists showed, the result obtains for legal as well as mathematical rules.[33]

Yet there is something askew in this conclusion. After all, we know that no test maker would accept (*c*) as an answer, and indeed we can be fairly confident that test makers would not include both (*a*) and (*b*) as possible answers, because the underlying rules that generate them are so obvious as to make the question fatally ambiguous.[34] Another example may sharpen the point. The examination for people seeking driver's licenses in the District of Columbia once included this question: "What is responsible for most automobile accidents? (*a*) the car; (*b*) the driver; (*c*) road conditions." Anyone who does not know immediately that the answer is (*b*) does not understand what the testing enterprise is all about.[35]

In these examples we know something about the rule to follow only because we are familiar with the social practices of intelligence testing and drivers' education. That is, the answer does not follow from a rule that can be uniquely identified without specifying something about the substantive practices. Similarly, although we can use standard techniques of legal argument to draw the conclusion from the decided cases that the Constitution requires substantial equality in the distribution of wealth, . . . we know that no judge will in the near future draw that conclusion. The failure to reach that result is not ensured because the practice of "following rules" or neutral application of the principles inherent in the decided cases precludes a judge from doing so. Rather it is ensured because judges in contemporary America are selected in a way that keeps them from thinking that such arguments make sense. This branch of the argument thus makes a sociological point about neutral principles. Neither the principles nor any reconstructed version of a theory that takes following rules as its focus can be neutral in the sense required by the liberal tradition, because taken by itself, an injunction to follow the rules tells us nothing of substance. If such a theory constrains judges, it does so only because they have implicitly accepted some version of what the rules in controverted cases ought to be before they apply those rules in the case at hand.[36]

The theory of neutral principles is attractive because it affirms the openness of the courts to all reasonable arguments drawn from the decided cases. But if the courts are indeed open to such arguments, the theory allows judges to do whatever they want. If it is only a consequence of the pressures exerted by a highly developed, deeply entrenched, homeostatic social structure that judges seem to eschew conclusions grossly at odds with the values of liberal capitalism, sociological analysis ought to destroy the attraction of the theory. Principles are "neutral" only in the sense that they are, as a matter of contingent fact, unchallenged, and the contingencies have obvious historical limits.[37]

. . .

Craft + neutrality

Endnotes

[1] Other possible definitions are discussed in Mark Tushnet, "Following the Rules Laid Down: A Critique of Interpretivism and Neutral Principles," 96 *Harvard Law Review* 781, 805–6 (1983).

[2] A comprehensive survey of the argument that law cannot be made certain is Anthony D'Amato, "Legal Uncertainty," 71 *California Law Review* 1 (1983).

[3] Principles cannot be neutral in content because they necessarily specify, in general terms, who will prevail in a dispute.

[4] Perry, "Why the Supreme Court Was [Plainly Wrong in the Hyde Amendment Case: A Brief Comment on Harris v. McRae," 32 *Stanford Law Review* 1113, 1127 (1980)].

[5] *Legitimacy* has another possible meaning, common in the sociological literature on government: legitimate actions are those that are accepted by the relevant public. For a brief discussion, see Mark Tushnet, "Perspectives on the Development of American Law," 1977 *Wisconsin Law Review* 81, 100–102. See also Alan Hyde, "The Concept of Legitimation in the Sociology of Law," 1983 *Wisconsin Law Review* 379. Decisions that lack legitimacy in this empirical sense are undesirable, because a court's main resource in effectuating its decisions is public acceptance, and illegitimate decisions deplete its limited capital. (This is the thesis of Jesse Choper, *Judicial Review and the National Political Process: A Functional Reconsideration of the Role of the Supreme Court* [1980].) It is implausible, however, that neutral application of principles is an important source of public acceptance of judicial decisions. The general public is unlikely to

care very much about a court's reasoning process, which is the focus of neutral principles theory; its concern is with results. Of course, to the extent that influential publicists—columnists for the *New York Times*, for example—accept the theory, they may invoke it to criticize the Court. The criticisms might then affect elite readers, from whom the effect might, so to speak, trickle down to the public. See Henry Monaghan, "Book Review," 94 *Harvard Law Review* 296, 310–11 (1980). The extent to which such criticisms affect the public and the Court's legitimacy is an empirical question, the investigation of which would require us to distinguish between the trickle-down effect of views about reasoning and the effects of views about the merits of decisions. Skepticism seems warranted by the few studies that point to the areas of interest. (The evidence is summarized in Austin Sarat, "Studying American Legal Culture: An Assessment of Survey Evidence," 11 *Law and Society Review* 427, 438–41, 466–69 [1977].) Hyde argues that there is no reason to think that legitimation is a significant dimension of law's social effect.

[6] This links the theory to general theories of precedent-based adjudication in nonconstitutional areas.

[7] 410 U.S. 113 (1973).

[8] Harris v. McRae, 448 U.S. 297 (1980).

[9] Perry, "Why the Supreme Court Was Wrong," pp. 1114, 1120, 1115–16.

[10] Id., p. 1117.

[11] [Id.,] pp. 1116–17.

[12] Perry presumably thinks that such a principle is inconsistent with other areas of constitutional law, for it recognizes a kind of acceptance of civil disobedience that is not recognized elsewhere in constitutional law. Westen gives the example of Coker v. Georgia, in which the Court held that, although Georgia could make unaggravated rape—if such there be—a crime because it is morally wrong, it was not constitutional to make it a capital offense. Coker v. Georgia, 433 U.S. 584 (1977); Westen, "Correspondence," [33 *Stanford Law Review* 1187, 1188 (1981)]. Perry rejects the "counterexample" of Brandenburg v. Ohio, 395 U.S. 444 (1969), in which the Court protected certain kinds of advocacy from criminal prosecution even though it could "take [other] action predicated on the view that such advocacy is morally objectionable." He argues that the advocacy in *Brandenburg* is protected to avoid a chilling effect on truly protected speech. Thus *Brandenburg's* real protection is given to "interests *distinct from*" the interest in advocating unlawful activity. Perry, "Why the Supreme Court Was Wrong," pp. 1118, 1119.

The same argument can be developed in the abortion context, however. Consider the narrow principle that government may not take action predicated on the view that abortions are immoral in cases in which the woman has not consented to the sexual contact that caused the pregnancy. *Roe v. Wade* might then be defended on the ground that governmental inquiries into whether consent had been given, particularly in light of the obvious controversy over what consent might mean, would intrude on the independent interest in informational privacy. Because refusal to fund abortions does not intrude on that interest, it is permissible according to this interpretation of *Roe*.

[13] Sandalow, "Constitutional Interpretation," [79 *Michigan Law Review* 1033, 1064–65 (1981)].

[14] Indeed, if it did not so depart we ought to wonder why the later case was litigated at all. Compare George Priest, "The Common Law Process and the Selection of Efficient Rules," 6 *Journal of Legal Studies* 65 (1977), with George Priest, "Selective Characteristic of Litigation," 9 *Journal of Legal Studies* 399 (1980).

[15] 381 U.S. 479 (1965).

[16] 268 U.S. 510 (1925).

[17] 262 U.S. 390 (1923).

[18] 395 U.S. 444 (1969).

[19] 341 U.S. 494 (1951).

[20] *Brandenburg* applied a categorical test that looks to the character of the words uttered—they must be an "incitement" and nothing else—and to the immediate circumstances in which they are uttered. *Dennis* used an approach that is explicitly more variable: Speech that very likely would lead to a less serious evil might be punished, as might speech that had a small probability of leading to an extremely serious evil. Of course, if categories proliferated, the *Brandenburg* approach would blend into the *Dennis* one. . . .

[21] Charles Black, *Decision according to Law* 81 (1981). See also id., pp. 21–24; Sandalow, "Constitutional Interpretation."

[22] See, e.g., Dershowitz and Ely, "*Harris v. New York*"; Tushnet, "Critical Legal Studies and Constitutional Law," pp. 631–33.

[23] Black, *Decision according to Law*, p. 82.

[24] Much turns here on the definition of *interesting*. Cases decided by the Supreme Court would fit any reasonable definition. See Frederick Schauer, "Easy Cases," 58 *Southern California Law Review* 399, 408–10 (1985). . . .

[25] See, e.g., John Hart Ely, "The Wages of Crying Wolf: A Comment on *Roe v. Wade*," 82 *Yale Law Journal* 920 (1973); Richard Epstein, "Substantive Due Process by Any Other Name: The Abortion Cases," 1973 *Supreme Court Review* 159; Laurence Tribe, "Toward a Model of Roles in the Due Process of Life and Law," 87 *Harvard Law Review* 1, 2–5 (1973).

[26] 410 U.S. 113, 153 (1973).

[27] Ely, "Wages," pp. 929–30.

[28] Donald Regan, "Rewriting *Roe v. Wade*," 77 *Michigan Law Review* 1569 (1979).

[29] See, e.g., Louis Henkin, "Shelley v. Kraemer: Notes for a Revised Opinion," 110 *University of Pennsylvania Law Review* 473 (1962); Louis Pollak, "Racial Discrimination and Judicial Integrity," 108 *University of Pennsylvania Law Review* 1 (1959).

[30] Dworkin observes that a person asked to add one chapter "in the best possible way" to a collaborative novel-in-progress faces limits similar to those that precedents place on judges. Ronald Dworkin, " 'Natural' Law Revisited," 34 *University of Florida Law Review* 165, 167 (1982). He fails to appreciate that, by disrupting our expectations about what fits best, the creative author may force us both to reinterpret all that has gone before and to expand our understanding of what a "novel" is. . . .

[31] This example is suggested by Winch, *Idea of Social Science*, at 29–32, who draws on Ludwig Wittgenstein, *Philosophical Investigations* (G. E. M. Anscombe trans. 3d ed. 1958). See also "Spiro" (pseud.), "Elastic Aptitude Test," 8 : 4 *Games Magazine* 22–23 (Apr. 1984) (including the question "What are the next three terms in the following series? 1, 3, 5, 7, . . . , . . . , . . . ," and defending the answer "8, 9, 10" by explaining that it is the series of positive numbers with the letter *e*).

[32] One possible rule is $f(1) = 1$; for n greater than 1, if n is divisible by 5, then $f(n) = n^2$; if $(n - 1)$ is divisible by 5, then $f(n) = f(n - 1) - f(n - 2)$; if neither n nor $(n - 1)$ is divisible by 5, $f(n) = 2n - 1$.

Schauer, "Easy Cases," p. 427, responds to this example by "adding a number of other choices," including "(*d*) 9, 11, 13; . . . (*i*) Reggie Jackson, Babe Ruth; (*j*) Cleveland, Newark," and claiming that these answers are "clearly incorrect, at least in this world." This misunderstands the structure of the example. The issue confronting the test taker is not "Are these answers within the range of possible ones?" but is rather "Given that these answers are listed among the possible answers, how could a rational test giver think that they are in the ballpark so as to make it sensible to include them on the list of answers?"

A test taker could sensibly resolve that issue as to every one of the answers that Schauer thinks is obviously wrong. For example, given that "Cleveland, Newark" appears on the list, the test taker could reasonably think that the inclusion of these answers demonstrates that the test giver is a numerologist and would then convert the suggested answers to the corresponding number and develop an appropriate mathematical rule. As to "9, 11, 13," the test giver might be following a rule whereby *pair* means "three numbers," a possibility familiar in the philosophical literature from Nelson Goodman, *Fact, Fiction, and Forecast* 74–81 (2d ed. 1965), where it appears as *grue*, meaning "green until now, and blue hereafter." Or—the alternative I prefer—the test giver likes to play with words, notices that *pair* sounds like *pear,* and thinks that, as the numbers appear on a page, "9, 11, 13" looks like a pear.

The hypothetical in the text demonstrates that we cannot resolve the ambiguities by recourse to the meaning of the words *pair of numbers;* we must also know something about the social practice of giving tests. The hypothetical explanations of strange answers are cousins to, though not expressly derived from, the social practice of administering literacy tests to southern blacks in the 1950s. See also Sanford Levinson, "What Do Lawyers Know (And What Do They Do with Their Knowledge)?: Comments on Schauer and Moore," 58 *Southern California Law Review* 441, 449 n. 38 (1985).

[33] This is a standard point in post-Wittgensteinian philosophy. See, e.g., *Wittgenstein: To Follow a Rule* (Steven Holtzman and Christopher Leich eds. 1981); Saul Kripke, *Wittgenstein on Rules and Private Language* (1982).

[34] But see Winch, *Idea of Social Science,* pp. 30–31 (assuming that the problem has no ambiguity). One can also imagine a fiendish test maker regarding (*c*) as the correct answer precisely because the ambiguity precludes the test taker from deciding between (*a*) or (*b*).

[35] Coaching the Scholastic Aptitude Test is geared to this way of understanding multiple choice tests. See David Owen, *None of the Above: Beyond the Myth of Scholastic Aptitude* 121–40 (1985) (describing method of analyzing choices by considering how "Joe Bloggs" would

assess them). See also Charles Taylor, *Philosophy and the Human Sciences* 29–30 (1985) (survey research into goals and values must consider "how did we design our questionnaire?," which relied on implicit understanding of those goals and values in its formulation of questions to ask).

[36] Recent work in literary theory emphasizes the role that interpretive communities play in determining the authoritative meaning of texts, and some of that work questions the basis on which an interpretive community gains its authority. For introductions, see Stanley Fish, *Is There a Text in This Class?: The Authority of Interpretive Communities* (1980); *The Politics of Interpretation* (William Mitchell ed. 1983); Christopher Butler, *Interpretation, Deconstruction, and Ideology: An Introduction to Some Current Issues in Literary Theory* (1984). A helpful discussion of some of the ambiguities in Fish's arguments is David Luban, "Fish v. Fish or, Some Realism about Idealism," 7 *Cardozo Law Review* 693 (1986).

[37] On the contingency of neutral categories, see Steven Collins, "Categories, Concepts, or Predicaments? Remarks on Mauss's Use of Philosophical Terminology," in *The Category of the Person* 46 (Michael Carrithers, Steven Collins, and Steven Lukes eds. 1985); Louis Dumont, "A Modified View of Our Origins: The Christian Beginnings of Modern Individualism," id., p. 93; John Comaroff and Simon Roberts, *Rules and Processes* (1981) (stressing the construction of disputes by rules).

On Reading the Constitution

LAURENCE H. TRIBE

. . . What does it mean to *read* this Constitution? What is it that we do when we *interpret* it? Why is there so much controversy over *how* it should be interpreted—and why is so much of that controversy, these days in particular, not limited to the academy or to the profession, but so public that it

From *The Tanner Lectures on Human Values,* Vol. IX (Salt Lake City: University of Utah Press, 1988), pp. 3–34. Reprinted with permission of the University of Utah Press.

makes the evening news and the front pages? It's no secret, of course, that the Supreme Court's school prayer decisions in the 1960s, its abortion decision in 1973, its reaffirmation of those controversial decisions in the mid-1980s, and its refusal to accept the Reagan administration's quite stark anti-affirmative-action views have all given administration spokesmen—particularly Attorney General Edwin Meese and William Bradford Reynolds, the assistant attorney general for civil rights—and those who sympathize with them ample incentive to criticize the Court's interpretation of the Constitution. But that is hardly new. Disagreement with the Supreme Court's laissez-faire rulings of the early twentieth century and the Court's invalidation of key New Deal measures into the 1930s provided ample motive for people to attack the Court during those years. Disagreement with the desegregation and the reapportionment decision decades later spurred loud reactions against the jurisprudence of the Warren Court. But the *level* and *tone* of the public debate has reached, I think, something of a new pitch—one that has not been heard at this intensity in so sustained a way since Franklin D. Roosevelt's assault in the "Nine Old Men" in the presidential election of 1936.

In any case, it is my intention to take the dispute seriously—not to regard it simply as a mask for disagreement with the Court's results on particular issues, or as a mere excuse to oppose one or another judicial nominee, although to some extent it *is* simply a matter of whose ox has most recently been gored. Recognizing that such substantive disagreement plays a large role in bringing critics out into the open, in other words, does not justify inattention to the content of that disagreement. So I proceed from the premise that there is a real dispute over ways of interpreting the Constitution, and I want to try to understand what the structure of that dispute is.

If there is genuine controversy over how the Constitution should be read, certainly it cannot be because the disputants have access to different bodies of information. After all, they all have exactly the same text in front of them, and that text has exactly one history, however complex, however multifaceted. Is it that different people believe different things about how that history *bears* on the enterprise of constitutional interpretation?

Thomas Grey . . . asks[1] provocatively whether some individuals regard the history of the Constitution, both prior to its adoption and immediately thereafter, and even the history subsequent to that, as somehow a *part* of the Constitution—in much the same way that some theologians consider tradition, sacrament, and authoritative pronouncements to be part of the Bible. And he asks whether perhaps others regard the history, and certainly the post-adoption tradition and the long line of precedent, as standing entirely apart from the Constitution, shedding light on what it means, but not becoming *part* of that meaning—in much

the way other theologians consider the words of the Bible to be the sole authoritative source of revelation, equally accessible to all who read it, in no need of the intervention of specialized interpreters and thus not to be mediated by any priestly class.

Perhaps the disputants agree, or at least many of them do, on what *counts* as "The Constitution" but simply approach the same body of textual and historical materials with different visions, different premises, different convictions. But that assumption raises obvious questions: How are those visions and premises and convictions relevant to how this brief text ought to be read? Is reading the text just a *pretext* for expressing the reader's vision in the august, almost holy terms of constitutional law? Is the Constitution simply a mirror in which one sees what one wants to see?

The character of contemporary debate might appear to suggest as much. Liberals characteristically accuse conservatives of reading into the Constitution their desires to preserve wealth and privilege and the prevailing distribution of both. Conservatives characteristically accuse liberals of reading into the Constitution their desires to redistribute wealth, to equalize the circumstances of the races and the sexes, to exclude religion from the public realm, and to protect personal privacy. A once largely scholarly debate conducted almost exclusively in the pages of the law journals and the journals of cognate disciplines, and occasionally in the pages of the *United States Reports,* where Supreme Court opinions appear, now erupts regularly into a flurry of charges and countercharges between persons no less august than the attorney general of the United States and a growing list of Supreme Court justices speaking outside their accustomed role as authors of formal opinions. How are we to understand such charges and countercharges?

. . .

. . . [T]he "conservatives" on the Court, no less than the "liberals," talk as though reading the Constitution required something much more than passively discovering a fixed meaning planted there generations ago. Those who wrote the document, and those who voted to ratify it, were undoubtedly projecting their wishes into an indefinite future. If writing is wish-*projection*, is reading merely an exercise in wish-*fulfillment*—not fulfillment of the wishes of the *authors*, who couldn't begin to have foreseen the way things would unfold, but fulfillment of the wishes of *readers*, who perhaps use the language of the Constitution simply as a mirror to dress up their own political or moral preferences in the hallowed language of our most fundamental document? Justice Joseph Story feared that that might happen when he wrote in 1845: "How easily men satisfy themselves that the Constitution is exactly what they wish it to be."[2]

To the extent that is so, it is indefensible. The authority of the Constitution, its claim to obedience, and the force that we permit it to exercise in our law and over our lives would lose all legitimacy if it really were only a mirror for the readers' ideas and ideals. We *have* to reject as completely unsatisfactory the idea of an empty, or an infinitely malleable, Constitution. We must find principles of interpretation that can anchor the Constitution in some more secure, determinate, and external reality. But that is no small task.

One basic problem is that the text itself leaves so much room for the imagination. Simply consider the preamble, which speaks of furthering such concepts as "Justice" and the "Blessings of Liberty." It is not hard, in terms of concepts that fluid and that plastic, to make a linguistically plausible argument in support of more than a few surely incorrect conclusions. Perhaps a rule could be imposed that it is improper to refer to the preamble in constitutional argument on the theory that it is only an introduction, a preface, and not part of the Constitution *as enacted*. But even if one were to invent such a rule, which has no apparent grounding in the Constitution itself, it is hardly news that the remainder of the document is filled with lively language about "liberty," "due process of law," the "privileges or immunities" of citizens, and the guarantee of a "Republican Form of Government"—words that, although not *infinitely* malleable, are capable of supporting meanings at opposite ends of virtually any legal, political, or ideological spectrum.

It is therefore not surprising that readers on both the right and left of the American political center have invoked the Constitution as authority for strikingly divergent conclusions about the legitimacy of existing institutions and practices, and that neither wing has found it difficult to cite chapter and verse in support of its "reading" of our fundamental law. As is true of other areas of law,

the materials of constitutional law require construction, leave room for argument over meaning, and tempt the reader to import his or her vision of the just society into the meaning of the materials being considered.

In a recent book . . . I argued that as a result of this fluidity, judges *have* to acknowledge, as they read the Constitution, that they cannot avoid making at least *some* basic choices in giving it content.[3] . . .

In this sense, although I agree with much of what Ronald Dworkin has written in his powerful new book, *Law's Empire*, I am troubled by the breadth of his notion of interpretation. In his view, to "interpret" a cultural or social practice, or a legal text, is to make of it the best thing of its kind that one believes it is capable of being. As Dworkin would have it, for example, the interpreter of a play or a poem seeks to understand it so that it becomes the best play or the best poem that it can be. And so he urges that the interpreter of a constitutional concept like "due process of law" or "equal protection of the laws" should seek to understand that concept in accord with the interpreter's larger vision of what a good constitution should be like. This approach is certainly not excluded in any a priori way by the meaning of the concept of "interpretation"; work in interpretive theory, or hermeneutics, suggests that the concept is indeed broad enough to take in what writers like Dworkin have in mind.

Yet I believe that the enterprise we are or should be about when we advance an argument in the Constitution's name must be more bounded and less grandiose than all that. The moment you adopt a perspective as open as Dworkin's, the line between what, perhaps to your dismay, you think the Constitution *says* and what you wish it *would* say, becomes so tenuous that it is extraordinarily difficult, try as you might, to maintain that line at all. The question becomes how one can maintain the line—given the ambiguity of the Constitution's text, the plasticity of its terms, the indeterminacy of its history, and the possibility of making noises in the Constitution's language that *sound* like an argument for just about anything. What does it mean to suggest that the Constitution imposes constraints on choice—serious constraints? How can one maintain, in other words, a stance in which reading the Constitution differs from writing one?

One thing that is plain is that there would *be*

no real difference between those two enterprises if what we meant by "the Constitution" included not only the text and the history and tradition of its interpretation but also something as vague and ineffable as the essence of the American spirit—what Thomas Grey has described as the "grand and cloudy Constitution that stands in our minds for the ideal America, earth's last best hope, the city on the hill."[4] Well, *that* Constitution, which seems to me to be the one that some commentators . . . evoke even when they purport to be discussing something more modest, may be the stuff of bicentennial celebrations, but it is hard for me to think of it as binding law—law that unelected judges should be entrusted to expound in an enforceable way. I am evidently regarded by some as an admirer of that gauzy sort of Constitution. Indeed, I figure as one of the chief villains in such derisive works as Henry Monaghan's essay, "Our Perfect Constitution."[5] Monaghan there accuses me of always seeing a silver lining even in the gray and sometimes bleak language of the document. But I want to distance myself from anything quite as mystical as all that. "Mysterious," as Justice Stevens would have it, the Constitution may be. Mysterious, but not mystical—and not even lost in the mists of the ideal.

Still, there is the haunting fact that linguistic possibility cannot be denied: the words of the Constitution are broad enough to make the loftiest claims possible. Now enter Edwin Meese and others of the "originalist" or "intentionalist" school. They say: "We have a solution. Our solution is to domesticate the words of the Constitution with the addition of history. History will do the trick." But notice what they do with history. *Brown v. Board of Education*, Mr. Meese says, is a wonderful example of a correct decision.[6] Notice the more than slight embarrassment: the history doesn't particularly support it; the history shows that those who wrote and ratified the Fourteenth Amendment thought, as I indicated earlier, that segregated public education was perfectly fine. So how does history solve the problem if one has a convenient bit of amnesia when history doesn't point to results that one feels in retrospect are surely right?[7] The history would also suggest that it is permissible to disqualify the clergy, to say that priests and ministers cannot serve in state legislatures or hold public office. That history, too, we would have to forget.

The fact is that history, including the history of

what people expected or wished for or intended or feared—especially when it is a history of *collective* beliefs, beliefs of hundreds of members of Congress who proposed an amendment and hundreds of state legislators who voted to ratify it—is fundamentally indeterminate and can be described at a great many levels of generality and abstraction. It seems to me that, however helpful it is—and although it is indefensible to ignore it—history alone cannot serve to domesticate, discipline, and bind down text. History alone cannot eliminate in an airtight and demonstrable way the possibility of constructing out of the Constitution's phrases an argument of sorts for nearly any desired conclusion.

I say an argument "of sorts." But it would not necessarily be an argument that would deserve to be taken seriously, much less an argument that could fairly persuade. That really is the point. It may not be possible to "prove," in the way you prove a mathematical conjecture to be true or false, that a particular fanciful, ingenious argument about the Constitution simply doesn't count as a plausible interpretation. But from the impossibility of that sort of proof, all that follows is that law, like literature, is not mathematics—that judicial deliberation, like all legal discussion, cannot be reduced to scientific processes of deduction and induction. And that should not be terribly surprising, although some people apparently continue to be surprised by it.

The impossibility of that kind of airtight "proof" does not, however, translate—as some seem to believe it does—into a claim of such total indeterminacy that *all* interpretations of the Constitution are equally acceptable and that the only test of which interpretation you favor should be whether it advances or retards your vision of the good society. I think it is possible to do much better than that, although not nearly as well as some might wish.

Part of the answer . . . is in no sense peculiar to *constitutional* law but relates, rather, to the deep and abiding problem of how to imagine, conceptualize, and understand the process and the practice of giving reasons—of engaging in rational persuasion—without leaning on notions of timeless, universal, and unquestionable truth. A great many people have lost faith in the idea of the timeless, the universal, and the unquestionable. And yet somehow, in their ordinary lives, they can still distinguish what sounds like a good argument from what sounds like a spurious argument. And it does not require placing judges or other interpreters of the Constitution on a phony, quasi-mathematical pedestal to conclude that, for reasons of a practical kind, it makes sense to entrust to people removed from the political fray the process of reason-giving, even in an environment where we lack the metric—the external measure—to prove conclusively that reason X is no good, that reason Y is decisive. A number of philosophers, most notably Hilary Putnam, have made extremely useful contributions to the enterprise of elaborating what reason-giving consists of in a world unbolstered by ultimate truth.[8] But the processes of constitutional interpretation and adjudication obviously cannot be called off while that enterprise is being pursued, especially if you believe, as I do, that that enterprise will go on forever.

The part of the answer that *is* peculiar to constitutional interpretation depends not on any general thesis about knowledge or interpretation but rather on features of the Constitution that we actually have. And in beginning to sort out good and bad ways of arguing about what *this* Constitution means, I think we can make considerable headway by inquiring what it is about some modes of discourse, some modes of conversation that are put forth as "constitutional argument," that makes them suspect from the start. What is it about some purported modes of constitutional analysis that makes them implausible candidates for ways of reading the Constitution we actually have?

In effect, I want to offer some *negative* observations about ways *not* to read the Constitution, before turning in the second of these lectures to the more affirmative project of *reading* the Constitution, against the backdrop of several actual cases and two hypothetical cases I will posit. Two ways *not* to read the Constitution are readily apparent. I call them reading by *dis*-integration and reading by *hyper*-integration.

When I say reading by "*dis*-integration," I mean approaching the Constitution in ways that ignore the salient fact that its parts are linked into a whole—that it is a *constitution*, and not merely an unconnected bunch of separate clauses and provisions with separate histories, that must be interpreted.

When I say reading by "*hyper*-integration," I mean approaching the Constitution in ways that ignore the no less important fact that the whole contains distinct parts—parts that were, in some instances, added at widely separated points in American history; parts that were favored and opposed by greatly disparate groups; parts that reflect quite distinct, and often radically incompatible, premises. In the beginning the Constitution as proposed by Congress in 1787 was ratified by the requisite number of states in 1787 and 1788. Twenty-six amendments were added, ten of them in 1791, the remainder from 1795 to 1971—and so became "valid," under Article V, "to all intents and purposes, as part of this Constitution." The Constitution of the United States is thus simultaneously a single entity or structure *and* a collection of enactments by the people; the whole is not a unitary, seamless proclamation. These observations may seem too obvious to be worth making. But they serve to disqualify much of what passes as constitutional argument and interpretation. Those who try to see in this complicated collage of compromise over time one single vision, and who then proceed to argue from that vision, have lost sight of the constraints imposed by our experience under a written constitution. They are not reading the Constitution we *have*, but a hyper-integrated constitution for which they yearn.

. . .

. . . The basic point . . . is that whatever our overarching theories about knowledge and interpretation might be, we can make real progress in reading the Constitution by eliminating at the start arguments that are not eligible for treatment as constitutional interpretation because they entail reading not *this* Constitution, but a desiccated, disintegrated version of it.

At the other extreme there stands the fallacy of *hyper*-integration—of treating the Constitution as a kind of seamless web, a "brooding omnipresence" that speaks to us with a single, simple, sacred voice expressing a unitary vision of an ideal political society. Of course, that would have been an impossible view to maintain early in our history: the fugitive slave clause; the Constitution's prohibition on any interference by Congress with the slave trade until the year 1808; the apportionment formula for the House of Representatives, which regarded a slave as equal to three-fifths of a person; and the other accommodations to the institution of slavery that were written into the text would have been difficult to square with many of the ideals found elsewhere in the document.

But it would be a fundamental mistake to suppose that, after ratification of the Civil War amendments, all such basic contradictions were eliminated from the Constitution, which suddenly became a coherent, consistent document. Conflicting visions—of liberal individualism on the one hand and civic republicanism on the other; of national supremacy as opposed to states' rights; of positivism as opposed to natural law—pervade the Constitution throughout its many parts. The notion that the Constitution embodies an immanent, unitary, changeless set of underlying values or principles—whether procedural or substantive or structural—seems an extraordinary intellectual conceit, one inconsistent with the character of the Constitution's various provisions as concrete political enactments that represent historically contingent, and not always wholly coherent, compromises in a document which was made in stages, incrementally, over a period of two centuries.

. . .

There is a suggestive analogy from the fields of algebraic topology and algebraic geometry, in which I once worked. The multidimensional curved space in which we find ourselves probably has no unified simple geometry. Locally, the space may have a Euclidian structure while globally, at large distances, its structure may be Riemannian or Lobachevskian. It may even be that the local topology is very different from the global topology. The Constitution is similarly multidimensional, and its global structure need be no more congruent with its local structure than is that of physical space. The web is not seamless. The parts do not always cohere. Anyone who says "I have here a little hologram embodying the essence of the Constitution, which can be turned round and round, revealing a seamless web," should incur your suspicion.

That insight has significance well beyond the negative. Instead of simply serving to *disqualify* otherwise attractive candidates for methods of constitutional interpretation, the insight might also provide something of an answer to those who would attack particular approaches in interpretation as subject to internal contradictions and anomalies. Many critical legal scholars, for example, have developed elaborate and often very insightful analyses designed ultimately to show that what they call "liberal constitutional scholarship" cannot meet various demands of coherence—it will have an internal contradiction here and there.[9] And it has been a commonplace in constitutional commentary for a long time to deride various approaches as insufficiently democratic or insufficiently majoritarian in character and, therfore, as contradicting some supposed need of the Constitution *as a whole* to affirm democracy.[10] But where is that "need" of the Constitution "as a whole"? When all of the supposed unities are exposed to scrutiny, criticisms of that kind become considerably less impressive. Not all need be reducible to a single theme. Inconsistency—even inconsistency with democracy—is hardly earth-shattering. Listen to Walt Whitman: "Do I contradict myself? Very well then, I contradict myself." "I am large, I contain multitudes," the Constitution replies.[11]

. . .

Endnotes

[1] Grey, "The Constitution as Scripture," 37 *Stan. L. Rev.* 1 (1984). . . .

[2] Michael Kammen, *A Machine That Would Go of Itself: The Constitution in American Culture* (New York: Knopf, 1986). [xxiii].

[3] Laurence Tribe, *Constitutional Choices* (Cambridge, Mass.: Harvard University Press, 1985).

[4] Grey, "The Constitution as Scripture," [19].

[5] Monaghan, "Our Perfect Constitution," 56 *N.Y.U. L. Rev. 353* (1981).

[6] 347 U.S. 483 (1954).

[7] Some have proposed ignoring as a mere assumption, or as a clearly subordinate intent, the ratifiers' expectation that racial segregation in public schools would not be outlawed by the Fourteenth Amendment. See, e.g., Bork, "Neutral Principles and Some First Amendment Problems," 47 *Ind. L.J.* 1, 14–15 (1971).

[8] See Hilary Putnam, *Reason, Truth and History* (Cambridge: Cambridge University Press, 1981); Michelman, "Justification (and Justifiability) of Law in a Contra-

dictory World," in *NOMOS: Justification,* vol. 28, ed. J. R. Pennock and J. Chapman (New York: New York University Press, 1986). Cf. the discussion of nihilism in Friedrich Nietzsche, *The Will to Power,* trans. A Ludovic (New York: Russell and Russell, 1964).

[9] See, e.g., Tunshnet, "The Dilemmas of Liberal Constitutionalism," 42 *Ohio St. L.J.* 411 (1981).

[10] For a brief review of such commentary, see Brest, "The Fundamental Rights Controversy: The Essential Contradictions of Normative Constitutional Scholarship," *90 Yale L.J.* 1063 (1981).

[11] Walt Whitman, "Song of Myself," *Leaves of Grass,* 9th ed. (1891–92), lines 1324–26. Cf. Emerson, "Self-Reliance," *Essays: First Series* (1841) ("A foolish consistency is the hobgoblin of little minds, adored by little statesmen and philosophers and divines").

Study Questions

1. Does Justice Douglas's appeal to the "penumbras and emanations" of the Bill of Rights in *Griswold* constitute good constitutional interpretation, in your view? Is such an appeal a license to ignore the text of the Constitution? Why or why not? Take note of the Third Amendment, which prohibits the quartering of soldiers in someone's home without the owner's consent, and of the Fourth Amendment, which guarantees the right "of the people to be secure in their person, houses, papers, and effects, against unreasonable searches and seizures." Note that the kind of intrusion prohibited by both amendments is a physical intrusion, not a regulation of behavior. Is it stretching the meaning of these amendments to make them prohibit statutes regulating behavior, as the Connecticut statute did?

2. At various points throughout the privacy cases, appeal has been made to the Ninth Amendment: "The enumeration in the Constitution, of certain rights, shall not be construed to deny or disparage others retained by the people." The suggestion has been made that privacy is one of these "retained" rights. But the Ninth is the focus of controversy. Some scholars argue that its appearance in the text of the Constitution is prophylactic only: at the time of adoption there was some concern that the inclusion of a bill of rights would be taken to imply that the federal power (granted in section 8 of Article I) is not limited but extends all the way up to the edge of the rights enumerated; that is, that the federal government has the power to do everything except infringe upon those listed rights. The Ninth Amendment was meant merely to preclude that inference. On its face, however, the Ninth seems to be a clear invitation to look beyond the text and structure of the Constitution to locate fundamental rights still retained by the people. The difficulty, of course, is that we are not told where to look for such rights; the text of the amendment provides no guidelines. How would you determine to what rights the Ninth Amendment refers? Should the Ninth be relied upon at all in interpreting the Constitution?

3. Concurring in *Griswold,* Justice Goldberg asserted that privacy in the marital relation is a fundamental part of our nation's traditions. Is he right? Is it part of our traditions that couples be allowed to use birth control? Do any aspects of our history dispute this?

4. Justice Blackmun, in dissent in *Bowers,* argued that the Court should protect our fundamental interests in "controlling the nature of [our] intimate associations with others." Bork objects to this formulation of the right of privacy as it would make it impossible consistently to criminalize adultery, incest, or other sex crimes so long as they are committed in the home. Is Bork correct?

5. Tushnet claims that, since a court in one case can always say that the principle or rule for which another, earlier case was previously taken to stand is in fact not the "truly" operative principle, interpretive activity loses its constraining force. Is this claim borne out by Tushnet's criticism of the Court's privacy decisions?

6. Read the text of the United States Constitution. Does anything in the document itself indicate how it is to be interpreted? If not, how should this silence be construed?

7. The official record of the Constitutional Convention at Philadelphia was purposely destroyed by the delegates. One explanation offered for this holds that the framers did not want future interpretation of the Constitution to be dogmatized by what they thought. Is this convincing? If so, what larger conclusions can be drawn from their action?

B. *Legal Reasoning*

Introduction

This section takes a step back from the specific concerns about privacy that occupied us in the previous section and turns to an exploration of several perspectives on the aims and methods of judicial decision making.

Law professor Steven Burton opens the discussion with an analysis of legal reasoning undertaken from the standpoint of a person trying to determine how a court will likely deal with a case. Burton starts by characterizing *rules* and *cases,* the primary materials of legal reasoning, and by explaining why the idea of applying a rule to (or following a rule within) a particular set of factual circumstances is not simply a straightforward exercise.

Burton then turns to a fuller examination of the two basic forms of legal reasoning, *reasoning by analogy* and *deductive reasoning.* He outlines the steps involved in reasoning by analogy and relates these to the process of common law adjudication (legal decision making by judges applying "rules" developed by other judges in prior cases); he indicates the ways in which these rules differ from other kinds of rules, for example, legislative enactments. A central concern in common law adjudication is with establishing the *precedential value* of a given case, that is, establishing the rule for which the cases stands, which rule can then serve as a guide to the decision of future cases that are similar or analogous to the present one in "relevant" ways. Burton's discussion reveals the parameters of this difficulty through a review of more specific issues: What does it mean to "follow a precedent"? What distinguishes the "holding" of a case from mere *"dicta"*? What does it mean to say that two factual situations are "alike in important respects"?

Lastly, Burton focuses on the role of deductive reasoning in legal decision making. Here he shows the ways in which reasoning deductively from an enacted law, such as a statute or constitutional provision, raises problems of interpretation, and the ways in which the techniques of analogical reasoning can be employed to facilitate such interpretation.

Legal Reasoning and Intuition

Joseph Hutcheson's "The Judgement Intuitive" was first published in 1929 and quickly became a classic statement of a conception of legal reasoning associated with a broader perspective on the law called *legal realism.* (For more on the general theory of legal realism, see Chapter One.) As their name suggests, the realists stressed a down-to-earth approach to legal decision making and regarded with some disdain the more traditional understanding of legal reasoning as a dispassionate and rational analysis of the applicable rules and cases that issues in a correct and sound resolution of any and all legal disputes.

Central to the realist criticism of the view that legal reasoning is a rational procedure bound by rules was the conviction, expressed by Supreme Court Justice Oliver Wendell Holmes, that "general propositions do not decide concrete cases." Cases, not rules, were, for the realists, the only source of law. Hutcheson's essay recounts how he came to accept this view. He confesses that he had initially been trained in and had adopted the belief in "slot-machine" jurisprudence, the belief in the exactitude and precision of legal reasoning, carried out through "logomachy," or a war of words, a kind of verbal sparing. Eventually, however, his many years in the courtroom brought him to see the human side of the law; the side represented by the jury, faced with a difficult case and struggling to do justice. With this revelation came another: that good judges, like good jurors, "feel" their way to a just decision by waiting for the "hunch" or flash of insight that will light the way, the intuition that will point in the right direction. In this, Hutcheson agrees with other realists, many of whom argued that judges deciding particular disputes should be guided by the aim of responding to the real human needs before them, not by slavishly following inferences from the abstract categories and distinctions in the "rules."

The judge's judgment, then, is purely the product of a hunch. The rest of what the judge typically does, the lengthy opinion that he or she provides as a preface to the decision, is, according to Hutcheson, mere rhetoric—an "apologia." Supporting the judicial hunch with appropriate legal jargon is necessary, however, to disguise its arbitrary nature. The task of the judge is therefore to reason backward from an intuition of the "desirable" result to a rationalization that will justify it.

And since the decision or judgment itself, rather than the verbiage surrounding it, accurately reflects the judge's intuition in a given case, those seeking to predict what the judge will do in the future should look to any and all of these factors likely to influence his or her hunch. This conclusion led some realists to advocate an empirical or even anthropological study of judges and their decisions, focusing on the collection of data regarding their life-style, social status, political affiliation, and even diet, in an effort to account for all those factors that could conceivably influence a judge's behavior.

"Legal reasoning," for many of the realists then, is something of a misnomer. What a judge does when faced with a difficult case is something much more like an art or craft than compliance with a statable, logical procedure.

Basic Forms of Legal Reasoning

STEVEN J. BURTON

Cases and Rules

Most laypersons probably think of the law as a system of rules. The study of law in U.S. law schools, however, normally begins with the reading of a law case. The law student reads and reasons primarily from cases throughout law school. Thinking about cases is an important intellectual activity throughout one's legal career, though legal rules, too, play a major role in legal thought. Before undertaking the main discussion of legal reasoning, three basic questions will be

From *An Introduction to Law and Legal Reasoning* (Boston: Little, Brown, 1985), pp. 1, 19–39, 41–43, 68–73, 76–77. Reprinted with permission of Little, Brown and Company.

posed in this chapter: What is a case? What is a rule? Why do we study primarily cases?

. . .

[A.] Using Cases and Rules

Expressions of the law take the form of both rules (generalizations) and cases (examples). To develop skill at making lawyerly predictions and persuasions, it is better to emphasize a study of cases than a study of rules. Rules are deceptively simple in appearance. Cases are complex and rich in variety. Consequently, predicting or persuading from rules alone is often unreliable in a world that is more complex and varied than even the cases.

1. Rules in Problem Cases

Rules, it was said, are abstract or general statements of what the law permits or requires of classes of persons in classes of circumstances. Rules are cast in general language and apply to more than one case but less than all cases. A rule itself may say little or nothing about how it should be interpreted and analyzed in a particular case. Using a rule, as a basis for making predictions and persuasions, often requires intensive analysis and considerable interpretation.

Consider, for example,[1] a simple rule that provides that "No person shall sleep in a city park." Imagine two problem cases.[2] In the first, a gentleman was found sitting upright on a park bench at noon, his chin was resting on his chest, and his eyes were closed. The gentleman was snoring audibly. In the second, a disheveled tramp was found lying on the same bench at midnight, a pillow was beneath his head, and a newspaper was spread over his body as if it were a blanket. The tramp, however, had insomnia. Both were arrested under the rule and brought before a court for trial. Would you predict that the gentleman will be convicted and the tramp acquitted? That the gentleman will be acquitted and the tramp convicted? That both will be convicted? That both will be acquitted? There is no fifth alternative. Does your answer follow from the language of the rule itself?

Consider, for a second example, a rule that provides that "No person shall bring a vehicle into a city park." Imagine some possible problem cases. An ambulance was driven into the park to reach a jogger who collapsed with an apparent heart attack. The local Jaycees put a World War II tank in the park as a monument to the town's war dead. Some teenagers held a car race in the park, a go-cart race, a bicycle race, or a roller-skating race. A tree surgeon drove his truck into the park to load and remove the branches of a dead tree under contract with the city. Surely some of these incidents would not be violations of the rule, yet all might plausibly be said to involve a person bringing a vehicle into the park. Consequently, merely *saying* in any of these cases that a person brought a vehicle into a park would not be sufficient to persuade someone that the rule had been trangressed.

In almost any case, knowing the rules leaves more intellectual work to be done because rules are expressed imperfectly and projected into an uncertain future. The language of a rule does not itself determine whether many particular cases come within the class of cases designated by the rule. Whoever states a rule to govern future cases rarely, if ever, will anticipate all of the future cases that might plausibly be described in the language of the rule but that should not be within the class designated by the rule, or that could not plausibly be described in the language of the rule but that should be within the class. Consequently, a lawyer must go beyond the rules themselves to predict what a court will do or persuade someone of what a court will or should do in a particular case. A lawyer must analyze and interpret the rules in light of possible cases. Karl Llewelyn put it more colorfully in his lectures of 1929–1930 introducing Columbia students to the study of law:

> We have discovered in our teaching of the law that general propositions are empty. We have discovered that students who come eager to learn the rules and who do learn them, *and who learn nothing more*, will take away the shell and not the substance. We have discovered that rules *alone*, mere forms of words, are worthless. We have learned that the concrete instance, the heaping up of concrete instances, the present, vital memory of a multitude of concrete instances, is necessary in order to make any general proposition, be it rule of law or any other, *mean* anything at all. Without the concrete instances the general proposition is baggage, impedimenta, stuff about the feet. It not only does not help. It hinders.[3]

2. Decided Cases in Problem Cases

A case, it was said, is a short story of an incident in which the state acted or may act to settle a particular dispute. Decided cases tell a story with a beginning, a middle, and an end—a story that occurred once and resulted in the settlement of a particular dispute by the coercive dispute settlement machinery of the state. Using decided cases, as a basis for making predictions and persuasions in problem cases, involves a perhaps less familiar intellectual process than that seemingly required by rules. Though often difficult to grasp, learning this way of thinking is well worth the effort. Lawyers in practice generally will care less about the law in the abstract than in its practical implications for particular existing or possible future disputes involving a particular client. Judges generally do not enact rules; they decide cases.

Effective legal planning requires a keen sense of the variety of disputes that can arise in the future. A lawyer engaged in planning a client's activities is engaged partly in imagining the particular disputes that might arise from the client's activities and taking precautions to minimize losses the client may suffer in such disputes. Elegantly drafted contract language, for example, may be worthy of praise for its style but will earn none if a foreseeable dispute arises and was not anticipated in the drafting. The world was a habit of confounding even those with perspicacious insights and vivid imaginations. A study of the cases stimulates and supplements the imagination so that better precautions can be taken for a greater variety of disputes that might arise from a client's activities.

Once a dispute has arisen, the lawyer will be engaged in predicting what the court will do or persuading someone of what the court will or should do in that case. Pyrrhic victories, as when a court accepts a lawyer's preferred general rule but concludes that the client loses under that rule, usually are of little interest to the lawyer and less to the client. To predict what the court will do in one case, a lawyer can look to what courts have done in other similar cases. To persuade a court of what it should do in one case, a lawyer can point out what courts have done in other, similar cases. A practice of comparing and contrasting cases may have advantages over rules because the cases supply particularities that general rules leave untreated. Cases are the grist for the legal reasoning mill.

Consider again, for example, the rule that prohibits any person from bringing a vehicle into a city park. Assume that a judge must decide whether a tree surgeon violated that rule by bringing his truck into the park to load and carry away dead tree branches under contract with the city. As has been seen, it could be said that the tree surgeon violated the rule because he is a person and brought a vehicle into the park. It also could be said that the city, not a "person" within the meaning of the rule, brought the vehicle into the park through its contract with the tree surgeon. At this point, the language of the rule gives no further guidance. The lawyers and judges must look elsewhere.

Assume further, then, that from a previously decided case we know, or from common sense all involved would agree, that it is no violation of the rule for an ambulance to enter the park to minister aid to a stricken jogger. Assume also that we know or can agree that it is a violation of the rule for teenagers to race cars in the park. Now the question may be posed: Is the tree surgeon's truck case more like the ambulance case or more like the teenagers' racing cars case?

It would seem that one can reach a reasoned answer to the question, though the reasons do not line up to produce that answer as numbers line up to produce a sum. The ambulance case shows that the statute cannot be interpreted literally, as prohibiting all persons from bringing any vehicle into any city park under any circumstances. There is room for interpretation. The teenagers' racing cars case suggests, by inference in light of common sense, that the rule seeks to protect the park and those who seek rest and recreation in the park from noisy and dangerous activities involving vehicles. Like the rule, the city and the tree surgeon were maintaining the park for the benefit of persons who use it. A city park is not a national wilderness area, in which virtually no intrusion whatsoever may be allowed. The short intrusion on the tranquillity of the park is small in relation to the benefits. It would be absurd in this day to require the tree surgeon to carry the tree branches out of the park by manual labor or horse-drawn cart (if that is not a "vehicle"). Accordingly, the tree surgeon should not be punished under the rule as properly interpreted.

From a different perspective, a further reason can be given for emphasizing the study of cases: They force lawyers and judges to think *hard* about justice in society. To a large extent in the U.S. legal system, it is thought that justice will emerge from the arguments of adversaries before a judge. Lawyers not only are engaged in protecting a client's interest but also participate in the search for justice, which likely will concern the court because the judge is disinterested as between the parties and isolated from the political process. Predicting what a judge will do or persuading a judge of what should be done requires the lawyer to appeal to the justice of the case.

Moreover, the action of the state to settle a dispute, the decision in a law case, is coercive action by the state involving at least the threatened use of physical force by the state. The law that determines when that power may be used—when the sheriff may deprive an individual of liberty or property pursuant to judicial decree—also determines the limits of freedom from a major form of state compulsion. The law at the same time defines the legitimate use of force by the state and the scope of individual liberty, in a major respect. It is an effort to rule out arbitrary or oppressive uses of power by the state while allowing justifiable uses of that power. The lawyer is society's expert on when (in what cases) the state may use its coercive powers legitimately.

Cases, much more than rules, press lawyers and judges to think hard about justice, the limits of proper governmental power, and the scope of individual freedom. It is easy to agree, for example, on a general rule that promises should be kept. But should the state enforce your promise to pay me $500 for the Eiffel Tower, should you decide not to keep your promise? Would it make a difference if the Eiffel Tower in mind were a stage prop I had delivered to you for use in a play? Again, should the state enforce your promise to join me for dinner at my lodge, should you decide not to keep your promise? Would it make a difference if I had paid you to give an after-dinner speech? What, exactly, should it mean to "enforce" that promise when the dinner is history?

Cases display the complexities with which the law must deal. Comparing and contrasting cases suppl[ies] the particularities that are needed for lawyers to predict intelligently what a court will do or persuade a court of what it should do in a particular case, and for judges to make reasoned decisions in problem cases. Comparing and contrasting cases requires hard, rigorous thinking about justice and the proper role of government in a free and democratic society. As one philosopher suggested in a different context:

> Principles and laws may serve us well.
> They can help us to bring to bear on what
> is now in question, what is not now in
> question. They help us to connect one
> thing with another and another. But at the
> bar of reason, always the final appeal is to
> cases.[4]

The Analogical Form of Legal Reasoning

Legal problems in the United States may be governed by the common law, enacted law, or both kinds of law. In a pure common law system, official lawmaking is by judges on a case-by-case basis. Legal reasoning starts with a decided case and largely takes the form of an analogy. In a pure system of enacted law, official lawmaking is by an

official body (e.g., a legislature) that enacts general rules (e.g., constitutions, statutes, codes, or regulations). Legal reasoning starts with a rule and largely takes a deductive form. . . .

This [section] will show that the analogical form of legal reasoning makes a significant contribution to the rationality of legal thought. It establishes a framework for analysis that serves in appropriate cases to identify the proper starting points for reasoning, organize the relevant materials, and frame the issues for predictions, persuasions, or decisions. However, the analogical form itself is not sufficient for making good predictions, persuasions, and decisions. It leaves unclear which of the many facts in a case are reasons and will or should lead a court to decide the case one way or the other. The problem of deciding which facts in a case thus are the important facts (the "problem of importance") requires that the analogical form of legal reasoning be supplemented.

A. The Analogical Form

The central tenet of the common law is the principle of stare decisis, which means roughly that like cases should be decided alike. It is sometimes expressed as the doctrine of precedent or the principle of equal treatment under the law. Reasoning under the principle of stare decisis is reasoning by analogy, or by example.

Analogical reasoning is familiar in a number of everyday nonlegal situations. For example, when Mother allows Older Brother to stay up until 9:00 P.M. and Younger Brother claims the same treatment, Younger Brother probably is claiming that he is like Older Brother because both are children (a fact). He thinks that therefore they are alike and should be treated alike. When Mother rejects his claim and explains that older children need less sleep than younger children (another fact), she is asserting that there is an important difference between the two children and that therefore they should not be treated alike. For a second example, Mother's view that one simply cannot invite to the wedding Cousin Matilda, who lives in town, without also inviting Cousin Wilbur, who lives in Europe, reflects some underlying belief that the two cousins should be treated alike because they both are cousins. Daughter's response that only persons who live nearby should be invited reflects her claim that Cousin Matilda and Cousin Wilbur are not alike in an important respect and therefore should not be treated alike.

In the abstract, analogical reasoning in any setting requires three steps. First, one must start with a *base-point* situation from which to reason (the treatment of Older Brother, Cousin Matilda) and assume that the treatment of the base-point situation was in some sense correct under the circumstances. Second, one must describe those factual respects in which the base-point situation and the problem situation (Younger Brother, Cousin Wilbur) are *similar* (childhood status, cousinhood status); and those factual respects in which the two situations are *different* (age, geographical proximity). Third, one must determine whether the factual similarities or the differences are more *important* under the circumstances and thus should control the decision in the problem situation.

The second and third steps are made necessary by the simple logic of analogies. No two persons, acts, or things ever will be aike in all factual respects. The claim that two persons, acts, or things are alike is not a claim that they are identical (as in the arithmetical conception of equality). If identical, they would not be two and could not be compared or contrasted at all. Nor will any two persons, acts, or things ever be different in all factual respects. If different in all factual respects, they could not both be persons, acts, or things, and comparing or contrasting them would be pointless. Therefore, analogical reasoning requires careful consideration of both the similarities and the differences between two situations and then a judgment whether the similar respects or different respects are more important under the circumstances.

Analogical reasoning is highly situational, or dependent on context. It is largely pointless to ask whether Older Brother and Younger Brother are alike or unalike in the abstract: They are both. Likeness or unalikeness in an important respect makes sense only in a concrete setting, as in the example involving bedtime. Even then, the ascription of likeness or unalikeness may change with the circumstances. Given the fact of a three-year difference in age, for example, the two brothers may be unalike for purposes of bedtime at ages 3 and 6 but alike for the same purposes some years later. And they may be different for purposes of bedtime while similar for purposes of distributing Christmas presents fairly.

Analogical reasoning in most familiar nonlegal settings also is highly informal. What will count as

a base point, or an important similarity or difference under the circumstances, is determined by the individuals involved for whatever reasons they find appealing. Their imaginations are left free rein; their intuitions are left unbridled. Rarely are they quite aware that they are reasoning "by analogy" or are analyzing (1) the propriety of a base point, (2) the factual similarities and differences between two situations, and (3) the relative importance of the factual similarities and differences under the circumstances.

B. The Analogical Form of Legal Reasoning

Legal reasoning in the analogical form is not fundamentally different from analogical reasoning in most familiar nonlegal situations. It is more formal and consequently is more self-conscious, rigorous, and uniform in expression than is reasoning in everyday life. Underlying good legal reasoning of this kind are certain well-accepted rules of the game that help identify the proper base points for argument, a vocabulary and method that encourage rigorous consideration of both similarities and differences between a decided case and a problem case, and a form of expression for framing the issue to be decided when making predictions, persuasions, and decisions. The analogical form, however, does not solve the problem of importance; that is, it does not indicate whether the factual similarities or the differences between two cases are more important under the circumstances and thus will or should lead a court to decide the case one way or the other.

1. Precedents

The first step in analogical reasoning is the selection of a proper base point with which to compare and contrast the problem situation. The doctrine of precedent gives a special status as base points to law cases that were decided in the past by the highest court in the jurisdiction in which a problem case arises.[5] The U. S. legal system includes a federal jurisdiction in which federal courts are primarily responsible for certain matters of national interest, and the U. S. Supreme Court is the highest court for these matters. It also includes fifty state jurisdictions in which state courts carry primary responsibility for most other matters. Each state has a highest court, usually called the supreme court of the state. The cases decided in the past by these courts are the best *precedents* for the decision of future cases within their respective jurisdictions. That is, the precedents of the highest court in a jurisdiction are the most authoritative base points for reasoning in the analogical form concerning legal problems within that jurisdiction.

Of less, but considerable, significance are other cases that can serve as useful base points. The precedents of any court (including foreign courts) may be used as the base point for analogical argument before any other court. If the case is not a precedent of the relevant jurisdiction, it nonetheless may be a well-reasoned decision that the court will find persuasive. Hypothetical cases found in the scholarly literature of the American Law Institute's Restatements of the Law similarly may be used as persuasive base points when reasoning in the analogical form. Additionally, lawyers and judges sometimes use hypothetical cases of their own construction when the result in such cases is not controversial among all relevant persons.

This explanation of the relevant base points in common law adjudication simplifies the rules of the game. For example, it is open to the highest court in a problem case to *overrule* its own precedents. The case that overrules earlier cases then becomes the proper base point for future cases, in place of the earlier cases, thereby effecting a change in the law. Overruling is not a common occurrence, though the possibility is ever-present. The complex relationships among courts are treated in several law school courses in far greater detail than is appropriate to this introduction. It suffices here to understand that legal reasoning proceeds on the basis of formal rules of the game that identify the authoritative and otherwise acceptable base points for legal reasoning in the analogical form.

2. *Factual Similarities and Differences*

The second step in analogical reasoning is the identification of factual similarities and differences between the base-point situation and a problem situation. Legal reasoning in the analogical form uses a vocabulary and rhetoric that emphasizes the need for rigorous attention to both relationships. In controversial cases, which are the problem cases that require lawyerly skill because reasonable arguments are available to both parties, there will be many precedents that are facially similar to the problem case but that seem to cut both ways. By

rigorous analysis of the facts of the cases the legal analyst will proceed to identify the many plausible points of factual similarity and difference. A judgment whether the similarities or differences are more important under the circumstances can be made intelligently only after identifying the range of plausible points of comparison and contrast.

A judge or decision *follows precedent* when the facts of a previously decided case are sufficiently similar to those of a problem case for justice to require like treatment of the two cases (unless the earlier case is overruled). A judge or case *distinguishes precedent* when the facts of a previously decided case are sufficiently different for justice to require different treatment of the two cases. There is no reason to presume in advance of rigorous analysis that a facially similar precedent should be followed or distinguished. The principle that like cases should be decided alike implies that unalike cases should be decided unalike if the differences are more important under the circumstances. Stare decisis requires as much that judges distinguish unalike precedents as that they follow like precedents.

In principle, then, the doctrine of precedent requires the judge to treat each relevant authoritative precedent in one of three ways: The judge may follow a precedent, distinguish it, or overrule it. A judge may not in good conscience ignore a relevant authoritative precedent, though this sometimes happens and becomes a ground for criticizing the judge. In their arguments, lawyers similarly are expected to advocate that each relevant authoritative precedent be followed, distinguished, or, less commonly, overruled.[6] Legal arguments are seriously vulnerable if they ignore a relevant authoritative precedent that does not support the point.

Whether a judge should follow or distinguish a precedent depends in part on a careful analysis of the facts of the precedent in relation to the facts of a problem case. The facts of a case consist of a description of the events in the world that set the stage for the dispute, how the parties came to find themselves in dispute, and sometimes what the parties did to try to resolve the dispute on their own. These are all events that normally occur before a court is called on to settle the dispute and mostly can be described in ordinary, nontechnical language. The facts of a case also include a description of the legal proceedings in the lower courts, if any, as necessary to identify the legal point (the *legal issue*) that was or may be appealed to the higher court. The issue on appeal always involves the question whether the trial judge erred in making some particular decision under the factual circumstances in the particular case. The facts and the legal issue establish the context in which the judgment of importance will be made at the third step.

A legal analyst compiles the facts of the problem case, as they have been or may be proved in court, and analyzes them until they are understood with great particularity. A detailed mastery of the legally provable facts is necessary because the presence or absence of a particular fact may become the point on which a precedent is determined to be alike or unalike in an important respect: One does not know which facts will matter, at the early stages of legal analysis. Good lawyers err on the side of compiling more facts in greater detail than they are likely to need in the course of legal proceedings.

The legal analyst using the analogical form then locates (by thoughtful legal research) the facially similar precedents and analyzes the facts of the precedents. Here again, it is necessary to gain a masterful understanding of the facts in great detail, though the facts as summarized in the official reports of decided cases normally are sufficient for this purpose. The lawyer does not yet know which facts will or should matter when a court decides to follow or distinguish each facially similar precedent. The judge will want to know all plausible similarities and differences before deciding which are more important under the circumstances.

Only then can the analyst identify the factual similarities and differences between a precedent and a problem case. Doing so, of course, is not a mechanical matter of finding identical statements in the descriptions of the cases. Lawyers often summarize the facts in their own language. This allows room for creativity and insight into relationships among the facts that overly technical or thoughtless descriptions sometimes mask. It also allows room for some distortion of the facts, though opposing counsel, higher courts, and fellow judges can be expected to point out such distortions.

Highly rigorous analysis of the facts thus is encouraged by the practice of following or distinguishing all facially similar precedents that are not overruled. Whether two cases will be regarded as alike or unalike in the more important respects depends on the facts of the problem case, the facts of the precedents, and the plausible relationships of similarity or difference between the congeries of facts. Prior to such an analysis of the facts, it should not be thought that a facially similar precedent is more likely to be followed or distinguished in any problem case. Accordingly, mastery of the facts to identify all plausible factual relationships is an essential step in analogical legal reasoning.

3. The Problem of Importance

The third step for analogical reasoning is determining whether the factual similarities or the differences between the two situations are more important under the circumstances. Legal reasoning in the analogical form similarly requires a judgment whether facially similar precedents should be followed or distinguished (assuming away any question of overruling). The judge in a law case, however, is not free to assign importance to the similarities or differences between cases on any ground whatsoever. The judge's duty is to decide that question in accordance with the law. But it is most difficult to give a satisfactory account of what it might mean in common law adjudication to decide *in accordance with the law.* This is where the problem of importance arises.

A natural inclination is to think that deciding in accordance with the law means following the common law rules at this third step and, thus, to depart from the analogical form of legal reasoning. The common law rules are rules announced by judges in their opinions in cases governed by the common law. These rules, one might think, should perform two functions: They should identify the legally important facts in advance of a case and what legal consequences follow if the important facts are present in a case. For example, a common law rule might provide that "If a man dies without a will, then his property shall become the property of his eldest son." The man's death without a will would be a possible fact. The legal consequence of its occurrence would be the transfer of his property to the eldest son. The law would make the judgment of important in advance of the materialization of a case; the important fact would be that of a man's death without a will. The judge in a case would not be free to decide that any other fact is important enough to justify a different legal consequence.

To elaborate, such a common law rule would take the form (or be translatable into the form) of an "if . . . , then . . ." statement. For example: If facts *a, b,* and *c* are present but fact *d* is not, then the defendant shall be held liable for the plaintiff's damages. A legal rule in this form would tell an analyst that facts *a, b, c* and *d* are important in cases governed by the rule that the presence of *a, b* and *c* together with the absence of *d* shall result in the defendant's liability. The "if . . ." clause would state the necessary and sufficient factual conditions that require invoking the legal consequence stated in the "then . . ." clause. Common law rules often are expressed or may be translated into a form approximating this simple scheme.

This form of expression can be illustrated, and its serious difficulties in common law adjudication exposed, by an extended example.[7] Five hypothetical cases will be described in an order in which they might be decided in a common law jurisdiction. The statement of facts and legal reasoning are

given in a simplified form that represents what a court might write in a published opinion. Each story starts with Costello, the original owner of five horses and a somewhat naive and too-trusting friend of Abbott's. Each horse came by theft or fraud into the hands of Abbott, and Costello sought to recover possession of the horse from Abbott or someone who came into possession of the horse after Abbott sold it. To help the reader keep the facts straight, a diagram of the factual relationships in each case appears [in the figure].

CASE 1

Abbott stole a horse belonging to Costello and sold it to Holliday, who did not know and had no reason to know it had been stolen from Costello. Costello sued Holliday to recover the horse. Costello won.

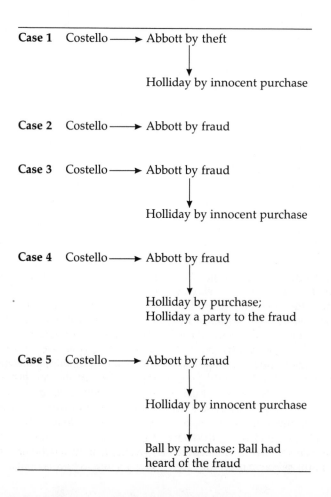

Case 1   Costello ⟶ Abbott by theft

Holliday by innocent purchase

Case 2   Costello ⟶ Abbott by fraud

Case 3   Costello ⟶ Abbott by fraud

Holliday by innocent purchase

Case 4   Costello ⟶ Abbott by fraud

Holliday by purchase;
Holliday a party to the fraud

Case 5   Costello ⟶ Abbott by fraud

Holliday by innocent purchase

Ball by purchase; Ball had
heard of the fraud

The court in Case 1 might give as its reasoning a general rule: A person who purchases property from a seller who did not own the property does not acquire ownership and must return the property to the rightful owner. The court then might apply the rule to the facts of the case: Holliday purchased the horse from Abbott, a thief who did not own it. This evidently yields as a conclusion: Holliday did not acquire ownership of the horse from Abbott and must return it to Costello.

CASE 2

Abbott bought a horse from Costello, giving as payment a forged check on another person's account. Abbott knew the check was forged. After delivering the horse to Abbott, Costello discovered the fraud and sued Abbott to recover the horse. Costello won.

The court in Case 2 might give as its reasoning another general rule: A person who acquires possession of property by fraudulent purchase does not acquire ownership and must return the property to the rightful owner. Application of the rule: Abbott acquired possession of the horse by purchase with a fraudulent check. Conclusion: Abbott did not acquire ownership of the horse and must return it to Costello. So far, so good.

CASE 3

The facts are similar to Case 2, except that Abbott sold the horse to Holliday. Holliday knew that Abbott had bought the horse from Costello, but did not know or have reason to know that Abbott paid with a forged check. Costello sued Holliday to recover the horse. Holliday won.

If the rules announced in the precedents were "the law" that determines the results in future cases, Case 3 would have to go the other way. The combination of the rules announced in Cases 1 and 2 would seem to require that Costello win. Case 2 announces as a rule that people who fraudulently acquire possession of property do not acquire ownership; Case 1 announces as a rule that a person without ownership of property cannot transfer ownership to another. In Case 3, Abbott did not acquire ownership of the horse, under the rule in Case 2. By finding for Holliday, however, the court seems to ignore the rule in Case 1, for it finds Holliday owns the horse when Abbott did not.

There are many cases on the books that decide Case 3 for Holliday, in jurisdictions that decide Cases 1 and 2 for Costello and that also recognize a general rule like that in Case 1.

The court in Case 3 could craft a new rule that is consistent with the results in all three cases. It could announce, for example, that an owner of property who loses possession of the property by another's wrongful act may recover possession only from the perpetrator or from a subsequent purchaser if the wrongful act was theft. But surely this is quite a change from the rule given in Case 1. Moreover, this new rule would be announced *after* the decision in Case 3; the judgment of importance would be made by the court in Case 3 rather than by the rule in advance of Case 3. The new rule would not have been on the books for the lawyers to use in predicting what the court would do in Case 3 or persuading the court of what it should do in Case 3.

How reliable, then, would be the rule of Case 3 for predicting or persuading in Cases 4 and 5?

CASE 4

The facts are similar to Case 3, except that Holliday had helped Abbott perpetrate a fraud on Costello. Costello sued Holliday to recover the horse.

CASE 5

The facts are similar to Case 3, except that after buying the horse from Abbott, Holliday sold and delivered it to Ball. Ball had heard rumors of the fraud worked on Costello by Abbott. Costello sued Ball to recover the horse.

The court in Case 3 modified the rule of Case 1 to do justice in Case 3. The court in Case 4 similarly could modify the rule of Case 3 to do justice in Case 4. And the same is true in Cases 5 et seq.

The form of expression that purports to treat the results in common law cases as a consequence of preexisting rules thus does not reflect accurately the process of common law decision. As Professor Edward H. Levi put it, "[t]he rules change as the rules are applied. More important, the rules arise from a process which, while comparing fact situations, creates the rules and then applies them."[8] Judges in common law cases may write as if the law has always been what it has come to be, but this is well known to be a fiction.

An inclination to regard the judgment of importance as a function of preexisting legal rules of this sort is misleading in a further way. Despite its common use in common law cases, this form of expression is not at all compatible with reasoning analogically. Indeed, reasoning by analogy would be analytically superfluous if there were rules of this sort and they worked as their form of expression seems to suggest. Such a rule could simply be applied to the facts of a new case. There would be no need to search out the precedents or analyze the facts of the precedents to identify similarities and differences between the precedents and the problem case. The principle of stare decisis itself would serve no purpose, nor would studying cases be so important. Rather, we would study primarily rules and collect them in textbooks that contain little other than the rules.

To avoid this undesired result, a basic principle of common law adjudication is that a judge is empowered to decide the case before the court and only the case before the court. A judge has no authority at common law to enact an authoritative general rule to govern parties and situations that were not before the court. The judge in Case 1 could not decide how Case 3 must be decided, however broadly she may craft a rule to explain the decision in Case 1. In all likelihood, the judge in Case 1 had not considered the facts of Cases 3 et seq. when crafting the general rule. Its mechanical application in later cases may yield a thoughtless and arbitrary result. Moreover, the parties in the later cases are entitled to their days in court. They should not have their disputes resolved on the basis of the facts and arguments put before the court by others in Case 1 only because the language employed by the court in its opinion in Case 1 was sufficiently general to be so used.

This principle is reinforced by the practice of distinguishing between the *holding* of a precedent and its *dicta*. The holding is a statement that captures in a sentence or two the probable significance of a single precedent as a base point for reasoning by analogy in future cases. It summarizes the important facts in the precedent case—the facts that are likely to become a point of important similarity or difference between the precedent and a problem case, largely as perceived by the court in the precedent case. It also states the legal consequence that followed from those facts in that case. A holding technically is less general than a common law rule, which may be stated in a court's opinion but does not contain the particularities needed to convey the short story of the particular case. As will be seen, a common law rule may be used as a major premise in legal reasoning in the deductive form; a holding is used as a base point in analogical legal reasoning.

A holding summarizes what was decided in a single case in which the judge did not and could not decide an entire class of cases. It does not purport to determine the result in other cases involving different parties under different circumstances. Those cases will be decided when they materialize and will be treated in accordance with the holding of a precedent if they then are determined to be like the precedent in important respects. A holding may have broad implications for a class of future cases, but whether a problem case is within that class or not will be decided when the case materializes and is brought before a court.

Common law rules largely are part of the dicta of a case. The dicta include those statements in the court's opinion that go beyond what was necessary to decide the case before the court. Dicta lack the full status of law because they purport to exceed the powers of a common law judge. Dicta can be quite useful when predicting what the court will do or persuading someone of what that court should do in future cases because they often express truthfully the court's inclinations on matters it expects to come before it. But the holding of a case has the privileged status of "the law"; dicta merely forecast, in a vague and less reliable way, what the law is likely to become.

For example, the holding of Case 1 above is that an owner of property who is the victim of a theft can recover possession of the property from a purchaser who bought it from the thief, even if the purchaser did not know or have reason to know that it was buying stolen property. Without casting doubt on the holding in Case 1, the court in Case 3 properly can hold that an owner of property who is the victim of a fraud cannot recover possession of the property from a purchaser who, not knowing or having reason to know of the fraud, bought it from the perpetrator of the fraud. It thus decides that the difference between fraud and theft is an important difference that requires different treatment of the cases. Similarly, the court in Case 4 can hold that a purchaser who helped perpetrate a fraud on the original owner is not like the purchaser in Case 3, which decided only that the owner cannot recover possession of the property from an innocent purchaser—one who did not know and had no reason to know of the fraud. It thus decides that Case 4 is more like Case 2, in which the owner sued the perpetrator of the fraud himself, than it is like Case 3, in which the owner sued a subsequent purchaser who was not complicit in the fraud.

In each case as the law unfolds, the general rule announced in a prior case may be given effect only to the extent that the holding of the precedent and the principle of stare decisis are determined to require. It all depends on the finding of similarity or difference in the more important respects between the facts of the precedent and the facts of the problem case, not necessarily on the announced general rules that stand in substantial part as dicta. The general rule announced in Case 1 ("A person who purchases property from a seller who did not own the property does not acquire ownership and must return the property to the rightful owner") can be disregarded properly in Case 3 because it is dictum insofar as it is more general than the holding ("An owner of property who is the victim of a theft can recover possession of the property from a purchaser who bought it from the thief, even if the purchaser did not know or have reason to know that it was buying stolen property").

The analogical form captures significant aspects of legal reasoning at common law (and, it will be seen, in other settings). The horse trading illustration shows how the analogical form provides a vocabulary and frames an issue for decision and thus contributes to the rationality of legal thought. In Case 5, for example, a judge must decide whether one who, having heard rumors of the fraud, buys a horse from an innocent purchaser who bought it from one who took possession by fraud, is *more like* one who bought a horse fraudulently (Case 2) or from a thief (Case 1), or *more like* one who, not knowing or having reason to know of the fraud, bought a horse from one who took possession by fraud (Case 3). Legal arguments in Case 5 can be expected to address that legal issue, posed in the analogical form, through an analysis of factual similarities and differences in the cases.

But what does lead a court to determine that, for example, the difference between fraud and theft in Cases 1 and 3 is an important difference that requires different results in those two cases? Fraud and theft are alike in some respects because both are wrongful in the eyes of the law. But they are unlike in other respects because fraud at common law most often is a civil wrong, not punished by imprisonment, while theft at common law is more serious and is treated as a criminal wrong, punished by imprisonment. The courts often regard the difference here as more important than the similarity, at least when the subsequent purchaser is an innocent one. Similarly, the precedents are like Case 5 in some respects because the original owner is the victim of wrongful behavior in all of these cases. They are unlike Case 5 in other respects because none involved a purchaser who had heard of the wrongful behavior and bought the horse from a purchaser who was wholly innocent and herself would win in a suit by the original owner, as in Case 3. The resolution of the key issues remains a mystery, so far as the formal analysis of analogical legal reasoning takes one.

The analogical form of legal reasoning leaves the crucial third step—the judgment of importance under the circumstances—wholly unaddressed. As Professor H. L. A. Hart put it:

> [T]hough "Treat like cases alike and different cases differently" is a central element in the idea of justice, it is by itself incomplete and, until supplemented, cannot afford any determinate guide to conduct. . . . [U]ntil it is established what resemblances and differences are relevant, "Treat like cases alike" must remain an empty form. To fill it we must know when, for the purposes in hand, cases are to be regarded as alike and what differences are relevant.[9]

. . .

The Deductive Form of Legal Reasoning

Legal reasoning in the deductive form is most closely associated with reasoning from enacted law, which principally consists of general rules. Such rules are found in a variety of official legal documents, such as constitutions, statutes, codes, regulations, and executive orders.[10] They usually are enacted and published by a group of people who are authorized to make law, such as the Congress, a state legislature, or executive and administrative agencies. For convenience, this [section] will speak primarily of statutes enacted by Congress or a state legislature, though what is said largely applies to other enacted rules (and, as will be seen in the next chapter, common law rules).

Legal reasoning in the deductive form from enacted rules differs from analogical legal reasoning in a number of key respects. First, the enactment of a rule usually occurs before any case governed by the rule materializes. The starting point for reasoning is the rule, not a case. Second, the principle of legislative supremacy, founded on principles of constitutional democracy, generally requires judges to play a subordinate role to the more democratic branches of government, which enact many rules, because the judges generally are less controllable by the electorate.[11] Accordingly, a judge has no authority to modify the language of a duly enacted rule as the case law interpreting that rule unfolds. Its expression remains static, as it was enacted, until the nonjudicial lawmaker amends it or repeals it. Nor may a judge ignore an applicable enacted rule, which displaces any inconsistent common law. Third, the static expression of enacted rules in abstract language leads legal reasoning from such rules to focus heavily on problems of language interpretation. The judicial task largely is to decide on the membership of a particular problem case in abstract classes of cases designated, in principle, by the language of the enacted rules.

A. The Deductive Form

Like analogical reasoning, deductive reasoning[12] is familiar in a variety of everyday nonlegal contexts. A common point of comparison is to the rules of a game. In the board game "Monopoly," for example, it is a rule that any player who passes "Go" receives $200 unless that player is on his way to "Jail." It is easy to determine when a player named Oscar passes "Go," not being on his way to "Jail." Oscar's entitlement to $200 then follows automatically. Deductive reasoning also is used extensively in more serious settings. A teacher may announce that (only and all) students who answer 90 percent or more of the questions correctly on a test will receive an "A." If Martha then answers 92 percent correctly on a test, it should follow automatically that she is entitled to an "A." It follows as automatically that she is not so entitled if she answers correctly fewer than 90 percent of the questions on the test.

In the abstract, this version of deductive reasoning requires three steps. First, having reviewed the factual situation superficially, one must establish a relevant *major premise* (if a player passes "Go," not being on the way to "Jail," then the player gets $200; only if a student answers correctly 90 percent or more of the questions on a test shall the student receive an "A"). Second, one must formulate a *minor premise* in the language of the major premise (Oscar passed "Go," not being on his way to jail; Martha scored 92 percent on a test). Third, one must use the relationship of the major and minor premises to yield a necessary *conclusion* (Oscar is entitled to $200; Martha is entitled to an "A").

Logicians call this form of reasoning a *syllogism*. The conclusion of a valid syllogism follows necessarily from the premises. Thus,

MAJOR PREMISE:	All men are mortal;
MINOR PREMISE:	Socrates is a man;
CONCLUSION:	Socrates is mortal.

A syllogism is "valid" if the conclusion must be true *if* the premises are true. In other words, only someone who is crazy or stupid would deny that Socrates is mortal while accepting both that all men are mortal and that Socrates is a man. A syllogism is "sound" when it is valid and the premises in fact are true. A conclusion that is supported by a sound syllogism is true because a logically valid syllogism transfers the truth of the premises to the conclusion. If supported only by a valid syllogism, the truth of the conclusion remains contingent on the unknown truth of the premises.

. . .

B. Cases within the Deductive Form

. . . [L]egal reasoning in the deductive form requires that lawyers and judges (1) identify an authoritative rule that serves as a major premise, (2) characterize the facts of a problem case in language that serves as a minor premise, and (3) interpret the rule in relation to the facts to reach a sound conclusion. At least in controversial cases, however, the conclusion to a legal syllogism based on enacted law cannot be necessarily sound from a logical point of view. The rules refer to abstract classes of cases and do not themselves supply the particularities that are needed to decide a problem case. The membership of a particular case within an abstract class of cases designated by the rule must be decided through a judgment of importance.

Reasoning in the analogical form may be employed by good lawyers and judges to help interpret an enacted rule in relation to the facts of a problem case and thus to decide how the rule applies in a particular case. Enacted rules, however, differ from common law rules because they lack roots in the case law; they supersede earlier decided cases and normally are announced before any problem case governed by the rule materializes. Consequently, no judicial precedents using the rule exist to serve as base points until some time after enactment. Reasoning analogically in a case governed by enacted law requires that other meaningful base points be found with which to compare and contrast a problem case.

The base points that are used when reasoning analogically to interpret and apply enacted law are both real and hypothetical situations. Of course, not just any real or hypothetical situation will shed light on the meaning of the Constitution, for example. There must be some reason for thinking that the base points are examples of what the Constitution permits or requires. There are several kinds of base points that can be employed meaningfully, even though such base points cannot have quite the authority that a precedent does at common law.

The text of an enacted rule is a starting point for finding meaningful base points. The text has a context that includes examples of its "intended" or accepted effect in concrete situations. The context includes the ordinary meanings of the terms used in the text and thus examples that come to the mind of a speaker of the English language. Such examples can be used as base points, though it is usually unnecessary to spell out these analogies. The ordinary meanings tend to be helpful to a lawyer or judge only in easier cases. The cases that require lawyerly skill are those in which analogies with contradictory implications can be drawn from the ordinary meanings of the text. Consequently, a legal analyst often must find base points that are more closely linked to the words of a text, as they are used in the text.

The context also includes precedent cases that interpret and apply the text, noncontroversial hypothetical cases, cases or situations governed by other rules within the same enactment, historical events or situations linked to the enactment of the rule, contemporary historical, economic, and social practices at the time of enactment, and examples given in the legislative history. These features of context, more than the ordinary meanings, may shed light directly on the words of an enacted text, as they are used in the text. The remainder of this section will illustrate how base points found in each of these features of the context can be used to interpret and apply a text.

Consider the freedom of speech clause of the first amendment to the U.S. Constitution: "Congress shall make no law . . . abridging the freedom of speech. . . . " Any lawyer reasoning from this general rule in the deductive form can be seriously misled. For example, the language on its face expresses a prohibition only on certain acts by Congress, but it also effectively prohibits such acts by the states.[13] There is no need to digress to explain how that came about, however, since it is almost universally accepted, at least for the time being. A more straightforward problem will be posed.

Assume two problem cases.[14] In one, a state enacted a penal statute that made it a crime for any person to hang the governor in effigy. Peter Protest was prosecuted under the statute for hanging the governor in effigy, which he admitted doing. Protest was convicted and sentenced to a jail term. He argued unsuccessfully in state court that his conviction was unconstitutional and should be set aside because the statute violated the freedom of speech clause. Protest appealed to the U.S. Supreme Court on that ground. In the second case, a state enacted a penal statute that made it a crime for any person to hang the governor. Neil Nihil was prosecuted under the statute for hanging the governor, which he admitted doing. Nihil was convicted and sentenced to a jail term. He argued unsuccessfully in state court that his conviction was unconstitutional and should be set aside because the statute violated the freedom of speech clause. Nihil, too, appealed to the U.S. Supreme Court on that ground.

By coincidence, the two cases reach the Supreme Court at the same time. It is reasonably certain that the Supreme Court would and should set aside Protest's conviction but not Nihil's. It would be expected to do so because a penal statute against hanging the governor in effigy unconstitutionally abridges the freedom of speech, but a penal statute against hanging the governor does not. The problem is to explain the reasoning that would justify these conclusions by, in necessary part, drawing a distinction between the two cases. One cannot justify setting aside Protest's conviction by an argument that as plausibly requires setting aside Nihil's conviction, nor can one justify upholding Nihil's conviction by an argument that as plausibly requires upholding Protest's conviction.

It is not possible to justify the two decisions by reasoning deductively from the text of the freedom of speech clause alone. That might lead to the conclusion that both convictions should be upheld. Neither hanging the governor in effigy nor hanging the governor are *speech,* if *speech* is interpreted in its ordinary sense to mean talking or using words. By this approach, neither act would be protected by the first amendment.

The Supreme Court, however, has given the freedom of speech clause a broader interpretation. In *Tinker v. Des Moines School District,*[15] for example, the Court held that a high school student who wore a black armband to a public school in 1965 to protest the Vietnam War could not be suspended from school for that reason. This protest was "symbolic speech" within the protection of the freedom of speech clause. In other cases, the Court has said that the first amendment generally protects freedom of expression. Paintings, photographs, music, and other forms of expression thus may be constitutionally protected, along with lectures criticizing official policies, campaign speeches, and other more obviously protected forms of expression. *Speech* within the meaning of the first amendment is not given its ordinary meaning.

The two decisions cannot be justified by giving *speech* the meaning *expression* (or *political expression*) and then reasoning deductively from a statement of the meaning of the freedom of speech clause. That would require that both convictions be set aside:

MAJOR PREMISE: If a state imposes a penalty on a person for engaging in expression, then the penalty shall be set aside as a violation of the first amendment.

MINOR PREMISE$_1$: Protest's conviction was a penalty imposed for engaging in expression.

CONCLUSION$_1$: Protest's conviction shall be set aside.

MINOR PREMISE$_2$: Nihil's conviction was a penalty imposed for engaging in expression.

CONCLUSION$_2$: Nihil's conviction shall be set aside.

Both hanging the governor in effigy and hanging the governor are ways of expressing one's political views. The latter is but a way to express them

forcefully. The mere fact that expression, even political expression, is a part of Protest's situation does not justify setting aside Protest's conviction. The same argument as plausibly justifies setting aside Nihil's conviction.

The two decisions can be more satisfactorily distinguished by reasoning in the analogical form. For example, the enacted rule, the freedom of speech clause, could be interpreted and applied in light of an analogy between the problem cases and a precedent case that interpreted the same enacted rule, such as the *Tinker* case. Thus, the court might defend its decision to set aside Protest's conviction by drawing an analogy between hanging the Governor in effigy and wearing a black armband to protest the Vietnam War. The *Tinker* case and Protest's case are alike in an important respect because both involve expressions of dissenting political views by symbolic means. The differences between wearing a black armband and hanging a governor in effigy probably are not important in this context. The difference between these symbolic expressions and Nihil's act of hanging the governor, however, probably is important because Nihil's act was violent.

Additionally, the Court might reason in the analogical form from noncontroversial hypothetical cases. It might reason that actually hanging the governor is in an important respect different from hanging the governor in effigy because the former is, after all, forceful and a breach of the peace. Hanging the governor in effigy is more like giving a public lecture criticizing the governor's policies. No one would suggest that such a lecture is not protected by the first amendment. By contrast, hanging the governor is more like hanging one's spouse, usually a clear case of murder. Hanging one's spouse, too, is "expression" in some respects. Ask a psychoanalyst. Yet no one would suggest plausibly that the first amendment protects murder.

The Court in Protest's and Nihil's cases might reason analogically from a third kind of base point—cases or situations governed by other rules within the same enactment. For example, the freedom of speech clause of the first amendment is conjoined in that amendment with the freedom of the press clause: "Congress shall make no law . . . abridging the freedom of speech, or the press. . . ." Neither Protest nor Nihil was exercising the freedom of the press in any plausible sense, so that clause does not itself apply. It probably would apply, however, to protect a published political cartoon depicting the governor hanging from a tree, in effigy or in the flesh. The Court in the two problem cases might reason that hanging the governor in effigy is in important respects like such a published political cartoon. Hanging the governor is not. It thus would look to cases or situations governed by other rules within the same enactment and thus within the context of the freedom of speech clause. Such base points would be meaningful when applying the first amendment because the Constitution should be interpreted as a whole to give it a coherent meaning.

Historical events or situations that are linked to the enactment of a rule are another kind of meaningful base point for reasoning in the analogical form to interpret and apply the rule. The history of events that inspired the first amendment is well known and is part of its context. A colonial government's suppression of Peter Zenger's expressions of political criticism, for example, is widely regarded as a prime example of the sort of thing the first amendment was enacted to prevent. The suppression of Zenger's press was referred to during the debates preceding ratification of that amendment and often compared to English practices in the colonies after 1760.[16] The Court might justify its decisions in the Protest and Nihil cases by reasoning that hanging the Governor in effigy is like what Zenger did but hanging the Governor is not, and all might agree. Some such reasoning might underlie the *Tinker* case. Wearing a black armband to protest the Vietnam War is in an important respect like what Zenger did.

. . .

It has been seen, then, that analysis of enacted law begins in any case with the language of the authoritative rule—the text. This starting point usefully identifies the issues that must be decided and establishes a uniform language for analysis and argument. The rule itself, however, stops short of determining the membership of a problem case within the abstract class of cases designated by the rule. The decision in a particular case governed by an enacted rule often is made by reasoning in the analogical form to interpret and apply the text.

Because enacted rules lack roots in the case law, such analogical reasoning requires that lawyers and judges look for base points in a number of settings that are related to the enactment—the con-

text. In addition to the examples suggested by the ordinary meanings of the words of an enactment, there are at least six features of the context that may contain useful base points. First, one may use judicial precedents applying the same enacted rule, much as one would use precedents at common law (the *Tinker* case.)[17] Second, one may use noncontroversial hypothetical cases (giving a lecture criticizing the governor's policies; hanging one's spouse). Third, one may use cases or situations governed by other rules in the same enactment (the published political cartoon). Fourth, one may use historical events or situations that are linked to the enactment of the rule (what Zenger did). Fifth, one may use contemporary historical, economic, and social practices at the time of enactment (importation of "cheap immigrant labor"). Sixth, one may use the legislative history (same). There is, of course, no guarantee that conflicting analogies may not be drawn from these many sources, or that any or all would be helpful in every case.

Endnotes

[1] This example and the next are adapted from Fuller, Positivism and Fidelity to Law: A Reply to Professor Hart, 71 Harv. L. Rev. 630, 662–666 (1958).

[2] The shorthand descriptions of cases may be thought of as "short, short stories," which rely on common images to fill in the details.

[3] K. Llewelyn, The Bramble Bush 12 (1951).

[4] J. Wisdom, A Feature of Wittgenstein's Technique, in J. Wisdom, Paradox and Discovery 90, 102 (1965).

[5] *Jurisdiction* refers to the scope of a court's power to decide cases lawfully. It may be defined in territorial, citizenship, functional, or other terms.

[6] The American Bar Association's Code of Professional Responsibility (1976) sets forth a comprehensive set of ethical considerations and disciplinary rules governing the practice of law in those jurisdictions in which it is adopted. Under EC 7-23, a lawyer who knows of "legal authority in the controlling jurisdiction directly adverse" to his client's position must disclose it.

[7] The illustrations are adapted from Fuller, The Forms and Limits of Adjudication, 92 Harv. L. Rev. 353, 375–376 (1978).

[8] E. Levi, An Introduction to Legal Reasoning 3–4 (1948).

[9] H. Hart, The Concept of Law 155 (1961).

[10] This form of reasoning also is employed with rules "enacted" by private persons in the form of contracts,

wills, corporate charters, and the like. What is said in this [section] applies to private law of this kind with some modifications.

[11] The principle of constitutional supremacy and the doctrine of judicial review make out an important exception to this statement. . . .

[12] The term *deductive reasoning* is used here to refer primarily to deduction in the form of a syllogism. Other forms of deduction are possible but seem to capture less well the most notable forms of legal reasoning.

[13] Technically, the freedom of speech clause is "incorporated" by judicial interpretation into the due process clause of the fourteenth amendment, which applies by its terms to the states. See Gitlow v. New York, 268 U.S. 652 (1925); Whitney v. California, 274 U.S. 357 (1927).

[14] This analysis is adapted from Burton, Comment on "Empty Ideas": Logical Positivist Analyses of Equality and Rules, 91 Yale L.J. 1136, 1139–1146 (1982).

[15] 393 U.S. 503 (1969).

[16] Z. Chaffee, Free Speech in the United States 21 (1969).

[17] Note, however, that the force of precedent need not be the same in common law, statutory, and constitutional cases. See Levi, The Sovereignty of the Courts, 50 U. Chi. L. Rev. 679 (1983).

The Judgment Intuitive

JOSEPH HUTCHESON, JR.

Many years ago, at the conclusion of a particularly difficult case both in point of law and of fact, tried to a court without a jury, the judge, a man of great learning and ability, announced from the Bench that since the narrow and prejudiced modern view of the obligations of a judge in the decision of causes prevented his resort to the judgment aleatory by the use of his "little, small dice" he would take the case under advisement, and, brooding over it, wait for his hunch.

To me, a young, indeed a very young lawyer, picked, while yet the dew was on me and I had just begun to sprout, from the classic gardens of a University, where I had been trained to regard the law as a system of rules and precedents, of categories and concepts, and the judge had been spoken of as an administrator, austere, remote, "his intellect a cold logic engine," who, in that rarified atmosphere in which he lived coldly and logically determined the relation of the facts of a particular case to some of these established precedents, it appeared

From *Cornell Law Quarterly*, Vol. 14 (1929), pp. 274–288.

that the judge was making a jest, and a very poor one, at that.

I had been trained to expect inexactitude from juries, but from the judge quite the reverse. I exalted in the law its tendency to formulize. I had a slot machine mind. I searched out categories and concepts and, having found them, worshiped them.

I paid homage to the law's supposed logical rigidity and exactitude. A logomachist, I believed in and practiced logomancy. I felt a sense of real pain when some legal concept in which I had put my faith as permanent, constructive and all-embracing opened like a broken net, allowing my fish to fall back into the legal sea. Paraphrasing Huxley, I believed that the great tragedy of the law was the slaying of a beautiful concept by an ugly fact. Always I looked for perfect formulas, fact proof, concepts so general, so flexible, that in their terms the jural relations of mankind could be stated, and I rejected most vigorously the suggestion that there was, or should be, anything fortuitous or by chance in the law. Like Jurgen I had been to the Master Philologist and with words he had conquered me.

I had studied the law in fragments and segments, in sections and compartments, and in my mind each compartment was nicely and logically arranged so that every case presented to me only the problem of arranging and re-arranging its facts until I could slip it into the compartment to which it belonged. The relation of landlord and tenant, of principal and agent, of bailor and bailee, of master and servant, these and a hundred others controlled my thinking and directed its processes.

Perceiving the law as a thing fullgrown, I believed that all of its processes were embraced in established categories, and I rejected most vigorously the suggestion that it still had life and growth, and if anyone had suggested that the judge had a right to feel, or hunch out a new category into which to place relations under his investigation, I should have repudiated the suggestion as unscientific and unsound, while as to the judge who dared to do it, I should have cried "Away with him! Away with him!"

I was too much influenced by the codifiers, by John Austin and Bentham, and by their passion for exactitude. I knew that in times past the law had grown through judicial action; that rights and processes had been invented by the judges, and that under their creative hand new remedies and new rights had flowered.

I knew that judges "are the depositories of the laws like the oracles, who must decide in all cases of doubt and are bound by an oath to decide according to the law of the land,"[1] but I believed that creation and evolution were at an end, that in modern law only deduction had place, and that the judges must decide "through being long personally accustomed to and acquainted with the judicial decisions of their predecessors."[2]

I recognized, of course, that in the preparation of the facts of a case there was room for intuition, for feeling; that there was a sixth sense which must be employed in searching out the evidence for clues, in order to assemble facts and more facts, but all of this before the evidence was in. I regarded the solution of the problem when the evidence was all in as a matter for determination by the judge by pure reason and reflection, and while I knew that juries might and did arrive at their verdicts by feeling, I repudiated as impossible the idea that good judges did the same.

I knew, of course, that some judges did follow "hunches,"—"guesses" I indignantly called them. I knew my Rabelais, and had laughed over without catching the true philosophy of old Judge Bridlegoose's trial, and roughly, in my youthful, scornful way, I recognized four kinds of judg-ments; first the cogitative, of and by reflection and logomancy; second, aleatory, of and by the dice; third, intuitive, of and by feeling or "hunching;" and fourth, asinine, of and by an ass; and in that same youthful, scornful way I regarded the last three as only variants of each other, the results of processes all alien to good judges.

As I grew older, however, and knew and understood better the judge to whom I have in this opening referred; as I associated more with real lawyers, whose intuitive faculties were developed and made acute by the use of a trained and cultivated imagination; as I read more after and came more under the spell of those great lawyers and judges whose thesis is that "modification is the life of the law,"[3] I came to see that "as long as the matter to be considered is debated in artificial terms, there is danger of being led by a technical definition to apply a certain name and then to deduce consequences which have no relation to the grounds on which the name was applied;"[4] that "the process of inclusion and exclusion so often applied in developing a rule, cannot end with its first enunciation. The rule announced must be deemed tentative. For the many and varying facts to which it will be applied cannot be foreseen."[5]

I came to see that "every opinion tends to become a law."[6] That "regulations, the wisdom, necessity and validity of which as applied to, existing conditions, are so apparent that they are now uniformly sustained, a century ago, or even half a century ago, would probably have been rejected as arbitrary and oppressive, . . . and that in a changing world it is impossible that it should be otherwise."[7]

I came to see that "resort to first principles is, in the last analysis, the only safe way to a solution of litigated matters."[8]

I came to see that instinct in the very nature of law itself is change, adaptation, conformity, and that the instrument for all of this change, this adaptation, this conformity, for the making and the nurturing of the law as a thing of life, is the power of the brooding mind, which in its very brooding makes, creates and changes jural relations, establishes philosophy, and drawing away from the outworn past, here a little, there a little, line upon line, precept upon precept, safely and firmly, bridges for the judicial mind to pass the abysses between that past and the new future.[9]

So, long before I came to the Bench, and while I was still uncertain as to the function of the judge, his office seeming pale and cold to me, too much concerned with logomachy; too much ruled by logomancy, I loved jury trials, for there, without any body of precedent to guide them, any established judicial recognition of their right so to do, nay, in the face of its denial to them, I could see those twelve men bringing equity, "the correction of that wherein by reason of its universality the law is deficient," into the law.

There they would sit, and hearing sometimes the "still, sad music of humanity," sometimes "catching sight through the darkness of the fateful threads of woven fire which connect error with its retribution," wrestling in civil cases with that legal Robot, "the reasonably prudent man," in criminal cases with that legal paradox, "beyond a reasonable doubt," would hunch out just verdict after verdict by the use of that sixth sense, that feeling, which flooding the mind with light, gives the intuitional flash necessary for the just decision.

Later, when I became more familiar with the practices in admiralty and in equity, more especially when, a judge in such cases, I felt the restless, eager ranging of the mind to overcome the confusion and the perplexities of the evidence, or of constricting and outworn concepts, and so to find the hidden truth, I knew that not only was it the practice of good judges to "feel" their way to a decision of a close and difficult case, but that in such cases any other practice was unsound. "For it is no paradox to say that in our most theoretical moods we may be nearest to our most practical applications."

I knew that "general propositions do not decide concrete cases. The decision will depend on a judgment or intuition more subtle than any articulate major premise."[10]

And so, after eleven years on the Bench following eighteen at the Bar, I, being well advised by observation and experience of what I am about to set down, have thought it both wise and decorous to now boldly affirm that "having well and exactly seen, surveyed, overlooked, reviewed, recognized, read and read over again, turned and tossed about, seriously perused and examined the preparitories, productions, evidences, proofs, allegations, depositions, cross speeches, contradictions . . . and other such like confects and spiceries, both at the one and the other side, as a good judge ought to do, I posit on the end of the table in my closet all the pokes and bags of the defendants—that being done I thereafter lay down upon the other end of the same table the bags and satchels of the plaintiff."[11]

Thereafter I proceed "to understand and resolve the obscurities of these various and seeming contrary passages in the law, which are laid claim to by the suitors and pleading parties," even just as Judge Bridlegoose did, with one difference only. "That when the matter is more plain, clear and liquid, that is to say, when there are fewer bags," and he would have used his "other large, great dice, fair and goodly ones," I decide the case more or less off hand and by rule of thumb. While when the case is difficult or involved, and turns upon a hairsbreadth of law or of fact, that is to say, "when there are many bags on the one side and on the other" and Judge Bridlegoose would have used his "little small dice," I, after canvassing all the available material at my command, and duly cogitating upon it, give my imagination play, and brooding over the cause, wait for the feeling, the hunch—that intuitive flash of understanding which makes the jump-spark connection between question and decision, and at the point where the path is darkest for the judicial feet, sheds its light along the way.

And more, "lest I be stoned in the street" for this admission, let me hasten to say to my brothers of the Bench and of the Bar, "my practice is therein the same with that of your other worships."[12]

For let me premise here, that in feeling or "hunching" out his decisions, the judge acts not differently from, but precisely as the lawyers do in working on their cases, with only this exception; that the lawyer, having a predetermined destination in view,—to win his law suit for his client—looks for and regards only those hunches which keep him in the path that he has chosen, while the judge, being merely on his way with a roving commission to find the just solution, will follow his hunch wherever it leads him, and when, following it, he meets the right solution face to face, he can cease his labors and blithely say to his troubled mind—"Trip no farther, pretty sweeting, journeys end in lovers meeting, as every wise man's son doth know."

Further, at the outset, I must premise that I speak now of the judgment or decision, the solution itself, as opposed to the apologia for that decision; the decree, as opposed to the logomachy, the effusion of the judge by which that decree is explained or excused. I speak of the judgment pronounced, as opposed to the rationalization by the judge on that pronouncement.

I speak, in short, of that act of definitive sentence of which Trinquamelle and Bridlegoose discoursed.

"But when you do these fine things" quoth Trinquamelle, "how do you, my fine friend, award your decrees and pronounce judgment?" "Even as your other worships," quoth Bridlegoose, "for I give out sentence in his favor unto whom hath befallen the best chance by the dice, judiciary, tribunian, pretorial, which comes first. So doth the law command."[13]

And not only do I set down boldly that I, "even as your other worships do," invoke and employ hunches in decisions, but I do affirm, and will presently show, that it is that tiptoe faculty of the mind which can feel and follow a hunch which makes not only the best gamblers, the best detectives, the best lawyers, the best judges, the materials of whose trades are the most chancey because most human, and the results of whose activities are for the same cause the most subject to uncertainty and the best attained by approximation, but it is that same faculty which has guided and will continue to guide the great scientists of the world,[14] and even those august dealers in certitude, the mathematicians themselves, to their most difficult solutions, which have opened and will continue to open hidden doors; which have widened and will ever widen man's horizon.

"For facts are sterile until there are minds capable of choosing between them and discerning those which conceal something, and recognizing that which is concealed. Minds which under the bare fact see the soul of the fact."[15]

I shall further affirm, and I think maintain, that the judge is, in the exercise of this faculty, popularly considered to be an attribute of only the gambler and the short story detective, in the most gallant of gallant companies; a philosopher among philosophers, and I shall not fear to stand, unrebuked and unashamed before my brothers of the Bench and Bar.

I remember once, in the trial of a patent case, where it was contended with great vigor on the one side that the patent evidenced invention of the highest order, and with equal vigor on the other that the device in question was merely a mechanical advance, I announced, almost without any sense of incongruity, that I would take the case under advisement, and after "having well and exactly seen and surveyed, overlooked, reviewed, read and read over again" etc., all of the briefs,

authorities and the record, would wait awhile before deciding to give my mind a chance to hunch it out, for if there was the flash of invention in the device my mind would give back an answering flash; while if there were none, my mind would, in a dully cogitative way, find only mechanical advance.

One of the lawyers, himself a "huncher," smiled and said—"Well, Your Honor, I am very grateful to you for having stated from the Bench what I have long believed, but have hesitated to avow, that next to the pure arbitrament of the dice in judicial decisions, the best chance for justice comes through the hunch." The other lawyer, with a different type of mind, only looked on as though impatient of such foolery.

But I, proceeding according to custom, got my hunch, found invention and infringement, and by the practice of logomachy so bassworded my opinion in support of my hunch that I found myself in the happy situation of having so satisfied the intuitive lawyer by the correctness of the hunch, and the logomachic lawyer by the spell of my logomancy, that both sides accepted the result and the cause was ended.

Now, what is this faculty? What are its springs, what its uses? Many men have spoken of it most beautifully. Some call it "intuition"—some, "imagination," this sensitiveness to new ideas, this power to range when the track is cold, this power to cast in ever widening circles to find a fresh scent, instead of standing baying where the track was lost.

"Imagination, that wondrous faculty, which properly controlled by experience and reflection, becomes the noblest attribute of man, the source of poetic genius, the instrument of discovery in science."[16]

"With accurate experiment and observation to work upon , imagination becomes the architect of physical theory. Newton's passage from a falling apple to a falling moon was an act of the prepared imagination without which the laws of Keppler could never have been traced to their foundations.

"Out of the facts of chemistry the constructive imagination of Dalton formed the atomic theory. Scientific men fight shy of the word because of its ultra-scientific connotations, but the fact is that without the exercise of this power our knowledge of nature would be a mere tabulation of co-existences and sequences."[17]

Again—"There is in the human intellect a

power of expansion, I might almost call it a power of creation, which is brought into play by the simple brooding upon facts. The legend of the spirit brooding over chaos may have originated in experience of this power."[18]

It is imagination which, from assembled facts, strikes out conclusions and establishes philosophies. "Science is analytical description. Philosophy is synthetic interpretation. The philosopher is not content to describe the fact; he wishes to ascertain its relation to experience in general, and thereby to get at its meaning and its worth. He combines things in interpretative synthesis. To observe processes and to construct means is science. To criticize and coordinate ends is philosophy. For a fact is nothing except in relation to desire; it is not complete except in relation to a purpose and a whole. Science, without philosophy, facts without perspective and valuation cannot save us from havoc and despair. Science gives us knowledge, but only philosophy can give us wisdom."[19] Cardozo expresses it most beautifully.

"Repeatedly, when one is hard beset, there are principles and precedents and analogies which may be pressed into the service of justice, if one has the perceiving eye to use them. It is not unlike the divinations of the scientist. His experiments must be made significant by the flash of a luminous hypothesis. For the creative process in law, and indeed in science generally, has a kinship to the creative process in art. Imagination, whether you call it scientific or artistic, is for each the faculty that creates."

"Learning is indeed necessary, but learning is the springboard by which imagination leaps to truth. The law has its piercing intuitions, its tense, apocalyptic moments. We gather together our principles and precedents and analogies, even at times our fictions, and summon them to yield the energy that will best attain the jural end. If our wand has the divining touch, it will seldom knock in vain. So it is that the conclusion, however deliberate and labored, has often the aspect of a lucky find."

" 'When I once asked the best administrator whom I knew,' writes Mr. Wallas, 'how he formed his decisions, he laughed, and with the air of letting out for the first time a guilty secret, said: "Oh, I always decide by feeling. So and so always decides by calculation, and that is no good." When again I asked an American judge, who is widely admired both for his skill and for his impartiality,

how he and his fellows formed their conclusions, he also laughed, and said that he would be stoned in the street if it were known that, after listening with full consciousness to all the evidence, and following as carefully as he could all the arguments, he wated until he "felt" one way or the other. He had elided the preparation and the brooding, or at least had come to think of them as processes of faint kinship with the state of mind that followed.' 'When the conclusion is there', says William James, 'we have already forgotten most of the steps preceding its attainment.' "[20]

Collision cases in admiralty furnish excellent illustrations of the difficulty of arriving at a sound fact conclusion by mere reasoning upon objective data. In these cases, as every trier knows, the adherents of the respective ships swear most lustily in true seagoing fashion for their side, and if a judge were compelled to decide the case by observing the demeanor of the witnesses alone, he would be in sad plight, for at the end of eleven years upon the Bench I am more convinced than ever that the shrewdest, smartest liars often make the most plausible and satisfactory witnesses, while the humblest and most honest fellows often, upon the witness stand, acquit themselves most badly.

Now, in such circumstances, deprived of the hunch which is the clue to judgment, "the intuition more subtle than any major premise," it would be better for the judge either to resort to the device of summoning the litigants "to personally compear before him a precise hundred years thereafter to answer to some interrogatories touching certain points which were not contained in the verbal defense"[21] or to use the "little small dice" in which Judge Bridlegoose placed so much confidence in tight cases, than to try to decide the case by rule of thumb upon the number of witnesses, or the strength of their asseverations.

Fortunately, however, in these cases the judge may, reconciling all the testimony reconcilable, and coming to the crux of the conflict, having a full and complete picture of the scene itself furnished by the actors, re-enact the drama and as the scene unfolds with the actors each in the place assigned by his own testimony, play the piece out, watching for the joints in the armor of proof, the crevices in the structure of the case or its defense. If the first run fails, the piece may be played over and over until finally, when it seems perhaps impossible to work any consistent truth out of it, the hunch comes, the scenes and the players are rearranged in accordance with it, and lo, it works successfully and in order.

If in other causes this faculty of "feeling" the correct decision is important to the successful trier of facts, it is doubly so in patent cases for "it is not easy to draw the line which separates the ordinary skill of a mechanic versed in his art, from the exercise of patentable invention, and the difficulty is especially great in the mechanic arts, where the successive steps in improvements are numerous, and where the changes and modifications are introduced by practical mechanics."[22]

Mr. Roberts, in his scholarly and exhaustive treatise on *Patentability and Patent Interpretation*, has this to say of the Krementz case:

"How the court could have arrived at the conclusion that this case furnished an instance of patentable invention is very difficult to understand in view of its attitude toward many other cases. . . . The explanation must be sought in the fact that no objective criteria has ever been recognized as decisive of the question of patentability, and that accordingly each case has had to be decided upon consideration of what the judicial mind could determine to be, on the whole, just and fair under the particular circumstances which happened to be present."[23]

Nevertheless, says Roberts, "There have frequently been unmistakable indications of perplexity on the part of the judges when endeavoring to assign reasons for their decision one way or another in cases where patentable invention was doubtful" and commenting further on the remarks of Mr. Justice Shiras in the Krementz case at page 559, parts of which are quoted herein, he concludes:—

"This was not a logical conclusion founded upon well established premises; it was only a confession of doubt, and a guess induced by special considerations which could not furnish a rule for the determination of any other question of a similar kind."[24]

To relieve this "perplexity" and to avoid these "confessions of doubt" and "guesses induced by special considerations" Mr. Roberts proposes to substitute for the subjective determination which breeds these undesirable conditions, decisions upon purely objective criteria, wholly dependent upon objective evidence, and wholly free from the influence of subjective bias.

"In short," says Roberts, "it is utterly futile to attempt to settle questions of patentability by resorting to merely subjective tests. All changes effected in the industrial arts are the production of thought, but it is impossible to discover any certain gauge for their rank in the inventive scale by simply contemplating the mental processes which have accomplished their origination."[25]

Mr. Roberts' effort, while vigorous and sustained, and supported by a wealth of learning, leaves me, as to the proposition that questions of invention may in all cases be decided upon purely objective criteria, without "the intuition more subtle than any major premise," cold.

Judges who have tried many patent cases, who have heard the testimony of experts, the one affirming the matter to be merely an advance in mechanical steps, the other to be invention of the highest order; the one affirming prior use, the other denying it; the one affirming it to be the flight of genius into new fields, the other, the mere dull trudging of an artisan, know that for a just decision of such causes no objective criteria can be relied on. They well know that there must be in the trier something of the same imaginative response to an idea, something of that same flash of genius that there is in the inventor, which all great patent judges have had, that intuitive brilliance of the imagination, that luminous quality of the mind, that can give back, where there is invention, an answering flash for flash.

Time was when judges, lawyers, law writers and teachers of the law refused to recognize in the judge this right and power of intuitive decision. It is true that the trial judge was always supposed to have superior facilities for decision, but these were objectivized in formulas, such as—the trial judge has the best opportunity of observing the witnesses, their demeanor,—the trial judge can see the play and interplay of forces as they operate in the actual clash of the trial.

Under the influence of this kind of logomachy, this sticking in the "skin" of thought, the trial judge's superior opportunity was granted, but the real reason for that superior position, that the trial creates an atmosphere springing from but more than the facts themselves, in which and out of which the judge may get the feeling which takes him to the desired end, was deliberately suppressed.

Later writers, however, not only recognize but emphasize this faculty, nowhere more attractively than in Judge Cardozo's lectures before the law schools of Yale University, in 1921[26] and Columbia University in 1927,[27] while Max Radin, in 1925, in a most sympathetic and charming way, takes the judge's works apart, and shows us how his wheels go round.[28]

He tells us, first, that the judge is a human being; that therefore he does not decide causes by the abstract application of rules of justice or of right, but having heard the cause and determined that the decision ought to go this way or that way, he then takes up his search for some category of the law into which the case will fit.

He tells us that the judge really feels or thinks a certain result seems desirable, and he then tries to make his decision accomplish that result. "What makes certain results seem desirable to a judge?" he asks, and answers his question that that seems desirable to the judge which, according to his training, his experience, and his general point of view, strikes him as the jural consequence that ought to flow from the facts, and he advises us that what gives the judge the struggle in the case is the effort so to state the reasons for his judgment that they will pass muster.

Now what is he saying except that the judge really decides by feeling, and not by judgment; by "hunching" and not by ratiocination, and that the ratiocination appears only in the opinion?

Now what is he saying but that the vital, motivating impulse for the decision is an intuitive sense of what is right or wrong for that cause, and that the astute judge, having so decided, enlists his every faculty and belabors his laggard mind, not only to justify that intuition to himself, but to make it pass muster with his critics?

There is nothing unreal or untrue about this picture of the judge, nor is there anything in it from which a just judge should turn away. It is true, and right that it is true, that judges really do try to select categories or concepts into which to place a particular case so as to produce what the judge regards as a righteous result, or, to avoid any confusion in the matter of morals, I will say a "proper result."

This is true. I think we should go further, and say it ought to be true. No reasoning applied to practical matters is ever really effective unless motivated by some impulse.

"Occasionally and frequently, the exercise of the judgment ought to end in absolute reservation.

We are not infallible, so we ought to be cautious."[29] "Sometimes," however, "if we would guide by the light of reason, we must let our minds be bold."[30]

The purely contemplative philosopher may project himself into an abstract field of contemplation where he reasons, but practical men, and in that judges must be included, must have impulses. The lawyer has them, and because he has them his work is tremendously important. If a lawyer merely reasoned abstractly and without motive he would do the judge no good. But the driving impulse to bring about his client's success not only makes him burrow industriously for precedents, and as industriously bring them forth, but also makes him belabor and cudgel the brains of the listening judge to bring him into agreement.

It is this factor in our jurisprudence, and only this, that clients have lawyers and that lawyers are advocates, which has made and will continue to make it safe for judges not only to state, but sometimes to make the law. "A thorough advocate in a just cause,—a penetrating mathematician facing the starry heavens, alike bear the semblance of divinity."

If the judge sat upon the Bench in a purely abstract relation to the cause, his opinion in difficult cases would be worth nothing. He must have some motive to fire his brains, to "let his mind be bold."

By the nature of his occupation he cannot have advocacy for either side of the case as such, so he becomes an advocate, an earnest one, for the—in a way—abstract solution. Having become such advocate, his mind reaches and strains and feels for that result. He says with Elihu, the son of Barachel, the Buzite, of the family of Ram—"There is a spirit in man, and the breath of the Almighty giveth him understanding. It is not the great that are wise, nor the aged that understand justice.——Hearken to me; I also will show mine opinion. For I am full of matter; the spirit within me constraineth me. Behold my belly is as wine which hath no vent. Like new wineskins it is ready to burst."[31]

And having travailed and reached his judgment, he struggles to bring up and pass in review before his eager mind all of the categories and concepts which he may find useful directly or by analogy, so as to select from them that which in his opinion will support his desired result.

For while the judge may be, he cannot appear to be, arbitrary. He must at least appear reasonable, and unless he can find a category which will at least "semblably" support his view, he will feel uncomfortable.

Sometimes he must almost invent a category, but he can never do quite that thing, for as we have seen, the growth of the law is interstitial, and the new category cannot be new enough wholly to avoid contact and placement in the midst of prior related categories.

But whether or not the judge is able in his opinion to present reasons for his hunch which will pass jural muster, he does and should decide difficult and complicated cases only when he has the feeling of the decision, which accounts for the beauty and the fire of some, and the labored dullness of many dissenting opinions.

All of us have known judges who can make the soundest judgments and write the dullest opinions on them; whose decisions were hardly ever affirmed for the reasons which they gave. Their difficulty was that while they had the flash, the intuitive power of judgment, they could not show it forth. While they could by an intuitive flash leap to a conclusion, just as an inventor can leap to his invention, just as often as an inventor cannot explain the result or fully understand it, so cannot and do not they.

There is not one among us but knows that while too often cases must be decided without that "feeling" which is the triumphant precursor of the just judgment, that just as "sometimes a light surprises the Christian while he sings," so sometimes, after long travail and struggle of the mind, there does come to the dullest of us, flooding the brain with the vigorous blood of decision, the hunch that there is, or is not invention; that there is or is not, anticipation, that the plaintiff should be protected by a decree, or should be denied protection. This hunch, sweeping aside hesitancy and doubt, takes the judge vigorously on to his decision; and yet, the cause decided, the way thither, which was for the blinding moment a blazing trail, becomes wholly lost to view.

Sometimes again that same intuition or hunch, which warming his brain and lighting his feet produced the decision, abides with the decider "while working his judgment backward" as he blazes his trail "from a desirable conclusion back to one or another of a stock of logical premises."[32]

It is such judicial intuitions, and the opinions lighted and warmed by the feeling which produced them, that not only give justice in the cause, but like a great white way, make plain in the wilderness the way of the Lord for judicial feet to follow.

If these views are even partly sound, and if to great advocacy and great judging the imaginative, the intuitional faculty is essential, should there not be some change in the methods of the study and of the teaching of the law in our great law schools? Should there not go along with the plain and severely logical study of jural relations study and reflection upon, and an endeavor to discover and develop, those processes of the mind by which such decisions are reached, those processes and faculties which, lifting the mind above the mass of constricting matter whether of confused fact or precedent that stands in the way of just decision, enable it by a kind of apocalyptic vision to "trace the hidden equities of divine reward, and to catch sight through the darkness, of the fateful threads of woven fire which connect error with its retribution?"[33]

Endnotes

[1] I Bl. Comm. 169.

[2] *Ibid.*

[3] Carter, Law, its Origin, Growth and Function (1907). "Modification implies growth. It is the life of the law." Washington v. Dawson, 264 U.S. 219, 236, 44 Sup. Ct. 302 (1924), Brandeis, J., dissenting.

[4] Guy v. Donald, 203 U.S. 399, 406, 27 Sup. Ct. 63 (1926).

[5] Washington v. Dawson, *supra* note [3].

[6] Lochner v. New York, 198 U.S. 45, 76, 25 Sup. Ct. 539 (1905).

[7] Euclid Valley v. Ambler, 272 U.S. 365, 47 Sup. Ct. 114 (1926).

[8] Old Colony Trust Co. v. Sugarland Industries, 296 Fed. 129, 138 (S. D. Tex. 1924).

[9] "Judges do and must legislate, but they can do so only interstitially. They are confined from Molar to molecular motions. A common law judge could not say, I think the doctrine of consideration a bit of historical nonsense, and shall not enforce it in my court. No more could a judge exercising the limited jurisdiction of admiralty say I think well of the common law rules of master and servant, and propose to introduce them here *en bloc.*" Southern Pacific v. Jensen, 244 U.S. 205, 221, 37 Sup. Ct. 524 (1917), Holmes, J., dissenting.

[10] *Ibid.*

[11] Rabelais, Book III, c. 39.

[12] *Ibid.*

[13] *Ibid.*

[14] "The method of science indeed is the method of the Chancery Court—it involves the collection of all available evidence and the subjection of all such evidence to the most searching examination and cross examination." Gregory, Discovery, the Spirit and Service of Science 166, quoting H. E. Armstrong.

[15] *Ibid.*, at 170, quoting Henri Poincare.

[16] Address to the Royal Society of England, November 3, 1859, Sir Benjamin Brodie, quoted from Fragments of Science, 109.

[17] "Scientific use of the Imagination" Address delivered before the British Association at Liverpool, Sept. 16, 1860 by Tyndall, quoted from Fragments of Science, 111.

[18] *Ibid.*, at 114.

[19] Durant, Story of Philosophy.

[20] Cardozo, Paradoxes of Legal Science (1928) 59, 60.

[21] Rabelais, Book III, c. 44.

[22] Krementz v. S. Cottle Co., 148 U.S. 559.

[23] Roberts, Patentability, and Patent Interpretation 181.

[24] *Ibid.*, at 181.

[25] *Ibid.*, at 247.

[26] Cardozo, the Nature of the Judicial Process (1921).

[27] *Supra* note [20].

[28] Radin, *Theory of Judicial Decision* (1925), 2 Am. B. A. J. 359.

[29] *Op. cit. supra* note [14], at 36, quoting Faraday.

[30] Burns v. Bryan, 264 U.S. 504, 520, 44 Sup. Ct. 412 (1923), Brandeis, J., dissenting.

[31] Job, Chapter 32, verses 9, 10, 18, 19.

[32] *Supra* note 28.

[33] Ruskin, Sesame and Lilies.

Study Questions

1. Hutcheson cautions that, even though judicial decisions are always arbitrary, they cannot be allowed to *appear* that way. What danger is there in allowing judges openly and candidly to follow their feelings and hunches? What if their feelings lead to evil decisions? Does Hutcheson assume that judges' hunches will guide them to just and "right" results? If so, is the assumption likely to be correct?

2. What (if any) are the differences between Hutcheson's criticisms of the traditional, formalistic, and apolitical conception of legal reasoning and the criticisms of Tushnet (in Section A)? Are both claiming that judicial decisions rest on the personal views and values of the judge? Would Tushnet be willing to trust the "hunches" of Hutcheson's judge?

3. Based on your reading of the material in this chapter, how would you decide Burton's Cases 4 and 5? How would you decide what "rules" Cases 1, 2, and 3 stand for? And how would your understanding of those cases guide your resolution of 4 and 5?

Cases for Further Reflection

Home Building and Loan Association v. Blaisdell
290 U.S. 398 (1934)
United States Supreme Court

While the specific point of law at stake in this case is not as dramatic as those raised in other cases we have encountered, *Blaisdell* directly confronts one of the core questions put by this chapter: To what degree should discerning the meaning of the Constitution rely on the intent of those who wrote it, as oppposed to the perceived changing demands and needs of a later society? Consider, while you read, these questions: If the "original intent" of the authors of the "contract clause" so clearly applies to the facts of this case, how can Chief Justice Hughes justify ignoring it? Should any deference be paid to that original intent at all? What is it that had changed between 1787 and 1931 to permit Hughes to decide as he did? What is left of a written constitution if the "plain meaning" of the document can be disregarded?

[In 1933, Minnesota enacted the Mortgage Moratorium Law. The law was intended to place limitations on the rights of banks and other lending institutions to foreclose on clients who had defaulted on their mortgages. The law was designed as an emergency measure to help protect homeowners from the ravages of the Great Depression. The Blaisdells defaulted on their loan payments to Home Building and Loan, and the company tried to foreclose; the Blaisdells blocked foreclosure by invoking the moratorium law. The company then went to court, arguing that the law violated the "contracts clause" of Article I, Section 10 of the Constitution: "No State shall . . . pass any . . . Law impairing the Obligation of Contracts." The Minnesota Supreme Court upheld the law and the company appealed to the U.S. Supreme Court.]

Hughes [Chief Justice] . . .

In determining whether the provision for this temporary and conditional relief exceeds the power of the State by reason of the clause in the Federal Constitution prohibiting impairment of the obligations of contracts, we must consider the relation of emergency to constitutional power, the historical setting of the contract clause, the development of the jurisprudence of this Court in the construction of that clause, and the principles of construction which we may consider to be established.

Emergency does not create power. Emergency does not increase granted power or remove or diminish the restrictions imposed upon power granted or reserved. The Constitution was adopted in a period of grave emergency. Its grants of power to the Federal Government and its limitations of the power of the States were determined in the light of emergency and they are not altered by emergency. . . .

The constitutional question presented in the light of an emergency is whether the power possessed embraces the particular exercise of it in response to particular conditions. . . . When the provisions of the Constitution, in grant of restriction, are specific, so particularized as not to admit of construction, no question is presented. Thus, emergency would not permit a State to have more than two Senators in the Congress, or permit the election of President by a general popular vote without regard to the number of electors to which the States are respectively entitled, or permit the States to "coin money" or to "make anything but gold and silver coin a tender in payment of debts." But where constitutional grants and limitations of power are set forth in general clauses, which afford a broad outline, the process of construction is essential to fill in the details. That is true of the contract clause. . . .

In the construction of the contract clause, the debates in the Constitutional Convention are of little aid. But the reasons which led to the adoption of that clause, and of the other prohibitions of Section 10 of Article I, are not left in doubt and have frequently been described with eloquent emphasis. The widespread distress following the revolutionary period, and the plight of debtors, had called forth in the States an ignoble array of legislative schemes for the defeat of creditors and the invasion of contractual obligations. Legislative interferences had been so numerous and extreme that the confidence essential to prosperous trade had been undermined and the utter destruction of credit was threatened "The sober people of America" were convinced that some "thorough reform" was needed which would "inspire a general prudence and industry, and give a regular course to the business of society." The Federalist, No. 44. It was necessary to interpose the restraining power of a central authority in order to secure the foundations even of "private faith." . . .

But full recognition of the occasion and general purpose of the clause does not suffice to fix its precise scope. Nor does an examination of the details of prior legislation in the States yield criteria which can be considered controlling. To ascertain the scope of the constitutional prohibition we examine the course of judicial decisions in its application. These put it beyond question that the prohibition is not an absolute one and is not to be read with literal exactness like a mathematical formula. . . .

The obligation of a contract is "the law which binds the parties to perform their agreement." This Court has said that " . . . [n]othing can be more material to the obligation than the means of enforcement. . . . The ideas of validity and remedy are inseparable, and both are parts of the obligation, which is guaranteed by the Constitution against invasion." . . . [But it] "is competent for the States to change the form of the remedy, or to modify it otherwise, as they may see fit, provided no substantial right secured by the contract is thereby impaired. No attempt has been made to fix definitely the line between alterations of the remedy, which are to be deemed legitimate, and those which under the form of modifying the remedy, impair substantial rights. Every case must be determined upon its own circumstances" . . . [and] "[i]n all such cases the question becomes, therefore, one of reasonableness, and of that the legislature is primarily the judge." . . .

The policy of protection contracts against impairment presupposes the maintenance of a government by virtue of which contractual relations are worth while,—a government which retains adequate authority to secure the peace and good order of society. This principle of harmonizing the constitutional prohibition with the necessary residuum of state power has had progressive recognition in the decisions of this Court. . . .

The legislature cannot "bargain away the public health or the public morals." Thus, the constitutional provision against the impairment of contracts was held not to be violated by an amendment of the state constitution which put an end to a lottery theretofore authorized by the legislature. . . . A similar rule has been applied to the control by the State of the sale of intoxicating liquors. The States retain adequate power to protect the public health against the maintenance of nuisances despite insistence upon existing contracts. Legislation to protect the public safety comes within the same category of reserved power. . . .

The argument is pressed that in the cases we have cited the obligation of contracts was affected only incidentally. This argument proceeds upon a misconception. The question is not whether the legislative action affects contracts incidentally, or directly or indirectly, but whether the legislation is addressed to a legitimate end and the measures taken are reasonable and appropriate to that end. Another argument, which comes more closely to the point, is that the state power may be addressed directly to the prevention of the enforcement of contracts only when these are of a sort which the legislature in its discretion may denounce as being in themselves hostile to public morals, or public health, safety or welfare, or where the prohibition is merely of injurious practices; that interference with the enforcement of other and valid contracts acording to appropriate legal procedure, although the interference is temporary and for a public purpose, is not permissible. . . . Undoubtedly, whatever is reserved of state power must be consistent with the fair intent of the constitutional limitation of that power. . . . This principle precludes a construction which would permit the State to adopt as its policy the repudiation of debts or the destruction of contracts or the denial of means to enforce them. But it does not follow that conditions may not arise in which a temporary restraint of enforcement may be consistent with the spirit and purpose of the constitutional provision and thus be found to be within the range of the reserved power of the State to protect the vital interests of the community. . . .

Whatever doubt there may have been that the protective power of the State, its police power, may be exercised—without violating the true intent of the provision of the Federal Constitution—in directly preventing the immediate and literal enforcement of contractual obligations, by a temporary and conditional restraint, where vital public interests would otherwise suffer, was removed by our decisions relating to the enforcement of provisions of leases during a period of scarcity of housing. Marcus Brown Holding Co. v. Feldman, 256 U.S. 170 (1921); Edgar A. Levy Leasing Co. v. Siegel, 258 U.S. 242 (1922). . . . The statutes of New York, declaring that a public emergency existed, directly interfered with the enforcement of covenants for the surrender of the possession of premises on the expiration of leases. Within the City of New York and contiguous counties, the owners of dwellings, including apartment and tenement houses . . . , were wholly deprived until November 1, 1922, of all possessory remedies for the purpose of removing from their premises the tenants or occupants in possession when the laws took effect, . . . providing the tenants or occupants were ready, able and willing to pay a reasonable rent or price for their use and occupation. . . .

It is manifest from this review of our decisions that there has been a growing appreciation of public needs and of the necessity of finding ground for a rational compromise between individual rights and public welfare. The settlement and consequent contraction of the public domain, the pressure of a constantly increasing density of population, the interrelation of the activities of our people and the complexity of our economic interests, have inevitably led to an increased use of the organization of society in order to protect the very bases of individual opportunity. Where, in earlier days, it was thought that only the concerns of individuals or of classes were involved, and that those of the State itself were touched only remotely, it has later been found that the fundamental interests of the State are directly affected; and the question is no longer merely that of one party to a contract as against another, but of the use of reasonable means to safeguard the economic structure upon which the good of all depends.

It is no answer to say that this public need was not apprehended a century ago, or to insist that what the provision of the Constitution meant to the vision of that day it must mean to the vision of our time. If by the statement that what the Constitution meant at the time of its adoption it means to-day, it is intended to say that the great clauses of the Constitution must be confined to the interpretation which the framers, with the conditions and outlook of their time, would have placed upon them, the statement carries its own refutation. It was to guard against such a narrow conception that Chief Justice Marshal uttered the memorable warning— "We must never forget that it is a *constitution* we are expounding" (McCulloch v. Maryland, 4 Wheat. 316, 407)—"a constitution intended to endure for ages to come, and consequently, to be adapted to the various *crises* of human affairs." When we are dealing with the words of the Constitution, said this Court in Missouri v. Holland, 252 U.S. 416, 433, "we must realize that they have called into life a being the development of which could not have been foreseen completely by the most gifted of its begetters. . . . The case before us must be considered in the light of our whole experience and not merely in that of what was said a hundred years ago."

When we consider the contract clause and the decisions which have expounded it in harmony with the essential reserved power of the States to protect the security of their peoples, we find no warrant for the conclusion that the clause has been warped by these decisions from its proper signifi-

cance or that the founders of our Government would have interpreted the clause differently had they had occasion to assume that responsibility in the conditions of the later day. The vast body of law which has been developed was unknown to the fathers, but it is believed to have preserved the essential content and the spirit of the Constitution. With a growing recognition of public needs and the relation of individual right to public security, the court has sought to prevent the perversion of the clause through its use as an instrument to throttle the capacity of the States to protect their fundamental interests. This development is a growth from the seeds which the fathers planted. . . .

Applying the criteria established by our decisions we conclude:

1. An emergency existed in Minnesota which furnished a proper occasion for the exercise of the reserved power of the State to protect the vital interests of the community. . . . As the Supreme Court of Minnesota said, the economic emergency which threatened "the loss of homes and lands which furnish those in possession the necessary shelter and means of subsistence" was a "potent cause" for the enactment of the statute.

2. The legislation was addressed to a legitimate end, that is, the legislation was not for the mere advantage of particular individuals but for the protection of a basic interest of society.

3. In view of the nature of the contracts in question—mortgages of unquestionable validity— the relief afforded and justified by the emergency, in order not to contravene the constitutional provision, could only be of a character appropriate to that emergency and could be granted only upon reasonable conditions.

4. The conditions upon which the period of redemption is extended do not appear to be unreasonable. . . . The relief afforded by the statute has regard to the interest of mortgagees as well as to the interest of mortgagors. The legislation seeks to prevent the impending ruin of both by a considerate measure of relief. . . .

5. The legislation is temporary in operation. It is limited to the exigency which called it forth. . . .

We are of the opinion that the Minnesota statute as here applied does not violate the contract clause of the Federal Constitution. Whether the legislation is wise or unwise as a matter of policy is a question with which we are not concerned. . . .

Judgment affirmed.

Sutherland, [Justice,] joined by Van Devanter, McReynolds, and Butler, [Justices], dissenting. . . .

The whole aim of construction, as applied to a provision of the Constitution, is to discover the meaning, to ascertain and give effect to the intent, of its framers and the people who adopted it. The necessities which gave rise to the provision, the controversies which preceded, as well as the conflicts of opinion which were settled by its adoption, are matters to be considered to enable us to arrive at a correct result. The history of the times, the state of things existing when the provision was framed and adopted, should be looked to in order to ascertain the mischief and the remedy. As nearly as possible we should place ourselves in the condition of those who framed and adopted it. . . .

An application of these principles to the question under review removes any doubt, if otherwise there would be any, that the contract impairment clause denies to the several states the power to mitigate hard consequences resulting to debtors from financial or economic exigencies by an impairment of the obligation of contracts of indebtedness. A candid consideration of the history and circumstances which led up to and accompanied the framing and adoption of this clause will demonstrate conclusively that it was framed and adopted with the specific and studied purpose of preventing legislation designed to relieve debtors *especially* in time of financial distress. . . .

Following the Revolution, and prior to the adoption of the Constitution, the American people found themselves in a greatly impoverished condition. Their commerce had been well-nigh annihilated. They were not only without luxuries, but in great degree were destitute of the ordinary comforts and necessities of life. In these circumstances they incurred indebtedness in the purchase of imported goods and otherwise, far beyond their capacity to pay. . . .

In an attempt to meet the situation recourse was had to the legislatures of the several states under the Confederation; and these bodies passed, among other acts, the following: laws providing for the emission of bills of credit and making them legal tender for the payment of debts, and providing also for such payment by the delivery of specific property at a fixed valuation; instalment laws, authorizing payment of overdue obligations

at future intervals of time; stay laws and laws temporarily closing access to the courts; and laws discriminating against British creditors. . . .

In the midst of this confused, gloomy, and seriously exigent condition of affairs, the Constitutional Convention of 1787 met at Philadelphia. . . . Shortly prior to the meeting of the Convention, Madison had assailed a bill pending in the Virginia Assembly, proposing the payment of private debts in three annual instalments on the ground that "no legislative principle could vindicate such an interposition of the law in private contracts." . . .

In the plan of government especially urged by Sherman and Ellsworth there was an article proposing that the legislatures of the individual states ought not to possess a right to emit bills of credit, etc., "or in any manner to obstruct or impede the recovery of debts, whereby the interests of foreigners or the citizens of any other state may be affected." And on July 13, 1787, Congress in New York, acutely conscious of the evils engendered by state laws interfering with existing contracts, passed the Northwest Territory Ordinance, which contained the clause: "And, in the just preservation of rights and property, it is understood and declared, that no law ought ever to be made or have force in the said territory, that shall, in any manner whatever, interfere with or affect private contracts, or engagements, bona fide, and without fraud previously formed." It is not surprising, therefore, that, after the Convention had adopted the clauses, no state shall "emit bills of credit," or "make any thing but gold and silver coin a tender in payment of debts," Mr. King moved to add a "prohibition on the states to interfere in private contracts." This was opposed by Gouverneur Morris and Colonel Mason. Colonel Mason thought that this would be carrying the restraint too far; that cases would happen that could not be foreseen where some kind of interference would be essential. This was on August 28. But Mason's view did not prevail, for, on September 14 following, the first clause of Art. I, §10, was altered so as to include the provision, "No state shall . . . pass any . . . law impairing the obligation of contracts," and in that form it was adopted.

Luther Martin, in an address to the Maryland House of Delegates, declared his reasons for voting against the provision. He said that he considered there might be times of such great public calamity and distress as should render it the duty of a government in some measure to interfere by passing laws totally or partially stopping courts of justice, or authorizing the debtor to pay by instalments; that such regulations had been found necessary in most of all of the states "to prevent the wealthy creditor and the moneyed man from totally destroying the poor, though industrious debtor. Such times may again arrive." And he was apprehensive of any proposal which took from the respective states the power to give their debtor citizens "a moment's indulgence, however necessary it might be, and however desirous to grant them aid."

On the other hand, Sherman and Ellsworth defended the provision in a letter to the Governor of Connecticut. In the course of the Virginia debates, Randolph declared that the prohibition would be promotive of virtue and justice, and preventive of injustice and fraud; and he pointed out that the reputation of the people had suffered because of frequent interferences by the state legislatures with private contracts. . . .

The provision was strongly defended in The Federalist, both by Hamilton in No. 7 and Madison in No. 44. . . .

Contemporaneous history is replete with evidence of the sharp conflict of opinion with respect to the advisability of adopting the clause. . . .

If it be possible by resort to the testimony of history to put any question of constitutional intent beyond the domain of uncertainty, the foregoing leaves no reasonable ground upon which to base a denial that the clause of the Constitution now under consideration was meant to foreclose state action impairing the obligation of contracts *primarily and especially* in respect of such action aimed at giving relief to debtors *in time of emergency*. And if further proof be required to strengthen what already is inexpugnable, such proof will be found in the previous decisions of this court. . . .

The present exigency is nothing new. From the beginning of our existence as a nation, periods of depression, of industrial failure, of financial distress, of unpaid and unpayable indebtedness, have alternated with years of plenty. . . .

The defense of the Minnesota law is made upon grounds which were discountenanced by the makers of the Constitution and have many times been rejected by this court. That defense should not now succeed because it constitutes an effort to overthrow the constitutional provision by an appeal to facts and circumstances identical with those which brought it into existence. With due regard for the processes of logical thinking, it legitimately cannot be urged that conditions which produced the rule may now be invoked to destroy it. . . .

I quite agree with the opinion of the court that whether the legislation under review is wise or unwise is a matter with which we have nothing to do. Whether it is likely to work well or work ill presents a question entirely irrelevant to the issue. The only legitimate inquiry we can make is whether it is constitutional. If it is not, its virtues, if it have any, cannot save it; if it is, its faults cannot be invoked to accomplish its destruction. If the provisions of the Constitution be not upheld when they pinch as well as when they comfort, they may as well be abandoned. Being unable to reach any other conclusion than that the Minnesota statute infringes the constitutional restriction under review, I have no choice but to say so.

Cardozo, [Justice] [unpublished concurring opinion].

"We must never forget that it is *a constitution* we are expounding." Marshall, C.J., in McCulloch v. Maryland. . . . "A constitution [is] intended to endure for ages to come, and, consequently, to be adapted to the various *crises* of human affairs." Ibid. . . .

"The case before us must be considered in the light of our whole experience and not merely in that of what was said a hundred years ago." Holmes, J. in Missouri v. Holland. . . .

A hundred years ago when this court decided Bronson v. Kinzie . . . property might be taken without due process of law through the legislation of the states, and the courts of the nation were powerless to give redress, unless indeed they could find that a contract had been broken. Dartmouth College v. Woodward . . . ; Fletcher v. Peck. . . . The judges of those courts had not yet begun to speak of the police power except in an off hand way or in expounding the effect of the commerce clause upon local regulations. The License Cases. . . . Due process in the states was whatever the states ordained. In such circumstances there was jeopardy, or the threat of it, in encroachment, however slight, upon the obligation to adhere to the letter of a contract. Once reject that test, and no other was available, or so it might well have seemed. The states could not be kept within the limits of reason and fair dealing for such restraints were then unknown as curbs upon their power. It was either all or nothing.

The Fourteenth Amendment came, and with it a profound change in the relation betweeen the federal government and the governments of the states. No longer were the states invested with arbitrary power. Their statutes affecting property or liberty were brought within supervision of independent courts and subjected to the rule of reason. The dilemma of "all or nothing" no longer stared us in the face.

Upon the basis of that amendment, a vast body of law unknown to the fathers has been built in treatise and decision. The economic and social changes wrought by the industial revolution and by the growth of population have made it necessary for government at this day to do a thousand things that were beyond the experience or the thought of a century ago. With the growing recognition of this need, courts have awakened to the truth that the contract clause is perverted from its proper meaning when it throttles the capacity of the states to exert their governmental power in response to crying needs. Block v. Hirsh . . . ; Marcus Brown Co. v. Feldman . . . ; Levy Leasing Co. v. Siegel. . . . The early cases dealth with the problem as one affecting the conflicting rights and interests of individuals and classes. This was the attitude of the courts up to the Fourteenth Amendment; and the tendency to some extent persisted even later. Edwards v. Kearzey . . . ; Burnitz v. Beverly. . . . The rights and interests of the state itself were involved, as it seemed, only indirectly and remotely, if they were thought to be involved at all. We know better in these days, with the passing of the frontier and of the unpeopled spaces of the west. With these and other changes, the welfare of the social organism in any of its parts is bound up more inseparably than ever with the welfare of the whole. A gospel of laissez-faire—of individual initiative—of thrift and industry and sacrifice—may be inadequate in that great society we live in to point the way to salvation, at least for economic life. The state when it acts today by statutes like the one before us is not furthering the selfish good of individuals or classes as ends of ultimate validity. It is furthering its own good by maintaining the economic structure on which the good of all depends. Such at least is its endeavor, however much it miss the mark. The attainment of that end, so august and impersonal, will not be barred and thwarted by the obstruction of a contract set up along the way.

Looking back over the century, one perceives a process of evolution too strong to be set back. The decisions brought together by the Chief Justice [Hughes] show with impressive force how the court in its interpretation of the contract clause has been feeling its way toward a rational compromise between private rights and public welfare. From the beginning it was seen that something must be subtracted from the words of the Constitution in all their literal and stark significance. This was forcefully pointed out by Johnson, J., in Ogden v. Saunders, 12 Wheat. 213, 286. At first refuge was found in the distinction between right and remedy with all its bewildering refinements. Gradually the distinction was perceived to be inadequate. The search was for a broader base, for a division that would separate the lawful and the forbidden by lines more closely in correspondence with the necessities of government. The Fourteenth Amendment was seen to point the way. Contracts were still to be preserved. There was to be no arbitrary destruction of their binding force, nor any arbitrary impairment. There was to be no impairment, even though not arbitrary, except with the limits of fairness, or moderation, and the pressing and emergent need. But a promise exchanged between individuals was not to paralyze the state in its endeavor in times of direful crisis to keep its lifeblood flowing.

To hold this may be inconsistent with things that men said in 1787 when expounding to compatriots the newly written constitution. They did not see the changes in the relation between states and nation or in the play of social forces that lay hidden in the womb of time. It may be inconsistent with things that they believed or took for granted. Their beliefs to be significant must be adjusted to the world they knew. It is not in my judgment inconsistent with what they say today nor with what today they would believe, if they were called upon to interpret "in the light of our whole experience" the constitution that they framed for the needs of an expanding future.

With this supplemental statement I concur in all that has been written in the opinion of the court.

Cruzan v. Director, Missouri
Department of Health
88-1503; 58 U.S.L.W. 4916 (1989)
United States Supreme Court

This case, representing the Court's first foray into the legal and moral debate over the "right to die," created immediate and predictable controversy when it was handed down in June 1989. Of concern to us here are the various views offered by members of the Court on the legitimate basis of and proper scope to be given to a "constitutionally protected liberty interest in refusing unwanted medical treatment." Does the due process clause of the Fourteenth Amendment include such an interest? Or does the "right to refuse" treatment have no basis in the Constitution whatever? May such an interest be limited by the competing interest of the state in preserving human life? Or does this interest rise to the level of a fundamental right of "medical self-determination," deeply rooted in our nation's traditions? How would the theories of legal reasoning and constitutional interpretation discussed in this chapter approach these questions? What theories of interpretation are invoked in (or suggested by) the majority, concurring, and dissenting opinions in the case?

Chief Justice Rehnquist delivered the opinion of the Court.

Petitioner Nancy Beth Cruzan was rendered incompetent as a result of severe injuries sustained during an automobile accident. Co-petitioners Lester and Joyce Cruzan, Nancy's parents and co-guardians, sought a court order directing the withdrawal of their daughter's artificial feeding and hydration equipment after it became apparent that she had virtually no chance of recovering her cognitive faculties. The Supreme Court of Missouri held that because there was no clear and convincing evidence of Nancy's desire to have life-sustaining treatment withdrawn under such circumstances, her parents lacked authority to effectuate such a request. We granted certiorari, 492 U. S.——(1989), and now affirm.

On the night of January 11, 1983, Nancy Cruzan lost control of her car as she traveled down Elm Road in Jasper County, Missouri. The vehicle overturned, and Cruzan was discovered lying face down in a ditch without detectable respiratory or cardiac function. Paramedics were able to restore her breathing and heartbeat at the accident site, and she was transported to a hospital in an unconscious state. An attending neurosurgeon diagnosed her as having sustained probable cerebral contusions compounded by significant anoxia (lack of oxygen). The Missouri trial court in this case found that permanent brain damage generally results after 6 minutes in an anoxic state; it was estimated that Cruzan was deprived of oxygen from 12 to 14 minutes. She remained in a coma for approximately three weeks and then progressed to an unconscious state in which she was able to orally ingest some nutrition. In order to ease feeding and further the recovery, surgeons implanted a gastrostomy feeding and hydration tube in Cruzan with the consent of her then husband. Subsequent rehabilitative efforts proved unavailing. She now lies in a Missouri state hospital in what is commonly referred to as a persistent vegetative state: generally, a condition in which a person exhibits motor reflexes but evinces no indications of significant cognitive function. The State of Missouri is bearing the cost of her care.

After it had become apparent that Nancy Cruzan had virtually no chance of regaining her mental faculties her parents asked hospital employees to terminate the artificial nutrition and hydration procedures. All agree that such a removal would cause her death. The employees refused to honor the request without court approval. The parents then sought and received authorization from the state trial court for termination. The court found that a person in Nancy's condition had a fundamental right under the State and Federal Constitutions to refuse or direct the withdrawal of "death prolonging procedures." . . . The court also found that Nancy's "expressed thoughts at age twenty-five in somewhat serious conversation with a housemate friend that if sick or injured she would not wish to continue her life unless she could live at least halfway normally suggests that given her present condition she would not wish to continue on with her nutrition and hydration." . . .

The Supreme Court of Missouri reversed by a divided vote. . . .

We granted certiorari to consider the question of whether Cruzan has a right under the United States Constitution which would require the hospital to withdraw life-sustaining treatment for her under these circumstances.

At common law, even the touching of one person by another without consent and without legal justification was a battery. . . . Before the turn of the century, this Court observed that "[n]o right is held more sacred, or is more carefully guarded, by the common law, than the right of every individual to the possession and control of his own person, free from all restraint or interference of others, unless by clear and unquestionable authority of law." . . . This notion of bodily integrity has been embodied in the requirement that informed consent is generally required for medical treatment. Justice Cardozo, while on the Court of Appeals of New York, aptly described this doctrine: "Every human being of adult years and sound mind has a right to determine what shall be done with his own body; and a surgeon who performs an operation without his patient's consent commits an assault, for which he is liable in damages." . . . The informed consent doctrine has become firmly entrenched in American tort law. . . .

The logical corollary of the doctrine of informed consent is that the patient generally possesses the right not to consent, that is, to refuse treatment. Until about 15 years ago and the seminal decision in *In re Quinlan*, 70 N. J. 10, 355 A. 2d 647, cert. denied *sub nom., Garger* v. *New Jersey*, 429 U. S. 922 (1976), the number of right-to-refuse-treatment decisions were relatively few. Most of the earlier cases involved patients who refused medical treatment forbidden by their religious beliefs, thus implicating First Amendment rights as well as common law rights of self-determination. More recently, however, with the advance of medical technology capable of sustaining life well past the point where natural forces would have brought certain death in earlier times, cases involving the right to refuse life-sustaining treatment have burgeoned. . . .

In the *Quinlan* case, young Karen Quinlan suffered severe brain damage as the result of anoxia, and entered a persistent vegetative state. Karen's father sought judicial approval to disconnect his daughter's respirator. The New Jersey Supreme Court granted the relief, holding that Karen had a right of privacy grounded in the Federal Constitution to terminate treatment. *In re Quinlan*, 70 N. J., at 38–42, 355 A. 2d at 662–664. Recognizing that this right was not absolute, however, the court balanced it against asserted state interests. Noting that the State's interest "weakens and the individual's right to privacy grows as the degree of bodily

invasion increases and the prognosis dims," the court concluded that the state interests had to give way in that case. . . . The court also concluded that the "only practical way" to prevent the loss of Karen's privacy right due to her incompetence was to allow her guardian and family to decide "whether she would exercise it in these circumstances." . . .

After *Quinlan*, however, most courts have based a right to refuse treatment either solely on the common law right to informed consent or on both the common law right and a constitutional privacy right.

. . .

As these cases demonstrate, the common-law doctrine of informed consent is viewed as generally encompassing the right of a competent individual to refuse medical treatment. Beyond that, these decisions demonstrate both similarity and diversity in their approach to decision of what all agree is a perplexing question with unusually strong moral and ethical overtones. State courts have available to them for decision a number of sources—state constitutions, statutes, and common law—which are not available to us. In this Court, the question is simply and starkly whether the United States Constitution prohibits Missouri from choosing the rule of decision which it did. This is the first case in which we have been squarely presented with the issue of whether the United States Constitution grants what is in common parlance referred to as a "right to die." We follow the judicious counsel of our decision in *Twin City Bank* v. *Nebeker*, 167 U. S. 196, 202 (1897), where we said that in deciding "a question of such magnitude and importance . . . it is the [better] part of wisdom not to attempt, by any general statement, to cover every possible phase of the subject."

The Fourteenth Amendment provides that no State shall "deprive any person of life, liberty, or property, without due process of law." The principle that a competent person has a constitutionally protected liberty interest in refusing unwanted medical treatment may be inferred from our prior decisions. In *Jacobson* v. *Massachusetts*, 197 U. S. 11, 24–30 (1905), for instance, the Court balanced an individual's liberty interest in declining an unwanted smallpox vaccine against the State's interest in preventing disease. Decisions prior to the incorporation of the Fourth Amendment into the

Fourteenth Amendment analyzed searches and seizures involving the body under the Due Process Clause and were thought to implicate substantial liberty interests. See, e. g., *Breithaupt* v. *Abrams*, 352 U. S. 432, 439 (1957) ("As against the right of an individual that his person be held inviolable . . . must be set the interests of society . . . ").

Just this Term, in the course of holding that a State's procedures for administering antipsychotic medication to prisoners were sufficient to satisfy due process concerns, we recognized that prisoners possess "a significant liberty interest in avoiding the unwanted administration of antipsychotic drugs under the Due Process Clause of the Fourteenth Amendment." *Washington* v. *Harper*,——U. S.——,——(1990) . . . ("The forcible injection of medication into a nonconsenting person's body represents a substantial interference with that person's liberty"). Still other cases support the recognition of a general liberty interest in refusing medical treatment. *Vitek* v. *Jones*, 445 U. S. 480, 494 (1980) (transfer to mental hospital coupled with mandatory behavior modification treatment implicated liberty interests); *Parham* v. *J. R.*, 442 U. S. 584, 600 (1979) ("a child, in common with adults, has a substantial liberty interest in not being confined unnecessarily for medical treatment").

But determining that a person has a "liberty interest" under the Due Process Clause does not end the inquiry; "whether respondent's constitutional rights have been violated must be determined by balancing his liberty interests against the relevant state interests."

. . .

. . . Here, Missouri has in effect recognized that under certain circumstances a surrogate may act for the patient in electing to have hydration and nutrition withdrawn in such a way as to cause death, but it has established a procedural safeguard to assure that the action of the surrogate conforms as best it may to the wishes expressed by the patient while competent. Missouri requires that evidence of the incompetent's wishes as to the withdrawal of treatment be proved by clear and convincing evidence. The question, then, is whether the United States Constitution forbids the establishment of this procedural requirement by the State. We hold that it does not.

Whether or not Missouri's clear and convincing evidence requirement comports with the United States Constitution depends in part on what interests the State may properly seek to protect in this situation. Missouri relies on its interest in the protection and preservation of human life, and there can be no gainsaying this interest. As a general matter, the States—indeed, all civilized nations—demonstrate their commitment to life by treating homicide as serious crime. Moreover, the majority of States in this country have laws imposing criminal penalties on one who assists another to commit suicide. We do not think a State is required to remain neutral in the face of an informed and voluntary decision by a physically-able adult to starve to death.

But in the context presented here, a State has more particular interests at stake. The choice between life and death is a deeply personal decision of obvious and overwhelming finality. We believe Missouri may legitimately seek to safeguard the personal element of this choice through the imposition of heightened evidentiary requirements. It cannot be disputed that the Due Process Clause protects an interest in life as well as an interest in refusing life-sustaining medical treatment. . . .

In our view, Missouri has permissibly sought to advance these interests through the adoption of a "clear and convincing" standard of proof to govern such proceedings.

. . .

In sum, we conclude that a State may apply a clear and convincing evidence standard in proceedings where a guardian seeks to discontinue nutrition and hydration of a person diagnosed to be in a persistent vegetative state.

. . .

Justice Scalia, concurring.

The various opinions in this case portray quite clearly the difficult, indeed agonizing, questions that are presented by the constantly increasing power of science to keep the human body alive for longer than any reasonable person would want to inhabit it. The States have begun to grapple with these problems through legislation. I am concerned, from the tenor of today's opinions, that we are poised to confuse that enterprise as successfully as we have confused the enterprise of legislating concerning abortion—requiring it to be conducted against a background of federal constitutional imperatives that are unknown because they are being newly crafted from Term to Term. That would be a great misfortune.

While I agree with the Court's analysis today, and therefore join in its opinion, I would have preferred that we announce, clearly and promptly, that the federal courts have no business in this field; that American law has always accorded the State the power to prevent, by force if necessary, suicide—including suicide by refusing to take appropriate measures necessary to preserve one's life; that the point at which life becomes "worthless," and the point at which the means necessary to preserve it become "extraordinary" or "inappropriate," are neither set forth in the Constitution nor known to the nine Justices of this Court any better than they are known to nine people picked at random from the Kansas City telephone directory; and hence, that even when it is demonstrated by clear and convincing evidence that a patient no longer wishes certain measures to be taken to preserve her life, it is up to the citizens of Missouri to decide, through their elected representatives, whether that wish will be honored. It is quite impossible (because the Constitution says nothing about the matter) that those citizens will decide upon a line less lawful than the one we would choose; and it is unlikely (because we know no more about "life-and-death" than they do) that they will decide upon a line less reasonable.

The text of the Due Process Clause does not protect individuals against deprivations of liberty *simpliciter*. It protects them against deprivations of liberty "without due process of law." To determine that such a deprivation would not occur if Nancy Cruzan were forced to take nourishment against her will, it is unnecessary to reopen the historically recurrent debate over whether "due process" includes substantive restrictions.

. . . It is at least true that no "substantive due process" claim can be maintained unless the claimant demonstrates that the State has deprived him of a right historically and traditionally protected against State interference . . . *Bowers* v. *Hardwick*, 478 U. S. 186, 192 (1986). . . . That cannot possibly be established here.

At common law in England, a suicide—defined as one who "deliberately puts an end to his own existence, or commits any unlawful malicious act, the consequence of which is his own death," 4 W. Blackstone, Commentaries *189—was criminally liable. . . . Although the States abolished

the penalties imposed by the common law (*i. e.*, forfeiture and ignominious burial), they did so to spare the innocent family, and not to legitimize the act. Case law at the time of the Fourteenth Amendment generally held that assisting suicide was a criminal offense. . . .

. . . And most States that did not explicitly prohibit assisted suicide in 1868 recognized, when the issue arose in the 50 years following the Fourteenth Amendment's ratification, that assisted and (in some cases) attempted suicide were unlawful. . . . Thus, "there is no significant support for the claim that a right to suicide is so rooted in our tradition that it may be deemed 'fundamental' or 'implicit in the concept of ordered liberty.' "

. . .

The dissents of Justices Brennan and Stevens make a plausible case for our intervention here only by embracing—the latter explicitly and the former by implication—a political principle that the States are free to adopt, but that is demonstrably not imposed by the Constitution. "The State," says Justice Brennan, "has no legitimate general interest in someone's life, completely abstracted from the interest of the person living that life, that could outweigh the person's choice *to avoid medical treatment*." . . . The italicized phrase sounds moderate enough, and is all that is needed to cover the present case—but the proposition cannot *logically* be so limited. One who accepts it must also accept, I think, that the State has no such legitimate interest that could outweigh "the person's choice *to put an end to her life*." Similarly, if one agrees with Justice Brennan that "the State's general interest in life must accede to Nancy Cruzan's particularized and intense interest in self-determination *in her choice of medical treatment*," . . . he must also believe that the State must accede to her "particularized and intense interest in self-determination *in her choice whether to continue living or to die*." For insofar as balancing the relative interests of the State and the individual is concerned, there is nothing distinctive about accepting death through the refusal of "medical treatment," as opposed to accepting it through the refusal of food, or through the failure to shut off the engine and get out of the car after parking in one's garage after work. Suppose that Nancy Cruzan were in precisely the condition she is in today, except that she could be fed and digest food and water *without* artificial assistance. How is the State's "interest"in keeping her alive thereby increased, or her interest in deciding whether she wants to continue living reduced? It seems to me, in other words, that Justice Brennan's position ultimately rests upon the proposition that it is none of the State's business if a person wants to commit suicide. Justice Stevens is explicit on the point: "Choices about death touch the core of liberty. . . . [N]ot much may be said with confidence about death unless it is said from faith, and that alone is reason enough to protect the freedom to conform choices about death to individual conscience." . . . This is a view that some societies have held, and that our States are free to adopt if they wish. But it is not a view imposed by our constitutional traditions, in which the power of the State to prohibit suicide is unquestionable.

What I have said above is not meant to suggest that I would think it desirable, if we were sure that Nancy Cruzan wanted to die, to keep her alive by the means at issue here. I assert only that the Constitution has nothing to say about the subject. To raise up a constitutional right here we would have to create out of nothing (for it exists neither in text nor tradition) some constitutional principle whereby, although the State may insist that an individual come in out of the cold and eat food, it may not insist that he take medicine; and although it may pump his stomach empty of poison he has ingested, it may not fill his stomach with food he has failed to ingest. Are there, then, no reasonable and humane limits that ought not to be exceeded in requiring an individual to preserve his own life? There obviously are, but they are not set forth in the Due Process Clause. What assures us that those limits will not be exceeded is the same constitutional guarantee that is the source of most of our protection—what protects us, for example, from being assessed a tax of 100% of our income above the subsistence level, from being forbidden to drive cars, or from being required to send our children to school for 10 hours a day, none of which horribles is categorically prohibited by the Constitution. Our salvation is the Equal Protection Clause, which requires the democratic majority to accept for themselves and their loved ones what they impose on you and me. This Court need not, and has no authority to, inject itself into every field of human activity where irrationality and oppression may theoretically occur, and if it tries to do so it will destroy itself.

Justice Brennan, with whom Justice Marshall and Justice Blackmun join, dissenting.

. . .

Today the Court, while tentatively accepting that there is some degree of constitutionally protected liberty interest in avoiding unwanted medical treatment, including life-sustaining medical treatment such as artificial nutrition and hydration, affirms the decision of the Missouri Supreme Court. The majority opinion, as I read it, would affirm that decision on the ground that a State may require "clear and convincing" evidence of Nancy Cruzan's prior decision to forgo life-sustaining treatment under circumstances such as hers in order to ensure that her actual wishes are honored. . . . Because I believe that Nancy Cruzan has a fundamental right to be free of unwanted artificial nutrition and hydration, which right is not outweighed by any interests of the State, and because I find that the improperly biased procedural obstacles imposed by the Missouri Supreme Court impermissibly burden that right, I respectfully dissent. Nancy Cruzan is entitled to choose to die with dignity.

. . .

The starting point for our legal analysis must be whether a competent person has a constitutional right to avoid unwanted medical care. Earlier this Term, this Court held that the Due Process Clause of the Fourteenth Amendment confers a significant liberty interest in avoiding unwanted medical treatment. *Washington* v. *Harper*, 494 U. S.——, ——(1990). Today, the Court concedes that our prior decisions "support the recognition of a general liberty interest in refusing medical treatment." . . . The Court, however, avoids discussing either the measure of that liberty interest or its application by assuming, for purposes of this case only, that a competent person has a constitutionally protected liberty interest in being free of unwanted artificial nutrition and hydration. . . . Justice O'Connor's opinion is less parsimonious. She openly affirms that "the Court has often deemed state incursions into the body repugnant to the interests protected by the Due Process Clause," that there is a liberty interest in avoiding unwanted medical treatment and that it encompasses the right to be free of "artificially delivered food and water." . . .

But if a competent person has a liberty interest to be free of unwanted medical treatment, as both the majority and Justice O'Connor concede, it must be fundamental. "We are dealing here with [a decision] which involves one of the basic civil rights of man." *Skinner* v. *Oklahoma ex rel. Williamson,* 316 U.S. 535, 541 (1942) (invalidating a statute authorizing sterilization of certain felons). Whatever other liberties protected by the Due Process Clause are fundamental, "those liberties that are 'deeply rooted in this Nation's history and tradition'" are among them. *Bowers* v. *Hardwick,* 478 U. S. 186, 192 (1986) (quoting *Moore* v. *East Cleveland, supra,* at 503) (plurality opinion). "Such a tradition commands respect in part because the Constitution carries the gloss of history." *Richmond Newspapers, Inc.* v. *Virginia,* 448 U. S. 555, 589 (1980) (Brennan, [Justice], concurring in judgment).

The right to be free from medical attention without consent, to determine what shall be done with one's own body, *is* deeply rooted in this Nation's traditions, as the majority acknowledges. . . . This right has long been "firmly entrenched in American tort law" and is securely grounded in the earliest common law. . . . " 'Anglo-American law starts with the premise of thorough-going self determination. It follows that each man is considered to be master of his own body, and he may, if he be of sound mind, expressly prohibit the performance of lifesaving surgery, or other medical treatment.' " . . . "The inviolability of the person" has been held as "sacred" and "carefully guarded" as any common law right. . . . Thus, freedom from unwanted medical attention is unquestionably among those principles "so rooted in the traditions and conscience of our people as to be ranked as fundamental." . . .

That there may be serious consequences involved in refusal of the medical treatment at issue here does not vitiate the right under our common law tradition of medical self-determination. It is "a well-established rule of general law . . . that it is the patient, not the physician, who ultimately decides if treatment—any treatment—is to be given at all. . . . The rule has never been qualified in its

application by either the nature or purpose of the treatment, or the gravity of the consequences of acceding to or foregoing it." . . . See also *Downer* v. *Veilleux,* 322 A. 2d 82, 91 (Me. 1974) ("The rationale of this rule lies in the fact that every competent adult has the right to forego treatment, or even cure, if it entails what for him are intolerable consequences or risks, however unwise his sense of values may be to others").

. . .

Although the right to be free of unwanted medical intervention, like other constitutionally protected interests, may not be absolute, no State interest could outweigh the rights of an individual in Nancy Cruzan's position. Whatever a State's possible interests in mandating life-support treatment under other circumstances, there is no good to be obtained here by Missouri's insistence that Nancy Cruzan remain on life-support systems if it is indeed her wish not to do so. Missouri does not claim, nor could it, that society as a whole will be benefited by Nancy's receiving medical treatment. No third party's situation will be improved and no harm to others will be averted. . . .

The only state interest asserted here is a general interest in the preservation of life. But the State has no legitimate general interest in someone's life, completely abstracted from the interest of the person living that life, that could outweigh the person's choice to avoid medical treatment. "[T]he regulation of constitutionally protected decisions . . . must be predicated on legitimate state concerns *other than* disagreement with the choice the individual has made. . . . Otherwise, the interest in liberty protected by the Due Process Clause would be a nullity." . . . Thus, the State's general interest in life must accede to Nancy Cruzan's particularized and intense interest in self-determination in her choice of medical treatment. There is simply nothing legitimately within the State's purview to be gained by superseding her decision. . . .

Suggestions for Further Reading

Alexander, L., "Constrained by Precedent," *Southern California Law Review*, Vol. 63 (1989): 3–64.

Arthur, J., *The Unfinished Constitution* (Belmont, Calif.: Wadsworth, 1989).

Bickel, A. M., *The Least Dangerous Branch*, 2nd ed. (New Haven, Conn.: Yale University Press, 1962).

Bork, R., *The Tempting of America: The Political Seduction of the Law* (New York: Free Press, 1990).

Brest, P., "The Fundamental Rights Controversy: The Essential Contradictions of Normative Constitutional Scholarship," *Yale Law Journal*, Vol. 90 (1981): 1062–1109.

Brest, P., and Levinson, S., *Processes of Constitutional Decisionmaking*, 2nd ed. (Boston: Little, Brown, 1983).

Burton, S. J., *An Introduction to Law and Legal Reasoning* (Boston: Little, Brown, 1985).

Carter, L., *Reason in Law* (Glennville, Ill.: Scott, Foresman, 1988).

Dworkin, R., *Taking Rights Seriously* (Cambridge, Mass.: Harvard University Press, 1977).

Dworkin, R., *A Matter of Principle* (Cambridge, Mass.: Harvard University Press, 1985).

Dworkin, R., *Law's Empire* (Cambridge, Mass.: Harvard University Press, 1986).

Ely, J. H., *Democracy and Distrust: A Theory of Judicial Review* (Cambridge, Mass.: Harvard University Press, 1980).

Golding, M., *Legal Reasoning* (New York: Alfred A. Knopf, 1984).

Grey, T. C., "Do We Have an Unwritten Constitution?" *Stanford Law Review*, Vol. 27 (1975): 703–771.

Grey, T. C., "The Constitution as Scripture," *Stanford Law Review*, Vol. 37 (1984): 1–25.

Law, S., "Homosexuality and the Social Meaning of Gender," *Wisconsin Law Review* (1988): 187–235.

Levi, E. H., *An Introduction to Legal Reasoning* (Chicago: University of Chicago Press, 1949).

Levinson, S., *Constitutional Faith* (Princeton, N.J.: Princeton University Press, 1988).

Levinson, S., and Mailloux, S., *Interpreting Law and Literature* (Evanston, Ill.: Northwestern University Press, 1988).

Lyons, D., "A Preface to Constitutional Theory," *Northern Kentucky Law Review*, Vol. 15 (1988): 459–477.

Moore, M. S., "The Interpretive Turn in Modern Theory," *Stanford Law Review*, Vol. 41 (1989):871–957.

Perry, M. J., *The Constitution, the Courts, and Human Rights* (New Haven, Conn.: Yale University Press, 1982).

Perry, M. J., *Morality, Politics, and Law* (New York: Oxford University Press, 1988).

Schauer, F., "An Essay on Constitutional Language," *UCLA Law Review*, Vol. 29 (1982): 797–832.

Symposium on Interpretation, *Southern California Law Review*, Vol. 58 (1985): 1–725.

Symposium on Interpreting the Ninth Amendment, *Chicago-Kent Law Review*, Vol. 64 (1988): 1–268.

Tribe, L. H., *American Constitutional Law*, 2nd ed. (Mineola, New York: The Foundation Press, 1988).

Tribe, L. H., *Abortion: The Clash of Absolutes* (New York: W. W. Norton, 1990).

Tushnet, M., *Red, White, and Blue: A Critical Analysis of Constitutional Law* (Cambridge, Mass.: Harvard University Press, 1988).

Weinrib, E. J., "Legal Formalism: On the Immanent Rationality of Law," *Yale Law Journal*, Vol. 97 (1988): 949–1116.

West, R., "Adjudication Is Not Interpretation: Some Reservations About the Law-as-Literature Movement," *Tennessee Law Review*, Vol. 54 (1987): 203–278.

White, J. B., *Justice as Translation* (Chicago: University of Chicago Press, 1990).

Chapter III

Freedom of Expression and the Law

During the 1984 Republican National Convention in Dallas, a small group of protestors, including Gregory Lee Johnson, marched through the streets of Dallas, winding up at Dallas City Hall. There Johnson unfurled an American flag, which had been handed to him during the march, and proceeded to burn it while shouting "Reagan, Mondale which will it be? Either one means World War Three" and "Red, white, and blue, we spit on you; you stand for plunder, you will go under." Johnson was arrested by Dallas police and charged with violating a Texas statute that made it a crime to desecrate a state or national flag. The statute defined "desecration" as defacing, damaging, or otherwise physically mistreating the flag "in a way that the actor knows will seriously offend one or more persons likely to observe or discover his action." Johnson insisted that his conduct was protected by the First Amendment to the Constitution and that the Texas law was therefore unconstitutional, In *Texas v. Johnson*, the Supreme Court agreed and touched off a heated, national debate on the limits of constitutional freedom.

Must the law permit Johnson to burn the flag even if this activity offends many others? Why must his freedom take priority over their desire that it be curtailed? How much offensive or shocking behavior must our society tolerate? Does the guarantee of freedom of speech in the First Amendment to the Constitution protect all forms of speech? Is obscene language or pornographic literature properly regarded as a constitutionally protected form of "expression"? What about racist insults? The symbols and chants of hate groups and bigots? What justifies the law's attempt to draw lines dividing permissible from impermissible speech? May only speech that harms others be restricted? Suppose Johnson had claimed that the tenets of his religion required him to burn the flag. Does the language of the First Amendment, protecting the free exercise

of religion, immunize his activity from state interference? If Johnson's religion condemned all forms of deference to a flag, may the state compel him to salute the flag in a public school classroom?

Section A probes the limits of and justifications for freedom of speech, canvassing the arguments raised in *Johnson* and then broadening to a consideration of the classic theory of freedom of conscience and expression defended by philosopher John Stuart Mill. This section asks us to consider how Mill's view would handle the tough cases of hate groups and racially assaultive speech.

Section B turns to a more specific, recurrent, and divisive issue: the constitutional and moral status of obscene and pornographic speech. The essays by Joel Feinberg and Catherine MacKinnon debate the nature and consequences of pornography.

A. *Freedom of Expression*

Introduction

In his opinion for the majority in *Texas v. Johnson*, now retired Justice William Brennan begins by asking whether burning the American flag as a form of political protest qualifies as "speech" that could at least potentially be protected by the "free-speech" clause of the First Amendment. The federal courts have long held that the "speech" shielded by that amendment is not restricted to verbal commu-

nication: various forms of "symbolic speech," including wearing armbands and staging sit-ins, have been found deserving of free-speech protection because such conduct is "expressive," it seeks to convey a message, to communicate an idea. Brennan argues that Johnson's conduct was expressive in this sense.

Since Johnson's speech is arguably protected by the Constitution, the Court probes the reasons offered by Texas to suppress it. Texas gives two reasons: Flag burning can be prohibited in order to (1) prevent disturbances of the peace, and

(2) protect the American flag as a symbol of national unity. Following the decision in *Brandenburg v. Ohio*, the Court says that Texas may suppress Johnson's freedom of expression consistent with the first reason, if what he did amounted to inciting a riot or imminent lawless action and in fact came close to doing that. No evidence suggested this was the case. The central question, then, focuses on the second claim: that flag burning can be prohibited because of the unique nature of the flag as a symbol of our nation. To this Brennan responds that, however dear the flag may be to many Americans, Johnson destroyed it to make a point, and the government may not "prohibit the expression of an idea simply because society finds the idea itself offensive or disagreeable."

In a passionate dissent, Chief Justice Rehnquist recites both history and poetry in an effort to marshall support for the view that the flag is a special case, a unique and revered symbol that must be protected. The flag is not simply another viewpoint competing with others; it transcends First Amendment values. Moreover, Johnson's conduct in burning the flag did not, Rehnquist thinks, deserve to be called "speech," even if symbolic. Burning the flag is more like a "fighting word," an insult undeserving of constitutional protection. Rehnquist ends on a broader point, asserting that "surely one of the high purposes of a democratic society is to legislate against conduct that is regarded as evil and profoundly offensive to the majority of people—whether it be murder, embezzlement, pollution, or flag burning."

Mill and the Harm Principle

John Stuart Mill's famous essay "On Liberty" aims to give a broader philosophical justification for the wide-ranging freedom of expression applauded as a constitutional principle by the majority in *Johnson*. The core of Mill's position, stated in the opening paragraph of our selection, has come to be called the "harm principle." This states that the only justification for limiting a person's freedom of thought and action is to prevent that person from harming others. His or her own good is never a sufficient reason for restricting a person's freedom, either physically or through use of the law. (Mill recognizes only two narrow exceptions to this principle: children and "backward" peoples.) Only when actions threaten to harm others will interference be legitimate; where conduct is primarily "self-regarding," it cannot be prohibited. That which is primarily self-regarding defines the sphere of individual liberty.

Mill isolates three types of liberty: (1) liberty of "tastes and pursuits," the liberty to frame and pursue a plan of life, to make a variety of personal, career, and life-style choices; (2) liberty of "association," the freedom to come together with others for purposes anywhere from marriage to clubs, from church to business; and (3) liberty of "thought and feeling," the freedom of conscience and expression. Mill is especially concerned with the last of these, since he believes it contributes crucially both to the individual and to the social good. For all we know, Mill claims, any given opinion or view may express the truth; if we squelch that opinion we are robbed ourselves of the opportunity to learn the truth, thus harming ourselves. Furthermore, the collision of differing and contrasting points of view and life-styles will be helpful in challenging us to justify our own convictions to ourselves; views that must be defended are thereby invigorated. And finally, if an opinion is false or a choice a poor one, these facts will be discovered sooner or later in their clash with contending perspectives; the truth will win out in the end.

Mill's theory firmly repudiates the view known as *paternalism*, the idea that interference with a person's liberty is justified in order to protect that person's own welfare or needs or interests; a restriction of your freedom for your own good. No one, Mill believes, should be told what to do with his or her life, assuming of course that he or she is a competent adult. Each of us has the best knowledge of what is in our own interests. The evil of paternalistic interference far outweighs any evil that a person may visit upon himself. This does not mean that Mill argues for a callous egoism: we certainly should encourage and assist others to take better care of themselves, to give up dangerous habits, to enrich their lives. But we may not coerce them into such things with the instrument of the law. Where the majority seeks to coerce the minority, Mill observes, the result is frequently intolerance, prejudice, and pain.

Some writers have suggested that the decisions of courts in cases like *Johnson*, and in cases dealing with obscenity, pornography, religious freedom, and so on, illustrate how the First Amendment "constitutionalizes" Mill's harm principle, so that the Constitution is read as an endorsement of the conception of liberty articulated by Mill. When reading the material throughout this chapter, you should ask yourself whether this is the case and whether such a reading of the Constitution is desirable.

Is it possible, for example, to frame or draft statutes or interpret constitutional language in a way that adequately defines what is to count as "harm" to another? Certain forms of harm are of course obvious and uncontroversial: deprivation of property and physical injury, for example. But to limit harm to such obvious forms would be unacceptably narrow. Most of us would agree that the law should prohibit assault (placing another in reasonable fear of imminent bodily harm) or libel (publication of facts about another with the aim of injuring his or her reputation). Plainly there are ways of "harming" someone without stealing his stereo or punching him in the nose. Harm it seems must include certain forms of psychological injury or distress. But this gives rise to another difficulty: How to shape the law so that further harms fall within the prohibitions of the harm principle without weakening that standard altogether by counting as "harmful" anything that displeases or offends. The freedom to do only that to which no one has any objection is limited indeed.

the truth. And it is for this reason that Mill so adamantly insists that there can be no orthodoxy, no publicly endorsed values in a truly open society. It is therefore no surprise that Mill bases his individualistic theory of liberty on the utilitarian principle of the "greatest good"—freedom of conscience and action is right and desirable solely because it brings about greater happiness for us today than any other arrangement—rather than upon an appeal to basic human rights or ancient and venerated traditions; for each of these would require a basis in ultimate truth which we cannot ascertain.

The fundamental problem with Mill's society, Kendall seems to argue, is its artificiality: it regards human community as little more than a debating club, defined by an overriding interest in a "truth" that by its own terms is made virtually unattainable. Real human communities, Kendall insists, often rank preservation of traditions and customs, ways of life that are esteemed as valuable, as more important than abstract "truth." And it is because such customs and traditions are necessary to human society, Kendall thinks, that our own constitutional democracy (or any society), to the extent that it incorporates Mill's ideals, becomes unstable: in allowing everyone to "do their own thing," common understandings, customs, and practices that bind a people together erode and ultimately disappear.

Criticisms of Mill

Political scientist Wilmoore Kendall is not so much concerned to press the foregoing questions about Mill's harm principle as to raise more basic worries about the foundational assumptions of Mill's "open society." Kendall believes that the tolerance exhibited by the society Mill urges upon us is not merely incidentally related to the idea that we can never be sure which viewpoints or opinions express the truth; it is in fact squarely based on a profound *skepticism* about values in particular and about truth in general. The cornerstone of Mill's argument, says Kendall, is the presupposition that no one can ever really be certain that something is

The Skokie Case: Speech by Hate Groups

In April 1977, residents of the Chicago suburb of Skokie were shocked to learn that the National Socialist Party of America, commonly known as the American Nazi Party, was planning to stage a "white-power" rally on the steps of Skokie's village hall on May 1. Nearly half of Skokie's population was at that time Jewish, and as many as twelve hundred of those were actual survivors of Hitler's persecution of European Jews. The members of the community forced village officials to obtain a court order preventing the rally and to pass ordinances prohibiting the dissemination of any material "which promotes and incites hatred against persons by reason of their race, national origin, or religion" or to "incite violence, hatred, abuse or hostility toward anyone based on race, religion, or ethnicity." Skokie maintained that neo-Nazi chants and signs or armbands bearing the swastika were racial slurs, unprotected by the First Amendment. Frank Collin, the head of the Nazi Party, with the help of the American Civil Liberties Union (ACLU), challenged the ordinances in federal court and won. The court found that the ordinances impermissibly limited freedom of speech. Frank Collin is quoted as saying: "The key to Skokie is that the right to free speech was denied us here, in Marquette Park. We fought in the courts from 1975 onward. We were constantly denied. . . . I've got to come up with something within the law, to use the law against our enemy, the Jew. . . . I used it [the First Amendment] at Skokie. I planned the reaction of the Jews. They are hysterical."[1]

Typical of the Nazi rhetoric during the confrontation is this comment: "We want to reach the good people—get the fierce anti-Semites who have to live among the Jews to come out of the woodwork and stand up for themselves. . . . Good. I hope they're terrified [the survivors]. I hope they're shocked. Because we're coming to get them again. I don't care if someone's mother or father or brother dies in the gas chambers. The unfortunate thing is not that there were six million Jews who died. The unfortunate thing is that there were so many Jewish survivors."[2]

The essay by Carl Cohen discusses the larger issues raised by the Skokie case: How much freedom of speech should a society have to put up with? Assuming that we believe in (and that our law endorses) something close to Mill's theory of free expression, how much offensive or shocking behavior has to be tolerated? Cohen answers that nothing spoken or published (save that which is defamatory), no matter how offensive or insulting, can legitimately be prohibited in a legal regime committed to freedom of speech. Cohen reviews a number of grounds upon which the prohibition of offensive or shocking speech has often been argued for: that it presents a "clear and present danger"; that is is an incitement to riot; that it constitutes "fighting words"; that it is obscene. While each of these arguments may apply in a limited number of cases, none of them, Cohen argues, can legitimately be stretched to cover the Skokie situation.

Racist Speech

The final two selections in this chapter together form a debate over a more recent free-speech controversy. Many college campuses in the last few years have experienced an alarming increase in various racial incidents, from racial graffiti in dorms to abusive racial slurs and epithets in the quad. As a consequence, several campuses have experimented with policies prohibiting "discriminatory harassment" or "personal vilification." Critics have argued that such policies run afoul of the First Amendment; and in 1988, a federal court in Michigan struck down a policy of the University of Michigan that prohibited "stigmatizing or victimizing" individuals or groups on the basis of "race, ethnicity, religion, sex, sexual orientation, creed, national origin, ancestry, age, marital status, handicap or Vietnam-era veteran status" by creating an "intimidating, hostile, or demeaning" educational environment. The court claimed that the terms of the policy were so vague and broad as to fail to pass constitutional muster.[3]

Should universities restrict racist speech? Insisting that "racist speech inflicts real harm, and that this harm is not trivial," law professor Charles Lawrence maintains that racial insults and slurs do not deserve protection, even under Mill's stringent theory. Assaultive speech does not communicate ideas; rather, it uses words like weapons. Its purpose is to hurt, not to inform. This makes such speech very much like "fighting words," a recognized exception to the First Amendment carved out by the Supreme Court in *Chaplinsky v. New Hampshire*. Furthermore, racial graffiti in residence halls constitutes an invasion of privacy and may be prohibited, Lawrence suggests, on that ground.

Constitutional scholar Gerald Gunther, discussing a recent effort at Stanford University to institute a racist speech policy, argues that such efforts are misguided and dangerous. Pointing to the Court's argument in *Texas v. Johnson*, Gunther claims that the First Amendment must continue to stand in the way of silencing speech simply because it is offensive, even to many. Efforts to suppress disagreeable speech, Gunther contends, spring largely from the complacent majority and are aimed at individuals at the political extremes. Yet it is precisely such complacency that the First

Amendment was designed to challenge, by assuring minorities of all kinds a right to be heard.

Endnotes

[1] Quoted in Donald Alexander Downs, *Nazis in Skokie* (Notre Dame, Ind.: University of Notre Dame Press, 1985), p. 28.

[2] *Ibid.*, pp. 28–29.

[3] See *Doe v. University of Michigan* 721 F. Supp. 852 (1989).

Texas v. Johnson
109 S. Ct. 2533 (1989)
United States Supreme Court

Justice Brennan delivered the opinion of the Court.

After publicly burning an American flag as a means of political protest, Gregory Lee Johnson was convicted of desecrating a flag in violation of Texas law. This case presents the question whether his conviction is consistent with the First Amendment. We hold that it is not.

I

While the Republican National Convention was taking place in Dallas in 1984, respondent Johnson participated in a political demonstration dubbed the "Republican War Chest Tour." As explained in literature distributed by the demonstrators and in speeches made by them, the purpose of this event was to protest the policies of the Reagan administration and of certain Dallas-based corporations. The demonstrators marched through the Dallas streets, chanting political slogans and stopping at several corporate locations to stage "die-ins" intended to dramatize the consequences of nuclear war. On several occasions they spray-painted the walls of buildings and overturned potted plants, but Johnson himself took no part in such activities. He did, however, accept an American flag handed to him by a fellow protestor who had taken it from a flag pole outside one of the targeted buildings.

The demonstration ended in front of Dallas City Hall, where Johnson unfurled the American flag, doused it with kerosene, and set it on fire. While the flag burned, the protestors chanted, "America, the red, white, and blue, we spit on you." After the demonstrators dispersed, a witness to the flag-burning collected the flag's remains and buried them in his backyard. No one was physically injured or threatened with injury, though several witnesses testified that they had been seriously offended by the flag-burning.

Of the approximately 100 demonstrators, Johnson alone was charged with a crime. The only criminal offense with which he was charged was the desecration of a venerated object in violation of Tex. Penal Code Ann. § 42.09 (a)(3) (1989).[1] After a trial, he was convicted, sentenced to one year in prison, and fined $2,000. The Court of Appeals for the Fifth District of Texas at Dallas affirmed Johnson's conviction, . . . but the Texas Court of Criminal Appeals reversed, . . . holding that the State could not, consistent with the First Amendment, punish Johnson for burning the flag in these circumstances.

. . .

II

Johnson was convicted of flag desecration for burning the flag rather than for uttering insulting words. This fact somewhat complicates our consideration of his conviction under the First Amendment. We must first determine whether Johnson's burning of the flag constituted expressive conduct, permitting him to invoke the First Amendment in challenging his conviction . . .

The First Amendment literally forbids the abridgement only of "speech," but we have long recognized that its protection does not end at the spoken or written word. While we have rejected "the view that an apparently limitless variety of conduct can be labeled 'speech' whenever the person engaging in the conduct intends thereby to express an idea," . . . we have acknowledged that conduct may be "sufficiently imbued with elements of communication to fall within the scope of the First and Fourteenth Amendments." . . .

In deciding whether particular conduct possesses sufficient communicative elements to bring the First Amendment into play, we have asked whether "[a]n intent to convey a particularized message was present, and [whether] the likelihood was great that the message would be understood by those who viewed it." . . . Hence, we have recognized the expressive nature of students' wearing of black armbands to protest American military involvement in Vietnam . . . of a sit-in by blacks in a "whites only" area to protest segregation . . . of the wearing of American military uniforms in a dramatic presentation criticizing American involvement in Vietnam . . . and of picketing about a wide variety of causes.

Especially pertinent to this case are our decisions recognizing the communicative nature of conduct relating to flags. Attaching a peace sign to the flag . . . saluting the flag . . . and displaying a red flag, . . . we have held, all may find shelter under the First Amendment. . . . That we have had little difficulty identifying an expressive element in conduct relating to flags should not be surprising. The very purpose of a national flag is to serve as a symbol of our country; it is, one might say, "the one visible manifestation of two hundred years of nationhood." . . . Thus, we have observed:

> "[T]he flag salute is a form of utterance. Symbolism is a primitive but effective way of communicating ideas. The use of an emblem or flag to symbolize some system, idea, institution, or personality, is a short cut from mind to mind. Causes and nations, political parties, lodges and ecclesiastical groups seek to knit the loyalty of their followings to a flag or banner, a color or design."

Pregnant with expressive content, the flag as readily signifies this Nation as does the combination of letters found in "America."

The State of Texas conceded for purposes of its oral argument in this case that Johnson's conduct was expressive conduct, . . . and this concession seems to us prudent. . . . Johnson burned an American flag as part—indeed, as the culmination—of a political demonstration that coincided with the convening of the Republican Party and its renomination of Ronald Reagan for President. The expressive, overtly political nature of this conduct was both intentional and overwhelmingly apparent. At his trial, Johnson explained his reasons for burning the flag as follows: "The American Flag

was burned as Ronald Reagan was being renominated as President. And a more powerful statement of symbolic speech, whether you agree with it or not, couldn't have been made at that time. It's quite a just position [juxtaposition]. We had new patriotism and no patriotism." . . . In these circumstances, Johnson's burning of the flag was conduct "sufficiently imbued with elements of communication" . . . to implicate the First Amendment.

III

The Government generally has a freer hand in restricting expressive conduct than it has in restricting the written or spoken word.

. . .

. . . [W]e must decide whether Texas has asserted an interest in support of Johnson's conviction that is unrelated to the suppression of expression. . . . The State offers two separate interests to justify this conviction: preventing breaches of the peace, and preserving the flag as a symbol of nationhood and national unity. We hold that the first interest is not implicated on this record and that the second is related to the suppression of expression.

A

Texas claims that its interest in preventing breaches of the peace justifies Johnson's conviction for flag desecration. However, no disturbance of the peace actually occurred or threatened to occur because of Johnson's burning of the flag. Although the State stresses the disruptive behavior of the protestors during their march toward City Hall, . . . it admits actual breach of the peace occurred at the time of the flagburning or in response to the flagburning." . . . The State's emphasis on the protestors' disorderly actions prior to arriving at City Hall is not only somewhat surprising given that no charges were brought on the basis of this conduct, but it also fails to show that a disturbance of the peace was a likely reaction to *Johnson's* conduct. The only evidence offered by the State at trial to show the reaction to Johnson's actions was the testimony of several persons who had been seriously offended by the flag-burning. . . .

The State's position, therefore, amounts to a claim that an audience that takes serious offense at particular expression is necessarily likely to disturb the peace and that the expression may be prohibited on this bases. Our precedents do not countenance such a presumption. On the contrary, they recognize that a principal "function of free speech under our system of government is to invite dispute. It may indeed best serve its high purpose when it induces a condition of unrest, creates dissatisfaction with conditions as they are, or even stirs people to anger." . . .

. . . It would be odd indeed to conclude *both* that "if it is the speaker's opinion that gives offense, that consequence is a reason for according it constitutional protection" . . . *and* that the Government may ban the expression of certain disagreeable ideas on the unsupported presumption that their very disagreeableness will provoke violence.

Thus, we have not permitted the Government to assume that every expression of a provocative idea will incite a riot, but have instead required careful consideration of the actual circumstances surrounding such expression, asking whether the expression "is directed to inciting or producing imminent lawless action and is likely to incite or produce such action." *Brandenburg* v. *Ohio*, 395 U.S. 444, 447 (1969) (reviewing circumstances surrounding rally and speeches by Ku Klux Klan). To accept Texas'[s] arguments that it need only demonstrate "the potential for a breach of the peace," . . . and that every flag-burning necessarily possesses that potential, would be to eviscerate our holding in *Brandenburg.* This we decline to do.

Nor does Johnson's expressive conduct fall within that small class of "fighting words" that are "likely to provoke the average person to retaliation, and thereby cause a breach of the peace." *Chaplinsky* v. *New Hampshire*, 315 U.S. 568, 574 (1942). No reasonable onlooker would have regarded Johnson's generalized expression of dissatisfaction with the policies of the Federal Government as a direct personal insult or an invitation to exchange fisticuffs. . . .

We thus conclude that the State's interest in maintaining order is not implicated on these facts. . . .

IV

It remains to consider whether the State's interest in preserving the flag as a symbol of nationhood and national unity justifies Johnson's conviction.

. . . Johnson was not, we add, prosecuted for the expression of just any idea; he was prosecuted for his expression of dissatisfaction with the policies of this country, expression situated at the core of our First Amendment values. . . .

Moreover, Johnson was prosecuted because he knew that his politically charged expression would cause "serious offense." If he had burned the flag as a means of disposing of it because it was dirty or torn, he would not have been convicted of flag desecration under this Texas law: federal law designates burning as the preferred means of disposing of a flag "when it is in such condition that it is no longer a fitting emblem for display," 36 U.S.C. § 176(k), and Texas has no quarrel with this means of disposal. . . . The Texas law is thus not aimed at protecting the physical integrity of the flag in all circumstances, but is designed instead to protect it only against impairments that would cause serious offense to others. . . .

Whether Johnson's treatment of the flag violated Texas law thus depended on the likely communicative impact of his expressive conduct. Our decision in *Boos* v. *Barry* [485 U.S. 312 (1988)] tells us that this restriction on Johnson's expression is content-based. In *Boos,* we considered the constitutionality of a law prohibiting "the display of any sign within 50 feet of a foreign embassy if that sign tends to bring that foreign government into 'public odium' or 'public disrepute.' " . . . Rejecting the argument that the law was content-neutral because it was justified by "our international law obligation to shield diplomats from speech that offends their dignity," . . . we held that a "[t]he emotive impact of speech on its audience is not a 'secondary effect' " unrelated to the content of the expression itself. . . .

According to the principles announced in *Boos,* Johnson's political expression was restricted because of the content of the message he conveyed. We must therefore subject the State's asserted interest in preserving the special symbolic character of the flag to "the most exacting scrutiny." . . . [2]

Texas argues that its interest in preserving the flag as a symbol of nationhood and national unity survives this close analysis. Quoting extensively from the writings of this Court chronicling the flag's historic and symbolic role in our society, the State emphasizes the ' "special place' " reserved for the flag in our Nation. . . . The State's argument is not that it has an interest simply in maintaining the flag as a symbol of *something*, no matter what it symbolizes; indeed, if that were the State's position, it would be difficult to see how that interest is endangered by highly symbolic conduct such as Johnson's. Rather, the State's claim is that it has an interest in preserving the flag as a symbol of *nationhood* and *national unity*, a symbol with a determinate range of meanings. . . . According to Texas, if one physically treats the flag in a way that would tend to cast doubt on either the idea that nationhood and national unity are the flag's referents or that national unity actually exists, the message conveyed thereby is a harmful one and therefore may be prohibited.

If there is a bedrock principle underlying the First Amendment, it is that the Government may not prohibit the expression of an idea simply because society finds the idea itself offensive or disagreeable. . . .

We have not recognized an exception to this principle even where our flag has been involved. In *Street* v. *New York*, 394 U.S. 576 (1969), we held that a State may not criminally punish a person for uttering words critical of the flag. Rejecting the argument that the conviction could be sustained on the ground that Street had "failed to show the respect for our national symbol which may properly be demanded of every citizen," we concluded that "the constitutionally guaranteed 'freedom to be intellectually . . . diverse or even contrary,' and the 'right to differ as to things that touch the heart of the existing order,' encompass the freedom to express publicly one's opinions about our flag, including those opinions which are defiant or contemptuous." . . . Nor may the Government, we have held, compel conduct that would evince respect for the flag. "To sustain the compulsory flag salute we are required to say that a Bill of Rights which guards the individual's right to speak his own mind, left it open to public authorities to compel him to utter what is not in his mind." . . .

In holding in *Barnette* that the Constitution did not leave this course open to the Government, Justice Jackson described one of our society's defining principles in words deserving of their frequent repetition: "If there is any fixed star in our constitutional constellation, it is that no official, high or petty, can prescribe what shall be orthodox in politics, nationalism, religion, or other matters of opinion or force citizens to confess by word or act their faith therein." . . . In *Spence*, we held that the same interest asserted by Texas here was insufficient to support a criminal conviction under a flag-misuse statute for the taping of a peace sign to an American flag. "Given the protected character of [Spence's] expression and in light of the fact that no interest the State may have in preserving the physical integrity of a privately owned flag was significantly impaired on these facts," we held, "the conviction must be invalidated." 418 U.S., at 415. . . .

In short, nothing in our precedents suggests that a State may foster its own view of the flag by prohibiting expressive conduct relating to it. To bring its argument outside our precedents, Texas attempts to convince us that even if its interest in preserving the flag's symbolic role does not allow it to prohibit words or some expressive conduct critical of the flag, it does permit it to forbid the outright destruction of the flag. The State's argument cannot depend here on the distinction between written or spoken words and nonverbal conduct. That distinction, we have shown, is of no moment where the nonverbal conduct is expressive, as it is here, and where the regulation of that conduct is related to expression, as it is here. . . . In addition, both *Barnette* and *Spence* involved expressive conduct, not only verbal communication, and both found that conduct protected.

Texas'[s] focus on the precise nature of Johnson's expression, moreover, misses the point of our prior decisions: their enduring lesson, that the Government may not prohibit expression simply because it disagrees with its message, is not dependent on the particular mode in which one chooses to express an idea. If we were to hold that a State may forbid flag-burning wherever it is likely to endanger the flag's symbolic role, but allow it wherever burning a flag promotes that role—as where, for example, a person ceremoniously burns a dirty flag—we would be saying that when it comes to impairing the flag's physical integrity, the flag itself may be used as a symbol—as a substitute for the written or spoken word or a "short cut from mind to mind"—only in one direction. We would be permitting a State to "prescribe what shall be orthodox" by saying that one may burn the flag to convey one's attitude toward it and its referents only if one does not endanger the flag's representation of nationhood and national unity. . . .

. . . To conclude that the Government may permit designated symbols to be used to communicate only a limited set of messages would be to enter territory having no discernible or defensible boundaries. Could the Government, on this theory, prohibit the burning of state flags? Of copies of the Presidential seal? Of the Constitution? In evaluating these choices under the First Amendment, how would we decide which symbols were sufficiently special to warrant this unique status? To do so, we would be forced to consult our own political preferences, and impose them on the citizenry, in the very way that the First Amendment forbids us to do. . . .

There is, moreover, no indication—either in the text of the Constitution or in our cases interpreting it—that a separate juridical category exists for the American flag alone. Indeed, we would not be surprised to learn that the persons who framed our Constitution and wrote the Amendment that we now construe were not known for their reverence for the Union Jack. The First Amendment does not guarantee that other concepts virtually sacred to our Nation as a whole—such as the principle that discrimination on the basis of race is odious and destructive—will go unquestioned in the marketplace of ideas. . . . We decline, therefore, to create for the flag an exception to the joust of principles protected by the First Amendment.

It is not the State's ends, but its means, to which we object. It cannot be gainsaid that there is a special place reserved for the flag in this Nation, and thus we do not doubt that the Government has a legitimate interest in making efforts to "preserv[e] the national flag as an unalloyed symbol of our country." . . . We reject the suggestion, urged at oral argument by counsel for Johnson, that the Government lacks "any state interest whatsoever" in regulating the manner in which the flag may be displayed. . . . Congress has, for example, enacted precatory regulations describing the proper treatment of the flag, . . . and we cast no doubt on the legitimacy of its interest in making such recommendations. To say that the Govern-

ment has an interest in encouraging proper treatment of the flag, however, is not to say that it may criminally punish a person for burning a flag as a means of political protest. . . .

We are fortified in today's conclusion by our conviction that forbidding criminal punishment for conduct such as Johnson's will not endanger the special role played by our flag or the feelings it inspires. To paraphrase Justice Holmes, we submit that nobody can suppose that this one gesture of an unknown man will change our Nation's attitude towards its flag. See *Abrams* v. *United States*, 250 U.S. 616, 628 (1919) (Holmes, J., dissenting). Indeed, Texas'[s] argument that the burning of an American flag " ' is an act having a high likelihood to cause a breach of the peace,' " . . . and its statute's implicit assumption that physical mistreatment of the flag will lead to "serious offense," tend to confirm that the flag's special role is not in danger; if it were, no one would riot or take offense because a flag had been burned.

We are tempted to say, in fact, that the flag's deservedly cherished place in our community will be strengthened, not weakened, by our holding today. Our decision is a reaffirmation of the principles of freedom and inclusiveness that the flag best reflects, and of the conviction that our toleration of criticism such as Johnson's is a sign and source of our strength. Indeed, one of the proudest images of our flag, the one immortalized in our own national anthem, is of the bombardment it survived at Fort McHenry. It is the Nation's resilience, not its rigidity, that Texas sees reflected in the flag—and it is that resilience that we reassert today.

The way to preserve the flag's special role is not to punish those who feel differently about these matters. It is to persuade them that they are wrong. "To courageous, self-reliant men, with confidence in the power of free and fearless reasoning applied through the processes of popular government, no danger flowing from speech can be deemed clear and present, unless the incidence of the evil apprehended is so imminent that it may befall before there is opportunity for full discussion. If there be time to expose through discussion the falsehood and fallacies, to avert the evil by the processes of education, the remedy to be applied is more speech, not enforced silence." *Whitney* v. *California*, 274 U.S. 357, 377 (1927) (Brandeis, J., concurring). And, precisely because it is our flag that is involved, one's response to the flag-burner may exploit the uniquely persuasive power of the flag itself. We can imagine no more appropriate response to burning a flag than waving one's own, no better way to counter a flag-burner's message than by saluting the flag that burns, no surer means of preserving the dignity even of the flag that burned than by—as one witness here did—according its remains a respectful burial. We do not consecrate the flag by punishing its desecration, for in doing so we dilute the freedom that this cherished emblem represents.

V

Johnson was convicted for engaging in expressive conduct. The State's interest in preventing breaches of the peace does not support his conviction because Johnson's conduct did not threaten to disturb the peace. Nor does the State's interest in preserving the flag as a symbol of nationhood and national unity justify his criminal conviction for engaging in political expression. The judgment of the Texas Court of Criminal Appeals is therefore

Affirmed.

Justice Kennedy, concurring.

I write not to qualify the words Justice Brennan chooses so well, for he says with power all that is necessary to explain our ruling. I join his opinion without reservation, but with a keen sense that this case, like others before us from time to time, exacts its personal toll. This prompts me to add to our pages these few remarks.

The case before us illustrates better than most that the judicial power is often difficult in its exercise. We cannot here ask another branch to share responsibility, as when the argument is made that a statute is flawed or incomplete. For we are presented with a clear and simple statute to be judged against a pure command of the Constitution. The outcome can be laid at no door but ours.

The hard fact is that sometimes we must make decisions we do not like. We make them because they are right, right in the sense that the law and the Constitution, as we see them, compel the result. And so great is our commitment to the process

that, except in the rare case, we do not pause to express distaste for the result, perhaps for fear of undermining a valued principle that dictates the decision. This is one of those rare cases.

Our colleagues in dissent advance powerful arguments why respondent may be convicted for his expression, reminding us that among those who will be dismayed by our holding will be some who have had the singular honor of carrying the flag in battle. And I agree that the flag holds a lonely place of honor in an age when absolutes are distrusted and simple truths are burdened by unneeded apologetics.

With all respect to those views, I do not believe the Constitution gives us the right to rule as the dissenting members of the Court urge, however painful this judgment is to announce. Though symbols often are what we ourselves make of them, the flag is constant in expressing beliefs Americans share, beliefs in law and peace and that freedom which sustains the human spirit. The case here today forces recognition of the costs to which those beliefs commit us. It is poignant but fundamental that the flag protects those who hold it in contempt.

For all the record shows, this respondent was not a philosopher and perhaps did not even possess the ability to comprehend how repellent his statements must be to the Republic itself. But whether or not he could appreciate the enormity of the offense he gave, the fact remains that his acts were speech, in both the technical and the fundamental meaning of the Constitution. So I agree with the Court that he must go free.

Chief Justice Rehnquist, with whom Justice White and Justice O'Connor join, dissenting.

In holding this Texas statute unconstitutional, the Court ignores Justice Holmes'[s] familiar aphorism that "a page of history is worth a volume of logic." . . . For more than 200 years, the American flag has occupied a unique position as the symbol of our Nation, a uniqueness that justifies a governmental prohibition against flag burning in the way respondent Johnson did here.

At the time of the American Revolution, the flag served to unify the Thirteen Colonies at home, while obtaining recognition of national sovereignty abroad. Ralph Waldo Emerson's Concord Hymn describes the first skirmishes of the Revolutionary War in these lines:

"By the rude bridge that arched the flood
   Their flag to April's breeze unfurled,
"Here once the embattled farmers stood
   And fired the shot heard round the world."

During that time, there were many colonial and regimental flags, adorned with such symbols as pine trees, beavers, anchors, and rattle snakes, bearing slogans such as "Liberty or Death," "Hope," "An Appeal to Heaven," and "Don't Tread on Me." The first distinctive flag of the Colonies was the "Grand Union Flag"—with 13 stripes and a British flag in the left corner—which was flown for the first time on January 2, 1776, by troops of the Continental Army around Boston. By June 14, 1777, after we declared our independence from England, the Continental Congress resolved:

> "That the flag of the thirteen United States be thirteen stripes, alternate red and white: that the union be thirteen stars, white in a blue field, representing a new constellation." . . .

One immediate result of the flag's adoption was that American vessels harassing British shipping sailed under an authorized national flag. Without such a flag, the British could treat captured seamen as pirates and hang them summarily; with a national flag, such seamen were treated as prisoners of war.

During the War of 1812, British naval forces sailed up Chesapeake Bay and marched overland to sack and burn the city of Washington. They then sailed up the Patapsco River to invest the city of Baltimore, but to do so it was first necessary to reduce Fort McHenry in Baltimore Harbor. Francis Scott Key, a Washington lawyer, had been granted permission by the British to board one of their warships to negotiate the release of an American who had been taken prisoner. That night, waiting anxiously on the British ship, Key watched the British fleet firing on Fort McHenry. Finally, at daybreak, he saw the fort's American flag still flying; the British attack had failed. Intensely moved, he began to scribble on the back of an envelope the poem that became our national anthem:

"Oh! say can you see by the dawn's early light,
What so proudly we hailed at the twilight's last gleaming?
Whose broad stripes and bright stars, thro' the perilous fight,
O'er the ramparts we watched were so gallantly streaming?

And the rockets' red glare, the bombs bursting in air,
Gave proof thro' the night that our flag was still there.
Oh! say does that star-spangled banner yet wave
O'er the land of the free and the home of the brave?"

The American flag played a central role in our Nation's most tragic conflict, when the North fought against the South. The lowering of the American flag at Fort Sumter was viewed as the start of the war. . . . The Southern States, to formalize their separation from the Union, adopted the "Stars and Bars" of the Confederacy. The Union troops marched to the sound of "Yes We'll Rally Round The Flag Boys, We'll Rally Once Again." President Abraham Lincoln refused proposals to remove from the American flag the stars representing the rebel States, because he considered the conflict not a war between two nations but an attack by 11 States against the National Government. . . . By war's end, the American flag again flew over "an indestructible union, composed of indestructible states." . . .

One of the great stories of the Civil War is told in John Greenleaf Whittier's poem, Barbara Frietchie:

"Up from the meadows rich with corn,
Clear in the cool September morn,
"The clustered spires of Frederick stand
Green-walled by the hills of Maryland.
"Round about them orchards sweep,
Apple and pear tree fruited deep,
"Fair as the garden of the Lord
To the eyes of the famished rebel horde,
"On that pleasant morn of the early fall
When Lee marched over the mountain wall;
"Over the mountains winding down,
Horse and foot, into Frederick town.
"Forty flags with their silver stars,
Forty flags with their crimson bars,
"Flapped in the morning wind: the sun
Of noon looked down, and saw not one.
"Up rose old Barbara Frietchie then,
Bowed with her fourscore years and ten;
'Bravest of all in Frederick town,
She took up the flag the men hauled down,
"In her attic-window the staff she set,
To show that one heart was loyal yet.
"Up the street came the rebel tread,
Stonewall Jackson riding ahead.
"Under his slouched hat left and right
He glanced; the old flag met his sight.

" 'Halt!'—the dust-brown ranks stood fast.
'Fire!'—out blazed the rifle-blast.
"It shivered the window, pane and sash;
It rent the banner with seam and gash.
"Quick, as it fell, from the broken staff
Dame Barbara snatched the silken scarf.
"She leaned far out on the window-sill,
And shook it forth with a royal will.
" 'Shoot if you must, this old grey head,
But spare your country's flag,' she said.
"A shade of sadness, a blush of shame,
Over the face of the leader came;
"The nobler nature within him stirred
To life at that woman's deed and word;
" 'Who touches a hair of yon grey head
Dies like a dog! March on! he said.
"All day long through Frederick street
Sounded the tread of marching feet:
"All day long that free flag tost
Over the heads of the rebel host
"Ever its torn folds rose and fell
On the loyal winds that loved it well:
"And through the hill-gaps sunset light
Shone over it with a warm good-night.
"Barbara Frietchie's work is o'er,
And the rebel rides on his raids no more.
"Honor to her! and let a tear
Fall, for her sake, on Stonewall's bier.
"Over Barbara Frietchie's grave,
Flag of Freedom and Union, wave!
"Peace and order and beauty draw
Round thy symbol of light and law;
"And ever the stars above look down
On thy stars below in Frederick town!"

In the First and Second World Wars, thousands of our countrymen died on foreign soil fighting for the American cause. At Iwo Jima in the Second World War, United States Marines fought hand-to-hand against thousands of Japanese. By the time the Marines reached the top of Mount Suribachi, they raised a piece of pipe upright and from one end fluttered a flag. That ascent had cost nearly 6,000 American lives. The Iwo Jima Memorial in Arlington National Cemetery memorializes that event. President Franklin Roosevelt authorized the use of the flag on labels, packages, cartons, and containers intended for export as lend-lease aid, in order to inform people in other countries of the United States' assistance. . . .

During the Korean War, the successful amphibious landing of American troops at Inchon was marked by the raising of an American flag within an hour of the event. Impetus for the enactment of the Federal Flag Desecration Statute in 1967 came from the impact of flag burnings in the United States on troop morale in Vietnam. Representative L. Mendel Rivers, then chairman of the House Armed Services Committee, testified that, "The burning of the flag . . . has caused my mail to increase 100 percent from the boys in Vietnam, writing me and asking me what is going on in America." . . . Representative Charles Wiggins stated: "The public act of desecration of our flag tends to undermine the morale of American troops. That this finding is true can be attested by many Members who have received correspondence from servicemen expressing their shock and disgust of such conduct." . . .

The flag symbolizes the Nation in peace as well as in war. It signifies our national presence on battleships, airplanes, military installations, and public buildings from the United States Capitol to the thousands of county courthouses and city halls throughout the country. Two flags are prominently placed in our courtroom. Countless flags are placed by the graves of loved ones each year on what was first called Decoration Day, and is now called Memorial Day. The flag is traditionally placed on the casket of deceased members of the Armed Forces, and it is later given to the deceased's family. . . . Congress has provided that the flag be flown at half-staff upon the death of the President, Vice President, and other government officials "as a mark of respect to their memory." . . . The flag identifies United States merchant ships, . . . and "[t]he laws of the union protect our commerce wherever the flag of the country may float." . . .

No other American symbol has been as universally honored as the flag. In 1931, Congress declared "The Star Spangled Banner" to be our national anthem. . . . In 1949, Congress declared June 14th to be Flag Day. . . . In 1987, John Philip Sousa's "The Stars and Stripes Forever" was designated as the national march. . . . Congress has also established "The Pledge of Allegiance to the Flag" and the manner of its deliverance. . . . The flag has appeared as the principal symbol on approximately 33 United States postal stamps and in the design of at least 43 more, more times than any other symbol. . . .

Both Congress and the States have enacted numerous laws regulating misuse of the American flag. Until 1967, Congress left the regulation of misuse of the flag up to the States. Now, however, Title 18 U.S.C. § 700(a), provides that:

> "Whoever knowingly casts contempt upon any flag of the United States by publicly mutilating, defacing, defiling, burning, or trampling upon it shall be fined not more than $1,000 or imprisoned for not more than one year, or both."

Congress has also prescribed, *inter alia*, detailed rules for the design of the flag, . . . the time and occasion of flag's display, . . . the position and manner of its display, . . . respect for the flag, . . . and conduct during hoisting, lowering and passing of the flag . . . With the exception of Alaska and Wyoming, all of the States now have statutes prohibiting the burning of the flag. Most of the state statutes are patterned after the Uniform Flag Act of 1917, which in § 3 provides: "No person shall publicly mutilate, deface, defile, defy, trample upon, or by word or act cast contempt upon any such flag, standard, color, ensign or shield." . . . Most were passed by the States at about the time of World War I. . . .

The American flag, then, throughout more than 200 years of our history, has come to be the visible symbol embodying our Nation. It does not represent the views of any particular political party, and it does not represent any particular political philosophy. The flag is not simply another "idea" or "point of view" competing for recognition in the marketplace of ideas. Millions and millions of Americans regard it with an almost mystical reverence regardless of what sort of social, political, or philosophical beliefs they may have. I cannot agree that the First Amendment invalidates the Act of Congress, and the laws of 48 of the 50 States, which make criminal the public burning of the flag.

More than 80 years ago in *Halter* v. *Nebraska*, 205 U.S. 34 (1907), this Court upheld the constitutionality of a Nebraska statute that forbade the use or representations of the American flag for advertising purposes upon articles of merchandise. The Court there said:

> "For that flag every true American has not simply an appreciation but a deep affection. . . . Hence, it has often occurred that insults to a flag have been the cause of war, and indignities put upon it, in the

presence of those who revere it, have often been resented and sometimes punished on the spot." . . .

But the Court insists that the Texas statute prohibiting the public burning of the American flag infringes on respondent Johnson's freedom of expression. Such freedom, of course, is not absolute. . . . In *Chaplinsky* v. *New Hampshire*, 315 U.S. 568 (1942), a unanimous Court said:

> "Allowing the broadest scope to the language and purpose of the Fourteenth Amendment, it is well understood that the right of free speech is not absolute at all times and under all circumstances. There are certain well-defined and narrowly limited classes of speech, the prevention and punishment of which have never been thought to raise any Constitutional problem. These include the lewd and obscene, the profane, the libelous, and the insulting or 'fighting' words—those which by their very utterance inflict injury or tend to incite an immediate breach of the peace. It has been well observed that such utterances are no essential part of any exposition of ideas, and are of such slight social value as a step to truth that any benefit that may be derived from them is clearly outweighed by the social interest in order and morality." . . .

The Court upheld Chaplinsky's conviction under a state statute that made it unlawful to "address any offensive, derisive or annoying word to any person who is lawfully in any street or other public place." . . . Chaplinsky had told a local Marshal, "You are a God damned racketeer" and a "damned Fascist and the whole government of Rochester are Fascists or agents of Fascists." . . .

Here is may equally well be said that the public burning of the American flag by Johnson was no essential part of any exposition of ideas, and at the same time it had a tendency to incite a breach of the peace. Johnson was free to make any verbal denunciation of the flag that he wished; indeed, he was free to burn the flag in private. He could publicly burn other symbols of the Government or effigies of political leaders. He did lead a march through the streets of Dallas, and conducted a rally in front of the Dallas City Hall. He engaged in a "die-in" to protest nuclear weapons. He shouted out various slogans during the march, including: "Reagan, Mondale which will it be? Either one means World War III"; "Ronald Reagan, killer of the hour, Perfect example of U.S. power"; and "red, white and blue, we spit on you, you stand for plunder, you will go under." . . . For none of these acts was he arrested or prosecuted; it was only when he proceeded to burn publicly an American flag stolen from its rightful owner that he violated the Texas statute.

The Court could not, and did not, say that Chaplinsky's utterances were not expressive phrases—they clearly and succinctly conveyed an extremely low opinion of the addressee. The same may be said of Johnson's public burning of the flag in this case; it obviously did convey Johnson's bitter dislike of his country. But his act, like Chaplinsky's provocative words, conveyed nothing that could not have been conveyed and was not conveyed just as forcefully in a dozen different ways. As with "fighting words," so with flag burning, for purposes of the First Amendment: It is "no essential part of any exposition of ideas, and [is] of such slight social value as a step to truth that any benefit that may be derived from [it] is clearly outweighed" by the public interest in avoiding a probable breach of the peace. The highest courts of several States have upheld state statutes prohibiting the public burning of the flag on the grounds that it is so inherently inflammatory that it may cause a breach of public order. . . .

The result of the Texas statute is obviously to deny one in Johnson's frame of mind one of many means of "symbolic speech." Far from being a case of "one picture being worth a thousand words," flag burning is the equivalent of an inarticulate grunt or roar that, it seems fair to say, is most likely to be indulged in not to express any particular idea, but to antagonize others. Only five years ago we said . . . that "the First Amendment does not guarantee the right to employ every conceivable method of communication at all times and in all places." The Texas statute deprived Johnson of only one rather inarticulate symbolic form of protest—a form of protest that was profoundly offensive to many—and left him with a full panoply of other symbols and every conceivable form of verbal expression to express his deep disapproval of national policy. Thus, in no way can it be said that Texas is punishing him because his hearers—or any other group of people—were profoundly

opposed to the message that he sought to convey. Such opposition is no proper basis for restricting speech or expression under the First Amendment. It was Johnson's use of this particular symbol, and not the idea that he sought to convey by it or by his many other expressions, for which he was punished.

Our prior cases dealing with flag desecration statutes have left open the question that the Court resolves today.

. . .

But the Court today will have none of this. The uniquely deep awe and respect for our flag felt by virtually all of us are bundled off under the rubric of "designated symbols." . . . that the First Amendment prohibits the government from "establishing." But the government has not "established" this feeling; 200 years of history have done that. The government is simply recognizing as a fact the profound regard for the American flag created by that history when it enacts statutes prohibiting the disrespectful public burning of the flag.

The Court concludes its opinion with a regrettably patronizing civics lecture, presumably addressed to the Members of both Houses of Congress, the members of the 48 state legislatures that enacted prohibitions against flag burning, and the troops fighting under that flag in Vietnam who objected to its being burned: "The way to preserve the flag's special role is not to punish those who feel differently about these matters. It is to persuade them that they are wrong." . . . The Court's role as the final expositor of the Constitution is well established, but its role as a platonic guardian admonishing shcool children has no similar place in our system of government. The cry of "no taxation without representation" animated those who revolted against the English Crown to found our Nation—the idea that those who submitted to government should have some say as to what kind of laws would be passed. Surely one of the high purposes of a democratic society is to legislate against conduct that is regarded as evil and profoundly offensive to the majority of people—whether it be murder, embezzlement, pollution, or flag burning.

Our Constitution wisely places limits on powers of legislative majorities to act, but the declaration of such limits by this court "is, at all times, a question of much delicacy, which ought seldom, if ever, to be decided in the affirmative, in a doubtful case." . . . Uncritical extension of constitutional protection to the burning of the flag risks the frustration of the very purpose for which organized governments are instituted. The Court decides that the American flag is just another symbol, about which not only must opinions pro and con be tolerated, but for which the most minimal public respect may not be enjoined. The government may conscript men into the Armed Forces where they must fight and perhaps die for the flag, but the government may not prohibit the public burning of the banner under which they fight. I would uphold the Texas statute as applied in this case.

Endnotes

[1] Tex. Penal Code Ann. § 42.09 (1989) provides in full:
"§ 42.09. Desecration of Venerated Object

"(a) A person commits an offense if he intentionally or knowingly desecrates:
"(1) a public monument;
"(2) a place of worship or burial; or
"(3) a state or national flag.
"(b) For purposes of this section, 'desecrate' means deface, damage, or otherwise physically mistreat in a way that the actor knows will seriously offend one or more persons likely to observe or discover his action.
"(c) An offense under this section is a Class A misdemeanor."

[2] Our inquiry is, of course, bounded by the particular facts of this case and by the statute under which Johnson was convicted. There was no evidence that Johnson himself stole the flag he burned, . . . nor did the prosecution or the arguments urged in support of it depend on the theory that the flag was stolen. . . . Thus, our analysis does not rely on the way in which the flag was acquired, and nothing in our opinion should be taken to suggest that one is free to steal a flag so long as one later uses it to communicate an idea. We also emphasize that Johnson was prosecuted *only* for flag desecration—not for trespass, disorderly conduct, or arson.

On Liberty

JOHN STUART MILL

The object of this Essay is to assert one very simple principle, as entitled to govern absolutely the dealings of society with the individual in the way of compulsion and control, whether the means used be physical force in the form of legal penalties, or the moral coercion of public opinion. That principle is, that the sole end for which mankind are warranted, individually or collectively, in interfering with the liberty of action of any of their number, is self-protection. That the only purpose for which power can be rightfully exercised over any member of a civilized community, against his will, is to prevent harm to others. His own good, either physical or moral, is not a sufficient warrant. He cannot rightfully be compelled to do or forbear because it will be better for him to do so, because it will make him happier, because, in the opinions of others, to do so would be wise, or even right. There are good reasons for remonstrating with him, or reasoning with him, or persuading him, or entreating him, but not for compelling him, or visiting him with any evil, in case he do otherwise. To justify that, the conduct from which it is desired to deter

---

From *On Liberty*. Excerpts from Chapters I and II, and all of Chapter IV. First published in 1859.

him must be calculated to produce evil to some one else. The only part of the conduct of any one, for which he is amenable to society, is that which concerns others. In the part which merely concerns himself, his independence is, of right, absolute. Over himself, over his own body and mind, the individual is sovereign.

It is, perhaps, hardly necessary to say that this doctrine is meant to apply only to human beings in the maturity of their faculties. We are not speaking of children, or of young persons below the age which the law may fix as that of manhood or womanhood. Those who are still in a state to require being taken care of by others, must be protected against their own actions as well as against external injury. For the same reason, we may leave out of consideration those backward states of society in which the race itself may be considered as in its nonage. The early difficulties in the way of spontaneous progress are so great, that there is seldom any choice of means for overcoming them; and a ruler full of the spirit of improvement is warranted in the use of any expedients that will attain an end, perhaps otherwise unattainable. Despotism is a legitimate mode of government in dealing with barbarians, provided the end be their improvement, and the means justified by actually effecting that end. Liberty, as a principle, has no application to any state of things anterior to the time when mankind have become capable of being improved by free and equal discussion. Until then, there is nothing for them but implicit obedience to an Akbar or a Charlemagne, if they are so fortunate as to find one. But as soon as mankind have attained the capacity of being guided to their own improvement by conviction or persuasion (a period long since reached in all nations with whom we need here concern ourselves), compulsion, either in the direct form or in that of pains and penalties for noncompliance, is no longer admissible as a means to their own good, and justifiable only for the security of others.

It is proper to state that I forego any advantage which could be derived to my argument from the idea of abstract right, as a thing independent of utility. I regard utility as the ultimate appeal on all ethical questions; but it must be utility in the largest sense, grounded on the permanent interests of man as a progressive being. Those interests, I contend, authorize the subjection of individual spontaneity to external control, only in respect to those actions of each, which concern the interest of other people. If any one does an act hurtful to others, there is a *primâ facie* case for punishing him, by law, or, where legal penalties are not safely applicable, by general disapprobation. There are also many positive acts for the benefit of others, which he may rightfully be compelled to perform; such as, to give evidence in a court of justice; to bear his fair share in the common defence, or in any other joint work necessary to the interest of the society of which he enjoys the protection; and to perform certain acts of individual beneficence, such as saving a fellow creature's life, or interposing to protect the defenceless against ill-usage, things which whenever it is obviously a man's duty to do, he may rightfully be made responsible to society for not doing. A person may cause evil to others not only by his actions but by his inaction, and in either case he is justly accountable to them for the injury. The latter case, it is true, requires a much more cautious exercise of compulsion than the former. To make any one answerable for doing evil to others, is the rule; to make him answerable for not preventing evil, is, comparatively speaking, the exception. Yet there are many cases clear enough and grave enough to justify that exception. In all things which regard the external relations of the individual, he is *de jure* amenable to those whose interests are concerned, and if need be, to society as their protector. There are often good reasons for not holding him to the responsibility; but these reasons must arise from the special expediencies of the case: either because it is a kind of case in which he is on the whole likely to act better, when left to his own discretion, than when controlled in any way in which society have it in their power to control him; or because the attempt to exercise control would produce other evils, greater than those which it would prevent. When such reasons as these preclude the enforcement of responsibility, the conscience of the agent himself should step into the vacant judgment-seat, and protect those interests of others which have no external protection; judging himself all the more rigidly, because the case does not admit of his being made accountable to the judgment of his fellow-creatures.

But there is a sphere of action in which society, as distinguished from the individual, has, if any, only an indirect interest; comprehending all that portion of a person's life and conduct which affects only himself, or, if it also affects others, only with their free, voluntary, and undeceived consent and participation. When I say only himself, I mean directly, and in the first instance: for whatever affects himself, may affect others *through* himself; and the objection which may be grounded on this contingency, will receive consideration in the sequel. This, then, is the appropriate region of human liberty. It comprises, first, the inward domain of consciousness; demanding liberty of conscience, in the most comprehensive sense; liberty of thought and feeling; absolute freedom of opinion and sentiment on all subjects, practical or speculative, scientific, moral, or theological. The liberty of expressing and publishing opinions may seem to fall under a different principle, since it belongs to that part of the conduct of an individual which concerns other people; but, being almost of as much importance as the liberty of thought itself, and resting in great part on the same reasons, is practically inseparable from it. Secondly, the principle requires liberty of tastes and pursuits; of framing the plan of our life to suit our own character; of doing as we like, subject to such consequences as may follow; without impediment from our fellow-creatures, so long as what we do does not harm them, even though they should think our conduct foolish, perverse, or wrong. Thirdly, from this liberty of each individual, follows the liberty, within the same limits, of combination among individuals; freedom to unite, for any purpose not involving harm to others: the persons combining being supposed to be of full age, and not forced or deceived.

No society in which these liberties are not, on the whole, respected, is free, whatever may be its form of government; and none is completely free in which they do not exist absolute and unqualified. The only freedom which deserves the name, is that of pursuing our own good in our own way, so long as we do not attempt to deprive others of theirs, or impede their efforts to obtain it. Each is the proper guardian of his own health, whether bodily, or mental and spiritual. Mankind are greater gainers by suffering each other to live as seems good to themselves, than by compelling each to live as seems good to the rest. . . .

We have now recognized the necessity to the mental well-being of mankind (on which all their other well-being depends) of freedom of opinion, and freedom of the expression of opinion, on four distinct grounds; which we will now briefly recapitulate.

First, if any opinion is compelled to silence, that opinion may, for aught we can certainly know, be true. To deny this is to assume our own infallibility.

Secondly, though the silenced opinion be an error, it may, and very commonly does, contain a portion of truth; and since the general or prevailing opinion on any subject is rarely or never the whole truth, it is only by the collision of adverse opinions that the remainder of the truth has any chance of being supplied.

Thirdly, even if the received opinion be not only true, but the whole truth; unless it is suffered to be, and actually is vigorously and earnestly contested, it will, by most of those who receive it, be held in the manner of a prejudice, with little comprehension or feeling of its rational grounds. And not only this, but, fourthly, the meaning of the doctrine itself will be in danger of being lost, or enfeebled, and deprived of its vital effect on the character and conduct: the dogma becoming a mere formal profession, inefficacious for good, but cumbering the ground, and preventing the growth of any real and heartfelt conviction from reason or personal experience. . . .

Of the Limits to the Authority of Society over the Individual

What, then, is the rightful limit to the sovereignty of the individual over himself? Where does the authority of society begin? How much of human life should be assigned to individuality, and how much to society?

Each will receive its proper share, if each has that which more particularly concerns it. To individuality should belong the part of life in which it is chiefly the individual that is interested; to society, the part which chiefly interests society.

Though society is not founded on a contract, and though no good purpose is answered by inventing a contract in order to deduce social obligations from it, every one who receives the protection of society owes a return for the benefit, and the fact of living in society renders it indispensable that each should be bound to observe a certain line of conduct towards the rest. This conduct consists, first, in not injuring the interests of one another; or rather certain interests, which either by express legal provision or by tacit understanding, ought to be considered as rights; and secondly, in each person's bearing his share (to be fixed on some equitable principle) of the labors and sacrifices incurred for defending the society or its members from injury and molestation. These conditions society is justified in enforcing, at all costs to those who endeavor to withhold fulfillment. Nor is this all that society may do. The acts of an individual may be hurtful to others, or wanting in due consideration for their welfare, without going the length of violating any of their constituted rights. The offender may then be justly punished by opinion, though not by law. As soon as any part of a person's conduct affects prejudicially the interests of others, society has jurisdiction over it, and the question whether the general welfare will or will not be promoted by interfering with it, becomes open to discussion. But there is no room for entertaining any such question when a person's conduct affects the interests of no persons besides himself, or needs not affect them unless they like (all the persons concerned being of full age, and the ordinary amount of understanding). In all such cases there should be perfect freedom, legal and social, to do the action and stand the consequences.

It would be a great misunderstanding of this doctrine, to suppose that it is one of selfish indifference, which pretends that human beings have no business with each other's conduct in life, and that they should not concern themselves about the well-doing or well-being of one another, unless their own interest is involved. Instead of any diminution, there is need of a great increase of disinterested exertion to promote the good of others. But disinterested benevolence can find other instruments to persuade people to their good, than whips and scourges, either of the literal or the metaphorical sort. I am the last person to undervalue the self-regarding virtues; they are only second in importance, if even second, to the social. It is equally the business of education to cultivate both. But even education works by conviction and persuasion as well as by compulsion, and it is by the former only that, when the period of education is past, the self-regarding virtues should be inculcated. Human beings owe to each other help to distinguish the better from the worse, and encouragement to choose the former and avoid the latter. They should be forever stimulating each other to increased exercise of their higher faculties, and increased direction of their feelings and aims towards wise instead of foolish, elevating instead of degrading, objects and contemplations. But neither one person, nor any number of persons, is warranted in saying to another human creature of ripe years, that he shall not do with his life for his own benefit what he chooses to do with it. He is the person most interested in his own well-being: the interest which any other person, except in cases of strong personal attachment, can have in it, is trifling, compared with that which he himself has; the interest which society has in him individually (except as to his conduct to others) is fractional, and altogether indirect: while, with respect to his own feelings and circumstances, the most ordinary man or woman has means of knowledge immeasurably surpassing those that can be possessed by anyone else. The interference of society to overrule his judgment and purposes in what only regards himself, must be grounded on general presumptions; which may be altogether wrong, and even if right, are as likely as not to be misapplied to individual cases, by persons no better acquainted with the circumstances of such cases than those are who look at them merely from without. In this department, therefore, of human affairs, Individuality has its proper field of action. In the conduct of human beings towards one another, it is necessary that general rules should for the most part be observed, in order that people may know what they have to expect; but in each person's own concerns, his individual spontaneity is entitled to free exercise. Considerations to aid his judgment, exhortations to strengthen his will, may be offered to him, even obtruded on him, by others; but he, himself, is the final judge. All errors which he is likely to commit against advice and warning, are far outweighed by the evil of allowing others to constrain him to what they deem his good.

I do not mean that the feelings with which a person is regarded by others, ought not to be in any way affected by his self-regarding qualities or deficiencies. This is neither possible nor desirable. If he is eminent in any of the qualities which conduce to his own good, he is, so far, a proper object of admiration. He is so much the nearer to the ideal perfection of human nature. If he is grossly deficient in those qualities, a sentiment the opposite of admiration will follow. There is a degree of folly, and a degree of what may be called (though the phrase is not unobjectionable) lowness or depravation of taste, which, though it cannot justify doing harm to the person who manifests it, renders him necessarily and properly a subject of distaste, or, in extreme cases, even of contempt: a person would not have the opposite qualities in due strength without entertaining these feelings. Though doing no wrong to anyone, a person may so act as to compel us to judge him, and feel to him, as a fool, or as a being of an inferior order: and since this judgment and feeling are a fact which he would prefer to avoid, it is doing him a service to warn him of it beforehand, as of any other disagreeable consequence to which he exposes himself. It would be well, indeed, if this good office were much more freely rendered than the common notions of politeness at present permit, and if one person could honestly point out to another that he thinks him in fault, without being considered unmannerly or presuming. We have a right, also, in various ways, to act upon our unfavorable opinion of any one, not to the oppression of his individuality, but in the exercise of ours. We are not bound, for example, to seek his society; we have a right to avoid it (though not to parade the avoidance), for we have a right to choose the society most acceptable to us. We have a right, and it may be our duty to caution others against him, if we think his example or conversation likely to have a pernicious effect on those with whom he associates. We may give others a preference over him in optional good offices, except those which tend to his improvement. In these various modes a person may suffer very severe penalties at the hands of others, for faults which directly concern only himself; but he suffers these penalties only in so far as they are the natural, and, as it were, the spontaneous consequences of the faults themselves, not because they are purposely inflicted on him for the sake of punishment. A person who shows rashness, obstinacy, self-conceit—who cannot live within moderate means—who cannot restrain himself from hurtful indulgences—who pursues animal pleasures at the expense of those of feelings and intellect—must expect to be lowered in the opinion of others, and to have less share of their favorable sentiments, but of this he has no right to complain, unless he has merited their favor by special excellence in his social relations, and has thus established a title to their good offices, which is not affected by his demerits towards himself.

What I contend for is, that the inconveniences which are strictly inseparable from the unfavorable judgment of others, are the only ones to which a person should ever be subjected for that portion of his conduct and character which concerns his own good, but which does not affect the interests of others in their relations with him. Acts injurious to others require a totally different treatment. Encroachment on their rights; infliction on them of any loss or damage not justified by his own rights; falsehood or duplicity in dealing with them; unfair or ungenerous use of advantages over them; even selfish abstinence from defending them against injury—these are fit objects of moral reprobation, and, in grave cases, of moral retribution and punishment. And not only these acts, but the dispositions which lead to them, are properly immoral, and fit subjects of disapprobation which may rise to abhorrence. Cruelty of disposition; malice and ill-nature; that most anti-social and odious of all passions, envy; dissimulation and insincerity; irascibility on insufficient cause, and resentment disproportioned to the provocation; the love of domineering over others; the desire to engross more than one's share of advantages (the πλε νεξτα of the Greeks); the pride which derives gratification from the abasement of others; the egotism which thinks self and its concerns more important than everything else, and decides all doubtful questions in his own favor—these are moral vices, and constitute a bad and odious moral character: unlike the self-regarding faults previously mentioned, which are not properly immoralities, and to whatever pitch they may be carried, do not constitute wickedness. They may be proofs of any amount of folly, or want of personal dignity and self-respect; but they are only a subject of moral reprobation when they involve a breach of duty to others, for whose sake the individual is bound to have care for himself. What are called duties to ourselves are not socially obligatory, unless circumstances render them at the same time duties to others. The term duty to oneself, when it means anything more than prudence, means self-respect or self-development; and for none of these is any one accountable to his fellow-creatures, because for none of them is it for the good of mankind that he be held accountable to them.

The distinction between the loss of consideration which a person may rightly incur by defect of prudence or of personal dignity, and the reprobation which is due to him for an offence against the rights of others, is not a merely nominal distinction. It makes a vast difference both in our feelings

own affairs vs affairs of others

injury to self in effect injures someone else?!?

and in our conduct towards him, whether he displeases us in things in which we think we have a right to control him, or in things in which we know that we have not. If he displeases us, we may express our distaste, and we may stand aloof from a person as well as from a thing that displeases us; but we shall not therefore feel called on to make his life uncomfortable. We shall reflect that he already bears, or will bear, the whole penalty of his error; if he spoils his life by mismanagement, we shall not, for that reason, desire to spoil it still further: instead of wishing to punish him, we shall rather endeavor to alleviate his punishment, by showing him how he may avoid or cure the evils his conduct tends to bring upon him. He may be to us an object of pity, perhaps of dislike, but not of anger or resentment; we shall not treat him like an enemy of society: the worst we shall think ourselves justified in doing is leaving him to himself, if we do not interfere benevolently by showing interest or concern for him. It is far otherwise if he has infringed the rules necessary for the protection of his fellow-creatures, individually or collectively. The evil consequences of his acts do not then fall on himself, but on others; and society, as the protector of all its members, must retaliate on him; must inflict pain on him for the express purpose of punishment, and must take care that it be sufficiently severe. In the one case, he is an offender at our bar, and we are called on not only to sit in judgment on him, but, in one shape or another, to execute our own sentence: in the other case, it is not our part to inflict any suffering on him, except what may incidentally follow from our using the same liberty in the regulation of our own affairs, which we allow to him in his.

The distinction here pointed out between the part of a person's life which concerns only himself, and that which concerns others, many persons will refuse to admit. How (it may be asked) can any part of the conduct of a member of society be a matter of indifference to the other members? No person is an entirely isolated being; it is impossible for a person to do anything seriously or permanently hurtful to himself, without mischief reaching at least to his near connections, and often far beyond them. If he injures his property, he does harm to those who directly or indirectly derived support from it, and usually diminishes, by a greater or less amount, the general resources of the community. If he deteriorates his bodily or mental faculties, he not only

brings evil upon all who depended on him for any portion of their happiness, but disqualifies himself for rendering the services which he owes to his fellow-creatures generally; perhaps becomes a burden on their affection or benevolence; and if such conduct were very frequent, hardly any offence that is committed would detract more from the general sum of good. Finally, if by his vices or follies a person does no direct harm to others, he is nevertheless (it may be said) injurious by his example; and ought to be compelled to control himself, for the sake of those whom the sight or knowledge of his conduct might corrupt or mislead.

And even (it will be added) if the consequences of misconduct could be confined to the vicious or thoughtless individual, ought society to abandon to their own guidance those who are manifestly unfit for it? If protection against themselves is confessedly due to children and persons under age, is not society equally bound to afford it to persons of mature years who are equally incapable of self-government? If gambling, or drunkenness, or incontinence, or idleness, or uncleanliness, are as injurious to happiness, and as great a hindrance to improvement, as many or most of the acts prohibited by law, why (it may be asked) should not law, so far as is consistent with practicability and social convenience, endeavor to repress these also? And as a supplement to the unavoidable imperfections of law, ought not opinion at least to organize a powerful police against these vices, and visit rigidly with social penalties those who are known to practise them? There is no question here (it may be said) about restricting individuality, or impeding the trial of new and original experiments in living. The only things it is sought to prevent are things which have been tried and condemned from the beginning of the world until now; things which experience has shown to to be useful or suitable to any person's individuality. There must be some length of time and amount of experience, after which a moral or prudential truth may be regarded as established: and it is merely desired to prevent generation after generation from falling over the same precipice which has been fatal to their predecessors.

I fully admit that the mischief which a person does to himself, may seriously affect, both through their sympathies and their interests, those nearly connected with him, and in a minor degree, society at large. When, by conduct of this sort, a person is

question of treating unfit like kids.

led to violate a distinct and assignable obligation to any other person or persons, the case is taken out of the self-regarding class, and becomes amenable to moral disapprobation in the proper sense of the term. If, for example, a man, through intemperance or extravagance, becomes unable to pay his debts, or, having undertaken the moral responsibility of a family, becomes from the same cause incapable of supporting or educating them, he is deservedly reprobated, and might be justly punished; but it is for the breach of duty to his family or creditors, not for the extravagance. If the resources which ought to have been devoted to them, had been diverted from them for the most prudent investment, the moral culpability would have been the same. George Barnwell murdered his uncle to get money for his mistress, but if he had done it to set himself up in business, he would equally have been hanged. Again, in the frequent case of a man who causes grief to his family by addition to bad habits, he deserves reproach for his unkindness or ingratitude; but so he may for cultivating habits not in themselves vicious, if they are painful to those with whom he passes his life, or who from personal ties are dependent on him for their comfort. Whoever fails in the consideration generally due to the interests and feelings of others, not being compelled by some more imperative duty, or justified by allowable self-preference, is a subject of moral disapprobation for that failure, but not for the cause of it, nor for the errors, merely personal to himself, which may have remotely led to it. In like manner, when a person disables himself, by conduct purely self-regarding, from the performance of some definite duty incumbent on him to the public, he is guilty of a social offence. No person ought to be punished simply for being drunk; but a soldier or a policeman should be punished for being drunk on duty. Whenever, in short, there is a definite damage, or a definite risk of damage, either to an individual or to the public, the case is taken out of the province of liberty, and placed in that of morality or law.

But with regard to the merely contingent, or, as it may be called, constructive injury which a person causes to society, by conduct which neither violates any specific duty to the public, nor occasions perceptible hurt to any assignable individual except himself; the inconvenience is one which society can afford to bear, for the sake of the greater good of human freedom. If grown persons are to be

punished for not taking proper care of themselves, I would rather it were for their own sake, than under pretence of preventing them from impairing their capacity of rendering to society benefits which society does not pretend it has a right to exact. But I cannot consent to argue the point as if society had no means of bringing its weaker members up to its ordinary standard of rational conduct, except waiting till they do something irrational, and then punishing them, legally or morally, for it. Society has had absolute power over them during all the early portion of their existence: it has had the whole period of childhood and nonage in which to try whether it could make them capable of rational conduct in life. The existing generation is master both of the training and the entire circumstances of the generation to come; it cannot indeed make them perfectly wise and good, because it is itself so lamentably deficient in goodness and wisdom; and its best efforts are not always, in individual cases, its most successful ones; but it is perfectly well able to make the rising generation, as a whole, as good as, and a little better than, itself. If society lets any considerable number of its members grow up mere children, incapable of being acted on by rational consideration of distant motives, society has itself to blame for the consequences. Armed not only with all the powers of education, but with the ascendency which the authority of a received opinion always exercises over the minds who are least fitted to judge for themselves; and aided by the *natural* penalties which cannot be prevented from falling on those who incur the distaste or the contempt of those who know them; let not society pretend that it needs, besides all this, the power to issue commands and enforce obedience in the personal concerns of individuals, in which, on all principles of justice and policy, the decision ought to rest with those who are to abide the consequences. Nor is there anything which tends more to discredit and frustrate the better means of influencing conduct, than a resort to the worse. If there be among those whom it is attempted to coerce into prudence or temperance, any of the material of which vigorous and independent characters are made, they will infallibly rebel against the yoke. No such person will ever feel that others have a right to control him in his concerns, such as they have to prevent him from injuring them in theirs; and it easily comes to be considered a mark of spirit and courage to fly in the face of such usurped authority, and do with ostentation the exact opposite of what it enjoins; as in the fashion of grossness which succeeded, in the time of Charles II, to the fanatical moral intolerance of the Puritans. With respect to what is said of the necessity of protecting society from the bad example set to others by the vicious or the self-indulgent; it is true that bad example may have a pernicious effect, especially the example of doing wrong to others with impunity to the wrongdoer. But we are now speaking of conduct which, while it does no wrong to others, is supposed to do great harm to the agent himself: and I do not see how those who believe this, can think otherwise than that the example, on the whole, must be more salutary than hurtful, since, if it displays the misconduct, it displays also the painful or degrading consequences which, if the conduct is justly censured, must be supposed to be in all or most cases attendant on it.

But the strongest of all the arguments against the interference of the public with purely personal conduct, is that when it does interfere, the odds are that it interferes wrongly, and in the wrong place. On questions of social morality, of duty to others, the opinion of the public, that is, of an overruling majority, though often wrong, is likely to be still oftener right; because on such questions they are only required to judge of their own interests; of the manner in which some mode of conduct, if allowed to be practised, would affect themselves. But the opinion of a similar majority, imposed as a law on the minority, on questions of self-regarding conduct, is quite as likely to be wrong as right; for in these cases public opinion means, at the best, some people's opinion of what is good or bad for other people; while very often it does not even mean that; the public, with the most perfect indifference, passing over the pleasure or convenience of those whose conduct they censure, and considering only their own preference. There are many who consider as an injury to themselves any conduct which they have a distaste for, and resent it as an outrage to their feelings; as a religious bigot, when charged with disregarding the religious feelings of others, has been known to retort that they disregard his feelings, by persisting in their abominable worship or creed. But there is no parity between the feeling of a person for his own opinion, and the feeling of another who is offended at his holding it; no more than between the desire of a thief to take a purse,

and the desire of the right owner to keep it. And a person's taste is as much his own peculiar concern as his opinion or his purse. It is easy for any one to imagine an ideal public, which leaves the freedom and choice of individuals in all uncertain matters undisturbed, and only requires them to abstain from modes of conduct which universal experience has condemned. But where has there been seen a public which set any such limit to its censorship? or when does the public trouble itself about universal experience? In its interferences with personal conduct it is seldom thinking of anything but the enormity of acting or feeling differently from itself; and this standard of judgment, thinly disguised, is held up to mankind as the dictate of religion and philosophy, by nine tenths of all moralists and speculative writers. These teach that things are right because they are right; because we feel them to be so. They tell us to search in our own minds and hearts for laws of conduct binding on ourselves and on all others. What can the poor public do but apply these instructions, and make their own personal feelings of good and evil, if they are tolerably unanimous in them, obligatory on all the world?

The evil here pointed out is not one which exists only in theory; and it may perhaps be expected that I should specify the instances in which the public of this age and country improperly invests its own preferences with the character of moral laws. I am not writing an essay on the aberrations of existing moral feeling. That is too weighty a subject to be discussed parenthetically, and by way of illustration. Yet examples are necessary, to show that the principle I maintain is of serious and practical moment, and that I am not endeavoring to erect a barrier against imaginary evils. And it is not difficult to show, by abundant instances, that to extend the bounds of what may be called moral police, until it encroaches on the most unquestionably legitimate liberty of the individual, is one of the most universal of all human propensities.

As a first instance, consider the antipathies which men cherish on no better grounds than that persons [whose] religious opinions are different from theirs, do not practise their religious observances, especially their religious abstinences. To cite a rather trivial example, nothing in the creed or practice of Christians does more to envenom the hatred of Mahomedans against them, than the fact of their eating pork. There are few acts which

Christians and Europeans regard with more unaffected disgust, than Mussulmans regard this particular mode of satisfying hunger. It is, in the first place, an offence against their religion; but this circumstance by no means explains either the degree or the kind of their repugnance; for wine also is forbidden by their religion, and to partake of it is by all Mussulmans accounted wrong, but not disgusting. Thier aversion to the flesh of the "unclean beast" is, on the contrary, of that peculiar character, resembling an instinctive antipathy, which the idea of uncleanness, when once it thoroughly sinks into the feelings, seems always to excite even in those whose personal habits are anything but scrupulously cleanly, and of which the sentiment of religious impurity, so intense in the Hindoos, is a remarkable example. Suppose now that in a people, of whom the majority were Mussulmans, that majority should insist upon not permitting pork to be eaten within the limits of the country. This would be nothing new in Mahomedan countries.[1] Would it be a legitimate exercise of the moral authority of public opinion? and if not, why not? The practice is really revolting to such a public. They also sincerely think that it is forbidden and abhorred by the Deity. Neither could the prohibition be censured as religious persecution. It might be religious in its origin, but it would not be persecution for religion, since nobody's religion makes it a duty to eat pork. The only tenable ground of condemnation would be, that with the personal tastes and self-regarding concerns of individuals the public has no business to interfere.

To come somewhat nearer home: the majority of Spaniards consider it a gross impiety, offensive in the highest degree to the Supreme Being, to worship him in any other manner than the Roman Catholic; and no other public worship is lawful on Spanish soil. The people of all Southern Europe look upon a married clergy as not only irreligious, but unchaste, indecent, gross, disgusting. What do Protestants think of these perfectly sincere feelings, and of the attempt to enforce them against non-Catholics? Yet, if mankind are justified in interfering with each other's liberty in things which do not concern the interests of others, on what principle is it possible consistently to exclude these cases? or who can blame people for desiring to suppress what they regard as a scandal in the sight of God and man? No stronger case can be shown for prohibiting anything which is regarded as a personal immorality, than is made out for sup-

pressing these practices in the eyes of those who regard them as impieties; and unless we are willing to adopt the logic of persecutors, and to say that we may persecute others because we are right, and that they must not persecute us because they are wrong, we must be aware of admitting a principle of which we should resent as a gross injustice the application to ourselves.

The preceding instances may be objected to, although unreasonable, as drawn from contingencies impossible among us: opinion, in this country, not being likely to enforce abstinence from meats, or to interfere with people for worshipping, and for either marrying or not marrying, according to their creed or inclination. The next example, however, shall be taken from an interference with liberty which we have by no means passed all danger of. Wherever the puritans have been sufficiently powerful, as in New England, and in Great Britain at the time of the Commonwealth, they have endeavored, with considerable success, to put down all public, and nearly all private, amusements: especially music, dancing, public games, or other assemblages for purposes of diversion, and the theatre. There are still in this country large bodies of persons by whose notions of morality and religion these recreations are condemned; and those persons belonging chiefly to the middle class, who are the ascendant power in the present social and political condition of the kingdom, it is by no means impossible that persons of these sentiments may at some time or other command a majority in Parliament. How will the remaining portion of the community like to have the amusements that shall be permitted to them regulated by the religious and moral sentiments of the stricter Calvinists and Methodists? Would they not, with considerable peremptoriness, desire these intrusively pious members of society to mind their own business? This is precisely what should be said to every government and every public, who have the pretension that no person shall enjoy any pleasure which they think wrong. But if the principle of the pretension be admitted, no one can reasonably object to its being acted on in the sense of the majority, or other preponderating power in the country; and all persons must be ready to conform to the idea of a Christian commonwealth, as understood by the early settlers in New England, if a religious profession similar to theirs should ever succeed in regaining its lost ground, as religions supposed to be declining have so often been known to do.

To imagine [another] contingency, perhaps more likely to be realized than the one last mentioned. There is confessedly a strong tendency in the modern world towards a democratic constitution of society, accompanied or not by popular political institutions. It is affirmed that in the country where this tendency is most completely realized—where both society and the government are most democratic—the United States—the feeling of the majority, to whom any appearance of a more showy or costly style of living than they can hope to rival is disagreeable, operates as a tolerably effectual sumptuary law, and that in many parts of the Union it is really difficult for a person possessing a very large income, to find any mode of spending it, which will not incur popular disapprobation. Though such statements as these are doubtless much exaggerated as a representation of existing facts, the state of things they describe is not only a conceivable and possible, but a probable result of democratic feeling, combined with the notion that the public has a right to a veto on the manner in which individuals shall spend their incomes. We have only further to suppose a considerable diffusion of Socialist opinions, and it may become infamous in the eyes of the majority to possess more property than some very small amount, or any income not earned by manual labor. Opinions similar in principle to these, already prevail widely among the artisan class, and weigh oppressively on those who are amenable to the opinion chiefly of that class, namely, its own members. It is known that the bad workmen who form the majority of the operatives in many branches of industry, are decidedly of opinion that bad workmen ought to receive the same wages as good, and that no one ought to be allowed, through piecework or otherwise, to earn by superior skill or industry more than others can without it. And they employ a moral police, which occasionally becomes a physical one, to deter skilful workmen from receiving, and employers from giving, a larger remuneration for a more useful service. If the public have any jurisdiction over private concerns, I cannot see that these people are in fault, or that any individual's particular public can be blamed for asserting the same authority over his individual conduct, which the general public asserts over people in general.

But, without dwelling upon supposititious cases, there are, in our own day, gross usurpations upon the liberty of private life actually practised, and still greater ones threatened with some expectation of success, and opinions proposed which assert an unlimited right in the public not only to prohibit by law everything which it thinks wrong, but in order to get at what it thinks wrong, to prohibit any number of things which it admits to be innocent.

Under the name of preventing intemperance, the people of one English colony, and of nearly half the United States, have been interdicted by law from making any use whatever of fermented drinks, except for medical purposes: for prohibition of their sale is in fact, as it is intended to be, prohibition of their use. And though the impracticability of executing the law has caused its repeal in several of the States which had adopted it, including the one from which it derives its name, an attempt has notwithstanding been commenced, and is prosecuted with considerable zeal by many of the professed philanthropists, to agitate for a similar law in this country. The association, or "Alliance" as it terms itself, which has been formed for this purpose, has acquired some notoriety through the publicity given to a correspondence between its Secretary and one of the very few English public men who hold that a politician's opinions ought to be founded on principles. Lord Stanley's share in this correspondence is calculated to strengthen the hopes already built on him, by those who know how rare such qualities as are manifested in some of his public appearances, unhappily are among those who figure in political life. The organ of the Alliance, who would "deeply deplore the recognition of any principle which could be wrested to justify bigotry and persecution," undertakes to point out the "broad and impassable barrier" which divides such principles from those of the association. "All matters relating to thought, opinion, conscience, appear to me," he says, "to be without the sphere of legislation; all pertaining to social act, habit, relation, subject only to a discretionary power vested in the State itself, and not in the individual, to be within it." No mention is made of a third class, different from either of these, viz., acts and habits which are not social, but individual; although it is to this class, surely, that the act of drinking fermented liquors belongs. Selling fermented liquors, however, is trading, and trading is a social act. But the infringement complained of is not on the liberty of the seller, but on that of the buyer and consumer; since the State might just as well forbid him to drink wine, as purposely make it impossible for him to obtain it. The Secretary, however, says, "I claim, as a citizen, a right to legislate whenever my social rights are invaded by the social act of another." And now for the definition of these "social rights." "If anything invades my social rights, certainly the traffic in strong drink does. It destroys my primary right of security, by constantly creating and stimulating social disorder. It invades my right of equality, by deriving a profit from the creation of a misery, I am taxed to support. It impedes my right to free moral and intellectual development, by surrounding my path with dangers, and by weakening and demoralizing society, from which I have a right to claim mutual aid and intercourse." A theory of "social rights," the like of which probably never before found its way into distinct language—being nothing short of this—that it is the absolute social right of every individual, that every other individual shall act in every respect exactly as he ought; that whosoever fails thereof in the smallest particular, violates my social right, and entitles me to demand from the legislature the removal of the grievance. So monstrous a principle is far more dangerous than any single interference with liberty; there is no violation of liberty which it would not justify; it acknowledges no right to any freedom whatever, except perhaps to that of holding opinions in secret, without ever disclosing them: for the moment an opinion which I consider noxious, passes any one's lips, it invades all the "social rights" attributed to me by the Alliance. The doctrine ascribes to all mankind a vested interest in each other's moral, intellectual, and even physical perfection, to be defined by each claimant according to his own standard.

Another important example of illegitimate interference with the rightful liberty of the individual, not simply threatened, but long since carried into triumphant effect, is Sabbatarian legislation. Without doubt, abstinence on one day in the week, so far as the exigencies of life permit, from the usual daily occupation, though in no respect religiously binding on any except Jews, it is a highly beneficial custom. And inasmuch as this custom cannot be observed without a general consent to that effect among the industrious classes, therefore, in so far as some persons by working may impose the same necessity on others, it may be allowable and right that the law should guarantee to each, the observance by others of the custom, by

suspending the greater operations of industry on a particular day. But this justification, grounded on the direct interest which others have in each individual's observance of the practice, does not apply to the self-chosen occupations in which a person may think fit to employ his leisure; nor does it hold good, in the smallest degree, for legal restrictions on amusements. It is true that the amusement of some is the day's work of others; but the pleasure, not to say the useful recreation, of many, is worth the labor of a few, provided the occupation is freely chosen, and can be freely resigned. The operatives are perfectly right in thinking that if all worked on Sunday seven days' work would have to be given for six days' wages: but so long as the great mass of employments are suspended, the small number who for the enjoyment of others must still work, obtain a proportional increase of earnings; and they are not obliged to follow those occupations, if they prefer leisure to emolument. If a further remedy is sought, it might be found in the establishment by custom of a holiday on some other day of the week for those particular classes of persons. The only ground, therefore, on which restrictions on Sunday amusements can be defended, must be that they are religiously wrong; a motive of legislation which never can be too earnestly protested [against]. "Deorum injuriae Diis curae." It remains to be proved that society or any of its officers holds a commission from on high to avenge any supposed offence to Omnipotence, which is not also a wrong to our fellow-creatures. The notion that it is one man's duty that another should be religious, was the foundation of all the religious persecutions ever perpetrated, and if admitted, would fully justify them. Though the feeling which breaks out in the repeated attempts to stop railway travelling on Sunday, in the resistance to the opening of Museums, and the like, has not the cruelty of the old persecutors, the state of mind indicated by it is fundamentally the same. It is a determination not to tolerate others in doing what is permitted by their religion, because it is not permitted by the persecutor's religion. It is a belief that God not only abominates the act of the misbeliever, but will not hold us guiltless if we leave him unmolested.

I cannot refrain from adding to these examples of the little account commonly made of human liberty, the language of downright persecution which breaks out from the press of this country, whenever it feels called on to notice the remarkable phenomenon of Mormonism. Much might be said on the unexpected and instructive fact, that an alleged new revelation, and a religion founded on it, the product of palpable imposture, not even supported by the *prestige* of extraordinary qualities in its founder, is believed by hundreds of thousands, and has been made the foundation of a society, in the age of newspapers, railways, and the electric telegraph. What here concerns us is, that this religion, like other and better religions, has its martyrs; that its prophet and founder was, for his teaching, put to death by a mob; that others of its adherents lost their lives by the same lawless violence; that they were forcibly expelled, in a body, from the country in which they first grew up; while, now that they have been chased into a solitary recess in the midst of a desert, many of this country openly declare that it would be right (only that it is not convenient) to send an expedition against them, and compel them by force to conform to the opinion of other people. The article of the Mormonite doctrine which is the chief provocative to the antipathy which thus breaks through the ordinary restraints of religious tolerance, is its sanction of polygamy; which, though permitted to Mahomedans, and Hindoos, and Chinese, seems to excite unquenchable animosity when practised by persons who speak English, and profess to be a kind of Christians. No one has a deeper disapprobation than I have of this Mormon institution; both for other reasons, and because, far from being in any way countenanced by the principle of liberty, it is a direct infraction of that principle, being a mere riveting of the chains of one half of the community, and an emancipation of the other from reciprocity of obligation towards them. Still, it must be remembered that this relation is as much voluntary on the part of the women concerned in it, and who may be deemed the sufferers by it, as is the case with any other form of the marriage institution; and however surprising this fact may appear, it has its explanation in the common ideas and customs of the world, which teaching women to think marriage the one thing needful, make it intelligible that many a woman should prefer being one of several wives, to not being a wife at all. Other countries are not asked to recognize such unions, or release any portion of their inhabitants from their own laws on the score of Mormonite opinions. But when the dissentients have conceded to the hostile sentiments of others, far more than could justly be de-

manded; when they have left the countries to which their doctrines were unacceptable, and established themselves in a remote corner of the earth, which they have been the first to render habitable to human beings; it is difficult to see on what principles but those of tyranny they can be prevented from living there under what laws they please, provided they commit no aggression on other nations, and allow perfect freedom of departure to those who are dissatisfied with their ways. A recent writer, in some respects of considerable merit, proposes (to use his own words) not a crusade, but a *civilizade*, against this polygamous community, to put an end to what seems to him a retrograde step in civilization. It also appears so to me, but I am not aware that any community has a right to force another to be civilized. So long as the sufferers by the bad law do not invoke assistance from other communities, I cannot admit that persons entirely unconnected with them ought to step in and require that a condition of things with which all who are directly interested appear to be satisfied, should be put an end to because it is a scandal to persons some thousands of miles distant, who have no part or concern in it. Let them send missionaries, if they please, to preach against it; and let them, by any fair means (of which silencing the teachers is not one), oppose the progress of similar doctrines among their own people. If civilization has got the better of barbarism when barbarism had the world to itself, it is too much to profess to be afraid lest barbarism, after having been fairly got under, should revive and conquer civilization. A civilization that can thus succumb to its vanquished enemy must first have become so degenerate, that neither its appointed priests and teachers, nor anybody else, has the capacity, or will take the trouble, to stand up for it. If this be so, the sooner such a civilization receives notice to quit, the better. It can only go on from bad to worse, until destroyed and regenerated (like the Western Empire) by energetic barbarians.

Endnote

[1] The case of the Bombay Parsees is a curious instance in point. When this industrious and enterprising tribe, the descendants of the Persian fire-worshippers, flying from their native country before the Caliphs, arrived in Western India, they were admitted to toleration by the

Hindoo sovereigns, on condition of not eating beef. When those regions afterwards fell under the dominion of Mahomedan conquerors, the Parsees obtained from them a continuance of indulgence, on condition of refraining from pork. What was at first obedience to authority became a second nature, and the Parsees to this day abstain both from beef and pork. Though not required by their religion, the double abstinence has had time to grow into a custom of their tribe; and custom, in the East, is a religion.

The "Open Society" and Its Fallacies

WILMOORE KENDALL

A little over 100 years ago John Stuart Mill wrote in his essay *On Liberty* that " . . . there ought to exist the fullest liberty of professing and discussing, as a matter of ethical conviction, any doctrine, however immoral it may be considered."[1] The sentence from which this is taken is not *obiter:* Chapter Two of his book is devoted to arguments, putatively philosophical in character, which if they were sound would warrant precisely such a conclusion;[2] we have therefore every reason to assume that Mill meant by the sentence just what it says. The topic of Chapter Two is the entire "communications" process in civilized society ("advanced" society, as Mill puts it);[3] and the question he raises is whether there should be limitations on that process.[4] He treats that problem as the central problem of all civilized societies, the one to which all other problems are subordinate, because of the consequences, good or ill, that a society must bring upon itself according as it adopts this or that solution to it. And he has supreme confidence in the rightness of the solution he offers. Presumably to avoid all possible misunderstanding, he provides several alternative statements of it, each of which makes his intention abundantly clear, namely, that society must be so organized as to make that solution its supreme law. "Fullest," that is, absolute freedom of thought and speech, he asserts by clear implication[5] in the entire argument of the chapter, is not to be one of several competing goods society is to foster, one that on occasion might reasonably be sacrificed, in part at least, to the preservation of other goods; *i.e.,* he refuses to recognize any competing good in the name of which it can be limited. The silencing of dissenters on behalf of a received doctrine, of an accepted idea—this is an alternative statement—is *never* justified:[6] it can only do hurt, unwarranted hurt, alike to the person silenced, to the individual or group that silences, to the doctrine or idea on behalf of which the silencing is done, and to the society in the name of which the silencers silence.[7] The quotation I started with is, then, merely the strongest, the most intransigent, of several formulations of a general prescription he makes for advanced societies. We shall do well to examine it, phrase-by-phrase, before proceeding:

"There ought to exist"—*ought,* so that the prescription is put forward on ethical grounds—"the fullest liberty"—a liberty, *i.e.,* that no one (individual, group, government, even society as a whole) is entitled to interfere with—"of professing and discussing"—that is, of publicly propagating—"as a matter of ethical conviction"—which, however, as any reader can quickly satisfy himself by re-examining Chapter II, is not intended to exclude other types of conviction, "intellectual" conviction for example—"any doctrine"—and "doctrine" is not intended to exclude, either, since he uses the term synonymously with "idea" and "opinion"; usually, indeed, he prefers the word "opinion"—"however immoral it may be considered"—where "immoral" also is used merely to cover what Mill considers the extreme case, the case in which, he supposes, people are least likely to refrain from silencing; and he would be equally willing, as the

From *American Political Science Review,* Vol. 54 (1960), pp. 972–979. Reprinted with permission of the American Political Science Association.

context shows, to write "however wrong," that is, "however incorrect," "however dangerous," "however foolish," or even "however harmful," and where "it may be considered" is recognizably shorthand for "it may be considered by anyone whomsoever."

It is fashionable, these days, in part because of a fairly recent book by the scientist-philosopher K. R. Popper,[8] to call the kind of society Mill had in mind an "open society"—by at least implied contrast with a "closed" society, that is, an "hermetically sealed" society, in which Mill's grand principle is, by definition, *not* observed. And we are told, variously, by writers whom we may call (because they so call themselves) Liberals, that we have an open society and ought to protect it against the machinations of those who would like to close it; or that we have a closed society and ought, heeding Mill's arguments, to turn it forthwith into an open society; or that democracy, freedom, progress—any or all of them—must stand or fall, according as we maintain or inaugurate or return to an open society; or that all who are opposed to the idea of the open society are authoritarians, enemies of human freedom, totalitarians. We are told all this, however, at least in its application to civilized societies in general (as opposed to the United States in particular),[9] on grounds that have not varied perceptibly since Mill set them down in the *Essay*. We are still dealing, then, with Mill's issue; and we shall think more clearly about it, I believe, if we keep it stated as much as possible in his terms—for no subsequent pleader for the open society has possessed his clarity or vigor of mind—as follows: Ought there to exist in organized society—the United States, *e.g.*—that "fullest liberty of professing and discussing" that Mill argues for? On what theoretical grounds can that liberty be defended? Is openness of the kind Mill's society would possess one of the characteristics of the *good* society? Before attempting to deal with these questions, let me pause to clarify certain aspects of his position.

━━

I

First, Mill must not be understood as saying, over-all, something *more* extravagant than he is actually saying. He is fully aware of the necessity for laws against libel and slander, and does not deem them inconsistent with his doctrine.[10] He is aware, also, of organized society's need to protect its younger members against certain forms of expression;[11] which is to say that his "fullest liberty of professing and discussing" is to obtain only among adults. Laws prohibiting, *e.g.*, the circulation of obscene literature amongst school-children, or, *e.g.*, utterance calculated to undermine the morals (however the society chooses to define morals) of a minor, are presumably not proscribed. Nor does the doctrine outlaw sanctions against incitement to crime[12]—provided, one must hasten to add, nothing political is involved (Mill would permit punishment for incitement to, *e.g.*, tyrannicide, only if it could be shown to have resulted in an overt act).[13] And, finally—a topic about which, as it seems to me, there is much confusion amongst commentators on Mill—he would permit the police to disperse a mob where a riot is clearly imminent, even if its shoutings did bear upon some political, social, or economic issue; but not, he makes abundantly clear, on grounds of any official exception to the doctrinal tendency of the shoutings. The individuals concerned would be free to resume their agitation the following morning.[14]

This is an important point because the passage in question, dealing with the mob at the corn-merchant's house, has given Mill an undeserved reputation for having been an adherent of the clear-and-present-danger doctrine as we know it today. We may perhaps clear it up best as follows. The situations covered by the clear-and-present danger doctrine, as applied, *e.g.*, to the Communist "threat," and by parallel doctrines in contemporary political theory,[15] are those in which Mill was *most* concerned to maintain absolute liberty of discussion—those situations, namely, in which the ideas being expressed have a tendency dangerous to the established political, social, or economic order. We must not, then, suppose his society to be one in which anarchists, or defenders of polygamy, for example, could be silenced because of the likelihood of their picking up supporters and, finally, winning the day; since for Mill the likelihood of their picking up supporters is merely a further reason for letting them speak. *All* utterance with a bearing on public policy—political, social or economic—is to be permitted, no matter what some members of society, even the majority, even all the members save some lonely dissenter,[16] may happen to think of it. Mill must, then, also not be understood as saying something *less* extravagant than he is actually saying.

Second, what is at issue for Mill is not merely unlimited freedom of speech (as just defined) but, as he makes abundantly clear, unlimited freedom of thought as well, *and* a way of life appropriate to their maintenance. To put it otherwise: when we elevate freedom of thought and speech to the position of society's highest good, it ceases to be merely freedom of thought and speech, and becomes—with respect to a great many important matters—the society's ultimate standard of *order*.

Mill did not dwell upon the inescapable implications of this aspect of his position; it has been left to his epigones, expecially in the United States, to think the position out. The open society, they tell us repeatedly, *must* see to it that all doctrines start out equal in the market-place of ideas; for society to assign an advantaged position to these doctrines rather than those would be tantamount to suppressing those; society can, therefore, have no orthodoxy, no public truth, no standard, upon whose validity it is entitled to insist; outside its private homes, its churches, and perhaps its non-public schools, it therefore cannot indoctrinate; *all* questions are for it open questions, and must, publicly, be treated as open. If it has public schools and universities, it will be told (and with unexceptionable logic), these also must treat all questions as open—otherwise what happens to the freedom of thought and so, ultimately, to the freedom of speech of the student who might have thought differently had his teachers not treated some questions as closed? Even if in their hearts and souls all the members of the open society believe in a particular religion, or a particular church, each must nevertheless be careful in his public capacity to treat all religions and churches as equal, to treat dissent, when and as it occurs, as the peer of dogma, to treat the voodoo missionary from Cuba as on an equal plane with an Archbishop of his own church.[17] The open society's first duty (so its custodians will remind it, and if not those at home then those abroad)[18] is to freedom; and that means that it is *not* free to give public status to its beliefs, its standards, and its loyalties. Mill's disciples are completely faithful to the spirit of his thought when they insist that if we mean business about freedom, that is how it is going to have to be. The open society confers "freedom" upon its members; but it does so at the cost of its own freedom as a society.

Third, Mill denies the existence—that is to say, at any particular place and moment—not only of a public truth,[19] but of any truth whatever unless it be the truth of the denial itself. (Let us not press this last too far, however, lest it seem a mere "debater's" point; it is of course, the Achilles' heel of all skepticisms.) Reduced to its simplest terms, the argument of the *Essay* runs as follows: whenever and wherever men disagree about a teaching, a doctrine, an opinion, an idea, we have no way of knowing which party is correct; the man (or group) who moves to silence a teaching on the ground that it is incorrect attributes to himself a kind of knowledge (Mill says an "infallibility") that no one is ever entitled to claim short of (if then) the very case where the question is sure not to arise—that is, where there is unanimity, and so no temptation to silence to begin with. When, therefore, Mill's followers demand the elevation of skepticism to the status of a national religion, and the remaking of society in that image, they are not reading into his position something that is not there—for all that Mill himself, as I have intimated, preserves a discreet silence on the detailed institutional consequences of his position. They are, rather, only making specific applications of notions that, for Mill, are the point of departure for the entire discussion.

The *basic* position, in fine, is not that society must have no public truth, no orthodoxy, no preferred doctrines, *because* it must have freedom of speech; but that it must not have them *for the same reason* that it must have freedom of speech, namely: because, in any given situation, no supposed truth has any proper claim to special treatment, and this in turn because it may turn out to be incorrect—nay, *will* turn out to be at least partially incorrect, since each competing idea is at most a partial truth. Nor is that all: Mill's freedom-of-speech doctrine is not merely derivative from a preliminary assault upon truth itself;[20] it is *inseparable from* that assault and cannot, I contend, be defended on any other ground. It is incompatible with religious, or any other, belief.

Fourth, Mill is not saying that no man must be silenced because every man has a "right" to freedom of speech. Consistent skeptic that he is, he warns us—and from an early moment—that he disclaims any advantage that might accrue to his argument from an appeal to abstract right; he is going to justify his position in terms of "utility," in terms of "the permanent interest of a man [*sic*] as a progressive being,"[21] whatever that may mean; and he sticks scrupulously to at least the first half of the promise throughout the *Essay*. This raises interesting questions as to (a) what Mill could have meant—whether indeed he means anything at all that people committed to the idea of abstract right might find intelligible—by such words as "ethical," "immoral," etc.; as to (b) the pains Mill takes, throughout his main argument, to reduce the question, "Should some types of expression be prohibited in civilized society because the ideas they express are wicked?" to the question, "Should some types of expression be prohibited because they are intellectually incorrect?"; and as to (c) the kind of moral fervor his followers have poured into the propagation of his views. Everything reduces itself for Mill to intellectual argument, where you either win or draw or lose by the sheer appeal to reason—which, for Mill, excludes *ex hypothesi* any appeal to revelation or authority, for that would merely precipitate an endless discussion as to the status, from the standpoint of reason, of revelation and authority.

The notion of a "right" to freedom of speech, a capacity on the part of every man to say what he pleases that society must respect, because he is *entitled* to it—of a right that men have to live in the kind of society that Mill projects—is a later development. It occurs in different countries for different reasons and under different auspices; but to the extent that it is intended seriously it represents a complete break with Mill. Those who appeal to such a notion therefore have in his own shrewd example a warning that they must not attempt to do so on his grounds;[22] and much current confusion about the open society would be avoided if they would but take the warning to heart. In short, if we are going to speak of a *right* to freedom of speech, a *right* to live in an open society, we are going to have to justify it with arguments of a different character from Mill's, and so move the discussion onto a plane entirely different from Mill's. We are, above all, going to have to subordinate what we have to say to certain rules of discourse from which Mill, by his own fiat, is happily free. For any such right is inconceivable save as one component of a system or complex of rights, that mutually limit and determine one another and are meaningless save as they are deemed subject to the general proposition that we are not entitled to the exercise of *any* right unless we discharge the duties correlative to that right. Once we begin to argue

from premises of that sort we shall begin to talk sense, not nonsense, about freedom of speech and the open society. And the essence of the sense, I hasten to add, will be found to lie in the fact that we are no longer driving the roots of our doctrine into the soil of skepticism, because (as I have suggested already) once we speak of a right[23] we have already ceased to be skeptics. And nothing is more certain than that we shall come out with something quite different from Popper's conception of the open society.

Fifth, Mill was fully aware (as his disciples seem not to be) both of the novelty and of the revolutionary character of his proposal for a society organized around the notion of freedom of speech. Just as he deliberately cuts himself off from any appeal to the notion of abstract right, so does he cut himself off from any appeal to tradition. Not only had no one ever before taught his doctrine concerning freedom of speech. No one had ever taught a doctrine even remotely like his. No one, indeed, had ever discussed such a doctrine even as a matter of speculative fancy.[24] Hardly less than Machiavelli, and more than Hobbes, Mill is in full rebellion against both religion and philosophy, and so in full rebellion also against the traditional society that embodies them.[25] Hardly less than Machiavelli, he conceives himself a "new prince in a new state,"[26] obliged to destroy what has preceded him so that he may create what he feels stirring within him.[27] Hardly less than Machiavelli, again, he is a teacher of *evil*: all truths that have preceded his are (as we have noted in passing above) at most partial truths, and enjoy even that status only because Mill confers it upon them.[28] To reverse a famous phrase, Mill thinks of himself as standing not upon the shoulders of giants but of pygmies. He appeals to no earlier teacher,[29] identifies himself with nothing out of the past; and his doctrine of freedom of speech is, as I have intimated already, the unavoidable logical consequence of the denials from which his thought moves. Not, however, because it is in fact to be the public policy of the society he will found, not because it is to govern his followers' actions with respect to the freedom of thought of others, but because it is the perfect weapon—perfect because of its alleged connection with the quest for truth—to turn upon the traditional society that he must overthrow. For he who would destroy a society must first destroy the public truth it conceives itself as embodying; and Mill's doctrine of freedom of speech, to the extent that it gets itself accepted publicly, does precisely that. I do not, I repeat, believe it can be separated from the evil teaching that underlies it; and nothing could be more astonishing than the incidence of persons amongst us who because of their religious commitments must repudiate the evil teaching, yet continue to embrace the doctrine.

Sixth, Mill's most daring *démarche* in the *Essay* (and Popper's in the *Open Society and Its Enemies*) is that of confronting the reader with a series of false dilemmas: unlimited freedom of speech or all-out thought-control; the open society or the closed society; etc. I say "false" for two reasons: first, because unlimited freedom of speech and the open society are not real alternatives at all, as I hope shortly to show. And second, because the dilemmas as posed conceal the real choices available to us, which are always choices as to how-open-how-closed our society is to be, and thus not choices between two possibilities but choices among an infinite range of possibilities. Mill would have us choose between never silencing and declaring ourselves infallible, as Popper would have us believe that a society cannot be a little bit closed, any more than a woman can be a little bit pregnant. All our knowledge of politics bids us not to fall into that trap. Nobody wants all-out thought-control or the closed society; and nobody has any business pretending that somebody else wants them. For the real question is, how open can a society be and still remain open at all? Or, to put it differently, is there any surer prescription for arriving, willy nilly, in spite of ourselves, at the closed society, than is involved in current pleas for the open society?

II

That brings me to the central business of this article, which I may put as follows. Let us adjourn objections to open society doctrines on the ground that they are rooted in demonstrably evil teachings. Let us also suppose, *arguendo*, that we have organized a society in accordance with Mill's prescriptions, and for Mill's reasons. Have we then cause to suppose, as Mill thinks, that we shall end up forwarding the interests of truth? In other words, Mill offers us not only an exhortation but a prediction, and we wish merely to know what would in fact happen if we did what he tells us to do. My contention will be that, once the question is

put in that way,[30] we run up against some insuperable objections to his prescriptions in and of themselves—objections, moreover, that remain equally valid even if one starts out, unlike Mill, from a supposed "right," whether natural or constitutional, to freedom of speech. I shall argue the objections in a logical order such that if each in turn were overcome the remaining ones would still stand.

Mill's proposals have as one of their tacit premises a false conception of the nature of society, and are, therefore, unrealistic on their face. They assume that society is, so to speak, a *debating club* devoted above all to the pursuit of truth, and capable therefore of subordinating itself—and all other considerations, goods, and goals—to that pursuit. Otherwise, the proposals would go no further than to urge upon society the common-sense view that the pursuit of truth is *one* of the goods it ought to cherish (even perhaps that one which it is most likely, in the press of other matters, to fail to make sufficient provision for); that it will neglect this good only at its own peril (a point that could easily be demonstrated); and that, accordingly, it should give hard and careful thought to what kind of provision it can make for it without disrupting unduly the pursuit of other goods. But we know only too well that society is *not* a debating club—all our experience of society drives the point home—and that, even if it were one, like the UN General Assembly, say, the chances of its adopting the pursuit of truth as its supreme good are negligible. Societies, alike by definition and by the teaching of history, cherish a whole series of goods—among others, their own self-preservation, the *living* of the truth they believe themselves to embody already, and the communication of that truth (pretty much intact, moreover) to future generations, their religion, etc.—which they are not only likely to value as much as or more than the pursuit of truth, but *ought* to value as much as or more than the pursuit of truth, because these are *preconditions* of the pursuit of truth.

To put it a little differently, the proposals misconceive the strategic problem, over against organized society, of those individuals who *do* value the pursuit of truth above all other things. That strategic problem we may state as follows: *fortunate* that society that has even a small handful—a "select minority," in Ortega y Gasset's phrase—of persons who value the pursuit of truth in the way in which Mill imagines a society valuing it. *Fortu-*

nate that select minority in such a society, if it can prevail upon the society to provide it with the leisure and resources with which to engage in the pursuit of truth; or, failing that, at least not to stand in the way of its pursuit of truth. And *wise* that society whose decision-makers see deeply enough into things to provide that select minority—even in the context of guarantees against its abusing its privileges—the leisure and the resources it needs for the pursuit of truth. To ask more than that of society, to ask that it give that select minority freedom to treat publicly all questions as open questions, as open not only for itself in the course of its discharge of its own peculiar function but for everybody, is Utopian in the worst sense of the word; and so, certain to defeat the very purpose the asking is intended to serve. By asking for all, even assuming that all to be desirable, we imperil our chances of getting that little we might have got had we asked only for that little.

If we nevertheless waive that objection, we confront another, namely, that the proposals have as a further tacit premise a false conception of human beings, and how they act in organized society. Concretely, Mill not only assumes that speech (the professing and discussing of any doctrine, however immoral) is incapable of doing hurt in society. (He has to assume this, since he calls for non-interference with speech, while the overriding principle of the *Essay* is that society is always entitled to interfere in order to prevent hurt, whether to itself or to its individual members.) This is disturbing enough: Socrates, we recall, taught otherwise, namely, that he who teaches my neighbor evil does *me* hurt. But Mill also assumes (else again his proposal is romantic) that people can be persuaded either to *be* indifferent toward the possible tendency of what their neighbors are saying, or at least to *act* as if they were indifferent. We know nothing about people, I suggest, that warrants our regarding such an assumption, once it is brought out into the open, as valid. Thus his proposals, like all political proposals that call implicitly for the refashioning of human nature, can be enforced only through some large-scale institutional coercion. And I believe it to be this consideration, above all, that explains the failure of Mill's followers, to date, to persuade any organized society to adopt his proposals. We have no experience of unlimited freedom of speech as Mill defines it, of the open society as Popper defines it, unless, after a fashion and for a brief moment, in Weimar

Germany—an experience no organized society will be eager to repeat.

Let us now turn to still another objection. I contend that such a society will become *intolerant*, one in which the pursuit of truth can only come to a halt. Whatever the private convictions of the society's individual members concerning what Plato teaches us to call the important things (that is, the things with which truth is primarily concerned), the society itself is now, by definition, dedicated to a national religion of skepticism, to the suspension of judgment as *the* exercise of judgment *par excellence*. It can, to be sure, tolerate all expression of opinion that is predicated upon its own view of truth; but what is it to do with the man who steps forward to urge an opinion, to conduct an inquiry, *not* predicated on that view? What is it to do with the man who, with every syllable of faith he utters, challenges the very foundations of skeptical society? What can it say to him except, "Sir, you cannot enter into our discussions, because you and we have no common premises from which discussion between us can be initiated?" What can it do, in a word, but silence him, and look on helplessly as within its own bosom the opinions about the important things descend into an ever greater conforming dullness? Nor—unlike traditional society, which did *not* regard all questions as open questions—need it hesitate to silence him. The proposition that all opinions are equally—and hence infinitely—valuable, said to be the unavoidable inference from the proposition that all opinions are equal, is only one—and perhaps the less likely—of two possible inferences, the other being: all opinions are equally—and hence infinitely—*without* value, so what difference does it make if one, particularly one not our own, gets suppressed?[31] This we may fairly call the central paradox of the theory of freedom of speech. In order to practice tolerance on behalf of the pursuit of truth, you have first to value and believe in not merely the pursuit of truth but Truth itself, with all its accumulated riches to date. The all-questions-are-open-questions society cannot do that; it cannot, therefore, practice tolerance towards those who disagree with it. It must persecute—and so, on its very own showing, arrest the pursuit of truth.

I next contend that such a society as Mill prescribed will descend ineluctably into ever-deepening *differences of opinion*, into progressive breakdown of those common premises upon which alone a society can conduct its affairs by discussion, and so into the abandonment of the discussion process and the arbitrament of public questions by violence and civil war. This is the phenomenon—we may call it the dispersal of opinion—to which Rousseau, our greatest modern theorist of the problem, recurred again and again in his writings.[32] The all-questions-are-open-questions society cannot endeavor to arrest it, by giving preferred status to certain opinions and, at the margin, mobilizing itself internally for their defense; for by definition it places a *premium* upon dispersion by inviting irresponsible speculation and irresponsible utterance. As time passes, moreover, the extremes of opinion will—as they did in Weimar—grow further and further apart, so that (for the reason noted above) their bearers can less and less tolerate even the thought of one another, still less one another's presence in society. And again the ultimate loser is the pursuit of truth.

Still another tacit premise of the proposals is the extraordinary notion that the discussion process, which correctly understood does indeed forward the pursuit of truth, and does indeed call for *free* discussion, is one and the same thing with Mill's unlimited freedom of speech. They rest, in consequence, upon a false conception of the discussion process. What they will produce is not truth but rather only deafening noise and demoralizing confusion. For the essence of Mill's freedom of speech is the divorce of the right to speak from the duties correlative to the right; the right to speak is a right to speak *ad nauseam*, and with impunity. It is shot through and through with the egalitarian overtones of the French Revolution, which are as different from the measured aristocratic overtones of the pursuit of truth by discussion, as understood by the tradition Mill was attacking, as philosophy is different from phosphorus.

Of the latter point we may sufficiently satisfy ourselves, it seems to me, by recalling how the discussion process works in those situations in which men who are products of the tradition organize themselves for a serious venture in the pursuit of truth—as they do in, say, a branch of scholarship, an academic *discipline*, and the community of truth-seekers corresponding to it.[33]

Such men demonstrably proceed on some such principles as these: (a) The pursuit of truth is indeed forwarded by the exchange of opinions and ideas among many; helpful suggestions do indeed emerge sometimes from surprising quarters; but one does not leap from these facts to the conclusion that helpful suggestions may come from just anybody. (b) The man or woman who wishes to exercise the right to be heard has a logically and temporally prior obligation to *prepare* himself for participation in the exchange, and to prepare himself in the manner defined by the community. Moreover (c), from the moment he begins to participate in the exchange, he must make manifest, by his behavior, his sense of the duty to act is if the other participants had something to teach him—the duty, in a word, to see to it that the exchange goes forward in an atmosphere of courtesy and mutual self-respect. Next (d), the entrant must so behave as to show that he understands that scholarly investigation did not begin with his appearance on the scene, that there is a strong presumption that prior investigators have not labored entirely in vain, and that the community is the custodian of—let us not sidestep the *mot juste*—an *orthodoxy*, no part of which it is going to set lightly to one side. (e) That orthodoxy must be understood as concerning first and foremost the frame of reference within which the exchange of ideas and opinions is to go forward. That frame of reference is, to be sure, subject to change, but this is a matter of meeting the arguments that led originally to its adoption, and meeting them in recognition that the ultimate decision, as to whether or not to change it, lies with the community. (f) The entrant, insofar as he wishes to challenge the orthodoxy, must expect barriers to be placed in his way, and must not be astonished if he is punished, at least in the short term, by what are fashionably called "deprivations"; he must, indeed, recognize that the barriers and the deprivations are a necessary part of the organized procedure by which truth is pursued. (g) Access to the channels of communication that represent the community's central ritual (the learned journals, that is to say) is something that the entrant wins by performing the obligation to produce a craftsmanlike piece of work. (h) The ultimate fate of the entrant who disagrees with the orthodoxy but cannot persuade the community to accept his point of view is, quite simply, isolation within or banishment from the community.

No suggestion is made that this is a complete statement of the rules as we see them operating about us in the scholarly disciplines, or that the particular forms of words employed are the happiest, or most accurate, that could be found. They do, however, seem to me to suggest the broad outlines of the paradigm of the free discussion process as it goes forward in an academic community, and to drive home its differences from the freedom of speech process as Mill defines it. Nor, I think, could anything be more obvious than the answer to the question, which of the two is the more likely to forward the pursuit of truth? But this is not all. *The point about Mill's model is that by giving equal privileges to those who are in fact opposed to or ignorant of the discussion process, it constitutes a major onslaught against Truth. The two paradigms are not only different, but incompatible.*

It would not be easy, of course, to transfer the rules of the discussion process set forth here to the public forum of a society; nor is there any point in denying that the transfer would involve our openly conceding to society far greater powers, particularly as regards silencing the ill-mannered, the ignorant, the irrelevant, than it would ever enjoy under Mill's prescription. Here, however, two things must be kept in mind. First (however reluctant we may be to admit it), that society always has, and constantly exercises, the power to silence. And second, that no society is likely, within the foreseeable future, to remake itself in the image of either of the two paradigms. The question, always, is that of which of the two we accept as the ideal toward which we try to move. That is the real issue at stake between the proponents and opponents of the "open society."

Endnotes

[1] *On Liberty and Considerations on Representative Government*, ed. R. B. McCallum (Oxford, 1946), p. 14 fn.

[2] That is approximately how Mill himself puts it: the words preceding what I have quoted are, "If the arguments of the present chapter are of any validity, ..." The chapter is entitled "Of the Liberty of Thought and Discussion."

[3] *Cf. ibid.*, p. 9: " . . . we may leave out of consideration those backward states of society in which the race itself may be considered as in its nonage." The distinction seems to turn variously (*ibid.*) on whether "mankind have become capable of being improved by free and equal discussion" and whether they "have attained the capacity of being guided to their own improvement by conviction or persuasion." On the latter point he adds, perhaps a little optimistically: " . . . a period long since reached in all nations with whom we need here concern ourselves." *Cf. ibid.* p. 59, where he refers, astonishingly, to "the present low state of the

human mind," that being the point he needs to establish the thesis there in question.

[4] Who should be permitted, in the fashionable jargon of the "communications" literature, "to say what, and to whom."

[5] Those who regard "absolute" as too strong a term to be deemed a synonym of "fullest" may wish to be reminded of the following passage (*ibid.*, p. 11): " . . . the appropriate region of human liberty . . . comprises . . . liberty of conscience in the most comprehensive sense: liberty of thought and feeling; *absolute* freedom of opinion and sentiment on all subjects, practical or speculative, scientific, moral, or theological. [And the] liberty of expressing and publishing opinions . . . is practically inseparable from [liberty of thought] . . . ." (italics added). And *cf. ibid.*: "No society . . . is completely free in which [these liberties] . . . do not exist *absolute and unqualified*" (italics added).

[6] *Cf. ibid.*, p. 14: " . . . I deny the right of the people to exercise such coercion, either by themselves or their government. The power itself is illegitimate. The best government has no more title to it than the worst." The statement could hardly be more sweeping.

[7] Not to speak of "mankind." *Cf. ibid.*, pp. 14–15: " . . . the peculiar evil of silencing the expression of an opinion is, that it is robbing the human race; . . . those who dissent from the opinion, still more than those who hold it."

[8] K. R. Popper, *The Open Society and Its Enemies* (London, 1945), 2 vols. The term "open society" is of course much older (Bergson uses a distinction between "open" and "closed" society in *Les deux sources de la morale et de la religion*, though for a quite different purpose). Popper wedded the term "open society" to Mill's ideas, and the term "closed society" to those of his *bêtes noires*, Plato especially.

[9] The exception is necessary, because the American arguments are often based on the meaning of the Constitution of the United States, the First Amendment especially.

[10] *Cf. op. cit.*, p. 73: "Whenever, in short, there is a definite damage, or a definite risk of [definite?] damage, either to an individual or to the public, the case is taken out of the province of liberty, and placed in that of morality and law."

[11] *Cf. ibid.*, p. 72: " . . . protection against themselves is confessedly due to children and persons under age. . . . "

[12] *Cf. ibid.*, p. 49: " . . . even opinions lose their immunity when the circumstances in which they are expressed are such as to constitute their expression a positive instigation to some mischievous act." To this writer's mind a curious concession, which Mill ought *not* to have made. Once it is made, a society wishing to

silence this or that form of persuasive utterance has only to declare the behavior it is calculated to produce a crime, and it may silence—with Mill's blessing.

[13] *Cf. ibid.*, p. 14 fn.

[14] *Cf. ibid.*, p. 49.

[15] *E.g.*, the doctrine that enemies of liberty must not be permitted to take advantage of "civil liberties" in order to undermine and destroy them; or the doctrine that free society is entitled to interfere with free expression in order to perpetuate its own existence. Mill would certainly not have countenanced either doctrine.

[16] *Cf. ibid.*, p. 14: "If all mankind were of one opinion, and only one person were of the contrary opinion, mankind would be no more justified in silencing that one person, than he, if he had the power, would be justified in silencing all mankind."

[17] Who, after all, is to say which is right?

[18] As witness the sermons addressed by the New York press to the Trujillo regime.

[19] Except, we must remind ourselves, the public truth that there is no public truth.

[20] *Ibid., passim.*

[21] *Ibid.*, p. 9.

[22] We must distinguish here between a "natural" or "ethical" "right" to freedom of expression and a mere constitutional right. The case for the latter could of course be rested upon Mill's grounds, insofar as they are valid.

[23] Again, we must except the merely constitutional right.

[24] Plato, of course, contemplates a freedom of speech *situation* in Book IX of the *Republic;* but merely to show that it can result only in disaster.

[25] *Cf.* Leo Strauss, *Thoughts on Machiavelli* (Glencoe, 1958), ch. 4, *passim.*

[26] *Cf. ibid.*, p. 9.

[27] *Cf. ibid.*, ch. 2, *passim.*

[28] *Cf. op. cit.*, pp. 42–46.

[29] That he had broken sharply with his father and with Bentham is, I take it, a commonplace.

[30] *I.e.*, as a problem for "empirical" political theory.

[31] *Cf.* Bertrand de Jouvenel, *On Sovereignty* (Chicago: 1957), p. 288: "One of the strangest intellectual illusions of the nineteenth century was the idea that toleration could be ensured by moral relativism. . . . The relativist tells us that the man professing opinion A ought to respect opinion B, because his own opinion A has no more intrinsic value than B. But in that case B has no more than A. Attempts to impose either would be attempts to impose what had no intrinsic value; but also suppression of either would be suppression of what had no intrinsic value. And in that case there is no crime . . . in the suppression of contrary opinions." On equality of opinions in Mill, see note 16 *supra.* On the progress in Mill from "equally valuable" to "equally and infinitely valuable," *cf. op. cit.*, p. 46: ". . . truth has no chance but in proportion as every side of it, every opinion which embodies any fraction of the truth, not only finds advocates, but is so advocated as to be listened to." And the presumption, he insists, is that every opinion *does* contain some fraction of the truth: " . . . it is always probable that dissentients have something worth hearing . . . and that truth would lose something by their silence" (p. 42).

[32] See *Social Contract*, IV, i., as also *The Discourse on the Sciences and Arts, passim,* and Rousseau's famous letter of 1767 to the Marquis of Mirabeau. *Cf.* de Jouvenel, *op. cit.*, p. 286: "The whole of [Rousseau's] . . . large stock of political wisdom consists in contrasting the dispersion of feelings in a people morally disintegrated by the progress of the 'sciences and arts,' with the natural unity of a people in which dissociation has not occurred." As de Jouvenel notes (p. 287), Rousseau, though himself a Protestant, deplored the introduction of Protestantism into France, and on these grounds.

[33] A similar point might be developed over the difference between Mill's freedom of speech and the free discussion of the traditional American town-meeting.

Free Speech and Political Extremism: How Nasty Are We Free to Be?

CARL COHEN

I want to discuss the limits of freedom in speaking and publishing: what they are, and what they should be. I want to ask you and myself about the frontiers, the extemes, the uses of speech that seem barely tolerable, about uses of freedom that are, in fact, intolerable to many.

I am not thinking merely about controversial speech. That's easy. Or agitating speech. That's not very hard. I am thinking about speech that is nasty, vicious, wrongheaded, and downright evil or at least thought to be so. I am not sure what content or manner meets that description. We all know that when two parties are in bitter, mortal conflict, each one thinks the other is evil, nasty and morally wrong.

As an example, consider the war between Iran and Iraq recently in progress. Each party finds the other utterly vicious. But, you say, that is *war!* Right. We want to think about freedom within a civil society, a society divided, perhaps, even angry and bitter, but still civil. How far may speech go in such a setting? What is permissible?

Consider another example, within a civil society, closer to our target. In Miami, on Biscayne Boulevard, in March of 1986, there was a confrontation between a group of anti-Contra demonstrators, and a group of pro-Contra demonstrators— groups whose members detest and revile one another, as you know. [Note: The double negative "anti-Contra" sounds silly, but in this case is not readily avoidable; I use it for the sake of accuracy.] One of the pro-Contra folks was waving a placard at one of the anti-Contra speakers which read: "[So-and-so] is a bigot . . . " and then added more about Nicaragua. It was a nasty sign, and the police asked him to stop waving it. He replied, according to the lengthy report in *The Miami Herald*, "On top of that, he's an SOB" and then he added, "They say in war and love everything is permitted. And this is war!"

Let's think about this situation briefly, to learn from it. We may accept the premise about war, although it may be overstated; there are laws and rules governing warfare, too. In war, let us assume, no holds are barred. But, in that conflict of demonstrators, could nastiness in speech be justified by a state of war? Surely not. We were then, and we are now, not at war. In war we shoot and kill. Here in Miami we are in a civil society, seeking to govern ourselves, although divided, with order and fairness, and aiming to live decently.

Nothing is to be gained by saying: The rules are off! No rules! That simply makes brutes of us all. In that way we return ourselves to the animal world. I remember a sort of chant I learned, long ago, from my Spanish teacher at Miami High, in which the final line (if I recall correctly) was a petition to Santa Maria, to deliver us all from the reign of the animals. The philosophically interesting and politically interesting question is: What speech is permitted when the rules are *on*?

Now that pro-Contra demonstrator was wrong to justify his nasty words by the claims of war. But he was not necessarily wrong in seeking to justify his words *within* the rules. I do not address the merits of the argument—which side is right, whether anyone in the controversy is or was a bigot or an SOB. This is not my concern here, plainly. But saying such things of another demonstrator, or of the other group (that they are bigots, etc.)—is that permissible? Or should the police have taken away his sign?

I will put my cards on the table: I think that that particular speech was within the rules. The rules permit it, the good rules of a good society, the rules that protect speech and the freedom to speak to the furthest limit in a democratic civil community.

I will defend here an old, sound, conservative

From *Law and Philosophy*, Vol. 7 (1989), pp. 263–279. Reprinted with permission of Kluwer Academic Publishers.

proposition: in the realm of political speech, no content, no nastiness, no stupidity or evil, may be silenced. Even when we are convinced, to the bottom of our souls, that what they are saying is awful and ugly, we must protect their saying. That is the glory of a free society.

The argument defending this conclusion I am going to pursue with you in some detail. But I don't want to do that in the context of the pro-Contra/anti-Contra conflict. That's almost too easy, because we are all well aware that that conflict is a political one, and one on which there really are two sides, both vigorously argued. So I want to transpose the case into one that is harder, and one in which we (very probably) are all on the same political side.

In that same confrontation (according to the *Miami Herald* of 23 March 1986) one of the pro-Contra supporters said: "I'm Jewish, and what these people are doing is the same as if the Nazis were demonstrating in Miami Beach." And another participant also compared the anti-Contra protest to a Nazi march in a Jewish neighborhood in Miami Beach, or to a Ku Klux Klan rally in a black neighborhood.

That's an extreme comparison, perhaps, but a useful one. Let's think in those terms. We, you and I, will have no disagreement about the evils of Nazism, or the nastiness of racism. So, as an intellectual adventure with some electricity, let's ask: What limits are there on the nastiness of *those* nasty folks? In this matter I am as privileged as the person quoted in the demonstration; I'm Jewish too.

We Americans have some experience in these matters. Ten years ago, you will recall, in Skokie, Illinois,—also a very Jewish community, a northern suburb of Chicago—the Nazis planned a march. The Village government tried to stop them. The battle became a royal one, even reaching the United States Supreme Court. Let's think about the extremes of political speech in that context. In your minds, picture the American Nazis, jerks, square-heads, with uniforms and swastikas and placards, planning to march down Collins Avenue, or Washington Avenue, on Miami Beach, and then down Fifth St. [My parents, in their late years, lived in a condominium at the corner of Washington and Fifth. I remember my mother saying that when that building opened, a new Chapter of Hadassah came instantly into being!]

Now, many would say that such a Nazi march should not be permitted. They might say: "Look, we recognize the central importance of free speech. But free speech is like every other freedom in that it must have limits in a good society. The Nazis, saying what they say in the way they say it, exceed reasonable limits. Associating themselves with the annihilation of millions of Jews, they seek to advance their views, abrasively, in a community—Miami Beach—populated by many of the same people who had been tortured by Nazis. Some of these Jews, after narrow escape, actually sought refuge in this country, in Miami. We applaud the vigorous defense of free speech—but this is a case in which the constitutional protections of dissident opinions do not apply."

But that position is not sufficient as it stands. Certainly it is true that neither the Constitution, nor any sensible principle lying behind it, guarantees the right to say anything, anywhere, anytime. But if we are going to allow some speech to be restricted, those restrictions must be very narrowly drawn, and sustain a heavy burden of justification. So the Nazi-blockers [not "anti-Nazis" because that name would apply to many who would also protect the right of the Nazis to demonstrate] face the task of giving sound argument specifying the proper limits of free speech, limits that would be exceeded by the Nazis. I use the case of the Nazis precisely because it is as extreme as any I can imagine, and therefore the best test for the principles I shall put forward.

My enterprise, then, is to consider the limits and the arguments the Nazi-blockers put forward, and to see if we find them sound. And you will join me in this task, I trust. I will do this in six short "chapters."

Chapter 1. Danger

Grave danger is the basis of a kind of limit upon speech thought reasonable by many. You know the famous passage written by Justice Holmes in 1919: "The question in every case [he wrote] is whether the words used are used in such circumstances and are of such a nature to create a clear and present danger that they will bring about substantive evils that Congress has a right to prevent"

[*Schenck v. United States*, 249 US 47 at 52]. Now if the Nazis march on Collins Avenue the dangers are patently clear, and arise immediately as they march. So would not Justice Holmes's illustration apply? He continued: "The most stringent protection of free speech would not protect a man in falsely shouting fire in a theater, and causing a panic." Don't Nazis marching in Miami Beach, in effect, shout fire in a theater? If their speech is irresponsible, why must we permit it? Neither the shouter in the theater, nor the Nazi on Collins Avenue (says the Nazi-blocker) is entitled to the constitutional protection of free speech.

But the analogy with the theater is in fact not good at all. Whoever shouts fire in a theater is certainly not entitled to protection on grounds of free speech. But the circumstances of a Nazi demonstration differ from those in a theater in three fundamental respects:

a) The theater audience is captive, subjected against its will to the shout and the sequel. Not so any gathering for a Nazi parade. Those angered or offended are free to stay away, or to leave; they need have nothing to do with it. The panic in the theater traps and injures those who had come for reasons entirely unrelated to the shout. What is reasonably said in a theater depends, of course, upon what properly goes on there—an expectation reasonably imposed upon speech in the classroom as well. The shouted false alarm is not essentially speech in the theater at all; it is a warning of danger fraudulently given, no different from the fraudulent ringing of a fire alarm bell. But concerning the audience any Nazi march may draw, all of this simply cannot be said.

b) A shouted warning, or false alarm, permits no discussion. It is not the expression of opinion, but the signal for flight, giving no opportunity for reasoned reply. The other day, in Ann Arbor, some criminal fool released a tear gas cannister in a theater! The audience was presented with inescapable threat; it had no options. But we who find the Nazis hateful do have options; the Nazi demonstration may be answered with a counter-demonstration, as an anti-Contra demonstration may be answered with a pro-Contra demonstration. What is evil may be exposed, refuted, in print or by voice, then or later. Demonstrations by bigots, Nazis or others, cannot threaten immediate calamity at all comparable to a false alarm in a crowded theater.

c) The shouted alarm of fire is, by hypothesis, false. We would think very differently of an honest warning. No doubt Nazi views are also false—but being right is not a condition on which permission to demonstrate may be premised. If it were, who will decide who is right enough to speak?

So true enough, there are words in some special circumstances which, because of the grave danger they present, cannot claim free speech protection—like the shouting of "Fire!" falsely in a theater. But a political demonstration, in a park or on a major avenue, is nothing like that.

Chapter 2. Incitement to Riot

"But [the Nazi-blocker rejoins] you underestimate the seriousness of the threat this demonstration would immediately create. If the Nazis march with swastikas and brown shirts on Miami Beach they will almost certainly provoke a riot. Incitement to riot is a crime. When it is deliberate as in the case we envisage, when its violent consequences are highly probable and fully anticipated, such incitement cannot be defended as mere speech. It is conduct designed to breach the public peace, using the First Amendment as a shield. Citizens of Miami Beach have the right, even the duty, to protect themselves from that despicable design."

This argument is dangerous. It is often heard, but it seriously misapprehends the concept of "incitement to riot." That a message or a symbol excites an audience to furious antagonism gives no evidence whatever of criminal incitement. That crime consists in urging upon one's audience the commission of some unlawful act in a context in which it is probable that some in the audience will do what is being urged. Even then the speaker will not normally be guilty of criminal incitement unless persons in his audience do in fact engage in the unlawful conduct he urged upon them. Nothing like these conditions are present in the case of a Nazi march in Miami Beach, or an anti-Contra demonstration in Miami. In such demonstrations it is usual that no specific acts are urged at all, and Nazis are very careful never to urge illegal acts. They say things like: "Jews Not Wanted Here!" or, "White Power!" or, "America for the White Man!" Some in their audience may then break the law by attacking not the Jews but the Nazis themselves—but those whose symbols provoked their fury cannot be criminally responsible for that misconduct.

Incitement must be (and in the law it is) very narrowly delineated. When overt unlawful deeds are committed as a direct consequence of agitating speech, that speech becomes a part of the crime—as the planning of a robbery becomes part of the robbery itself; and persons whose inflammatory words lead to the very disorder they propose may be similarly culpable as part of the deliberate creators of that disorder. But Nazis, in Miami Beach, where no one in the audience will be inclined to do anything they may urge, could never be guilty of inciting to riot.

Chapter 3. Incitement and the General Intent to Breach the Peace

"You may be technically correct [the Nazi-blocker answers] about the requirements for that criminal charge, but you are blinded by technicalities. The Nazis delight in creating fright and havoc among Jews. In this country, in recent years, their demonstrations have several times actually resulted in riot. Nazis understand full well how maddening their symbols are to their intended victims; they plan that abrasion. It is a good principle in law that one may reasonably be held to intend the natural and anticipated consequences of one's acts. True, the riot will not be caused by an audience that complies with their urgings, so they may be innocent of some technical crime of incitement. They will nevertheless be guilty of engaging deliberately in conduct designed to infuriate, and calculated to result in a wholesale breach of the public peace. Incitement in that more general sense is what we have the right to protect ourselves against."

This argument has much appeal—but I contend that it is profoundly mistaken. The citizens of Miami Beach, or of Miami or of Skokie, may not silence infuriating speakers because of the response expected to their words. If they may silence speakers on that ground, no truly controversial position on an incendiary topic could be freely presented there. For in that case, whenever it could be shown that the probable reaction would be intem-

perate or disorderly, the advocacy of an unpopular position would have to be forbidden. Thus trying the permissibility of controversial speech to its expected reception establishes what has been called "the heckler's veto." A decent society, one that honors freedom concretely, cannot authorize that veto; it is those who respond illegally and violently who must be restrained.

Very unpopular causes may be as freely advocated under our Constitution as those in popular favor. Political advocates at the extremes, radical or reactionary, wise or crazy, will commonly meet with an angry and unruly reception. Communists, pacifists, Nazis, hawks and doves—those at the extremes—will be forever in need of defense. Their freedom is in our interest not only because rational judgment upon any position requires that that position be heard. Some lessons must be continually relearned, even by those who once taught them. If Nazis are not free to demonstrate because their Jewish audience will be hostile, the Jew will not be free to demonstrate when their Arab audience [and in Detroit we have a very large Arab-American community] promises equal hostility. When demonstrations to which sufficient anger may be threatened are not allowed, the hecklers have been given the veto—and then they may exercise it no matter what the content of their views.

This issue was fully tested, in our country, in a most interesting actual case. In Chicago, in 1949, a passionate message of racial hatred was delivered (by a Catholic priest under suspension) to a sizable audience in a large hall. Outside, a cordon of police struggled to control the infuriated counter-demonstrators, while Father Terminiello completed his speech. He was later convicted of creating a breach of the peace—a breach actually created not by him or his followers but by persons outside the hall, so maddened by his bigotry as to throw bottles and bricks at the windows as he spoke. Is Terminiello to be punished for speaking so? The judge in the trial court had instructed the jury that the words "breach of the peace" include speech that "stirs the public to anger, invites dispute, brings about a condition of unrest, or creates a disturbance. . . ." That, said the Supreme Court of the United States, was grave error. Justice Douglas wrote the majority opinion. He said: "[One] function of free speech under our system of government is to invite dispute. It may indeed best serve its high purpose when it induces a condition of unrest, creates dissatisfaction with conditions as they are, or even stirs people to anger. Speech is often provocative and challenging. It may strike at prejudices and preconceptions and have profound unsettling effects as it presses for acceptance of an idea. That is why freedom of speech, though not absolute, . . . is nevertheless protected against censorship or punishment, unless shown likely to produce a clear and present danger of a serious substantive evil that rises far above public inconvenience, annoyance, or unrest" [*Terminiello v. City of Chicago*, 337 US 1, at 4, 1949].

Ironically, the right of a racist to speak thus defended became a bulwark for the freedom of those they reviled. Years later, civil rights activists, convicted because of the tumultuous responses of their hostile audiences, had *their* convictions reversed also by the Supreme Court, relying on the precedent set in the Terminiello decision.

The pendulum swings for strong and weak alike. In Miami, in 1986, it was the *anti*-Contra demonstrators who were infuriating to the majority, and highly provocative. But in Cambridge, Massachusetts, in 1987, it was the *pro*-Contra speakers who were the object of a maddened attack. I have clipped a photograph from *The New York Times* of a hall at Harvard University, in which a Contra leader, Adolpho Calero, was speaking; an anti-Contra demonstrator, believing him a devil, is attacking the speaker physically to silence him [NY Times 4 Oct 87]. Shall we silence Calero for a breach of the peace, or collar that young man who does not grasp the point that disagreement, even when bitter, does not justify suppression? Plainly he must learn, and we must never forget, that even in the most hostile territory the right to political agitation for all parties (in our country) has been and will be secured.

And those who would forbid a demonstration before it begins have a much weaker case even than those who would convict Calero, or Terminiello. For in those cases, the attacks did take place; in the case of the envisioned march on Miami Beach, we cannot be certain that incivility and disorder will rule the day. You may recall that in the famous Pentagon Papers case, when the United States Government argued that the publication of those papers in the *New York Times* would lead to loss of life in Southeast Asia, the Supreme Court held that such an argument (even if the publication were ultimately found unlawful) may not serve as a ground for the suppression of the publication in advance. If that is true for stolen government papers, is it not all the more true in defense of speech in a public, political demonstration?

Chapter 4. Fighting Words

"Well [says the Nazi-blocker] it should be grounds for suppression, even if it isn't, if the speech in question has a very high probability of provoking violence. Of course we can't know with absolute certainty that a riot will ensue if the Nazis march with swastikas in Miami Beach, but we can be pretty confident when we predict it. Some words and symbols, by their plain meaning in known contexts, are so provocative as to cause decent and reasonable people to respond by fighting. Speech like that [they conclude] is rightly forbidden.

"And in this [they continue] the Supreme Court is on our side. Some years ago, in New Hampshire, a Jehovah's Witness named Chaplinsky was convicted, when stopped from preaching in the street, for shouting at a policemen thus: "You are a goddamned racketeer [and] a damned fascist and the whole government of Rochester [NH] are fascists or agents of fascists." He claimed freedom of speech as his shield, but the Supreme Court held that some utterances are not entitled to normal protection. They wrote: '[It] is well understood that the right of free speech is not absolute at all times and under all circumstances. There are certain well-defined and narrowly limited classes of speech, the prevention and punishment of which have never been thought to raise any constitutional problem. These include the lewd and obscene, the profane, the libelous, and the insulting or "fighting words"—those which by their very utterance inflict injury or tend to incite an immediate breach of the peace' " [*Chaplinsky v. New Hampshire*, 315 US 568, at 572, 1942].

So the Nazi-blocker concludes: "Not protecting 'fighting words' as though they were normal political controversy is plain good sense. In a community where live thousands of survivors of Nazi death camps, an aggressive Nazi demonstration is surely speech which, by its very utterance, inflicts injury and tends to incite an immediate breach of the peace."

But this argument simply does not apply to the case of the political demonstration here being discussed.

First, the doctrine, that words may be treated as equivalent to the first blows in a fight is highly suspect, and it is a view now almost completely abandoned in the courts. What words under what circumstances may be treated so must forever be uncertain and disputable. Words that infuriate you may merely amuse me. Words can hurt, surely,— but there is a great difference between verbal hurts and physical blows. That is why, honoring freedom generally, we place freedom of speech in the most protected of arenas. If words that sometimes provoke a fight are punished because of that danger, the uncertainty about *which* words may have that consequence must chill all debate, hedge all robust speaking in a vigorous contest. Words are not literal blows; the metaphor must not be allowed to confuse; the theory that, in a civil society, nasty words may justify physical retaliation is simply not tenable.

But, second, even if the "fighting words" doctrine had some appropriate application in some contexts, it would have to be so narrowly restricted to special circumstances as to have no bearing on a proposed demonstration by a political sect or party. It could, at best, be applied only to utterances by a specific person to the face of another, being defamatory in the extreme. Demonstrations before a general public—by the KKK, or the Black Panthers, or the anti-Contras, or the pro-Contras—are not one-to-one confrontations however maddening we may think their point.

Third, the doctrine could apply, if ever, only *after* those personal insults had been hurled, and a retaliatory blow struck—never as the ground for forbidding a demonstration in advance.

And finally, if the doctrine were ever applicable, it would certainly be restricted to cases of grave, personal offense; it has no application where the cause of agitation, however bitter, is political. This "fighting words" gambit cannot succeed.

Chapter 5. Obscenity

Finally, then, the Nazi-blocker must admit that it is not really harm to some persons that motivates him, or danger to all, or incitement to riot, or fighting words, or any such concern. It is the plain evil of those Nazi views—the racism and anti-semitism and general stupidity and bigotry—that he thinks deserves to be silenced. When all the other arguments have failed he comes in the end to question the principle of free speech itself, asking, in effect, whether that principle really does oblige us to protect all content, however damnable. This is his last resort.

"Some speech content [he argues at last]— speech utterly without redeeming social value—is not and ought not be protected by the First Amendment. Obscenity, of course, is normally associated with sexually explicit matter. But its essential, nonsexual characteristics are two: a) it is intolerably offensive in some setting; and b) it is totally worthless. Whatever may be permitted behind closed doors, there are some forms of language, and pictures, and acts—perverted behaviors, sexual intercourse—that are not permitted in public places. That prohibition is based on the recognition that thrusting specific content of that kind upon an unwilling audience in a public place is a gross imposition, and a cause of offense against which that audience, and all of us, have a right to be protected. Such obscene matter does not contribute in any way to the public forum. It is barren of ideas, and not at all the kind of stuff—opinion, argument, information—that the Supreme Court has insisted must be protected by our Constitution.

"Some political garbage—like that of the Nazis and the KKK, although not in the same way carnal, is just like that. Citizens of a decent community have a right to be shielded from it in precisely that spirit. Indeed, lascivious acts or pictures are offensive, but not nearly as offensive as some irrational racism, or anti-semitism. So we contend [the Nazi-blocker continues] that in a wide but accurate sense of the term, hate-mongering like that of the Nazis is obscene. As that category is used now in the law, the term might not apply. But it is still not an unreasonable stretch of language, or a concept, to prohibit Nazi speech on the same fundamental grounds."

And that is what it comes to, that is what all censorship comes to, in the end: some content is thought so very bad that it must not be heard or seen. I call this argument "the outrage override." With this we get to the root of the conflict between the blocker and the civil libertarian. The blocker believes in his heart that some things may be suppressed because the content of the views expressed are simply intolerable, "beyond the pale." The libertarian believes in his heart that giving to any the power to silence that they do not think it worthy to hear is more intolerable still. That is why Nazis and other racists provide a good illustrative case. Their views are thought manifestly worthless, and that is not in dispute—but they are laden with ideas. Of course some of those ideas are despicable, but sometimes just for that reason they are meaningful. No segment of society, I argue, is entitled to decide for the rest of us that some ideas are so lacking in worthy content that we will have no opportunity to evaluate them for ourselves.

Even where the matter in question has no political content, and is sexually explicit, and is known to give offense to some, we protect the freedom of others to see or hear it by obliging whose who are offended to shield themselves by turning it off, or turning away, or walking away. That was the very issue faced by the Supreme Court of the United States in another case—a Florida case, in fact [*Erznoznick v. City of Jacksonville*, 422 US 205 at 207, 1975]. The objectionable matter in question appeared on a drive-in movie screen, showing X-rated films and viewable from a road in the distance. But when it is possible for a viewer or hearer to turn away, said the Court, his being offended when he does not do so will not serve to cancel the rights of others to speak, or to listen or to watch.

Justice Powell, recently retired from the Court, wrote the majority opinion in *Erznoznick*, saying, in part: "When the government, acting as censor, undertakes selectively to shield the public from some kinds of speech on the ground that they are more offensive than others, the First Amendment strictly limits its power. . . . [R]estrictions have been upheld only when the speaker intrudes upon the privacy of the home . . . or the degree of captivity [of the audience] makes it impractical for the unwilling viewer or auditor to avoid exposure" (p. 209).

And sometimes the garbage is inextricably mixed with other stuff that deserves a hearing. In yet another case, in which a young man in a courthouse wearing a jacket with words on it ["Fuck the draft"] that I find uncomfortable to repeat in public, but words having a political message too, was arrested for obscene display, the Supreme Court vindicated him in the end:

> The ability of Government, consonant with the Constitution, to shut off discourse solely to protect others from hearing it

is . . . dependent upon a showing that substantial privacy interests are being invaded in an essentially intolerable manner. Any broader view of this authority would effectively empower a majority to silence dissidents simply as a matter of personal predilections [*Cohen v. California* 403 US 15, at 21; 1971].

So we have to ask: is the extreme political speech in question (say, the Nazi garbage) an invasion of the privacy of the citizens? Generally it is not. A Nazi march down Collins Avenue—or one by the anti-Contras on Biscayne Blvd.—would surely not be. Streets and parks are the common and proper places for political assembly. To some degree we cannot avoid encountering what happens in such places—but we do not have to stay, and we cannot expect to be insulated by law from all that we find intensely objectionable.

Justice Powell [in *Erznoznick*] continues:

> The plain, if at time disquieting truth is that in our pluralistic society, constantly proliferating new and ingenious forms of expression, "we are inescapably captive audiences for many purposes." . . . Much that we encounter offends our aesthetic, if not our political and moral sensibilities. Nevertheless, the Constitution does not permit government to decide which types of otherwise protected speech are sufficiently offensive to require protection for the unwilling listener or viewer. Rather, absent the narrow circumstances described above [in which exposure is entirely impossible to avoid] the burden normally falls upon the viewer to 'avoid further bombardment of his sensibilities simply by averting his eyes' [422 US 210]. . . . The limited privacy interests of persons on the public streets cannot justify . . . censorship of otherwise protected speech on the basis of its content.

"Well, [comes the last try from the Nazi-blocker] is this Nazi garbage 'otherwise protected speech'? Have we not agreed that it is utterly worthless, and offensive, and is it therefore not like hard-core obscenity, unentitled to protection? If so, we are justified in prohibiting it."

But it is not, not at all. The right of the public to see and hear Nazis, or Communists, or Contras, or anti-Contras, or any political view, however extreme, is at least as compelling as the right to read risque literature or look at bare breasts and buttocks on the screen. Even with respect to pornography, simply because some materials lack redeeming social value—whatever that is—does not justify prohibition. For material having any political content whatever, that argument could not possibly apply, and could not possibly be applied fairly.

Chapter 6. Conclusion

What then shall we conclude about political extremism and free speech? Are there any restrictions, of any kind, that may be applied to such speaking? Of course there are! The speaking that is bridled with criminal acts does become part of those later deeds. And, apart from criminality, there are reasonable restrictions that may be enforced upon the *manner* of speaking, and the *place* of it, and the *time* of it. We may permit rallies in the parks, and yet reserve some quiet arboretum as a place where no political demonstrations may be held. We may respect political demonstrations on downtown streets—and yet hold that, during the rush hours, political demonstrations will create more inconvenience than is tolerable. Or we may, as a community, protect residential streets from noisy demonstrations. The places may be restricted, the times may be restricted—and the manner too, eliminating, say, all electronic megaphones and super-noisy amplification. We may, within the rules, impose such regulations—but, and this is the key, *we may not do so selectively.* The restriction of manner or place that applies to one view applies to all. It may be unlawful to post stickers on public walls—but that applies to all stickers, not just those of the unfavored minority. And what we permit for the politics in wide favor —say, a march on Main Street—we must permit for the nastiest of the unfavored. By content we must, in a free society, make no exceptions. Freedom is not merely for those we can tolerate; it is for all.

Finally, then, please note: Robust, wide open political debate, uninhibited political debate, in parks and streets and lecture halls, is going to rouse anger, and give offense. Some public offensiveness, and some private distress, will be an inevitable cost of freedom. That is what a free, democratic society requires. It is not simply the kooks whom we protect, but ourselves. Citizens who would govern themselves—we—have the right to hear every opinion on our public business. The Nazis may be crazy, or vicious, but that does not cancel our need to pass judgment upon them; therefore the opportunity to hear them must be protected, partly in their interest, but mainly in ours.

And we cannot make exceptions for the specially nasty bits. Some say: "OK then, let them speak—but not with their infernal swastika!" But if the swastika is too offensive for some to tolerate today, the Star of David will be claimed equally intolerable by others tomorrow.

So, I say, the Nazis have the same right to sing the "Hort Wessel Lied," that others have to sing the "Internationale," and still others "We Shall Overcome." To the claim that some stuff is just too nasty to permit, I answer: no degree of nastiness can justify silencing speech in a free society.

Even on Miami Beach for the Nazis? And even in Miami for the anti-Contras? Yes, the effectiveness of political protest often depends critically upon the symbolic use of location. When the Nazis planned to demonstrate in Skokie ten years ago, whatever we may think of them, that location, being heavily Jewish, was part of their point. Civil rights demonstrators, as part of their point often carried their moral convictions, very offensive to the segregationist majority, to the heart of Jim Crow country—to Selma, Alabama, and Philadelphia, Mississippi. Blacks who demonstrate for fair housing opportunities often do so in the heart of middle-class suburban communities that would exclude them. The Nazis carry signs reading "White Power." If we do not permit them to do that in black neighborhoods, how can we justify Black Panthers carrying signs saying "Black Power" in white neighborhoods?

But the civil rights marchers carried a message of human equality and decency; the swastika is the symbol of unspeakable indecency. Yes. But that judgment of contents cannot be made antecedently, and can have no bearing upon the right to speak publicly. Our best hope that sound judgment will be passed upon nasty political views lies in the freedom of all to hear them, and the freedom of all to speak and write in reply.

I conclude: We learn from the extreme case. The Nazis, by presenting a case about as extreme as any we can conjure up, provide us with an instruc-tive test of our own principles. These are powerful principles, and sound ones; they are a tribute to our own civility, and—if I may be permitted to end on a slightly corny note—one of the most deeply satisfying marks of our own national culture, of which I am very proud.

Prohibiting Racist Speech: A Debate

CHARLES LAWRENCE AND GERALD GUNTHER

By Charles Lawrence

I have spent the better part of my life as a dissenter. As a high-school student, I was threatened with suspension for my refusal to participate in a civil-defense drill, and I have been a conspicuous con-sumer of my First Amendment liberties ever since. There are very strong reasons for protecting even speech that is racist. Perhaps the most important is that such protection reinforces our society's com-mitment to tolerance as a value. By protecting bad speech from government regulation, we will be forced to combat it as a community.

I have, however, a deeply felt apprehension about the resurgence of racial violence and the cor-responding increase in the incidence of verbal and symbolic assault and harassment to which blacks and other traditionally excluded groups are sub-jected. I am troubled by the way the debate has been framed in response to the recent surge of racist incidents on college and university campuses and in response to some universities' attempts to regulate harassing speech. The problem has been framed as one in which the liberty of free speech is in conflict with the elimination of racism. I believe this has placed the bigot on the moral high ground and fanned the rising flames of racism.

Above all, I am troubled that we have not listened to the real victims—that we have shown so little understanding of their injury, and that we have abandoned those whose race, gender, or sex-ual orientation continues to make them second-class citizens. It seems to me a very sad irony that the first instinct of civil libertarians has been to challenge even the smallest, most narrowly framed efforts by universities to provide black and other minority students with the protection the Consti-tutuion, in my opinion, guarantees them.

The landmark case of *Brown v. Board of Educa-tion* is not a case that we normally think of as a case about speech. But *Brown* can be broadly read as articulating the principle of equal citizenship. *Brown* held that segregated schools were inher-ently unequal because of the message that segrega-tion conveyed: that black children were an untou-chable caste, unfit to go to school with white children. If we understand the necessity of elimi-nating the system of signs and symbols that signal the inferiority of blacks, then we should hesitate before proclaiming that all racist speech that stops short of physical violence must be defended.

University officials who have formulated poli-cies to respond to incidents of racial harassment have been characterized in the press as "thought police," even though such policies generally do nothing more than impose sanctions against inten-tional face-to-face insults. Racist speech that takes the form of face-to-face insults, catcalls, or other assaultive speech aimed at an individual or small group of persons falls directly within the "fighting words" exception to the First Amendment

---

From "Good Speech, Bad Speech—Yes," and "Good Speech, Bad Speech—No," *Stanford Lawyer*, Vol. 24 (1990), pp. 6, 8, 40, and 7, 9, 41. Reprinted with per-mission of Charles Lawrence and Gerald Gunther.

protection. The Supreme Court has held in *Chaplinsky v. New Hampshire* that words which "by their very utterance inflict injury or tend to incite an immediate breach of the peace" are not protected by the First Amendment.

If the purpose of the First Amendment is to foster the greatest amount of speech, racial insults disserve that purpose. Assaultive racist speech functions as a preemptive strike. The invective is experienced as a blow, not as a proffered idea. And once the blow is struck, a dialogue is unlikely to follow. Racial insults are particularly undeserving of First Amendment protection, because the perpetrator's intention is not to discover truth or initiate dialogue but to injure the victim. In most situations, members of minority groups realize that they are likely to lose if they fight back, and are forced to remain silent and submissive.

Courts have held that offensive speech may not be regulated in public forums (such as streets, where the listener may avoid the speech by moving on). But the regulation of otherwise protected speech has been permitted when the speech invades the privacy of the unwilling listener's home, or when the unwilling listener cannot avoid the speech. Racist posters, fliers, and graffiti in dormitories, bathrooms, and other common living spaces would seem to fall within the reasoning of these cases. Minority students should not be required to remain in their rooms in order to avoid racial insult. Minimally, they should find a safe haven in their dorms and in all other common rooms that are a part of their daily routine.

I would also argue that the university's responsibility for ensuring that these students receive an equal educational opportunity provides a compelling justification for regulations that ensure them safe passage in all common areas. A minority student should not have to risk becoming the target of racially assaulting speech every time he or she chooses to walk across campus. Regulating vilifying speech that cannot be anticipated or avoided need not preclude announced speeches and rallies—situations that would give minority-group members and their allies the opportunity to organize counterdemonstrations or avoid the speech altogether.

The most commonly advanced argument against the regulation of racist speech proceeds something like this: We recognize that minority groups suffer pain and injury as the result of racist speech, but

we must allow this hate mongering for the benefit of society as a whole. Freedom of speech is the lifeblood of our democratic system. It is especially important for minorities, because often it is their only vehicle for rallying support for the redress of their grievances. It will be impossible to formulate a prohibition so precise that it will prevent the racist speech you want to suppress, without catching in the same net all kinds of speech that it would be unconscionable for a democratic society to suppress.

Such arguments seek to strike a balance between our concern, on the one hand, for the continued free flow of ideas and the democratic process dependent on that flow, and, on the other, our desire to further the cause of equality. There can, however, be no meaningful discussion of how we should reconcile our commitment to equality with our commitment to free speech, until it is acknowledged that racist speech inflicts real harm, and that this harm is far from trivial.

To engage in a debate about the First Amendment and racist speech without a full understanding of the nature and extent of that harm is to risk making the First Amendment an instrument of domination rather than a vehicle of liberation. We have not all known the experience of victimization by racist, misogynist, and homophobic speech, nor do we equally share the burden of the harm it inflicts. We are often quick to say that we have heard the cry of the victims when we have not.

The *Brown* case is again instructive, because it speaks directly to the psychic injury inflicted by racist speech by noting that the symbolic message of segregation affected "the hearts and minds" of Negro children "in a way unlikely ever to be undone." Racial epithets and harassment often cause deep emotional scarring and feelings of anxiety and fear that pervade every aspect of a victim's life.

Brown also recognized that black children did not have an equal opportunity to learn and participate in the school community when they bore the additional burden of being subjected to the humiliation and psychic assault contained in the message of segregation. University students bear an analogous burden when they are forced to live and work in an environment where at any moment they may be subjected to denigrating verbal harassment and assault. The same injury was addressed by the Supreme Court when it held that, under Title VII of the Civil Rights Act of 1964, sexual harassment which creates a hostile or abusive work environment violates the ban on sex discrimination in employment.

Carefully drafted university regulations could bar the use of words as assault weapons while at the same time leaving unregulated even the most heinous of ideas provided those ideas are presented at times and places and in manners that provide an opportunity for reasoned rebuttal or escape from immediate insult. The history of the development of the right to free speech has been one of carefully evaluating the importance of free expression and its effects on other important societal interests. We have drawn the line between protected and unprotected speech before without dire results. (Courts have, for example, exempted from the protection of the First Amendment obscene speech and speech that disseminates official secrets, defames or libels another person, or is used to form a conspiracy or monopoly.)

Blacks and other people of color are skeptical about the argument that even the most injurious speech must remain unregulated because, in an unregulated marketplace of ideas, the best ones will rise to the top and gain acceptance. Experience tells quite the opposite. People of color have seen too many demagogues elected by appealing to America's racism, and too many sympathetic politicians shy away from issues that might brand them as being too closely allied with disparaged groups.

Whenever we decide that racist speech must be tolerated because of the importance of maintaining societal tolerance for all unpopular speech, we are asking blacks and other subordinated groups to bear the burden for the good of all. We must be careful that the ease with which we strike the balance against the regulation of racist speech is in no way influenced by the fact that the cost will be borne by others. We must be certain that those who will pay that price are fairly represented in our deliberations and that they are heard.

At the core of the argument that we should resist all government regulation of speech is the ideal that the best cure for bad speech is good—that ideas that affirm equality and the worth of all individuals will ultimately prevail. This is an empty ideal unless those of us who would fight racism are vigilant and unequivocal in that fight. We must look for ways to offer assistance and support to students whose speech and political participation are chilled in a climate of racial harassment.

Civil rights lawyers might consider suing on behalf of blacks whose right to an equal education is denied by a university's failure to ensure a nondiscriminatory educational climate or conditions of employment. We must embark upon the development of a First Amendment jurisprudence grounded in the reality of our history and our contemporary experience. We must think hard about how best to launch legal attacks against the most indefensible forms of hate speech. Good lawyers can create exceptions and narrow interpretations that limit the harm of hate speech without opening the floodgates of censorship.

Everyone concerned with these issues must find ways to engage actively in actions that resist and counter the racist ideas that we would have the First Amendment protect. If we fail in this, the victims of hate speech must rightly assume that we are on the bigots' side.

By Gerald Gunther

I am deeply troubled by current efforts—however well-intentioned—to place new limits on freedom of expression at this and other campuses. Such limits are not only incompatible with the mission and meaning of a university; they also send exactly the wrong message from academia to society as a whole. University campuses should exhibit greater, not less, freedom of expression than prevails in society at large.

Proponents of new limits argue that historic First Amendment rights must be balanced against "Stanford's commitment to the diversity of ideas and persons." Clearly, there is ample room and need for vigorous University action to combat racial and other discrimination. But curbing freedom of speech is the wrong way to do so. The proper answer to bad speech is usually more and better speech—not new laws, litigation, and repression.

Lest it be thought that I am insensitive to the pain imposed by expressions of racial or religious hatred, let me say that I have suffered that pain and empathize with others under similar verbal assault. My deep belief in the principles of the First Amendment arises in part from my own experiences.

I received my elementary education in a public school in a very small town in Nazi Germany. There I was subjected to vehement anti-Semitic remarks from my teacher, classmates and others—"Judensau" (Jew pig) was far from the harshest. I can assure you that they hurt. More generally, I lived in a country where ideological orthodoxy reigned and where the opportunity for dissent was severely limited.

The lesson I have drawn from my childhood in Nazi Germany and my happier adult life in this country is the need to walk the sometimes difficult path of denouncing the bigots' hateful ideas with all my power, yet at the same time challenging any community's attempt to suppress hateful ideas by force of law.

Obviously, given my own experience, I do *not* quarrel with the claim that words *can* do harm. But I firmly deny that a showing of harm suffices to deny First Amendment protection, and I insist on the elementary First Amendment principle that our Constitution usually protects even offensive, harmful expression.

That is why—at the risk of being thought callous or doctrinaire—I feel compelled to speak out against the attempt by some members of the Stanford community to enlarge the area of forbidden speech under the Fundamental Standard. Such proposals, in my view, seriously undervalue the First Amendment and far too readily endanger its precious content. Limitations on free expression beyond those established by law should be eschewed in an institution committed to diversity and the First Amendment.

In explaining my position, I will avoid extensive legal arguments. Instead, I want to speak from the heart, on the basis of my own background and of my understanding of First Amendment principles—principles supported by an ever larger number of scholars and Supreme Court justices, especially since the days of the Warren Court.

Among the core principles is that any official effort to suppress expression must be viewed with the greatest skepticism and suspicion. Only in very narrow, urgent circumstances should government or similar institutions be permitted to inhibit speech. True, there are certain categories of speech that may be prohibited; but the number and scope of these categories has steadily shrunk over the last fifty years. Face-to-face insults are one such category; incitement to immediate illegal action is another. But opinions expressed in debates and arguments about a wide range of political and social issues should not be suppressed simply because of disagreement with those views, with the content of the expression.

Similarly, speech should not and cannot be banned simply because it is "offensive" to substantial parts or a majority of a community. The refusal to suppress offensive speech is one of the most difficult obligations the free speech principle imposes upon all of us; yet it is also one of the First Amendment's greatest glories—indeed it is a central test of a community's commitment to free speech.

The Supreme Court's 1989 decision to allow flag-burning as a form of political protest, in *Texas v. Johnson,* warrants careful pondering by all those who continue to advocate campus restraints on "racist speech." As Justice Brennan's majority opinion in *Johnson* reminded, "If there is a bedrock principle underlying the First Amendment, it is that the Government may not prohibit the expression of an idea simply because society finds the idea itself offensive or disagreeable." In refusing to place flag-burning outside the First Amendment, moreover, the *Johnson* majority insisted (in words especially apt for the "racist speech" debate): "The First Amendment does not guarantee that other concepts virtually sacred to our Nation as a whole —*such as the principle that discrimination on the basis of race is odious and destructive*—will go unquestioned in the marketplace of ideas. We decline, therefore, to create for the flag an exception to the joust of principles protected by the First Amendment." (Italics added.)

Campus proponents of restricting offensive speech are currently relying for justification on the Supreme Court's allegedly repeated reiteration that "fighting words" constitute an exception to the First Amendment. Such an exception has indeed been recognized in a number of lower court cases. However, there has only been *one* case in the history of the Supreme Court in which a majority of the Justices has ever found a statement to be a punishable resort to "fighting words." That was *Chaplinsky v. New Hampshire,* a nearly fifty-year-old case involving words which would very likely not be found punishable today.

More significant is what has happened in the nearly half-century since: Despite repeated appeals to the Supreme Court to recognize the applicability of the "fighting words" exception by affirming challenged convictions, the Court has in every instance refused. One must wonder about the strength of an exception that, while theoretically recognized, has for so long not been found apt in practice. (Moreover, the proposed Stanford rules are *not* limited to face-to-face insults to an addressee, and thus go well beyond the traditional, albeit fragile, "fighting words" exception.)

The phenomenon of racist and other offensive speech that Stanford now faces is not a new one in the history of the First Amendment. In recent decades, for example, well-meaning but in my view misguided majorities have sought to suppress not only racist speech but also antiwar and antidraft speech, civil rights demonstrators, the Nazis and the Ku Klux Klan, and left-wing groups.

Typically, it is people on the extremes of the political spectrum (including those who advocate overthrow of our constitutional system and those who would not protect their opponents' right to dissent were they the majority) who feel the brunt of repression and have found protection in the First Amendment; typically, it is well-meaning people in the majority who believe that their "community standards," their sensibilities, their sense of outrage, justify restraints.

Those in power in a community recurrently seek to repress speech they find abhorrent; and their efforts are understandable human impulses. Yet freedom of expression—and especially the protection of dissident speech, the most important function of the First Amendment—is an antimajoritarian principle. Is it too much to hope that, especially on a university campus, a majority can be persuaded of the value of freedom of expression and of the resultant need to curb our impulses to repress dissident views?

The principles to which I appeal are not new. They have been expressed, for example, by the most distinguished Supreme Court justices ever since the beginning of the Court's confrontations with First Amendment issues nearly seventy years ago. These principles are reflected in the words of so imperfect a First Amendment defender as Justice Oliver Wendell Holmes: "If there is any principle of the Constitution that more imperatively calls for attachment than any other it is the principle of free thought—not free thought for those who agree with us but freedom for the thought that we hate."

This is the principle most elaborately and eloquently addressed by Justice Louis D. Brandeis, who reminded us that the First Amendment rests on a belief "in the power of reason as applied through public discussion" and therefore bars "silence coerced by law—the argument of force in its worst form."

This theme, first articulated in dissents, has repeatedly been voiced in majority opinions in more recent decades. It underlies Justice Douglas's remark in striking down a conviction under a law banning speech that "stirs the public to anger": "A function of free speech [is] to invite dispute. . . . Speech is often provocative and challenging. That is why freedom of speech [is ordinarily] protected against censorship or punishment."

It also underlies Justice William J. Brennan's comment about our "profound national commitment to the principle that debate on public issues should be uninhibited, robust and wide-open, and that it may well include vehement, caustic and sometimes unpleasantly sharp attacks"—a comment he followed with a reminder that constitutional protection "does not turn upon the truth, popularity or social utility of the ideas and beliefs which are offered."

These principles underlie as well the repeated insistence by Justice John Marshall Harlan, again in majority opinions, that the mere "inutility or immorality" of a message cannot justify its repression, and that the state may not punish because of "the underlying content of the message." Moreover, Justice Harlan, in one of the finest First Amendment opinions on the books, noted, in words that Stanford would ignore at its peril at this time:

"The constitutional right of free expression is powerful medicine in a society as diverse and populous as ours. . . . To many, the immediate consequence of this freedom may often appear to be only verbal tumult, discord and even offensive utterance. These are, however, within established limits, in truth necessary side effects of the broader enduring values which the process of open debate permits us to achieve. That the air may at times seem filled with verbal cacophony is, in this sense, not a sign of weakness but of strength."

In this same passage, Justice Harlan warned that a power to ban speech merely because it is offensive is an "inherently boundless" notion, and added that "we think it is largely because governmental officials cannot make principled distinctions in this area that the Constitution leaves matters of taste and style so largely to the individual." (The Justice made these comments while overturning the conviction of an antiwar protestor for "offensive conduct." The defendant had worn, in a courthouse corridor, a jacket bearing the words "Fuck the Draft." It bears noting, in light of the ongoing campus debate, that Justice Harlan's majority opinion also warned that "we cannot indulge in the facile assumption that one can forbid particular words without also running the substantial risk of suppressing ideas in the process.")

I restate these principles and repeat these words for reasons going far beyond the fact that they are familiar to me as a First Amendment scholar. I believe—in my heart as well as my mind—that these principles and ideals are not only established but right. I hope that the entire Stanford community will seriously reflect upon the risks to free expression, lest we weaken hard-won liberties at Stanford and, by example, in this nation.

Study Questions

1. As Wilmoore Kendall indicates, Mill rested his case for the "harm principle" on a utilitarian moral and social theory: The harm principle is "right" just because it promotes the greatest good for society overall (or at least more good than any other arrangement). Can you see problems in attempting to justify such a stringent principle on utilitarian grounds?

2. Consider the following cases: (a) You enjoy listening to "rap" music, particularly music by rap groups that use what some people would consider violent and lewd lyrics. Your neighbor Joe knows that you listen to such music nightly (he never hears it, though, as you never play it too loudly), and this knowledge drives him to distraction. Joe hates rap music. He believes it is the root of all evil. He can't sleep at night, lying awake greatly distressed by the thought that you are polluting your mind with the hateful chatter. (b) One day, you take your portable stereo and your rap music tapes to the beach, set them up, and turn on the music while snoozing in the sun. Joe is a few yards away; he hears the music and is disgusted; his day is ruined. (c) A friend of yours joins you on the beach and is so taken by the music that she removes all her clothing and prances about the beach naked, moving to the music. Joe witnesses this display and is, predictably, distressed and offended. Question: Have you (or your friend) "harmed" Joe in any of these cases? If not, why not? What difference is there between the psychological distress produced by assaulting or defaming someone (which most of us, and certainly the law, recognize as real forms of harm) and the various forms of distress experienced by Joe? Many communities have ordinances prohibiting public nudity. Can such ordinances be justified on Mill's grounds?

3. Laws requiring drivers to wear seat belts and motorcyclists to wear helmets; laws making suicide and dueling illegal; laws forbidding gambling and certain forms of drug use, all are examples of paternalism in the law. Mill roundly condemned such paternalistic intervention in the lives of competent adults on the grounds that their knowledge of what is best for them is not as good as the government's; each person knows best, Mill seems to have thought, what is in his or her own best interest. Does Mill assume this and, if so, is he correct? How would you argue against him?

4. In June 1990, officials at Stanford University approved a modification to university policies regarding racist speech. The new policy prevents harassment by "personal vilification," defined as "words or nonverbal symbols . . . commonly understood to convey direct and visceral hatred or contempt for human beings on the basis of their sex, race, color, handicap, religion, sexual orientation, or national and ethnic origin." The harassing conduct must "be intended to stigmatize an individual or small number of individuals" and must be addressed directly to those it stigmatizes. Similar antiharassment policies have been implemented or are under consideration at many universities and colleges across the country. Should the Stanford policy be judged constitutionally permissible? Is it consistent with your understanding of the First Amendment? Is it consistent with the framers' understanding of the First Amendment?

5. Dissenting in *Texas v. Johnson*, Justice Stevens makes the following argument:

> The Court is . . . quite wrong in blandly asserting that [Johnson] was prosecuted for his expression of dissatisfaction with the policies of this country. . . . [He] was prosecuted because of the method he chose to express his dissatisfaction. . . . Had he chosen to spray-paint—or perhaps convey with a motion picture projector—his message of dissatisfaction on the facade of the Lincoln Memorial, there would be no question about the power of the government to

prohibit his means of expression. The prohibition would be supported by the legitimate interest in preserving the quality of an important national asset.

Is the analogy that Stevens seeks to make here sound? Why or why not?

6. Imagine that I am a budding genius at chemistry and that I discover a recipe for making a deadly nerve gas from household ingredients. I then decide to publish my results in a letter to the editor in the local newspaper. Should I be allowed to do so? On what grounds could my "speech" be curtailed?

7. What (or how much) must I be permitted to do in the name of exercising my freedom of religion? In 1878, a man named Reynolds, living in what is now the state of Utah, was charged and convicted of the offense of bigamy (entering into a state of marriage with a person when one already has a living spouse). On appeal, Reynolds argued that he was a member of the Mormon church and that polygamy was not only permissible by the tenets of that faith (at the time), but actually mandatory "where circumstances permit" under pain of "damnation in the life to come." He claimed that his right freely to exercise his religion under the First Amendment was thus being infringed by the antipolygamy law. The Supreme Court disagreed, noting that polygamy "has always been odious" among the civilized nations of Europe and the Americas. The Court concluded that

> [L]aws are made for the government of actions, and while they cannot interfere with mere religious belief and opinion, they may with practice. Suppose one believed that human sacrifices were a necessary part of religious worship. Would it be seriously contended that the civil government under which he lived could not interfere to

prevent a sacrifice? . . . Can a man excuse his practices [in violation of the law] because of his religious belief? To permit this would be to make the professed doctrines of religious belief superior to the law of the land, and in effect to permit every citizen to become a law unto himself. (*Reynolds v. United States* 98 U.S. 145 [1878])

Is there a principled way to decide which religious practices must be allowed and which must not be tolerated? What would Mill say of this case? (Note his discussion of the persecution of Mormons at the end of his selection.) What about a church in which the members believe that Scripture commands them to handle poisonous snakes? What of a church whose rituals involve the consumption of illegal substances? What of a church that denies medical care to children?

8. In 1987, the city of Hialeah, Florida, passed an ordinance outlawing ritual animal sacrifice. The ordinance was aimed at the worshippers of the church of "Santeria," a religious cult with roots in the Caribbean. Practitioners of Santeria, it is claimed, believe that animal sacrifices are necessary to cure illnesses and sanctify births, deaths, and marriages. Chickens, goats, turtles, and ducks, among other animals, are killed by being stabbed through the neck. Residents of the city claimed that the sacrifices could do psychological harm to the children of cult members; and they complained that animal carcasses were not always properly disposed of. Members of the church asserted that they must be allowed "freely to exercise" their religion. Should the Constitution be interpreted to protect Santeria members and their practices? What would the principle articulated in the *Reynolds* case (see question 7, above) say here? (See "To One City, It's Cruelty, To Cultists, It's Religion," *The National Law Journal*, Sept. 11, 1989, p. 8.)

B. *Obscenity and Pornography*

Introduction

Many people believe that speech that is "pornographic" or "obscene" (whether the two are the same is one of the topics of this chapter) should not be protected by the law. Such speech might include (but would not necessarily be limited to) (1) depictions, on film or in still pictures, of human genitalia, contact between genitals, anus, and mouth (in various combinations) or descriptions of such activities; (2) depictions or descriptions of homosexual intercourse; (3) depictions or descriptions of bestiality. Many would also include in such prohibited categories of "speech," depictions or descriptions of violence in connection with any of the above (for example, mutilation, binding and gagging, sexual penetration with implements, drawing of blood, infliction of pain).

The term *pornography* can be broadly defined to refer to any form of sexually explicit material. In this sense, any of the items falling within the categories listed above would be "pornographic." The focus of this section is what legal implications, if any, should flow from that description.

Legal Definitions

As all parties to the debate about the legality of pornography are willing to admit, existing law construes pornography as a special case of the "obscene"; and many of the pornography cases that have come before the courts in the past several decades have posed the issue of whether, and to what extent, obscenity is constitutionally protected speech. The basic standard governing current obscenity law was handed down by the Supreme Court in 1973 in *Miller v. California*. The Court held that "the basic guidelines for the trier of fact must

be: (a) whether 'the average person, applying contemporary community standards,' would find that the work, taken as a whole, appeals to the prurient interest, (b) whether the work depicts or describes in a patently offensive way, sexual conduct specifically defined by the applicable state law, and (c) whether the work, taken as a whole, lacks serious literary, artistic, political, or scientific value."[1]

The Court confined the permissible scope of the state regulation of the obscene to "works which depict or describe sexual conduct," and urged that "patently offensive representations or descriptions of ultimate sexual acts, normal or perverted, actual or simulated" or "patently offensive representations or descriptions of masturbation, excretory functions, and lewd exhibition of the genitals" would likely fall within the ambit of material deemed "obscene" by the *Miller* standard. State regulations of obscene materials have been upheld under the *Miller* test to protect audiences whose members are unwilling or "captive" (for example, prohibitions on showing pornographic films at drive-in movie theaters visible from the street or of the broadcast over the radio of "dirty words") or whose members are minors.[2] Zoning ordinances for "adult theaters" and restrictions on "live" sexual performances have also been permitted.[3] Nonetheless, a great many works that many people might find obscene (*Playboy*, *Hustler*, the "triple-X" film available at the local video store) are plainly at present constitutionally protected forms of expression.

Pornography and Harm

Should pornography be legally permissible? In his selection, philosopher Joel Feinberg explores various factors bearing on this question. Feinberg argues for a generally liberal position, consistent with the overall view of Mill: Pornographic works may be prohibited only if they can be shown to be directly harmful or at least profoundly offensive to many in a way that cannot be avoided. Feinberg criticizes what he takes to be the courts' confusion of pornography with the obscene. This has led, among other things, to the debates about the status of pornographic materials. Are they forms of art or literature? Or simply "sex aids"? The concept of the "obscene," according to Feinberg, encompasses that which is blatant, flagrant, or shameless. Can sex ever be described in these ways? Perhaps in some cases; but much pornography, Feinberg thinks, is not actually obscene.

Feinberg discusses two general grounds for banning or at least greatly restricting the production and distribution of pornographic materials: that they bring about violence and that they are profoundly offensive. With respect to the latter ground, Feinberg considers the suggestion that the prohibition of pornography could be defended by appeal to what he calls the "offense principle": the idea that conduct that is profoundly or extremely obscene, offensive, or revolting may legitimately be forbidden as a form of public nuisance (similar, for example, to creating a horrible stench), at least where the conduct is unavoidable by reasonable means. Here, of course, the question of the status of works of pornography as art or literature may be used to offset their offensiveness; but even pornography lacking any such "redeeming" characteristics, Feinberg maintains, rarely rises to the level of revulsion necessary to be preventable under the offense principle. And even if it does, such material is usually avoidable.

Does pornography cause harm? And if so, can its production and use be restricted on Mill's grounds? It is here that Feinberg takes up the challenge of feminist arguments in favor of banning pronography. The feminist critique of pornography is, as Feinberg sees it, defended on two grounds: Pornography harms women either by "defaming" them (holding them up to ridicule and derision) as a group or by inciting violence against them (for example, rape). Feinberg responds that neither the connection between pornography and defamation nor to instances of actual violence can be closely enough forged to pass muster under the harm principle, properly understood. If pornography depicts women as subordinate in a way that gives rise to a cause of action for defamation, then

so will many other things, from television shows to novels. On the other hand, to prohibit pornography on the ground that it brings about violence requires both a likelihood of serious harm and a direct link between the pornographic expression (the film or magazine) and the violence. The connection between pornography and violence can't be merely suggestive, it must be tight. Feinberg is doubtful that such a tight link can be established; the closest that one can come to such proof, he admits, is in the case of "violent" pornography, of which Feinberg provides several gruesome examples.

Yet even in the case of especially violent pornography the question can still be raised: Does it *cause* violence against women? No, says Feinberg; and the explanation is that the direction of causation is not from violent pornography to violent acts against women. It is, rather, that violent pornography and rape are both effects of a deeper, causal agency: the "cult of macho." Pornography and rape are both products of a set of underlying beliefs about and attitudes toward women which are associated with "machismo." Pornography is a symptom, and therefore its suppression will likely have little effect. Nor it is possible to argue, by analogy to concepts in the criminal law, that the makers or distributors of pornographic materials are guilty of "incitement" to violence or "solicitation" of rape, for vendors of pornography do not counsel or advise customers to rape—not, at least, in a way the law currently would recognize.

Finally, Feinberg rejects the feminist argument that the profound offense felt by women through bare awareness of degrading and humiliating pornographic films and magazines is sufficient to justify the suppression of pornography. Even if not reasonably avoidable, such feelings of offense "at the thought" that members of one's sex are being degraded fails to establish that anyone in particular is really being victimized by such portrayals.

The Feminist Critique of Pornography

In 1984, the city of Indianapolis, Indiana, enacted an unusual antipornography ordinance. The ordinance was based on the city council's finding that pornography is "a systematic practice of exploitation and subordination based on sex which differentially harms women," and pornography was accordingly defined as "the graphic sexually explicit subordination of women, whether in pictures or in words." Based on this conception of pornography, the ordinance prohibited a variety of activities, including "trafficking" in pornography and "forcing" pornography on a person in any place of employment, school, home, or public place. The ordinance further prohibited "coercion into pornographic performance." The law gave to any woman aggrieved by trafficking or coercion a right to file a complaint "as a woman acting against the subordination of women."[4]

In her essay, feminist legal scholar Catherine MacKinnon defends the general position taken by the Indianapolis ordinance (of which she was a principal author). Like Feinberg, MacKinnon also challenges the law's identification of pornography with the obscene, but for very different reasons. Assimilating pornography to obscenity, MacKinnon claims, obscures its true nature by representing it as just one more form of expression, one more way of conveying an idea, belief, or attitude. From a moral point of view, this reduces the debate about pornography to whether such material is in good or bad taste; legally it has the effect of making pornography an issue under the First Amendment. As against this, MacKinnon defends the "civil rights" conception of pornography implicit in the Indianapolis law: Pornography is a discriminatory practice, not simply a certain type of offensive picture or text; pornography is not a political or social or religious "idea," and as such it does not deserve First Amendment protection, any more than the now-outlawed practice of racial segregation. Displays of violent pornography are not invitations to engage in a dialogue with the "marketplace of ideas"; they are rather acts of disempowerment.

Pornography, MacKinnon believes, reflects and reinforces the way men in general tend to regard women; it is not linked only with a cult of macho: even men who don't think of themselves as especially macho nonetheless participate in a culture that regards women as essentially commodities for use by men. The problem with obscenity law is that it is made by men and reflects male ideals and standards. This is especially obvious, MacKinnon thinks, in the case of the *Miller* standards: the "average person" is a male; "community standards" are already infected with sexism; "lacking serious . . . merit" effectively permits much that is demeaning to women.

At a deeper level, MacKinnon challenges Feinberg's Millian premises as they apply to the pornography question. Mill and other liberal political philosophers assume that persons will not be silenced socially so long as no legal restrictions are placed upon their freedom of expression. But this, MacKinnon claims, is false: Permitting pornographers to "speak" silences women. Finally, MacKinnon argues that pornography does "contribute causally" to harm to women; and she urges that the law's understanding of "harm," derived from the simple transitive model of "A hit B," is unduly narrow and fails to account for a larger sense in which a discriminatory practice, whether it be pornography or racial segregation, can result in a "collective harm."

Endnotes

[1] 413 U.S. 15 (1973).

[2] See *Erznoznik v. Jacksonville* 422 U.S. 205 (1975); F.C.C. v. Pacific Foundation 438 U.S. 726 (1978); and *Pinkus v. United States* 436 U.S. 293 (1978).

[3] See *Young v. American Mini Theatres* 427 U.S. 50 (1976), and *California v. Larue* 409 U.S. 109 (1972).

[4] See *American Booksellers Assoc. v. Hudnut* in "Cases for Further Reflection" at the end of this chapter.

Obscenity as Pornography

JOEL FEINBERG

1. The Feminist Case Against Pornography[1]

In recent years a powerful attack on pornography has been made from a different quarter and on different, but often shifting grounds. Until 1970 or so, the demand for legal restraints on pornography came mainly from "sexual conservatives," those who regarded the pursuit of erotic pleasure for its own sake to be immoral or degrading, and its public depiction obscene. The new attack, however, comes not from prudes and bluenoses, but from women who have been in the forefront of the sexual revolution. We do not hear any of the traditional complaints about pornography from this group—that erotic states in themselves are immoral, that sexual titillation corrupts character, and that the spectacle of "appeals to prurience" is repugnant to moral sensibility. The new charge is rather that pornography degrades, abuses, and defames women, and contributes to a general climate of attitudes toward women that makes violent sex crimes more frequent. Pornography, they claim, has come to pose a threat to public safety, and its legal restraint can find justification either under the harm principle, or, by analogy with Nazi parades in Skokie and K.K.K. rallies, on some theory of profound (and personal) offense.

It is somewhat misleading to characterize the feminist onslaught as a new argument, or new emphasis in argument, against the same old thing. By the 1960s pornography itself had become in large measure a new and uglier kind of phenomenon. There had always been sado-masochistic elements in much pornography, and a small minority taste to be served with concentrated doses of it. There had also been more or less prominent ex-

pressions of contemptuous attitudes toward abject female "sex objects," even in much relatively innocent pornography. But now a great wave of violent pornography appears to have swept over the land, as even the mass circulation porno magazines moved beyond the customary nude cheesecake and formula stories, to explicit expressions of hostility to women, and to covers and photographs showing "women and children abused, beaten, bound, and tortured" apparently "for the sexual titillation of consumers."[2] When the circulation of the monthly porn magazines comes to 16 million and the porno industry as a whole does $4 billion a year in business, the new trend cannot help but be alarming.[3]

There is no necessity, however, that pornography *as such* be degrading to women. First of all, we can imagine easily enough an ideal pornography in which men and women are depicted enjoying their joint sexual pleasures in ways that show not a trace of dominance or humiliation of either party by the other.[4] The materials in question might clearly satisfy my previous definition of "pornography" as materials designed entirely and effectively to induce erotic excitement in observers, without containing any of the extraneous sexist elements. Even if we confine our attention to actual specimens of pornography—and quite typical ones—we find many examples where male dominance and female humiliation are not present at all. Those of us who were budding teenagers in the 1930s and '40s will tend to take as our model of pornography the comic strip pamphlets in wide circulation among teenagers during that period. The characters were all drawn from the popular legitimate comic strips—The Gumps, Moon Mullins, Maggie and Jiggs, etc.—and were portrayed in cartoons that were exact imitations of the originals. In the pornographic strips, however, the adventures were all erotic. Like all pornography, the cartoons greatly exaggerated the size of organs and appetites, and the "plot lines" were entirely predictable. But the episodes were portrayed with great good humor, a

From *Offense to Others* (New York: Oxford University Press, 1985), pp. 143–164.

kind of joyous feast of erotica in which the blessedly unrepressed cartoon figures shared with perfect equality. Rather than being humiliated or dominated, the women characters equalled the men in their sheer earthy gusto. (That feature especially appealed to teenage boys who could only dream of unrestrained female gusto.) The episodes had no butt at all except prudes and hypocrites. Most of us consumers managed to survive with our moral characters intact.

In still other samples of actual pornography, there is indeed the appearance of male dominance and female humiliation, but even in many of these, explanations of a more innocent character are available. It is in the nature of fantasies, especially adolescent fantasies, whether erotic or otherwise, to glorify imaginatively, in excessive and unrealistic ways, the person who does the fantasizing. When that person is a woman and the fantasy is romantic, she may dream of herself surrounded by handsome lovesick suitors, or in love with an (otherwise) magnificent man who is prepared to throw himself at her feet, worship the ground she walks on, go through hell for her if necessary—the clichés pile up endlessly. If the fantasizing person is a man and his reverie is erotic, he may dream of women who worship the ground *he* walks on, etc., and would do anything for the honor of making love with him, and who having sampled his unrivaled sexual talents would grovel at his feet for more, etc., etc. The point of the fantasy is self-adulation, not "hostility" toward the other sex.

Still other explanations may be available. "Lust," wrote Norman Mailer, "is a world of bewildering dimensions. . . ."[5] When its consuming fire takes hold of the imagination, it is likely to be accompanied by almost any images suggestive of limitlessness, any natural accompaniments of explosive unrestrained passion. Not only men but women too have been known to scratch or bite (like house cats) during sexual excitement, and the phrase "I could hug you to pieces"—a typical expression of felt "limitlessness"—is normally taken as an expression of endearment, not of homicidal fury. Sexual passion in the male animal (there is as yet little but conjecture on this subject) may be associated at deep instinctive or hormonal levels with the states that capture the body and mind during aggressive combat. Some such account may be true of a given man, and explain why a certain kind of pornography may arouse him, without implying anything at all about his settled attitudes toward women, or his general mode of behavior toward them. Then, of course, it is a commonplace that many "normal" people, both men and women, enjoy sado-masochistic fantasies from time to time, without effect on character or conduct. Moreover, there are pornographic materials intended for men, that appeal to their masochistic side exclusively, in which they are "ravished" and humiliated by some grim-faced amazon of fearsome dimensions. Great art these materials are not, but neither are they peculiarly degrading to women.

It will not do then to isolate the most objectionable kinds of pornography, the kinds that are most offensive and even dangerous to women, and reserve the label "pornographic" for them alone. This conscious redefinition is what numerous feminist writers have done, however, much to the confusion of the whole discussion. Gloria Steinem rightly protests against "the truly obscene idea that sex and the domination of women must be combined"[6] (*there* is a proper use of the word "obscene"), but then she manipulates words so that it becomes true by definition (hence merely trivially true) that *all* pornography is obscene in this fashion. She notes that "pornography" stems from the Greek root meaning "prostitutes" or "female captives," "thus letting us know that the subject is not mutual love, or love at all, but domination and violence against women."[7] Steinem is surely right that the subject of the stories, pictures, and films that have usually been called "pornographic" is not love, but it doesn't follow that they are all without exception about male domination over women either. Of course Steinem doesn't make that further claim as a matter of factual reporting, but as a stipulated redefinition. Her proposal can lead other writers to equivocate, however, and find sexist themes in otherwise innocent erotica that have hitherto been called "pornographic"— simply because they *are* naturally called by that name. Steinem adopts "erotica" as the contrasting term to "pornography" as redefined. Erotica, she concludes, is about sexuality, but "pornography is about power, and sex-as-a-weapon," conquerors dominating victims. The distinction is a real one, but better expressed in such terms as "degrading pornography" (Steinem's "pornography") as opposed to "other pornography" (Steinem's "erotica").

At least one other important distinction must be made among the miscellany of materials in the category of degrading pornography. Some degrading pornography is also violent, glorifying in physical mistreatment of the woman, and featuring "weapons of torture or bondage, wounds and bruises."[8] "One frightening spread from *Chic Magazine* showed a series of pictures of a woman covered with blood, masturbating with a knife. The title was 'Columbine Cuts Up.'"[9] A movie called "Snuff" in which female characters (and, it is alleged, the actresses who portrayed them) are tortured to death for the sexual entertainment of the audiences, was shown briefly in a commercial New York theatre. The widely circulated monthly magazine *Hustler* once had a cover picture of a nude woman being pushed head first into a meat grinder, her shapely thighs and legs poised above the opening to the grinder in a sexually receptive posture, while the rest comes out of the bottom as ground meat. The exaggeration of numbers in Kathleen Barry's chilling description hardly blunts its horror: "In movie after movie women are raped, ejaculated on, urinated on, anally penetrated, beaten, and, with the advent of snuff films, murdered in an orgy of sexual pleasure."[10] The examples, alas, are abundant and depressing.

There are other examples, however, of pornography that is degrading to women but does not involve violence. Gloria Steinem speaks of more subtle forms of coercion: "a physical attitude of conqueror and victim, the use of race or class difference to imply the same thing, perhaps a very unequal nudity with one person exposed and vulnerable while the other is clothed."[11] As the suggested forms of coercion become more and more subtle, obviously there will be very difficult line-drawing problems for any legislature brave enough to enter this area.

Yet the most violent cases at one end of the spectrum are as clear as they can be. They all glory in wanton and painful violence against helpless victims and do this with the extraordinary intention (sometimes even successful) of causing sexual arousal in male viewers. One could give every other form of pornography, degrading or not, the benefit of the doubt, and still identify with confidence all members of the violent extreme category. If there is a strong enough argument against pornography to limit the liberty of pornographers, it is probably restricted to this class of materials. Some

feminist writers speak as if that would not be much if any restriction, but that may be a consequence of their *defining* pornography in terms of its most revolting specimens.[12] A pornographic story or film may be degrading in Steinem's subtle sense, in that it shows an intelligent man with a stupid woman, or a wealthy man with a chambermaid, and intentionally exploits the inequality for the sake of the special sexual tastes of the presumed male consumer, but if that were the *only* way in which the work degraded women, it would fall well outside the extreme (violent) category. All the more so, stories in which the male and female are equals—and these materials too can count as pornographic—would fall outside the objectionable category.

May the law legitimately be used to restrict the liberty of pornographers to produce and distribute, and their customers to purchase and use, erotic materials that are violently abusive of women? (I am assuming that no strong case can be made for the proscription of materials that are merely degrading in one of the relatively subtle and nonviolent ways.) Many feminists answer, often with reluctance, in the affirmative. Their arguments can be divided into two general classes. Some simply invoke the harm principle. Violent pornography wrongs and harms women, according to these arguments, either by defaming them as a group, or (more importantly) by inciting males to violent crimes against them or creating a cultural climate in which such crimes are likely to become more frequent. The two traditional legal categories involved in these harm-principle arguments, then, are *defamation* and *incitement*. The other class of arguments invoke[s] the offense principle, not in order to prevent mere "nuisances," but to prevent profound offense analogous to that of the Jews in Skokie or the blacks in a town where the K.K.K. rallies.

2. *Violent Pornography, the Cult of Macho, and Harm to Women*

I shall not spend much time on the claim that violent and other extremely degrading pornography should be banned on the ground that it *defames* women. In a skeptical spirit, I can begin by pointing out that there are immense difficulties in applying the civil law of libel and slander as it is presently constituted in such a way as not to violate freedom of expression. Problems with *criminal* libel and slander would be even more unmanageable, and *group* defamation, whether civil or criminal, would multiply the problems still further. The argument on the other side is that pornography is essentially propaganda—propaganda against women. It does not slander women in the technical legal sense by asserting damaging falsehoods about them, because it *asserts* nothing at all. But it spreads an image of women as mindless playthings or "objects," inferior beings fit only to be used and abused for the pleasure of men, whether they like it or not, but often to their own secret pleasure. This picture lowers the esteem men have for women, and for that reason (if defamation is the basis of the argument) is sufficient ground for proscription even in the absence of any evidence of tangible harm to women caused by the behavior of misled and deluded men.

If degrading pornography defames (libels or slanders) women, it must be in virtue of some beliefs about women—false beliefs—that it conveys, so that in virtue of those newly acquired or reenforced false beliefs, consumers lower their esteem for women in general. If a work of pornography, for example, shows a woman (or group of women) in exclusively subservient or domestic roles, that may lead the consumer to *believe* that women, in virtue of some inherent female characteristics, are only fit for such roles. There is no doubt that much pornography does portray women in subservient positions, but if that is defamatory to women in anything like the legal sense, then so are soap commercials on TV. So are many novels, even some good ones. (A good novel may yet be about some degraded characters.) That some groups are portrayed in unflattering roles has not hitherto been a ground for the censorship of fiction or advertising. Besides, it is not clearly the *group* that is portrayed at all in such works, but only one individual (or small set of individuals) and fictitious ones at that. Are fat men defamed by Shakespeare's picture of Falstaff? Are Jews defamed by the characterization of Shylock? Could any writer today even hope to write a novel partly about a fawning corrupted black, under group defamation laws, without risking censorship or worse? The chilling effect on the practice of fiction-writing would amount to a near freeze.

Moreover, as Fred Berger points out,[13] the de-

grading images and defamatory beliefs pornographic works are alleged to cause are not produced in the consumer by explicit statements asserted with the intent to convince the reader or auditor of their truth. Rather they are caused by the stimulus of the work, in the context, on the expectations, attitudes, and beliefs the viewer brings with him to the work. That is quite other than believing an assertion on the authority or argument of the party making the assertion, or understanding the assertion in the first place in virtue of fixed conventions of language use and meaning. Without those fixed conventions of language, the work has to be interpreted in order for any message to be extracted from it, and the process of interpretation, as Berger illustrates abundantly, is "always a matter of judgment and subject to great variation among persons."[14] What looks like sexual subservience to some looks like liberation from sexual repression to others. It is hard to imagine how a court could provide a workable, much less fair, test of whether a given work has sufficiently damaged male esteem toward women for it to be judged criminally defamatory, when so much of the viewer's reaction he brings on himself, and viewer reactions are so widely variable.

It is not easy for a single work to defame successfully a group as large as 51% of the whole human race. (Could a misanthrope "defame" the whole human race by a false statement about "the nature of man"? Would every human being then be his "victim"?) Perhaps an unanswered barrage of thousands of tracts, backed by the prestige of powerful and learned persons without dissent might successfully defame any group no matter how large, but those conditions would be difficult to satisfy so long as there is freedom to speak back on the other side. In any case, defamation is not the true gravamen of the wrong that women in general suffer from extremely degrading pornography. When a magazine cover portrays a woman in a meat grinder, *all* women are insulted, degraded, even perhaps endangered, but few would naturally complain that they were *libelled* or *slandered*. Those terms conceal the point of what has happened. If women are harmed by pornography, the harm is surely more direct and tangible than harm to "the interest in reputation."[15]

The major argument for repression of violent pornography under the harm principle is that it promotes rape and physical violence. In the United States there is a plenitude both of sexual violence against women and of violent pornography. According to the F.B.I. Uniform Crime Statistics (as of 1980), a 12-year-old girl in the United States has one chance in three of being raped in her lifetime; studies only a few years earlier showed that the number of violent scenes in hard-core pornographic books was as high as 20% of the total, and the number of violent cartoons and pictorials in leading pornographic magazines was as much as 10% of the total.[16] This has suggested to some writers that there must be a direct causal link between violent pornography and sexual violence against women; but causal relationships between pornography and rape, if they exist, must be more complicated than that. The suspicion of direct connection is dissipated, as Aryeh Neier points out,

> . . . when one looks at the situation in other countries. For example, violence against women is common in . . . Ireland and South Africa, but pornography is unavailable in those countries. By contrast violence against women is relatively uncommon in Denmark, Sweden, and the Netherlands, even though pornography seems to be even more plentifully available than in the United States. To be sure, this proves little or nothing except that more evidence is needed to establish a causal connection between pornography and violence against women beyond the fact that both may exist at the same time. But this evidence . . . simply does not exist.[17]

On the other hand, there is evidence that novel ways of committing crimes are often suggested (usually inadvertently) by bizarre tales in films or TV . . . , and even factual newspaper reports of crimes can trigger the well-known "copy-cat crime" phenomenon. But if the possibility of copy-cat cases, by itself, justified censorship or punishment, we would have grounds for suppressing films of *The Brothers Karamozov* and the TV series *Roots* (both of which have been cited as influences on imitative crimes). "There would be few books left on our library shelves and few films that could be shown if every one that had at some time 'provoked' bizarre behavior were censored."[18] A violent episode in a pornographic work may indeed be a causally necessary condition for the commission of some specific crime by a specific perpetrator on a specific victim at some specific time and place. But for his reading or viewing that episode,

the perpetrator may not have done precisely what he did in just the time, place, and manner that he did it. But so large a part of the full causal explanation of his act concerns his own psychological character and predispositions, that it is likely that some similar crime would have suggested itself to him in due time. It is not likely that non-rapists are converted into rapists *simply* by reading and viewing pornography. If pornography has a serious causal bearing on the occurence of rape (as opposed to the trivial copy-cat effect) it must be in virtue of its role (still to be established) in implanting the appropriate cruel dispositions in the first place.

Rape is such a complex social phenomenon that there is probably no one simple generalization to account for it. Some rapes are no doubt ineliminable, no matter how we design our institutions. Many of these are the product of deep individual psychological problems, transferred rages, and the like. But for others, perhaps the preponderant number, the major part of the explanation is sociological, not psychological. In these cases the rapist is a psychologically normal person well adjusted to his particular subculture, acting calmly and deliberately rather than in a rage, and doing what he thinks is expected of him by his peers, what he must do to acquire or preserve standing in his group. His otherwise inexplicable violence is best explained as a consequence of the peculiar form of his socialization among his peers, his pursuit of a prevailing ideal of manliness, what the Mexicans have long called *machismo*, but which exists to some degree or other among men in most countries, certainly in our own.

The macho male wins the esteem of his associates by being tough, fearless, reckless, wild, unsentimental, hard-boiled, hard drinking, disrespectful, profane, willing to fight whenever his honor is impugned, and fight without fear of consequences no matter how extreme. He is a sexual athlete who must be utterly dominant over "his" females, who are expected to be slavishly devoted to him even though he lacks gentleness with them and shows his regard only by displaying them like trophies; yet he is a hearty and loyal companion to his "teammates" (he is always on a "team" of some sort.) Given the manifest harm the cult of macho has done to men,[19] women, and to relations between men and women, it is difficult to account for its survival in otherwise civilized nations. Perhaps it is useful in time of war, and war has been a preoccupation of most generations of young men, in most nations, up to the present. If so, then the persistence of *machismo* is one of the stronger arguments we have (among many others) for the obsolescence of war.

The extreme character of macho values must be understood before any sense can be made of the appeal of violent pornography. The violent porn does not appeal to prurience or lust as such. Indeed, it does not appeal at all to a psychologically normal male who is not in the grip of the macho cult. In fact these pictures, stories, and films have no other function but to express and reenforce the macho ideology. "Get your sexual kicks," they seem to say, "but make sure you get them by humiliating the woman, and showing her who's boss. Make sure at all costs not to develop any tender feelings toward her that might give her a subtle form of control over you and thus destroy your standing with the group. Remember to act in the truly manly manner of a 'wild and crazy guy.' "

In her brilliant article on this subject, Sarah J. McCarthy cites some horrible examples from *Penthouse* Magazine of the macho personality structure which is peculiarly receptive to, and a necessary condition for, the appeal of violent porn:

> "There's still something to be said for bashing a woman over the head, dragging her off behind a rock, and having her," said one of the guys in the February 1980 *Penthouse*. . . . "Women Who Flirt With Pain" was the cover hype for a *Penthouse* interview with an assortment of resident Neanderthals (a name that would swell them with pride).

> "We're basically rapists because we're created that way," proclaims Dale. "We're irrational, sexually completely crazy. Our sexuality is more promiscuous, more immediate, and more fleeting, possibly less deep. We're like stud bulls that want to mount everything in sight. . . . "

> The letters-to-the-editor in the February *Penthouse* contains an ugly letter from someone who claims to be a sophomore at a large midwestern university and is "into throat-fucking." He writes of Kathy and how he was "ramming his huge eleven-inch tool down her throat." [Sexual

bragging, pornography style.] Kathy "was nearly unconscious from coming." [Deceit and self-deception, pornography style.] Gloria Steinem writes in the May 1980 *Ms.*: "Since *Deep Throat*, a whole new genre of pornography has developed. Added to the familiar varieties of rape, there is now an ambition to rape the throat. . . . "

> Another issue of *Penthouse* contains an article about what they have cleverly called "tossing." A college student from Albuquerque, who drives a 1974 Cadillac and who is "attracted to anything in a skirt," tells how it's done. "How did you get into tossing?" the *Penthouse* interviewer asks. "It just happened," says Daryl. "I was doing it in high school two years ago and didn't know what it was. I'd date a chick once, fuck her in my car, and just dump her out. Literally."[20]

These repugnant specimens are not examples of make-believe violent pornography. Rather, they are examples of the attitudes and practices of persons who are antecedently prone to be appreciative consumers of violent pornography. These grisly sentiments are perhaps found more commonly among working class youths in military barracks and factories but they are only slightly more familiar than similar bravado heard by middle class Americans in fraternity houses and dormitories. These remarks are usually taken as meant to impress their male auditors; they are uttered with a kind of aggressive pride. The quotations from *Penthouse* capture the tone exactly. These utterly outrageous things are said publicly and casually, not in passion, not in hate, not in lust. They seem to say "That's just the way we machos are—for better or worse." Sarah McCarthy understands it perfectly—

> Though I'm sure male rage exists, just as female rage exists, it is probably not the main cause of rape. What we may be dealing with is the banality of rape, the sheer ordinariness of it as the logical end of macho, the ultimate caricature of our sexual arrangements. Some men may think that rape is just the thing to do. Its source could, in large part, be due to something as mundane as faulty sex education, rather

than a wellspring of rage of mythic proportions. In many subcultures within the
United States, violence against women has
become acceptable, expected, even
trendy. . . .[21]

There is probably no more typical pure macho
enterprise than gang rape, a kind of group rite
among cultish "individualists," in some ways like
a primitive puberty ritual in which insecure males
"prove themselves" to one another, and the victim
is but an incidental instrument to that end. In a
chapter on rape and war in her *Against Our Will*,[22]
Susan Brownmiller discusses the behavior of
American troops in Vietnam. Various veterans are
quoted to the effect that rape was widespread but
rarely reported. One veteran who denied his own
participation, had a terse explanation of the behavior of others: "They only do it when there are a lot
of guys around. You know, it makes them feel
good. They show each other what they can do.
They won't do it by themselves."[23] Macho values
thrive and spread in wartime battle zones. They
become part of the process by which soldiers celebrate their cynical toughness and try to convince
themselves and one another that they truly have it.

Would it significantly reduce sexual violence if
violent pornography were effectively banned? No
one can know for sure, but if the cult of macho is
the main source of such violence, as I suspect, then
repression of violent pornography, whose function
is to pander to the macho values already deeply
rooted in society, may have little effect. Pornography does not cause normal decent chaps, through
a single exposure, to metamorphoze into rapists.
Pornography-reading machos commit rape, but
that is because they already have macho values,
not because they read the violent pornography that
panders to them. Perhaps then *constant* exposure
to violent porn might turn a decent person into a
violence-prone macho. But that does not seem
likely either, since the repugnant violence of the
materials could not have any appeal in the first
place to one who did not already have some strong
macho predispositions, so "constant exposure"
could not begin to become established. Clearly,
other causes, and more foundational ones, must be
at work, if violent porn is to have any initial purchase. Violent pornography is more a symptom of
machismo than a cause of it, and treating symptoms
merely is not a way to offer protection to potential
victims of rapists. At most, I think there may be a

small spill-over effect of violent porn on actual violence. Sometimes a bizarre new sadistic trick (like
"throat-fucking"?) is suggested by a work of violent pornography and taken up by those prone to
cruel violence to begin with. More often, perhaps,
the response to an inventive violent porno scene
may be like that of the college *Penthouse* reader to
"tossing": "I was doing it in high school two years
ago, and I didn't know what it was." He read
Penthouse and learned "what it was," but his conduct, presumably, was not significantly changed.

If my surmise about causal connections is correct they are roughly as indicated in the . . . diagram.

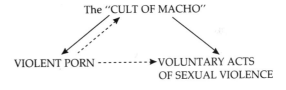

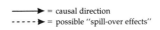

——▶ = causal direction
- - - -▶ = possible "spill-over effects"

The primary causal direction is not from violent
pornography to violent real-life episodes. Neither
is it from violent pornography to the establishment
and reenforcement of macho values. Rather, the
cult of macho expectations is itself the primary
cause *both* of the existence of violent porn (it provides the appreciative audience) and of the real-life
sexual violence (it provides the motive). The dotted
arrows express my acknowledgement of the point
that there might be some small spill-over effect
from violent pornography back on the macho
values that spawn it, in one direction, and on real-
life violence in the other, but the pornography cannot be the primary causal generator. Sexual violence will continue to fester so long as the cult of
macho flourishes, whether or not we eliminate legal violent pornography.

How then can we hope to weaken and then
extirpate the cultish values at the root of our problem? The criminal law is a singularly ill-adapted
tool for that kind of job. We might just as well
legislate against entrepreneurship on the grounds
that capitalism engenders "acquisitive personalities," or against the military on the grounds that it
produces "authoritarian personalities," or against

certain religious sects on the ground that they foster puritanism, as criminalize practices and institutions on the grounds that they contribute to *machismo*. But macho values are culturally, not instinctively, transmitted, and the behavior that expresses them is learned, not inherited, behavior. What is learned can be unlearned. Schools should play a role. Surely, learning to see through machismo and avoid its traps should be as important a part of a child's preparation for citizenship as the acquisition of patriotism and piety. To be effective, such teaching should be frank and direct, not totally reliant on general moral platitudes. It should talk about the genesis of children's attitudes toward the other sex, and invite discussion of male insecurity, resentment of women, cruelty, and even specific odious examples. Advertising firms and film companies should be asked (at first), then pressured (if necessary) to cooperate, as they did in the successful campaign to deglamorize cigarette smoking. Fewer exploitation films should be made that provide attractive models of youths flashing knives, playing chicken or Russian roulette, or "tossing" girls. Materials (especially films) should be made available to clergymen as well as teachers, youth counselors, and parole officers. A strong part of the emphasis of these materials should be on the harm that bondage to the cult of macho does to men too, and how treacherous a trap *machismo* can be. The new moral education must be careful, of course, not to preach dull prudence as a preferred style for youthful living. A zest for excitement, adventure, even danger, cannot be artificially removed from adolescent nature. Moreover, teamwork, camaraderie, and toughness of character need not be denigrated. But the cult of macho corrupts and distorts these values in ways that can be made clear to youths. The mistreatment of women, when its motivation is clearly revealed and understood, should be a sure way of eliciting the contempt of the group, not a means to greater prestige within it.

Rape is a harm and a severe one. Harm prevention is definitely a legitimate use of the criminal law. Therefore, if there is a clear enough causal connection to rape, a statute that prohibits violent pornography would be a morally legitimate restriction of liberty. But it is not enough to warrant supression that pornography as a whole might have some harmful consequences to third parties, even though most specific instances of it do not. "Communications from other human beings are

among the most important causes of human behavior," Kent Greenawalt points out, "but criminal law cannot concern itself with every communication that may fortuitously lead to the commission of a crime. It would, for example, be ludicrous to punish a supervisor for criticizing a subordinate, even if it could be shown that the criticism so inflamed the subordinate that he assaulted a fellow worker hours later."[24] An even stronger point can be made. Even where there is statistical evidence that a certain percentage of communications of a given type will predictably lead the second party to harm third parties, so that in a sense the resultant harms are not "fortuitous," that is not sufficient warrant for prohibiting all communications of that kind. It would be even more ludicrous, for example, for a legislature to pass a criminal statute against the criticism of subordinates, on the ground that inflamed employees sometimes become aggressive with their fellow workes.

A more relevant example of the same point, and one with an ironic twist, is provided by Fred Berger:

> A journal that has published studies often cited by the radical feminists . . . has also published an article that purports to show that the greater emancipation of women in western societies has led to great increases in criminal activity *by* women. Such crimes as robbery, larceny, burglary, fraud, and extortion have shown marked increase, as have arson, murder, and aggravated assault. But freedom of expression would mean little if such facts could be taken as a reason to suppress expression that seeks the further liberation of women from their secondary, dependent status with respect to men.[25]

Of course, one can deny that violent porn is a form of valuable free expression analogous to scholarly feminist articles, but the point remains that indirectly produced harms are not by themselves sufficient grounds for criminalizing materials, that some further conditions must be satisfied.

Those instances of sexual violence which may be harmful side-effects of violent pornography are directly produced by criminals (rapists) acting voluntarily on their own. We already have on the statute books a firm prohibition of rape and sexual assault. If, in addition, the harm principle permits the criminalization of actions only indirectly related to the primary harm, such as producing, displaying or selling violent pornography, then there is a danger that the law will be infected with unfairness; for unless certain further conditions are fulfilled, the law will be committed to punishing some parties for the entirely voluntary criminal conduct of other parties. . . . Suppose that *A* wrongfully harms (e.g. rapes) *B* in circumstances such that (1) *A* acts fully voluntarily on his own initiative, and (2) nonetheless, but for what *C* has communicated to him, he would not have done what he did to *B*. Under what further conditions, we must ask, can *C* be rightfully held criminally responsible along with *A* for the harm to *B*? Clearly *C* can be held responsible if the information he communicated was helpful assistance to *A* and intended to be such. In that case *C* becomes a kind of collaborator. Under traditional law, *C* can also incur liability if what he communicated to *A* was some kind of encouragement to commit a crime against. *B*. The clearest cases are those in which *C* solicits *A*'s commission of the criminal act by offering inducements to him. "Encouragement" is also criminal when it takes the form of active urging. Sometimes mere advice to commit the act counts as an appropriate sort of encouragement. When the encouragement takes a general form, and the harmful crime is recommended to "the general reader" or an indefinite audience, then the term "advocacy" is often used. Advocating criminal conduct is arguably a way of producing such conduct, and is thus often itself a crime. An article in a pornographic magazine advocating the practice of rape (as opposed to advocating a legislative change of the rape laws) would presumably be a crime if its intent were serious and its audience presumed to be impressionable to an appropriately dangerous degree.[26]

Violent pornography, however, does not seem to fit any of these models. Its authors and vendors do not solicit rapes; nor do they urge or advise rapes; nor do they advocate rape. If some of their customers, some of the time, might yet "find encouragement" in their works to commit rapes because rape has been portrayed in a way that happens to be alluring to them, that is their own affair, the pornographer might insist, and their own responsibility. The form of "encouragement" that is most applicable (if any are) to the pornography case is that which the common law has traditionally called "incitement." Sir Edward Coke wrote in 1628 that "all those that incite . . . set on, or stir up any other" to a crime are themselves

accessories.[27] Thus, haranguing an angry crowd on the doorsteps of a corn dealer, in Mill's famous example,[28] might be the spark that incites the mob's violence against the hated merchant, even though the speaker did not explicitly urge, advise, or advocate it. Yet, a similar speech, twenty-four hours earlier, to a calmer audience in a different location, though it may have made a causal contribution to the eventual violence, would not have borne a close enough relation to the harm to count as an "incitement," or "positive instigation" (Mill's term) of it.

Given that "communication" is a form of expression, and thus has an important social value, obviously it cannot rightly be made criminal simply on the ground that it may lead some others on their own to act harmfully. Even if works of pure pornography are *not* to be treated as "communication," "expression" or "speech" in the sense of the First Amendment), but as mere symbolic aphrodisiacs or sex aids without further content[29] . . . , they may yet have an intimate personal value to those who use them, and a social value derived from the importance we attach to the protection of private erotic experience. By virtue of that significance, one person's liberty can be invaded to prevent the harm other parties might cause to *their* victims only when the invaded behavior has a specially direct connection to the harm caused, something perhaps like direct "incitement." Fred Berger suggests three necessary conditions that expected harms must satisfy if they are to justify censorship or prohibition of erotic materials, none of which, he claims, is satisfied by pornography, even violent pornography.

> **1.** There must be strong evidence of a very likely and serious harm. [I would add—" that would not have occurred otherwise."]
>
> **2.** The harms must be clearly and directly linked with the expression.
>
> **3.** It must be unlikely that further speech or expression can be used effectively to combat the harm.[30]

Berger suggests that the false shout of "fire" in a crowded theatre is paradigmatically the kind of communication that satisfies these conditions. If so, then he must interpret the second condition to be something like the legal standard of incitement—setting on, stirring up, inflaming the other party (or mob of parties) to the point of hysteria or panic, so that their own infliction of the subsequent damage is something less than deliberate and fully voluntary. Their inciter in that case is as responsible as they are, perhaps even more so, for the harm that ensues. Surely, the relation between pornographers and rapists is nowhere near that direct and manipulative. If it were, we would punish the pornographers proportionately more severely, and blame the actual rapist (poor chap; he was "inflamed") proportionately less.

It may yet happen that further evidence will show that Berger's conditions, or some criteria similar to them, are satisfied by violent pornography. In that case, a liberal should have no hesitation in using the criminal law to prevent the harm. In the meantime, the appropriate liberal response should be a kind of uneasy skepticism about the harmful effects of pornography of third party victims, conjoined with increasingly energetic use of "further speech or expression" against the cult of macho, "effectively to combat the harm."

3. *Violent Pornography and Profound Offense*

The harm principle grounds for legally banning pornography do not appear sufficient. Does the offense principle do any better? Pornographic displays *can* be public nuisances, of course, and when the balancing tests tip in the nuisance direction, the offending activities may fairly be prohibited, or redirected to less offensive channels. The manner in which degrading and violent pornography offends women (and men who support women's rights) is substantially different from that in which erotica as such offend the prudish. The shame, embarrassment, shock, disgust, and irritation of the latter group can be effectively avoided if the erotic displays are concealed from their view. The offense to a woman's sensibilities when her whole sex is treated as grist for the meat grinder, however, is deeply repugnant to her moral sensibilities whether out of view or not. Feminist writers often make this point by means of analogies to racist literature and films.

Suppose some unscrupulous promoters decide that they can make large profits by pandering to the latent hatred against blacks which they sup-

pose to be endemic in a substantial minority of the white community. Since explicitly racist remarks and overt racist behavior are no longer widely acceptable in American society, many secret black-haters might enjoy an occasional night at the movies where they can enjoy to their heart's content specially made films that lampoon minstrel-style "darkies" "with wide eyes as white as moons, hair shot straight in the air like Buchwheat's, afraid of everything—spiders, [their] own shadows, ghosts."[31] So much for comic openers. The main features could be stories of uppity blacks put in their place by righteous whites, taunted and hounded, tarred and feathered, tortured and castrated, and in the climactic scenes, hung up on gallows to the general rejoicing of their betters. The aim of the films would be to provide a delicious catharsis of pent-up hatred. It would be prudent, on business gounds, to keep advertisements discreet, and to use euphemistic descriptions like "folk films" (analogous to "adult films").

I don't imagine that many blacks would be placated by the liberal lawmaker who argues in support of his refusal to enact prohibitive legislation that there is little evidence of actual harm done to blacks by the films, that they do not advocate violence to blacks or incite mobs to fury, and that for all we know they will make the racists less dangerous by providing a harmless outlet for their anti-social impulses. Neither would many blacks be assuaged by the liberal assurance that we should all be wary of possible harmful effects anyway, continue to look for evidence thereof, and use educational campaigns as a more effective means of exposing the evils of racism. "That is all well and good," the blacks might reply, "but first we must lance this painful boil on our sensibilities. The 'folk films,' whether we are in the audience or not, are morally abominable affronts to us. Their very existence in our midst is a perpetual laceration of our feelings. We aren't present to be humiliated, but they degrade the very atmosphere in which we breathe and move."

The analogy to violent pornographic films is close though not perfect. (It is an interesting fact to ponder that although there undoubtedly is a large racist underground in this country, no promoter has yet found a way of exploiting it in the manner of our example.) The pornographic films do serve an erotic interest of their customers, and that gives them, *ceteris paribus*, a personal value greater perhaps than that of the "folk films." The racist films, on the other hand, may be easier to disguise as genuine works of drama, thus making it much more difficult for a line to be drawn between them and genuine attempts at dramas about odious people and their victims. The bare-knowledge offense in the two cases seems almost equally profound, going well beyond anything called "mere nuisance," to touch the chord of moral sensibility.

It does not express an unsympathetic attitude toward the offended parties, however, to deny a basis in either the harm or offense principles for the use of legal force to "lance the boil." Profound offense . . . , is either an impersonal and disinterested moral outrage or else an aggrieved response on one's own behalf because of the unpleasant mental states one has been forced to experience. If it is an impersonal response, then it can warrant legal force against its cause only on the basis of the principle of legal moralism which is unacceptable to liberals. We would have to argue in that case that the very showing of violent films to appreciative audiences is an evil in itself and one of such magnitude that it can be rightly prevented by legal force if necessary, even though it is not the kind of evil that *wrongs* any one. . . . If, on the other hand, the profound offense is a felt personal wrong voiced on one's own behalf as its "victim," then the complaint is that the offending materials cause one to suffer unpleasant states that are a nuisance to avoid. But that offense will not have much weight on the scales if one is not forced to witness the showings, or lurid announcements of the showings, and is not forced to take irritating and inconveniencing detours to avoid them. The offense principle, in short, will not warrant legal prohibition of the films unless the offense they cause is not reasonably avoidable, and bare-knowledge offense, insofar as it is mere offensive nuisance, *is* reasonably avoidable. It is only in its character as disinterested moral outrage that it is not reasonably avoidable, but we cannot ban everything that is thought to be outrageous, whether right-violating or not, without recourse to legal moralism.

This argument, I conceded, is subject to two strong qualifications. . . . It may be possible in certain untypical situations to go between its horns and thus escape its dilemma. A profoundly offended state of mind may be both disinterested moral outrage and also involve a sense of personal grievance, as when the offending cause is an affront to the offended party himself or a group to which he belongs. To feel personally degraded or insulted before others may well be to feel personally *wronged*, even though one's interests are unaffected and one's unpleasant states easily avoidable. The more difficult question is whether one truly *is* personally wronged when this happens, whether one's own rights have in fact been violated. The difficult cases I have in mind fall in between more extreme cases on either side that are easier to make judgments about. Consider hypothetical cases 1, 2 (a and b), and 3. Cases 2a and b are the difficult ones I have in mind.

CASE 1

A desecrates in private an icon that *B* regards as inherently sacred. *B* is morally outraged later when he learns about it. We can assume for the sake of the argument that *A*'s action was morally wrong, but that it caused no harm to *B* (or anyone else). Neither was it, in any sense, directed at *B*. (*A* and *B* are total strangers.) Nevertheless, *B* suffers deep offense, as well as moral outrage, whenever he thinks about it. But *B* does not feel personally wronged. *A* did not violate *his* rights simply because he did something *B* morally disapproved of. *B* is neither the "target" of *A*'s morally wrongful action, nor its victim.

CASE 2A

B is morally outraged (in at least the disinterested way) when he learns that *A* and his friends, all of whom resent *B* for no good reason, frequently insult him when they gather together in private, and maliciously ridicule him behind his back. *A* and his friends act wrongly, but not in a manner that harms *B* (there is, for example, no incitement or defamation against him), but their conduct *is*, in a sense, directed at *B*, and *B* is deeply offended to learn about it. He *feels* personally wronged, but is he in fact wronged? Have his rights been violated? He was the "target" of morally wrongful behavior, but was he its *victim*? *A* and his friends might rebut his grievance by saying: "We all happen to dislike you (whether or not for good reason is beside the point), and we get great collective pleasure from sharing that dislike. How does that violate your rights? Do you have a right not to be disliked or not to have that dislike shared by those who have it? In fact, our little private party, while understandably not to your liking, was none of your business."

CASE 2B

A and his friends are anti-semitic Nazi sympathizers who gather together privately and in secret in A's apartment, and spend an evening regaling themselves with abusive and mocking stories about Jews, and top off their evening of fun by showing old Nazi propaganda films against Jews, and even newsreels of Jewish corpses discovered in the newly liberated concentration camps. The latter cause general hilarity except for one odd chap in a corner who masturbates excitely at depictions of torture instruments. We can safely assume that all of this is morally wrongful though not necessarily harmful behavior, and that it has Jews, as a class, as its "target." B is a Jew who learns of the party later, and is morally outraged, deeply offended, and in his estimation personally wronged by the immoral activities. But again we can admit that he was (part of) the target of those activities so that his offense was in a clear sense "personal," while doubting that he was the victim of those activities, one whose own rights were violated.

CASE 3

This is an easier case. A and his friends include at their party (in 2a) C, D, and E, who know nothing about B. A then deliberately lies to C, D, and E by telling them that B is an exconvict, a child molester, and bad check passer. This utterly destroys B's reputation for probity with C, D, and E, who eventually spread the libel widely among many other persons, including B's customers. B's business declines and his economic interests as well as his interest in his good name are harmed by the defamation. B later learns what has happened and is outraged. He was not only the target of wrongful behavior; he was its victim, the one whose rights were violated. He not only feels personally wronged; he clearly was personally wronged.

The moral I draw from these stories is that the targets of abuse in 2a and b were not in fact its victims, so that their profound offense, while both moral and personal, is not the sort of "wrongful offense" (a right-violating offense) that is a reason for criminal prohibition. I am realistic enough to expect that many readers will not share my "intuition," and that the matter is not easily settled by argument. Even if I concede, however, for the sake of the argument, that B's rights *were* violated in 2a and b as well as 3 (though not in 1), there will be little gain for those who would invoke legal action against A (without resorting to legal moralism) in those cases. It would be an extraordinary extension of the offense principle to punish such activities even on the supposition that some parties' rights were violated by their bare-knowledge offense. That would be to consider the quite avoidable offended feelings of those parties to have more weight on the balancing scales than the freedom of others to speak their minds to one another in private. B may be even more offended to learn that his enemies have insulted or ridiculed him to other parties who may not even know him, and this case, I admit, is a more plausible if not entirely convincing example of a violated right, even without defamation. But all that is conveyed by these comments to the strangers who hear them is that A has a low regard for B (which is his right). They may also infer from this that B has low regard for A. B surely will not be reluctant to express that disregard to any of A's auditors who inquire, which, I should think, would also be *his* right.

Racist and porno films do not directly insult specific individuals, but rather large groups, thus diluting the impact of the insult, or at least its directed personal character, proportionately. The "folk films" might be more serious affronts in this respect than the porno films since their target is a much smaller group than half of the human race, and one which has historically been brutalized by slavery and cruel repression. A black man might be more likely to feel a *personal* grievance at the folk film he does not witness than a woman would to a porno film she does not witness, for these reasons.[32] This personal aspect of his offense would overlay the more general disinterested moral indignation he shares with the women who are offended by their bare knowledge of the existence of violent pornographic displays. Nonetheless, understandable as the black's felt grievance may be, the insulting film shown to a willing audience in a private or commercial theatre is in the same boat as the insulting conversations among willing friends in a private home or club. In both cases the conduct is morally execrable, but in neither case do liberal principles warrant state intervention to punish the mischief. If, however, I concede for the sake of the argument what seems to me to be dubious, namely that undeserved insults *wrong* the insulted party (violate his rights), and further (what is not doubtful) that he can be inflamed by the bare knowledge of them even though they occur behind his back, then I must make the further concession that these are relevant reasons under the offense principle in support of criminal prohibition. They cite, after all, a wrongful offense of the appropriate kind. But unless the balancing tests that mediate the offense principle are satisfied (and in these cases that would require that the offending conduct be of a kind that has virtually no redeeming personal and social value whatever), that relevant consideration can never be a sufficient reason.

The second accommodation our theory must make for profound offense is to acknowledge that severe restrictions should be made on announcements and advertisements. A black need not suffer the direct humiliation and stinging affront to his dignity and self-respect that would come from his being forced into the audience for a "folk film." He can simply stay away, and avoid the worst of it. But if the city is blanketed with garish signs announcing the folk films, or worse than that, signs that dispense with euphemisms and advertise "shows that put niggers in their place," then the affronts are no longer private; the offense is no longer avoidable; and its nature no less profound. The signs . . . can be expected to inflame the blacks, who are the direct object of their insult, in the manner of fighting words, further frustrating them since violent response cannot be permitted. The offense of conspicuous advertisements, even nongraphic ones (though graphic ones are the worst), is so great that any restriction of them short of interference with the minimum basic right of communication is warranted.

In this and the preceding chapter we have distinguished three types of activities the bare knowledge of which can be profoundly offensive. The first category is illustrated by private desecration of cherished symbols like religious icons and national flags, and by the mistreatment in private of dead bodies. We are to think of these "private" activities as unwitnessed by others or witnessed only voluntarily by other participants or spectators. In the second category are the "Skokie-type cases," for example, a Nazi demonstration in Skokie or a K.K.K. march in Harlem. Spectators are deliberately sought out and taunted by the display of hated symbols of racial cruelty known to offend deeply those they insult. In the third category are racist "folk films" and violent porno films shown in privately owned and secluded places for the pleasure of anyone in the general public who wishes to buy a ticket. All three categories can cause bare-knowledge offense as well as equally "profound" offense to unwilling observers (if any). But they differ subtly in various other important respects.

The bare-knowledge offense taken at "private desecrations" is not personal; that is, the offense is not taken because the offended party thinks of *himself* as wronged. (In fact he may admit that no one is personally wronged by the conduct he finds odious.) If he demands that legal force be used to prevent the outrageous behavior (anyway), the offending party might challenge him thus: "What concern is my behavior to you? You are morally outraged at what I have done, but I've done nothing *to* you except to morally outrage you. The outrage may or may not be justifiable, but it's no business of *yours* (or of anyone [else's] for that matter) to intervene, either to enforce your moral judgment (which implies legal moralism) or simply because you find your own intense moral aversion unpleasant. You can always escape *that* unpleasantness by ceasing to dwell in your imagination upon unseen things. If you can't escape the annoyance that way, then you are suffering from a severe neurotic obsession and should seek help." The offense produced by the sacrilegious private conduct, in short, cannot be thought to be a wrong *to* anyone, even if it is morally wrong in itself. Hence, it cannot be rightly banned on liberal principles, no matter how repugnant it might be to think about.

In the other two categories, however, the bare-knowledge offense, while equally profound, is also personal. The folk film promoter's challenge "What concern is that to you?" can be answered by some people—" I am black. Your film mocks and insults blacks, and therefore mocks and insults me, my family, and my dear ones. That's how it concerns me." If it is plausible to think of a person as truly wronged by abusively insulting materials shown to others behind his back, (and I have doubted this) then the black person's bare-knowledge offense, and the woman's bare-knowledge offense at violent porn films, are not only profound, they are also wrongful (to them) in the sense required by the offense principle. There is then a reason of the appropriate kind for banning them, but that reason is not likely to be decisive in most cases when the actual offensive materials are not thrust upon any unwilling observers or advertised in prominent places and obtrusive ways. The offending materials usually have very little personal or social value, it is true, but they are instances of a general category (films or books) which we all have a very great stake in keeping free. The porno films, in addition, service certain erotic tastes, which kinky though they may be, are a source of important personal value to some, and an area of personal experience that has a strong claim to noninterference. Whatever minimal value the porno film may have, it is not nullified by any spiteful or malicious motives of its displayers. The theatre owner would prefer that women were never in the neighborhood to be offended. It is no part of his purpose to offend women; his whole aim is to make money from men. Indeed, it is in his commercial interest not to arouse the wrath of organized women's groups, for their unrelentingly pesky campaigns against him could in the end drive him out of business in search of a less stressful way of making money. If that happens in time to all violent porn displayers, the whole genre will be as empty as racial folk films are now, and for similar reasons. Even without the help of legislatures, the black community would make such a fuss about folk film theatres, that customers would prefer to stay at home with their own videotaped materials, and theatre owners would throw in the towel. But then the home films would be as clearly immune from criminal prohibition as insulting private conversations (no matter how abusive of third parties) and private voluntary sexual activity (no matter how kinky).

The third category, which includes the examples of Nazis in Skokie and Klansmen in Harlem, differ in two important respects from the second category. The offending behavior deliberately seeks out the audience that will be most intensely, most profoundly, and most personally offended, and imposes its offense on them as its sole motivating purpose. It is therefore spiteful and malicious through and through, thus lacking measurable social value. In the purest hypothetical cases, at least, where for some people the offense cannot possibly be avoided, and the menacing abuse of the dis-

played symbols is the sole "message" communicated, the offense principle clearly justifies prohibition, whether by preliminary injunction, by on the spot "cease and desist orders," or by general prohibitory statute. The difference between these cases and the violent porn cases are subtle; but small differences in mode and manner of offense can be the basis of large differences in the form of political response, and in the realm of criminal law policy, must inevitably be so. Wherever a line is drawn between permission and prohibition, there will be cases close to the line on both sides of it.

Endnotes

[1] I do not wish to imply that there is one position about the punishability or censorship of pornography that all writers called "feminists" hold. Some, like Ann Garry in "Pornography and Respect for Women" (*Social Theory and Practice*, vol. 4, 1978) deny that pornography is necessarily by its very nature degrading to women. Others, like Wendy Kaminer in "Pornography and the First Amendment: Prior Restraints and Private Actions" in *Take Back the Night: Women on Pornography*, ed. Laura Lederer (New York: William Morrow and Co., Inc., 1980), accept the analysis of pornography that I discuss in the text, but deny that it provides a sufficient ground for censorship. The view I attribute to "feminists" is simply one held by many leading radical feminists, and most frequently and plausibly defended by feminist writers in the 1970s and '80s.

[2] Lisa Lehrman, Preface to the Colloquium on Violent Pornography: "Degradation of Women Versus Right of Free Speech," *New York University Review of Law and Social Change* 8, (1978–79), p. 181.

[3] The figure estimates are from Sarah J. McCarthy, "Pornography, Rape, and the Cult of Macho," *The Humanist*, Sept./Oct. 1980, p. 11.

[4] Ann Garry, *op. cit.* (footnote 1) is persuasive on this point:

> Imagine the following situation, which exists only rarely today: Two fairly conventional people who love each other enjoy playing tennis and bridge together, and having sex together. In all these activities they are free from hang-ups, guilt, and tendencies to dominate or objectify each other. These two people like to watch tennis matches and old romantic movies on TV, like to watch Julia Child cook, like to read the bridge column in the newspaper, and like to watch pornographic movies. Imagine further that this couple is not at all uncommon in society and that non-sexist pornography is as common as this kind of nonsexist relationship. The situation sounds fine and

healthy to me. I see no reason to think that an interest in pornography would disappear in the circumstances. People seem to enjoy watching others experience or do (especially do well) what they enjoy experiencing, doing, or wish they could do themselves. We do not morally object to people watching tennis on TV: why would we object to these hypothetical people watching pornography? (p. 419)

I would qualify Garry's account in two ways. First, it is not essential to her point that the two people "love each other," provided only that they like and respect each other. Second, their pleasures will be possible only if the film is well done, in particular keeping at least minimal photographic distance from what is depicted. Otherwise it might arouse anti-erotic repugnance.

5 Norman Mailer, *The Prisoner of Sex* (New York: New American Library, 1971), p. 82.

6 Gloria Steinem, "Erotica and Pornography, A Clear and Present Difference," *Ms.*, November, 1978, p. 53.

7 *Ibid.*, p. 54. Susan Wendell proposes a similar definition according to which depictions of "unjustified physical coercion of human beings" with some exceptions will count as pornographic even if they are not in any way *sexual*. See David Copp and Susan Wendell, eds., *Pornography and Censorship, Scientific, Philosophical, and Legal Studies* (Buffalo, N.Y.: Prometheus Books, 1983), p. 167. Pornography [all pornography] is to Susan Brownmiller "the undiluted essence of anti-female propoganda"—*Against Our Will: Men, Women, and Rape* (New York: Simon and Schuster, 1975), p. 394. Lorenne Clark takes it to be essential to pornography that it portrays women "in humiliating, degrading, and violently abusive situations," adding that "it frequently depicts them willingly, even avidly, suffering and inviting such treatment." See her "Liberalism and Pornography" in the Copp-Wendell volume, *supra*.

8 Steinem, *op. cit.* (footnote 6), p. 54.

9 Lisa Lehrman, *op. cit* (footnote 2), pp. 181–82.

10 Kathleen Barry, *Female Sexual Slavery* (New York: Avon Books, 1979), p. 206.

11 Steinem, *op. cit.* (footnote 6), p. 54.

12 The most extreme of these definitions is that of Andrea Dworkin in her "Pornography and Grief" in *Take Back the Night: Women on Pornography*, ed. Laura Lederer (New York: William Morrow and Co., 1980), p. 288—"The eroticization of murder is the essence of pornography. . . ."

13 Fred R. Berger, "Pornography, Feminism, and Censorship," (Unpublished paper, Philosophy Department, University of California, Davis), pp. 17ff. I am greatly indebted to this scholarly and well-argued essay.

14 *Ibid.*, p. 18.

15 "Defamation [libel or slander] is an invasion of the interest in reputation and good name, by communications to others which tend to diminish the esteem in which the plaintiff is held, or to excite adverse feelings or opinions against him."—William L. Prosser, *Handbook of the Law of Torts* (St. Paul: West Publishing Co., 1955), p. 572.

16 The studies are cited by Berger, *op. cit.* (footnote 13), p. 38.

17 Aryeh Neier, "Expurgating the First Amendment," *The Nation*, June 21, 1980, p. 754.

18 *Loc. cit.*

19 The former major league baseball pitcher Ryne Duren had a brief but distinguished career despite his constant heavy drinking and rowdiness off the field. Only when he was nearing forty did he manage to reform himself with the help of a rehabilitation center. Why did he behave so irrationally—playing, for example, with a constant hangover? "The problem is the image of the macho man who defies everything," he says. "Most of the guys I played with admired anyone who could drink all night and play baseball the next afternoon." *Newsweek*, June 20, 1983, p. 13.

20 Sarah J. McCarthy, "Pornography, Rape, and the Cult of Macho," *The Humanist*, Sept./Oct., 1980, p. 15.

21 *Ibid.*, p. 17.

22 Susan Brownmiller, *Against Our Will: Men, Women, and Rape* (New York: Macmillan, 1975).

23 Quoted by McCarthy, *op. cit.* (footnote 20), p. 17.

24 Kent Greenawalt, "Speech and Crime," *American Bar Foundation Research Journal*, no. 4 (1980), p. 654.

25 Berger, *op. cit.* (footnote 13), pp. 23–24. The study cited by Berger is: Freda Adler, "The Interaction Between Women's Emancipation and Female Criminality: A Cross-cultural Perspective," *International Journal of Criminology and Penology*, 5 (1977):101–12.

26 The Supreme Court's standards of seriousness and dangerousness have been so extraordinarily high, however, that even a magazine article advocating (in a general way) rape might escape constitutionally valid punishment unless it urged *imminent* action against precise victims. In the landmark case *Brandenburg v. Ohio*, 395 U.S. 444 (1969), the court ruled that advocacy of illegal violence may be proscribed only when the advocacy amounts to *incitement* of imminent lawless action. Two conditions must be satisfied for liability. The advocacy must be (1) "directed to inciting or producing imminent lawless action," and (2) likely to succeed in inciting or producing such action.

27 Edward Coke, Second Part of the *Institutes of the Laws of England*, p. 182.

[28] John Stuart Mill, *On Liberty*, chap. 3, para. 1. Mill writes: "An opinion that corn dealers are starvers of the poor, or that private property is robbery, ought to be unmolested when simply circulated through the press, but may justly incur punishment when delivered orally to an excited mob assembled before the house of a corn dealer, or when handed about among the same mob in the form of a placard."

[29] This interpretation is persuasively argued by Frederick Schauer in his article "Speech and 'Speech'—Obscenity and 'Obscenity': An Exercise in the Interpretation of Constitutional Language," *Georgia Law Review* 67 (1979).

[30] Fred L. Berger, *op. cit.* (footnote 13), p. 28.

[31] Sarah J. McCarthy, *op. cit.* (footnote 20), p. 11.

[32] On the other hand, it is hard to know how typical is Andrea Dworkin's highly personal response to other people's pornography—". . . pornography silences me . . . pornography makes me sick every day of my life." Panel Discussion, "Effects of Violent Pornography" in "Colloquium on Violent Pornography," *op. cit.* (footnote 2), p. 239.

Pornography: On Morality and Politics

CATHERINE MACKINNON

Pornosec, the subsection of the Fiction Department which turned out cheap pornography for distribution among the proles . . . nicknamed Muck House by the people who worked it . . . produce[d] booklets in sealed packets with titles like "Spanking Stories" or "One Night in a Girls' School," to be bought furtively by proletarian youths who were under the impression that they were buying something illegal.
          —George Orwell, *1984*

Silence is a woman's ornament.
          —Sophocles

Possession and use of women through the sexualization of intimate intrusion and access to them is a central feature of women's social definition as inferior and feminine. Visual and verbal intrusion, access, possession, and use is predicated upon and produces physical and psychic intrusion, access, possession, and use. In contemporary industrial society, pornography is an industry that mass produces sexual intrusion on, access to, possession and use of women by and for men for profit. It exploits women's sexual and economic inequality for gain. It sells women to men as and for sex. It is a technologically sophisticated traffic in women.

This understanding of the reality of pornography must contend not only with centuries of celebratory intellectual obfuscation.[1] It must contend with a legal tradition of neutralization through abstraction from the realities of power, a tradition that has authoritatively defined pornography as not about women as such at all, but about sex, hence about morality, and as not about acts or practices, but about ideas. Uncovering gender in this area of law reveals women to be most invisible when most exposed and most silent when used in defense of speech. In both pornography and the law of obscenity, women are seen only as sex and heard only when mouthing a sexual script. When pornography and the law of pornography are investigated together, it becomes clear that pornography is to women's status, hence its critique is to feminism, as its preservation is to male supremacy in its liberal legal guise.

The law of obscenity[2] is the state's approach to addressing the pornography problem, which it construes as an issue of regulation of expression under the First Amendment.[3] Nudity, explicitness, excess of candor, arousal or excitement, prurience, unnaturalness—these qualities raise concerns under obscenity law when sex is depicted or portrayed. Abortion or birth control information or treatments for "restoring sexual virility" (whose, do you suppose?) have also been covered.[4] Sex forced on real women so that it can be sold at a profit to be forced on other real women; women's bodies trussed and maimed and raped and made into things to be hurt and obtained and accessed and this presented as the nature of women; the coercion that is visible and the coercion that has become invisible—this and more grounds the feminist concern with pornography. Obscenity as such probably does little harm.[5] Pornography contributes causally to attitudes and behaviors of violence and discrimination which define the treatment and status of half the population.[6]

Obscenity law is concerned with morality, meaning good and evil, virtue and vice. The concerns of feminism with power and powerlessness are first political, not moral. From the feminist perspective, obscenity is a moral idea; pornography is a political practice. Obscenity is abstract; pornography is concrete. Obscenity conveys moral condemnation as a predicate to legal condemnation. Pornography identifies a political practice that is predicated on power and powerlessness—a practice that is, in fact, legally protected. The two concepts represent two entirely different things.

In accounting for gender inequality as part of the socially constructed relationship between power—the political—on the one hand and knowledge of truth and reality—the epistemological—on the other, the classic description Justice Stewart once offered of the obscenity standard, "I know it when I see it,"[7] becomes even more revealing than it is usually taken to be. Taken as a statement that connects epistemology with power, if one asks, from the point of view of women's experience, does he know what women know when we see what we see, one has to doubt it, given what is on the newsstands. How does his point of view keep what is there, there? To liberal critics, his admission exposed the relativity, the partiality, the insufficient abstractness of the obscenity standard. Not to be emptily universal, to leave your concreteness showing, is a sin among men. Their problem with Justice Stewart's formulation is that it implies that anything, capriciously, could be suppressed. In fact, almost nothing is. The meaning of what his view permits, as it turns

out, is anything but capricious. It is entirely systematic and determinate. His statement is precisely descriptively accurate; its candor is why it has drawn so much criticism.[8] He admitted what courts do epistemologically all the time. In so doing, he both did it and gave it the stature of doctrine (if only dictum). That is, he revealed that the obscenity standard—and it is not unique—is built on what the male standpoint sees. The problem is, so is pornography. In this way, the law of obscenity reproduces the pornographic point of view of women on the level of constitutional jurisprudence.

Pornography, in the feminist view, is a form of forced sex, a practice of sexual politics, an institution of gender inequality.[9] In this perspective, pornography, with the rape and prostitution in which it participates, intitutionalizes the sexuality of male supremacy, which fuses the erotization of dominance and submission with the social construction of male and female. Gender is sexual. Pornography constitutes the meaning of that sexuality. Men treat women as whom they see women as being. Pornography constructs who that is. Men's power over women means that the way men see women defines who women can be. Pornography is that way. In this light, obscenity law can be seen to treat morals from the male point of view, meaning the standpoint of male dominance. The feminist critique of pornography, by contrast, proceeds from women's point of view, meaning the standpoint of the subordination of women to men.

One can be for or against this pornography without getting beyond liberalism. The critical yet formally liberal view of Susan Griffin, for example, conceptualizes eroticism as natural and healthy but corrupted and confused by "the pornographic mind."[10] Pornography distorts Eros, which preexists and persists, despite male culture's pornographic "revenge" upon it. Eros is, unaccountably, still there. Pornography mistakes it, mis-images it, misrepresents it. There is no critique of reality here, only objections to how it is seen; no critique of that reality that pornography imposes on women's real lives, those lives that are so seamlessly consistent with the pornography that it can be credibly defended by saying it is only a mirror of reality.

Contrast this with the feminist analysis of pornography by Andrea Dworkin, in which sexuality itself is a social construct, gendered to the ground. Male dominance here is not an artificial overlay upon an underlying inalterable substratum of uncorrupted essential sexual being. Sexuality free of male dominance will require change, not reconceptualization, transcendence, or excavation. Pornography is not imagery in some relation to a reality elsewhere constructed. It is not a distortion, reflection, projection, expression, fantasy, representation, or symbol either. It is sexual reality. Andrea Dworkin's *Pornography* presents a sexual theory of gender inequality of which pornography is a core constitutive practice. The way pornography produces its meaning constructs and defines men and women as such. Gender is what gender means.[11] It has no basis in anything other than the social reality its hegemony constructs. The process that gives sexuality its male supremacist meaning is therefore the process through which gender inequality becomes socially real.

In this analysis, the liberal defense of pornography as human sexual liberation, as derepression—whether by feminists, marxists, or neo-Freudians—is a defense not only of force and sexual terrorism, but of the subordination of women.[12] Sexual liberation in the liberal sense frees male sexual aggression in the feminist sense. What in the liberal view looks like love and romance looks a lot like hatred and torture to the feminist. Pleasure and eroticism become violation. Desire appears as lust for dominance and submission. The vulnerability of women's projected sexual availability is victimization. The acting that women are allowed is asking to be acted upon. Play conforms to scripted roles, fantasy expresses ideology not exemption from it, and admiration of natural physical beauty becomes objectification.

The experience of the (overwhelmingly) male audiences who consume pornography is therefore not fantasy or simulation or catharsis but sexual reality: the level of reality on which sex itself largely operates.[13] To understand this does not require noticing that women in pornography are real women to whom something real is being done.[14] It does not even require inquiring into the systematic infliction of pornographic sexuality upon women, although it helps.[15] The aesthetic of pornography itself, the way it provides what those who consume it want, is itself the evidence. Pornography turns a woman into a thing to be acquired and used.[16] When uncensored explicit—that is, the most pornographic—pornography tells all, all means what a distanced detached observer would report about who did what to whom. This is the turn-on. Why

does having sex as object, observing sex objectively presented, cause the male viewer to experience his own sexuality? Because his eroticism is, socially, a watched thing.[17]

If objectivity is the epistemological stance of which objectivication is the social process, the way the perceptual posture of a material position is embodied as a social form of power, the most sexually potent depictions and descriptions would be the most objective blow-by-blow re-presentations. Pornography participates in its audience's eroticism because it creates an accessible sexual object, the possession and consumption of which is male sexuality, to be consumed and possessed as which is female sexuality. In this sense, sex in life is no less mediated than it is in art. Men have sex with their image of a woman. Escalating explicitness, "exceeding the bounds of candor," is the aesthetic of pornography not because the materials depict objectified sex but because they create the experience of a sexuality which is itself objectified.[18] It is not that life and art imitate each other; in sexuality, they are each other.

The law of obscenity has literally nothing in common with this feminist critique. Men's obscenity is not women's pornography. Obscenity is more concerned with whether men blush, pornography with whether women bleed—both producing a sexual rush. One commentator has said, "Obscenity is not suppressed primarily for the protection of others. Much of it is suppressed for the purity of the 'consumer.' Obscenity, at bottom, is not a crime. Obscenity is a sin."[19] This is literally accurate. A sin is an idea that something is bad. Men are turned on by obscenity, including by its suppression, in the same way they are by sin. Animated by morality from the male standpoint, in which violation—of women and rules—is eroticized, obscenity law proceeds according to the interest of male power, robed in gender-neutral good and evil.

Morality in its specifically liberal form animates the organization of state power on the pornography issue. Its approach is premised upon a set of parallel distinctions which can be consistently traced through obscenity law. Although the posture this law adopts toward the problem it envisions has shifted over time, its fundamental norms remain consistent: public is opposed to private, ethics is opposed to morality, and factual is opposed to valued determinations. These distinctions are supposed gender neutral but are implicitly, socially, gender based: female is private, moral, valued, subjective; male is public, ethical, factual, objective.[20] To construe concern with pornography in these socially "feminine" terms, under male dominance, is to preclude legitimate state intervention. If such gendered concepts are constructs of the male experience, imposed from the male standpoint on society as a whole, liberal morality is an expression of male supremacist politics. That is, discourse conducted in terms of good and evil which does not expose the gendered foundations of these concepts proceeds oblivious to—and serves to disguise the presence and interest of—the position of power which underlies, and is furthered by, that discourse.

Obscenity law proposes to control what and how sex can be publicly shown. In practice, its standard centers upon the same features that feminism and pornography both reveal as key to male sexuality: the erect penis and penetration.[21] Historically, obscenity law was vexed by restricting such portrayals while protecting great literature. (Nobody considered protecting women.) Solving this problem by exempting works of perceived value, obscenity restrictions relaxed—some might say collapsed—revealing a significant shift in the last decade.[22] Under the old law, pornography was publicly repudiated yet privately consumed and actualized: do anything to women with impunity in private behind a veil of public denial and civility. Under the new law, in a victory for Freudian derepression, pornography is publicly celebrated.[23] The old private rules have become the new public rules. Women were sex and are still sex. Greater efforts of brutality have become necessary to eroticize the taboo—each taboo being a hierarchy in disguise—since the frontier of the taboo keeps vanishing as one crosses it. Put another way, more and more violence has become necessary to keep the progressively desensitized consumer aroused to the illusion that sex (and he) is daring and dangerous. Making sex with the powerless "not allowed" is a way of keeping "getting it" defined as an act of power, an assertion of hierarchy, which keeps it sexy in a sexual system in which hierarchy is sexy. In addition, pornography has become ubiquitous. Sexual terrorism has become democratized. Pornography has become truly available to women for the first time in history. Among other effects, this central mechanism of sexual subordi-

nation, this means of systematizing the definition of women as a sexual class, has now become available to its victims for scrutiny and analysis as an open public system, not just as a private secret abuse.[24] Hopefully, this was a mistake.

In obscenity law, the state has been perfected as the mirror of society. In pornography, women are sex. In obscenity law, women are sex. In pornography, women's bodies are dirty. In obscenity law, obscenity is filth. In pornography, the more explicit the sex, the more pornographic. In obscenity law, the more explicit the sex, the more obscene. In pornography, sex is a dirty secret. Obscenity law sees it, therefore helps keep it, that way. Pornography sees nothing wrong with what it does to women. Neither does obscenity law. Pornography is socially decried but socially permitted. Obscenity is the legal device through which it is legally repudiated but legally permitted.

On a deeper level, male morality sees that which maintains its power as good, that which undermines or qualifies it or questions its absoluteness as evil. Differences in the law over time—such as the liberalization of obscenity doctrine—reflect either changes in which group of men has power or shifts in perceptions of the best strategy for maintaining male supremacy—probably some of both. But it must be made to work. The outcome, descriptively analyzed, is that obscenity law prohibits what it sees as immoral, which from women's standpoint tends to be relatively harmless, while protecting what it sees as moral, which is often damaging to women. So it, too, is a politics, only covertly so. What male morality finds evil, meaning threatening to its power, feminist politics tends to find comparatively harmless. What feminist politics identifies as central in women's subordination—the erotization of dominance and submission—male morality tends to find relatively harmless or defend as affirmatively valuable, hence as protected speech.

In 1973, obscenity under law came to mean that which "the average person applying contemporary standards, would find that, taken as a whole, appeals to the prurient interest; that [which] depicts or describes, in a patently offensive way, sexual conduct as defined by the applicable state law; and that which, taken as a whole, lacks serious literary, artistic, political, or scientific value.[25] Feminism doubts whether "the average person," gender neutral, exists; has more questions about the content and process of definition of community standards than about deviations from them; wonders why prurience counts but powerlessness does not, why sensibilities are better protected from offense than women are from exploitation; defines sexuality, hence its violation and expropriation, more broadly than does any state law; and wonders why a body of law which cannot in practice tell rape from intercourse should be entrusted with telling pornography from anything less. In feminist perspective, one notices that although the law of obscenity says that sex on streetcorners is not supposed to be legitimated "by the fact that the persons are simultaneously engaged in a valid political dialogue,"[26] the requirement that the work be considered "as a whole" legitimates something very like that on the level of publications such as *Playboy*,[27] even though experimental evidence is beginning to support what victims have long known: legitimate settings diminish the injury perceived to be done to the women whose trivialization and objectification it contextualizes.[28] Besides, if a woman is subjected, why should it matter that the work has other value?[29] Perhaps what redeems a work's value among men enhances its injury to women. Existing standards of literature, art, science, and politics are, in feminist light, remarkably consonant with pornography's mode, meaning, and message. Finally and foremost, a feminist approach reveals that although the content and dynamic of pornography concerns women—the sexuality of women, women as sexuality—in the same way that the vast majority of "obscenities" refer specifically to women's bodies, women's invisibility has been such that the law of obscenity has never even considered pornography a women's issue.[30]

To appeal to "prurient interest" means to give a man an erection.[31] Men are scared to make it possible for some men to tell other men what they can and cannot have sexual access to, because men have power. Men believe that if you do not let them have theirs, they might not let you have yours. This is why the indefinability of pornography—all the "one man's this is another man's that"—is so central to pornography's definition.[32] It is not because all men are such great liberals, but because those other men might be able to do to them whatever *they* can do to *them*, which may explain why the liberal principle is what it is.

What this frame on the issue obscures, because the fought-over are invisible, is that the fight over a definition of pornography is a fight among men over the terms of access to women, hence over the best means to guarantee male power as a system. The tacit questions become: Whose sexual practices threaten this system? Are they men whose sexual access can be sacrificed in the interest of maintaining it for the rest? Public sexual access by men to anything other than women is far less likely to be protected speech. This is not to say that male sexual access to anything—children, other men, women with women, objects, animals—is not the real rule. The issue is rather how public, hence how express in law, that system will be.

In this light, the "prurient interest" prong of the obscenity standard has a built-in bind. To find prurience as a fact, someone has to admit sexual arousal by the materials;[33] but male sexual arousal signals the importance of protection. Men put themselves in this position and then wonder why they cannot agree. Sometimes it seems that what is obscene is what does not turn on the Supreme Court, or what revolts them more, which is rare, since revulsion is eroticized. Sometimes it seems that what is obscene is what turns on those men whom the men in power think they can afford to ignore. Sometimes it seems that what is obscene is what makes dominant men see themselves as momentary potential targets of male sexual aggression. Sometimes it seems that anything can be done to a woman, but obscenity is sex that makes male sexuality look bad.[34]

Courts' difficulties in framing workable standards to separate "prurient" from other sexual interest, commercial exploitation from art or advertising, sexual speech from sexual conduct, and obscenity from great literature make the feminist point. These lines have proved elusive in law because they do not exist in life. Commercial sex resembles art because both exploit women's sexuality. The liberal slippery slope is the feminist totality. Politically speaking, whatever obscenity may do, pornography converges with more conventionally acceptable depictions and descriptions just as rape does with intercourse, because both are acts within the same power relation. Just as it is difficult to distinguish literature or art against a background, a standard, of objectification, it is difficult to discern sexual freedom against a background, a standard, of sexual coercion. This does not mean that it cannot be done. It means that legal standards will be practically unenforceable, will reproduce this problem rather than solve it, until they address its fundamental issue—gender inequality—directly.

To define the pornographic as the "patently offensive" further misconstrues its harm. Pornography is not bad manners or poor choice of audience; obscenity is. Pornography is also not an idea; obscenity is. The legal fiction whereby the obscene is "not speech" has deceived few;[35] it has effectively avoided the need to adjudicate pornography's social etiology. But obscenity law got one thing right: pornography is more actlike than thoughtlike. The fact that pornography, in a feminist view, furthers the idea of the sexual inferiority of women, a political idea, does not make pornography a political idea. That one can express the idea a practice expresses does not make that practice an idea. Pornography is not an idea any more than segregation or lynching are ideas, although both institutionalize the idea of the inferiority of one group to another. The law considers obscenity deviant, antisocial. If it causes harm, it causes antisocial acts, acts against the social order.[36] In a feminist perspective, pornography is the essence of a sexist social order, its quintessential social act.

If pornography is an act of male supremacy, its harm is the harm of male supremacy made difficult to see because of its pervasiveness, potency, and success in making the world a pornographic place. Specifically, the harm cannot be discerned from the objective standpoint because it is so much of "what is." Women live in the world pornography creates, live its lie as reality. As Naomi Scheman has said, "lies are what we have lived, not just what we have told, and no story about correspondence to what is real will enable us to distinguish the truth from the lie."[37] So the issue is not what the harm of pornography is, but how the harm of pornography is to become visible. As compared with what? To the extent pornography succeeds in constructing social reality, it becomes invisible as harm.

The success, therefore the harm, of pornography, is invisible to the male state in its liberal guise and so has been defined out of the customary approach taken to, and the dominant values underlying, the First Amendment. The theory of the First Amendment under which most pornography is protected from governmental restriction proceeds from liberal assumptions[38] that do not apply to the situation of women. First Amendment theory, like virtually all liberal legal theory, presumes the validity of the distinction between public and private: the "role of law [is] to make and guard the line between the sphere of social power, organized in the form of the state, and the arena of private right."[39] On this basis, courts distinguish between obscene billboards ("thrust upon the unwilling viewer") and the private possession of obscenity at home.[40] The problem is that not only the public but also the private is a "sphere of social power" of sexism. On paper and in life, pornography is thrust upon unwilling women in their homes.[41] The distinction between public and private does not cut the same for women as for men. As a result, it is men's right to inflict pornography upon women in private that is protected.

The liberal theory underlying First Amendment law proceeds on the belief that free speech, including pornography, helps discover truth. Censorship, in its view, restricts society to partial truths. Laissez-faire might be an adequate theory of the social preconditions for knowledge in a nonhierarchical society. In a society of gender inequality, the speech of the powerful impresses its view upon the world, concealing the truth of powerlessness under a despairing acquiescence that provides the appearance of consent and makes protest inaudible as well as rare. Pornography can invent women because it has the power to make its vision into reality, which then passes, objectively, for truth. So while the First Amendment supports pornography on the belief that consensus and progress are facilitated by allowing all views, however divergent and unorthodox, it fails to notice that pornography (like the racism, including anti-Semitism, of the Nazis and the Klan) is not at all divergent or unorthodox. It is the ruling ideology. Feminism, the dissenting view, is suppressed by pornography. Thus, while defenders of pornography argue that allowing all speech, including pornography, frees the mind to fulfill itself, pornography freely enslaves women's minds and bodies inseparably, normalizing the terror that enforces silence on women's point of view.

In liberalism, speech must never be sacrificed for other social goals.[42] But liberalism has never understood this reality of pornography: the free so-called speech of men silences the free speech of women. It is the same social goal, just other people. This is what a real inequality, a real conflict, a real disparity in social power looks like. First, women do not simply have freedom of speech on a social level. The most basic assumption underlying First Amendment adjudication is that, socially, speech is free. The First Amendment itself says, "Congress shall make no law . . . abridging the freedom of speech." Free speech exists. The problem for government is to avoid constraining that which, if unconstrained by government, is free. This tends to presuppose that whole segments of the population are not systematically silenced socially, prior to government action. Second, the law of the First Amendment comprehends that freedom of expression, in the abstract, is a system but fails to comprehend that sexism (and racism), in the concrete, are also systems. As a result, it cannot grasp that the speech of some silences the speech of others in a way that is not simply a matter of competition for airtime. That pornography chills women's expression is difficult to demonstrate empirically because silence is not eloquent. Yet on no more of the same kind of evidence, the argument that suppressing pornography might chill legitimate speech has supported its protection.

First Amendment logic has difficulty grasping harm that is not linearly caused in the "John hit Mary" sense. The idea is that words or pictures can be harmful only if they produce harm in a form that is considered an action. Words work in the province of attitudes, actions in the realm of behavior. Words cannot constitute harm in themselves— never mind libel, invasion of privacy, blackmail, bribery, conspiracy, most sexual harassment, and most discrimination. What is saying "yes" in Congress—a word or an act? What is saying "Kill" to a trained guard dog? What is its training? What is saying "You're fired" or "We have enough of your kind around here"? What is a sign that reads "Whites Only?" What is a real estate advertisement that reads "Churches Nearby?" What is a "Help Wanted—Male" ad? What is a letter that states: "Constituent interests dictate that the understudy to my administrative assistant be a man"? What is "Sleep with me and I'll give you an 'A' "? These words, printed or spoken, are so far from legally protecting the cycle of events they actualize that they are regarded as evidence that acts occurred, in some cases as actionable in themselves.[43] Is a woman raped by an attitude or a behavior? Which is sexual arousal? Which is cross burning? The difficulty of the distinction in the abstract has not prevented the law from acting when the consequences were seen to matter. When words are tantamount to acts, they are treated as acts.

The ascendancy of the positivistic idea of causality as used in First Amendment absolutism,[44] which in pure form would prohibit all restrictions by government on everything classified as expression, dates from around the time when it was believed conclusively proved that it is impossible to prove conclusively that pornography causes harm. This notion of causality did not first appear in this law at this time, however.[45] As Judge Jerome Frank said in a footnote in *Roth,* "According to Judge Bok, an obscenity statute may be validly enforced when there is proof of a causal relation between a particular book and undesirable conduct. Almost surely, such proof cannot ever be adduced."[46] Criticizing old ideas of atomic physics in light of Einstein's theory of relativity, Werner Heisenberg stated the conditions that must exist for a causal relation to make sense. "To co-ordinate a definite cause to a definite effect has sense only when both can be observed without introducing a foreign element disturbing their interrelation. The law of causality, because of its very nature, can only be defined for isolated systems."[47] Among the influences that disturb the isolation of systems are observers.

The law of obscenity has never been required to show a causal relation between the obscene and anything else, by this standard or any other. Underlying the adoption of such a causality standard in debates on the merits of state intervention in the pornography area is a rather hasty analogy between the regularities of physical and social systems, an analogy that has seldom been explicitly justified or even updated as the physical sciences have altered their epistemological foundations. Social systems are not isolated systems. Experimental research, in which it has been scientifically shown that pornography has harmful effects, minimizes what will always be "foreign elements" at some cost of simulating social reality. Yet whenever field experiments are done for verisimilitude, it is said that the interactions are insufficiently isolated to prove pure causality. If pornography is systemic, it may not be isolable from the system in which it exists.[48] This does not mean that no harm exists. It does mean that because the harm is so pervasive, it cannot be sufficiently isolated to be perceived as existing according to this model of causality, a model that is neither the existing legal standard, the only scientific standard, a standard used in other policy areas (like the relation between smoking and cancer or driving drunk and having accidents). Nor is it a social or political standard in which the experiences of victims have any weight. In other words, if pornography is seen as harmful only if it causes harm by this model, and if pornography's harm cannot be isolated from society's organization itself, its harm will not be perceptible within the episteme.

The dominant view is that pornography must cause harm just as car accidents cause harm, or its effects are not cognizable as harm. The trouble with this individuated, atomistic, linear, exclusive, isolated, narrowly tortlike—in a word, positivistic —conception of injury is that the way pornography targets and defines women for abuse and discrimination does not work like this. It does hurt individuals, just not as individuals in a one-at-a-time sense, but as members of the group women. Individual harm is caused one woman and not another essentially as one number rather than another is caused in roulette; but on a group basis, the harm is absolutely selective and systematic. Its causality is essentially collective and totalistic and contextual. To reassert atomistic linear causality as a sine qua non of injury—you cannot be harmed unless you are harmed through this etiology—is to refuse to respond to the true nature of this specific kind of harm. Such refusals call for explanation. Morton Horowitz has written that the issue of causality in tort law is "one of the pivotal ideas in a system of legal thought that sought to separate private law from politics and to insulate the legal system from the threat of redistribution."[49] Perhaps causality in the law of obscenity is an attempt to privatize the injury pornography does to women in order to insulate the same system from the threat of gender equality.

Women are known to be brutally coerced into pornographic performances. But so far it is only with children, usually male children, that courts see that the speech of pornographers was once someone else's life.[50] Courts and commissions and legislatures and researchers have searched largely in vain for the injury of pornography in the mind of the (male) consumer or in "society," or in empirical correlations between variations in levels of "antisocial" acts and liberalization in obscenity laws.[51] Speech can be regulated "in the interests of unwilling viewers, captive audiences, young children, and beleaguered neighborhoods,"[52] but the normal level of sexual force—force that is not seen as force because it is inflicted on women and called sex—has never been a policy issue in the pornography area. Until the last few years experimental research never approached the question of whether pornographic stimuli might support sexual aggression against women or whether violence per se might be sexually stimulating or have sexual sequelae.[53] Research is just beginning on the consequences for women of sexual depictions that show consensual dominance and submission.[54] We know the least about the impact of female-only nudity, depictions of specific acts like penetration, or sex that appears mutual in a social context of gender inequality. We know even less about why sex—that is, women—*must*, seemingly, be experienced through a traffic in pictures and words.

Beyond offensiveness or prurience, to say that pornography is "dehumanizing" is an attempt to articulate its harm. But "human being" is a social concept with many possible meanings. If one looks at liberal meanings of personhood through a feminist political analysis of what pornography does to women, the inadequacy of the liberal dehumanization critique becomes clear. In a feminist perspective, pornography dehumanizes women in a culturally specific and empirically descriptive—not liberal moral—sense. In the same act, pornography dispossesses women of the same power of which it possesses men: the power of sexual, hence gender, definition. The power to tell one who one is and the power to treat one accordingly. Perhaps a human being, for gender purposes, is someone who controls the social definition of sexuality.

By distinction, a person in one Kantian view is a free and rational agent whose existence is an end in itself, as opposed to instrumental.[55] In pornography, women exist for the end of male pleasure. Kant sees "human" as characterized by universal abstract rationality, with no component of individual or group differences, and as a "bundle of rights."[56] Pornography purports to define what a woman is. It does this on a group basis, including when it raises individual qualities to sexual stereotypes, as in the strategy of *Playboy's* "Playmate of the Month." Perhaps pornography derives much of its sexual power, as well as part of its justification, from the implicit assumption that the Kantian notion of person actually describes the condition of women in this society, so that if we are there, we are freely and rationally there, when the fact is that women—in pornography and in part because of pornography—have no such rights.

Other views of the person include one of Wittgenstein's statements that the best picture of the human soul is the human body.[57] Apparently this depends upon what picture of the human body one has in mind. Marx's work offers various concepts of personhood deducible from his critique of various forms of productive organization. Whatever material conditions the society values defines a person there, so that in a bourgeois society, a person might be a property owner.[58] But women are the property that constitute the personhood, understood as the masculinity, of men under capitalism. Thinking further in marxian terms, one wonders whether women in pornography are more properly fetishes or objects. Does pornography more attribute lifelikeness to that which is dead—as in fetishism—or make deathlike that which is alive—as in objectification? Probably this depends upon whether, socially speaking, women are more dead than alive.

In Hume's concept of a person as a bundle or collection of sense perceptions, such that the feeling of self-identity over time is a persistent illusion,[59] one finds a view of the human that coincides with the view of women in pornography. The empiricist view of person is the pornographic view of women. No critique of dominance or subjection, certainly not of objectification, can be grounded in a vision of reality in which all sense perceptions are just sense perceptions. This is one way an objectivist epistemology supports the unequal holding and wielding of power in a society in which the persistent illusion of selfhood of half the population is materially supported and maintained at the expense of the other half. Those who are socially allowed a self are also allowed the luxury of postulating its illusoriness and having that called a philosophical position. Whatever self they ineluctably have, they do not lose by saying it is an illusion. On this level, taken as high male ideology, much of Western culture becomes descriptive even if not particularly explanatory. Thus Hume defines the human in the same terms feminism uses to define women's dehumanization: for women in pornography, the self is, precisely, a persistent illusion.

According to ordinary-language philosopher Bernard Williams, "person" ordinarily entails valuing self-respect and feeling pain.[60] As principal author of the *Williams Report* on obscenity in England, Williams found women deprived of none of his values of "person" in or by pornography. Of course, how self is defined, what respect attaches to, stimuli of pleasure, and to an extent stimuli and thresholds of pain are cultural variables. Women in pornography are turned on by being put down and feel pain as pleasure. We want it, we beg for it, we get it. To argue that this is dehumanizing is not to take respect as an ahistorical absolute or to treat pain as socially or personally invariant or uniformly negative. Rather, it is to say that the acceptance of the social definition of these values—the acceptance of self-respect and the avoidance of pain as values—permits the erotization of their negative—debasement and torture—in pornography. It is only to the extent that each of these values is socially accepted as human within a given culture that their negation becomes a quality of sex and is eroticized in and as "woman." Only when self-respect is accepted as human does debasement become sexy and female; only when the avoidance of pain is accepted as human does torture become sexy and female. In this way, women's sexuality as expressed in pornography precisely negatives her status as human. But there is more: exactly what is defined as degrading to a human being, however that is socially defined, is exactly what is sexually arousing to the male point of view in the pornography, just as the one to whom it is done is the girl regardless of sex. In this way, it is specifically women whom pornography identifies with and by sexuality—a painful, debasing sexuality of torture, a sexuality of humiliation and use—as the erotic is equated with the dehumanizing.

To define the pornographic as that which is violent, not sexual, as liberal moral analyses tend to, is to trivialize and evade the essence of this critique while seeming to express it. As with rape, where the issue is not the presence or absence of force but what sex is as distinct from coercion, the question for pornography is what eroticism is distinct from the subordination of women. This is not a rhetorical question. Under male dominance, whatever sexually arouses a man is sex. In pornography, the violence is the sex. The inequality is sex. The humiliation is sex. The debasement is sex. The intrusion is sex. Pornography does not work sexually without gender hierarchy. If there is no inequality, no violation, no dominance, no force, there is no sexual arousal. Obscenity law does the pornographers a real favor by obscuring this, pornography's central dynamic, under the coy gender-neutral abstraction of "prurient interest" while adding the dominance interest of state prohibition.

Calling rape and pornography violent, not sexual (the banner of much antirape and antipornography work), is an attempt to protest that women do not find rape pleasurable or pornography stimulating while avoiding claiming this rejection as women's point of view. The concession to the objective stance, the attempt to achieve credibility by covering up the specificity of viewpoint, not only abstracts from women's experience; it lies about it. Women and men both know men find rape sexual and pornography erotic. It therefore is. Women and men both know that sexuality is commonly violent without being any the less sexual. To deny this sets up the situation so that when women are aroused by sexual violation, experience it as women's sexuality, the feminist analysis is seen to be contradicted. But it is not contradicted, it is proved. The male supremacist definition of female sexuality as lust for self-annihilation has won. It would be surprising, feminist analysis would be wrong, and sexism would be trivial if this were merely exceptional.[61] To reject forced sex in the name of women's point of view requires an account of women's experience of being violated by the same acts both sexes have learned as natural and fulfilling and erotic when no critique, no alternatives, and few transgressions have been permitted.

The depersonalization critique and the "violence not sex" critique expose a double standard of sex and of personhood but do not attack the masculinity of the standards for personhood and for sex which pornography sets. The critiques are thus useful, to some extent deconstructive, but beg the deeper questions of the place of pornography in sexuality and of sexuality in the construction of women's definition and status. They act as if women can be "persons" by interpretation—as if the concept is not, in every socially real way, defined by and in terms of and reserved for men, and as if sexuality is not itself a construct of male power. To do this is to act as if pornography did not exist or were impotent. Deeper than the personhood question or the violence question is the question of the mechanism of social causation by which pornography constructs women and sex, defining

what "woman" means and what sexuality is in terms of each other, hence excluding women's social reality from the substantive definition of personhood.

The law of obscenity at times says that sexual expression is only talk, and therefore cannot be intrinsically harmful. Yet somehow pornographic talk is vital to protect. If pornography is a practice of gender inequality, especially to the degree that pornography works on the ideological level and gender *is* an ideology, if pornography is sex and gender is sexual, the question of the relation between pornography and life is nothing less than the question of the dynamic of the subordination of women to men. If "objectification . . . is never trivial," girls *are* ruined by books.[62] Consciousness of this process—connecting thought and life, mind and body with social power, point of view with politics—has been obstructed by fear of repressive state use of any critique of any form of expression, by the power of pornographers to create a climate hostile to inquiry into their power and profits, and by the power of pornography to create women in its image of their use.

Because obscenity law so evades the reality of pornography, it is difficult to show that the male state, hegemonically liberal whether in the hands of conservatives or of liberals, actually protects pornography. The deception that the state is hostile to sexual derepression and eager to repress pornography, the fantasy that an authoritarian state restricts pornography rather than protects it, lay clearly exposed when the courts were confronted with the real damage pornography does to women's status and treatment as the basis for making it civilly actionable to its victims. The courts accepted the harm but held the pornography more important than those it harms—hence protected it as speech. In *American Bookseller Assn. Inc. v. Hudnut* the Seventh Circuit Court of Appeals held that an ordinance that makes the injuries of pornography actionable as sex inequality is unconstitutional under the First Amendment because it prohibits expression of a point of view.[63]

Acts became ideas and politics became morals as the court transformed coercion, force, assault, and trafficking in subordination into "thought control" and second-class citizenship on the basis of gender into "ideas that can be expressed about sexuality."[64] Obscenity law, which is based upon nothing but value judgments about morality, was presented as the standard for constitutional point-of-viewlessness. The court saw legal intervention against acts (most of which are already crimes) as "point of view" discrimination without doubting the constitutionality of state intervention against obscenity, which has no connection with acts and is expressly defined on the basis of point of view about sex. The court saw civil action by individual women as censorship threatening freedom, yet saw no threat to freedom and no censorship in criminal prosecutions of obscenity. When is a point of view not a point of view? When it is yours—especially when your words, like those of the pornographers, are words in power. In the epistemologically hermetic doublethink of the male point of view, prohibiting advances toward sex equality under law is state neutrality. From the male standpoint, it looks neutral because the state mirrors the inequality of the social world. Under the aegis of this neutrality, state protection of pornography becomes official policy.[65]

The law of pornography thus has the same surface theme and the same underlying theme as pornography itself. Superficially both involve morality: rules made and transgressed for purposes of sexual arousal. Actually, both are about power: the equation between the erotic and the control of women by men, *women* made and transgressed for purposes of sexual arousal. It seems essential to the kick of pornography that it be to some degree against the rules, but never truly unavailable or truly illegitimate. Thus obscenity law, like the law of rape, preserves both the value and the ability to get what it purports to devalue and restrict access to by prohibition. Obscenity law helps keep pornography sexy by putting state power—force, hierarchy—behind its purported prohibition on what men can have sexual access to. The law of obscenity is to pornography as pornography is to sex: a map that purports to be a mirror, a practice that pretends to represent a practice, a legitimation and authorization and set of directions and guiding controls that project themselves onto social reality, while purporting merely to reflect an image of what is already there. Pornography presents itself as fantasy or illusion or idea, which can be good or bad as it is accurate or inaccurate while it actually, hence accurately, distributes power. Liberal morality cannot deal with illusions that constitute reality because its theory of reality, lacking a substantive critique of the distribution of social power, cannot get behind the empirical word, truth by correspon-

dence. On the surface, both pornography and the law of obscenity are about sex. But it is the status of women that is at stake.

Endnotes

[1] Andrea Dworkin, *Pornography: Men Possessing Women* (New York: Perigee, 1981), reviews and demolishes this tradition.

[2] To the body of law ably encompassed and annotated by W. B. Lockhart and R. McClure, "Literature, The Law of Obscenity, and the Constitution," 38 *Minnesota Law Review* 295 (1961); and idem, "Censorship of Obscenity," 45 ibid. 5 (1960), I add only the most important cases since then: Stanley v. Georgia, 394 U.S. 557 (1969); U.S. v. Reidel, 402 U.S. 351 (1971); Miller v. California, 413 U.S. 15 (1973); Paris Adult Theatre I v. Slaton, 413 U.S. 49 (1973); Hamling v. U.S., 418 U.S. 87 (1974); Jenkins v. Georgia, 418 U.S. 153 (1974); Splawn v. California, 431 U.S. 595 (1977); Ward v. Illinois, 431 U.S. 767 (1977); Lovisi v. Slayton, 539 F.2d 349 (4th Cir. 1976); U.S. v. 12 200-Ft. Reels of Super 8MM Film, 413 U.S. 123 (1973); Erznoznik v. City of Jacksonville, 422 U.S. 205 (1975); New York v. Ferber, 458 U.S. 747 (1982).

[3] "Congress shall make no law . . . abridging the freedom of speech, or of the press . . ." Amendment I, U.S. Constitution (1791). First Amendment absolutism has been the conscience of the First Amendment. Justice Black, at times joined by Justice Douglas, took the position that the Constitution, including the First Amendment, was "absolute." Hugo Black, "The Bill of Rights," 35 *New York University Law Review* 865, 867 (1960); idem, *A Constitutional Faith* (New York: Alfred A. Knopf, 1968); Edmond Cahn, "Justice Black and First Amendment 'Absolutes': A Public Interview," 37 ibid. 549 (1962). For a discussion, see Harry Kalven, "Upon Rereading Mr. Justice Black on the First Amendment," 14 *UCLA Law Review* 428 (1967). For one exchange in the controversy surrounding the "absolute" approach to the First Amendment, as opposed to the "balancing" approach, see, e.g., Wallace Mendelson, "On the Meaning of the First Amendment: Absolutes in the Balance," 50 *California Law Review* 821 (1962); L. Frantz, "The First Amendment in the Balance," 71 *Yale Law Journal* 1424 (1962); idem, "Is the First Amendment Law?—A Reploy to Professor Mendelson," 51 *California Law Review* 729 (1963); Wallace Mendelson, "The First Amendment and the Judicial Process: A Reply to Mr. Frantz," 17 *Vanderbilt Law Review* 479 (1964). In the pornography context, see, e.g., Roth v. U.S., 354 U.S. 476, 514 (1957) (Douglas, J.,

joined by Black, J., dissenting); Smith v. California, 361 U.S. 147, 155 (1959) (Black., J., concurring); Miller v. California, 413 U.S. 15, 37 (1973) (Douglas, J., dissenting). It is not the purpose of this chapter to criticize absolutism as such, but rather to identify and criticize some widely and deeply shared implicit beliefs that underlie both the absolutist view and the more mainstream flexible approaches.

[4] Canadian Criminal Code, 1983, Offences Tending to Corrupt Morals, Section 159(1) (c) and (d); People v. Sanger, 222 N.Y. 192 (1918).

[5] *The Report of the Commission on Obscenity and Pornography* (Washington, D.C.: U.S. Government Printing Office, 1970) (majority report). Which is not to ignore (a) the widespread criticism from a variety of perspectives of the commission's methodology, e.g., Lane V. Sunderland, *Obscenity: The Court, the Congress and the President's Commission* (Washington, D.C.: American Enterprise Institute for Public Policy Research, 1975); E. Donnerstein, "Pornography Commission Revisited: Aggression—Erotica and Violence against Women," *Journal of Personality and Social Psychology* 39 (1980): 269–277; A. Garry, "Pornography and Respect for Women," *Social Theory and Practice* 4 (Summer 1978); I. Diamond, "Pornography and Repression," *Signs: Journal of Women in Culture and Society* 5 (Summer 1980): 686–701; V. Cline, "Another View: Pornography Effects, the State of the Art," in *Where Do You Draw the Line? An Exploration into Media Violence, Pornography, and Censorship*, ed. V. B. Cline (Provo, Utah: Brigham Young University Press, 1974); P. Bart and M. Jozsa, "Dirty Books, Dirty Films, and Dirty Data," in *Take Back the Night: Women on Pornography*, ed. L. Lederer (New York: William Morrow, 1980), pp. 209–217; (b) the data the commission found and minimized (like the fact that a substantial minority of men were stimulated to aggression by exposure to what the commission studied (*Report of Obscenity Commission*, vol. 8, p. 377) or ignored the significance of (like Mosher's findings on the differential effects of exposure by gender); or (c) the fact that the commission did not focus questions about gender, did its best to eliminate "violence" from its materials (so as not to overlap with the Violence Commission), and propounded unscientific theories like "puritanism" to explain women's negative responses to the materials; or (d) no scientific causality is required to legally validate even an obscenity regulation. The Supreme Court, in an opinion by Chief Justice Burger, stated: "But, it is argued, there is no scientific data which conclusively demonstrate that exposure to obscene materials adversely affects men and women or their society. It is [urged] that, absent such a demonstration, any kind of state regulation is 'impermissible.' We reject this argument. It is not for us to resolve empirical uncertainties underlying state legislation, save in the exceptional case where that legislation plainly impinges upon rights protected by the constitution itself. . . . Although there is no conclusive proof of a connection between antisocial behavior and obscene material, the legislature of Georgia could quite reasonably determine that such a connection does or might exist." Paris Adult Theatre I v. Slaton, 413 U.S. 49, 60–61 (1973).

[6] Some of pornography's harm to women is documented in studies. The findings are that exposure to pornography increases normal men's willingness to aggress against women under laboratory conditions; makes both women and men substantially less able to perceive accounts of rape as accounts of rape; makes normal men more closely resemble convicted rapists psychologically; increases all the attitudinal measures that are known to correlate with rape, such as hostility toward women, propensity to rape, condoning rape, and predicting that one would rape or force sex on a woman if one knew one would not get caught; and produces other attitude changes in men like increasing the extent of their trivialization, dehumanization, and objectification of women. Diana E. H. Russell, "Pornography and Rape: A Causal Model," *Political Psychology* 9 (1988): 41–74; idem, "Pornography and Violence: What Does the New Research Say?" in Lederer, *Take Back the Night*, p. 218; N. Malamuth and E. Donnerstein, eds., *Pornography and Sexual Aggression* (Orlando, Fla.: Academic Press, 1984); D. Zillman, *Connection between Sex and Aggression* (Hillsdale, N.J.: Erlbaum, 1984); J. V. P. Check, N. Malamuth, and R. Stille, "Hostility to Women Scale" (Manuscript, York University, Toronto, 1983); E. Donnerstein, "Pornography: Its Effects on Violence against Women," in Malamuth and Donnerstein, *Pornography and Sexual Aggression*, pp. 53–82; N. Malamuth, "Rape Proclivity among Males," *Journal of Social Issues* 37 (1981): 138–157; N. Malamuth and J. Check, "The Effects of Mass Media Exposure on Acceptance of Violence against Women: A Field Experiment," *Journal of Research in Personality* 15 (1981): 436–446; N. Malamuth and B. Spinner, "A Longitudinal Content Analysis of Sexual Violence in the Best-Selling Erotica Magazines," *Journal of Sex Research* 16 (August 1980): 226–237; D. L. Mosher and H. Katz, "Pornographic Films, Male Verbal Aggression against Women, and Guilt," in *Technical Report of the Commission on Obscenity and Pornography*, vol. 8 (Washington, D.C.: U.S. Government Printing Office, 1971). Also D. Mosher, "Sex Callousness towards Women," in ibid.; D. Zillman and J. Bryant, "Effects of Massive Exposure to Pornography," in Malamuth and Donnerstein, *Pornography and Sexual Aggression*, pp. 115–138; M. McManus, ed., *Final Report of the Attorney General's Commission on Pornography* (Nashville: Rutledge Hill Press, 1986).

[7] Jacobellis v. Ohio, 378 U.S. 184, 197 (1964) (Stewart, J., concurring).

[8] Justice Stewart is said to have complained that this single line was more quoted and remembered than anything else he ever said.

[9] The following are illustrative, not exhaustive: Dworkin, *Pornography;* D. Leidholdt, "Where Pronography Meets Facism," *WIN News,* March 15, 1983, p. 18; G. Steiner, "Night Words: High Pornography and Human Privacy," in *The Case against Pornography,* ed. D. Holbrook (La Salle, Ill: Open Court, 1973); Susan Brownmiller, *Against Our Will: Men, Women, and Rape* (New York: Simon and Schuster, 1975), p. 394; R. Morgan, "Theory and Practice: Pornography and Rape," in *Going Too Far: The Personal Chronicle of a Feminist* (New York: Random House, 1977); Kathleen Barry, *Female Sexual Slavery* (Englewood Cliffs, N.J.: Prentice-Hall, 1979); R. R. Linden, D. R. Pagano, D. E. H. Russell, and S. L. Star, eds., *Against Sadomasochism: A Radical Feminist Analysis* (Palo Alto, Calif.: Frog in the Well, 1982), especially articles by Ti-Grace Atkinson, Judy Butler, Andrea Dworkin, Alice Walker, John Stoltenberg, Audre Lorde, and Susan Leigh Star; Alice Walker, "Coming Apart," in Lederer, *Take Back the Night,* pp. 95–104; and other articles in that volume with the exception of the legal ones; Gore Vidal, "Women's Liberation Meets the Miller-Mailer-Manson Man," in *Homage to Daniel Shays: Collected Essays 1952–1972* (New York: Random House, 1972), pp. 389–402; Linda Lovelace and Michael McGrady, *Ordeal* (New York: Berkley, 1980); Kate Millett, *Sexual Politics* (Garden City, N.Y.: Doubleday, 1977); F. Rush, *The Best-Kept Secret: Sexual Abuse of Children* (Englewood Cliffs, N.J.: Prentice-Hall, 1980). Colloquium, "Violent Pornography: Degradation of Women versus Right of Free Speech," 8 *New York University Review of Law and Social Change* 181 (1978–79), contains both feminist and nonfeminist argument. Also of real interest is Susan Sontag, "The Pornographic Imagination," *Partisan Review* 34 (1967): 181–214.

[10] Susan Griffin, *Pornography and Silence: Culture's Revenge against Nature* (New York: Harper & Row, 1981).

[11] In addition to Dworkin, *Pornography,* see Andrea Dworkin, "The Root Cause," in *Our Blood: Prophesies and Discourses on Sexual Politics* (New York: Harper & Row, 1976), pp. 96–111.

[12] The position that pornography is sex—whatever you think of sex, you think of pornography—underlies nearly every treatment of the subject. In particular, nearly every nonfeminist treatment proceeds on the implicit or explicit assumption, argument, criticism, or suspicion that pornography is sexually liberating. See D. H. Lawrence, "Pornography and Censorship," in *Sex, Literature and Censorship,* ed. Harry T. Moore (New York: Viking 1975); Hugh Hefner, "The Playboy Philosophy," pts. 1 and 2, *Playboy,* December 1962, p. 73, and February 1963, p. 10; Henry Miller, "Obscenity and the Law of Reflection," *Tricolor,* 48 (February

1945), reprinted in *The Air Conditioned Nightmare II* (New York: New Directions, 1947), pp. 274, 286; D. English, "The Politics of Porn: Can Feminists Walk the Line?" *Mother Jones,* April 1980, pp. 20–23, 43–44, 48–50; J. B. Elshtain, "The Victim Syndrome: A Troubling Turn in Feminism," *The Progressive,* June 1982, pp. 40–47. For example, "In opposition to the Victorian view that narrowly defines proper sexual function in a rigid way analogous to ideas of excremental regularity and moderation, pornography builds a model of plastic variety and joyful excess in sexuality. In opposition to the sorrowing Catholic dismissal of sexuality as an unfortunate and spirtually superficial concomitant of propagation, pornography affords the alternative idea of the independent status of sexuality as a profound and shattering ecstasy." David A. J. Richards, "Free Speech and Obscenity Law: Toward a Moral Theory of the First Amendment," 123 *University of Pennsylvania Law Review* 45, 81 (1974).

[13] The contents of adult bookstores and pornographic movies, the pornographers (who, like all smart pimps, do some form of market research), and the pornography itself confirm that pornography is for men. That women may consume it does not make it any less for men, any more than the observation that men mostly consume pornography means that pornography does not harm women. See also M. Langelan, "The Political Economy of Pornography," *Aegis: Magazine on Ending Violence against Women* 5 (Autumn 1981): 5–7; James Cook, "The X-Rated Economy," *Forbes,* September 18, 1978, p. 18. From personal observation, women tend to avoid pornography as much as possible—which is not all that much, as it turns out.

The "fantasy" and "catharsis" hypotheses, together, assert that pornography cathects sexuality on the level of fantasy fulfillment. The work of Donnerstein, particularly, shows that the opposite is true. The more pornography is viewed, the more pornography—and the more brutal pornography—is both wanted and required for sexual arousal. What occurs is desensitization requiring progressively more potent stimulation, not catharsis. See the works cited in note 9, above, and M. Straus, "Leveling, Civility, and Violence in the Family," *Journal of Marriage and the Family* 36 (1974): 13–29.

[14] Lovelace and McGrady, *Ordeal,* provides an account by one coerced pornography victim. See also the brilliant chapter 6, "The Use of Performers in Commercial Pornography," in M. McManus, ed., *Final Report of the Attorney General's Commission on Pornography* (Nashville: Rutledge Hill Press, 1986).

[15] Diana E. H. Russell, in a random sample of 930 San Francisco households, found that 10 percent of women had ever "been upset by anyone trying to get you to do what they'd seen in pornographic pictures, movies or books"; *Sexual Exploitation,* pp. 125–127. Obviously,

this figure could include only those who knew that the pornography was the source of the sex, which makes it conservative. See also Russell, *Rape in Marriage* (New York: Macmillan, 1982), pp. 83–84 (24 percent of rape victims answered "yes" to the question). The hearings held by the Minneapolis City Council's Committee of Government Operations (with which Andrea Dworkin and I assisted) produced many accounts of the use of pornography to force sex on women and children; *Public Hearings on Ordinances to Add Pornography as Discrimination against Women* (Minneapolis, December 12–13, 1983).

[16] A parallel observation is made by Frederic Jameson of tourism in relation to landscape: "the American tourist no longer lets the landscape 'be in its being' as Heidegger would have said, but takes a snapshot of it, thereby graphically transforming space into its own material image. The concrete activity of looking at a landscape . . . is thus comfortably replaced by *the act of taking possession of it* and converting it into a form of personal property"; "Reification and Utopica in Mass Culture," *Social Text 1* (Winter 1979): 131 (emphasis added).

[17] Laura Mulvey has observed that Freud's "scopophilia" means "taking other people as objects, subjecting them to a controlling and curious gaze," the sexuality of which is "pleasure in using another person as an object of sexual stimulation through sight"; "Visual Pleasure and Narrative Cinema," *Screen* 16, no. 3 (1982). As he so often did, Freud interpreted a male norm as an isolated abnormality. Of course, mass media technology has generalized such behaviors.

[18] "Explicitness" of accounts is a central issue in both obscenity adjudications and audience access standards adopted voluntarily by self-regulated industries as well as by boards of censor (e.g., Ontario). See, e.g., "complete candor and realism" discussed in Grove Press v. Christenberry, 175 F. Supp. 488, 489 (S.D.N.Y. 1959); "directness," Grove Press v. Christenberry, 276 F. 2d 433, 438 (2nd Cir. 1960); "show it all," Mitchum v. State, 251 So.2d 298, 301 (Fla. 1971); Kaplan v. California, 413 U.S. 115, 118 (1973). How much sex the depiction shows is implicitly thereby correlated with how sexual (i.e., how sexually arousing to the male) the material is. See, e.g., Justice White's dissent in Memoirs v. Massachusetts, 383 U.S. 413, 460 (1966); R. D. Hefner, "What G, PG, R and X Really Means," *Congressional Record*, December 8, 1980, pp. 126, 172. Andrea Dworkin brilliantly gives the reader the experience of this aesthetic in her blow-by-blow account in *Pornography*.

[19] L. Henkin, "Morals and the Constitution: The Sin of Obscenity," 63 *Columbia Law Review* 391, 394 (1963).

[20] It may seem odd to denominate "moral" as female in this discussion of male morality. Under male supremacy, men define things; I describe that. Men define women as "moral." This is the male view of women. Thus this analysis, a feminist critique of the male standpoint, terms "moral" the concept that pornography is about good and evil. The term *female* refers to men's attributions of women, which I am analyzing as "male."

[21] A reading of case law supports the reports in Woodward and Armstrong, *The Brethren* (New York: Simon and Schuster, 1979), p. 194, to the effect that this is a bottom-line criterion for at least some justices. The interesting question is why male supremacy would change from keeping the penis hidden so it could be covertly glorified to having it everywhere on display, overtly glorified. This suggests at least that a major shift from private terrorism to public terrorism has occurred. What used to be perceived as a danger to male power, the exposure of the penis, has now become a strategy in maintaining it.

[22] One possible reading of Lockhart and McClure, "Literature, the Law of Obscenity, and the Constitution," is that this exemption was their agenda, and that their approach was substantially adopted in the third prong of the *Miller* doctrine. For the law's leading attempt to grapple with this issue, see Memoirs v. Massachusetts, 383 U.S. 413 (1966), and as overturned in Miller v. California, 413 U.S. 15 (1973), with citations therein to Lockhart and McClure. See also U.S. v. One Book Entitled "Ulysses," 5 F. Supp. 182 (S.D.N.Y. 1933) and 72 F.2d 705 (2nd Cir. 1934).

[23] Andrea Dworkin and I developed this analysis together. See also her argument about how pornography is an issue of sexual access to women, producing a fight among men, in "Why So-Called Radical Men Love and Need Pornography," in Lederer, *Take Back the Night*, p. 141.

[24] Those termed "fathers" and "sons" in ibid. we came to term "the old boys," whose strategy for male dominance involves keeping pornography and the abuse of women private, and "the new boys," whose strategy for male dominance involves making pornography and the abuse of women public. Freud and the accepted generalization of his depression hypothesis to the culture at large are intellectually central in "the new boys' " approach and success. To conclude, as some have, that women have benefited from the public availability of pornography, so should be grateful and have a stake in its continuing availability, is to say that open condoned oppression is so beneficial compared with covert condoned oppression that it should be allowed to continue. This position ignores the alternative of ending the oppression. The benefit of pornography's open availability is that it becomes easier for women to know whom and what we are dealing with, in order to end it.

[25] Miller v. California, 413 U.S. 15 (1973).

[26] Paris Adult Theatre I v. Slayton, 413 U.S. 49, 67 (1973). See also "A quotation from Voltaire in the fly-leaf of a book will not constitutionally redeem an otherwise obscene publication." Kois v. Wisconsin, 408 U.S. 229, 231 (1972), quoted in Miller v. California, 413 U.S. at 25 n. 7.

[27] Penthouse International v. McAuliffe, 610 F.2d 1353 (5th Cir. 1980). For a study in enforcement, see Coble v. City of Birmingham, 389 So.2d 527 (Ala. Ct. App. 1980).

[28] Malamuth and Spinner, "Longitudinal Content Analysis." "The portrayal of sexual aggression within such 'legitimate' magazines as *Playboy* and *Penthouse* may have a greater impact than similar portrayals in hard-core pornography"; N. Malamuth and E. Donnerstein, "The Effects of Aggressive-Pornographic Mass Media Stimuli," *Advances in Experimental Social Psychology* 15 (1982): 103–136 and n. 130. This result is apparently emerging even more clearly in Neil Malamuth's ongoing experiments.

[29] Some courts, under the obscenity rubric, seem to have understood that the quality of artistry does not undo the damage. "This court will not adopt a rule of law which states that obscenity is suppressible but well-written [or a technically well produced] obscenity is not." People v. Fritch, 13 N.Y.2d 119, 126, 243 N.Y.S.2d 1, 7, 192 N.E.2d 713 (bracketed words added by the court in People v. Mature Enterprises, 343 N.Y.S.2d 911 [1973]). More to the point of my argument here is Justice O'Connor's observation: "The compelling interests identified in today's opinion . . . suggest that the Constitution might in fact permit New York to ban knowing distribution to works depicting minors engaged in explicit sexual conduct, regardless of the social value of the depictions. For example, a 12-year-old child photographed while masturbating surely suffers the same psychological harm whether the community labels the photography 'edifying' or 'tasteless.' The audience's appreciation of the depiction is simply irrelevant ot New York's asserted interest in protecting children from psychological, emotional, and mental harm." New York v. Ferber, 458 U.S. 747 (1982) (concurring). Put another way, how does it make a harmed child not harmed that what was produced by harming him is great art?

[30] Women typically get mentioned in obscenity law only in the phrase "women and men," used as a synonym for "people." At the same time, exactly who the victim of pornography is has long been a great mystery. The few references in obscenity litigation to "exploitation" occur in contexts like the reference to "a system of commercial exploitation of people with sado-masochistic sexual aberrations," meaning the customers (all of whom were male) of women dominatrixes. State v. Von Cleef, 102 N.J. Super. 104 (1968). Also, of course, the male children in *Ferber*. Or Justice

Frankfurter's reference to the "sordid exploitation of man's nature and impulses" as part of his conception of pornography in Kingsley Pictures Corp. v. Regents, 360 U.S. 684, 692 (1958).

[31] Miller v. California, 413 U.S. at 24 (1973).

[32] See, e.g., "What shocks me may be sustenance for my neighbor." 413 U.S. at 40–41 (Douglas, J., dissenting); "[What] may be trash to me may be prized by others." U.S. v. 12 200-Ft. Reels of Super 8MM Film, 413 U.S. 123, 137 (1973) (Douglas, J., dissenting). As put by Chuck Traynor, the pimp who forced Linda "Lovelace" into pornography, "I don't tell you how to write your column. Don't tell me how to treat my broads"; quoted in Goria Steinem, "The Real Linda Lovelace," in *Outrageous Acts and Everyday Rebellions* (New York: Holt, Rinehart, and Winston, 1983), p. 252.

[33] See the *Mishkin* resolution of this for nonstandard sexuality, 383 U.S. 502 (1966).

[34] Hopefully, it is obvious that this is not a comment about the personal sexuality or principles of any judicial individual, but rather an analysis that emerges from a feminist attempt to interpret the deep social structure of a vast body of case law on the basis of a critique of gender. Further research should systematically analyze the contents of the pornography involved in the cases. Is it just chance that the first film to be found obscene by a state Supreme Court depicts male masturbation? Landau v. Fording, 245 C.A.2d 820, 54 Cal. Rptr. 177 (1966). Given the ubiquity of the infantilization of women and the sexualization of little girls, would *Ferber* have been decided the same if twelve-year-old girls had been shown masturbating? See Commonwealth of Massachusetts v. Oakes, 410 Mass. 602, 518 N.E. 2d 836 (1988), *cert. granted* 100 L. Ed. 2d 226 (1988). Is the depiction of male sexuality in a way that men think it is dangerous for women and children to see the reason works like *Lady Chatterley's Lover* and *Tropic of Cancer* got in trouble?

[35] Roth v. U.S., 354 U.S. 476 (1957); but cf. Stanley v. Georgia, 394 U.S. 557 (1969), in which the right to private possession of obscene materials is protected as a First Amendment speech right. (One justice noticed this incongruity in the oral argument in *Stanley*; see P. Kurland and G. Casper, eds., *Landmark Briefs and Arguments of the Supreme Court of the United States: Constitutional Law*, vol. 67 [Virginia: University Publications of America, 1975], 850.)

[36] See, e.g., the charge to the Pornography Commission to study "the effect of obscenity and pornography upon the public and particularly minors and its relation to crime and other antisocial behavior" (McManus, *Final Report*, p. 1).

[37] Naomi Scheman, "Making It All Up" (Manuscrpt, Minneapolis, January 1982), p. 7.

[38] For the general body of work to which I refer, which

is usually taken to be diverse, see Thomas I. Emerson, *Toward a General Theory of the First Amendment* (New York: Vintage, 1967); idem, *The System of Freedom of Expression* (New York: Vintage, 1970); A Meiklejohn, *Free Speech and Its Relation to Self-Government* (New York: Harper & Brothers, 1948); Brandeis, J., concurring in Whitney v. California, 274 U.S. 357, 375 (1927) (joined by Holmes, J.); T. Scanlon, "A Theory of Freedom of Expression," *Philosophy & Public Affairs* 1 (1972): 204–226; John Ely, "Flag Desecration: A Case Study in the Roles of Categorization and Balancing in First Amendment Analysis," 88 *Harvard Law Review* 1482 (1975); Z. Chafee, *Free Speech in the United States* (Cambridge, Mass.: Harvard University Press, 1941), p. 245. This literature is ably summarized and anatomized by Ed Baker, who proposes an interpretive theory that goes far toward responding to my objections here, without really altering the basic assumptions I criticize. See C. Edwin Baker, "Scope of the First Amendment Freedom of Speech," 25 *UCLA Law Review* 964 (1978); and idem, "The Process of Change and the Liberty Theory of the First Amendment," 55 *Southern California Law Review* 293 (1982).

[39] Stanley v. Georgia, 394 U.S. 557 (1969).

[40] Erzonznik v. City of Jacksonville, 422 U.S. 205 (1975); Stanley v. Georgia. See also Breard v. Alexandria, 341, U.S. 622 641–645 (1951); Kovacs v. Cooper, 336 U.S. 77, 87–89 (1949).

[41] See Walker, "Coming Apart," in Lederer, *Take Back the Night*; Diana E. H. Russell, ed. "Testimony against Pornography: Witness from Denmark," ibid.; *Public Hearings on Ordinances.* Cf. Justice Douglas, dissenting in Paris Adult Theatre I v. Slayton: "[In] a life that has not been short, I have yet to be trapped into seeing or reading something that would offend me." 413 U.S. 49, 71 (1973). He probably hadn't.

[42] Emerson, *Toward a General Theory*, pp. 16–25, and *System of Freedom of Expression*, p. 17.

[43] Law contains many examples of pure speech treated as actionable acts. A crime of bribery, for example, is typically defined to occur when a person "confers, or offers or agrees to confer, any benefit upon a public servant upon an agreement or understanding that such public servant's vote, opinion, judgment, action, decision or exercise of discretion as a public servant will thereby be influenced." Section 200.00 N.Y. Penal Law. Offers, agreements, and influence are verbal. A vote is a word. Discretion is exercised, decisions made and executed, through words. In regulating opinions, judgments, and understandings, bribery statutes attempt thought control. Another example is the federal regulation of discrimination in housing, which makes it actionable "to make, print, or publish . . . any notice, statement, or advertisement, with respect to the sale or rental of a dwelling" on a discriminatory basis. 42 U.S.C. Section 3604(c) (1982). Here, the speech is the

discriminatory act. Similarly, antiunion speech is an unfair labor practice under the National Labor Relations Act, Section 8, 29 U.S.C. 158. See N.L.R.B. v. Gissel Packing Company, 395 U.S. 575, 617 (1969). Most sexual harassment is done through words. See C. MacKinnon, *Sexual Harassment of Working Women* (New Haven: Yale University Press, 1979), for examples. See also Davis v. Passman, 442 U.S. 228 (1979) (letter treated as actionable sex discrimination); P. Seator, "Judicial Indifference to Pornography's Harm: American Booksellers v. Hudnut," 17 *Golden Gate University Law Review* 297, 320, 330 (1987).

[44] The absolutist position on the entire Constitution was urged by Justice Black. See, e.g., Hugo Black, "The Bill of Rights," 35 *New York University Law Review* 865, 867 (1968), focusing at times on the First Amendment; and E. Cahn, "Justice Black and First Amendment 'Absolutes': A Public Interview," 37 *New York University Law Review* 549 (1962). Justice Douglas as well as Justice Black emphatically articulated the absolutist postion in the obscenity context. See, e.g., Miller v. California, 413 U.S. 15, 37 (1973) (Douglas, J., dissenting); Smith v. California, 361 U.S. 147, 155 (1959) (Black, J., concurring); Roth v. United States, 354 U.S. 476, 514 (1957) (Douglas, J., joined by Black, J., dissenting). Absolutist-influenced discontent with obscenity law is clear in Justic Brennan's dissent in Paris Adult Theatre I v. Slaton, 413 U.S. 49, 73 (1973).

[45] See, e.g., U.S. v. Roth, 237 F.2d 796, 812–817 (2nd Cir. 1956)(Frank, J., concurring).

[46] 237 F.2d 796, 826 n. 70 (Frank, J., concurring).

[47] Werner Heisenberg, *The Physical Principles of Quantum Theory* (Chicago: University of Chicago Press, 1930), p. 63.

[48] Pornography and harm are not two separate events anyway if pornography is a harm.

[49] Morton Horowitz, "The Doctrine of Objective Causation," in *The Politics of Law*, ed. D. Kairys (New York: Pantheon 1982), p. 201. The pervasiveness of the objectification of women has been considered as a reason why pandering should not be constitutionally restricted: "The advertisements of our best magazines are chock-full of thighs, ankles, calves, bosoms, eyes, and hair, to draw the potential buyer's attention to lotions, tires, food, liquor, clothing, autos, and even insurance policies." Ginzburg v. U.S., 383 U.S. 463, 482 (1966) (Douglas, J., dissenting). Justice Douglas thereby illustrated, apparently without noticing, that somebody in addition to the entire advertising industry knows that associating sex, that is, women's bodies, with things causes people to act on that association.

[50] Two boys' masturbating with no showing of explicit force demonstrates the harm of child pornography in New York v. Ferber, 458 U.S. 747 (1982), while shoving money up a woman's vagina, among other acts, raises

serious questions of "regulation of 'conduct' having a communicative element" in live sex adjudications. California v. LaRue, 409 U.S. 109 (1972) (live sex can be regulated by a state in connection with serving alcoholic beverages). "Snuff" films, in which a woman is actually murdered to produce a film for sexual entertainment, are known to exist. People v. Douglas and Hernandez, Felony Complaint # NF8300382, Municipal Court, Judicial District, Orange County, California, August 5, 1983, alleges the murder of two young girls to make a pornographic film. Douglas was convicted of murder but the film was never found.

[51] Both Susan Griffin (*Pornography and Silence*) and the oldest Anglo-Saxon obscenity cases locate the harm of pornography in the mind of the consumer, where it is thought to start and stop. Regina v. Hicklin, 3 Q.B. 360 (1868) ("tendency to deprave and corrupt those whose minds are open to such immoral influences and into whose hands a publication of this sort may fall"). The data of Court and of Kutchinsky, both correlational, reach contrary conclusions on the issue of the relation of pornography's availability to crime statistics; B. Kutchinsky, "Towards an Explanation of the Decrease in Registered Sex Crimes in Copenhagen," in *Technical Report*, p. 7; idem, "The effect of Easy Availability of Pornography on the Incidence of Sex Crimes: The Danish Experience," *Journal of Social Issues* 29 (1973): 163–182; cf. J. H. Court, "Pornography and Sex Crimes: A Re-evaluation in the Light of Recent Trends around the World," *International Journal of Criminology and Penology* 5 (1976): 129ff. More recent investigations into correlations focused on rape in the United States have reached still other conclusions. L. Baron and M. Straus have found a strong correlation between state-to-state variations in the rare of reported rape and the numbers of readers of *Playboy* and *Hustler*; "Sexual Stratification, Pornography, and Rape" (Manuscript, Family Research Laboratory and Department of Sociology, University of New Hampshire, 18 November 1983). The authors conclude: "the findings suggest that the combination of a society which is characterized by a struggle to secure equal rights for women, by a high readership of sex magazines which depict women in ways which may legitimize violence, and by a context in which there is a high level of non-sexual violence, constitutes a mix of societal characteristics which precipitate rape" (p. 16). See also *Report of the Committee on Obscenity and Film Censorship* (London: HMSO, 1979) and the opinions of Justice Harlan on the injury to "society" as a permissible basis for legislative judgments in this area. Alberts v. U.S., 354 U.S. 476, 501–502 (1956) (concurring in companion case to Roth).

[52] Lawrence Tribe, *American Constitutional Law* (Mineola, N.Y.: Foundation Press, 1978), p. 662.

[53] I am conceiving rape as sexual aggression. . . . The work of Neil Malamuth is the leading research in this area. See Malamuth, "Rape Proclivity among Males"; idem, "Rape Fantasies as a Function of exposure to Violent Sexual Stimuli," *Archives of Sexual Behavior* 10 (1981): 33; Malamuth, Haber, and Seymour Feshbach, "Testing Hypotheses regarding Rape: Exposure to Sexual Violence, Sex Differences, and the 'Normality' of Rapists," *Journal of Research in Personality* 14 (1980): 121–137; Malamuth, M. Heim, and S. Feshbach, "Sexual Responsiveness of College Students to Rape Depictions: Inhibitory and Disinhibitory Effects," *Journal of Personality and Social Psychology* 38 (1980): 399–408. See also the work by Malamuth cited in note 6, above. Of course, there are difficulties in measuring rape as a direct consequence of laboratory experiments, difficulties that have led researchers to substitute other measures for willingness to aggress.

Apparently, it is impossible to make a film for experimental purposes which portrays violence or aggression by a man against a woman and which a substantial number of normal male experimental subjects do not perceive as sexual; conversation with E. Donnerstein.

[54] By this I do not mean erotica, which could be defined as sexually explicit sex premised on equality. See also Zillman and Bryant, "Effects of Massive Exposure to Pornography."

[55] See also the "original position" of John Rawls, *A Theory of Justice* (Cambridge, Mass.: The Belknap Press of Harvard University Press, 1971), and idem, "Kantian Constructivism in Moral Theory," *Journal of Philosophy* 9 (1980): 515, 533–535.

[56] Immanuel Kant, *Fundamental Principles of the Metaphysics of Morals*, trans. T. Abbott (Indianapolis: Bobbs-Merrill, 1947); Arthur Danto, "Persons," in *Encyclopedia of Philosophy*, vol. 6, ed. P. Edwards (New York: Macmillan, 1967), 10; Margaret Radin, "Property and Personhood," 34 *Stanford Law Review* 957 (1982).

[57] Ludwig Wittgenstein, *Philosophical Investigations*, trans. G. Anscombe, 2d ed. (Oxford: Blackwell, 1958), p. 178.

[58] E.g., *Capital*.

[59] David Hume, "Of Personal Identity," in *A Treatise on Human Nature* (Oxford: Clarendon Press, 1986), bk. 1, pt. 4, sec. 6.

[60] Bernard Williams, "Are Persons Bodies?" "Personal Identity and Individualization," and "Bodily Continuity and Personal Identity," all in *Problems of the Self* 1 (1973).

[61] One might ask at this point, not why some women embrace explicit sadomasochism, but why any women do not.

[62] Dworkin, *Pornography*, p. 115. "Echoing Macaulay, 'Jimmy' Walker remarked that he had never heard of a woman seduced by a book." U.S. v. Roth, 237 F.2d

796, 812 (2nd Cir. 1956) (appendix to concurrence of
Frank, J.). Much of what is usually called seduction,
feminists might consider rape or forced sex.

[63] American Booksellers Assn., Inc. v. Hudnut, 771
F.2d 323 (7th Cir. 1985).

[64] 771 F.2d at 328.

[65] In this case, official policy has been expressed
through the device of "summary affirmance" of the
Hudnut result by the U.S. Supreme Court. Hudnut v.
American Booksellers Assn., Inc., 475 U.S. 1001 (1986).
A summary affirmance resolves a case without briefs or
arguments by letting stand a result reached in a court
of appeals. Lower courts reviewing the identical issues
are bound by the result but not by the reasoning of the
decision that is affirmed. Where the issues are not
identical, or where the decision departs from established precedent, or where intervening legal developments suggest that the Court would reach a different
result, lower courts may not be bound by the result.
The Supreme Court may grant full review to the issues
without being bound by the previous summary affirmance. Mandel v. Bradley, 432 U.S. 173 (1977); Hicks
v. Miranda, 422 U.S. 332 (1975). So while this result is
a significant state behavior, it need not be the last word
on the subject.

Study Questions

1. Read the court's opinion in *American Booksellers
v. Hudnut* (reprinted in this chapter's "Cases" section). Do you agree with the court's reasons for
striking down the Indianapolis antipornography
ordinance as unconstitutional? The court held that
the ordinance could not be permitted to take effect
since it constituted discrimination on the basis of
viewpoint: Only those expressing the "approved"
view of women will be allowed to speak. Is this a
persuasive rationale?

2. MacKinnon criticizes the court's reasoning
in *Hudnut*, which found that the Indianapolis law
impermissibly endorsed a specific viewpoint and
thereby failed to be "content neutral." MacKinnon
responds by pointing out that current obscenity
law does not represent a neutral viewpoint either:
it only seems that way to men because it represents
their view point. Do you agree? Disagree? What are
your reasons?

3. Feminist critiques of pornography often assume that all women are, by extension, virtual participants in pornography, since it is "their" body
which is being "objectified," turned into a thing, a
vehicle for (male) pleasure. In this sense, all
women are, or at least can be, "harmed" by pornography, even though many of them may not
realize it. Is this a defensible position?

4. In October 1990, a jury in Cincinnati acquitted Cincinnati's Contemporary Arts Center
and its director, Dennis Barrie, of the misdemeaner
charge of pandering obscenity. The charge arose
out of the Center's exhibition of a 175-photo retrospective of the work of homosexual artist and pho-
tographer Robert Mapplethorpe. Five of the photos, from Mapplethorpe's "X Portfolio," depicted
homoerotic and sadomasochistic images, including a man's fist up another man's rectum and a
bullwhip protruding from a man's anus. Can such
material be displayed for *bona fide* educational and
cultural purposes? Can a case be made for the suppression of homoerotic images based on the position defended by Joel Feinberg? Does MacKinnon's feminist critique of pornography have any
applicability to such images? Also, consider: Existing obscenity law deems obscene patently offensive works that, "taken as a whole," lack literary,
artistic, political, or scientific merit. The court in
this case ruled that the "work as a whole" in question consisted only of the five photos under consideration, rather than the entire 175-photo exhibition. Was this a defensible interpretation of the
Miller standard?

Cases for Further Reflection

State v. Bradbury
9 A. 2d 657 (1939)
Supreme Court of Maine

The holding in this case is representative of an entire body of Anglo-American common law according to which the treatment of human remains contrary to "common decency" is an offense. Can such laws be squared with Mill's harm principle? Assuming many people feel strongly about such matters, does that fact show that Mill's theory must be rejected as a way of distinguishing between legitimate and illegitimate restrictions on freedom of action?

Thaxter, Justice.

The respondent, Frank E. Bradbury, lived with an unmarried sister, Harriet, in a two and a half story building situated on Main Street in the City of Saco. They were old people and the last survivors of their family. In June 1938 Harriet was in failing health. She appeared to have suffered some injury from a fall and during the night of June 9th she remained in a reclining chair in the front room of their home. About four o'clock in the morning of June 10th she died. The respondent thereupon built a hot fire in the furnace in the basement of the house, tied a rope around the legs of his sister's body, dragged it down the cellar stairs, shoved it into the furnace and burned it. It was impossible to get it all into the fire box at once, but as the head and shoulders were consumed, he forced it farther and farther until he was able to close the furnace door. Reverend Ward R. Clark, who lived in the next door, testified that during the morning of June 10th a heavy, dark smoke, with a very disagreeable odor poured from the chimney of the house. The next day an investigation was made by the authorities, who asked the respondent to show them the remains of his sister. Going to the basement of the house, he took down the crank used for shaking down the furnace, turned over the grates, shovelled out the ashes and said:

"If you want to see her, there she is." A few bones were found; the rest of the body had been consumed.

The indictment charged that the respondent "with force and arms, unlawfully and indecently did take the human body of one Harriet P. Bradbury, and then and there indecently and unlawfully put and placed said body in a certain furnace, and then and there did dispose of and destroy the said body of the said Harriet P. Bradbury by burning the same in said furnace, to the great indecency of Christian burial, in evil example to all others in like case offending, against the peace of said State and contrary to the laws of the same."

The offence is not covered by the provisions of Rev. Stat. 1930, Ch. 135, Sec. 47, which makes it an offence to disinter, to conceal, to indecently expose, to throw away or to abandon a human body; and it is important to note that the indictment does not charge the violation of any statute. The question for us to decide is whether this was a crime under the common law.

Judge Holmes, in speaking of the common law as applicable to crimes, has well said: "The first requirement of a sound body of law is, that it should correspond with the actual feelings and demands of the community, whether right or wrong." Holmes, Common Law, p. 41. And in Pierce v. Proprietors of Swan Point Cemetery, 10 R. I. 227, a case involving rights of sepulture, the court discusses the application thereto of the principles of the common law and quotes from a report published in 1836 by Joseph Story, Simon Greenleaf and others on the Codification of the Laws of Massachusetts. With reference to the common law, this says in part: "In truth, the common law is not in its nature and character an absolutely fixed, inflexible system, like the statute law, providing only for cases of a determinate form, which fall within the letter of the language, in which a particular doctrine or legal proposition is expressed. It is rather a system of elementary principles and of general juridical truths, which are continually expanding with the progress of society, and adapting themselves to the gradual changes of trade and commerce, and the mechanic arts, and the exigencies and usages of the country."

It is because the common law gives expression to the changing customs and sentiments of the people that there have been brought within its scope such crimes as blasphemy, open obscenity, and kindred offenses against religion and morality, in short those acts which, being highly indecent, are contra bonos mores. *Rex v. Lynn.*

The proper method for disposal of the dead has been regulated by law from earliest times, on the continent of Europe by the canon law, and in England by the ecclesiastical law. . . . But even in England where the subject has been largely committed to the ecclesiastical courts, the principles of the common law have been held applicable and the courts have not hesitated to apply them to give effect to the well recognized customs of the day and age. *Rex v. Lynn*, supra.

In *Reg. V. Stewart*, the rule is broadly laid down in the following language: "We have no doubt, therefore, that the common law casts on some one the duty of carrying to the grave, decently covered, the dead body of any person dying in such a state of indigence as to leave no funds for that purpose. The feelings and the interest of the living require this, and create the duty. . . ."

In this country the subject is governed quite largely by statute and where no statutory provision is applicable by the principles of the common law; and the general doctrine laid down in *Reg. V. Stewart*, supra, modified only by changing usages, has been almost universally followed.

In our own state some time before the decision in *Reg. v. Stewart*, it was held that the indecent disposal of a human body was an offence at common law. *Kanavan's* Case, 1 Me, 226. The second count of the indictment in this case charged that the respondent "unlawfully and indecently took the body" of a child "and threw it into the river, against common decency." The respondent maintained that the offence was not indictable at common law and filed a motion in arrest of judgment. The indictment was held good. The court said: "From our childhood, we all have been accustomed to pay a reverential respect to the sepulchres of our fathers, and to attach a character of sacredness to the grounds dedicated and enclosed as the cemeteries of the dead. Hence, before the late statute of Massachusetts was enacted, it was an of-

fence at common law to dig up the bodies of those who had been buried, for the purpose of dissection. It is an outrage upon the public feelings, and torturing to the afflicted relatives of the deceased. If it be a crime thus to disturb the ashes of the dead, it must also be a crime to deprive them of a decent burial, by a disgraceful exposure or disposal of the body, contrary to usages so long sanctioned, and which are so grateful to the wounded hearts of friends and mourners."

This case seems to lay down the doctrine that any disposal of a dead body which is contrary to common decency is an offense at common law. But counsel for the respondent in the case before us argues that cremation is now a well recognized method of disposing of a dead body and cites the case of *Reg. v. Price*, as an authority that on the facts of the instant case no crime has been committed. If this case upholds the doctrine for which he contends, it does not represent the law in this country. A careful reading of it, however, satisfies us that the court did not intend to lay down any such principle. The question considered was a very narrow one, "whether," to use the language of the court, "to burn a dead body instead of burying it is in itself an illegal act." The question is answered as follows: "I am of the opinion that a person who burns instead of burying a dead body does not commit a criminal act, unless he does it in such a manner as to amount to a public nuisance at common law." And in the case before us the essence of the offense charged and proved is, not that the body was burned, but that it was indecently burned, in such a manner that, when the facts should in the natural course of events become known, the feelings and natural sentiments of the public would be outraged.

Wisconsin v. Yoder
406 U.S. 205 (1972)
United States Supreme Court

A landmark decision in the law of the "free exercise" clause, this case illustrates the conflict between the right of individuals to entertain beliefs on religious grounds and to educate their children accordingly, and the authority of the state to override the claims of these beliefs by working to instill certain values and attitudes in the classroom. The reasoning of the Court in this case should be compared with that of the Court in the "peyote case" (included at the end of this section). To what other religious groups might the Court's reasoning here apply? What would Mill and Kendall say of this case?

Mr. Chief Justice Burger delivered the opinion of the Court.

[We granted certiorari] to review a decision of the Wisconsin Supreme Court holding that respondents' convictions of violating the State's compulsory school-attendance law were invalid under the Free Exercise Clause. [We affirm.]

Respondents Jonas Yoder and Wallace Miller are members of the Old Order Amish Religion, and respondent Adin Yutzy is a member of the Conservative Amish Mennonite Church. . . . Wisconsin's compulsory school-attendance law required them to cause their children to attend public or private school until reaching age 16 but the respondents declined to send their children, ages 14 and 15, to public school after they completed the eighth grade. [Respondents were convicted under the compulsory-attendance law and were fined $5 each.] Trial testimony showed that they believed that by sending their children to high school, they [would] endanger their own salvation and that of their children. The State stipulated that respondents' religious beliefs were sincere. . . .

Formal high school education beyond the eighth grade is contrary to Amish beliefs, not only because it places Amish children in an environment hostile to Amish beliefs with increasing emphasis on competition in class work and sports and with pressure to conform to the styles, manners, and ways of the peer group, but also because it takes them away from their community, physically and emotionally, during the crucial and formative adolescent period of life. During this period, the children must acquire Amish attitudes favoring manual work and self-reliance and the specific skills needed to perform the adult role of an Amish farmer or housewife. . . .

[An expert] testified that compulsory high school attendance could not only result in great psychological harm to Amish children, because of the conflicts it would produce, but would also, in his opinion, ultimately result in the destruction of the Old Order Amish church community as it exists in the United States today. The testimony of [another expert] also showed that the Amish succeed in preparing their high school age children to

be productive members of the Amish community. [The] evidence also showed that the Amish have an excellent record as law-abiding and generally self-sufficient members of society. . . .

[A] State's interest in universal education, however highly we rank it, is not totally free from a balancing process when it impinges on fundamental rights and interests, such as those specifically protected by the Free Exercise Clause of the First Amendment, and the traditional interest of parents with respect to the religious upbringing of their children. . . . It follows that in order for Wisconsin to compel school attendance beyond the eighth grade against a claim that such attendance interferes with the practice of a legitimate religious belief, it must appear either that the State does not deny the free exercise of religious belief by its requirement, or that there is a state interest of sufficient magnitude to override the interest claiming protection under the Free Exercise Clause. [O]nly those interests of the highest order and those not otherwise served can overbalance legitimate claims to the free exercise of religion. . . .

. . . In evaluating [respondents'] claims we must be careful to determine whether the Amish religious faith and their mode of life are, as they claim, inseparable and interdependent. A way of life, however virtuous and admirable, may not be interposed as a barrier to reasonable state regulation of education if it is based on purely secular considerations; to have the protection of the Religion Clauses, the claims must be rooted in religious belief. Although a determination of what is a "religious" belief or practice entitled to a constitutional protection may present a most delicate question, the very concept of ordered liberty precludes allowing every person to make his own standards on matters of conduct in which society as a whole has important interests. Thus, if the Amish asserted their claims because of the subjective evaluation and rejection of the contemporary secular values accepted by the majority, much as Thoreau rejected the social values of his time and isolated himself at Walden Pond, their claim would not rest on a religious basis. Thoreau's choice was philosophical and personal rather than religious, and such belief does not rise to the demands of the Religion Clause.

Giving no weight to such secular considerations, however, we see that the record in this case abundantly supports the claim that the traditional way of life of the Amish is not merely a matter or personal preference, but one of deep religious conviction, shared by an organized group, and intimately related to daily living. That the Old Order Amish daily life and religious practice stem from their faith is shown by the fact that it is in response to their literal interpretation of the Biblical injunction from the Epistle of Paul to the Romans, ''be not conformed to this world. . . .'' This command is fundamental to the Amish faith. Moreover, for the Old Order Amish, religion is not simply a matter of theocratic belief. As the expert witnesses explained, the Old Order Amish religion pervades and determines virtually their entire way of life, regulating it with the detail of the Talmudic diet through the strictly enforced rules of the church community. . . .

The impact of the compulsory-attendance law on respondents' practice of the Amish religion is not only severe, but inescapable, for the Wisconsin law affirmatively compels them, under threat of criminal sanction, to perform acts undeniably at odds with fundamental tenets of their religious beliefs. See [Braunfeld]. Nor is the impact of the compulsory-attendance law confined to grave interference with important Amish religious tenets from a subjective point of view. It carries with it precisely the kind of objective danger to the free exercise of religion which the First Amendment was designed to prevent. [It raises] a very real threat of undermining the Amish community and religious practice as they exist today; they must either abandon belief and be assimilated into society at large, or be forced to migrate to some other and more tolerant region. [In sum], enforcement of the State's requirement of compulsory formal education after the eighth grade would gravely endanger if not destroy the free exercise of respondents' religious beliefs.

. . . [The State does not challenge] the claim that the Amish mode of life and education is inseparable from and a part of the basic tenets of their religion—indeed, as much a part of their religious belief and practices as baptism, the confessional, or a sabbath may be for others. The Court must not ignore the danger that an exception from a general obligation of citizenship on religious grounds may run afoul of the Establishment Clause, but that danger cannot be allowed to prevent any exception no matter how vital it may be to the protection of values promoted by the right of free exercise. . . .

The State advances two primary arguments in support of its system of compulsory education. It notes, as Thomas Jefferson pointed out early in our history, that some degree of education is necessary to prepare citizens to participate effectively and intelligently in our open political system if we are to preserve freedom and independence. Further, education prepares individuals to be self-reliant and self-sufficient participants in society. We accept these propositions.

However, the evidence adduced by the Amish in this case is persuasively to the effect that an additional one or two years of formal high school for Amish children in place of their long-established program of informal vocational education would do little to serve those interests. . . . It is one thing to say that compulsory education for a year or two beyond the eighth grade may be necessary when its goal is the preparation of the child for life in modern society as the majority live, but it is quite another if the goal of education be viewed as the preparation of the child for life in the separated agrarian community that is the keystone of the Amish faith.

The State attacks respondents' position as one fostering ''ignorance'' from which the child must be protected by the State. [But] this record strongly shows that the Amish community has been a highly successful social unit within our society, even if apart from the conventional ''mainstream.'' Its members are productive and very law-abiding members of society; they reject public welfare in any of its usual modern views. The Congress itself recognized their self-sufficiency by authorizing exemption of such groups as the Amish from the obligation to pay social security taxes.[1] A way of life that is odd or even erratic but interferes with no rights or interests of others is not to be condemned because it is different.

The State, however, supports its interest in providing an additional one or two years of compulsory high school education to Amish children because of the possibility that some such children will choose to leave the Amish community, and that if this occurs they will be ill-equipped for life. . . . However, on this record, that argument is highly speculative. . . .

Contrary to the suggestion [in Justice Douglas's dissent], our holding today in no degree depends on the assertion of the religious interest of the child as contrasted with that of the parents. It is the parents who are subject to prosecution here [and] it is their right of free exercise, not that of their children, that must determine Wisconsin's power to impose criminal penalties on the parent. The dissent argues that a child who expresses a desire to attend public high school in conflict with the wishes of his parents should not be prevented from doing so. There is no reason for the Court to consider that point since it is not an issue in the case. The children are not parties to this litigation. The State has at no point tried this case on the theory that respondents were preventing their children from attending school against their expressed desires, and indeed the record is to the contrary.[2] . . .

Our holding in no way determines the proper resolution of possible competing interests of parents, children, and the State in an appropriate state court proceeding in which the power of the State is asserted on the theory that Amish parents are preventing their minor children from attending high school despite their expressed desires to the contrary. Recognition of the claim of the State in such a proceeding would, of course, call into question traditional concepts of parental control over the religious upbringing and education of their minor children recognized in this Court's past decisions. It is clear that such an intrusion by a State into family decisions in the area of religious training would give rise to grave questions of religious freedom. . . . On this record we neither reach nor decide those issues.[3]

. . . It cannot be over-emphasized that we are not dealing with a way of life and mode of education by a group claiming to have recently discovered some "progressive" or more enlightened process for rearing children for modern life. [In light of the "convincing showing" by the Amish here,] one that probably few other religious groups or sects could make, and weighing the minimal difference between what the State would require and what the Amish already accept, it was incumbent on the State to show with more particularity how its admittedly strong interest in compulsory education would be adversely affected by granting an exemption to the Amish. Sherbert v. Verner. . . .[4]

Affirmed.

December 13, 1950, from the obligation to pay social security taxes if they are, by reason of the tenets of their sect, opposed to receipt of such benefits and agree to waive them, provided the Secretary finds that the sect makes reasonable provision for its dependent members. . . .

The record in this case establishes without contradiction that the Green County Amish had never been known to commit crimes, that none had been known to receive public assistance, and that none were unemployed. [Footnote by the Court.]

[2] The only relevant testimony in the record is to the effect that the wishes of the one child who testified corresponded with those of her parents. Testimony of Frieda Yoder, Tr. 92–94, to the effect that her personal religious beliefs guided her decision to discontinue school attendance after the 8th grade. The other children were not called by either side. [Footnote by the Court.]

[3] What we have said should meet the suggestion that the decision of the Wisconsin Supreme Court recognizing an exemption for the Amish from the State's system of compulsory education constituted an impermissible establishment of religion. . . . Accommodating the religious beliefs of the Amish can hardly be characterized as sponsorship or active involvement. The purpose and effect of such an exemption are not to support, favor, advance, or assist the Amish, but to allow their centuries-old religious society, here long before the advent of any compulsory education, to survive free from the heavy impediment compliance with the Wisconsin compulsory-education law would impose. Such an accommodation "reflects nothing more than the governmental obligation of neutrality in the face of religious differences, and does not represent that involvement of religious with secular institutions which it is the object of the Establishment Clause to forestall." [Sherbert v. Verner.] [Footnote by the Court.]

[4] Several States have now adopted plans to accommodate Amish religious beliefs through the establishment of an "Amish vocational school." These are not schools in the traditional sense of the word. . . . There is no basis to assume that Wisconsin will be unable to reach a satisfactory accommodation with the Amish in light of what we now hold, so as to serve its interests without impinging on respondents' protected free exercise of their religion. [Footnote by the Court.]

Endnotes

[1] 26 U.S.C. § 1402(h) authorizes the Secretary of Health, Education, and Welfare to exempt members of "a recognized religious sect" existing at all times since

American Booksellers Association v. Hudnut
771 F. 2d 323 (1985)
United States Court of Appeals, Seventh Circuit

In an opinion by Judge Frank Easterbrook, the federal appellate court in this case affirmed a lower court's decision that Indianapolis's antipornography ordinance was unconstitutional under the First Amendment. Easterbrook's arguments should be assessed alongside the positions defended by Joel Feinberg and Catherine MacKinnon.

Easterbrook, Circuit Judge.

Indianapolis enacted an ordinance defining "pornography" as a practice that discriminates against women. "Pornography" is to be redressed through the administrative and judicial methods used for other discrimination. The City's definition of "pornography" is considerably different from "obscenity," which the Supreme Court has held is not protected by the First Amendment.

. . . To be "obscene" under *Miller v. California*, 413 U.S. 15 . . . (1973), "a publication must, taken as a whole, appeal to the prurient interest, must contain patently offensive depictions or descriptions of specified sexual conduct, and on the whole have no serious literary, artistic, political, or scientific value." . . . Offensiveness must be assessed under the standards of the community. Both offensiveness and an appeal to something other than "normal, healthy sexual desires" . . . are essential elements of "obscenity."

"Pornography" under the ordinance is "the graphic sexually explicit subordination of women, whether in pictures or in words, that also includes one or more of the following:

1. Women are presented as sexual objects who enjoy pain or humiliation; or

2. Women are presented as sexual objects who experience sexual pleasure in being raped; or

3. Women are presented as sexual objects tied up or cut up or mutilated or bruised or physically hurt, or as dismembered or truncated or fragmented or severed into body parts; or

4. Women are presented as being penetrated by objects or animals; or

5. Women are presented in scenarios of degradation, injury, abasement, torture, shown as filthy or inferior, bleeding, bruised, or hurt in a context that makes these conditions sexual; or

6. Women are presented as sexual objects for domination, conquest, violation, exploitation, possession, or use, or through postures or positions of servility or submission or display."

The Indianapolis ordinance does not refer to the prurient interest, to offensiveness, or to the standards of the community. It demands attention to particular depictions, not to the work judged as a whole. It is irrelevant under the ordinance whether the work has literary, artistic, political, or scientific value. The City and many amici point to these omissions as virtues. They maintain that pornography influences attitudes, and the statute is a way to alter the socialization of men and women rather than to vindicate community standards of offensiveness. And as one of the principal drafters of the ordinance has asserted, "if a woman is subjected, why should it matter that the work has other value?" Catherine A. MacKinnon, *Pornography, Civil Rights, and Speech*, 20 Harv.Civ.Rts.— Civ.Lib.L. Rev. 1, 21 (1985).

Civil rights groups and feminists have entered this case as amici on both sides. Those supporting the ordinance say that it will play an important role in reducing the tendency of men to view women as sexual objects, a tendency that leads to both unacceptable attitudes and discrimination in the workplace and violence away from it. Those opposing the ordinance point out that much radical feminist literature is explicit and depicts women in ways forbidden by the ordinance and that the ordinance would reopen old battles. It is unclear how Indianapolis would treat works from James Joyce's *Ulysses* to Homer's *Iliad*; both depict women as submissive objects for conquest and domination.

We do not try to balance the arguments for and against an ordinance such as this. The ordinance discriminates on the ground of the content of the speech. Speech treating women in the approved way—in sexual encounters "premised on equality" (MacKinnon, *supra*, at 22)—is lawful no matter how sexually explicit. Speech treating women in the disapproved way—as submissive in matters sexual or as enjoying humiliation—is unlawful no matter how significant the literary, artistic, or political qualities of the work taken as a whole. The state may not ordain preferred viewpoints in this way. The Constitution forbids the state to declare one perspective right and silence opponents.

The ordinance contains four prohibitions. People may not "traffic" in pornography, "coerce" others into performing in pornographic works, or "force" pornography on anyone. Anyone injured by someone who has seen or read pornography has a right of action against the maker or seller. Trafficking is defined in § 16–3(g)(4) as the "production, sale, exhibition, or distribution of pornography." The offense excludes exhibition in a public or educational library, but a "special display" in a library may be sex discrimination. Section 16–3(g)(4)(C) provides that the trafficking paragraph "shall not be construed to make isolated passages or isolated parts actionable."

"Coercion into pornographic performance" is defined in § 16–3(g)(5) as "[c]oercing, intimidating or fraudulently inducing any person . . . into performing for pornography. . . . " The ordinance specifies that proof of any of the following "shall not constitute a defense: I. That the person is a woman; . . . VI. That the person has previously posed for sexually explicit pictures . . . with anyone . . . ; . . . VIII. That the person actually consented to a use of the performance that is changed into pornography; . . . IX. That the person knew that the purpose of the acts or events in question was to make pornography; . . . XI. That the person signed a contract, or made statements affirming a willingness to cooperate in the production of pornography; XII. That no physical force, threats, or weapons were used in the making of the pornography; or XIII. That the person was paid or otherwise compensated."

"Forcing pornography on a person," according to § 16–3(g)(5), is the "forcing of pornography on any woman, man, child, or transsexual in any place of employment, in education, in a home, or in any public place." The statute does not define forcing, but one of its authors states that the definition reaches pornography shown to medical students as part of their education or given to language students for translation. MacKinnon, *supra*, at 40–41.

Section 16–3(g)(7) defines as a prohibited practice the "assault, physical attack, or injury of any woman, man, child, or transsexual in a way that is directly caused by specific pornography."

For purposes of all four offenses, it is generally "not . . . a defense that the respondent did not know or intend that the materials were pornography. . . ." Section 16–3(g)(8). But the ordinance provides that damages are unavailable in trafficking cases unless the complainant proves "that the respondent knew or had reason to know that the materials were pornography." It is a complete defense to a trafficking case that all of the materials in question were pornography only by virtue of category (6) of the definition of pornography. In cases of assault caused by pornography, those who seek damages from "a seller, exhibitor or distributor"

must show that the defendant knew or had reason to know of the material's status as pornography. By implication, those who seek damages from an author need not show this.

A woman aggrieved by trafficking in pornography may file a complaint "as a woman acting against the subordination of women" with the office of equal opportunity. Section 16–17(b). A man, child, or transsexual also may protest trafficking "but must prove injury in the same way that a woman is injured. . . . " *Ibid.* Subsection (a) also provides, however, that "any person claiming to be aggrieved" by trafficking, coercion, forcing, or assault may complain against the "perpetrators." We need not decide whether § 16–17(b) qualifies the right of action in § 16–17(a).

The office investigates and within 30 days makes a recommendation to a panel of the equal opportunity advisory board. The panel then decides whether there is reasonable cause to proceed (§ 16–24(2)) and may refer the dispute to a conciliation conference or to a complaint adjudication committee for a hearing (§§ 16–24(3), 16–26(a)). The committee uses the same procedures ordinarily associated with civil rights litigation. It may make findings and enter orders, including both orders to cease and desist and orders "to take further affirmative action . . . including but not limited to the power to restore complainant's losses. . . . " Section 16–26(d). Either party may appeal the committee's decision to the board, which reviews the record before the committee and may modify its decision.

Under Indiana law an administrative decision takes effect when rendered, unless a court issues a stay. . . . The board's decisions are subject to review in the ordinary course. . . . Judicial review in pornography cases is to be de novo . . . , which provides a second complete hearing. When the board finds that a person has engaged in trafficking or that a seller, exhibitor, or distributor is responsible for an assault, it must initiate judicial review of its own decision, . . . and the statute prohibits injunctive relief in these cases in advance of the court's final decision. . . .

The district court held the ordinance unconstitutional. . . . The court concluded that the ordinance regulates speech rather than the conduct involved in making pornography. The regulation of speech could be justified, the court thought, only by a compelling interest in reducing sex discrimination, an interest Indianapolis had not established. The ordinance is also vague and overbroad, the court believed, and establishes a prior restraint of speech.

. . . "If there is any fixed star in our constitutional constellation, it is that no official, high or petty, can prescribe what shall be orthodox in politics, nationalism, religion, or other matters of opinion or force citizens to confess by word or act their faith therein." *West Virginia State Board of Education v. Barnette*, 319 U.S. 624, 642 . . . (1943). Under the First Amendment the government must leave to the people the evaluation of ideas. Bald or subtle, an idea is as powerful as the audience allows it to be. A belief may be pernicious—the beliefs of Nazis led to the death of millions, those of the Klan to the repression of millions. A pernicious belief may prevail. Totalitarian governments today rule much of the planet, practicing suppression of billions and spreading dogma that may enslave others. One of the things that separates our society from theirs is our absolute right to propagate opinions that the government finds wrong or even hateful. . . .

Under the ordinance graphic sexually explicit speech is "pornography" or not depending on the perspective the author adopts. Speech that "subordinates" women and also, for example, presents women as enjoying pain, humiliation, or rape, or even simply presents women in "positions of servility or submission or display" is forbidden, no matter how great the literary or political value of the work taken as a whole. Speech that portrays women in positions of equality is lawful, no matter how graphic the sexual content. This is thought control. It establishes an "approved" view of women, of how they may react to sexual encounters, of how the sexes may relate to each other. Those who espouse the approved view may use sexual images; those who do not, may not.

Indianapolis justifies the ordinance on the ground that pornography affects thoughts. Men who see women depicted as subordinate are more likely to treat them so. Pornography is an aspect of dominance. It does not persuade people so much as change them. It works by socializing, by establishing the expected and the permissible. In this view pornography is not an idea; pornography is the injury.

There is much to this perspective. Beliefs are also facts. People often act in accordance with the images and patterns they find around them. People raised in a religion tend to accept the tenets of that religion, often without independent examination. People taught from birth that black people are fit only for slavery rarely rebelled against that creed; beliefs coupled with the self-interest of the masters established a social structure that inflicted great harm while enduring for centuries. Words and images act at the level of the subconscious before they persuade at the level of the conscious. Even the truth has little chance unless a statement fits within the framework of beliefs that may never have been subjected to rational study. . . .

Yet this simply demonstrates the power of pornography as speech. All of these unhappy effects depend on mental intermediation. Pornography affects how people see the world, their fellows, and social relations. If pornography is what pornography does, so is other speech. Hitler's orations affected how some Germans saw Jews. Communism is a world view, not simply a *Manifesto* by Marx and Engels or a set of speeches. Efforts to suppress communist speech in the United States were based on the belief that the public acceptability of such ideas would increase the likelihood of totalitarian government. Religions affect socialization in the most pervasive way. The opinion in *Wisconsin v. Yoder*, 406 U.S. 205 . . . 1526 . . . (1972), shows how a religion can dominate an entire approach to life, governing much more than the relation between the sexes. Many people believe that the existence of television, apart from the content of specific programs, leads to intellectual laziness, to a penchant for violence, to many other ills. The Alien and Sedition Acts passed during the administration of John Adams rested on a sincerely held belief that disrespect for the government leads to social collapse and revolution—a belief with support in the history of many nations. Most governments of the world act on this empirical regularity, suppressing critical speech. In the United States, however, the strength of the support for this belief is irrelevant. . . .

Racial bigotry, anti-semitism, violence on television, reporters' biases—these and many more influence the culture and shape our socialization. None is directly answerable by more speech, unless that speech too finds its place in the popular culture. Yet all is protected as speech, however insidious. Any other answer leaves the government in control of all of the institutions of culture, the great censor and director of which thoughts are good for us.

Sexual responses often are unthinking responses, and the association of sexual arousal with the subordination of women therefore may have a substantial effect. But almost all cultural stimuli provoke unconscious responses. Religious ceremonies condition their participants. Teachers convey messages by selecting what not to cover; the implicit message about what is off limits or unthinkable may be more powerful than the messages for which they present rational argument. Television scripts contain unarticulated assumptions. People may be conditioned in subtle ways. If the fact that speech plays a role in a process of conditioning were enough to permit governmental regulation, that would be the end of freedom of speech.

It is possible to interpret the claim that the pornography is the harm in a different way. Indianapolis emphasizes the injury that models in pornographic films and pictures may suffer. The record contains materials depicting sexual torture, penetration of women by red-hot irons and the like. These concerns have nothing to do with written materials subject to the statute, and physical injury can occur with or without the "subordination" of women. . . . [A] state may make injury in the course of producing a film unlawful independent of the viewpoint expressed in the film.

The more immediate point, however, is that the image of pain is not necessarily pain. In *Body Double*, a suspense film directed by Brian DePalma, a woman who has disrobed and presented a sexually explicit display is murdered by an intruder with a drill. The drill runs through the woman's body. The film is sexually explicit and a murder occurs—yet no one believes that the actress suffered pain or died. In *Barbarella* a character played by Jane Fonda is at times displayed in sexually explicit ways and at times shown "bleeding, bruised, [and] hurt in a context that makes these conditions sexual"—and again no one believes that Fonda was actually tortured to make the film. In *Carnal Knowledge* a woman grovels to please the sexual whims of a character played by Jack Nicholson; no one believes that there was a real sexual submission, and the Supreme Court held the film protected by the First Amendment. . . . And this works both ways. The description of women's sexual domination of men in *Lysistrata* was not real dominance. Depictions may affect slavery, war, or sexual roles, but a book about slavery is not itself slavery, or a book about death by poison a murder.

Much of Indianapolis's argument rests on the belief that when speech is "unanswerable," and

the metaphor that there is a "marketplace of ideas" does not apply, the First Amendment does not apply either. The metaphor is honored; Milton's *Aeropagitica* and John Stuart Mill's *On Liberty* defend freedom of speech on the ground that the truth will prevail, and many of the most important cases under the First Amendment recite this position. The Framers undoubtedly believed it. As a general matter it is true. But the Constitution does not make the dominance of truth a necessary condition of freedom of speech. To say that it does would be to confuse an outcome of free speech with a necessary condition for the application of the amendment.

A power to limit speech on the ground that truth has not yet prevailed and is not likely to prevail implies the power to declare truth. At some point the government must be able to say (as Indianapolis has said): "We know what the truth is, yet a free exchange of speech has not driven out falsity, so that we must now prohibit falsity." If the government may declare the truth, why wait for the failure of speech? Under the First Amendment, however, there is no such thing as a false idea, *Gertz v. Robert Welch, Inc.*, 418 U.S. 323 . . . (1974), so the government may not restrict speech on the ground that in a free exchange truth is not yet dominant.

. . .

Employment Division, Department of Human Resources of Oregon v. Smith

88-1213; 58 U.S. LW. 4435 (1990)
United States Supreme Court

May a state prohibit an individual from ingesting an illegal drug when he does so as part of a *bona fide* religious practice? This is the question confronted by the Court here; in an opinion by Justice Scalia, the answer given is yes. Does Scalia's position constitute a return to the stark "belief/practice" distinction announced in the Mormon "polygamy" case (*Reynolds*)? What arguments does Scalia give for the Court's decision? How does he explain the very different result reached by the Court in the Amish school case (*Yoder*)? How do the dissenters respond?

Justice Scalia delivered the opinion of the Court.

This case requires us to decide whether the Free Exercise Clause of the First Amendment permits the State of Oregon to include religiously inspired peyote use within the reach of its general criminal prohibition on use of that drug, and thus permits the State to deny unemployment benefits to persons dismissed from their jobs because of such religiously inspired use. . . .

Respondents Alfred Smith and Galen Black were fired from their jobs with a private drug rehabilitation organization because they ingested peyote for sacramental purposes at a ceremony of the Native American Church, of which both are members. When respondents applied to petitioner Employment Division for unemployment compensation, they were determined to be ineligible for benefits because they had been discharged for work-related "misconduct."

. . .

The Free Exercise Clause of the First Amendment, which has been made applicable to the States by incorporation into the Fourteenth Amendment . . . , provides that "Congress shall make no law respecting an establishment of religion, or *prohibiting the free exercise thereof*. . . ." U.S. Const. Am. I (emphasis added). The free exercise of religion means, first and foremost, the right to believe and profess whatever religious doctrine one desires. . . .

But the "exercise of religion" often involves not only belief and profession but the performance of (or abstention from) physical acts: assembling with others for a worhip service, participating in sacramental use of bread and wine, proselytizing, abstaining from certain foods or certain modes of transportation. It would be true, we think (though no case of ours has involved the point), that a state would be "prohibiting the free exercise [of religion]" if it sought to ban such acts or abstentions only when they are engaged in for religious reasons, or only because of the religious belief that they display. It would doubtless be unconstitutional, for example, to ban the casting of "statues that are to be used for worship purposes," or to prohibit bowing down before a golden calf.

Respondents in the present case, however, seek to carry the meaning of "prohibiting the free exercise [of religion]" one large step further. They contend that their religious motivation for using peyote places them beyond the reach of a criminal law that is not specifically directed at their religious practice, and that is concededly constitutional as applied to those who use the drug for other reasons. They assert, in other words, that "prohibiting the free exercise [of religion]" includes requiring any individual to observe a generally applicable law that requires (or forbids) the performance of an act that his religious belief forbids (or requires). As a textual matter, we do not think the words must be given that meaning. It is no more necessary to regard the collection of a general tax, for example, as "prohibiting the free exercise [of religion]" by those citizens who believe support of organized government to be sinful, than it is to regard the same tax as "abridging the freedom . . . of the press" of those publishing companies that must pay the tax as a condition of staying in business. It is a permissible reading of the text, in the one case as in the other, to say that if prohibiting the exercise of religion (or burdening the activity of printing) is not the object of the tax but merely the incidental effect of a generally applicable and otherwise valid provision, the First Amendment has not been offended. . . .

Our decisions reveal that the latter reading is the correct one. We have never held that an individual's religious beliefs excuse him from compliance with an otherwise valid law prohibiting conduct that the State is free to regulate. On the contrary, the record of more than a century of our free exercise jurisprudence contradicts that proposition. As described succinctly by Justice Frankfurter in *Minersville School Dist. Bd. of Educ.* v. *Gobitis*, 310 U.S. 586, 594–595 (1940): "Conscientious scruples have not, in the course of the long struggle for religious toleration, relieved the individual from obedience to a general law not aimed at the promotion or restriction of religious beliefs. The mere possession of religious convictions which contradict the relevant concerns of a political society does not relieve the citizen from the discharge of political responsibilities (footnote omitted)." We first had occasion to assert that principle in *Reynolds* v. *United States*, 98 U.S. 145 (1879), where we rejected the claim that criminal laws against polygamy could not be constitutionally applied to those whose religion commanded the practice. "Laws," we said, "are made for the government of actions, and while they cannot interfere with mere religious belief and opinions, they may with practices. . . . Can a man excuse his practices to the contrary because of his religious belief? To permit this would be to make the professed doctrines of religious belief superior to the law of the land, and in effect to permit every citizen to become a law unto himself."

. . .

The only decisions in which we have held that the First Amendment bars application of a neutral, generally applicable law to religiously motivated action have involved not the Free Exercise Clause alone, but the Free Exercise Clause in conjunction with other constitutional protections, such as freedom of speech and of the press. . . .

The present case does not present such a hybrid situation, but a free exercise claim unconnected with any communicative activity or parental right. Respondents urge us to hold, quite simply, that when otherwise prohibitable conduct is accompanied by religious convictions, not only the convictions but the conduct itself must be free from governmental regulation. We have never held that, and decline to do so now. There being no contention that Oregon's drug law represents an attempt to regulate religious beliefs, the communication of religious beliefs, or the raising of one's children in those beliefs, the rule to which we have adhered ever since *Reynolds* plainly controls.

. . .

Because respondents' ingestion of peyote was prohibited under Oregon law, and because that prohibition is constitutional, Oregon may, consistent with the Free Exercise Clause, deny respondents unemployment compensation when their dismissal results from use of the drug. The decision of the Oregon Supreme Court is accordingly reversed.

It is so ordered.

. . .

Justice Blackmun, with whom Justice Brennan and Justice Marshall join, dissenting. . . .

Until today, I thought this was a settled and inviolate principle of this Court's First Amendment jurisprudence. The majority, however, perfunctorily dismisses it as a "constitutional anomaly." . . . As carefully detailed in Justice O'Connor's concurring opinion, . . . the majority is able to arrive at this view only by mischaracterizing this Court's precedents. The Court discards

leading free exercise cases such as *Cantwell* v. *Connecticut*, 310 U.S. 296 (1940), and *Wisconsin* v. *Yoder*, 406 U.S. 205 (1972), as "hybrid." . . . The Court views traditional free exercise analysis as somehow inapplicable to criminal prohibitions (as opposed to conditions on the receipt of benefits), and to state laws of general applicability (as opposed, presumably, to laws that expressly single out religious practices). . . . The Court cites cases in which, due to various exceptional circumstances, we found strict scrutiny inapposite, to hint that the Court has repudiated that standard altogether. . . . In short, it effectuates a wholesale overturning of settled law concerning the Religion Clauses of our Constitution. One hopes that the Court is aware of the consequences, and that its result is not a product of overreaction to the serious problems the country's drug crisis has generated.

This distorted view of our precedents leads the majority to conclude that strict scrutiny of a state law burdening the free exercise of religion is a "luxury" that a well-ordered society cannot afford, . . . and that the repression of minority religions is an "unavoidable consequence of democratic government." . . . I do not believe the Founders thought their dearly bought freedom from religious persecution a "luxury," but an essential element of liberty—and they could not have thought religious intolerance "unavoidable," for they drafted the Religion Clauses precisely in order to avoid that intolerance. . . .

In weighing respondents' clear interest in the free exercise of their religion against Oregon's asserted interest in enforcing its drug laws, it is important to articulate in precise terms the state interest involved. It is not the State's broad interest in fighting the critical "war on drugs" that must be weighed against respondents' claim, but the State's narrow interest in refusing to make an exception for the religious, ceremonial use of peyote. . . .

. . . Failure to reduce the competing interests to the same plane of generality tends to distort the weighing process in the State's favor. . . .

Similarly, this Court's prior decisions have not allowed a government to rely on mere speculation about potential harms, but have demanded evidentiary support for a refusal to allow a religious exception. . . .

. . . In this case, the State's justification for refusing to recognize an exception to its criminal laws for religious peyote use is entirely speculative.

The State proclaims an interest in protecting the health and safety of its citizens from the dangers of unlawful drugs. It offers, however, no evidence that the religious use of peyote has ever harmed anyone. . . .

The carefully circumscribed ritual context in which respondents used peyote is far removed from the irresponsible and unrestricted recreational use of unlawful drugs. The Native American Church's internal restrictions on, and supervision of, its members' use of peyote substantially obviate the State's health and safety concerns. . . .

Moreover, just as in *Yoder*, the values and interests of those seeking a religious exemption in this case are congruent, to a great degree, with those the State seeks to promote through its drug laws. . . .

. . . Not only does the Church's doctrine forbid nonreligious use of peyote; it also generally advocates self-reliance, familial responsibility, and abstinence from alcohol. . . .

. . . There is considerable evidence that the spiritual and social support provided by the Church has been effective in combatting the tragic effects of alcoholism on the Native American population.

. . .

Respondents believe, and their sincerity has *never* been at issue, that the peyote plant embodies their deity, and eating it is an act of worship and communion. Without peyote, they could not enact the essential ritual of their religion. . . .

If Oregon can constitutionally prosecute them for this act of worship, they, like the Amish, may be "forced to migrate to some other and more tolerant region." *Yoder*, 406 U.S., at 218. This potentially devastating impact must be viewed in light of the federal policy—reached in reaction to many years of religious persecution and intolerance—of protecting the religious freedom of Native Americans. . . .

For these reasons, I conclude that Oregon's interest in enforcing its drug laws against religious use of peyote is not sufficiently compelling to outweigh respondents' right to the free exercise of their religion. Since the State could not constitutionally enforce its criminal prohibition against respondents, the interests underlying the State's drug laws cannot justify its denial of unemployment benefits. . . .

. . . The State of Oregon cannot, consistently with the Free Exercise Clause, deny respondents unemployment benefits.

I dissent.

Suggestions for Further Reading

Brest, P., and Vandenburg, A. "Politics, Feminism, and the Constitution: The Antipornography Movement in Minneapolis," *Stanford Law Review*, Vol. 39 (1987): 607–661.

Devlin, P., *The Enforcement of Morals* (London: Oxford University Press, 1965).

Downs, D. A., *Nazis in Skokie: Freedom, Community, and the First Amendment* (Notre Dame, Ind.: University of Notre Dame Press, 1985).

Feinberg, J., *The Moral Limits of the Criminal Law*, 4 vols. (New York: Oxford University Press, 1984); esp. Vols. 1 and 2.

Gracyk, T. A., "Pornography as Representation: Aesthetic Considerations," *Journal of Aesthetic Education*, Vol. 21 (1987): 103–121.

Greenawalt, K., *Conflicts of Law and Morality* (New York: Oxford University Press, 1989).

Greenawalt, K., "O'er the Land of the Free: Flag Burning as Speech," *UCLA Law Review*, Vol. 37 (1990): 925–947.

Grey, T. C., *The Legal Enforcement of Morality* (New York: Alfred A. Knopf, 1983).

Gubar, S., and Hoff, J., *For Adult Users Only: The*

Dilemma of Violent Pornography (Bloomington: Indiana University Press, 1989).

Hart, H. L. A., *Law, Liberty, and Morality* (Stanford, Calif.: Stanford University Press, 1963).

Husak, D. N., "What Is So Special About Free Speech?" *Law and Philosophy*, Vol. 4 (1985): 1–15.

Kappeler, S., *The Pornography of Representation* (Minneapolis: University of Minnesota Press, 1986).

Lawrence, C., "If He Hollers Let Him Go: Regulating Racist Speech on Campus," *Duke Law Journal* (1990): 431–483.

Levinson, S., "Freedom of Expression in Contemporary American Constitutional Law," in P. S. Cook (Ed.), *Liberty of Expression* (Washington, D. C.: Wilson Center Press, 1990): 45–63.

Richards, D. A. J., *Sex, Drugs, Death and the Law* (Totowa, N. J.: Rowman & Littlefield, 1982).

Ryan, A. (Ed.), *The Idea of Freedom* (Oxford: Oxford University Press, 1979).

Schauer, F., *Free Speech: A Philosophical Enquiry* (Cambridge: Cambridge University Press, 1982).

Wolff, R. P., *The Poverty of Liberalism* (Boston: Beacon Press, 1968).

Chapter IV

Equality and the Law

The ideals of equality and justice are among the most powerful of those by which we purport to live. Many believe that the highest purpose of our law is to bring about justice and to treat persons equally; the central place given to these principles in the Constitution and the Declaration of Independence is testament to their importance. Yet, as with the guarantees of freedom of speech and religion, the aspiration to equality brings with it a host of profound and perplexing philosophical problems, problems pervasive in the law. Chapter Four introduces us to them.

Just what is the condition of "equality"? And can the law bring it about? The material in Section A investigates these questions, focusing on the constitutional requirement of "equal protection" and its implementation through antidiscrimination law and programs of preferential treatment or "affirmative action." What kind of equality does the Constitution guarantee? Should it tolerate any differences in treatment based on race or sex? Should it be "color-blind"? Gender-blind? The *Bakke* case frames the legal issues involved and sets up the discussion pursued by the contributors to this section.

Section B looks at discrimination based on sex and gender. What conception of sexual equality does the Constitution endorse? What forms of gender bias exist in the law? And should all distinctions based upon sex be impermissible? This section begins with the unusual claim made by the defendant in *Michael M. v. Superior Court of Sonoma County* and ends with one contributor's conception of a society of complete gender equality.

A. Constitutional Equality and Preferential Treatment

Introduction

The ultimate source and focus for the philosophically difficult legal issues regarding equality is the Fourteenth Amendment to the Constitution, and in particular, the so-called *equal protection* clause, guaranteeing that no state shall "deny to any person within its jurisdiction the equal protection of the laws." A brief discussion of the background to and subsequent development of this clause will set the stage for an understanding of the difficulties it poses.

The Fourteenth Amendment

Following the Civil War, the Congress passed a number of constitutional amendments with the aim of "reconstructing" the South and healing the union. The Thirteenth Amendment prohibited slavery and gave Congress the power to take steps to eradicate it. In response, many of the Southern states passed harsh and restrictive laws applying to blacks, curtailing their civil rights in various ways, though short of an outright return to slavery. To eliminate these "Black Codes," Congress enacted the Civil Rights Act of 1866. This act granted to newly freed blacks a small number of specifically enumerated but limited rights: to enter into contracts, to sue, to hold and convey property, to move about without threat of arrest. While the original draft language of the act apparently included a reference to general "civil rights and immunities," this was later dropped.

According to some scholars, the majority of the supporters of the 1866 act were against the idea of full political and social equality for blacks, and this may have been a factor in the passage of the Fourteenth Amendment. According to legal historian Raoul Berger, one group of legislators, concerned that the act have a proper foundation in the Constitution, proposed the Fourteenth Amendment to serve that purpose; and it was their view that the equal protection clause guaranteed to blacks no more than the few specific rights listed in the act. Other factions, however, seemingly had larger ambitions and may have intended that "equal protection of the law" be broadly read to ensure full political and social equality for blacks.

Throughout the rest of the nineteenth century and well into this one, the narrow conception of equality predominated in the courts. In 1896, in *Plessy v. Fergusen*,[1] the Supreme Court held that the segregation of blacks and whites on public transit facilities (and by implication in various other public facilities) did not violate the guarantee of equal protection, provided that such separate facilities were roughly similar; and the Court noted that many of the states that supported the Fourteenth Amendment had, for example, segregated their schools and prohibited racial intermarriage. This "separate-but-equal" doctrine prevailed until 1954 and the landmark case *Brown v. Board of Education*.[2] Finding that the practice of segregation stamped blacks with "a badge of inferiority," the Court concluded that separate but equal "is inherently unequal." Later cases prohibited racial segregation in a whole variety of public facilities and settings.

The significance for us of the history just sketched is twofold. First, it seems clearly to show that the understanding of equality now endorsed by the courts, and presumably by the great majority of Americans, moves well beyond any views reasonably attributable to the framers of the Fourteenth Amendment; they, it appears, may well have regarded *Plessy* as correctly decided and *Brown* as a misinterpretation of the amendment's language. Second, the fact of two such divergent interpretations as *Plessy* and *Brown* reveals just how flexible and open-ended the language of the equal protection clause is. If we acknowledge that the guarantee of equality may mean more than what its authors took it to mean, and if we recognize the breadth and sweep of the text itself, we are brought to the edge of a basic issue in social and political philosophy: What is equality? What conception of equality should we understand our law to endorse? Why is equality desirable?

The Concept of Equality

Why is it important to treat persons equally? Suppose that you and I are both hungry. We have both gone without food for the same length of time and for the same reasons. We are physically quite alike and both extremely weak. What gives each of us an equal claim to a piece of food? The answer given by many philosophers going back to Aristotle invokes a basic moral principle that has been thought by some to be self-evidently true: *Those who are the same in relevant respects ought to be treated the same with regard to those respects;* or, *Those similarly situated should be similarly treated.* This *formal principle of equality* reveals an important feature of the concept of equality: When we ask whether two things or two people are "equal," we must always be assumed to be asking this question relative to some aspect of the things or people that we judge to be relevant. It is not enough simply to ask "Are A and B equal?" The question makes no sense until we further specify the traits in which A and B are to be judged equal or unequal. Are A and B equal in respect of height, weight, shoe size, intelligence, bravery, moral worth? We must have in mind, in other words, the parameters within which they are to be judged similar or dissimilar, the relevant respects in which they are the same or different.

One way to understand the equal protection clause of the Constitution is as a confirmation or implementation of the formal principle of equality: The clause says that legislatures must treat similarly those who are similarly situated with respect to the purposes of the laws they pass. Once a legislature decides which persons are to be affected by a new law, for example, it must further ensure that those persons are treated equally with respect to that law.

The problem in all this, of course, is that the formal principle of equality, and the equal protection clause understood simply as a guarantee of formal equality, say nothing by themselves about which are the traits that matter. They merely lay down a requirement of fair administration, prohibiting differences in treatment among those who have already been determined to be the same in the relevant way.

Generally speaking, the law has sought to solve the problem of specifying which traits are relevant through a negative approach: Instead of trying to settle on all those ways in which, ideally, persons should be regarded as similarly situated, the law has contented itself with seeking to identify and root out those respects that should *not* matter, those traits or characteristics that do not justify differences in treatment. This approach derives support from the basic aim of the post–Civil War amendments to the Constitution: to prohibit at least some forms of discrimination against blacks; "race, color, or previous condition of servitude" are traits on which the Constitution says it is unfair or unjust to base differences in treatment. Other parts of the Constitution, and of our law generally, would add national origin, religious affiliation, and status as an illegitimate child to the list of proscribed traits. Any law that classifies persons on the basis of these traits automatically becomes "suspect" and must be subjected to "strict scrutiny" to determine if it is justified by a "compelling" interest of the state. To treat persons differently or unequally on the basis of these characteristics without such a compelling reason is to practice discrimination.

Many of us think of discrimination on the basis of race or religion as the most fundamental violation of equality; yet the concept of discrimination is not without its own difficulties. How is discrimination to be identified and remedied? When does a practice that disadvantages a particular population or group become "discriminatory"? Should antidiscrimination law be color-blind, forbidding the use of race or ethnicity in all laws, no matter how ill or well intended? And how should acts of discrimination be dealt with by the law? Should the victims of past discrimination be given some kind of favored treatment? Should a firm or other employer, shown to have discriminated in the past, be required to hire up to a fixed percentage of its work force from among members of the minority group against which it discriminated? Should it matter if the actual minority persons hired were not the individuals originally turned down for jobs? These questions are dealt with in the essay by philosopher Kent Greenawalt.

Greenawalt begins with a review of the concepts of "discrimination" and "reverse discrimination," and of the general framework of moral and ethical concepts relevant to the assessment of the rights and wrongs of antidiscrimination law. Greenawalt then turns to more specific concerns about the law's handling of racial discrimination. Greenawalt supports the general trend in antidiscrimination law of expanding the understanding of what is discriminatory and of fashioning broad remedies for it. He argues that the law should not be color-blind, but may correctly use racial criteria, for example, in redrawing school attendance zones or in instituting busing programs to achieve integration. Greenawalt also argues in favor of the principle upheld in *Griggs v. Duke Power Co.*: If an employment practice can be shown to have a disproportionate or "disparate" impact upon particular minority groups, such as blacks,

this of itself is sufficient to require the employer to justify the practice as a "business necessity."

Lastly, Greenawalt believes that requiring a government or employer found guilty of past discrimination to hire a percentage of its future workers from among the pertinent ethnic group, some of whose members were its original victims, is justifiable, since this may discourage further discrimination. Even though the new hires were not themselves denied jobs, they may nonetheless have suffered because of the general sense of discouragement and hopelessness often produced by a long-running regime of segregation and discrimination.

Further Issues

The remainder of Chapter Four pursues two specific issues relating to the law's aspiration to equality. First, is it *always* impermissible to use traits such as ethnic or national origin as factors on the basis of which to treat persons differently or unequally? This query has been sharply posed in recent years by the proliferation of "preferential treatment" or "affirmative action" policies in education and employment. Supporters argue that such programs are required by ideas of fairness and the greater social good; opponents contend that such practices disserve the ideal of equality.

Second, even if we agree that characteristics like race and ethnicity should be among the (generally) prohibited dimensions along which government must judge and compare its citizens, what other traits should be added to the list? Should sex be among these characteristics? What conception of sexual equality should be pursued by the law? And what means can permissibly be used to realize it?

Equality and Preferential Treatment

An understanding and assessment of both the moral and the legal issues raised by programs of preferential treatment or affirmative action turn on the interplay of two types of considerations: *social utility* or the overall good and *justice* (both distributive and compensatory). These terms and their relevance to the debate over preferential treatment are spelled out in the selection by Kent Greenawalt. The distinctions between act and rule utilitarianism and between distributive and compensatory justice are, as we shall see, centrally important to understanding what is at stake in the debate over affirmative action.

Though it was decided some years ago, the *Bakke* case remains a useful introduction to the legal dimensions of the preferential treatment controversy. The medical school at the University of California at Davis ran two admissions programs, one for "regular" applicants and one for "special," disadvantaged students. Sixteen of the one hundred seats in the entering class were set aside for students from the special program, which had a lower minimum grade point average requirement than the regular program. Alan Bakke was twice rejected under the regular program, though students with lower overall scores were admitted through the special program. Bakke sued the university, alleging that he was unjustifiably excluded from the medical school in violation of both the equal protection clause of the Constitution and the Civil Rights Act of 1964. The trial court agreed with Bakke but refused to order the school to admit him; this was done by the Supreme Court of California.

The United States Supreme Court split badly on the issues involved in *Bakke*, with Justice Powell emerging as the key figure. (Powell voted against "quotas" but in favor of using race as a factor in medical school admissions. Four other justices held that the Civil Rights Act, and by implication the equal protection clause, prohibits any consideration of race as a relevant factor, joining with Powell to make a majority against quotas; another four justices held that Davis-type preferential treatment programs are permissible under both the act and the Constitution, joining with Powell in asserting that consideration of race and ethnicity is allowable.) Since Powell was the key vote, our selection focuses upon his opinion.

As we saw earlier, the courts have long held that any ordinance, policy, or practice that treats a person's race as a factor relevant to how he or she is to be treated by the government must be subjected to "strict scrutiny," meaning that the law must be shown necessary to the realization of a "compelling" objective if it is to have any hope of being upheld. Justice Powell argues that such scrutiny must be applied to the Davis program, and he carefully reviews the various arguments given by Davis to support preferential treatment: to increase the representation of minority students in medical school; to "cure" societal discrimination; to better serve the health needs of the minority community. Powell rejects these as constitutionally permissible grounds for preferential treatment but argues that another purpose—to promote diversity—is legitimate and may permit the use of race as one factor among many in admissions decisions. The Constitution will not tolerate, however, policies that unduly burden the rights of particular, innocent individuals, like Bakke, simply to further the social standing of certain groups.

The *Bakke* case gives rise to larger questions of social policy and morality; these are taken up in the essays by Bernard Boxill, Lisa Newton, and Charles Murray. Two of the arguments most commonly offered in support of preferential treatment programs are based on the idea of justice. The first argument appeals to the obvious inequalities of material condition and opportunity presently existing between whites and members of certain minority groups and claims that such differences are the result of *distributive injustice,* an unequal distribution of benefits stemming from the use of race as a relevant factor in the distribution of social wealth: jobs, educational opportunities, and so forth. Preferences are therefore needed now in order to place blacks and other minorities in positions they would have had but for the discrimination, positions they would presumably have attained under conditions of fair competition.

Bernard Boxill presents a different argument. He maintains that the case for preferential treatment rests squarely on the notion of *reparation*. We must institute such programs to aid minorities, not because we want to achieve some ideal of equal opportunity but because the present condition of blacks in America is a direct result of a history of injustices committed against them by whites. It is not enough merely that whites compensate such individuals: for compensation need involve no recognition of a prior injustice. Reparation is not forward looking but backward looking: it responds to the violation of a person's right. Boxill insists that reparation, so understood, is owed by whites as a group to blacks as a group, and he endeavors in several ways to make this model plausible.

Lisa Newton invokes the concept of justice not to support but to challenge the correctness of preferential treatment. Reaching back to Aristotle,

Newton clarifies what she takes to be two understandings of justice, both political and ideal; and she attempts to show how each incorporates the idea that many of us have in mind when we speak of "equality before the law." Newton draws out the implications of this notion in an effort to demonstrate that any form of discrimination— including that involved in preferential treatment— is inconsistent with political justice. She concludes by posing two further difficulties bearing on the feasibility of preferential treatment practices: Just who or what are the groups to whom special treatment is owing? And how can it be ascertained how much special treatment is enough? Newton argues that neither question has a clear answer.

As Greenawalt makes clear in his selection, arguments based upon the notion of social utility, or overall social good, frequently complement arguments for or against preferential treatment based on considerations of justice. Utilitarian supporters of preferential treatment have urged, for example, that such programs are necessary to bring larger numbers of minorities into the professions, thereby enriching and benefiting the lives of those who participate in them. The presence of women and people of color in universities and professional schools, for example, will enhance the likelihood that important perspectives on life will not go unrepresented in the classroom. It is further claimed, as by U. C. Davis in *Bakke*, that greater numbers of minorities in medical, law, and business schools will result in improved service to minority communities currently underserved by these professions. And it is asserted that those "successful" minority persons who have been aided by preferential treatment can serve as valuable role models for young people from disadvantaged backgrounds.

Opponents of affirmative action respond that such programs will not bring about the greatest good for society as a whole. They point to the potential for resentment among those members of nonpreferred groups who, like Bakke, are passed over in favor of minority individuals; and they raise the concern that minority graduates of professional schools who are admitted with lower grade averages and test scores may not be as qualified as those passed over to dispense services that are beneficial, and sometimes vital, to society.

In his essay, contributor Charles Murray argues in yet a different way that preferential treatment is a poor social policy. Murray's thesis is that preferential treatment has spawned a "new racism." It perpetuates the view (sustained by the "old racism" and never quite eliminated) that blacks are inferiors who need help and who can never be quite as good as whites. Various social inequalities, including significant disparities in educational opportunity, mean that few blacks are as well prepared for college or careers as whites. Yet aggressive affirmative action policies demand that blacks be admitted or hired anyway, with the consequence that few if any white students or workers encounter blacks who are adequately prepared or experienced for the tasks they are called upon to perform. Moreover, the need to have a "token" black on the corporate board or in the partnership reduces blacks to the status of being valuable only *as* blacks and leads to insufficient on-the-job training and a patronizing attitude on the part of white colleagues. In these ways, preferential treatment does more harm than good.

Endnotes

[1] 163 U.S. 537 (1896).

[2] 347 U.S. 483 (1954).

Justice, Utility, and Discrimination

KENT GREENAWALT

A Brief Summary of Some Features of Law and Legal Institutions Relevant to Discrimination and Reverse Discrimination

. . . [A]n examination of legal materials on discrimination and reverse discrimination can generate considerable confusion about what is at stake in a particular case unless one has in mind some cardinal features of the American polity and judicial system. The aim here is to provide sufficient background to make clear the particular context in which various questions of discrimination arise.

A. The Federal Constitution, Congress, the State Legislatures, and Administrative Bodies

As the framework for the American system of government, the Constitution controls the powers exercised by both the federal government and the state governments. The national government has limited powers, Congress in theory being permitted to legislate only for designated subjects, such as raising armies and regulating interstate commerce. The federal government is free to spend money in any way that promotes the general welfare of citizens, but attempts to further the general welfare by other means are left to the states, which are not restricted in the scope of their powers. This is the original theory of the Constitution, but it has evolved somewhat differently. The commerce power has been so broadly interpreted that a great many things Congress wishes to do in regulating the lives of citizens can be justified as an exercise of

that power. And federal financing of state and private institutions has become so pervasive that the federal government can exercise a high degree of control by demanding that requirements be met as a condition for the receipt of federal money. Much antidiscrimination legislation has been grounded either in the commerce power or in the spending power. The federal bar on discrimination by private employers, for instance, is a regulation of commerce, and the restraint on discrimination in university hiring derives from the spending power. The third significant source of federal power to combat discrimination is found in the Thirteenth and Fourteenth amendments, which give Congress the power to enforce their provisions, including the guarantee of equal protection of the laws.

Federal administrative agencies, such as the Labor Department, are responsible for administering the laws that Congress enacts. Typically, they will prescribe much more detailed regulations and procedures than Congress has provided. These administrative regulations may help guide courts as to what Congress intended, when that is in doubt. And so long as the regulations are consistent with the statute they enforce, they become a subsidiary source of federal law, to be enforced by the courts if that becomes necessary.

Although some subjects, such as the waging of war, are of exclusive federal concern and some other subjects have been barred to the states by congressional action, congressional involvement in an area does not ordinarily preclude state legislative activity. In respect to antidiscrimination laws, state and local efforts in many northern states preceded federal legislation, and federal law in many places actually defers to enforcement by state and local authorities. For matters left open by federal statutes and regulations, state legislatures, local governments, or such specialized bodies as state universities may make decisions about desirable rules and policies. What a state may not do, however, is adopt or enforce any legislation or policy that conflicts with federal law. The federal gov-

From *Discrimination and Reverse Discrimination* (New York: Knopf, 1983), pp. 12–49. Copyright © 1983 by Alfred A. Knopf, Inc. Reprinted with permission of Alfred A. Knopf, Inc.

ernment is supreme, and if it has acted validly, any inconsistent state practices must yield.

Both federal and state government bodies are restricted in another way. They may not act in a manner that violates individual rights guaranteed by the federal Constitution. A few of these guarantees, such as a rule against retroactive criminal legislation, are found in the original Constitution; but the most significant individual rights are contained in the Bill of Rights, adopted two years later, and in the Thirteenth, Fourteenth, and Fifteenth amendments, passed after the Civil War. Although the Bill of Rights was additionally addressed only against the federal government, and the Civil War amendments were directed mainly against the states, the course of interpretation has almost entirely merged the restrictions on federal and state governments. For our purposes, we can assume that the relevant limits are identical. Because constitutional limits generally apply only against governments, private persons and institutions cannot, with few exceptions, violate the Constitution, although they may violate statutes that place similar restrictions on the private sector.

We are now in a position to understand, for example, the various challenges that can be made to a state university decision to prefer applicants for admission who are members of minority groups. It may be argued that such a policy violates a state statute or the state constitution, since a university that is an organ of the state is bound to comply with valid state constitutional and statutory law. It may be argued that the policy violates a federal statute or the equal protection clause of the Fourteenth Amendment. In *University of California Regents v. Bakke,* both of these challenges were made under federal law, and a state constitutional claim was also made.

B. The United States Supreme Court and Federal and State Courts

The United States has parallel federal and state courts; at the apex of each of these two pyramidal structures is the United States Supreme Court. Cases that involve a federal issue, such as the legitimacy under a federal statute or under the federal Constitution of admissions preferences for blacks, can begin in either a federal or a state trial court. Once the facts are determined and the trial court has reached a decision, the losing litigant may appeal the decision to an appellate court. If the case

has started in a federal district court the appeal goes to the federal court of appeals; if the case has started in a state trial court, the appeal proceeds through the state appellate system that is provided. The appellate courts must accept the facts as found by the trial court; their job is to review the legal determinations made by the trial judge. After the case has been decided by the federal court of appeals or the state supreme court, the only recourse left is to the United States Supreme Court. With some exceptions, the Supreme Court has discretion to choose the cases it wishes to hear, which it does formally by granting certiorari. It will take a case from a state court only if an issue of federal law is crucial to the decision; as far as purely state law questions are concerned, the state supreme court is the ultimate interpreter. When the Supreme Court takes a case, it then receives full written arguments, called briefs, from the lawyers in the case, as well as amicus curiae briefs (friends of the court) from other interested organizations. It also hears oral argument. Sometime later it renders its decision, typically with opinions that explain the outcome.

What the Supreme Court says about federal law is authoritative in future cases for all the lower courts, state as well as federal; and in practical terms, the Constitution means what the Supreme Court says it means. The Supreme Court treats its own prior decisions with great respect and will usually attempt to decide a new case consistently with the decisions in cases that have preceded it. But it can change its mind and overrule an earlier case, indicating that a decision is no longer authoritative. More often, it will narrow the scope of an earlier decision without rejecting it outright. Thus major constitutional issues are open to continuing reexamination, and one can never be quite sure what weight an earlier decision will carry.

"Discrimination," "Reverse Discrimination," and Related Concepts

When one deals with a sensitive topic, one must be as careful as one can about the use of related terms, since variant connotations can themselves be the source of serious misunderstanding. In one sense, "to discriminate" is merely to perceive a difference ("she can discriminate between persons of Chinese origin and those of Korean origin") or to treat differently ("in setting a regimen for practice, the coach discriminates among his players, giving each the work he needs to develop his special skills"). In these usages, no implication need be present that one person or group is treated worse than another. But in most discussions of social issues, to say that discrimination exists is to suggest that one group of people is treated worse than another. Moreover, the term usually implies that the grounds for unfavorable treatment bear no close relation to the benefit or burden involved; we are more likely to speak of an employer's discrimination against blacks or in favor of veterans than of its discrimination against stupid or clumsy people. Ordinarily, if the basis for differentiation is not closely related to the benefit, the differentiation is not justified, and the term "discrimination" often signals that negative evaluation; but to describe veterans' preferences in public employment as discrimination in favor of veterans is not necessarily to condemn the preferences.

When I use the term "discrimination" standing alone in this essay, I mean only that a difference of treatment is to the disadvantage of members of some group. I shall analyze the crucial questions—whether the disadvantage bears significant relation to the benefit or burden and whether it is unjustified—without making application of the word "discrimination" turn on my conclusion.

"Reverse discrimination" means a difference in treatment that reverses the pattern of earlier discrimination. Typically, more favorable treatment, say in admission to an academic institution or in employment, is given to members of groups that have been discriminated against in the past. Some people who support such programs object to the term "reverse discrimination" because they fear that the label will tar such programs with the assumption of unjustifiability that accompanies other practices called discrimination. In many sorts of discussions, use of a different, less freighted, vocabulary may be wise; but I hope that here, where terms are set out with some care, the reader will understand that I do not mean to smuggle in normative conclusions by referring to "reverse discrimination."

Like "discrimination," the term "preferential treatment" is usually applied when the reasons for giving persons an advantage do not relate directly to the relevant benefit or burden; one does not think of professional teams giving preferential treatment to the most skilled athletes. Because it does not carry some of the more negative connotations of "discrimination," a phrase such as "preferential treatment for minorities" may convey the nature of a program in a more neutral way than does "reverse discrimination." True reverse discrimination or preferential treatment goes beyond merely measuring qualifications by a more accurate yardstick than has traditionally been used. If, for example, it could be shown that aptitude tests consistently underpredicted the performance of blacks in universities, then it would not be reverse discrimination to discount their relevance for black applicants.

"Affirmative action" is a phrase that refers to attempts to bring members of underrepresented groups, usually groups that have suffered discrimination, into a higher degree of participation in some beneficial program. Some affirmative action efforts include preferential treatment; others do not. Publicizing the availability of jobs more broadly than had been done previously and changing hiring practices to minimize the risks of discrimination against blacks may be done without affording blacks any employment advantage.

Two other terms that often appear in discussions of reverse discrimination and affirmative action are "quotas" and "goals." They will be treated in context as the discussion proceeds.

Discrimination and Reverse Discrimination: Justice and Utility

The pattern of the rest of this essay is to weave ethical analysis with legal development. . . . Within the past two and a half decades, the movement of the law has been from resolution of the easier ethical issues concerning discrimination to the more difficult ones, so that the progressive explication of the law fits naturally with the development of ethical issues from relatively simple to more complex. Arguments about the law's intervention in matters of discrimination fall into two broad categories, arguments about consequences and deontological arguments; or, more roughly, arguments of utility and arguments of justice.

The proper place of various sorts of moral arguments is, of course, one of the central inquiries in moral philosophy. The following summarized and oversimplified account is not intended as a satisfactory treatment of that inquiry, which many students will already have undertaken in some depth. For them, these passages can serve as a reminder of the way in which the broader theoretical issues bear on social problems of responding to unjustified discrimination. For the readers for whom these theoretical issues are new, this discussion can highlight the way in which perplexities over a practical social question can lead one to examine much more general doubts about the appropriate standards of human action.

A. Consequences and Utility

The moral significance of likely consequences is a long-debated issue. Some thinkers have asserted that when people say X is right, what they *mean* is simply that X will be more conducive to desirable consequences than any alternative. These thinkers also claim that the desirability of consequences is the final test of whether an act is immoral or moral. Other thinkers join them in this second claim, without believing that the standard of consequences is necessarily what is meant when people speak of right or wrong. Thinkers who accept this second proposition, whether or not they accept the first, may be called consequentialists, or utilitarians.

In the utilitarian philosophy developed by Beccaria and Bentham, a cardinal tenet was that the ultimate standard of good consequences is the greatest happiness of the greatest number. But utilitarianism is now often understood in a broader sense. Thus one who believes that the spread of knowledge and the maximum development of human faculties are desirable consequences, quite apart from whether or not they contribute to happiness, could be a "utilitarian" in this sense, although his theory would depart from Bentham's in a fundamental respect. I follow that usage rather than employing the less familiar word "consequentialist."

The modern disagreement between act-utilitarians and rule-utilitarians is important for our purposes and requires brief explication. An act-utilitarian believes that the criterion for evaluating any particular act is whether the consequences of that act will be beneficial or harmful. A rule-utilitarian says that the criterion is whether the act conforms to a standard or rule that, if followed generally, would lead to desirable consequences. Thus the act-utilitarian would ask if a particular lie will have desirable consequences; the rule-utilitarian would inquire whether lies, or this sort of lie, would generally have good consequences. This way of putting the distinction makes it more stark than it is likely to be in practice. A sophisticated act-utilitarian will take into account for any given act the desirable consequences of stability from following a settled rule and the consequences of example for future actors. Thus an act-utilitarian might oppose euthanasia in even the most appealing cases on the ground that the example of killing innocent persons in such circumstances poses too great a danger of diminishing respect for life generally. A sophisticated rule-utilitarian, on the other hand, must sensibly admit some qualifications to simple rules. He may say lying is wrong, *unless* the lie prevents physical harm to innocent people (as in the example of the prospective killer looking for a gun) or saves someone from unproductive emotional trauma (a terminally ill person clearly unequipped to deal with the prospect of imminent death asks if he will get better), etc. As the rules of the rule-utilitarian become more and more refined, there is less and less to distinguish him or her from the act-utilitarian.

Whichever approach is more sound from the standpoint of moral philosophy, when legislators and judges take a utilitarian perspective regarding the establishment and interpretation of legal rules, they usually function like rule-utilitarians, asking whether the rule they make or employ will have generally desirable consequences.

B. Deontology and Justice

A deontological theory of ethics asserts that some practices are to be done or avoided for their own sakes, independent of the consequences they produce. Thus a lie, or some subclass of lies, may be regarded as wrong even if likely to promote happiness or other desirable results. A person who concludes that some acts are intrinsically wrong may still have to choose between an approach that is consequentialist in a sense and one that is not. He or she may face an occasion in which the commission of one intrinsically wrong act will reduce the total number of intrinsically wrong acts—as, for example, when the telling of one lie will prevent the telling of more lies. Then the person will have to decide whether his or her moral responsibility is to tell the truth in this instance or to promote truth-telling. Those who approach ethics from a deontological perspective have typically focused on the individual's duty not to commit inherently wrongful acts; but one might count as morally relevant the contribution of one's action toward the moral quality of subsequent acts by oneself or others.

Whether or not one believes that acts can be intrinsically wrongful independent of their potential to produce beneficial results, one may think that the pursuit of desirable consequences must be constrained by distributive principles; that, for example, a distribution that is more equal or in which benefits are more closely correlated to moral desert is to be preferred to a distribution that includes a higher total of beneficial consequences but is less equal or correlates benefits less closely to moral desert.

Nonutilitarian arguments about government intervention to stop discrimination, and about reverse discrimination, can, with a little stretching, all be classed as arguments of justice. Either they are arguments about the distribution of benefits and burdens, in which event, as explained below, they obviously concern justice; or they are arguments about rights the government should accept or support. Although usage here may be a little less clear, government violations of moral rights, and government failures to support moral rights that it should support, constitute forms of injustice.

The two notions of justice that have most obvious application to problems of reverse discrimination are distributive justice and compensatory justice. Since the time of Aristotle, the idea of distributive justice has been held to require that equals be treated equally and unequals unequally. This principle precludes arbitrary distinctions based on irrelevant characteristics. More broadly, we might say that members of society should have a fair share of the benefits and burdens of a social order. Neither the notion that equals should be treated equally nor the notion of a fair share gets us very far by itself. We must know by what criteria people are to be judged equal or unequal and also decide what will count as equality of benefit or burden. Suppose two berry pickers work equally hard but one is able to pick twice as many berries as the other. Should he be paid twice as much or the same amount? If one person requires $100 a week for medical care to keep in excellent health and

another requires an expensive machine costing $200 per week even to stay alive, are they being treated equally or unequally if each gets a check for $100 each week? To fill in the formula about equals being treated equally or about a fair share, we require a rather complete account of the qualities that should matter, and how much each should matter, in respect to a wide range of benefits and burdens. And if we are talking about treatment by the government, we also require a philosophy about the proper extent of government involvement in the private order. For one alternative almost always is for the government to leave as is whatever private ordering occurs. For example, as far as the berry pickers are concerned, the government may simply leave wages to be determined by the private employer.

Reaching agreement on all the qualities that should count is typically much more difficult than reaching agreement on some qualities that should not count, and here the formulas of distributive justice can be helpful. Suppose it is agreed that for the distribution of civic benefits and burdens, such as government jobs and taxes, one's religion should not be relevant. We are then in a position to say that no one should suffer in competition for a job or have to pay higher taxes because of his or her religion. This is the sort of position that is commonly asserted not only about religion, but also about race, national or ethnic origin, and increasingly, gender.

Someone is being denied distributive justice when he or she loses a benefit because of an irrelevant characteristic. In the clearest instance, this occurs at the moment an arbitrary choice is made. But the claim can be somewhat more complex. It may be that because of decisions on the basis of irrelevant characteristics at an earlier stage, a person has been deprived of the opportunity to acquire traits that are relevant to receipt of the benefit. Highly developed writing and analytical skills are, for example, valuable for lawyers. Organizations hiring lawyers and law schools choosing students understandably care whether applicants possess these skills. Let us suppose that a group in society has been systematically and unjustifiably denied the chance to develop these skills and that, therefore, opportunities in law, which carry substantial income, prestige, and power, are not available to members of that group. Even if it were true that no law school and no employers of lawyers discriminated on arbitrary grounds, nevertheless members of the group in question might say their inability to become lawyers represents a denial of distributive justice. The assertion would seem especially powerful if they were blocked from other positions of power and wealth for the same reasons. If persons have thus far suffered disabilities because of distributive injustice, they have a claim of distributive justice to be given the share that they would have had but for the original wrong.

The second concept of justice that is important to us is compensatory justice. The notion here is that if one is unjustly deprived of something one rightfully possesses, one should be paid back. In the simple case, A steals B's bicycle. Principles of compensatory justice require A to return the bicycle to B, or if the bike is no longer around, to give B enough money to buy a replacement. Persons who have suffered because they have been wrongly treated on the basis of some arbitrary characteristic may claim that those who wronged them should pay them back for the harm done. To a substantial extent, the demands of compensatory justice will coincide with demands of distributive justice: that people be placed in positions they would have obtained in the absence of original wrongs. But the principle of compensatory justice may go further. Suppose Adam is a shiftless man of thirty years who has never worked and does not plan to. He barely survives on welfare. The local sheriff knowingly "frames" him for a theft, and as a consequence, Adam goes for five years to prison, where he is miserable. As soon as he is out, he returns to his previous existence. As far as distributive justice is concerned, he *now* has no complaint concerning the sheriff's behavior. Although Adam undoubtedly had a complaint of distributive injustice while in prison (i.e., he was being made to suffer harm he did not deserve), he would now be, we are assuming, penniless and living on welfare whether or not he had been framed. But Adam does still have a claim of compensatory justice against the sheriff; he wants to be paid back for the hellish existence and loss of liberty that he has had to endure for five years.

I have suggested that a third concept of justice is that moral rights be adequately recognized by the government. Restrictions on private discrimination may be said, for example, to violate the basic rights of liberty and property of persons who choose to discriminate. On the other hand, discrimination of many kinds may be thought to offend a moral right to compete for benefits on the basis of one's relevant skills. Such a right would be directly violated by governmental discrimination; governmental inaction against private discrimination might be considered an unjust failure to support the moral right to compete that private individuals have against other private individuals and enterprises. This particular claimed right could also be interposed against remedies for past discrimination that include preferential treatment for members of groups previously victimized. A frequent part of discussions of discrimination is a claimed right to adequate or equal opportunity. What is often meant is something more than a fair chance to compete on the basis of one's present skills; namely, a claim that the government should afford minimally satisfactory, or equal, opportunities to develop talents and skills. Such claims may be understood as one point of view about what distributive justice requires in respect to opportunity— opportunity being a special kind of benefit that a society may distribute in various ways. In instances of reverse discrimination, both sides can present arguments based on equal opportunity. Members of previously harmed groups may say that present preferences help make up for earlier deprivations; those who lose a benefit because of a preferential program may say they are being presently denied equal opportunity.

Yet another notion of justice, procedural justice, is very important in the law and bears on problems of discrimination and reverse discrimination. Most straightforwardly, once it is determined what characteristics are to count as relevant for distributions of burdens and benefits and what sorts of injuries warrant compensation, then a fair way of determining who qualifies is required if these accepted principles of justice are to be realized in practice. The relationship between procedure and substantive principle is more complicated, however. "Ideal" substantive principles may have to be tempered to some degree in the interest of having standards that can be applied fairly and at acceptable expense.

It may also be thought that justice requires a fair input into social decisions about how benefits will be allocated. Since we know that political decision makers are often not disinterested and are responsive to pressures, and since we know also that various decisions about distribution will affect people differently, we can conclude that if members of a group are unfairly represented in the political process, the chances that their claims of justice will be disregarded are increased. In practical terms, the realization of other aspects of justice depends heavily on a degree of political justice.

C. Utility and Justice

How do considerations of justice relate to utility? At least three possibilities suggest themselves. The first is that all proper considerations of justice are reducible to utilitarian benefits. The second is that principles of justice set "side constraints" on the pursuit of utilitarian objectives. The third is that when principles of justice conflict with utilitarian considerations, the decision maker must resolve on some ad hoc basis which principles are to be satisfied. A utilitarian might say that the way to fill out the formulas of justice is to ask what criteria of initial distribution will promote the most desirable consequences for members of society, and what standards of compensation will reduce insecurity and unhappiness for those who suffer loss and will deter those tempted to take things from others. For the utilitarian, principles of justice would be merely useful subcategories of more general principles of utility.

We can, however, conjure up some instances in which utility would not seem to be served by adhering to principles of justice. Suppose it could be shown that in families, all members are happier and psychologically healthier if there is a clear hierarchy that eliminates any competitive wrangling among supposed equals. Imagine twins identical in every respect except a small birthmark on one that allows the parents to tell them apart. Should the parents arbitrarily choose one and raise him to a higher status over the other? Calculations of utility would suggest doing so, but distributive justice would appear to be violated. Perhaps a similar, and certainly more realistic, example concerns doing experimentation in which otherwise similar patients are intentionally treated differently. Is any principle of justice violated when some patients receive probably valuable medicine and others get a placebo—a practice that in the long run helps develop the best possible medicines and saves lives? Compensatory justice may not serve utility when we know that the only compensation available will be misused. Suppose Adam, the jobless man framed and put in jail, will, if he receives monetary compensation from the sheriff, waste it

on drink, which makes him miserable; further suppose that the sheriff has undergone a reformation and now donates all his money except modest living expenses to worthwhile charities. Adam deserves compensation under principles of justice but his getting it will disserve utility. The rigorous act-utilitarian must say that if principles of justice, or other claimed principles of moral right, actually conflict with the aim of achieving the most desirable consequences (and this conflict is obvious to those making the choice), the principles must yield.

A rule-utilitarian may urge that the *rules* of compensatory and distributive justice do serve utility, and that isolated exceptions are beside the point. Perhaps he or she would recognize some rulelike exception that covers experimentation, in which the practice of treating equals unequally is at the heart of the method.

A position that straddles between the typical utilitarian and deontological views is one in which what philosophers should judge to be the most adequate set of moral standards is the set whose acceptance will produce the most desirable consequences, that set turning out to be largely nonutilitarian because societies will actually achieve the best consequences if their members adopt some other set of standards. The person who adopts such a stance shares with the utilitarian the ultimate criterion for judging moral practices, but he or she rejects the utilitarian's view about how actual people should approach moral problems and evaluate social institutions.

If one concludes that valid claims of justice have a weight that is not reducible to utilitarian considerations, one must decide how conflicts between justice and utility are to be resolved. Some people believe that a true claim of justice must take priority; that desirable consequences may be pursued only if no injustice is done. Others believe that utility can override valid claims of justice if the consequential considerations are powerful enough. As the earlier discussion of deontological standards indicates, the issue about consequences can arise even if one focuses on justice alone. One might believe that doing justice for some present victims of injustice will actually reduce the possibilities for justice in the future, by, for example, creating such resentment among those who have to pay the price that they will be disposed to inflict new wrongs on the original victims or on others. Should one perceive such a conflict, one would have to choose between doing justice and promoting justice.

As you address the problems of discrimination and reverse discrimination, you will want to consider carefully whether you think claims of justice carry weight independent of the likely consequences of recognizing them, and if so, how conflicts between doing justice in the present and promoting desirable consequences (possibly including encouraging justice in the future) should be resolved. Your decisions on these points may or may not affect your view of the circumstances, if any, in which discrimination and reverse discrimination are warranted.

Whatever their ultimate moral significance, certain principles of justice are commonly dealt with by legislators and judges, who usually will not try to work out systematically the social consequences of following them. For the legislator, the explanation may be that the principles are widely accepted or simply that they appear to be of obvious moral weight. For the judge, the principles may be deeply reflected in the legal materials with which he or she works, and the judge may accept them as authoritative without reflecting on whether their pursuit will in particular instances promote a better society. There is even some question whether such reflections are the judge's business. Some scholars believe that in every case, the judge's duty is simply to decide in which direction the existing legal materials point; that the side that would win on this basis has an institutionalized *right* to a decision in its favor. In this view, general weighings of considerations of social advantage are to be left to the legislature. The competing view is that at least in very close cases, for which the legal materials produce no clear answer, a judge does appropriately take into account the same sorts of considerations of social policy that influence legislators. Since proponents of the "rights thesis" acknowledge that some legal standards do direct judges to make decisions about social desirability and moral acceptability, and since proponents of the view that judges appropriately weigh considerations of policy and morality agree that the legal standards often preclude such inquiry in particular cases, the theoretical disagreement, in practical terms, seems to come down to how often such matters may be taken into account. Such questions about the appropriate role of judges lurk in the background of many lawsuits over discrimination and reverse discrimination. In any event, the main point here is that even if concepts of justice are largely reducible to utilitarian considerations, it may be that for judges, these concepts should often be taken as givens of the legal system not demanding further justification.

. . .

We shall proceed in a moment to the more perplexing problem of the remedies for school segregation, but we may note that a fixed principle for discussions of reverse discrimination is the immorality and unconstitutionality of racial separation that occurs at the behest of the majority and dominant group of whites and systematically suppresses the opportunities in life of members of a minority.

State denial of benefits, such as jobs, to members of a racial minority is even more obviously improper, morally and constitutionally, because in that situation there is not even the veneer of equal treatment which the "separate but equal" formula for segregated facilities suggests. Yet such denials are not wholly without conceivable justification. Apart from the argument that racial harmony will be promoted by excluding blacks from certain jobs, a claim just considered in regard to school segregation, it might be said that a significant correlation exists between racial identity and performance in the relevant position, and that since most blacks will perform less well than most whites, it makes sense to choose whites. Such a justification strikes us now as hollow and hypocritical; but if we take the claim more seriously than it may deserve, we can learn something about our moral judgments concerning discrimination. Initially, we would be skeptical that the claimed correlation exists; but even if it were proven, the conclusion that whites should be chosen would not follow. The state can engage in a more careful evaluation of individual qualifications. If it were urged that picking whites is more convenient, we might respond that disqualifying people because of immutable characteristics such as race cannot be justified on the basis of administrative ease. Suppose the proponent of such a policy challenged us to explain whether we would accept choosing people on the basis of intelligence if the correlation to performance were no greater than in respect to race and the difficulty of making more individualized assessments of capacity the same. We might of course say no, that intelligence alone should never be used as a basis for choosing people unless the correlation between measured general intelligence and actual performance is very high. But we might also distinguish intelligence from race. Testable intelligence is not a wholly immutable characteristic; people can make themselves more intelligent. More important, if blacks generally perform less well than whites, we strongly suspect that the historical reason is the cruel suppression of blacks by government and society. To exclude all blacks, some of whom may be perfectly able to perform, because the level of performance of most blacks has been lowered by past unjust discrimination seems obviously unfair. Finally, when blacks have been denied job opportunities, these denials have not been isolated incidents in respect to particular jobs, they have been part of a pattern of system-wide discrimination against a clearly identifiable segment of society that has a powerful sense of group consciousness. Such discrimination perpetuates notions of class inferiority and racism, and forecloses opportunities for advancement for future generations. Whatever marginal gains in administrative ease might be achieved by excluding blacks could not possibly justify that practice.

Does this analysis lead to the conclusion that whenever a state imposes substantial disadvantages only on a minority group, its actions are unjustified? Not necessarily. If a grave threat is posed by some members of a minority and authorities are genuinely unable to determine which persons these are, perhaps they may take preventive steps against all members of the group. So at least thought the Supreme Court when, during World War II, it sustained a curfew on the West Coast for all people of Japanese ancestry and then approved the much more drastic step of their exclusion from the area. . . . Many, including myself, believe that the showing of danger of espionage and sabotage was much too weak to warrant such treatment of American citizens of Japanese descent; but the situation illustrates the possible conflict of considerations of general welfare on the one hand and the claims to equal treatment and recognition of rights of one part of the community on the other. If someone believes that such treatment of minorities can ever be justified, he or she must acknowledge that very pressing utilitarian needs can override what would otherwise be the unchallengeable demands of justice.

. . .

Remedies for Specific and Illegal Past Discrimination and the Problem of de Facto Segregation

I come now to the question of remedies for discrimination that [violate] the Constitution or statutes, discussing also the thorny problems of whether discrimination can occur that is not intentional, and voluntary efforts to integrate schools. I spend as much time as I do on these subjects because of their close relationship to what are thought of as typical instances of reverse discrimination, which is, after all, usually conceived of as a broadly directed attempt to remedy discrimination. More particularly, classification by race or sex is often used to remedy specific violations of law, and racial criteria may be used to counteract de facto segregation. Further, a point that is often overlooked, claims of justification that are central to reverse discrimination may be required to support certain remedies for clear violations of law or uncompelled efforts to integrate schools. One who is trying to develop a coherent approach to the ethical and legal problems of reverse discrimination must, therefore, come to terms with the ethical and legal problems that accompany remedies for specific breaches of law and decisions on how to respond to de facto segregation.

A. Racial Segregation

For too many years, *Brown v. Board of Education* was simply disregarded altogether by most southern school districts, although the Supreme Court's opinion on implementation had approved only brief delay. . . . Inaction represented a kind of accommodation to public resistance in the South, but unfortunately it contributed to that resistance by encouraging some people to believe that the day of reckoning could be indefinitely postponed. Even in those districts where remedies were applied, they were rather halting, allowing students to transfer to schools of their choice and producing little real change in segregated school systems. Approximately a decade after *Brown*, the Supreme Court made it clear that effective integration of a school system was the only acceptable remedy for school segregation, and that effective integration meant racially mixed schools, to be achieved by redesigning school zones or by busing if that was necessary to accomplish the goal.

If we are to ask whether this remedial requirement is ethically and constitutionally defensible, it helps to consider first what has come to be called de facto segregation. In many northern cities, the school system has not been administered with a segregative purpose, or at least no such purpose has been provable in court. Yet because of housing patterns, school attendance zones drawn by geographical area produce schools whose students are entirely or almost entirely of one race. Typically, past government action of various sorts may have contributed to the housing patterns; but such patterns are mostly the product of private discrimination, and in any event, school administrators are not to blame for them.

What are the responsibilities of the school officials in such a setting? Part of the legal answer is that according to the Supreme Court, the Constitution has not been violated unless there has been intentional discrimination; and courts have generally declined to require school boards to remedy the indirect effect of housing patterns for which other government bodies may have borne some responsibility. So school boards are not constitutionally required to do anything about de facto segregation, even if action by other government agencies has helped cause that segregation. But a few school districts have thought that even in the absence of prior discrimination more integrated schools would be desirable, and they have voluntarily taken steps in that direction, sometimes using racial categorizations of pupils for purposes of school assignment. In some states it is, or was, part of the general policy of the state education department that school districts should try to achieve "racial balance."

What is the ethical status of these attempts? We should first draw a distinction. One way of integrating schools is by redrawing or combining attendance zones. A line between zones is redrawn to bring more whites into a school that was previously mostly black and to bring more blacks into a school that was previously mostly white. Or, say, in the instance of two elementary schools, zones are combined so that all children go to grades 1–3 at one school and grades 4–6 at the other school. When administrators redraw lines and combine zones, they will have the racial composition of the neighborhoods in mind, and to that extent, they are not acting in a color-blind way; but no individual pupil is assigned to a particular school because of his or her race. Busing programs are typically race-conscious in a stronger sense. Suppose one school is 90 percent white and 10 percent black, and another is 90 percent black and 10 percent white. Only white students will be bused from the "white" school to the "black" one, and only black students will be bused in the other direction. Thus the treatment of these individual students is determined by their race. Because this practice comes much closer to reverse discrimination, we shall consider attempts to achieve racial balance in this most controversial form.

A busing program is, of course, likely to involve some extra degree of inconvenience for pupils who are sent away from their neighborhoods. For this reason and perhaps others—such as the possible benefits of having school friends who can be playmates away from school—deviations from the idea of neighborhood schools involve costs, and at some point these costs will become so great they will outweigh possible benefits. No one, for example, has suggested busing small children two hours each way in order to achieve integration. But the fundamental moral question is most sharply posed if we imagine a program that is relatively cost-free in these terms.

Against such a program, it may be said that the district is distinguishing pupils on the arbitrary ground of race. One pupil is sent to school A because he is black; another pupil, alike in every relevant respect except for his whiteness, is sent to school B. Assuming that the white pupil is dissatisfied with his assignment, he may argue that he is being denied what he or his parents consider a benefit on no ground other than his race, and that this practice both directly violates principles of distributive justice and involves the state in perpetuating distinctions based on race.

In favor of the program, it may be said that blacks will benefit from being educated in a setting where they encounter whites, who make up by far the largest racial group in society. Indeed, if the Court was right in *Brown v. Board of Education* that blacks do not learn as effectively in segregated schools, blacks in schools that are segregated de facto may suffer about as much as those segregated by the design of school authorities. Moreover, it is desirable for whites also to learn in an integrated setting, since they should realize early in their lives that they live in a multiracial society. There is a twofold response to the claim of the white pupil that he is being denied a benefit on the basis of the arbitrary characteristic of race. First, it may be said that since he is being sent to a school of comparable quality and receiving what the school board regards as the value of an integrated education, he is not, whatever his own perceptions may be, being denied a significant benefit. Even if the quality of schooling is by some standard less good than in his neighborhood school, he may have no special claim to receive schooling of that quality. Second, it can be argued that because the arbitrary characteristic of race has played such a crucial role in our society, persons, black and white, now think largely in racial terms; and the only way to ameliorate the effects of centuries of unjust treatment of members of minority races and to moderate the possibility of future discrimination is now to recognize race temporarily to achieve racially mixed education and contribute to a truly integrated society.

You will have to decide for yourself which position you find more compelling. My own view is that, assuming a race-conscious classification can accomplish integrated schools without great cost and that other techniques will not be effective, the use of such classification is justified. In *Swann v. Charlotte-Mecklenburg Board of Education* [402 U.S. 1(1971)], a case not actually presenting this issue, the entire membership of the Supreme Court indicated that as far as the Constitution is concerned a school board can, if it chooses, use racial categorizations to integrate schools that are segregated de facto. Thus the Constitution neither requires nor forbids race-conscious programs to correct de facto segregation and promote integration.

It is time now to return to the remedies for de jure segregation. The Supreme Court, in the *Swann* opinion, insisted that districts previously segregated de jure—whether by law or by the actions of school officials—must be genuinely integrated by whatever steps are required, including busing if necessary. The practical effect of this ruling is that southern school districts, and the many northern districts found to have engaged in de jure segregation, must attain a degree of integration considerably greater than that which exists in most northern cities and greater than would have existed had the district never had segregated schools. We can assume that housing patterns alone would have produced a good bit of racial division in southern schools as well as northern ones. But southern districts are not permitted now simply to draw school assignments on geographical nonracial

lines, as may most northern districts; they must actually accomplish integration. Not surprisingly, the scope of the remedies for prior segregation, typically requiring race-conscious action, has caused some people to think the respective treatment of de jure and de facto segregation is itself unjust.

If we believe that race-conscious action is warranted to correct de facto segregation, we will not object to its use to cure de jure segregation, although we may still question whether a court should demand it. But whatever our views about de facto segregation, there are strong reasons supporting the Supreme Court's position on de jure systems. We know that housing patterns would have produced some segregation of southern schools regardless of school policies, but how much? That is the rub. Actual housing patterns are, of course, linked to the historical locations of segregated schools, so there is no way of knowing what the housing patterns would now be if schools had been integrated. A court is simply not in a position to say how far de facto segregation would have occurred in any event. So it imposes a remedy that will do as much as is feasible to correct segregation caused by the actions of school authorities. An order of as full integration as seems practical is the only remedy that can assuredly be said to do so.

B. Employment Discrimination

The remedies in employment discrimination cases raise more directly the central issues of reverse discrimination. The Supreme Court has interpreted the federal statute . . . to bar the use of tests for employment that have a disproportionate impact on a minority group unless they are justified by "business necessity." Say, for example, an employer has used a general aptitude test to screen for all jobs in his firm, and blacks tend to do worse on the test than whites. If an applicant's test results have little bearing on his or her ability to perform a certain job, then as to that job, the employer has "discriminated" against blacks under the meaning of the statute, whether or not that was the intention. In order to comply with the statute, employers thus have a burden that goes beyond refraining from intentional discrimination. If they use tests to screen for employment or promotions, they must first ascertain whether there is any disproportionate impact; whether certain groups—for example, blacks, women, or Catholics—score worse on the tests than do other groups and are, therefore, disproportionately excluded from the positions in question. If there is a disproportionate impact, the employer must determine if the test serves "business necessity," that is, if there is a demonstrable correlation between performance on the test and performance on the job. If there is such a correlation, continued use of the test is acceptable, the theory being that the group whose members score less well on the test really has fewer members qualified for the position. If the test does not serve business necessity, the employer must stop relying on it, its use being viewed as an indirect way of excluding members of a group from jobs for which they may well be qualified.

Assuming that the law properly forbids intentional discrimination in employment, is this disproportionate impact[/]business necessity standard also proper? If what were involved were criminal penalties, penalizing an employer for guessing wrong about whether a test serves business necessity might be thought unfair. But that problem is much less significant when only civil remedies are involved. If the sole standard for administration of the statute were intentional discrimination, many employers who used tests intentionally as a method to discriminate would go undetected, for it would be hard to prove an employer's bad motive for using a test neutral on its face. Other powerful reasons support attacking the tests. The poor performance of blacks on many tests is largely the product of previous educational disadvantage, much of it caused by intentional discrimination. Part of the purpose of fair employment laws is to avoid perpetuation of prior discrimination and to bring disadvantaged groups more nearly into the mainstream of the economy. These aims warrant the prohibition of tests that hurt members of disadvantaged groups and serve no real need of the employers. Since employers must decide what tests to use, they may fairly bear the burden of ensuring that tests with a disproportionate impact are genuinely needed. The point is not so much that employers who intend no discrimination are necessarily to blame for using improper tests, although they might be accused of insufficient sensitivity to a social problem; rather, their slight interest in choosing methods of screening is required to give way to the broader need for equal opportunity.

When courts have determined that employers have discriminated, either intentionally or by the use of unjustified tests, they have not ordered employers to fire existing white employees; but they have sometimes, in addition to other remedies, required that in the future a certain percentage of the group discriminated against be hired and that identifiable victims of discrimination be put, when possible, in the position they would have had but for discrimination. Thus a black employee improperly denied seniority may be placed on the seniority scale in the position that he or she would have had but for being a victim of discrimination.

Each of these remedies incorporates the possibility that the best-qualified applicant for a position at a particular point in time will not get the job. Does that applicant have a good argument that he or she is being unjustly treated? (I assume here and throughout the following discussion that the original discrimination was intentional. You may want to consider how far the analysis holds for unintentional discrimination.)

Let us first take the narrowest remedy: only blacks who earlier applied and would have gotten the job had there not been illegal discrimination are now given jobs; and a white who is better qualified than some of those blacks is denied a job. Each black who is given a job is put in no better a position than he or she would have been in had the employer acted correctly in the first place. Such treatment seems minimally appropriate compensation for the original wrong (perhaps the employer should also pay him back something for the years when he did not have the job), and distributive justice may also call for a person to occupy the position he or she would have occupied had no wrong to him or her been done. Whatever the strength of a general claim to be considered on the basis of one's qualifications, it does not override the claim for redress for past wrongs by the employer. Employers must take care of such wrongs before they can be viewed as having positions open to new applicants.

Still, the present white applicant appears to be an innocent victim of the employer's original wrong. The beneficiary is another white, the white who was earlier hired because of discrimination; but by now this employee may be an experienced and skilled worker who has built up strong expectations based on years at the job. Firing that worker to satisfy the claim of justice of the new white applicant would defeat his or her own claim of justice not to have reasonably formed expectations frustrated; and from the utilitarian perspective it would be highly undesirable both to productivity and to psychological security to replace such experienced workers with novices. (Indeed if he or she could now compete freshly for the job, the experienced worker might well be the best qualified; or would his or her qualifications have to be disregarded because earned as a result of the employer's original discrimination?) However one approaches the issue, the possible claims of the well-qualified white applicant seem weaker than the claims of the victims of discrimination and of those presently employed.

Note that when remedies are given only to the very persons who suffered illegal discrimination, reverse discrimination by race is not really involved. These people are now favored only because a denial of their rights has been established, not (except indirectly) because they are black.

The analysis becomes more complicated, and the conclusion less clear, if the remedy requires an employer to hire or advance a certain percentage of blacks, plainly benefiting some blacks who were not previously victimized by this employer. To respond to the question whether excluded white applicants have a legitimate claim that they are not being accorded distributive justice, we need to consider what purposes an order to hire a specific percentage of blacks might serve. First, the percentage requirement may be the most accurate way of redressing the wrongs of those who suffered from the employer's past discrimination. Often blacks will not even have bothered to apply to employers who were known to refuse to hire blacks; their claim to compensatory and distributive justice hardly seems weaker than that of the unsuccessful applicant, if it is a fact that they would have applied and been chosen had there been no discrimination. Once the class of victims is broadened in this way, the impossibility of designating each one accurately is plain. Many of those who seek a job may well be among those who previously failed to apply because of discrimination. Forcing the employer to hire a set percentage of blacks makes it more likely that those who suffered will be hired, without their having to face competition with all present applicants.

Second, a set percentage may constitute a guarantee against continued discrimination. Identifying intentional discrimination is not always easy, especially in respect to jobs that require complex qualifications. If an employer has been proved to have discriminated, it may be prudent to estab-

lish objective goals in hiring that will effectively preclude further discrimination against the same group. Of course, such goals *may* be an unnecessary or unwise way to try to stop discrimination; but if they are the best society can do to ensure nondiscrimination, a "best-qualified" white who happens on one occasion to lose out does not have a well-founded objection, since any alternative scheme will do a worse job overall of choosing the best qualified.

Third, the effects of prior discrimination may not have exhausted themselves. Awareness of jobs is often by word-of-mouth, and hiring is frequently affected by the recommendations of present employees. If most employees are now white because of prior discrimination, these influences may serve to diminish the chances of blacks for jobs, even if the employer ceases to discriminate. These concerns may be met to a degree by minimizing the role of employee recommendations in hiring decisions and by widely publicizing available jobs; but the requirement to hire a specified percentage may arguably be a way to ensure that the lingering influences of past discrimination do not defeat fair employment opportunity in the present. Whether any particular percentage really satisfies these purposes will be questionable; but if the order to hire a percentage of minority employees is actually necessary to accomplish them, it seems a legitimate corrective of past discrimination and a safeguard against future wrongdoing. It is a form of reverse discrimination, because persons are favored on the basis of their membership in a minority group; but it is covered by the same corrective justification that applies most clearly when the individual victim of discrimination is preferred.

Suppose the percentage of minority group members to be hired is justified on a different theory: that the minority group should have the proportion of persons in the work force that it would have had if there had never been discrimination. We shall consider here a police force whose discrimination was unconstitutional even before any fair employment statutes were passed. Imagine that there has been systematic discrimination against black applicants for a period of thirty years and that, as a consequence, 5 percent of the police force is black instead of 25 percent. Suppose the court orders that half of those hired must be black until the representation of blacks on the force has reached 25 percent. Since only relatively recent black victims of past discrimination will actually now be qualified and interested in becoming police officers, a job that attracts young persons, the percentage of blacks to be hired appears too high even for the combined purposes of correcting past discrimination for actual victims of that discrimination and ensuring future nondiscriminatory hiring free of the effects of prior discrimination. One justification that might be offered is that since blacks as a group suffered discrimination, the remedy properly applies to blacks as a group. As stated, this justification appears to be based on fallacious reasoning. Because some blacks at an earlier period were victimized by discrimination is not a good reason to grant undeserved benefits to other blacks at a later period simply because they are black. The justification could become plausible only if some greater connection were asserted between the blacks who lost out and the blacks who now benefit. A second possible justification is that the community needs a police force that is 25 percent black. It might be urged, for example, that black citizens will respond better to black officers and will respect the force as a whole more if they see a reasonable proportion of black police. Each of these general justifications is also advanced for reverse discrimination that does not respond to specific violations; and they will be discussed more fully in that context. The important point to note here, however, is that unless some version of the group redress justification is persuasive, the hypothetical remedy goes beyond what can legitimately be considered corrective of previous discrimination; and unless either that or the desirable proportion justification holds, the white applicant's claim that he or she has been unjustly deprived of a benefit because the remedy exceeds the scope of the violation appears to be valid.

Broader Efforts to Stop Discrimination and the Encouragement of Reverse Discrimination

Corrective measures against illegal discrimination are not always based on a determination that a particular organization has discriminated. Rather, a whole class of organizations may be subject to remedial devices imposed by the nonjudicial branches of government, and these may include specified percentages of minority group members and women to be chosen. Using reported instances of individual discrimination and general statistical data about potential applicants and successful applicants, the executive branch, or possibly the legislature, concludes that discrimination, say in employment, occurs frequently. Rather than simply telling all employers to refrain from discriminating, the agency requires that employers set targets or "goals" if their present number of minority or female employees falls below that which would generally be appropriate in that area. The federal government has instituted such goals for government contractors under its power to determine how public money is spent. If the government contractors fail to satisfy the Office of Federal Contract Compliance Programs (OFCCP), under the Labor Department, that they are not engaging in discrimination, federal financial support is terminated. One controversial government effort of this sort has concerned universities. Since virtually all major universities receive a substantial amount of their budget from various federal government sources, the threat of a cutoff of funds has been virtually equivalent to compulsion. In addition to mandating open hiring practices, including advertising, and elaborate reporting techniques to uncover possible discrimination, the government (until late 1978 the Department of Health, Education, and Welfare but now the OFCCP) has directed universities to set goals for how many minority group members and women should be hired. The precise status of these goals has been a matter of acute controversy. Officials have said that they are not rigid quotas and that their only aim is nondiscriminatory hiring: if a university does not meet its goals, it will not be penalized if it can prove that it has not discriminated. Nevertheless, it is obvious that if the goals are met, university officials will have a lot less explaining to do than if they are not met, and the risks of meeting the goals seem far fewer than the risks of not meeting them. The goals thus operate as something considerably more significant than a rough statistical projection of what nondiscriminatory hiring would be expected to yield. Since academic appointments turn on a host of subtle and essentially unmeasurable factors, such as potential for creative scholarship and ability to communicate effectively to students, saying in any particular instance whether discrimination against or in favor of a minority group member has occurred is very hard. A university may thus perceive that if it does not meet, or come very close to meeting, its goals, establishing that it did not discriminate will be difficult. Whatever the theory of the goals, they can place pressure on some universities, and their branches, to engage in reverse discrimination. Programs such as the guidelines for universities may be justified as more effective, less narrowly focused, efforts to stop discrimination by institutions that have discriminated and might otherwise continue to discriminate. They may also be a way of combating the influence of past discriminatory practices on present hiring. If, for example, white males have acquired superior academic "credentials" through past discrimination, present nondiscriminatory hiring that gives heavy emphasis to those credentials may be unfair to blacks and women who are actually better qualified but can present less sparkling resumes. Seen in this light, the goals are not dissimilar to the corrective orders given by courts, save that in particular instances some employers may be required, or encouraged, to hire a proportion of minorities or women even though they have never discriminated in the past and would not discriminate in the future. As to

such employers, and as to the white male applicants to such employers who do not get jobs because of the goals, the setting of goals might be justified as a perhaps unfortunate but necessary concomitant of having an effectively administrable approach. Whether goals of this sort really are needed to prevent discrimination and the unfair effects of past discrimination is sharply disputed. If other more modest techniques would suffice, these justifications alone do not override the claims of white males to be evaluated fairly on the basis of their qualifications.

Other qualifications might be offered for hiring goals that operate in the fashion described. It might be claimed that for some reason having more minority and women employees is socially desirable, or that advancing the positions of members of groups that have suffered previous discrimination is appropriate even when that advancement exceeds what would occur under nondiscriminating hiring policies.

. . .

Regents of the University of California v. Bakke

438 U.S. 265 (1978)
United States Supreme Court

Powell, [Justice].

This case presents a challenge to the special admissions program of the petitioner, the Medical School of the University of California at Davis, which is designed to assure the admission of a specified number of students from certain minority groups. The Superior Court of California sustained respondent's challenge, holding that petitioner's program violated the California Constitution, Title VI of the Civil Rights Act of 1964 . . . , and the Equal Protection Clause of the Fourteenth Amendment. The court enjoined petitioner from considering respondent's race or the race of any other

applicant in making admissions decisions. It refused, however, to order respondent's admission to the Medical School, holding that he had not carried his burden of proving that he would have been admitted but for the constitutional and statutory violations. The Supreme Court of California affirmed those portions of the trial court's judgment declaring the special admissions program unlawful and enjoining petitioner from considering the race of any applicant. It modified that portion of the judgment denying respondent's requested injunction and directed the trial court to order his admission.

For the reasons stated in the following opinion, I believe that so much of the judgment of the California court as holds petitioner's special admissions program unlawful and directs that respondent be admitted to the Medical School must be affirmed. For the reasons expressed in a separate opinion, my Brothers The Chief Justice, Mr. Justice Stewart, Mr. Justice Rehnquist, and Mr. Justice Stevens concur in this judgment.

I also conclude for the reasons stated in the following opinion that the portion of the court's judgment enjoining petitioner from according any consideration to race in its admissions process must be reversed. For reasons expressed in separate opinions, my Brothers Mr. Justice Brennan, Mr. Justice White, Mr. Justice Marshall, and Mr. Justice Blackmun concur in this judgment.

Affirmed in part and reversed in part.

I

The Medical School of the University of California at Davis opened in 1968 with an entering class of 50 students. In 1971, the size of the entering class was increased to 100 students, a level at which it remains. No admissions program for disadvantaged or minority students existed when the school opened, and the first class contained three Asians but no blacks, no Mexican-Americans, and no American Indians. Over the next two years, the faculty devised a special admissions program to increase the representation of "disadvantaged" students in each medical school class. The special program consisted of a separate admissions system operating in coordination with the regular admissions process.

Under the regular admissions procedure, a candidate could submit his application to the Medical School beginning in July of the year preceding the academic year for which admission was sought. Because of the large number of applications, the admissions committee screened each one to select candidates for further consideration. Candidates whose overall undergraduate grade point averages fell below 2.5 on a scale of 4.0 were summarily rejected. About one out of six applicants was invited for a personal interview. Following the interviews, each candidate was rated on a scale of 1 to 100 by his interviewers and four other members of the admissions committee. The rating embraced the interviewers' summaries, the candidate's overall grade point average, grade point average in

science courses, scores on the Medical College Admissions Test (MCAT), letters of recommendation, extracurricular activities, and other biographical data. The ratings were added together to arrive at each candidate's "benchmark" score. Since five committee members rated each candidate in 1973, a perfect score was 500; in 1974, six members rated each candidate, so that a perfect score was 600. The full committee then reviewed the file and scores of each applicant and made offers of admission on a "rolling" basis. The chairman was responsible for placing names on the waiting list. They were not placed in strict numerical order; instead, the chairman had discretion to include persons with "special skills."

The special admissions program operated with a separate committee, a majority of whom were members of minority groups. On the 1973 application form, candidates were asked to indicate whether they wished to be considered as "economically and/or educationally disadvantaged" applicants; on the 1974 form the question was whether they wished to be considered as members of a "minority group," which the Medical School apparently viewed as "Blacks," "Chicanos," "Asians," and "American Indians." If these questions were answered affirmatively, the application was forwarded to the special admissions committee. No formal definition of "disadvantaged" was ever produced but the chairman of the special committee screened each application to see whether it reflected economic or educational deprivation. Having passed this initial hurdle, the applications then were rated by the special committee in a fashion similar to that used by the general admissions committee, except that special candidates did not have to meet the 2.5 grade point average cutoff applied to regular applicants. About one-fifth of the total number of special applicants were invited for interviews in 1973 and 1974. Following each interview, the special committee assigned each special applicant a benchmark score. The special committee then presented its top choices to the general admissions committee. The latter did not rate or compare the special candidates against the general applicants, but could reject recommended special candidates for failure to meet course requirements or other specific deficiencies. The special committee continued to recommend special applicants until a number prescribed by faculty vote were admitted. While the overall class size was still 50, the prescribed number was 8; in 1973 and 1974, when the class size had doubled to 100, the prescribed number of special admissions also doubled, to 16.

From the year of the increase in class size—1971—through 1974, the special program resulted in the admission of 21 black students, 30 Mexican-Americans, and 12 Asians, for a total of 63 minority students. Over the same period, the regular admissions program produced 1 black, 6 Mexican-Americans, and 37 Asians, for a total of 44 minority students. Although disadvantaged whites applied to the special program in large numbers, none received an offer of admission through that process. Indeed, in 1974, at least, the special committee explicitly considered only "disadvantaged" special applicants who were members of one of the designated minority groups.

Allan Bakke is a white male who applied to the Davis Medical School in both 1973 and 1974. In both years Bakke's application was considered under the general admissions program, and he received an interview. . . .

In both years, applicants were admitted under the special program with grade point averages, MCAT scores, and benchmark scores significantly lower than Bakke's.

After the second rejection, Bakke filed the instant suit in the Superior Court of California. . . .

Declaring that the University could not take race into account in making admissions decisions, the trial court held the challenged program violative of the Federal Constitution, the state constitution, and Title VI. The court refused to order Bakke's admission, however, holding that he had failed to carry his burden of proving that he would have been admitted but for the existence of the special program.

Bakke appealed from the portion of the trial court judgment denying him admission, and the University appealed from the decision that its special admissions program was unlawful and the order enjoining it from considering race in the processing of applications. . . . Because the special admissions program involved a racial classification, the Supreme Court held itself bound to apply strict scrutiny. It then turned to the goals the University presented as justifying the special program. Although the court agreed that the goals of integrating the medical profession and increasing the number of physicians willing to serve members of minority groups were compelling state interests, it concluded that the special admissions program was not the least intrusive means of achieving those goals. Without passing on the state constitutional or the federal statutory grounds cited in the trial court's judgment, the California court held that the Equal Protection Clause of the Fourteenth Amendment required that "no applicant may be rejected because of his race, in favor of another who is less qualified, as measured by the standards applied without regard to race."

Turning to Bakke's appeal, the court ruled that since Bakke had established that the University had discriminated against him on the basis of his race, the burden of proof shifted to the University to demonstrate that he would not have been admitted even in the absence of the special admissions program. . . . In its petition for rehearing below, however, the University conceded its inability to carry that burden. The California court thereupon amended its opinion to direct that the trial court enter judgment ordering Bakke's admission to the Medical School.

. . .

II

A

At the outset we face the question whether a right of action for private parties exists under Title VI. . . . We assume, only for the purposes of this case, that respondent has a right of action under Title VI.

B

The language of § 601, 78 Stat. 252, like that of the Equal Protection Clause, is majestic in its sweep:

> No person in the United States shall, on the ground of race, color, or national origin, be excluded from participation in, be denied the benefits of, or be subjected to discrimination under any program or activity receiving Federal financial assistance.

The concept of "discrimination," like the phrase "equal protection of the laws," is susceptible of varying interpretations, for as Mr. Justice Holmes declared, "[a] word is not a crystal, transparent and unchanged, it is the skin of a living thought and may vary greatly in color and content according to the circumstances and the time in which it is used." We must, therefore, seek whatever aid is available in determining the precise meaning of the statute before us. . . .

In view of the clear legislative intent, Title VI must be held to proscribe only those racial classifications that would violate the Equal Protection Clause or the Fifth Amendment.

III

A

. . . The parties . . . disagree as to the level of judicial scrutiny to be applied to the special admissions program. Petitioner argues that the court below erred in applying strict scrutiny, as this inexact term has been applied in our cases. That level of review, petitioner asserts, should be reserved for classifications that disadvantage "discrete and insular minorities." . . . Respondent, on the other hand, contends that the California court correctly rejected the notion that the degree of judicial scrutiny accorded a particular racial or ethnic classification hinges upon membership in a discrete and insular minority. . . .

En route to this crucial battle over the scope of judicial review, the parties fight a sharp preliminary action over the proper characterization of the special admissions program. Petitioner prefers to view it as establishing a "goal" of minority representation in the Medical School. Respondent, echoing the courts below, labels it a racial quota.

This semantic distinction is beside the point: The special admissions program is undeniably a classification based on race and ethnic background. To the extent that there existed a pool of at least minimally qualified minority applicants to fill the 16 special admissions seats, white applicants could compete only for 84 seats in the entering class, rather than the 100 open to minority applicants. Whether this limitation is described as a quota or a goal, it is a line drawn on the basis of race and ethnic status.

The guarantees of the Fourteenth Amendment extend to all persons. Its language is explicit: "No State shall . . . deny to any person within its jurisdiction the equal protection of the laws." It is settled beyond question that the "rights created by the first section of the Fourteenth Amendment are, by its terms, guaranteed to the individual. The rights established are personal rights." The guar-

antee of equal protection cannot mean one thing when applied to one individual and something else when applied to a person of another color. If both are not accorded the same protection, then it is not equal.

Nevertheless, petitioner argues that the court below erred in applying strict scrutiny to the special admissions program because white males, such as respondent, are not a "discrete and insular minority" requiring extraordinary protection from the majoritarian political process. . . . This rationale, however, has never been invoked in our decisions as a prerequisite to subjecting racial or ethnic distinctions to strict scrutiny. Nor has this Court held that discreteness and insularity constitute necessary preconditions to a holding that a particular classification is invidious. These characteristics may be relevant in deciding whether or not to add new types of classifications to the list of "suspect" categories or whether a particular classification survives close examination. Racial and ethnic classifications, however, are subject to stringent examination without regard to these additional characteristics. . . .

B

This perception of racial and ethnic distinctions is rooted in our Nation's constitutional and demographic history. The Court's initial view of the Fourteenth Amendment was that its "one pervading purpose" was "the freedom of the slave race, the security and firm establishment of that freedom, and the protection of the newly-made freeman and citizen from the oppressions of those who had formerly exercised dominion over him." . . . The Equal Protection Clause, however, was "[v]irtually strangled in infancy by post-civil-war judicial reactionism." It was relegated to decades of relative desuetude while the Due Process Clause of the Fourteenth Amendment, after a short germinal period, flourished as a cornerstone in the Court's defense of property and liberty of contract. . . . In that cause, the Fourteenth Amendment's "one pervading purpose" was displaced. See e.g., Plessy v. Ferguson, 163 U.S. 537 (1896). It was only as the era of substantive due process came to a close . . . that the Equal Protection Clause began to attain a genuine measure of vitality. . .

By that time it was no longer possible to peg the guarantees of the Fourteenth Amendment to the struggle for equality of one racial minority. During the dormancy of the Equal Protection Clause, the United States had become a Nation of minorities. Each had to struggle—and to some extent struggles still—to overcome the prejudices not of a monolithic majority, but of a "majority" composed of various minority groups of whom it was said—perhaps unfairly in many cases—that a shared characteristic was a willingness to disadvantage other groups. As the Nation filled with the stock of many lands, the reach of the Clause was gradually extended to all ethnic groups seeking protection from official discrimination. . . . The guarantees of equal protection, said the Court in Yick Wo, "are universal in their application, to all persons within the territorial jurisdiction, without regard to any differences of race, of color, or of nationality; and the equal protection of the laws is a pledge of the protection of equal laws." . . .

Although many of the Framers of the Fourteenth Amendment conceived of its primary function as bridging the vast distance between members of the Negro race and the white "majority," . . . supra, the Amendment itself was framed in universal terms, without reference to color, ethnic origin, or condition of prior servitude. As this Court recently remarked in interpreting the 1866 Civil Rights Act to extend to claims of racial discrimination against white persons, "the 39th Congress was intent upon establishing in the federal law a broader principle than would have been necessary simply to meet the particular and immediate plight of the newly freed Negro slaves." . . . And that legislation was specifically broadened in 1870 to ensure that "all persons," not merely "citizens," would enjoy equal rights under the law. Indeed, it is not unlikely that among the Framers were many who would have applauded a reading of the Equal Protection Clause that states a principle of universal application and is responsive to the racial, ethnic, and cultural diversity of the Nation.

Over the past 30 years, this Court has embarked upon the crucial mission of interpreting the Equal Protection Clause wih the view of assuring to all persons "the protection of equal laws" . . . in a Nation confronting a legacy of slavery and racial discrimination. . . . Because the landmark decisions in this area arose in response to the continued exclusion of Negroes from the mainstream of American society, they could be characterized as involving discrimination by the "majority" white race against the Negro minority. But they need not

be read as depending upon that characterization for their results. It suffices to say that "[o]ver the years, this Court has consistently repudiated '[d]istinctions between citizens solely because of their ancestry' as being 'odious to a free people whose institutions are founded upon the doctrine of equality.'" . . .

Petitioner urges us to adopt for the first time a more restrictive view of the Equal Protection Clause and hold that discrimination against members of the white "majority" cannot be suspect if its purpose can be characterized as "benign." The clock of our liberties, however, cannot be turned back to 1868. It is far too late to argue that the guarantee of equal protection to *all* persons permits the recognition of special wards entitled to a degree of protection greater than that accorded others. "The Fourteenth Amendment is not directed solely against discrimination due to a 'two-class theory'— that is, based upon differences between 'white' and Negro."

Once the artificial line of a "two-class theory" of the Fourteenth Amendment is put aside, the difficulties entailed in varying the level of judicial review according to a perceived "preferred" status of a particular racial or ethnic minority are intractable. The concepts of "majority" and "minority" necessarily reflect temporary arrangements and political judgments. As observed above, the white "majority" itself is composed of various minority groups, most of which can lay claim to a history of prior discrimination at the hands of the State and private individuals. Not all of these groups can receive preferential treatment and corresponding judicial tolerance of distinctions drawn in terms of race and nationality, for then the only "majority" left would be a new minority of white Anglo-Saxon Protestants. There is no principled basis for deciding which groups would merit "heightened judicial solicitude" and which would not. Courts would be asked to evaluate the extent of the prejudice and consequent harm suffered by various minority groups. Those whose societal injury is thought to exceed some arbitrary level of tolerability then would be entitled to preferential classifications at the expense of individuals belonging to other groups. Those classifications would be free from exacting judicial scrutiny. As these preferences began to have their desired effect, and the consequences of past discrimination were undone, new judicial rankings would be necessary. The kind of variable sociological and political analysis necessary to produce such rankings simply does not lie within the judicial competence—even if they otherwise were politically feasible and socially desirable.

Moreover, there are serious problems of justice connected with the idea of preference itself. First, it may not always be clear that a so-called preference is in fact benign. . . . Second, preferential programs may only reinforce common stereotypes holding that certain groups are unable to achieve success without special protection based on a factor having no relationship to individual worth. Third, there is a measure of inequity in forcing innocent persons in respondent's position to bear the burdens of redressing grievances not of their making.

By hitching the meaning of the Equal Protection Clause to these transitory considerations, we would be holding, as a constitutional principle, that judicial scrutiny of classifications touching on racial and ethnic background may vary with the ebb and flow of political forces. Disparate constitutional tolerance of such classifications well may serve to exacerbate racial and ethnic antagonisms rather than alleviate them. Also, the mutability of a constitutional principle, based upon shifting political and social judgments, undermines the chances for consistent application of the Constitution from one generation to the next, a critical feature of its coherent interpretation. In expounding the Constitution, the Court's role is to discern "principles sufficiently absolute to give them roots throughout the community and continuity over significant periods of time, and to lift them above the level of the pragmatic political judgments of a particular time and place." . . .

If it is the individual who is entitled to judicial protection against classifications based upon his racial or ethnic background because such distinctions impinge upon personal rights, rather than the individual only because of his membership in a particular group, then constitutional standards may be applied consistently. Political judgments regarding the necessity for the particular classification may be weighed in the constitutional balance . . . , but the standard of justification will remain constant. This is as it should be, since those political judgments are the product of rough compromise struck by contending groups within the democratic process. When they touch upon an individual's race or ethnic background, he is entitled to a judicial determination that the burden he is asked to bear on that basis is precisely tailored to serve a compelling governmental interest. . . .

C

Petitioner contends that on several occasions this Court has approved preferential classifications without applying the most exacting scrutiny. Most of the cases upon which petitioner relies are drawn from three areas: school desegregation, employment discrimination, and sex discrimination. Each of the cases cited presented a situation materially different from the facts of this case.

The school desegregation cases are inapposite. Each involved remedies for clearly determined constitutional violations. . . . Racial classifications thus were designed as remedies for the vindication of constitutional entitlement. Moreover, the scope of the remedies was not permitted to exceed the extent of the violations. Here, there was no judicial determination of constitutional violation as a predicate for the formulation of a remedial classification.

The employment discrimination cases also do not advance petitioner's cause. For example, in Franks v. Bowman Transportation Co., 424 U.S. 747 (1976), we approved a retroactive award of seniority to a class of Negro truckdrivers who had been the victims of discrimination—not just by society at large, but by the respondent in that case. . . . But we have never approved preferential classifications in the absence of proved constitutional or statutory violations.

Nor is petitioner's view as to the applicable standard supported by the fact that gender-based classifications are not subjected to this level of scrutiny. . . . [T]he Court has never viewed such classification as inherently suspect or as comparable to racial or ethnic classifications for the purpose of equal protection analysis. . . .

In this case, unlike *Lau* and *United Jewish Organizations,* there has been no determination by the legislature or a responsible administrative agency that the University engaged in a discriminatory practice requiring remedial efforts. Moreover, the operation of petitioner's special admissions program is quite different from the remedial measures approved in those cases. It prefers the designated minority groups at the expense of other individuals who are totally foreclosed from competition for the 16 special admissions seats in every Medical School class. . . .

IV

We have held that in "order to justify the use of a suspect classification, a State must show that its purpose or interest is both constitutionally permissible and substantial, and that its use of the classification is 'necessary . . . to the accomplishment' of its purpose or the safeguarding of its interest." . . . The special admissions program purports to serve the purposes of: (i) "reducing the historic deficit of traditionally disfavored minorities in medical schools and in the medical profession," (ii) countering the effects of societal discrimination; (iii) increasing the number of physicians who will practice in communities currently underserved; and (iv) obtaining the educational benefits that flow from an ethnically diverse student body. It is necessary to decide which, if any, of these purposes is substantial enough to support the use of a suspect classification.

A

If petitioner's purpose is to assure within its student body some specified percentage of a particular group merely because of its race or ethnic origin, such a preferential purpose must be rejected not as insubstantial but as facially invalid. Preferring members of any one group for no reason other than race or ethnic origin is discrimination for its own sake. This the Constitution forbids.

B

The State certainly has a legitimate and substantial interest in ameliorating, or eliminating where feasible, the disabling effects of identified discrimination. . . .

We have never approved a classification that aids persons perceived as members of relatively victimized groups at the expense of other innocent individuals in the absence of judicial, legislative, or administrative findings of constitutional or statutory violations. After such findings have been made, the governmental interest in preferring members of the injured groups at the expense of others is substantial, since the legal rights of the victims must be vindicated. In such a case, the extent of the injury and the consequent remedy will have been judicially, legislatively, or adminis-

tratively defined. Also, the remedial action usually remains subject to continuing oversight to assure that it will work the least harm possible to other innocent persons competing for the benefit. . . .

Petitioner does not purport to have made, and is in no position to make, such findings. Its broad mission is education, not the formulation of any legislative policy or the adjudication of particular claims of illegality. For reasons similar to those stated in Part III of this opinion, isolated segments of our vast governmental structures are not competent to make those decisions, at least in the absence of legislative mandates and legislatively determined criteria.[1] . . . Before relying upon these sorts of findings in establishing a racial classification, a governmental body must have the authority and capability to establish, in the record, that the classification is responsive to identified discrimination. . . .

C

Petitioner simply has not carried its burden of demonstrating that it must prefer members of particular ethnic groups over all other individuals in order to promote better health-care delivery to deprived citizens. Indeed, petitioner has not shown that its preferential classification is likely to have any significant effect on the problem.

D

The fourth goal asserted by petitioner is the attainment of a diverse student body. This clearly is a constitutionally permissible goal for an institution of higher education. Academic freedom, though not a specifically enumerated constitutional right, long has been viewed as a special concern of the First Amendment. The freedom of a university to make its own judgments as to education includes the selection of its student body. . . .

The atmosphere of "speculation, experiment and creation"—so essential to the quality of higher education—is widely believed to be promoted by a diverse student body. . . .

Thus, in arguing that its universities must be accorded the right to select those students who will contribute the most to the "robust exchange of ideas," petitioner invokes a countervailing constitutional interest, that of the First Amendment. In this light, petitioner must be viewed as seeking to achieve a goal that is of paramount importance in the fulfillment of its mission.

It may be argued that there is greater force to these views at the undergraduate level than in a medical school where the training is centered primarily on professional competency. But even at the graduate level, our tradition and experience lend support to the view that the contribution of diversity is substantial. . . . Physicians serve a heterogeneous population. An otherwise qualified medical student with a particular background— whether it be ethnic, geographic, culturally advantaged or disadvantaged—may bring to a professional school of medicine experiences, outlooks, and ideas that enrich the training of its student body and better equip its graduates to render with understanding their vital service to humanity.

. . . As the interest of diversity is compelling in the context of a university's admissions program, the question remains whether the program's racial classification is necessary to promote this interest.

V

A

. . . The diversity that furthers a compelling state interest encompasses a far broader array of qualifications and characteristics of which racial or ethnic origin is but a single though important element. Petitioner's special admissions program, focused *solely* on ethnic diversity, would hinder rather than further attainment of genuine diversity. . . .

The experience of other university admissions programs, which take race into account in achieving the educational diversity valued by the First Amendment, demonstrates that the assignment of a fixed number of places to a minority group is not a necessary means toward that end. An illuminating example is found in the Harvard College program:

> In recent years Harvard College has expanded the concept of diversity to include students from disadvantaged economic, racial and ethnic groups. Harvard College now recruits not only Californians or Louisianans but also blacks and Chicanos and other minority students. . . .

In practice, this new definition of diversity has meant that race has been a factor in some admission decisions. When the Committee on Admissions reviews the large middle group of applicants who are "admissible" and deemed capable of doing good work in their courses, the race of an applicant may tip the balance in his favor just as geographic origin or a life spent on a farm may tip the balance in other candidates' cases. A farm boy from Idaho can bring something to Harvard College that a Bostonian cannot offer. Similarly, a black student can usually bring something that a white person cannot offer. . . .

In Harvard college admissions the Committee has not set target-quotas for the number of blacks, or of musicians, football players, physicists or Californians to be admitted in a given year. . . . But that awareness [of the necessity of including more than a token number of black students] does not mean that the Committee sets a minimum number of blacks or of people from west of the Mississippi who are to be admitted. It means only that in choosing among thousands of applicants who are not only "admissible" academically but have other strong qualities, the Committee, with a number of criteria in mind, pays some attention to distribution among many types and categories of students.

In such an admissions program, race or ethnic background may be deemed a "plus" in a particular applicant's file, yet it does not insulate the individual from comparison with all other candidates for the available seats. The file of a particular black applicant may be examined for his potential contribution to diversity without the factor of race being decisive when compared, for example, with that of an applicant identified as an Italian-American if the latter is thought to exhibit qualities more likely to promote beneficial educational pluralism. Such qualities could include exceptional personal talents, unique work or service experience, leadership potential, maturity, demonstrated compassion, a history of overcoming disadvantage, ability to communicate with the poor, or other qualifications deemed important. In short, an admissions program operated in this way is flexible enough to consider all pertinent elements of diversity in light of the particular qualifications of each applicant, and to place them on the same footing for consideration, although not necessarily according them the same weight. Indeed, the weight attributed to a particular quality may vary from year to year depending upon the "mix" both of the student body and the applicants for the incoming class.

This kind of program treats each applicant as an individual in the admissions process. The applicant who loses out on the last available seat to another candidate receiving a "plus" on the basis of ethnic background will not have been foreclosed from all consideration for that seat simply because he was not the right color or had the wrong surname. It would mean only that his combined qualifications, which may have included similar nonobjective factors, did not outweigh those of the other applicant. His qualifications would have been weighed fairly and competitively, and he would have no basis to complain of unequal treatment under the Fourteenth Amendment.

It has been suggested that an admissions program which considers race only as one factor is simply a subtle and more sophisticated—but no less effective—means of according racial preference than the Davis program. A facial intent to discriminate, however, is evident in petitioner's preference program and not denied in this case. No such facial infirmity exists in an admissions program where race or ethnic background is simply one element—to be weighed fairly against other elements—in the selection process. "A boundary line," as Mr. Justice Frankfurter remarked in another connection, "is none the worse for being narrow." . . . And a court would not assume that a university, professing to employ a facially nondiscriminatory admissions policy, would operate it as a cover for the functional equivalent of a quota system. . . .

B

In summary, it is evident that the Davis special admissions program involves the use of an explicit racial classification never before countenanced by this Court. It tells applicants who are not Negro, Asian, or Chicano that they are totally excluded from a specific percentage of the seats in an entering class. No matter how strong their qualifications, quantitative and extracurricular, including their own potential for contribution to educational diversity, they are never afforded the chance to compete with applicants from the preferred groups for the special admissions seats. At the same time, the preferred applicants have the opportunity to compete for every seat in the class.

The fatal flaw in petitioner's preferential program is its disregard of individual rights as guaranteed by the Fourteenth Amendment. . . .

C

In enjoining petitioner from ever considering the race of any applicant, however, the courts below failed to recognize that the State has a substantial interest that legitimately may be served by a properly devised admissions program involving the competitive consideration of race and ethnic origin. For this reason, so much of the California court's judgment as enjoins petitioner from any consideration of the race of any applicant must be reversed.

VI

With respect to respondent's entitlement to an injunction directing his admission to the Medical School, petitioner has conceded that it could not carry its burden of proving that, but for the existence of its unlawful special admissions program, respondent still would not have been admitted. Hence, respondent is entitled to the injunction, and that portion of the judgment must be affirmed.

Endnote

[1] For example, the University is unable to explain its selection of only the four favored groups—Negroes, Mexican-Americans, American Indians, and Asians—for preferential treatment. The inclusion of the last group is especially curious in light of the substantial numbers of Asians admitted through the regular admissions process.

The Morality of Reparation

BERNARD BOXILL

In "Black Reparations—Two Views," Michael Harrington rejected and Arnold Kaufman endorsed James Forman's demand for $500 million in reparation from Christian churches and Jewish Synagogues for their part in the exploitation of black people. Harrington's position involves two different points; he argues that reparation is irrelevant and unwarranted because even if it were made, it would do little to "even up incomes"; and he maintains that the *demand* for reparation will be counterproductive, since it will "divert precious political energies from the actual struggle" to even up incomes. Now, though Kaufman seemed to show good reason that, contra Harrington, the demand for reparation could be productive, I shall in the ensuing, completely disregard that issue. Whether the demand for reparation is counterproductive or not is a question the answer to which depends on the assessment of a large number of consequences which cannot be answered by philosophy alone.

In this paper I shall take issue with what I have distinguished as the fist of Harrington's points, viz. that reparation is unwarranted and irrelevant because it would do little to even up incomes. I assume that, by implication, Harrington is not averse to special compensatory programs which will effectively raise the incomes of the poor; what he specifically opposes is reparation. By a discussion of the justification and aims of reparation and compensation, I shall now try to show that, though both are parts of justice, they have different aims, and hence compensation cannot replace reparation.

Let me begin with a discussion of how compensation may be justified. Because of the scarcity of positions and resources relative to aspiring individuals, every society that refuses to resort to paternalism or a strict regimentation of aspirations must incorporate competition among its members for scarce positions and resources. Given that freedom of choice necessitates at least the possibility of competition, I believe that justice requires that appropriate compensatory programs be instituted both to ensure that the competition is fair, and that the losers be protected.

If the minimum formal requirement of justice is that persons be given equal consideration, then it is clear that justice requires that compensatory programs be implemented in order to ensure that none of the participants suffers from a removable handicap. The same reasoning supports the contention that the losers in the competition be given, if necessary, sufficient compensation to enable them to reenter the competition on equal terms with the others. In other words, the losers can demand equal opportunity as well as can the beginners.

In addition to providing compensation in the above cases, the community has the duty to provide compensation to the victims of accident where no one was in the wrong, and to the victims of "acts of God" such as floods, hurricanes, and earthquakes. Here again, the justification is that such compensation is required if it is necessary to ensure equality of opportunity.

Now, it should be noted that, in all the cases I have stated as requiring compensation, no prior injustice need have occurred. This is clear, of course, in the case of accidents and "acts of God"; but it is also the case that in a competition, even if everyone abides by the rules and acts fairly and justly, some will necessarily be losers. In such a case, I maintain, if the losers are rendered so destitute as to be unable to compete equally, they can demand compensation from the community. Such a right to compensation does not render the competition nugatory; the losers cannot demand success—they can demand only the minimum necessary to reenter the competition. Neither is it the case that every failure has rights of compensation against the community. As we shall see, the right to compensation depends partly on the conviction that every individual has an equal right to pursue what he considers valuable; the wastrel or indolent

From *Social Theory and Practice*, Vol. 2 (1972), pp. 113–122. Reprinted with permission of Bernard Boxill.

man has signified what he values by what he has freely chosen to be. Thus, even if he seems a failure and considers himself a failure, he does not need or have a right of compensation. Finally, the case for compensation sketched is not necessarily paternalistic. It is not argued that society or government can decide what valuable things individuals should have and implement programs to see to it that they have them. Society must see to it that its members can pursue those things they consider valuable.

The justification of compensation rests on two premises: first, each individual is equal in dignity and worth to every other individual, and hence has a right, equal to that of any other, to arrange his life as he sees fit, and to pursue and acquire what he considers valuable; and second, the individuals involved must be members of a community. Both premises are necessary in order to show that compensation is both good and, in addition, mandatory or required by justice. One may, for example, concede that a man who is handicapped by some infirmity should receive compensation; but if the man is a member of no community, and if his infirmity is due to no injustice, then one would be hard put to find the party who could be legitimately forced to bear the cost of such compensation. Since persons can be legitimately compelled to do what justice dictates, then it would seem that in the absence of a community, and if the individual has suffered his handicap because of no injustice, that compensation cannot be part of justice. But given that the individual is a member of a community, then I maintain that he can legitimately demand compensation from that community. The members of a community are, in essential respects, members of a joint undertaking; the activities of the members of a community are interdependent and the community benefits from the efforts of its members even when such efforts do not bring the members what they individually aim at. It is legitimate to expect persons to follow the spirit and letter of rules and regulations, to work hard and honestly, to take calculated risks with their lives and fortunes, all of which helps society generally, only if such persons can demand compensation from society as a whole when necessary.

The case for rights of compensation depends, as I have argued above, on the fact that the individuals involved are members of a single community the very existence of which should imply a tacit agreement on the part of the whole to bear the costs of compensation. The case for reparation I shall try to show is more primitive in the sense that it depends only on the premise that every person has an equal right to pursue and acquire what he values. Recall that the crucial difference between compensation and reparation is that whereas the latter is due only after injustice, the former may be due when no one has acted unjustly to anyone else. It is this relative innocence of all the parties concerned which made it illegitimate, in the absence of prior commitments, to compel anyone to bear the cost of compensation.

In the case of reparation, however, this difficulty does not exist. When reparation is due, it is not the case that no one is at fault, or that everyone is innocent; in such a case, necessarily, someone has infringed unjustly on another's right to pursue what he values. This could happen in several different ways, dispossession being perhaps the most obvious. When someone possesses something, he has signified by his choice that he values it. By taking it away from him one infringes on his equal right to pursue and possess what he values. On the other hand, if I thwart, unfairly, another's legitimate attempt to do or possess something, I have also acted unjustly; finally, an injustice has occurred when someone makes it impossible for others to pursue a legitimate goal, even if these others never actually attempt to achieve that goal. These examples of injustice differ in detail, but what they all have in common is that no supposition of prior commitment is necessary in order to be able to identify the parties who must bear the cost of reparation; it is simply and clearly the party who has acted unjustly.

The argument may, perhaps, be clarified by the ideas of a state of nature and a social contract. In the state of nature, as John Locke remarks, every man has the right to claim reparation from his injurer because of his right of self-preservation; if each man has a duty not to interfere in the rights of others, he has a duty to repair the results of his interference. No social contract is required to legitimize compelling him to do so. But when compensation is due, i.e., when everyone has acted justly, and has done his duty, then a social contract or a prior agreement to help must be appealed to in order to legitimately compel an individual to help another.

The case for reparation thus requires for its justification less in the way of assumptions than the case for compensation. Examination of the justifications of reparation and compensation also reveals the difference in their aims.

The characteristic of compensatory programs is that they are essentially "forward looking"; by that I mean that such programs are intended to alleviate disabilities which stand in the way of some *future* good, *however* these disabilities may have come about. Thus, the history of injustices suffered by black and colonial people is quite irrelevant to their right to compensatory treatment. What is strictly relevant to this is that such compensatory treatment is necessary if some future goods such as increased happiness, equality of incomes, and so on, are to be secured. To put it another way, given the contingency of causal connections, the present condition of black and colonial people could have been produced in any one of a very large set of different causal sequences. Compensation is concerned with the remedying of the present situation however it may have been produced; and to know the present situation, and how to remedy it, it is not, strictly speaking, necessary to know just how it was brought about, or whether it was brought about by injustice.

On the other hand, the justification of reparation is essentially "backward looking"; reparation is due only when a breach of justice *has* occurred. Thus, as opposed to the case of compensation, the case for reparation to black and colonial people depends precisely on the fact that such people have been reduced to their present condition by a history of injustice. In sum, while the aim of compensation is to procure some future good, that of reparation is to rectify past injustices; and rectifying past injustices may not insure equality of opportunity.

The fact that reparation aims precisely at correcting a prior injustice suggests one further important difference between reparation and compensation. Part of what is involved in rectifying an injustice is an acknowledgment on the part of the transgressor that what he is doing is required of him because of his prior error. This concession of error seems required by the premise that every person is equal in worth and dignity. Without the acknowledgment of error, the injurer implies that the injured has been treated in a manner that befits him; hence, he cannot feel that the injured party is his equal. In such a case, even if the unjust party repairs the damage he has caused, justice does not yet obtain between himself and his victim. For, if it is true that when someone has done his duty nothing can be demanded of him, it follows that if, in my estimation, I have acted dutifully even when someone is injured as a result, then I must feel that nothing can be demanded of me and that any repairs I may make are gratuitous. If justice can be demanded, it follows that I cannot think that what I am doing is part of justice.

It will be objected, of course, that I have not shown in this situation that justice cannot obtain between injurer and victim, but only that the injurer does not *feel* that justice can hold between himself and the one he injures. The objection depends on the distinction between the objective transactions between the individuals and their subjective attitudes, and assumes that justice requires only the objective transactions. The model of justice presupposed by this objection is, no doubt, that justice requires equal treatment of equals, whereas the view I take is that justice requires equal consideration between equals; that is to say, justice requires not only that we *treat* people in a certain way, for whatever reason we please, but that we treat them as equals precisely because we believe they are our equals. In particular, justice requires that we acknowledge that our treatment of others can be required of us; thus, where an unjust injury has occurred, the injurer reaffirms his belief in the other's equality by conceding that repair can be demanded of him, and the injured rejects the allegation of his inferiority contained in the other's behavior by demanding reparation.

Consequently, when injustice has reduced a people to indigency, compensatory programs alone cannot be all that justice requires. Since the avowed aim of compensatory programs is forward looking, such programs *necessarily* cannot affirm that the help they give is required because of a prior injustice. This must be the case even if it is the unjustly injuring party who makes compensation. Thus, since the acknowledgment of error is required by justice as part of what it means to give equal consideration, compensatory programs cannot take the place of reparation.

In sum, *compensation* cannot be substituted for *reparation* where reparation is due, because they satisfy two differing requirements of justice. In addition, practically speaking, since it is by demanding and giving justice where it is due that the members of a community continually reaffirm their belief in each other's equality, a stable and equitable society is not possible without reparation being given and demanded when it is due.

Consider now the assertion that the present generation of white Americans owe the present generation of black Americans reparation for the injustices of slavery inflicted on the ancestors of the black population by the ancestors of the white population. To begin, consider the very simplest instance of a case where reparation may be said to be due: Tom has an indisputable moral right to possession of a certain item, say a bicycle, and Dick steals the bicycle from Tom. Here, clearly, Dick owes Tom, at least the bicycle and a concession of error, in reparation. Now complicate the case slightly; Dick steals the bicycle from Tom and "gives" it to Harry. Here again, even if he is innocent of complicity in the theft, and does not know that his "gift" was stolen, Harry must return the bicycle to Tom with the acknowledgment that, though innocent or blameless, he did not rightfully possess the bicycle. Consider a final complication; Dick steals the bicycle from Tom and gives it to Harry; in the meantime Tom dies, but leaves a will clearly conferring his right to ownership of the bicycle to his son, Jim. Here again we should have little hesitation in saying that Harry must return the bicycle to Jim.

Now, though it involves complications, the case for reparation under consideration is essentially the same as the one last mentioned: the slaves had an indisputable moral right to the products of their labour; these products were stolen from them by the slave masters who ultimately passed them on to their descendants; the slaves presumably have conferred their rights of ownership to the products of their labour to their descendants; thus, the descendants of slave masters are in possession of wealth to which the descendants of slaves have rights; hence, the descendants of slave masters must return this wealth to the descendants of slaves with a concession that they were not rightfully in possession of it.

It is not being claimed that the descendants of slaves must seek reparation from those among the white population who happen to be descendants of slave owners. This perhaps would be the case if slavery had produced for the slave owners merely specific hoards of gold, silver or diamonds, which could be passed on in a very concrete way from father to son. As a matter of fact, slavery produced not merely specific hoards, but wealth which has been passed down mainly to descendants of the white community to the relative exclusion of the descendants of slaves. Thus, it is the white com-

munity as a whole that prevents the descendants of slaves from exercising their rights of ownership, and the white community as a whole that must bear the cost of reparation.

The above statement contains two distinguishable arguments. In the first argument the assertion is that each white person, individually, owes reparation to the black community because membership in the white community serves to identify an individual as a recipient of benefits to which the black community has a rightful claim. In the second argument, the conclusion is that the white community as a whole, considered as a kind of corporation or company, owes reparation to the black community.

In the first of the arguments sketched above, individuals are held liable to make reparation even if they have been merely passive recipients of benefits; that is, even if they have not deliberately chosen to accept the benefits in question. This argument invites the objection that, for the most part, white people are simply not in a position to choose to receive or refuse benefits belonging to the descendants of slaves and are, therefore, not culpable or blameable and hence not liable to make reparation. But this objection misses the point. The argument under consideration simply does not depend on or imply the claim that white people are culpable or blameable; the argument is that merely by being white, an individual receives benefits to which others have at least partial rights. In such cases, whatever one's choice or moral culpability, reparation must be made. Consider an extreme case: Harry has an unexpected heart attack and is taken unconscious to the hospital. In the same hospital Dick has recently died. A heart surgeon transplants the heart from Dick's dead body to Harry without permission from Dick's family. If Harry recovers, he must make suitable reparation to Dick's family, conceding that he is not in rightful possession of Dick's heart even if he had no part in choosing to receive it.

The second of the arguments distinguished above concluded that for the purpose in question, the white community can be regarded as a corporation or company which, as a whole, owes reparation to the sons of slaves. Certainly the white community resembles a corporation or company in some striking ways; like such companies, the white community has interests distinct from, and opposed to, other groups in the same society, and joint action is often taken by the members of the white community to protect and enhance their interests. Of course, there are differences; people are generally born into the white community and do not deliberately choose their membership in it; on the other hand, deliberate choice is often the standard procedure for gaining membership in a company. But this difference is unimportant; European immigrants often deliberately choose to become part of the white community in the United States for the obvious benefits this brings, and people often inherit shares and so, without deliberate choice, become members of a company. What is important here is not how deliberately one chooses to become part of a community or a company; what is relevant is that one chooses to continue to accept the benefits which circulate exclusively within the community, sees such benefits as belonging exclusively to the members of the community, identifies one's interests with those of the community, viewing them as opposed to those of others outside the community, and finally, takes joint action with other members of the community to protect such interests. In such a case, it seems not unfair to consider the present white population as members of a company that incurred debts before they were members of the company, and thus to ask them justly to bear the cost of such debts.

It may be objected that the case for reparation depends on the validity of inheritance; for, only if the sons of slaves inherit the rights of their ancestors can it be asserted that they have rights against the present white community. If the validity of inheritance is rejected, a somewhat different, but perhaps even stronger, argument for reparation can still be formulated. For if inheritance is rejected with the stipulation that the wealth of individuals be returned to the whole society at their deaths, then it is even clearer that the white community owes reparation to the black community. For the white community has appropriated, almost exclusively, the wealth from slavery in addition to the wealth from other sources; but such wealth belongs jointly to all members of the society, white as well as black; hence, it owes them reparation. The above formulation of the argument is entirely independent of the fact of slavery and extends the rights of the black community to its just portion of the total wealth of the society.

Reverse Discrimination as Unjustified

LISA NEWTON

I have heard it argued that "simple justice" requires that we favor women and blacks in employment and educational opportunities, since women and blacks were "unjustly" excluded from such opportunities for so many years in the not so distant past. It is a strange argument, an example of a possible implication of a true proposition advanced to dispute the proposition itself, like an octopus absent-mindedly slicing off his head with a stray tentacle. A fatal confusion underlies this argument, a confusion fundamentally relevant to our understanding of the notion of the rule of law.

Two senses of justice and equality are involved in this confusion. The root notion of justice, progenitor of the other, is the one that Aristotle (*Nichomachean Ethics* 5.6; *Politics* 1.2; 3.1) assumes to be the foundation and proper virtue of the political association. It is the condition which free men establish among themselves when they "share a common life in order that their association bring them self-sufficiency"—the regulation of their relationship by law, and the establishment, by law, of equality before the law. Rule of law is the name and pattern of this justice; its equality stands against the inequalities—of wealth, talent, etc.—

From *Ethics*, Vol. 83 (1973), pp. 308–312. Reprinted with permission of The University of Chicago Press and Lisa Newton.

otherwise obtaining among its participants, who by virtue of that equality are called "citizens." It is an achievement—complete, or, more frequently, partial—of certain people in certain concrete situations. It is fragile and easily disrupted by powerful individuals who discover that the blind equality of rule of law is inconvenient for their interests. Despite its obvious instability, Aristotle ssumed that the establishment of justice in this sense, the creation of citizenship, was a permanent possibility for men and that the resultant association of citizens was the natural home of the species. At levels below the political association, this rule-governed equality is easily found; it is exemplified by any group of children agreeing together to play a game. At the level of the political association, the attainment of this justice is more difficult, simply because the stakes are so much higher for each participant. The equality of citizenship is not something that happens of its own accord, and without the expenditure of a fair amount of effort it will collapse into the rule of a powerful few over an apathetic many. But at least it has been achieved, at some times in some places; it is always worth trying to achieve, and eminently worth trying to maintain, wherever and to whatever degree it has been brought into being.

Aristotle's parochialism is notorious; he really did not imagine that persons other than Greeks could associate freely in justice, and the only form of association he had in mind was the Greek *polis*. With the decline of the *polis* and the shift in the center of political thought, his notion of justice underwent a sea change. To be exact, it ceased to represent a political type and became a moral ideal: the ideal of equality as we know it. This ideal demands that all men be included in citizenship— that one Law govern all equally, that all men regard all other men as fellow citizens, with the same quarantees, rights, and protections. Briefly, it demands that the circle of citizenship achieved by any group be extended to include the entire human race. Properly understood, its effect on our associations can be excellent: it congratulates us on our achievement of rule of law as a process of government but refuses to let us remain complacent until we have expanded the associations to include others within the ambit of the rules, as often and as far as possible. While one man is a slave, none of us may feel truly free. We are constantly prodded by this ideal to look for possible unjustifiable discrimination, for inequalities not absolutely required for the functioning of the society and advantageous to all. And after twenty centuries of pressure, not at all constant, from this ideal, it might be said that some progress has been made. To take the cases in point for this problem, we are now prepared to assert, as Aristotle would never have been, the equality of sexes and of persons of different colors. The ambit of American citizenship, once restricted to white males of property, has been extended to include all adult free men, then all adult males including ex-slaves, then all women. The process of acquisition of full citizenship was for these groups a sporadic trail of half-measures, even now not complete; the steps on the road to full equality are marked by legislation and judicial decisions which are only recently concluded and still often not enforced. But the fact that we can now discuss the possibility of favoring such groups in hiring shows that over the area that concerns us, at least, full equality is presupposed as a basis for discussion. To that extent, they are full citizens, fully protected by the law of the land.

It is important for my argument that the moral ideal of equality be recognized as logically distinct from the condition (or virtue) of justice in the political sense. Justice in this sense exists *among* a citizenry, irrespective of the number of the populace included in that citizenry. Further, the moral ideal is parasitic upon the political virtue, for "equality" is unspecified—it means nothing until we are told in what respect that equality is to be realized. In a political context, "equality" is specified as "equal rights"—equal access to the public realm, public goods and offices, equal treatment under the law— in brief, the equality of citizenship. If citizenship is not a possibility, political equality is unintelligible. The ideal emerges as a generalization of the real condition and refers back to that condition for its content.

Now, if justice (Aristotle's justice in the political sense) is equal treatment under law for all citizens, what is injustice? Clearly, injustice is the violation of that equality, discriminating for or against a group of citizens, favoring them with special immunities and privileges or depriving them of those guaranteed to the others. When the southern employer refuses to hire blacks in white-collar jobs, when Wall Street will only hire women as secretaries with new titles, when Mississippi high schools routinely flunk all black boys above ninth grade, we have examples of injustice, and we work to restore the equality of the public realm by ensuring that equal opportunity will be provided in such cases in the future. But of course, when the employers and the schools *favor* women and blacks, the same injustice is done. Just as the previous discrimination did, this reverse discrimination violates the public equality which defines citizenship and destroys the rule of law for the areas in which these favors are granted. To the extent that we adopt a program of discrimination, reverse or otherwise, justice in the political sense is destroyed, and none of us, specifically affected or not, is a citizen, a bearer of rights—we are all petitioners for favors. And to the same extent, the ideal of equality is undermined, for it has content only where justice obtains, and by destroying justice we render the ideal meaningless. It is, then, an ironic paradox, if not a contradiction in terms, to assert that the ideal of equality justifies the violation of justice; it is as if one should argue, with William Buckley, that an ideal of humanity can justify the destruction of the human race.

Logically, the conclusion is simple enough: all discrimination is wrong prima facie because it violates justice, and that goes for reverse discrimination too. No violation of justice among the citizens may be justified (may overcome the prima facie objection) by appeal to the ideal of equality, for that ideal is logically dependent upon the notion of justice. Reverse discrimination, then, which attempts no other justification than an appeal to equality, is wrong. But let us try to make the conclusion more plausible by suggesting some of the implications of the suggested practice of reverse discrimination in employment and education. My argument will be that the problems raised there are insoluble, not only in practice but in principle.

We may argue, if we like, about what "discrimination" consists of. Do I discriminate against blacks if I admit none to my school when none of the black applicants are qualified by the tests I always give? How far must I go to root our cultural bias from my application forms and tests before I can say that I have not discriminated against those of different cultures? Can I assume that women are not strong enough to be roughnecks on my oil rigs, or must I test them individually? But this controversy, the most popular and well-argued aspect of the issue, is not as fatal as two others which cannot be avoided: if we are regarding the blacks as a "minority" victimized by discrimination, what is a "minority"? And for any group—blacks, women, whatever—that has been discriminated against,

what amount of reverse discrimination wipes out the initial discrimination? Let us grant as true that women and blacks were discriminated against, even where laws forbade such discrimination, and grant for the sake of argument that a history of discrimination must be wiped out by reverse discrimination. What follows?

First, are there other groups which have been discriminated against? For they should have the same right of restitution. What about American Indians, Chicanos, Appalachian Mountain whites, Puerto Ricans, Jews, Cajuns, and Orientals? And if these are to be included, the principle according to which we specify a "minority" is simply the criterion of "ethnic (sub) group," and we're stuck with every hyphenated American in the lower-middle class clamoring for special privileges for *his* group—and with equal justification. For be it noted, when we run down the Harvard roster, we find not only a scarcity of blacks (in comparison with the proportion in the population) but an even more striking scarcity of those second-, third-, and fourth-generation ethnics who make up the loudest voice of Middle America. Shouldn't they demand *their* share? And eventually, the WASPs will have to form their own lobby, for they too are a minority. The point is simply this: there is no "majority" in America who will not mind giving up just a bit of their rights to make room for a favored minority. There are only other minorities, each of which is discriminated against by the favoring. The initial injustice is then repeated dozens of times, and if each minority is granted the same right of restitution as the others, an entire area of rule governance is dissolved into a pushing and shoving match between self-interested groups. Each works to catch the public eye and political popularity by whatever means of advertising and power politics lend themselves to the effort, to capitalize as much as possible on temporary popularity until the restless mob picks another group to feel sorry for. Hardly an edifying spectacle, and in the long run no one can benefit: the pie is no larger—it's just that instead of setting up and enforcing rules for getting a piece, we've turned the contest into a free-for-all, requiring much more effort for no larger a reward. It would be in the interests of all the participants to reestablish an objective rule to govern the process, carefully enforced and the same for all.

Second, supposing that we do manage to agree in general that women and blacks (and all the others) have some right of restitution, some right to a privileged place in the structure of opportunities for a while, how will we know when that while is up? How much privilege is enough? When will the guilt be gone, the price paid, the balance restored? What recompense is right for centuries of exclusion? What criterion tells us when we are done? Our experience with the Civil Rights movement shows us that agreement on these terms cannot be presupposed: a process that appears to some to be going at a mad gallop into a black takeover appears to the rest of us to be at a standstill. Should a practice of reverse discrimination be adopted, we may safely predict that just as some of us begin to see "a satisfactory start toward righting the balance," others of us will see that we "have already gone too far in the other direction" and will suggest that the discrimination ought to be reversed again. And such disagreement is inevitable, for the point is that we could not *possibly* have any criteria for evaluating the kind of recompense we have in mind. The context presumed by any discussion of restitution is the context of rule of law: law sets the rights of men and simultaneously sets the method for remedying the violation of those rights. You may exact suffering from others and/or damage payments for yourself if and only if the others have violated your rights; the suffering you have endured is not sufficient reason for them to suffer. And remedial rights exist only where there is law: primary human rights are useful guides to legislation but cannot stand as reasons for awarding remedies for injuries sustained. But then, the context presupposed by any discussion of restitution is the context of preexistent full citizenship. No remedial rights could exist for the excluded; neither in law nor in logic does there exist a right to *sue* for a standing to sue.

From these two considerations, then, the difficulties with reverse discrimination become evident. Restitution for a disadvantaged group whose rights under the law have been violated is possible by legal means, but restitution for a disadvantaged group whose grievance is that there was no law to protect them simply is not. First, outside of the area of justice defined by the law, no sense can be made of "the group's rights," for no law recognizes that group or the individuals in it, qua members, as bearers of rights (hence *any* group can constitute itself as a disadvantaged minority in some sense and demand similar restitution). Second, outside of the area of protection of law, no sense can be made of the violation of rights (hence the amount of the recompense cannot be decided by any objective criterion). For both reasons, the practice of reverse discrimination undermines the foundation of the very ideal in whose name it is advocated; it destroys justice, law, equality, and citizenship itself, and replaces them with power struggles and popularity contests.

Affirmative Racism

CHARLES MURRAY

A few years ago, I got into an argument with a lawyer friend who is a partner in a New York firm. I was being the conservative, arguing that preferential treatment of blacks was immoral; he was being the liberal, urging that it was the only way to bring blacks to full equality. In the middle of all this he

From *The New Republic* (December 31, 1984), pp. 18–23. Reprinted with permission of *The New Republic*.

abruptly said, "But you know, let's face it. We must have hired at least ten blacks in the last few years, and none of them has really worked out." He then returned to his case for still stronger affirmative action, while I wondered what it had been like for those ten blacks. And if he could make a remark like that so casually, what remarks would he be able to make some years down the road, if by that time it had been fifty blacks who hadn't "really worked out"?

My friend's comment was an outcropping of a new racism that is emerging to take its place alongside the old. It grows out of preferential treatment for blacks, and it is not just the much-publicized reactions, for example, of the white policemen or firemen who are passed over for promotion because of an affirmative action court order. The new racism that is potentially most damaging is located among the white elites—educated, affluent, and occupying the positions in education, business, and government from which this country is run. It currently focuses on blacks; whether it will eventually extend to include Hispanics and other minorities remains to be seen.

The new racists do not think blacks are inferior. They are typically longtime supporters of civil rights. But they exhibit the classic behavioral symptom of racism: they treat blacks differently from whites, because of their race. The results can be as concretely bad and unjust as any that the old racism produces. Sometimes the effect is that blacks are refused an education they otherwise could have gotten. Sometimes blacks are shunted into dead-end jobs. Always, blacks are denied the right to compete as equals.

The new racists also exhibit another characteristic of racism: they *think* about blacks differently from the way they think about whites. Their global view of blacks and civil rights is impeccable. Blacks must be enabled to achieve full equality. They are still unequal, through no fault of their own (it is the fault of racism, it is the fault of inadequate opportunity, it is the legacy of history). But the new racists' local view is that the blacks they run across professionally are not, on the average, up to the white standard. Among the new racists, lawyers have gotten used to the idea that the brief a black colleague turns in will be a little less well-rehearsed and argued than the one they would have done. Businessmen expect that a black colleague will not read a balance sheet as subtly as they do. Teachers expect black students to wind up toward the bottom of the class.

The new racists also tend to think of blacks as a commodity. The office must have a sufficient supply of blacks, who must be treated with special delicacy. The personnel problems this creates are more difficult than most because whites barely admit to themselves what's going on.

What follows is a foray into very poorly mapped territory. I will present a few numbers that

explain much about how the process gets started. But the ways that the numbers get translated into behavior are even more important. The cases I present are composites constructed from my own observations and taken from firsthand accounts. All are based on real events and real people, stripped of their particularities. But the individual cases are not intended as evidence, because I cannot tell you how often they happen. They have not been the kind of thing that social scientists or journalists have wanted to count. I am writing this because so many people, both white and black, to whom I tell such stories know immediately what I am talking about. It is apparent that a problem exists. How significant is it? What follows is as much an attempt to elicit evidence as to present it.

As in so many of the crusades of the 1960s, the nation began with a good idea. It was called "affirmative action," initiated by Lyndon Johnson through Executive Order 11246 in September 1965. It was an attractive label and a natural corrective to past racism: actively seek out black candidates for jobs, college, or promotions, without treating them differently in the actual decision to hire, admit, or promote. The term originally evoked both the letter and the spirit of the order.

Then, gradually, affirmative action came to mean something quite different. In 1970 a federal court established the legitimacy of quotas as a means of implementing Johnson's executive order. In 1971 the Supreme Court ruled that an employer could not use minimum credentials as a prerequisite for hiring if the credential acted as a "built-in headwind" for minority groups—even when there was no discriminatory intent and even when the hiring procedures were "fair in form." In 1972 the Equal Employment Opportunity Commission acquired broad, independent enforcement powers.

Thus by the early 1970s it had become generally recognized that a good-faith effort to recruit qualified blacks was not enough—especially if one's school depended on federal grants or one's business depended on federal contracts. Even for businesses and schools not directly dependent on the government, the simplest way to withstand an accusation of violating Title VII of the Civil Rights Act of 1964 was to make sure not that they had not just interviewed enough minority candidates, but that they had actually hired or admitted enough of them. Employers and admissions committees arrived at a rule of thumb: if the blacks who are available happen to be the best candidates, fine; if not, the best available black candidates will be given some sort of edge in the selection process. Sometimes the edge will be small; sometimes it will be predetermined that a black candidate is essential, and the edge will be very large.

Perhaps the first crucial place where the edge applies is in admission to college. Consider the cases of the following three students: John, William, and Carol, 17 years old and applying to college, are all equal on paper. Each has a score of 520 in the mathematics section of the Scholastic Aptitude Test, which puts them in the top third—at the 67th percentile—of all students who took the test. (Figures are based on 1983 data.)

John is white. A score of 520 gets him into the state university. Against the advice of his high school counselor, he applies to a prestigious school, Ivy U. where his application is rejected in the first cut—its average white applicant has math scores in the high 600s.

William is black, from a middle-class family who sent him to good schools. His score of 520 puts him at the 95th percentile of all blacks who took the test. William's high school counselor points out that he could probably get into Ivy U. William applies and is admitted—Ivy U. uses separate standards for admission of whites and blacks, and William is among the top blacks who applied.

Carol is black, educated at an inner-city school, and her score of 520 represents an extraordinary achievement in the face of terrible schooling. An alumnus of Ivy U. who regularly looks for promising inner-city candidates finds her, recruits her, and sends her off with a full scholarship to Ivy U.

When American universities embarked on policies of preferential admissions by race, they had the Carols in mind. They had good reason to be optimistic that preferential treatment would work—for many years, the best universities had been weighting the test scores of applicants from small-town public schools when they were compared against those of applicants from the top private schools, and had been giving special breaks to students from distant states to ensure geographic distribution. The differences in preparation tended to even out after the first year or so. Blacks were being brought into a long-standing and successful tradition of preferential treatment.

In the case of blacks, however, preferential treatment ran up against a large black-white gap in academic performance combined with ambitious goals for proportional representation. This gap has been the hardest for whites to confront. But though it is not necessary or even plausible to believe that such differences are innate, it is necessary to recognize openly that the differences exist. By pretending they don't, we begin the process whereby both the real differences and the racial factor are exaggerated.

The black-white gap that applies most directly to this discussion is the one that separates blacks and whites who go to college. In 1983, for example, the mean Scholastic Aptitude Test score for all blacks who took the examination was more than 100 points below the white score on both the verbal and the math sections. Statistically, it is an extremely wide gap. To convert the gap into more concrete terms, think of it this way: in 1983, the same Scholastic Aptitude Test math score that put a black at the 50th percentile of all blacks who took the test put him at the 16th percentile of all whites who took the test.

These results clearly mean we ought to be making an all-out effort to improve elementary and secondary education for blacks. But that doesn't help much now, when an academic discrepancy of this magnitude is fed into a preferential admissions process. As universities scramble to make sure they are admitting enough blacks, the results feed the new racism. Here's how it works:

In 1983, only 66 black students nationwide scored above 700 in the verbal section of the Scholastic Aptitude Test, and only 205 scored above 700 in the mathematics section. This handful of students cannot begin to meet the demand for blacks with such scores. For example, Harvard, Yale, and Princeton have in recent years been bringing an aggregate of about 270 blacks into each entering class. If the black students entering these schools had the same distribution of scores as that of the freshman class as a whole, then every black student in the nation with a verbal score in the 700s, and roughly 70 percent of the ones with a math score in the 700s, would be in their freshman classes.

The main problem is not that a few schools monopolize the very top black applicants, but that these same schools have much larger implicit quotas than they can fill with those applicants. They fill out the rest with the next students in line—students who would not have gotten into these schools if they were not black who otherwise would have been showing up in the classrooms of the nation's less glamorous colleges and universities. But the size of the black pool does not expand appreciably at the next levels. The number of blacks scoring in the 600s on the math section in 1983, for example, was 1,531. Meanwhile, 31,704 nonblack students in 1983 scored in the 700s on the math section and 121,640 scored in the 600s. The prestige schools cannot begin to absorb these numbers of other highly qualified freshmen, and they are perforce spread widely throughout the system.

At schools that draw most broadly from the student population, such as the large state universities, the effects of this skimming produce a situation that confirms the old racists in everything they want most to believe. There are plenty of outstanding students in such student bodies (at the University of Colorado, for example, 6 percent of the freshmen in 1981 had math scores in the 700s and 28 percent had scores in the 600s), but the skimming process combined with the very small raw numbers means that almost none of them are black. What students and instructors see in their day-to-day experience in the classroom is a disproportionate number of blacks who are below the white average, relatively few blacks who are at the white average, and virtually none who are in the first rank. The image that the white student carries away is that blacks are less able than whites.

I am not exalting the SAT as an infallible measure of academic ability, or pointing to test scores to try to convince anyone that blacks are performing below the level of whites. I am simply using them to explain what instructors and students already notice, and talk about, among themselves.

They do not talk openly about such matters. One characteristic of the new racism is that whites deny in public but acknowledge in private that there are significant differences in black and white academic performance. Another is that they dismiss the importance of tests when black scores are at issue, blaming cultural bias and saying that test scores are not good predictors of college performance. At the same time, they watch anxiously over their own children's test scores.

The differences in academic performance do not disappear by the end of college. Far from narrowing, the gap separating black and white academic achievement appears to get larger. Various studies, most recently at Harvard, have found that during the 1970s blacks did worse in college (as measured by grade point average) than their test scores would have predicted. Moreover, the black-white gap in the Graduate Record Examination is larger than the gap in the Scholastic Aptitude Test. The gap between black and white freshmen is a bit less than one standard deviation (the technical measure for comparing scores). Black and white seniors who take the Graduate Record Examination reveal a gap of about one and a quarter standard deviations.

Why should the gap grow wider? Perhaps it is an illusion—for example, perhaps a disproportionate number of the best black students never take the examination. But there are also reasons for suspecting that in fact blacks get a worse education in college than whites do. Here are a few of the hypotheses that deserve full exploration.

Take the situation of William—a slightly above-average student who, because he is black, gets into a highly competitive school. William studies very hard during the first year. He nonetheless gets mediocre grades. He has a choice. He can continue to study hard and continue to get mediocre grades, and be seen by his classmates as a black who cannot do very well. Or he can explicitly refuse to engage in the academic game. He decides to opt out, and his performance gets worse as time goes on. He emerges from college with a poor education and is further behind the whites than he was as a freshman.

If large numbers of other black students at the institution are in the same situation as William, the result can be group pressure not to compete academically. (At Harvard, it is said, the current term among black students for a black who studies like a white is "incognegro.") The response is not hard to understand. If one subpopulation of students is conspicuously behind another population and is visibly identifiable, then the population that is behind must come up with a good excuse for doing poorly. "Not wanting to do better" is as good as any.

But there is another crucial reason why blacks might not close the gap with whites during college: they are not taught as well as whites are. Racist teachers impeding the progress of students? Perhaps, but most college faculty members I know tend to bend over backward to be "fair" to black students—and that may be the problem. I suggest that inferior instruction is more likely to be a manifestation of the new racism than the old.

Consider the case of Carol, with outstanding abilities but deprived of decent prior schooling: she struggles the first year, but she gets by. Her academic skills still show the aftereffects of her inferior preparation. Her instructors diplomatically point out the more flagrant mistakes, but they ignore minor lapses, and never push her in the aggressive way they push white students who have her intellectual capacity. Some of them are being patronizing (she is doing quite well, considering). Others are being prudent: teachers who criticize black students can find themselves being called racists in the classroom, in the campus newspaper, or in complaints to the administration.

The same process continues in graduate school. Indeed, because there are even fewer blacks in graduate schools than in undergraduate schools, the pressures to get black students through to the degree, no matter what, can be still greater. But apart from differences in preparation and ability that have accumulated by the end of schooling, the process whereby we foster the appearance of black inferiority continues. Let's assume that William did not give up during college. He goes to business school, where he gets his Masters degree. He signs up for interviews with the corporate recruiters. There are 100 persons in his class, and William is ranked near the middle. But of the 5 blacks in his class, he ranks first (remember that he was at the 95th percentile of blacks taking the Scholastic Aptitude Test). He is hired on his first interview by his first-choice company, which also attracted the very best of the white students. He is hired alongside 5 of the top-ranking white members of the class.

William's situation as one of 5 blacks in a class of 100 illustrates the proportions that prevail in business schools, and business schools are by no means one of the more extreme examples. The pool of black candidates for any given profession is a small fraction of the white pool. This works out to a 20-to-1 edge in business; it is even greater in most of the other professions. The result, when many hiring institutions are competing, is that a major gap between the abilities of new black and white employees in any given workplace is highly likely. Everyone needs to hire a few blacks, and the edge that "being black" confers in the hiring decision warps the sequence of hiring in such a way that a scarce resource (the blacks with a given set of qualifications) is exhausted at an artificially high rate, producing a widening gap in comparison with the remaining whites from which an employer can choose.

The more aggressively affirmative action is enforced, the greater the imbalance. In general, the first companies to hire can pursue strategies that minimize or even eliminate the difference in ability between the new black and white employees. IBM and Park Avenue law firms can do very well, just as Harvard does quite well in attracting the top black students. But the more effectively they pursue these strategies, the more quickly they strip the population of the best black candidates.

To this point I have been discussing problems that are more or less driven by realities we have very little hope of manipulating in the short term except by discarding the laws regarding preferential treatment. People do differ in acquired abilities. Currently, acquired abilities in the white and black populations are distributed differently. Schools and firms do form a rough hierarchy when they draw from these distributions. The results follow ineluctably. The dangers they represent are not a matter of statistical probabilities, but of day-to-day human reactions we see around us.

The damage caused by these mechanistic forces should be much less in the world of work than in the schools, however. Schools deal in a relatively narrow domain of skills, and "talent" tends to be assigned specific meanings and specific measures. Workplaces deal in highly complex sets of skills, and "talent" consists of all sorts of combinations of qualities. A successful career depends in large part upon finding jobs that elicit and develop one's strengths.

At this point the young black professional must sidestep a new series of traps laid by whites who need to be ostentatiously nonracist. Let's say that William goes to work for the XYZ Corporation, where he is assigned with another management trainee (white) to a department where much of the time is spent preparing proposals for government contracts. The white trainee is assigned a variety of scut work—proofreading drafts, calculating the costs of minor items in the bid, making photocopies, taking notes at conferences. William gets more dignified work. He is assigned portions of the draft to write (which are later rewritten by more experienced staff), sits in on planning sessions, and even goes to Washington as a highly visible part of the team to present the bid. As time goes on, the white trainee learns a great deal about how the company operates, and is seen as a go-getting young member of the team. William is perceived to be a bright enough fellow, but not much of a detail man and not really much of a self-starter.

Even if a black is hired under terms that put him on a par with his white peers, the subtler forms of differential treatment work against him. Particularly for any corporation that does business with the government, the new employee has a specific, immediate value purely because he is black. There are a variety of requirements to be met and rituals to be observed for which a black face is helpful. These have very little to do with the long-term career interests of the new employee; on the contrary, they often lead to a dead end as head of the minority-relations section of the personnel department.

Added to this is another problem that has nothing to do with the government. When the old racism was at fault (as is often still is), the newly hired black employee was excluded from the socialization process because the whites did not want him to become part of the group. When the new racism is at fault, it is because many whites are embarrassed to treat black employees as badly as they are willing to treat whites. Hence another reason that whites get on-the-job training that blacks do not: much of the early training of an employee is intertwined with mental assignments and mild hazing. Blacks who are put through these routines often see themselves as racially abused (and when a black is involved, old-racist responses may well have crept in). But even if the black is not unhappy about the process, the whites are afraid that he is, and so protect him from it. There are many variations, all having the same effect: the black is denied an apprenticeship that the white has no way of escaping. Without serving the apprenticeship, there is no way of becoming part of the team.

Carol suffers a slightly different fate. She and a white woman are hired as reporters by a major newspaper. They both work hard, but after a few months there is no denying it: neither one of them can write. The white woman is let go. Carol is kept on, because the paper cannot afford to have any fewer blacks than it already has. She is kept busy with reportorial work, even though they have to work around the writing problem. She is told not to worry—there's lots more to being a journalist than writing.

It is the mascot syndrome. A white performing at a comparable level would be fired. The black is kept on, perhaps to avoid complications with the Equal Employment Opportunity Commission (it can be very expensive to fire a black), perhaps out of a more diffuse wish not to appear discriminatory. Everybody pretends that nothing is wrong—but the black's career is at a dead end. The irony, of course, is that the white who gets fired and has to try something else has been forced into accepting a chance of making a success in some other line of work whereas the black is seduced into *not* taking the same chance.

Sometimes differential treatment takes an even more pernicious form: the conspiracy to promote a problem out of existence. As part of keeping Carol busy, the newspaper gives her some administrative responsibilities. They do not amount to much. But she has an impressive title on a prominent newspaper and she is black—a potent combination. She gets an offer from a lesser paper in another part of the country to take a senior editorial post. Her current employer is happy to be rid of an awkward situation and sends along glowing references. She gets a job that she is unequipped to handle—only this time, she is in a highly visible position, and within a few weeks the deficiencies that were covered up at the old job have become the subject of jokes all over the office. Most of the jokes are openly racist.

It is important to pause and remember who Carol is: an extremely bright young woman, not (in other circumstances) a likely object of condescension. But being bright is no protection. Whites can usually count on the market to help us recognize egregious career mistakes and to prevent us from being promoted too far from a career line that fits our strengths, and too far above our level of readiness. One of the most prevalent characteristics of white differential treatment of blacks has been to exempt blacks from these market considerations, substituting for them a market premium attached to race.

The most obvious consequence of preferential treatment is that every black professional, no matter how able, is tainted. Every black who is hired by a white-run organization that hires blacks preferentially has to put up with the knowledge that many of his co-workers believe he was hired because of his race; and he has to put up with the suspicion in his own mind that they might be right.

Whites are curiously reluctant to consider this a real problem—it is an abstraction, I am told, much less important than the problem that blacks face in getting a job in the first place. But black professionals talk about it, and they tell stories of mental breakdowns; of people who had to leave the job altogether; of long-term professional paralysis. What white would want to be put in such a situation? Of course it would be a constant humiliation to be resented by some of your co-workers and condescended to by others. Of course it would affect your perceptions of yourself and your self-confidence. No system that produces such side effects—as preferential treatment *must* do—can be defended unless it is producing some extremely important benefits.

And that brings us to the decisive question. If the alternative were no job at all, as it was for so many blacks for so long, the resentment and condescension are part of the price of getting blacks into the positions they deserve. But is that the alternative today? If the institutions of this country were left to their own devices now, to what extent would they refuse to admit, hire, and promote people because they were black? To what extent are American institutions kept from being racist by the government's intervention?

It is another one of those questions that are seldom investigated aggressively, and I have no evidence. Let me suggest a hypothesis that bears looking into: that the signal event in the struggle for black equality during the last thirty years, the one with real impact, was not the Civil Rights Act of 1964 or Executive Order 11246 or any other governmental act. It was the civil rights movement itself. It raised to a pitch of acute and lasting discomfort the racial consciousness of the generations of white Americans who are now running the country. I will not argue that the old racism is dead at any level of society. I will argue, however, that in the typical corporation or in the typical admissions office, there is an abiding desire to be not-racist. This need not be construed as brotherly love. Guilt will do as well. But the civil rights movement did its job. I suggest that the laws and the court decisions and the continuing intellectual respectability behind preferential treatment are not holding many doors open to qualified blacks that would otherwise be closed.

Suppose for a moment that I am right. Suppose that, for practical purposes, racism would not get in the way of blacks if preferential treatment were abandoned. How, in my most optimistic view, would the world look different?

There would be fewer blacks at Harvard and Yale; but they would all be fully competitive with the whites who were there. White students at the state university would encounter a cross-section of blacks who span the full range of ability, including the top levels, just as whites do. College remedial courses would no longer be disproportionately black. Whites rejected by the school they wanted would quit assuming they were kept out because a less-qualified black was admitted in their place. Blacks in big corporations would no longer be shunted off to personnel-relations positions, but would be left on the main-line tracks toward becoming comptrollers and sales managers and chief executive officers. Whites would quit assuming that black colleagues had been hired because they were black. Blacks would quit worrying that they had been hired because they were black.

Would blacks still lag behind? As a population, yes, for a time, and the nation should be mounting a far more effective program to improve elementary and secondary education for blacks than it has mounted in the last few decades. But in years past virtually every ethnic group in America has at one time or another lagged behind as a population, and has eventually caught up. In the process of catching up, the ones who breached the barriers were evidence of the success of that group. Now blacks who breach the barriers tend to be seen as evidence of the inferiority of that group.

And that is the evil of preferential treatment. It perpetuates an impression of inferiority. The system segments whites and blacks who come in contact with each other so as to maximize the likelihood that whites have the advantage in experience and ability. The system then encourages both whites and blacks to behave in ways that create self-fulfilling prophecies even when no real differences exist.

It is here that the new racism links up with the old. The old racism has always openly held that blacks are permanently less competent than whites. The new racism tacitly accepts that, in the course of overcoming the legacy of the old racism, blacks are temporarily less competent than whites. It is an extremely fine distinction. As time goes on, fine distinctions tend to be lost. Preferential treatment is providing persuasive evidence for the old racists, and we can already hear it *sotto voce:* "We gave you your chance, we let you educate them and push them into jobs they couldn't have gotten on their own and coddle them every way you could. And see: they still aren't as good as whites, and you are beginning to admit it yourselves." Sooner or later this message is going to be heard by a white elite that needs to excuse its failure to achieve black equality.

The only happy aspect of the new racism is that the corrective—to get rid of the policies encouraging preferential treatment—is so natural. Deliberate preferential treatment by race has sat as uneasily with America's equal-opportunity ideal during the post-1965 period as it did during the days of legalized segregation. We had to construct tortuous rationalizations when we permitted blacks to be kept on the back of the bus—and the rationalizations to justify sending blacks to the head of the line have been just as tortuous. Both kinds of rationalization say that sometimes it is all right to treat people of different races in different ways. For years, we have instinctively sensed this was wrong in principle but intellectualized our support for it as an expedient. I submit that our instincts were right. There is no such thing as good racial discrimination.

Study Questions

1. Do the reasons leading us to believe that racial discrimination against blacks and others is wrong and unconstitutional also apply in the case of the discrimination involved in affirmative action practices? Should the classifications utilized in such programs ("being a black," "being a woman," etc.) be subjected to "strict scrutiny"? What would be the result?

2. Does Justice Powell in his opinion in *Bakke* really apply strict scrutiny? Would even the "Harvard Plan" pass such scrutiny? Powell seems to think that it makes a difference whether an applicant is turned down for medical school because of a quota system or because race is used as a factor in an admissions policy. Is he right? Why should that matter to someone like Bakke who, after all, loses out either way and apparently as a consequence of his race?

3. Consider the example of a state that enacts a law requiring a passing score on a literacy test as a prerequisite to registration as a voter. The test has the effect of disqualifying many of the Hispanics in the state, but nearly all whites pass the exam. How should a law that has a disproportionate racial impact but is nonetheless nondiscriminatory "on its face" be viewed? Should it be automatically presumed invalid? Should it be taken as evidence of racial prejudice operating behind the scenes? Should the fact that it is color-blind on its face be sufficient to let it stand? Should such a literacy test be allowed to stand when confronted with an equal protection challenge? Does the formal principle of equality give us any guidance here?

4. Are programs of preferential treatment an appropriate way of making reparation? One feature of reparatory justice as it usually conceived is that the wrongdoer does the paying back. Does the fact that the burden of preferential practices typically falls on "innocent" persons such as Bakke weaken Boxill's arguments? Is Bakke innocent? Has Bakke benefitted from discrimination against blacks? How would Boxill respond?

B. Sex, Gender, and Equality

Introduction

In 1978, a jury in Sonoma County, California, convicted a young man named Michael M. (his last name being withheld to shield his identity) for violation of section 261.5 of the California Penal Code: unlawful sexual intercourse "accomplished with a female not the wife of the perpetrator, where the female is under the age of eighteen years." California, like most states, criminalizes "statutory rape," so called since the act is unlawful even if both parties consent to it. Appealing to reverse his conviction, Michael M. made an unusual and intriguing argument: The California law is unconstitutional and violates the guarantee of equal protection since only men can be held criminally liable for its violation. California's statutory rape law is an example of sex discrimination.

In his opinion for the United States Supreme Court, Chief Justice Rehnquist began by stating what the Court (and California) took to be the purpose of the statute: to prevent illegitimate teenage pregnancy. The Court found that this is an important objective (citing statistics regarding teenage pregnancy and its attendant social effects). Can the state seek to meet this objective by punishing only the male? The court answered yes, since most of the burden of the pregnancy falls on the female. A gender-neutral statute, permitting the punishment of the female as well as the male, would frustrate the law's enforcement, since the female is unlikely to notify the authorities if she too faces a penalty. The statute therefore does not violate the equal protection guarantee. Males and females are not similarly situated with respect to the risks of sex and pregnancy and therefore it is not a violation of equal protection to treat them differently.

Justice Brennan, in a dissenting opinion, countered that even if the goal here is an important one, the statute is not "substantially related"— does not come close enough—to the achievement of that goal. Other states have switched to gender-neutral statutes without much difficulty; and a gender-neutral law might well have a greater deterrent effect, since both participants would be liable. It is irrational, the dissenters seem to believe, to take illicit sexual activity so seriously and yet exempt from punishment 50 percent of the violators.

Sexism in the Law

The *Michael M.* case serves as a useful point of departure for an exploration of the whole question of "equality between the sexes" and what that means (or should mean) under our Constitution and laws. In what ways are men and women equal or the same? In what ways are they different? And what should be made of these differences?

In their article, Nadine Taub and Elizabeth Schneider summarize the history and development of sex discrimination law, with the aim of showing how the law continues to justify discrimination against women by invoking what are thought to be "legitimate" or "real" differences between the sexes. These are in fact, Taub and Schneider argue, unfair stereotypes and burdens that have been socially imposed upon women. As they see it, until the 1970s the law was dominated by a "separate sphere" theory, according to which women have a separate, distinct, and immutable "nature" that makes them unfit for many of the positions and occupations traditionally held by men; women properly belong to a separate social and legal realm, consisting primarily if not exclusively of domestic life and child rearing. In the past, the law excluded women from many aspects of public life and left them unprotected within the private, domestic world. Only recently have the courts begun consistently to strike down gender-based classifications as violative of women's equal protection rights. But even here, Taub and Schneider point out, the courts have generally refused to require that laws which distinguish between persons on the basis of their sex must be "strictly scrutinized." Instead, they have settled on a weaker, intermediate standard of review: It is enough if such laws are "substantially related to an important governmental interest."

The authors then turn to *Michael M.* They are suspicious of the declared purpose in retaining the statutory rape law. Is it to prevent teenage pregnancy? If so, then why not punish both persons involved? Taub and Schneider suggest a more sinister purpose. On a deeper level, they claim, the statute reinforces a range of damaging and morally unacceptable sexual stereotypes: that men are always the aggressors in sexual encounters; that women are submissive and naive; that women need to have their chastity protected. In short, say Taub and Schneider, the Court assumes that the problem of teenage pregnancy is important and thereby acquiesce in a sexist law. The Court invokes the physiological difference of pregnancy, together with socially imposed sex-role expectations, with the consequence that deeper and potentially more damaging prejudices against women are retained.

Sexism and the Political Power of Women

As we have seen, one of the focal questions regarding the law of equal protection is: What traits or characteristics are impermissible to use when treating persons in one way or another? One suggested answer is this: If, by virtue of grouping people on the basis of a certain characteristic or trait, one thereby identifies that group as a "discrete and insular minority," any law classifying people in that way violates the constitutional demand of equality. To be a discrete and insular minority means to be isolated as a group from the rest of the population, cut off from effective political action or social participation, and made the focus of prejudice. In this way, race (for example, being black) or religious affiliation (for example, being Mormon) can clearly serve to mark off an insular minority.

What would this general approach say of women and of discrimination based upon sex?

Have laws made women a "discrete and insular minority"? Constitutional scholar John Hart Ely takes up these questions and finds that they are not easily answered. In one obvious sense, Ely observes, women are not a "minority": numerically at least they are presently a "majority," in the United States at any rate. But what follows from this? Have women as a group been unfairly isolated from political and social action because of unequal treatment?

Ely's answer is a qualified no. It is true, he admits, that many women do not enjoy, on a level equal with that of men, various of the goods our society has to offer (jobs, prestige, political office); but this may not be unfair, as many women may simply prefer this unequal state of affairs. Nor is it plausible, Ely contends, to argue that women have a "slave mentality," submissively enduring an unequal regime; at least, this is not plausible without more evidence than the mere lack of a "women's uprising," analogous to a slave revolt. Ely suggests that the courts deal with cases of alleged sex discrimination by looking to the date at which the allegedly discriminatory law was enacted. Why? If the law was passed in an earlier era, when people were not as aware of sexist assumptions involved in certain practices and attitudes, and at a time when women could not vote, then the courts should strike down the legislation on the grounds that, for the purposes of such a law, women *were* the disempowered victims of prejudice, unable to affect their fate. On the other hand, recent gender-based laws, Ely believes, should be allowed to stand by the courts. They should not be viewed as violations of equal protection since women as a group are now able to protect themselves; if they don't choose to do so, it is not because they can't. We may disagree with their choice to remain in the back seat, but it remains their choice.

The Assimilationist Ideal

Philosopher and lawyer Richard Wasserstrom closes this chapter by exploring a broader question: In what way would differences in race, and in particular in sex, be viewed in an "ideal" society? Wasserstrom investigates and compares three possibilities.

The first, or "assimilationist," ideal seeks a society in which differences among the races or between the sexes are treated like differences in eye color. Since no one thinks that eye color should be relevant in any way to the distribution of social benefits or burdens, the assimilationist society would be one in which nothing turns on one's race or sex. The second ideal, that of "diversity," analogizes sex and race to the current legal status of religion. One's religious identity, we believe, should make no difference to political rights and benefits; yet we still permit (and encourage) people to recognize and celebrate their differing religious identities. Similarly, on this view people could still define themselves in terms of gender differences, though no political or social stigma would be attached to doing so. The last of the three ideals would take sexual equality much as we have it now, with considerable sex-role differentiation.

Which ideal is the most attractive? Would assimilationism be too radical a break with our current set of beliefs and traditions? These questions cannot be answered, Wasserstrom thinks, without facing the further question of whether the "differences" between the sexes are "natural" or "social." Wasserstrom argues that they are largely, if not entirely, social in origin, as almost none of the obvious physical differences between men and women really make a difference in our technologically advanced society. He then constructs a positive case for the assimilationist ideal: The assimilationist society allows all its members a degree of individual autonomy that cannot be present in a society that, like ours, defines people's prospects and limits their possibilities ahead of time, simply by confining them to "preprogrammed" sex roles.

Michael M. *v.* Superior Court of Sonoma County

United States Supreme Court
450 U.S. 464 (1981)

Justice Rehnquist announced the judgment of the Court and delivered an opinion, in which The Chief Justice, Justice Stewart, and Justice Powell joined.

The question presented in this case is whether California's "statutory rape" law, § 261.5 of the Cal. Penal Code Ann . . . violates the Equal Protection Clause of the Fourteenth Amendment. Section 261.5 defines unlawful sexual intercourse as "an act of sexual intercourse accomplished with a female not the wife of the perpetrator, where the female is under the age of 18 years." The statute thus makes men alone criminally liable for the act of sexual intercourse.

In July 1978, a complaint was filed in the Municipal Court of Sonoma County, Cal., alleging that petitioner, then a 17 1/2-year-old male, had had unlawful sexual intercourse with a female under the age of 18, in violation of § 261.5. The evidence adduced at a preliminary hearing showed that at approximately midnight on June 3, 1978, petitioner and two friends approached Sharon, a 16 1/2-year-old female, and her sister as they

waited at a bus stop. Petitioner and Sharon, who had already been drinking, moved away from the others and began to kiss. After being struck in the face for rebuffing petitioner's initial advances, Sharon submitted to sexual intercourse with petitioner. Prior to trial, petitioner sought to set aside the information on both state and federal constitutional grounds, asserting that § 261.5 unlawfully discriminated on the basis of gender. The trial court and the California Court of Appeal denied petitioner's request for relief and petitioner sought review in the Supreme Court of California.

The Supreme Court held that "section 261.5 discriminates on the basis of sex because only females may be victims, and only males may violate the section." . . . The court then subjected the classification to "strict scrutiny," stating that it must be justified by a compelling state interest. It found that the classification was "supported not by mere social convention but by the immutable physiological fact that it is the female exclusively who can become pregnant." . . . Canvassing "the tragic human costs of illegitimate teenage pregnancies," including the large number of teenage abortions, the increased medical risk associated with teenage pregnancies, and the social consequences of teenage childbearing, the court concluded that the State has a compelling interest in preventing such pregnancies. Because males alone can "physiologically cause the result which the law properly seeks to avoid," the court further held that the gender classification was readily justified as a means of identifying offender and victim. For the reasons stated below, we affirm the judgment of the California Supreme Court.

As is evident from our opinions, the Court has had some difficulty in agreeing upon the proper approach and analysis in cases involving challenges to gender-based classifications. . . .

. . . Unlike the California Supreme Court, we have not held that gender-based classifications are "inherently suspect" and thus we do not apply so-called "strict scrutiny" to those classifications. . . . Our cases have held, however, that the traditional minimum rationality test takes on a somewhat "sharper focus" when gender-based classifications are challenged. See *Craig v. Boren* 429 U.S. 190, 210 (1976). . . . In *Reed* v. *Reed*, 404 U.S. 71 (1971), for example, the Court stated that a gender-based classification will be upheld if it bears a "fair and substantial relationship" to legitimate state ends, while in *Craig* v. *Boren* . . . the Court restated the test to require the classification to bear a "substantial relationship" to "important governmental objectives."

Underlying these decisions is the principle that a legislature may not "make overbroad generalizations based on sex which are entirely unrelated to any differences between men and women or which demean the ability or social status of the affected class." . . . But because the Equal Protection Clause does not "demand that a statute necessarily apply equally to all persons" or require " 'things which are different in fact . . . to be treated in law as though they were the same,' " . . . this Court has consistently upheld statutes where the gender classification is not invidious, but rather realistically reflects the fact that the sexes are not similarly situated in certain circumstances. . . . As the Court has stated, a legislature may "provide for the special problems of women." . . .

Applying those principles to this case, the fact that the California Legislature criminalized the act of illicit sexual intercourse with a minor female is a sure indication of its intent or purpose to discourage that conduct. Precisely why the legislature desired that result is of course somewhat less clear.

This Court has long recognized that "[i]nquiries into congressional motives or purposes are a hazardous matter." . . .

. . . Here, for example, the individual legislators may have voted for the statute for a variety of reasons. Some legislators may have been concerned about preventing teenage pregnancies, others about protecting young females from physical injury or from the loss of "chastity," and still others about promoting various religious and moral attitudes towards premarital sex.

The justification for the statute offered by the State and accepted by the Supreme Court of California, is that the legislature sought to prevent illegitimate teenage pregnancies.

. . .

We are satisfied not only that the prevention of illegitimate pregnancy is at least one of the "purposes" of the statute, but also that the State has a strong interest in preventing such pregnancy. At the risk of stating the obvious, teenage pregnancies, which have increased dramatically over the last two decades,[1] have significant social, medical, and economic consequences for both the mother and her child, and the State.[2]

. . .

. . . Of particular concern to the State is that approximately half of all teenage pregnancies end in abortion.[3] And of those children who are born, their illegitimacy makes them likely candidates to become wards of the State.

We need not be medical doctors to discern that young men and young women are not similarly situated with respect to the problems and the risks of sexual intercourse. Only women may become pregnant, and they suffer disproportionately the profound physical, emotional, and psychological consequences of sexual activity. The statute at issue here protects women from sexual intercourse at an age when those consequences are particularly severe.[4]

The question thus boils down to whether a State may attack the problem of sexual intercourse and teenage pregnancy directly by prohibiting a male from having sexual intercourse with a minor female. We hold that such a statute is sufficiently related to the State's objectives to pass constitutional muster.

Because virtually all of the significant harmful and inescapably identifiable consequences of teenage pregnancy fall on the young female, a legislature acts well within its authority when it elects to punish only the participant who, by nature, suffers few of the consequences of his conduct. It is hardly unreasonable for a legislature acting to protect minor females to exclude them from punishment. Moreover, the risk of pregnancy itself constitutes a substantial deterrence to young females. No similar natural sanctions deter males. A criminal sanction imposed solely on males thus serves to roughly "equalize" the deterrents on the sexes.

We are unable to accept petitioner's contention that the statute is impermissibly underinclusive and must, in order to pass judicial scrutiny, be *broadened* so as to hold the female as criminally liable as the male. It is argued that this statute is not *necessary* to deter teenage pregnancy because a gender-neutral statute, where both male and female would be subject to prosecution, would serve that goal equally well. The relevant inquiry, however, is not whether the statute is drawn as precisely as it might have been, but whether the line chosen by the California Legislature is within constitutional limitations. . . .

In any event, we cannot say that a gender-neutral statute would be as effective as the statute California has chosen to enact. The State persuasively contends that a gender-neutral statute would frustrate its interest in effective enforcement. Its view is that a female is surely less likely to report violations of the statute if she herself would be subject to criminal prosecution.[5] In an area already fraught with prosecutorial difficulties, we decline to hold that the Equal Protection Clause requires a legislature to enact a statute so broad that it may well be incapable of enforcement.[6]

We similarly reject petitioner's argument that § 261.5 is impermissibly overbroad because it makes unlawful sexual intercourse with prepubescent females, who are, by definition, incapable of becoming pregnant. Quite apart from the fact that the statute could well be justified on the grounds that very young females are particularly susceptible to physical injury from sexual intercourse . . . , it is ludicrous to suggest that the Constitution requires the California Legislature to limit the scope of its rape statute to older teenagers and exclude young girls.

There remains only petitioner's contention that the statute is unconstitutional as it is applied to him because he, like Sharon, was under 18 at the time of sexual intercourse. Petitioner argues that the statute is flawed because it presumes that as

between two persons under 18, the male is the culpable aggressor. We find petitioner's contentions unpersuasive. Contrary to his assertions, the statute does not rest on the assumption that males are generally the aggressors. It is instead an attempt by a legislature to prevent illegitimate teenage pregnancy by providing an additional deterrent for men. The age of the man is irrelevant since young men are as capable as older men of inflicting the harm sought to be prevented.

In upholding the California statute we also recognize that this is not a case where a statute is being challenged on the grounds that it "invidiously discriminates" against females. To the contrary, the statute places a burden on males which is not shared by females. But we find nothing to suggest that men, because of past discrimination or peculiar disadvantages, are in need of the special solicitude of the courts. Nor is this a case where the gender classification is made "solely for . . . administrative convenience" . . . , or rests on "the baggage of sexual stereotypes." . . . As we have held, the statute instead reasonably reflects the fact that the consequences of sexual intercourse and pregnancy fall more heavily on the female than on the male. . . .

Accordingly the judgment of the California Supreme Court is

Affirmed.

· · ·

Justice Brennan, with whom Justices White and Marshall join, dissenting. . . . It is disturbing to find the Court so splintered on a case that presents such a straightforward issue: Whether the admittedly gender-based classification in Cal. Penal Code Ann. § 261.5 . . . bears a sufficient relationship to the State's asserted goal of preventing teenage pregnancies to survive the "mid-level" constitutional scrutiny mandated by *Craig* v. *Boren*. . . . Applying the analytical framework provided by our precedents, I am convinced that there is only one proper resolution of this issue: the classification must be declared unconstitutional. I fear that the plurality opinion . . . reach[es] the opposite result by placing too much emphasis on the desirability of achieving the State's asserted statutory goal—prevention of teenage pregnancy—and not enough emphasis on the fundamental question of whether the sex-based discrimination in the California statute is *substantially* related to the achievement of that goal.

· · ·

The State of California vigorously asserts that the "important governmental objective" to be served by § 261.5 is the prevention of teenage pregnancy. It claims that its statute furthers this goal by deterring sexual activity by males—the class of persons it considers more responsible for causing those pregnancies. But even assuming that prevention of teenage pregnancy is an important governmental objective and that it is in fact an objective of § 261.5 . . . , California still has the burden of proving that there are fewer teenage pregnancies under its gender-based statutory rape law than there would be if the law were gender neutral. To meet this burden, the State must show that because its statutory rape law punishes only males, and not females, it more effectively deters minor females from having sexual intercourse.

The plurality assumes that a gender-neutral statute would be less effective than § 261.5 in deterring sexual activity because a gender-neutral statute would create significant enforcement problems. . . .

. . . However, a State's bare assertion that its gender-based statutory classification substantially furthers an important governmental interest is not enough to meet its burden of proof under *Craig* v. *Boren*. Rather, the State must produce evidence that will persuade the court that its assertion is true. . . .

The State has not produced such evidence in this case. Moreover, there are at least two serious flaws in the State's assertion that law enforcement problems created by a gender-neutral statutory rape law would make such a statute less effective than a gender-based statute in deterring sexual activity. . . .

. . . There are now at least 37 States that have enacted gender-neutral statutory rape laws. . . .

. . . California has introduced no evidence that those States have been handicapped by the enforcement problems the plurality finds so persuasive.[7] . . .

The second flaw in the State's assertion is that even assuming that a gender-neutral statute would be more difficult to enforce, the State has still not shown that those enforcement problems would make such a statute less effective than a gender-based statute in deterring minor females from engaging in sexual intercourse.[8] Common sense, however, suggests that a gender-neutral statutory rape law is potentially a *greater* deterrent of sexual activity than a gender-based law, for the simple

reason that a gender-neutral law subjects both men and women to criminal sanctions and thus arguably has a deterrent effect on twice as many potential violators. Even if fewer persons were prosecuted under the gender-neutral law, as the State suggests, it would still be true that twice as many persons would be *subject* to arrest. The State's failure to prove that a gender-neutral law would be a less effective deterrent than a gender-based law, like the State's failure to prove that a gender-neutral law would be difficult to enforce, should have led this Court to invalidate § 261.5 . . .

. . . Until very recently, no California court or commentator had suggested that the purpose of California's statutory rape law was to protect young women from the risk of pregnancy. Indeed, the historical development of § 261.5 demonstrates that the law was intially enacted on the premise that young women, in contrast to young men, were to be deemed legally incapable of consenting to an act of sexual intercourse. Because their chastity was considered particularly precious, those young women were felt to be uniquely in need of the State's protection. In contrast, young men were assumed to be capable of making such decisions for themselves; the law therefore did not offer them any special protection.

It is perhaps because the gender classification in California's statutory rape law was initially designed to further these outmoded sexual stereotypes, rather than to reduce the incidence of teenage pregnancies, that the State has been unable to demonstrate a substantial relationship beween the classification and its newly asserted goal. . . . But whatever the reason, the State has not shown that Cal. Penal Code § 261.5 is any more effective than a gender-neutral law would be in deterring minor females from engaging in sexual intercourse. It has therefore not met its burden of proving that the statutory classification is substantially related to the achievement of its asserted goal.

I would hold that § 261.5 violates the Equal Protection Clause of the Fourteenth Amendment, and I would reverse the judgment of the California Supreme Court.

Endnotes

[1] In 1976 approximately one million 15-to-19-year-olds became pregnant, one-tenth of all women in that age group. Two-thirds of the pregnancies were illegitimate.

Illegitimacy rates for teenagers (births per 1,000 unmarried females ages 14 to 19) increased 75% for 14-to-17-year-olds between 1961 and 1974 and 33% for 18-to-19-year-olds. Alan Guttmacher Institute, 11 Million Teenagers 10, 13 (1976); C. Chilman, Adolescent Sexuality In a Changing American Society 195 (NIH Pub. No. 80–1426, 1980).

[2] The risk of maternal death is 60% higher for a teenager under the age of 15 than for a women in her early twenties. The risk is 13% higher for 15-to-19-year-olds. The statistics further show that most teenage mothers drop out of school and face a bleak economic future. See, *e.g.*, 11 Million Teenagers, *supra*, at 23, 25; Bennett & Bardon, The Effects of a School Program On Teenager Mothers and Their Children, 47 Am. J. Orthopsychiatry 671 (1977); Phipps-Yonas, Teenage Pregnancy and Motherhood, 50 Am. J. Orthopsychiatry 403, 414 (1980).

[3] This is because teenagers are disproportionately likely to seek abortions. Center for Disease Control, Abortion Surveillance 1976, pp. 22–24 (1978). In 1978, for example, teenagers in California had approximately 54,000 abortions and 53,800 live births. California Center for Health Statistics, Reproductive Health Status of California Teenage Women 1, 23 (Mar. 1980).

[4] Although petitioner concedes that the State has a "compelling" interest in preventing teenage pregnancy, he contends that the "true" purpose of § 261.5 is to protect the virtue and chastity of young women. As such, the statute is unjustifiable because it rests on archaic stereotypes. What we have said above is enough to dispose of that contention. The question for us—and the only question under the Federal Constitution—is whether the legislation violates the Equal Protection Clause of the Fourteenth Amendment, not whether its supporters may have endorsed it for reasons no longer generally accepted. Even if the preservation of female chastity were one of the motives of the statute, and even if that motive be impermissible, petitioner's argument must fail because "[i]t is a familiar practice of constitutional law that this court will not strike down an otherwise constitutional statute on the basis of an alleged illicit legislative motive."

[5] Petitioner contends that a gender-neutral statute would not hinder prosecutions because the prosecutor could take into account the relative burdens on females and males and generally only prosecute males. But to concede this is to concede all. If the prosecutor, in exercising discretion, will virtually always prosecute just the man and not the woman, we do not see why it is impermissible for the legislature to enact a statute to the same effect.

[6] The question whether a statute is *substantially* related to its asserted goals is at best an opaque one. It can be

plausibly argued that a gender-neutral statute would produce fewer prosecutions than the statute at issue here. . . . Justice Brennan's dissent argues, on the other hand, that

"even assuming that a gender-neutral statute would be more difficult to enforce, . . . [c]ommon sense . . . suggests that a gender-neutral statutory rape law is potentially a greater deterrent of sexual activity than a gender-based law, for the simple reason that a gender-neutral law subjects both men and women to criminal sanctions and thus arguably has a deterrent effect on twice as many potential violators." . . .

Where such differing speculations as to the effect of a statute are plausible, we think it appropriate to defer to the decision of the California Supreme Court, "armed as it was with the knowledge of the facts and circumstances concerning the passage and potential impact of [the statute], and familiar with the milieu in which that provision would operate." . . .

[7] There is a logical reason for this. In contrast to laws governing forcible rape, statutory rape laws apply to consensual sexual activity. Force is not an element of the crime. Since a woman who consents to an act of sexual intercourse is unlikely to report her partner to the police—whether or not she is subject to criminal sanctions—enforcement would not be undermined if the statute were to be made gender neutral. See n. 8, *infra.*

[8] As it is, § 261.5 seems to be an ineffective deterrent of sexual activity. . . . According to statistics provided by the State, an average of only 61 juvenile males and 352 adult males were arrested for statutory rape each year between 1975 and 1978. Brief for Respondent 19. During each of those years there were approximately one million Californian girls between the ages of 13–17. Cal. Dept. of Finance, Population Projections for California Counties, 1975–2020, with Age Sex Detail to 2000, Series E–150 (1977). Although the record in this case does not indicate the incidence of sexual intercourse involving those girls during that period, the California State Department of Health estimates that there were almost 50,000 pregnancies among 13-to-17-year-old girls during 1976. Cal. Dept. of Health, Birth and Abortion Records, and Physician Survey of Office Abortions (1976). I think it is fair to speculate from this evidence that a comparison of the number of arrests for statutory rape in California with the number of acts of sexual intercourse involving minor females in that State would likely demonstrate to a male contemplating sexual activity with a minor female that his chances of being arrested are reassuringly low. I seriously question, therefore, whether § 261.5 as enforced has a substantial deterrent effect. . . .

Perspectives on Women's Subordination and the Role of the Law

NADINE TAUB AND ELIZABETH SCHNEIDER

The Anglo-American legal tradition purports to value equality, by which it means, at a minimum, equal application of the law to all persons. Nevertheless, throughout this country's history, women have been denied the most basic rights of citizenship, allowed only limited participation in the marketplace, and otherwise denied access to power, dignity, and respect. Women have instead been largely occupied with providing the personal and household services necessary to sustain family life.

The work women perform in the domestic sphere is barely acknowledged, let alone valued. Institutional arrangements that preclude women's economic and sexual autonomy ensure that this work will be done primarily by women. Often, though not always, these institutions are expressed in legal form.

· · ·

The Legal Ideology of Sexual Inequality

As we have seen, the law has enforced male dominance through its direct impact on the lives of individual women and men, and its symbolic devaluation of women and their functions. The law has also perpetuated inequality through the articulation of an ideology that camouflages the fundamental injustice of existing sexual relations. Because the law purports to be the embodiment of justice, morality, and fairness, it is particularly effective in performing this ideological function.

Historically, women's subservient status has

From David Kairys (ed.), *The Politics of Law: A Progressive Critique* (New York: Pantheon, 1982), pp. 117, 124–135, 137–139. Compilation copyright © 1982 by David Kairys. Reprinted with permission of Pantheon Books, a Division of Random House, Inc.

been associated with a view of differences between the sexes and differential legal treatment. A succession of Supreme Court decisions[1] has legitimized that subservient status by upholding laws which, on their face, mandate that the sexes be treated differently. This section examines the prinkcipal doctrinal bases used by the Court by focusing on three illustrative Supreme Court decisions.[2] In an 1873 decision, differences between men and women were expressed in terms of gross overgeneralizations reflecting moral or religious views of women's nature and proper role. The ideology masked women's inferior treatment by glorifying women's separate role. In 1908, the differences focused to a much greater extent on the "facts" of women's physical limitations necessitated by their reproductive functions and their consequent dependence on men. These deficiencies called for special treatment for women to be on an equal footing with men. Present-day ideology is even more subtle. The Supreme Court espouses a concern for sexual equality and purports to reject stereotypical overgeneralizations about the sexes; yet it refuses to recognize classifications based on reproductive capacity as sex-based, and it regards legal and social disabilities that have been imposed on women as realistic differences sufficient to justify differential treatment. By continuing to make differential treatment appear fair, the current Court provides a rationale for present inequalities.

Women's "Separate Sphere": Bradwell v. Illinois

In *Bradwell* v. *Illinois*,[3] the Supreme Court upheld the Illinois Supreme Court's decision to refuse Myra Bradwell admission to the Illinois bar because she was a woman.[4] She studied law under her husband's tutelage; raised four children; ran a private school; was involved in civic work; and founded a weekly newspaper, the *Chicago Legal News*, which became an important legal publication. A feminist active in women's suffrage organizations, Myra Bradwell played an important role in obtaining Illinois legislation that removed women's legal disabilities. She took her case to the Supreme Court, arguing that admission to practice law was guaranteed by the privileges and immunities clause of the recently adopted Fourteenth Amendment.

The *Bradwell* litigation took place within the context of a particular conception of sex roles. Although women were in no way the equals of men during the colonial and Revolutionary periods, the nature of their subordination, particularly in the middle classes, changed dramatically between the end of the eighteenth century and the middle of the nineteenth century.[5] The early stages of industrial capitalism involved increasing specialization and the movement of production out of the home, which resulted in heightened sex segregation. Men went out of the house to work; and women's work, influence, and consciousness remained focused at home. Although women continued to be dependent on and subservient to men, women were no longer placed at the bottom of a hierarchy dominated by men. Rather, they came to occupy women's "separate sphere," a qualitatively different world centered on home and family. Women's role was by definition incompatible with full participation in society.

"Separate-sphere" ideology clearly delineated the activities open to women. Women's role within the home was glorified, and women's limited participation in paid labor outside the home[6] was most often in work that could be considered an extension of their work within the home. For example, native-born mill girls in the 1820s and 1830s, and immigrant women in the 1840s and 1850s, worked in largely sex-segregated factories manufacturing textiles, clothing, and shoes. Likewise, after a period of time, teaching became a woman's occupation. Unpaid charitable and welfare activities, however, were encouraged as consistent with women's domestic responsibilities.

Although ultimately quite constraining, the development of women's separate sphere had some important benefits. While the emphasis on women's moral purity and the cult of domesticity tended to mask women's inferior position, it also allowed women a certain degree of autonomy. It gave them the opportunity to organize extensively into religious and secular welfare associations, afforded access to education, and provided them with a basis for uniting with other women. Evaluations of the cult of domesticity and women's separate sphere by feminist historians have consequently ranged from the view that women were victims of this ideology to the recognition that women found a source of strength and identity in their separate world.[7]

The development of separate-sphere ideology appears in large measure to have been a consequence of changes in the conditions of production. Behavior was then further channeled by a vast cultural transformation promoted through books and magazines. The law does not seem to have played an overt role in the initial articulation of the separate-sphere ideology; but to the extent that the ideological transformation that occurred in the early part of the nineteenth century was a reaction to a strict hierarchy imposed by the previous legal order, the legal system may well have played an important part at the outset.

In any event, the law appears to have contributed significantly to the perpetuation of this ideology. Immediately following the Civil War, feminists attempted to have women expressly included in the protections of the Fourteenth and Fifteenth Amendments. The failure of the Fourteenth and Fifteenth Amendments to address the needs of women, and indeed for the first time to write the word "men" into the Constitution, resulted in a long-lasting division in the women's movement, which reflected differences regarding both ends and means, and which lasted at least until the 1890s. Feminists aligned with the Republican Party stressed black suffrage and saw women suffrage as coming through a constitutional amendment at some future time. The more militant and effective National Woman Suffrage Association favored legal and political efforts to obtain a judicial or congressional declaration that the Wartime Amendments also secured rights for women.[8] Although Myra Bradwell's legal challenge was not known to be part of an organized strategy, her attempt to use the Fourteenth Amendment to challenge state prohibitions on occupational choices legally reflected this tack. By invoking the cult of domesticity as a legal rationale for rejecting this demand, the courts enshrined and reinforced separate-sphere ideology while deferring women's rights.

In rejecting Myra Bradwell's challenge to Illinois's prohibition on occupational choice, the Supreme Court had two options: to construe the new constitutional guarantees narrowly so as to defeat all comers, or to find special reasons for treating women differently. The majority adopted the first approach. It held that the decision was controlled by the Court's decision (the day before) in the *Slaughter-House Cases*,[9] which held that, even after the adoption of the Fourteenth Amendment, states retained the unmediated right to regulate occupations.

However, Justice Joseph Bradley, who dissented in *Slaughter-House*, opted for the second approach. His concurring opinion is the embodiment of the separate-sphere ideology:

> [T]he civil law as well as nature itself, has always recognized a wide difference in the respective spheres and destinies of man and woman. Man is, or should be woman's protector and defender. The natural and proper timidity and delicacy which belongs to the female sex evidently unfits it for many of the occupations of civil life. . . . The constitution of the family organization, which is founded in the divine ordinance, as well as in the nature of things, indicates the domestic sphere as that which properly belongs to the domain and functions of womanhood. The harmony, not to say identity, of interests and views which belong, or should belong, to the family institution is repugnant to the idea of a woman adopting a distinct and independent career from that of her husband. . . .
>
> It is true that many women are unmarried and not affected by any of the duties, complications, and incapacities arising out of the married state, but these are exceptions to the general rule. The paramount destiny and mission of woman are to fulfill the noble and benign offices of wife and mother. This is the law of the Creator. And the rules of civil society must be adapted to the general constitution of things, and cannot be based upon exceptional cases.[10]

Glorification of women's destiny serves to soften any sense of unfairness in excluding women from the legal profession. Since this "paramount destiny and mission" of women is mandated by "nature," "divine ordinance," and "the law of the Creator," the civil law need not recognize the claims of women who deviate from their proper role. By conceiving of the law as the means of enforcing reality as it "is or should be," Bradley can concede that some women do live apart from men—or even that some women who live with men are capable of

functioning in the public domain—without exposing the law as unreasonable.

Women's Physical Differences: Muller v. Oregon

In the nineteenth century, the persisting separate-sphere ideology legitimized and reinforced women's marginal and secondary status in the work force. Working women were suspicious, inferior, and immoral. Those women who joined the work force were predominantly single or widowed, and confined to "women's jobs," serving as a reserve supply of cheap labor. The primary identification of women with the home also provided an ideological basis for keeping women out of unions.

With industrialization and urbanization in the late nineteenth century came deplorable work conditions for all workers, which prompted unions and social reformers to press for legislation regulating conditions of work, hours, and wages. By the turn of the century, both sex-neutral and sex-based protective laws had been passed and sustained against legal challenge. Women-only protective laws were enacted with the express support of such reform groups as the National Women's Trade Union League, the General Federation of Women's Clubs, and the National Consumers' League, which merged the energies of wealthy and working women. Although sex-based legislation might have conflicted with suffragists' initial argument that women were entitled to the role because they were fundamentally equal to men, it was entirely consistent with the more expedient position they had adopted in the 1890s, to the effect that women should be given the vote because their special perspective would benefit society.

Protective-labor legislation was countered legally by conservatives who, led by the American Bar Association, revived the natural-law notion of freedom of contract and located it in the due process clause of the Fourteenth Amendment. The effort culminated in *Lochner* v. *New York*,[11] a decision that, in striking down maximum-hour legislation for bakers by relying on the "common understanding" that baking and most other occupations did not endanger health, cast doubt on the validity of all protective legislation.

Advocates of state "protective" legislation for women could take two routes after *Lochner*: one, to displace the "common understanding" in *Lochner* with scientific evidence that all industrial jobs, when performed more than ten hours a day, were dangerous to a worker's health; or two, by arguing that women's need for special protection justified an exception to *Lochner*.[12] In *Muller* v. *Oregon*[13] the Supreme Court was faced with a challenge to an Oregon statute that prohibited women from working more than ten hours a day in a laundry. The National Consumers' League, which played the major role in the middle- and upper-class reform movement, filed an *amicus* brief, written by Louis Brandeis, Josephine Goldmark, and Florence Kelly,[14] which attempted to combine both approaches. The brief portrayed as common knowledge pseudo-scientific data regarding physical differences between men and women, emphasizing the "bad effects" of long hours on women workers' health, "female functions," childbearing capacity, and job safety, and on the health and welfare of future generations. Adopting the view urged by the *amici*, the Court upheld the challenged legislation:

> [T]hat woman's physical structure and the performance of maternal functions place her at a disadvantage in the struggle for subsistence is obvious. This is especially true when the burdens of motherhood are upon her. Even when they are not, by abundant testimony of the medical fraternity continuance for a long time on her feet at work, repeating this from day to day, tends to injurious effects upon the body, and as healthy mothers are essential to vigorous offspring, the physical well-being of woman becomes an object of public interest and care in order to preserve the strength and vigor of the race. . . .
>
> Still again history discloses the fact that woman has always been dependent upon man. . . . As minors, though not to the same extent, she has been looked upon in the courts as needing special care that her rights may be preserved. . . . Though limitations upon personal and contractual rights may be removed by legislation, there is that in her disposition and habits of life which will generate against a full assertion of these rights. She will still be where some legislation to protect her seems necessary to secure a real equality of right. . . . Differentiated by these matters from the other sex, she is properly placed in a class by

herself, and legislation designed for her protection may be sustained, even when the legislation is not necessary for men and could not be sustained.[15]

Muller expresses a view of women as different from and more limited than men because of their "physical structure" and "natural functions." Although this view of women is every bit as fixed as that expressed in *Bradwell*, it purports to be grounded in physical fact. Legal reforms, such as the removal of "limitations upon personal and contractual rights," would be ineffective in changing women's rights because of women's "disposition and habits of life." These differences in physical structure and childbearing capacity are thus sufficient for women to be "properly placed in a class by themselves." Women's primary function as mother is now seen as physically incompatible with the demands of equal participation in the work force. Special work conditions for women are therefore justified.

Both social reformers and legal realists regarded the statute's survival and the Supreme Court's recognition of economic and social facts as important victories. However, as organized labor lost interest in protective legislation for men, the primary legal legacy of *Muller* was a view of women that justified excluding women from job opportunities and earning levels available to men.[16] The Court's focus on the apparently immutable facts of women's physique obscured the exploitation of workers generally and the social discrimination that assigned full-time responsibility for the household to women. As an ideological matter, the notion that women's different physiology requires special protection continues to legitimize a division of labor in which men are primary wage earners entitled to draw on the personal services of their wives, and women remain marginal workers available to replace more expensive male workers.[17]

Unequal Equal Protection: Michael M. v. Sonoma County

Although Supreme Court opinions of the 1960s began to acknowledge some changes in woman's position,[18] it took the rebirth of an active women's movement in the 1960s and the development of a legal arm to obtain a definitive legal determination that sex-based discrimination violated the equal-protection clause of the Fourteenth Amendment.

In 1971, the Supreme Court, in *Reed* v. *Reed*,[19] for the first time invalidated a statute on the ground that it denied women equal protection. The Court unanimously struck down an Idaho statute preferring males to females in the performance of estate administration, refusing to find generalizations about women's business experience adequate to sustain the preference. Although the actual dispute involved a relatively trivial duty, a statute that already had been repealed, and facts that presented no major threat to the established social order, the opinion appeared to voice a view of women that seemed radically different from previous judicial expressions.

Equal protection rests on the legal principle that people who are similarly situated in fact must be similarly treated by the law.[20] In *Reed* the Court for the first time held that women and men are similarly situated. The Court recognized the social reality, through "judicial notice," that "in this country, presumably due to the greater longevity of women, a large proportion of estates . . . are administered by women."[21] By recognizing a departure from traditional social roles as so obvious as to be able to rely on judicial notice, the Court appeared to presage the erosion of the "differences" ideology.

Over the last ten years, in upholding equal-protection challenges to sex-based legislation, the Supreme Court has repeatedly rejected over-generalizations based on sex.[22] For example, in *Frontiero* v. *Richardson*,[23] the Court upheld an equal-protection challenge to the military's policy of denying dependency benefits to male dependents of female servicewomen. The plurality opinion criticized *Bradwell* as reflective of an attitude of "romantic paternalism" that "in practical effect, put women not on a pedestal but in a cage."[24] Similarly, in *Stanton* v. *Stanton*,[25] the Court upheld an equal-protection challenge to a state statute specifying a greater age of majority for males than females with respect to parental obligation for support. In so doing, the Court appeared to understand the effect of stereotypes in perpetuating discrimination and the detrimental impact that differential treatment has on women's situation.[26]

However, the Supreme Court's developing application of equal protection has not lived up to its initial promise. The Court has adopted a lower standard of review for sex-based classifications[27] than for race-based classifications, reflecting its view that race discrimination is a more serious so-cial problem than sex discrimination. The Court has rejected only those stereotypes that it perceives as grossly inaccurate. Indeed, the Court has developed a new and more subtle view of "realistically based differences," which encompasses underlying physical distinctions between the sexes, distinctions created by law, and socially imposed differences in situation, and frequently confuses the three. In these cases, the Court simply reasons that equal protection is not violated because men and women are not "similarly situated."

The paradigmatic physical distinction between the sexes, women's reproductive capacity, has been consistently viewed by courts as a proper basis for differential treatment. The present Court does so by refusing to recognize that classifications based on pregnancy involve sex discrimination and by ignoring the similarities between pregnancy and other temporary disabilities. In *Geduldig* v. *Aiello*,[28] the Supreme Court rejected an equal-protection challenge to California's disability insurance system, which paid benefits to persons in private employment who were unable to work but excluded from coverage disabilities resulting from pregnancy. The Court noted that

> [w]hile it is true that only women become pregnant, it does not follow that every legislative classification concerning pregnancy is a sex-based classification like those considered in *Reed, supra* and *Frontiero, supra*. Normal pregnancy is an objectively identifiable physical condition with unique characteristics. Absent a showing that distinctions involving pregnancy are mere pretexts designed to effect an invidious discrimination against the members of one sex or the other, lawmakers are constitutionally free to include or exclude pregnancy from the coverage of legislation such as this on any reasonable basis, just as with respect to any other physical condition.[29]

This position was effectively reaffirmed in *General Electric* v. *Gilbert*,[30] in which the exclusion of pregnancy from General Electric's disability program was upheld in the face of a challenge under Title VII of the Civil Rights Act.

Similarly, the present Court finds differential treatment justified by women's special circumstances, even when those circumstances reflect legislatively[31] or socially imposed burdens.[32] In *Parham* v. *Hughes*,[33] a plurality of the Court upheld a Georgia statute that allowed an unwed mother to sue for the wrongful death of her child, but disallowed such suits by an unwed father unless he had procured a court order legitimating the child. The Court found that treating men and women differently in this fashion did not constitute impermissible sex discrimination because the two sets of parents were not similarly situated in two respects. First, under Georgia law, unwed fathers, but not unwed mothers, could legitimate their children by a unilateral act. This difference is, of course, imposed by law, not by biological necessity. Second, the Court pointed to the difficulty in ascertaining the father's identity. Here the difference in situation results primarily from socially imposed differences in child-rearing patterns, since, as a physiological matter, unless the woman is observed giving birth, there is little reason to put more faith in a woman's claim to be a particular child's parent than in a man's claim to be that child's parent. The Court's reliance on these societally imposed differences reflects its present willingness to uphold distinctions that are generally accurate though unfair to individuals and likely to perpetuate existing sex roles.

The most recent expression of the Court's current ideology of equality is a 1981 Supreme Court case, *Michael M.* v. *Sonoma County*,[34] upholding California's statutory rape law, challenged by a seventeen-year-old male, which punished males having sex with a female under eighteen. The thrust of his attack on the statute was that it denied him equal protection since he, not his partner, was criminally liable.

Statutory rape laws have rested historically on the legal fiction that young women are incapable of consent. They exalt female chastity and reflect and reinforce archaic assumptions about the male initiative in sexual relations and the weakness and naïveté of young women.[35] Nevertheless, the Court in *Michael M.* found no violation of equal-protection guarantees and upheld the differential treatment as reasonably related to the goal of eliminating teenage pregnancy.

Although the Court in *Michael M.* cited its prior decisions rejecting sex-based classifications without proof of a "substantial relationship" to "important governmental objectives," it did not, in fact, apply them. No legislative history was produced in California or elsewhere to show that the purpose of the sex-based classification was to eliminate teenage pregnancy. Moreover, the experi-

ence of other jurisdictions showed that the criminalization of male, but not female, conduct bore little relation to the goal of eliminating teenage pregnancy. Instead, the Court simply stated that because females become pregnant and because they bear the consequences of pregnancy, "equalization" via differential punishment is reasonable.

> We need not be medical doctors to discern that young men and young women are not similarly situated with respect to the problems and risks of sexual intercourse. Only women may become pregnant and they suffer disproportionately the profound physical, emotional and psychological consequences of sexual activity.[36]

Thus, the Court asserts, the sex-based classification, which "serves roughly to 'equalize' the deterrents on the sexes,"[37] realistically reflects the fact that the sexes are not similarly situated.

Justice Potter Stewart's concurring opinion in *Michael M.* develops the crux of this new ideology of realistically based classifications:

> The Constitution is violated when government, state or federal, invidiously classifies similarly situated people on the bases of the immutable characteristic with which they were born. . . . [W]hile detrimental gender classifications by government often violate the Constitution, they do not always do so, for the reason that there are differences between males and females that the Constitution necessarily recognizes. In this case we deal with the most basic of these differences: females can become pregnant as the result of sexual intercourse; males cannot. . . .
>
> "[A] State is not free to make overbroad generalizations based on sex which are entirely unrelated to any differences between men and women or which demean the ability or social status of the protected class." Gender-based classifications may not be based upon administrative convenience or upon archaic assumptions about the proper role of the sexes. . . . But we have recognized that in certain narrow circumstances men and women are *not* similarly situated and in these circumstances a gender classification based on clear differences between the sexes is not invidious,

and a legislative classification realistically based upon these differences is not unconstitutional. . . .

Applying these principles to the classification enacted by the California legislature, it is readily apparent that [the statute] does not violate the Equal Protection Clause. Young women and men are not similarly situated with respect to the problems and risks associated with intercourse and pregnancy, and the statute is realistically related to the legitimate state purpose of reducing those problems and risks.[38]

Yet, the classification at issue in *Michael M.* had very little to do with biological differences between the sexes. As is seen from the total absense of supportive legislative history, the statute was not designed to address the problem of teenage pregnancy. Moreover, as Justice John Paul Stevens points out, if criminal sanctions are believed to deter the conduct leading to pregnancy, a young woman's greater risk of harm from pregnancy is, if anything, a reason to subject her to sanctions. The statute instead embodies and reinforces the assumption that men are always responsible for initiating sexual intercourse and females must always be protected against their aggression. Nevertheless, the Court's focus on the physical fact of reproductive capacity serves to obscure the social bases of its decision. Indeed, it is striking that the Court entirely fails to treat pregnancy as sex discrimination when discrimination really is in issue, while using it as a rationale in order to justify differential treatment when it is not in issue.

Like *Bradwell* and *Muller, Michael M.* affirms that there are differences between the sexes, both the physical difference of childbearing capacity and women's social role, which should result in differential legal treatment. However, because this affirmation comes at the same time as the Court claims to reject "overbroad generalizations unrelated to differences between men and women or which demean [women's] ability or social status," the Court's approval of differential treatment is especially pernicious. The fact of and harms caused by teenage pregnancy are used by the Court to avoid close analysis of the stereotypes involved and careful scrutiny of the pregnancy rationale. The role that the challenged statute plays in reinforcing those harms is never examined. The Court accepts as immutable fact that men and women are

not similarly situated, particularly when pregnancy is involved. The Court then appears to favor equal rights for women, but for one small problem—pregnancy.

As an ideological matter, the separation of pregnancy and child-bearing capacity, social discrimination, and even legally imposed discrimination from "invidious" discrimination, in which differential treatment is unrelated to "real" differences between men and women, perform an important function of legitimizing discrimination through the language of equality.[39] Although its doctrinal veneer is different, the Court's current approach has the same effect as *Bradwell* and *Muller.* If both pregnancy and socially imposed differences in role always keep men and women from being similarly situated—thereby excluding sex-based differences from the purview of equal protection—then the real substance of sex discrimination can still be ignored. Childbearing capacity is the single greatest basis of differential treatment for women—it is a major source of discrimination in both work and family life, and the critical distinction on which the ideology of both separate spheres and physical differences rests. Yet, by appearing to reject gross generalizations about proper roles of the sexes exemplified by both *Bradwell* and *Muller,* current ideology attempts to maintain credibility by "holding out the promise of liberation."[40] By emphasizing its reliance on a reality that appears more closely tied to physical differences and the hard facts of social disadvantage, e.g., the consequences of teenage pregnancy for young girls, the Court appears sensible and compromising. Indeed, the message of the Court's approach is merely to reject "ultra feminist" androgyny while favoring equality generally. However, by excluding the core of sex discrimination, the Court is effectively removing women entirely from the reach of equal protection.

This new ideological approach must be viewed, as were *Bradwell* and *Muller,* in its historical context. Although the women's movement provided the triggering change in consciousness, and an understanding of the nature and forms of sex stereotyping on which the sex-discrimination challenges of this period have been based,[41] many of the sex-discrimination cases decided by the Supreme Court have not arisen from feminist struggles and have been presented to the Court by men, not women. As a result, these cases, including *Michael M.,* did not always develop the harm perceived by women for the Court, either as a factual or legal matter. Moreover, in the absence of a sustained mass movement, the Supreme Court has been able to use feminist formulations to justify the status quo. Over the last several years, with the advent of a visible right-wing, anti-feminist, and anti-abortion movement, the women's movement appears to be garnering less public support. Indeed, a strategy of these groups to separate superficial claims for parity, such as equal pay, from more fundamental demands, such as the Equal Rights Amendment and reproductive control, has already had some impact on the women's movement, where issues of reproductive control have not always been viewed as sex discrimination.[42] The Court's new approach tends to strengthen this separation of issues within the women's movement and reward the most conservative tendencies.

Although the legal ideology of equality shows some progression from *Bradwell* to *Michael M.*, there is less than might be expected. Certainly the Court's view of women, and the ways in which it sees the sexes, has moved from an overt view of women's separate roles to a more subtle view of limited differences, but this new view is more dangerous precisely because it appears so reasonable. The Court's perception of differences that suffice to justify discrimination has altered somewhat, but it remains equally fixed. The Court continues to validate inequality by legitimizing differential treatment.

Endnotes

[1] The Supreme Court is by no means the exclusive source of legal ideology. Indeed, it is arguable that in the area of women's rights, Supreme Court opinions are not the best or most accurate source of prevailing views of women, since few Supreme Court cases prior to 1970 involved assertions of equal rights by women.

[2] Much of the material regarding the first two cases has been drawn from Barbara A. Babcock et al., *Sex Discrimination and the Law: Causes and Remedies* (Boston: Little, Brown, 1975), pp. 782–800.

[3] Bradwell v. Illionois, 83 U.S. (16 Wall.) 130 (1873).

[4] Arabella Mansfield, in Iowa, had become the first woman regularly admitted to practice law in the United States in 1869.

[5] See Mary Ryan, [*Womanhood in America*, 2d ed. (New York: New Viewpoints, 1979); Alice Kessler-Harris,

Women Have Always Worked: A Historical Overview (Old Westbury: The Feminist Press, 1981), pp. 70, 147; and Nancy F. Cott, *The Bonds of Womanhood* (New Haven: Yale University Press, 1977).]

[6] Only about 10 percent of all women worked in the paid labor force in the mid-1840s. The percentage did not rise above 20 percent before 1900. Kessler-Harris, *supra* note 5, at 61, 70.

[7] *See* Cott, *supra* note 5, at 197–99.

[8] *See generally* Ellen C. DuBois, *Elizabeth Cady Stanton and Susan B. Anthony: Correspondence, Writings and Speeches* (New York: Schocken, 1981).

[9] 83 U.S. (16 Wall.) 130 (1873).

[10] *Id*. at 141–42.

[11] Lochner v. New York, 198 U.S. 45 (1905).

[12] Babcock et al., *supra* note 2, at 28.

[13] Muller v. Oregon, 208 U.S. 412 (1908).

[14] This brief has mistakenly come to be known as the first Brandeis brief, since Louis Brandeis actually filed it, although Josephine Goldmark, Florence Kelly, and other volunteers assembled the data. Babcock et al., *supra* note 2, at 29.

[15] Muller v. Oregon, 208 U.S. at 421–22.

[16] Sex-based protective legislation was considered valid until a series of court decisions between 1968 and 1973 invalidated such statutes. A few statutes, however, remain on the books today.

[17] *See* Heidi Hartmann, "Capitalism, Patriarchy and Job Segregation by Sex," 1 *SIGNS* 137 (1976).

[18] *See, e.g.,* Hoyt v. Florida, 368 U.S. 57 (1961).

[19] Reed v. Reed, 404 U.S. 71 (1971).

[20] *See generally* Joseph Tussman and Jacobus TenBroek, "The Equal Protection of the Laws," 37 *California Law Review* 341 (1949).

[21] Reed v. Reed, 404 U.S. at 75.

[22] Most of these cases have involved assumptions built into government benefit statutes that the male was the breadwinner and the female the dependent at home. *See* Frontiero v. Richardson, 411 U.S. 677 (1973); Weinberger v. Wiesenfeld, 420 U.S. 636 (1975); Califano v. Goldfarb, 430 U.S. 199 (1977); and Califano v. Westcott, 443 U.S. 76 (1979).

[23] Frontiero v. Richardson, 411 U.S. 677 (1973).

[24] *Id*. at 684.

[25] Stanton v. Stanton, 421 U.S. 7 (1975).

[26] *Id*. at 14–15.

[27] In Craig v. Boren, 429 U.S. 190, 197 (1976), the Court articulated the standard that "to withstand constitutional challenge, . . . classifications by gender must serve important governmental objectives and must be

substantially related to achievement of those objectives."

[28] Geduldig v. Aiello, 417 U.S. 484 (1974).

[29] *Id.* at 496, n.20.

[30] General Electric v. Gilbert, 429 U.S. 125 (1976). The Supreme Court's view of pregnancy expressed in *Gilbert* was promptly rejected by Congress. The Pregnancy Discrimination Act, 26 U.S.C. §3304(a) (12) (1976), was passed by Congress to overturn the *Gilbert* decision. This suggests that the Supreme Court's ideology concerning pregnancy as a permissible basis for differential treatment in employment was not widely accepted. It underscores the tenuousness of relying on Supreme Court opinions as a source of prevailing views on women. *See* note 1 *supra.*

[31] For example, in both Schlesinger v. Ballard, 419 U.S. 498 (1975), and Rostker v. Goldberg, 101 S. Ct. 2646, the Supreme Court rejected equal-protection challenges to sex discrimination in the military on the grounds that since sex-based differential treatment already existed in the military, men and women were not "similarly situated" to begin with. In *Rostker,* the Court particularly emphasized that since the perpetuation of this differential treatment was fully considered by Congress and not "unthinking," it was permissible. *Supra* at 2655.

[32] Ironically, despite his actual vote, Justice Potter Stewart's dissent in Caban v. Mohammed, 441 U.S. 380, 398 (1979), at least gives lip service to the need to differentiate between inherent physical differences and societally imposed differences in roles.

[33] Parham v. Hughes, 441 U.S. 347 (1979).

[34] Michael M. v. Sonoma County, 450 U.S. 464 (1981).

[35] Note, "The Constitutionality of Statutory Rape Laws," 27 *UCLA Law Review* 757, 761 (1980); Michael M. v. Sonoma County, 159 California Reporter 340, 601 P.2d 572 (1979); (Mosk, J., dissenting). Leigh Bienen,

"Rape III: National Developments in Rape Reform Legislation," 6 *Women's Rights Law Reporter* 170, 189 (1981). However, as Bienen points out, the women's movement has sometimes been ambivalent as to whether these laws helped or hurt women. Bienen, *supra* at 180.

[36] Michael M. v. Sonoma County, 450 U.S. at 471.

[37] *Id.* at 473.

[38] *Id.* at 477–79.

[39] *See* in particular, chapter 5; Alan Freeman, "Legitimizing Racial Discrimination Through Antidiscrimination Law: A Critical Review of Supreme Court Doctrine," 62 *Minnesota Law Review* 1050 (1978).

[40] *Id.* at 1052.

[41] Indeed, feminist legal strategies are still evolving. For a thorough presentation of the principle that each person is entitled to equal treatment based on equal performance without regard to sex, *see* Barbara Brown et al., "The Equal Rights Amendment: A Constitutional Basis for Equal Rights for Women," 80 *Yale Law Journal* 871 (1971). Concern that the equal-rights approach allows a few exceptional women to satisfy the criteria for success and thus escape subordination while their individual success serves to justify the reality that most women remain in an inferior position has been expressed in [Kathryn Powers, "Sex Segregation and the Ambivalent Directions of Sex Discrimination Law," *Wisconsin Law Review* 55 (1979)]; Catherine MacKinnon, *Sexual Harassment of Working Women: A Case of Sex Discrimination* (New Haven: Yale University Press, 1979); and Ann E. Freedman, "Housework, Childcare and the Limits of Equality Theory" (Paper presented at the Critical Legal Studies Conference, Minniapolis, Minnesota, May 1981). For a discussion of alternate formulations, see these sources and Nadine Taub, Book Review, 80 *Columbia Law Review* 1686 (1980).

[42] *See* Mary Dunlap, "Harris v. McRae," 6 *Women's Rights Law Reporter* 165 (1981).

Sexism and the Political Power of Women

JOHN HART ELY

The case of women is timely and complicated.[1] Instances of first-degree prejudice are obviously rare,[2] but just as obviously exaggerated stereotyping—typically to the effect that women are unsuited to the work of the world and therefore belong at home—has long been rampant throughout the male population and consequently in our almost exclusively male legislatures in particular. It may all be in apparent good humor, even perceived as protective, but it has cost women dearly. Absent a strong demonstration of mitigating factors, therefore, we would have to treat gender-based classifications that act to the disadvantage of women as suspicious. If the stereotyping has been clear, however, so has the noninsularity of the group affected. The degree of contact between men and women could hardly be greater, and neither, of course, are women "in the closet" as homosexuals historically have been. Finally, lest you think I missed it, women have about half the votes, apparently more. As if it weren't enough that they're not discrete and insular, they're not even a minority!

Despite that seeming avalanche of rebuttal, there remains something that seems right in the claim that women have been operating at an unfair disadvantage in the political process, though it's tricky pinning down just what gives rise to that intuition. It is tempting to observe that although women may be a majority, they haven't in any real sense *consented* to the various instances of gender-based legislation. Voters, female and male alike, are typically confronted not with single-issue referenda but rather with packages of attitudes, packages we call candidates. Most women are not injured in any direct way by laws that classify on the basis of sex—depriving women, say, of the opportunity to tend bar, guard railroad crossings, or administer estates—and the fact that they help elect representatives who are unprepared to repeal such

laws may mean only that there are other issues about which they feel more strongly. This may indeed be so, but the argument changes the rules.[3] Once we start to shift from a focus on whether something is blocking the opportunity to correct the stereotype reflected in the legislation, to one that attempts to explain why those who have that opportunity have chosen to pursue other goals instead, we begin to lose our way, to permit our disagreement with the substantive merits of the legislation to take the place of what is *constitutionally* relevant, an inability to do anything about it. That answer triggers a more promising inquiry, though—whether it is fair to say that women have "chosen" not to avail themselves of their opportunities, either by voting or by personally influencing those men with whom they come in contact, to correct the exaggerated stereotype that many men hold and on the basis of which they have often legislated. A major reason for lack of action on either of these fronts, or so at least it can be plausibly be argued, has been that many women have *accepted* the overdrawn stereotype and thus have seen nothing to "correct" by vote or a personal persuasion, and by their example may even have acted so as to reinforce it. That could, of course, imply that it wasn't so exaggerated a stereotype after all, but it could mean something else too, that our society, including the women in it, has been so pervasively dominated by men that women quite understandably have accepted men's stereotypes, of women as well as on other subjects.[4]

The general idea is one that in some contexts has merit. A sufficiently pervasive prejudice can block its own correction not simply by keeping its victims "in the closet" but also by convincing even them of its correctness. In *Castaneda v. Partida*, decided in 1977, the Court held that a prima facie case of intentional discrimination against Mexican-Americans in the selection of grand jurors was not constitutionally affected by the fact that Mexican-Americans enjoyed "governing majority" status in the county involved. Concurring, Justice Marshall gave the reason why: "Social scientists agree that members of minority groups frequently respond to

From *Democracy and Distrust: A Theory of Judicial Review* (Cambridge: Harvard University Press, 1980), pp. 164–170.

discrimination and prejudice by attempting to dis- associate themselves from the group, even to the point of adopting the majority's negative attitudes towards the minority."[5] Nor does this insight seem relevant only to numerical minorities: slaves out- numbered masters in the antebellum South, and outnumbered whites generally in some states, but that apparently didn't keep many of them from assimilating much of the mythology used to legiti- mate their enslavement.[6]

To apply all this to the situation of women in America in 1980, however, is to strain a metaphor past the breaking point. It is true that women do not generally operate as a very cohesive political force, banding together to elect candidates pledged to the "woman's point of view." Constitutional suspiciousness should turn on evidence of blocked access, however, not on the fact that elections are coming out "wrong." There is an infinity of groups that do not act as such in the political marketplace, but we don't automatically infer that they have a "slave mentality." The cause, more often, is that (sensibly or not) the people involved are not in agreement over the significance of their shared characteristic. Thus in assessing suspiciousness it cannot be enough simply to note that a group does not function as a political bloc. A further reference to the surrounding conditions must be had, to see if there are systemic bars (and I'm obviously not suggesting they need be official ones) to access. On that score it seems important that today discussion about the appropriate "place" of women is com- mon among both women and men, and between the sexes as well. The very stereotypes that gave rise to laws "protecting" women by barring them from various activities are under daily and pub- licized attack, and are the subject of equally spirited defense. (That the common stereotypes are so openly described and debated, as they are not in the case of racial minorities, is itself some evidence of the comparatively free and non- threatening nature of the interchange.) Given such open discussion of the traditional stereotypes, the claim that the numerical majority is being "domi- nated," that women are in effect "slaves" who have no realistic choice but to assimilate the stereo- types, is one it has become impossible to maintain except at the most inflated rhetorical level. It also renders the broader argument self-contradictory, since to make such a claim in the context of the current debate one must at least implicitly grant the validity of the sterotype, that women are in effect

mental infants who will believe anything men tell them to believe. Many women do seem to prefer the old stereotype to the new liberation. You and I may think that's a mistaken choice. But once we begin regarding serious disagreement with a choice as proof that those who made it aren't in control of their minds, we've torn up the rulebook and made substantive wrongheadedness the test of unconstitutionality.

However, most laws classifying by sex weren't passed this morning or even the day before yester- day: in fact it is rare to see a gender-based classifi- cation enacted since the New Deal. In general women couldn't even *vote* until the Nineteenth Amendment was ratified in 1920, and most of these laws probably predate even that: they should be invalidated. Throughout this discussion, however, I have been concerned with factors more subtle than the lack of a vote, and it can at least be argued that until quite recently there persisted throughout America's female population a "*Casteneda*-like" ac- ceptance of the prejudices of males, unventilated by more than token airing of their validity. Given what appropriately makes a classification suspi- cious, it is not necessarily a unitary question whether discrimination against a certain group should be so regarded, and the case of women seems one where the date of enactment should be important. It surely seems more helpful than any- thing the Court has come up with on the question of whether those who passed the law in issue were proceeding on the basis of an "archaic and over- broad generalization"[7] or whether, say, they were genuinely trying to protect women from certain physical risks to which in statistical terms they are unusually subject, realized there were counterex- amples and estimated their incidence about right, but nonetheless felt the costs of identifying the exceptions were simply too high. I noted above how dangerously subjective direct attempts to judge whether a given law was generated by an overdrawn stereotype can be, since the face of the statute will inevitably be consistent with either of these descriptions of the decision process, and the legislative history will inevitably be partial and subject to manipulation. The date of passage seems a somewhat more solid datum, one that can at least begin to anchor the judicial inquiry. That's an aside, however, since the date of passage seems unquestionably relevant to what our analysis has suggested is a more promising approach to the question of suspiciousness—one geared to the existence of official or unofficial blocks on the opportunities of those the law disadvantages to counter by argument or example the overdrawn stereotypes we might, from the demography of the decision-making body, otherwise suspect were operative.

The case of women can be further put in perspective by exploring what should follow from a judicial determination that the suspiciousness of a given classification has not been allayed and that it therefore is unconstitutional. Here too the answer is not unitary: we have looked at several indicia of suspiciousness, and their remedial implications differ. Where a law is suspect because of what I have been calling first-degree prejudice, or indeed where it has been infected by a subtler form of stereotyping under conditions where the negatively affected group was barred from effective access at the time of passage *and still is,* the only appropriate remedy is to void the classification and insist—if the legislature wishes to continue to classify—on a different, generally more finely tuned, test of qualification. The obvious alternative to this is to have the judiciary restrike the substantive balance, attempting not to let the prejudices that apparently influenced the legislature play a part, and invalidate the classification only if in some sense it still ends up unacceptable on its merits. You will not be surprised to learn that I regard that approach as quite inappropriate. We can cite occasions on which our judiciary has displayed a lesser susceptibility to bare-knuckled first-degree prejudice than our elected officials, but we also can cite some where it hasn't. Moreover, instances of such prejudice, for reasons it is not necessary to review, are almost invariably instances of self-serving comparison as well. Judges tend to belong to the same broad categories as legislators—most of them, for example, are white heterosexual males comfortably above the poverty line—and there isn't any reason to suppose that they are immune to the usual temptations to self-aggrandizing generalization. When in a given situation you can't be trusted to generalize and I can't be trusted to generalize, the answer, if possible, is not to generalize, which suggests that the Supreme Court has chosen wisely in insisting generally that a classification whose suspiciousness has not been allayed simply cannot be employed. Where in fact it was largely the product of a simple desire to disadvantage those disqualified, it probably will just be abandoned, which seems a desirable outcome. Where,

however, a classification of some sort does seem necessary (though the one the legislature employed was constitutionally unacceptable), the remedy of flat-out disallowance will impose costs in both time and money, as it will generally necessitate a somewhat more individualized test of qualification. However, legislatures often incur those costs voluntarily, and courts on other occasions have forced them to do so where constitutionally protected interests will be threatened by an imperfectly fitting classification. The unusual dangers of distortion in situations of self-aggrandizing generalization seem also to demand that we bear the increased costs of more individualized justice.

A case like that of women, where access was blocked in the past but can't responsibly be said to be so any longer, seems different in a way that suggests that a less drastic remedy may be appropriate. In cases of first-degree prejudice, or self-serving stereotyping where the access of the disadvantaged group remains blocked, the alternative of "remanding" the question to the political processes for a "second look"[8] would not be acceptable: we don't give a case back to a rigged jury. Here, however, such a "second look" approach seems to make sense. Technically the Court's judgment would be the same in all situations of unallayed suspiciousness: "due process of lawmaking" having been denied, the law that emerged would have to be declared unconstitutional. The difference would emerge in the event—unlikely, precisely because access is no longer blocked—that the legislature after such a declaration of unconstitutionality reconsidered and repassed the same or a similar law. The fact that due process of lawmaking was denied in 1908 or even in 1939 needn't imply that it was in 1982 as well, and consequently the new law should be upheld as constitutional.[9] In fact I may be wrong in supposing that because women now are in a position to protect themselves they will, that we are thus unlikely to see in the future the sort of official gender discrimination that has marked our past.[10] But if women don't protect themselves from sex discrimination in the future, it won't be because they can't. It will rather be because for one reason or another—substantive disagreement or more likely the assignment of a low priority to the issue—they don't choose to. Many of us may condemn such a choice as benighted on the merits, but that is not a constitutional argument.

. . .

Endnotes

[1] Ratification of the Equal Rights Amendment would moot the issue. At the moment that seems unlikely. It is true, however, that much of the state legislation that would otherwise be in issue (notably that mandating employment discriminations) has been preempted by federal legislation (notably Title VII of the Civil Rights Act of 1964).

[2] "Some of my best friends are Negro" got to be a parody of white hypocrisy, but *the* best friend of most men really is a woman, which eliminates the real hostility and fear that persists among the races. It is also instructive to contrast white resistance, often literally murderous, to the enforcement of the Fifteenth Amendment with the uneventful enforcement of the Nineteenth Amendment, which obviously had to be fought for but once ratified was accepted with apparent good grace. See also Wasserstrom, "Racism, Sexism, and Preferential Treatment: An Approach to the Topics," 24 *U.C.L.A. L. Rev.* 581, 589 (1977).

[3] It is also undercut, in a way the one that follows it is not, by polls indicating that a higher percentage of men than women support the Equal Rights Amendment (a fairly good referendum on the sorts of laws we are talking about). See, e.g., *Washington Post*, August 16, 1978, at A5, col. 6 (NBC News poll); *People*, March 5, 1979, at 33.

[4] See J. Pole, *The Pursuit of Equality in American History* 320, 322 (1978).

[5] 430 U.S. 483, 503 (1977) (Marshall, J., concurring), citing G. [Allport, *The Nature of Prejudice* 78 (1954) at 150–53]; A. Rose, *The Negro's Morale* 85–96 (1949); G. Simpson and J. Yinger, *Racial and Cultural Minorities* 192–95, 227, 295 (4th ed. 1972); Bettelheim, "Individual and Mass Behavior in Extreme Situations," 38 *J. Abnormal and Social Psych.* 417 (1943). See also L. Tribe, *American Constitutional Law* 1044 n. 12 (1978); Simon, ["Racially Prejudiced Governmental Actions: A Motivation Theory of the Constitutional Ban against Racial Discrimination," 15 *San Diego L. Rev.* 1041 at 1079 n. 87]; G. Allport, supra, at 142 ("One's reputation, whether false or true, cannot be hammered, hammered, hammered, into one's head without doing something to one's character"), 159–60; Brown v. Board of Education, 347 U. S. 483, 494 (1954): "To separate them from others of similar age and qualifications solely because of their race generates a feeling of inferiority as to their status in the community that may affect their hearts and minds in a way unlikely ever to be undone."

[6] See A. de Tocqueville, *Democracy in America* 319 (Anchor ed. 1959).

[7] E.g., Schlesinger v. Ballard, 419 U.S. 498, 508 (1975).

[8] Cf. Bickel and Wellington, "Legislative Purpose and the Judicial Process: The Lincoln Mills Case," 71 *Harv. L. Rev.* 1 (1957).

[9] To put on the group affected the burden of using its recently unblocked access to get the offending laws repealed would be to place in their path an additional hurdle that the rest of us do not have to contend with in order to protect ourselves—hardly an appropriate response to the realization that they have been unfairly blocked in the past.

[10] Although more men than women appear to favor the Equal Rights Amendment, a majority of each appears to (albeit apparently a majority insufficient to assure ratification).

The Assimilationist Ideal

RICHARD WASSERSTROM

Just as we can and must ask what is involved in our or any other culture in being of one race or one sex rather than the other, and how individuals are in fact viewed and treated, we can also ask a different

From *Philosophy and Social Issues* (Notre Dame: University of Notre Dame Press, 1980), pp. 23–43.

question, namely, what would the good or just society make of an individual's race or sex, and to what degree, if at all, would racial and sexual distinctions ever properly be taken into account there? Indeed, it could plausibly be argued that we could not have a wholly adequate idea of whether a society was racist or sexist unless we had some conception of what a thoroughly nonracist or nonsexist society would look like. This question is an extremely instructive as well as an often neglected one. Comparatively little theoretical literature that deals with either racism or sexism has concerned itself in a systematic way with this issue, but as will be seen it is in some respects both a more important and a more complicated one where sex is concerned than where race is involved.[1] Moreover, as I shall argue, many discussions of sexual differences which touch upon this question do so inappropriately by concentrating upon the relatively irrelevant question of whether the differences between males and females are biological rather than social in origin.

The inquiry that follows addresses and seeks to answer two major questions. First, what are the major, plausible conceptions of what the good society would look like in respect to the race and sex of individuals, and how are these conceptions to be correctly characterized and described? And second, given a delineation of the alternatives, what is to be said in favor or against one or another of them? Here, the focus is upon two more specific issues. One concerns the relevance and force of the various arguments founded upon nature and the occurrence of natural differences for the preservation of sex roles and sexual or racial differences in the good society. The other concerns some of the central moral arguments for the elimination of sex roles and the diminution, if not elimination, of the importance of distinctions connected with one's sex or race.

In order to ask more precisely what some of the possible ideals are of desirable racial or sexual differentiation, it is necessary to ask: Differentiation in respect to what? And one way to do this is to distinguish in a crude way among three levels or areas of social and political arrangements and activities. First, there is the area of basic political rights and obligations, including such things as the rights to vote and to travel, and the obligation to pay taxes. Second, there is the area of important, but perhaps less primary institutional benefits and burdens of both governmental and nongovernmental types. Examples are access to and employment in the significant economic markets, the opportunity to acquire and enjoy housing in the setting of one's choice, the right of persons who want to marry each other to do so, and the duties (nonlegal as well as legal) that persons acquire in getting married. And third, there is the area of individual, social interaction, including such matters as whom one will marry, have as friends, and, perhaps, what aesthetic preferences one will cultivate and enjoy.

As to each of these three areas we can ask, for example, whether in a nonracist or a nonsexist society it would be thought appropriate ever to take the race or sex of an individual into account. It is, for instance, a widely held, but by no means unanimously accepted, view that we would have the good society in respect to race if race were to be a wholly unimportant characteristic of individuals —if, that is, race were to function in the lives of individuals in the way in which eye color now does.

Thus, one conception of a nonracist society is that which is captured by what I shall call the assimilationist ideal: a nonracist society would be one in which the race of an individual would be the functional equivalent of the eye color of individuals in our society today.[2] In our society no basic political rights and obligations are determined on the basis of eye color. No important institutional benefits and burdens are connected with eye color. Indeed, except for the mildest sort of aesthetic preferences, a person would be thought odd who even made private, social decisions by taking eye color into account. It would, of course, be unintelligible, and not just odd, were a person to say today that while he or she looked blue-eyed, he or she regarded himself or herself as really a brown-eyed person. Because eye color functions differently in our culture than does race, there is no analogue to passing for eye color. Were the assimilationist ideal to become a reality, the same would be true of one's race. In short, according to the assimilationist ideal, a nonracist society would be one in which an individual's race was of no more significance in any of these three areas than is eye color today.

What is a good deal less familiar is an analogous conception of the good society in respect to sexual differentiation—one in which an individual's sex were to become a comparably unimportant characteristic. An assimilationist society in respect to sex would be one in which an individual's sex was of no more significance in any of the three areas than is eye color today. There would be no analogue to transsexuality, and, while physiological or anatomical sex differences would remain, they would possess only the kind and degree of significance that today attaches to the physiologically distinct eye colors persons possess.

It is apparent that the assimilationist ideal in respect to sex does not seem to be as readily plausible and obviously attractive here as it is in the case of race. In fact, many persons invoke the possible realization of the assimilationist ideal as a reason for rejecting the Equal Rights Amendment and indeed the idea of women's liberation itself. The assimilationist ideal may be just as good and just as important an ideal in respect to sex as it is in respect to race, but it is important to realize at the outset that this appears to be a more far-reaching proposal when applied to sex rather than race and that many more persons think there are good reasons why an assimilationist society in respect to sex would not be desirable than is true for the comparable racial ideal. Before such a conception is assessed, however, it will be useful to provide a somewhat fuller characterization of its features.

To begin with, it must be acknowledged that to make the assimilationist ideal a reality in respect to sex would involve more profound and fundamental revisions of our institutions and our attitudes than would be the case in respect to race. On the institutional level we would, for instance, have to alter significantly our practices concerning marriage. If a nonsexist society is a society in which one's sex is no more significant than eye color in our society today, then laws which require the persons who are getting married to be of different sexes would clearly be sexist laws.

More importantly, given the significance of role differentiation and ideas about the psychological differences in temperament that are tied to sexual identity, the assimilationist ideal would be incompatible with all psychological and sex-role differentiation. That is to say, in such a society the ideology of the society would contain no proposition asserting the inevitable or essential attributes of masculinity or feminity; it would never encourage or discourage the ideas of sisterhood or brotherhood; and it would be unintelligible to talk about the virtues or the disabilities of being a woman or a man. In addition, such a society would not have any norms concerning the appropriateness of different social behavior depending upon whether one were male or female. There would be no conception of the existence of a set of social tasks that were more appropriately undertaken or performed by males or by females. And there would be no expectation that the family was composed of one adult male and one adult female, rather than, say, just two adults—if two adults

seemed the appropriate number. To put it simply, in the assimilationist society in respect to sex, persons would not be socialized so as to see or understand themselves or others as essentially or significantly who they were or what their lives would be like because they were either male or female. And no political rights or social institutions, practices, and norms would mark the physiological differences between males and females as important.[3]

Were sex like eye color, these kinds of distinctions would make no sense. Just as the normal, typical adult is virtually oblivious to the eye color of other persons for all significant interpersonal relationships, so, too, the normal, typical adult in this kind of nonsexist society would be equally as indifferent to the sexual, physiological differences of other persons for all significant interpersonal relationships. Bisexuality, not heterosexuality or homosexuality, would be the typical intimate, sexual relationship in the ideal society that was assimilationist in respect to sex.[4]

To acknowledge that things would be very different is, of course, hardly to concede that they would thereby be undesirable—or desirable for that matter. But still, the problem is, perhaps, with the assimilationist ideal. And the assimilationist ideal is certainly not the only possible, plausible ideal.

There is, for instance, another one that is closely related to, but distinguishable from that of the assimilationist ideal. It can be understood by considering how religion rather than eye color tends to be thought about in our culture today and incorporated within social life today. If the good society were to match the present state of affairs in respect to one's religious identity, rather than the present state of affairs in respect to one's eye color, the two societies would be different, but not very greatly so. In neither would we find that the allocation of basic political rights and duties ever took an individual's religion into account. And there would be a comparable indifference to religion even in respect to most important institutional benefits and burdens—for example, access to employment in the desirable vocations, the opportunity to live where one wished to live, and the like. Nonetheless, in the good society in which religious differences were to some degree socially relevant, it would be deemed appropriate to have some institutions (typically those which are connected in an intimate way with these religions) which did in a variety of ways properly take the religion of members of the society into account. For example, it would be thought both permissible and appropriate for members of a religious group to join together in collective associations which have religious, educational, and social dimensions, and when it came to the employment of persons who were to be centrally engaged in the operation of those religious institutions (priests, rabbis and ministers, for example), it would be unobjectionable and appropriate explicitly to take the religion of job applicants into account. On the individual, interpersonal level, it might also be thought natural and possibly even admirable, were persons to some significant degree to select their associates, friends, and mates on the basis of their religious orientation. So there is another possible and plausible ideal of what the good society would look like in respect to a particular characteristic in which differences based upon that characteristic would be to some degree maintained in some aspects of institutional and interpersonal life. The diversity of the religious beliefs of individuals would be reflected in the society's institutional and ideological fabric in a way in which the diversity of eye color would not be in the assimilationist society. The picture is a more complex, somewhat less easily describable one than that of the assimilationist ideal.

There could be at least two somewhat different reasons why persons might think it preferable to have some ideal different from that of the assimilationist one in respect to religion. They might, for instance, think that heterodoxy in respect to religious belief and practice was a positive good. On this view they would see it as a loss—they would think it a worse society—were everyone to be a member of the same religion. Or they might, instead, view heterodoxy in respect to religious belief and practice more as a necessary, lesser evil. On this view they would see nothing intrinsically better about diversity rather than uniformity in respect to religion, but they might also think that the evils of achieving anything like homogeneity far outweighed the possible benefits. That is to say, persons holding this position might believe, for instance, that there was one correct religion and that it would be good were everyone to accept and be a member of that religion, but they might also believe that it would be undesirable and wrong to try to structure the social and political institutions, or the socialization of persons in the society, in such a way that social benefits and burdens were

distributed in accordance with one's religion or that significantly different norms of social behavior ought to be connected with being of one religion or the other. Because persons favoring religious diversity for either reason would desire and expect different religions to exist in the good society, and because religions themselves are composed of and require certain institutional structures of varying degrees of formality and complexity, the good society modeled upon this ideal would necessarily contain some acceptable social and interpersonal differentiation based upon the religious identity of the individuals in the society. As such, the rendering of the precise description of the right degree of differentiation based upon religion would be a more complex and more difficult undertaking than is true for the assimilationist ideal.

Nonetheless, it may be that in respect to sex, and conceivably, in respect to race, too, something more like this ideal of diversity in respect ro religion is the right one. But one problem then—and it is a more substantial one than is sometimes realized—is to specify with a good deal of precision and care what the ideal really comes to in the matter of sexual or racial identity and degree of acceptable sexual or racial differentiation. Which institutional and personal differentiations would properly be permissible and which would not be? Which attiudes, beliefs, and role expectations concerning the meaning and significance of being male or female would be properly introduced and maintained in the good society and which would not be? Which attitudes, beliefs, and role expectations continue in the good society to constitute the meaning of ethnicity as a racial concept and which would have to be purged? Part, but by no means all, of the attractiveness of the assimilationist ideal is its clarity and simplicity. In the good society of the assimilationist sort we would be able to tell easily and unequivocally whether any law, practice, attitude, or form of socialization was in any respect either racist or sexist. Part, but by no means all, of the unattractiveness of any more pluralistic ideal concerning sex or race is that it makes the question of what is racist or sexist a much more difficult and complicated one to answer. But although simplicity and lack of ambiguity may be virtues, they are not the only virtues to be taken into account in deciding among competing ideals. We quite appropriately take other considerations to be relevant to an assessment of the value and worth of alternative, possible conceptions of nonracist and nonsexist societies. What has been said so far by no means settles the question.

Nor do I even mean to suggest that all persons who reject the assimilationist ideal in respect to sex would necessarily embrace something like the kind of pluralistic ideal I have described as matching something like our present arrangements and ideas concerning the relevance of religious identity—although these do seem to exhaust the plausible ideals in respect to race. Some persons might think the right ideal was one in which substantially greater sexual differentiation and sex-role identification were retained than would be the case within a good society of that general type. Thus, someone might believe, for instance, that the good society was, perhaps, essentially like the one they think we now have in respect to sex: equality of basic political rights, such as the right to vote, but all of the sexual differentiation in both legal and nonlegal, formal and informal institutions, all of the sex-role socialization and all of the differences in matters of temperament that are characteristic of the way in which our society has been and still is ordered. And someone might also believe that the prevailing ideological concomitants of these arrangements are the correct and appropriate ones to perpetuate.[5]

This could, of course, be regarded as a version of the pluralistic ideal described above, with the emphasis upon the extensive character of the institutional, normative, and personal differences connected with sexual identity. Whether it is a form of this pluralistic ideal or a different ideal altogether turns, I think, upon two things: first, how pervasive the sexual differentiation is in terms of the number, importance, and systemic interconnectedness of the institutions and role expectations connected with being of one sex or the other, and, second, whether the ideal contains within it a conception of the appropriateness of significant institutional and interpersonal inequality, e.g., that the woman's job is in large measure to serve and be dominated by the male. The more either or both of these features is present, the clearer is the case for regarding this as an ideal, distinctively different from either of the other two described so far. I shall indicate later why I think these two features make such a difference.

But the next question is that of how a choice is rationally to be made among these different, possible ideals. One general set of issues concerns the empirical sphere, because the question of whether something is a plausible and attractive ideal does turn in part on the nature of the empirical world. If it is true, for example, that any particular characteristic, such as an individual's race or sex, is not only a socially significant category in our culture but that it is largely a socially created one as well, then for many people a number of objections to the assimilationist ideal appear immediately to disappear. The other general set of issues concerns the relevant normative considerations. Here the key questions concern the principles and considerations by which to assess and evaluate different conceptions of how persons ought to be able to live and how their social institutions ought to be constructed and arranged. I begin with the empirical considerations and constraints, although one heuristic disadvantage in doing so is that this decision may appear to give them greater weight than, as I shall argue, they in fact deserve.

What opponents of assimilationism and proponents of schemes of strong sexual differentiation seize upon is that sexual difference appears to be a naturally occurring category of obvious and inevitable relevance for the construction of any plausible conception of the nature of the good society.[6] The problems with this way of thinking are twofold. To begin with, a careful and thorough analysis of the social realities would reveal, I believe, that it is the socially created sexual differences which constitute most of our conception of sex differences and which tend in fact to matter the most in the way we live our lives as persons of one sex or the other. For, it is, I think, sex-role differentiation and socialization, not the physiological and related biological differences—if there are any— that make men and women as different as they are from each other, and it is these same sex-role-created differences which are invoked to justify the necessity or the desirability of most sexual differentiation proposed to be maintained at any of the levels of social arrangements and practices described earlier.[7]

It is important, however, not to attach any greater weight than is absolutely necessary to the truth or falsity of this causal claim about the source of the degree of sexual distinctions that exist[s] in our or other cultures. For what is significant, although seldom recognized, is the fact that the answer to that question almost never goes very far in settling the question of what the good society should look like in respect to any particular characteristic of individuals. And the answer certainly does not go as far as many persons appear to believe it does to settle that question of the nature of the good society.

Let us suppose that there are what can be called "naturally occurring" sexual differences and even that they are of such a nature that they are in some sense of direct prima facie social relevance. It is essential to see that this would by no means settle the question of whether in the good society sex should or should not be as minimally significant as eye color. Even if there are major or substantial biological differences between men and women that are in this sense "natural" rather than socially created, this does not determine the question of what the good society can and should make of these differences—without, that is, begging the question by including within the meaning of "major" or "substantial" or "natural" the idea that these are things that ought to be retained, emphasized, or otherwise normatively taken into account. It is not easy to see why, without begging the question, it should be thought that this fact, if it is a fact, settles the question adversely to anything like the assimilationist ideal. Persons might think that truths of this sort about nature or biology do affect, if not settle, the question of what the good society should look like for at least two different reasons.

In the first place, they might think the differences are of such a character that they substantially affect what would be *possible* within a good society of human persons. Just as the fact that humans are mortal necessarily limits the features of any possible good society, so, they might argue, the fact that males and females are physiologically or biologically different limits in the same way the features of any possible good society.[8]

In the second place, they might think the differences are of such a character that they are relevant to the question of what would be *desirable* in the good society. That is to say, they might not think that the differences determine or affect to a substantial degree what is possible, but only that the differences are appropriately taken into account in any rational construction of an ideal social existence.

The second reason seems to be a good deal more plausible than the first. For there appear to be very few, if any, respects in which the ineradicable, naturally occurring differences between males and females *must* be taken into account. The industrial revolution has certainly made any of the general differences in strength between the sexes capable of being ignored by the good society for virtually all significant human activities.[9] And even if it were true that women are naturally better suited than men to care for and nurture children, it is also surely the case that men can be taught to care for and nurture children well.[10] Indeed, the one natural or biological fact that seems *required* to be taken into account is the fact that reproduction of the human species requires that the fetus develop *in utero* for a period of months. Sexual intercourse is not necessary, for artificial insemination is available. Neither marriage nor the nuclear family is necessary either for conception or child rearing. Given the present state of medical knowledge and what might be termed the natural realities of female pregnancy, it is difficult to see why any important institutional or interpersonal arrangements are constrained to take the existing biological differences as to the phenomenon of *in utero* pregnancy into account.

But to say all this is still to leave it a wholly open question to what degree the good society *ought* to build upon any ineradicable biological differences, or to create ones in order to construct institutions and sex roles which would thereby maintain a substantial degree of sexual differentiation. The way to answer that question is to consider and assess the arguments for and against doing so. What is significant is the fact that many of the arguments for doing so are less persuasive than they appear to be upon the initial statement of this possibility.

It might be argued, for instance, that the fact of menstruation could be used as a premise upon which to base the case for importantly different social roles for females than for males. But this could only plausibly be proposed if two things were true: first, that menstruation would be debilitating to women and hence relevant to social role even in a culture which did not teach women to view menstruation as a sign of uncleanliness or as a curse;[11] and, second, that the way in which menstruation necessarily affected some or all women was in fact necessarily related in an important way to the role in question. But even if both of these were true, it would still be an open question whether any sexual differentiation ought to be built upon these facts. The society could still elect to develop institutions that would nullify the effect of these natural differences and it would still be an open question whether it ought to do so. Suppose, for example, what seems implausible—that some or all women will not be able to perform a particular task while menstruating, e.g., guard the border of a country. It would be possible, even easy, if the society wanted to, to arrange for substitute guards for the women who were incapacitated. We know that persons are not good guards when they are sleepy, and we make arrangements so that persons alternate guard duty to avoid fatigue. The same could be done for menstruating women, even given the implausibly strong assumptions about menstruation.

The point that is involved here is a very general one that has application in contexts having nothing to do with the desirability or undesirability of maintaining substantial sexual differentiation. It has to do with the fact that humans possess the ability to alter their natural and social environment in distinctive, dramatic, and unique ways. An example from the nonsexual area can help bring out this too seldom recognized central feature. It is a fact that some persons born in human society are born with congenital features such that they cannot walk or walk well on their legs. They are born naturally crippled or lame. However, humans in our society certainly possess the capability to devise and construct mechanical devices and institutional arrangements which render this natural fact about some persons relatively unimportant in respect to the way they and others will live together. We can bring it about, and in fact are in the process of bringing it about, that persons who are confined to wheelchairs can move down sidewalks and across streets because the curb stones at corners of intersections have been shaped so as to accommodate the passage of wheelchairs. And we can construct and arrange buildings and events so that persons in wheelchairs can ride elevators, park cars, and be seated at movies, lectures, meetings, and the like. Much of the environment in which humans live is the result of their intentional choices and actions concerning what that environment shall be like. They can elect to construct an environment in which the natural incapacity of some persons to walk or walk well is a major difference or a difference that will be effectively nullified vis-à-vis the lives that they, too, will live.

Nonhuman animals cannot do this in anything like the way humans can. A fox or an ape born lame is stuck with the fact of lameness and the degree to which that will affect the life it will lead. The other foxes or apes cannot change things. This capacity

of humans to act intentionally and thereby continuously create and construct the world in which they and others will live is at the heart of what makes studies of nonhuman behavior essentially irrelevant to and for most if not all of the normative questions of social, political, and moral theory. Humans can become aware of the nature of their natural and social environment and then act intentionally to alter the environment so as to change its impact upon or consequences for the individuals living within it. Nonhuman animals cannot do so. This difference is, therefore, one of fundamental theoretical importance. At the risk of belaboring the obvious, what it is important to see is that the case against any picture of the good society of an assimilationist sort—if it is to be a defensible critique—ought to rest on arguments concerned to show why some other ideal would be preferable; it cannot plausibly rest in any significant respect upon the claim that the sorts of biological differences typically alluded to in contexts such as these require that the society not be assimilationist in character.

There are, though, several other arguments based upon nature, or the idea of the "natural" that also must be considered and assessed. First, it might be argued that if a way of doing something is natural, then it ought to be done that way. Here, what may be meant by "natural" is that this way of doing the thing is the way it would be done if culture did not direct or teach us to do it differently. It is not clear, however, that this sense of "natural" is wholly intelligible; it supposes that we can meaningfully talk about how humans would behave in the absence of culture. And few if any humans have ever lived in such a state. Moreover, even if this is an intelligible notion, the proposal that the natural way to behave is somehow the appropriate or desirable way to behave is strikingly implausible. It is, for example, almost surely natural, in this sense of "natural," that humans would eat their food with their hands, except for the fact that they are, almost always, socialized to eat food differently. Yet, the fact that humans would naturally eat this way, does not seem in any respect to be a reason for believing that that is thereby the desirable or appropriate way to eat food. And the same is equally true of any number of other distinctively human ways of behaving.

Second, someone might argue that substantial sexual differentiation is natural not in the sense that it is biologically determined nor in the sense that it would occur but for the effects of culture, but rather in the sense that substantial sexual differentiation is a virtually universal phenomenon in human culture. By itself, this claim of virtual universality, even if accurate, does not directly establish anything about the desirability or undesirability of any particular ideal. But it can be made into an argument by the addition of the proposition that where there is a widespread, virtually universal social practice or institution, there is probably some good or important purpose served by the practice or institution. Hence, given the fact of substantial sex-role differentiation in all, or almost all, cultures, there is on this view some reason to think that substantial sex-role differentiation serves some important purpose for and in human society.

This is an argument, but it is hard to see what is attractive about it. The premise which turns the fact of sex-role differentiation into any kind of a strong reason for sex-role differentiation is the premise of conservatism. And it is no more or less convincing here than elsewhere. There are any number of practices or institutions that are typical and yet upon reflection seem without significant social purpose. Slavery was once such an institution; war perhaps still is.

More to the point, perhaps, the concept of "purpose" is ambiguous. It can mean in a descriptive sense "plays some role" or "is causally relevant." Or, it can mean in a prescriptive sense "does something desirable" or "has some useful function." If "purpose" is used descriptively in the conservative premise, then the argument says nothing about the continued desirability of sex-role differentiation or the assimilationist ideal. If "purpose" is used prescriptively in the conservative premise, then there is no reason to think that premise is true.[12]

To put it another way, the question that seems fundamentally to be at issue is whether it is desirable to have a society in which sex-role differences are to be retained in the way and to the degree they are today—or even at all. The straightforward way to think about the question is to ask what would be good and what would be bad about a society in which sex functioned like eye color does in our society; or alternatively, what would be good and what would be bad about a society in which sex functioned in the way in which religious identity does today; or alternatively, what would be good and what would be bad about a society in which sex functioned in the way in which it does today.

We can imagine what such societies would look like and how they might work. It is hard to see how thinking about answers to this question is substantially advanced by reference to what has typically or always been the case. If it is true, for instance, that the sex-role-differentiated societies that have existed have tended to concentrate power and authority in the hands of males, have developed institutions and ideologies that have perpetuated that concentration, and have restricted and prevented women from living the kinds of lives that persons ought to be able to live for themselves, then this, it seems to me, says far more about what may be wrong with any strongly nonassimilationist ideal than does the conservative premise say what may be right about any strongly nonassimilationist ideal.

This does not, however, exhaust the reasons why persons might think that the question of whether sex differences are naturally occurring differences is an important or relevant one. There are at least two others. First, if the differences are natural, rather than socially created, it might be thought that there is less of an obligation to correct or alter the impact or effect that those differences will play in the lives people will be able to live in the society. That is to say, if it is nature, or biology, that accounts for the differences that result, then the society is not causally responsible and for that reason is not to blame for or accountable for those differences. The cause is not society, but nature. If society were the cause, and if the differences produced arrangements that seemed unequal or unfair, then the fault would be society's and its obligation to remedy the situation would be clearer, more direct, and more stringent. But since it is not, the causal chain is different and society is, for this reason, off the hook of accountability. An argument such as this one is seldom made explicit, but it underlies, I suspect, much of the motivation for the belief in the relevance of the search for natural as opposed to social causation.

The difficulty here is that only if the question is cast in terms of a certain very particular conception of compensatory justice does the causal issue assume genuine relevance or importance. What remains unexplained is why that perspective should be seen to be the obviously correct or appropriate one from which to look at matters. For if the question were to be cast, instead, in terms of a conception of distributive justice—one that was, say, founded upon the importance of a *resulting* equality of distributional treatment—then the cause of the initial differences or inequalities becomes a substantially less significant issue. And, if the focus were to be on the more general question of what kind of society it would be desirable to have, then the correct causal explanation would be still less important. Consider again the fact that some persons are born lame while others are not. Even though social institutions did not cause the lameness at all, it is difficult to understand how that is at all decisive to the question of what the good society would do in the way of seeking to nullify the natural consequences of lameness through having certain institutions and arrangements rather than others. If the cause of undesirable existing inequalities or differences is socially created, then there is an additional argument of a compensatory sort for requiring that the society make the alterations necessary to change the operative social mechanisms. But the absence of such an argument in no way implies that things may therefore be appropriately or justly left the way nature has produced them.

The other argument is that if the differences are natural, then there are considerations of efficiency that come into play. If some persons are naturally less equipped or suited to do some things, then it will be less efficient than would otherwise be the case to bring it about that they will end up being able to do those things—either because they will not be able to do them as well as others, or because it will be most costly to bring it about that they will be able to do them as well as others who are differently endowed can do them. Here, too, there is, I think, something to the argument, but not as much as is typically supposed. If it is possible to arrange things so that the natural differences can be nullified, and if there are reasons of justice (or reasons of morality) for doing so, then it is as hard here, as elsewhere, to see why considerations of efficiency should necessarily be thought overriding.

There are, in fact, several different issues and arguments that may be involved here, and it is worthwhile trying to disentangle them. One issue is whether what underlies this line of thought is the view that all persons ought to be *required* to do whatever it is they are naturally endowed to do, and that, therefore, the social institutions should be designed so as to bring that state of affairs into being. On this view, if a person were naturally endowed to be a brain surgeon, or a garbage col-

lector, the social institutions ought to at least direct if not require the person to end up in that role or place—irrespective of the person's desires and irrespective of the kind and quality of life allotted to the persons with differing natural endowments. A society organized in this fashion would, doubtless, be highly efficient in terms of the correspondence between natural endowments and places in society and the degree to which each person was living the life he or she was "naturally" suited for, but I do not see how one could easily argue that such a "naturally" ordered society would be either just or morally desirable. Apart from everything else, if one wanted a nice philosophical example of a case of viewing persons wholly as a means—a case of using persons as objects—a society organized and justified along these lines would seem to be an obvious candidate.

But the argument about nature and efficiency may not be this sweeping. Perhaps instead the claim is only that in the good society at least those persons who are especially able or competent ought to be permitted to do what they are naturally able or competent to do. This is a substantially weaker thesis, and I shall assume for purposes of argument that it is defensible. This thesis is not, however, fundamentally at issue. The primary question is whether the society ought to be organized so that the less well endowed will be able to do things, live their lives, in a way that is more fully adequate and satisfactory. If some are naturally able to do certain things well, while others are less able naturally to do them, one complaint the better endowed could have about attempts to increase the abilities and opportunities of the less well endowed is that based upon the overall social cost involved in doing so. But the better endowed do not have a claim that, just because they happen to be better endowed by nature, they *alone* should have the opportunity to participate in institutions that depend upon or require certain abilities, talents, dispositions, and the like. They can claim that different social structures may be less efficient in terms of overall cost of having those social structures than ones in which they alone participate. But if there are considerations of justice or morality that favor these alternative "more expensive" arrangements, it seems plausible that considerations of efficiency should at least to some degree give way.

Perhaps, though, they have one other argument, namely, that if alternative social arrangements are to be preferred, then the society will be one in which the institutions do not permit them to utilize their natural talents to the fullest extent. This may be just a restatement of the argument from efficiency, or it may be an argument that the better endowed deserve to be able always to utilize their natural talents to the fullest.[13]

I do not think they can claim to deserve to be able always to utilize their natural talents to the fullest. They cannot claim this because, *ex hypothesi* since these are natural talents or capabilities, they manifestly did nothing to deserve these natural attributes. And while it may be good to permit them to utilize their talents—in terms of the happiness of those who are naturally better endowed—there is no reason to give their claims any greater weight than the claims of others on the ground that their talents or characteristics are naturally rather than socially produced. And it even seems plausible, for reasons analogous to those offered by Rawls for the difference principle, that if there are sacrifices of any sort to be made, it is fairer that they be made or borne by the naturally better rather than naturally worse off.

So, even supposing that there is a clear sense of natural endowments or capabilities based on sexual physiology, and even supposing that the natural differences between males and females were as strongly present "in nature" as the preceding arguments require, the conclusions to be drawn vis-à-vis the character of the good society would be appreciably weaker and more indeterminate than is typically supposed by those who focus upon the possible existence of biological differences between the sexes. The primary point that emerges is that the question of whether there are natural differences (in any of the above senses) between males and females (or even persons of different races) tends to get disputed on the wrong grounds. The debate tends to focus upon whether biology or society is the cause of the differences. The debate ought to attend instead to the question of why it matters. The debaters ought to address first the unasked question of within what theoretical inquiry the issue is even relevant. When the question is one of ideals, of what the good society would make of sexual or racial characteristics, the issue of natural as opposed to social causation is a strikingly irrelevant one. There do not, therefore, appear to be any very powerful, let alone conclusive, arguments against something like the assimilationist society that can be based on any of the different, possible appeals to nature and the natural.

If the chief thing to be said in favor of something like the assimilationist society in respect to sex is that some arguments against it are not very relevant, that does not by itself make a very convincing case. Such is not, however, the way in which matters need be left. There is an affirmative case of sorts for something like the assimilationist society.

One strong, affirmative moral argument on behalf of the assimilationist ideal is that it does provide for a kind of individual autonomy that a substantially nonassimilationist society cannot provide. The reason is because any substantially nonassimilationist society will have sex roles, and sex roles interfere in basic ways with autonomy. The argument for these two propositions proceeds as follows.

Any nonassimilationist society must have some institutions and some ideology that distinguishes between individuals in virtue of their sexual physiology, and any such society will necessarily be committed to teaching the desirability of doing so. That is what is implied by saying it is nonassimilationist rather than assimilationist. And any substantially nonassimilationist society will make one's sexual identity an important characteristic so that there will be substantial psychological, role, and status differences between persons who are male and those who are female. That is what is implied by saying that it is substantially nonassimilationist. Any such society will necessarily have sex roles, a conception of the places, characteristics, behaviors, etc., that are appropriate to one sex or the other but not both. That is what makes it a *sex* role.

Now, sex roles are, I think, morally objectionable on two or three quite distinct grounds. One such ground is absolutely generic and applies to all sex roles. The other grounds are less generic and apply only to the kinds of sex roles with which we are familiar and which are a feature of patriarchal societies, such as our own. I begin with the more contingent, less generic objections.

We can certainly imagine, if we are not already familiar with, societies in which the sex roles will be such that the general place of women in that society can be described as that of the servers of men. In such a society individuals will be socialized in such a way that women will learn how properly to minister to the needs, desires, and interests of men; women and men will both be taught that it is right and proper that the concerns and affairs of men are more important than and take precedence over those of women; and the norms and supporting set of beliefs and attitudes will be such that this role will be deemed the basic and appropriate role for women to play and men to expect. Here, I submit, what is objectionable about the connected set of institutions, practices, and ideology—the structure of the prevailing sex role—is the role itself. It is analogous to a kind of human slavery. The fundamental moral defect—just as is the case with slavery—is not that women are being arbitrarily or capriciously assigned to the social role of server, but that such a role itself has no legitimate place in the decent or just society. As a result, just as is the case with slavery, the assignment on *any* basis of individuals to such a role is morally objectionable. A society arranged so that such a role is a prominent part of the structure of the social institutions can be properly characterized as an *oppressive* one. It consigns some individuals to lives which have no place in the good society, which restrict unduly the opportunities of these individuals, and which do so in order improperly to enhance the lives and opportunities of others.

But it may be thought possible to have sex roles and all that goes with them without having persons of either sex placed within a position of general, systemic dominance or subordination. Here, it would be claimed, the society would not be an oppressive one in this sense. Consider, for example, the kinds of sex roles with which we are familiar and which assign to women the primary responsibilities for child rearing and household maintenance. It might be argued first that the roles of child rearer and household maintainer are not in themselves roles that could readily or satisfactorily be eliminated from human society without the society itself being deficient in serious, unacceptable ways. It might be asserted, that is, that these are roles or tasks that simply must be filled if children are to be raised in a satisfactory way. Suppose this is correct, suppose it is granted that society would necessarily have it that these tasks would have to be done. Still, if it is also correct that, relatively speaking, these are unsatisfying and unfulfilling ways for humans to concentrate the bulk of their energies and talents, then, to the degree to which this is so, what is morally objectionable is that if this is to be a *sex* role, then women are unduly and unfairly allocated a disproportionate share of what

is unpleasant, unsatisfying, unrewarding work. Here the objection is the degree to which the burden women are required to assume is excessive and unjustified vis-à-vis the rest of society, i.e., the men. Unsatisfactory roles and tasks, when they are substantial and pervasive, should surely be allocated and filled in the good society in a way which seeks to distribute the burdens involved in a roughly equal fashion.

Suppose, though, that even this feature were eliminated from sex roles, so that, for instance, men and women shared more equally in the dreary, unrewarding aspects of housework and child care, and that a society which maintained sex roles did not in any way have as a feature of that society the systemic dominance or superiority of one sex over the other, there would still be a generic moral defect that would remain. The defect would be that any set of sex roles would necessarily impair and retard an individual's ability to develop his or her own characteristics, talents, capacities, and potential life-plans to the extent to which he or she might desire and from which he or she might derive genuine satisfaction. Sex roles, by definition, constitute empirical and normative limits of varying degrees of strength—restrictions on what it is that one can expect to do, be, or become. As such, they are, I think, at least prima facie objectionable.

To some degree, all role-differentiated living is restrictive in this sense. Perhaps, therefore, all role differentiation in society is to some degree troublesome, and perhaps all strongly role-differentiated societies are objectionable. But the case against sex roles and the concomitant sexual differentiation they create and require need not rest upon this more controversial point. For one thing that distinguishes sex roles from many other roles is that they are wholly involuntarily assumed. One has no choice about whether one shall be born a male or female. And if it is a consequence of one's being born a male or a female that one's subsequent emotional, intellectual, and material development will be substantially controlled by this fact, then it is necessarily the case that substantial, permanent, and involuntarily assumed restraints have been imposed on some of the most central factors concerning the way one will shape and live one's life. The point to be emphasized is that this would necessarily be the case, even in the unlikely event that substantial sexual differentiation could be maintained without one sex or the other becoming dominant and developing oppressive institutions and an ideology to support that dominance and oppression. Absent some far stronger showing than seems either reasonable or possible that potential talents, abilities, interests, and the like are inevitably and irretrievably distributed between the sexes in such a way that the sex roles of the society are genuinely congruent with and facilitative of the development of those talents, abilities, interests, and the like that individuals can and do possess, sex roles are to this degree incompatible with the kind of respect which the good or the just society would accord to each of the individual persons living within it. It seems to me, therefore, that there are persuasive reasons to believe that no society which maintained what I have been describing as *substantial* sexual differentiation could plausibly be viewed as a good or just society.

What remains more of an open question is whether a society in which sex functioned in the way in which eye color does (a strictly assimilationist society in respect to sex) would be better or worse than one in which sex functioned in the way in which religious identity does in our society (a nonoppressive, more diversified or pluralistic one). For it might be argued that especially in the case of sex and even in the case of race much would be gained and nothing would be lost if the ideal society in respect to these characteristics succeeded in preserving in a nonoppressive fashion the attractive differences between males and females and the comparably attractive differences among ethnic groups. Such a society, it might be claimed, would be less bland, less homogeneous and richer in virtue of its variety.

I do not think there is any easy way to settle this question, but I do think the attractiveness of the appeal to diversity, when sex or race are concerned, is less alluring than is often supposed. The difficulty is in part one of specifying what will be preserved and what will not, and in part one of preventing the reappearance of the type of systemic dominance and subservience that produces the injustice of oppression. Suppose, for example, that it were suggested that there are aspects of being male and aspects of being female that are equally attractive and hence desirable to maintain and perpetuate: the kind of empathy that is associated with women and the kind of self-control associated with men. It does not matter what the characteristic is, the problem is one of seeing why the characteristic should be tied by the social institu-

tions to the sex of the individuals of the society. If the characteristics are genuinely ones that all individuals ought to be encouraged to display in the appropriate circumstances, then the social institutions and ideology ought to endeavor to foster them in all individuals. If it is good for everyone to be somewhat empathetic all of the time or especially empathetic in some circumstances, or good for everyone to have a certain degree of self-control all of the time or a great deal in some circumstances, then there is no reason to preserve institutions which distribute these psychological attributes along sexual lines. And the same is true for many, if not all, vocations, activities, and ways of living. If some, but not all persons would find a life devoted to child rearing genuinely satisfying, it is good, surely, that that option be open to them. Once again, though, it is difficult to see the argument for implicitly or explicitly encouraging, teaching, or assigning to women, as opposed to men, that life simply in virtue of their sex. Thus, while substantial diversity in individual characteristics, attitudes, and ways of life is no doubt an admirable, even important feature of the good society, what remains uncertain is the necessity or the desirability of continuing to link attributes or behaviors such as these to the race or sex of individuals. And for the reasons I have tried to articulate there are significant moral arguments against any conception of the good society in which such connections are pursued and nourished in the systemic fashion required by the existence and maintenance of *sex* roles.

. . .

Endnotes

1 One of the few thorough and valuable explorations of this question as it relates to sexual difference is Jaggar's "On Sexual Equality," 84 *Ethics* 275 (1974). The article also contains a very useful analysis of the views of other feminist writers who have dealt with this topic.

2 There is a danger in calling this ideal the "assimilationist" ideal. That term often suggests the idea of incorporating oneself, one's values, and the like into the dominant group and its practices and values. No part of that idea is meant to be captured by my use of the term. Mine is a stipulative definition.

3 Jaggar describes something fairly close to the assimilationist view in this way:

"The traditional feminist answer to this question [of what the features of a nonsexist society would be] has been that a sexually egalitarian society is one in which virtually no public recognition is given to the fact that there is a physiological sex difference between persons. This is not to say that the different reproductive function of each sex should be unacknowledged in such a society nor that there should be no physicians specializing in female and male complaints, etc. But it is to say that, except in this sort of context, the question whether someone is female or male should have no significance. . . .

". . . In the mainstream tradition, the nonsexist society is one which is totally integrated sexually, one in which sexual differences have ceased to be a matter of public concern." Jaggar, *supra* note 1, at 276–77.

[4] In describing the assimilationist society in this fashion, I do not mean thereby to be addressing the question of how government and laws would regulate all these matters, or even whether they would. I am describing what laws, practices, attitudes, conventions, ideology, behavior, and the like one would expect to find. These might be reasons, for example, why it would be undesirable to have laws that regulated interpersonal relationships and personal preferences. We have no such laws concerning eye color and interpersonal relationships and yet it is generally irrelevant in this area. If the entire cultural apparatus were different from what it now is in respect to race or sex, we can imagine that race and sex would lose their significance in the analogous ways, even in the absence of laws which regulated all dimensions of social life.

[5] Thus, for example, a column appeared a few years ago in the *Washington Star* concerning the decision of the Cosmos Club to continue to refuse to permit women to be members. The author of the column (and a member of the club) defended the decision on the ground that women appropriately had a different status in the society. Their true distinction was to be achieved by being faithful spouses and devoted mothers. The column closed with this paragraph:

"In these days of broken homes, derision of marriage, reluctance to bear children, contempt for the institution of the family—a phase in our national life when it seems more honorable to be a policewoman, or a model, or an accountant than to be a wife or mother—there is a need to reassert a traditional scale of values in which the vocation of homemaker is as honorable and distinguished as any in political or professional life. Such women, as wives and widows of members, now enjoy in the club the privileges of their status, which includes [*sic*] their own drawing rooms, and it is of interest that they have been among the most outspoken opponents of the proposed changes in club structure." Groseclose,

"Now—Shall We Join the Ladies?" *Washington Star*, Mar. 13, 1975.

[6] This is not to deny that certain people believe that race is linked with characteristics that prima facie are relevant. Such beliefs persist. They are, however, unjustified by the evidence. *See, e.g.,* Block & Dworkin, "IQ, Heritability and Inequality," *3 Phil & Pub. Aff.* 331 (1974); 4 *id.* 40 (1974). More to the point, even if it were true that such a linkage existed, none of the characteristics suggested would require that political or social institutions, or interpersonal relationships, would have to be structured in a certain way.

[7] See, e.g., [Hochschild, "A Review of Sex Role Research," 78 *Am J. Soc.* 1011 (1973), which reviews and very usefully categorizes the enormous volume of literature on this topic. *See also* Stewart, "Social Influences on Sex Differences in Behavior," in Teitelbaum (ed.) *Sex Differences* (Garden City, N.Y.: Anchor Press/ Doubleday, 1976); Weitzman, "Sex-Role Socialization" in Freeman (ed.), *Women: A Feminist Perspective* (Palo Alto, Cal.: Mayfield Publishing Co., 1975), p. 105. A number of the other pieces in *Women: A Feminist Perspective* also describe and analyze the role of women in the culture, including the way they are thought of by the culture.

The Women's Room by Marilyn French (New York: Harcourt Brace Jovanovich, 1977) is a powerful literary portrayal of a number of these same matters]; Mead, *Sex and Temperament in Three Primitive Societies* (New York: Morrow, 1935).

"These three situations [the cultures of the Anapesh, the Mundugumor, and the Tchambuli] suggest, then, a very definite conclusion. If those temperamental attitudes which we have traditionally regarded as feminine—such as passivity, responsiveness, and a willingness to cherish children—can so easily be set up as the masculine pattern in one tribe, and in another to be outlawed for the majority of women as well as for the majority of men, we no longer have any basis for regarding such aspects of behaviour as sex-linked. . . .

". . . We are forced to conclude that human nature is almost unbelievably malleable, responding accurately and contrastingly to contrasting cultural conditions. . . . Standardized personality differences between the sexes are of this order, cultural creations to which each generation, male and female is trained to conform." *Id.*, at 190–91.

A somewhat different view is expressed in Sherman, *On the Psychology of Women* (Springfield, Ill.: C. C. Thomas, 1975). There the author suggests that there are "natural" differences of a psychological sort between men and women, the chief ones being aggressiveness and strength of sex drive. *See id.* at 238. However, even if she is correct as to these biologically based differences, this does little to establish what the good society should look like. . . .

Almost certainly the most complete discussion of this topic is Macoby & Jacklin, *The Psychology of Sex Differences* (Stanford, Cal.: Stanford U. Press, 1974). The authors conclude that the sex differences which are, in their words, "fairly well established," are: (1) that girls have greater verbal ability than boys; (2) that boys excel in visual-spacial ability; (3) that boys excel in mathematical ability; and (4) that males are aggressive. *Id.* at 351–52. They conclude, in respect to the etiology of these psychological sex differences, that there appears to be a biological component to the greater visual-spacial ability of males and to their greater aggressiveness. *Id.* at 360.

[8] As H. L. A. Hart has observed in a different context, if humans had a different physical structure such that they were virtually invulnerable to physical attack or assault by other humans, this would alter radically the character or role of substantial segments of the criminal and civil law. Hart, *The Concept of Law* (Oxford: At the Clarendon Press, 1961), p. 190. But humans are, of course, not like this at all. The fact that humans are vulnerable to injury by others is a natural fact that affects the features of any meaningful conception of the good society.

[9] As Sherman observes, "Each sex has its own special physical assets and liabilities. The principal female liability of less muscular strength is not ordinarily a handicap in a civilized, mechanized, society. . . . There is nothing in the biological evidence to prevent women from taking a role of equality in a civilized society." Sherman, *supra* note 7, at 11.

There are, of course, some activities that would be sexually differentiated in the assimilationist society, namely, those that were specifically directed toward, say, measuring unaided physical strength. Thus, I think it likely that even in this ideal society, weight-lifting contests and boxing matches would in fact be dominated, perhaps exclusively so, by men. But it is hard to find any significant activities or institutions that are analogous. And it is not clear that such insignificant activities would be thought worth continuing, especially since sports function in existing patriarchal societies to help maintain the dominance of males. *See,* [Millett, *Sexual Politics* (Garden City, N.Y.: Doubleday & Co., 1970)], at 48–49.

It is possible that there are some nontrivial activities or occupations that depend sufficiently directly upon unaided physical strength that most if not all women would be excluded. Perhaps being a lifeguard at the ocean is an example. Even here, though, it would be important to see whether the way lifeguarding had traditionally been done could be changed to render such physical strength unimportant. If it could be changed, then the question would simply be one of whether the increased cost (or loss of efficiency) was worth the gain in terms of equality and the avoidance

of sex-role differentiation. In a nonpatriarchal society very different from ours, where sex was not a dominant social category, the argument from efficiency might well prevail. What is important, once again, is to see how infrequent and peripheral such occupational cases are.

[10] Once again, though, I believe there is substantial evidence that to sex-role socialization and not to biology is far more plausibly attributed the dominant causal role in the relative child-rearing capacities and dispositions of men and women in our and other societies.

[11] *See, e.g.,* Paige, "Women Learn to Sing the Menstrual Blues," in C. Tavis (ed.), *The Female Experience* (Del Mar, Cal.: CRM, Inc., 1973), p. 17.

"I have come to believe that the 'raging hormones' theory of menstrual distress simply isn't adequate. All women have the raging hormones, but not all women have menstrual symptoms, not do they have the same symptoms for the same reasons. Nor do I agree with the 'raging neurosis' theory, which argues that women who have menstrual symptoms are merely whining neurotics, who need only a kind pat on the head to cure their problems.

"We must instead consider the problem from the perspective of women's subordinate social position, and of the cultural ideology that so narrowly defines the behaviors and emotions that are appropriately 'feminine.' Women have perfectly good reasons to react emotionally to reproductive events. Menstruation, pregnancy and childbirth—so sacred, yet so unclean—are the woman's primary avenues of achievement and self-expression. Her reproductive abilites define her femininity; other routes to success are only second-best in this society. . . .

". . . My current research on a sample of 114 societies around the world indicates that ritual observances and taboos about menstruation are a method of controlling women and their fertility. Men apparently use such rituals, along with those surrounding pregnancy and childbirth, to assert their claims to women and their children.

". . . The hormone theory isn't giving us much mileage, and it's time to turn it in for a better model, one that looks to our beliefs about menstruation and women. It is no mere coincidence that women get the blue meanies along with an event they consider embarrassing, unclean—and a curse." *Id.* at 21.

[12] *See also,* Joyce Trebilcot, "Sex Roles: The Argument from Nature," 85 *Ethics* 249 (1975).

[13] Thomas Nagel suggests that the educationally most talented deserve, as a matter of "educational justice," the opportunity to develop their talents to the fullest. Thomas Nagel, "Equal Treatment and Compensatory Discrimination," 2 *Phil. & Pub. Aff.* 348, 356 (1973).

I do not find the concept of educational justice a clear or even wholly intelligible one. Nor, I think, has Nagel adequately explained why this is a matter of desert at all.

Study Questions

1. In what ways is California's statutory rape law "sexist"? Reread the text of the statute (in Hrenquist's opinion in *Michael M.*) and then consider the following: Under the statute, intercourse with a female under the age of eighteen is criminal but intercourse with a male under eighteen is not. Therefore, any female under eighteen who has sex with an older male participates in an unlawful activity (even though she cannot be punished for it); whereas any male under eighteen, as long as he has sex with a woman above that age, participates in a perfectly lawful activity. Teenage boys, in other words, seem to have more sexual freedom than teenage girls. Was this an intended consequence of the statute? How can we tell? Is this further evidence of prejudice against women? What would Taub and Schneider's analysis say?

2. Is sex discrimination bad or wrong for the same reasons as racial discrimination? Is sex discrimination rooted in assumptions of inferiority and prejudice? Do the various familiar stereotypes of women (that they are weak, overly emotional, dependent, less intellectual than men) add up to the suspicion that laws that maintain (or even encourage) these stereotypes are motivated by a hatred of women, similar to race hatred in the case of blacks?

3. In 1972, the Congress proposed an amendment to the Constitution stating that "equality of rights under the law shall not be denied or abridged by the United States or by any State on account of sex." Because it was not ratified by a sufficient number of states (some even withdrew their initial support), the Equal Rights Amendment or ERA failed to become part of the Constitution. What changes might it have made to the law of sex discrimination? If you had been a judge faced with interpreting the amendment, what would you have taken to be its meaning? It is worth noting that some opponents of the ERA sought to defeat it by arguing that it would lead ultimately to some of the same consequences that Wasserstrom says

would follow in an "assimiliationist" society. Would the ERA have required an assimilationist society? Does the equal protection clause of the Fourteenth Amendment require assimilationism?

4. Ely claims that women have acquiesced in any of the gender-based laws treating women differently from men that were passed since women got the vote. Therefore, Ely asserts, these laws should not be ruled unconstitutional. What assumptions underlie Ely's claim? How would Taub and Schneider respond?

5. By the end of its 1990–1991 term, the United States Supreme Court was expected to hand down its ruling in *International Union v. Johnson Controls*. Johnson Controls, Inc. is a Milwaukee-based manufacturer of automotive batteries, the main ingredient of which is lead. Studies have shown that exposure to certain levels of lead can seriously impair female reproductive abilities and injure developing fetuses. During the 1980s, Johnson Controls, along with many other large manufacturing corporations, instituted a fetal protection policy. Under the policy, all female employees, unless they provide proof of sterility, are barred from any job with a level of lead exposure alleged to pose reproductive hazards. The plaintiffs in the case, a group of female workers, alleged that the policy effectively excluded women workers from virtually all of the typically higher-paying manufacturing jobs in the company's plants and hence constituted sex discrimination. The plaintiffs argued that such policies—which do not consider a woman's personal situation, such as her plans to have children or her age (some policies include women up to sixty years old)—are simply an expression of paternalism: They presume that women workers are not capable of deciding for themselves whether to accept a certain job risk. The plaintiffs used the Pregnancy Disability Act of 1978—which forbids employers from treating female workers differently from male workers simply on the basis of pregnancy unless the condition affects the woman's ability to do the job—to support their position. However, Johnson Controls argued that it had both a moral and legal obligation to provide a safe working environment and that this obligation extended to protecting fetal life from workplace hazards. Does the Johnson Controls policy constitute sex discrimination, in your view? Why or why not? If you believe that such policies are discriminatory, do they discriminate overtly and consciously? Or

do they instead have a discriminatory effect, or "disparate impact"? Under existing law, a policy that is consciously discriminatory can be retained only if it is based on a "bona fide occupational qualification" necessary to the normal operation of the business. Is being a male a genuine occupational qualification for jobs with high lead-exposure levels? Is protecting the health and safety of third parties, such as fetuses, part of a company's normal operations?

Cases for Further Reflection

City of Richmond v. Croson
109 S. Ct. 706 (1989)
United States Supreme Court

This case represents one of the Court's latest confrontations over affirmative action plans and the Constitution's guarantee of equality. The following excerpt contains portions of the principal opinion by Justice O'Connor, the concurrence of Justice Scalia, and the dissent of Justice Marshall. To what extent does O'Connor echo the views of Justice Powell in *Bakke*? Does the Constitution forbid only acts of "identified discrimination"? What evidence convinces Marshall that the city's affirmative action plan is responding to past racial discrimination? Also note O'Connor's discussion of Ely's views in connection with the political power of Richmond's blacks. How does Marshall respond? And compare Scalia's position with that defended by Lisa Newton.

Justice O'Connor announced the judgment of the Court. . . .

In this case, we confront once again the tension between the Fourteenth Amendment's guarantee of equal treatment to all citizens, and the use of race-based measures to ameliorate the effects of past discrimination on the opportunities enjoyed by members of minority groups in our society. . . .

On April 11, 1983, the Richmond City Council adopted the Minority Business Utilization Plan (the Plan). The Plan required prime contractors to

whom the city awarded construction contracts to subcontract at least 30% of the dollar amount of the contract to one or more Minority Business Enterprises (MBEs). . . .

. . . The 30% set-aside did not apply to city contracts awarded to minority-owned prime contractors. . . .

The Plan defined an MBE as "[a] business at least fifty-one (51) percent of which is owned and controlled . . . by minority group members." . . . "Minority group members" were defined as "[c]itizens of the United States who are Blacks, Spanish-speaking, Orientals, Indians, Eskimos, or Aleuts." . . . There was no geographic limit to the Plan; an otherwise qualified MBE from anywhere in the United States could avail itself of the 30% set-aside. The Plan declared that it was "remedial" in nature, and enacted "for the purpose of promoting wider participation by minority business enterprises in the construction of public projects."

. . .

There was no direct evidence of race discrimination on the part of the city in letting contracts or any evidence that the city's prime contractors had discriminated against minority-owned subcontractors.

. . .

On September 6, 1983, the city of Richmond issued in invitation to bid on a project for the provision and installation of certain plumbing fixtures at the city jail. On September 30, 1983, Eugene

Bonn, the regional manager of J. A. Croson Company (Croson), a mechanical plumbing and heating contractor, received the bid forms. The project involved the installation of stainless steel urinals and water closets in the city jail. Products of either of two manufacturers were specified, Acorn Engineering Company (Acorn) or Bradley Manufacturing Company (Bradley). Bonn determined that to meet the 30% set-aside requirement, a minority contractor would have to supply the fixtures. The provision of the fixtures amounted to 75% of the total contract price.

. . .

[Though Croson turned out to be the low bidder, it encountered difficulties in meeting the MBE requirement, and eventually asked that it be waived. The City refused; Croson sued, challenging the constitutionality of the Plan—Ed.]

. . .

The Equal Protection Clause of the Fourteenth Amendment provides that "[N]o State shall . . . deny to *any person* within its jurisdiction the equal protection of the laws" (emphasis added). As this Court has noted in the past, the "rights created by the first section of the Fourteenth Amendment are, by its terms, guaranteed to the individual. The rights established are personal rights." *Shelly* v. *Kraemer*, 334 U.S. 1, 22 (1948). The Richmond Plan denies certain citizens the opportunity to compete for a fixed percentage of public contracts based solely upon their race. To whatever racial group these citizens belong, their "personal rights" to be treated with equal dignity and respect are implicated by a rigid rule erecting race as the sole criterion in an aspect of public decisionmaking.

Absent searching judicial inquiry into the justification for such race-based measures, there is simply no way of determining what classifications are "benign" or "remedial" and what classifications are in fact motivated by illegitimate notions of racial inferiority or simple racial politics. Indeed, the purpose of strict scrutiny is to "smoke out" illegitimate uses of race by assuring that the legislative body is pursuing a goal important enough to warrant use of a highly suspect tool. The test also ensures that the means chosen "fit" this compelling goal so closely that there is little or no possibility that the motive for the classification was illegitimate racial prejudice or stereotype.

Classifications based on race carry a danger of stigmatic harm. Unless they are strictly reserved for remedial settings, they may in fact promote notions of racial inferiority and lead to a politics of racial hostility. . . .

. . . We thus reaffirm the view . . . that the standard of review under the Equal Protection Clause is not dependent on the race of those burdened or benefited by a particular classification.

. . .

Even were we to accept a reading of the guarantee of equal protection under which the level of scrutiny varies according to the ability of different groups to defend their interests in the representative process, heightened scrutiny would still be appropriate in the circumstances of this case. One of the central arguments for applying a less exacting standard to "benign" racial classifications is that such measures essentially involve a choice made by dominant racial groups to disadvantage themselves. If one aspect of the judiciary's role under the Equal Protection Clause is to protect "discrete and insular minorities" from majoritarian prejudice or indifference . . . , some maintain that these concerns are not implicated when the "white majority" places burdens upon itself. See J. Ely, Democracy and Distrust 170 (1980).

In this case, blacks comprise approximately 50% of the population of the city of Richmond. Five of the nine seats on the City Council are held by blacks. The concern that a political majority will more easily act to the disadvantage of a minority based on unwarranted assumptions or incomplete facts would seem to militate for, not against, the application of heightened judicial scrutiny in this case. See Ely, The Constitutionality of Reverse Racial Discrimination, 41 U. Chi. L. Rev. 723, 739, n. 58 (1974) ("Of course it works both ways: a law that favors Blacks over Whites would be suspect if it were enacted by a predominantly Black legislature").

. . .

. . . The District Court found the city council's "findings sufficient to ensure that, in adopting the Plan, it was remedying the present effects of past discrimination in the *construction industry*." . . . Like the "role model" theory . . . , a generalized assertion that there has been past discrimination in an entire industry provides no guidance for a legislative body to determine the precise scope of the injury it seeks to remedy. It "has no logical stopping point." . . . "Relief" for such an ill-defined wrong could extend until the percentage of public contracts awarded to MBEs in Richmond mirrored the percentage of minorities in the population as a whole.

Appellant argues that it is attempting to remedy various forms of past discrimination that are alleged to be responsible for the small number of minority businesses in the local contracting industry. Among these the city cites the exclusion of blacks from skilled construction trade unions and training programs. This past discrimination has prevented them "from following the traditional path from laborer to entrepreneur." . . .

While there is no doubt that the sorry history of both private and public discrimination in this country has contributed to a lack of opportunities for black entrepreneurs, this observation, standing alone, cannot justify a rigid racial quota in the awarding of public contracts in Richmond, Virginia. Like the claim that discrimination in primary and secondary schooling justifies a rigid racial preference in medical school admissions, an amorphous claim that there has been past discrimination in a particular industry cannot justify the use of an unyielding racial quota.

It is sheer speculation how many minority firms there would be in Richmond absent past societal discrimination, just as it was sheer speculation how many minority medical students would have been admitted to the medical school at Davis absent past discrimination in educational opportunities. Defining these sorts of injuries as "identified discrimination" would give local governments license to create a patchwork of racial preferences based on statistical generalizations about any particular field of endeavor.

These defects are readily apparent in this case. The 30% quota cannot in any realistic sense be tied to any injury suffered by anyone.

. . .

In sum, none of the evidence presented by the city points to any identified discrimination in the Richmond construction industry. We, therefore, hold that the city has failed to demonstrate a compelling interest in apportioning public contracting opportunities on the basis of race. To accept Richmond's claim that past societal discrimination alone can serve as the basis for rigid racial prefer-

ences would be to open the door to competing claims for "remedial relief" for every disadvantaged group. The dream of a Nation of equal citizens in a society where race is irrelevant to personal opportunity and achievement would be lost in a mosaic of shifting preferences based on inherently unmeasurable claims of past wrongs. . . .

. . . We think such a result would be contrary to both the letter and spirit of a constitutional provision whose central command is equality.

. . .

Justice Scalia, concurring in the judgment.

I agree with much of the Court's opinion, and, in particular, with its conclusion that strict scrutiny must be applied to all governmental classification by race, whether or not its asserted purpose is "remedial" or "benign." . . . I do not agree, however, with the Court's dicta suggesting that, despite the Fourteenth Amendment, state and local governments may in some circumstances discriminate on the basis of race in order (in a broad sense) "to ameliorate the effects of past discrimination." . . . The benign purpose of compensating for social disadvantages, whether they have been acquired by reason of prior discrimination or otherwise, can no more be pursued by the illegitimate means of racial discrimination than can other assertedly benign purposes we have repeatedly rejected. . . .

. . . The difficulty of overcoming the effects of past discrimination is as nothing compared with the difficulty of eradicating from our society the source of those effects, which is the tendency—fatal to a nation such as ours—to classify and judge men and women on the basis of their country or origin or the color of their skin. A solution to the first problem that aggravates the second is no solution at all.

. . . At least where state or local action is at issue, only a social emergency rising to the level of imminent danger to life and limb—for example, a prison race riot, requiring temporary segregation of inmates . . . can justify an exception to the principle embodied in the Fourteenth Amendment that "[o]ur Constitution is color-blind, and neither knows nor tolerates classes among citizens," *Plessy* v. *Ferguson*, 163 U.S. 537, 559 (1896) (Harlan, J., dissenting).

. . .

It is plainly true that in our society blacks have suffered discrimination immeasurably greater than any directed at other racial groups. But those who believe that racial preferences can help to "even the score" display, and reinforce, a manner of thinking by race that was the source of the injustice and that will, if it endures within our society, be the source of more injustice still. The relevant proposition is not that it was blacks, or Jews, or Irish who were discriminated against, but that it was individual men and women, "created equal," who were discriminated against. And the relevant resolve is that that should never happen again. Racial preferences appear to "even the score" (in some small degree) only if one embraces the proposition that our society is appropriately viewed as divided into races, making it right that an injustice rendered in the past to a black man should be compensated for by discriminating against a white. Nothing is worth that embrace. Since blacks have been disproportionately disadvantaged by racial discrimination, any race-neutral remedial program aimed at the disadvantaged *as such* will have a disproportionately beneficial impact on blacks. Only such a program, and not one that operates on the basis of race, is in accord with the letter and the spirit of our Constitution. . . .

Justice Marshall, with whom Justice Brennan and Justice Blackmun join, dissenting.

It is a welcome symbol of racial progress when the former capital of the Confederacy acts forthrightly to confront the effects of racial discrimination in its midst. In my view, nothing in the Constitution can be construed to prevent Richmond, Virginia, from allocating a portion of its contracting dollars for businesses owned or controlled by members of minority groups. . . .

A majority of this Court holds today, however, that the Equal Protection Clause of the Fourteenth Amendment blocks Richmond's initiative. The essence of the majority's position is that Richmond has failed to catalogue adequate findings to prove that past discrimination has impeded minorities from joining or participating fully in Richmond's construction contracting industry. I find deep irony in second-guessing Richmond's judgment on this point. As much as any municipality in the United States, Richmond knows what racial discrimination is; a century of decisions by this and other federal courts has richly documented the city's disgraceful history of public and

private racial discrimination. In any event, the Richmond City Council *has* supported its determination that minorities have been wrongly excluded from local construction contracting. Its proof includes statistics showing that minority-owned businesses have received virtually no city contracting dollars and rarely if ever belonged to area trade associations; testimony by municipal officials that discrimination has been widespread in the local construction industry; and . . . exhaustive and widely publicized federal studies . . . , which showed that pervasive discrimination in the Nation's tight-knit construction industry had operated to exclude minorities from public contracting. These are precisely the types of statistical and testimonial evidence which, until today, this Court had credited in cases approving of race-conscious measures designed to remedy past discrimination.

. . .

Today, for the first time, a majority of this Court has adopted strict scrutiny as its standard of Equal Protection Clause review of race-conscious remedial measures. . . . This is an unwelcome development. A profound difference separates governmental actions that themselves are racist, and governmental actions that seek to remedy the effects of prior racism or to prevent neutral governmental activity from perpetuating the effects of such racism.

. . .

I am also trouble by the majority's assertion that, even if it did not believe generally in strict scrutiny of race-based remedial measures, "the circumstances of this case" require this Court to look upon the Richmond City Council's measure with the strictest scrutiny. . . . The sole such circumstance which the majority cites, however, is the fact that blacks in Richmond are a "dominant racial grou[p]" in the city.

. . .

It cannot seriously be suggested that nonminorities in Richmond have any "history of purposeful unequal treatment." . . . Nor is there any indication that they have any of the disabilities that have characteristically afflicted those groups this Court has deemed suspect.

. . .

The majority today sounds a full-scale retreat from the Court's longstanding solicitude to race-conscious remedial efforts "directed toward deliverance of the century-old promise of equality of economic opportunity." . . . The new and restrictive tests it applies scuttle one city's effort to surmount its discriminatory past, and imperil those of dozens more localities. I, however, profoundly disagree with the cramped vision of the Equal Protection Clause which the majority offers today and with its application of that vision to Richmond, Virginia's, laudable set-aside plan. The battle against pernicious racial discrimination or its effects is nowhere near won. I must dissent.

Personnel Administrator of Massachusetts v. Feeney
442 U.S. 256 (1979)
United States Supreme Court

The facts of this case raise a number of issues discussed in this chapter: What is discrimination? When does a practice that unequally affects a given group or population, disadvantaging it relative to others, become discriminatory and thus impermissible? To be illegal, must such unequal treatment be motivated by a desire to bring it about? Or is the unequal state of affairs enough by itself? Do you agree with Justice Stewart that an intent to exclude women was not present in this case?

[Feeney, a woman who was not a veteran, worked for twelve years as a state employee. She had taken and passed a number of civil service exams for better jobs, but because of Massachusetts's veterans' preference law, she was each time ranked below male veterans who had earned lower test scores than herself. Under the Massachusetts law, all veterans who qualified for state civil service jobs had to be considered for appointment ahead of any qualified nonveteran. The law defined a veteran as "any person, male or female, including a nurse," who was honorably discharged from the armed forces after at least ninety days of active service, at least one day of which was during "wartime." The law operated to the overwhelming advantage of males. Feeney brought suit in federal court, alleging that the state's absolute preference for veterans constituted discrimination and thus violated the

equal protection clause of the Fourteenth Amendment. The federal district court agreed with Feeney; Massachusetts then appealed to the Supreme Court.]

Stewart, [Justice]. . . .

Notwithstanding the apparent attempts by Massachusetts to include as many military women as possible within the scope of the preference, the statute today benefits an overwhelmingly male class. This is attributable in some measure to the variety of federal statutes, regulations, and policies that have restricted the number of women who could enlist in the United States Armed Forces, and largely to the simple fact that women have never been subjected to a military draft.

When this litigation was commenced, then, over 98% of the veterans in Massachusetts were male; only 1.8% were female. And over one-quarter of the Massachusetts population were veterans. During the decade between 1963 and 1973 when the appellee was actively participating in the State's merit selection system, 47,005 new permanent appointments were made in the classified official service. Forty-three percent of those hired were women, and 57% were men. Of the women appointed, 1.8% were veterans, while 54% of the men had veteran status. A large unspecified percentage of the female appointees were serving in lower paying positions for which males traditionally had not applied.

At the outset of this litigation appellants conceded that for "many of the permanent positions for which males and females have competed" the veterans' preference has "resulted in a substantially greater proportion of female eligibles than male eligibles" not being certified for consideration. The impact of the veterans' preference law upon the public employment opportunities of women has thus been severe. This impact lies at the heart of the appellee's federal constitutional claim.

———

II

The sole question for decision on this appeal is whether Massachusetts, in granting an absolute lifetime preference to veterans, has discriminated against women in violation of the Equal Protection Clause of the Fourteenth Amendment.

A

The equal protection guarantee of the Fourteenth Amendment does not take from the States all power of classification. . . .

Certain classifications, however, in themselves supply a reason to infer antipathy. Race is the paradigm. A racial classification, regardless of purported motivation, is presumptively invalid and can be upheld only upon an extraordinary justification. This rule applies as well to a classification that is ostensibly neutral but is an obvious pretext for racial discrimination. But, as was made clear in Washington v. Davis, 426 U.S. 229, and Arlington Heights v. Metropolitan Housing Dev. Corp., 429 U.S. 252, even if a neutral law has a disproportionately adverse effect upon a racial minority, it is unconstitutional under the Equal Protection Clause only if that impact can be traced to a discriminatory purpose.

Classifications based on gender, not unlike those based upon race, have traditionally been the touchstone for pervasive and often subtle discrimination. This Court's recent cases teach that such classifications must bear a close and substantial relationship to important governmental objectives, and are in many settings unconstitutional. . . . [A]ny state law overtly or covertly designed to prefer males over females in public employment would require an exceedingly persuasive justification to withstand a constitutional challenge under the Equal Protection Clause of the Fourteenth Amendment.

B

The cases of Washington v. Davis, supra, and Arlington Heights v. Metropolitan Housing Dev. Corp., supra, recognize that when a neutral law has a disparate impact upon a group that has historically been the victim of discrimination, an unconstitutional purpose may still be at work. But those cases signaled no departure from the settled rule that the Fourteenth Amendment guarantees equal laws, not equal results. . . .

When a statute gender-neutral on its face is challenged on the ground that its effects upon women are disproportionably adverse, a twofold inquiry is thus appropriate. The first question is whether the statutory classification is indeed neutral in the sense that it is not gender based. If the classification itself, covert or overt, is not based upon gender, the second question is whether the adverse effect reflects invidious gender-based discrimination. In this second inquiry, impact provides an "important starting point," but purposeful discrimination is "the condition that offends the Constitution." . . .

If the impact of this statute could not be plausibly explained on a neutral ground, impact itself would signal that the real classification made by the law was in fact not neutral. But there can be but one answer to the question whether this veteran preference excludes significant numbers of women from preferred state jobs because they are women or because they are nonveterans. Apart from the fact that the definition of "veterans" in the statute has always been neutral as to gender and that Massachusetts has consistently defined veteran status in a way that has been inclusive of women who have served in the military, this is not a law that can plausibly be explained only as a gender-based classification. Indeed, it is not a law that can rationally be explained on that ground. . . . Too many men are [adversely] affected by ch. 31, §23, to permit the inference that the statute is but a pretext for preferring men over women. . . .

The dispositive question, then, is whether the appellee has shown that a gender-based discriminatory purpose has, at least in some measure, shaped the Massachusetts veterans' preference legislation. . . . [S]he points to two basic factors which in her view distinguish ch. 31, §23, from the neutral rules at issue in the Washington v. Davis and *Arlington Heights* cases. The first is the nature of the preference, which is said to be demonstrably gender-biased in the sense that it favors a status reserved under federal military policy primarily to men. The second concerns the impact of the absolute lifetime preference upon the employment opportunities of women, an impact claimed to be too inevitable to have been unintended. The appellee contends that these factors, coupled with the fact that the preference itself has little if any relevance to actual job performance, more than suffice to prove the discriminatory intent required to establish a constitutional violation. . . .

To the extent that the status of veteran is one that few women have been enabled to achieve, every hiring preference for veterans, however modest or extreme, is inherently gender-biased. If Massachusetts by offering such a preference can be said intentionally to have incorporated into its state employment policies the historical gender-based federal military personnel practices, the degree of the preference would or should make no constitutional difference. Invidious discrimination does not become less so because the discrimination accomplished is of a lesser magnitude. Discriminatory intent is simply not amenable to calibration. It either is a factor that has influenced the legislative choice or it is not. The District Court's conclusion that the absolute veterans' perference was not originally enacted or subsequently reaffirmed for the purpose of giving an advantage to males as such necessarily compels the conclusion that the State intended nothing more than to prefer "veterans." Given this finding, simple logic suggests that an intent to exclude women from significant public jobs was not at work in this law. To reason that is was, by describing the preference as "inherently nonneutral" or "gender-biased," is merely to restate the fact of impact, not to answer the question of intent.

To be sure, this case is unusual in that it involves a law that by design is not neutral. The law overtly prefers veterans as such. As opposed to the written test at issue in *Davis*, it does not purport to define a job-related characteristic. To the contrary, it confers upon a specifically described group—perceived to be particularly deserving—a competitive headstart. . . .

The appellee's ultimate argument rests upon the presumption, common to the criminal and civil law, that a person intends the natural and foreseeable consequences of his voluntary actions. . . .

The decision to grant a preference to veterans was of course "intentional." So, necessarily, did an adverse impact upon nonveterans follow from that decision. And it cannot seriously be argued that the Legislature of Massachusetts could have been unaware that most veterans are men. It would thus be disingenuous to say that the adverse consequences of this legislation for women were unintended, in the sense that they were not volitional or in the sense that they were not foreseeable.

"Discriminatory purpose," however, implies more than intent as volition or intent as awareness of consequences. It implies that the decisionmaker, in this case a state legislature, selected or reaffirmed a particular course of action at least in part "because of," not merely "in spite of," its adverse effects upon an indentifiable group. Yet nothing in the record demonstrates that this preference for veterans was originally devised or subsequently re-enacted because it would accom-

plish the collateral goal of keeping women in a stereotypic and predefined place in the Massachusetts Civil Service.

To the contrary, the statutory history shows that the benefit of the preference was consistently offered to "any person" who was a veteran. That benefit has been extended to women under a very broad statutory definition of the term veteran. . . . When the totality of legislative actions establishing and extending the Massachusetts veterans' preference are considered, the law remains what it purports to be: a preference for veterans of either sex over nonveterans of either sex, not for men over women.

. . .

Marshall, [Justice], joined by Brennan, [Justice], dissenting.

Although acknowledging that in some circumstances, discriminatory intent may be inferred from the inevitable or foreseeable impact of a statute, the Court concludes that no such intent has been established here. I cannot agree. In my judgment, Massachusetts' choice of an absolute veterans' preference system evinces purposeful gender-based discrimination. And because the statutory scheme bears no substantial relationship to a legitimate governmental objective, it cannot withstand scrutiny under the Equal Protection Clause. . . .

That a legislature seeks to advantage one group does not, as a matter of logic or of common sense, exclude the possibility that it also intends to disadvantage another. Individuals in general and lawmakers in particular frequently act for a variety of reasons. . . . [T]he critical constitutional inquiry is not whether an illicit consideration was the primary or but-for cause of a decision, but rather whether it had an appreciable role in shaping a given legislative enactment. . . .

. . . [S]ince reliable evidence of subjective intentions is seldom obtainable, resort to inference based on objective factors is generally unavoidable. To discern the purposes underlying facially neutral policies, this Court has therefore considered the degree, inevitability, and foreseeability of any disproportionate impact as well as the alternatives reasonably available.

In the instant case, the impact of the Massachusetts statute on women is undisputed. . . . Because less than 2% of the women in Massachusetts are veterans, the absolute preference formula has rendered desirable state civil service employment an almost exclusively male prerogative.

As the District Court recognized, this consequence follows foreseeably, indeed inexorably, from the long history of policies severely limiting women's participation in the military. Although neutral in form, the statute is anything but neutral in application. . . . Where the foreseeable impact of a facially neutral policy is so disproportionate, the burden should rest on the State to establish that sex-based considerations played no part in the choice of the particular legislative scheme.

Clearly, that burden was not sustained here. The legislative history of the statute reflects the Commonwealth's patent appreciation of the impact the preference system would have on women, and an equally evident desire to mitigate that impact only with respect to certain traditionally female occupations. Until 1971, the statute and implementing civil service regulations exempted from operation of the preference any job requisitions "especially calling for women." In practice, this exemption, coupled with the absolute preference for veterans, has created a gender-based civil service hierarchy, with women occupying low-grade clerical secretarial jobs and men holding more responsible and remunerative positions.

Thus, for over 70 years, the Commonwealth has maintained, as an integral part of its veterans' preference system, an exemption relegating female civil service applicants to occupations traditionally filled by women. Such a statutory scheme both reflects and perpetuates precisely the kind of archaic assumptions about women's roles which we have previously held invalid. Particularly when viewed against the range of less discriminatory alternatives available to assist veterans. Massachusetts' choice of a formula that so severely restricts public employment opportunities for women cannot reasonably be thought gender-neutral. . . .

Watkins v. U.S. Army
837 F. 2d 1428 (1988)
United States Court of Appeals,
Ninth Circuit

Should sexual orientation be included among those "immutable" traits or characteristics like race or birth status upon which unequal treatment may never be predicated, at least without a "compel-

ling" reason? This is the question put by *Watkins*. In 1982, the Army sought to discharge Watkins, an admitted homosexual, pursuant to regulations making ineligible for reenlistment those personnel "of questionable moral character and a history of antisocial behavior, sexual perversion or homosexuality." The regulations defined a homosexual as "a person, regardless of sex, who desires bodily contact between persons of the same sex, actively undertaken or passively permitted, with the intent to obtain or give sexual gratification." The regulations went on to add that "any official, private, or public profession of homosexuality may be considered in determining whether a person is an admitted homosexual."[1] Take note of the court's discussion of *Bowers v. Hardwick* (reprinted in Chapter Two): If states may permissibly criminalize homosexual sodomy, how, according to the majority, can regulations penalizing homosexuals nonetheless violate the principle of equal treatment? The law penalizes and thus "discriminates" against burglars. How, given *Bowers*, is the case of gays different? Why does Judge Reinhardt dissent, given his belief that gays and lesbians have been the victims of intolerance and prejudice? (Compare also Reinhardt's remarks about following the precedent of *Bowers* with the material on legal reasoning in Chapter Two.) Why does the court hold that laws classifying persons on the basis of sexual orientation must be subject to "strict scrutiny"?

NORRIS, Circuit Judge:

In August 1967, at the age of 19, Perry Watkins enlisted in the United States Army. In filling out the Army's pre-induction medical form, he candidly marked "yes" in response to a question whether he had homosexual tendencies. The Army nonetheless considered Watkins "qualified for admission" and inducted him into its ranks. Watkins served fourteen years in the Army, and became, in the words of his commanding officer, "one of our most respected and trusted soldiers." . . .

Even though Watkins'[s] homosexuality was always common knowledge, . . . the Army has never claimed that his sexual orientation or behavior interfered in any way with military functions. To the contrary, an Army review board found "there is no evidence suggesting that his behavior has had either a degrading effect upon unit performance, morale or discipline, or upon his own job performance." . . .[2]

In 1981 the Army promulgated new regulations which mandated the disqualification of all homosexuals from the Army without regard to the length or quality of their military service. Pursuant to these new regulations, the Army notified Watkins that he would be discharged and denied reenlistment because of his homosexuality. In this federal court action, Watkins challenges the Army's actions and new regulations on various statutory and constitutional grounds.

. . .

We now turn to the threshold question raised by Watkins'[s] equal protection claim: Do the Army's regulations discriminate based on sexual orientation?

. . .

We conclude that these regulations, on their face, discriminate against homosexuals on the basis of their sexual orientation. Under the regulations any homosexual act or statement of homosexuality gives rise to a presumption of homosexual orientation, and anyone who fails to rebut that presumption is conclusively barred from Army service. In other words, the regulations target homosexual orientation itself. The homosexual acts and statements are merely relevant, and rebuttable, indicators of that orientation.

. . .

. . . The Army . . . argues that the Supreme Court's decision in *Bowers v. Hardwick*, 478 U.S. 186 . . . (1986), forecloses Watkins'[s] equal protection challenge to its regulations. In *Hardwick*, the Court rejected a claim by a homosexual that a Georgia statute criminalizing sodomy deprived him of his liberty without due process of law in violation of the Fourteenth Amendment. More specifically, the Court held that the constitutionally protected right to privacy—recognized in cases such as *Griswold v. Connecticut*, 381 U.S. 479 . . . (1965), and *Eisenstadt v. Baird*, 405 U.S. 438 . . . (1972)—does not extend to acts of consensual homosexual sodomy. . . . The Court's holding was limited to this due process question. The parties did not argue and the Court explicitly did not decide the question whether the Georgia sodomy statute might violate the equal protection clause. . . .

The Army nonetheless argues that it would be "incongruous" to hold that its regulations deprive

gays of equal protection of the laws when *Hardwick* holds that there is no constitutionally protected privacy right to engage in homosexual sodomy. . . . We disagree. First, while *Hardwick* does indeed hold that the due process clause provides no substantive privacy protection for acts of private homosexual sodomy, nothing in *Hardwick* suggests that the state may penalize gays for their sexual orientation. . . .

. . . Second, although *Hardwick* held that the due process clause does not prevent states from criminalizing acts of homosexual sodomy, . . . nothing in *Hardwick* actually holds that the state may make invidious distinctions when regulating sexual conduct. . . .

. . . We cannot read *Hardwick* as standing for the proposition that government may outlaw sodomy only when committed by a disfavored class of persons. Surely, for example, *Hardwick* cannot be read as a license for the government to outlaw sodomy only when committed by blacks. If government insists on regulating private sexual conduct between consenting adults, it must, at a minimum, do so evenhandedly—prohibiting all persons from engaging in the proscribed sexual acts rather than placing the burden of sexual restraint solely on a disfavored minority.[3]

. . .

We now address the merits of Watkins'[s] claim that we must subject the Army's regulations to strict scrutiny because homosexuals constitute a suspect class under equal protection jurisprudence. The Supreme Court has identified several factors that guide our suspect class inquiry.

The first factor the Supreme Court generally considers is whether the group at issue has suffered a history of purposeful discrimination. . . .

. . . As the Army concedes, it is indisputable that "homosexuals have historically been the object of pernicious and sustained hostility." . . .

. . . Homosexuals have been the frequent victims of violence and have been excluded from jobs, schools, housing, churches, and even families. . . .

The second factor that the Supreme Court considers in suspect class analysis is difficult to capsulize and may in fact represent a cluster of factors grouped around a central idea—whether the discrimination embodies a gross unfairness that is sufficiently inconsistent with the ideals of equal protection to term it invidious. Considering this additional factor makes sense. After all, discrimination exists against some groups because the animus is warranted—no one could seriously argue that burglars form a suspect class.

. . .

. . . In giving content to this concept of gross unfairness, the Court has considered (1) whether the disadvantaged class is defined by a trait that "frequently bears no relation to ability to perform or contribute to society," *Frontiero*, 411 U.S. at 686 . . . (plurality); (2) whether the class has been saddled with unique disabilities because of prejudice or inaccurate stereotypes; and (3) whether the trait defining the class is immutable.

. . .

Sexual orientation plainly has no relevance to a person's "ability to perform or contribute to society." Indeed, the Army makes no claim that homosexuality impairs a person's ability to perform military duties. Sergeant Watkins'[s] exemplary record of military service stands as a testament to quite the opposite. . . . Moreover, as the Army itself concluded, there is not a scintilla of evidence that Watkins'[s] avowed homosexuality "had either a degrading effect upon unit performance, morale or discipline, or upon his own job performance." . . .

This irrelevance of sexual orientation to the quality of a person's contributuion to society also suggests that classifications based on sexual orientation reflect prejudice and inaccurate stereotypes—the second indicia of a classification's gross unfairness.

[The] Army suggests that the public opprobrium directed towards gays does not constitute prejudice in the pejorative sense of the word, but rather represents appropriate public disapproval of persons who engage in immoral behavior. The Army equates homosexuals with sodomists and justifies its regulations as simply reflecting a rational bias against a class of persons who engage in criminal acts of sodomy. In essence, the Army argues that homosexuals, like burglars, cannot form a suspect class because they are criminals.

The Army's argument, essentially adopted by the dissent, rests on two false premises. First, the class burdened by the regulations is defined by the sexual *orientation* of its members, not by their sex-

ual conduct. . . . To our knowledge, homosexual orientation itself has never been criminalized in this country. Moreover, any attempt to criminalize the status of an individual's sexual orientation would present grave constitutional problems. . . .

Second, little of the homosexual *conduct* covered by the regulations is criminal. The regulations reach many forms of homosexual conduct other than sodomy such as kissing, handholding, caressing, and hand-genital contact. Yet, sodomy is the only consensual adult sexual conduct that Congress has criminalized. . . .

Finally, we turn to immutability as an indicator of gross unfairness. . . .

. . . Although the Supreme Court considers immutability relevant, it is clear that by "immutability" the Court has never meant strict immutability in the sense that members of the class must be physically unable to change or mask the trait defining their class. People can have operations to change their sex. Aliens can ordinarily become naturalized citizens. The status of illegitimate children can be changed. People can frequently hide their national origin by changing their customs, their names, or their associations. Lighter skinned blacks can sometimes "pass" for white, as can Latinos for Anglos, and some people can even change their racial appearance with pigment injections. . . . At a minimum, then, the Supreme Court is willing to treat a trait as effectively immutable if changing it would involve great difficulty, such as requiring a major physical change or a traumatic change of identity. Reading the case law in a more capacious manner, "immutability" may describe those traits that are so central to a person's identity that it would be abhorrent for government to penalize a person for refusing to change them, regardless of how easy that change might be physically. Racial discrimination, for example, would not suddenly become constitutional if medical science developed an easy, cheap, and painless method of changing one's skin pigment. . . .

Under either formulation, we have no trouble concluding that sexual orientation is immutable for the purposes of equal protection doctrine. Although the causes of homosexuality are not fully understood, scientific research indicates that we have little control over our sexual orientation and that, once acquired, our sexual orientation is largely impervious to change. . . . Scientific proof aside, it seems appropriate to ask whether heterosexuals feel capable of changing *their* sexual orientation. Would heterosexuals living in a city that passed an ordinance banning those who engaged in or desired to engage in sex with persons of the *opposite* sex find it easy not only to abstain from heterosexual activity but also to shift the object of their sexual desires to persons of the same sex? It may be that some heterosexuals and homosexuals can change their sexual orientation through extensive therapy, neurosurgery or shock treatment. . . .

. . . But the possibility of such a difficult and traumatic change does not make sexual orientation "mutable" for equal protection purposes. To express the same idea under the alternative formulation, we conclude that allowing the government to penalize the failure to change such a central aspect of individual and group identity would be abhorrent to the values animating the constitutional ideal of equal protection of the laws.

. . .

Having concluded that homosexuals constitute a suspect class, we must subject the Army's regulations facially discriminating against homosexuals to strict scrutiny. Consequently, we may uphold the regulations only if ' "*necessary* to promote a *compelling* governmental interest.' "

. . .

[Even] granting special deference to the policy choices of the military, we must reject many of the Army's asserted justifications because they illegitimately cater to private biases.

. . .

The Army's defense of its regulations, however, goes beyond its professed fear of prejudice in the ranks. Apparently, the Army believes that its regulations rooting out persons with certain sexual tendencies are not merely a response to prejudice, but are also grounded in legitimate moral norms. In other words, the Army believes that its ban against homosexuals simply codifies society's moral consensus that homosexuality is evil. Yet, even accepting *arguendo* this proposition that anti-homosexual animus is grounded in morality (as opposed to prejudice masking as morality), equal protection doctrine does not permit notions of majoritarian morality to serve as

compelling justification for laws that discriminate against suspect classes. . . .

. . . Although courts may sometimes have to accept society's moral condemnation as a justification even when the morally condemned activity causes no harm to interests outside notions of morality, . . . our deference to majoritarian notions of morality must be tempered by equal protection principles which require that those notions be applied evenhandedly. Laws that limit the acceptable focus of one's sexual desires to members of the opposite sex, like laws that limit one's choice of spouse (or sexual partner) to members of the same race, cannot withstand constitutional scrutiny absent a compelling governmental justification.

. . .

Reversed and remanded.
Reinhardt, Circuit Judge, dissenting.

With great reluctance, I have concluded that I am unable to concur in the majority opinion. Like the majority, I believe that homosexuals have been unfairly treated both historically and in the United States today. Were I free to apply my own view of the meaning of the Constitution and in that light to pass upon the validity of the Army's regulations, I too would conclude that the Army may not refuse to enlist homosexuals. I am bound, however, as a circuit judge to apply the Constitution as it has been interpreted by the Supreme Court and our own circuit, whether or not I agree with those interpretations. Because of this requirement, I am sometimes compelled to reach a result I believe to be contrary to the proper interpretation of constitutional principles. This is, regrettably, one of those times.

In this case we consider the constitutionality of a regulation which bars homosexuals from enlisting in the Army. Sergeant Perry Watkins challenges that regulation under the Equal Protection Clause. The majority holds that homosexuals are a suspect class, and that the regulation cannot survive strict scrutiny. Because I am compelled by recent Supreme Court and Ninth Circuit precedent to conclude first, that homosexuals are not a suspect class and second, that the regulation survives both rational and intermediate level scrutiny, I must dissent. . . .

Bowers v. Hardwick . . . is the landmark case involving homosexual conduct. In *Hardwick*, the Supreme Court decided that homosexual sodomy is not protected by the right to privacy, and thus that the states are free to criminalize that conduct. Because Hardwick did not challenge the Georgia sodomy statute under the Equal Protection Clause, and neither party presented that issue in its briefs or at oral argument, the Court limited its holding to due process and properly refrained from reaching any direct conclusion regarding an equal protection challenge to the statute. . . . However, the fact that *Hardwick* does not address the equal protection question directly does not mean that the case is not of substantial significance to such an inquiry.

. . .

In my opinion, *Hardwick must* be read as standing precisely for the proposition the majority rejects. To put it simply, I believe that after *Hardwick* the government may outlaw homosexual sodomy even though it fails to regulate the private sexual conduct of heterosexuals. In *Hardwick* the Court took great care to make clear that it was saying only that *homosexual* sodomy is not constitutionally protected, and not that all sexual acts—both heterosexual and homosexual—that fall within the definition of sodomy can be prohibited.

. . .

The majority opinion concludes that under the criteria established by equal protection case law, homosexuals must be treated as a suspect class. . . . Were it not for *Hardwick* (and other cases discussed *infra*), I would agree, for in my opinion the group meets all the applicable criteria. . . . However, after *Hardwick*, we are no longer free to reach that conclusion.

The majority opinion treats as a suspect class a group of persons whose defining characteristic is their desire, predisposition, or propensity to engage in conduct that the Supreme Court has held to be constitutionally unprotected, an act that the states can—and approximately half the states have—criminalized. Homosexuals are different from groups previously afforded protection under the equal protection clause in that homosexuals are defined by their conduct—or, at the least, by their desire to engage in certain conduct. With other groups, such as blacks or women, there is no connection between particular conduct and the definition of the group. When conduct that plays a

central role in defining a group may be prohibited by the state, it cannot be asserted with any legitimacy that the group is specially protected by the Constitution.[4]

. . .

. . . Laws against sodomy do not affect homosexuals and heterosexuals equally. Homosexuals are more heavily burdened by such legislation, even if we ignore the governmental tendency to prosecute general sodomy statutes selectively against them. . . . Oral sex, a form of sodomy, is the primary form of sexual activity among homosexuals; however, sexual intercourse is the primary form of sexual activity among heterosexuals. If homosexuals were in fact a suspect class, a statute criminalizing both heterosexual sodomy and homosexual sodomy would still not survive equal protection analysis. For the prohibition to be equal, the government would have to prohibit sexual intercourse—conduct as basic to heterosexuals as sodomy is to homosexuals. This, obviously, the government would not and could not do. Therefore, if equal protection rules apply (i.e., if homosexuals are a suspect class), a ban on homosexual sodomy could not stand no matter how the statute was drawn. *Hardwick* makes it plain that the contrary is true. . . .

Before concluding my discussion of *Hardwick*, I wish to record my own view of the opinion. I have delayed doing so until I have applied the case as I believe we have a duty to apply it. Now, I must add that as I understand our Constitution, a state simply has no business treating any group of persons as the State of Georgia and other states with sodomy statutes treat homosexuals. In my opinion, invidious discrimination against a group of persons with immutable characteristics can never be justified on the grounds of society's moral disapproval. No lesson regarding the meaning of our Constitution could be more important for us as a nation to learn. I believe that the Supreme Court egregiously misinterpreted the Constitution in *Hardwick*. In my view, *Hardwick* improperly condones official bias and prejudice against homosexuals, and authorizes the criminalization of conduct that is an essential part of the intimate sexual life of our many homosexual citizens, a group that has historically been the victim of unfair and irrational treatment. I believe that history will view *Hardwick* much as it views *Plessy v. Ferguson*, 163 U.S. 537

. . . (1896). And I am confident that, in the long run, *Hardwick*, like *Plessy*, will be overruled by a wiser and more enlightened Court.

. . .

Endnotes

[1] *Watkins v. U.S. Army* 837 F. 2d 1428 (9th Cir. 1988), p. 1434–1436.

[2] In this opinion we use the term "sexual orientation" to refer to the orientation of an individual's sexual preference, not to his actual sexual conduct. Individuals whose sexual orientation creates in them a desire for sexual relationships with persons of the opposite sex have a heterosexual orientation. Individuals whose sexual orientation creates in them a desire for sexual relationships with persons of the same sex have a homosexual orientation.

In contrast, we use the terms "homosexual conduct" and "homosexual acts" to refer to sexual activity between two members of the same sex whether their orientations are homosexual, heterosexual, or bisexual, and we use the terms "heterosexual conduct" and "heterosexual acts" to refer to sexual activity between two members of the opposite sex wheter their orientations are homosexual, heterosexual, or bisexual.

Throughout this opinion, the terms "gay" and "homosexual" will be used synonymously to denote persons of homosexual orientation.

[3] The dissent's interpretation of *Hardwick*—that it authorizes the state to single out homosexual conduct for criminal sanction *because* that conduct is committed by homosexuals—is wide of the mark. *Hardwick* explicitly focused on the question whether the right to privacy extends constitutional protection to the commission of homosexual sodomy. . . . In essence, the dissent shifts *Hardwick's* focus away from substantive due process and the right to privacy towards the right of homosexuals to enjoy equal treatment under the laws. Such an expansively anti-homosexual reading of *Hardwick* is unsupported and unfair both to homosexuals and the Supreme Court.

We also cannot agree with the dissent's assertion that the equal protection clause is entirely "procedural in nature" and that, therefore, our equal protection analysis is coherent "[o]nly if heterosexual sodomy is *not* protected by the right to privacy." . . . However the Supreme Court defines the right to privacy—whether that definition includes a right to engage in heterosexual sodomy, homosexual sodomy, neither, or both—the equal protection clause imposes an independent obligation on government not to draw invidious distinctions among its citizens. . . . We do not read *Hardwick* as in any way eroding that principle.

[4] Thus, it is not even necessary to decide whether the majority's view of *Hardwick*—that it is based on a condemnation of sodomy rther than of homosexuality—is correct. Whatever the explanation for the Court's willingness to allow sodomy to be criminalized—whether its decision is based on its views as to the morality of homosexuality or on its disapproval of sodomy, including the heterosexual variety—that willingness is inconsistent with affording special constitutional protection to homosexuals—a group whose primary form of sexual activity, the Court tells us, may be declared criminal.

Suggestions for Further Reading

Aristotle, *Nichomachean Ethics* (various translations).

Berger, R., *Government by Judiciary: The Transformation of the Fourteenth Amendment* (Cambridge, Mass.: Harvard University Press, 1977).

Brandt, R. (Ed.), *Social Justice* (Englewood Cliffs, N.J.: Prentice-Hall, 1962).

Cohen, M., *et al.*, *Equality and Preferential Treatment* (Princeton, N.J.: Princeton University Press, 1977).

Cover, R. M., *Justice Accused: Antislavery and the Judicial Process* (New Haven, Conn.: Yale University Press, 1975).

Dworkin, R., "What Is Equality: Parts 1 and 2," *Philosophy and Public Affairs*, Vol. 10 (1981): 185–246; 283–344.

Dworkin, R., "What Is Equality: Part 3," *Iowa Law Review*, Vol. 73 (1987): 1–54.

Freeman, A. D., "Legitimizing Racial Discrimination Through Antidiscrimination Law," *Minnesota Law Review*, Vol. 62 (1978): 1049–1119.

Greenawalt, K., *Discrimination and Reverse Discrimination* (New York: Alfred A. Knopf, 1983).

Kluger, R., *Simple Justice* (New York: Vintage Books, 1975).

Lewis, A., *Gideon's Trumpet* (New York: Random House, 1964).

MacKinnon, C., *Toward a Feminist Theory of the State* (Cambridge, Mass.: Harvard University Press, 1989).

Nozick, R., *Anarchy, State, and Utopia* (New York: Basic Books, 1974).

Okin, S. M., "Justice and Gender," *Philosophy and Public Affairs*, Vol. 16 (1987): 42–72.

Rawls, J., *A Theory of Justice* (Cambridge, Mass.: Harvard University Press, 1971).

Rhode, D., "Occupational Inequality," *Duke Law Journal* (1988): 1207–1241.

Tussman, J., and tenBroek, J., "The Equal Protection of the Laws," *California Law Review*, Vol. 37 (1949): 341–381.

Williams, B., "The Idea of Equality," in B. Williams (Ed.), *Problems of the Self* (Cambridge: Cambridge University Press, 1973).

Chapter V
Criminal Law

Many of us are better acquainted with the basic language and aims of the criminal law than with any other part of our jurisprudence. Unfortunately, most of that familiarity fails to extend much beyond the latest television courtroom drama or movie mystery, and this is regrettable. For the criminal law raises some of the most troubling and yet fascinating philosophical difficulties anywhere in the law—problems sharpened in their urgency by the obvious extent to which the criminal law can affect the course of a human life, or, in the extreme case, end it.

A few days before Christmas 1984, a slightly built man named Bernhard Goetz entered a subway car in New York City. Four youths, apparently looking for trouble, asked him for money. Goetz responded with a .38 caliber revolver, wounding each of the four and paralyzing one of them. The media quickly branded Goetz the "subway vigilante," and his eventual trial on multiple counts of assault and attempted murder raised difficult issues: Did Goetz intend to kill the youths? Could he be convicted of "attempted" murder? Did he act in self-defense?

Did he endanger others unjustifiably? Should he be punished? These questions prompt larger ones: Under what conditions should a person be held responsible for his or her acts? Under what conditions may one be excused? Suppose I simply made a mistake? Or was merely careless? Or was mentally unstable? Is it fair to punish me for a harm I caused but did not intend? If I try but fail to commit a crime should I be punished as severely as if I had succeeded? What is the aim of punishment in the first place? Must the punishment always "fit" the crime? Is that always possible? If, for example, my crime consists in subjecting you to a chance of injury, would it be fair to subject me in similar fashion to a risk of harm? Are there punishments that ought never to be inflicted?

Section A begins our exploration of these issues through a study of liability for criminal "attempts." George Fletcher identifies two different approaches to the question of attempts and relates them to the specific issues raised in the Goetz case. David Lewis then asks how severely should attempts to commit a crime be punished.

Sections B and C examine the role of the "mental element" in crime. The readings in B consider strict-liability offenses in the criminal law. George Fletcher argues that one form of strict criminal liability—the felony-murder rule—is indefensible on moral grounds. Mark Kelman canvasses the traditional reasons for strict criminal liability and offers an alternative justification. The selections in C take up the question of the insanity defense, Norval Morris arguing for its abolition, Sanford Kadish for its retention.

Section D turns to larger issues about punishment. Both Marvin Frankel and Richard Wasserstrom tackle the problem of how the practice of criminal punishment can be justified and whether it should be abandoned for a regime of "therapy." Other readings deal with the limits of the constitutional prohibition on "cruel and unusual" punishments.

A. What Is a Crime?

Introduction

Bernhard Goetz was accused of having committed at least four separate and distinct crimes, all arising out of his use of a gun on the subway that morning: possessing a loaded gun in public, recklessly endangering the lives of others, criminal assault, and attempted murder. How can one action produce such a wealth of "crimes"? The answer is that each offense was based upon one or another aspect of Goetz'a conduct together with his state of mind at the time of the incident. A central feature of the criminal law is its attempt to rest liability upon the conjunction of these two elements: outward behavior and inner state of mind. Since these concepts will figure prominently in the material for this section, it will be useful to pause a moment over them.

The two basic elements of criminality are marked by their Latin names: *actus reus* and *mens rea*. *Actus reus* refers to an act of wrongdoing: running a red light, shooting someone, taking their television set without their permission (and not returning it). The criminal law is concerned with conduct, with things people *do*. You might wonder why this is so. Must something be *done* before the criminal law can respond? Why not (for example) focus on thoughts or emotions? Why not subject to punishment those who possess, though they have not yet manifested, "poor character"? Why can't a person be punished for having "evil thoughts"? (Consider in this connection that, several centuries ago, it was a criminal offense in England to "imagine the King's death.") It is of course difficult to prove what thoughts or feelings a person has (unless they are willing to tell you), and perhaps thoughts, by themselves, are less dangerous than actual conduct. Certainly they are difficult to control; whereas acts are, at least usually, something over which we have some power.

Even if we agree that the criminal law should confine its attention to acts, this still leaves the problem of understanding what an "act" is. Acts can be difficult to define. How many "acts" did Bernhard Goetz commit? Is "imagining the King's death" an "act"? The Model Penal Code (MPC), a proposed uniform criminal statute written by a number of lawyers and legal scholars, defines an "act" as a "muscular movement under conscious control." Is "possessing a loaded gun" an "act" under this definition?

The expression *"mens rea"* literally means "guilty mind" or "evil mind," and is generally taken to refer to the *mental* element of a crime. The basic idea is that one must have had a culpable or blameworthy state of mind before one can be said to have committed a crime. This requirement is frequently explained in terms of the idea that a criminal acts with the *intent to commit the offense*. It doesn't take much reflection to see that this requirement raises a whole range of fresh difficulties and problems: How can it be determined what X intended or thought or believed or wanted? Aren't there different states of mind that a person can have when he or she performs an action that constitutes an *actus reus*? Should all states of mind be regarded as equally culpable? If not, then how do we distinguish between the relevant states of mind and grade them appropriately? What states of mind excuse persons from liability altogether?

Plainly there are some conditions under which a person cannot be held accountable for an act of wrongdoing. This ties *mens rea* to the notion of an *excuse*: a factor that, if proven, establishes that the actor did not have the required state of mind and is therefore not properly subject to the sanctions of the criminal law. Typical excuses include infancy (being a minor), duress (being forced or pressured by another), mistake (being unaware of crucial facts or circumstances), and insanity (suffering from some kind of mental disability or defect).

In order to have before us a useful framework for the analysis of problems having to do with states of mind, consider the manner in which the drafters of the Model Penal Code sought to handle the mental element. The code proposes that every criminal offense be specified in terms of a breakdown of its constituent elements. Take burglary as an example. Most jurisdictions define burglary in this way: Knowingly breaking and entering the dwelling house of another with the intent to commit a felony therein. This crime has several elements: (1) breaking and entering; (2) dwelling house; (3) of another; (4) intent to commit a felony. The code proposes that, in order to be convictable of this offense, I must have the requisite state of mind with respect to each element of the offense. In this case, that means that I must, with intent or conscious purpose, have broken in and entered onto property; have done so in the awareness that it was a dwelling house, and the dwelling house of another; and have intended to commit a felony once I got inside. Failure to possess the relevant state of mind in conjunction with any of the elements would mean that I could not be convicted of the offense. Suppose I leave my house late at night, intending to burglarize some homes down the street. It is unusually dark and foggy; I break into my own house. Have I committed burglary? No; though I acted with the purpose or conscious intent to enter, I did not do so with respect to the dwelling house *of another*. (I may be convictable of *attempting* burglary, of course, but that is a separate matter.) Frustrated, I try again the next night. Hours of effort and no success wear me out and I decide to return home. It is dark and even foggier than the night before. I walk through the unlocked door of what I think is my house. But it is not my house. Have I committed burglary? No; though I entered the dwelling of another, I did not act with the "purpose to enter the house of another"; I acted with the purpose to go home, even though that's not where I wound up.

Conflicting Conceptions of Criminal Wrongdoing

In the issues posed by the Goetz case, law professor George Fletcher sees a clash between two general approaches to understanding the aims and purposes of the criminal law. The debate formed by that conflict turns on a basic question: Why should consequences matter in defining a criminal offense? The traditional approach focuses upon the *suffering* of the crime victim, the actual harm done. This concern was reflected in the charges brought against Goetz for assault. The traditional view is less inclined to consider, for example, the imposition of a risk of harm—reflected in the reckless endangerment charge—as deserving of criminal punishment. But if an injury occurs, even if it was not specifically intended by the perpetrator, the suffering of the victim demands a response. In this way, the traditional view construes the mental element or "intent" requirement broadly: If the "natural and probable" consequence of shooting at a man at close range is that you might sever his spinal cord, then if that results, you "intended" it, even if there was no conscious purpose to bring about that consequence. The traditional approach, Fletcher points out, is also closely linked with a *retributive* conception or understanding of the aim of punishment: The suffering of the victim demands that the perpetrator "pay" for his wicked deed. (Retributivism is discussed in detail in Section D.)

In contrast to the traditional view, the newer or modern approach, as Fletcher refers to it, is reflected in the charges brought against Goetz for attempted murder and reckless endangerment. Here the concern is not with the harm done to the victim but with the assailant's act itself, with the act that caused the harm, and with the degree of control the assailant had over that act. If I shoot at you, intending to kill you but I miss, why should the absence of a victim mitigate the seriousness of what I have done? Am I not just as guilty of endangering your life, putting you at risk? The modern view thus settles on a rationale for punishing the

attempt to commit a crime and to punish such attempts with equal severity as successfully completed crimes.

Which approach to defining and responding to criminality is best? Which is morally right? Fletcher is worried about the headlong flight of the law in the direction set by the modern approach, and his concerns can be most easily understood in terms of the category of attempt crimes. It is to these that the other readings in this section turn.

Liability and Punishment for Attempts

In "The Punishment That Leaves Something to Chance," philosopher David Lewis asks: Why punish (unsuccessful) attempts to commit a crime less severely than the commission of the completed crime itself? That this has been the general practice of our law is indisputable; but the reasons for it are less clear.

Imagine that two people shoot at me. One hits me; the other misses by inches. Both tried equally hard and acted with equal malice (evil intent). Insofar as we want to punish the wicked or deter the dangerous, both my attackers would seem to merit equal punishment. Lewis recounts and questions various explanations for punishing the person who missed the target less harshly than the one who got the "bull's eye." Does it make sense to punish one more severely merely because he actually succeeded? Is the one who missed more likely to try again? Does the fact that both tried and only one succeeded show that the successful attempter tried harder—was "wholehearted" in his efforts—so that he deserves more punishment or so that he manifests greater danger?

Lewis rejects the foregoing rationales and suggests another: Punishing (unsuccessful) attempters less harshly than those who complete the crime represents a form of *penal lottery*, subjecting a person to a risk of harm. Attempts to commit a crime, whether or not they succeed, do impose risks (perhaps of death) on their intended victims. So, Lewis proposes, our law appropriately deals with attempters in the same way, exposing *them* to a risk of greater punishment (perhaps even death): the risk that they may hit the target rather than miss and wind up in the electric chair rather than a jail cell. The law makes the severity of their punishment turn on chance.

Lewis proposes that we make the element of chance operating in the law of attempt more explicit and overt by instituting a penal lottery in which those convicted of attempt draw lots, the loser being, say, executed. The worse the crime you attempt, the worse the odds for you.

Is a penal lottery unfair or unjust? And if so, how? Is it fair to subject all attempters, successful or not, to a risk of death? Does it matter that we subject them *equally* to such a risk of death? If people's lives are affected by chance in a whole variety of other ways (which they indisputably are), why not in this way? Lewis is partial to the penal lottery; but he stops short of committing himself to it.

The facts of *People v. Dlugash* introduce a further dimension to the debate over attempts. During an argument in the early morning hours, Joe Bush shoots Mike Geller three times in the chest. Roughly five minutes later, Bush's companion, Dlugash, walks over the prone Geller and empties five shots in and about the head and vital organs. Dlugash later testifies that he acted because he was "afraid of Joe Bush." Dlugash is convicted of murder; but an appellate court reverses the conviction on the grounds that the state did not prove beyond a reasonable doubt that Geller was alive at the time Dlugash pulled the trigger. But Dlugash was also convicted of the "lesser included offense" of attempted murder. Dlugash now presents the appellate court with an unusual question: Can you attempt to murder a man who is already dead?

The common law of England—many of the central principles and distinctions of which were adopted by the early states in this country—made it a criminal offense to attempt to commit a crime: the unsuccessful effort to bring about the intended harm. As with most crimes, attempt has both *actus reus* and *mens rea* components. The *mens rea* requirement for attempts is fairly straightforward: One must have acted with the purpose to commit the object crime. (There are some difficult cases here, though. If I throw a bomb at a car, hoping and desiring to kill the driver but killing the passenger instead, did I intend the passenger's death?) The *actus reus* requirement for attempts is more complex, the principal difficulty being how to draw a line successfully between merely *preparing* to commit a crime (for example, buying burglar's

tools) and *beginning the attempt* (heading off to the bank with the tools in my backpack). How much do I have to do, how far do I have to go in order to have "made the attempt"?

Certainly the thorniest problem in the law of attempts, however, has been that posed by the following question: If what you are trying to do would constitute a crime if completed, should you be convicted of attempt if the crime was impossible to commit? Should it matter why the crime could not be committed? One obvious sort of reason for the "impossibility" involved here is that the facts might not be as you take them to be: X shoots at a shape lying under the blankets on a bed, intending to kill the person he believes to be asleep on it; but the lump under the sheets is merely a pile of pillows. Y is a pickpocket looking for easy prey; he reaches into your pocket, intending to steal your wallet, but the pocket is empty. Has X attempted murder or simply engaged in target practice with the bedclothes? Should Y be convicted of attempted robbery or merely admonished to keep his hands to himself?

What if the facts that make it impossible to complete your attempt relate to the legal definition or classification of a thing? Z tries to buy what he thinks are stolen goods from a "fence"; yet the goods are not stolen but really Z's own. Must Z be acquitted on the grounds that no amount of effort exerted in "buying" one's own things will make that conduct into the crime of receiving stolen property? Or should Z be judged guilty, since only an unforeseeable contingency (no thanks to him) kept his act from being a crime? If we let every such contingency exonerate the attempter, does that mean that the only attempts punishable will be (paradoxically) the successful ones? Traditionally, the law called the impossibility faced by X and Y "factual" and that facing Z "legal." The grounds for this distinction are not clear; they are explored by the court in *Dlugash*.

In *Dlugash*, the court notes that the law of attempt in New York has been modified to reflect the position adopted by the Model Penal Code. MPC section 5.01 effectively does away with the legal/factual impossibility distinction. It focuses on what the defendant intended or believed, not what actually obtained. How then does this approach apply to Dlugash? If he believed the victim to be alive at the moment of the shooting, he is guilty of attempted murder, even if Geller was in fact dead at the time. And, the Court holds, there is evidence here to support the claim that Dlugash *did* believe Geller to be alive. (It is also worth noting that the MPC, unlike many states, would punish Dlugash's attempt with the same degree of severity as the crime that was his object.)

The Significance of Suffering

GEORGE P. FLETCHER

December 22, 1984, the Saturday before Christmas, about 1:00 P.M., Bernhard Goetz leaves his apartment at 55 West 14th Street and walks to the subway station at the corner of Seventh Avenue and 14th Street. He enters a car on the number 2 line, the IRT express running downtown, and sits down close to four black youths. The youths, seeming drifters on the landscape of the city, are noisy and boisterous, and the 15 to 20 other passengers have moved to the other end of the car. Goetz is white, 37 years old, slightly built, and dressed in dungarees and a windbreaker. Something about his appearance beckons. One of the four, Troy Canty, lying nearly prone on the long bench next to the door, asks Goetz as he enters, "How are ya?" Canty and possibly a second youth, Barry Allen, then approach Goetz, and Canty asks him for five dollars. Goetz asks him what he wants. Canty repeats: "Give me five dollars."[1] Suddenly, the moving car resounds with gunshots, one aimed at each of the young blacks.

At this point the story becomes uncertain. According to Goetz's subsequent confession, he pauses, goes over to a youth sitting in the two-seater by the conductor's cab at the end of the car, looks at him, and says, "You seem to be [doing] all right; here's another,"[2] and fires a fifth shot that empties his five-shot Smith & Wesson .38 revolver. The bullet enters Darrell Cabey's body on his left side, traverses the back, and severs his spinal cord.

There are other interpretations of these events, particularly an argument that Goetz hit Cabey on the fourth rather than the fifth shot, but in the early days after the shooting these alternative accounts are not widely disseminated.

Someone pulls the emergency brake and the train screeches to a halt. The passengers flee the car, but two women remain, immobilized by fear. Goetz says some soothing words to the fearful women, and then a conductor approaches and asks him whether he is a cop. The gunman replies, "They tried to rip me off." He refuses to hand over his gun and quietly walks to the front of the car, enters the platform between cars, patiently unfastens the safety chain, jumps to the tracks below, and disappears into the dark of the subway tunnel. Three young black kids lie bleeding on the floor of the train; Darrell Cabey sits wounded and paralyzed in the end seat.

A mythical figure is born—an unlikely avenger for the fear that both unites and levels all urban dwellers in the United States. If the four kids had mugged a passenger, newspaper reporters would have sighed in boredom. There are, on the average, 38 crimes a day on the New York subways. If a police officer had intervened and shot four kids who were hassling a rider for money, protests of racism and police brutality would have been the call of the day. This was different. A common man had emerged from the shadows of fear. He shot back when others only fantasize their responses to shakedowns on the New York subways.

Like the Lone Ranger, the mysterious gunman subdues the criminals and disappears into the night. If he had been apprehended immediately, the scars and flaws of his own personality might have checked the public's tendency to romanticize him. The analogy to Charles Bronson's avenging crime in *Death Wish* is on everyone's lips. The *Times* remains cautious, but the *Post*, from the beginning, dubs the unknown gunman the "subway vigilante." The police participate in this posturing of the case by setting up an "avenger hotline." They expect to receive tips leading to an arrest and eventually they get one, but at first they are swamped with calls supporting the "avenger." Though Mayor Ed Koch condemns the violence, he too inflates the incident by describing it as the act of a vigilante. No common criminal, this one. An everyman had come out of the crowd and etched his actions, right or wrong, in the public imagination.

With no offender to bear down on, the press has only the four black kids to portray in the news; the picture they present is not attractive. Uneducated, with criminal records, on the prowl for a few dollars, they exemplify the underclass of teenage criminals feared by both blacks and whites. In October of the same year, Darrell Cabey, age 19, had been arrested in the Bronx on charges of armed robbery. In 1983, James Ramseur, age 18, and Troy Canty, age 19, had both served short sentences for petty thievery. Barry Allen, age 18, had twice pled guilty to charges of disorderly conduct. James Ramseur and Darrell Cabey are found with a total of three screwdrivers in their pockets—the tools of their petty thievery. The few witnesses who come forward describe the behavior of the four youths before Goetz entered the car as "boisterous."

The emerging information supports the picture that frustrated New Yorkers want to believe in. Four stereotypical muggers who harass and hound a frail-looking middle-class "whitey." That he should turn out, against all odds, to be armed confirms the extraordinary nature of true, spontaneous justice. It is not often that things turn out right, and here in the season of religious miracles comes an event in which good triumphs over evil.

A willingness to accept a rumor of "sharpened screwdrivers" testifies to the widespread bias in favor of the romanticized gunman. The *Times* reported the day after the shooting that two of the victims were found with screwdrivers in their jackets. There was no suggestion that they were "sharpened." Somehow, however, the story got abroad that the screwdrivers were sharpened weapons rather than merely tools for opening sealed metal boxes. On the "Donahue" show, a week after the event, the discussion was of "sharp-

ened" screwdrivers. In an article in the *Times* surveying the first week's events, the writer reports the supposed fact: "three of the youths were found to be carrying sharpened screwdrivers."[3] Some journalists resist the popular rumor that the screwdrivers were specially prepared weapons of assault.[4] On the whole, however, the press and the public want to believe the worst about the subway victims.

Goetz makes an effort to go underground. On the day of the shooting he rents a car and drives north to Vermont and New Hampshire. As he later describes it, "heading north, is the way to go if there's a problem."[5] The countryside in New England may remind him reassuringly of his early years in rural upstate New York.[6] He thinks "the system would interpret it as one more crime. I just figured I'd get away for two days, I wanted to come back."[7] When he does come back to New York a few days later, he learns that the police, acting on a tip that Goetz meets the description of the slight blond gunman, left notes for him in his mailbox and on his door. They want to talk to him, but they are far from having singled him out as a serious suspect. Nonetheless, he fears apprehension and returns to Vermont and New Hampshire. He agonizes for almost two days and then walks into the police station in Concord, New Hampshire, shortly after noon on December 31.

He delivers several lengthy confessions. One two-hour interview with the New Hampshire police is recorded on audiotape; another of equal length, with New York authorities, is videotaped. Neither of these is fully disclosed to the public until after the trial begins. Goetz is turned over to the New York authorities on January 3, 1985, and spends a few days at Rikers Island prison. When he is released January 7 on $50,000 bail, his popular support is at its peak.

From the very beginning, the Goetz proceedings are caught in a political dialectic between the rush of popular support for the "subway vigilante" and the official attitude of outrage that anyone would dare usurp the state's task of keeping law and order. While the public calls into the newly established police hotline to express support for the wanted man, public officials, ranging from President Reagan to black leaders to Mayor Koch, come out strongly against "vigilantism" on the streets. The general public might applaud a little man's striking back against uncontrolled violence, but the President speaks of the "breakdown of

— Cabey — Allen
— Ramseur — Canty

civilization" when people like Bernhard Goetz "take the law into their own hands." Hazel Dukes of the NAACP calls Goetz a 21st-century version of a Ku Klux Klan "nightrider."

These pitted, hostile forces eventually find their way into well-prepared channels of legal argument and customary patterns of legal maneuvering. The legal system converts our ill-understood rage into a stylized mode of debate about broader issues of criminal responsibility and fair procedure. The "breakdown of civilization" never comes to pass, precisely because the issue of defending oneself against a threat in the subway can be formulated as a question beyond passion and instinctual conflict.

. . .

The second grand jury concluded that the prosecution had a sound basis for bringing Goetz to trial and convincing the jury beyond a reasonable doubt that Goetz's responses in the subway were unreasonable under the circumstances. Thus they indicted Goetz for a variety of crimes, 10 distinct offenses in all, based not only on the possession of the gun but on shooting the four youths without justification. If there was no self-defense, Goetz committed a crime by pulling his gun and firing five shots, injuring each of the youths once. But precisely what was the crime? There is no crime called "shooting in a subway" nor even a crime of shooting a gun. The criminal law seeks to specify particular aspects of violent and aggressive behavior that make the conduct wrongful and worthy of punishment.

In a single act of shooting at Troy Canty, Goetz might have committed three distinct offenses, each offense focusing on a different aspect of the violent outburst. The crime of attempted murder stresses Goetz's allegedly murderous intent in shooting. The crime of assault zeroes in on the actual suffering inflicted on Troy Canty. The newly devised crime of "reckless endangerment" consists exclusively in creating a risk of harm to Canty as well as the other passengers on the train. These three perspectives are hardly consistent. If the essence of the crime is Goetz's shooting with murderous intent, why should it matter whether the bullet rips through Canty's flesh? And if the crime inheres in wounding Canty, why should we inquire whether, in addition, Goetz endangered him by creating a risk of wounding him?

A single volley of shots generated nine felony charges, one count of attempted murder and of assault against each of the four victims and an additional charge of endangering others. It makes good sense to distinguish among the four victims, to recognize the humanity of each and thus to hinge distinct offenses on each of the wounding shots. It is far more questionable to apply three overlapping offenses to each of these shots.

The multiplicity of charges camouflages basic uncertainty in the legal system about why an act of shooting should be treated as a crime. Two conflicting schools of thought have emerged about the essential nature of criminal wrongdoing. A traditional approach emphasizes the victim's suffering and the actor's responsibility for bringing about irreversible damage. A modern approach to crime takes the act—the range of the actor's control over what happens—as the core of the crime. It is a matter of chance, the modernists say, whether a shot intended to kill actually hits its target. It is purely fortuitous, as the argument goes, that Goetz failed to kill one of his four intended victims. It is a matter of providence, as Gregory Waples later argued to the jury, that the volley of shots did not injure an innocent bystander on the train.

The traditionalists root their case in the way we feel about crime and suffering. Modernists hold to arguments of rational and meaningful punishment. Despite what we might feel, the modernist insists, reason demands that we limit the criminal law to those factors that are within the control of the actor. The occurrence of harm is beyond his control and therefore ought not to have weight in the definition of crime and fitting punishment. The tension between these conflicting schools infects virtually all of our decisions in designing a system of crime and punishment.

Historically, it is hard to deny the relevance of actual harm and suffering in our thinking about crime. The criminal law would never have come into being unless people actually harmed each other. Our thinking about sin and crime begins with a change in the natural order, a human act that leaves a stain on the world. The sin of Eden was not looking at the apple, not possessing it, but eating it. Oedipus's offense against the gods was not lusting, but actually fornicating with his mother. Cain's crime was not endangering Abel, but spilling his blood. The notions of sin and crime are rooted in the harms that humans inflict on each other.[8]

The classical conception of retributive punishment, the *lex talionis*, reenacts the crime on the person of the offender. This is expressed metaphorically in the biblical injunction to take an eye for an eye, a tooth for a tooth, and life for a life. In *Discipline and Punish*, the philosopher Michel Foucault argues that classically, punishment symbolically *expiated* the crime by replicating on the body of the criminal the harm he inflicted on another. It is hard even to think about punishment without perceiving the relationship between the harm wrought by the criminal and the harm he suffers in return.

From this perspective the salient fact in Goetz's crime, then, is his actually injuring the four youths. And the greater the injury, the greater the crime. If one of the four youths had died, even a year later, the crime would have fallen into a different category. Causing death is the ultimate evil, at least in the prevailing secular worldview. Homicide is the only crime for which, in some of its variations, capital punishment is still constitutional. The feature of homicide that makes it so heinous is not only the intention, not only the risk implicit in the defendant's act, but the inescapable fact of death. We no longer speak about the victim's blood crying out for revenge. But sensitivity to death and other irreversible harms represents an enduring afterglow of the biblical passion for punishing violations of the natural order.

This is not the way many or perhaps most policy makers think about crime in the modern world. Sometime in the last two or three centuries, our scientific thinking about crime began to shift from the harm done to the act that brings about the harm. The fortuitous connection between acts and their consequences did not trouble the great jurists of the past, but today, in the thinking of the moderns, a great divide separates the actor and his deed from the impact of his act on others. "There is many a slip 'twixt the cup and the lip."[9] And all those slips, all those matters of chance, have undermined the unity we once felt between a homicidal act and the death of the victim.

The notions of risk, probability, and chance circumscribe the modern way of thinking about action and harm. Instead of seeing harm first and the action as the means for bringing about the harm, we are now inclined to see the action first and the harm as a contingent consequence of the action. And if we see the action first and the harm second, we invite the question, Why should we consider the harm at all in assessing the criminal evil of shooting someone in the subway? Many radical reformers hold that indeed the harm is totally irrelevant. If you shoot and miss, you should be punished as though you had killed someone. All that matter are the acts that you can control. And you cannot control the bullet after it leaves the barrel. Power may come from the barrel of a gun, as Chairman Mao said, but according to the modernists, you exhaust your power as soon as you fire the gun.

Modernists pride themselves on the rationality of their theory. If the purpose of punishment is *either* to punish wickedness *or* to influence and guide human behavior, the criminal law should limit its sights to conduct and circumstances within human control. There is nothing wicked about the way things fortuitously turn out. The actor's personal culpability is expressed in his actions—not in the accidents of nature that determine the consequences of his actions. And so far as the purpose of punishment is to set an example and deter future offenders, the only conduct that can be deterred is that within our control. The arguments of reason seem almost unbeatable.

The shift toward arresting and prosecuting those who merely attempt crimes reflects a practical concern as well. The legal system should arguably not only react to crimes already committed, but should intervene before the harm is done. The police should arrest the would-be offender before he has a chance to realize the harm his conduct bespeaks. Crimes should be defined and jail sentences inflicted not only to expiate previous wrongs and deter future offenders, but to prevent harm from occurring. This makes a good deal of sense in a world in which we try to manage the resources of government in order to maximize the welfare of all. This approach to punishment is typically called "preventive" as opposed to the traditional "retributive" practice of punishing past crimes, measure for measure.

The rationalists have held sway over English and American criminal law for most of the period since World War II. The prevailing view is that criminal law should serve social goals, rationally determined and efficiently pursued. Punishment should serve the goal of control either by rehabilitating offenders or, when we despair of changing criminals with doses of therapy, by deterring people in the future from choosing crime as a profitable career. The modern approach to crime dismisses as subrational the argument that people simply *feel* that actually killing someone is far worse than trying to kill. The Model Penal Code, a rationalist document that reflects the attitudes of reform-minded lawyers in the 1950s, goes so far as to recommend punishing attempted murder the same way we punish murder.[10] Yet the concern for the suffering of victims is too deep-seated to be rejected simply because the reformers have so limited a conception of fair and decent punishment.

We punish convicted criminals not only because as social planners we see a need to deter crime in the future, but because we recognize the irrepressible need of victims to restore their faith in themselves and in the society in which they live. The imperative to do justice requires that we heed the suffering of the victims, that we inquire at trial whether the defendant is responsible for that suffering, and we adjudge him guilty, if the facts warrant it, not for antiseptically violating the rules of the system, but for inflicting a wrong on the body and to the dignity of the victim. If Goetz was guilty for having shot at Troy Canty, Barry Allen, James Ramseur, and Darrell Cabey, his guilt consisted primarily in having brought these young men to their knees in pain, in leaving lead in their flesh and scars on their bodies, and, in Darrell Cabey's case, in severing his spinal cord, causing him to be paralyzed and to suffer brain damage for the rest of his life.

Whether the defendant actually causes the harm to the victim becomes, therefore, a pivotal question in every trial responding to the fact of suffering. Usually there is no particular problem in establishing the toll a gunshot takes on its victim, but unexpectedly, the question whether Goetz's shooting Cabey actually caused Cabey's brain damage became a hotly contested issue in the Goetz trial.

The prosecutor, Gregory Waples, returned repeatedly to the theme of the permanent disabilities that Goetz inflicted on Cabey. As Waples stressed in his opening statement, as a result of the cold-blooded fifth shot when Cabey was sitting defenseless in his seat, Cabey could "look forward to the rest of his life . . . living in a wheel chair."[11] It would be hard to deny that Goetz's shot severed Cabey's spinal cord, but did the same shot also produce the brain damage? Cabey incurred damage to his brain because, as Waples explained:[12]

> while he was in the hospital struggling, fighting for his life, struggling to recover

from the gunshot wound the defendant inflicted which paralyzed him for life . . . medical complications set in and . . . three weeks after he was shot, [as a result of] these medical complications, he suffered a respiratory arrest. Darrell Cabey actually stopped breathing while in the hospital and was deprived of oxygen . . . [and he] plunged into a deep coma . . . . a persistent vegetating state.

When Waples called the doctor who ministered to Cabey, one Claude Macaluso, and questioned the doctor about the coma, the defense protested vigorously. It is clear why [defense attorney] Slotnick would want to avoid burdening his client with the stigma of having caused this misery. Goetz may not have killed anyone, but his actions allegedly reduced Cabey to a "vegetating state" even worse than suffering paralysis from the waist down. If Waples's accusation proved to be correct, Goetz's shooting Cabey would appear in the worst possible light, worse even than swiftly and painlessly killing. Whatever the legal implications of this responsibility, portraying Goetz as someone who wreaked this human damage would obviously weigh heavily in the jury's mind.

The defense's objection generated an arcane but significant legal debate, out of the presence of the jury, in which both lawyers questioned Dr. Macaluso about the details of the treatment afforded Cabey in the hospital. Slotnick tried to elicit an admission from the doctor that the coma occurred because the doctors waited too long to put Cabey on an artificial respirator. Perhaps they did. Dr. Macaluso conceded that they could have prevented the coma if they had intervened sooner, but in response to Waples's follow-up question, he insisted that there was nothing irregular or improper about the procedures followed in Cabey's treatment.

The thrust of the defense was that Cabey suffered the brain-damaging coma not because Goetz shot him, but because the hospital doctors were negligent in not putting him on a respirator sooner and thereby preventing the coma. The case was analogous, in the defense's theory, to a hypothetical situation in which Cabey lay recuperating in the hospital and someone came along and hurt him for reasons totally unconnected to the subway shooting. Slotnick and Baker maintained that if the doctors were at fault, Goetz was not causally responsible and therefore not to blame for Cabey's brain damage. This aspect of Cabey's suffering should not, the defense reasoned, be presented to the jury as a consequence of the shooting.

The defense's maneuver foundered on Dr. Macaluso's testimony that there was nothing out of the ordinary about the treatment accorded Cabey. Even if, in theory, the doctors might have intervened sooner, his vital signs did not indicate the use of a respirator; there was nothing negligent about the procedures used. If there was nothing unusual in the hospital treatment, Goetz had to stand responsible for the consequences. His shooting Cabey triggered the treatment, which in turn resulted in the coma and the brain damage. He initiated a foreseeable chain of consequences, and these consequences were to be reckoned as part of his deed. As the matter was resolved, Waples could question Dr. Macaluso in front of the jury about the details of the coma and the resulting brain damage.

An analogous debate ran through the trial about whether Goetz hit Cabey and severed his spinal cord with the fourth or fifth shot fired. The prosecution argued that the fifth shot, fired after the pause and the comment "You seem to be [doing] all right; here's another,"[13] did the damage. The defense developed the countertheory that the fourth shot was the one that hit home. The reason for this maneuver is apparent: Goetz had a better claim of self-defense on the fourth shot than he had on the fifth shot. Therefore, the defense wanted the jury to think that the fourth shot, following immediately after the first three, caused the permanent injuries. Even if the fifth was fired in cold blood, against a sitting, defenseless Cabey, the act of firing that bullet would be seen as less heinous if the bullet missed Cabey and careened into the cab wall.

The question that united these two debates is why consequences should matter at all in defining a criminal offense. The traditional approach to crime, stressing the consequences more than the actor's intention, still shapes the law of New York, and even more significantly, it controls the way ordinary people sitting as jurors make decisions about how wrong, how criminal, a shooting should be regarded. A shooting that results in brain damage is worse than one that merely wounds. And a shot that inflicts permanent injuries is harder to justify on grounds of self-defense than one that misses altogether.

Each of the two competing theories, the traditional and modern, generated one of the primary charges levied against Goetz. The traditional theory expresses itself in the crime of assault, which is hinged to the harm, the serious physical injury, suffered by each of the victims. The modern theory comes to the fore in the charge of attempted murder, a crime that inheres in an unsuccessful effort to bring about an intended harm. The attempter is liable even if he has not caused harm to anyone. He can stab and miss, put poison in food that is never eaten, point a gun that unbeknownst to him is unloaded—in all of these cases he can be guilty of attempted murder. The charge of attempted murder against Goetz did not require proof that his bullets struck anyone.

The crime of assault, traditionally called assault and battery, dates back to the earliest stages of the common law of crimes. The core of the crime is the physical injury inflicted on the victim. The actor must act in some way to bring about this injury, and it cannot be the case that the injury is purely accidental. In a general way, we can say that the injury must be intentional.

The crime of attempt is an innovation of the early 19th century. It comes into the law in the same period that the preventive theory of crime takes hold in the minds of reformers and the use of the modern prison replaces forms of punishment like flogging and modes of execution that reenacted the crime on the body of the criminal. As homicide and assault embody the old order, the crime of attempt is the flagship of modern, rational penology.

The external aspects of both assault and attempted murder—apart from the question of Goetz's intention, motive, and subjective state—lent themselves to easy proof. Assault merely requires that the actor cause physical harm to the victim. It is true the New York statute distinguishes among levels of injury. Reflecting the influence of the traditional school, the statute requires a "serious physical injury" for the crime of assault in the first degree.[14] Causing mere "physical injury" can never be worse than assault in the third degree.[15] There is not much learning about the difference between regular and serious physical injury, but presumably, a gunshot would be serious under anyone's definition.

The external side of attempted murder was equally easy to prove. The New York statute defines a criminal attempt in general terms suitable to any offense. All that is required is "any conduct which tends to effect the commission"[16] of the crime. There is no doubt that shooting represents some conduct tending . . . "to effect the commission" of homicide.

Generally we can determine when particular crimes occur. An assault occurs when injury sets in—in Goetz's case, when the bullet strikes the flesh of each of the victims. Attempted crimes are different, for there is no way, in theory or in fact, to know when the actor crosses the threshold of punishable, criminal conduct. Let us suppose that Goetz decided in 1981, after being mugged and beaten, that he would arm himself and shoot the first group of black kids who made any move at all toward harassing him. That act of arming himself would not, everyone would agree, be sufficient to constitute attempted murder. But then let us consider the events of December 22, 1984. At what point did Goetz commit the crime of attempt—when did he complete the act that "tended to effect the commission" of homicide? When he entered the subway car? When he sat down amid the four youths? When he stood up in response to Cabey's asking him for five dollars? When he pulled the gun? When he aimed it? There is simply no way of drawing the line, even in theory. Unmoored from the traditional anchor of criminality—the suffering of the victim—the boundaries of attempted crime have remained hopelessly vague.

. . .

The vague contours of attempted murder also trigger increased attention to the intention required for it to be said that someone attempts to kill. Both the traditional crime of assault and the modern offense of attempted murder require intentional conduct, but the requirement is construed more narrowly for the latter. The difference between the narrow view and broad view of intention emerges from reflecting about the intention of Lee Harvey Oswald in firing two shots in the apparent aim of assassinating President Kennedy. One shot hit Governor Connally, who was sitting in front of Kennedy. Oswald knew that it was likely that he would hit Connally as well as the President. Did he intend to kill, or at least to injure, Connally as well as to kill Kennedy? Many lawyers would say yes. Others would insist that Oswald was, at most, reckless in hitting Connally, that he did not intend to injure him.

The moral doctrine of double effect distinguishes between two results of an action—the conscious object of the action and an expected side effect on the basis of what is important to the actor. The actor *intends* only the result in which his desires and personality are invested. Expected but undesired side effects are therefore not within the scope of the actor's intention. Accordingly, killing a fetus as an undesired side effect of removing it from a fallopian tube would not be an intentional killing. Destroying a schoolhouse and killing children as the by-product of bombing a railroad depot would not qualify as an intentional killing. Nor would injuring Connally be regarded as intentional. Oswald had neither an interest in injuring Connally nor a desire to injure him; in this strict sense he did not intentionally hit him with the shot intended for Kennedy.

The intention required for common law assault and battery has always been more expansive than this narrow linking of intention with the desired end of one's action. Intentional assault includes knowingly causing harm as a side effect. If the required intent is understood in this broader sense, Oswald was guilty of an intentional assault against Connally. Lawyers capture this point by saying that the intent required for assault need not be specific or purposeful, but may be general.

In contrast, the intention required for attempted murder is narrowly construed. Because attempted murder lacks the element of harm inflicted on a specific victim, the burden of the wrong is expressed in a pointed, narrowly construed intent to kill. The required intention is so demanding because that is all there is to the crime. Accordingly, few lawyers would say that Oswald intended to kill Connally. The notion of an assault is compatible with lesser degrees of focus on causing harm, such as the element of recklessness sufficient for assault in the second degree. But the law of attempts remains linked to intended wrongdoing, narrowly understood.

This restrictive approach to liability makes sense, for the crime of attempted murder has already gone far toward an innovative, atypical form of liability. It insists neither on the suffering of a specific victim nor on a precisely defined boundary as a fair warning to those who might trespass on the interests of others. The least that the law can require is a precisely defined intention.

From a moral perspective as well, the crime of attempted murder demands a more rigorous intention than does the traditional crime of assault. Assault requires an intent to injure; murder officially requires an intent to kill. Jurors might well be inclined, however, to take the name of the attempted crime—murder—as the object of the required intent. A critical conceptual difference divides killing from murder. The sixth commandment does not say: thou shalt not kill. It says: thou shalt not murder. Killing in self-defense underscores the difference. If justified by self-defense, a killing is not murder, but it is a killing nonetheless.

If the jurors thought about attempted murder as turning on an intent to murder, they might well think that Goetz's claim of self-defense precluded his having this vicious intent. If, in his own view of what was going on, he was motivated by a desire to save himself, then one could not say that he desired to kill as an end in itself. His end would not be to murder, but to save himself from a threatened attack. If his intent was morally sound and not evil in itself, jurors might balk at treating it as an intent to murder or even to kill.

This way of thinking about attempted murder makes perfectly good sense, even though New York judges would be loath to instruct a jury to integrate the issue of self-defense with the analysis of intention. The standard instruction in New York defines intention, dryly, as merely the "conscious end or object" of the act. Even a killing in self-defense is the conscious end of the defense act, and therefore the killing is intended—even if thought to be necessary to personal survival. Yet, in the final analysis, lay jurors invariably follow their commonsense understanding of an intent to murder. If the jurors thought of this intent as necessarily vicious, they might well take any belief in the necessity of self-defense as logically incompatible with the required intent.

The irony of this logic would be that they would, in effect, bring in the subjective standard of self-defense by the back door. The prolonged pretrial appeal in the Goetz case rejected the subjective standard in favor of the standard of reasonableness, but conceptualizing viciousness as an element of the required intent to kill turns out to have the same logical implications as the subjective standard of self-defense. Both imply that a good faith belief in self-defense precludes liability for attempted murder, in one case because the intent is not vicious and in the other because the claim of self-defense is subjectively sound.

The charges levied against Bernhard Goetz reflect the traditional harm-oriented as well as the modern act-oriented approaches to crime. The grand jury faulted him both for causing suffering (assault in the first degree) and for acting with the potential of causing even greater intended suffering (attempted murder).

The tension between these two philosophical positions reappears in the field of reckless conduct. As intentional conduct can be considered criminal, with or without resulting harm, so reckless conduct can be faulted, apart from the harm that may eventuate. When harm occurs, the proper charges are reckless homicide[17] or reckless assault[18]—depending, of course, on the victim's fate. If no one is hurt, the reckless act itself might support a charge of reckless endangerment.

Intentional crimes are admittedly more serious than reckless offenses; in the former case, the offender identifies himself with the evil he tries to bring about. He chooses it; he wants it. The evil is his. But in a case of recklessness, the actor chooses only to create a *risk* of injury. He does not identify with the harm that may eventuate from the risk. He chooses merely the risk.[19]

Obviously some risks are beneficial. We choose to create and expose ourselves and others to risks of driving, flying, using fireplaces, smoking, and, these days, of sexual intercourse. In order to talk about reckless behavior, we need to distinguish the bad risks that render conduct reckless from the good risks we accept as the price of modern living. The conventional approach to this distinction is to insist that a reckless risk be both substantial and unjustifiable.[20] The point of the "substantiality" requirement is simply to set a threshold of seriousness. The issue of "justifiable" risk speaks to the question whether the risk was worth running under the circumstances.

On the charges of recklessly assaulting the four youths, there was not much question at the trial whether the risk was substantial. After all, Goetz shot at them. The burden of analysis on those charges fell on the question whether the risk was "justified" under the circumstances. As self-defense could justify an intentional assault, it could do the same for reckless assault. Thus the issue of self-defense would control liability for reckless as well as for intentional assault.

As 19th-century penology generated the crime of attempt, 20th-century thinking yielded a crime of recklessness in which no one is hurt. This crime of pure risk-taking first crystallized in American legal thought in the 1950s, when the Model Penal Code proposed its adoption. In 1965 the New York legislature improvised on the theme introduced in the model code by distinguishing misdemeanor and felony versions of reckless endangerment. The former, reckless endangerment in the second degree, requires merely that the actor recklessly create a "substantial risk of serious physical injury to another person."[21] The latter, the first-degree charge, is more demanding in several respects[22] and most significantly in requiring that the defendant's act evince "a depraved indifference to human life."

These two offenses closely track the wording of manslaughter in the second degree and murder in the second degree. Take manslaughter in the second degree, committed by "recklessly causing the death of another person,"[23] then subtract the element of suffering and death. The remainder is the misdemeanor of reckless endangerment.[24] Take murder in the second degree[25] without the consequence of actual harm, and the balance is reckless endangerment in the first degree.[26]

This offense aptly captured the alleged danger that Goetz's shooting generated toward the other passengers on the train. Though the felony of reckless endangerment technically speaks to the risk Goetz created to the four youths as well as the other passengers, the prosecution treated the offense as addressing the potential harm to the non-involved bystanders. It was a matter of "providence," Gregory Waples argued, that shooting five times in a crowded subway car did not injure one of the other passengers. In contrast, the defense maintained that the bullets were fired either directly into the bodies of the victims or, in the case of the one stray bullet, into the steel side panel of the car. Despite the suggestion of one witness,[27] no bullet ricocheted through the car; no one except the four targets, the defense maintained, was in fact endangered by the shooting.

These argumentative forays never, as lawyers say, "joined issue." With Waples relying on the potential of harm and the defense stressing what actually happened, these arguments passed each other by. Waples relied on an abstract conception of risk-taking, defined generally as shooting in a crowded subway car. Baker and Slotnick relied on a more concrete notion of the relevant risk, defined by this suspect's shooting under these unique circumstances.

There are in fact an infinite number of ways of describing the risk that Goetz created. It would also be correct to say that he fired the gun in a crowded place, without specifying that it was a moving train, or that he fired a weapon, without distinguishing between a machine gun and a pistol. One could get more concrete and fill in details about where the passengers were sitting, the speed of the train, and the force of air currents at the time of the shooting. All these factors are relevant to the likelihood that a bystander would be hit. In the end, the danger of Goetz's shooting posed a problem of physics not of providence.

Yet as soon as we pin down all the physical variables and predict the path of the bullets, a paradox arises. It turns out that bullets that do not strike innocent bystanders *could not* have struck them, for the path of the bullet is physically determined at the moment of firing. If a bullet did not in fact strike a particular passenger, it was physically impossible that it strike him. According to this logic, if the bullet did not strike a bystander, it did not endanger him. In a physically determined world (that we can know in principle) it is not clear that it makes sense to talk about recklessly endangering but not injuring another.

The only way to avoid this paradox is to retreat from the quest for a total description of the physical variables. We have to think about classes of cases, such as those of firing in the direction of a passenger, or in the vicinity of a passenger or in the same subway car the passenger is sitting in.[28] In these cases, the marksman's accuracy may vary. The physical forces may vary. An element of chance enters into the analysis. And in a world of chance, we can say that perhaps someone could have been hit who was not hit.

As with many other theoretical conundrums raised by the Goetz case, Justice Crane never had to cut through to the core of the problem. He rejected the defense's motion to dismiss on the ground that there was no risk at all to anyone other than the four kids, but he never had to formulate a view on the correct description of the risk. He avoided the issue by instructing the jury in the language of the statute. It was up to the jury to decide precisely what risk Goetz took by firing the gun under those circumstances.

Even those who sympathized with Goetz in his struggle to vindicate himself relative to the four youths thought that he might have a weak case on the charge of reckless endangerment. That he was justified relative to four apparent aggressors does not mean that he was justified in scaring the daylights out of the 15 to 20 other passengers in the car. They, after all, were totally innocent bystanders. How can the provocative behavior of four youths on the train justify depriving innocent people of their peace and security on the subway? The prosecution developed an ingenious argument about why the argument of justification as to bystanders could not be based on the criteria of self-defense.

Waples argued that self-defense should be limited to cases of justification relative to the alleged aggressors. So far as a risk is justified relative to innocent bystanders, the argument should be grounded in the statutory provision on necessity, an innovation in the 1965 Penal Law.[29] The difference between the two provisions, as Waples developed his theory, is that the provision on self-defense generates a full justification any time the defender reasonably believes that he is under attack—whether in fact he is being attacked or not. The provision on necessity seems to require that an "imminent public or private injury" actually be "about to occur."[30] If the four youths were not in fact about to attack Goetz, that fact would not preclude a claim of self-defense, but it would bar—at least under Waples's plausible reading of the statue—a claim of necessity. Thus Waples sensed an important advantage in seeking a ruling that the proper justification in cases of reckless endangerment is not self-defense, but necessity.

Neither the defense nor Justice Crane adequately responded to Waples's argument on this point.[31] The defense never countered the theoretical thrust of the argument and they never had to; for tactical reasons, Waples decided midtrial that he preferred that the question whether the four youths were actually committing a robbery not be treated as a relevant issue in the case.

The defense may have sensed that they had a weak case on the charge of reckless endangerment, for after the impaneling of the jury in the trial, they approached Gregory Waples with an offer to plead guilty to two felony charges, possessing a loaded gun in public and reckless endangerment in the first degree.[32] This plea would have seemed to vindicate Goetz in his confrontation with the four youths[33] and yet satisfy the public interest in condemning and deterring violent conduct on the subway. But the District Attorney refused the deal. It was too important, in his view, to try the case and let a jury of ordinary New Yorkers resolve the issues.

The law remains ambivalent about the relevance of human suffering in defining criminal conduct. Both kinds of charges—those of actual harm and those of potential harm—were levied against Bernhard Goetz. There would be no plea bargain, no plea of guilty. The jury would have to make the ultimate decision about whether Goetz acted in self-defense and, if he did not, how his victims' suffering should be gauged.

The relevance of the victim's suffering in the criminal law poses a serious hurdle to the struggle for reasoned principles in the law. Generations of theorists have sought to explain why we punish actual homicide more severely than attempted homicide, the real spilling of blood more severely than the unrealized intent to do so. Our combined philosophical work has yet to generate a satisfactory account of why the realization of harm aggravates the penalty. Yet the practice persists in every legal system of the Western world. We cannot adequately explain why harm matters, but matter it does.

The law can and should go only so far to implement a rule of reason abstracted from the sensibilities of common people. It is after all common people, speaking in the voice of the jury, who ultimately decide whether an accused offender is guilty under the law. This is not to say that the law should surrender to the irrational passions that thrive in racial antagonism and the lust for vengeance. But neither should the drive for reason in the law make us forget that the law serves human beings. Oliver Wendell Holmes captured this elementary point in the best-known aphorism of American law: "The life of the law has not been logic; it has been experience."[34] The collected wisdom of tradition is expressed in the learned arguments of those who seek to refine the law on the basis of reason, but it also demands continual reinforcement from the jurors who bring to criminal trials their common sense and intuitive sense of justice.

. . .

Endnotes

[1] In the first week after the shooting, the story was widely recounted that prior to the shooting, the gunman said, "I have five dollars for each of you." See *New York Times*, December 24, 1984, p. 1. In one of his confessions recorded on December 31, 1984, Goetz insisted that instead, he said, "I have five dollars for you." See transcript of the videotaped confession (hereafter referred to as video transcript). . . .

[2] There are two confessions. On the audiotaped confession, given to the New Hampshire police in the early evening of December 31, he says, "You seem to be doing all right; here's another." On the videotaped confession, given later the same evening to New York authorities, he says, "You seem to be all right; here's another." This ambiguity is retained by indicating the word "doing" in brackets throughout the text.

[3] Article by David Sanger, *New York Times*, December 30, 1984, section IV, p. 6. A reference to "sharpened screwdrivers" also appears the day before, December 29, 1984, in an Op-Ed piece, Schanberg, "A New Morality Play."

[4] For coverage of the victims' side of the story, see the articles by Margo Hornblower, *Washington Post*, January 11, 1985, p. A3, and Jimmy Breslin, *New York Daily News*, December 30, 1984, p. 6.

[5] Transcript of tape-recorded confession (hereafter referred to as audio transcript). . . .

[6] For the best summary of Goetz's early years, see the article by Carol Agus, "Wimp or Wolf," *New York Newsday*, December 15, 1985, pp. 12–51.

[7] Audio transcript, p. 38.

[8] I concede the contrary Christian tradition, expressed in Matthew 5:28, that takes the intent for the deed.

[9] Bartlett identifies this saying as "epigram 32" in Paladas [fl. 400] in 10 *The Greek Anthology* (J. W. MacKail ed., 1906).

[10] MPC § 5.05(1).

[11] Record at 4762–63.

[12] Record at 4773.

[13] See . . . note 2.

[14] NYPL § § 120.05, 120.10.

[15] NYPL § 120.00.

[16] NYPL § 110.00.

[17] NYPL § 125.15(1).

[18] NYPL § 120.05(4) ("by means of a deadly weapon or a dangerous instrument").

[19] Recklessness is conventionally distinguished from negligence, where the actor creates the risk but neither chooses it nor knows of it. See Model Penal Code § 2.02(2).

[20] New York, NYPL § 15.5(3) (recklessness requires [1] that the risk be substantial and unjustifiable and [2] that choosing to run the risk "constitutes a gross deviation from the standard of conduct that a reasonable person would observe in the situation").

[21] NYPL § 120.20.

[22] See NYPL § 120.25 (requires "grave risk of death" rather than merely "substantial risk of serious physical injury").

[23] NYPL § 125.15 (1).

[24] The difference in punishment is worth noting. Manslaughter in the second degree is a class C felony, punished by a maximum term of 15 years, NYPL 70.00(2)(c); reckless endangerment in the second degree is a class A misdemeanor, punished by a maximum of one year, NYPL 70.15(1). The only difference between the two offenses is whether the reckless act results in death.

[25] NYPL § 125.25.(2) ("Under circumstances evincing a depraved indifference to human life, he recklessly engages in conduct which creates a grave risk of death . . . and thereby causes the death of another person").

[26] NYPL § 120.25 (the wording is identical to NYPL § 125.25[3] except for the last clause on causing death). The fortuitous occurrence of death, a result beyond the actor's control, raises the penalty from a maximum of seven years to life imprisonment.

[27] Victor Flores testified as follows (Record at 5887):
WAPLES: Did you hear any other sound when the shooting was going on?
FLORES: There was the sound from ceiling of the car. I heard a sound.
WAPLES: What sound did you hear?
FLORES: Like something hit metal.
WAPLES: And where was that in relation to where you were?
FLORES: That was very close to where I was sitting.
WAPLES: You're talking about the ceiling of the car now?
FLORES: Ceiling.

[28] Significantly, the Model Penal Code presumes recklessness where one person knowingly points a gun "at or in the direction of another." MPC § 211.1

[29] NYPL § 35.05.

[30] Id.

[31] If Justice Crane had been forced to decided the issue, he probably would have rejected Waples's argument on the basis of a footnote in the Court of Appeals opinion in People v. Goetz, 868 NY2d 96, 104 n.2, which says that "justification is a defense to [i.e., reckless endangerment]." The footnote does not distinguish, however, between different types of justification and is therefore consistent with Waples's contention that the proper justification for reckless endangerment is necessity rather than self-defense.

[32] Gregory Waples disclosed this to me in an interview on June 18, 1987. So far as I know, it has not been reported in the press.

[33] Neither of these guilty pleas would have hurt Goetz in his defense against the civil tort actions brought by the shooting victims.

[34] Oliver Wendell Holmes, Jr., *The Common Law* 1 (1881).

The Punishment That Leaves Something to Chance

DAVID LEWIS

1

We are accustomed to punish criminal attempts much more severely if they succeed than if they fail. We are also accustomed to wonder why. It is hard to find any rationale for our leniency toward the unsuccessful. Leniency toward aborted attempts, or mere preparation, might be easier to understand. (And whether easy or hard, it is not my present topic.) But what sense can we make of leniency toward a completed attempt—one that puts a victim at risk of harm, and fails only by luck to do actual harm?

Dee takes a shot at his enemy, and so does Dum. They both want to kill; they both try, and we may suppose they try equally hard. Both act out of malice, without any shred of justification or excuse. Both give us reason to fear that they might be ready to kill in the future. The only difference is that Dee hits and Dum misses. So Dee has killed, he is guilty of murder, and we put him to death.[1] Dum has not killed, he is guilty only of attempted murder, and he gets a short prison sentence.

Why? Dee and Dum were equally wicked in their desires. They were equally uninhibited in pursuing their wicked desires. Insofar as the wicked deserve to be punished, they deserve it equally. Their conduct was equally dangerous: they inflicted equal risks of death on their respective victims. Insofar as those who act dangerously deserve to be punished, again they deserve it equally. Maybe Dee's act was worse than Dum's act, just because of Dee's success; but it is not the act that suffers punishment, it is the agent. Likewise, if we want to express our abhorrence of wickedness or of dangerous conduct, either exemplar of what we abhor is fit to star in the drama of crime and punishment. Further, Dee and Dum have equally engaged in conduct we want to prevent by deterrence. For we prevent successful attempts by preventing attempts generally. We cannot deter success separately from deterring attempts, since attempters make no separate choice about whether to succeed. Further, Dee and Dum have equally shown us that we might all be safer if we defended ourselves against them; and one function of punishment (at any rate if it is death, imprisonment, or transportation) is to get dangerous criminals off the streets before they do more harm. So how does their different luck in hitting or missing make any difference to considerations of desert, expression, deterrence, or defense? How can it be just, on any credible theory of just punishment, to punish them differently?

Here is one rationale for our peculiar practice. If the gods see innocent blood shed, they will be angry; if they are angry, none of us will be safe until they are propitiated; and to propitiate the gods, we must shed guilty blood. Whereas if by luck no innocent blood is shed, the gods will not be angered just by the sight of unsuccessful wickedness, so there will be no need of propitiation.— This rationale would make sense, if its premises were true. And if we put "the public" or "the victim's kin" for "the gods" throughout it still makes sense; and that way, maybe the premises are true, at least sometimes and to some extent. But this rationale does nothing at all to defend our practice *as just*. If our practice is unjust, then the ways of the gods (or the public; or the kin) are unjust, although if the powers that be want to see injustice done, it might be prudent to ignore justice and do their bidding.

A purely conservative rationale is open to the same complaint. Maybe it is a good idea to stay with the practice we have learned how to operate, lest a reform cause unexpected problems. Maybe it is good for people to see the law go on working as they are accustomed to expect it to. Maybe a reform would convey unintended and disruptive

From *Philosophy & Public Affairs*, Vol. 18 (1989), pp. 53–67. Copyright © 1989 Princeton University Press. Reprinted with permission of Princeton University Press.

messages: as it might be, that we have decided to take murder less seriously than we used to. These considerations may be excellent reasons why it is prudent to leave well enough alone, and condone whatever injustice there may be in our present practice. They do nothing at all to defend our practice as just.

Another rationale concerns the deterrence of second attempts. If at first you don't succeed, and if success would bring no extra punishment, then you have nothing left to lose if you try, try again. "If exactly the same penalty is prescribed for successes as for attempts, there will be every reason to make sure that one is successful."[2] It cannot hurt to have some deterrence left after deterrence has failed. Maybe the experience of having tried once will make the criminal more deterrable than he was at first.—But why is this any reason for punishing successful attempts more severely? It might as well just be a reason for punishing two attempts more severely than one, which we could do regardless of success. If each separate attempt is punished, and if one share of punishment is not so bad that a second share would be no worse, then we have some deterrence against second attempts.

Another rationale sees punishment purely as a deterrent, and assumes that we will have deterrence enough if we make sure that crime never pays. If so, there is no justification for any more penal harm than it takes to offset the gains from a crime. Then a failed attempt needs no punishment: there are no gains to be offset, so even if unpunished it still doesn't pay.—I reply that in the first place, this system of minimum deterrence seems likely to dissuade only the most calculating of criminals. In the second place, punishment is not just a deterrent. I myself might not insist on retribution per se, but certainly the expressive and defensive functions of punishment are not to be lightly forsaken.

Another rationale invokes the idea of "moral luck."[3] Strange to say, it can happen by luck alone that one person ends up more wicked than another. Perhaps that is why the successful attempter, by luck alone, ends up deserving more severe punishment?—I [reply], first, that to some extent this suggestion merely names our problem. We ask how Dee can deserve more severe punishment just because his shot hits the mark. Call that "moral luck" if you will; then we have been asking all along how this sort of moral luck is possible. But, second, it may be misleading to speak of the

moral luck of the attempter, since it may tend to conflate this case with something quite different. The most intelligible cases of moral luck are those in which the lucky and the unlucky alike are disposed to become wicked if tempted, and only the unlucky are tempted. But then, however alike they may have been originally, the lucky and the unlucky do end up different in how they are and in how they act. Not so for the luck of hitting or missing. It makes no difference to how the lucky and the unlucky are, and no difference to how they act.[4]

Finally, another rationale invokes the difference between wholehearted and halfhearted attempts.[5] Both are bad, but wholehearted attempts are worse. A wholehearted attempt involves more careful planning, more precautions against failure, more effort, more persistence, and perhaps repeated tries. *Ceteris paribus*, a wholehearted attempt evinces more wickedness—stronger wicked desires, or less inhibition about pursuing them. *Ceteris paribus*, a wholehearted attempt is more dangerous. It is more likely to succeed; it subjects the victim, knowingly and wrongfully, to a greater risk. Therefore it is more urgently in need of prevention by deterrence. *Ceteris paribus*, the perpetrator of a wholehearted attempt is more of a proven danger to us all, so it is more urgent to get him off the streets. So from every standpoint—desert, expression, deterrence, defense—it makes good sense to punish attempts more severely when they are wholehearted. Now, since wholehearted attempts are more likely to succeed, success is some evidence that the attempt was wholehearted. Punishing success, then, is a rough and ready way of punishing wholeheartedness.

I grant that it is just to punish wholehearted attempts more severely—or better, since "heartedness" admits of degrees, to proportion the punishment to the heartedness of the attempt. And I grant that in so doing we may take the probability of success—in other words, the risk inflicted on the victim—as our measure of heartedness. That means not proportioning the punishment simply to the offender's wickedness, because two equally wicked attempters may not be equally likely to succeed. One may be more dangerous than the other because he has the advantage in skill or resources or information or opportunity. Then if we proportion punishment to heartedness measured by risk, we may punish one attempter more severely not because he was more wicked, but because his conduct was more dangerous. From a purely retributive standpoint, wickedness might seem the more appropriate measure; but from the expressive standpoint, we may prefer to dramatize our abhorrence not of wickedness per se but of dangerous wickedness; and from the standpoint of deterrence or defense, clearly it is dangerous conduct that matters.

So far, so good; but I protest that it is unjust to punish success as a rough and ready way of punishing wholeheartedness. It's just too rough and ready. Success is some evidence of wholeheartedness, sure enough. But it is very unreliable evidence: the wholehearted attempt may very well be thwarted, the half- or quarterhearted attempt may succeed. And we can have other evidence that bears as much or more on whether the attempt was wholehearted. If what we really want is to punish wholeheartedness, we have no business heeding only one unreliable fragment of the total evidence, and then treating that fragment as if it were conclusive. Suppose we had reason—*good* reason—to think that on average the old tend to be more wholehearted than the young in their criminal attempts. Suppose even that we could infer wholeheartedness from age somewhat more reliably than we can infer it from success. Then if we punished attempters more severely in proportion to their age, that would be another rough and ready way of punishing wholeheartedness. *Ex hypothesi*, it would be less rough and ready than what we do in punishing success. It would still fall far short of our standards of justice.

II

In what follows, I shall propose a new rationale. *I do not say that it works.* I do say that the new rationale works better than the old ones. It makes at least a prima facie case that our peculiar practice is just, and I do not see any decisive rebuttal. All the same, I think that the prima facie case is probably not good enough, and probably there is no adequate justification for punishing attempts more severely when they succeed.

Our present practice amounts to a disguised form of *penal lottery*—a punishment that leaves something to chance. Seen thus, it *does* in some sense punish all attempts alike, regardless of suc-

cess. It is no less just, and no more just, than an undisguised penal lottery would be. Probably any penal lottery is seriously unjust, but it is none too easy to explain why.

By a penal lottery, I mean a system of punishment in which the convicted criminal is subjected to a risk of punitive harm. If he wins the lottery, he escapes the harm. If he loses, he does not. A pure penal lottery is one in which the winners suffer no harm at all; an impure penal lottery is one in which winners and losers alike suffer some harm, but the losers suffer more harm. It is a mixture: part of the punishment is certain harm, part is the penal lottery.

An overt penal lottery is one in which the punishment is announced explicitly as a risk—there might be ways of dramatizing the fact, such as a drawing of straws on the steps of the gallows. A covert penal lottery is one in which the punishment is not announced as a risk, but it is common knowledge that it brings risk with it. (A covert lottery must presumably be impure.)

A historical example of an overt penal lottery is the decimation of a regiment as punishment for mutiny. Each soldier is punished for his part in the mutiny by a one-in-ten risk of being put to death. It is a fairly pure penal lottery, but not entirely pure: the terror of waiting to see who must die is part of the punishment, and this part falls with certainty on all the mutineers alike.

Covert and impure penal lotteries are commonplace in our own time. If one drawback of prison is that it is a place where one is exposed to capricious violence, or to a serious risk of catching AIDS,[6] then a prison sentence is in part a penal lottery. If the gulag is noted for its abysmal standards of occupational health and safety, then a sentence of forced labor is in part a penal lottery.

III

What do we think, and what should we think, of penal lotteries? Specifically, what should we think of a penal lottery, with death for the losers, as the punishment for all attempts at murder, regardless of success? Successful or not, the essence of the crime is to subject the victim, knowingly and wrongfully, to a serious risk of death. The proposed punishment is to be subjected to a like risk of death.

We need a standard of comparison. Our present system of leniency toward the unsuccessful is too problematic to make a good standard, so let us instead compare the penal lottery with a hypothetical reformed system. How does the lottery compare with a system that punishes all attempts regardless of success, by the certain harm of a moderate prison term? A moderate term, because if we punished successful and unsuccessful attempts alike, we would presumably set the punishment somewhere between our present severe punishment of the one and our lenient punishment of the other.(Let the prison be a safe one, so that in the comparison case we have no trace of a penal lottery.) Both for the lottery and for the comparison case, I shall assume that we punish regardless of success. In the one case, success per se makes no difference to the odds; in the other case, no difference to the time in prison. This is not to say that every convicted criminal gets the very same sentence. Other factors might still make a difference. In particular, heartedness (measured by the risk inflicted) could make a difference, and success could make a difference to the extent that it is part of our evidence about heartedness.

Now, how do the two alternatives compare?

The penal lottery may have some practical advantages. It gets the case over and done with quickly. It is not crime school. A prison costs a lot more than a gallows plus a supply of long and short straws.[7]

(Likewise a prison with adequate protection against random brutality by guards and fellow inmates costs more than a prison without. So it seems that we have already been attracted by the economy of a system that has at least some covert admixture of lottery.)

Like a prison term (or fines, or flogging) and unlike the death penalty *simpliciter,* the penal lottery can be graduated as finely as we like. When we take the crime to be worse, we provide fewer long straws to go with the fatal short straws. In particular, that is how we can provide a more severe punishment for the more wholehearted attempt that subjected the victim to a greater risk.

From the standpoint of dramatizing our abhorrence of wicked and dangerous conduct, a penal lottery seems at least as good as a prison sentence. Making the punishment fit the crime, Mikado-fashion, is *poetic* justice. The point we want to dramatize, both to the criminal and to the public, is that what we think of the crime is just like

what the criminal thinks of his punishment. If it's a risk for a risk, how can anybody miss the point?

From the standpoint of deterrence, there is no doubt that we are sometimes well deterred by the prospect of risk.[8] It happens every time we wait to cross the street. It is an empirical question how effective a deterrent the penal lottery might be. Compared with the alternative punishment of a certain harm, such as a moderate prison term, the lottery might give us more deterrence for a given amount of penal harm, or it might give us less. Whether it gives us more or less might depend a lot on the details of how the two systems operate. If the lottery gave us more, that would make it preferable from the standpoint of deterrence.

(We often hear about evidence that certainty is more deterring than severity. But to the extent that this evidence pertains only to the uncertainty of getting caught, getting convicted, and serving the full sentence, it is scarcely relevant. The criminal might think of escaping punishment as a game of skill—his skill, or perhaps his lawyer's. For all we know, a risk of losing a game of chance might be much more deterring than an equal risk of losing a game of skill.)

From the standpoint of defense, the penal lottery gets some dangerous criminals off the streets forever, while others go free at once. Moderate prison terms would let all go free after a longer time, some of them perhaps reformed and some of them hardened and embittered. It is another empirical question which alternative is the more effective system of defense. Again, the answer may depend greatly on the details of the two systems, and on much else that we cannot easily find out.[9]

IV

So far we have abundant uncertainties, but no clear-cut case against the penal lottery. If anything, the balance may be tipping in its favor. So let us turn finally to the standpoint of desert. Here it is a bit hard to know what to make of the penal lottery. If the court has done its job correctly, then all who are sentenced to face the same lottery, with the same odds, are equally guilty of equally grave crimes. They deserve equal treatment. Do they get it?—Yes and no.

Yes. We treat them alike because we subject them

all to the very same penal lottery, with the very same odds. And when the lots are drawn, we treat them alike again, because we follow the same predetermined contingency plan—death for losers, freedom for winners—for all of them alike.

No. Some of them are put to death, some are set free, and what could be more unequal than that?

Yes. Their fates are unequal, of course. But that is not our doing. They are treated unequally by Fortune, not by us.

No. But it is we who hand them over to the inequity of Fortune. We are Fortune's accomplices.

Yes. Everyone is exposed to the inequity of Fortune, in ever so many ways. However nice it may be to undo some of these inequities, we do not ordinarily think of this as part of what is required for equal treatment.

No. It's one thing not to go out of our way to undo the inequities of Fortune; it's another thing to go out of our way to increase them.

Yes. We do that too, and think it not at all contrary to equal treatment. When we hire astronauts, or soldiers or sailors or firemen or police, we knowingly subject these people to more of the inequities of Fortune than are found in ordinary life.

No. But the astronauts are volunteers . . .

Yes. . . . and so are the criminals, when they commit the crimes for which they know they must face the lottery. The soldiers, however, sometimes are not.

No. Start over. We agreed that the winners and losers deserve equal punishment. That is because they are equally guilty. Then they deserve to suffer equally. But they do not.

Yes. They do not suffer equally; but if they deserve to, that is not our affair. We seldom think that equal punishment means making sure of equal suffering. Does the cheerful man get a longer prison sentence than the equally guilty morose man, to make sure of equal suffering? If one convict gets lung cancer in prison, do we see to it that the rest who are equally guilty suffer equally? When we punish equally, what we equalize is not the suffering itself. What we equalize is our contribution to expected suffering.

No. This all seems like grim sophistry. Surely, equal treatment has to mean more than just treating people so that some common description of what we are doing will apply to them all alike.

Yes. True. But we have made up our minds already, in other connections, that lotteries count as equal treatment, or near enough. When we have an indivisible benefit or burden to hand out (or even one that is divisible at a significant cost) we are very well content to resort to a lottery. We are satisfied that all who have equal chances are getting equal treatment—and not in some queer philosophers' sense, but in the sense that matters to justice.

It seems to me that "Yes" is winning this argument, but that truth and justice are still somehow on the side of "No." The next move, dear reader, is up to you. I shall leave it unsettled whether a penal lottery would be just. I shall move on to my second task, which is to show that our present practice amounts to a covert penal lottery. If the penal lottery is just, so is our present practice. If not, not.

V

To show that they do not matter, I shall introduce the differences between an overt penal lottery and our present practice one at a time, by running through a sequence of cases. I claim that at no step is there any significant difference of justice between one case and the next. Such differences as there are will be practical advantages only, and will come out much in favor of our present practice.

Case I is the overt penal lottery as we have imagined it already, with one added stipulation, as follows. We will proportion the punishment to the heartedness of the attempt, as measured by the risk of death[10] the criminal knowingly and wrongfully inflicted on the victim. We will do this by sentencing the criminal to a risk equal to the one he inflicted on the victim. If the criminal subjected his victim to an 80 percent risk of death, he shall draw his straw from a bundle of eight short and two long; whereas if he halfheartedly subjected the victim to a mere 40 percent risk, he shall draw from four short and six long; and in this way his punishment shall fit his crime. Therefore the court's task is not limited to ascertaining whether the defendant did knowingly and wrongfully subject the victim to a risk of death.

Case 2 is like Case I, except that we skip the dramatic ceremony on the steps of the gallows and draw straws ahead of time. In fact, we have the drawing even before the trial. It is not the defendant himself who draws, but the Public Drawer. The Drawer is sworn to secrecy; he reveals the outcome only when and if the defendant has been found guilty and sentenced to the lottery. If the defendant is acquitted and the drawing turns out to have been idle, no harm done. Since it is not known ahead of time whether the sentence will be eight and two, four and six, or what, the Drawer must make not one but many drawings ahead of time. He reveals the one, if any, that turns out to be called for.

Case 3 is like Case 2, except without the secrecy. The Drawer announces at once whether the defendant will win or lose in case he is found guilty and sentenced. (Or rather, whether he will win or lose if he is sentenced to eight and two, whether he will win or lose if he is is sentenced to four and six, and so on.) This means that the suspense in the courtroom is higher on some occasions than others. But that need not matter, provided that the court can stick conscientiously to the task of ascertaining whether the defendant did knowingly and wrongfully subject the victim to risk, and if so how much risk. It is by declaring that a criminal deserves the lottery that the court expresses society's abhorrence of the crime. So the court's task is still worth doing, even when it is a foregone conclusion that the defendant will win the lottery if sentenced (as might happen if he had won all the alternative draws). But the trial may seem idle, and the expression of abhorrence may fall flat, when it is known all along that, come what may, the defendant will never face the lottery and lose.

Case 4 is like Case 3, except that we make the penal lottery less pure. Losers of the penal lottery get death, as before; winners get a short prison sentence. Therefore it is certain that every criminal who is sentenced to the lottery will suffer at least some penal harm. Thus we make sure that the trial and the sentence will be taken seriously even when it is a foregone conclusion that the defendant, if sentenced, will win the lottery.

Case 1 also was significantly impure. If the draw is held at the last minute, on the very steps of the gallows, then every criminal who is sentenced to face the lottery must spend a period of time— days? weeks? years?—in fear and trembling, and imprisoned, waiting to learn whether he will win

or lose. This period of terror is a certain harm that falls on winners and losers alike. Case 2 very nearly eliminates the impurity, since there is no reason why the Drawer should not reveal the outcome very soon after the criminal is sentenced. Case 3 eliminates it entirely. (In every case, a defendant must spend a period in fear as he waits to learn whether he will be convicted. But this harm cannot count as penal, because it falls equally on the guilty and the innocent, on those who will be convicted and those who will be acquitted.) Case 4 restores impurity, to whatever extent we see fit, but in a different form.

Case 5 is like Case 4, except that the straws are replaced by a different chance device for determining the outcome of the lottery. The Public Drawer conducts an exact reenactment of the crime. If the victim in the reenactment dies, then the criminal loses the lottery. If it is a good reenactment, the risk to the original victim equals the risk to the new victim in the reenactment, which in turn equals the risk that the criminal will lose the lottery; and so, as desired, we punish a risk by an equal risk.

If the outcome of the lottery is to be settled before the trial, as in Cases 2, 3, and 4, then it will be necessary for the Drawer to conduct not just one but several reenactments. He will entertain all reasonable alternative hypotheses about exactly how the crime might have happened—exactly what the defendant might have done by way of knowingly and wrongfully inflicting risk on the victim. He will conduct one reenactment for each hypothesis. The court's task changes. If the court finds the defendant guilty of knowingly and wrongfully inflicting a risk of death, it is no longer required also to measure the amount of risk. Nobody need ever figure out whether it was 80 percent, 40 percent, or what. Instead, the court is required to ascertain which hypothesis about exactly how the crime happened is correct. Thereby the court chooses which of all the hypothetical reenactments is the one that determines whether the criminal wins or loses his lottery. If the court finds that the criminal took careful aim, then the chosen reenactment will be one in which the criminal's stand-in also took careful aim, whereas if the court finds that the criminal halfheartedly fired in the victim's general direction, the chosen reenactment will be one in which the stand-in did likewise. So the criminal will be more likely to lose his lottery in the first case than in the second.

The drawbacks of a lottery by reenactment are plain to see. Soon we shall find the remedy. But first, let us look at the advantages of a lottery by reenactment over a lottery by drawing straws. We have already noted that with straws, the court had to measure how much risk the criminal inflicted, whereas with reenactments, the court has only to ascertain exactly how the crime happened. Both tasks look well-nigh impossible. But the second must be easier, because the first task consists of the second plus more besides. The only way for the court to measure the risk would be to ascertain just what happened, and then find out just how much risk results from such happenings.

Another advantage of reenactments over straws appears when we try to be more careful about what we mean by "amount of risk." Is it (1) an "objective chance"? Or is it (2) a reasonable degree of belief for a hypothetical observer who knows the situation in as much minute detail as feasible instruments could permit? Or is it (3) a reasonable degree of belief for someone who knows just as much about the details of the situation as the criminal did? Or is it (4) the criminal's actual degree of belief, however unreasonable that might have been? It would be nice not to have to decide. But if we want to match the criminal's risk in a lottery by straws to the victim's risk, then we must decide. Not so for a lottery by reenactment. If the reenactment is perfect, we automatically match the amount of risk in all four senses. Even if the reenactment is imperfect, at least we can assure ourselves of match in senses (3) and (4). It may or may not be feasible to get assured match in senses (1) and (2), depending on the details of what happened. (If it turns out that the criminal left a bomb hooked up to a quantum randomizer, it will be comparatively easy. If he committed his crime in a more commonplace way, it will be much harder.) But whenever it is hard to get assured match in senses (1) and (2), it will be harder still to measure the risk and get assured match in a lottery by straws. So however the crime happened, and whatever sense of match we want, we do at least as well by reenactment as by straws, and sometimes we do better.

Case 6 is like Case 5, except that enactment replaces *re*enactment. We use the original crime, so to speak, as its own perfect reenactment. If the criminal is sentenced to face the lottery, then if his victim dies, he loses his lottery and he dies too, whereas if the victim lives, the criminal wins, and

he gets only the short prison sentence. It does not matter when the lottery takes place, provided only that it is not settled so soon that the criminal may know its outcome before he decides whether to commit his crime.

The advantages are many: we need no Drawer to do the work; we need not find volunteers to be the stand-in victims in all the hypothetical reenactments; the "reenactment" is automatically perfect, matching the risk in all four senses; we spare the court the difficult task of ascertaining exactly how the crime happened. If we want to give a risk for a risk, and if we want to match risks in any but a very approximate and uncertain fashion, the lottery by enactment is not only the easy way, it is the only remotely feasible way.

The drawback is confusion. When a criminal is sentenced to face the lottery by straws, nobody will think him more guilty or more wicked just because his straw is short. And when a criminal is sentenced to face the lottery by reenactment, nobody will think him more guilty just because the stand-in victim dies. But if he is sentenced to the lottery by enactment, then one and the same event plays a double role: if his victim dies, that death is at once the main harm done by his crime and also the way of losing his lottery. If we are not careful, we are apt to misunderstand. We may think that the successful attempter suffers a worse fate because he is more guilty when he does a worse harm, rather than because he loses his lottery. But it is not so: his success is irrelevant to his guilt, his wickedness, his desert, and his sentence to face the lottery—exactly as the shortness of his straw would have been, had he been sentenced to the lottery by straws.

VI

I submit that our present practice is exactly Case 6: punishment for attempts regardless of success, a penal lottery by enactment, impurity to help us take the affair seriously even when the lottery is won, and the inevitable confusion. We may not understand our practice as a penal lottery—confused as we are, we have trouble understanding it at all—but, so understood, it does make a good deal of sense. It is another question whether it is really just. Most likely it isn't, but I don't understand why not.

Endnotes

[1] I do not wish to enter the debate about whether the traditional death penalty is ever justified. If you think not, substitute throughout whatever you think is the correct maximum penalty; my argument will go through almost without change.

[2] John Kleinig, *Punishment and Desert* (The Hague: Martinus Nijhoff, 1973), p. 132. Kleinig does not take this to afford an adequate justification.

[3] See Thomas Nagel, "Moral Luck," *Proceedings of the Aristotelian Society,* supp. vol. 50 (1976): 141, repr. in Nagel, *Mortal Questions* (Cambridge: Cambridge University Press, 1979), p. 29. Nagel distinguishes, as he should, between the "moral luck" of the attempter and the different sort of moral luck that makes some genuine difference to how one is and how one acts.

[4] The luck of hitting and missing does make a difference to how their actions of shooting may be described: Dee's is a killing, Dum's is not. Dee's causes harm and thereby invades the victim's rights in a way that Dum's does not. (Dee invades the victim's right not to be harmed, as well as his right not to be endangered; Dum invades only the latter right.) But this is no difference in how they act, since the description of an action in terms of what it causes is an extrinsic description. The actions themselves, events that are finished when the agent has done his part, do not differ in any intrinsic way.

You might protest that a killing is not over when the killer has done his part; it is a more prolonged event that ends with the death of the victim; so there is, after all, an intrinsic difference between Dee's action of killing and Dum's action of shooting and missing.— No; an action of killing is different from the prolonged event of someone's getting killed, even though "the killing" can denote either one.

[5] See Lawrence C. Becker, "Criminal Attempt and the Theory of the Law of Crimes," *Philosophy & Public Affairs* 3, no. 3 (Spring 1974): 288. Becker does not take this to afford an adequate justification.

[6] See A. Hough and D. M. Schwartz, "AIDS and Prisons," in *Meeting the Challenge: Papers of the First National Conference on AIDS,* ed. Adam Carr (Canberra: Australian Government Publishing Service, 1986), pp. 171–80.

[7] This point would disappear if something less cheap and quick than death were the penalty for losers of the lottery.

[8] See Thomas C. Schelling, "The Threat That Leaves Something to Chance," in his book *The Strategy of Conflict* (Cambridge: Harvard University Press, 1960). Schelling does not discuss penal lotteries as such, but much of his discussion carries over. What does not carry over, or not much, is his discussion of chancy threats as a way to gain credibility when one has strong reason not to fulfill one's threat.

[9] This question would have to be reconsidered if something other than death were the maximum penalty, and so the penalty for losers of the lottery. It would remain an empirical question, and probably a difficult one, which is the more effective system of defense.

[10] I note a complication once and for all, but I shall ignore it in what follows. The relevant risk is not really the victim's risk of death, but rather the risk of being killed—that is, of dying a death which is caused, perhaps probabilistically, and in the appropriate insensitive fashion, by the criminal's act. Likewise for the criminal's risk in the penal lottery.

People v. Dlugash

363 N. E. 2d 1155 (1977)
Court of Appeals of New York

Jasen, Judge.

The criminal law is of ancient origin, but criminal liability for attempt to commit a crime is comparatively recent. At the root of the concept of attempt liability are the very aims and purposes of penal law. The ultimate issue is whether an individual's intentions and actions, though failing to achieve a manifest and malevolent criminal purpose, constitute a danger to organized society of sufficient magnitude to warrant the imposition of criminal sanctions. Difficulties in theoretical analysis and concomitant debate over very pragmatic questions of blameworthiness appear dramatically in reference to situations where the criminal attempt failed to achieve its purpose solely because the factual or legal context in which the individual acted was not as the actor supposed them to be. Phrased somewhat differently, the concern centers on whether an individual should be liable for an attempt to commit a crime when, unknown to him, it was impossible to successfully complete the crime attempted. For years, serious studies have been made on the subject in an effort to resolve the continuing controversy when, if at all, the impossibility of successfully completing the criminal act should preclude liability for even making the futile attempt. The 1967 revision of the Penal law approached the impossibility defense to the inchoate crime of attempt in a novel fashion. The statute provides that, if a person engages in conduct which would otherwise constitute an attempt to commit a crime, "it is no defense to a prosecution for such attempt that the crime charged to have been attempted was, under the attendant circumstances, factually or legally impossible of commission, if such crime could have been committed had the attendant circumstances been as such person believed them to be." (Penal Law, §110.10.) This appeal presents to us, for the first time, a case involving the application of the modern statute. We hold that, under the proof presented by the People at trial, defendant Melvin Dlugash may be held for attempted murder, though the target of the attempt may have already been slain, by the hand of another, when Dlugash made his felonious attempt.

On December 22, 1973, Michael Geller, 25 years old, was found shot to death in the bedroom of his Brooklyn apartment. The body, which had literally been riddled by bullets, was found lying face up on the floor. An autopsy revealed that the victim had been shot in the face and head no less than seven times. Powder burns on the face indicated that the shots had been fired from within one foot of the victim. Four small caliber bullets were recovered from the victim's skull. The victim had also been critically wounded in the chest. One heavy caliber bullet passed through the left lung, penetrated the heart chamber, pierced the left ventricle of the heart upon entrance and again upon exit, and lodged in the victim's torso. Although a second bullet was damaged beyond identification, the bullet tracks indicated that these wounds were also inflicted by a bullet of heavy caliber. A tenth bullet, of unknown caliber, passed through the thumb of the victim's left hand. The autopsy report listed the cause of death as "[m]ultiple bullet wounds of head and chest with brain injury and massive bilateral hemothorax with penetration of [the] heart." Subsequent ballistics examination established that the four bullets recovered from the victim's head were .25 caliber bullets and that the heart-piercing bullet was of .38 caliber.

Detective Joseph Carrasquillo of the New York City Police Department was assigned to investigate the homicide. On December 27, 1973, five days after the discovery of the body, Detective Carrasquillo and a fellow officer went to the defendant's residence in an effort to locate him. The officers arrived at approximately 6:00 P.M. The defendant answered the door and, when informed that the officers were investigating the death of Michael Geller, a friend of his, defendant invited the officers into the house. Detective Carrasquillo informed defendant that the officers desired any information defendant might have regarding the death of Geller and, since defendant was regarded as a suspect, administered the standard preinterrogation warnings. The defendant told the officers that he and another friend, Joe Bush, had just returned from a four- or five-day trip "upstate someplace" and learned of Geller's death only upon his return. Since Bush was also a suspect in the case and defendant admitted knowing Bush, defendant agreed to accompany the officers to the station house for the purposes of identifying photographs of Bush and of lending assistance to the investigation. Upon arrival at the police station, Detective Carrasquillo and the defendant went directly into an interview room. Carrasquillo advised the defendant that he had witnesses and information to the effect that as late as 7:00 P.M. on the day before the body was found, defendant had been observed carrying a .25 caliber pistol. Once again, Carrasquillo administered the standard preinterrogation statement of rights. The defendant then proceeded to relate his version of the events which culminated in the death of Geller. Defendant stated that, on the night of December 21, 1973, he, Bush and Geller had been out drinking. Bush had been staying at Geller's apartment and, during the course of the evening, Geller several times demanded that Bush pay $100 towards the rent on the apartment. According to defendant, Bush rejected these demands, telling Geller that "you better shut up or you're going to get a bullet." All three returned to Geller's apartment at approximately midnight, took seats in the bedroom, and continued to drink until sometime between 3:00 and 3:30 in the morning. When Geller again pressed his demand for rent money, Bush drew his .38 caliber pistol, aimed it at Geller and fired three times. Geller fell to the floor. After the passage of a few minutes, perhaps two, perhaps as much as five, defendant walked over to the fallen Geller, drew his .25 caliber pistol, and fired approximately five shots in the victim's head and face. Defendant contended that, by the time he fired the shots, "it looked like Mike Geller was already dead." After the shots were fired, defendant and Bush walked to the apartment of a female acquaintance. Bush removed his shirt, wrapped the two guns and a knife in it, and left the apartment, telling Dlugash that he intended to dispose of the weapons. Bush returned 10 or 15 minutes later and stated that he had thrown the weapons down a sewer two or three blocks away.

After Carrasquillo had taken the bulk of the statement, he asked the defendant why he would do such a thing. According to Carrasquillo, the defendant said, "gee, I really don't know." Carrasquillo repeated the question 10 minutes later, but received the same response. After a while, Carrasquillo asked the question for a third time and defendant replied, "well, gee, I guess it must have been because I was afraid of Joe Bush."

At approximately 9:00 P.M., the defendant repeated the substance of his statement to an Assistant District Attorney. Defendant added that at the time he shot at Geller, Geller was not moving and his eyes were closed. While he did not check for a pulse, defendant stated that Geller had not been doing anything to him at the time he shot because "Mike was dead."

Defendant was indicted by the Grand Jury of Kings County on a single count of murder in that, acting in concert with another person actually present, he intentionally caused the death of Michael Geller. At the trial, there were four principal prosecution witnesses: Detective Carrasquillo, the Assistant District Attorney who took the second admission, and two physicians from the office of the New York City Chief Medical Examiner. For proof of defendant's culpability, the prosecution relied upon defendant's own admissions as related by the detective and the prosecutor. From the physicians, the prosecution sought to establish that Geller was still alive at the time de-

fendant shot at him. Both physicians testified that each of the two chest wounds, for which defendant alleged Bush to be responsible, would have caused death without prompt medical attention. Moreover, the victim would have remained alive until such time as his chest cavity became fully filled with blood. Depending on the circumstances, it might take 5 to 10 minutes for the chest cavity to fill. Neither prosecution witness could state, with medical certainty, that the victim was still alive when, perhaps five minutes after the initial chest wounds were inflicted, the defendant fired at the victim's head. The defense produced but a single witness, the former Chief Medical Examiner of New York City. This expert stated that, in his view, Geller might have died of the chest wounds "very rapidly" since, in addition to the bleeding, a large bullet going through a lung and the heart would have other adverse medical effects. "Those wounds can be almost immediately or rapidly fatal or they may be delayed in there, in the time it would take for death to occur. But I would say that wounds like that which are described here as having gone through the lungs and the heart would be fatal wounds and in most cases they're rapidly fatal."

The jury found the defendant guilty of murder. The defendant then moved to set the verdict aside. He submitted an affidavit in which he contended that he "was absolutely, unequivocally and positively certain that Michael Geller was dead before [he] shot him." This motion was denied.[1]

On appeal, the Appellate Division reversed the judgment of conviction on the law and dismissed the indictment. The court ruled that "the People failed to prove beyond a reasonable doubt that Geller had been alive at the time he was shot by defendant; defendant's conviction of murder thus cannot stand." Further, the court held that the judgment could not be modified to reflect a conviction for attempted murder because "the uncontradicted evidence is that the defendant, at the time that he fired the five shots into the body of the decedent, believed him to be dead, and . . . there is not a scintilla of evidence to contradict his assertion in that regard."

While the defendant admitted firing five shots at the victim approximately two to five minutes after Bush had fired three times, all three medical expert witnesses testified that they could not, with any degree of medical certainty, state whether the victim had been alive at the time the latter shots were fired by the defendant. Thus, the People failed to prove beyond a reasonable doubt that the victim had been alive at the time he was shot by the defendant. Whatever else it may be, it is not murder to shoot a dead body.

The distinction between "factual" and "legal" impossibility is a nice one indeed and the courts tend to place a greater value on legal form than on any substantive danger the defendant's actions pose for society. The approach of the draftsmen of the Model Penal Code was to eliminate the defense of impossibility in virtually all situations. Under the code provision, to constitute an attempt, it is still necessary that the result intended or desired by the actor constitute a crime. However, the code suggested a fundamental change to shift the locus of analysis to the actor's mental frame of reference and away from undue dependence upon external considerations. The basic premise of the code provision is that what was in the actor's own mind should be the standard for determining his dangerousness to society and, hence, his liability for attempted criminal conduct.

In the belief that neither of the two branches of the traditional impossibility arguments detracts from the offender's moral culpability, the Legislature substantially carried the code's treatment of impossibility into the 1967 revision of the Penal Law. Thus, a person is guilty of an attempt when, with intent to commit a crime, he engages in conduct which tends to effect the commission of such crime. (Penal Law, §110.10.) Thus, if defendant believed the victim to be alive at the time of the shooting, it is no defense to the charge of attempted murder that the victim may have been dead.

Turning to the facts of the case before us, we believe that there is sufficient evidence in the record from which the jury could conclude that the defendant believed Geller to be alive at the time defendant fired shots into Geller's head. Defendant admitted firing five shots at a most vital part of the victim's anatomy from virtually point blank range. Although defendant contended that the victim had already been grievously wounded by another, from the defendant's admitted actions, the jury could conclude that the defendant's purpose and intention was to administer the coup de grace.

Defendant argues that the jury was bound to accept, at face value, the indications in his admissions that he believed Geller dead. Certainly, it is true that the defendant was entitled to have the entirety of the admissions, both the inculpatory and the exculpatory portions, placed in evidence before the trier of facts.

However, the jury was not required to automatically credit the exculpatory portions of the admissions. The general rule is, of course, that the credibility of witnesses is a question of fact and the jury may choose to believe some, but not all, of a witness' testimony.

In this case, there is ample other evidence to contradict the defendant's assertion that he believed Geller dead. There were five bullet wounds inflicted with stunning accuracy in a vital part of the victim's anatomy. The medical testimony indicated that Geller may have been alive at the time defendant fired at him. The defendant voluntarily left the jurisdiction immediately after the crime with his coperpetrator. Defendant did not report the crime to the police when left on his own by Bush. Instead, he attempted to conceal his and Bush's involvement with the homicide. In addition, the other portions of defendant's admissions make his contended belief that Geller was dead extremely improbable. Defendant, without a word of instruction from Bush, voluntarily got up from his seat after the passage of just a few minutes and fired five times point blank into the victim's face, snuffing out any remaining chance of life that Geller possessed. Certainly, this alone indicates a callous indifference to the taking of a human life. His admissions are barren of any claim of duress[2] and reflect, instead, an unstinting co-operation in efforts to dispose of vital incriminating evidence. Indeed, defendant maintained a false version of the occurrence until such time as the police informed him that they had evidence that he lately possessed a gun of the same caliber as one of the weapons involved in the shooting. From all of this, the jury was certainly warranted in concluding that the defendant acted in the belief that Geller was yet alive when shot by defendant.

The jury convicted the defendant of murder. Necessarily, they found that defendant intended to kill a live human being. Subsumed within this finding is the conclusion that defendant acted in the belief that Geller was alive. Thus, there is no need for additional fact findings by a jury. Although it was not established beyond a reasonable doubt that Geller was, in fact, alive, such is no defense to attempted murder since a murder would have been committed "had the attendant circumstances been as [defendant] believed them to be." (Penal Law, §110.10.) The jury necessarily found that defendant believed Geller to be alive when defendant shot at him.

The appellate Division erred in not modifying the judgment to reflect a conviction for the lesser included offense of attempted murder. An attempt to commit a murder is a lesser included offense of murder and the Appellate Division has the authority, where the trial evidence is not legally sufficient to establish the offense of which the defendant was convicted, to modify the judgment to one of conviction for a lesser included offense which is legally established by the evidence.

Endnotes

[1] It should be noted that Joe Bush pleaded guilty to a charge of manslaughter in the first degree. At the time he entered his plea, Bush detailed his version of the homicide. According to Bush, defendant Dlugash was a dealer in narcotic drugs and Dlugash claimed that Geller owed him a large sum of money from drug purchases. Bush was in the kitchen alone when Geller entered and threatened him with a shotgun. Bush pulled out his .38 caliber pistol and fired five times at Geller. Geller slumped to the floor. Dlugash then entered, withdrew his .25 caliber pistol and fired five shots into the deceased's face. Bush, however, never testified at Dlugash's trial.

[2] Notwithstanding the Appellate Division's implication to the contrary, the record indicates that defendant told the Assistant District Attorney that Bush, after shooting Geller, kept his gun aimed at Geller, and not at Dlugash. As defendant stated, "this was after Joe had his .38 on him, I started shooting on him."

Study Questions

1. Victor is unhappily married to Esmerelda. In fact, Victor so despises his wife that he has on more than one occasion seriously thought of killing her. Victor was raised on a small island in the Caribbean and, as a young boy, was initiated into the black-magic cults of the native peoples. Victor still retains deep beliefs in the power of voodoo magic. One day, when he feels he can stand his wife no longer, Victor retires to his secret workshop, where he has over the years meticulously collected the accoutrements of the black arts. Carefully he prepares a tiny, doll-like replica of the despised Esmerelda. When at last the doll is finished, Victor takes a deep breath and, with nervous fingers and a look of hatred, viciously and repeatedly stabs the doll with "sacred" needles. Exhausted by his deed, Victor collapses. When he awakens, he is overcome with remorse and disgust at what he has done. He promptly leaves his workshop, marches to the local police station, and turns himself in, believing, with all sincerity, that he has murdered his wife. Question: Is Victor guilty of attempted murder? Why not? Consider the language of the Model Penal Code, section 5.01:

(1) *Definition of Attempt.* A person is guilty of an attempt to commit a crime if, acting with the kind of culpability otherwise required for commission of the crime, he:

(a) purposely engages in conduct which would constitute the crime if the attendant circumstances were as he believes them to be; or

(b) when causing a particular result is an element of the crime, does or omits to do anything with the purpose of causing or with the belief that it will cause such result without further conduct on his part; or

(c) purposely does or omits to do anything which, under the circumstances as he believes them to be, is an act or omission constituting a substantial step in a course of conduct planned to culminate in his commission of the crime.

Is Victor convictable of attempt under this language?

2. Can the aim of deterrence—infliction of punishment for the purpose of scaring others into compliance with the law—serve as a rationale for punishing attempters with equal severity as those who successfully complete a crime?

B. *Strict Criminal Liability*

Introduction

A basic principle of our law has always been that punishment must be deserved. And this principle has been interpreted to require a finding of *mens rea*: Only where I have acted with the intent to commit an offense against the law, and have therefore acted with a culpable or blameworthy state of mind, should I be subjected to the possibility of punishment. Common as this principle is, there are important and controversial exceptions to it, and the doctrine of felony-murder, at stake in the case of *People v. Hickman*, is one of them.

As they emerged from a burglary at a liquor warehouse, defendants Rock and Hickman were surprised by police officers. The defendants attempted to escape by running toward some bushes near the parking lot. One of the officers lost sight of them, then moments later saw a man with a handgun running toward him along the bushes. Believing the armed man to be one of the burglars, the officer warned and then fired upon the shadowy figure. The unknown man turned out to be a police detective. Rock and Hickman, at this point some distance away, were charged with the detective's murder under the *felony-murder doctrine*.

Generally speaking, to be convictable of murder, one must either have acted with the intent to kill, or have exhibited extreme recklessness with regard to human life, say, by emptying a revolver into a crowded room. To be convicted of first-degree murder, it is usually necessary to have acted in a premeditated fashion, or that the killing have taken place under circumstances presumed to be premeditated, for example, by administering poison. The felony-murder doctrine is an exception to these requirements. This doctrine says that if, in the course of the commission of a felony a killing occurs, all accomplices in the felony are chargeable with murder. X, Y, and Z decide to rob a bank. Z waits in the getaway car while X and Y commit the holdup. A security guard makes a menacing ges-

ture and Y shoots him. Z is guilty of felony-murder even if he was nowhere near the scene and did not pull the trigger.

The felony-murder concept has numerous permutations and complexities. Suppose that, after X and Y leave the bank, one of the tellers dies of a fright-induced heart attack? California has held that Z is guilty of felony-murder.[1] What if X turns on Y in the bank and shoots him? Some states, again including California, have held that Z can be convicted for this murder as well.[2] Finally, what if neither the person killed nor the person doing the killing is one of the felons? This is the situation in *Hickman* and the Illinois court held that "there can be no doubt" about the justice of holding Hickman and Rock liable for the murder of the police detective.

Objections to Felony-Murder

The moral argument against the felony-murder doctrine is made in our selection by George Fletcher. Fletcher contrasts the positions on felony-murder taken in recent state court cases, such as the ones mentioned above, with the position adopted by the Model Penal Code. The code would pull back from the expansive scope given to felony-murder by the states, and it is not surprising therefore that no state has adopted the code's view. Fletcher speculates that many states have retained the felony-murder doctrine for the practical reason that it is a powerful tool for inflicting severe punishment on felons. But these same courts have thereby failed, objects Fletcher, to focus on the crucial moral question: What did any of the defendants in these cases do to endanger human life?

Fletcher suggests two rationales that could explain the felony-murder rule. First, it could be argued that persons like Hickman, by beginning a series of events that terminates in the death of another, incur a kind of moral stain or taint that must then be expiated through punishment appropriate to the crime of murder. Alternatively, it might be urged that those who commit felonies must run the risk if things turn out worse than they expected. Fletcher rejects both rationales on the ground that each violates a basic precept of justice, namely, that the punishment must be proportioned to the gravity of the offense.

Statutory rape (unlawful intercourse with a female minor), bigamy (being married to more than one person at a time), and various "public welfare" offenses (for example, mishandling or mislabeling drug products), along with the felony-murder rule, have traditionally been among those offenses imposing *strict criminal liability*, the defining feature of which is the refusal to require proof of the actor's state of mind as a prerequisite to liability. The principal justifications offered for the creation of strict-liability offenses have generally been utilitarian in nature, appealing to the supposed good consequences of imposing such liability. Those who favor strict criminal liability on these grounds argue that it will deter crime by inducing those contemplating felonious conduct to think again and that it will protect the public by provoking those who engage in dangerous but socially beneficial activities (such as drug manufacture) to be especially cautious. Others argue that strict liability is more efficient than the traditional emphasis upon the requirement of *mens rea* since it is burdensome to inquire into a defendant's state of mind. Opponents object that it is wrong and unfair to thus use the defendant as an expedient to promote the greater good. Persons should be punished, the critics insist, only when they manifest a culpable state of mind for the offense with which they have been charged.

In his essay, Mark Kelman reviews the history of strict-liability offenses and canvasses many of the foregoing arguments. He then offers his own argument in favor of strict criminal liability.

The opponents of strict liability, Kelman believes, build their case against it on the basis of a misleading image: the defendant as a "hapless victim," unable to avoid the imposition of an unfair sentence. But, Kelman counters, the defendant's situation only appears unfair if one looks at his conduct and options within a narrow time frame. In *Hickman*, during the time when the officer shot the detective, the defendants were elsewhere and could have done little to prevent the tragedy; in the standard case of statutory rape, the defendant can hardly be expected to have done anything to ascertain the age of his companion. Kelman responds that if we assess or evaluate a defendant's conduct within an expanded time frame, it becomes much more difficult to say that he or she could not easily have taken steps to avoid liability. Those in Hickman's position have voluntarily assumed a certain role and are on notice that they may be held strictly liable. The moral, according to Kelman, is: Don't take the job if you fear you can't prevent (further) violations of the law (above and beyond any you have already committed).

Endnotes

[1] *People v. Stampe* 2 Cal. App. 3d 203 (1969).

[2] *People v. Cabaltero* 31 Cal. App. 2d 52 (1939).

People v. Hickman

297 N.E. 2d 582 (1973)
Appellate Court of Illinois, Third District

Scott, Justice.

Robert Bruce Papes, Anthony Rock and Glenn Hickman were indicted by the Grand Jury of Will County for the offenses of murder and burglary. After trial by jury the defendants Rock and Hickman were found guilty of the crimes of murder, burglary and criminal damage to property. Papes was found guilty of burglary and criminal damage to property but not guilty of murder. The defendants Hickman and Rock filed a motion to arrest the judgment of guilty of murder and burglary.

This motion was partially granted by the trial court in that the judgment of guilty for the crime of murder was arrested.

Papes was placed on probation for a term of two years for the offense of burglary and as a term of probation was ordered to serve six months at the Illinois State Farm at Vandalia. The defendant Rock was sentenced by the trial court to a term of not less than one (1) year nor more than one (1) year and one (1) day in the penitentiary for the offense of burglary. The defendant Hickman was placed on probation for the offense of burglary for a period of two years and as a term of probation he was ordered to serve nine months in the Illinois State Farm at Vandalia.

The State has appealed from the order of the trial court arresting the judgment of murder as to the defendants Rock and Hickman.

The factual situation which resulted in the trial of the defendants occurred on the evening of April 2, 1970, at which time seventeen policemen from the police force of the city of Joliet were participating in a surveillance of a building known as the Illinois Wine and Liquor Warehouse. Among the officers involved in the surveillance was Sergeant James Cronk, who shortly before 10:15 P.M. noticed Robert Bruce Papes and the defendant Anthony Rock pass by the warehouse several times in a Cadillac automobile. Later several officers saw a Chevrolet automobile enter an alley south of the warehouse and stop at a side door of the building. Several people left the automobile and disappeared from sight into the doorway. The driver of this vehicle, who was Papes, walked a short distance, made a surveillance of the area, returned to the automobile and then drove out of the sight of the officers. After several minutes Papes was again seen walking in the alley and after once more looking over the area he again disappeared from the sight of the police officers when he went to the location of the side doorway of the warehouse. It was within a matter of a few seconds of Papes'[s] disappearance that Sergeant Cronk saw three individuals exit from the side doorway of the warehouse, at which time he signaled the officers to close in from various directions towards a concrete parking lot which was to the rear and west of the warehouse.

Papes and the defendants Rock and Hickman upon seeing the officers approaching them proceeded to run. Papes ran in a southwesterly direction and the defendants Rock and Hickman in a northwesterly direction towards some bushes located at the northwest corner of the parking lot. Papes was apprehended when a Sergeant Erwin pointed a shotgun at him. Papes submitted to an arrest and upon his person was found a loaded pistol and additional cartridges. As the defendant Rock was running he was carrying a small object in his hand. The defendant Hickman was carrying an attache case as he was fleeing.

The defendants Rock and Hickman ran through the bushes while in the meantime Sergeant Cronk ran to the rear of the warehouse where he noticed two people running in a northwesterly direction. Sergeant Cronk yelled "halt—police" several times but his commands were ignored. He lost sight of the two fleeing individuals but within seconds thereafter saw a man carrying a handgun running towards the bushes at the northwest corner of the parking lot. Sergeant Cronk, believing that this approaching individual was one of the burglars of the Illinois Wine and Liquor Warehouse, and referring to the handgun, ordered the person to "drop it." When there was no compliance to this warning Sergeant Cronk fired his shotgun at the individual, who was later discovered to be Detective William Loscheider of the Joliet police force. Loscheider was killed by this shot from his fellow officer's gun.

Approximately one-half hour later the defendants Rock and Hickman were arrested as they were walking on a street approximately two and a half blocks from the warehouse. Neither of the defendants had a weapon on his person.

Subsequent to the fatal shooting of Loscheider the police officers discovered that entry to the warehouse had been made by removing a panel from the side door and also by removal of the lock from the door.

During the trial of the defendants an analyst from the Illinois Bureau of Identification Crime Laboratory testified that the tool marks found on the side door of the warehouse were made by a screwdriver found in an attache case which was discovered on the parking lot to the rear of the warehouse.

During the course of the trial the court struck from the murder count of the indictment as to the defendants Rock and Hickman all allegations as to the defendants arming themselves in furtherance of a conspiracy to burglarize the Illinois Wine and Liquor Warehouse.

The foregoing constitutes a brief summary of

the unusual factual situation which led to this appeal and which presents to us the question as to whether or not the trial court erred when it entered an order arresting a judgment of guilty of murder against the defendants Rock and Hickman which had been returned against them by the jury.

More narrowly presented we must determine whether the actual shooting which caused the death of an innocent victim must have been performed by the defendants or someone acting in concert with them in order to comply with the requirements of the felony-murder doctrine.

Our criminal code contains the statutory provisions relating to the felony-murder doctrine, being Ch. 38, Sec. 9–1(a)(3), Ill. Rev. Stat., which provides:

> "(a) A person who kills an individual without lawful justification commits murder if, in performing the acts which cause the death:
>
>   . . .
>
> (3) He is attempting or committing a forcible felony other than voluntary manslaughter."

The defendants urge an interpretation of this statute to the effect that the person who kills or performs the acts which cause death must be the same person as the one who is attempting or committing a forcible felony before liability for murder can be imposed.

. . . While the syntax of the words involved in our felony-murder statute could be interpreted on the restrictive and narrow lines urged by the defendants, we do not believe that in statutory construction we are bound to consider only the wording used in the statute. The court in construing a statute may consider the notes and reports of the commission pursuant to which the statutory provision was adopted. . . . Turning our attention to the committee comments in regard to the statute in question we find on page 9 of Smith Hurd Ill. Ann. Stat., Ch. 38, the following comments in regard to the application of Sec. 9–1(a)(3), the felony-murder provision:

> "It is immaterial whether the killing in such a case is intentional or accidental, or is committed by a confederate without the connivance of the defendant. . . . or even by a third person trying to prevent the commission of the felony."

In support of the committee comment that one can be guilty of murder where the killing resulted from the act of a third person trying to prevent the commission of a felony, there is cited the case of People v. Payne. . . .

In *Payne* we have a factual situation where armed robbers entered the home of two brothers. One of the brothers discharged a weapon to prevent the robbery as did one of the robbers. The other brother was killed and it could not be determined whether he was killed by his brother or the robber. Our Supreme Court in affirming the defendant's conviction of murder stated:

> "Where several persons conspire to do an unlawful act, and another crime is committed in the pursuit of the common object, all are alike guilty of the crime committed, if it is a natural and probable consequence of the execution of the conspiracy. . . . It reasonably might be anticipated that an attempted robbery would meet with resistance, during which the victim might be shot either by himself or someone else in attempting to prevent the robbery, and those attempting to perpetrate the robbery would be guilty of murder."

There are other cases in Illinois where our reviewing courts have recognized that a defendant may be criminally responsible for the killing of another during the commission of a forcible felony even though no certainty exists that the defendant or his cohorts performed the fatal act. . . . Our Supreme Court in the *Payne* case, however, was confronted with a factual situation quite similar to the one presented to us in the instant case and in *Payne* the court clearly adopted the theory that a defendant and co-conspirators acting in concert with him can be held responsible for a killing of an innocent third party during the commission of a forcible felony even though the killing was not actually done by a person acting in concert with the defendant or his co-conspirators.

. . . We hold it to be of no consequence that in the instant case Detective Loscheider was killed at a time when the defendants were attempting to escape. Our Supreme Court has held that the period of time involved in an escape with immediate pursuit after committing a crime becomes part of the crime itself . . . :

> . . . (W)here two or more persons engage in a conspiracy to commit robbery and an

officer is murdered while in immediate pursuit of either or both of the offenders who are attempting to escape from the scene of the crime with the fruits of the robbery, each of the conspirators is guilty of murder, for the crime had not been completed at the time inasmuch as the conspirators had not won their way to a place of safety. We pointed out that a plan to commit robbery would be futile if it did not comprehend an escape with the proceeds of the crime, and that unless the plan was to kill any person attempting to apprehend the conspirators at the time of or immediately upon gaining possession of the property, the plan would be inane."

The defendants both in the trial court and in this appeal urge that the applicable law is set forth in the case of People v. Morris. . . . In *Morris* the defendant and two cohorts entered a restaurant armed for the purpose of committing a robbery. A struggle ensued between a patron and one of the cohorts during which gunfire erupted and the cohort was killed. The defendant Morris, one of the would-be robbers, was charged with murder of his co-conspirator under the theory of the felony-murder doctrine and was convicted of the crime of murder by the trial court. The reviewing court reversed the trial court holding that the felony-murder doctrine is not applicable against a surviving felon when a co-felon is justifiably killed during commission of a forcible felony.

. . . We do not believe that the rationale of the *Morris* case is controlling in the instant case since *Morris* presented a factual situation which differed in one very significant detail. In *Morris,* unlike the case before us, the victim was not an innocent third party. In *Morris* the victim was not free from culpability but was in fact an individual who was attempting to commit a felony. We do not hold that the character of the victim is controlling merely because he was a felon, nor do we indulge in the fanciful theory that the victim being a felon assumed the risk and thereby constructively con-

sented to his death, but we do hold that he assisted in setting in motion a chain of events which was the proximate cause of his death and therefore in the criminal law as in the civil law there is no redress for the victim.

Clearly the case of People v. Payne . . . and the case now before us are distinguishable from *Morris* in that unlike *Morris,* innocent parties were killed. We interpret *Payne* as setting forth the rule that he whose act causes in any way, directly or indirectly, the death of an innocent victim is guilty of murder by virtue of the felony-murder doctrine.

We are aware of the conflicting views from other jurisdictions concerning the application of the felony-murder doctrine in cases such as we are now considering, but we are only concerned with following the law as it has been established in our own state, and therefore hold that *Payne* is controlling in the instant case and that the defendants are guilty of the crime of murder. There should be no doubt about the "justice" of holding a felon guilty of murder who engages in a robbery followed by an attempted escape and thereby inevitably calls into action defensive forces against him, the activity of which results in the death of an innocent human being.

Mr. Justice Cardozo in "The Nature of the Judicial Process", pages 66, 67, said, and we believe wisely, that "When they (Judges) are called upon to say how far existing rules are to be extended or restricted, they must let the welfare of society fix the path, its direction and its distance. . . . The final cause of law is the welfare of society."

Following the precepts of Justice Cardozo we need not extend the existing rules in order to protect society, but are only required to follow the law as set forth in the case of *Payne*. This we do and accordingly direct that the order of the trial court of Will County arresting the judgment of murder as to the defendants in this case be reversed and that further this case is remanded for sentencing of the defendants for the crime of murder.

Reversed and remanded.

Reflections on Felony-Murder

GEORGE P. FLETCHER

Of all the reforms proposed by the Model Penal Code, perhaps none has been less influential than the Model Code's recommendation on the perennial problem of felony-murder.[1] As found in our nineteenth-century criminal codes, the rule has several variations. The basic scheme is to hold the accused liable for murder if the killing is connected in any way with the attempt to commit a felony or the flight from the scene of a felony. It does not matter whether the accused or an accomplice causes the death. Nor does it matter whether the killing occurs accidentally and non-negligently. According to one popular rationalization, the felon's intent in committing the felony attaches, fictitiously, to the killing and somehow becomes transformed into the malice aforethought required for murder.[2]

The drafters of the Model Penal Code attempted to crack this fictitious connection between the culpability of committing an ordinary felony and the culpability required for the most egregious felony of murder. The Code stands for the principle that the minimal culpability required for murder is greater even than reckless killing. The killing must be not only reckless, but, in addition, committed under circumstances "manifesting extreme indifference to the value of human life."[3] The Code recognizes that the prosecution might prove this required degree of recklessness by showing that the killing occurred in the course of a felony especially dangerous to human life.[4] There is no doubt that many killings committed in the course of robbery, rape, arson, or burglary are reckless, and indeed they might be committed under circumstances manifesting extreme indifference to the value of human life. But that is surely not the case with all killings that occur in the course of these felonies. Suppose that an arsonist carefully checks

the premises for signs of human life before setting fire, yet as the blaze erupts, an independently motivated burglar breaks into the house and perishes. One would be hard-pressed to regard the arsonist as having acted recklessly toward the unexpected burglar. Or suppose that an unarmed burglar encounters an occupant with a weak heart; though the burglar attempts to calm the occupant, the latter dies of shock. It is obvious that in some cases a felon might be reckless in taking the risk of homicide; but in other cases he might be free from significant fault in bringing on the death. The Model Penal Code suggests that killing in the course of a dangerous felony should be merely presumptive of the culpability required for homicide.[5] The point is that the presumption does not always hold, and when it does not, there is no reason to regard a killing in the course of a felony as different from other killings.

As a general matter, the Model Penal Code has stimulated an extraordinary level of legislative activity. In the last two decades thirty-four states have adopted at least some portion of the recommendations embodied in the Model Code. The most popular provisions are those defining the four kinds of culpability, those on lesser evils, insanity, duress, and, of course, the provision that adorns any criminal code: the requirement of a voluntary act. And the least popular recommendation: the proposed revision of the felony-murder rule.

Not a single state has adopted the Model Penal Code's proposed reformulation of the felony-murder rule. This is not to say that all the reformed statutes retain the felony-murder rule. A few states have redefined murder to require proof of culpability in the particular case. Alaska, Hawaii, and Kentucky all insist upon an intentional or knowing killing. Several states use a restricted version of the felony-murder rule in defining aggravating circumstances justifying the death penalty. By and large, however, the states that have reformed their criminal codes since 1960 have, first, ignored the recommendation of the Model Penal Code and, second, retained the felony-murder rule as a

From *Southwestern University Law Review*, Vol. 12 (1980), pp. 413–429. Reprinted with permission of the *Southwestern University Law Review*.

criterion of liability for the highest degree of criminal homicide.

The concern of this article is to probe the legislative romance with the felony-murder rule. Only a few jurisdictions in the Western world rely on this heavy-handed approximation of malice in killing. No evidence of the rule has been found in French or German law.[6] In 1957 England abolished the felony-murder rule and all forms of constructive or fictitious malice.[7] The English had never incorporated the rule in legislation, and indeed their common law never carried the notion of fictitious malice to the extent now legislatively recognized in the United States.

The precise problem with the felony-murder rule is that it represents a formal approximation of extremely reckless homicide. No one quarrels with imposing severe punishment on those who, for criminal purposes, generate a high risk of homicide. The problem derives from regarding the commission of the felony as conclusive on the question whether the defendant acted recklessly toward the victim. So far as the test is formal, the jury does not inquire whether in fact the defendant took an excessive risk of killing another; the inquiry falls rather on whether the defendant committed the underlying felony. If so, the only relevant question is whether the death occurred in the course of perpetrating, attempting to perpetrate, or escaping from the scene of the felony.

The intrinsic injustice of formal tests of liability becomes clear in cases like *People v. Fuller,*[8] a 1978 decision by a California court of appeal. At 8:30 A.M. on a Sunday morning in Fresno, a patrolling police officer saw two men rolling two tires each toward a parked Plymouth. The officer made a U-turn; the two suspects apparently noticed the police car, dropped the tires, got into the Plymouth and attempted to elude the pursuing officer. In the resulting chase, the driver of the Plymouth ran a red light and crashed into another car, killing the other driver. As it happened, the two men had stolen the tires from inside four unoccupied Dodge vans.

What crimes did the escaping suspects commit? They were presumably guilty of theft, either grand or petty, depending on the value of the tires. The driver of the Plymouth was presumably guilty of vehicular homicide; absent a conspiracy to run the red light, it would be difficult to hold the second defendant, who merely was a passenger in the car, to a charge of criminal homicide. This is the outcome of the case that one would expect in most jurisdictions, and it is the outcome that we could have expected under the California criminal code as it was enacted in 1872.

Yet in California—and several other states—a curious thing has happened to the crime of burglary. The common law crime of burglary required a nighttime breaking and entering of a dwelling house. This was the dangerous felony to which the California felony-murder rule was originally hitched. Law reformers in this century, however, have relentlessly expanded the contours of burglary, first by dropping the requirement of a breaking, then by including daytime as well as nighttime entries, and finally, in California, by expanding the "buildings" that can be burglarized to include motor vehicles with locked doors. Thus, it turns out, that if the two men entered the vans with the intent to take the tires, they were guilty of burglary. If they were fleeing the scene of burglary, the accident at the intersection became a killing in perpetration of the burglary and thus would support a charge of first-degree murder, not only against the driver but against the passenger as well.

With a little imagination, the court of appeal could have avoided this absurd result; it could have restricted felony-murder based on burglary to circumstances in which the commission of the particular burglary was dangerous to human life.[9] But the judges preferred instead to reason formalistically and to tie the issue of first-degree murder to the independent question whether entering the Dodge vans was burglary. Suppose the thieves had broken into the trunk of a car rather than the passenger compartment of a van. That probably would not have been burglary under the statute and there would have been no liability under the felony-murder rule. Distinctions as fragile as this one derive from losing sight of the relevant question in a prosecution for murder: what did the defendant do to endanger human life? A *formal* test for murder ignores the questions of actual risk and culpability and focuses instead on the commission of the underlying felony.

The taste for formal rules of first-degree murder has become an American idiosyncrasy. Our attachment to this heavy-handed doctrine resembles our attachment to the death penalty—an institution that separates us even more from other jurisdictions of the Western world. Those who complain about the peculiarly American devotion to the exclusionary rule should recall our penchant for felony-murder and the death penalty. We are severe not only toward constables who blunder, but toward felons who blunder and accidentally cause the deaths of others.

There is no doubt that law enforcement has much to gain both from the threat of the death penalty and from expansive tests of first-degree murder. These tough rules at the top of the scale bludgeon defendants into pleading to lesser charges. Also, in California at least, felony-murder has become the sole category of murder insulated from claims of diminished capacity. Because law enforcement has much to gain from retaining this joker in its hand, we should not be surprised by efforts to keep the rule as broad as possible. In the *Fuller* case, for example, a trial judge had decided that the automobile accident would not support an information for murder; the prosecution won on appeal. It would be naive to expect law enforcement to welcome anything less than the most expansive possible reading of the felony-murder rule.

What is surprising, however, is that neither state legislatures nor the courts have sought to bring the felony-murder rule into line with well-accepted criteria of individual accountability and proportionate punishment. The legislative romance with felony-murder takes many forms. Some states go so far as to recognize any felony as sufficient to classify a related killing as murder; others restrict the relevant felonies to those that, in the abstract, are "forcible" or "clearly dangerous to human life." The most restrictive mode, one that dates back to the nineteenth-century codes, is simply to specify the felonies that are formally conclusive on the issue of malice. Of the thirty-four codes revised in the last two decades, eighteen rely on this technique. Of course, the list of dangerous felonies varies. Some states include deviant sexual conduct, felonious escape, or kidnapping; others make do with the core felonies of rape, robbery, arson, and, alas, burglary.

The only new legislative technique to enter the ring in this round of law reform is New York's effort in 1965 to curtail the liability of accomplices. Recall that our passenger in the car running the red light would be guilty of first-degree murder. Every conspirator is liable for the substantive crimes, even the unexpected crimes, of his partners. This arbitrary rule derives from the fiction that the conspirators support each other's acts and, therefore, become complicitous in each other's substantive crimes. Yet killings and deaths sometimes occur without any contribution by co-conspirators; the arbitrariness of vicarious liability must give pause to even the most sanguinary advocate of law enforcement. The New York legislature sought to avoid extreme cases of injustice by defining a complicated four-part defense, which has since gained adoption in at least a half-dozen states.

To see how this affirmative defense works, let us analyze the case of the passenger in the *Fuller* case. The driver, as noted, is guilty of first-degree murder. Though an accomplice in the burglary, the passenger will not be liable if the following four conditions are satisfied:

1. He has neither committed the homicidal act nor aided its commission in any way. Unless he urged the driver to go through the red light, it would be hard to classify the passenger's sitting in the car as "aiding" in the homicidal act.

2. He is not armed with a deadly weapon. Let us suppose that the passenger did not have a gun on him. The problem in this case, however, is that the car itself is a deadly weapon. Is riding in the car tantamount to being armed with the weapon? Let us assume that this fanciful argument would not disqualify our passenger.

3. The accomplice has no reasonable ground to believe that the perpetrator was armed with a deadly weapon. This condition would give us difficulty. If the car constitutes such a weapon, our passenger loses the benefit of the affirmative defense.

4. The accomplice has no reasonable ground to believe the perpetrator would intentionally engage in dangerous conduct, in this case, to run the red light. This fourth condition poses a difficult hurdle, for our passenger presumably had grounds to believe the driver would run a traffic light if necessary to elude the police car.

This examination of the affirmative defense reveals how difficult it would be to find a set of facts that qualified an accomplice for exclusion. Nonetheless, the recognition of this affirmative defense has important symbolic value. The negative implication of the exclusion is that, in principle, co-conspirators should be judged only on their own culpability and their contribution to the homicidal act. This exclusion should be seen as but the beginning of law reform, a wedge against injustice that highlights the arbitrariness of punishing accomplices who fall just short of the legislative standard.

If this is all that legislative reform has accomplished in thirty-four states, perhaps we might expect more of the courts—those agents of the law that are thought to be sympathetic to criminal defendants.[10] Unfortunately, the courts have done very little[11] to bring us into line with the principles of homicide liability that prevail in the rest of the world.

It is true that the 1960s witnessed a sustained and sometimes successful attack on some excesses of the felony-murder rule. The leading cases—largely from Pennsylvania and California—raised the hopes of those seeking to refine the substantive criminal law. Yet these monuments of legal reasoning—*Redline*,[12] *Washington*,[13] *Phillips*,[14] *Satchell*,[15] and others—hardly speak to current issues in felony-murder. They all responded to particular excesses with respect to the felony-murder rule. . . .

In fact, the historical roots of felony-murder are tenuous and ill defined. The sources of the rule are not judicial decisions but scholarly commentaries. The earlier commentators, Coke and Hale, stressed the role of the unlawful act as a rejoinder to a defense of *per infortunium*. It was only with the eighteenth century commentators, Hawkins and Foster, that the argument shifted to the positive thesis that a felonious intent renders an incidental killing murder.

These commentators cast the felony-murder rule as an abstract generalization. They tell us little about the particular felonies that support the rule.

. . .

There is yet another approach to the felony-murder rule, which, if valid, would justify full enforcement. In this alternative conception the principle of felony-murder reflects two unrefined ways of thinking about criminal responsibility. One mode of thought stresses the taint that inheres in causing death, whether the homicide is culpable or not. The second mode of thought takes the preliminary act of wrongdoing, the felony, as a rationale for holding the felon accountable for the deadly consequences of his actions. Both of these modes of thought require explication and criticism, for

they both enjoy far more influence than they deserve.

The principle of tainting dates back to the origins of prosecution for criminal homicide. In thirteenth-century England, the assumption was that if one person caused the death of another, the killing itself upset the natural order; some response was necessary to expiate the killing and thus to expunge the taint.[16] As the Bible demands the sacrifice of a heifer in cases of homicides by unknown persons,[17] English law extracted two forfeitures in every case of manslaying. First, the instrument of death was forfeited to the Crown as deodand. Second, the killer forfeited his lands and his goods. These forfeitures applied in every case of unjustified killing. If, in addition, the killing occurred without excuse, that is absent the conditions of *se defendendo* and *per infortunium*, the slayer was subject to the death penalty for murder.

The model of taint and expiation haunts the way our courts think about criminal homicide. The felon must answer for a human death for no reason other than that he or his accomplice causes it. The felon is tainted by causing and the state responds by seeking expiation. It is important to distinguish expiating the taint of killing from justly punishing for faultfully causing death. The taint arises regardless of fault or blame; punishment is just only so far as it is proportional to fault. The notion of expiating a taint reflects a conception of the world that, if brought to consciousness, most lawyers would vehemently reject. Yet the notion of tainting might be one of the subconscious props for the contemporary persistence of the felony-murder rule.

The other unrefined mode of thought behind the rule begins not with the deadly outcome, but with the felonious background. That someone engages in a felony lowers the threshold of moral responsibility for the resulting death. If there is a principle behind this way of thinking, it is that a wrongdoer must run the risk that things will turn out worse than she expects.[18] The same principle has motivated common law courts and legislatures to reject the claim of mistake in cases of abducting infants,[19] statutory rape,[20] and assaulting a police officer. If the act is wrong, even as the defendant conceives the facts to be, then she presumably has no grounds for complaining if the facts turn out to be worse than she expects. In *United States v. Feola*,[21] defendant committed an assault against someone who turned out to be a police officer. He was convicted for assaulting a police officer, without regard to the reasonableness of his mistake. The United States Supreme Court upheld the conviction because "from the very outset . . . his planned course of conduct [was] wrongful." Therefore, the offender had to "take his victim as he [found] him." If wrongdoing justifies disregarding mistakes about aggravating circumstances, then felonious wrongdoing can justify disregarding whether the deadly outcome of the felony is accidental or culpable. . . .

These two modes of thought—the practice of tainting and the principle that the wrongdoer runs the risk—violate a basic principle of just punishment. Punishment must be proportional to wrongdoing. When the felony-murder rule converts an accidental death into first-degree murder, then punishment is rendered disproportionate to the wrong for which the offender is personally responsible. Tainting is no substitute for criteria of moral responsibility, and the principle that the wrongdoer must run the risk explicitly obscures the question of actual responsibility for the harmful result.

The theory of just punishment is called the retributive theory. Before we criticize retribution and the *lex talionis*[22] as outmoded, we should realize how much worse it is to make the punishment fit not the crime, but the result for which the offender is not personally to blame.

It may be that in the thinking of many people, the felony-murder rule finds its warrant in principles of deterrence as well as in the residual influence of early common law notions of taint and expiation. But of course, deterrence is not an apology for treating like cases differently; if there is no sound basis for distinguishing between thieves killing in an automobile accident and others doing so, then the remote possibility of deterring thieves from escaping the scene of the crime hardly justifies convicting Fuller of first-degree murder.

There may be an apology for the felony-murder rule, but it is one that could easily excuse too much injustice in our substantive criminal law. If we compare our combined system of substantive law and procedural rights with the total system that prevails in a Continental jurisdiction, say, in West Germany, we could hazard the following generalization. American law achieves a balance of advantage between defense and prosecution by bestowing extraordinary procedural protections on the accused and yet compensating the prosecution with rules of strict liability, felony-murder, conspiracy, and vicarious liability. German law, in contrast, offers fewer procedural protections—no jury, no exclusionary rule in our sense, fewer restrictions on hearsay evidence[23]—yet the German substantive law is more refined and more consistent with principles of individual responsibility.[24] This overall comparison between the two systems exceeds our present concerns. The point is simply that we should be more humble about the grandeur of American law. What the law of procedure grants the accused, the law of substance takes away. And if law enforcement in the United States fights to eliminate the fourth amendment exclusionary rule, then the defense should fight even harder to eliminate the unjust rules of vicarious liability and felony-murder.

Endnotes

[1] Model Penal Code § 210.2(1)(b) reads in pertinent part:

(1) Except as provided in Section 210.3(1)(b), criminal homicide constitutes murder when . . .

. . . .

(b) it is committed recklessly under circumstances manifesting extreme indifference to the value of human life. Such recklessness and indifference are presumed if the actor is engaged or is an accomplice in the commission of, or an attempt to commit, or flight after committing or attempting to commit, robbery, rape or deviate sexual intercourse by force or threat of force, arson, burglary, kidnapping or felonious escape.

[2] M. Foster, A Report of Some Proceedings of the Commissioner for the Trial of the Rebels in the Year 1746 in the County of Surrey and of Other Crown Cases 259 (1762).

[3] Model Penal Code § 210.2(1)(b).

[4] *Id.* (robbery, rape, deviate sexual intercourse by force or threat of force, arson, burglary, kidnapping, or felonious escape.)

[5] *Id.*

[6] For a survey of the French, German, and Soviet laws of homicide, see G. Fletcher, Rethinking Criminal Law 321–40 (1978) [hereinafter cited as Fletcher].

[7] English Homicide Act of 1957, ch. 11, § 1.

[8] 86 Cal. App. 3d 618, 150 Cal. Rptr. 515 (1978).

[9] *Cf.* People v. Nichols, 3 Cal. 3d 150, 474 P.2d 673, 89 Cal. Rptr. 721 (1970), which limits felony-murder based on arson to cases in which the defendant intentionally set the fire causing the death.

[10] The supposed sympathy of American courts to criminal defendants is limited to procedural protections such as the exclusionary rule, restrictions on station-house interrogation, and the right to counsel. . . .

[11] Shortly after the delivery of this lecture, the Michigan Supreme Court held in People v. Aaron, 409 Mich. 672, 299 N.W.2d 304 (1980), that the intent to commit a felony other than homicide is no longer sufficient to establish the malice required for murder. This decision may have a far-reaching impact.

[12] Commonwealth v. Redline, 391 Pa. 486, 137 A.2d 472 (1958).

[13] People v. Washington, 62 Cal. 2d 777, 402 P.2d 130, 44 Cal. Rptr. 442 (1965).

[14] People v. Phillips, 64 Cal. 2d 574, 414 P.2d 353, 51 Cal. Rptr. 225 (1966).

[15] People v. Satchell, 6 Cal. 3d 28, 489 P.2d 1361, 98 Cal. Rptr. 33 (1971).

[16] For a more general account of this development, see Fletcher, *supra* note 6, at 344–47.

[17] *Deuteronomy* 21:1–9.

[18] For a further development of this issue, *see generally* Fletcher, *supra* note 6.

[19] Regina v. Prince, L.R., 2 Cr. Cas. Res. 154 (1875).

[20] *See, e.g.*, Conn. Gen. Stat. Ann. § 53a–67 (West Supp. 1981); La. Rev. Stat. Ann. § 14:80 (West Supp. 1981); N.Y. Penal Law §§ 15.20(3), 130.25(2) (McKinney 1975).

[21] 420 U.S. 671 (1975).

[22] *Exodus* 21:23–25 (an eye for an eye).

[23] *See generally* J. Langhein, Comparative Criminal Procedure: Germany (1977).

[24] See Fletcher, *supra* note 6, at 736–58 (German approach to mistake of law), 818–29 (German theory of necessity as an excuse).

Strict Liability: An Unorthodox View

MARK KELMAN

What Is Strict Liability?

One cannot understand what strict liability in the criminal law means—much less understand why it is so generally considered anomalous and morally objectionable by the commentators—without first considering how a defendant's blameworthiness, or mental fault (mens rea), is usually assessed and, more particularly, the usual relevance of a defendant's mistakes in determining blameworthiness.

It is perhaps easiest to understand the criminal law's scheme if one focuses on an example where the law is not implicated at all: a child admits to his parents that he has hurt his younger sister, fully aware that hurting her is precisely the sort of untoward result that the parents would want him to avoid. In their blaming and punishing practices, most parents would differentiate between situations in which the child truthfully informed them: (1) "I hit her on purpose, in order to harm her"; (2) "I took actions that I knew would harm her although that was not my aim"; (3) "I was reckless as to whether she would be harmed; that is, I was subjectively aware that I was taking high risks that she would be hurt without any corresponding benefits to my activity"; (4) "I was not subjectively aware that I was risking harm, but a reasonably prudent person would not have acted as I did, not have acted with a negligent disregard for the risk of harm"; and (5) "Although I know I caused harm, I neither did it on purpose nor knew it would happen, nor was I aware of a risk it would happen; moreover, the ordinary reasonable person would not have been aware of the risk either."

Essentially, courts or legislatures must decide, in each instance, whether it is a sufficient excuse for a defendant to argue, as to each element of his

5 types of hitting your sister

offense, "I did not act intentionally" (that is, with purpose or knowledge), "I did not act recklessly," or "I was not negligent." Where the legal system deems it insufficient to exculpate the defendant on the ground that he was neither intentional, reckless, nor negligent in causing a particular aspect of the proscribed harm, the defendant is said to be strictly liable as to a particular element of an offense.

The excuses that defendants offer can invariably be described in terms of mistaken perceptions. A statute proscribes the sale of adulterated milk; the defendant admits that he sold milk which was in fact adulterated. As to one element of the offense—an element that will rarely be contested, that is, whether or not he sold the milk—he admits that he acted with purpose. But as to the generally crucial and controversial element of the offense—whether the milk was adulterated or not—he could claim that he mistakenly believed the milk was wholesome. Even if fact finders accept that the defendant genuinely did mistakenly believe the milk was unadulterated, the defendant would not necessarily be exculpated. Even if the crime requires recklessness as to this element, the defendant would be convicted if he had been subjectively aware of an unreasonable risk that the milk was adulterated. If the defendant need only be negligent as to this element, conviction would be easier: if the reasonably prudent milk seller had been aware of the unreasonable risk that the milk was adulterated, it would not help the defendant to have been subjectively unaware of this risk. Finally, if the statute is construed as a strict-liability statute (in the sense that with regard to the element of the offense in which mistakes are generally pleaded, even a reasonable mistake will not be forgiven), the mistake would simply be irrelevant.

The Historical and Modern Operation of Strict Liability

The maxim "actus non facit neum nisi mens sit rea" (a harmful act without a blameworthy mental state is not punishable) dates back to 1641 (Coke, p. 107). There have long been pockets in the criminal law, however, where the defendant has not been allowed to excuse his harmful behavior by pointing to the fact that if the circumstances were actually

those that he reasonably but mistakenly believed were present, he would not have violated criminal sanctions in taking the steps he took. Most prominently, in "morals crimes" that predate the regulatory state (bigamy, adultery, and statutory rape), and in the felony-murder area, the fact that an offense was not committed intentionally, recklessly, or negligently has traditionally not been a defense (*Commonwealth v. Mash*, 48 Mass. (7 Met.) 472 (1844) (holding that a person can be convicted of bigamy although he reasonably but mistakenly believes his first wife to be dead); cf. *Regina v. Tolson*, 23 Q.B.D 168 (1889) and *Commonwealth v. Elwell*, 43 Mass. (2 Met.) 190 (1840) (defendant can be convicted of adultery although he might reasonably believe he is having sexual relations with an unmarried woman)).

To some extent, however, a modern reader of these early strict-liability cases is likely to find them somewhat ambiguous. Most nineteenth-century judges seemed to believe that if mens rea, or blameworthiness, is requisite, the defendant must be subjectively aware of wrongdoing. Thus, the significant line for these judges was between blameworthy subjectively grounded liability (what in the late twentieth century would be called intention combined with recklessness) and faultless objectively grounded liability (what in the late twentieth century would be called strict liability *combined with* negligence, where a subjectively unaware defendant is held to the standards of a reasonable person). Today, the law is far more prone to view the relevant line between fault and blamelessness as that between liability grounded in the defendant's deviance from the behavior of a normal blameless citizen (intentional wrongdoing, recklessness, or abnormal inattention or inadvertence, represented by the sort of gross negligence required for criminal liability) and liability that will be imposed even on the defendant who behaves reasonably, like the average person (strict liability). Nonetheless, most modern practitioners and theorists tend to interpret these early cases as upholding strict liability and, as a practical matter, a court would almost certainly feel constrained to overrule the older cases to justify excusing someone who made a non-negligent mistake.

In the felony-murder area, the most significant pocket of strict liability, a defendant who kills another person during the perpetration of a felony may be punished as severely as an intentional killer, even if the killing was not negligent (*People v.*

Stamp, 2 Cal. App. 3d 203 . . . (1969) (although the victim dies of an unforeseeable heart attack during the course of an armed robbery, no finding need be made that the defendant should have been aware of that risk of death)). The fact that a felon is strictly liable for a death once he is committing one of a large number of statutorily enumerated or judicially described "dangerous" felonies is certainly controversial, but it has long been the law in most jurisdictions.

Generally, however, when commentators focus on strict-liability offenses, they are concerned not with moral crimes or felony-murder but with the public welfare or regulatory offenses that grew up in England and America with industrialization. Justice Robert Jackson described the trend toward strict criminal liability in his well-known opinion in *Morissette v. United States*, 342 U.S. 246, 253–256 (1952):

> The industrial revolution multiplied the number of workmen exposed to injury from increasingly powerful . . . mechanisms. . . . Traffic . . . came to subject the wayfarer to intolerable casualty risks if owners and drivers were not to observe new cares and uniformities of conduct. Congestion of cities . . . called for health and welfare regulations undreamed of in simpler times. Wide distribution of goods became an instrument of wide distribution of harm. . . . Such dangers have engendered . . . detailed regulations which heighten the duties of those in control of particular industries, trades, properties, or activities that affect public health, safety, or welfare. . . .
>
> While such offenses do not threaten the security of the state in the manner of treason, they may be regarded as offenses against its authority, for their occurrence impairs the efficiency of controls deemed essential to the social order as presently constituted. In this respect, whatever the intent of the violator, the injury is the same. . . . Hence, legislation applicable to such offenses does not specify intent as a necessary element.

Viewing the mens rea requirement as depending entirely upon what the legislature intended, courts have tended to interpret public welfare offenses as implying strict liability—at least so long as penalties for violation are mild, the legislative history and language of the statute imply an intention to dispense with traditional fault categories, and the harm to the public done by the action is relatively severe (*United States v. Balint*, 258 U.S. 250 (1922); *United States v. Dotterweich*, 320 U.S. 277 (1943)).

The Traditional Critique of Strict Liability

Although the courts have been relatively free in interpreting these sorts of legislative enactments as implying strict liability, the commentators have been remarkably uniform in attacking the propriety, and sometimes even the constitutionality, of imposing imprisonment rather than fines, when the defendant is not at least negligent. The Model Penal Code expresses this consensus position: its Section 2.05 mandates that only "violations" can be interpreted as strict-liability offenses. Violations can be punished only by a fine, forfeiture, or other civil penalty, and none of the disabilities based on conviction of a criminal offense can follow from conviction of a violation.

The arguments against punishing persons who have not at least made unreasonable mistakes about the circumstances in which they have acted harmfully fall into two broad classes: those believed to flow from theories of just punishment, and those believed to flow more directly from ideals of fairness.

Most commentators on the criminal law justify the infliction of punishment either because of its deterrent effect, or because of the need to exact retribution. Strict retributionists believe that the criminal deserves punishment because of his proved immoral conduct, regardless of the impact of punishment on his own or others' future conduct. Strict utilitarian-deterrence theorists believe that the criminal should be punished so as to diminish the number of future criminal acts, because each of these acts would be perceived as more costly by the criminal himself and other would-be criminals if punishment is imposed. Many commentators are utilitarians in terms of general justifying aim, but retributionists in terms of punishment distribution: they believe that the general justification of the social practice of punishment is to reduce the number of harmful incidents, but they also believe that it is inappropriate to punish a particular person, even if that would serve to reduce the number of crimes, unless he is blameworthy.

The strict retributionists and the distributive retributionists claim that punishing someone who has not intentionally, recklessly, or negligently caused the sorts of harms that are proscribed is unjust. Harm-causing conduct is generally an index of a morally flawed character, but when that conduct is accidental and when the actor neither was nor should have been aware that he was inflicting socially proscribed results, there is no reason to believe that he is anything worse than unlucky, and no reason to single him out for disapproval. (A fourth strand of theorists, the incapacitationists, stress only the need to isolate dangerous persons from nonimprisoned potential victims. They may oppose strict-liability crimes for the parallel reason that there is no particular reason to think that the non-negligent actor is especially prone to be dangerous in the future just because he has inflicted harm.)

Many deterrence-oriented theorists believe that it is inefficacious to punish people unless they are subjectively aware that they are causing harm, that is, unless they act intentionally or recklessly, since in the absence of such subjective awareness it is difficult to argue that someone can decide not to harm after weighing the benefits of causing harm against the costs the state will impose. But at least in the case of negligence-based liability, some deterrence-oriented theorists sense that whereas an actor may be unaware of the risks he poses at the moment he is causing harm, the imposition of liability will generally tend to make people more attentive and less prone to be unaware. In the case of strict-liability offenses, the argument is often made that the defendant is already behaving as well as can be expected and cannot be induced to be more careful.

The final argument slides into a conceptually separable fairness argument against the imposition of strict liability, an argument that is blatantly unfair—a sort of Kafkaesque nightmare—to punish people who have done all we would expect to avoid criminality, but who simply happen to cause harm. H. L. A. Hart's words are typical:

The reason why . . . strict liability is odious . . . is that those whom we punish should have had, when they acted, the normal capacities . . . for doing what the law requires and abstaining from what it forbids. . . . The moral protest is that it is morally wrong to punish because "he could not have helped it" or "he could not have done otherwise" or "he had no real choice" [*Punishment and Responsibility* (Oxford: Clarendon Press, 1968, p. 152)].

The vision of punishing a hapless, choiceless defendant is perhaps the most powerful buttress of the argument against strict liability.

Arguments for Strict Liability

Arguments made by judges. Generally speaking, the explicit arguments made by judges interpreting statutes as imposing strict liability are rather weak, far weaker than they need be.

Often, the judges implicitly acknowledge the critics' contention that the imposition of strict liability is obviously unjust, but they stress that the legislature was centrally interested in eradicating a certain harm and had chosen to err on the side of injustice to the individual. For example, in *Balint*, Chief Justice William Howard Taft wrote that "Congress weighed the possible injustice of subjecting an innocent seller [of opium] to a penalty against the evil of exposing innocent purchasers to danger from the drug, and concluded that the latter was the result preferably to be avoided" (254). This argument seems puzzlingly incomplete, however: if the deterrence-oriented critics of strict liability are right in asserting that punishing the non-negligent will not effectively reduce the incidence of harm, then one is violating one's principles against punishing the innocent without gaining corresponding benefits.

A better argument made by judges is that the imposition of strict liability is justified on the ground that proof of states of mind is administratively burdensome. Judge Oliver Wendell Holmes, in *Commonwealth v. Smith*, . . . 44 N.E. 503, 504 (1896), noted that it may be reasonable for the legislature conclusively to presume malice when harm is caused, because "actual knowledge [is] a matter difficult to prove."

Finally, judges often argue that the strictly liable defendant, although unaware that the conduct he is engaging in violates the explicit prohibitory norm that the legislature has announced, is perfectly aware of violating more general moral norms which are not specifically legally proscribed. Thus, for example, the strictly liable statutory rapist may not have reason to be aware that he is having sexual relations with a girl below the age of consent, but he is aware that he is engaged in the morally, if not legally, condemned act of fornication with a young person. Once the defendant engages in immoral activity, so the argument goes, he cannot justly complain if the activity turns out to be illegal as well (*Regina v. Prince*, L.R. 2 Cr. Cas. Res. 154 (1875)).

Generally speaking, the dominant view in the Anglo-American legal culture is that it is arbitrary and unreasonable to punish the person who is unlucky enough to have in fact had intercourse with an underage girl when one does not punish those who have intercourse with girls who seem no older. Similarly, most commentators believe there are "legal process" reasons to avoid the imposition of strict liability in these circumstances: if the legislature views sexual relations with overage girls as illicit, the court should force it to outlaw such relations explicitly, and not just to make them risky, so that opponents of such morals legislation will have the opportunity to address their concerns squarely.

On the other hand, proponents of the claim that even a reasonable mistake as to the victim's age is no defense could make the following argument: if the legislature were unconstrained by the difficulties of administering vague standards, the statutory rape law it would enact would state, in effect, "Don't have intercourse with innocent girls." Because it is feared that there is inadequate social consensus on how to apply the descriptive term *innocent* to particular cases, the legislature selects an exact age of consent and avoids inconsistant or prejudicial jury verdicts and excessive prosecutorial discretion. Some men may be lucky enough to escape prosecution because the innocent girls they have sexual relations with happen to be overage according to the administrable rule. They are beneficiaries of our desire to restrain arbitrary, biased, and excessive state power, as are the beneficiaries of evidentiary exclusionary rules, who may be acquitted although guilty of an offense because society wants to deter the police from gathering evidence in a fashion that is generally abusive of private rights. But there is no necessary reason to acquit the defendant who in fact cause. the legislatively proscribed harm and can be convicted without excessive state discretion.

Some alternative arguments for strict liability. A strong case could be made that proponents of strict liability have far too readily conceded the anomaly of strict criminal liability. In essence, the key to seeing strict liability as less deviant in the criminal justice system is to dissipate the powerful metaphoric picture of the defendant as "hapless victim" and to see the real policy fight as a rather balanced one over the relative merits and demerits of precise rules (conclusive presumptions) and vague, ad hoc standards (case-by-case determinations of negligence).

H. L. A. Hart's argument that the defendant convicted of a strict-liability offense "could not have helped" committing the crime depends on the use of a rationally indefensible narrow time frame in focusing on the defendant's conduct. *Whenever* one thinks about criminality, one has available narrow time-frame interpretations of the relevant data—in which one learns all one can about the appropriateness of punishment by looking at some alleged criminal *incident*. One also has available broader time frames in which one incorporates data about the defendant's general personal history (as in the insanity defense), the "history" of the incident (as in the defenses of duress, entrapment, and provocation), or the defendant's conduct subsequent to the incident (as in the defense of abandonment of an attempt). It may well be the case that if one looks only at the precise *moment* at which harm is consummated, the strictly liable actor may seem powerless to avoid criminality, but it is invariably the case that the actor could have avoided liability by taking earlier steps which were hardly impossible. Chief Justice Warren Burger made precisely this point in upholding a strict-liability interpretation of statutes proscribing the shipment of adulterated drugs, on the ground that the parties who were held strictly accountable could refuse to take "responsible" managerial positions if they were afraid they would not be able to prevent violations.

> *Dotterweich* and the cases which have followed reveal that in providing sanctions which reach and touch the individuals who execute the corporate mission . . . the Act imposes not only a positive duty to seek out and remedy violations when they occur

[handwritten margin notes: "moral issues"; "statutory rape"; "innocent under age"; "Exclusionary rule"; "time frame"; "adulterated drugs Ex."]

but also, and primarily, a duty to implement measures that will insure violations will not occur. The requirements of foresight and vigilance imposed on responsible corporate agents are beyond question demanding, and perhaps onerous, *but they are no more stringent than the public has the right to expect of those who voluntarily assume positions of authority* in business enterprises whose services and products affect the health and well-being of the public that supports them [*United States v. Park*, 421 U.S. 658, 672–673 (1975)].

It is significant to note that only by constructing the underlying material in the strict-liability situations with a very narrow time frame that the distinction between liability predicated on negligence, and strict liability, maintains its practical import in many critical situations.

An example is the familiar problem of "reasonable" (non-negligent) mistakes as to the victim's age in the statutory rape setting. Is one's view of a "reasonable" belief to be ascertained solely by reference to perceptions available to the defendant during the purportedly illegal seduction (she "*looked*" sixteen or "she told me she was sixteen"), or does one require that some checks prior to seduction be taken, such as checking birth certificates or asking parents? Of course, if one is hostile to statutory rape laws in general, it is perfectly reasonable to negate them by defining negligent perceptions in terms of the girl's physical appearance—that is, in terms of judgments which can be made at the narrow time-framed moment of the allegedly criminal incident. But it is hardly conceivable that a defendant ought to attract serious sympathy as someone unable to avoid crime when he has certainly had the opportunity to check on the legal appropriateness of his companion as an object of sexual desire.

If one really cared about using statutory rape laws to protect the chastity of the young, one would have to insist that people take steps to avoid mistakes of age, not simply that they refrain from sexual relations once they believe or know that the girl is underage. It is difficult to imagine that a strict-liability interpretation ensnares many defendants who have taken extensive steps to avoid mistakes: for example, in *People v. Hernandez*, . . . 393 P.2d 673 (1964), the much-heralded California case overturning the imposition of strict liability as to

the victim's age in the statutory rape context, the defendant had known the prosecutrix for several months before they had sexual relations, but the court chose to focus instead on how mature the prosecutrix appeared.

Once one dissipates the opponent's rhetorical move—the image of the hopelessly ensnared, powerless victim of state power—one can come to see the proper debate in the area rather differently than it has been seen. As a "policy" matter, the legislative decision whether to condemn a defendant only where negligence is shown, or to condemn wherever harm is caused, is nothing more than the outcome of a perfectly traditional balance of interests between strict, easily applied rules and vaguer, ad hoc standards.

If the legislature enacts a negligence standard so that, for example, a manufacturer is liable for shipping adulterated food only if he acted unreasonably, or a liquor license holder is liable for selling to underage customers only if he screened customers unreasonably, two rather poor, although different, sets of bad consequences can result. If the negligence standard is defined vaguely, so that each jury is simply instructed to determine whether the particular defendant was reasonable, jury verdicts will be inconsistent, unpredictable, and biased. Moreover, if the particular jury equates reasonable behavior with ordinary behavior, an entire industry may free itself of responsibility by uniformly acting less carefully than the legislature would like.

On the other hand, the legislature (or a court or administrative body "interpreting" the legislature) might *predefine* what constitutes "reasonable care," setting out a precise series of steps that the defendant must take to be found non-negligent. The problem, of course, is that this centralized command may be imperfectly tuned to the precise circumstances of each potential defendant. The defendant might know a cheaper, more effective way of averting harm. But, of course, it may be in the defendant's selfish interest to adopt the preordained non-negligent technique, even if it will cause more harm.

For example, if a liquor license holder faces a $100 fine for each violation of the sale-to-minors proscription, under strict liability he would adopt the system best suited to his particular circumstances (System A), which costs $400 to implement and which would result in five violations. (The net private *and* social cost is $900.) In a regime of negligence, however, he might adopt instead the system the legislature has preordained as non-negligent (System B), although it costs $600 to implement and will result in ten violations. If it is assumed that he is certain he will be found non-negligent using System B and that he is fairly certain that his System A (although in fact better in his circumstances at avoiding the socially feared result) will be judged negligent by juries, given a preordained description of reasonable care, then he will adopt B. Although B's social cost is $1,600 rather than $900, B's private cost will be only $600, whereas System A will cost him $900. (Nothing here turns on the cost being one of fines: if, for example, a person were jailed whenever he had violated the "no sales" act more than five times, the defendant in a negligence system would adopt the high-harm but no-violation preordained non-negligent system, although it was both more costly and harmful.)

Switching to strict liability—essentially making a conclusive presumption that causing harm is blameworthy—has its costs, too, which "policy" analysts would readily note. Like all conclusive presumptions, it is bound to be inaccurate in particular situations: there will doubtless be cases where someone is blamed who, on closer analysis, society would not have wanted to blame. But that is true in the "rule-like" form of negligence too, where society demands that actors take predefined steps even though others who take different steps may have behaved at least as carefully.

It is possible that someone might be condemned simply because he failed to take the steps he had been ordered to take. But it is to be suspected that few would feel comfortable in condemning someone who could honestly claim that he so strongly shared the legislative goal of minimizing the incidence of some proscribed harm, such as sales of liquor to minors, that he had taken steps which were designed to, and in fact did, lower the incidence of that harm. Not only will the "rule-like" form of negligence be unjust when it occasionally condemns these especially good citizens, but even worse, it may frequently induce socially irrational behavior. The standard-like form of negligence should also, according to the prevailing supposition about vague statutes, convict some innocents too, but it may convict innocents for *bad* reasons (such as the race prejudice of juries) rather than for *no* reasons, that is, the accidental overinclusiveness of the conclusive presumption.

Conclusion

The uniformity of commentators' opposition to imprisoning persons whom fact finders, focusing on their particular cases and unaided by presumptions, have not explicitly found negligent, reckless, or intentional makes it seem at least plausible that strict liability will disappear as a significant criminal law category. For the time being, however, defendants remain unable to plead their mistakes in public welfare offenses and a number of traditional morals crimes.

The uniformity of commentators' hostility results less from reasoned consideration of the actual issues than from a misleading rhetorical ploy which implies that the strictly liable defendant was unable to avoid criminality, and from a failure to take account of perfectly standard liberal legalist arguments against ad hoc standards. The root of this blindness to the case for strict liability is most likely the desire to reassure oneself that only the blameworthy are punished; obviously, the most significant attack on the claim that society is punishing only the wicked comes from general determinists who see criminality as grounded in adverse socioeconomic conditions. One way of blocking out the degree to which we are all more or less drawn to the determinists' position is to show how ultrasensitive we are to punishing the blameless, without paying much heed to how blamelessness is defined. The ritual attack on strict-liability crime, then, is largely an exercise in mutual flattery of our moral solemnity and deflects attention from the serious charges of moral inadequacy.

Study Questions

1. Supreme Court Justice Frank Murphy, dissenting in a case holding the president of a drug company strictly liable for some mislabeling infractions said: "It is a fundamental principle of Anglo-Saxon jurisprudence that guilt is personal and that it ought not lightly to be imputed to a citizen who, like the respondent, has no evil intention or consciousness of wrongdoing . . . [I]t is inconsistent with established canons of criminal law to rest liability on an act in which the accused did not participate and of which he had no personal knowledge"

(*U.S. v. Dotterweich* 320 U.S. 277 [1943]). Do you agree with Murphy? Why or why not?

2. Various commentators have condemned the felony-murder rule as "barbaric," "primitive,"

"unenlightened and uncivilized." Do you agree with Fletcher that the felony-murder rule is very likely morally indefensible?

C. *Insanity and Excuse*

Introduction

In everyday life, most of us are willing to excuse a friend who arrives late for an important meeting or a student who turns in a late paper, but only of course if the excuse is reasonable under the circumstances (the teacher gets to decide what's reasonable!). The law is willing to listen to excuses too.

Suppose that I am charged with the robbery of an elderly man in a city park. It would be a recognized defense or legitimate excuse under the law to such a charge that: I was *entrapped* into committing the crime, a police officer having planted the idea of it in my mind, an idea to which I was not otherwise predisposed; I was *coerced* into the robbery through a threat of death or serious bodily harm; I was a *minor* under the age of seven. In *Richardson v. U.S.*,[1] the defendant was charged with robbery for having stopped a man named Snowden and removed $98 from his (Snowden's) wallet. On appeal from his conviction, Richardson said that Snowden owed him (Richardson) a long-standing gambling debt, amounting to $270, which Richardson had been seeking to collect for some time. Richardson's conviction was reversed on the grounds that he had made an honest mistake: he thought that, as a result of the outstanding debt, the money in Snowden's wallet was his (Richardson's) property. To engage in robbery, one must act with the intent (purpose) to take the property of another; since Richardson thought the property belonged to him, his mistake negated the *mens rea* required for the offense. Mistakes can excuse.

The law recognizes a number of excuses, many of which pose difficult questions for judges and juries. Was Patty Hearst really coerced into terrorism by the Symbionese Liberation Army?

Was former Washington, D.C., mayor Marion Barry really entrapped by the police in a drug bust? No claim of excuse has provoked such a contentious debate, however, as the claim that a defendant must be acquitted, even for a wrongdoing he plainly committed, because at the time of the offense he was *insane*.

The legal effort to excuse the insane has given rise to at least two prominent issues, each discussed in this section. How is "insanity" to be understood? And why should insanity be an excuse at all? The *Cameron* case serves as a point of departure for these questions.

Cameron and the Development of the Insanity Defense

The facts of Marie Cameron's gruesome murder need no elaboration. Marie's stepson, Gary, was arrested and charged with the crime. At trial, he raised the defense that he was insane at the time of the murder, and evidence was introduced to show he was a "paranoid schizophrenic." As is always the case in a criminal proceeding before a jury, the closing arguments of the prosecution and the defense are followed by that phase of the trial in which the judge "instructs" the jury, in which, that is, he or she informs the jury of the rules of the law that they must apply to their determination of the facts of the case. In *Cameron*, the trial judge instructed the jury as to the rules governing the defense of insanity, as these rules were then structured by the law of Washington state. Applying the judge's instructions, the jury convicted Cameron and the appellate court affirmed the conviction.

Cameron appealed to the Supreme Court of Washington, alleging that the instructions given to the jury incorrectly stated the "law" governing the insanity plea. Before we delve more deeply into the issues raised by Cameron's appeal, we must understand something of the broader history of the insanity defense and the various attempts to fashion and define an appropriate test for insanity.

Insanity is a legal rather than a medical term; and the efforts to clarify its meaning have been many and varied. The modern law of insanity begins with the famed *M'Naghten* case, decided by the British House of Lords in 1843. Daniel M'Naghten had been charged with shooting and killing one Edward Drummond, whom M'Naghten mistakenly believed to be the prime minister of England, Sir Robert Peel. M'Naghten pled not guilty, his lawyer insisting that M'Naghten suffered from delusions that undermined his perception of right and wrong. Upon considering the matter, the House of Lords articulated what came to be called the M'Naghten Rule, as intended to govern pleas of insanity. They held that

> in all cases a man is presumed to be sane and to possess sufficient degree of reason to be responsible for his crimes, until the contrary be proved to the juror's satisfaction; and to establish a defense on the grounds of insanity it must be clearly proved that, at the time of committing the act, the party accused was laboring from such a defect of reason, from a disease of the mind, as not to know the nature and quality of the act he was doing; or, if he did know it, that he did not know he was doing what was wrong.[2]

The substance of the M'Naghten Rule can be reduced to four elements: (1) defect of reason; (2) disease of the mind; (3) failure to know the nature and quality of one's act; and (4) failure to know that the act was wrong. As the rule is generally interpreted, elements 1 and 2 are necessary for a determination of insanity; either 3 or 4, together with 1 and 2, is sufficient. Typically, the "mental disease" spoken of in 2 must be a comparatively permanent condition, including such things as congenital defects and traumatic injury. There are at least two divergent interpretations of "know" as it is employed in 3 and 4. One view holds that "know" refers only to formal cognition or intellectual awareness (as in "I know that two plus two equal four"); the other holds that "know" is to be understood in a wider sense to mean that one appreciates the total setting (including the feelings and emotions of oneself and others) in which one's actions take place, and that one can evaluate the impact of one's actions upon others (as in "He knew that the match would cause a fire and the people would be burned").

The M'Naghten Rule was widely adopted throughout the jurisdictions of the common law world as the appropriate test for legal insanity; and many states, including Washington state at the time of *Cameron*, rely on some variant of it. Yet the M'Naghten Rule has been subjected to severe criticism over the years. Contemporary criminologists and jurists argue that it relies heavily on an outmoded psychology according to which the mental life of a person can be neatly divided into "cognitive," "affective," and "volitional" components. Such a model ignores the complexity of our psychic lives, the degree to which how we seek to understand the world and what we believe about it both influence and are influenced by our deepest desires, goals, and feelings. Other critics point out that *M'Naghten* stresses only cognitive impairment as relevant to insanity, with the result that the insanity defense often is unavailable to those who are seriously disturbed even though cognitively they may function on a near-normal level; a person suffering from kleptomania, for instance, would be such a case. It was for these reasons that, early on, some jurisdictions sought to supplement *M'Naghten* with an "irresistible impulse" test: One is exempt from criminal liability if one either fits the *M'Naghten* definition or at the time of the offense could not control the urge to act as one did. This ancillary test was not without critics of its own. Is it really possible for a jury to ascertain whether a given "impulse" was irresistible? How can we tell when someone could have resisted if only he or she had tried a little harder? How do we know that he or she *could* have tried harder?

An alternative test for insanity was proposed by federal judge David Bazelon in 1954 in *Durham v. U.S.*[3] Durham was a habitual offender who underwent numerous psychiatric treatments, none of which seemed to be effective. When arrested and convicted for yet another offense, Judge Bazelon took advantage of Durham's appeal to state a new test: The accused is not criminally responsible if his or her unlawful act was the "product of mental disease or mental defect." The court believed this rule to be superior to those it supplanted, as it treated the mind as a functional unit, thus bringing the legal standards up to date with developments in modern psychiatry and psychology and allowing experts to present all the relevant scientific and medical data to the jury. *Durham* represented a sharp departure from the old tests of criminal insanity; nevertheless, several jurisdictions adopted it. The rule created problems, however, and was ultimately rejected by the U.S. Supreme Court. The most frequent criticism of the rule was that it gave no standards or guidelines to the jury. As a result of its breadth, inordinate weight was given to the testimony of "experts," whose conflicting testimony often left juries in a state of bewilderment. Is the defendant crazy or not?

The test for insanity proposed by the Model Penal Code is rapidly gaining acceptance as a remedy for the defects of the *M'Naghten, Durham,* and irresistible impulse tests. Section 4.01 of the code provides that "a person is not responsible for criminal conduct if at the time of such conduct as a result of mental disease or defect he lacks substantial capacity either to appreciate the criminality [wrongfulness] of his conduct or to conform his conduct to the requirements of the law."

The central issue in *Cameron* has to do with the applicability of the M'Naghten Rule to the defendant's conduct and, in particular, to the third and fourth elements of the test: Did Cameron understand the nature and quality of his actions? Plainly, he understood in some sense what he was doing and comprehended its implications (why else would one stab a victim over seventy times?). On the other hand, he may have thought he was killing Satan. Did Cameron know that what he was doing was wrong? The narrow issue in the case centers on the trial court's definition of "wrong," which it took to be knowledge that the act was "contrary to law." Did Cameron realize that what he was doing violated the law? Perhaps. The Supreme Court of Washington reversed Cameron's conviction, holding that one who believes he is acting under a divine command is no less insane because he knows or realizes (in some sense) that murder is against the law.

Should the Insanity Defense Be Abolished?

Some people are outraged that a person such as Cameron should be found "not guilty by reason of insanity." The deliberate and vicious nature of the crime seems to them to demand a guilty verdict. Dissatisfaction with the realities of the insanity defense, together with the obvious difficulty in framing an acceptable and workable test for it, have moved some to condemn the defense as misconceived from the outset and to push for its abolition. The debate over abolition is joined here in the selections by Norval Morris and Sanford Kadish.

Morris defends the abolitionist position. What does this actually amount to and what are the arguments for it? Under existing law, a plea of insanity is a special defense. This means that it excuses an individual from responsibility for conduct that otherwise satisfies the [*actus reus* and *mens rea*] requirements for a crime. Morris proposes that the special defense of insanity be eliminated. In his view, mental illness would be relevant to a person's guilt or innocence only insofar as it might show that the defendant lacked the specific *mens rea* for the offense with which he or she is charged. An example serves to illustrate Morris's scheme and how it would differ from the current regime: In *People v. Wetmore,*[4] the victim of a burglary returned home after a three-day absence to find the defendant living in his (the victim's) apartment. The defendant, Wetmore, was wearing the victim's clothes and cooking his food. The lock on the door had been broken and the place was a shambles. Psychiatric examiners found that the homeless Wetmore suffered from the delusion that he "owned" property and that he was "directed" to the victim's apartment, where he promptly moved in. Wetmore's conviction on burglary charges was reversed, the court finding that Wetmore could not be held accountable for breaking and entering the house of another if he thought it was his own.

Wetmore's mental illness precluded his having the state of mind necessary for the offense with which he was charged. But mental illness will not always have this effect, and Cameron's case shows us why: In spite of his illness, it is beyond dispute that Cameron acted with the intent and purpose to kill. Under the abolitionist proposal, then, Wetmore is acquitted but Cameron is not. This is the difference between eliminating and retaining the insanity plea as a special defense.

Should the law distinguish in this way between Wetmore and Cameron? Why should the special defense be abolished? As Morris indicates, the principal argument made for eliminating the defense asserts that it is simply unworkable. "Insanity" defies any attempt at a meaningful definition; it confuses judges and juries; and it is very costly. Moreover, Morris alleges, the special defense is rarely raised and then only in connection with particularly heinous crimes. Morris concludes on a larger theme: The very idea of attempting to draw a bright line between the sick and the bad is misguided because it obscures the reality that social factors and determinants of behavior impair the capacity of persons to conform to the law much more severely than insanity ever does.

What are the objections to Morris's proposal? As Kadish claims, the abolition of the special defense of insanity will have the consequence that people like Cameron are convicted. But, one might ask, what is the real difference here? After all, whether or not he is found "guilty," Cameron is not likely simply to "go free." Mentally ill individuals who are acquitted, like Wetmore, frequently are taken into custody again under the procedure of "civil commitment" and subjected to treatment. If they wind up in custody in either case, what is the difference between the law's handling of Wetmore and Cameron? Kadish replies that the difference is this: Criminal conviction and a verdict of guilty, unlike civil commitment, carry with them a *moral stigma*; they represent a judgment that the individual's conduct is evil or wicked, properly deserving of blame and condemnation. This way of understanding a guilty verdict is reflected elsewhere in our law, for instance, in the refusal to permit convicted felons to vote. Yet if persons such as Cameron truly are "sick," Kadish reasons, they should not be blamed or condemned in this way. Cameron is not a proper object of that kind of moral response. And all this is quite independent of whether Cameron should be detained for his and others' safety.

To better appreciate the intuition animating Kadish's position, consider the following: It seems that for many centuries in Europe, from the early Middle Ages through the close of the eighteenth century, animals were routinely tried, convicted, and punished for a variety of "crimes," including eating crops, destroying livestock, and attacking humans.[5] Typical of these animal cases is that of the dog, Provetie. (See "Cases for Further Reflection" at the conclusion of this chapter.) On May 5, 1595, Provetie bit the hand of a young child, who was carrying a piece of meat. The child died and

Provetie was apprehended, tried, and convicted of murder. In passing sentence, the judge proclaimed that Provetie must be severely punished "as an example to others and more especially to evilly disposed dogs," and in consequence he ordered Provetie to be hanged "at the plain of Gravesteijn . . . where evildoers are customarily punished." (In this case the dog got off easily; other punishments routinely involved torture.)

Various hypotheses have been offered to explain this bizarre chapter of legal history but its relevance for us lies in this: While many of us might want this dog off the streets, few if any of us would regard the procedure of charging and convicting the dog, condemning it as an evildoer, and hanging it in order to deter other dogs as anything but silly. Most of us would find something peculiarly inappropriate about such treatment of a dog. Such conduct is inappropriate because it reflects a way of regarding dogs that seems simply to be mistaken: Dogs are not capable of understanding the requirements of law or good morals, nor are they able to conform their behavior to such standards. Those opposing the abolition of the insanity defense ask us to imagine a case involving a person who, with respect to the law, is in substantially the same position as the dog, that is, someone who is unable either to understand fully its requirements or to conform his or her behavior to them.

Morris concedes that there is something to the claim that conviction in a case like *Cameron* is inappropriate; but he regards this claim as vague and ill-founded. We punish persons every day whose capacity to conform their behavior to the law is impaired by a variety of factors: parental neglect, social and economic deprivation, and the like. Yet no one thinks, he points out, that we should have a special defense of "growing up in a ghetto."

Endnotes

[1] 403 F. 2d 574 (1968).

[2] 8 Eng. Rep. 718 (1843).

[3] 214 F. 2d 862 (D.C. Cir. 1954).

[4] 149 Cal. Rptr. 265 (1978).

[5] For a thorough and entertaining discussion see E. P. Evans, *The Criminal Prosecution and Capital Punishment of Animals* (London: Faber and Faber, 1987).

State v. Cameron

100 Wash. 2d 520 (1983)
Supreme Court of Washington

Petitioner, Gary Cameron, was charged with the premeditated first degree murder of his step-mother, Marie Cameron. His principal defense was that he was insane at the time he committed the offense. The Court of Appeals affirmed a guilty verdict and this court granted Cameron's petition for review. We reverse the trial court and the Court of Appeals. In doing so, we shall discuss only those issues on which reversal is granted.

At the outset it should be noted that petitioner does not challenge the charge that he stabbed Marie Cameron numerous times or that she died as a result of those wounds. Further, there does not seem to be any serious question that, except for the defense of insanity, the stabbing was done with an intent to kill. Rather, the challenge focuses on three errors alleged to have denied him a fair trial: (1) the definition of insanity in such a way as to prevent the jury's consideration of his insanity defense; (2) the admission of foreign pubic hairs found on the victim's body; and (3) the admission of hearsay evidence of an alleged statement made by the victim 2 months prior to her murder. . . .

Turning first to the insanity defense, it is clear there is evidence running counter to petitioner's contention. This, however, does not detract from petitioner's challenge to the trial court's insanity instruction. The question is whether there is evidence of insanity which the jury could have considered but for the court's instruction. We hold there is.

The basic facts reveal that on the morning of June 9, 1980, petitioner stabbed Marie Cameron in excess of 70 times, leaving the knife sticking in her heart. The body was left in the bathtub with no apparent attempt to conceal it. Later that day a police officer saw petitioner in downtown Shelton wearing only a pair of women's stretch pants, a woman's housecoat, a shirt and no shoes. He was stopped and questioned. After first giving a false name, he corrected it and explained he was dressed that way because "I just grabbed what I could . . . My mother-in-law turned vicious." He also stated he was headed for California. Having no known reason to detain petitioner, the officer released him to continue hitchhiking.

The next day petitioner was detained by the Oregon State Police as he wandered along the shoulder of Interstate 5 near Salem. Since he was wearing only the stretch pants and one shoe he was thought to be an escapee from a nearby mental hospital. A check revealed petitioner was wanted in Shelton for the death of Marie Cameron.

Petitioner was arrested and informed of his constitutional rights. He then gave two confessions, the first being a tape-recorded oral confession and the second a signed written confession. Neither is challenged by petitioner.

In the oral confession petitioner stated generally that he was living in or about the home of his father and stepmother. He left home dressed as he was because his stepmother had become violent. "[S]he's into different types of sorcery. She's just strictly a very evil person . . . and she became very violent with me, with a knife in her hand, and so, uh, I don't deny that I'm the one that did what went on out there." He indicated that when he walked into the bathroom he had not expected her. When he saw her, she had the knife which he was able to take from her easily by bending her wrist back. Then, as he stated, "I took the knife and really stabbed her."

In describing the stabbing, petitioner related: "I just kept stabbing her and stabbing her, because she wasn't feeling . . . it was as if she was laughing . . . as if she was up to something that morning, and I don't know . . . she plays around with witchcraft and that stuff . . ." The last place he saw her was in the bathtub about which he said "she kept moving and moving and moving, and kind of grabbed me like this, but laughing, as if she was enjoying . . . and it was kind of sickening, but it was really maddening to me, because of her offense towards me, it was like . . . you know, it was almost like she was mechanical . . . I mean, the thing was set up that, that's what she wanted to happen. . . . I feel that deep inside she was asking somebody to put her out of her misery . . . she was very symbolic with the 'Scarlet Whore Beast' she was very much into sorcery very, uh, anti-God, not really anti-God but takes the God's truth and twists it into sorcery."

Concerning his feelings about the incident petitioner said: "I felt confused . . . I felt no different from the beginning than the end there was no difference . . . legally I know, that it is against the law, but as far as right and wrong in the eye of God, I would say I felt no particular wrong."

When asked further about the incident petitioner responded: "I washed the blood off me, and I changed clothes, and then I looked back at her and she was, uh, she was still moving around, after being stabbed, what I thought was in the heart, and the throat . . . about seven or eight times, and she just . . . she kept moving. It was like . . . there was a smile on her face, she kept lunging for me, while she was dead . . . I wasn't trying to be vicious . . . it would look that way, but that wasn't the intent, but she kept lunging at me, over and over again, and the nature of her attack, I was, ah, mad enough I wanted to kill her. I felt that I was justified in self-defense at that point . . ." The last petitioner saw of the knife "I tried to stick it in her heart . . . she's some kind of an animal."

Petitioner explained further "she's into a very strong sorcery trip, and that's why so many stab wounds . . . I'm not a goring [sic] person . . . I've never been violent in my life, but for some reason . . . there was some evil spirit behind her that was . . . it was like, it was like there was something within her that, that wasn't really part of her body . . . she was smiling . . . she was almost like enjoying playing and it was disgusting."

When petitioner subsequently gave the written confession he added: "My attack wasn't a vicious attack the first time. I was trying to stop the spirit that was moving in her. She kept saying, 'Gary, Gary, Gary,' as if she was enjoying it." When she stopped moving he washed himself, changed his clothes and then "My stepmother started moving again as if a spirit was in her. I took the knife and started stabbing her again. When I realized there was something in her that wouldn't stop moving, I started stabbing her in the head and heart. I wanted to kill the spirit that seemed to be attacking my spirit." Once again he changed his clothes but again found her moving and again stabbed her numerous times until all movement

stopped. He then changed clothes once more and left.

As with the petitioner's testimony we note the testimony of the psychiatrists and psychologists is not without some disparity. Nevertheless, there is ample evidence which, under a proper insanity instruction, could have been considered by the jury as a matter of defense.

Prior to trial, petitioner made a motion to acquit on the ground of insanity pursuant to RCW 10.77.080. Three psychiatrists, Doctors Jarvis, Allison and Bremner and a psychologist, Dr. Trowbridge, were called to testify. They agreed petitioner suffered from paranoid schizophrenia both at the time of the killing and at the time of trial. Although stating it differently, all four appeared to agree that petitioner believed he was an agent of God, required to carry out God's directions. They also agreed that petitioner believed God commanded him to kill his stepmother and that he was therefore obligated to kill the "evil spirit." Consequently, all doctors concurred he was legally insane at the time of the murder.

The trial court denied the motion for acquittal and submitted the issue of insanity to the jury. At trial, the four doctors repeated their earlier testimony. All agreed that at the time of the killing, and at the time of trial, petitioner suffered from the mental disease of paranoid schizophrenia. While expressing their views in slightly different ways, they agreed petitioner understood that, as a mechanical thing, he was killing his stepmother and knew it was against the laws of man. They stressed, however, that at the time, he was preoccupied with the delusional belief that his stepmother was an agent of satan who was persecuting him, as were others like Yasser Arafat and the Ayatollah Khomeini. He believed he was being directed by God to kill satan's angel and that by so doing, he was obeying God's higher directive or law. At this time he believed himself to be a messiah and in fact compared himself with Jesus Christ.

The doctors pointed out, in different ways, that because of his delusional beliefs, petitioner felt God had directed him to send her from this life to another. He had no remorse over the killing. He felt it was justified by God and that he was merely doing a service. "He felt he would generally be protected from any difficulties . . . because 'God would not allow it to happen.'"

Concerning the legal tests for insanity the

mental health experts opined that while he understood it was against the law to kill, he believed he was responding to God's directive and thus had an obligation to rid the world of this "demon," "sorceress" or "evil spirit." Thus, while technically he understood the mechanical nature of the act, he did not have the capacity to discern between right and wrong with reference to the act. Some of the doctors expressed the clear view that at the time of the killing, he was unable to appreciate the nature and quality of his acts. No doctor contended otherwise.

Concerning petitioner's insanity defense the trial court gave standard . . . pattern jury instruction . . . but, over petitioner's exception, added a last paragraph which defines "right and wrong."

> In addition to the plea of not guilty, the defendant has entered a plea of insanity existing at the time of the act charged.
>
> Insanity existing at the time of the commission of the act charged is a defense.
>
> For a defendant to be found not guilty by reason of insanity you must find that, as a result of mental disease or defect, the defendant's mind was affected to such an extent that the defendant was unable to perceive the nature and quality of the acts with which the defendant is charged or was unable to tell right from wrong with reference to the particular acts with which defendant is charged.
>
> *What is meant by the terms "right and wrong" refers to knowledge of a person at the time of committing an act that he was acting contrary to the law.*

(Italics ours.) Petitioner, on the other hand, proposed the use of [an alternative] jury instruction . . . which does not contain the last paragraph.

Petitioner argues that the trial court should have left the term "right and wrong" undefined as provided by the Legislature in RCW 9A.12.010. At the very least, it is urged, "right and wrong" should not have been defined in such a way as to exclude from the jury's deliberation the consideration of "right and wrong" in terms of one's ability to understand the moral qualities of the act.

[The court held that the instruction was wrong.]

At the time this case was tried, the Court of Appeals had just issued State v. Crenshaw . . . 617 P.2d 1041 (1980) which approved the instruction challenged herein. Subsequent thereto this court affirmed the Court of Appeals opinion. . . .

Insofar as the instant case is concerned, however, our discussion of *Crenshaw* also recognized an exception to the alternative grounds set forth therein. That exception is controlling here:

> A narrow exception to the societal standard of moral wrong has been drawn for instances wherein a party performs a criminal act, knowing it is morally and legally wrong, but believing, because of a mental defect, that the act is ordained by God: such would be the situation with a mother who kills her infant child to whom she is devotedly attached, believing that God has spoken to her and decreed the act. Although the woman knows that the law and society condemn the act, it would be unrealistic to hold her responsible for the crime, since her free will has been subsumed by her belief in the deific decree.

. . . Consequently, as we held in *Crenshaw*, one who believes that he is acting under the direct command of God is no less insane because he nevertheless knows murder is prohibited by the laws of man. Indeed, it may actually emphasize his insanity. . . .

In the instant case there is considerable evidence (although not unanimous) from which the jury could have concluded that petitioner suffered from a mental disease; that he believed his stepmother was satan's angel or a sorceress; that he believed God directed him to kill his stepmother; that because of the mental disease it was impossible for him to understand that what he was doing was wrong; and . . . that his free will had "been subsumed by [his] belief in the deific decree." The last paragraph of the trial court's challenged instruction precluded the jury's consideration of these factors and thus runs afoul of the *Crenshaw* exception. In short, the instruction prevented the jury from considering those essential relevant facts that formed petitioner's theory of the case. To this extent the trial court erred by adding the definitional paragraph to the instruction.

The Abolition of the Insanity Defense

NORVAL MORRIS

III. *The Abolition of the Special Defense of Insanity*

Abolition of the defense of insanity has received exhaustive attention in the literature; the informed reader is entitled, therefore, to be notified of where the argument leads so that he may avoid the sharper irritations of redundancy. In accordance with the thesis of separation of the mental health law and the criminal-law powers to incarcerate, I propose the abolition of the special defense of insanity. A fall-back alternative position, in no way conflicting with the separation thesis, is for the abolition of the special defense and for legislative substitution of a qualified defense of diminished responsibility to a charge of murder having the effect, if successful, of a conviction of manslaughter with the usual sentencing discretion attached to that crime.

The argument will be presented in broad perspective, the nuances of difference between the competing defenses of insanity being glossed over. The sequence will be (a) the general argument for abolition, (b) an analysis of how the law would operate under the proposed abolition and the alternative substitution of diminished responsibility, and (c) a consideration and repudiation of the main criticisms of the abolition proposal.

The problem is to cut through the accumulated cases, commentaries, and confusions to the issues of principle underlying the responsibility of the mentally ill for conduct otherwise criminal. The issues are basically legal, moral, and political, not medical or psychological, though, of course, the developing insights of psychiatry and psychology

are of close relevance to those legal, moral, and political issues.

A glance at the history of the common-law relationship between guilt and mental illness may help to structure the discussion. Until the nineteenth century, criminal-law doctrines of *mens rea* (criminal intent) handled the entire problem. Evidence of mental illness was admitted on the question of intent, and as the infant discipline of psychiatry claimed an increased understanding of mental processes such evidence on the question of intent grew in importance. Psychiatrists, then generally known as "alienists" (separating, alienating, the citizen from the community because of mental illness), claimed increasing competence to classify, explain the origins, and predict the course of mental illnesses, with and without diverse treatment interventions. The dramatic events of major criminal trials became important battlegrounds for psychiatry and psychiatrists, public dramatic ceremonials in which professional standing was proclaimed and tested. Inexorably, conflict developed between the disciplines of law and psychiatry with their distinct supporting epistemologies, the language and concepts of the law—free will, moral choice, guilt, and innocence—confronting those of psychiatry—determinism, degrees of cognitive and volitional control, classification of diseases, and definition of treatments. Complicating these inherent confrontations were the different consequences of the application of the two competing systems: the binary system of the law, guilt or innocence, and, if the former, punishment to close the equation; the continuum of psychiatry, degrees of illness and opportunities for "cure," to be determined in the last resort only by the fact of nondestructive life in the community.

In a multipurposive society these epistemological and purposive differences between law and psychiatry are to be welcomed but they carried, and still carry, the seeds of confusion. The pre-*McNaughtan* position was correct and clear: the psychiatrist could contribute useful evidentiary

From *Madness and the Criminal Law* (Chicago: University of Chicago Press), pp. 53–69. Reprinted with permission of The University of Chicago Press and Norval Morris.

Pre-McNaughton

insights to the issues correctly defined by the common law of crime—did the accused intend the prohibited harm? But by the time of *McNaughtan* (1843) this clear position was frustrated by the increasing tendency of lawyers, psychiatrists, public opinion, and legislators to turn questions of evidence into matters of substance, to transmute medical evidence about legal issues into substantive legal rules. *McNaughtan* was just such a substantive rule, confusing the evidence for a proposition with the proposition itself.

How would the pre-nineteenth-century position now stand, taking into account advances in the discipline of psychiatry? The sick mind of the accused would be relevant to his guilt since he may, because of sickness, have lacked the state of mind required for conviction of the offense with which he has been charged or of any other offense of which he may be convicted on such a charge (in the language of the trade, "lesser included offenses"). If guilty of such a crime, his sick mind is relevant to fair sentencing. If innocent, that is all the criminal law has to do with the matter though, of course, like any other citizen he may be civilly committed if he is mentally ill and is a danger to himself or others or is incapable of caring for himself. On many of these issues the psychiatrist has useful insights; on none should psychiatry frame the operative rule, define the dividing line between guilt and innocence, between detention and freedom. Whenever this happens, the law is perverted in practice, and psychiatry is brought into disrepute. The English and American judges went wrong in the nineteenth century; it is time we returned to older and truer principles.

I must stress that in advocating the abolition of the special defense of insanity, the nuances of difference among the *McNaughtan* Rules, the *Durham* Rule, the rules offered by the American Law Institute and accepted in *Brawner* and in many state criminal codes, the irresistible impulse test, the recommendations of the Group for the Advancement of Psychiatry, and other suggested special defenses, though important in practice and meriting close analysis, are not essential to the present discussion. All vary around the following structure: a definition of mental illness, as a threshold to the invocation of the defense, and a statement of a required causal relationship between that "mental illness" and the otherwise criminal behavior of the accused. My thesis stands,

whatever definition of illness and whatever language to capture a causal relationship are offered. And, of course, variations on where the burdens of proof are placed on those two issues, and on how heavy are those burdens, are also irrelevant.

It would be a mistake to read these dogmatisms as an attack on psychiatry. The lawyers have been quite content to strap a mattress to the back of any psychiatrist willing to appear in court to answer questions like: at the time of the killing did the accused "know the nature and quality of the act"? did he "know that it was wrong"? did he have "substantial capacity to appreciate the criminality of his conduct"? did he have "substantial capacity to control his conduct"? Wiser psychiatrists and those not tempted by the bright focus of public interest have avoided these philosophically impossible questions. Nor does it assist materially to direct the psychiatrist to give information to the jury to help them answer these elusive questions but to avoid offering answers himself, since it is the question themselves that are philosophically in error that pretend to a precision beyond present knowledge.

Why, then, go beyond the simple rule, to give mental illness the same exculpatory effect as, say, blindness or deafness? Evidence of the latter afflictions may be admitted as indicative of lack of both the *actus reus* (prohibited act) and the *mens rea* of a crime. Why go further? The answer lies in the pervasive moral sense that when choice to do ill is lacking, it is improper to impute guilt. And hence there is pressure for a special defense of insanity, just as there is pressure for a special defense of infancy or duress. Let us consider what has been offered by way of larger statements of the ends to be served by a special defense of insanity.

The major commissions of inquiry in the United States and in England have been less than compelling on the underlying justifications of this defense. Here is the American Law Institute's rationale for the special defense of insanity which now dominates the field:

> What is involved specifically is the drawing
> of a line between the use of public agencies
> and public force to *condemn* the offender by
> conviction, with resultant sanctions in
> which there is inescapably a punitive ingre-
> dient (however constructive we may at-
> tempt to make the process of correction)

and modes of disposition in which that ingredient is absent, even though restraint may be involved. To put the matter differently, the problem is to discriminate between the cases where a punitive-correctional disposition is appropriate and those in which a medical-custodial disposition is the only kind that the law should allow.[1]

This seems to me descriptive of what is to be done and not at all a justification of the doing.

The justification for the special defense of insanity offered by the English Royal Commission on Capital Punishment carries the matter no further. It says it has long been so; therefore it should continue to be. Should you doubt me, here are the commission's words:

> It has for centuries been recognized that, if a person was, at the time of his unlawful act, mentally so disordered that it would be unreasonable to impute guilt to him, he ought not to be held liable to conviction and punishment under the criminal law. Views have changed and opinions have differed, as they differ now, about the standards to be applied in deciding whether an individual should be exempted from criminal responsibility for this reason; but the principle has been accepted without question.[2]

The Butler Committee Report[3] in 1975 expressly accepted this "reason is since reason long has been" argument[4] even though, in their words, "the insanity defense is in fact almost unheard of nowadays," which, as we shall see, is the present situation in England. They regarded retention of a special defense as "right in principle"[5] though they carefully eschewed any definition of that principle, but they so whittled away the defense in practice in England as to make it a quaint historical survival rather than a contemporary and operative rule of law.

In *Durham,* Judge Bazelon put the matter curtly and clearly: "Our collective conscience does not allow punishment where it cannot impose blame."[6] Such a rationale claims too much, assumes our possession of finely calibrated moral scales, and flies in the face of observation of the dross daily work of our criminal courts. It is hortatory rather than descriptive but it does state a justification that a generous mind may accept as an aim though doubt as a reality.

Historically, of course, the special defense made good sense in relation to one punishment. Criminal punishment infused it with meaning. But even perfervid advocates of capital punishment do not favor the execution of the mentally ill, and this justification for the special defense is now sufficiently covered by the rules and practices of sentencing.

One is left, therefore, with the feeling that the special defense is a genuflection to a deep-seated moral sense that the mentally ill lack freedom of choice to guide and govern their conduct and that therefore blame should not be imputed to them for their otherwise criminal acts nor should punishment be imposed. To the validity of this argument we will several times return, but it is important not to assume that those who advocate the abolition of the special defense of insanity are recommending the wholesale punishment of the sick. They are urging rather that mental illness be given the same exculpatory effect as other adversities that bear upon criminal guilt. And they add the not unfair criticism of the conventional position that they observe the widespread conviction and punishment of the mentally ill, the special defense being an ornate rarity, a tribute to our capacity to pretend to a moral position while pursuing profoundly different practices.

The number held as not guilty by reason of insanity in the United States as a whole and in some states will illustrate the relative rarity of the special defense. Nationally, in the 1978 census of state and federal facilities, 3,140 persons were being held as not guilty by reason of insanity.[7] In Illinois, at the time of writing, 127 are so held. In New York, between 1965 and 1976 inclusive, 278 persons were found not guilty by reason of insanity (53 in the first five years, 225 in the second six years—the increase being explicable presumably by constitutionally imposed relaxation of the *Brawner* rules for, and processes of, releasing those found not guilty by reason of insanity). No one acquainted with the work of the criminal courts can think that these numbers remotely approximate the relationship between serious mental illness and criminal conduct. The defense is pleaded only where it may be advantageous to the accused and that balance of advantage fluctuates with sentencing practice and rules and practices relating to the release of those found not guilty by reason of insanity. Hence statistics will not lead us to principle in this matter; a more fundamental inquiry is necessary.

A useful entering wedge to principle is to inquire, What is the irreducible minimum relationship between mental illness and criminal guilt? What is the least the criminal law could do in this matter?

It is unthinkable that mental illness should be given a lesser reach than drunkenness. If a given mental condition (intent, recklessness) is required for the conviction of a criminal offense, then, as a proposition requiring no discussion, in the absence of that mental condition there can be no conviction. This holds true whether the absence of that condition is attributable to blindness, deafness, drunkenness, mental illness or retardation, linguistic difficulties, or, if it could be established, hypnotic control. But this states basic principles of criminal law, not a special defense. The main reasons for defining a "special defense" beyond the traditional common-law relationship between mental illness and the *actus reus* and *mens rea* of crime are, I think, twofold: expediency in crime control and fairness.

The expediency rationale can be quickly advanced and disposed of; the fairness rationale is more difficult.

In an important article in 1963, "Abolish 'The Insanity Defense'—Why Not?"[8] J. Goldstein and J. Katz accurately perceived that "the insanity defense is not a defense, it is a device for triggering indeterminate restraint"[9] of those who were mentally ill at the time of the crime but are not civilly committable now. In considerable part, that has been its role since 1800 when the emergence of the special defense in England led to the Criminal Lunatics Act of 1800, which provided indeterminate custody for those found not guilty by reason of insanity, with similar legislation spreading in the states and federal systems in this country.

[handwritten margin note: Original intent of ruling]

Few are prepared any longer to justify the special defense on this crime control basis, as a means of confining the dangerous though not civilly committable. It would be a strange "defense," an unusual benevolence, whose purpose is confinement of those who could not otherwise be confined.

Hence we are brought to the central issue—the question of fairness, the sense that it is unjust and unfair to stigmatize the mentally ill as criminals and to punish them for their crimes. The criminal law exists to deter and to punish those who would or who do choose to do wrong. If they cannot exercise choice, they cannot be deterred and it is a moral outrage to punish them.[10] The argument sounds powerful but its premise is weak.

Choice is neither present nor absent in the typical case where the insanity defense is currently pleaded; what is at issue is the degree of freedom of choice on a continuum from the hypothetically entirely rational to the hypothetically pathologically determined—in states of consciousness neither polar condition exists.

The moral issue sinks into the sands of reality. Certainly it is true that in a situation of total absence of choice it is outrageous to inflict punishment; but the frequency of such situations to the problems of criminal responsibility becomes an issue of fact in which tradition and clinical knowledge and practice are in conflict. The traditions of being possessed of evil spirits, of being bewitched, confront the practices of a mental health system which increasingly fashions therapeutic practices to hold patients responsible for their conduct. And suppose we took the moral argument seriously and eliminated responsibility in those situations where we thought there had been a substantial impairment of the capacity to choose between crime and no crime (I set aside problems of strict liability and of negligence for the time being). Would we not have to, as a matter of moral fairness, fashion a special defense of gross social adversity? The matter might be tested by asking which is the more criminogenic, psychosis or serious social deprivation? In an article in 1968 on this topic I raised the question of whether there should be a special defense of dwelling in a black ghetto.[11] Some literal-minded commentators castigated me severely for such a recommendation, mistaking a form of argument, the *reductio ad absurdum,* for a recommendation. But let me again press the point. If one were asked how to test the criminogenic effect of any factor in man or in the environment, the answer would surely follow empirical lines. One would measure and try to isolate the impact of that factor on behavior, with particular reference to criminal behavior. To isolate genetic pressure toward crime one might pursue twin studies or cohort studies, one might look at patterns of adoption and the criminal behavior of natural fathers and adoptive fathers and see whether they were related to the criminal behavior of their children.[12] Somewhat

[handwritten margin note: ghetto defense]

similar measuring techniques would be followed if one were trying to search out the relationship between unemployment and criminality, or a Bowlby-like study of the effects of maternal separation or maternal deprivation on later criminal behavior. Our answers to the question of the determining effects of such conditions would be found empirically and not in a priori arguing about their relationships to crime, though there may be ample room for argument involved in the empirical studies.

Hence, at first blush, it seems a perfectly legitimate correlational and, I submit, causal inquiry, whether psychosis, or any particular type of psychosis, is more closely related to criminal behavior than, say, being born to a one-parent family living on welfare in a black inner-city area. And there is no doubt of the empirical answer. Social adversity is grossly more potent in its pressure toward criminality, certainly toward all forms of violence and street crime as distinct from white-collar crime, than is any psychotic condition. As a factual matter, the exogenous pressures are very much stronger than the endogenous.

But the argument feels wrong. Surely there is more to it than the simple calculation of criminogenic impact. Is this unease rationally based? I think not, though the question certainly merits further consideration. As a rational matter it is hard to see why one should be more responsible for what is done to one than for what one is. Yet major contributors to jurisprudence and criminal-law theory insist that it is necessary to maintain the denial of responsibility on grounds of mental illness to preserve the moral infrastructure of the criminal law.[13] For many years I have struggled with this opinion by those whose work I deeply respect, yet I remain unpersuaded. Indeed, they really don't try to persuade, but rather affirm and reaffirm with vehemence and almost mystical sincerity the necessity of retaining the special defense of insanity as a moral prop to the entire criminal law.

And indeed I think that much of the discussion of the defense of insanity is the discussion of a myth rather than of a reality. It is no minor debating point that in fact we lack a defense of insanity as an operating tool of the criminal law other than in relation to a very few particularly heinous and heavily punished offenses. There is not an operating defense of insanity in relation to burglary or theft, or the broad sweep of index crimes generally;

the plea of not guilty on the ground of insanity is rarely to be heard in city courts of first instance which handle the grist of the mill of the criminal law—though a great deal of pathology is to be seen in the parade of accused and convicted persons before these courts. As a practical matter we reserve this defense for a few sensational cases where it may be in the interest of the accused either to escape the possibility of capital punishment (though in cases where serious mental illness is present, the risk of execution is slight) or where the likely punishment is of a sufficient severity to make the indeterminate commitment of the accused a preferable alternative to a criminal conviction. Operationally the defense of insanity is a tribute, it seems to me, to our hypocrisy rather than to our morality.

To be less aggressive about the matter and to put aside anthropomorphic allegations of hypocrisy, the special defense of insanity may properly be indicted as producing a morally unsatisfactory classification on the continuum between guilt and innocence. It applies in practice to only a few mentally ill criminals, thus omitting many others with guilt-reducing relationships between their mental illness and their crime; it excludes other powerful pressures on human behavior, thus giving excessive weight to the psychological over the social. It is a false classification in the sense that if a team of the world's most sensitive and trained psychiatrists and moralists were to select from all those found guilty of felonies and those found not guilty by reason of insanity any given number who should not be stigmatized as criminals, very few of those found not guilty by reason of insanity would be selected. How to offer proof of this? The only proof, I regret, is to be found by personal contact with a flow of felony cases through the courts and into the prisons. No one of serious perception will fail to recognize both the extent of mental illness and retardation among the prison population and the overwhelming weight of adverse social circumstances on criminal behavior. This is, of course, not an argument that social adversities should lead to acquittals; they should be taken into account in sentencing. And the same is true of the guilt and sentencing of those pressed by psychological adversities. The special defense is thus a morally false classification. And it is a false classification also in the sense that it does not select from the prison population those most in need of psychiatric treatment.

It may help to resolve these moral complexities to consider briefly how the law would work in practice where the special defense abolished, and then to offer an acceptable compromise position for those who strain at the simple solution of abolition.

Actus reus qualifications

Were the special defense abolished, mental illness would remain relevant and admissible on the question of the *actus reus* of crime. [Such situations] are rare . . . but when they occur, acquittal is the proper verdict since the criminal law can seek to control only voluntary acts and not those achieved in fugue states. Manifestly, the epileptic in a *grand mal* whose clonic movements strike and injure another commits no crime; but we need no special defense of insanity to reach that result, well-established *actus reus* doctrines suffice.

The *mens rea* question is more complex though the principle is easy to state: evidence of mental illness is admissible to show that the accused lacked the prohibited *mens rea*. For states of mind defined as "purpose" or "intent" there is no analytic difficulty. For "recklessness," insofar as a definition of "recklessness" requires that it be shown that the accused in fact foresaw the risk of this type of harm, there is again no analytic difficulty; but when recklessness may be achieved by "gross negligence," by failure to live up to an objective standard of care, then difficulties do come in the abolition position which will be addressed later in this chapter. But in the broad run of cases, certainly in those where the special defense is now pleaded, ordinary *mens rea* principles can well carry the freight.

One interesting aspect of the relationship between *mens rea* and mental illness was prescribed by the American Law Institute and widely copied by those states that have relied on the Model Penal Code in framing their criminal codes. For example, Illinois was in 1961 the first state to build its criminal law on the American Law Institute Model and in section 9-2-(b) of the Criminal Code provided:

> A person who intentionally or knowingly kills an individual commits voluntary manslaughter if at the time of the killing he believes the circumstances to be such that, if they existed, would justify or exonerate the killing under the principles stated in Article 7 of this Code, but his belief is unreasonable.[14]

The relevance to mental illness is immediately obvious. Mental illness may well lead an accused person to believe he has justification for his conduct when objectively this is not the case. Unless that belief be disproved beyond reasonable doubt by the prosecution, one accused of murder having such a belief will be convicted of manslaughter and sentenced accordingly, taking into account his mental illness in sentencing.[15]

It must be admitted that the mental illness–*mens rea* relationship can be corrupted and confounded, as can most other legal doctrines, and that it has been corrupted and confounded in a line of California cases, *Wells-Gorshen-Conley-White*.[16] Sound principle, that mental illness may be relevant to disproving the presence of a state of mind necessary to first degree murder or necessary to the "malice aforethought" that is the distinguishing characteristic of murder in California, has been pushed to an unacceptable complexity and confusion in the law of homicide in that state. It is not necessary here to trace those developments; the largest part of the difficulty these cases present is to be found in the central role still accorded "malice aforethought" in the California doctrine of "diminished capacity" and in the elusive emphases given in *Gorshen* and *Conley* to the accused's capacity to identify to some degree with the suffering of his victim as a precondition to the full possession of a prohibited mental state. Structures of talmudic complexity have been built around the relationship between mental illness and "malice aforethought"; the problem is readily avoidable by the clear definitions of the *mens rea* of crime being followed throughout the common-law world by all law-reform commissions and legislatures acquainted with the work of the American Law Institute's Model Penal Code. This relationship between mental illness and *mens rea* has in various formulations been judicially recognized in twenty-one states, in the federal system, and in the District of Columbia.[17]

The California case law on this topic has, regrettably, often been confused with the doctrine of diminished responsibility offered as an alternative proposal in this chapter, although in fact that doctrine lies closer in practice to provisions like section 9-2-(b) of the Illinois Code earlier discussed.

No state has as yet accepted the central proposal in this chapter. Many commentators support it, many oppose it;[18] many federal and state legislative bills have been drafted incorporating its thesis. Its time will come. At present, unsatisfactory compromises like those in Michigan, Indiana, and Illinois of "guilty but mentally ill," considered hereunder, are in vogue, but they are unprincipled.

The two commissions of inquiry—one in England and one in New York—have not accepted the abolitionist position in its entirety but they have moved far toward it.

The Butler Committee in 1975 recommended the substantial reduction of the reach of the special defense, placing their main reliance on diminished responsibility to solve the problems with which that defense was meant to grapple. To closely similar effect, but going further in the direction of complete abolition of the special defense than the Butler Committee did, a report entitled "The Insanity Defense in New York" made in 1978 by a distinguished committee and prepared under the direction of William A. Carnahan, deputy commissioner and counsel to the New York Department of Mental Hygiene (hereinafter the Carnahan Report), recommended the abolition of the special defense of insanity and the adoption of a rule of "diminished capacity under which evidence of abnormal mental condition would be admissible to affect the degree of crime for which an accused could be convicted."[19]

The Butler Committee recommended the retention of a special defense of insanity in a few very rare cases of "severe mental illness" and "severe subnormality." They recommended, "a specific exemption from conviction of any defendant who, at the time of the act or omission charged, was suffering from severe mental illness or severe subnormality . . . notwithstanding technical proof of *mens rea*."[20] The Butler Committee definitions of "severe mental illness" and "severe subnormality" are extensive and difficult.[21] They certainly narrowly confine the defense. And part of the reason for the Butler Committee compromise here is the statistical reality of what has happened in England and Wales to the special defense of insanity pursuant to the legislative introduction of diminished responsibility in the Homicide Act of 1957. That Act provided in section 2(1):

> Where a person kills or is party to the killing of another, he shall not be convicted of murder if he was suffering from such abnormality of mind . . . as substantially impaired his mental responsibility for his acts and omissions in doing or being a party to the killing.

Prior to 1957, of all persons committed for trial for murder in England about 20 percent were found unfit to stand trial and diverted from criminal process and about 20 percent were found not guilty by reason of insanity (the terminology is adapted from English to American usage). As that Act has had its impact, by the late 1970s, about 2 percent are unfit and diverted, less than 1 percent are found not guilty by reason of insanity, and about 37 percent fall under the diminished responsibility provisions.[22]

The same thing would happen in this country. The Butler Committee's recommendation of a restricted retention of a special defense of insanity is thus almost a *de minimis* inconsequential recognition of an extremely severely mentally ill or retarded group who need not be brought within criminal processes.

There are three points to be made in favor of a legislatively introduced rule of "diminished responsibility" in this country of the type now well tested by English juries.

First, for some exceptional murder charges *mens rea* principles and even rules like the Illinois 9-2-(b) may not suffice to reduce murder to manslaughter in cases where such a reduction is desirable. I hypothesize an accused who is clearly psychotic and paranoiac believing he is commanded by God to kill, as Hadfield and some others have believed. He has heard voices to that effect and is in no doubt of his moral duty. He probably does not fall within any *mens rea* provisions which would reduce his crime from murder to manslaughter (unless one sets out on the unacceptable path of California case law) and does not fall within analogues of Illinois section 9-2-(b) since he does not believe he has a defense to a criminal charge. Yet such cases are, it is submitted, better treated and sentenced as manslaughter than as murder. A legislative provision modeled on the English Homicide Act of 1957 would achieve that result.

Secondly, where states impose mandatory sentences on those convicted of murder, some escape mechanisms from those sentences for the mentally ill (other than frustration by charge bargaining) is desirable. The evil to be remedied here lies in the mandatory sentence, not in the criminal law relating to mentally ill criminals; but the only politically acceptable remedy may be legislative enunciation of a doctrine of diminished responsibility.

Thirdly, diminished responsibility is, on close analysis, apart from the two special problems in the two previous paragraphs, a shift of sentencing discretion to a degree from judge to jury, the jury under diminished responsibility lowering the maximum (and sometimes the minimum) sentencing range within which the judge will impose sentence. In some states there may be advantages in such a limitation of judicial discretion.

I now try to draw the analysis to a close. For the reasons offered above I urge the legislative abolition of the special defense of insanity. For those who find persuasive the three reasons last offered for a special legislatively introduced doctrine of diminished responsibility to flush out ordinary *mens rea* doctrines I recommend a formula akin to that in the English Homicide Act of 1957 with the accused who falls within it being convicted of and sentenced for manslaughter, his sentence taking into account his mental illness at the time of the crime.

. . .

Endnotes

[1] American Law Institute, Model Penal Code, sec. 4.01 Comment (Tentative Draft 4, 1955).

[2] Royal Commission on Capital Punishment, 1949–53 Report, Cmd. 8932, at 98 (1953).

[3] Report of the Committee on Mentally Abnormal Offenders, Cmd. 6244 (1974).

[4] *Id.*, §18.2 at 216 and §18.10 at 219.

[5] *Id.*, §18.10 at 219.

[6] 214 F.2d 862, 876 (D.C. Cir. 1954).

[7] Steadman, Monahan, Hartstone, Davis & Clark, "Mentally Disordered Offenders: A National Survey of Patients and Facilities," *Law and Human Behavior* (in press).

[8] 72 *Yale L. J.* 853 (1963).

[9] *Id.* at 868.

[10] Arguments for the retention of the special defense of insanity as a moral foundation of the criminal law are offered by Herbert Wechsler (see, for example, 37 F.R.D. 365 (2d Cir. 1964)) and by Sanford Kadish ("The

Decline of Innocence," 26 *Camb. L. J.* 273 (1968)). A more cautious support of retention is advanced by Francis A. Allen (*Law, Intellect and Education,* at 114–18 (1979)). Contrary views, generally supporting the abolitionist position taken in this chapter, are advanced by H. L. A. Hart, Chief Justice Weintraub, Lady Barbara Wooton, Joel Feinberg, Dr. Seymour Halleck, and Dr. Thomas Szasz. (Their views are summarized in the appendix to N. Morris, "Psychiatry and the Dangerous Criminal," 41 *S. Cal. L. Rev.* 514 (1968), prepared by Gary Lowenthal; see n. 13 of that article). The lists of those favoring abolition lengthens with the Butler Committee Report (see note 3 *supra*) and the Carnahan Report (see note 19 *infra*), as well as the apparently unending debates of the various proposals for a Federal Criminal Code. [Report of the Committee on Mentally Abnormal Offenders, Cmd. 6244 (1975).]

[11] Morris, note 10 *supra.*

[12] Mednick & Volovka, "Biology and Crime," in 2 *Crime and Justice* (N. Morris & M. Tonry, eds., 1980).

[13] See note 10 *supra.*

[14] Ill. Rev. Stat., ch. 38, §9-2(b).

[15] This relationship links closely to the alternative proposal of diminished responsibility discussed hereunder.

[16] People v. Wells, 33 Cal.2d 330, 202 P.2d 53 (1949), *cert. denied,* 338 U.S. 863 (1949); People v. Gorshen, 51 Cal.2d 761, 336 P.2d 492 (1959); People v. Conley, 64 Cal.2d 310, 411 P.2d 911, 49 Cal. Rptr. 815 (1966); People v. White, 117 Cal. App. 2d 270, 172 Cal. Rptr. 612 (Cal. Ct. App. 1981).

[17] See the Carnahan Report (text at n. 19 *infra*), at 144 n.15.

[18] For a summary statement of these views in 1968, see Morris, note 10 *supra,* the appendix by Gary Lowenthal, and see n.13 of that article.

[19] *Op. cit.,* at 9.

[20] *Supra* note 3, at 222.

[21] *Id.* at 229 and app. 10.

[22] These figures are adapted from app. 9 of the Butler Committee Report, itself relying on 1 Nigel Walker, *Crime and Insanity in England* 159 (1968).

The Decline of Innocence

SANFORD KADISH

The criminological positivists at the turn of the century started a good deal of creative rethinking about the criminal law.[1] Some of their proposals have gained widespread acceptance in the criminal law as we know it today. Others made no headway at all. One particular proposal, and a very fundamental one indeed, began a controversy which has ebbed and flowed regularly since. That is the proposal to eliminate from the criminal law the whole apparatus of substantive principles, or at least some of them, such as the legal insanity defence, which owe their presence to the law's traditional concern for distinguishing the guilty and the innocent in terms of their blameworthiness. The essence of the proposal is that innocence in this sense, moral innocence, if you will, should not disqualify a person from the consequences of the penal law. Moral innocence should, it is urged, give way to social dangerousness as the basis for a criminal disposition.

In recent years there has been a resurgence of the controversy produced by serious proposals to eliminate the defence of legal insanity and, more radical still, to eliminate across the board the requirements of *mens rea* from the definition of criminal offences and defences. If I may raise my colours at the outset, I am frankly a friend to neither proposal. In this brief paper I would like to discuss the implications of these suggested reforms and to develop my reasons for believing that the case has not been made.

The term "*mens rea*" is rivalled only by the term "jurisdiction" for the varieties of senses in which it has been used and for the quantity of obfuscation it has created. A few introductory paragraphs on usage is inescapable if minds are to meet on the genuine issues.

The criminal law constitutes a description of harms which a society seeks to discourage with the threat of criminal punishment for those who commit those harms. At the same time the criminal law comprises an elaborate body of qualifications to these prohibitions and threats. It used to be common, and it still is not unknown, to express all of these qualifications to liability in terms of the requirement of *mens rea*. This is the thought behind the classic maxim, "Actus non facit reum, nisi mens sit rea." Or in Blackstone's translation, "An unwarrantable act without a vicious will is no crime at all." The vicious will was the *mens rea*. Reduced to its essence it referred to the choice to do a blameworthy act. The requirement of *mens rea* was rationalised on the common sense view of justice that blame and punishment were inappropriate and unjust in the absence of that choice.

It is more helpful (and also more usual today) to speak more discriminatingly of the various classes of circumstances in which criminal liability is qualified by the requirement of blameworthiness. Putting aside the circumstances of justification and excuse (they are relevant but not central to the controversy) there are two principal categories of *mens rea* which should be distinguished.

The *first* category we can call *mens rea* in its special sense. In this special sense *mens rea* refers only to the mental state which is required by the definition of the offence to accompany the act which produces or threatens the harm. An attempt to commit a crime consists of an act which comes close to its commission done *with the purpose that the crime be committed*. Unlawful assembly is joining with a group in a public place *with intent to commit unlawful acts*. Larceny consists of the appropriation of another's property *knowing* it is not your own with *intent* to deprive the owner or possessor of it permanently. Receiving stolen goods is a crime when one receives those goods *knowing they are stolen*. Manslaughter is the killing of another by an act done with *awareness* of a substantial and unjustifiable risk of doing so.

That the absence of the *mens rea*, in this special sense of the required mental state, precludes liability in all of these cases is of course the merest tautology. This is the way these crimes are defined.

From *Cambridge Law Journal*, Vol. 26 (1968), pp. 273–290. Reprinted with permission of the Cambridge University Press and Sanford Kadish.

But it is important to see that they are so defined because the special *mens rea* element is crucial to the description of the conduct we want to make criminal. And description is crucial in so far as it is regarded as important to exclude from the definition of criminality what we do not want to punish as criminal. To revert to the examples just given, it would not be regarded as appropriate to make criminal the taking of another's property where the taker believed honestly that he was taking his own property. Neither would it make sense to make a person guilty of receiving stolen goods where he neither knew nor had occasion to know that the goods were stolen. And surely we should see nothing criminal in joining a group in a public place, apart from the intent to commit unlawful acts.

The *second* category of *mens rea* qualifications to liability is that of legal responsibility, which includes the familiar defences of legal insanity and infancy. These qualifications differ in several particulars from the *mens rea* qualifications of the first category. In requiring *mens rea* in the first, special, sense the law is saying that it does not hold a person where he has shown himself by his conduct, judged in terms of its totality, including his mental state, to be no different than the rest of us, or not different enough to justify the criminal sanction. In requiring *mens rea* in the sense of legal responsibility, the law absolves a person precisely because his deficiencies of temperament, personality or maturity distinguish him so utterly from the rest of us to whom the law's threats are addressed that we do not expect him to comply.

Proposals to eliminate the defence of legal insanity entail the abolition of *mens rea* in this latter sense of legal responsibility. The elimination of *mens rea* in its special sense raises more radical challenges to the traditional criminal law. Let me start with legal insanity.

I

Devising an appropriate definition of legal insanity has been the subject of most of the argument concerning this defence. The modern starting point in England and the United States is the M'Naghten test formulated in 1843 which asks whether at the time of the act the accused was labouring under such a disease of the mind as not to know the nature and quality of the act he was doing, or that it was wrong.[2]

The justification for this formulation is that it does in fact exclude from liability a category of persons who by definition could not be deterred by the prospect of punishment, simply because they were incapable of choice, and whom, in consequence, it would be futile as well as unjust to punish. The definition of the exculpation, therefore, coincides with the rationale of the traditional requirement of *mens rea*. Nonetheless, the M'Naghten test has been vigorously and consistently criticised since its formulation. One can roughly identify four major themes of criticism, which, half-seriously, I want to refer to as the themes of reaction, liberal reform, radical reform and neo-reaction.

The reactionary criticism is based on the premise that the defence of legal insanity provides a loophole through which those who deserve punishment can too easily manage to escape. Therefore, the protection of the public requires that the defence be eliminated altogether,[2a] or at least be made so difficult to establish (for example, by placing the burden upon the defendant to prove his insanity beyond reasonable doubt[3]) that very few will escape.

The liberal reform criticism is that the M'Naghten test does not go far enough. Inconsistently with its own premise of exculpating the blameless the test fails to cover classes of defendants who merit exculpation as much as those it does exculpate. The major class of such defendants comprises those whose ability to choose to conform is destroyed even though their cognitive capacity is sufficiently intact to disqualify them under M'Naghten. Another class consists of those who *knew* on a superficial intellectual level what they were doing and that it was wrong, but did not really understand with the full emotional affect that gives meaning to knowledge. This criticism produced a number of changes in the legal insanity defence in American jurisdictions, notably the addition of the irresistible impulse defence and a broadening in the conception of the requirement of knowledge.[4] It has also produced the increasingly influential proposal of the American Law Institute's Model Penal code: "A person is not responsible for criminal conduct if at the time of such conduct as a result of mental disease or defect he lacks substantial capacity either to appreciate the criminality of his conduct or to conform his conduct to the requirements of law."[5]

The radical critique of M'Naghten is that it is wrongheaded, not simply inadequate, because it is based upon particular symptoms of mental disease in large part meaningless in the medical conception of mental illness. In short, it is a mistake to attempt to impose a legal definition upon what is inevitably a medical phenomenon. As a consequence of this criticism such proposals emerged as those of the Royal Commission on Capital Punishment in 1953 which put the test of legal insanity in terms of whether an accused was suffering from mental disease or deficiency to such a degree that he ought not to be held responsible.[6] It also produced the famous Durham test in 1954 which inquires whether the unlawful act of the accused was the product of mental disease or defects.[7] Such proposals have found virtually no acceptance either in England or in the United States.

The neo-reactionary criticism recommends that efforts to find improved definitions of the test of legal insanity be abandoned and that legal insanity as a defence be eliminated from the criminal law. The justification for this view differs from the reactionary case for abolition. Both end up proposing undiscriminating penalisation of the sick and the bad. But the new criticism, or much of it, does so as a first step toward penalising neither. This more sophisticated proposal for abolition has been advanced by a variety of persons for a variety of reasons.[8] Let me try to summarise what I understand to be the major arguments.

The first is that the administration of the tests of insanity—all tests—have been a total failure. It has proven impossible to administer the defence rationally and equitably. In the end the jury's determination is largely governed by the credentials and presentation of the psychiatric experts; and the defendant's ability to pay determines the quality of the psychiatric evidence he can present. Moreover, psychiatric testimony is worth little—it is the softest of the soft sciences, psychiatrists disagree on key concepts and their conclusions and analyses turn on their own value judgments. Finally, the whole enterprise is an elaborate search after something that does not exist—there is not and cannot be a workable distinction between the responsible and the irresponsible, particularly when the distinction is drawn in terms of the issue of volitional capacity.

Secondly, it is argued that the defence of legal insanity is of little practical importance. To be sure the defence has real bite in cases of capital punishment. But the death penalty has been abolished in England and is fast becoming otiose in the United States. In the United States legal insanity is pleaded in no more than about 2 per cent of the jury cases which go to trial.[9] In England the situation is similar. With increasing frequency, issues of the mental abnormality of the offender are being taken into account after conviction rather than before. For example, mental abnormality questions in England are taken into consideration in probation orders with mental treatment as a condition, in hospital orders under section 60 or 65 of the Mental Health Act of 1959 and in transfers of prisoners from prisons to mental hospitals. As a consequence of these developments in recent years only in about 1 or 2 per cent of cases is the mental abnormality of an offender taken into account by finding the defendant not guilty because of legal insanity.[10]

Finally, and of central importance, it is believed that the retention of the distinction between those to be punished and those only to be treated is unfortunate and invidious because in point of fact it is in all cases, not only in some, that persons who do harms should be treated and held in the interest of the public protection. The incidence of gross psychopathy among criminal offenders is enormous, ranging over the widest classes of offenders, and only the smallest fraction are covered by the legal insanity tests. The effect of maintaining the dichotomy between the sick and the bad (essentially a false one anyway) is to block public and legislative perception that in most crimes psychical and social determinants inhibit the capacity of the actors to control their behaviour. As a consequence effective development and use of psychiatric therapeutic resources for the vast majority of offenders are thwarted.

In the last analysis this case for abolition makes two claims—the first, that the present situation is bad; the second, that abolition would make it better. My own view is that the first claim is supportable although somewhat overdrawn. The second claim I believe is unfounded.

I am ready to concede that the record of the administration of the legal insanity defence is very bad indeed. And to some extent I am inclined to believe that the softness of psychiatry as a science and the inherent difficulty of the issue which the defence presents are partly responsible. But several necessary qualifications tend to blunt the point made by this criticism. The insanity defence is scarcely the only feature of our criminal justice system which is badly administered in practice. For example, inefficiency and inequity are endemic to a system committed to an adversary process but not committed to supplying the resources of legal contest to the typically penurious who make up the bulk of criminal defendants. But I would hope that the lesson of all this would not be to abandon the adversary method on that score, but to improve its operation. Likewise with the insanity defence, improvement of its operation rather than its abolition would seem the more appropriate response. The difficulty is not all produced by psychiatrists and the nature of the issue. To the extent that the difficulty is due to inadequate defence resources, to persistent, if not perverse, misunderstandings by psychiatrists of what the law's concern is, to unjustifiable restrictions on the scope of psychiatric testimony—and I believe it is due to all of these factors to some extent—it seems at least equally plausible to address those causes as to eliminate the feature of the law which allows them to operate. And even to the extent that the causes of the difficulty are incorrectible because inherent in the insanity defence, the case for abolition is not made out, any more than the case for abolishing the jury or the defence of unintentionality or ignorance would be made out by pointing to the grave problems of administration they produce. This dispositive issue is whether we would achieve a net gain in doing without the troublesome element in the law. And this I will come to shortly.

As to the argument founded on the infrequency of the defence, in one sense it cuts the other way. For to the extent that the case for abolition rests on the inequitableness and irrationality of its administration, the very infrequency of the invocation of that defence reduces the import of the criticism. But in any event the infrequency of a defence is not an argument for its elimination. The defences of necessity or duress surely are invoked in a minute fraction of criminal cases. Yet few would regard this as a reason for abandoning them. The function of a legal defence is not measured by its use but by its usefulness in the total framework of the criminal justice system.

Finally, we face the claim that the perpetuation of the insanity defence has tended to reduce the flow of psychiatric and other resources for treatment of the great mass of offenders. Certainly the flow has been far too small. We need more research and more resources in the effective treatment of offenders. But whether the presence of the insanity defence has contributed to this situation (and substantially so, according to the charge) is a question of fact which I have not seen the slightest evidence to support. Indeed there is evidence to the contrary—witness the proliferation in England of alternative routes for the disposition of psychologically disturbed offenders[11] which abolitionists often use to show the otioseness of the defence of legal insanity.

Now for the second claim. Would we achieve a net advantage in eliminating the defence? As a start let us try to get clear what would follow if the defence of legal insanity were abolished. Certainly what would follow would depend on the formulation of the defence. But for present purposes we can confine ourselves to M'Naghten. Since other tests include the cases which it covers, what is true of eliminating the M'Naghten defence is true of eliminating the other formulations as well.

It will be remembered that M'Naghten authorises the defence of legal insanity when the effect of the defendant's mental disease is to destroy his cognitive capacity, to make him unable to know the nature and quality of his act. When this is so the defence of legal insanity is made out and the defendant becomes subject to the variety of provisions governing commitment of the criminally insane. Now if this defence were eliminated what would be the position of a defendant charged with a crime? Apparently it would depend upon the *mens rea*, in the special sense, required by the definition of the crime. If the crime were one like attempt, requiring a purpose by the defendant to achieve an object; or if it were one like larceny, requiring knowledge of a particular matter of fact; or if it were one like manslaughter, requiring knowledge of a particular risk, would it not be the case that the defendant has a complete defence? A total inability to know the nature and quality of the act quite plainly precludes convicting a defendant of any crime whose definition requires that he have that knowledge. And any crime which requires intent, or knowledge or recklessness surely posits that knowing. If it were not for the special, pre-emptive defence of legal insanity, therefore, the defendant would have a complete defence on the merits to any such crime—namely, the lack of *mens rea*. What the insanity defence does is to deprive a defendant of his normal *mens rea* defence (which would be unqualified and lead to discharge) and to require that he be acquitted on this special ground with its consequences for indeterminate commitment.

If, on the other hand, the crime required only negligence, the absence of an insanity defence would leave the defendant with no defence at all, since all that is required is that the defendant has fallen substantially below the standard of the reasonable man, and this, by definition, a M'Naghten defendant has done. (Except, of course, to the extent that the subjective feature of the concept of negligence—requiring that *some* special characteristics of the defendant be considered in defining the standard, as, for example, his inability to see or to hear—were enlarged to embrace his special cognitive disabilities.)

Now precisely these consequences are apparently intended, or at least accepted, by some abolitionists.[12] But it is difficult to see the force of their case. The whole spirit of the proposal is to put social defence on a surer ground; to assure that those who constitute threats to personal and social security be effectively channelled into a preventive system which authorises the state to subject them to restraint in the public interest and to provide them with a therapeutic regimen both in the public interest and in their own. The effect of eliminating the insanity defence is to do the opposite precisely for those offenders who have done the greatest harm—those defined by crimes requiring *mens rea* of intent, knowledge or recklessness. (As for crimes of negligence, to which insane defendants might still be liable, this objection does not apply, of course. Here the difficulty created is the conviction of the innocent, a matter I will consider subsequently.)

This self-defeating consequence of eliminating the insanity defence simpliciter has moved other abolitionists to add another branch to their proposal. This entails enactment of a provision which would preclude all evidence bearing on the absence of *mens rea* which is founded on the mental abnormality of the accused.[13] This was the form, for example, that the earliest abolitionist enactment in the United States took. In 1909 the State of Washington amended its law to provide that it should no longer be a defence that the defendant by reason of his insanity was unable to comprehend the nature and quality of the act committed. But the statute then continued: "nor shall any testimony or other proof thereof be admitted in evidence."[14] In addition, it is interesting to note, the statute, consistent with the positivist premise and with more modern proposals, provided for indeterminate commitment in a state hospital for the insane or "the insane ward of the state penitentiary" for those convicted who are found by the judge to meet the M'Naghten test of insanity.

To the abolitionist proposal on this footing there are two principal objections—the first technical, the second fundamental.

The technical objection is this. For the reasons put earlier evidence of the defendant's mental abnormality may be directly relevant to the presence of the *mens rea* of the crime charged, without proof of which a conviction is not possible. If *some* evidence which is relevant to the issue of *mens rea* is excluded the judge must have a standard to distinguish the admissible from the inadmissible evidence. This standard, of course, under the Washington statute, as well as under similarly grounded formulations, would presumably be whether the evidence goes to establish the inability of the defendant, as the result of a mental disease, to understand the nature and the quality of his acts. The upshot would be, therefore, that the test of legal insanity having been ejected through one door would re-enter through another, now presenting itself as a rule of evidence rather than as a substantive defence. And a good deal, if not all, of the messy and unsettling business of bringing psychiatrists into the courtroom and in exposing the guilt-innocent determination to those inherently inconclusive medical arguments over the operation of men's minds, which it is one of the important objectives of the abolitionist proposals to eliminate, would not be eliminated after all. For how else could the parties address themselves to the issue of whether certain *mens rea* evidence, somehow touching the defendant's mental abnormality, is or is not part of the forbidden case bearing on legal insanity?

And there is another consideration which makes the picture even darker for the success of this proposal. That is the unlikelihood of finally working to screen out any substantial amount of psychiatric evidence from the trial on the issue of guilt or innocence. California's experience with the bifurcated trial teaches a dismaying lesson. In order to clarify and simplify the issues before the jury, the California law was amended in 1927 to require separate trials whenever the defendant raises defences on the merits as well as the defence of legal insanity. At the first trial, the defendant's sanity is presumed, and evidence bearing on legal insanity is excluded.[15] The lower courts struggled for years in an attempt to distinguish between admissible and inadmissible evidence at the first trial. But it was hopeless. Evidence of mental insanity tending to establish legal insanity will usually do double service as also tending to establish the absence of the specific *mens rea* required. Finally the Supreme Court ended the agony by holding that any evidence of defendant's mental abnormality was admissible at the trial of the issue of his guilt, so long as it was relevant to the existence of a mental state required by the crime.[16] The experiment was a failure—issues of guilt and of mental condition proved to be inseparable.[17] Abolishing the legal insanity defence is no more likely to keep the trial free of psychiatry and its preceptors and their probing into the mental condition of the accused than is the requirement of the separate trial of the issue of insanity. You can change the name of the game, but you cannot avoid playing it so long as *mens rea* is required.

I turn now to what I referred to as the fundamental objection to this proposal. Essentially it is that it opens to the condemnation of a criminal conviction a class of persons who, on any commonsense notion of justice, are beyond blaming and ought not to be punished. The criminal law as we know it today does associate a substantial condemnatory onus with conviction for a crime. So long as this is so a just and humane legal system has an obligation to make a distinction between those who are eligible for this condemnation and those who are not. It is true, as has been argued,[18] that a person adjudicated not guilty but insane suffers a substantial social stigma. It is also true that this is hurtful and unfortunate, and indeed, unjust. But it results from the misinterpretation placed upon the person's conduct by people in the community. It is not, like the conviction of the irresponsible, the paradigmatic affront to the sense of justice in the law which consists in the deliberative act of convicting a morally innocent person of a crime, of imposing blame when there is no occasion for it.

This sentiment of justice has attained constitutional stature in decisions of the United States Supreme Court. Obviously I do not bring the Supreme Court into this for its legal authority in the U.K. What is relevant is that in these decisions the

court was responding to a fundamental sense of justice, which, unlike the mandate of the court, does not stop at national boundaries. The animating principle in several recent decisions was that to convict a person of a crime in circumstances in which it was impossible for him to conform violates a fundamental principle of justice. It was this principle which led the court to hold that it constituted an unconstitutional imposition of cruel and unusual punishment to make it a crime for a person "to be" a narcotic addict.[19] The same principle persuaded the court in another case to find a violation of due process of law in the conviction of a person for failing to register as a previously convicted offender upon arrival in Los Angeles in the absence of any circumstances calculated to give notice of her obligation to do so.[20] As observed recently by Mr. Justice Fortas: "Our morality does not permit us to punish for illness. We do not impose punishment for involuntary conduct, whether the lack of volition results from 'insanity,' or addiction to narcotics, or from other illnesses."[21]

Of course the spirit behind these proposals to abolish the insanity defence is humane rather than punitive: what is contemplated is that persons, once convicted, who are insane would then receive all the care and treatment appropriate to their condition, as indeed would all persons who commit crime. The answer was given by the Washington Supreme Court when it declared unconstitutional the abolition amendment to which I earlier referred: "Yet the stern and awful fact still remains, and is patent to all men, that the status and condition in the eyes of the world, and under the law, of one convicted of crime is vastly different from that of one simply adjudged insane. We cannot shut our eyes to the fact that the element of punishment is still in our criminal laws."[22]

A common rejoinder is that we convict and punish persons daily whose ability to conform is impaired by a variety of circumstances—by youthful neglect, by parental inadequacy, by the social and psychical deprivations of growing up in a grossly underprivileged minority subculture, or by countless other contingencies of life.[22a] This is perfectly true, but I fail to see that it supports eliminating the insanity defence. First, the argument logically is an argument for extension of the defence of lack of responsibility, not for its abolition. It is never a reason for adding to injustice that we are already guilty of some. Second, confining the defence to patent and extreme cases of irresponsibility is not a whimsical irrationality. There may well be an injustice in it, but it rests upon the practical concern to avoid vitiating the deterrent impact of the criminal law upon those who are more or less susceptible to its influences. As Professor Wechsler has observed: "The problem is to differentiate between the wholly non-deterrable and persons who are more or less susceptible to influence by law. The category must be so extreme that to the ordinary man burdened by passion and beset by large temptations, the exculpation of the irresponsibles bespeaks no weakness in the law. He does not identify with them; they are a world apart."[23] We may accept as a necessary evil—necessary, that is, given our commitment to a punishment system—the criminal conviction of persons whose ability to conform is somewhat impaired and still protest that it is unacceptable for a society to fail to make a distinction for those who are utterly and obviously beyond the reach of the law.

At the heart of a good deal of the argument for abolition is, and must be, the rejection of the punishment system altogether. To the extent this is the case the rejoinder I have just been discussing makes more sense. The refusal to punish defined classes of offenders is an assertion of the propriety of punishing the rest. As Professor Morris has rightly observed, "one group's exculpation from criminal responsibility confirms the inculpation of other groups."[24] On this footing my reservations to the abolitionist proposal is twofold. In the first place it is far from self-evident that the best way to achieve the end of penalisation is by penalising all rather than by expanding the definition of the irresponsible. Secondly, and more fundamentally, the decline of guilt—which is what penalisation is about—also means, and necessarily, the decline of innocence. This brings us squarely to the remaining major issue I want to deal with.

II

To this point I have been speaking of abolishing the insanity defence as a relatively conservative proposal that would leave the rest of the substantive criminal law intact. I turn now to more radical proposals, like those of Lady Wootton, which see this reform rather as one part of a larger radical transformation of the law which would tear up, root and branch, all manifestations of *mens rea* towards the end of extirpating blame and punishment from the criminal law.

Lady Wootton proposes (others have as well, but none so persuasively) that the entire body of qualifications to criminal liability embraced in the *mens rea* principle be eliminated.[25] She sometimes uses *mens rea* loosely, but it seems clear enough that she has in mind not only the defence of legal insanity, but also *mens rea* in its special sense as denoting the mental state required by the definition of particular crimes. Under her scheme there would be two separate stages of determinations made in the case of a person accused of crime. At the first stage there would be decided only whether the defendant committed the act prohibited by the criminal law, without regard to whether he acted intentionally, knowingly, recklessly and even negligently, or whether he had the capacity to conform to the law under the circumstances. His mental state would be altogether irrelevant. The second stage would arise if it were found that he committed the prohibited act. Now the issue would be to decide what ought to be done with the defendant considering all we know and can find out about him—from psychiatrists, from social workers or from any other source—including, but not limited to, his mental and emotional state at the time he acted. The choice of the disposition would be governed by whatever is desirable to protect the public from his further criminality, whether what is required be medical or psychiatric treatment, training, a permissive or a rigorous environment, punishment or incarceration. Presumably if the offender did not pose a danger he would be released immediately. If he did, he would be held whether he was a villain or a helpless victim of his own incapacities, and for as long as he continued to pose the danger. Thus, according to Lady Wootton, a forward looking approach would be substituted for a backward one we now use, a preventive system for a punitive one.

We should note at the outset what implications such a proposal would have for the whole body of substantive criminal law as we know it. Plainly it would not do to leave the criminal law as it is with only the mental element removed, because under our present law (the instances of strict liability apart) *mens rea* is crucial to the description of the behaviour we want to prevent. Perjury without knowledge of the lie is simply making an incorrect statement under oath. An unlawful assembly without the intent to do unlawful acts is simply joining a group of people in a public place. An attempt to commit a crime without the intent to do so would be incoherent. It would follow under Lady Wootton's proposal that the substantive law of crimes would ultimately have to be rewritten to consist entirely in the specification of harms, somewhat on the order of the following hypothetical provision dealing with crimes against the person:

"A person commits a crime" (or perhaps "subjects himself to the compulsory régime of social prevention and personal betterment") "who engages in conduct (in the sense only of bodily movements) as a factual consequence of which:

1. another person's life is lost; or,

2. another person is physically injured; or

3. another person's life or physical well-being is imperilled."

Now such a "criminal code" would eliminate many of the perplexities which confront the judge, the practitioner and the student of the criminal law, but I venture to say that that would be its only redeeming feature. Let me try to indicate why I think this is so.

Presumably I am not allowed to say that the proposal would end up punishing innocent persons, because what is contemplated is the abandonment of punishment and of the significance of guilt and innocence in the criminal law. But what may be said is that the abandonment of the significance of that distinction can be accomplished more easily in legal form than in fact. The compulsory subjection of people to incarceration or other forms of restriction upon their liberty on account of their conduct is viewed by others and by the person as punishment despite all efforts of circumlocution. We have seen this happen in America with the juvenile delinquency laws. "Juvenile delinquency" in a very short time simply became another word for crime committed by youth.

Furthermore, as Professor Hart has observed, people in their own conduct and in relation to others do not view themselves as objects of circumstances but as responsible authors of conduct.[26] What often matters most in relating to others is the motivation and intention of the actors rather than the objective effects of their conduct. It would surely be damaging for the law to run counter to this pervasive human orientation to morality and social life in general.

And even if these basic human outlooks would in time be changed the consequence would be even more damaging. Much of our commitment to the democratic values, to human dignity and self-determination, to the value of the individual, turns on the pivot of a view of man as a responsible agent entitled to be praised or blamed depending upon his free choice of conduct. A view of men "merely as alterable, predictable, curable or manipulatable things"[27] is the foundation of a very different social order indeed. The ancient notion of free will may well in substantial measure be a myth. But even a convinced determinist should reject a governmental regime which is founded on anything less in its system of authoritative disposition of citizens. Whether the concept of man as responsible agent is fact or fancy is a very different question from whether we ought to insist that the government in its coercive dealings with individuals must act on that premise.

It is no answer that under the Wootton proposal *mens rea* would not be eliminated but simply taken into account, albeit with many other factors, after conviction rather than before. What is crucial is that it would cease to be relevant on the issue of guilt or innocence. That is the point at which it functions to distinguish the responsible from the irresponsible, the blameworthy from the blameless. To use *mens rea* simply as additional data in manipulating deviants is no concession at all.

There is also at stake the value of protection against crime. If the effectiveness of crime prevention through general deterrence, operating through the condemnation and conviction of offenders as a means of reinforcing habits and commitments of law abidingness, has never really been proven, neither has it been disproven. Given how little we really yet know of these matters it would be folly to abandon the traditional tools of social protection in favour of complete reliance on a system which works solely through the treatment of the actual offender and sacrifices the deterrent possibilities of the penal system upon those who might, but have not, offended.

There are objections also on another level. The proposed reconstitution of the criminal law would create insecurity in the general community when the central function of the criminal law is to create that security. The Wootton fallacy is to see only the negative side of the criminal law—the punishment of persons found guilty of criminal conduct. But it is crucial to keep in mind as well the positive side of the criminal law. It not only provides for the punishment of the guilty, it also protects the rest of us against official interference in the conduct of our lives and does so primarily through the much maligned concept of innocence. Where a person has behaved as well as a human being can behave, the requirement of *mens rea*, in its special sense, protects him. To abandon *mens rea* and to substitute a Wootton code—in which, as I tried to show, the occurrence of the harm as a purely factual consequence of a person's physical movements suffices for conviction—removes this essential safeguard. Even the best of us may be swept into the net, for the test of our eligibility for sanctions is not our responsible acts and the consequences for which we may fairly be held responsible, but sheer accident; and accident, by definition, may befall us all. Nor is it any comfort that we will no longer be exposed to condemnation and punishment as such. Whatever it is called we will be exposed to coercive intervention by the state in our daily lives regardless of our most dutiful efforts to comply with what is required of us. Even if the proposal would more effectively deal with the threat of crime (which, as I said, there is no reason to believe) it would do so by substituting what most of us would consider a greater threat to our security and liberty.

Of course the police and the prosecutors usually would not prosecute and the judges would not convict (or whatever the word would be) and the dispositional authorities would promptly release—when convinced that the person presented no danger. But they would have an unfettered discretion to do so or not in the case of potentially every person in the community. Of so unfettered a discretion we have seen enough even in the way the law is administered under our present system. We do not have to guess at the dangers. We know them. The discretion would constitute an invitation to abusive and discriminatory exercise of authority against the disliked or the unpopular on political or other grounds. To speak only of my own country, ghetto Blacks and long-haired hippies are singled out for police and prosecutorial reprisals even under our presently structured criminal law. Consider the rich possibilities for the play of prejudice a Wootton criminal law would provide.

Moreover, feelings of outrage and injustice over great wrongs are human. One may doubt how far a non-punitive law would go in eradicating such feelings. There would be no restriction on the expert dispositional authorities acting vindictively whenever the circumstances of particular crimes enraged them. At least our present criminal law serves in some measure to channel and confine the punitive sentiment.

Even when decisions of the dispositional experts were conscientious and enlightened those decisions would rest entirely upon judgments of prediction of future behaviour, a shaky foundation upon which to rest an entire system in the present imperfect state of our knowledge. The dispositional judgments would be based in addition upon the assumption that we have the ability to alter anti-social proclivities. This is an equally perilous premise in light of the substantial lack of knowledge, techniques, resources and manpower to effect changes in people along these lines.

Moreover, the natural and logical implications of proposals like those of Lady Wootton would multiply further the evils I have tried to describe. Even if people, like Lady Wootton, stop short of those natural implications it is hard to see why. Why should there be any limit on the duration of the detention of persons brought within the system? The legislative gradations of maximum punishments are, after all, a product of the punishment-blame system and hardly serve the purposes of a preventive-therapeutic one. Why need there be any requirement to await some outward conduct which produces the harm? Surely it should be enough that experts find the seeds of anti-social behaviour in personality tests and family relationships.

In the last analysis, what is entailed in the abolition of *mens rea* and the decline of innocence is only with slight exaggeration the conversion of the status of the entire population into that of persons on release on parole from mental institutions under an indeterminate commitment.[28]

In the criminal law of England and the United States today there are many small-scale enactments of proposals like those of Lady Wootton. We have strict liability in many offences. Hospital orders in Britain and sexual psychopath laws in the United States, indeterminate sentence laws and, to some extent, juvenile delinquency laws in the United States all exhibit some features of the Wootton *mens rea* proposal. One would hope that the direction of creative reform would not be to remake the criminal law after the model of these special and largely unsuccessful exceptions to the fundamental criminal law principles, but rather to devise legal principles and mechanisms for subjecting the process of treatment and social prevention to the restraints of law. But this is the subject of another paper.

Endnotes

[1] See Radzinowicz, *Ideology and Crime* (1966), p. 56.

[2] (1843) 8 Eng.Rep. 718.

[2a] See *State v. Strasburg*, 60 Wash. 106, 110 Pac. 1020 (1910), especially concurring opinion at 110 Pac. at 1029, speaking of the State of Washington's elimination of the defence of legal insanity: "No defense has been so much abused and no feature of the administration of our criminal law has so shocked the law-loving and the law-abiding citizen as that of insanity, put forward not only as a shield to the poor unfortunate bereft of mind or reason, but more frequently as a cloak to hide the guilty for whose act astute and clever counsel can find neither excuse, justification, nor mitigating circumstances, either in law or in fact. It is therefore not strange that there should be found a legislative body seeking to destroy this evil and wipe out this scandal upon the administration of justice."

[3] See the Oregon statute at issue in *Leland v. Oregon*, 343 U.S. 790 (1952).

[4] See, *e.g.*, *People v. Wolff*, 61 Cal. 2d 795, 394 P. 2d 959 (1964).

[5] A.L.I., Model Penal Code, Proposed Official Draft (1962), § 4.01.

[6] Royal Commission on Capital Punishment, 1949–1953, Report, § 333 (Cmd. 8932 (1953).

[7] *Durham v. United States*, 214 F. 2d 862 (1954).

[8] See, *e.g.*, N. Morris, "Psychiatry and the Dangerous Criminal" (1968) 41 So.Calif.L.Rev. 514; Wootton, *Crime and the Criminal Law* (1963), Chaps. 2 and 3; Hart, *The Morality of the Criminal Law* (1965), pp. 24–25; Weintraub, "Remarks" (1964) 37 F.R.D. 369; Halleck, *Psychiatry and the Dilemmas of Crime* (1967), pp. 205–229.

[9] Kalven and Zeisel, *The American Jury* (1966), p. 330.

[10] Walker, "The Mentally Abnormal Offender in the English Penal System," *The Sociological Review Monograph* No. 9 (1965), 133.

[11] *Ibid.*

[12] See N. Morris, *supra*, note 8 at 518–519.

[13] See *Hart, supra*, note 8.

[14] See *State v. Strasburg*, 60 Wash. 106, 110 Pac. 1020 (1910). See also *State v. Lang*, 168 La. 958, 123 So. 639

(1929); *Sinclair v. State*, 161 Miss. 142, 132 So. 581 (1931).

[15] Calif. Penal Code, § 1016.

[16] *People v. Wells*, 33 Cal. 2d 330, 202 P. 2d 53 (1949); *People v. Gorshen*, 51 Cal. 2d 716, 333 P. 2d 492 (1959).

[17] Louisell and Hazard, "Insanity as a Defense: The Bifurcated Trial" (1961) 49 Calif.L.Rev. 805, 830.

[18] N. Morris, *supra*, note 8 at 524–525.

[19] *Robinson v. California*, 370 U.S. 660 (1962).

[20] *Lambert v. California*, 355 U.S. 225 (1957).

[21] *Budd v. California*, 385 U.S. 909, 912–913 (1966) (dissenting opinion).

[22] *State v. Strasburg*, 110 Pac. 1020, 1025 (1910).

[22a] See N. Morris, *supra*, note 8, at 520.

[23] "The Criteria of Criminal Responsibility" (1955) 22 Univ. of Chi.L.Rev. 367, 374.

[24] *Supra*, note 8, at 520.

[25] Wootton, *Crime and the Criminal Law* (1963), Chaps. 2 and 3; Marshall, *Intention—in Law and Society* (1968); Campbell, "A Strict Acountability Approach to Criminal Responsibility" (Dec. 1965) 29 Fed.Prob. 33. See Ancel, *Social Defense* (Eng. ed. 1965); Glueck, *Law and Psychiatry* (1963) Chap. 4.

[26] Hart, *Punishment and Responsibility* (1968), p. 182.

[27] *Id.*

[28] For a like-minded, but fuller, critique of the Wootton proposal see Packer, *The Criminal Sanction* (1968).

Study Questions

1. In response to growing frustration with the existing tests for insanity, some jurisdictions, rather than abolish the defense altogether, have created a new verdict—"guilty but mentally ill"—as an alternative to the traditional options, "guilty" and "not guilty by reason of insanity." This verdict allows the jury to find that a person was sufficiently culpable to be said to have committed the crime, but at the same time to have suffered from a mental illness. Under this verdict, the accused is convicted and sentenced as a normal offender; he or she may then be moved to a treatment facility for all or part of the sentence; any time remaining after the completion of treatment must be spent back in prison. Does this compromise verdict make sense? Is it morally defensible?

2. How do the two conceptions of criminality, traditional and modern, identified by George

Fletcher (in his essay in Section A) bear on the issue of abolishing or retaining the special defense of insanity?

3. In 1985, a woman of Japanese ancestry walked into the ocean near Santa Monica, California, with her two children after learning that her husband was having an affair. Though she survived, the children drowned. Experts testified at trial that the woman's actions were consistent with the traditional practice of *oyako-shinju*, or parent-child suicide, for which she would be charged with involuntary manslaughter in Japan today. The first-degree murder charge initially filed against her was dropped and she was allowed to plead guilty to voluntary manslaughter. She received five years of probation with psychiatric treatment (see "Cultural Defenses Draw Fire," *The National Law Journal*, [April 17, 1989]: 3, 28). Should a person's cultural background be invocable to show that he or she did not have the *mens rea* for a crime with which he or she is charged? What problems do you see with such "cultural defenses"? Suppose I engage in conduct which, by the terms of my culture, I do not even recognize as "criminal"? Should this kind of "ignorance of the law" be an excuse?

4. What standards should courts employ when faced with novel insanity defenses? Consider four such cases: (1) In May 1979, while working at a pub in England, the defendant, a woman, got into a fight with a barmaid and stabbed her to death. Charged with murder, her record indicated a history of uncontrolled behavior, resulting in nearly thirty convictions in the preceding ten years. It was noticed that her uncontrollable disruptive behavior followed a definite monthly pattern. Doctors later diagnosed her condition as "premenstrual syndrome" (see D. Brahams, "Premenstrual Syndrome: A Disease of the Mind," *The Lancet*, Vol. 11 [Nov. 28, 1981]: 1238–1240). (2) In 1984, a defendant was charged with attempted bank robbery and larceny. In defense, he pled insanity in the form of a "pathological gambling disorder" (*U.S. v. Gould* 741 F. 2d 45 [4th Cir.

1984]). (3) Ann Green was charged with murder in the suffocation deaths of her two infants. She testified that she had seen hands she did not recognize holding pillows over the infants' faces. In 1989, a jury found Ms. Green "not responsible" for the deaths on the grounds that she suffered from "postpartum psychosis." (4) In 1989, Terrence Frank successfully avoided a conviction for first-degree murder in the shooting deaths of two persons on a Navajo reservation in Arizona. Mr. Frank's attorney convinced the jury that his client was "temporarily insane" at the time of the killing as a result of brain damage he had sustained from childhood exposure to uranium radiation leaking from mines surrounding his home. Frank's father and grandfather had both died from radiation-induced cancer; an abnormally high rate of birth defects were recorded in the area. (Frank was convicted of second-degree, unpremeditated murder. See "Toxin Defense' Successful," *The National Law Journal* [May 1, 1989]: 5). Which, if any, of these conditions should be acknowledged as disorders rising to the level of legal "insanity"? How should judges and juries weigh evidence of conditions yet to be widely received and accepted by the scientific community?

5. In March 1991, a jury convicted Norma Valentin on drug possession charges despite a defense based on the claim that she suffered from multiple personality disorder. According to Ms. Valentin, her other personalities include "Vicki," a drug dealer, "Ayessa," an Indian fortune-teller, and "Virginia," the personality involved in relationships with men. Ms. Valentin's counsel had contended that her "core" personality should not be criminally liable for crimes committed by one of her "secondary" personalities (see "Don't Try This Defense," *The National Law Journal*, [March 25, 1991], p. 6). Assuming that Ms. Valentin's multiple personality disorder is genuine, as attested by psychiatrists, should the law attempt to apportion responsibility among the various personalities "housed" within a single body? Why or why not?

D. *The Aims and Limits of Criminal Punishment*

Introduction

The final phase of a criminal proceeding involves the sentencing of the defendant (assuming of course that he or she has been found guilty). It is here that the penalties of the law, whether in the form of fines, imprisonment, or in the extreme case, death, are brought to bear upon the person then before the court. Though some states are now trying to tighten the reins, for the most part judges retain considerable discretion in the sentencing decision, usually within fairly broad parameters which are set, for example, in the form of minimum and maximum prison terms stipulated by the legislature. What sorts of considerations should figure in a sentencing decision?

Often the sentencing judge will announce the sentence, together with an argument supporting it, in the form of a memorandum of the court. Such is the case with Judge Marvin Frankel's fascinating memorandum in *U.S. v. Bernard Bergman*. Frankel's memorandum is an excellent example of an attempt to approach, through application to a specific case, an understanding of several philosophical theories of the nature and justification of criminal punishment. These theories, and their implications for novel forms of punishment, are discussed in this section.

Bergman and the Goals of Punishment

Rabbi Bernard Bergman was indicted in New York in 1975 on charges of conspiracy to defraud the government through the use of padded Medicaid claims made in connection with a number of nursing homes he operated. Bergman entered a plea of guilty and came before Judge Frankel for sentenc-

ing. Bergman's attorney argued before the court that no legitimate purpose would be served by punishing him. Weighing this contention, Judge Frankel embarked upon a general consideration of the various purposes that criminal punishment is alleged to serve and their applicability to Bergman and his crime.

Frankel first considers the claim that the only legitimate concern of a system of criminal justice is with the *rehabilitation* of the offender. The purpose of fixing responsibility, in this view, is simply to locate those individuals who need preventative detention and therapy. Frankel rejects this as a dubious goal, for prisons do anything but rehabilitate. Frankel next considers the theory of *deterrence*. He explains the important distinction between *specific* and *general deterrence*, insisting that the latter is the basic aim of punishment: The law seeks to induce others to avoid acting as the offender did. To this, Bergman's counsel raised an objection, invoking a third major theory of punishment, the *retributive* view of philosopher Immanuel Kant. Relying on Kant's claims that punishment must always be deserved and that one must never use an individual merely as a means—an instrument—for furthering some larger goal, Bergman's counsel sought to undermine the permissibilty of appeals to deterrence as a ground for punishing the defendant. Frankel responds that he is not simply or merely using Bergman's punishment in this way; he is also respecting the choice Bergman himself made "between keeping the law required for society's protection or paying the penalty." Our system, says Frankel, presupposes that persons make choices and are accountable for them. In this way, both general deterrence and retribution, as basic aims of punishment, have a role in the judgment passed on Bergman.

Having said all this, however, Frankel is still left with the difficult judgment of what specific punishment to dole out in this case. What would deterrence require here? Alternatively, what punishment would "fit" the crime?

Theories of Punishment

The various considerations raised by Frankel in his memorandum tend to align themselves with one or the other of two general moral and social theories: *utilitarianism* and *deontological ethics*, the view associated with Kant. On the most abstract level, utilitarianism is one of a family of views that takes the *consequences* or results produced or likely to be produced by an act or a policy as the measure of its moral correctness. Deontological ethics, in contrast, measures the rightness or correctness of conduct by the degree to which it conforms to duties or obligations we have to treat others in appropriate ways. As mentioned above, Kant holds a deontological theory of punishment called retributivism. This can be formulated more precisely as the view that punishing a person is justifiable if and only if it gives to him or her what he or she deserves.

The utilitarian argues that punishing a person is justifiable if and only if doing so has (or is likely to have) better consequences than not doing so; and as we have seen, there are several ways in which punishment might be thought to yield good consequences: through deterring others from committing the same offence; by incapacitating the offender, thereby preventing him or her from engaging in further undesirable behavior; and, perhaps, by contributing to the individual's rehabilitation.

Initially, both views of punishment possess some degree of attractiveness. The utilitarian holds that it is necessary for an instance of punishment to be justified that it do some good. Suppose a man steals some bread from a supermarket to feed his hungry children. The utilitarian asks us to temper the reaction to punish the man for his choice and to consider the larger circumstances within which he acted: What good will it do to penalize him? The problem with Kant's retributivism, the utilitarian might say, is that it requires that we punish such persons even where this clearly won't do any good, and this is inconsistent with a humane and enlightened approach to criminality. The Kantian, on the other hand, claims that it is necessary that punishment be deserved, but that this is an imperative that the utilitarian will not always observe. Suppose we inform you that we have decided to punish you with life imprisonment for the crime of running a stop sign. We are doing this not because you deserve or merit such a punishment but rather

to use you as an example to others (tired of the widespread failure to obey stop signs, we reason that the frequency of such lawlessness will decrease dramatically at the sight of your awful plight). Even assuming that subjecting you to such punishment would serve the goal of deterrence, surely you would demand to know what gives us the right to use you in this way—and it is this demand that lies at the heart of the retributivist insistence that punishment must be deserved. The difficulty with the utilitarian preoccupation with deterrence, it seems, is that it may allow persons to be punished out of all proportion to their guilt or even in the absence of any guilt whatever, when it serves the interests of society.

The details of the debate between these and other approaches to the topic of punishment are explored more fully in the selection by Jeffrie Murphy.

The Elimination of Punishment

Philosopher Richard Wasserstrom describes and then argues against the view that punishment, understood as a deliberate deprivation (e.g., the infliction of pain or some other evil), ought never to be resorted to but instead replaced with a regime in which the accused is subjected to therapy and rehabilitated. Wasserstrom raises serious questions for such a view: How does being "sick" relate to a person's conduct? Why should being sick relieve one of responsibility for what one does? Are criminals always sick? Is criminal behavior itself a sickness? Will focusing solely on curing the offender serve the goal of deterring others? Whose behavior do we wish to modify, the offender's or that of others in society? Wasserstrom concludes that until these questions are satisfactorily answered the rehabilitationist position remains unconvincing.

Cruel and Unusual Punishments

Bernard Bergman was sentenced to a punishment of four months imprisonment for his crime of fraud. Many crimes are punished in a similar way, through imposition of a jail sentence, payment of fines, or a combination of both. Recently, however, courts in various parts of the United States have begun to experiment with other, novel forms of punishment. *Goldschmitt v. Florida* is an example.

Arthur Goldschmitt was convicted of driving under the influence of alcohol. The trial court placed Goldschmitt on probation (releasing him into the community under the supervision of a court officer) on the grounds that Goldschmitt comply with a condition: that he place on his car a bumper sticker reading "Convicted D.U.I.— Restricted License." Goldschmitt objected to this condition on several grounds, relying primarily on the claim that the humiliation and disgrace of forcing him to display such a message on his car amounted to a form of "cruel and unusual" punishment, in violation of the Eighth Amendment to the Constitution.

In one of his most famous stories, the nineteenth-century American author Nathaniel Hawthorne described the punishment inflicted upon an adulteress in early America: She was forced for the rest of her days to wear on her chest a scarlet letter A, plainly visible to all, as a sign of her crime. Judicial "scarlet letters" are becoming increasingly common and they raise troublesome questions: Is humiliation a useful form of punishment? Is subjecting a person to disgrace and public ridicule justifiable in any acceptable theory of punishment? Do such sentences constitute cruel and unusual punishment? What makes a particular sentence cruel and unusual? Are there some forms of punishment that our law should never inflict?

Philosopher Jeffrie Murphy takes up the question of the meaning of the Eighth Amendment's ban on certain forms of punishment. Murphy reviews and rejects several proposals for fleshing out the meaning of "cruel and unusual." It might be suggested, for example, that the language simply be taken at face value. Murphy rejects this suggestion as absurd: A punishment does not become licit if only done painlessly and often. A further suggestion turns to the constitutional theory of original intent (see the discussion in Chapter Two) and urges that "cruel and unusual" means whatever the framers of the Constitution thought it meant, that is, whatever *they* would have deemed cruel and unusual. Murphy rejects this idea as well, countering that it is subject to all the problems confronting originalism as a general interpretive method. Nor is it reasonable to let the meaning of "cruel and unusual" reflect the consensus of public opinion at any one time, since the Eighth and simi-

lar amendments were supposed to serve as a check or constraint on the sentiments of the majority, not an implementation of them. Lastly, Murphy considers the utilitarian position that a punishment is cruel and unusual only when it levies a penalty in excess of what is warranted by the goal of bringing about the greatest happiness, say, by deterring others. The problem here, says Murphy, is that the language and subsequent interpretation of the clause make it clear that it was meant to rule out certain punishments altogether, even if they would have an extra deterrent effect if carried out.

Murphy proposes that the determination of which punishments are cruel and unusual be made in light of the Kantian, retributive conception of punishment. Cruel and unusual punishments are those that may not be inflicted, no matter how advantageous to society, because they are inconsistent with a proper regard for human dignity and a respect for persons as autonomous and responsible beings. The clause thus acts as a "side constraint," setting the permissible outer boundaries of social policy.

As Murphy points out, many who reject retributivism as a theory of punishment do so because they equate it with a primitive and thinly disguised lust for vengeance. Retributivists argue that this reaction is confused. Retributivism is not the view that punishment is justifiable as a means of satisfying the emotional response of vengefulness. Rather, the motivation is the desire to do justice, to see that the moral balance is restored and the debt repaid. One of the principal architects of retributivism, Immanuel Kant, appealed to what he called the "principle of equality" (or, perhaps less confusingly) *reciprocity*, a returning of like for like. The principle holds that "any undeserved evil that you inflict on someone else among the people is one that you do to yourself. If you vilify him, you vilify yourself; if you steal from him, you steal from yourself; if you kill him, you kill yourself. Only the law of retribution (*jus talonis*) can determine exactly the kind and degree of punishment."[1] Retributivism does not treat persons as mere objects upon which to vent our emotions: Kant argued that the law of retribution is inextricably bound to the idea of a person's inherent worth or dignity.

Central to the retributive theory is the *principle of proportionality*. This states that the severity of the punishment inflicted must be proportional to the gravity of the offense; the punishment, in other words, must fit the crime. Familiar as this saying is, the principle it represents is not entirely clear, and it raises problems both for retributivism and for courts confronted with claims under the Eighth Amendment. Questions about how the requirement of proportionality is supposed to work are raised in the *Coker* case.

Coker *and Proportionality*

While serving time in prison for murder and other violent crimes, Erlich Coker escaped from a Georgia facility and raped a woman. He was tried, convicted, and sentenced to death on the rape charge, the jury finding that death was an appropriate punishment given the presence of certain "aggravating factors." The Supreme Court overturned Coker's conviction, arguing that death as a punishment for rape is grossly disproportionate and thus violates the Eighth Amendment. A brief digression on the impact of the Eighth Amendment on the death penalty will allow us to see the issues here more clearly.

It is widely agreed that the Constitution itself certainly contemplates the death penalty, which was commonly used in the eighteenth century, even for crimes other than murder. In 1972, however, the Supreme Court, in *Furman v. Georgia*,[2] struck down all state capital punishment laws as they then operated. Differing explanations were given for the ruling. Some justices took the position that death, for whatever crime, is always cruel and unusual, since it fails to comport with "evolving standards of decency." The plurality took the view that death is not unconstitutional *per se* but that the unbridled discretion then given to juries to impose death as a punishment had resulted in a racially prejudicial administration of the punishment, making its imposition "arbitrary and capricious," and violating the Eighth Amendment on that ground.

Subsequent to *Furman*, most states enacted statutes to control jury deliberations in death penalty cases, providing for "guided discretion." These new procedural laws created a separate "penalty phase" in any trial resulting in conviction for a capital offense, permitting juries to recommend execution only if they found "aggravating circumstances" (for example, that the murder was committed for monetary gain or by a prisoner under a sentence of life imprisonment.) These laws were later upheld by the Court.

The Supreme Court in *Coker* divides on the question of how to understand and apply the retributive requirement of proportionality. This problem surfaces in at least two forms in the Court's opinion. First, should the aggravating factors here, including the previous crimes Coker had committed, bear on the appropriate punishment for his act of rape? And second, does death itself fit the crime? How strictly should Kant's law of equality be interpreted? The Court reads it strictly: Even though rape is a brutal and violent crime, it does not involve taking a life; death is appropriate as a punishment only in return for death.

In his writings on the state of Virginia, Thomas Jefferson recorded among other things some proposed revisions to the state's criminal code.[3] The revised code assigned specific punishments to types of offenses: treason and murder were to be punished with death; rape and sodomy were to be punished with "dismemberment"; and maiming and disfiguring with "retaliation." The proposed penal code constituted an attempt to carry out the retributive requirement that the punishment fit the crime on at least two levels. First, the schedule of proposed punishments attempted to ensure that the mode or kind of punishment be appropriate to the crime committed: reparation for larceny; physical beatings for battery, and so on. Second, the principle of equality was applied concretely to the specific manner in which crimes and their matching punishments were to be carried out: murder by poison, for example, was to be punished with death by poison.

How closely must punishment match crime? Would it be possible to carry out the logic of the Virginia code across the board? In some cases, this would be impossible, as with the blind man who attacks and blinds another; he can't be blinded in return. But are there certain punishments that must remain unacceptable even if they are literally workable as a return of like for like? May we torture the torturer? Rape the rapist? (Neither Kant nor the Virginia code are willing to insist upon literal sameness here: both recommend castration as a punishment for rape.) Jeffrie Murphy answers that retributivism should be understood to recommend only that crimes and punishments be ranked in severity, with the most serious crime getting the most serious punishment, the second most serious crime getting the second most serious punishment, and so on; with no further requirement that the crime be precisely mirrored, detail for detail, in the punishment.

Endnotes

[1] Immanuel Kant, *The Metaphysical Elements of Justice,* (trans. J. Ladd) (Indianapolis, Ind.: Bobbs-Merrill, 1965), p. 101.

[2] 408 U.S. 238 (1972).

[3] Thomas Jefferson, *Notes on the State of Virginia: Proposed Revised Code of Virginia,* reprinted in S. Presser and J. Zainalden (eds.), *Law and American History: Cases and Materials* (St. Paul, Minn.: West, 1980).

Sentencing Memorandum U.S. v. Bergman

MARVIN E. FRANKEL

The sentencing proceeding is unusual in some respects. It has been the subject of more extensive submissions, written and oral, than this court has ever received upon such an occasion. The court has studied some hundreds of pages of memoranda and exhibits, plus scores of volunteered letters. A broad array of issues has been addressed. Imaginative suggestions of law and penology have been tendered. A preliminary conversation with counsel, on the record, preceded the usual sentencing hearing. Having heard counsel again and the defendant speaking for himself, the court postponed the pronouncement of sentence for further reconsideration of thoughts generated during the days of studying the briefs and oral pleas. It seems fitting now to report in writing the reasons upon which the court concludes that defendant must be sentenced to a term of four months in prison.[1]

I. *Defendant and His Crimes*

Defendant appeared until the last couple of years to be a man of unimpeachably high character, attainments, and distinction. A doctor of divinity and an ordained rabbi, he has been acclaimed by people around the world for his works of public philanthropy, private charity, and leadership in educational enterprises. Scores of letters have come to the court from across this and other countries reporting debts of personal gratitude to him for numerous acts of extraordinary generosity. (The court has also received a kind of petition, with fifty-odd signatures, in which the signers, based upon learning acquired as newspaper readers, denounce the defendant and urge a severe sentence. Unlike the pleas for mercy, which appear to reflect unquestioned facts inviting compassion, this document should and will be disregarded.) In addition to his good works, defendant has managed to amass considerable wealth in the ownership and operation of nursing homes, in real estate ventures, and in a course of substantial investments.

Beginning about two years ago, investigations of nursing homes in this area, including questions of fraudulent claims for Medicaid funds, drew to a focus upon this defendant among several others. The results that concern us were the present indictment and two state indictments. After extensive pretrial proceedings, defendant embarked upon elaborate plea negotiations with both state and federal prosecutors. A state guilty plea and the instant plea were entered in March of this year. (Another state indictment is expected to be dismissed after defendant is sentenced on those to which he has pled guilty.) As part of the detailed plea arrangements, it is expected that the prison sentence imposed by this court will comprise the total covering the state as well as the federal convictions.[2]

For purposes of the sentence now imposed, the precise details of the charges, and of defendant's carefully phrased admissions of guilt, are not matters of prime importance. Suffice it to say that the plea on Count One (carrying a maximum of five years in prison and a $10,000 fine) confesses defendant's knowing and wilful participation in a scheme to defraud the United States in various ways, including the presentation of wrongfully padded claims for payments under the Medicaid program to defendant's nursing homes. Count Three, for which the guilty plea carries a theoretical maximum of three more years in prison and another $5,000 fine, is a somewhat more "technical" charge. Here, defendant admits to having participated in the filing of a partnership return which was false and fraudulent in failing to list people who had bought partnership interests from him in one of his nursing homes, had paid for such interests, and had made certain capital withdrawals.

The conspiracy to defraud, as defendant has admitted it, is by no means the worst of its kind; it is by no means as flagrant or extensive as has been portrayed in the press; it is evidently less grave than other nursing-home wrongs for which others have been convicted or publicized. At the same time, the sentence, as defendant has acknowledged, is imposed for two federal felonies including, as the more important, a knowing and purposeful conspiracy to mislead and defraud the Federal Government.

II. *The Guiding Principles of Sentencing*

Proceeding through the short list of the supposed justifications for criminal sanctions, defense counsel urge that no licit purpose could be served by defendant's incarceration. Some of these arguments are plainly sound; others are not.

The court agrees that this defendant should not be sent to prison for "rehabilitation." Apart from the patent inappositeness of the concept to this individual, this court shares the growing understanding that no one should ever be sent to prison for rehabilitation. That is to say, nobody who would not otherwise be locked up should suffer that fate on the incongruous premise that it will be good for him or her. Imprisonment is punishment. Facing the simple reality should help us to be civilized. It is less agreeable to confine someone when we deem it an affliction rather than a benefaction. If someone must be imprisoned—for other, valid reasons—we should seek to make re-

habilitative resources available to him or her. But the goal of rehabilitation cannot fairly serve in itself as grounds for the sentence to confinement.[3]

Equally clearly, this defendant should not be confined to incapacitate him. He is not dangerous. It is most improbable that he will commit similar, or any, offenses in the future. There is no need for "specific deterrence."

Contrary to counsel's submissions, however, two sentencing considerations demand a prison sentence in this case:

1. *First*, the aim of *general deterrence*, the effort to discourage similar wrongdoing by others through a reminder that the law's warnings are real and that the grim consequence of imprisonment is likely to follow from crimes of deception for gain like those defendant has admitted.

2. *Second*, the related, but not identical, concern that any lesser penalty would, in the words of the Model Penal Code, §7.01(1)(c), "depreciate the seriousness of the defendant's crime."

Resisting the first of these propositions, defense counsel invoke Immanuel Kant's axiom that "one man ought never to be dealt with merely as a means subservient to the purposes of another."[4] In a more novel, but equally futile, effort, counsel urge that a sentence for general deterrence "would violate the Eighth Amendment proscription against cruel and unusual punishment." Treating the latter point first, because it is a short subject, it may be observed simply that if general deterrence as a sentencing purpose were now to be outlawed, as against a near unanimity of views among state and federal jurists, the bolt would have to come from a place higher than this.[5]

As for Dr. Kant, it may well be that defense counsel mistake his meaning in the present context.[6] Whether or not that is so, and without pretending to authority on that score, we take the widely accepted stance that a criminal punished in the interest of general deterrence is not being employed "merely as a means. . . ." Reading Kant to mean that every man must be deemed *more* than the instrument of others, and must "always be treated as an end in himself,"[7] the humane principle is not offended here. Each of us is served by the enforcement of the law—not least a person like the defendant in this case, whose wealth and privileges, so long enjoyed, are so much founded upon law. More broadly, we are driven regularly in our ultimate interests as members of the community to use ourselves and each other, in war and in peace, for social ends. One who has transgressed against the criminal laws is certainly among the more fitting candidates for a role of this nature. This is no arbitrary selection. Warned in advance of the prospect, the transgressor has chosen, in the law's premises, "between keeping the law required for society's protection or paying the penalty."[8]

But the whole business, defendant argues further, is guesswork; we are by no means certain that deterrence "works." The position is somewhat overstated; there is, in fact, some reasonably "scientific" evidence for the efficacy of criminal sanctions as deterrents, at least as against some kinds of crimes.[9] Moreover, the time is not yet here when all we can "know" must be quantifiable and digestible by computers. The shared wisdom of generations teaches meaningfully, if somewhat amorphously, that the utilitarians have a point; we do, indeed, lapse often into rationality and act to seek pleasure and avoid pain.[10] It would be better, to be sure, if we had more certainty and precision. Lacking these comforts, we continue to include among our working hypotheses a belief (with some concrete evidence in its support) that crimes like those in this case—deliberate, purposeful, continuing, non-impulsive, and committed for profit—are among those most likely to be generally deterrable by sanctions most shunned by those exposed to temptation.[11]

The idea of avoiding depreciation of the seriousness of the offense implicates two or three thoughts, not always perfectly clear or universally agreed upon, beyond the idea of deterrence. It should be proclaimed by the court's judgment that the offenses are grave, not minor or purely technical. Some attention must be paid to the demand for equal justice; it will not do to leave the penalty of imprisonment a dead letter as against "privileged" violators while it is employed regularly, and with vigor, against others. There probably is in these conceptions an element of retributiveness, as counsel urge. And retribution, so denominated, is in some disfavor as a reason for punishment. It remains a factor, however, as Holmes perceived,[12] and as is known to anyone who talks to judges, lawyers, defendants, or people generally. It may become more palatable, and probably more humanely understood, under the rubric of "deserts" or "just deserts."[13] However the concept is formulated, we have not yet reached a state, supposing

we ever should, in which the infliction of punishments for crime may be divorced generally from ideas of blameworthiness, recompense, and proportionality.

III. *An Alternative, "Behavioral Sanction"*

Resisting prison above all else, defense counsel included in their thorough memorandum on sentencing two proposals for what they call a "constructive," and therefore a "preferable" form of "behavioral sanction." One is a plan for Dr. Bergman to create and run a program of Jewish vocational and religious high school training. The other is for him to take charge of a "Committee on Holocaust Studies," again concerned with education at the secondary school level.

A third suggestion was made orally at yesterday's sentencing hearing. It was proposed that Dr. Bergman might be ordered to work as a volunteer in some established agency as a visitor and aide to the sick and the otherwise incapacitated. The proposal was that he could read, provide various forms of physical assistance, and otherwise give comfort to afflicted people.

No one can doubt either the worthiness of these proposals or Dr. Bergman's ability to make successes of them. But both of the carefully formulated "sanctions" in the memorandum involve work of an honorific nature, not unlike that done in other projects to which the defendant has devoted himself in the past. It is difficult to conceive of them as "punishments" at all. The more recent proposal is somewhat more suitable in character, but it is still an insufficient penalty. The seriousness of the crimes to which Dr. Bergman has pled guilty demands something more than "requiring" him to lend his talents and efforts to further philanthropic enterprises. It remains open to him, of course, to pursue the interesting suggestions later on as a matter of unforced personal choice.

IV. *"Measuring" the Sentence*

In cases like this one, the decision of greatest moment is whether to imprison or not. As reflected in the eloquent submissions for defendant, the prospect of the closing prison doors is the most appalling concern; the feeling is that the length of the sojourn is a lesser question once that threshold is passed. Nevertheless, the setting of a term remains to be accomplished. And in some respects it is a subject even more perplexing, unregulated, and unprincipled.

Days and months and years are countable with a sound of exactitude. But there can be no exactitude in the deliberations from which a number emerges. Without pretending to a nonexistent precision, the court notes at least the major factors.

The criminal behavior, as has been noted, is blatant in character and unmitigated by any suggestion of necessitous circumstance or other pressures difficult to resist. However metaphysicians may conjure with issues about free will, it is a fundamental premise of our efforts to do criminal justice that competent people, possessed of their faculties, make choices and are accountable for them. In this sometimes harsh light, the case of the present defendant is among the clearest and least relieved. Viewed against the maxima Congress ordained, and against the run of sentences in other federal criminal cases, it calls for more than a token sentence.[14]

On the other side are factors that take longer to enumerate. Defendant's illustrious public life and works are in his favor, though diminished, of course, by what this case discloses. This is a first, probably a last, conviction. Defendant is 64 years old and in imperfect health, though by no means so ill, from what the court is told, that he could be expected to suffer inordinately more than many others of advanced years who go to prison.

Defendant invokes an understandable, but somewhat unworkable, notion of "disparity." He says others involved in recent nursing home fraud cases have received relatively light sentences for behavior more culpable than his. He lays special emphasis upon one defendant whose frauds appear indeed to have involved larger amounts and who was sentenced to a maximum of six months' incarceration, to be confined for that time only on week nights, not on week days or weekends. This court has examined the minutes of that sentencing proceeding and finds the case distinguishable in material respects. But even if there were a threat of such disparity as defendant warns against, it could not be a major weight on the scales.

Our sentencing system, deeply flawed, is characterized by disparity. We are to seek to "individualize" sentences, but no clear or clearly agreed standards govern the individualization. The lack of meaningful criteria does indeed leave sentencing judges far too much at large. But the result, with its nagging burdens on conscience, cannot be meaningfully alleviated by allowing any handful of sentences in a short series to fetter later judgments. The point is easy, of course, where Sentence No. 1 or Sentences 1–5 are notably harsh. It cannot be that a later judge, disposed to more leniency, should feel in any degree "bound." The converse is not identical, but it is not totally different. The net of this is that this court has considered and has given some weight to the trend of the other cited sentences (though strict logic might call for none), but without treating them as forceful "precedents" in any familiar sense.

How, then, the particular sentence adjudged in this case? As has been mentioned, the case calls for a sentence that is more than nominal. Given the other circumstances, however—including that this is a first offense, by a man no longer young and not perfectly well, where danger of recidivism is not a concern—it verges on cruelty to think of confinement for a term of years. We sit, to be sure, in a nation where prison sentences of extravagant length are more common than they are almost anywhere else. By that light, the term imposed today is not notably long. For this sentencing court, however, for a nonviolent first offense involving no direct assaults or invasions of others' security (as in bank robbery, narcotics, etc.), it is a stern sentence. For people like Dr. Bergman, who might be disposed to engage in similar wrongdoing, it should be sufficiently frightening to serve the major end of general deterrence. For all but the profoundly vengeful, it should not depreciate the seriousness of his offenses.

V. *Punishment in or for the Media*

Much of defendant's sentencing memorandum is devoted to the extensive barrage of hostile publicity to which he has been subjected during the years before and since his indictment. He argues, and it appears to be undisputed, that the media (and people desiring to be featured in the media) have vilified him for many kinds of evildoing of which he has in fact been innocent. Two main points are made on this score with respect to the problem of sentencing.

First, as has been mentioned, counsel express the concern that the court may be pressured toward severity by the force of the seeming public outcry. That the court should not allow itself to be affected in this way is clear beyond discussion.[15] Nevertheless, it is not merely permissible, but entirely wholesome and responsible, for counsel to bring the expressed concern out in the open. Whatever our ideals and mixed images about judges, it would be naive to doubt that judges have sometimes been swept by a sense of popular demand toward draconian sentencing decisions. It cannot hurt for the sentencing judge to be reminded of this and cautioned about it. There can be no guarantees. The sentencer must confront and regulate himself. But it bears reaffirmance that the court must seek to discount utterly the fact of notoriety in passing its judgment upon the defendant. Defense counsel cite reported opinions of this court reflecting what happens in a large number of unreported cases, by the present sentencer and many others, in which "unknown" defendants have received prison sentences, longer or shorter than today's, for white-collar or comparably nonviolent crimes. The overall run of cases, with all their individual variations, will reflect, it is hoped, earnest efforts to hew to the principle of equal treatment, with or without publicity.

Defendant's second point about his public humiliation is the frequently heard contention that he should not be incarcerated because he "has been punished enough." The thought is not without some initial appeal. If punishment were wholly or mainly retributive, it might be a weighty factor. In the end, however, it must be a matter of little or no force. Defendant's notoriety should not in the last analysis serve to lighten, any more than it may be permitted to aggravate, his sentence. The fact that he has been pilloried by journalists is essentially a consequence of the prestige and privileges he enjoyed before he was exposed as a wrongdoer. The long fall from grace was possible only because of the height he had reached. The suffering from loss of public esteem reflects a body of opinion that the esteem had been, in at least some measure, wrongly bestowed and enjoyed. It is not possible to justify the notion that this mode of nonjudicial punishment should be an occasion for leniency not

given to a defendant who never basked in such an admiring light at all. The quest for both the appearance and the substance of equal justice prompts the court to discount the thought that the public humiliation serves the function of imprisonment.

Writing, as judges rarely do, about a particular sentence concentrates the mind with possibly special force upon the experience of the sentencer as well as the person sentenced. Consigning someone to prison, this defendant or any other, "is a sad necessity."[16] There are impulses of avoidance from time to time—toward a personally gratifying leniency or toward an opposite extreme. But there is, obviously, no place for private impulse in the judgment of the court. The course of justice must be sought with such objective rationality as we can muster, tempered with mercy, but obedient to the law, which, we do well to remember, is all that empowers a judge to make other people suffer.

Endnotes

[1] The court considered, and finally rejected, imposing a fine in addition to the prison term. Defendant seems destined to pay hundreds of thousands of dollars in restitution. The amount is being worked out in connection with a state criminal indictment. Apart from defendant's further liabilities for federal taxes, any additional money exaction is appropriately left for the state court.

[2] This is not absolutely certain. Defendant has been told, however, that the imposition of any additional prison sentence by the state court will be an occasion for reconsidering today's judgment.

[3] This important point, correcting misconceptions still widely prevalent, is developed more fully by Dean Norval Morris in *The Future of Imprisonment* (1974).

[4] Quoting from I. Kant, *Philosophy of Law* 198 (Hastie trans. 1887).

[5] To a large extent the defendant's Eighth Amendment argument is that imprisoning him because he has been "newsworthy" would be cruelly wrong. This thought is accepted by the court without approaching the Constitution. (See below.) The reference at this point is meant to acknowledge, if only to reject, a seemingly broader submission.

[6] See H. L. A. Hart, *Punishment and Responsibility* 243–44 (1968).

[7] Andenaes, *The Morality of Deterrence*, 37 U. Chi. L. Rev. 649 (1970). See also O. Holmes, *Common Law* 43–44, 46–47 (1881).

[8] H. L. A. Hart, *supra* note 6, at 23.

[9] See, e.g., F. Zimring and G. Hawkins, *Deterrence* 168–71, 282 (1973).

[10] See Andenaes, *supra* note 7, at 663–64.

[11] For some supporting evidence that "white-collar" offenses are somewhat specially deterrable, see Chambliss, *Types of Deviance and the Effectiveness of Legal Sanctions*, 1967 Wis. L. Rev. 703, 708–10.

[12] See O. Holmes, *Common Law* 41–42, 45 (1881).

[13] See A. von Hirsch, *Doing Justice* 45–55 (1976); see also N. Morris, *The Future of Imprisonment* 73–77 (1974).

[14] Despite Biblical teachings concerning what is expected from those to whom much is given, the court has not, as his counsel feared might happen, held Dr. Bergman to a higher standard of responsibility because of his position in the community. But he has not been judged under a lower standard either.

[15] Cf. Andenaes, *supra* note 7, at 656.

[16] Andenaes, *supra* note 7, at 653.

The Therapeutic Model

RICHARD WASSERSTROM

There is a view, held most prominently but by no means exclusively by persons in psychiatry, that we ought never punish persons who break the law and that we ought instead to do something much more like what we do when we treat someone who has a disease. According to this view, what we ought to do to all such persons is to do our best to bring it about that they can and will function in a satisfactory way within society. The functional equivalent to the treatment of a disease is the rehabilitation of an offender, and it is a rehabilitative system, not a punishment system, that we ought to have if we are to respond, even to criminals, in anything like a decent, morally defensible fashion.

Karl Menninger has put the proposal this way:

> If we were to follow scientific methods, the convicted offender would be detained indefinitely pending a decision as to whether and how to reintroduce him successfully into society. All the skill and knowledge of modern behavior science would be used to examine his personality assets, his liabilities and potentialities, the environment from which he came, its effects upon him, and his effects upon it.
>
> Having arrived at some diagnostic grasp of the offender's personality, those in charge can decide whether there is a chance that he can be redirected into a mutually satisfactory adaptation to the world. If so, the most suitable techniques in education, industrial training, group administration, and psychotherapy should be selectively applied. All this may be best done extramurally or intramurally. It may require maximum "security" or only minimum "security." If, in due time, perceptible change occurs, the process should be expedited by finding a suitable spot in society and industry for him, and getting him out of prison control and into civil status (with parole control) as quickly as possible.[1]

It is important at the outset to see that there are two very different arguments which might underlie the claim that the functional equivalent of a system of treatment is desirable and in fact always ought to be preferred to a system of punishment.

The first argument fixes upon the desirability of such a system over one of punishment in virtue of the fact that, because no offenders are responsible for their actions, no offenders are ever justifiably punished. The second argument is directed towards establishing that such a system is better than one of punishment even if some or all offenders are responsible for their actions. A good deal of the confusion present in discussions of the virtues of a system of treatment results from a failure to get clear about these two arguments and to keep the two separate. The first is superficially the more attractive and ultimately the less plausible of

From *Philosophy and Social Issues* (Notre Dame, Ind.: University of Notre Dame Press, 1980), pp. 122–130.

the two. Each, though, requires its own explication and analysis.

One way in which the first argument often gets stated is in terms of the sickness of offenders. It is, so the argument begins, surely wrong to punish someone for something that he or she could not help, for something for which he or she was not responsible. No one can help being sick. No one ought, therefore, ever be punished for being sick. As the Supreme Court has observed: "Even one day in prison would be cruel and unusual punishment for the 'crime' of having a common cold."[2] Now, it happens to be the case that everyone who commits a crime is sick. Hence, it is surely wrong to punish anyone who commits a crime. What is more, when a response is appropriate, the appropriate response to sickness is treatment. For this reason what we ought to do is to treat offenders, not punish them.

One difficulty with this argument is that the relevance of sickness to the rightness or wrongness of the punishment of offenders is anything but obvious. Indeed, it appears that the conclusion depends upon a non sequitur just because we seldom, if ever, seek to punish people for being sick. Instead we punish them for actions they perform. On the surface, at least, it would seem that even if someone is sick, and even if the person cannot help being sick, this in no way implies that none of his or her actions could have been other than what it was. Thus, if the argument against ever punishing the guilty criminal is to be at all persuasive, it must be shown that for one reason or another, the sickness which afflicts all criminals must affect their actions in such a way that they are thereby prevented ever from acting differently. Construed in this fashion, the argument is at least coherent and responsive. Unfortunately, there is now no reason to be persuaded by it.

It might be persuasive were there any reason to believe that all criminal acts were, for example, instances of compulsive behavior; if, that is, we thought it likely to be true that all criminals were in some obvious and distinguishable sense afflicted by or subjected to irresistible impulses which compelled them to break the law. For there are people who do seem to be subjected to irresistible impulses and who are thereby unable to keep themselves from, among other things, committing crimes. And it is surely troublesome if not clearly wrong to punish them for these actions. Thus, the kleptomaniac or the person who is truly already

addicted to narcotics does seem to be suffering from something resembling a sickness and, moreover, to be suffering from something which makes it very difficult if not impossible for such a person to control the actions so compelled. Pity not blame seems appropriate, as does treatment rather than punishment.[3]

Now, the notion of compulsive behavior is not without difficulties of its own. How strong, for instance, does a compulsion have to be before it cannot be resisted? Would someone be a kleptomaniac only if such an individual would steal an object even though a policeman were known by the person to be present and observing every move? Is there anything more that is meant by compulsive behavior than the fact that it is behavior which is inexplicable or unaccountable in terms of the motives and purposes people generally have? More importantly, perhaps, why do we and why should we suppose that the apparently "motiveless" behavior must be the product of compulsions which are less resistible than those to which we all are at times subjected? As has been observed, ". . . it is by no means self-evident that [a wealthy] person's yearnings for valueless [items] are inevitably stronger or more nearly irresistible than the poor man's hunger for a square meal or for a pack of cigarettes."[4]

But while there are problems such as these, the more basic one is simply that there is no reason to believe that all criminal acts are instances of compulsive behavior. Even if there are persons who are victims of irresistible impulses, and even if we ought always to treat and never to punish such persons, it surely does not follow that everyone who commits a crime is doing a compulsive act. And because this is so, it cannot be claimed that all criminals ought to be exempted from punishment—treated instead—because they have a sickness of this sort.

It might be argued, though, that while compulsive behavior accounts only for some criminal acts, there are other sicknesses which account for the remainder. At this juncture the most ready candidate to absorb the remaining cases is that of insanity. The law, for example, has always been willing to concede that a person ought never be punished if the person was so sick or so constituted that he or she did not know the nature or quality of the act, or if this were known, that the person did not know that the act was wrong. And more recently, attempts have been made, sometimes successfully, to expand this exemption to include any person whose criminal action was substantially the product of mental defect or disease.[5]

Once again, though, the crucial point is not the formulation of the most appropriate test for insanity, but the fact that it is far from evident, even under the most "liberal" test imaginable, that it would be true that everyone who commits a crime would be found to be sick and would be found to have been afflicted with a sickness which in some sense rendered the action in question unavoidable. Given all of our present knowledge, there is simply every reason to suppose that some of the people who do commit crimes are neither subject to irresistible impulses, incapable of knowing what they are doing, nor suffering from some other definite mental disease. And, if this is so, then it is a mistake to suppose that the treatment of criminals is on this ground always to be preferred to their punishment.

There is, though, one final version of the claim that every criminal action is excusable on grounds of the sickness of the actor. And this version does succeed in bringing all the remaining instances of criminality, not otherwise excusable, within the category of sickness. It does so only by making the defining characteristic or symptom of mental illness the commission of an illegal act. All criminals, so this argument goes, who are not insane or subject to irresistible impulses are sociopaths—people afflicted with that mental illness which manifests itself exclusively through the commission of antisocial acts. This sickness, like any other sickness, should be treated rather than punished.

Once this stage of the discussion is reached, it is important to be aware of what has happened. In particular, there is no longer the evidentiary claim that all criminal acts are caused by some sickness. Instead there is the bare assertion that this must be so—an assertion, moreover, of a somewhat deceptive character. The illness which afflicts these criminals *is simply* the criminal behavior itself. The disease which is the reason for not punishing the action is identical with the action itself. At this point any attempt to substantiate or disprove the existence of a relationship between sickness and crime is ruled out of order. The presence of mental illnesses of these kinds cannot, therefore, be reasons for not punishing, or for anything else. Thus, even if it is true that we ought never to punish and that we ought always to treat someone whose criminal action was unavoidable because the prod-

uct of some mental or physical disease—even if we concede all this—it has yet to be demonstrated, without begging the question, that all persons who commit crimes are afflicted with some disease or sickness of this kind. And, therefore, if it is always wrong to punish people, or if it is always preferable to treat them, then an argument of a different sort must be forthcoming.

In general form that different argument is this: The legal system ought to abandon its attempts to assess responsibility and punish offenders and it ought instead to focus solely on the question of how most appropriately the legal system can deal with, i.e., rehabilitate if possible, the person presently before the court—not, however, because everyone is sick, but because no good comes from punishing even those who are responsible.

One such proponent of this view is Lady Barbara Wootton.[6] Her position is an ostensibly simple one. What she calls for is the "elimination" of responsibility. The state of mind, or *mens rea*, of the actor at the time he or she committed the act in question is no longer to be determinative—in the way it now is—of how he or she shall be dealt with by society. Rather, she asserts, when someone has been accused of violating the law we ought to have a social mechanism that will ask and answer two distinct questions: Did the accused in fact do the act in question? If he or she did, given all that we know about this person, what is the appropriate form of social response to him or her?

Lady Wootton's proposal is for a system of social control that is thoroughly forward-looking, and in this sense, rehabilitative in perspective. With the elimination of responsibility comes the elimination of the need by the legal system to distinguish any longer between wickedness and disease. And with the eradication of this distinction comes the substitution of a forward-looking, treatment system for the backward-looking, punitive system of criminal law.

The mental state or condition of the offender will continue to be important but in a different way. "Such conditions . . . become relevant, not to the question of determining the measure of culpability but to the choice of the treatment most likely to be effective in discouraging him from offending again. . . ."[7]

> . . . one of the most important consequences must be to obscure the present rigid distinction between the penal and the

medical institution. . . . For purposes of convenience offenders for whom medical treatment is indicated will doubtless tend to be allocated to one building, and those for whom medicine has nothing to offer to another; but *the formal distinction between prison and hospital will become blurred, and, one may reasonably expect, eventually obliterated altogether. Both will be simply "places of safety" in which offenders receive the treatment which experience suggests is most likely to evoke the desired response.*[8]

Thus, on this view even if a person was responsible when he or she acted and blameworthy for having so acted, we still ought to behave toward him or her in roughly the same way that we behave toward someone who is sick—we ought, in other words, to do something very much like treating him or her. Why? Because this just makes more sense than punishment. The fact that he or she was responsible is simply not very relevant. It is wrong of course to punish people who are sick; but even with those who are well, the more humane and civilized approach is one that concerns itself solely with the question of how best to effect the most rapid and complete rehabilitation or "cure" of the offender. The argument is not that no one is responsible or blameworthy; instead, it is that these descriptions are simply irrelevant to what, on moral grounds, ought to be the only significant considerations, namely, what mode of behavior toward the offender is most apt to maximize the likelihood that he or she will not in the future commit those obnoxious or dangerous acts that are proscribed by the law. The only goal ought to be rehabilitation (in this extended sense of "rehabilitation"), the only issue how to bring about the rehabilitation of the offender.

The moral good sense of this approach can be percieved most clearly, so the argument goes on, when we contrast this thoroughly forward-looking point of view with punishment. For if there is one thing which serves to differentiate any form of punishment from that of treatment, it is that punishment necessarily permits the possibility and even the desirability that punishment will be imposed upon an offender even though he or she is fully "cured"—even though there is no significant likelihood that he or she will behave improperly in the future. And, in every case in which a person is punished—in every case in which the infliction of the punishment will help the offender not at all

(and may in fact harm him or her immeasurably)—the act of punishment is, on moral grounds, seriously offensive. Even if it were true that some of the people who commit crimes are responsible and blameworthy, and even if it were the case that we had meaningful techniques at our disposal for distinguishing those who are responsible from those who are not—still, every time we inflict a punishment on someone who will not be benefited by it, we commit a seriously immoral act. This claim, or something like it, lies, I think, at the base of the case which can be made against the punishment even of the guilty. For it is true that any system of punishment does require that some people will be made to suffer even though the suffering will help them not at all. It is this which the analogue to a system of treatment, a rehabilitative system such as Lady Wootton's, expressly prevents, and it is in virtue of this that such a system might be thought preferable.[9]

There are, I think, both practical and theoretical objections to a proposal such as this. The practical objections concern, first, the possibility that certain "effective" treatments may themselves be morally objectionable, and, second, the possibility that this way of viewing offenders may create a world in which we all become indifferent to the characteristics that distinguish those who are responsible from those who are not. The ease, for example, with which someone like Menninger tends to see the criminal not as an adult but as a "grown-up child"[10] says something about the ease with which a kind of paternalistic manipulativeness could readily pervade a system composed of "places of safety."[11]

These are, though, contingent rather than necessary worries. A system organized in accordance with this rehabilitative ideal could have a view that certain therapies were impermissible on moral grounds, just as it could also treat all of the persons involved with all of the respect they deserved as persons. Indeed, it is important when comparing and contrasting proposals for rehabilitative systems with punishment to make certain that the comparisons are of things that are comparable. There are abuses present in most if not all institutional therapeutic systems in existence today, but there are also abuses present in most if not all institutional penal systems in existence today. And the practical likelihood of the different abuses is certainly worth taking seriously in trying to evaluate the alternatives. What is not appropriate, however, is to contrast either an ideal of the sort proposed by Wootton or Menninger with an existing penal one, or an ideal, just penal system with an existing therapeutic one.[12]

These matters to one side, one of the chief theoretical objections to a proposal of the sort just described is that it ignores the whole question of general deterrence. Were we to have a system such as that envisioned by Lady Wootton or Menninger, we would ask one and only one question of each person who violated the law: What is the best, most efficacious thing to do to this individual to diminish substantially the likelihood that he or she will misbehave in this, or similar fashion, again? If there is nothing at all that need be done in order for us to be quite confident that he or she will not misbehave again (perhaps because the person is extremely contrite, or because we are convinced it was an impulsive, or otherwise unlikely-to-be-repeated act), then the logic of this system requires that the individual be released forthwith. For in this system it is the future conduct of the actor, and it alone, that is the only relevant consideration. There is simply no room within this way of thinking to take into account the achievement of general deterrence. H. L. A. Hart has put the matter this way in explaining why the *reform* (when any might be called for) of the prisoner cannot be the general justifying aim of a system of punishment.

> The objection to assigning to Reform this place in punishment is not merely that punishment entails suffering and Reform does not: but that Reform is essentially a remedial step for which ex hypothesi there is an opportunity only at the point where the criminal law has failed in its primary task of securing society from the evil which breach of the law involves. Society is divisile at any moment into two classes: (i) those who have actually broken a given law and (ii) those who have not yet broken it but may. *To take Reform as the dominant objective would be to forego the hope of influencing the second—and in relation to the more serious offences—numerically much greater class. We should thus subordinate the prevention of the first offences to the prevention of recidivism.*[13]

A system of punishment will on this view find its justification in the fact that the announcement of penalties and their infliction upon those who break the laws induces others to obey the laws. The question why punish anyone at all *is* answered by Hart. We punish because we thereby deter potential offenders from becoming actual offenders. For Hart, the case for punishment as a general social practice or institution rests on the prevention of crime; it is not to be found either in the inherent appropriateness of punishing offenders or in the contingently "corrective" or rehabilitative powers of fines or imprisonments on some criminals.

Yet, despite appearances, the appeal to general deterrence is not as different as might be supposed from the appeal to a rehabilitative ideal. In both cases, the justification for doing something (or nothing) to the offender rests upon the good consequences that will ensue. General deterrence just as much as rehabilitation views what should be done to offenders as a question of *social control*. It is a way of inducing those who can control their behavior to regulate it in such a way that it will conform to the dictates of the law. The disagreement with those who focus upon rehabilitation is only over the question of whose behavioral modification justifies the imposition of deprivations upon the criminals. Proponents of general deterrence say it is the modification of the behavior of the noncriminals that matters; proponents of rehabilitation say it is the modification of the behavior of the criminals that is decisive. Thus, a view such as Hart's is less a justification of punishment than of a system of threats of punishment. For if the rest of society could be convinced that offenders would be made to undergo deprivations that persons would not wish to undergo we would accomplish all that the deterrent theory would have us achieve through our somewhat more visible applications of these deprivations to offenders. This is so because it is the belief that punishment will follow the commission of an offense that deters potential offenders. The actual punishment of persons is necessary to keep the threat of punishment credible.

To put matters this way is to bring out the fact that the appeal to general deterrence, just as much as the appeal to rehabilitation, appears to justify a wholly forward-looking system of social control. . . .

Endnotes

[1] Menninger, "Therapy Not Punishment," reprinted in Murphy (ed.), *Punishment and Rehabilitation* (Belmont, California: Wadsworth Publishing Co., 1973), p. 136.

[2] Robinson v. California, 370 U.S. 660 (1962).

[3] The Supreme Court has worried about this problem in, for example, the case of chronic alcoholism, in Powell v. Texas, 392 U.S. 514 (1968). The discussion in this and related cases is neither very clear nor very illuminating.

[4] Barbara Wootton, *Social Science and Social Pathology* (London: G. Allen & Unwin, 1959), p. 235.

[5] *See, e.g.,* Durham v. United States, 214 F. 2d 862 (D.C. Cir., 1954); United States v. Brawner, 471 F. 2d 969 (D.C. Cir., 1972); and Model Penal Code § 4.01.

[6] Barbara Wootton, *Crime and the Criminal Law* (London: Stevens, 1963).

[7] *Ibid.,* p. 77.

[8] *Ibid.,* pp. 79–80 (emphasis added).

[9] There are some additional, more practical arguments that might be offered in support of such a proposal.

To begin with, by making irrelevant the question of whether the actor was responsible when he or she acted, the operation of the criminal law could be greatly simplified. More specifically, by "eliminating" the issue of responsibility we thereby necessarily eliminate the requirement that the law continue to attempt to make those terribly difficult judgments of legal responsibility which our system of punishment requires to be made. And, as a practical matter, at least, this is no small consideration. For surely there is no area in which the techniques of legal adjudication have functioned less satisfactorily than in that of determining the actor's legal responsibility as of the time he violated the law. The attempts to formulate and articulate satisfactory and meaningful criteria of responsibility; the struggles to develop and then isolate specialists who can meaningfully and impartially relate these criteria to the relevant medical concepts and evidence; and the difficulties encountered in requiring the traditional legal fact-finding mechanism—the jury—ultimately to resolve these issues—all of these bear impressive witness, it could plausibly be claimed, for the case for ceasing to make the effort.

In addition, it is no doubt fair to say that most people do not like to punish others. They may, indeed, have no objection to the punishment of others; but the actual task of inflicting and overseeing the infliction of an organized set of punishments is distasteful to most. It is all too easy, therefore, and all too typical, for society to entrust the administration of punishments to those who, if they do not actually enjoy it, at least do not find it unpleasant. Just as there is no necessary reason for punishments ever to be needlessly severe, so there is no necessary reason for those who are charged with the duty of punishing to be brutal or unkind. Nonetheless, it is simply a fact that it is difficult, if not impossible, to attract sensitive, kindly or compassionate persons to assume this charge. No such analogous problem, it might be argued, attends the call for treatment.

[10] "What might deter the reader from conduct which his neighbors would not like does not necessarily deter the grown-up child of vastly different background. . . .

"It is not the successful criminal upon whom we inflict our antiquated penal system. It is the unsuccessful criminal, the criminal who really doesn't know how to commit crimes and who gets caught. . . . The clumsy, the desperate, the obscure, the friendless, the defective, the diseased—these men who commit crimes that do not come off—are bad actors, indeed. But they are not the professional criminals, many of whom occupy high places." Menninger, *op. cit., supra* note 1, pp. 134–35.

[11] These are discussed persuasively and in detail by Morris in his important article, "Persons and Punishment," 52 *The Monist* 475 (1968), pp. 476–90.

[12] *Ibid.* I think that Morris at times indulges in an improper comparison of the two.

[13] H. L. A. Hart, *The Concept of Law* (Oxford: Clarendon Press, 1961), p. 181 (emphasis added).

Goldschmitt v. Florida

490 So. 2d 123 (Fla. App. 2 Dist. 1986)
District Court of Appeal of Florida, Second District

Per Curiam.
Appellant, Arthur Goldschmitt, was convicted of driving under the influence of alcohol to the extent his normal faculties were impaired (D.U.I.). Goldschmitt appeals the trial court's order placing him on probation and requiring as a special condition of probation that he affix to his personal vehicle a bumper sticker reading "Convicted D.U.I.—Restricted License."

. . . We first consider whether section 316.193(4)(a), Florida Statutes (1985), permits the imposition of this or any other special conditions of probation. Goldschmitt urges that the statute authorizes probation for first-time D.U.I. offenders solely to ensure compliance with the concomitant statutory provision that the offender perform fifty hours of community service. Appellee responds that while the community service condition is a special, *additional* penalty created by the legislature, D.U.I. probation otherwise is no different than any other form of probation.[1] We agree. Section 948.03(4), Florida Statutes (1985), which permits the sentencing court to fashion special conditions of probation, does not distinguish between felony, misdemeanor, and criminal traffic offenses, or between county and circuit courts.

. . . Goldschmitt's argument that the bumper sticker constitutes a judicially developed, new penalty finds additional basis in the fact that this particular condition has become standard for all first-time D.U.I. offenders sentenced by two of the county's four judges. We would be quicker to accept his argument if we could be persuaded that any of the judges felt duty bound by local custom or rule to require the sticker despite their personal desire to the contrary. However, this obviously is not the case since half the local judiciary disdain the use of the sticker. While we are skeptical of special probation conditions imposed across-the-board, as opposed to being tailored to the needs and circumstances of the individual probationer, we cannot say that a judge may not impose a special condition of probation any time he or she chooses if that special condition otherwise is lawful.[2] Those who do require the bumper sticker apparently are of the opinion the sticker serves some useful purpose and that every first-time offender should have one.

. . . Next, we turn to the various constitutional objections raised by Goldschmitt. First, he advances the theory that the trial court has infringed upon his first amendment rights by forcing him to broadcast an ideological message via the bumper sticker. His principal authority for this proposition is *Wooley v. Maynard*, 430 U.S. 705, 97 . . . (1977), wherein a New Hampshire Jehovah's Witness found objectionable and taped over the "Live Free or Die" motto on his automobile license plate. Suffice it to say we agree with appellee that the message involved in the present case is "no more ideological than a permit to park in a handicapped parking space" as required by section 320.0848, Florida Statutes (1985). Further, in *Wooley v. Maynard*, the issue was whether New Hamp-

shire's interest in broadcasting its state motto sufficiently overrode the defendant's objections to the motto that criminal penalties could be imposed for defacing the tag. Here, the criminal behavior has already been committed prior to the requirement that the message be displayed as a form of penance and a warning to other potential wrongdoers.

. . . Goldschmitt's second constitutional argument is that the bumper sticker constitutes cruel and unusual punishment and is therefore violative of the eighth amendment. He likens the sticker to the pillory of colonial times, a form of publicly suffered punishment that most would agree is cruel and unusual by modern standards. . . . However, the differences between the degrading physical rigors of the pillory and a small strip of colorful adhesive far outweigh the similarities. The mere requirement that a defendant display a "scarlet letter" as part of his punishment is not necessarily offensive to the Constitution.

The deterrent, and thus the rehabilitative, effect of punishment may be heightened if it "inflicts disgrace and contumely in a dramatic and spectacular manner." *United States v. William Anderson Co., Inc.*, 698 F.2d 911, 913 (8th Cir.1983). The court in *William Anderson* expressed approval of behavioral sanctions imposed as conditions of probation for certain white-collar criminals, including speeches before civic groups on the evils of price fixing. "Measures are effective which have the impact of the 'scarlet letter' described by Nathaniel Hawthorne or the English equivalent of 'wearing papers' in the vicinity of Westminster Hall like a sandwich-man's sign describing the culprit's transgressions." . . . And, in *United States v. Carlston*, 562 F.Supp. 181 (N. D. Cal.1983), a defendant convicted of tax evasion was ordered to purchase computers and teach their use to probationers and parolees, the court noting that by association with street criminals he would be "constantly reminded that his conduct was legally and socially wrong." . . . Appellee refers to this philosophy, in the context of the present case, as "Pavlovian conditioning."

Of course, such innovative dispositions can be carried to extremes which might offend constitutional standards. In *Bienz v. State*, 343 So.2d 913 (Fla. 4th DCA 1977), a probationer was ordered into a halfway house with directions to obey all instructions. A supervisor accused him of behaving like a baby and directed him to wear diapers over his regular clothing. While the case was resolved on other grounds, the court commented:

"[S]uffice it to say that a command . . . that an adult male wear diapers in public would certainly be demeaning in the minds of so-called reasonable men . . . not surprisingly, prior decisions involving such bizarre incidents are sparse." . . . On the other hand, the requirement that a purse snatcher wear taps on his shoes whenever he left his residence was approved in *People v. McDowell*, 59 Cal. App.3d 807 . . . (1976), despite the defendant's plea that this was tantamount to a sign saying "I am a thief."

In the final analysis, we are unable to state as a matter of law that Goldschmitt's bumper sticker is sufficiently humiliating to trigger constitutional objections or, perhaps more to the point, that the lower court's belief that such a sticker is "rehabilitative" is so utterly without foundation that we are empowered to substitute our judgment for its.[3]

Accordingly, we affirm the judgment and order of probation of the trial court.

Endnotes

[1] One additional distinguishing feature of probation for the first-time D.U.I. offenders is that it is mandatory, whereas probation generally is but a matter of grace. *Robinson v. State*, 442 So.2d 284 (Fla. 2d DCA 1983).

[2] For example, the condition should bear some relationship to the nature of the offense of conviction and should have some reasonable rehabilitative basis. . . .

[3] Initially we were concerned by the possibility that innocent persons might be punished by the bumper sticker, insofar as appellant's vehicle might be owned or operated by others. However, at oral argument the parties advised that the bumper stickers come equipped with a special Velcro strip that enables the "Convicted—D.U.I." message to be obscured when persons other than the probationer are using the vehicle.

Cruel and Unusual Punishments

JEFFRIE MURPHY

> Excessive bail shall not be required, nor excessive fines imposed, nor cruel and unusual punishments inflicted.
>
> Amendment VIII
> *The Constitution of The United States of America*

This constitutional statement of right, like that of the English Bill of Rights (1689) from which its language was drawn, should be viewed as placing an absolute ban on certain punitive practices.[1] Indeed, this is an instructive way (at least initially and primarily) to view all bans contained in the Bill of Rights—as side constraints on permissible legislative enactment.[2] In the language of moral theory, one can say that a constitutional bill of rights is the attempt to formulate reasonable deontological restrictions (restrictions of principle) on the pursuit of social utility.[3] The constitutional provisions tell citizens what their rights are, and it is wrong in principle (not just bad policy) to pursue even laudable social goals in violation of such rights. As Ronald Dworkin has suggested, "The Constitution . . . injects an extraordinary amount of our political morality into the issue of whether a law is valid."[4] Thus if one can mount a good argument that to treat a person in a certain way is gravely unjust or would violate some basic human right of his, this is also and necessarily a good argument that it is unconstitutional to treat him in this way. The

From *Retribution, Justice, and Therapy* (Dordrecht: D. Reidel, 1979), pp. 223–249. Reprinted with permission of Kluwer Academic Publishers.

Constitution is a document of moral principle and is in this sense anti-democratic.

This essentially deontological or principled conception of constitutional rights (as absolute bans on certain means a majority might be tempted to employ to maximize social utility) will be presupposed in the following discussion of cruel and unusual punishments.[5] In other words, my basic questions will be the following: Are there certain punishments which one would want to oppose in principle, as unjust violations of the rights of the person being punished, regardless of the social utility (e.g., deterrence) which might flow from such punishments? Since I believe that the answer to this question obviously is *yes* (will anyone stand up for torture and mutilation?), another and much more difficult question must next be confronted—namely, what is it about such punishments which make them cruel and unusual in the sense of being wrong in principle? When an answer to this question has been developed, I shall turn to the final question I wish to explore in this essay: Is there any good reason for believing that *death* is cruel and unusual, that capital punishment should be opposed in principle? Attempting to answer this final question will require a consideration of recent Supreme Court cases in which the death penalty has been discussed in terms of the Eighth Amendment.

What does it mean to say that the infliction of some punishment *P* is wrong *in principle*? Getting at this question is, as I have suggested, to get at the core of the Eighth Amendment ban on cruel and unusual punishments. I shall argue that the best way to explicate the concept of a punishment's being wrong in principle is through a *retributive* conception and justification of punishment—i.e., a conception and justification resting upon the concepts of justice; rights and desert (and *not* social utility). Before arguing positively for this, however, let me first briefly suggest why other ways of proceeding (other conceptions of cruel and unusual) will not work.

(1) *Literalism.* The only punishments banned are those which cause great physical suffering and which happen with statistical infrequency—i.e., punishments which satisfy the literal meaning of the words "cruel" and "unusual."[6]

This analysis, of course, is absurd. Would anyone seriously maintain that radical mutilation or disfigurement will become acceptable as a punishment if we do it under anesthetic and several times

a week? Surely not. And does anyone seriously maintain that we can meet all the reasonable objections of those who believe that the death penalty violates the Eighth Amendment by suggesting that we execute painlessly and with great frequency? Physical suffering is a relevant factor and, if severe enough, may even be a sufficient condition for calling a punishment cruel. It is not, however, reasonable to regard it as a *necessary* condition—as the case of anesthetized mutilation demonstrates. (Psychological suffering poses interesting problems because it is present in many punishments—e.g., long-term imprisonment—which most persons would be reluctant to regard as cruel and unusual. The extent to which, if at all, this reluctance is justified is a question I shall explore later in the essay).

(2) *Historical Authority.* The only punishments banned are those which the Founding Fathers regarded as cruel and unusual at the time the Constitution was enacted.[7]

Surely this will not do either. Suppose that the Founding Fathers banned punishment *P1* because of their realization that *P1* had horrendous property *Q*. Suppose further that punishment *P2* also has horrendous property *Q* but that the Founding Fathers did not realize this. Are we then to be prohibited from attacking *P2* on constitutional grounds even though we realize that it has the very same property the Founding Fathers most wanted to oppose? This would be a stange kind of historical piety indeed. (For this reason it seems to me incorrect to suppose that the issue of whether the death penalty is cruel and unusual punishment is closed merely because the Founding Fathers did not explicitly ban it.) In my view of constitutional intent, the Founding Fathers should be viewed as intending to formulate reasonable deontological side constraints or restrictions of principle on the pursuit of majoritarian utilitarianism. Thus, whenever we can mount a good argument for a principled restriction, we are at least not wildly far afield of their intent—as we would clearly be if we tried to interpret the Constitution in terms, not of principle, but of some notion of wise or useful or efficient social policy. The Bill of Rights is not a document of policy; it is a document attempting to give us just or fair ground rules for the pursuit of policy.

(3) *Consensus.* The only punishments to be banned are those which would be rejected as inconsistent with the moral conscience of the citizens

of the society at a certain time in history—namely, the time at which the Court is actually considering the constitutional permissibility of a certain punishment. This is at least part of what it means to claim that the Clause "must draw its meaning from the evolving standards of decency that mark the progress of a maturing society."[8]

This consensus test is open to two interpretations. On one, it is irrational; on the other, it is redundant. First, let us suppose that the consensus is the sort one could discover by taking a random sample of citizen preferences—e.g., an opinion poll. It is, of course, ludicrous to regard the Constitution as sanctifying this kind of consensus. Probably the best test of what the citizens will find morally tolerable is that which is enacted by their representatives. But to say that a punishment passes the Eighth Amendment test if it has been enacted into law by a legislature is simply to abandon constitutional review of legislative enactments—i.e., to abandon the very point of having a Bill of Rights. One cannot use a right to check majoritarian excess if that right is interpreted in terms of majoritarian preference of tolerance. If tomorrow an opinion poll reveals (as I fear it might if such a poll were taken) that Americans are tolerant or even in favor of torture and mutilation, the Eighth Amendment will not have to be reinterpreted in light of that fact. Thus this kind of appeal to consensus is irrational.

A second interpretation of the consensus test is the following: A punishment will be rejected as cruel and unusual if it would be rejected as shocking the conscience, not of a majority of people selected at random, but of those citizens who are truly informed, educated, and morally sensitive.[9] There are two problems with this elitist consensus. First, it is very likely that the characterization of the elite will be circular and question-begging—i.e., we shall count as members of the relevant elite only those persons who hold the view we want to appeal to consensus to defend (opposition to the death penalty, perhaps).[10] Second, and more important, is the following problem: If genuinely enlightened persons all agree that some punishment *P* is evil and shocking to the conscience, it must be because of some property *Q* (pain, unfairness, degradation, etc.) which they have found in *P*. But then *P* is wrong because of property *Q*, not because of a consensus of enlightened judges. *P* is not wrong because there is a consensus against it; there is a consensus against it because it is wrong and

can be demonstrated to be so by argument (the showing that *P* contains *Q*).[11] This reveals that the consensus is morally redundant. We can go directly to *P* and condemn it as wrong because we can see that it bears morally obnoxious property *Q*—i.e., we can be brought to see whatever it is about *P* that the elite sees which makes them form a consensus against it.[12]

(4) *Utilitarianism.* A punishment is to be banned as cruel and unusual only if it is more extreme than that required for the pursuit of a legitimate state end or goal. As Bentham might put it, the purpose of punishment is to cause pain to the criminal as a means of deterring him and others from engaging in anti-social conduct, conduct which undermines the general welfare. Any pain inflicted beyond what is required for these goals is simply the gratuitous infliction of suffering and constitutes cruelty.[13]

In American law, the utilitarian interpretation of the cruel and unusual punishment clause has taken the form of the so-called "least restrictive alternative" test—i.e., a punishment is cruel and unusual (in the sense of being "excessive"—a crucial work in the total language of the Eighth Amendment) if it is more restrictive or intrusive than necessary to accomplish a legitimate state purpose.[14] For example: Capital punishment will be cruel and unusual if the same legitimate state purpose (deterrence of murder, say) could be accomplished with a less restrictive or intrusive punishment—e.g., long-term imprisonment.

There is insight in this test, and it can be reformulated in retributive language so as to represent a demand of justice rather than utility. For example, I shall later suggest that "excessive" can be interpreted as "lacking a reasonable *proportionality* to the seriousness of the offense"—where the legitimate state purpose is conceived to be, not simply deterring murder, but also insuring that the punishment for murder will be of a gravity justly proportional to the gravity of murder. And so too for other crimes and punishments.[15] When interpreted in a strictly utilitarian manner, however, the test simply will not work as an interpretation of the Eighth Amendment—and this for one very simple reason: It will not account for the paradigms, for the cases of punishments which everyone would agree are cruel and unusual: torture and mutilation. The Eighth Amendment does not tell us that torture and mutilation may be used only when required by a legitimate state purpose; it tells us rather that torture and mutilation may never be used *at all,* regardless of the state's purpose. It is this absolute or side constraint nature of a constitutional ban which no utilitarian outlook can capture. Constitutional bans are not policies; they are constraints on policies. Thus they cannot be explicated in terms of policy considerations.

The above comments have been far too sketchy, but I hope that they have at least provided grounds for suspicion against some common and initially tempting analyses of the Eighth Amendment ban on cruel and unusual punishments. I now wish to move to more positive considerations. I wish to develop a retributive account of the concepts of cruel and unusual punishment which will account for why the ban on such punishments must be regarded as a side constraint or principled restriction on policy. A retributive theory of punishment is one which characterizes punishment primarily in terms of the concepts of justice, rights and desert—i.e., is concerned with the just punishment, the punishment the criminal deserves, the punishment society has a right to inflict (and the criminal has the right to expect). In this way the theory makes central the special moral status of persons—unique individuals who, because they are autonomous and responsible creatures, must not be used for the benefit of others (as we use objects or animals) but who must be regarded as inviolate. Human persons have that special value which Kant (the most illustrious defender of retributivism) called *dignity*—a value which we respect when we address ourselves to them in terms of their unique characters and acts (i.e., what those characters and acts *deserve*) and not in terms of the general usefulness of treating them in certain ways.[16] The retributivist obviously does not want to ignore such utilitarian matters as deterrence and rehabilitation and incapacitation, but he insists that these values be pursued only after the values he regards as primary (rights, justice, and desert) have been secured. The intuitive idea, then, is that a cruel and unusual punishment is among the class of unjust punishments, of undeserved punishments, of punishments we have no right to inflict—regardless of utility. A general theory of the *just punishment* is thus what is required. For reasons I have already suggested, such a theory will have a strong bearing upon constitutional interpretation. But, given that every reasonable person of every nationality must care about the restrictions demanded by justice on the pursuit of utility,

it should also be of interest to those with no particular concern for American constitutional law.

Worries about the justification of particular kinds of punishment normally presuppose, of course, a belief that punishment in general is justified. Though I do not hold that this belief is obviously correct,[17] I shall assume its correctness for purposes of the present discussion. Otherwise, the discussion of the nature of certain punishments (torture, mutilation, and other cruel and unusual punishments) might be boringly brief—i.e., one might argue that these are wrong simply in virtue of their being punishments at all. Of course, even if one thought this, one might still want to argue that certain punishments have *something else* wrong with them. Just because one believes that all members of a series of acts *A1. . . . An* are bad, one is not committed to believing that they are *equally* bad. So even the person who thinks that all punishments are evil might still reasonably believe that torture is a worse instance of this kind of evil than, say, a small fine.

Thus our basic worry is not whether punishment of any kind is ever justified, but is rather the following: Given that we are going to punish in some way, are there certain *kinds* of punishment or certain *amounts* of punishment or certain *procedures* surrounding punishment which are so objectionable as to be banned outright or severly limited for reasons other than utilitarian deterrence? All of these worries—kind, amount, procedure—may plausibly be regarded as covered in the Eighth Amendment—a claim (controversial with respect to procedure) for which I shall argue later in the paper. *P* is intrinsically the sort of thing (torture perhaps) which we simply should not do to a person. *P* is not intrinsically evil but this amount of *P* (30 years in prison for possession of one marijuana cigarette, perhaps) is too much of *P* for this sort of conduct. *P* is the kind of punishment which is likely to be administered in an arbitrary and capricious way.[18] These are the three primary ways we are inclined to object to a particular punishment on grounds of justice (and thus oppose it in principle) and thus are the primary ingredients of the Eighth Amendment ban on cruel and unusual punishments.

Stating all this, of course, is not to solve anything—but is only to set the problems for discussion. *Why* are certain punishments intrinsically objectionable? *How much* punishment is too much (or too little)? All punishments certainly can be administered in an arbitrary and capricious way, so what is it about certain punishments which make such administration more likely?

Here traditional retributive theories are not as precisely helpful as one would like though they do give us a start in the right direction. Retributivism, as a general justification for punishment, proceeds in the following way—a way drawn from the theory of Immanuel Kant:[19] Punishment is justified primarily by backward looking considerations—i.e., the criminal, having engaged in wrongful conduct in the past, *deserves* his punishment. It would be unjust for him not to receive it. In receiving it, he pays a kind of *debt* to his fellow citizens—to those other members of the community who, unlike him, have satisfied the social obligation of reciprocity, have made the sacrifice of obedience that is required for any just legal system to work. Since all persons benefit from the operation of a just legal system, and since such systems require general obedience to work, it is only fair or just that each person so benefiting make the sacrifice (obedience or self-restraint) required and thereby do his part. Those who do not must pay in some other way (receive punishment) because it would be unfair to those who have been obedient if the criminal were allowed to profit from his own wrongdoing. (In this view a certain kind of profit—not bearing the burden of self-restraint—is intrinsic to criminal wrongdoing.) Hegel, who elaborated this Kantian retributive theory, argued that the criminal, who as a rational person could see that even he derived benefits from participation in a community of law, could be regarded as rationally willing (though not empirically desiring) his own punishment.[20] This being so, he deserves it in the sense that he has a *right* to it.[21] It is important to see that this theory grounds punishment on justice or fairness (i.e., justice demands that we inflict the punishment deserved, that we have the right to inflict, that the criminal has the right to receive), *not* on utility. The basic principle is that no person should profit from his own wrongdoing, and retribution keeps this from happening. If a person does profit from his own wrongdoing, from his disobedience, this is *unfair* or *unjust*, not merely to his victim, but to all members of the community who have been obedient—one reason why crime is an offense against the *state*. Now it may be, as the utilitarian might argue, that such unfairness—if widespread—would have socially undesirable consequences. But this is not Kant's argument. His argument is that the *injustice or unfairness itself*, regardless of consequences, demands retribution. As H. L. A. Hart has argued, "a theory of punishment which disregarded these moral convictions [about justice] or viewed them simply as factors, frustration of which made for socially undesirable excitement, is a different kind of theory from one which *out of deference to those convictions themselves* [justifies] punishment."[22] Kant's theory is clearly of this latter sort.

I have attempted to defend this retributive outlook in detail in other essays, and I shall not go over this ground again here except to mention three general points in an attempt to counter the bad press the theory usually gets:[23] (1) The theory is not an attempt to give approval to such barbaric motives as a desire for vengeance or vindictiveness. The only motive behind it is the desire to do justice. Thus retributivism is not an irrational cry for more and nastier punishments. Indeed, if retributivism were followed consistently, we should probably punish less and in more decent ways; for we now treat many criminals in ways harsher than, in justice, they deserve. (2) Retributivism is built around a rather attractive (if controversial) model of human beings as free or autonomous creatures, as enjoying rights, and responsible for what they do. Surely this is more attractive than the "you are sick and helpless or like a child" model behind a therapeutic response to crime or the "you can be used and manipulated for the common good" model behind utilitarian deterrence theory.[24] (3) Even many people who do not like the *name* "retributivist" are persuaded by considerations that are clearly retributive in nature. Suppose it was suggested that we punish negligent vehicular homicide with life imprisonment and first-degree murder with a couple of years in jail, and suppose this suggestion was justified with the following utilitarian reason: Conduct of the first sort is much more common and dangerous than conduct of the latter sort (we are much more likely to be killed by a negligent driver than by someone who kills us with the primary object of killing us), and thus we should use the most severe deterrents against those who are genuinely dangerous. If we object to this suggestion, as most of us would want to, that this would be unjust or unfair because it would not be apportioning punishment to fault or desert, we should be making a retributive argument. Thus even if the label "retributivist" repels most people, many of the actual doctrines of the theory do not.

Let us grant for present purposes, then, that the retributive outlook sketched above can provide a reasonable general justification of punishment in terms of its being unjust or unfair to allow criminals to be free-riders or parasites on schemes of social cooperation—something which would occur if they were not made to sacrifice in some way for not having made the required sacrifice of self-restraint. How will this help us in determining the *kinds* or *amounts* of punishment which will be tolerable—i.e., what alternative methods of sacrifice will be allowed, and which ones will be prohibited?

Here the guidance provided by the retributive theory is not as clear as one would like. Some version of the *jus talionis* ("like for like") principle seems initially tempting; but even Kant—one of its staunchist defenders—cannot consistently maintain it to the end. One immediate problem is that the principle cannot with sense be taken literally in all cases. Hegel observes "It is easy enough . . . to exhibit the retributive character of punishment as an absurdity (theft for theft, robbery for robbery, an eye for an eye, a tooth for a tooth—and then you can go on to suppose that the criminal has only one eye or no teeth)."[25] Kant also sees that there is a problem in applying *jus talionis* to "punishments that do not allow reciprocation because they are either impossible in themselves or would themselves be punishable crimes against humanity in general."[26] With respect to rape, pederasty and bestiality, for example, Kant believes that imprisonment is inadequate as a punishment but that a literal return of like for like would either be immoral (e.g., the rape of the rapist) or impossible (e.g., we cannot by definition commit bestiality upon a human criminal). Thus he proposes castration for the former two offenses and expulsion from society for the latter. He admits, however, that this is not a literal application of *jus talionis* but only in some sense captures the intuitive "spirit" of the principle.

What is it to capture the "spirit" of the principle? Perhaps something like the following: The principle of *jus talionis*, though requiring likeness of punishment, does not require *exact* likeness in all respects. There is no reason in principle (though there are practical difficulties) against trying to specify in a general way what the costs in life and labor of certain kinds of crime might be, and how the costs of punishment might be calculated, so that retribution could be understood as preventing criminal profit.[27]

There are still serious difficulties here, however—the chief being that, once a literal reading of *jus talionis* is abandoned, its application "in spirit" seems to be largely a matter of intuition unguided by any systematic theory. Kant's favorite example of *jus talionis* is the penalty of death for the crime of murder—this in spite of the fact that the punishment for *almost everything else* is imprisonment, a punishment which can literally satisfy "like for like" only for the offenses of false imprisonment or kidnapping. And speaking explicitly of the death penalty, Kant argues that this punishment must be "kept entirely free from any maltreatment that would make an abomination of the humanity residing in the person suffering it."[28] The criminal's "innate personality," he claims, protects the criminal against any morally indecent treatment.[29] In suggesting that the state should never do anything to a criminal that humiliates and degrades his dignity as a person, Kant seems to be working toward a ban on those punishments that have been described as cruel and unusual—i.e., a principled ban on certain punishments (torture and mutilation?) even when the "like for like" principle would seem to require them. There is insight here, but how the insight is to be squared with his support of castration as a punishment is a mystery to me.

The principle of *jus talionis* has thus produced a bit of a muddle, and the explanation for this is the following: Though a conception of reciprocity explains why the guilty should be punished, it is not clear that this same principle will explain why like should be returned for like or even that the evil inflicted on the criminal should be of equal gravity with that which the criminal has inflicted on his victim. The criminal has acted unfairly and that is why he must be punished. But unfairness is unfairness, murder being no more *unfair* than robbery. Thus if murder if worse than robbery (and thus deserves a worse punishment), this cannot be shown on the basis of purely formal considerations. Consider, again, the punishment for rape if the "like for like" position is adopted. If it be argued that the position does not entail that we rape the rapist but only do to him something of *equal* evil, it can be replied that the question "What evils *are* equal?" does not admit of a purely formal answer. Thus a retributivism grounded on fairness can at most demand a kind of *proportionality* between crime and punishment—i.e., demand that we rank acceptable punishments on a scale of seriousness, rank criminal offenses on a scale of seriousness, and then guarantee that the most serious punishments will be matched with the most serious crimes, the next most serious punishments with the next most serious crimes, and so on. This ranking must be reasonable, of course, but there is no reason to suppose that it will be determined solely or even primarily by considerations of fairness—i.e., no reason to suppose that seriousness can be totally analyzed in terms of fairness. In particular, considerations of fairness alone will not answer the question of which punishments will be allowed as the most serious. There will be substantive reasons for not allowing certain punishments (e.g., torture) even if these would satisfy a fairness principle of proportionality.

Let me say one other thing at this point about the concept of proportionality as applied to punishment. It can mean either (a) doing to the criminal something of equal gravity to what he has done to his victim or (b) making sure that the most serious punishments are applied to the most serious offenses, etc. So if the most serious punishment in a particular legal system is 20 years in prison and if this punishment is applied to the crime of murder, it could plausibly be argued that the proportionality demand stated in (b) has been satisfied, but not that stated in (a). And my argument thus far has been that (b), but not (a), can reasonably be derived from Kant's theory. At most a constrained variant of (a) might be derivable: (a*) do to the criminal something of equal gravity to what he has done to his victim unless this would require our doing something (e.g., torturing) to which there are serious substantive moral objections. If we allow such substantive restrictions, however, we shall be forced to admit that the decision to allow or not to allow *death* to remain as a system's most severe punishment cannot—contrary to Kant—be based simply on considerations of fairness or proportionality. We must at least reflect upon the possibility that our choice of this as a punishment will be constrained by other morally relevant properties of death.[30]

So far, then, we can get this much from Kant's theory: A punishment will be unjust (and thus banned on principle) if it is of such a nature as to be degrading or dehumanizing (inconsistent with human dignity). The values of justice, rights and desert make sense, after all, only on the assumption that we are dealing with creatures who are autonomous, responsible, and deserving of the special kind of treatment due that status. This is why

animals can be treated wrongly but cannot be wronged, cannot be treated unjustly, cannot have their rights violated. A theory of the just punishment, then, must keep this special status of persons and the respect it deserves at the center of attention. And there are at least two ways suggested by Kant whereby, in punishing, we can fail to do this: First, we can employ a punishment which is in itself degrading, which treats the prisoner as an animal instead of a human being, which perhaps even is an attempt to *reduce* him to an animal or a mere thing. Torture is of this nature. Using Kantian language, one might say that torture is addressed exclusively to the sentient or heteronomous—i.e., *animal*—nature of a person. Sending painful voltage through a man's testicles to which electrodes have been attached, or boiling him in oil, or eviscerating him, or gouging out his eyes—these are not *human* ways of relating to another person. He could not be expected to understand this while it goes on, have a view about it, enter into discourse about it, or conduct any other characteristically human activities during the process—a process whose very point is to reduce him to a terrified, defecating, urinating, screaming animal. I cannot, of course, *prove* that it is wrong to treat people in this way; for the wrongness of doing this is more obvious than any premises which could be given to justify its being wrong. Anyone who did not see this could not be made to understand anything else about morality. For we have here a paradigm of not treating a person as a person—and thus an undermining of that very value (autonomous human personhood) upon which any conception of justice must rest.[31] It is unjust to be tortured, everyone has a right not to be tortured, no one has a right to torture, no one deserves torture—all these claims flow from a theory of punishment (such as retributivism) which takes seriously and makes central the special status of persons.

A second way in which a punishment can fail to show respect for the status of autonomous persons is through radical lack of proportionality.[32] An autonomous person has a right that his punishment be *addressed* to that status—to those unique features of his individual, responsible conduct which occasion the punishment. A punishment radically disproportionate to the seriousness of the offense is not addressed to that for which he is responsible and blameworthy and deserving of punishment but is necessarily addressed to something else—e.g., society's mere *dislike* of him or his conduct.[33] This, in my view, is how the concept of "excessive" found in the Eighth Amendment should be interpreted.[34] To the degree that a person is being punished out of reasonable proportion to the seriousness of his offense, then to that degree is he being *used*—not being punished as justice would demand.

But is not the amount of punishment prescribed for an offense a criterion for how serious the offense is? That is, is it not almost true by definition that the most serious offenses will carry the most serious punishments—the prescription of the punishment by society being an index of how seriously society deplores the conduct? This challenge, in my judgment, is to be met in the following way: A just society cannot criminalize conduct simply because it deplores that conduct; its grounds for deploring the conduct must be *reasonable*. Conduct such as homosexuality does not cease to be morally trivial and become morally serious simply because a majority of people *think* it is morally serious and deplore it. As the Supreme Court correctly held in the *Robinson* case: if narcotic addiction is a disease, then no reasonable society may criminalize it—no matter how much it may represent a status detested and deplored by many persons.[35] In a just society, therefore, punishment must be proportional to the *objective* seriousness of the conduct, not to its subjective seriousness—i.e., the degree to which it is held in disapproval by the society at large.

[At] present, of course, we lack a coherent theory of objective seriousness. Thus, except in extreme cases, it will be practically difficult if not impossible to guarantee just proportionality in punishing. For one who cares about justice, however, this lack will stimulate research and thinking in order that a reasonable theory on these matters may be developed. The alternative is simply to stop caring about doing justice—hardly an acceptable outcome.[36] As I indicated previously, a theory of justice alone may not be able to tell us which offenses are most serious; it may require supplementation by a consideration of the substantive or intrinsic character of certain kinds of conduct. A theory of justice, however, can at least demand the following: that everyone has the right to have offenses graded in terms of individual fault or blameworthiness (i.e., desert) and not mere social utility, that other even substantive bases for grading be reasonable,[37] that punishments be graded on a comparable basis, and that there be a matching between seriousness of punishment and seriousness of offense. A theory of justice may not be able to supply all the details for ranking, but it can supply the framework.

Thus (by a process of deduction, variation, and free association) I have extracted the following from a generally Kantian account of retributive sentencing: A punishment will be banned in principle if (1) it represents a direct assault on the dignity of persons or (2) it is radically disproportional to the seriousness (the *objective* seriousness) of the conduct criminalized. Consideration (1) is, of course, more basic than (2)—i.e., certain punishments might pass the proportionality test but would still be rejected because they fail what might be called the "respect for persons" test. Thus the punishment of torture by an act of torture could hardly be faulted on grounds of proportionality, but it would still be rejected as an intrinsically inhuman method of punishment.

Both of the above notions—intrinsic heinousness and radical lack of proportionality—have a secure place in the interpretation of the Eighth Amendment. A ban on the first is clearly a part of the original meaning,[38] and a ban on the second has been prominent in twentieth century Eighth Amendment cases—including the recent *Coker* case where it was held (incorrectly in my judgment) that death was too severe a penalty for the crime of rape.[39]

Now what has gone on so far, even if one does not agree with the theoretical background, has probably done nothing more than produce *conclusions* which almost everyone would regard as noncontroversially reasonable—namely, that justice demands absolute side constraints against punishments which are intrinsically heinous or radically disproportionate. This is required if we are to respond to criminals as *people*—as individuals with unique characters and degrees of responsibility. (We are not to think of them simply in terms of dangerousness—as on a par with wild animals, or such natural disasters as earthquakes, or even madmen.)[40]

What I wish to do now is to move this general account I have been giving into an area of genuine controversy—namely, the penalty of *death*. Given the above sketch of the concepts of cruel and unusual punishments, is it reasonable to regard the punishment of death as falling under this description? That is, are there good reasons why, on grounds of justice or respect for rights (rather than utility), we should accept an absolute ban or principled restriction against the penalty of death? Does it belong, in other words, in the same camp as torture, mutilation, or punishments of radical disproportionality? We have the right not to be treated as animals—in a dehumanizing way. We have the right to be punished with sanctions proportional to our offenses. Do we also have the right not to be punished with death? If so, is this because death is necessarily a dehumanizing punishment or because it necessarily lacks proportionality with all possible offenses (or both)—or for some new reason entirely?

It should be obvious at the outset that there is no reason to believe that a punishment of death will always fail to satisfy the proportionality requirement. It would, of course, fail to satisfy this requirement for many offenses—but surely not for at least some acts of *murder*. (Kant's intuition seems correct here.) It is often said that, by making the criminal wait for a long time in terror and uncertainty before execution, we do something worse to him than any murderer does to a victim.[41] But this is just not so. What about the killers of Moro? Or suppose Patty Hearst's abductors had finally killed her? Are these acts not quite proportional to capital punishment? (It is also perhaps worth noting that much of the waiting is *chosen by the prisoner* while he files appeals.) Or what if the murderer tortured and mutilated his victim before the murder? We think of these activities as so horrible that we shall not even allow them as punishments, so surely their horribleness plus killing could be proportional to capital punishment—if anything, capital punishment might seem disproportionally *little* here. (A query: If torture and mutilation are so terrible that we will not allow them as punishments even when we do allow death, why then do we rank murder as an offense as *more serious* than torture and mutilation?)[42] Thus, if the concept of proportionality can be worked out at all, it seems that it should be possible to work it out for some acts of murder punishable by death.

Even when proportionality is satisfied, however, we shall not use a certain punishment if it is intrinsically degrading to the humanity of the criminal—e.g., we shall not torture the torturer. Is there perhaps, then, something intrinsically degrading, showing lack of respect for persons as persons, in the punishment of death—so that it too

could be banned even in cases where it satisfies the proportionality demand?[43]

Now it is easy to think that capital punishment is intrinsically degrading if we allow ourselves to be dominated by a certain picture of what capital punishment is like—e.g., the final part of Truman Capote's *In Cold Blood*.[44] But all that this may show is that brutalization may preceed and may accompany (as surrounding circumstances) the punishment of death.[45] This would be a reason for objecting to and changing those circumstances. But it would not be an objection to death *simpliciter* as a punishment. For suppose we consider another picture: the final scene of Plato's dialogue *Phaedo*, depicting the execution of Socrates by self-administered painless poison amid discourse with friends and family—all those around, even the jailer, showing great respect. This seems, at least intuitively, to depict a humanized death—a civilized execution. In this way, thus, does death seem to differ from torture. Is it conceptually possible to depict Socrates at a civilized torture session, a humanized case of evisceration of Socrates, a way of sending high voltage through Socrates's testicles which shows respect for him as a person? The answer seems *no*.[46] In a variety of social contexts (e.g., euthanasia) people are now rallying around the slogan "Death with Dignity." This suggests that they intuitively grasp some distinction between death *simpliciter* (which is surely bad) and circumstances which could surround death which would make it, not just bad, but degrading. But can we imagine anyone, who understands language and knows how to think, suggesting the slogan "Torture with Dignity" as part of a campaign against the excesses of certain political regimes? Death may be brought about in a degrading way; torture *must* be brought about in a degrading way. Thus we could imagine devising ways to humanize executions, to design them so that respect for the criminal would be shown. We cannot (*logically* cannot) imagine devising humanized or civilized torture sessions.[47]

Thus it seems to me that it is by no means obvious that execution *in itself* is necessarily—like torture—a way of showing lack of respect for a person, a way of treating him as or reducing him to an animal. Thus death may pass both the proportionality test and the respect for persons test. If so does this then show that the punishment of death cannot legitimately be opposed in principle, that we have no general right not to be executed by the state, and that opposition to the death penalty on principle is, at best, a kind of well-meaning sentimentality or, at worst, merely an illegitimate attempt to legislate our preferences for policy through the vehicle of constitutional law?[48]

In the remaining part of this essay, I shall present a defense for an answer *no* to this question. That is, I shall argue that a basic right of citizens in just societies is compromised by the death penalty and thus that there are grounds for a side constraint or principled restriction against it. My argument will support, in broad outline, a primary portion of the majority reasoning in *Furman v. Georgia* and later capital punishment cases.[49]

In what way did the Court hold capital punishment to be unconstitutional? Many arguments were given, but the one which comes through most clearly is the following: The death penalty is applied in an *arbitrary* and *capricious* way[50]—e.g., it tends to be used upon the poor and blacks and on almost no one else. Thus we are required on constitutional grounds to do *one* of the following: (a) devise ways to keep capital punishment from being applied in an arbitrary and capricious manner or (b) ban it outright.[51] Against the general thrust of this argument, two charges are immediately to be made: (1) *All* punishments (including imprisonment) are arbitrary and capricious in the way noted, but it is absurd to say that all punishments are unconstitutional. And yet the Court decision might seem to commit us to this absurd conclusion.[52] (2) To call capital punishment arbitrary and capricious is to make a *procedural* objection to it, one which could best be expressed by the Fourteenth Amendment "due process of law" or "equal protection" clauses. Why then drag in the Eighth Amendment, as the court did, in support of its decision? The Eighth Amendment, in banning cruel and unusual punishments, is surely *substantive* and not procedural in nature; and bringing it in simply muddies the waters.[53]

What I should like to do now is the following: Develop a principle relevant to the capital punishment issue which (a) breaks down a sharp substance-procedure distinction and thus renders the Eighth Amendment relevant and (b) distinguishes death from other punishments—especially imprisonment. That is, I want to meet both of the above objections and thus vindicate the major thrusts of the Court's reasoning.

What will the principle be? Recall that I am concerned with principles which rest on *rights* (i.e., with principles proper) and not with useful social policies. And what possible rights could be relevant to the kinds of punishment permissible other than the ones already mentioned (right not to be dehumanized; right to proportionality) and tentatively rejected for the death penalty? I shall suggest the following: *the right not to be dealt with negligently by one's government,* the right not to have one's basic interests threatened in casual and irresponsible ways by the state.[54] But is this not simply a statement of procedure; and, as such, how can it bridge the substance-procedure gap? To answer this objection, we can do no better than to turn to the writings of Judge Learned Hand whose discussion of negligence in tort law will be useful for our present purposes:

> The degree of care demanded of a person by an occasion is the resultant of three factors: the likelihood that his conduct will injure others, taken with the seriousness of the injury if it happens, and balanced against the interest which he must sacrifice to avoid the risk.[55]

In other words, there is no such thing as negligence *per se* or in the abstract. Whether the steps I take to reduce risk (the *procedures* of my acting) are negligent or not will depend in part on the (*substantive*) gravity of the harm that might result. Thus what constitutes due care as a precaution against my hurting your mailbox may not come close to what constitutes due care as a precaution against hurting your eyes. And, in the criminal area, what constitutes due process with respect to a parking fine may not come close to what constitutes due process for a long jail term.[56]

How does this apply to capital punishment? In the following way: All trial, conviction, and sentencing procedures are subject to *error*—to the possibility that they will convict the innocent. And there are two kinds of innocence at stake here: those totally innocent of any wrongdoing and those whose conduct, though meriting convicting of something (e.g., manslaughter), does not merit conviction of an offense of supreme gravity (e.g., murder in the first degree). Due process is an attempt to guard against both sorts of error. And what will be responsible (i.e., non-arbitrary and non-capricious) principles of due process for various criminal sanctions? How is the state to exercise due care instead of negligence in dealing with its citizens in terms of penal sanctions? Obviously, if Hand is correct, this question can be answered sensibly only if we have a reasonable view of the gravity of the (substantive) *harm* that might result from the error. Thus we have broken down the sharp line which supposedly separated substance and procedure, and the Eighth Amendment at least has a foot in the door. One objection to the Court's reasoning is thus met. But what about the other objection—that the Court's condemning of capital punishment as cruel and unusual because arbitrary and capricious logically must condemn *all* punishments in our society (even imprisonment) as cruel and unusual? Obviously, the objection can be met in only one way—namely, by showing that death is a *graver harm* than loss of liberty and that, therefore, higher standards of due care (due process) must surround the former sanction.

Can this be shown? Perhaps not in all cases—particularly in the case of life or extremely long-term imprisonment. Studies on the effects of long-term incarceration in "total institutions" indicate that long-term confinement develops in persons an "institutional personality"—i.e., a personality with diminished affect, neurotic dependencies, loss of autonomy and mental competence generally: in short, a kind of death (of personhood).[57] If these studies are correct, then long-term incarceration will be a kind of slow torture and psychic mutilation and *should* no doubt be banned on Eighth Amendment grounds (something the courts may be moving toward in declaring whole prison systems in violation of the Eighth Amendment).[58] This being so, it is a *virtue* of the Court's analysis that its arguments against death also apply to long-term incarceration. If they applied to all incarceration (or even to long-term incarceration if it does not have the above consequence), however, this would indeed be an absurdity. So what is it about death *simpliciter* which makes it a graver harm than loss of liberty *simpliciter*? Is it that people *fear* death more?—surely not, since many people fear death less than loss of liberty ("Give me liberty or give me death!") because they value liberty as a primary good of greater value than life.[59] Is it because death must entail intolerable suffering or degradation? No. As I have previously argued, certain manners of death may have this defect, but not necessarily death itself. What then?

One of the most common claims made in defense of the claim that death is worse than loss of liberty is the claim that death is *irrevocable*. But this will not do. Everything that is past is irrevocable. If I kill you in error, I have indeed done you an irrevocable injury. But so too if I imprison you falsely for five years. Margaret Radin, in her excellent discussion of capital punishment, attempts to meet this worry in the following way:

> Of course, even one day in prison is irrevocable in the sense that all past events and their resultant effects on human beings are irrevocable. Yet, although it might be difficult to articulate, most people intuitively recognize a distinction between the irrevocability of everything and the irrevocability of death or mutilation. The latter is the strong sense of irrevocability referred to here. It encompasses irreversible deprivations of attributes or capacities essential to, or at least closely connected with, complete personhood.[60]

This will not work. Radin is trying to show that death is a greater evil than loss of liberty because death is irrevocable—that is, she is supposed to be analyzing "grave harm" in terms of "irrevocability." But she is actually reasoning quite the other way around—i.e., analyzing irrevocability (in the "strong sense") in terms of grave harm. But if we already know the harm of death is greater than the harm of loss of liberty, we do not need the concept of irrevocability at all. One suspects that her analysis is unhelpfully circular—a suspicion reinforced when we notice that a synonym for "irrevocable" ("irreversible") is used in the analysis.

Let me then simply step in at this point and offer my own suggestion: Death is a greater harm than loss of liberty because it [(a) is] totally *incompensable* and (b) represents *lost opportunity* of a morally crucial kind. First, the concept of incompensability.[61] This is a concept which obviously admits of degrees. Some harms which we do to people are of such a nature—e.g., damage to their property or income—that it makes sense to speak of totally compensating them for their loss. For other harms, we cannot totally compensate; but we can at least make a reasonable attempt. Loss of liberty seems to me of this nature. In a culture such as ours, we know what it is like—and it intuitively seems reasonable and acceptable—to set a monetary value on my time and labor. Indeed, I can reasonably *bargain* these away for money—as when I work for a living. Thus if I am imprisoned by the state in error, it is at least not intuitively absurd to suggest that damages be paid as a way of compensating for the resulting harm. (We cannot totally compensate, of course, but we can in some sense make a reasonable stab at it.) But what would it be like to be paid anything even resembling adequate compensation for being tortured, radically mutilated, or debased in some other way—for being deprived of my status of honor or dignity as a person? If these have a price, this means that in a very real sense I do not have them to begin with—a man whose honor has a price simply being a man without honor. Suits in tort law may be brought and won here, of course, but how many winners would really believe that they had been even close to adequately compensated? How many would have bargained for this "price" in advance? Let us now move to death: On a scale of incompensability, death does indeed seem at the top. It is both logically and empirically impossible to compensate me if I am executed in error. (A wrongful death action may pay off someone, but necessarily *not me*). In contract law, we do not even *allow* people to bargain away for money their life or their personal integrity against torture and mutilation; but we do allow them to bargain away almost totally their personal liberty—e.g., by joining a volunteer army.[62] Should we punish people by doing S to them when we shall not even allow them to do S to themselves—even for pay?

The question, of course, is rhetorical; and I shall move from it to present the upshot of what I have been saying thus far. I have argued that death is like torture and mutilation (and unlike loss of liberty) in at least one important respect: that when we injure someone by killing him in error, we have done him an injury which is incompensable. Not so with imprisonment in error; for this is at least compensable to a significant degree. Thus in at least this one respect death is a graver harm than loss of liberty, and thus it is reasonable to require greater standards of due care or due process to prevent error in its application as a punishment. The Court was thus correct: the procedures which surround the punishment of death may properly be called arbitrary and capricious even if those same procedures are adequate for imprisonment.

But is this all? Is the only reason that death is worse than loss of liberty the fact that the former (when done in error) is totally incompensable and the latter (when done is error) is only partially incompensable? This does not seem correct—not as the *whole* story. Surely death is a worse injury than loss of liberty even when the punishment is *correctly* administered (i.e., not in error)—this being the very point, after all, of having death as the most severe sanction in one's arsenal of responses to crime. What this shows is that the person in favor of the death penalty for the most serious crimes (and reserving imprisonment for lesser crimes) *cannot consistently oppose the Court's reasoning in Furman v. Georgia*! For by his own admission, the death penalty *is* more serious than imprisonment; and thus, unless he wants (unreasonably) to quarrel with the claim that standards of due care or due process are in part a function of gravity of harm, he must agree with the Court that higher standards of review are required for the death penalty than for any other.

Why, then, might death reasonably be regarded as substantively more serious than loss of liberty? An answer to this question might help provide an interesting reason for why death is an incompensable injury—i.e., a reason more interesting than "You cannot compensate Jones if Jones is no longer around to be compensated."

Thus I shall now turn to the second point I want to make about death—that it represents *lost opportunity* of a morally crucial kind.[63] What I shall say here will be very brief; and it may also seem rather old-fashioned and romantically sentimental. Be that as it may, here it is: the most important thing within a human life (something stressed by philosophers from Socrates through Kant and by such other admirable and insightful individuals as Jesus and Tolstoy) is the *development of one's own moral character*, the development of oneself in such a way that one's life can honestly be said to be coherent, meaningful, and perhaps even admirable. To use the language of Plato and Socrates, one might say that what is most important in a human life is not what happens when the *body* is confined but is rather any harm that may come to the *soul*—or, to use less metaphysically provocative language, harm that may come to those crucial attributes of moral character and integrity which are most essential to personhood. The development of a morally coherent personality is the most crucial task or project of any human life—a project which we all muddle through with various degrees of success or failure (mostly failure) for our lifetimes. To block or interrupt this project (or to preclude one's ever having an opportunity to have a change of heart, reflect on one's life, and *start* such a project) is, in my judgment, the gravest harm that one can do to a person. Imprisonment (unless of such a nature or duration as to have profound effects on the inmate's mental health) will not do an individual this kind of harm—witness the number of inmates who in a very real sense have become "new people" while serving prison terms. But death, alas, provides no such opportunities and thus can certainly harm a person in this highly significant (one could say spiritual) way.[64] For death is the *loss* of significant opportunity (the opportunity to accomplish certain things, to treat people differently, to become a new person); and for many persons this must be the most terrifying thing about it.

> His mental sufferings were due to the fact that that night, as he looked at Gerasim's sleepy, good-natured face with its prominent cheekbones, the question suddenly occurred to him: 'What if my whole life has been wrong?' It occurred to him that what had appeared perfectly impossible before, namely that he had not spent his life as he should have done, might after all be true. It occurred to him that his scarcely perceptible attempts to struggle against what was considered good by the most highly placed people, those scarcely noticeable impulses which he had immediately suppressed, might have been the real thing, and all the rest false. . . . 'But if that is so,' he said to himself, 'and I am leaving this life with the consciousness that I have lost all that was given me and it is impossible to rectify it—what then?' (Leo Tolstoy, *The Death of Ivan Ilych*)

Given the exceptional moral gravity of having one's prospects for a morally significant and meaningful life interrupted, one might well want to deny the state any right to do this—i.e., one might adopt a direct absolute ban on the penalty of death. For it is by no means clear that one can show respect for the dignity of a person as a person if one is willing to interrupt and end his most uniquely human capacities and projects. Thus, contrary to initial and plausible impressions of the kind sketched previously, there is perhaps a case to be made that the punishment of death is degrading after all.

Even if one does not buy this, however, one must at the very least—given the considerations I have noted—have strong sympathy with the disjunctive position articulated by the Court—namely, that granting the supreme gravity of the penalty of death, the Constitution requires either (a) significantly more stringent standards of review for this penalty than for any other or (b) an outright ban on the penalty. Recent Court decisions requiring an elaborate consideration of mitigating and aggravating circumstances before a sentence of death may be imposed are an attempt to work with (a).[65] If this attempt fails—i.e., if it turns out that the standards of review surrounding imprisonment are really the best we can do—then we may be led indirectly into an outright ban on the death penalty. I am hoping for failure.

> I have no pleasure in the death of the wicked; but that the wicked turn from his way and live. *Ezekiel XXXIII, II*

Endnotes

[1] The best general treatment of the constitutional issues surrounding an application of the Eighth Amendment—with special focus on the death penalty—will be found in Margaret Jane Radin, 'The Jurisprudence of Death: Evolving Standards for the Cruel and Unusual Punishments Clause,' *University of Pennsylvania Law Review*, Volume 126, No. 5, May, 1978, pp. 989–1064. My own treatment of this topic has been enormously influenced by her essay.

[2] The notion of side constraints (as opposed to patterns or end results) as basic in moral theory has been developed by Robert Nozick, *Anarchy, State and Utopia* (New York: Basic Books, 1974), Chapter 3.

[3] See John Rawls, *A Theory of Justice* (Cambridge: Harvard University Press, 1971), all references under the headings 'Constitution' and 'Constitutional convention' on 591 of Index.

[4] Ronald Dworkin, *Taking Rights Seriously* (Cambridge: Harvard University Press, 1977), p. 215.

[5] I realize that these matters are more complex than I am suggesting here. What I wish to explore in this essay, however, is how far one can go with a purely deontological conception of constitutional restrictions and a purely retributive conception of punishment. It turns out, I think, that one can go pretty far.

[6] See Chief Justice Burger's discussion (with respect to cruelty) in *Furman v. Georgia*, 408 U.S. 238, 392 (1972) (Burger, C. J., dissenting).

[7] *Furman v. Georgia*, 408 U.S. 238, 418 (Powell, J., dissenting).

[8] *Trop v. Dulles*, 356 U.S. 86, 101 (1958) (plurality opinion) (Warren, C. J.).

[9] *Furman v. Georgia*, 408 U.S. 360 ff. (Marshall, J., concurring). Justice Marshall considers and rejects the opinion poll model and adopts a version of an elitist model involving a prediction of what people would deplore if fully informed.

[10] One is reminded of John Stuart Mill's "competent judge" test in *Utilitarianism* (Chapter 2). Mill attempts to show that contemplative pleasures are superior to sensual pleasures because persons who have experienced both (competent judges) prefer the former to the latter. Any person who has experienced both and does *not* judge in this way, however, would obviously pose a problem for Mill's test. How does he deal with this? In the following circular way: such persons reveal that they have lost their capacities for finer feelings and thus lose their status of competence.

[11] This, of course, is logically similar to Socrates's puzzle in Plato's dialogue *Euthyphro:* Is that which is pious pious because the gods approve of it; or do the gods approve of it because it is pious?

[12] The elite, of course, may be *epistemologically* relevant—i.e., they may get us to see or appreciate some morally relevant feature which we otherwise might have missed but for their insight. Their attitude toward the feature is not what *makes* it relevant, however.

[13] Jeremy Bentham, *The Principles of Morals and Legislation* (1789), especially Chapter XIV.

[14] "There is no reason to believe that [capital punishment] serves any penal purpose more effectively than the less severe punishment of imprisonment" (*Furman v. Georgia*, 408 U.S. 305) (Brennan, J., concurring). The general constitutional notion of the least restrictive alternative is articulated in *Shelton v. Tucker*, 364 U.S. 479.

[15] Consider persons in an "original position" of the kind described by John Rawls, *supra* note 3. It seems reasonable to suppose that they would choose a system in which penalties were no more severe than necessary to accomplish whatever purpose they set as reasonable. If Rawls is correct in claiming that choices in such a constrained setting yield principles of justice, then we have a non-utilitarian foundation for a least restrictive alternative principle.

[16] For more on this, see my 'Rights and Borderline Cases,' *Arizona Law Review* 19, Number 1 (1977) 228–241.

[17] See my 'Marxism and Retribution,' *Philosophy and Public Affairs* 2 Number 3 (Spring 1973) 217–243.

[18] It has been argued, for example, that capital cases bring out the worst and the most irrational in juries and judges. See Charles L. Black, Jr., *Capital Punishment: The Inevitability of Caprice and Mistake* (New York: Norton, 1974).

[19] I have elaborated this Kantian account more fully in my 'Marxism and Retribution,' *supra* Note 17. See also my *Kant: The Philosophy of Right* (London: Macmillan, 1970).

[20] See my 'Marxism and Retribution,' *supra* note 17.

[21] For more on punishment as a *right* of the criminal, see Herbert Morris, 'Persons and Punishment,' *The Monist*, 52, No. 4 (1968) 475–501. This is reprinted in my *Punishment and Rehabilitation* (Belmont, Calif.: Wadsworth, 1973).

[22] "Murder and the Principles of Punishment," *Punishment and Responsibility* (Oxford: Oxford University Press, 1968), p. 79.

[23] The retributive theory of punishment is, fortunately in my judgment, undergoing a bit of a renaissance at the moment. For a careful discussion which generally deplores this, see Hugo Bedau's essay in the 'Symposium: The New Retributivism,' *The Journal of Philosophy* LXXV, Number 11 (November 1978) 601 ff.

[24] For an argument that utilitarianism also tends to treat persons as children, see Adrian M. S. Piper, 'Utility, Publicity, and Manipulation,' *Ethics*, 88, No. 3 (April 1978) 189–206.

[25] *Philosophy of Right*, translated by T.M. Knox (Oxford: Oxford University Press, 1952), p. 72.

[26] *The Metaphysical Elements of Justice*, translated by John Ladd (Indianapolis: Bobbs-Merrill, 1965), p. 132.

[27] One interesting attempt to work something like this out may be found in Claudia Card, 'Retributive Penal Liability,' *American Philosophical Quarterly Monographs*, No. 7, 1973. According to Card, a retributively just punishment exposes the offender to hardship that is comparable to the worst that anyone could reasonably expect to suffer from such conduct were it to become general in the community. As Andrew von Hirsch has pointed out, however, this will not do "because it gives disproportionate emphasis to the potential harmfulness of the conduct, and relegates culpability to the role of a limiting principle" ('Symposium: The New Retributivism,' *supra* note 23). Von Hirsch's essay is a reply to Bedau.

[28] *Supra* note 26, p. 102.

[29] *Supra* note 26, p. 100.

[30] As I shall later argue, the mere fact (if it is a fact) that people tend to *believe* that death is horrendous is not a morally relevant property of death. (What people believe about death is surely not a property of death at all.) Such beliefs about death, however, might be relevant in a Rawlsian "original position" (*supra* note 15) in that they might prompt the rational choosers to place special constraints on its intentional causation.

[31] For an expansion of this sort of argument (or of a defense for not giving an argument), see my 'The Killing of the Innocent,' *The Monist* 57, No. 4, (October 1973) 527–550. . . .

[32] I say *radical* for the following reason: Any departure from proportionality is less than ideal justice would demand, but it may be impossible to grade these matters in a very fine way. We should still want to condemn, however, cases where the gap in seriousness between punishment and offense is clearly too wide.

[33] Obvious examples here are severe punishment for drug use, or consensual homosexual activity among adults, or any other "victimless crimes."

[34] See *Lockett v. Ohio*, 98 S. Ct. 2981 (1978) (White, J. dissenting in part and concurring in part). Justice White articulates both the utilitarian and the retributive analyses of "excessive."

[35] *Robinson v. California*, 370 U.S. 660 (1962).

[36] Andrew von Hirsh has made a start toward developing a framework for a theory of objective seriousness. See *supra* note 27 and his *Doing Justice: The Choice of Punishments* (New York: Hill and Wang, 1976). Though von Hirsch believes that such devices as the Sellin-Wolfgang survey technique for measuring degrees of seriousness have a use, he sees clearly that objective criteria for seriousness cannot be ultimately based on popular judgments. Von Hirsch has not (as I believe he would be the first to admit) given us very much, but he has given us a start—and a start in the *right direction* (toward just retribution).

[37] "Reasonable" may equal "would be chosen by parties in a Rawlsian original position." See *supra* note 15.

[38] For an excellent survey of the history of the Eighth Amendment and its interpretation, see *Furman v. Georgia*, 408 U.S. 314 (Marshall, J., concurring).

[39] *Coker v. Georgia*, 433 U.S. 584 (1977). In my judgment, the Court erred in not considering *degrees* of rape and aggravating circumstances which might render a punishment of death proportional—a point well made by Justice Powell in the dissenting part of his judgment.

[40] Some criminals (e.g., the psychopathic killer) are perhaps best regarded as wild animals or other non-responsible natural forces of destruction. Such a way of looking at them is not to regard them as persons; but this is all right because, from the moral point of view, *they are not persons*. If drastic steps (e.g., execution) are advocated for them, this cannot coherently be regarded as capital punishment (since they are not responsible and thus not legitimately open to *punishment*) but must be regarded simply as painless extermination— something done in the same spirit in which we destroy a mad dog. I see nothing *intrinsically* wrong about such

steps (i.e., see no reason for believing that psychopaths have a moral right to life); but the *practical* dangers of acting in this way (i.e., letting legal authorities—as in Nazi Germany—decide who is and who is not a person) are so grave that it is irresponsible even to consider this as a legal option. For more on this, see my 'Moral Death: A Kantian Essay on Psychopathy,' *Ethics* 82, Number 4 (July 1972) 284–298.

[41] Albert Camus argued in this way in his essay 'Reflections on the Guillotine.' One other serious problem about long delays is the following: during the delay a prisoner can in a very real sense become a "new person" by morally transforming himself. Is it fair that this new person be executed for a crime committed by a different and previous self? As I shall argue later in the paper, the possibility of self-transformation is a very good reason against the penalty of death.

[42] There is, of course, the utilitarian reason: we wish to give the torturer an incentive for not killing his victim after the torture session is over.

[43] There are three bad arguments (addressed to me in various public discussions) that the infliction of the death penalty is intrinsically wrong which—since they may be widely used—are perhaps worth a brief attack. (1) Punishing people by killing them *degrades us*—we are demeaned in the process. But we shall be demeaned by doing this only if doing it is wrong; it cannot be wrong *because* it demeans us. This begs the question. (2) "Two wrongs do not make a right"—a favorite cliché of Americans, particularly undergraduate students. This of course, begs the question also. The very point at issue is whether capital punishment is a wrong. (3) We must defend the value of the "sanctity of human life"—a value compromised when we execute. This bare slogan is of little help, because it can plausibly cut both ways on the capital punishment issue. Looking at the condemned person, we shall cite sanctity of life as a reason for not killing him. If we look at the *victim* (of murder), however, we could just as well cite sanctity of life as a reason *for* capital punishment—i.e., our use of a punishment this serious is our way of expressing how seriously we take the crime of murder. With analysis, however, this slogan can be turned into an argument—one which I shall develop later in the paper. Even analyzed, however, it will rest on a controversial assumption—namely that killing is morally worse than letting die. For a defense of this assumption, see my 'The Killing of the Innocent,' *supra* note 31.

[44] This book (based on a factual murder and execution) was made into a successful Hollywood movie. Both the book and the movie depict two marginal human beings of unclear responsibility who, after being convicted of murder and sentenced to death, arouse our pity and

compassion as they reveal both their humanity and animality in touching ways. Their route to death (except for their contact with Capote) is cold and impersonal.

[45] For more on the distinction between death and the terrible circumstances which may surround death, see my 'Rationality and the Fear of Death,' The Monist 59, Number 2 (April 1976) 187–203.

[46] This is not to say that some persons—e.g., Church martyrs, soldiers who will not betray comrades under torture, etc.—cannot rise above the inherent degradation of what is being done to them. Their animal nature is being addressed, but they hold out for a very long time (perhaps until death) before allowing that nature to answer. I am grateful to Merrilee Salmon for discussing these matters with me.

[47] We would be more inclined to regard as insane a person who voluntarily tortured himself than a person who voluntarily took his own life.

[48] This is the suspicion expressed by Justice Rehnquist in his dissent in Furman v. Georgia—a suspicion shared by some of the other dissenting Justices.

[49] The major relevant cases, other than Furman v. Georgia, are: Gregg v. Georgia, 428 U.S. 153 (1976); Woodson v. North Carolina, 428 U.S. 280 (1976); Roberts v. Louisiana, 428 U.S. 325 (1976); Jurek v. Texas, 428 U.S. 276 (1976); Coker v. Georgia, supra note 39; and Lockett v. Ohio, supra note 34.

[50] This is also the central argument of Charles Black's widely read book on capital punishment, supra note 18.

[51] The Justices are clearly divided on which alternative is preferable.

[52] Again, see Black (supra note 18) for a clear statement of and an attempt to meet this objection.

[53] "The Eighth Amendment was included in the Bill of Rights to assure that certain types of punishments would never be imposed, not to channelize the sentencing process. The approach of these concurring opinions has no antecedent in the Eighth Amendment cases. It is essentially and exclusively a procedural due process argument [dealt with and dismissed in McGautha v. California, 402 U.S. 207] . . . and it would be disingenuous to suggest that today's ruling has done anything less than overrule McGautha in the guise of an Eighth Amendment adjudication" (Furman v. Georgia, 408 U.S. 399 and 400) (Burger, C. J., dissenting).

[54] Again, it is perhaps worth noting (for those who are impressed, as I am, by his theoretical machinery) that Rawls's contractors (supra note 3) would surely adopt such a principle in the original position.

[55] Conway v. O'Brien (2 Cir. 1940) 111 F. 2d 611, 612.

See Also United States v. Carroll Towing Co. (2 Cir. 1947) 159 F. 2d 169.

[56] Mr. Justice Harlan wrote: "I do not concede that whatever process is 'due' an offender faced with a fine or a prison sentence necessarily satisfies the requirements of the Constitution in a capital case" (Reid v. Covert, 354 U.S. 1) (1957).

[57] See Erving Goffman, Asylums (New York: Doubleday, 1961). See also my 'Rationality and the Fear of Death,' supra note 45.

[58] It is not uncommon for federal court to declare the prison systems of entire states (e.g. Arizona) to be in violation of the Eighth Amendment—the primary reason usually being overcrowding. But what is the matter with overcrowding? Presumably the effects it has on prisoners. But what if long-term incarceration has the same or similar effects?

[59] As noted above (supra note 30) attitudes toward death as opposed to other punishments could be relevant in the Rawlsian original position; but, unless these attitudes are absolutely uniform for all persons, it is hard to see how the application of the punishment could be fair—i.e., some will be more hurt by it than others. Again, one needs an objective account.

[60] Radin, supra note 1, p. 1022. Irrevocability is probably the most frequently cited reason in defense of the claim that death is more serious than loss of liberty. See Black, supra note 18. And Justice Marshall: "Death is irrevocable; life imprisonment is not" (Furman v. Georgia, 408 U.S. 346).

[61] For an excellent discussion of the distinction between compensable and incompensable injuries, see Nozick, supra note 2, Chapter 4.

[62] We do, of course, have the concept of a Faustian contract. But we also take these to be perverse.

[63] I have elaborated this point in great detail in my "Rationality and the Fear of Death," supra note 45. I am very grateful to Ellen Canacakos for discussion of this closing portion of the paper.

[64] I say can instead of must because some persons (e.g., Socrates and other exceptionally rare individuals) seem to have attained personal excellence prior to their execution. The Justices in Furman v. Georgia who seem to me closest to the view I am here articulating are Marshall and Brennan. Marshall (at 346) writes "Death, of course, makes rehabilitation impossible." And Brennan (at 272, 273) writes: "When we consider why [certain punishments] have been condemned, however, we realize that the pain involved is not the only reason. The true significance of these punishments is that they treat members of the human race as nonhumans, as objects to be toyed with and discarded."

[65] *Lockett v. Ohio, supra* note 34. There is, of course, a social cost of having stricter procedures to prevent error—Hand's third factor in his algebra of negligence. The primary social costs for criminal due process will be expense, court time, and—of course—the greater possibility that guilty and dangerous persons will be freed to prey again upon innocent victims and that others will be less effectively deterred from crime. I have had little to say about these matters—not because I think they are unimportant but because (as indicated in note 5) I wanted to see how far one could go via a different route.

Coker v. Georgia

433 U.S. 584 (1977)
United States Supreme Court

Syllabus[1]

While serving various sentences for murder, rape, kidnaping, and aggravated assault, petitioner escaped from a Georgia prison and, in the course of committing an armed robbery and other offenses, raped an adult woman. He was convicted of rape, armed robbery, and the other offenses and sentenced to death on the rape charge, when the jury found two of the aggravating circumstances present for imposing such a sentence, *viz*, that the rape was committed (1) by a person with prior capital-felony convictions and (2) in the course of committing another capital felony, armed robbery. The Georgia Supreme Court affirmed both the conviction and sentence. *Held:* The judgment upholding the death sentence is reversed and the case is remanded.

Mr. Justice White, joined by Mr. Justice Stewart, Mr. Justice Blackmun, and Mr. Justice Stevens, concluded that the sentence of death for the crime of rape is grossly disproportionate and excessive punishment and is therefore forbidden by the Eighth Amendment as cruel and unusual punishment.

(a) The Eighth Amendment bars not only those punishments that are "barbaric" but also those that are "excessive" in relation to the crime committed, and a punishment is "excessive" and unconstitutional if it (1) makes no measurable contribution to acceptable goals of punishment and hence is nothing more than the purposeless and needless imposition of pain and suffering; of (2) is grossly out of proportion to the severity of the crime.

(b) That death is a disproportionate penalty for rape is strongly indicated by the objective evidence of present, public judgment, as represented by the attitude of state legislatures and sentencing juries, concerning the acceptability of such a penalty, it appearing that Georgia is currently the only State authorizing the death sentence for rape of an adult woman, that it is authorized for rape in only two other States but only when the victim is a child, and that in the vast majority (9 out of 10) of rape convictions in Georgia since 1973, juries have not imposed the death sentence.

(c) Although rape deserves serious punishment, the death penalty, which is unique in its severity and irrevocability, is an excessive penalty for the rapist who, as such and as opposed to the murderer, does not unjustifiably take human life.

(d) The conclusion that the death sentence imposed on petitioner is disproportionate punishment for rape is not affected by the fact that the jury found the aggravating circumstances of prior capital felony convictions and occurrence of the rape while committing armed robbery, a felony for which the death sentence is also authorized, since the prior convictions do not change the fact that the rape did not involve the taking of life, and since the jury did not deem the robbery itself deserving of the death penalty, even though accompanied by the aggravating circumstances of prior capital felony convictions.

(e) That under Georgia law a deliberate killer cannot be sentenced to death, absent aggravating circumstances, argues strongly against the notion that, with or without such circumstances, a rapist who does not take the life of his victim should be punished more severely than the deliberate killer.

Mr. Justice Brennan concluded that the death penalty is in all circumstances cruel and unusual punishment prohibited by the Eighth and Fourteenth Amendments.

Mr. Justice Marshall concluded that the death penalty is a cruel and unusual punishment prohibited by the Eighth and Fourteenth Amendments.

Mr. Justice Powell concluded that death is disproportionate punishment for the crime of raping an adult woman where, as here, the crime was not committed with excessive brutality and the victim did not sustain serious or lasting unjury.

Dissenting Opinion

Mr. Chief Justice Burger, with whom Mr. Justice Rehnquist joins, dissenting.

In a case such as this, confusion often arises as to the Court's proper role in reaching a decision. Our task is not to give effect to our individual views on capital punishment; rather, we must determine what the Constitution permits a State to do under its reserved powers. In striking down the death penalty imposed upon the petitioner in this case, the Court has overstepped the bounds of proper constitutional adjudication by substituting its policy judgment for that of the state legislature. I accept that the Eighth Amendment's concept of disproportionality bars the death penalty for minor crimes. But rape is not a minor crime; hence the Cruel and Unusual Punishment Clause does not give the Members of this Court license to engraft their conceptions of proper public policy onto the considered legislative judgments of the States. Since I cannot agree that Georgia lacked the constitutional power to impose the penalty of death for rape, I dissent from the Court's judgment.

1

On December 5, 1971, the petitioner, Ehrlich Anthony Coker, raped and then stabbed to death a young woman. Less than eight months later Coker kidnapped and raped a second young woman. After twice raping this 16-year-old victim, he stripped her, severely beat her with a club, and dragged her into a wooded area where he left her for dead. He was apprehended and pleaded guilty to offenses stemming from these incidents. He was sentenced by three separate courts to three life terms, two 20-year terms, and one eight-year term of imprisonment.[2] Each judgment specified that the sentences it imposed were to run consecutively rather than concurrently. Approximately one and one-half years later, on September 2, 1974, petitioner escaped from the state prison where he was serving these sentences. He promptly raped another 16-year-old woman in the presence of her husband, abducted her from her home, and threatened her with death and serious bodily harm. It is this crime for which the sentence now under review was imposed.

The Court today holds that the State of Georgia may not impose the death penalty on Coker. In so doing, it prevents the State from imposing any effective punishment upon Coker for his latest rape. The Court's holding, moreover, bars Georgia from guaranteeing its citizens that they will suffer no further attacks by this habitual rapist. In fact, given the lengthy sentences Coker must serve for the crimes he has already committed, the Court's holding assures that petitioner—and others in his position—will henceforth feel no compunction whatsoever about committing further rapes as frequently as he may be able to escape from confinement and indeed even within the walls of the prison itself. To what extent we have left States "elbow room" to protect innocent persons from depraved human beings like Coker remains in doubt.

2

My first disagreement with the Court's holding is its unnecessary breadth. The narrow issue here presented is whether the State of Georgia may constitutionally execute this petitioner for the particular rape which he has committed, in light of all the facts and circumstances shown by this record. The plurality opinion goes to great lengths to consider societal mores and attitudes toward the generic crime of rape and the punishment for it; however, the opinion gives little attention [to] the special circumstances which bear directly on whether imposition of the death penalty is an appropriate societal response to Coker's criminal acts: (a) On account of his prior offenses, Coker is already serving such lengthy prison sentences that imposition of additional periods of imprisonment would have no incremental punitive effect; (b) by his life pattern Coker has shown that he presents a particular danger to the safety, welfare and chastity of women, and on his record the likelihood is therefore great that he will repeat his crime at first opportunity; (c) petitioner escaped from prison, only a year and a half after he commenced serving his latest sentences; he has nothing to lose by further escape attempts; and (d) should he again succeed in escaping from prison, it is reasonably predictable that he will repeat his pattern of attacks on women—and with impunity since the threat of added prison sentences will be no deterrent.

Unlike the Court, I would narrow the inquiry in this case to the question actually presented: Does the Eighth Amendment's ban against cruel and unusual punishment prohibit the State of Georgia from executing a person who has, within the space of three years, raped three separate women, killing one and attempting to kill another, who is serving prison terms exceeding his probable lifetime and who has not hesitated to escape confinement at the first available opportunity? Whatever one's view may be as to the State's constitutional power to impose the death penalty upon a rapist who stands before a court convicted for the first time, this case reveals a chronic rapist whose continuing danger to the community is abundantly clear.

Mr. Justice Powell would hold the death sentence inappropriate in *this* case because "there is no indication that petitioner's offense was committed with excessive brutality or that the victim sustained serious or lasting injury."[3] Apart from the reality that rape is inherently one of the most egregiously brutal acts one human being can inflict upon another, there is nothing in the Eighth Amendment that so narrowly limits the factors which may be considered by a state legislature in determining whether a particular punishment is grossly excessive. Surely recidivism, especially the repeated commission of heinous crimes, is a factor which may properly be weighed as an aggravating circumstance, permitting the imposition of a punishment more severe than for one isolated offense. For example, as a matter of national policy, Congress

has expressed its will that a person who has committed two felonies will suffer enhanced punishment for a third one, 18 U.S.C. § 3575(e)(1); Congress has also declared that a second conviction for assault on a mail carrier may be punished more seriously than a first such conviction, *id*, § 2114. Many States provide an increased penalty for habitual criminality. See, *e. g.,* Wis. Stat. § 939.62; . . .[4] As a factual matter, the plurality opinion is correct in stating that Coker's "prior convictions do not change the fact that the instant crime being punished is rape not involving the taking of life," . . . however, it cannot be disputed that the existence of these prior convictions make Coker a substantially more serious menace to society than a first-time offender:[5]

"There is a widely held view that those who present the strongest case for severe measures of incapacitation are not murderers as a group (their offenses often are situational) *but rather those who have repeatedly engaged in violent, combative behavior.* A well-demonstrated propensity for life-endangering behavior is thought to provide a more solid basis for infliction of the most severe measures of incapacitation than does the fortuity of a single homicidal incident." Packer, Making the Punishment Fit the Crime, 77 Harv. L. Rev. 1071, 1080 (1964). (Emphasis added.)

In my view, the Eighth Amendment does not prevent the State from taking an individual's "well demonstrated propensity for life-endangering behavior" into account in devising punitive measures which will prevent inflicting further harm upon innocent victims. See *Gregg v. Georgia,* 428 U.S. 153, 183 n. 28 . . . (1976). Only one year ago Mr. Justice White succinctly noted: "death finally forecloses the possibility that a prisoner will commit further crimes, whereas life imprisonment does not." *Roberts v. Louisiana,* 428 U.S. 325, 354 . . . (1976) (White, J., dissenting); see also *Furman v. Georgia,* 408 U.S., at 310 . . . (White, J., concurring).

In sum, once the Court has held that "the punishment of death does not invariably violate the Constitution," *Gregg v. Georgia,* 428 U.S., at 169 . . . it seriously impinges upon the State's legislative judgment to hold that it may not impose such sentence upon an individual who has shown total and repeated disregard for the welfare, safety, personal integrity and human worth of others, and who seemingly cannot be deterred from continuing such conduct.[6] I therefore would hold that the death sentence here imposed is within the power reserved to the State and leave for another day the question of whether such sanction would be proper under other circumstances. The dangers which inhere whenever the Court casts its constitutional decisions in terms sweeping beyond the facts of the case presented, are magnified in the context of the Eighth Amendment. In *Furman v. Georgia*, 408 U.S., at 431, . . . Mr. Justice Powell, in dissent stated:

> "where, as here, the language of the applicable [constitutional] provision provides great leeway and where the underlying social policies are felt to be of vital importance, the temptation to read personal preference into the Constitution is understandably great. *It is too easy to propound our subjective standards of wise policy under the rubric of more or less universally held standards of decency.*" (Emphasis added.)

Since the Court now invalidates the death penalty as a sanction for all rapes of adults at all times under all circumstances,[7] I reluctantly turn to what I see as the broader issues raised by this holding.

3

The plurality . . . acknowledges the gross nature of the crime of rape. A rapist not only violates a victim's privacy and personal integrity, but inevitably causes serious psychological harm as well as physical harm in the process. The long-range effect on the victim's life may be gravely affected, and this in turn may have a serious detrimental effect upon her husband and any children she may have. I therefore wholly agree with Mr. Justice White's conclusion as far as it goes—that "[s]hort of homicide, [rape] is the 'ultimate violation of the self.'" . . . Victims may recover from the physical damage of knife or bullet wounds, or a beating with fists or a club, but recovery from such a gross assault on the human personality is not healed by medicine or surgery. To speak blandly, as the plurality does, of rape victims which are "unharmed," or, as the concurrence, to classify the human outrage of rape in terms of "excessively brutal," . . . versus "moderately brutal," takes too little account of the profound suffering the crime imposes upon the victims and their loved ones.

Despite its strong condemnation of rape, the Court reaches the inexplicable conclusion that "the death penalty . . . is an excessive penalty" for the perpetrator of this heinous offense.[8] This, the Court holds, is true even though in Georgia the death penalty may be imposed only where the rape is coupled with one or more aggravating circumstances. The process by which this conclusion is reached is as startling as it is disquieting. It represents a clear departure from precedent by making this Court "under the aegis of the Cruel and Unusual Punishment Clause, the ultimate arbiter of the standards of criminal responsibility in diverse areas of the criminal law, throughout the country." *Powell v. Texas*, 392 U.S. 514, 533 . . . (1968) (Opinion of Marshall, J.)[9] This seriously strains and distorts our federal system, removing much of the flexibility from which it has drawn strength for two centuries.

The analysis of the plurality opinion is divided into two parts: (a) an "objective" determination that most American Jurisdictions do not presently make rape a capital offense, and (b) a subjective judgment that death is an excessive punishment for rape because the crime does not, in and of itself, cause the death of the victim. I take issue with each of these points.

a

The plurality opinion basis its analysis, in part, on the fact that "Georgia is the sole jurisdiction in the United States at the present time that authorizes the sentence of death when the rape victim is an adult woman." . . . Surely, however, this statistic cannot be deemed determinative, or even particularly relevant. As the opinion concedes, . . . two other States—Louisiana and North Carolina—have enacted death penalty statutes for adult rape since this Court's 1972 decision in *Furman v. Georgia*, 408 U.S. 238. . . . If the Court is to rely on some "public opinion" process, does this not suggest the beginning of a "trend?"

More to the point, however, it is myopic to base sweeping constitutional principles upon the narrow experience of the past five years. Considerable uncertainty was introduced into this area of the law by this Court's *Furman* decision. A large number of States found their death penalty statutes invalidated; legislatures were left in serious doubt by the expressions vacillating between discretionary and mandatory death penalties, as to whether this Court would sustain *any* statute imposing death as a criminal sanction.[10] Failure of

520 Chapter V Criminal Law

more States to enact statutes imposing death for rape of an adult woman may thus reflect hasty legislative compromise occasioned by time pressures following *Furman,* a desire to wait on the experience of those States which did enact such statutes, or simply an accurate forecast of today's holding.

In any case, when considered in light of the experience since the turn of this century, where more than one-third of American jurisdictions have consistently provided the death penalty for rape, the plurality's focus on the experience of the immediate past must be viewed as truly disingenuous. Having in mind the swift changes in positions of some Members of this Court in the short span of five years, can it rationally be considered a relevant indicator of what our society deems "cruel and unusual" to look solely to what legislatures have *refrained* from doing under conditions of great uncertainty arising from our less than lucid holdings on the Eighth Amendment? Far more representative of societal mores of the 20th Century is the accepted practice in a substantial number of jurisdictions preceding the *Furman* decision. "The problem . . . is the suddenness of the Court's perception of progress in the human attitude since decisions of only a short while ago." *Furman v. Georgia,* 408 U.S., at 410 . . . (Blackmun, J., dissenting). Cf. *Rudolph v. Alabama,* 375 U.S. 889 . . . (1963).

However, even were one to give the most charitable acceptance to the plurality's statistical analysis, it still does not, to my mind, support its conclusion. The most that can be claimed is that for the past year Georgia has been the only State whose adult rape death penalty statute has not otherwise been invalidated; two other state legislatures had enacted rape death penalty statutes in the last five years, but these were invalidated for reasons unrelated to rape under the Court's decisions last Term. *Woodson v. North Carolina,* 428 U.S. 280 . . . (1976); *Roberts v. Louisiana,* 428 U.S. 325 . . . (1976). Even if these figures could be read as indicating that no other States view the death penalty as an appropriate punishment for the rape of an adult woman, it would not necessarily follow that Georgia's imposition of such sanction violates the Eighth Amendment.

The Court has repeatedly pointed to the reserve strength of our federal system which allows state legislatures, within broad limits, to experiment with laws, both criminal and civil, in the

effort to achieve socially desirable results. See, *e. g., Whalen v. Roe,*———U.S.———,———, and n. 22 . . . (1977); *Johnson v. Louisiana,* 406 U.S. 356 . . . (1972) (opinion of Powell, J.); *California v. Green,* 399 U.S. 149 . . . (1970) (Harlan J., concurring); *Fay v. New York,* 332 U.S. 261 . . . (1947). Various provisions of the Constitution, including the Eighth Amendment and the Due Process Clause, of course place substantive limitations on the type of experimentation a State may undertake. However, as the plurality admits, the crime of rape is second perhaps only to murder in its gravity. It follows then that Georgia did not approach such substantive constraints by enacting the statute here in question. . . .

Statutory provisions in criminal justice applied in one part of the country can be carefully watched by other state legislatures, so that the experience of one State becomes available to all. Although human lives are in the balance, it must be remembered that failure to allow flexibility may also jeopardize human lives—those of the victims of undeterred criminal conduct. . . . Our concern for the accused ought not (to) foreclose legislative judgments showing a modicum of consideration for the potential victims.

Three state legislatures have, in the past five years, determined that the taking of human life and the devastating consequences of rape will be minimized if rapists may, in a limited class of cases, be executed for their offenses.[11] That these states are presently a minority does not, in my view, make their judgment less worthy of deference. Our concern for human life must not be confined to the guilty; a state legislature is not to be thought insensitive to human values because it acts firmly to protect the lives and related values of the innocent. In this area the choices for legislatures are at best painful and difficult and deserve a high degree of deference. Only last Term Mr. Justice White observed:

"It will not do to denigrate these legislative judgments as some form of vestigial savagery or as purely retributive in motivation; for they are solemn judgments, reasonably based, that imposition of the death penalty will save the lives of innocent persons. This concern for life and human values and sincere efforts of the States to pursue them are matters of the greatest moment *with which the judiciary should be most reluctant to interfere."* Roberts v. Louisiana, 428 U.S., at 355 . . . (White, J., Dissenting). (Emphasis added.)

The question of whether the death penalty is an appropriate punishment for rape is surely an open one. It is arguable that many prospective rapists would be deterred by the possibility that they could suffer death for their offense; it is also arguable that the death penalty would have only minimal deterrent effect.[12] It may well be that rape victims would become more willing to report the crime and aid in the apprehension of the criminals if they knew that community disapproval of rapists was sufficiently strong to inflict the extreme penalty; or perhaps they would be reluctant to cooperate in the prosecution of rapists if they knew that a conviction might result in the imposition of the death penalty. Quite possibly, the occasional, well-publicized execution of egregious rapists may cause citizens to feel greater security in their daily lives,[13] or, on the contrary, it may be that members of a civilized community will suffer the pangs of a heavy conscience because such punishment will be perceived as excessive.[14] We cannot know which among this range of possibilities is correct, but today's holding forecloses the very exploration we have said federalism was intended to foster. It is difficult to believe that Georgia would long remain alone in punishing rape by death if the next decade demonstrated a drastic reduction in its incidence of rape, and increased cooperation by rape victims in the apprehension and prosecution of rapists, and a greater confidence in the rule of law on the part of the populace.

In order for Georgia's legislative program to develop it must be given time to take effect so that data may be evaluated for comparison with the experience of States which have not enacted death penalty statutes. Today, the Court repudiates the State's solemn judgment on how best to deal with the crime of rape before anyone can know whether the death penalty is an effective deterrent for one of the most horrible of all crimes. And this is done a few short years after Justice Powell's excellent statement:

> "In a period in our country's history when the frequency of [rape] is increasing alarmingly, it is indeed a grave event for the Court to take from the States whatever deterrent and retributive weight the death penalty retains." *Furman v. Georgia*, 408

U.S., at 459 . . . (Powell, J., dissenting) (footnote omitted).

To deprive States of this authority as the Court does, on the basis that "the current judgment with respect to the death penalty for rape . . . weighs very heavily on the side of rejecting capital punishment as a suitable penalty for raping an adult woman," . . . is impermissibly rash. The current judgment of some Members of this Court has undergone significant change in the short time since *Furman*.[15] Social change on great issues generally reveals itself in small increments, and the "current judgment" of many States could well be altered on the basis of Georgia's experience, were we to allow its statute to stand.[16]

b

The subjective judgment that the death penalty is simply disproportionate for the crime of rape is even more disturbing than the "objective" analysis discussed *supra*. The plurality's conclusion on this point is based upon the bare fact that murder necessarily results in the physical death of the victim, while rape does not. . . . However, no Member of the Court explains why this distinction has relevance, much less constitutional significance. It is, after all, not irrational—nor constitutionally impermissible—for a legislature to make the penalty more severe than the criminal act it punishes[17] in the hope it would deter wrongdoing:

> "We may not require the legislature to select the least severe penalty possible so long as the penalty selected is not cruelly inhuman or disproportionate to the crime involved." *Gregg v. Georgia*, 428 U.S., at 175. . . . Accord, *Furman v. Georgia*, 408 U.S., at 451 . . . (Powell, J., dissenting).

It begs the question to state, as does the plurality opinion:

> "Life is over for the victim of the murderers; for the rape victim, life may not be nearly so happy as it was, but is not over and normally is not beyond repair." . . .

Until now, the issue under the Eighth Amendment has not been the state of any particular victim after the crime, but rather whether the punishment imposed is grossly disproportionate to the evil committed by the perpetrator. See, *Gregg v. Georgia*, 428

U.S., at 173 . . . ; *Furman v. Georgia*, 408 U.S. . . . (Powell, J., dissenting). As a matter of constitutional principle, that test cannot have the primitive simplicity of "life for life, eye for eye, tooth for tooth." Rather States must be permitted to engage in a more sophisticated weighing of values in dealing with criminal activity which consistently poses serious danger of death or grave bodily harm. If innocent life and limb is to be preserved I see no constitutional barrier in punishing by death all who engage in such activity, regardless of whether the risk comes to fruition in any particular instance. See Packer, *supra*, 77 Harv.L.Rev., at 1077–1079.

Only one year ago the Court held it constitutionally permissible to impose the death penalty for the crime of murder, provided that certain procedural safeguards are followed. Compare *Gregg v. Georgia, supra; Profitt v. Florida*, 428 U.S. 242 . . . (1976), and *Jurek v. Texas*, 418 U.S. 262 . . . (1976), with *Roberts v. Louisiana, supra*, and *Woodson v. North Carolina, supra*. Today, the Court readily admits that "[s]hort of homicide, [rape] is the 'ultimate violation of self.' " Moreover, as stated by Mr. Justice Powell,

> "[t]he threat of serious injury is implicit in the definition of rape; the victim is either forced into submission by physical violence or by the threat of violence." *Furman v. Georgia*, 408 U.S., at 460. . . .

Rape thus is not a crime "light-years" removed from murder in the degree of its heinousness; it certainly poses a serious potential danger to the life and safety of innocent victims—apart from the devastating psychic consequences. It would seem to follow therefore that, affording the States proper leeway under the broad standard of the Eighth Amendment,[18] murder is properly punishable by death, rape should be also, if that is the considered judgment of the legislators.

The Court's conclusion to the contrary is very disturbing indeed. The clear implication of today's holding appears to be that the death penalty may be properly imposed only as to crimes resulting in death of the victim. This casts serious doubt upon the constitutional validity of statutes imposing the death penalty for a variety of conduct which, though dangerous, may not necessarily result in any immediate death, *e.g.*, treason, airplane hijacking, and kidnapping. In that respect, today's holding does even more harm than is initially apparent. We cannot avoid judicial notice that crimes such as airplane hijacking, kidnapping, and mass terrorist activity constitute a serious and increasing danger to the safety of the public. It would be unfortunate indeed if the effect of today's holding were to inhibit States and the Federal Government from experimenting with various remedies—including possibly imposition of the penalty of death—to prevent and deter such crimes.

Some sound observations, made only a few years ago, deserve repetition:

> "Our task here, as must so frequently be emphasized and re-emphasized, is to pass upon the constitutionality of legislation that has been enacted and that is challenged. This is the sole task for judges. We should not allow our personal preferences as to the wisdom of legislative and congressional action, or our distaste for such action, to guide our judicial decision in cases such as these. The temptations to cross that policy line are very great. In fact, as today's decision reveals, they are almost irresistible." *Furman v. Georgia*, 408 U.S., at 411 . . . (Blackmun, J., dissenting).

Whatever our individual views as to the wisdom of capital punishment, I cannot agree that it is constitutionally impermissible for a state legislature to make the "solemn judgment" to impose such penalty for the crime of rape. Accordingly, I would leave to the States the task of legislating in this area of the law.

Endnotes

[1] The syllabus constitutes no part of the opinion of the Court but has been prepared by the Reporter of Decisions for the convenience of the reader.

[2] On March 12, 1973, the Superior Court of Richmond County, Ga., sentenced Coker to 20 years' imprisonment for the kidnapping of petitioner's second victim, and to life imprisonment for one act of rape upon her. On May 28, 1973, the Superior Court of Taliaferro County, Ga., sentenced Coker to eight years' imprisonment for aggravated assault upon the same victim, and to life imprisonment for the second rape upon her. On April 6, 1973, the Superior Court of Clayton County, Ga., sentenced Coker to 20 years' imprisonment for the rape of petitioner's first victim, and to life imprisonment for her murder. . . .

[3] The position today adopted by Mr. Justice Powell constitutes a disquieting shift from the view he em-

braced several Terms ago in *Furman v. Georgia*, 408 U.S. 238, 460–461 . . . (1972), where he stated:

"While I reject each of [petitioners'] attempts to establish specific categories of cases in which the death penalty may be deemed excessive, I view them as groping toward what is for me the appropriate application of the Eighth Amendment. While in my view *the disproportionality test may not be used either to strike down the death penalty for rape altogether or to install the Court as a tribunal for sentencing review, that test may find its application in the peculiar circumstances of specific cases. Its utilization should be limited to the rare case in which the death penalty is rendered for a crime technically falling within the legislatively defined class but factually falling outside the likely legislative intent in creating the category."* (Emphasis added.)

While Mr. Justice Powell purports to dissent from the broadest sweep of the Court's holding, I cannot see that his view differs materially from that of the plurality. He suggests two situations where it might be proper to execute rapists: (1) where the "offense [is] committed with excessive brutality"; and (2) where "the victim sustained serious or lasting injury." The second part of this test was rejected by Mr. Justice Powell himself in *Furman*, and with good reason: "the emotional impact [upon the rape victim] may be impossible to gauge at any particular point in time. The extent and duration of psychological trauma may not be known or ascertainable prior to trial." *Id.*, at 460. . . . Can any Member of the Court state with confidence that a 16-year-old woman who is raped in the presence of her husband three weeks after giving birth to a baby "sustained [no] serious or lasting injury?" This bifurcation of rape into categories of harmful and nonharmful eludes my comprehension.

The difficulty with the first part of Mr. Justice Powell's test is that rape is inherently an aggravated offense; in Mr. Justice Powell's own words, "the threat of both [physical and psychological] injury is always present." *Id.*, at 459. . . . Therefore the "excessive brutality" requirement must refer to something more, I assume, than the force normally associated with physically coercing or overpowering the will of another. Rather, what must be meant is that the rapist has engaged in torture or has committed an aggravated battery upon the victim. See, *ante*, at 2863 and n. 1. However, torture and aggravated battery are offenses separate from rape, and ordinarily are punished separately. The clear negative inference of Mr. Justice Powell's analysis therefore appears to be that where rape alone is committed, *i. e.*, rape unaccompanied by any other criminal conduct, the death penalty may never be imposed.

[4] This court has consistently upheld the constitutional validity of such punishment-enhancing statutes. See, *e. g.*, *Spencer v. Texas*, 385 U.S. 554, 559–560 . . . (1967):

"No claim is made here that recidivist statutes are . . . unconstitutional, nor could there be under our cases. Such statutes and other enhanced-sentence laws, and procedures designed to implement their underlying policies, have been enacted in all the States, and by the Federal Government as well. . . . Such statutes . . . have been sustained in this Court on several occasions against contentions that they violate constitutional strictures dealing with double jeopardy *ex post facto* laws, *cruel and unusual punishment*, due process, equal protection, and privileges and immunities." (Footnote and citations omitted; emphasis added.) Accord, *Oyler v. Boles*, 368 U.S. 448, 451 . . . (1962).

[5] This special danger is demonstrated by the very record in this case. After trying and gagging the victim's husband, and raping the victim, petitioner sought to make his getaway in their automobile. Leaving the victim's husband tied and gagged in his bathroom, Coker took the victim with him. As he started to leave, he brandished the kitchen knife he was carrying and warned the husband that "if he would get pulled over or the police was following him in any way that he would kill—he would kill my wife. *He said he didn't have nothing to lose—that he was in prison for the rest of his life, anyway. . . .*" Testimony of the victim's husband, Appendix, at 121 (emphasis added).

[6] Professor Packer addressed this:

"What are we to do with those whom we cannot reform, and in particular, those who by our failure are thought to remain menaces to life? Current penal theories admit, indeed insist upon, the need for permanent incapacitation in such cases. Once this need is recognized, the death penalty as a means for incapacitation for the violent psychopath can hardly be objected to on grounds that will survive rational scrutiny, *if the use of the death penalty in any situation is to be permitted.* And its use in rape cases as a class, while inept, is no more so than its use for any other specific offense involving danger to life and limb." 77 Harv.L. Rev., at 1081. (Emphasis added.)

[7] I find a disturbing confusion as to this issue in the plurality opinion. The issue is whether Georgia can, under any circumstances and for any kind of rape— "mild" or "gross"—impose the death penalty. Yet the plurality opinion opens its discussion, apparently directed at demonstrating that this was not an "aggravated" rape, saying that following the rape and kidnapping, "Mrs. Carver was unharmed." . . . If the Court is holding that no rape can ever be punished by death, why is it relevant whether Mrs. Carver was "unharmed"?

[8] While only three Justices have joined Mr. Justice White in this portion of his opinion, see separate opinion of Mr. Justice Powell, *ante*. I take this to be the

view of the Court in light of Mr. Justice Brennan's and Mr. Justice Marshall's statements joining the judgment.

[9] Only last term in *Gregg v. Georgia*, 428 U.S. 153 . . . (1976), Mr. Justice Stewart, Mr. Justice Powell, and Mr. Justice Stevens warned that "the requirement of the Eighth Amendment must be applied with an awareness of the limited role to be played by the courts," and noted that "we may not act as judges as we might as legislators." *Id.*, at 174–175. . . . Accord, *Roberts v. Louisiana*, 428 U.S., at 355–356 . . . (White, J., dissenting). The plurality further noted that "[t]he deference we owe to decisions of the state legislatures under our federal system, [*Furman v. Georgia*, 407 U.S.] at 465–470 . . . (Rehnquist, J., Dissenting), is enhanced where the specification of punishments is concerned, for *these are peculiarly questions of legislative policy.' Gore v. United States*, 357 U.S. 386, 393 . . . (1958)." 428 U.S., at 176 . . . (emphasis added).

[10] I take no satisfaction in my predictive caveat in *Furman:*

"Since there is no majority of the Court on the ultimate issue presented in these cases, the future of capital punishment in this country has been left in an uncertain limbo. Rather than providing a final and unambiguous answer on the basic constitutional question, the collective impact of the majority's ruling is to demand an undetermined measure of change from the various state legislatures and the Congress." *Furman v. Georgia*, 408 U.S., at 403 . . . (Burger, C.J., dissenting).

[11] The statute here in question does not provide the death penalty for any and all rapists. Rather, the jury must find that at least one statutorily defined aggravated circumstance is present. Ga.Code Ann. §§ 26–3102, 27–2534.1(b)(1), (2) and (7).

[12] "The value of capital punishment as a deterrent of crime is a complex factual issue the resolution of which properly rests with the legislatures, which can evaluate the results of statistical studies in terms of their own local conditions and with a flexibility of approach that is not available to the courts. *Furman v. Georgia* [408 U.S.], at 403–405 . . . (Burger, C. J., dissenting)." *Gregg v. Georgia*, 428 U.S., at 186 . . . (plurality opinion).

[13] "There are many cases in which the sordid, heinous nature of a particular [rape], demeaning, humiliating, and often physically or [psychologically] traumatic, will call for public condemnation." *Furman v. Georgia*, 408 U.S. 459 . . . (Powell, J., dissenting).

[14] Obviously I have no special competence to make these judgments, but by the same token no other Member of the Court is competent to make a contrary judgment. This is why our system has, until now, left these difficult policy choices to the state legislatures, who may be no wiser, but surely are more attuned to the mores of their communities, than are we.

[15] Indeed as recently as 1971—a year before *Furman*—a majority of this Court appeared to have no doubt about the constitutionality of the death penalty. See *McGautha v. California*, 402 U.S. 183 . . . (1971).

[16] To paraphrase Mr. Justice Powell, "[w]hat [the Court is] saying, in effect, is that the evolutionary process has come suddenly to an end; that the ultimate wisdom as to the appropriateness of capital punishment [for adult rape] under all circumstances, and for all future generations, has somehow been revealed." *Furman v. Georgia*, 408 U.S., at 431 . . . (Powell, J., dissenting).

[17] For example, hardly any thief would be deterred from stealing if the only punishment upon being caught were return of the money stolen.

[18] Mr. Justice Stewart, Mr. Justice Powell, and Mr. Justice Stevens in *Gregg v. Georgia* noted that "in assessing a punishment selected by a democratically elected legislature against the constitutional measure [of the Eighth Amendment], we presume its validity. . . . *A heavy burden rests on those who would attack the judgment of the representative of the people.*" 428 U.S., at 175 . . . (emphasis added). Accord, *Furman v. Georgia*, 408 U.S., at 451 . . . (Powell, J., dissenting).

The reasons for this special deference to state legislative enactments was described:

"This is true in part because the constitutional test is intertwined with an assessment of contemporary standards and the legislative judgment weighs heavily in ascertaining such standards. '[I]n a democratic society legislatures, not courts, are constituted to respond to the will and consequently the moral values of the people.' *Furman v. Georgia* [408 U.S.], at 383 . . . (Burger, C. J., dissenting)." 428 U.S., at 175–176. . . .

Study Questions

1. Do you agree with Wasserstrom's arguments against the rehabilitative alternative to a regime of punishment? Why or why not?

2. In a famous passage in his *Metaphysics of Morals*, Kant gave the following argument to demonstrate the necessity of death as a punishment for murder:

If . . . he has committed a murder, he must die. In this case, there is no substitute that will satisfy the requirements of legal justice. There is no sameness of kind between death and remaining alive even under the most miserable conditions, and consequently there is also no equality between the crime and the retribution unless the criminal is put to death. . . . Even if a civil society were to dissolve itself by common agreement of all its members (for example, if the people inhabiting an island decided to separate and disperse themselves around the world), the last murderer remaining in prison must first be executed, so that everyone will duly receive what his actions are worth. (John Ladd, trans., *The Metaphysical Elements of Justice* [Indianapolis, Ind.: Bobbs-Merrill, 1965], p. 102)

In what respects is this argument convincing? In what respects not?

3. In October 1975, Windell McDowell was convicted in a California court of purse snatching and was placed on probation on the condition that he not go out of his house without wearing shoes with metal taps on the soles. (*People v. McDowell* 59 Cal. App. 3d 807 [1976]. In Oregon in 1986, Thomas Kirby pled guilty to a charge of first-degree burglary and was placed on probation on the condition that he publish, at his own expense, an advertisement, accompanied with a picture, in the local newspaper. The ad was to read "Criminal's Apology." (*State v. Kirby* No. 85-1649 [Or. Cir. Ct. for Lincoln County, Oregon, March 7, 1986]). Richard Bateman was convicted on two counts of first-degree sexual abuse in 1985. Though he faced a maximum sentence of five years in prison and a large fine, an Oregon court instead suspended Bateman's sentence and placed him on probation. As one of the conditions of his sentence, Bateman was required to place, on the door of his residence and on both doors of any vehicle he might drive, in three-inch lettering, the words "Dangerous Sex Offender—No Children Allowed" (*State v. Bateman* Nos. C85-08-33209 and C85-10-34220 [Or. Cir. Ct. for Multnomah County, Oregon, June 17, 1986]). Are any of these "scarlet-letter" punishments "cruel and unusual"? Which ones? And why? What are these sentences supposed to accomplish? Are those purposes consistent with defensible goals of criminal punishment? What would Murphy's analysis say of such cases?

4. Growing frustration with drug-related crimes have prompted several state legislators to introduce bills with harsh punishments. One such bill, introduced recently in the Texas legislature, would have punished convicted drug dealers by cutting off their fingers, one finger for each conviction. A bill introduced in Delaware would have required felony drug offenders to receive "no fewer than five nor more than 40 lashes well laid on" on a bare back. Should either mutilation or flogging be permissible punishments for such offenses?

Cases for Further Reflection

People v. Burroughs
35 Cal. 3d 824, 678 p. 2d 894 (1984)
Supreme Court of California

This case deals with the purposes of the felony-murder rule and whether they make any sense in application to Burroughs, an unlicensed physician whose patient died during treatment. The narrow issue at stake in the case turns on California's restriction of the felony-murder rule to those cases in which the felony is "inherently dangerous to human life." What alleged purposes of the felony-murder rule are identified in the majority and dissenting opinions? If those purposes make sense, why shouldn't the rule be applicable to *any* felony? Setting aside the felony-murder rule, do you think Burroughs deserves to treated as a murderer?

Grodin, Justice.

Defendant Burroughs, a 77-year-old self-styled "healer," appeals from a judgment convicting him of unlawfully selling drugs, compounds, or devices for alleviation or cure of cancer (Health & Saf. Code, § 1707.1); felony practicing medicine without a license (Bus. & Prof. Code, § 2141.5, now § 2053); and second degree felony murder (Pen. Code, § 187) in the treatment and death of Lee Swatsenbarg.

Burroughs challenges his second degree murder conviction by contending the felonious unlicensed practice of medicine is not an "inherently dangerous" felony, as that term has been used in our previous decisions to describe and limit the kinds of offenses which will support application of the felony-murder rule. We conclude that while the felonious unlicensed practice of medicine can, in many circumstances, pose a threat to the health of the individual being treated, commission of that crime as defined by statute does not inevitably pose danger to human life. Under well-established principles it cannot, therefore, be made the predicate for a finding of murder, absent proof of malice. As a consequence, we must reverse defendant's second degree felony-murder conviction. . . .

Lee Swatsenbarg had been diagnosed by the family physician as suffering from terminal leukemia. Unable to accept impending death, the 24-year-old Swatsenbarg unsuccessfully sought treatment from a variety of traditional medical sources. He and his wife then began to participate in Bible study, hoping that through faith Lee might be cured. Finally, on the advice of a mutual acquaintance who had heard of defendant's ostensible successes in healing others, Lee turned to defendant for treatment.

During the first meeting between Lee and defendant, the latter described his method of curing cancer. This method included a consumption of a unique "lemonade," exposure to colored lights, and a brand of vigorous massage administered by defendant. Defendant remarked that he had successfully treated "thousands" of people, including a number of physicians. He suggested the Swatsenbargs purchase a copy of his book, Healing for the Age of Enlightenment. If after reading the book Lee wished to begin defendant's unorthodox treatment, defendant would commence caring for Lee immediately. During the 30 days designated for the treatment, Lee would have to avoid contact with his physician.

Lee read the book, submitted to the conditions delineated by defendant, and placed himself under defendant's care. Defendant instructed Lee to drink the lemonade, salt water, and herb tea, but consume nothing more for the ensuing 30 days. At defendant's behest, the Swatsenbargs bought a lamp equipped with some colored plastic sheets, to bathe Lee in various tints of light. Defendant also agreed to massage Lee from time to time, for an additional fee per session.

Rather than improve, within two weeks Lee's condition began rapidly to deteriorate. He developed a fever, and was growing progressively weaker. Defendant counseled Lee that all was proceeding according to plan, and convinced the young man to postpone a bone marrow test urged by his doctor.

During the next week Lee became increasingly ill. He was experiencing severe pain in several areas, including his abdomen, and vomiting frequently. Defendant administered "deep" abdominal massages on two successive days, each time telling Lee he would soon recuperate.

Lee did not recover as defendant expected, however, and the patient began to suffer from convulsions and excruciating pain. He vomited with increasing frequency. Despite defendant's constant attempts at reassurance, the Swatsenbargs began to panic when Lee convulsed for a third time after the latest abdominal massage. Three and a half weeks into the treatment, the couple spent the night at defendant's house, where Lee died of a massive hemorrhage of the mesentery in the abdomen. The evidence presented at trial strongly suggested the hemorrhage was the direct result of the massages performed by defendant. . . .

Defendant's conviction of second degree felony murder arose out of the jury's determination that Lee Swatsenbarg's death was a homicide committed by defendant while he was engaged in the felonious unlicensed practice of medicine. The trial court ruled that an underlying felony of unlicensed practice of medicine could support a felony-murder conviction because such practice was a felony "inherently dangerous to human life."[1]

Consequently, the trial judge instructed the jury that if the homicide resulted directly from the commission of this felony, the homicide was felony murder of the second degree.[2] This instruction was erroneous as a matter of law.

When an individual causes the death of another in furtherance of the perpetration of a felony, the resulting offense may be felony murder. This court has long held the felony-murder rule in disfavor. "We have repeatedly stated that felony murder is a 'highly artificial concept' which 'deserves no extension beyond its required application.' "

. . . For the reasons stated below, we hold that to apply the felony-murder rule to the facts of the instant case would be an unwarranted extension of this highly "anachronistic"[3] notion . . .

At the outset we must determine whether the underlying felony is "inherently dangerous to human life." . . . We formulated this standard because "[i]f the felony is not inherently dangerous, it is highly improbable that the potential felon will be deterred; he will not anticipate that injury or death might arise solely from the fact that he will commit the felony." . . .

In assessing whether the felony is inherently dangerous to human life, "we look to the elements of the felony in the abstract, not the particular 'facts' of the case." This form of analysis is compelled because there is a killing in every case where the rule might potentially be applied. If in such circumstances a court were to examine the particular facts of the case prior to establishing whether the underlying felony is inherently dangerous, the court might well be led to conclude the rule applicable despite any unfairness which might redound to the defendant by so broad an application: the existence of the dead victim might appear to lead inexorably to the conclusion that the underlying felony is exceptionally hazardous. We continue to resist such unjustifiable bootstrapping. . . .

The primary element of the offense in question here is the practice of medicine without a license. The statute defines such practice as "treating the sick or afflicted." One can certainly conceive of treatment of the sick or afflicted which has quite innocuous results—the affliction at stake could be a common cold, or a sprained finger, and the form of treatment an admonition to rest in bed and drink fluids or the application of ice to mild swelling. Thus, we do not find inherent dangerousness at this stage of our investigation.

. . .

[The court considers several factors involved in felonious practice of medicine and finds that none is "inherently dangerous to human life."—Ed.]

. . .

Consequently, we are disinclined to rule today that the risks set forth in §2053 are so critical as to render commission of this felony of necessity inherently dangerous to human life. . . .

Moreover, our analysis of precedent in this area reveals that the few times we have found an underlying felony inherently dangerous (so that it would support a conviction of felony murder), the offense has been tinged with malevolence totally absent from the facts of this case. In People v. Mattison (1971) 4 Cal. 3d 177, . . . we held that poisoning food, drink, or medicine with intent to injure was inherently dangerous. The wilful and malicious burning of an automobile (located in a garage beneath an occupied home) was ruled inherently dangerous in People v. Nichols (1970) 3 Cal. 3d 150. . . . Finally, we held kidnapping to be such an offense in People v. Ford, . . . 60 Cal. 2d 772, 795. . . .

To hold, as we do today, that a violation of §2053 is not inherently so dangerous that by its very nature, it cannot be committed without creating a substantial risk that someone will be killed, is consistent with our previous decisions in which the underlying felony has been held not inherently hazardous. We have so held where the underlying felony was felony false imprisonment . . . possession of a concealable firearm by an ex-felon . . . escape from a city or county penal facility . . . and in other, less potentially threatening circumstances.

Finally, the underlying purpose of the felony-murder rule, to encourage felons to commit their offenses without perpetrating unnecessary violence which might result in a homicide, would not be served by applying the rule to the facts of this case. Defendant was or should have been aware he was committing a crime by treating Swatsenbarg in the first place. Yet, it is unlikely he would have been deterred from administering to Lee in the manner in which he did for fear of a prosecution for murder, given his published beliefs on the efficacy of massage in the curing of cancer. Indeed, nowhere is it claimed that defendant attempted to perform any action with respect to Swatsenbarg other than to heal him—and earn a fee for doing so.

This clearly is a case in which conviction of felony murder is contrary to our settled law, as well as inappropriate as a matter of sound judicial policy. The instruction regarding felony murder was erroneous.

Accordingly, defendant's second degree murder conviction is reversed.

. . .

Richardson, Justice, dissenting.

I respectfully dissent. In my view, the unauthorized practice of medicine "under circumstances or conditions which cause or create a risk of great bodily harm, serious physical or mental illness, or death" (Bus. & Prof. Code, § 2053) fully supports application of the second degree felony-murder rule.

Relying on hypertechnical and irrelevant distinctions between great bodily harm, serious physical and mental injury, and the risk of death, the majority ignores the "rational function that [the felony-murder rule] is designed to serve." . . . As we have frequently reiterated, that purpose "is to deter those engaged in felonies from killing negligently or accidentally."

. . .

[In *People v. Nichols,*] we declared that "the burning of a motor vehicle, which usually contains gasoline and which is usually found in close proximity to people, is inherently dangerous to human life. We therefore conclude that the wilful and malicious burning of a motor vehicle calls into play the second degree felony-murder rule." (3 Cal. 3d at p. 163. . . .) How can the underlying felony at issue here be less "inherently dangerous to human life" than the burning of an automobile?

In enacting Business and Professions Code section 2053, the Legislature clearly sought to impose a greater penalty in those cases where the unauthorized practice of medicine causes significant risks that may lead to death. The use of the felony-murder rule in this context clearly furthers the goal of deterring such conduct. The underlying conduct proscribed by section 2053 is manifestly "inherently dangerous to life." Viewed in the abstract, improper treatment of the "sick and afflicted" under the dangerous circumstances and conditions specified in that section is almost synonymous with inherently dangerous conduct.

I would affirm the judgment of conviction.

Endnotes

[1] Felony practicing medicine without a license violates section 2053 of the Business and Professions Code (formerly §2141.5) which states:

Any person who willfully, under circumstances or conditions which cause or create a risk of great bodily harm, serious physical or mental illness, or death, practices or attempts to practice, or advertises or holds himself or herself out as practicing, any system or mode of treating the sick or afflicted in this state, or diagnoses, treats, operates for, or prescribes for any ailment, blemish, deformity, disease, disfigurement, disorder, injury, or other physical or mental condition of any person, without having at the time of so doing a valid, unrevoked or suspended certificate as provided in this chapter, or without being authorized to perform such act pursuant to a certificate obtained in accordance with some other provision of law, is punishable by imprisonment in the county jail for not exceeding one year or in the state prison.

[2] Second degree felony murder was defined for the jury as,

The unlawful killing of a human being, whether intentional, unintentional or accidental, which occurs as a direct causal result of the commission of or attempt to commit a felony inherently dangerous to human life, namely, the crime of practicing medicine without a license under circumstances or conditions which cause or create risk of great bodily harm, serious mental or physical illness, or death, and where there was in the mind of the perpetrator the specific intent to commit such crime, is murder of the second degree.

The specific intent to commit such felony, i.e., practicing medicine without a license under circumstances or conditions which cause or create risk of great bodily harm, serious mental or physical illness, or death, and the commission of or attempt to commit such crime must be proved beyond any doubt.

[3] People v. Phillips, 64 Cal. 2d 574, 583, n.6, 51 Cal. Rptr. 225, 414 P. 2d 353 (1966). "The felony-murder doctrine has been censured not only because it artificially imposes malice as to one crime because of defendant's commission of another but because it anachronistically resurrects from a bygone age a 'barbaric' concept that has been discarded in the place of its origin."

In People v. Dillon, 34 Cal. 3d 441, 462–472, 194 Cal. Rptr. 390, 668 P. 2d 697 (1983) we reaffirmed the first degree felony-murder rule despite serious reservations as to its rationality and moral vitality, because we regarded ourselves bound by the explicit statutory provision (Pen. Code § 189) from which that rule derived. The second degree felony-murder rule, by contrast, is a creature of judicial invention, and as the Chief Justice's concurring opinion suggests the time may be ripe to reconsider its continued vitality. We decline to do so here, however, since that issue has not been raised, briefed, or argued.

In Re Yamashita
327 U.S. 1 (1946)
United States Supreme Court

In this case the Supreme Court considered the petition of former Japanese General Yamashita, who had been captured, tried, and sentenced to death for various war crimes by a U.S. Army military commission in December 1945. Yamashita claimed that he had been unlawfully tried and convicted in that, among other things, he had no personal involvement with or knowledge of the atrocities allegedly committed by his troops. Was Yamashita subjected to a form of strict criminal liability? The majority holds that Yamashita "permitted his troops to commit" the crimes. Is this a justification for strict liability? How is what Yamashita did different from negligence: failure to fulfill one's duty of care for the safety of others? Is all negligence then a type of strict liability? If there are strong moral arguments against strict criminal liability, do similar arguments cut against liability for criminal negligence?

Mr. Chief Justice Stone delivered the opinion of the Court.

. . . The charge, so far as now relevant, is that petitioner, between October 9, 1944 and September 2, 1945, in the Philippine Islands, "while commander of armed forces of Japan at war with the United States of America and its allies, unlawfully disregarded and failed to discharge his duty as commander to control the operations of the members of his command, permitting them to commit brutal atrocities and other high crimes against people of the United States and of its allies and dependencies, particularly the Philippines; and he . . . thereby violated the laws of war."

Bills of particulars, filed by the prosecution by order of the commission, allege a series of acts, one hundred and twenty-three in number, committed by members of the forces under petitioner's command during the period mentioned. The first item specifies the execution of "a deliberate plan and purpose to massacre and exterminate a large part of the civilian population of Batangas Province, and to devastate and destroy public, private and religious property therein, as a result of which more than 25,000 men, women and children, all unarmed noncombatant civilians, were brutally mistreated and killed, without cause or trial, and entire settlements were devastated and destroyed wantonly and without military necessity." Other items specify acts of violence, cruelty and homicide inflicted upon the civilian population and prisoners of war, acts of wholesale pillage and the wanton destruction of religious monuments.

It is not denied that such acts directed against the civilian population of an occupied country and against prisoners of war are recognized in international law as violations of the law of war. . . . But it is urged that the charge does not allege that petitioner has either committed or directed the commission of such acts, and consequently that no violation is charged as against him. But this overlooks the fact that the gist of the charge is an unlawful breach of duty by petitioner as an army commander to control the operations of the members of his command by "permitting them to commit" the extensive and widespread atrocities specified. The question then is whether the law of war imposes on an army commander a duty to take such appropriate measures as are within his power to control the troops under his command for the prevention of the specified acts which are violations of the law of war and which are likely to attend the occupation of hostile territory by an uncontrolled soldiery, and whether he may be charged with personal responsibility for his failure to take such measures when violations result. That this was the precise issue to be tried was made clear by the statement of the prosecution at the opening of the trial.

It is evident that the conduct of military operations by troops whose excesses are unrestrained by the orders or efforts of their commander would almost certainly result in violations which it is the purpose of the law of war to prevent. Its purpose to protect civilian populations and prisoners of war from brutality would largely be defeated if the commander of an invading army could with impunity neglect to take reasonable measures for their protection. Hence the law of war presupposes that its violation is to be avoided through the control of the operations of war by commanders who are to some extent responsible for their subordinates.

. . .

We do not make the laws of war but we respect them so far as they do not conflict with the commands of Congress or the Constitution. There is no contention that the present charge, thus read, is without the support of evidence, or that the commission held petitioner responsible for failing to take measures which were beyond his control or inappropriate for a commanding officer to take in the circumstances.[1] We do not here appraise the evidence on which petitioner was convicted. We do not consider what measures, if any, petitioner took to prevent the commission, by the troops under his command, of the plain violations of the law of war detailed in the bill of particulars, or whether such measures as he may have taken were appropriate and sufficient to discharge the duty imposed upon him. These are questions within the peculiar competence of the military officers composing the commission and were for it to decide. . . . It is plain that the charge on which petitioner was tried charged him with a breach of his duty to control the operations of the members of his command, by permitting them to commit the specified atrocities. This was enough to require the commission to hear evidence tending to establish the culpable failure of petitioner to perform the duty imposed on him by the law of war and to pass upon its sufficiency to establish guilt.

. . .

Mr. Justice, Murphy, dissenting.

The significance of the issue facing the Court today cannot be overemphasized. An American military commission has been established to try a fallen military commander of a conquered nation for an alleged war crime. The authority for such action grows out of the exercise of the power conferred upon Congress by Article I, § 8, Cl. 10 of the Constitution to "define and punish . . . Offences against the Law of Nations. . . ." The grave issue raised by this case is whether a military commission so established and so authorized may disregard the procedural rights of an accused person as guaranteed by the Constitution, especially by the due process clause of the Fifth Amendment.

The answer is plain. The Fifth Amendment guarantee of due process of law applies to "any person" who is accused of a crime by the Federal Government or any of its agencies. No exception is made as to those who are accused of war crimes or as to those who possess the status of an enemy belligerent. Indeed, such an exception would be contrary to the whole philosophy of human rights which makes the Constitution the great living document that it is. The immutable rights of the individual, including those secured by the due process clause of the Fifth Amendment, belong not alone to the members of those nations that excel on the battlefield or that subscribe to the democratic ideology. They belong to every person in the world, victor or vanquished, whatever may be his race, color or beliefs. They rise above any status of belligerency or outlawry. They survive any popular passion or frenzy of the moment. No court or

legislature or executive, not even the mightiest army in the world, can ever destroy them. Such is the universal and indestructible nature of the rights which the due process clause of the Fifth Amendment recognizes and protects when life or liberty is threatened by virtue of the authority of the United States.

. . .

A military commission was appointed to try the petitioner for an alleged war crime. The trial was ordered to be held in territory over which the United States has complete sovereignty. No military necessity or other emergency demanded the suspension of the safeguards of due process. Yet petitioner was rushed to trial under an improper charge, given insufficient time to prepare an adequate defense, deprived of the benefits of some of the most elementary rules of evidence and summarily sentenced to be hanged. In all this needless and unseemly haste there was no serious attempt to charge or to prove that he committed a recognized violation of the laws of war. He was not charged with personally participating in the acts of atrocity or with ordering or condoning their commission. Not even knowledge of these crimes was attributed to him. It was simply alleged that he unlawfully disregarded and failed to discharge his duty as commander to control the operations of the members of his command, permitting them to commit the acts of atrocity. The recorded annals of warfare and the established principles of international law afford not the slightest precedent for such a charge. This indictment in effect permitted the military commission to make the crime whatever it willed, dependent upon its biased view as to petitioner's duties and his disregard thereof, a practice reminiscent of that pursued in certain less respected nations in recent years.

. . .

If we are ever to develop an orderly international community based upon a recognition of human dignity it is of the utmost importance that the necessary punishment of those guilty of atrocities be as free as possible from the ugly stigma of revenge and vindictiveness. Justice must be tempered by compassion rather than by vengeance. In this, the first case involving this momentous problem ever to reach this Court, our responsibility is both lofty and difficult. We must insist, within the confines of our proper jurisdiction, that the highest standards of justice be applied in this trial of an enemy commander conducted under the authority of the United States. Otherwise stark retribution will be free to masquerade in a cloak of false legalism. And the hatred and cynicism engendered by that retribution will supplant the great ideals to which this nations is dedicated.

. . .

. . . I find it impossible to agree that the charge against the petitioner stated a recognized violation of the laws of war.

It is important, in the first place, to appreciate the background of events preceding this trial. From October 9, 1944, to September 2, 1945, the petitioner was the Commanding General of the 14th Army Group of the Imperial Japanese Army, with headquarters in the Philippines. The reconquest of the Philippines by the armed forces of the United States began approximately at the time when the petitioner assumed this command. Combined with a great and decisive sea battle, an invasion was made on the island of Leyte on October 20, 1944. "In the six days of the great naval action the Japanese position in the Philippines had become extremely critical. Most of the serviceable elements of the Japanese Navy had been committed to the battle with disastrous results. The strike had miscarried, and General MacArthur's land wedge was firmly implanted in the vulnerable flank of the enemy. . . . There were 260,000 Japanese troops scattered over the Philippines but most of them might as well have been on the other side of the world so far as the enemy's ability to shift them to meet the American thrusts was concerned. If General MacArthur succeeded in establishing himself in the Visayas where he could stage, exploit, and spread under cover of overwhelming naval and air superiority, nothing could prevent him from overrunning the Philippines." Biennial Report of the Chief of Staff of the United States Army, July 1, 1943, to June 30, 1945, to the Secretary of War, p. 74.

By the end of 1944 the island of Leyte was largely in American hands. And on January 9, 1945, the island of Luzon was invaded. "Yamashita's inability to cope with General MacArthur's swift moves, his desired reaction to the deception measures, the guerrillas, and General Kenney's aircraft combined to place the Japanese in an impossible situation. The enemy was forced into a piecemeal commitment of his troops." . . . It was at this time and place that most of the alleged atrocities took place. Organized resistance around Manila ceased on February 23. Repeated land and air assaults pulverized the enemy and within a few months there was little left of petitioner's command except a few remnants which had gathered for a last stand among the precipitous mountains.

. . .

. . . Nowhere was it alleged that the petitioner personally committed any of the atrocities, or that he ordered their commission, or that he had any knowledge of the commission thereof by members of his command.

The findings of the military commission bear out this absence of any direct personal charge against the petitioner. The commission merely found that atrocities and other high crimes "have been committed by members of the Japanese armed forces under your command . . . that they were not sporadic in nature but in many cases were methodically supervised by Japanese officers and noncommissioned officers; . . . That during the period in question you failed to provide effective control of your troops as was required by the circumstances."

In other words, read against the background of military events in the Philippines subsequent to October 9, 1944, these charges amount to this: "We, the victorious American forces, have done everything possible to destroy and disorganize your lines of communication, your effective control of your personnel, your ability to wage war. In those respects we have succeeded. We have defeated and crushed your forces. And now we charge and condemn you for having been inefficient in maintaining control of your troops during the period when we were so effectively besieging and eliminating your forces and blocking your ability to maintain effective control. Many terrible atrocities were committed by your disorganized troops. Because these atrocities were so widespread we will not bother to charge or prove that you committed, ordered or condoned any of them. We will assume that they must have resulted from your inefficiency and negligence as a commander.

In short, we charge you with the crime of inefficiency in controlling your troops. We will judge the discharge of your duties by the disorganization which we ourselves created in large part. Our standards of judgment are whatever we wish to make them."

Nothing in all history or in international law, at least as far as I am aware, justifies such a charge against a fallen commander of a defeated force. To use the very inefficiency and disorganization created by the victorious forces as the primary basis for condemning officers of the defeated armies bears no resemblance to justice or to military reality.

. . .

Endnote

[1] In its findings the commission took account of the difficulties "faced by the Accused with respect not only to the swift and overpowering advance of American forces, but also to the errors of his predecessors, weaknesses in organization, equipment, supply . . . , training, communication, discipline and morale of his troops," and the "tactical situation, the character, training and capacity of staff officers and subordinate commanders as well as the traits of character . . . of his troops." It nonetheless found that petitioner had not taken such measures to control his troops as were "required by the circumstances." We do not weigh the evidence. We merely hold that the charge sufficiently states a violation against the law of war, and that the commission, upon the facts found, could properly find petitioner guilty of such a violation.

The Case of the Dog "Provetie"

As explained in Section C, the following case is one among many "animal trials" recorded throughout Europe from the late middle ages up to the eighteenth century. What does our reaction to such cases say about the objectives of criminal punishment? (Also, how did they make the dog "confess"?)

Reported in *The South African Law Journal*, Vol. 24 (1907): 232–234.

Claim and Conclusion made and taken in the matter of Lot Huygens Gael, Schout of the Town of Leiden, against and in respect of the dog of Jan Jansse van der Poel, named Provetie, with moreover the sentence of the court.

Lot Huygens Gael, Schout of the Town of Leiden, prosecutor on behalf of his lordship [the Count of Holland] in criminal matters, accuses in the open Court of the Schepenes of the Town of Leiden the dog of Jan Jansse van der Poel, named Provetie, or by whatsoever other name he may be called, now a prisoner, and says that he, the said Provetie, did not scruple on Sunday last, being the 5th of May, 1595, to bite the child of Jan Jacobsz van der Poel, which child was then playing at his uncle's house and had a piece of meat in his hand, and the said Provetie snapping at it did bite the said child and thus inflicted a wound in the second finger of the right hand, going through the skin to the flesh in such manner that the blood flowed therefrom, and the child a few days after died in consequence of fright, for which cause the prosecutor apprehended the said Provetie, all of which appears from the prisoner's own confession, made by him without torture or being put in irons . . .

Sentence: The Schepenen of Leiden, having seen the claim and conclusion made and taken by Lot Huygens Gael, Schout of this town, against and to the charge of the dog of Jan Jansse van der Poel, named Provetie, or by whatsoever other name or surname he may be known, the prisoner being present, having seen, moreover, the information obtained by the prosecutor for the purpose, besides the prisoner's own confession made without torture or being placed in irons, doing justice in the name of, etc., have condemned and hereby do condemn him to be led and taken to the plain of Gravesteijn in this town, where evildoers are customarily punished, and that he be there hanged by the executioner to the gallows with a rope until death ensues, that further his dead body be dragged on a hurdle to the gallows-field, and that he there remain hanging to the gallows, to the deterring of other dogs and to all as an example; moreover, they declare all his goods, should he have any, to be confiscated and forfeited for the benefit of the countship.

This done in the open court, all schepenen being present, the 15th May, 1595.

Rummel v. Estelle
445 U.S. 263 (1980)
United States Supreme Court

The opposing evaluations of the punishment given in this case should be read in light of the discussion of cruel and unusual punishments in Section D. What purpose is Texas's "three-time-loser" statute supposed to serve? Is there evidence that it works? "Recidivist" statutes, such as this one, are directed at "habitual criminals." Is it reasonable to expect to deter such persons? Does the moral and constitutional requirement of proportionality apply only to *types* of crimes and punishments (so that, for example, death is proportional to murder, though not to rape) but not to particular sentences *within a given type* (so that any length of imprisonment is permissible as long as some imprisonment is proportional)? Is the majority in *Rummel* making this argument?

Mr. Justice Rehnquist delivered the opinion of the Court.

Petitioner William James Rummel is presently serving a life sentence imposed by the State of Texas in 1973 under its "recidivist statute," . . . which provided that "[w]hoever shall have been three times convicted of a felony less than capital shall on such third conviction be imprisoned for life in the penitentiary." On January 19, 1976, Rummel sought a writ of habeas corpus in the United States District Court for the Western District of Texas, arguing that life imprisonment was "grossly disproportionate" to the three felonies that formed the predicate for his sentence and that therefore the sentence violated the ban on cruel and unusual punishments of the Eighth and Fourteenth Amendments. The District Court and the United States Court of Appeals for the Fifth Circuit rejected Rummel's claim, finding no unconstitutional disproportionality. We granted certiorari . . . and now affirm.

In 1964 the State of Texas charged Rummel with fraudulent use of a credit card to obtain $80 worth of goods or services. Because the amount in question was greater than $50, the charged offense was a felony punishable by a minimum of 2 years and a maximum of 10 years in the Texas Department of Corrections. Rummel eventually pleaded guilty to the charge and was sentenced to three years' confinement in a state penitentiary.

In 1969 the State of Texas charged Rummel with passing a forged check in the amount of $28.36, a crime punishable by imprisonment in a penitentiary for not less than two nor more than five years. Rummel pleaded guilty to this offense and was sentenced to four years' imprisonment.

In 1973 Rummel was charged with obtaining $120.75 by false pretenses. Because the amount obtained was greater than $50, the charged offense was designated "felony theft," which, by itself, was punishable by confinement in a penitentiary for not less than 2 nor more than 10 years. The prosecution chose, however, to proceed against Rummel under Texas'[s] recidivist statute, and cited in the indictment his 1964 and 1969 convictions as requiring imposition of a life sentence if Rummel were convicted of the charged offense. A jury convicted Rummel of felony theft and also found as true the allegation that he had been convicted of two prior felonies. As a result, on April 26, 1973, the trial court imposed upon Rummel the life sentence mandated by Art. 63 [of the Texas Penal Code].

. . .

This Court has on occasion stated that the Eighth Amendment prohibits imposition of a sentence that is grossly disproportionate to the severity of the crime. In recent years this proposition has appeared most frequently in opinions dealing with the death penalty.

. . .

Because a sentence of death differs in kind from any sentence of imprisonment, no matter how long, our decisions applying the prohibition of cruel and unusual punishments to capital cases are of limited assistance in deciding the constitutionality of the punishment meted out to Rummel.

Outside the context of capital punishment, successful challenges to the proportionality of particular sentences have been exceedingly rare. In Weems v. United States [217 U.S. 349 (1910)], a case coming to this Court from the Supreme Court of the Philippine Islands, petitioner successfully attacked the imposition of a punishment known as "cadena temporal" for the crime of falsifying a public record. . . . The mandatory "remedy" for this offense was *cadena temporal*, a punishment described graphically by the Court:

Its minimum degree is confinement in a penal institution for twelve years and one day, a chain at the ankle and wrist of the offender, hard and painful labor, no assistance from friend or relative, no marital authority or parental rights or rights of property, no participation even in the family council. These parts of his penalty endure for the term of imprisonment. From other parts there is no intermission. His prison bars and chains are removed, it is true, after twelve years, but he goes from them to a perpetual limitation of his liberty. He is forever kept under the shadow of his crime, forever kept within voice and view of the criminal magistrate, not being able to change his domicil without giving notice to the "authority immediately in charge of his surveillance," and without permission in writing. Id., at 366. . . .

Although Rummel argues that the length of Weems's imprisonment was, by itself, a basis for the Court's decision, the Court's opinion does not support such a simple conclusion. The opinion consistently referred jointly to the length of imprisonment and its "accessories" or "accompaniments" . . .

. . .

In an attempt to provide us with objective criteria against which we might measure the proportionality of his life sentence, Rummel points to certain characteristics of his offenses that allegedly render them "petty." He cites, for example, the absence of violence in his crimes. But the presence or absence of violence does not always affect the strength of society's interest in deterring a particular crime or in punishing a particular criminal. A high official in a large corporation can commit undeniably serious crimes in the area of antitrust, bribery, or clean air or water standards without coming close to engaging in any "violent" or short-term "life-threatening" behavior. Additionally, Rummel cites the "small" amount of money taken in each of his crimes. But to recognize that the State of Texas could have imprisoned Rummel for life if he had stolen $5,000, $50,000, or $500,000, rather than the $120.75 that a jury convicted him of stealing, is virtually to concede that the lines to be drawn are indeed "subjective," and therefore properly within the province of legislatures, not

courts. Moreover, if Rummel had attempted to defraud his victim of $50,000, but had failed, no money whatsoever would have changed hands; yet Rummel would be no less blameworthy, only less skillful, than if he had succeeded.

In this case, however, we need not decide whether Texas could impose a life sentence upon Rummel merely for obtaining $120.75 by false pretenses. Had Rummel only committed that crime, under the law enacted by the Texas Legislature he could have been imprisoned for no more than 10 years. In fact, at the time that he obtained the $120.75 by false pretenses, he already had committed and had been imprisoned for two other felonies, crimes that Texas and other States felt were serious enough to warrant significant terms of imprisonment even in the absence of prior offenses. Thus the interest of the State of Texas here is not simply that of making criminal the unlawful acquisition of another person's property; it is in addition the interest, expressed in all recidivist statutes, in dealing in a harsher manner with those who by repeated criminal acts have shown that they are simply incapable of conforming to the norms of society as established by its criminal law. By conceding the validity of recidivist statutes generally, Rummel himself concedes that the State of Texas, or any other State, has a valid interest in so dealing with that class of persons.

. . .

. . . Thus, under Art. 63, a three-time felon receives a mandatory life sentence, with possibility of parole, only if commission and conviction of each succeeding felony followed conviction for the preceding one, and only if each prior conviction was followed by actual imprisonment. Given this necessary sequence, a recidivist must twice demonstrate that conviction and actual imprisonment do not deter him from returning to crime once he is released. One in Rummel's position has been both graphically informed of the consequences of lawlessness and given an opportunity to reform, all to no avail. Article 63 thus is nothing more than a societal decision that when such a person commits yet another felony, he should be subjected to the admittedly serious penalty of incarceration for life, subject only to the State's judgment as to whether to grant him parole.[1]

. . .

Mr. Justice Powell, with whom Mr. Justice Brennan, Mr. Justice Marshall, and Mr. Justice Stevens join, dissenting.

. . .

The scope of the Cruel and Unusual Punishments Clause extends not only to barbarous methods of punishment, but also to punishments that are grossly disproportionate. Disproportionality analysis measures the relationship between the nature and number of offenses committed and the severity of the punishment inflicted upon the offender. The inquiry focuses on whether a person deserves such punishment, not simply on whether punishment would serve a utilitarian goal. A statute that levied a mandatory life sentence for overtime parking might well deter vehicular lawlessness, but it would offend our felt sense of justice. The Court concedes today that the principle of disproportionality plays a role in the review of sentences imposing the death penalty, but suggests that the principle may be less applicable when a noncapital sentence is challenged. Such a limitation finds no support in the history of Eighth Amendment jurisprudence.

The principle of disproportionality is rooted deeply in English constitutional law. The Magna Carta of 1215 insured that "[a] free man shall not be [fined] for a trivial offence, except in accordance with the degree of the offence; and for a serious offence he shall be [fined] according to its gravity." By 1400, the English common law had embraced the principle, not always followed in practice, that punishment should not be excessive either in severity or length.

. . .

In sum, a few basic principles emerge from the history of the Eighth Amendment. Both barbarous forms of punishment and grossly excessive punishments are cruel and unusual. A sentence may be excessive if it serves no acceptable social purpose, or is grossly disproportionate to the seriousness of the crime. The principle of disproportionality has been acknowledged to apply to both capital and noncapital sentences.

. . .

Examination of the objective factors traditionally employed by the Court to assess the proportionality of a sentence demonstrates that petitioner suffers a cruel and unusual punishment. Petitioner has been sentenced to the penultimate criminal penalty because he committed three offenses defrauding others of about $230. The nature of the crimes does not suggest that petitioner ever engaged in conduct that threatened another's person, involved a trespass, or endangered in any way the peace of society. A comparison of the sentence petitioner received with the sentences provided by habitual offender statutes of other American jurisdictions demonstrates that only two other States authorize the same punishment. A comparison of petitioner to other criminals sentenced in Texas shows that he has been punished for three property-related offenses with a harsher sentence than that given first-time offenders or two-time offenders convicted of far more serious offenses. The Texas system assumes that all three-time offenders deserve the same punishment whether they commit three murders or cash three fraudulent checks.

The petitioner has committed criminal acts for which he may be punished. He has been given a sentence that is not inherently barbarous. But the relationship between the criminal acts and the sentence is grossly disproportionate. For having defrauded others of about $230, the State of Texas has deprived petitioner of his freedom for the rest of his life. The State has not attempted to justify the sentence as necessary either to deter other persons or to isolate a potentially violent individual. Nor has petitioner's status as a habitual offender been shown to justify a mandatory life sentence. My view, informed by examination of the "objective indicia that reflect the public attitude toward a given sanction," is that this punishment violates the principle of proportionality contained within the Cruel and Unusual Punishments Clause.

. . .

Endnote

[1] Thus, it is not true that, as the dissent claims, the Texas scheme subjects a person to life imprisonment "merely because he is a three-time felon." On the contrary, Art. 63 mandates such a sentence only after shorter terms of actual imprisonment have proved ineffective.

Suggestions for Further Reading

Becker, L. C., "Criminal Attempt and the Theory of the Law of Crimes," *Philosophy and Public Affairs,* Vol. 3 (1974):262–294.

Bedau, H., *The Death Penalty in America,* 3rd ed. (Oxford: Oxford University Press, 1982).

Crump, D., and Crump, S., "In Defense of the Felony Murder Doctrine," *Harvard Journal of Law and Public Policy,* Vol. 8 (1990):359–398.

Dershowitz, A. M., *The Best Defense* (New York: Vintage Books, 1983).

Estrich, S., *Real Rape* (Cambridge, Mass.: Harvard University Press, 1987).

Fingarette, H., *The Meaning of Criminal Insanity* (Berkeley: University of California Press, 1972).

Fletcher, G. P., *Rethinking Criminal Law* (Boston: Little, Brown, 1978).

Frankel, M. E., *Criminal Sentences: Law Without Order* (New York: Hill & Wang, 1972).

Goldstein, A., *The Insanity Defense* (New Haven, Conn.: Yale University Press, 1967).

Gross, H., *A Theory of Criminal Justice* (New York: Oxford University Press, 1979).

Hart, H. L. A., *Punishment and Responsibility* (Oxford: Clarendon Press, 1968).

Kant, I., *The Metaphysical Elements of Justice* (trans. John Ladd) (Indianapolis, Ind.: Bobbs-Merrill, 1965).

Kaplan, J., and Weisberg, R. (Eds.), *Criminal Law: Cases and Materials* (Boston: Little, Brown, 1986).

Kelman, M., "Interpretive Construction in Substantive Criminal Law," *Stanford Law Review,* Vol. 33 (1981):591–673.

Menninger, K., *The Crime of Punishment* (New York: Viking Press, 1966).

Morris, H., *On Guilt and Innocence* (Berkeley: University of California Press, 1976).

Murphy, J. G., *Retribution, Justice and Therapy* (Dordrecht, the Netherlands: D. Reidel, 1979).

Murphy, J. G., *Punishment and Rehabilitation,* 2nd ed. (Belmont, Calif.: Wadsworth, 1985).

Nagel, T., "Moral Luck," in T. Nagel (Eds.), *Mortal Questions* (Cambridge: Cambridge University Press, 1979).

Packer, H., *The Limits of the Criminal Sanction* (Stanford, Calif.: Stanford University Press, 1968).

Perkins, R. M., "Criminal Liability Without Fault: A Disquieting Trend," *Iowa Law Review,* Vol. 68 (1983):1067–1081.

Szasz, T., *The Myth of Mental Illness* (New York: Hoeber-Harper, 1961).

Williams, B., *Moral Luck* (Cambridge: Cambridge University Press, 1981).

Chapter VI

Tort Law

Imagine the following: You have just landed a new job downtown. As your first day at the new office approaches, you become excited and a bit nervous. The night before your first meeting with the boss, you make sure that your alarm clock is set to go off early, because you want to be at the office on time to make a good first impression. But as fate would have it, the clock malfunctions during the night; the alarm doesn't go off and you leap out of bed in the morning with only a few minutes to get downtown. You catch an express bus to the business district. The bus driver seems to be in a hurry too; in fact, the bus is traveling at an illegal speed. This is all for the good, you think, until the bus approaches a major intersection, rounding the corner at the precise moment when a construction crew, lifting a steel beam with a crane, loses control of its rig and sends the beam crashing through the side of the bus at just the point where you are seated.

Fanciful as this may seem, accidents equally bizarre and equally costly occur daily.

Now, in Mercy Hospital—with broken bones, intravenous tubes, and a mounting medical bill—you have lost your job. Is anyone but yourself responsible for your plight? The construction crew? The bus company? The driver? The alarm-clock manufacturer? And if any of them are responsible in some way, what can you do about it? Have you been wronged by any or all these parties in a way the law might recognize? The answer is yes. Any one of these parties (with the probable exception of the alarm-clock maker) may have committed a *tort:* a personal harm or wrong to an individual for which the law provides redress.

But what does this really mean? What sort of "wrong" is a tort? Why not simply say, for example, that the wrong here is a *criminal* wrong; that the bus driver and the construction crew have committed crimes for which they deserve to be punished? The answer is that, though they may have committed certain crimes as well, being convictable of a crime is not the same thing as being liable under the law of tort. In the criminal law, the state or the "people" collectively seek to enforce basic standards of behavior by acting to pay a wrongdoer back for his wrongful deed and working to discourage similar, future conduct. In the law of tort, it is you, the individual victim of another's wrongdoing, who brings a suit against the perpetrator. This difference between crime and tort marks a deeper difference in the fundamental purposes of the two branches of law.

The aim of the criminal law is, broadly, to ensure compliance with those rules and standards deemed essential to the preservation of society as a whole. When these rules are broken, people are often hurt. But the criminal law concerns itself with that hurt only insofar as it is reflected in the disrespect shown for society's rules. It is not a necessary condition of criminality that there be an identifiable

"victim" in the sense that you, in your hospital bed, believe that you have been made a victim. Some crimes (conspiracy, illegal possession, unsuccessful attempts) do not have victims who suffer loss in this way; and even those that do (robbery, rape, sexual abuse) do not concern themselves with making good that loss, nor with annulling the criminal's gain. Thus arises the need for a body of law specifically concerned with the wrongdoer's gain and the victim's loss—an institutional mechanism for determining where the burden of losses, intentionally or even unintentionally created, should fall. This is the role fulfilled by tort law. You, the plaintiff, seek to have the losses or burdens that have befallen you (medical bills, lost wages, "pain and suffering") shifted to and compensated by someone else. A central question, of course, is when and under what circumstances this should be done.

In large part, the existing body of tort law is a response to the vast array of injuries to which all of us are exposed—and some of us unlucky enough to experience—as a consequence of living in a complex, highly industrialized society. Tort law deals, in fact, primarily with unintended harm, particularly negligent harm, the risks of which seem steadily to be growing.

Negligence is by far the most pervasive and most litigated category of torts; and since we will be focusing on negligence cases throughout this chapter, we need to be clear on its meaning. One is negligent if one fails to exercise due care or regard for the safety of others, thereby exposing them to an unreasonable risk of harm. To say that one is negligent is not necessarily to say that one is forgetful or inattentive (though this may be the case). Rather, to be negligent means to fall below the acceptable level of care for the welfare of others that society expects of us all.

Liability in negligence is based on the idea

of *fault:* negligence law declares that I should be liable for those consequences of my conduct that are my "fault." But how, exactly, is this to be understood? Is fault to be understood "subjectively," requiring always a personal moral shortcoming in the defendant? Or is fault to be construed "objectively," measured in terms of a failure to live up to a general, publicly set standard of behavior? The law has adopted the objective test. Suppose you leave a banana peel on the stairway. I slip on the peel and am injured. When it asks whether you acted negligently, the law does not assess the faultiness of your conduct exclusively from your own (subjective) point of view, taking into account your particular weaknesses or inabilities. It doesn't inquire into whether you personally realized the danger presented by the banana peel—perhaps you are slow and just never thought about it. Instead, it asks whether a reasonable person would have appreciated the danger.

Why should negligence be measured by an objective test? Many jurists answer, in utilitarian fashion, that cooperative social life requires a certain minimum standard of average care upon which everyone can rely. People who, because of their constitution, cannot live up to this standard may be forgiven by an enlightened conscience; but since their conduct still poses a threat or danger, they must be held to that average, objective standard.

Return now to the construction crew in our hypothetical case. Suppose the crew was required by industry standards (in addition to common sense) to hoist the steel beams with a cable of sufficient tensile strength to handle the load. Instead, the crew used a cheaper, substandard cable—a clear example of a failure to exercise proper care for the safety of others, exposing workers, pedestrians, motorists, and their passengers to a risk of serious harm. Does this mean that you can sue the company for its negligence? Not of itself. To establish a *prima facie* case of negligent harm, the law requires a plaintiff to prove, by a preponderance (majority) of the evidence, that: (1) the defendant (here the construction company) did have a duty to exercise reasonable care in the context within which it acted (lifting heavy steel girders); (2) that the defendant violated or breached that duty (used cheap, unsafe cable and thereby created a genuine hazard); and (3) the breach of that duty caused harm to you (permitted the girder to escape and strike you, resulting in injuries).

It is around these basic elements of the law of negligence that significant philosophical issues have formed. Just what duties do I have to others? How far do these duties extend? Do I (should I) have a duty to *help* others as well as to refrain from *harming* them? Is it fair that I be required always to act reasonably? How is "reasonableness" to be measured? What determines whether my conduct has caused your injury? Am I responsible for all the harm that I cause? If I fail to help you and you are hurt, did I cause that? How relevant to my responsibility for your harm is the fact that I caused it? Or that I was at fault or blameworthy in acting as I did?

The selections in Section A of this chapter begin by pursuing questions about causation in the law of tort. The *Lynch* and *Palsgraf* cases present contrasting perspectives on the law's response to the question "When can one thing be said to have caused another?" The essays by W. Page Keeton, H. L. A. Hart and A. M. Honoré, and Judith Thomson try to provide some answers. The readings in Section B then take up a more specific but related issue: liability for omissions, or failures to act, and the legal status of a duty to rescue.

A. Causation and Liability

Introduction

In *Lynch v. Fisher,* the defendant ran out of gas while driving his truck down the highway. He negligently parked the truck on the road, failing either to move it completely to the side or to set out flares. He then left the scene in search of a service station. A couple, Mr. and Mrs. Gunter, rounded the corner at excessive speed, were unable to avoid collision with the truck, and were injured, Mrs. Gunter severely. Plaintiff Lynch, traveling in the opposite direction, encountered the accident scene soon after the incident occurred and went to aid the Gunters. Helping Mrs. Gunter out of the car, he then went to the driver's side. When Mr. Gunter got out, Lynch leaned inside to remove the floor pad to use as a cushion. There he found a loaded pistol, which he handed to Mr. Gunter. As Lynch prepared to tend to the wife, Mr. Gunter, now temporarily deranged from shock, mistook Lynch for an assailant and shot him in the foot. Finally, truck driver Fisher returned to find a confusion of wrecked vehicles, an unconscious woman, a trigger-happy madman, and a footsore Good Samaritan, who promptly slapped him with a hefty podiatrist bill.

Helen Palsgraf purchased a ticket to ride the train from Brooklyn to Rockaway Beach. While she waited on the railway platform, various trains to other destinations arrived and departed. As one of these was pulling away, a man carrying a plain-wrapped package emerged from the crowd and sprinted down the platform to catch the train. He appeared to be losing ground when two of the railroad's employees came to his assistance, pulling and pushing him onto the moving train. In so doing, the package—which contained large fireworks—fell to the ground, slid under the tracks, and, ignited by a spark from the train, exploded. Either the explosion of the fireworks themselves, or else a stampede caused by the explosion (the facts are still unclear, despite what Judge Cardozo says), caused some scales located some distance away on the platform to topple over onto poor Mrs. Palsgraf. She sued the railroad, alleging that it caused her injuries. (Why didn't she sue the man with the package?)

Should the defendants in either of these cases be held liable for the injuries involved? As we have seen, the law of negligence makes the answer to this question turn on another one: Did either of these defendants *cause* the injuries? This is not easy to answer.

Cause, Effect, and the Law

When is an act or event the cause of some further act or event? Indeed, when is an act or event even relevant to a question of causation? Suppose that you sneeze and that immediately following this an elderly man in Peoria has a heart attack. Absent any further knowledge of the matter, a reasonable person would surely deny that these two events were in any way causally linked or related. One way both to explain and support this obvious reaction would be to point out that the injury (heart attack) would certainly have occurred even if you hadn't sneezed. (After all, what possible connection could there be?) This observation strongly suggests that, for one act or event, A, to be causally relevant to the occurrence of some other act or event, B, it must at least be the case that A is a *necessary condition* for the occurrence of B; that is, B would not have happened if A hadn't.

Unfortunately, this conclusion won't get us very far. Consider the tragic circumstances surrounding the death of former president John Kennedy. Many people still believe (whether correctly or incorrectly we may never know) that the pulling of a trigger on a rifle by a man named Lee Harvey Oswald led to Kennedy's death; and if they are right, then Oswald's pulling of that trigger at that moment on that day in Dallas was a necessary condition, or *sine qua non* ("that without which there is not") of Kennedy's death. But consider: If the sun hadn't been shining. Oswald would not have been able to see the presidential motorcade; if the motorcade hadn't kept to its prescribed route, it would not have arrived at the point opposite Oswald's location; if the trigger on Oswald's rifle hadn't been working properly . . . if Oswald had not gained entry to the building from which he shot . . . if Kennedy hadn't made it to Dallas or hadn't been elected president . . . if Oswald hadn't been born. . . . The point is obvious enough. If we look into the past of any given event, we will find numerous (perhaps infinitely many?) conditions such that, had they not occurred as they did, the event in question would never have arisen. And for each of these conditions, a seemingly endless number of further events serve as necessary conditions, and on and on. Insofar as each is a necessary condition or *sine qua non* of its successor in the chain, all would seem to have an equal claim to being called a "cause," and we are left with an abundance of potential defendants.

A related difficulty in understanding legal causation can be seen in a similar way. Presumably, for any given act I perform, that act will continue having consequences indefinitely; that is, it will stand as a necessary condition for the occurrence of an entire series of other acts or events. Take, for example, my act of preparing this book. That act is a necessary condition for you reading it. Suppose, reading this book with such enthusiasm, you stay up too late one night and sleep in too late the next morning; you miss class and the final exam; you flunk the course; your grade point average is ruined, and you can't get into law school, as you had planned. Because of this, you don't meet the young attorney who would have been your spouse; and so on. Does it make sense to say that I am responsible for you not having a spouse or a legal career? When do I cease being responsible for what I do, for chains of cause and effect that I initiate?

I start a fire in my fireplace, negligently leaving it unattended. A spark ignites my draperies and spreads from there to the wall; soon the entire house is ablaze. From my home, the fire grows and spreads to neighboring houses and eventually to the entire town. Would it make sense to hold me liable for all the resulting injury and damage? Plainly, some limitations must be placed on liability for harm that is, loosely speaking, a "consequence" of one's conduct, if for no other reason than that failing to do so would seem to undermine at least one animating purpose of the tort system. If my conduct results in the destruction of an entire town, it would be pointless to hold me liable in tort (though there might be reason for charging me with a crime), because the purpose of fixing liability in tort is to see to it that the victim's losses are compensated. Obviously I can't compensate the entire town. How, then, can these limits be drawn in a philosophically defensible fashion?

Judge Benjamin Cardozo (later to sit on the U.S. Supreme Court), writing for the New York Court of Appeals in *Palsgraf*, puts the central question in the case this way: Was the railroad's act a wrong to *Mrs. Palsgraf* (even if it was a wrong to the man with the package)? Cardozo insists that negligence requires a *relationship* between the parties involved: The negligent act must have been directed to a specific person before that individual may recover from the defendant. To have a "cause of action" (basis for a suit), Mrs. Palsgraf must show that the railroad breached a duty it had to her. Cardozo claims that this did not occur: "The risk reasonably to be perceived defines the duty to be obeyed." Nothing in this case would have suggested to a reasonable person that the parcel wrapped in plain paper posed a risk to the health or safety of the plaintiff. The railroad does, of course, have certain duties to Mrs. Palsgraf, but these all amount to duties not to harm her in *foreseeable* ways. Since she was not harmed in a foreseeable way, none of those duties were violated.

Judge Andrews, dissenting from Cardozo's majority opinion, asserts that negligence is not a relationship between a person and those whom he "might reasonably be expected" to injure but rather to all those whom he "in fact" injures. Andrews rejects the restriction of negligence to the domain of the foreseeable. Such restrictions are vague and ill-defined questions of policy. What we know is that the negligence of the railroad workers was a necessary condition of the resulting harm and that the accident was a direct consequence of the defendant's actions, neither remote in time nor space.

The majority in *Lynch* make much the same argument: Though the injury arose in a bizarre and unforeseeable manner, it remains true that Lynch would not have been injured but for the negligence of Fisher; and while it is true that Gunter did the shooting, he cannot be accounted the "cause" of the wounded foot, since he was not acting deliberately or voluntarily at the time. The court, concluding that the "chain [linking Fisher's negligence to Lynch's injuries] is complete and whole—link by link," finds Fisher liable.

Proximate Cause and Foreseeability

As tort scholar W. Page Keeton indicates in his essay, the question of placing limits upon those consequences of my conduct that, for the purposes of tort law, I can correctly be said to have caused, has been transformed by the law into the requirement that plaintiff prove *two* kinds of cause: "factual" and "legal" or "cause in fact" and "proximate cause." The first or "factual" requirement is simply the familiar one of a *sine qua non:* Plaintiffs must show that their injuries would not have arisen had defendants not acted as they did. The second, *proximate cause,* marks the concern of the courts to contain the limits of causal liability within reasonable, fair, or just boundaries. D's conduct is the proximate cause of P's injury if and only if the act and the injury are "closely enough" related to make it fair or just to hold D liable. Over the years the courts have devised various limiting principles under the heading of proximate cause, appealing, for example, to whether the injury was a foreseeable result of the defendant's conduct or whether another cause "intervened" to bring about the harm.

Keeton probes the perplexities of factual and legal causation. Upon whom, for example, should the burden of proof be placed in regard to issues of causation? Should the law require the plaintiff to prove it more likely than not that, had the defendant not acted, the plaintiff would not have been injured? (How are such "contrary to fact" conditional statements to be proven?) Or should it be enough if the plaintiff can show that the defendant's act substantially increased the likelihood that the plaintiff would be injured? Keeton also reviews two important types of exceptions to the principle that the basic burden of proving causation rests with the plaintiff: the "alternative liability" and "market-share" doctrines. These doc-

trines, and the difficulties they raise, are also discussed in the contribution by Judith Thomson.

Lastly, Keeton attempts to summarize the criteria governing the determination of proximate or legal cause: The defendant's conduct is the proximate cause of the plaintiff's injury only if (1) harm to a person like the plaintiff was foreseeable; (2) the actual injury sustained by the plaintiff was of the same general type as that which was foreseeable; and (3) no new, independent cause intervened to bring about the harm. Keeton points to further questions that these criteria invite. Is it always clear, for example, which harms would and which would not be foreseeable by a reasonable person? And how are the foreseeable risks to be defined? Did Fisher's conduct in *Lynch* impose the clearly recognizable risk of *injury to motorists,* making Lynch's injury directly traceable to Fisher's conduct, so that he is liable? Or did his conduct impose the unforeseeable (and very small) risk of *bullet wounds to rescuers of deranged and gun-packing injured motorists,* with the result that Fisher cannot be held liable? Keeton clarifies the legal framework within which a number of worries about causation arise.

In the excerpt from their book *Causation in the Law,* philosophers H. L. A. Hart and A. M. Honoré take us deeper into the philosophical analysis and justification of causal language in the law. Hart and Honoré begin with the obvious fact that we all use causal language to describe the world: "He broke the window," "Oswald killed Kennedy," and so on. We make these kinds of judgments continually—in assigning responsibility, in reconstructing the past. Hart and Honoré defend the thesis that this ordinary causal language, our everyday, working understanding of "cause," includes distinctions and nuances that place limits on what I can truly be said to have caused. Hence, they reject the conclusion of Judge Andrews in *Palsgraf* that drawing such lines or defining such limits is purely a matter of arbitrary policy. The law both can and ought to reflect these commonsense ways of thinking.

Hart and Honoré begin their search for the implicit limiting principles of causal attribution with a paradigm case of causation: A throws a lighted match on some dry brush and soon a fire is blazing. Can the fire properly be attributed to A's conduct despite the presence of other factors (oxygen in the air, wind, dryness), each of which were equally necessary to the final result? And if so, why? We would all agree that A's conduct caused the fire. But why are we justified in this conviction? Because, Hart and Honoré answer, the wind and other factors are merely part of the background circumstances, part of the total context in which A acted. The wind and oxygen are mere conditions, rather than causes. And what is the difference? Conditions such as oxygen in the air are not unusual or out of the ordinary. The same tacit appeal to "normal" background conditions explains, so Hart and Honoré argue, the following kind of case: A hits B who falls to the ground, stunned. At precisely that moment, a tree topples on B and kills him. The collapse of the tree at that precise moment was not a normal condition but rather a part of an abnormal conjunction of events, a coincidence for which A cannot be blamed. The same idea can be applied in a third kind of case: A throws a lighted match on some dry brush; just before the flames die out, B arrives and creates a blaze by pouring gasoline on the smoldering embers. Here we would not be inclined to classify B's act as a mere condition or circumstance through which A acted. Why? Because B is an independent agent acting in the world. His voluntary and deliberate intervention "breaks" the causal chain linking A to the fire.

In Hart and Honoré's view, then, an act is the cause of harm if it is both necessary to the occurrence of the harm and sufficient to produce it without the cooperation of the voluntary or deliberate acts of others or abnormal conjunctions of events. In other words, if your conduct was a *sine qua non* of some harm, then you caused it unless another person voluntarily and deliberately intervened to produce the harm, or an unusual combination of events conspired to give rise to the harm.

The Decline of Cause

As we have seen, the law of tort has traditionally required that a plaintiff who wishes to recover against a defendant establish three things: (1) that the plaintiff was injured; (2) that the defendant failed to exercise his or her duty of reasonable care; and (3) that, as a result, the defendant caused the plaintiff's injuries.

There continue to be exceptions recognized by the law to the second requirement; these are pockets of strict liability, in which defendants can find themselves liable for injuries brought on by their actions, even if they were not "at fault" in failing to act reasonably and to exercise care for the well-being of others. Prominent among those cases in which strict tort liability is imposed are those involving "ultrahazardous" activities (such as blasting) and those dealing with the manufacture and distribution of consumer goods (product liability). Strict tort liability endorses a view that Hart and Honoré call "causal maximalism": the view that the question "Who is responsible for this injury" is to be settled exclusively by reference to causal criteria.[1]

What about exceptions to the last of the requirements stated above, the requirement that D caused P's injury? To abandon this requirement would be to embrace "causal minimalism": the idea that judgments about who caused an injury should play little or no role in determining who is to be held responsible or liable for it. You might think that this is a demand the law could not sensibly endorse. But as Judith Thomson chronicles, a small but growing number of recent cases have taken just this position. The *Summers* and *Sindell* cases, explored in detail by Thomson, illustrate this trend. Moreover, as Thomson notes, a growing number of contemporary legal theorists have dismissed the causation requirement as unimportant, once the true goals and aims of tort law are placed in proper perspective.

The theorists to whom Thomson refers argue that the fundamental purpose of tort law is *economic:* to bring about an efficient allocation of social resources, a cost-justified level of accidents and safety. In this view, tort law treats the occurrence of accidents as a problem of overall *social cost.*[2] Suppose O is the owner of a steel mill. The mill produces a useful commodity (steel) and an undesirable by-product (pollution). H is a homeowner living adjacent to the mill. H sues O for failure to abate the nuisance of filthy smoke and other pollutants drifting across his (H's) property. Should O be held liable? It is of course true that the nuisance to H would not have occurred but for the conduct of O; yet it is equally true that H's decision to live where he does is also a *sine qua non* of the injury. And it will get us nowhere, the economic theorists reason, to ask whether O proximately caused H's loss, as this is just a disguised way of re-asking the basic question of whether O should be made to pay. The idea of holding liable the one who *caused* the injury is therefore of little help. What the courts must do instead is view the problem as one of social cost: to adjust the law's response to suits like H's by attempting to strike a cost-efficient balance between the amount of benefit conferred by the factory's total product—steel-plus-pollution—against the amount of costs generated, the most efficient allocation of the joint resources of O and H.

A simple example illustrates how the economic theory is supposed to work. Suppose that O receives $5,000 per ton for the first one hundred tons of steel manufactured; and suppose that this one hundred tons of steel imposes a total cost upon H and his neighbors of $500 per ton. Clearly the net result for society as a whole is a benefit of $4,500. Under these circumstances, the economic theory says the courts should find that O has not been negligent and should not be liable for damage to H. Suppose, on the other hand, that the manufacture of ten thousand tons of steel brings only $1,500 per ton for O (given the marginal decline in the value of every extra lot of one hundred tons produced), but that, because the factory's pollution-control equipment becomes less efficient at higher volume, it imposes a cost upon residents of the surrounding community of $1,800 per ton. Here the production of so much polluting steel is not cost-justified on an overall basis, and so the law must find O liable as a way of forcing O to absorb the excess cost imposed upon the community and thereby return the overall level of social expenditures to an efficient point. The question of whether the defendant caused the plaintiff's injury drops out of the picture altogether.

Assuming that cause is thus "declining" in the law, is this a good or bad thing from a moral point of view? Thomson's essay sets out to answer this question by taking note of a parallel trend: the decline of cause in moral theory. Thomson is suspicious of both trends and tries to identify the source of her unease.

The ruling in *Summers v. Tice*, Thomson believes, illustrates the declining importance of cause in tort doctrine. The case involved two defendants, Tice and Simonson, who were both quail hunting. A quail was flushed and both defendants fired negligently in the direction of Summers; one shot struck him in the eye. The defendants were roughly equidistant from Summers and were using the same type of gun and shot; it was not possible to determine from which gun the pellet in Summers' eye had come. The Supreme Court of California argued that the standard practice of placing the burden of proof upon the plaintiff to establish that a specific person caused his injury had to be abandoned in this case, because to stick with it would leave Summers without a remedy. The burden must be shifted to the defendants to prove that they did not cause the injury; if they cannot then each is liable.

Thomson tries to articulate the moral position of those who agree with *Summers* and similar decisions: It doesn't matter that Tice didn't cause Summers' injury (if in fact it wasn't him) or that Simonson didn't cause Summers' injury (if in fact it wasn't him). What matters is that they both acted (equally) badly; and for that they should each have to pay. Thomson seeks to relate this view to the Kantian position that one's intention, one's "will," and not the results or effects of one's conduct should matter to its moral worth.

Responding to those who support the waning of cause, both in law and in our moral outlook, Thomson attempts to isolate the basis of the conviction that cause does matter. We simply *do* judge more harshly a person who, while acting badly, causes injury or death than a person who, acting equally badly, does not cause injury or death. Why? Because the first, but not the second, is to blame for what he or she has caused. Thomson tries to blunt the criticism that enhancing or enlarging the liability of the bad actor who just happens to hit the target rather than miss makes liability turn on sheer luck. It is more than sheer bad luck that makes one bad actor the cause of the injury and another not: The actor's own negligence helped to produce that result.

Endnotes

[1] See *Causation in the Law*, 2nd ed. (Oxford: Clarendon Press, 1985), pp. lxxiii–lxxvii.

[2] See, e.g., Richard Posner, *The Economic Analysis of Law*, 3rd ed. (Boston: Little, Brown, 1986).

Lynch v. Fisher

34 So. 2d 513 (1949)
Louisiana Court of Appeal

Hardy, Judge.

This matter comes before us on appeal from judgment of the Eleventh Judicial District Court of Louisiana sustaining exceptions of no cause or right of action filed on behalf of all defendants and dismissing plaintiff's action as of nonsuit.

The allegations of the petition which are placed at issue as to their sufficiency in setting forth the cause of action in the exceptions referred to, and which set forth the facts upon which plaintiff's action is based, may be summarized as follows:

That about 9:00 p.m. on July 3, 1945, an employee of the defendants, Wheless and Fisher, (whose insurer is the defendant, Lumbermen's Mutual Casualty Company of Chicago, Ill.) at the time engaged within the general scope and course of his employment, parked a pulpwood truck which he was driving on the right-hand side of highway No. 171, some twelve miles north of Mansfield, De Soto Parish, Louisiana;

That, while said truck was thus parked, a passenger car owned and driven by the defendant, Robert Joe Gunter, collided violently with the rear end thereof;

That the driver of the parked truck was guilty of negligence, imputable to his employers, on numerous grounds, specifically in parking the truck entirely on the highway without leaving a clearance of fifteen feet on the pavement; in failing to have warning lights on the parked truck; in leaving the truck parked on the highway, thereby constituting a menace to traffic, and in failing to set out flares, or to have same available and ready for service.

That the negligence of the defendant, Robert Joe Gunter, consisted of driving and operating his automobile at an excessive, unreasonable and unlawful rate of speed; in failing to keep and maintain a proper lookout; operating his vehicle without adequate brakes; and failing to take any action to avoid the collision;

That the concurrent acts of negligence of the driver of the truck and the driver of the passenger car were the proximate causes of the accident;

That plaintiff seeing the collision ran to the scene thereof, succeeded in opening the doors of the badly damaged Gunter car, and, with the aid of another party, extricated both Mrs. Gunter and the defendant, Robert Joe Gunter, from the automobile, which had meanwhile caught fire;

That, in the effort to further assist the fatally injured Mrs. Gunter, plaintiff attempted to pull a floor mat out of the car to be used as a cushion for her head as she lay upon the roadside; that in the performance of this act plaintiff found a pistol on the floor of the car and handed the same to the defendant Gunter, who, being delirious and temporarily mentally deranged by reason of the shock of the accident, fired the pistol at plaintiff, the bullet passing through plaintiff's left ankle and inflicting serious injuries, for which damages are claimed in this action.

. . .

Determination of the issue of proximate cause must of necessity be considered with relation to the allied doctrine of intervening cause which is clearly material under the alleged facts of this case.

It is quite true, as contended by learned counsel for defendants, as a general proposition of law that only that negligence which directly causes the injury is deemed to be proximate. But a resolution of this point must perforce depend upon the particular facts of each case.

In the matter before us there are three elements that must be determined:

(a) Did the original negligence of the driver of the parked truck set in motion a chain of circumstances following consecutively one upon the other which led to plaintiff's injury?

(b) Was the act of original negligence superseded by an intervening act breaking the chain of causation leading to plaintiff's injury?

(c) Is the fact that plaintiff's injuries resulted from an improbable and unforeseeable incident sufficient to eliminate the original act of negligence from consideration as a proximate cause?

The answer to these queries will dispose of all the claims based upon the doctrines of proximate and intervening causes and foreseeability.

Upon the basis of the allegations there is no room for any reasonable contravention of the proposition that the circumstances following the negligent parking of the truck down to the removal of the pistol from the car by plaintiff were natural, probable and reasonably to be expected. But at this point an imponderable enters into consideration. The rescuer hands a pistol to the rescued and is shot by the latter. Certainly under the general rule, this action could not be within the reasonable contemplation of any normal individual and the specific incident therefore could not be imputed to the negligent truck driver as a probable result flowing from his negligence. But, unfortunately, the proposition does not admit of being disposed of so easily, for it is well established in the jurisprudence of the State of Louisiana and a majority of other jurisdictions that the general rule must yield to specific instances.

Of course, no Court could reasonably hold that the driver of a vehicle, no matter how gross his negligence, could have contemplated the shooting of a third party as a normal and natural result of such negligence. Nor, indeed, could the rescuer himself be held to have assumed the risk of such a strange, unnatural and unusual result flowing from his gallant efforts.

But, if the results of accidents were normal, usual and predictable, the burden of both Bar and Bench would be made immeasurably lighter.

To determine whether or not the shooting incident is susceptible of being distinguished and set apart from the general law of proximate cause, we must base our conclusions not upon those elements which would be applicable as between parties to the collision itself but as affecting the injury inflicted upon an innocent third party, himself without fault.

Let us assume that plaintiff in this cause, rushing to the aid of helpless parties occupying the automobile involved in the collision, in the darkness of night, and wrenching open the door of the vehicle, had been severely bitten by a dog which was accompanying the occupants of the car and which had been so frightened or injured by the shock of the collision as to have lost its accustomed gentleness. Could it be said that such a result was proximately caused by the negligence of the truck driver because such a possibility was normally an expectable or foreseeable result of such negligence? The answer is obvious. Scores of cars might have collided with the rear end of this particular truck on this particularly well-traveled

main highway without producing such a result.

Similarly, the laws of probability were overwhelmingly against the occurrence of the character and nature of the incident and resulting injury to plaintiff under the actual facts of this case. But, certainly, plaintiff is without fault, and, certainly, the negligence of some party or the concurrent negligence of several parties combined to set up the unfortunate situation which resulted in his injury.

In our opinion the general doctrine of proximate cause cannot be applied under the alleged facts and chain of circumstances herein presented. Under the tenor of the allegations it is quite clear that plaintiff would not have been shot if originally the truck driver had not negligently parked his truck in such manner as to constitute a menace and hazard to vehicles rightfully traveling the highway.

. . . The proximate cause of the injury to one who voluntarily interposes to save the lives of persons imperiled by the negligence of others is the negligence which causes the peril. . . .

. . . In determining the question as to the efficiency of the intervening act, that is, in this case, the shooting of plaintiff by one of the defendants, we must consider the well-established principle that an intervening cause is not necessarily a superseding cause. The intervening cause, in order to supersede original negligence, must have alone produced injury.

Under paragraph (B) of the Comment on Section 440 of the Restatement of the Law of Torts this proposition is set forth: "Therefore, if in looking back from the harm and tracing the sequence of events by which it was produced, it is found that a superseding cause has operated, there is no need of determining whether the actor's antecedent conduct was or was not a substantial factor in bringing about the harm."

In the instant case there is no question but that in tracing back from the point of the actual injury to plaintiff we would ordinarily be compelled to conclude that the shooting by one of the defendants was unquestionably a superseding cause were it not for the allegation that the defendant inflicting the injury at the time was temporarily insane by reason of shock resulting from the collision caused by the initial negligence of the truck driver.

Section 455 of the Restatement of the Law of Torts submits the principle:

"If the actor's negligent conduct so brings about the delirium or insanity of another as to make the actor liable for it, the actor is also liable for harm done by the other to himself while delirious or insane, if his delirium or insanity.

(a). Prevents him from realizing the nature of his act. . . .

. . . We think it must logically and inevitably follow that under such circumstances the actor is not only liable for harm done in a fit of delirium or insanity by such deranged person to himself, but also for any harm caused by him to another.

In discussing proximate cause the opinion in Cruze v. Harvey & Jones . . . : "The nearest independent cause which is adequate to, and does, produce the result, is the proximate cause of the accident, and supersedes all remote causes."

From this principle, with respect to the facts applicable to the case under consideration, the opinion stated: "The nearest independent cause which produced the death of this mule was the open, unprotected well, and this supersedes all other remote causes, among which may have been the open gap through which the mule escaped."

In Lee v. Powell Bros. & Sanders Co., . . . the Court said: "For severing the legal connection between the negligence by which such an imminent danger was created and the injury that has resulted from it the intervening voluntary act of some person responsible for his acts would have to be shown."

In every consideration of the point which has come to our attention in the study of this case, the qualities of the relieving or superseding act are repeatedly and unfailingly designated as being intervening and voluntary, by a person responsible for his acts.

. . . Since we must accept the well pleaded allegations of the petition as being true for the purpose of determining the exception, we are constrained to hold that plaintiff has met the requirements established by these several factors and has negatived the possibility that the act which immediately resulted in the harm was the voluntary action of a person responsible for his acts.

Under the allegations of the petition it is inescapable that plaintiff has properly alleged that the defendant Gunter was mentally deranged and rendered temporarily insane as the result of the collision of his car with the parked truck. Plaintiff by his allegations has further definitely asserted that such a condition was brought about by the concurrent negligence of the several defendants. In order to affirm the holding of the lower court it would be necessary for us to find that the temporary insanity

of the defendant Gunter, which led to the shooting, was not caused by the collision. Clearly, this is a question of fact to be determined by trial on the merits, and, meanwhile, any conclusion must be governed by the plain allegations of the petition.

Any attempt to determine at what point, with relation to the actual injury to plaintiff, the negligence of the original actor, namely, the driver of the truck, ceased and a new and independent tortious act intervened and superseded the original negligence, conclusively impresses us with the impossibility of such a severance of causes. The chain is complete and whole, link by link, and though tested with the utmost care no break is revealed in the succession of circumstances.

The consecutive order of the related circumstances and events may be briefly outlined:

(1) Negligence of the truck driver in parking his truck on the highway, resulting in

(2) Collision, superinduced by the concurrent negligence of the defendant Gunter, resulting in

(3) (a) Attempted rescue by the plaintiff.

(b) Temporary mental derangement of the defendant Gunter as a result of the shock of the collision, resulting in

(4) The shooting of plaintiff and the injury sustained thereby.

If there is any break in the continuity of the incidents flowing from the original act of negligence, we are unable to point out such a circumstance.

. . .

We make no attempt to minimize the unusual and improbable character of the incident which is alleged to have occurred in the case before us.

The facts set forth are additional evidence of the truth of the adage that "truth is stranger than fiction."

We do not believe that the theory of foreseeability is applicable to the facts of this case. Referring again to the Restatement of the Law of Torts, we find in Section 435 a plain and unambiguous statement of the principle which refutes the requirement of foreseeability: "If the actor's conduct is a substantial factor in bringing about harm to another, the fact that the actor neither foresaw nor should have foreseen the extent of the harm or the manner in which it occurred does not prevent him from being liable."

. . .

Palsgraf v. Long Island Railroad

248 N.Y. 339 (1928)
New York Court of Appeals

Cardozo, [Chief Judge]. Plaintiff was standing on a platform of defendant's railroad after buying a ticket to go to Rockaway Beach. A train stopped at the station, bound for another place. Two men ran forward to catch it. One of the men reached the platform of the car without mishap, though the train was already moving. The other man, carrying a package, jumped aboard the car, but seemed unsteady as if about to fall. A guard on the car, who had held the door open, reached forward to help him in, and another guard on the platform pushed him from behind. In this act, the package was dislodged, and fell upon the rails. It was a package of small size, about fifteen inches long, and was covered by a newspaper. In fact it contained fireworks, but there was nothing in its appearance to give notice of its contents. The fireworks when they fell exploded. The shock of the explosion threw down some scales at the other end of the platform, many feet away. The scales struck the plaintiff, causing injuries for which she sues.

The conduct of the defendant's guard, if a wrong in its relation to the holder of the package, was not a wrong in its relation to the plaintiff, standing far away. Relatively to her it was not negligence at all. Nothing in the situation gave notice that the falling package had in it the potency of peril to persons thus removed. Negligence is not actionable unless it involves the invasion of a legally protected interest, the violation of a right. "Proof of negligence in the air, so to speak, will not do." "Negligence is the absence of care, according to the circumstances." The plaintiff as she stood upon the platform of the station might claim to be protected against intentional invasion of her bodily security. Such invasion is not charged. She might claim to be protected against unintentional invasion by conduct involving in the thought of reasonable men an unreasonable hazard that such invasion would ensue. These, from the point of view of the law, were the bounds of her immunity, with perhaps some rare exceptions, survivals for the most part of ancient forms of liability, where conduct is held to be at the peril of the actor (*Sullivan v. Dunham* . . .). If no hazard was apparent to the eye of ordinary vigilance, an act innocent and harmless, at least to outward seeming, with reference to her, did not take to itself the quality of a tort because it happened to be a wrong, though apparently not one involving the risk of bodily insecurity, with reference to some one else. "In every instance, before negligence can be predicated of a given act, back of the act must be sought and found a duty to the individual complaining, the observance of which would have averted or avoided the injury." "The ideas of negligence and duty are strictly correlative." (Bowen, L. J., in *Thomas v. Quartermaine* . . .). The plaintiff sues in her own right for a wrong personal to her, and not as the vicarious beneficiary of a breach of duty to another.

A different conclusion will involve us, and swiftly too, in a maze of contradictions. A guard stumbles over a package which has been left upon a platform. It seems to be a bundle of newspapers. It turns out to be a can of dynamite. To the eye of ordinary vigilance, the bundle is abandoned waste, which may be kicked or trod on with impunity. Is a passenger at the other end of the platform protected by the law against the unsuspected hazard concealed beneath the waste? If not, is the result to be any different, so far as the distant passenger is concerned, when the guard stumbles over a valise which a truckman or a porter has left upon the walk? The passenger far away, if the victim of a wrong at all, has a cause of action, not derivative, but original and primary. His claim to be protected against invasion of his bodily security is neither greater nor less because the act resulting in the invasion is a wrong to another far removed. In this case, the rights that are said to have been violated, the interests said to have been invaded, are not even of the same order. The man was not injured in his person nor even put in danger. The purpose of the act, as well as its effect, was to make his person safe. If there was a wrong to him at all, which may very well be doubted, it was a wrong to a property interest only, the safety of his package. Out of this wrong to property, which threatened injury to nothing else, there has passed, we are told, to the plaintiff by derivation or succession a right of action for the invasion of an interest of another order, the right to bodily security. The diversity of interests emphasizes the futility of the effort to build the plaintiff's right upon the basis of a wrong to some one else. The gain is one of emphasis, for a like result would follow if the interests were the same. Even then, the orbit of the danger as disclosed to the eye of reasonable vigilance would be the orbit of the duty. One who jostles one's neighbor in a crowd does not invade the rights of others standing at the outer fringe when the unintended contact casts a bomb upon the ground. The wrongdoer, as to them is the man who carries the bomb, not the one who explodes it without suspicion of the danger. Life will have to be made over, and human nature transformed, before prevision so extravagant can be accepted as the norm of conduct, the customary standard to which behavior must conform.

The argument for the plaintiff is built upon the shifting meanings of such words as "wrong" and "wrongful," and shares their instability. What the plaintiff must show is "a wrong" to herself, *i.e.*, a violation of her own right, and not merely a wrong to some one else, nor conduct "wrongful" because unsocial, but not "a wrong" to any one. We are told that one who drives at reckless speed through a crowded city street is guilty of a negligent act and, therefore, of a wrongful one irrespective of the consequences. Negligent the act is, and wrongful in the sense that it is unsocial, but wrongful and unsocial in relation to other travelers, only because the eye of vigilance perceives the risk of damage. If the same act were to be committed on a speedway or a race course, it would lose its wrongful quality. The risk reasonably to be perceived defines the duty to be obeyed, and risk imports relation; it is risk to another or to others within the range of apprehension. . . . This does not mean, of course, that one who launches a destructive force is always relieved of liability if the force, though known to be destructive, pursues an unexpected path. It was not necessary that the defendant should have had notice of the particular method in which an accident would occur, if the possibility of an accident was clear to the ordinarily prudent eye. . . . Some acts such as shooting, are so imminently dangerous to any one who may come within reach of the missile, however unexpectedly, as to impose a duty of prevision not far from that of an insurer. Even today, and much oftener in earlier stages of the law, one acts sometimes at one's peril. Under this head, it may be, fall certain cases of what is known as transferred intent, an act willfully dangerous to A resulting by misadventure in injury to B. These cases aside, wrong is defined in terms of the natural or probable, at least when unintentional. The range of reasonable apprehension is at times a question for the court, and at times, if varying inferences are possible, a question for the jury. Here, by concession, there was nothing in the situation to suggest to the most cautious mind that the parcel wrapped in newspaper would spread wreckage through the station. If the guard had thrown it down knowingly and willfully, he would not have threatened the plaintiff's safety, so far as appearances could warn him. His conduct would not have involved, even then, an unreasonable probability of invasion of her bodily security. Liability can be no greater where the act is inadvertent.

Negligence, like risk, is thus a term of relation. Negligence in the abstract, apart from things related, is surely not a tort, if indeed it is understandable at all. Negligence is not a tort unless it results in the commission of a wrong, and the commission of a wrong imports the violation of a right, in this case, we are told, the right to be protected against interference with one's bodily security. But bodily security is protected, not against all forms of interference or aggression, but only against some. One who seeks redress at law does not make out a cause of action by showing without more that there has been damage to his person. If the harm was not willful, he must show that the act as to him had possibilities of danger so many and apparent as to entitle him to be protected against the doing of it though the harm was unintended. Affront to personality is still the keynote of the wrong. Confirmation of this view will be found in the history and development of the action on the case. Negligence as a basis of civil liability was unknown to mediaeval law. For damage to the person, the sole remedy was trespass, and trespass did not lie in the absence of aggression, and that direct and personal. Liability for other damage, as where a servant without orders from the master does or omits something to the damage of another, is a plant of later growth. When it emerged out of the legal soil, it was thought of as a variant of trespass, an offshoot of the parent stock. This appears in the form of action, which was known as trespass on the case. The victim does not sue derivatively, or by right of subrogation, to vindicate an interest invaded in the person of another. Thus to view his cause of action is to ignore the fundamental difference between tort and crime. He sues for breach of a duty owing to himself.

The law of causation, remote or proximate, is thus foreign to the case before us. The question of liability is always anterior to the question of the measure of the consequences that go with liability. If there is no tort to be redressed, there is no occasion to consider what damage might be recovered if there were a finding of a tort. We may assume, without deciding, that negligence, not at large or in the abstract, but in relation to the plaintiff, would entail liability for any and all consequences, however novel or extraordinary. There is room for argument that a distinction is to be drawn according to the diversity of interests invaded by the act, as where conduct negligent in that it threatens an insignificant invasion of an interest in property results in an unforeseeable invasion of an interest of another order, as *e.g.*, one of bodily security. Perhaps other distinctions may be necessary. We do not go into the question now. The consequences to be followed must first be rooted in a wrong.

The judgment of the Appellate Division and that of the Trial Term should be reversed, and the complaint dismissed, with costs in all courts.

· · ·

Andrews, [Judge] (dissenting). Assisting a passenger to board a train, the defendant's servant negligently knocked a package from his arms. It fell between the platform and the cars. Of its contents the servant knew and could know nothing. A violent explosion followed. The concussion broke some scales standing a considerable distance away. In falling they injured the plaintiff, an intending passenger.

Upon these facts may she recover the damages she has suffered in an action brought against the master? The result we shall reach depends upon our theory as to the nature of negligence. Is it a relative concept—the breach of some duty owing to a particular person or to particular persons? Or where there is an act which unreasonably threatens the safety of others, is the doer liable for all its proximate consequences, even where they result in injury to one who would generally be thought to be outside the radius of danger? This is not a mere dispute as to words. We might not believe that to the average mind the dropping of the bundle

would seem to involve the probability of harm to the plaintiff standing many feet away whatever might be the case as to the owner or to one so near as to be likely to be struck by its fall. If, however, we adopt the second hypothesis we have to inquire only as to the relation between cause and effect. We deal in terms of proximate cause, not of negligence.

Negligence may be defined roughly as an act or omission which unreasonably does or may affect the rights of others, or which unreasonably fails to protect oneself from the dangers resulting from such acts. Here I confine myself to the first branch of the definition. Nor do I comment on the word "unreasonable." For present purposes it sufficiently describes that average of conduct that society requires of its members.

There must be both the act or the omission, and the right. It is the act itself, not the intent of the actor, that is important. In criminal law both the intent and the result are to be considered. Intent again is material in tort actions, where punitive damages are sought, dependent on actual malice—not on merely reckless conduct. But here neither insanity nor infancy lessens responsibility.

As has been said, except in cases of contributory negligence, there must be rights which are or may be affected. Often though injury has occurred, no rights of him who suffers have been touched. A licensee or trespasser upon my land has no claim to affirmative care on my part that the land be made safe. Where a railroad is required to fence its tracks against cattle, no man's rights are injured should he wander upon the road because such fence is absent. An unborn child may not demand immunity from personal harm.

But we are told that "there is no negligence unless there is in the particular case a legal duty to take care, and this duty must be one which is owed to the plaintiff himself and not merely to others." This, I think too narrow a conception. Where there is the unreasonable act, and some right that may be affected there is negligence whether damage does or does not result. That is immaterial. Should we drive down Broadway at a reckless speed, we are negligent whether we strike an approaching car or miss it by an inch. The act itself is wrongful. It is a wrong not only to those who happen to be within the radius of danger but to all who might have been there—a wrong to the public at large. Such is the language of the street. Such the language of the courts when speaking of contributory negligence. Such again and again their language in speaking of the duty of some defendant and discussing proximate cause in cases where such a discussion is wholly irrelevant on any other theory. As was said by Mr. Justice Holmes many years ago, "the measure of the defendant's duty in determining whether a wrong has been committed is one thing, the measure of liability when a wrong has been committed is another." Due care is a duty imposed on each one of us to protect society from unnecessary danger, not to protect A, B or C alone.

It may well be that there is no such thing as negligence in the abstract. "Proof of negligence in the air, so to speak, will not do." In an empty world negligence would not exist. It does involve a relationship between man and his fellows. But not merely a relationship between man and those whom he might reasonably expect his act would injure. Rather, a relationship between him and those whom he does in fact injure. If his act has a tendency to harm some one, it harms him a mile away as surely as it does those on the scene. We now permit children to recover for the negligent killing of the father. It was never prevented on the theory that no duty was owing to them. A husband may be compensated for the loss of his wife's services. To say that the wrongdoer was negligent as to the husband as well as to the wife is merely an attempt to fit facts to theory. An insurance company paying a fire loss recovers its payment of the negligent incendiary. We speak of subrogation—of suing in the right of the insured. Behind the cloud of words is the fact they hide, that the act, wrongful as to the insured, has also injured the company. Even if it be true that the fault of father, wife or insured will prevent recovery, it is because we consider the original negligence not the proximate cause of the injury.

In the well-known *Polemis Case* (1921, 3 K. B. 560), Scrutton, L. J., said that the dropping of a plank was negligent for it might injure "workman or cargo or ship." Because of either possibility the owner of the vessel was to be made good for his loss. The act being wrongful the doer was liable for its proximate results. Criticized and explained as this statement may have been, I think it states the law as it should be and as it is.

The proposition is this. Every one owes to the world at large the duty of refraining from those acts that may unreasonably threaten the safety of others. Such an act occurs. Not only is he wronged to whom harm might reasonably be expected to result, but he also who is in fact injured, even if he be outside what would generally be thought the danger zone. There needs to be duty due the one complaining but this is not a duty to a particular individual because as to him harm might be expected. Harm to some one being the natural result of the act, not only that one alone, but all those in fact injured may complain. We have never, I think, held otherwise. Indeed in the *Di Caprio* case we said that a breach of a general ordinance defining the degree of care to be exercised in one's calling is evidence of negligence as to every one. We did not limit this statement to those who might be expected to be exposed to danger. Unreasonable risk being taken, its consequences are not confined to those who might probably be hurt.

If this be so, we do not have a plaintiff suing by "derivation or succession." Her action is original and primary. Her claim is for a breach of duty to herself—not that she is subrogated to any right of action of the owner of the parcel or of a passenger standing at the scene of the explosion.

The right to recover damages rests on additional considerations. The plaintiff's rights must be injured, and this injury must be caused by the negligence. We build a dam, but are negligent as to its foundations. Breaking, it injures property down stream. We are not liable if all this happened because of some reason other than the insecure foundation. But when injuries do result from our unlawful act we are liable for the consequences. It does not matter that they are unusual, unexpected, unforeseen and unforeseeable. But there is one limitation. The damages must be so connected with the negligence that the latter may be said to be the proximate cause of the former.

These two words have never been given an inclusive definition. What is a cause in a legal sense, still more what is a proximate cause, depend in each case upon many considerations, as does the existence of negligence itself. Any philosophical doctrine of causation does not help us. A boy throws a stone into a pond. The ripples spread. The water level rises. The history of that pond is altered to all eternity. It will be altered by other causes also. Yet it will be forever the resultant of all causes combined. Each one will have an influence. How great only omniscience can say. You may speak of a chain, or if you please, a net. An analogy is of little aid. Each cause brings about future events. Without each the future would not be the same. Each is proximate in the sense it is essential. But that is not what we mean by the word. Nor on the other hand do we mean sole cause. There is no such thing.

Should analogy be thought helpful, however, I prefer that of a stream. The spring, starting on its journey, is joined by tributary after tributary. The river, reaching the ocean, comes from a hundred sources. No man may say whence any drop of water is derived. Yet for a time distinction may be possible. Into the clear creek, brown swamp water flows from the left. Later, from the right comes water stained by its clay bed. The three may remain for a space, sharply divided. But at last, inevitably no trace of separation remains. They are so commingled that all distinction is lost.

As we have said, we cannot trace the effect of an act to the end, if end there is. Again, however, we may trace it part of the way. A murder at Serajevo may be the necessary antecedent to an assassination in London twenty years hence. An overturned lantern may burn all Chicago. We may follow the fire from the shed to the last building. We rightly say the fire started by the lantern caused its destruction.

A cause, but not the proximate cause. What we do mean by the word "proximate" is, that because of convenience, of public policy, of a rough sense of justice, the law arbitrarily declines to trace a series of events beyond a certain point. This is not logic, it is practical politics. Take our rule as to fires. Sparks from my burning haystack set on fire my house and my neighbor's. I may recover from a negligent railroad. He may not. Yet the wrongful act as directly harmed the one as the other. We may regret that the line was drawn just where it was, but drawn somewhere it had to be. We said the act of the railroad was not the proximate cause of our neighbor's fire. Cause it surely was. The words we used were simply indicative of our notions of public policy. Other courts think differently. But somewhere they reach the point where they cannot say the stream comes from any one source.

Take the illustration given in an unpublished manuscript by a distinguished and helpful writer on the law of torts. A chauffeur negligently collides with another car which is filled with dynamite, although he could not know it. An explosion follows. A, walking on the sidewalk nearby, is killed. B, sitting in a window of a building opposite, is cut by flying glass. C, likewise sitting in a window a block away, is similarly injured. And a further illustration. A nursemaid, ten blocks away, startled by the noise, involuntarily drops a baby from her arms to the walk. We are told that C may not recover while A may. As to B it is a question for court or jury. We will all agree that the baby might not. Because, we are again told, the chauffeur had no reason to believe his conduct involved any risk of injuring either C or the baby. As to them he was not negligent.

But the chauffeur, being negligent in risking the collision, his belief that the scope of the harm he might do would be limited is immaterial. His act unreasonably jeopardized the safety of any one who might be affected by it. C's injury and that of the baby were directly traceable to the collision. Without that, the injury would not have happened. C had the right to sit in his office, secure from such dangers. The baby was entitled to use the sidewalk with reasonable safety.

The true theory is, it seems to me, that the injury to C, if in truth he is to be denied recovery, and the injury to the baby is that their several injuries were not the proximate result of the negligence. And here not what the chauffeur had reason to believe would be the result of his conduct, but what the prudent would foresee, may have a bearing. May have some bearing, for the problem of proximate cause is not to be solved by any one consideration.

It is all a question of expediency. There are no fixed rules to govern our judgment. There are simply matters of which we may take account. We have in a somewhat different connection spoken of "the stream of events." We have asked whether that stream was deflected—whether it was forced into new and unexpected channels. This is rather rhetoric than law. There is in truth little to guide us other than common sense.

There are some hints that may help us. The proximate cause, involved as it may be with many other causes, must be, at the least, something without which the event would not happen. The court must ask itself whether there was a natural and continuous sequence between cause and effect. Was the one a substantial factor in producing the other? Was there a direct connection between them, without too many intervening causes? Is the effect of cause on result not too attenuated? Is the cause likely, in the usual judgment of mankind, to produce the result? Or by the exercise of prudent foresight could the result be foreseen? Is the result too remote from the cause, and here we consider remoteness in time and space, where we passed upon the construction of a contract—but something was also said on this subject. Clearly we must so consider, for the greater the distance either in time or space, the more surely do other causes intervene to affect the result. When a lantern is overturned the firing of a shed is a fairly direct consequence. Many things contribute to the spread of the conflagration—the force of the wind, the direction and width of streets, the character of intervening structures, other factors. We draw an uncertain and wavering line, but draw it we must as best we can.

Once again, it is all a question of fair judgment, always keeping in mind the fact that we endeavor to make a rule in each case that will be practical and in keeping with the general understanding of mankind.

Here another question must be answered. In the case supposed it is said, and said correctly, that the chauffeur is liable for the direct effect of the explosion although he had no reason to suppose it would follow a collision. "The fact that the injury occurred in a different manner than that which might have been expected does not prevent the chauffeur's negligence from being in law the cause of the injury." But the natural results of a negligent act—the results which a prudent man would or should foresee—do have a bearing upon the decision as to proximate cause. We have said so repeatedly. What should be foreseen? No human foresight would suggest that a collision itself might injure one a block away. On the contrary, given an explosion, such a possibility might be reasonably expected. I think the direct connection, the foresight of which the courts speak, assumes prevision of the explosion, for the immediate results of which, at least, the chauffeur is responsible.

It may be said this is unjust. Why? In fairness he should make good every injury flowing from his negligence. Not because of tenderness toward him we say he need not answer for all that follows his wrong. We look back to the catastrophe, the fire kindled by the spark, or the explosion. We trace the consequences—not indefinitely, but to a certain point. And to aid us in fixing that point we ask what might ordinarily be expected to follow the fire or the explosion.

This last suggestion is the factor which must determine the case before us. The act upon which defendant's liability rests is knocking an apparently harmless package onto the platform. The act was negligent. For its proximate consequences the defendant is liable. If its contents were broken, to the owner; if it fell upon and crushed a passenger's foot, then to him. If it exploded and injured one in the immediate vicinity, to him also as to A in the illustration. Mrs. Palsgraf was standing some distance away. How far cannot be told from the record—apparently twenty-five or thirty feet. Perhaps less. Except for the explosion, she would not have been injured. We are told by the appellant in his brief "it cannot be denied that the explosion was the direct cause of the plaintiff's injuries." So it was a substantial factor in producing the result—there was here a natural and continuous sequence—direct connection. The only intervening cause was that instead of blowing her to the ground the concussion smashed the weighing machine which in turn fell upon her. There was no remoteness in time, little in space. And surely, given such an explosion as here it needed no great foresight to predict that the natural result would be to injure one on the platform at no greater distance from its scene than was the plaintiff. Just how no one might be able to predict. Whether by flying fragments, by broken glass, by wreckage of machines or structures no one could say. But injury in some form was most probable.

Under these circumstances I cannot say as a matter of law that the plaintiff's injuries were not the proximate result of the negligence. That is all we have before us. The court refused to so charge. No request was made to submit the matter to the jury as a question of fact, even would that have been proper upon the record before us.

The judgment appealed from should be affirmed, with costs.

Pound, Lehman and Kellogg, [Judges], concur with Cardozo, [Chief Judge], Andrews, [Judge], dissents in opinion in which Crane and O'Brien, [Judges], concur.

Judgment reversed, etc.

Causation

W. PAGE KEETON

The subject of causation in tort law is broad and complex. Although much has been written about causation—the necessity of a reasonably close connection between the defendant's tortious conduct and the plaintiff's injury—no one has succeeded in devising terminology that can be applied without a great deal of uncertainty and difference of opinion.[1] Contributing to the controversy is the issue of whether causation is a question of law for the judge or a question of fact for the jury. Leon Green, a distinguished torts scholar, was of the view that issues pertaining to the labels of proximate cause or producing cause (as distinguished from actual cause) should not be regarded as issues for the jury to resolve. Although theoretically the resolution of proximate or producing cause issues may be left to the court, such is not the case in practice.

II. *Negligence and Proximate Cause*

The following analysis will consider first the tort action for negligence. In negligence cases the harm suffered in a damaging event is not the consequence of an intentional interference with a legally protected interest, or a type of activity that would constitute a basis for strict liability. Rather, the harm suffered is the consequence of an "omission to do something which a reasonable man, guided by those ordinary considerations . . . would do . . . ."[2] There are four elements in a claimant's prima facie case of negligence. These generally recognized elements are: (1) a duty of reasonable care, (2) a breach of that duty, (3) proximate causation, and (4) damages.[3] An explanation of the terms duty and breach of duty is necessary to

identify the issues underlying each of the elements and the problems arising in connection with proximate cause.

A. *Duty of Reasonable Care*

The law would be relatively simple, albeit unfair and contrary to the best interests of people as a whole, if a negligent actor were subject to liability for anything and everything that substantially increased the likelihood of harm to a claimant. The law, however, does not go that far. Rather, it imposes on an actor the responsibility of using reasonable care. Negligence is simply the failure to exercise reasonable care. Reasonable care in some contexts, such as professional activity, is articulated in a more complicated manner, and in many situations, the actor's duty of care is limited as a matter of law. Reasonable care will be used in this article to describe the relationship between individuals that imposes upon one a legal obligation based on policy considerations and practical institutional problems related to the judicial process.[4]

A duty in the negligence context may be defined as an obligation to conform to particular conduct. There are three factors related to this duty of care: (1) the relationship between the parties (such as occupier of land and trespasser or director of a corporation and stockholder); (2) the nature of the defendant's activity (such as common carrier or innkeeper); and (3) the type of loss the plaintiff suffers (such as intangible economic loss or personal injury). Based on these considerations, the term duty will identify the kind of conduct that will serve as a basis for the imposition of liability on an actor.

B. *Causation*

Generally, two elements are required to establish that the negligence of a defendant is the proximate cause of a plaintiff's injury: factual causation and legal causation. Factual causation refers to the requirement that the act and the injury be related.

From *South Texas Law Review,* Vol. 28 (1986), pp. 231–240. Reprinted with permission of the *South Texas Law Review.*

Legal causation refers to the requirement that the act and the injury be *reasonably* related.[5]

1. Factual Causation

Because the objective of tort law is to shift losses from injured persons to others, misconduct that is clearly unrelated to a claimant's injury should not subject the actor to liability. The requirement that factual causation be established before defendant is held liable ensures that such misconduct is not erroneously punished. Factual causation, or cause in fact, denotes that the negligent act or omission substantially contributed to the injury and without which no harm would be incurred.[6] Often, however, factual causation of a plaintiff's injury is uncertain, which raises the question: What must be the affinity of causal likelihood for the claimant to recover?

Courts agree that a tortious act does not result in liability to a claimant unless there is some likelihood that the injury complained of was factually caused by the tortious act. The general rule is that a claimant has the burden of proving that a tortious act was a proximate cause of his injury. Therefore, the plaintiff must have some evidence in the record that, if believed, would justify a reasonable person's conclusion that *it is more likely than not* that the tortious act was the factual cause of the plaintiff's injury. The affinity of causal likelihood must preponderate in favor of causation.[7]

Circumstantial evidence, expert testimony, or common knowledge may provide a basis from which the causal relationship may be inferred. However, the causal relationship should not be inferred unless, as a matter of common knowledge, it could be reasonably found by the fact finder as being more likely than not. It is this commentator's judgment that finding a preponderance of evidence favoring causation is only a starting point in consideration of the proximate cause issue.[8]

The issue of factual causation arose in *Nixon v. Mr. Property Management Co.*,[9] a recent, highly publicized rape case. The majority stated that "a reasonable inference exists that, but for [defendant's] failure to comply with the ordinance regarding maintenance of its apartment complex, this crime [rape] would have never taken place."[10] Thus, the majority held that the defendant's negligence was a proximate cause of the crime. The court concluded that "[w]ith a litany of prior crimes, includ-

ing *other* violent and assaultive crime, at [the] [a]partments, and with deposition testimony that vagrants frequented the area, a material fact question exists on the foreseeability of this crime as it relates to the proximate cause issue."[11] By analogy, the dissent concluded that "[p]roperty crimes and domestic disputes are not of the same general character as a rape,"[12] and that rape was not within the risk that the defendant was negligent in failing to guard against. The dissent took the position that, when viewing the evidence in the light most favorable to the claimant, the matter of factual causation remained one of pure conjecture or speculation.

It has been suggested that it should be enough, in some situations, for a claimant to recover all his claimed damages simply by proving that the defendant's tortious act substantially increased the likelihood of the claimant's injury.[13] If this lower standard of proof had been applicable to the facts in *Nixon,* the jury would have had to determine what it regarded as the percentage of likelihood that the defendant's negligence was a cause of the rape, and then award the plaintiff a like percentage for damages.[14]

While ordinarily the burden of proof of causation is on the claimant, in exceptional situations it is shifted to the defendant who must prove that his conduct was not a proximate cause, even though his conduct could have been a factual cause. Shifting the burden is based on the notion that the risk of loss from all or part of the plaintiff's injury should be allocated to the defendant when the causative agency or agencies cannot be established. For example, in *Technical Chemical Co. v. Jacobs,*[15] the Texas Supreme Court created a presumption that the plaintiff would have read a warning label on an explosive product if it had been attached to the product.

Two approaches have arisen in connection with shifting the burden of proof to the defendant in exceptional situations. With respect to both, courts have created a presumption in favor of the claimant. The two approaches are the alternative liability doctrine and the market-share liability doctrine. The alternative liability doctrine permits a claimant to join two or more defendants and prove that one or the other of the joined defendants caused a damaging event resulting in claimant's indivisible injury. Absent exculpating evidence, the claimant may recover the entire amount of damages from either joined defendant.[16] Perhaps the most interesting and far-reaching application of the alternative liability doctrine occurred in *Anderson v. Somberg*.[17] The plaintiff in *Anderson* was injured during back surgery when a forceps-like instrument broke off and lodged in his spine. The Supreme Court of New Jersey held that the surgeon (who may have been negligent in using the surgical instrument), the hospital (which may have been negligent in supplying the instrument), and the manufacturer of the instrument could be joined in one action. The court concluded that each could be held liable for the entire amount of damages in the absence of exculpatory evidence.

The doctrine of market-share liability, which varies according to jurisdiction, has been considered by a number of state courts, but was first applied by the California Supreme Court in *Sindell v. Abbott Laboratories*.[18] The following four requirements were adopted in *Sindell* to establish market-share liability: (1) the injury or illness must be occasioned by a fungible product made by all defendants joined in the lawsuit; (2) the injury or illness must be due to a design hazard, with each defendant having been found to have sold the product in a manner that made it unreasonably dangerous (because of either a failure to warn or an unreasonably dangerous design); (3) the specific manufacturer of the product or products that caused the injury cannot be identified by the plaintiff; and (4) the plaintiff must join enough of the manufacturers of the product to represent a substantial share of the market.[19]

Finally, mention should be made of the "creeping-illness" problem presented by the numerous claims against the manufacturers and suppliers of products containing various amounts of asbestos. Realistically, in the creeping-illness cases, the most a plaintiff can establish is that each exposure to a product containing asbestos involved a risk of contributing to the severity of a disease such as asbestosis or cancer. There is, however, uncertainty both as to whether a particular defendant's product contributed at all to the injury and what the percentage of contribution might have been. In the leading case on this subject, *Borel v. Fibreboard Paper Products Corp.*, the Fifth Circuit held each of several manufacturers liable for all damages.[20]

The existence of these doctrines suggests that in the interest of fairness and justice, the courts have, in a number of ways, relieved the claimant of proving that his or her injury was factually caused, in whole or in part, by the defendant's negligent or other tortious conduct. The courts have allocated among several defendants the liability of harm in a variety of situations where the tortious conduct of the defendant(s) could have caused some or all of the claimed injury.

2. Legal Causation

A court will examine, before finding a negligent actor liable for all consequences of his misconduct, any freakish nature of the consequences, any misconduct of others, or any other time and space considerations. Generally, the jurisprudence of most courts is that the negligence of an actor should be reasonably related to a plaintiff's injury; or, related in such a way as to make it just and practical to hold the defendant liable.

Two main issues arise within the context of legal causation. First, should the defendant be held liable for a consequence that was not foreseeable? Second, should the defendant be held liable for a consequence that would not have occurred but for the intervention of another cause, particularly the intervening conduct of another tortious actor?[21] Thus, two primary problems exist. First, concerning unforeseeable consequences, to what extent is the defendant liable for results that he reasonably could not have been expected to foresee? Second, concerning intervening causes, should the defendant be relieved of liability by some new cause of external origin coming into operation at a time subsequent to the defendant's conduct? Should the new cause be treated as superseding the defendant's *responsibility*?

Legal causation can be delineated in three general propositions for proximate causation where factual causation is presumably established. First, an actor's negligence is a proximate cause of harm to the plaintiff only if harm to one similarly situated to plaintiff was reasonably foreseeable.[22] Second, an actor's act or omission is a proximate cause of harm to the plaintiff only if the harm arose out of a damaging event or accident of the same general character as that which was reasonably foreseeable.[23] Finally, an actor's conduct is a proximate cause of harm to the plaintiff only if the harm was not brought about by a new and independent cause (a superseding cause).[24]

The first proposition requiring reasonable foreseeability as an element of proximate causation was elaborated upon in the celebrated case of *Palsgraf v. Long Island Railroad*,[25] and was accepted almost immediately thereafter by the American Law Institute in the *Restatement of Torts*.[26] The Restatement position is probably the current law in Texas.[27] Notwithstanding the general rule, virtually all courts would hold that where a rescuer is injured while attempting to rescue a person whom the defendant placed in danger, the defendant may be held liable to the rescuer as danger invites rescue. Even though the defendant may not have foreseen the coming of a rescuer, he is accountable as if he had.[28]

The second proposition that liability is limited to the scope of the foreseeable hazard is fairly settled, but it is not easily applied. In one sense, almost nothing is entirely unforeseeable, while in another sense no event is entirely foreseeable, because the exact details of the way and manner in which an accident occurs cannot be predicted.[29] The Texas Supreme Court in *Carey v. Pure Distributing Co.*[30] defined the scope of the foreseeable hazard in this way: an accident of the *same general kind* as that which occurred in the chain of events leading to the plaintiff's injury must have been anticipated.

In *Carey*, the defendant's truck driver, with knowledge of the truck's defective fastener, was hauling ten-gallon cans of oil in the truck. One of the cans fell when the fastener came loose—a clearly foreseeable event. The can struck the ground and the top blasted off, flew through the air, and struck plaintiff who was lying on a cot some twenty feet from the road. The court of civil appeals concluded that no reasonably prudent person would have predicted the top coming off, flying through the air, and hitting someone; therefore, the defendant was not liable.[31] But the Texas Supreme Court said that the damaging event must be of the *same general character* as might reasonably have been anticipated.[32]

The question now becomes: How would a reasonable person have described, in advance, the kind of occurrence or accident that likely would result from the defendant's conduct? The defendant is liable for all the direct consequences of that kind of accident, however unforeseeable some of the consequences might be. The most frequently used illustration of an event for which a negligent defendant is not liable is taken from the *Restatement (Second) of Torts*.[33] A defendant who gave a child a gun was exculpated from liability for the child's injury, caused not by firing a shot, but by dropping the gun on his toe. Another good example relates to the negligence of a defendant in permitting a passenger to get off a bus at a nonscheduled stop, a place where she was likely to get hit by a car. Instead of being hit, the passenger stepped on a banana peel and broke her hip. These are relatively easy cases that demonstrate the soundness of the idea that the defendant should be liable only for consequences resulting from an accident of the kind that he was negligent in failing to guard against.

A defendant ordinarily would be held liable for all the direct consequences of an accident of the kind that he was negligent in failing to guard against, even if the accident was caused by an unforeseeable force or conduct of another. The problem is illustrated by a well-known federal case, *Johnson v. Kosmos Portland Cement Co.*[34] In *Johnson*, the defendant failed to clean the residue from inside an oil barge tied to a dock, leaving it full of explosive gas. This is an example of negligence and a breach of duty to those likely to be harmed by fire or explosion. A bolt of lightning struck the barge, exploded the gas, and injured workmen on the premises. Consequently, the defendant was held liable. Even if it is assumed that lightning was an unforeseeable cause, the result (fire or explosion) was nevertheless to be anticipated.

However, an unforeseeable intervening cause, particularly conduct of another, can so change the nature of a damaging event that ought to have been anticipated and guarded against that the event becomes unforeseeable. Suppose the defendant is negligent in leaving a loaded gun where children are likely to be, and the gun is seized by a thief who murders another. The event that the defendant was negligent in failing to guard against was that of a child mishandling the gun and unintentionally discharging it. Courts and judges often disagree about whether an event brought about by unforeseeable conduct of another so changes the event as to make it different in kind from the one that the defendant was negligent in failing to guard against.[35]

Frequently a plaintiff is injured upon the occurrence of a secondary damaging event arising from defendant's original negligence. The damaging event may occur in the form of plaintiff's or another's subsequent conduct. Some examples of subsequent damaging events include where an injured victim commits suicide; where an injured victim is handicapped and, as a consequence of the handicap, suffers an additional injury; or where a physician, in attempting to heal the injured victim, negligently injures him further. These are a few of a variety of situations, and courts have created rules to deal with such specific happenings. In general, if the second occurrence was a reasonably foreseeable outgrowth of the first occurrence, the defendant will be subject to liability until the injured party, or another, has had a reasonable opportunity to reduce the likelihood of further harm.

. . .

Endnotes

[1] W. Prosser & W. Keeton, Prosser and Keeton on The Law of Torts § 41, at 263 (5th ed. 1984).

[2] Black's Law Dictionary 930 (5th ed. 1979).

[3] W. Prosser & W. Keeton, *supra* note 1, § 30 *passim*. The claimant normally has the burden of proof on all four elements.

[4] *Id.* § 53, at 356.

[5] Clark v. Waggoner, 452 S.W.2d 437, 439 (Tex. 1970).

[6] Missouri Pac. Ry. Co. v. American Statesman, 552 S.W.2d 99, 103 (Tex. 1977).

[7] McClure v. Allied Stores, 608 S.W.2d 901, 904 (Tex. 1980).

[8] See W. Prosser & W. Keeton, *supra* note 1, § 32, at 188–89.

[9] 690 S.W.2d 546 (Tex. 1985).

[10] *Id.* at 549.

[11] *Id.* at 551 (emphasis added).

[12] *Id.* at 558.

[13] *See generally* Malone, *Ruminations on Cause-in-Fact*, 9 Stan. L. Rev. 60 (1956).

[14] *See* Herskovits v. Group Health Coop., 664 P.2d 474 (Wash. 1983).

[15] 480 S.W.2d 602, 606 (Tex. 1972).

[16] *See* Summers v. Tice, 199 P.2d 1 (Cal. 1948), Ybarra v. Spangard, 154 P.2d 687 (Cal. 1944), Nichols v. Nold, 258 P.2d 317 (Kan. 1953); Anderson v. Somberg, 338 A.2d 1 (N.J.), *cert. denied*, 423 U.S. 929 (1975); Loch v. Confair, 93 A.2d 451 (Pa. 1953).

[17] 338 A.2d 1 (N.J.), *cert. denied*, 423 U.S. 929 (1975).

[18] 607 P.2d 924 (Cal.), *cert. denied*, 449 U.S. 912 (1980).

[19] Due to the limited scope of this article, I will not be discussing the ramifications of this doctrine and the extent to which it has been or will be accepted. *See* Hardy v. Johns-Manville Sales Corp., 509 F. Supp. 1353 (E.D. Tex. 1981), *rev'd*, 681 F.2d 334 (5th Cir. 1982); Collins v. Eli Lilly Co., 342 N.W.2d 37 (Wis.), *cert. denied*, 105 S. Ct. 107 (1984).

[20] Borel v. Fibreboard Paper Prods. Corp., 493 F.2d 1076 (5th Cir. 1973), *cert. denied*, 419 U.S. 869 (1974).

[21] The second overlaps the first, as will be indicated.

[22] Palsgraf v. Long Island R.R., 162 N.E. 99 (N.Y. 1928); City of Dallas v. Maxwell, 248 S.W. 667 (Tex. Comm'n App. 1923, holding approved).

[23] Nixon v. Mr. Property Management Co., 690 S.W.2d 546 (Tex. 1985); Carey v. Pure Distrib. Corp., 133 Tex. 31, 124 S.W.2d 847 (1939).

[24] I purposely have not defined what constitutes a superseding cause but will comment on this.

[25] 162 N.E. 99 (N.Y. 1928).

[26] Restatement of Torts § 281 comment c (1934).

[27] 1 State Bar of Texas, Texas Pattern Jury Charges PJC 2.02 (1969).

[28] Wagner v. International Ry., 133 N.E. 437 (N.Y. 1921).

[29] W. Prosser & W. Keeton, *supra* note 1, § 43, at 297.

[30] 133 Tex. 31, 35, 124 S.W.2d 847, 849 (1939).

[31] Pure Distrib. Co. v. Carey, 97 S.W.2d 768, 770 (Tex. Civ. App.—San Antonio, 1936), *rev'd*, 133 Tex. 31, 124 S.W.2d 847 (1939).

[32] Carey v. Pure Distrib. Co., 133 Tex. 31, 35, 124 S.W.2d 847, 849 (1939).

[33] Restatement (Second) of Torts § 281 comment f, illustration 3 (1965).

[34] 64 F.2d 193 (6th Cir.), *cert. denied*, 290 U.S. 641 (1933).

[35] *See supra* notes 9–12 and accompanying text.

Tracing Consequences

H. L. A. HART AND A. M. HONORÉ

II. *Tracing Consequences*

'To consequences no limit can be set': 'Every event which would not have happened if an earlier event had not happened is the consequence of that earlier event.' These two propositions are not equivalent in meaning and are not equally or in the same way at variance with ordinary thought. They have, however, both been urged sometimes in the same breath by the legal theorist and the philosopher: they are indeed sometimes said by lawyers to be 'the philosophical doctrine' of causation. It is perhaps not difficult even for the layman to accept the first proposition as a truth about certain physical events; an explosion may cause a flash of light which will be propagated as far as the outer nebulae; its effects or consequences continue indefinitely. It is, however, a different matter to accept the view that whenever a man is murdered with a gun his death was the consequence of (still less an 'effect' of or 'caused by') the manufacture of the bullet. The first tells a perhaps unfamiliar tale about unfamiliar events; the second introduces an unfamiliar, though, of course, a possible way of speaking about familiar events. It is not that this unrestricted use of 'consequence' is unintelligible or never found; it is indeed used to refer to bizarre or fortuitous connections or coincidences: but the point is that the various causal notions employed for the purposes of explanation, attribution of responsibility, or the assessment of contributions to the course of history carry with them implicit limits which are similar in these different employments.

It is, then, the second proposition, defining consequence in terms of 'necessary condition', with which theorists are really concerned. This proposition is the corollary of the view that, if we

look into the past of any given event, there is an infinite number of events, each of which is a necessary condition of the given event and so, as much as any other, is its cause. This is the 'cone'[1] of causation, so called because, since any event has a number of simultaneous conditions, the series fans out as we go back in time. The justification, indeed only partial, for calling this 'the philosophical doctrine' of causation is that it resembles Mill's doctrine that 'we have no right to give the name of cause to one of the conditions exclusive of the others of them.' It differs from Mill's view in taking the essence of causation to be 'necessary condition' and not 'the sum total'[2] of the sufficient conditions of an event.

Legal theorists have developed this account of cause and consequence to show what is 'factual,' 'objective,' or 'scientific' in these notions: this they call 'cause in fact' and it is usually stressed as a preliminary to the doctrine that any more restricted application of these terms in the law represents nothing in the facts or in the meaning of causation, but expresses fluctuating legal policy or sentiments of what is just or convenient. Moral philosophers have insisted in somewhat similar terms that the consequences of human action are 'infinite': this they have urged as an objection against the Utilitarian doctrine that the rightness of a morally right action depends on whether its consequences are better than those of any alternative action in the circumstances. 'We should have to trace as far as possible the consequences not only for the persons affected directly but also for those indirectly affected and to these no limit can be set.'[3] Hence, so the argument runs, we cannot either inductively establish the Utilitarian doctrine that right acts are 'optimific' or use it in particular cases to discover what is right. Yet, however vulnerable at other points Utilitarianism may be as an account of moral judgment, this objection seems to rest on a mistake as to the sense of 'consequence.' The Utilitarian assertion that the rightness of an action depends on its consequences is not the same as the assertion that it depends on all those later occurrences which

From *Causation in the Law, 2nd ed.* (Oxford: Clarendon Press, 1985), pp. 68–83. © H. L. A. Hart and A. M. Honoré. Reprinted with permission of Oxford University Press.

would not have happened had the action not been done, to which indeed 'no limit can be set.' It is important to see that the issue here is not the linguistic one whether the word 'consequence' would be understood if used in this way. The point is that, though we could, we do not think in this way in tracing connections between human actions and events. Instead, whenever we are concerned with such connections, whether for the purpose of explaining a puzzling occurrence, assessing responsibility, or giving an intelligible historical narrative, we employ a set of concepts restricting in various ways what counts as a consequence. These restrictions colour *all* our thinking in causal terms; when we find them in the law we are not finding something invented by or peculiar to the law, though of course it is for the law to say when and how far it will use them and, where they are vague, to supplement them.

No short account can be given of the limits thus placed on 'consequences' because these limits vary, intelligibly, with the variety of causal connection asserted. Thus we may be tempted by the generalization that consequences must always be something intended or foreseen or at least foreseeable with ordinary care: but counter-examples spring up from many types of context where causal statements are made. If smoking is shown to cause lung cancer this discovery will permit us to describe past as well as future cases of cancer as the effect or consequence of smoking even though no one foresaw or had reasonable grounds to suspect this in the past. What is common and commonly appreciated and hence foreseeable certainly controls the scope of consequences in certain varieties of causal statement but not in all. Again the voluntary intervention of a second person very often constitutes the limit. If a guest sits down at a table laid with knife and fork and plunges the knife into his hostess's breast, her death is not in any context other than a contrived one[4] thought of as caused by, or the effect or result of the waiter's action in laying the table; nor would it be linked with this action as its consequence for any of the purposes, explanatory or attributive, for which we employ causal notions. Yet as we have seen there are many other types of case where a voluntary action or the harm it does are naturally treated to the consequence of to some prior neglect of precaution. Finally, we may think that a simple answer is already supplied by Hume and Mill's doctrine that causal connection rests on general laws asserting regular

connection; yet, even in the type of case to which this important doctrine applies, reference to it alone will not solve our problem. For we often trace a causal connection between an antecedent and a consequent which themselves very rarely go together: we do this when the case can be broken down into intermediate stages, which themselves exemplify different generalizations, as when we find that the fall of a tile was the cause of someone's death, rare though this be. Here our problem reappears in the form of the question: When can generalizations be combined in this way?

We shall examine first the central type of case where the problem is of this last-mentioned form. Here the gist of the causal connection lies in the general connection with each other of the successive stages; and is not dependent on the special notions of one person providing another with reasons or exceptional opportunities for actions. This form of causal connection may exist between actions and events, and between purely physical events, and it is in such cases that the words 'cause' and 'causing' used of the antecedent action or event have their most obvious application. It is convenient to refer to cases of the first type where the consequence is harm as cases of 'causing harm,' and to refer to cases where harm is the consequence of one person providing another with reasons or opportunities for doing harm as cases of 'inducing' or 'occasioning' harmful acts. In cases of the first type a voluntary act, or a conjunction of events amounting to a coincidence, operates as a limit in the sense that events subsequent to these are not attributed to the antecedent action or event as its consequence even though they would not have happened without it. Often such a limiting action or coincidence is thought of and described as 'intervening': and lawyers speak of them as 'superseding' or 'extraneous' causes 'breaking the chain of causation.' To see what these metaphors rest on (and in part obscure) and how such factors operate as a limit we shall consider the detail of three simple cases.

(i) A forest fire breaks out, and later investigation shows that shortly before the outbreak *A* had flung away a lighted cigarette into the bracken at the edge of the forest, the bracken caught fire, a light breeze got up, and fanned the flames in the direction of the forest. If, on discovering these facts, we hesitate before saying that *A*'s action caused the forest fire this would be to consider the alternative hypothesis that in spite of appearances the fire only succeeded A's action in point of time, that the bracken flickered out harmlessly and the forest fire was caused by something else. To dispose of this it may be necessary to examine in further detail the process of events between the ignition of the bracken and the outbreak of fire in the forest and to show that these exemplified certain types of continuous change. If this is shown, there is no longer any room for doubt: A's action *was* the cause of the fire, whether he intended it or not. This seems and is the simplest of cases. Yet it is important to notice that even in applying our general knowledge to a case as simple as this, indeed in regarding it as simple, we make an implicit use of a distinction between types of factor which constitute a limit in tracing consequences and those which we regard as mere circumstances 'through' which we trace them. For the breeze which sprang up after A dropped the cigarette, and without which the fire would not have spread to the forest, was not only subsequent to his action but entirely independent of it: it was, however, a common recurrent feature of the environment, and, as such, it is thought of not as an 'intervening' force but as merely part of the circumstances in which the cause 'operates.' The decision so to regard it is implicitly taken when we combine our knowledge of the successive stages of the process and assert the connection.

It is easy here to be misled by the natural metaphor of a causal 'chain,' which may lead us to think that the causal process consists of a series of single events each of which is dependent upon (would not have occurred without) its predecessor in the 'chain' and so is dependent upon the initiating action or event. In truth in any causal process we have at each phase not single events but complex sets of conditions, and among these conditions are some which are not only subsequent to, but independent of the initiating action or event. Some of these independent conditions, such as the evening breeze in the example chosen, we classify as mere conditions in or on which the cause operates; others we speak of as 'interventions' or 'causes.' To decide how such independent elements shall be classified is also to decide how we shall combine our knowledge of the different general connections which the successive stages exemplify, and it is important to see that nothing *in* this knowledge itself can resolve this point. We may have to go to science for the relevant general knowledge before we can assert with proper confidence that A's ac-

tion did cause the fire, but science, though it tells us that an air current was required, is silent on the difference between a current in the form of an evening breeze and one produced by someone who deliberately fanned the flames as they were flickering out in the bracken. Yet an air current in this deliberately induced form is not a 'condition' or 'mere circumstance' through which we can trace the consequence; its presence would force us to revise the assertion that A caused the fire. Conversely if science helped us to identify as a necessary factor in producing the fire some condition or element of which we had previously been totally ignorant, e.g., the persistence of oxygen, this would leave our original judgment undisturbed if this factor were a common or pervasive feature of the environment or of the thing in question. There is thus indeed an important sense in which it is true that the distinction between cause and conditions is not a 'scientific' one. It is not determined by laws or generalizations concerning connections between events.

When we have assembled all our knowledge of the factors involved in the fire, the residual question which we then confront (the attributive question) may be typified as follows: Here is A's action, here is the fire: can the fire be attributed to A's action as its consequence given that there is also this third factor (the breeze or B's intervention) without which the fire would not have happened? It is plain that, both in raising questions of this kind and in answering them, ordinary thought is powerfully influenced by the analogy between the straightforward cases of causal attribution (where the elements required for the production of harm in addition to the initiating action are all 'normal' conditions) and even simpler cases of responsibility which we do not ordinarily describe in causal language at all but by the simple transitive verbs of action. These are the cases of the direct manipulation of objects involving changes in them or their position: cases where we say 'He pushed it,' 'He broke it,' 'He bent it.' The cases which we do confidently describe in causal language ('The fire was caused by his carelessness,' 'He caused a fire') are cases where no other human action or abnormal occurrence is required for the production of the effect, but only normal conditions. Such cases appear as mere long-range or less direct versions or extensions of the most obvious and fundamental case of all for the attribution of responsibility: the case where we can simly say 'He did it.' Conversely in attaching importance to thus causing harm as a distinct ground of responsibility and in taking certain kinds of factor (whether human interventions or abnormal occurrences), without which the initiating action would not have led to harm, to preclude the description of the case in simple causal terms, common sense is affected by the fact that here, because of the manner in which the harm eventuates, the outcome cannot be represented as a mere extension of the initiating action; the analogy with the fundamental case for responsibility ('He did it') has broken down.

When we understand the power exerted over our ordinary thought by the conception that causing harm is a mere extension of the primary case of doing harm, the interrelated metaphors which seem natural to lawyers and laymen, in describing various aspects of causal connection, fall into place and we can discuss their factual basis. The persistent notion that some kinds of event required in addition to the initiating action for the production of harm 'break the chain of causation' is intelligible, if we remember that though such events actually *complete* the *explanation* of the harm (and so *make* rather than *break* the causal explanation) they do, unlike mere normal conditions, break the *analogy* with cases of simple actions. The same analogy accounts for the description of these factors as 'new actions' (*novus actus*) or 'new causes,' 'superseding,' 'extraneous,' 'intervening forces': and for the description of the initiating action when 'the chain of causation' is broken as 'no longer operative,' 'having worn out,' *functus officio*.[5] So too when the 'chain' is held not to be 'broken' the initiating action is said to be still 'potent,'[6] 'continuing,' 'contributing,' 'operative,' and the mere conditions held insufficient to break the chain are 'part of the background,'[7] 'circumstances in which the cause operates,'[8] 'the stage set,' 'part of the history.'

(ii) *A* throws a lighted cigarette into the bracken which catches fire. Just as the flames are about to flicker out, *B*, who is not acting in concert with *A*, deliberately pours petrol on them. The fire spreads and burns down the forest. *A*'s action, whether or not he intended the forest fire, was not the cause of the fire: *B*'s was.

The voluntary intervention of a second human agent, as in this case, is a paradigm among those factors which preclude the assimilation in causal judgments of the first agent's connection with the eventual harm to the case of simple direct manipu-

lation. Such an intervention displaces the prior action's title to be called the cause and, in the persistent metaphors found in the law, it 'reduces' the earlier action and its immediate effects to the level of 'mere circumstances' or 'part of the history.' *B* in this case was not an 'instrument' through which *A* worked or a victim of the circumstances *A* has created. He has, on the contrary, freely exploited the circumstances and brought about the fire without the co-operation of any further agent or any chance coincidence. Compared with this the claim of *A*'s action to be ranked the cause of the fire fails. That this and not the moral appraisal of the two actions is the point of comparison seems clear. If *A* and *B* both intended to set the forest on fire, and this destruction is accepted as something wrong or wicked, their moral wickedness, judged by the criterion of intention, is the same. Yet the causal judgment differentiates between them. If their moral guilt is judged by the outcome, this judgment though it would differentiate between them cannot be the source of the causal judgment; for it presupposes it. The difference just is that *B* has caused the harm and *A* has not. Again, if we appraise these actions as good or bad from different points of view, this leaves the causal judgments unchanged. *A* may be a soldier of one side anxious to burn down the enemy's hide-out: *B* may be an enemy soldier who has decided that his side is too iniquitous to defend. Whatever is the moral judgment passed on these actions by different speakers it would remain true that *A* had not caused the fire and *B* had.

There are, as we have said, situations in which a voluntary action would not be thought of as an intervention precluding causal connection in this way. These are the cases discussed further below where an opportunity commonly exploited for harmful actions is negligently provided, or one person intentionally provides another with the means, the opportunity, or a certain type of reason for wrongdoing. Except in such cases a voluntary intervention is a limit past which consequences are not traced. By contrast, actions which in any of a variety of different ways are less than fully voluntary are assimilated to the means by which or the circumstances in which the earlier action brings about the consequences. Such actions are not the outcome of an informed choice made without pressure from others, and the different ways in which human action may fall short in this respect range from defective muscular control, through lack of consciousness or knowledge, to the vaguer notions of duress and of predicaments, created by the first agent for the second, in which there is no 'fair' choice.

In considering examples of such actions and their bearing on causal judgments there are three dangers to avoid. It would be folly to think that in tracing connections through such actions instead of regarding them, like voluntary interventions, as a limit, ordinary thought has clearly separated out their non-voluntary aspect from others by which they are often accompanied. Thus even in the crude case where A lets off a gun (intentionally or not) and startles B, so that he makes an involuntary movement of his arm which breaks a glass, the commonness of such a reaction as much as its compulsive character may influence the judgment that A's action was the cause of the damage.

Secondly we must not impute to ordinary thought all the fine discriminations that could be made and in fact are to be found in a legal system, or an equal willingness to supply answers to complex questions in causal terms. Where there is no precise system of punishment, compensation or reward to administer, ordinary men will not often have faced such questions as whether the injuries suffered by a motorist who collides with another in swerving to avoid a child are consequences attributable to the neglect of the child's parents in allowing it to wander on to the road. Such questions courts have to answer and in such cases common judgments provide only a general, though still an important indication of what are the relevant factors.

Thirdly, though very frequently non-voluntary actions are assimilated to mere conditions or means by which the first agent brings about the consequences, the assimilation is never quite complete. This is manifested by the general avoidance of many causal locutions which are appropriate when the consequences are traced (as in the first case) through purely physical events. Thus even in the case in which the second agent's role is hardly an 'action' at all, e.g., where A hits B, who staggers against a glass window and breaks it, we should say that A's blow made B stagger and break the glass, rather than that A's blow caused the glass to break, though in any explanatory or attributive context the case would be *summarized* by saying that A's action was the cause of the *damage*.

In the last two cases where B's movements are involuntary in the sense that they are not part of

any action which he chose or intended to do, their connection with A's action would be described by saying that A's blow *made B* stagger or *caused* him to stagger or that the noise of A's shot *made* him jump or *caused* him to jump. This would be true, whether A intended or expected B to react in this way or not, and the naturalness of treating A's action as the cause of the ultimate damage is due to the causal character of this part of the process involving B's action. The same is, however, true where B's actions are not involuntary movements but A is considered to have made or caused B to do them by less crude means. This is the case if, for example, A uses threats or exploits his authority over B to make B do something, e.g., knock down a door. At least where A's threats are of serious harm, or B's act was unquestionably within A's authority to order, he too has made or forced or (in formal quasi-legal parlance) 'caused' B to act.

Outside the area of such cases, where B's will would be said either not to be involved at all, or to be overborne by A, are cases where A's act creates a predicament for B *narrowing* the area of choice so that he has either to inflict some harm on himself or others, or sacrifice some important interest or duty. Such cases resemble coercion in that A narrows the area of B's choice but differ from it in that this predicament need not be intentionally created. A sets a house on fire (intentionally or unintentionally): B to save himself has to jump from a height involving certain injury, or to save a child rushes in and is seriously burned. Here, of course, B's movements are not involuntary; the 'necessity' of his action is here of a different order. His action is the outcome of a choice between two evils forced on him by A's action. In such cases, when B's injuries are thought of as the consequence of the fire, the implicit judgment is made that his action was the lesser of two evils and in this sense a 'reasonable' one which he was obliged to make to avoid the greater evil. This is often paradoxically, though understandably, described by saying that here the agent 'had no choice' but to do what he did. Such judgments involve a comparison of the importance of the respective interests sacrificed and preserved, and the final assertion that A's action was the cause of the injuries rests on evaluations about which men may differ.

Finally, the ground for treating some harm which would not have occurred without B's action as the consequence of A's action may be that B acted in ignorance of or under a mistake as to some feature of the situation created by *A*. Poisoning offers perhaps the simplest example of the bearing on causal judgments of actions which are less than voluntary in this Aristotelian sense. If *A* intending *B*'s death deliberately poisons *B*'s food and *B*, knowing this, deliberately takes the poison and dies, *A* has not, unless he coerced *B* into eating the poisoned food, caused *B*'s death: if, however, *B* does not know the food to be poisoned, eats it, and dies, *A* has caused his death, even if he put the poison in unwittingly. Of course only the roughest judgments are passed in causal terms in such cases outside law courts, where fine degrees of 'appreciation' or 'reckless shutting of the eyes' may have to be discriminated from 'full knowledge.' Yet, rough as these are, they indicate clearly enough the controlling principles.

Though in the foregoing cases *A*'s initiating action might often be described as 'the cause' of the ultimate harm, this linguistic fact is of subordinate importance to the fact that, for whatever purpose, explanatory, descriptive, or evaluative, consequences of an action are traced, discriminations are made (except in the cases discussed later) between free voluntary interventions and less than voluntary reactions to the first action or the circumstances created by it.

(iii) The analogy with single simple actions which guides the tracing of consequences may be broken by certain kinds of conjunctions of physical events. *A* hits *B* who falls to the ground stunned and bruised by the blow; at that moment a tree crashes to the ground and kills *B*. *A* has certainly caused *B*'s bruises but not his death: for though the fall of the tree was, like the evening breeze in our earlier example, independent of and subsequent to the initiating action, it would be differentiated from the breeze in any description in causal terms of the connection of *B*'s death with *A*'s action. It is to be noticed that this is not a matter which turns on the intention with which *A* struck *B*. Even if *A* hit *B* inadvertently or accidentally his blow would still be the cause of *B*'s bruises: he would have caused them, though unintentionally. Conversely even if *A* had intended his blow to kill, this would have been an attempt to kill but still not the cause of *B*'s death, unless *A* knew that the tree was about to fall just at that moment. On this legal and ordinary judgments would be found to agree; and most legal systems would distinguish for the purposes of punishment an attempt with a fatal upshot, issuing by such chance or anomalous events, from

'causing death'—the terms in which the offences of murder and manslaughter are usually defined.

Similarly the causal description of the case does not turn on the moral appraisal of *A*'s action or the wish to punish it. *A* may be a robber and a murderer and *B* a saint guarding the place *A* hoped to plunder. Or *B* may be a murderer and *A* a hero who has forced his way into *B*'s retreat. In both cases the causal judgment is the same. *A* had caused the minor injuries but not *B*'s death, though he tried to kill him. *A* may indeed be praised or blamed but not for causing *B*'s death. However intimate the connection between responsibility and causation, it does not determine causal judgments in this simple way. Nor does the causal judgment turn on a refusal to attribute grave consequences to actions which normally have less serious results. Had *A*'s blow killed *B* outright and the tree, falling on his body, merely smashed his watch we should still treat the coincidental character of the fall of the tree as determining the form of causal statement. We should then recognize *A*'s blow as the cause of *B*'s death but not the breaking of the watch.

The connection between *A*'s action and *B*'s death in the first case would naturally be described in the language of *coincidence*. 'It was a coincidence: it just happened that, at the very moment when *A* knocked *B* down, a tree crashed at the very place where he fell and killed him.' The common legal metaphor would describe the fall of the tree as an 'extraneous' cause. This, however, is dangerously misleading, as an analysis of the notion of coincidence will show. It suggests merely an event which is subsequent to and independent of some other contingency, and of course the fall of the tree has both these features in relation to *A*'s blow. Yet in these respects the fall of the tree does not differ from the evening breeze in the earlier case where we found no difficulty in tracing causal connection. The full elucidation of the notion of a coincidence is a complex matter for, though it is very important as a limit in tracing consequences, causal questons are not the only ones to which the notion is relevant. The following are its most general characteristics. We speak of a coincidence whenever the conjunction of two or more events in certain spatial or temporal relations (1) is very unlikely by ordinary standards and (2) is for some reason significant or important, provided (3) that they occur without human contrivance and (4) are independent of each other. It is therefore a coincidence if two persons known to each other in London meet without design in Paris on their way to separate independently chosen destinations; or if two persons living in different places independently decide to write a book on the same subject. The first is a coincidence of time and place ('It just happened that we were at the same place at the same time'), and the second a coincidence of time only ('It just happened that they both decided to write on the subject at the same time').

Use of this general notion is made in the special case when the conjunction of two or more events occurs in temporal and/or spatial relationships which are significant, because, as our general knowledge of causal processes shows, this conjunction is required for the production of some given further event. In the language of Mill's idealized model, they form a necessary part of a complex set of jointly sufficient conditions. In the present case the fall of the tree just as B was struck down within its range satisfies the four criteria for a coincidence which we have enumerated. First, though neither event was of a very rare or exceptional kind, their conjunction would be rated very unlikely judged by the standards of ordinary experience. Secondly, this conjunction was causally significant for it was a necessary part of the process terminating in B's death. Thirdly, this conjunction was not consciously designed by A; had he known of the impending fall of the tree and hit B with the intention that he should fall within its range B's death would not have been the result of any coincidence. A would certainly have caused it. The common-sense principle that a contrived conjunction cannot be a coincidence is the element of truth in the legal maxim (too broadly stated even for legal purposes) that an intended conequence cannot be too 'remote.' Fourthly, each member of the conjunction in this case was independent of the other; whereas if B had fallen against the tree with an impact sufficient to bring it down on him, this sequence of physical events, though freakish in its way, would not be a coincidence and in most contexts of ordinary life, as in the law, the course of events would be summarized by saying that in this case, unlike that of the coincidence, A's act was the cause of B's death, since each stage is the effect of the preceding stage. Thus, the blow forced the victim against the tree, the effect of this was to make the tree fall and the fall of the tree killed the victim.

One further criterion in addition to these four must be satisfied if a conjunction of events is to rank as a coincidence and as a limit when the consequences of the action are traced. This further criterion again shows the strength of the influence which the analogy with the case of the simple manipulation of things exerts over thought in causal terms. An abnormal *condition* existing at the time of a human intervention is distinguished both by ordinary thought and, with a striking consistency, by most legal systems from an abnormal event or conjunction of events subsequent to that intervention; the former, unlike the latter, are not ranked as coincidences or 'extraneous' causes when the consequences of the intervention come to be traced. Thus A innocently gives B a tap over the head of a normally quite harmless character, but because B is then suffering from some rare disease the tap has, as we say, 'fatal results.' In this case A has caused B's death though unintentionally. The scope of the principle which thus distinguishes contemporaneous abnormal conditions from subsequent events is unclear; but at least where a human being initiates some physical change in a thing, animal, or person, abnormal physical states of the object affected, existing at the time, are ranked as part of the circumstances in which the cause 'operates.' In the familiar controlling imagery these are part of 'the stage already set' before the 'intervention.'

Judgments about coincidences, though we often agree in making them, depend in two related ways on issues incapable of precise formulation. One of these is patent, the other latent but equally important. Just how unlikely must a conjunction be to rank as a coincidence, and in the light of what knowledge is likelihood to be assessed? The only answer is: 'very unlikely in the light of the knowledge available to ordinary men.' It is, of course, the indeterminacies of such standards, implicit in causal judgments, that make them inveterately disputable, and call for the exercise of discretion or choice by courts. The second and latent indeterminacy of these judgments depends on the fact that the things or events to which they relate do not have pinned to them some uniquely correct description always to be used in assessing likelihood. It is an important pervasive feature of all our empirical judgments that there is a constant possibility of more or less specific description of any event or thing with which they are concerned. The tree might be described not simply as a 'tree' but as a 'rotten tree' or as a 'fir tree' or a 'tree sixty feet tall.' So too its fall might be described not as a 'fall' but as a fall of a specified distance at a specified velocity. The likelihood of conjunctions framed in these different terms would be differently assessed. The criteria of appropriate description like the standard of likelihood are supplied by consideration of common knowledge. Even if the scientist knew the tree to be rotten and could have predicted its fall with accuracy, this would not change the judgment that its fall at the time when B was struck down within its range was a coincidence; nor would it make the description 'rotten tree' appropriate for the assessment of the chances involved in this judgment. There are other controls over the choice of description derived from the degree of specificity of our interests in the final outcome of the causal process. We are concerned with the fall of an object sufficient to cause 'death' by impact and the precise force or direction which may account for the detail of the wounds is irrelevant here.

Opportunities and Reasons

Opportunities. The discrimination of voluntary interventions as a limit is no longer made when the case, owing to the commonness or appreciable risk of such harmful intervention, can be brought within the scope of the notion of providing an opportunity, known to be commonly exploited for doing harm. Here the limiting principles are different. When A leaves the house unlocked the range of consequences to be attributed to this neglect, as in any other case where precautions are omitted, depends primarily on the way in which such opportunities are commonly exploited. An alternative formulation of this idea is that a subsequent intervention would fall within the scope of consequences if the likelihood of its occurring is one of the reasons for holding A's omission to be negligent.

It is on these lines that we would distinguish between the entry of a thief and of a murderer; the opportunity provided is believed to be sufficiently commonly exploited by thieves to make it usual and often morally or legally obligatory not to provide it. Here, in attributing consequences to prior actions, causal judgments are directly controlled by the notion of the risk created by them. Neglect of such precautions is both unusual and reprehensible. For these reasons it would be hard to separate the two ways in which such neglect deviates from the 'norm.' Despite this, no simple identification can be made of the notion of responsibility with the

causal connection which is a ground for it. This is so because the provision of an opportunity commonly taken by others is ranked as the cause of the outcome independently of the wish to praise or blame. The causal judgment may be made simply to assess a contribution to some outcome. Thus, whether we think well or ill of the use made of railways, we would still claim that the greater mobility of the population in the nineteenth century was a consequence of their introduction.

It is obvious that the question whether any given intervention is a sufficiently common exploitation of the opportunity provided to come within the risk is again a matter on which judgments may differ, though they often agree. The courts, and perhaps ordinary thought also, often describe those that are sufficiently common as 'natural' consequences of the neglect. They have in these terms discriminated the entry of a thief from the entry of a man who burnt the house down, and refused to treat the destruction of the house as a 'natural' consequence of the neglect.[9]

We discuss later in Chapter IX the argument that this easily intelligible concept of 'harm within the risk,' overriding as it does the distinctions between voluntary interventions and others, should be used as the general test for determining what subsequent harm should be attributed for legal purposes to prior action. The merits of this proposal to refashion the law along these simple lines are perhaps considerable, yet consequences of actions are in fact often traced both in the law and apart from it in other ways which depend on the discrimination of voluntary interventions from others. We distinguish, after all, as differing though related grounds of responsibility, causing harm by one's own action and providing opportunities for others to do harm, where the guiding analogy with the simple manipulation of things, which underlies causal thought, is less close. When, as in the examples discussed above, we trace consequences through the non-voluntary interventions of others our concern is to show that certain stages of the process have a certain type of connection with the preceding stages, and not, as when the notion of risk is applied, to show that the ultimate outcome is connected in some general way with the initiating action. Thus, when A's shot makes B start and break a glass it is the causal relationship described by the expression 'made B start' that we have in mind and not the likelihood that on hearing a shot someone may break a glass.

Causal connection may be traced in such cases though the initiating action and the final outcome are not contingencies that commonly go together.

Apart from these conceptual reasons for distinguishing these related grounds for responsibility, it is clear that both in the law . . . and apart from it we constantly treat harm as caused by a person's action though it does not fall 'within the risk.' If, when B broke the glass in the example given above, a splinter flew into C's eye, blinding him, A's action is indeed the cause of C's injury though we may not always blame him for so unusual a consequence.

Reasons. In certain varieties of interpersonal transactions, unlike the case of coercion, the second action is quite voluntary. A may not threaten B but may bribe or advise or persuade him to do something. Here, A does not 'cause' or 'make' B do anything: the strongest words we should use are perhaps that he 'induced' or 'procured' B's act. Yet the law and moral principles alike may treat one person as responsible for the harm which another free agent has done 'in consequence' of the advice or the inducements which the first has offered. In such cases the limits concern the range of those actions done by B which are to rank as the consequence of A's words or deeds. In general this question depends on A's intentions or on the 'plan of action' he puts before B. If A advises or bribes B to break in and steal from an empty house and B does so, he acts in consequence of A's advice or bribe. If he deliberately burns down the house this would not be treated as the consequence of A's bribe or advice, legally or otherwise, though it may in some sense be true that the burning would not have taken place without the advice or bribe. Nice questions may arise, which the courts have to settle, where B diverges from the detail of the plan of action put before him by A.

. . .

Endnotes

[1] Glanville Williams, *Joint Torts and Contributory Negligence,* p. 239.

[2] Mill, Book III, chap. v, s. 2.

[3] Ross, *The Right and the Good,* p. 36.

[4] E.g., if the guest was suspected of being a compulsive stabber and the waiter had therefore been told to lay only a plastic knife in his place.

[5] *Davies* v. *Swan Motor Co.* [1947] 2 KB 291, 318.

[6] *Minister of Pensions* v. *Chennell* [1947] KB 250, 256. Lord Wright (1950), 13 MLR 3.

[7] *Norris* v. *William Moss & Son Ltd.* [1954] I WLR 46, 351.

[8] *Minister of Pensions* v. *Chennell* [1947] KB 250, 256.

[9] *Bellows* v. *Worcester Storage Co.* (1937) 297 Mass. 188, 7 NE 2d 588.

The Decline of Cause

JUDITH JARVIS THOMSON

I

Once upon a time there was a simple way of characterizing tort law. It could in those days be said that the defendant will be declared liable for the plaintiff's loss if and only if the plaintiff proves the following three things: (1) that he suffered a loss, (2) that an act or failure to act on the part of the defendant was proximate cause of the plaintiff's suffering that loss, and (3) that the defendant was at fault in so acting or failing to act. Proximate cause was a messy business, of course, but one thing that was clear was that a person's act or omission was not proximate cause of another person's loss unless it caused the loss.

So much for once upon a time. Fault went first: it began to be possible in certain kinds of cases for a plaintiff to win his suit if he proved (1) that he suffered a loss, and (2) that an act or failure to act on the part of the defendant proximately caused his loss, even though he did not prove (3) that the defendant was at fault in so acting or failing to act. Now cause is going. In a number of cases in recent years the plaintiff has won his suit on proof (1) that he suffered a loss, and (3) that there was a faulty act or omission on the part of the defendant, but without proving (2) that the defendant's faulty act or omission caused the loss. No doubt the plaintiff has to prove *some* connection between his loss and the defendant's faulty act. If I prove I lost my legs this morning, and that you hit your little brother with a brick yesterday, *that* certainly will not suffice for me to win a suit against you for damages for the loss of my legs. The plaintiff has to connect the faulty act with the loss. But in the kind of case I

have in mind, the connection he makes need not be causation.

Which kind of case? A good example is *Sindell v. Abbott Laboratories*,[1] which was decided by the California Supreme Court in 1980. The plaintiff alleged she could prove that she developed cancer as a result of the DES taken by her mother while pregnant; she alleged she could prove also that the defendants—eleven drug companies—knew or should have known that DES would cause cancer in the daughters of mothers who took it. In other words, she alleged she could prove (1) that she was harmed, and (3) that the defendant drug companies were at fault. But she was unable to prove, after the passage of so many years, which drug company had marketed the very DES her mother took, so she was unable to prove about any of the drug companies (2) that *its* acts had caused the harm she suffered. All the same, she won the right to get a jury on the fact she alleged she could prove, and the right to win if she could prove them.

An earlier California case—*Summers v. Tice*,[2] decided in 1948—presented the problem that confronted the plaintiff in *Sindell* much more starkly and cleanly. The plaintiff Summers had gone hunting with the two defendants, Tice and Simonson. A quail was flushed, and, as Summers alleged, the defendants fired negligently in Summers' direction; as he also alleged, one of the two wounded him. But he was unable to prove which, since the defendants had fired similar pellets from similar guns. Loss yes, fault yes, but causality could not be proved. However he too won his suit.

My own impression is that cases like *Summers* and *Sindell*—in which loss and fault are clear, but causality cannot be proved—were very rarely won until recently. Why are they being won now? It is an excellent question, with, I am sure, a great many answers. Chief among them is probably a mix of four things: first, the very fact that causality *is* hard to prove in them; together with, second, the felt need to regulate the increasing number of activities which impose risk as a byproduct of technological

From *The Georgetown Law Journal*, Vol. 76 (1987), pp. 137–150. © 1987 The Georgetown Law Journal Association. Reprinted with permission of *The Georgetown Law Journal*.

advance; third, an increasing public acceptance of egalitarianism; and fourth, the absence as yet of a mechanism other than the tort suit to regulate those activities and secure a measure of compensation for those who may be being victimized by them.[3]

II

A related phenomenon—at least I think it really must be related—is the increasing dismissiveness about causality that can be seen in legal theorizing. Here are Landes and Posner in an article published in 1983: "causation in the law is an inarticulate groping for economically sound solutions. . . ."[4] In an article published in 1975, Calabresi defends the idea that certain concepts related to causality have a role to play in law, but his defense of that idea would have puzzled many lawyers fifty years ago. He says:

> [I]n law the term "cause" is used in different guises but always to identify those pressure points that are most amenable to the social goals we wish to accomplish. . . . [U]se of such [causal] concepts has great advantages over explicit identification and separation of the goals. Terms with an historical, common law gloss [like "cause"] permit us to consider goals (like spreading) that we do not want to spell out or too obviously assign to judicial institutions.[5]

This dismissiveness about causality is not visible only in those whose legal theorizing is influenced by economics.[6]

III

I am not competent to speak to the question why the law and legal theory have been developing in these ways, or even to the question exactly what forms these developments have taken. What I want to do instead is to mull over one of the sources of the welcome with which these developments have been received by many of the moral philosophers who have taken note of them.

What I have in mind is that there has been a phenomenon equally entitled to be called "The Decline of Cause" in moral theorizing.

The moral sophisticate nowadays is nowhere near as enamored of causality as the ignorant rest of us. Here is an example. Yesterday, Alfred backed his car out of his driveway without looking. Bad of him!—one ought not do that. Today, Bert backed his car out of his driveway without looking, but lo and behold there was a child at the end of the driveway, and Bert ran over the child and crushed its legs. Horrendous—much worse. Or so many people think.

The moral sophisticate regards that as a vulgar error. "Look," he says, "both Alfred and Bert behaved negligently, indeed equally negligently. Bert crushed a child's legs and Alfred did not, but that was just bad luck for Bert, and good luck for Alfred. After all, it wasn't Bert's fault that there was a child at the foot of his driveway; all Bert was at fault for is exactly what Alfred was at fault for, namely backing his car out of his driveway without looking. So Bert acted no worse than Alfred did, and—other things being equal—Bert is no worse a person than Alfred is."

The moral sophisticate may concede that the law does well to mark a difference between Alfred and Bert in the following two ways: (1) imposing a more severe punishment on Bert than on Alfred, and (2) making Bert, and not Alfred, compensate the child's parents. But if so, he says it is for reasons extraneous to the *moral* valuation proper to them and their acts.

It is clear that the moral sophisticate is going to hold this same view in other pairs of cases too. Murder and attempted murder, of course. Yesterday Charles fired a gun at a man, to kill him; Charles'[s] intended victim was wearing a bullet proof vest, so Charles did not kill him. Today David fired a gun at a man, to kill him; David's intended victim was not wearing a bullet proof anything, so David did kill him. David murdered a man, and Charles only attempted murder, but the moral sophisticate says that David acted no worse than Charles did—for after all, it was just bad luck for Charles that his intended victim was wearing that vest, and thus nothing that Charles can take any credit for.

It seems to me three principles lie behind this moral attitude. The first concerns itself with *acts*. What we do in the world depends on the world as well as on us. If you fire a gun at a man to kill him, then the question whether you do not merely fire a gun at him, but also kill him turns on whether the world cooperates—thus on whether the bullet actually reaches him, as it might not if some third party intervenes, and on whether it enters him when it reaches him, as it might not if he is wearing bullet proof clothes. The first principle I have in mind says that the moral value of what you do in the world turns on and only on that part of it which is *entirely* under your control. When you fire a gun at a man, what is under your control is at most such things as the kind of gun you fire, the time and place at which you fire it, the direction in which you fire it, and the intention with which you fire it—merely to scare your victim, or merely to wound him, or positively to kill him. The rest that happens is up to the world, and is not something that has any bearing on the moral value of your act.

I said "at most." Let us look again at the kind of gun you fire. Is it new? Is it clean? Is it sufficiently powerful to do the work you want it to do? Strictly speaking, that the gun you fire does or does not have these features is not entirely under your control. What is under your control is only that you have made an effort to be sure that you are firing a suitable gun and now think you are: After all, somebody might have secretly replaced your carefully chosen gun with a different one—whether a person did or did not do this is not under your control. Similarly for the time and place at which you fire the gun, and the direction in which you fire it: Somebody might have secretly altered your clocks and roadmaps, and substituted distorting glasses for the glasses you normally wear— whether a person did or did not do this is also not under your control.

Strictly speaking, all that is entirely under your control are your intentions in acting—what you are at any given time setting yourself to be doing. That is not to say that setting yourself to do this or that is all you actually *do;* it is to say that the normal value of what you do *by* setting yourself to act in this or that way turns entirely on the moral value of those settings of yourself to act.

The second of the three principles concerns itself with *failures to act*, or omissions, for short. Consider two switchmen on different railways, Edward and Frank. Both were under a duty to throw a switch at ten this morning, and both failed to do so because they did not want to be bothered. Edward's omission caused a terrible train crash;

Frank's omission caused nothing untoward at all, since the train Frank's switch-throwing was to turn had luckily stalled before the fork in the track. If you think murder no worse than attempted murder, you will surely think Edward's omission no worse than Frank's. It was, after all, no credit to Frank, it was merely good luck for him, that his train had stalled. The second principle says that the moral value of an omission—as of an act—turns on and only on what is entirely under the agent's control. If you could have set yourself to do a thing, and ought to have done so, then your failure to do so is equally bad no matter what your omission does or does not cause.

The cases of Alfred and Bert with which I began are cases to which both principles apply. Alfred and Bert both acted, for they backed their cars down their driveways; and both failed to act, for they failed to look while doing so. Given the two principles, the fact that Bert's acting while failing to act caused a child's legs to be crushed has no bearing at all on the moral value of what he did.

The third of the three principles has to do with the moral value of *persons*. We do think of some people as morally better than others; on what does this judgment turn? Presumably in part on the moral value of what a person does or fails to do. Given the first two principles, however, that is a function only of the moral value of a person's settings of himself to do this or that, and his failures to set himself to do this or that.

But only in part, for there is something else that a friend of these ideas should think bears on a person's moral value. What I have in mind is that if you think that good and bad luck has no bearing on the moral value of an act or omission *or* person, then you should grant that the truth or falsehood of certain counterfactuals is relevant. For example, I do not drive, and a fortiori have never backed a car out of a driveway with *or* without looking. If I had driven, would I on occasion have backed my car out of my driveway without looking? Isn't that relevant to the question how good or bad a person I am?

I am sure that all of us have faced temptations to act badly, and that many of those temptations we have resisted, though some we have not. Most people, however, are lucky enough never to be tempted to do something truly dreadful. For example, I am sure that none of us has ever been in a position of power over prisoners in a concentration camp. I am sure that none of us has been lost at sea in a lifeboat with no provisions other than a plump cabin boy. We have been lucky. How would we behave if we were in such situations? Surely that we would or would not behave in this or that way has a bearing on our moral value as people. One reason why Stanley Milgram's experiments[7] were found so shocking was that they uncovered the fact that a lot of perfectly ordinary people were quite ready to set themselves to cause others a great deal of pain simply on being told by an authority figure in a white coat to do so. Milgram's readers did not think for a moment that the actual absence of pain excused the subjects of the experiments; and they took it that what Milgram had shown was a deep moral failing which may be present in perfectly ordinary people, though without ever in fact showing itself.

How good a person are you? The third principle tells us that to the extent to which you do not know what you would set yourself to do in situations you have been so far lucky as not to have faced, you just do not know how good a person you are.

I described the person who holds these views as the "moral sophisticate," because I think we do think these views more sophisticated than those which tell us to look merely at what happens, more sophisticated even than those which tell us to look *both* at what happens *and* at what is internal to a person—what he sets himself to do, and what he would set himself to do if he were in situations he has never faced. But I might just as well have described the person who holds these views as a Kantian, because it is directly from Kant that they come down to us today. Kant said: "The good will is not good because of what it effects or accomplishes or because of its adequacy to achieve some proposed end; it is good only because of its willing, i.e., it is good of itself. . . . Usefulness or fruitlessness can neither diminish or augment [its] worth."[8] And so similarly for the bad will: it is not bad because of what it causes, but only of itself. We might redescribe the decline of cause in moral philosophy as the triumph of Kant.

That Kant has triumphed seems clear enough. For example, I rather fancy that all of you have at least some inclination to agree with the three principles I drew attention to. I certainly do.

It is of interest to notice that these Kantian ideas are visible even in contemporary defenders of the most un-Kantian moral theory of all. I

have Utilitarianism in mind, of course. Classical Utilitarians—such as John Stuart Mill and G. E. Moore—took the view that you have acted wrongly if and only if your act causes there to be less good in the world than you could have caused by choosing some other alternative act which was open to you at the time. Whether you knew it or not. Mill did explicitly grant that a man's intentions in acting do have a bearing on the moral evaluation proper to *him*; but Mill insisted that the morality of a man's *act* turns on, and only on, a comparison between what it does in fact cause, and what his other available alternatives would have caused. But hardly anyone is a Classical Utilitarian nowadays. Those in favor of its spirit say that the morality of a man's act turns, not on what it in fact causes, but on what he expects it to cause. In short, the morality of action turns, not on actual, but on expected utilities.

Now I think that these Kantian ideas are one source of the welcome with which many moral philosophers have received those developments in law and legal theory that I mentioned at the outset. For example, they think that all of the defendants were at fault in *Sindell* and *Summers*—equally at fault, regardless of whoever in fact caused the harm. So they think that no one can object, on *moral* grounds, to the plaintiffs' winning, and to the defendants' therefore having to share in the plaintiffs' costs.[9]

IV

What should *we* think of all this? It is swimming upstream to try to fight it, but my own feeling is that it smells too much of the study and too little of the open air. Adam Smith said, very plausibly, I think,

> But how well soever we may seem to be persuaded of the truth of [these ideas], when we consider [them] after this manner, in abstract, yet when we come to particular cases, the actual consequences which happen to proceed from any action, have a very great effect upon our sentiments concerning its merit or demerit, and almost always either enhance or diminish our sense of both.[10]

Alfred backed his car out of his driveway without looking, and luckily for him, nothing untoward happened in consequence. Bad of him, we think. But not horrendous. People do that kind of thing often enough. They ought not, but they do, and it seems no great sin. Bert also backed his car out of his driveway without looking, but *he* ran a child down and crushed its legs. As Adam Smith said, we just *do* think that what Bert did was worse than what Alfred did. How can any philosophy be right which tells us we are mistaken in thinking this?

On the other hand, I think that Adam Smith's remark would not have been at all plausible if he had not said "almost always." He said: "the actual consequences which happen to proceed from any action, have a very great effect upon our sentiments concerning its merit or demerit, and *almost always* either enhance or diminish our sense of both."[11] There seem to me to be two kinds of case in which they do not.

To get at the first kind, let me draw your attention to the fact that in every example I have given, right from the outset, the agent whose act did cause a harm was at fault. In the two court cases I began with, all of the defendants were at fault, the drug companies in *Sindell*, the negligent hunters in *Summers*. Alfred and Bert were both careless. Charles and David, each of whom shot at a man to kill him, were both at least attempting murder. And so on. But what of an agent who causes someone to suffer a harm, but not by negligence or intention or by any wrong at all? A child runs out into the street and is run down by a truck driver who is entirely without fault—he has taken all due care to ensure that his truck, and in particular, his brakes, were in good order, and he was driving with all due care. The child simply ran too suddenly, too close, into the path of his truck. Does the very fact that he caused harm to the child diminish our sense of the merit of his actions? I think not. This example comes from Thomas Nagel, and he says about it: "The driver, if he is entirely without fault, will feel terrible about his role in the event, but will not have to reproach himself."[12] Nor will we reproach him. There is nothing to reproach him for. So here is a case of the first kind I had in mind: it is a case in which an agent was not at fault at all in acting, and that a bad consequence happens to flow from his action does not affect our sense of its merit or demerit. In particular, the bad consequence does not make us think worse of his driving

than we would have thought had that bad consequence not flowed from it.

Symmetrically, we might imagine someone who does something of no particular merit, and something good just happens to flow from his doing it. For example, suppose a man is standing at a street corner, waiting for a bus. As he waits, he is idly tapping his foot. Through some freak of nature, his tapping his foot causes three lives to be saved. This good consequence does not affect our sense of the merit or demerit of his tapping his foot. In particular, it does not make us think better of his tapping his foot than we would have thought had that good consequence not flowed from it.

Let us go back to that truck driver, whom I will call Unlucky No Fault Driver. His not having been at fault must be the crucial fact about him which makes him an exception to Adam Smith's remarks. For let us now contrast him with two other truck drivers. Both of them were at fault. They were supposed to check their brakes before leaving the garage, but did not want to be bothered. So both went out with bad brakes. In the case of the first, nothing untoward happened, and I will call him Lucky Fault Driver. I will call the second Unlucky Fault Driver. A child ran in front of Unlucky Fault Driver's truck and he ran it down. I want to have it be clear about Unlucky Fault Driver that he ran the child down not because the child ran too suddenly, too close into the path of his truck, but because his brakes were not in good working order. Had his brakes been in good working order, he would have been able to stop his truck in time; but they were not, so he was not. Lucky Fault Driver acted badly, of course; but I think we do feel that Unlucky Fault Driver acted worse. The fact that a bad consequence flowed from his action does seem to affect our sense of its demerit.

Why? I think the answer is quite simply that Unlucky Fault Driver is to blame for the death he caused. Unlucky No Fault Driver also caused a death; but he is not to blame for it, since he was in no way at fault for causing it. It seems right to say that that is why the bad consequence which flowed from Unlucky No Fault Driver's action does not make us think it worse than we would have thought had that bad consequence not flowed from it. More generally, it seems right to say that a bad consequence of an action makes that action worse *only* where the agent is to blame for that bad consequence which his action causes.

I am sure that the Kantian moral sophisticate would say at this point, "But surely it was mere bad luck for Unlucky Fault Driver that he caused a child's death. And surely one can't plausibly think a man to blame for something that he caused merely out of bad luck." There is a mistake here, and I think it the main source of the trouble. For it was not *mere* bad luck for Unlucky Fault Driver that he caused a child's death. We need a clearer grip on how bad luck figures in these cases. Unlucky No Fault Driver was in two ways unlucky. It was a piece of bad luck for him that a child ran into his path; and second, it was a piece of bad luck for him that a child ran into his path; but it was not a piece of bad luck for him that he was unable to stop his truck in time. Unlucky Fault Driver was unlucky in only the first of those two ways. It was a piece of bad luck for him that he was unable to stop his truck in time. His being unable to stop his truck in time was due to his bad brakes, and thus to his own negligence. Lucky Fault Driver did not have that first piece of bad luck, so it remains a counterfactual truth about him that *if* he had had it, then he too would have been unable to stop his truck in time. His being unable to stop would not have been a mere piece of bad luck for him, but would, instead, have been due to his negligence.

And it is the very same thing—namely Unlucky Fault Driver's negligence—that makes it not *mere* bad luck for him that he caused the child's death, that also makes him to blame for the child's death. Unlucky No Fault Driver, by contrast, was not at fault; and that is why it was mere bad luck for him that he caused a child's death, and therefore also why he is not to blame for the death of the child he killed.

The Kantian moral sophisticate could of course insist that a man cannot be thought to blame for something if bad luck entered *in any way at all* into the history of his bringing it about. But that seems to me even on its face implausible. Consider, for example, a man who is brought to trial for murder. "Look," his lawyer says to the court, "I grant that the victim's death is not *mere* bad luck for my client, since my client fired a gun at him with the intention of killing him. But the victim's death is in part due to my client's bad luck. For unbeknownst to my client, the victim almost always wore a bullet proof vest, and it was just bad luck for my client that the victim's bullet proof vest happened to be at the cleaners' on the day my client shot at him. So my client cannot be thought to blame for his victim's death." Whatever else will work in a court, *that* won't.

Let us go back now and look again at the first of the three principles that I said lie behind the moral attitude of the Kantian moral sophisticate. The first principle is: the moral value of what you do in the world turns on and only on that part of it which is entirely under your control. That seems to me to be false, and for the reason I have pointed to. Admittedly the two faulty drivers, Lucky Fault Driver and Unlucky Fault Driver, both acted equally negligently, and the difference between them has its source in the fact that one had good luck, the other bad luck. All the same, the difference which has that source is a moral difference, and of a very grave order. For the one is *by* his negligence to blame for a death, and the other is not.

A similar point surely holds of failures to act. Edward and Frank both failed to throw the switch; Edward's (but not Frank's) negligence caused a crash, for which he is therefore to blame. That, I think, is why we think that what he did was worse than what Frank did.

It seems to me, however, that we should be more sympathetic to the third of the three principles I mentioned, which yields that Unlucky Fault Driver is no worse a person than Lucky Fault Driver is, and that Edward is no worse a person than Frank. Counterfactual truths about what people would have done and been to blame for if they had been in circumstances which they were lucky enough to have avoided really are important to us in assessing how good a person is—as important, I think, as truths about what they in fact did and in fact are to blame for.

This difference between our judgments of acts on the one hand and the people who perform them on the other hand may perhaps be due to the fact that different kinds of consequences flow from our arriving at these two different kinds of judgments. When we learn that someone is a bad person—untrustworthy, unreliable, prone to acting without thought for others—what flows from this judgment? Well, our attitude toward him changes, and in consequence we will behave differently toward him in many more or less delicate ways in the future. This reaction is appropriate whether the judgment is provoked by what he actually did *or* by what we have come to learn he would do if he were in circumstances he has not in fact been in. By contrast, some of the consequences of learning that a person has actually acted badly are backward looking. If we learn he is to blame for a dreadful outcome, we do not merely alter our behavior toward him in future, we may also lock him up for what he did, or exact compensation for it from him, or both.[13]

V

Candor, however, compels me to mention a difficulty for what I have been saying. Let us go back to Adam Smith. He said: "the actual consequences which happen to proceed from any action, have a great effect upon our sentiments concerning its merit or demerit, and *almost always* either enhance or diminish our sense of both."[14] I mentioned one class of exceptions. Unlucky No Fault Driver, for example, was merely unlucky. He caused a child's death, but because this was through no fault of his own, we do not think the worse of his actions. Where there is fault, however, I said that consequences do make a difference. We do think worse of Unlucky Fault Driver's actions than of Lucky Fault Driver's actions, and that is because the one is, and the other is not, to blame for a bad outcome.

But there is yet another class of exceptions to Adam Smith's remarks, which makes trouble for any simple treatment of these issues. The simplest example comes from a case I mentioned at the outset, namely *Summers v. Tice.*[15] (That is a wonderful case. If it had not occurred, we would have had to invent it.) The two defendants, Tice and Simonson, both fired negligently in Summers' direction, and one of them shot Summers, but we cannot tell which. Who should pay Summers' bills? Most people feel it right that Tice and Simonson should split the costs. The actual outcome in court was joint and several liability, but arguably that comes to roughly the same thing given the possibility of a suit for contribution, and in any case there are reasons to think that outcome fairer to Summers than a division of the costs. So far so good, nothing puzzling yet.

Now for the source of the puzzlement. Suppose that during the course of the trial evidence had come forward which made it as certain as empirical matters ever are that the pellet that caused Summers' injury came from Tice's gun, so that it is Tice who is to blame for Summers' injury. We do, I think, take it to be clear that Simonson should now be dismissed from the suit: no doubt he acted badly, but he is not to blame for the injury, and hence he is not appropriately held liable for its costs.[16] But our *moral* assessment of Tice and Simonson does not shift. We do not think the worse of Tice, or even of Tice's acts, because he, as it turns out, is to blame for the harm; and we do not think the better of Simonson, or of Simonson's acts, because *he*, as it turns out, is not to blame for the harm. Our moral attitude does not shift in any way by virtue of the discovery that it is Tice who actually caused the harm. So we really seem to have a second kind of exception to Adam Smith's remarks.

It could of course be said that it is just irrational on our part to fail to distinguish between Tice and Simonson in the way in which we do distinguish between Lucky and Unlucky Fault Drivers. But it does not *feel* irrational. And the moral views of the man and woman in the street are deserving of great respect: they ought not be dismissed as irrational unless it really does turn out that there is no rationale for them.

What bubbles up in us men-and-women-in-the-street is, I think, this: "Simonson nearly caused the very same harm that Tice caused." It is not true of Lucky Fault Driver that he nearly caused the very same harm that Unlucky Fault Driver caused. Or at least you were not thinking of him as having done so. One driver goes out in one part of town, the other in another; they both have bad brakes; a child runs in front of one, no child runs in front of the other. So far so good. One is to blame for a death and the other is not, and we feel very differently about what they did.

But now let the two drivers set out from the same part of town, down the same street. A child runs in front of both. Both come to a long screeching halt. The child is hit by one truck and not by the other. If the child had been running *ever* so slightly slower, it would have been hit by the other truck. Now the drivers seem to us like Tice and Simonson: we think no worse of what the one did than of what the other did.

This suggests that something else is at work in these cases, possibly two things, in fact.

In the first place, Tice and Simonson did not merely act equally negligently; they each imposed roughly the same risk of harm on a person. Similarly for the two truck drivers who set out from the same part of town, and in front of both of whom one child runs. Not so for two truck drivers who set out from different parts of town. If they both set out with bad brakes, they acted equally negligently; but if a child runs in front of one, and no child so much as gets near the other, they do not in fact impose even roughly the same risk of harm on anyone.

This does make a difference to us. Suppose you back your car out of your driveway without looking, but no child was anywhere near you. Perhaps you will feel bad later on thinking the matter over: after all, it is negligent to back out without looking. But you will not *dwell* on what you did; it would be irrational to lie awake at night shuddering at the thought of what you *might* have caused. But suppose you back your car out of your driveway without looking, and there was a child in the vicinity; indeed, you nearly hit it, and would have hit it but for the child's having noticed a penny up ahead and run faster to get to it. Here the shudder is not out of place. We all know what that terrible, nagging thought is like: it is not merely of what you might have caused, but of what you nearly did cause. You do not feel as bad as you would if you had actually hit the child; but you do feel considerably worse than you would if there had been no child in the vicinity at all.

Adam Smith said that the bad consequences of an act affect our sense of its merit or demerit, and I agreed that this is so if the act was faulty: for the bad things an act causes are things that its agent is to blame for, if his act was faulty. What seems to come out here is that it is not merely the actual bad consequences of an act that affect our sense of its demerit: the higher the risk of bad consequences that the act actually imposes on others, the greater the demerit of the act.

It is puzzling that this should be so, however. Your negligence in backing out of your driveway without looking is no greater or worse if there is a child in the vicinity than if there is not; and since you did not actually hit the child, [you] cannot explain [your] feeling that what you did was worse by appeal to the fact that you are to blame for a harm to the child. *Nobody* was harmed. So there is a gap here, and I hope you will find it as interesting a question as I do just how it is to be filled.

I said it is possible that there are two further things at work in these cases. The second of them is this: Tice and Simonson did not merely act equally negligently, and they did not merely each impose roughly the same risk of harm on *a* person; they each imposed roughly the same risk of harm on one and the same person, namely Summers. Similarly for the two truck drivers who set out from the same part of town, and in front of both of whom one child runs. Does *that* matter to us? I do not find it clear that it does. Dickenson fired his shotgun negligently last Wednesday, and nearly hit someone. He feels awful about what he did, and we think it right that he feel awful about it. Do we think worse of what Simonson did, given he nearly hit someone on Thursday, *and* given also that the person Simonson nearly hit was in fact hit by Tice? Perhaps so. But it is even harder, I think, to see why that should be so—if it is.

VI

Let me now try to pull this material together just briefly. I began by drawing attention to two phenomena in law—more precisely, one in law itself, the other in legal theory—which seem to warrant saying that as far as tort law is concerned at any rate, there has been a decline of cause. Many people think that if cause declines in law, law to that extent departs from morality. It therefore seemed to me worth drawing attention to the fact that there has been a decline of cause in moral theory too. That decline in part explains why moral theorists who interest themselves in law have welcomed those developments in law and legal theory. But it is of interest for its own sake. As Adam Smith said, when you think about these matters in the abstract, the philosophers seem to be right; but when you come out of the study, they seem to be wrong. Moral theorists must of course ask themselves why that is, and whether there is a rationale for it; that is the job of the moral theorist. But I hope that lawyers will find these questions of interest too. The law certainly is not, and need not be, an exact reflection of the morality of those governed by it; but responsible government tries to be sure it has a sound rationale whenever it departs from that morality, and therefore does well to try to become clear about what that morality is.

Endnotes

[1] 26 Cal. 3d 88, 163 Cal. Rptr. 132, 607 P.2d 924, *cert. denied*, 449 U.S. 912 (1980).

[2] 33 Cal. 2d 80, 199 P.2d 1 (1948).

[3] For an interesting discussion of these and related matters, which brings out their bearing on a particular case, see P. Shuck, Agent Orange on Trial, Mass Toxic Disasters in the Courts (1986).

[4] Landes & Posner, *Causation in Tort Law: An Economic Approach*, 12 J. L. Stud. 109, 131 (1983).

[5] Calabresi, *Concerning Cause and the Law of Torts: An Essay for Harry Kalven, Jr.*, 43 U. Chi. L. Rev. 69, 106–07 (1975) (emphasis in original).

[6] *See, e.g.*, Kelman, *The Necessary Myth of Objective Causation Judgments in Liberal Political Theory*, 63 Chi-Kent L Rev 579 (1987).

[7] *See* S. Milgram, Obedience to Authority (1974) (summarizing results of Milgram's experiments).

[8] I. Kant, Foundations of the Metaphysics of Morals 12–13 (Bobbs-Merrill ed. 1969).

[9] *See, e.g.*, Fischer & Ennis, *Causation and Liability*, 15 Phil. & Pub. Affairs 33 (1986); Kagan, *Causation, Liability, and Internalism*, 15 Phil. & Pub. Affairs 41 (1986).

[10] A. Smith, The Theory of Moral Sentiments 134 (Arlington House ed. 1969).

[11] The emphasis is mine.

[12] T. Nagel, Mortal Questions 28–29 (1979).

[13] As I wrote in part III, the moral sophisticate may say that while the law does well to mark a difference between Alfred and Bert (punishing Bert more severely than Alfred, exacting compensation for the injury from Bert), this is for reasons extraneous to the moral valuation proper to them and their acts. I think it is one thing to say the moral valuation proper to *them* does not warrant differential legal consequences: Bert is surely no worse a person than Alfred is. But it is another thing to say the moral valuation proper to *their* acts does not warrant differential legal consequences: Bert, after all, is to blame for a harm and Alfred is not, so there really is a moral difference between what Bert did and what Alfred did.

[14] A. Smith, *supra* note 10, at 134. The emphasis is mine.

[15] 33 Cal. 2d 80, 199 P.2d 1 (1948).

[16] Why this should be so is discussed in Thomson, *Remarks on Causation and Liability*, 13 Phil. & Pub. Affairs 101 (1984). Criticism of that discussion may be found in Fischer & Ennis, *supra* note 9, and in Kagan, *supra* note 9.

Study Questions

1. The *Lynch* and *Palsgraf* cases represent two competing views of causation in tort law. *Lynch* stands for the first and somewhat older principle that my liability for those events that would not have occurred except for my negligent conduct extends to any such consequences directly traceable to me, to my causal agency; under *Lynch*, in other words, I am liable for any consequences of my conduct traceable through a series of events back to me, as long as that chain is unbroken by the causal contribution of an intervening actor. This principle is preserved in the maxim "You take your victim as you find him (or her)": A hits B with a force that would normally only bruise a person; but, unknown to A, B has a very thin skull or is a hemophiliac; B dies. Under the *Lynch* view, A is liable for B's death. The second, newer principle is represented by Cardozo's opinion in *Palsgraf*: My liability extends only to those whom I might foreseeably harm through my negligent conduct. A number of causation cases line up on either side. Which view seems to you to make more sense? Can these principles be reconciled?

2. Elsewhere in their book, Hart and Honoré maintain that their analysis of causal attribution agrees with the law's position on the "thin-skull" cases (see question 1, above): They distinguish between a state of a person or thing *existing at the time* of a wrongful act and a later or *subsequent* event or state. Existing abnormal states (thin skulls, hemophilia, and so on) are "mere circumstances" or conditions on which the cause operates and do not "break" the chain of causation, so that the defendant is liable for the entire harm produced. But, they add, subsequent abnormal events or conditions *do* break the chain. They put it this way:

> Suppose plaintiff is run over through defendant's negligence. If on the way to the hospital he is hit by a falling tree, that is a coincidence [for which defendant is not liable]. If, just previously to being run over, he had been hit by a [falling] tree and severely injured, that is a circumstance existing at the time of the running over and will not negative the causal connection between the running over and the victim's death, [so the defendant is liable] even if the vic-

tim would not have died from the running down but for the previous blow from the tree. (*Causation in the Law*, 2nd ed., p. 161)

Does this make sense? Is it consistent with the basic outlines of Hart and Honoré's analysis?

3. What result would Hart and Honoré's analysis of causal attribution yield in *Lynch*? Does that result seem to you to count for or against their view?

4. Do you agree with Thomson that the decline of cause is an undesirable trend? How would you recommend that the courts handle cases like *Summers* and *Sindell*?

5. Negligence law takes the position that, with respect to certain qualities—general skill, intelligence, and judgment—everyone is presumed to be equal, and equally reasonable, and is held to that standard. If you fall below that standard, this will not excuse you. However, as Oliver Wendell Holmes notes, certain specific conditions, for example, blindness or other physical disabilities, are such that we adjust our expectations accordingly. Blind persons are judged against what a "reasonable blind person" would have done in a given situation. Are there other conditions that should be included on this list? Children, for instance, have traditionally been judged on the standard of reasonable conduct for persons of their actual age, intelligence, and experience. What about the elderly? The infirm? Do the fact of these exceptions to the objective test of reasonableness show that the standard is itself suspicious?

6. With the increasing complexity of our society, both the principles and doctrines of the law, and the courts that seek to apply them, have been strained to the limit with negligence litigation. Why not ameliorate this situation by simply abandoning the existing regime of negligence law? We could, for example, impose a tax on all those who act negligently, whether or not their conduct actually results in harm. The money thus obtained could be placed into a general fund out of which accident victims could be compensated, bypassing altogether the need for a lawsuit. Alternatively, we could require each individual to insure him or herself against accidents arising through the carelessness of others (schemes of "no-fault" auto insurance are a specific instance of this proposal). Would there be anything morally objectionable about such systems of "loss distribution"?

B. *Acts, Omissions, and the Duty to Rescue*

Introduction

We are all familiar with situations in which the law imposes upon us a duty to *refrain* from acting in ways harmful to other persons or their property, with prohibitions on murder, theft, assault, and so on. But what of situations in which the *failure* to act constitutes a breach of duty? Are there such cases? It is true that the law does recognize certain instances in which *omitting* to do something *for* someone, as opposed to *doing* something *to* him, is a breach of duty: where, for example, that person is your child or your spouse; or where you have entered into a contract to care for another. In other words, cases involving an otherwise legally recognized relationship.

As a general matter, the law's approach to the question of duty is governed by two principles: Everyone has a general duty of reasonable care for *misfeasance,* but no one (with few exceptions) has a duty of care for *nonfeasance.* What do these terms mean? *Misfeasance* refers to the infliction of harm, or acting in a way that inflicts harm. *Nonfeasance* refers to the failure to prevent harm. So all of us are under a general legal duty not to inflict harm upon one another, but none of us (again with few exceptions) are under a legal duty to prevent harm from befalling another.

Misfeasance and Nonfeasance

The concepts of misfeasance and nonfeasance are difficult ones. Part of the difficulty, as several of our selections in this chapter make clear, is that the distinction itself is not unproblematic. The difference between misfeasance and nonfeasance is supposed to mark the difference between *acts* (or *commissions*) and *omissions.* But what makes something one rather than the other? Take this, for example: It is Monday morning and my daughter needs to be ready for school by 7:00 A.M. I wake her up early, even though she did not get much sleep the night before. Have I performed the *act* of "getting my daughter ready for school"? Or have I *omitted* to perform the act of "letting her sleep in"? (I know how she will see it!) Some who have thought about this question argue that the answer depends upon how the situation is described, and that how we describe it turns on our *evaluation* of the alternatives:

> — Unless the defendant has a duty to act, an omission is not culpable. Of course, the line between omissions and commissions is blurry. There is considerable circularity in claiming that a defendant can be culpable only if he had committed an act, when we often describe an event in active conduct terms rather than passively if we have already (somehow) determined that the party is culpable. For instance, a parent who does *does not feed* a child may readily be said to *starve* the child—to commit an act—while a stranger would be said to *fail to feed*—a passive nonact.[1]

You would be more inclined to say "Adams (selflessly) got his daughter ready for (a wonderful day at) school" than to say "Adams (inexcusably) for-

got to wake his daughter," the more you are inclined to view one positively and the other negatively; and this is revealed by the (loaded) way in which each alternative is described.

Another suggestion, defended in our selection from Ernest Weinrib, distinguishes misfeasance from nonfeasance on the ground that the former always involves a situation in which the defendant has played some role in creating the risk to which the plaintiff has been exposed; whereas in situations of pure nonfeasance this is not the case. Weinrib contrasts these cases:

1. Driver (defendant) fails to apply his brakes in time and Pedestrian (plaintiff) is hurt.

2. One person (defendant) sees another (plaintiff) drowning in a pool and fails to throw him an easily available rope.

Here, our conviction that case 1 is an instance of misfeasance whereas case 2 is "mere" nonfeasance can be explained by seeing that Driver plays a role in creating the danger to which Pedestrian is exposed; whereas presumably this is not true of the defendant in case 2.

What significance does the misfeasance/nonfeasance distinction have for the question of which duties the law imposes upon us? The collective meaning of the two principles stated above is this: If you find a stranger in a position of peril, perhaps even of imminent death—a situation you did nothing to create—and you do nothing to help that person (even where this would be no risk to you), your conduct is mere nonfeasance and you generally are *not* legally liable for that person's injuries or death. The law's position is starkly summarized by the language of an older case:

> Actionable negligence is the neglect of a legal duty. The defendants are not liable unless they owed to the plaintiff a legal duty which they neglected to perform. With purely moral obligations the law does not deal. For example, the priest and Levite who passed by on the other side were not, it is supposed, liable at law for the continued suffering of the man who fell among thieves, which they might and morally ought to have prevented or relieved. Suppose A, standing close by a railroad, sees a two-year-old babe on the track and a car approaching. He can easily rescue the child with entire safety to himself, and the in-

stincts of humanity require him to do so. If he does not, he may, perhaps, justly be styled a ruthless savage and a moral monster; but he is not liable in damages for the child's injury, or indictable under the statute for its death. . . . There is a wide difference—a broad gulf—both in reason and in law, between causing and preventing an injury; between doing by negligence or otherwise a wrong to one's neighbor, and preventing him from injuring himself; between protecting him against injury by another and guarding him from injury that may accrue to him from the condition of the premises which he has unlawfully invaded. The duty to do no wrong is a legal duty. The duty to protect against wrong is, generally speaking and excepting certain intimate relations in the nature of a trust, a moral obligation only, not recognized or enforced by law.[2]

McFall v. Shimp

The impact of the misfeasance/nonfeasance distinction as it bears on the scope and limits of the duty of care owed to others is dramatically illustrated in the tragic case of Robert McFall.

Thirty-nine-year-old McFall suffered from aplastic anemia, a disease in which the patient's bone marrow fails to manufacture certain necessary blood components. McFall's condition was diagnosed in July of 1978 and a search was immediately undertaken to locate a bone marrow donor. Transfusions of bone marrow require that there be a high degree of genetic compatibility between patient and donor, so McFall's relatives were looked to first. Initial tests of McFall's immediate family failed to produce a donor; but, eventually, the medical team located McFall's first cousin, David Shimp. Preliminary tests indicated a high compatibility rating, and Shimp was scheduled for further testing during the third week of July. He failed to appear, stating in a later interview that his wife had asked him to not go through with the procedure. Running out of time and with no one else to turn to, McFall hired an attorney and filed a suit, asking the court for an *injunction* ordering Shimp to submit to the transfusion procedure.

Counsel for McFall could cite little in the way of prior authority dealing with this case, beyond an invocation of the court's equitable powers, and ended its arguments with a plea: "The time for study is over. The exigencies require action in order to save a human life. Our noblest traditions as a free people and our common sense of decency, society and morality all point to the proper result in this case. We respectfully suggest that it is time our law did likewise."

Judge Flaherty denied the injunction on two grounds. First, there is no legal duty to save another, he conceded, and this is perhaps as it should be; to force Shimp to submit to the procedure would be to usher in a new rule with no limitations. Second, the forcible intrusion into the body contemplated here is wholly impermissible. Flaherty's ruling was announced on July 26. Robert McFall died on August 10.

. . .

. . . The essay by legal philosopher Ernest Weinrib reviews the legal and moral dimensions of the debate over the "no-duty-to-rescue" rule. Those who defend the law's stance toward rescue raise several points. To the degree that the law is correct in requiring that your liability for another's injuries depends upon whether you *caused* harm to that person, it must follow that there can be no duty to rescue in cases of pure nonfeasance, as these are just those cases in which you have not caused the harm in question. Furthermore, regardless of which of several possible formulations of a general duty to rescue one selects, it remains the case that no principled limits could be placed on the invasion of individual liberty that would follow from the imposition of such a duty. By encroaching upon individual liberties in this way, a general duty of rescue would require "forced exchanges" between persons.

As Weinrib indicates, proponents of a legal duty to rescue commonly make the utilitarian argument that a general legal duty to come to the aid of those in peril is required by the goal of promoting the overall welfare. Critics of a legal duty to rescue have sought to build a moral case for their position by aligning themselves with the moral theory of Kant. Kant argued that the moral value of an act depends, not upon the consequences or results it produces, but solely upon the motive or "will" from which it springs. The moral worth of an action turns exclusively upon the moral acceptability of the principle on the basis of which one acts: doing the right thing because it is the right thing to do. This view seems to imply that to compel acts of rescue through the law would be to destroy their moral worth; for then my reason for coming to the aid of another would not simply be to "do my duty for duty's sake" but to do so to avoid punishment. Thus, the world would in a sense be made a morally worse place for having a legal duty to rescue. Those opposed to requiring rescue also raise a common complaint about utilitarianism: Since the sole concern of the utilitarian is with producing good results—maximizing the overall welfare—individuals are under a moral obligation to do whatever they can to achieve this maximization. But this, the critics allege, leaves no room in our moral life for "saints" or "heroes," for those who act "above and beyond the call of duty." For the utilitarian, any act that conduces to greater net good is already required; it is not something for which one can be lionized as a hero. The opponents of a duty to rescue regard this as a loss to our collective moral life.

The case for a general duty of rescue is made here by Weinrib. He endeavors to respond to the critics' fundamental objection that to impose upon all a general duty of rescue is to make all help obligatory and destroy individual moral freedom and choice. Why, Weinrib asks, is it more of a deprivation of liberty to be told that you have to call the police if you see a person in obvious danger than to be told that you must stop at a red light? The critics worry that a general duty of rescue might mean that a solvent person could be held civilly liable for refusing to supply the means of subsistence to someone who might otherwise starve. But what is the difference between this and our familiar system of social welfare programs?

More fundamentally, Weinrib tries to show that preoccupation with the infringement of liberty as an objection to a duty to rescue is misplaced. The values supporting our deep concern with individual liberty operate most visibly, Weinrib maintains, in the law of contract. Contract law assumes parties can reach agreements incurring only minimal transaction costs; that negotiations are possible and manageable; and that the parties occupy roughly equal bargaining positions. Where these conditions hold, and where the proposed arrangements are not otherwise illegal, the liberty of the parties to make such agreements as they see fit is accorded maximum scope. But, cautions Weinrib, there are situations—and rescue is one of them—where these "contract" values are conspicuously absent, so that a limited duty of "easy rescue," creating an affirmative obligation to aid another in an emergency where little or no inconvenience is posed for the rescuer, is consistent with liberty values. Weinrib tries to show that a duty of easy rescue could be explained and accounted for on either utilitarian or Kantian grounds.

Endnotes

[1] Mark Kelman, "Interpretive Construction in the Substantive Criminal Law," *Stanford Law Review*, Vol. 33 (1981), p. 637.

[2] *Buch v. Amory Mfg. Co.*, 44 A. 809 (1897).

McFall v. Shimp

No. 78-177711 (1978)
10th Penn. District, Allegheny County

Flaherty, [Judge], July 26, 1978. The Plaintiff, Robert McFall, suffers from a rare bone marrow disease and the prognosis for his survival is very dim, unless he receives a bone marrow transplant from a compatible donor. Finding a compatible donor is a very difficult task, and limited to a selection among close relatives. After a search and certain tests, it has been determined that only the Defendant is suitable as a donor. The defendant refuses to submit to the necessary transplant, and before the Court is a request for a preliminary injunction which seeks to compel the defendant to submit to further tests, and, eventually, the bone marrow transplant.

Although a diligent search has produced no authority, the Plantiff cites the ancient statute of King Edward I, St. Westminster 2, 13 Ed. I, c 24, pointing out, as is the case, that this Court is a successor to the English courts of Chancery and derives power from this statute, almost 700 years old. The question posed by the Plaintiff is that, in order to save the life of one of its members by the only means available, may society infringe upon one's absolute right to his "bodily security"?

The common law has consistently held to a rule which provides that one human being is under no legal compulsion to give aid or to take action to save that human being or to rescue. A great deal has been written regarding this rule which, on the surface, appears to be revolting in a moral sense. Introspection, however, will demonstrate that the rule is founded upon the very essence of our free society. It is noteworthy that counsel for the Plaintiff has cited authority which has developed in other societies in support of the Plaintiff's request in this instance. Our society, contrary to many others, has as its first principle, the respect for the individual, and that society and government exist to protect the individual from being invaded and hurt by another. Many societies adopt a contrary view which has the individual existing to serve the society as a whole. In preserving such a society as we have it is bound to happen that great moral conflicts will arise and will appear harsh in a given instance. In this case, the chancellor is being asked to force one member of society to undergo a medical procedure which would provide that part of that individual's body would be removed from him and given to another so that the other could live. Morally, this decision rests with the Defendant, and, in the view of the Court, the refusal of the Defendant is morally indefensible. For our law to *compel* the Defendant to submit to an intrusion of his body would change the very concept and principle upon which our society is founded. To do so would defeat the sanctity of the individual, and would impose a rule which would know no limits, and one could not imagine where the line would be drawn. This request is not to be compared with an action at law for damages, but rather is an action in equity before a Chancellor, which, in the ultimate, if granted, would require the [forcible] submission to the medical procedure. For a society, which respects the rights of *one* individual, to sink its teeth into the jugular vein or neck of one of its members and suck from it sustenance for *another* member, is revolting to our hard-wrought concepts of jurisprudence. [Forcible] extraction of living body tissue causes revulsion to the judicial mind. Such would raise the spectre of the swatstika and the inquisition, reminiscent of the horrors this portends.

This court makes no comment on the law regarding the Plaintiff's right in an action at law for damages, but has no alternative but to deny the requested equitable relief. An Order will be entered denying the request for a preliminary injunction.

The Case for a Duty to Rescue

ERNEST WEINRIB

From *The Yale Law Journal*, Vol. 90 (1980), pp. 247–293. Reprinted with permission of The Yale Law Journal Company and Fred B. Rothman & Company.

No observer would have any difficulty outlining the current state of the law throughout the common-law world regarding the duty to rescue. Except when the person endangered and the potential rescuer are linked in a special relationship, there is no such duty. This general rule rests on the law's distinction between the infliction of harm and the failure to prevent it. The distinction between misfeasance and nonfeasance in turn reflects deeply rooted intuitions about causation, and it has played a critical role in the development of the common-law notions of contract and tort and of the boundary between them. In large part because this distinction is so fundamental to the common law, the courts have uniformly refused to enunciate a general duty to rescue, even in the face of repeated criticisms that the absence of such a duty is callous. Nonetheless, recent developments, both judicial and academic, justify a reconsideration of the common-law position.

On the judicial side, many of the outposts of the doctrine that there is no general duty to rescue have fallen. Recognizing the meritoriousness of rescue and the desirability of encouraging it, the courts have increasingly accorded favorable treatment to injured rescuers. When a rescuer sues for compensation for his injuries, voluntary assumption of risk cannot be interposed as a defense, contributory negligence comes into play only if the plaintiff has been reckless, and a broad range of rescue attempts are deemed reasonably foreseeable by the defendant. Moreover, the courts have increased the number of special relationships that require one person to aid another in peril. These developments have made the general absence of a duty to rescue seem more eccentric and isolated. They have also raised the possibility that the general rule is in the process of being consumed and supplanted by the widening ambit of the exceptions and that the relationship between the general rule and the exceptions may be fundamentally incoherent.

On the academic side, recent writing has given new life to the debate on rescue. Professor Coase's approach, for example, implies that, from an economic point of view, the distinction between misfeasance and nonfeasance that supports the common-law rule is without significance. For Coase, the real issue is whether the alleged tortfeasor is to be allowed to impose the cost of his physical activity on the plaintiff, or whether the plaintiff, by his invocation of the legal process, will be allowed to harm the alleged tortfeasor.[1] For this approach, only the resulting distribution of costs matters; whether this result is accomplished by the defendant's operations in the physical world or by the plaintiff's operations in the legal world is not itself important. The refusal to accord a special recognition to the role of the court, and the assimilation of the court to an agency for the distribution of costs, has implications for the position of a person seeking judicial intervention. Because distinctions based on causation are obliterated in Coase's model of reciprocal harm, a plaintiff can claim no special consideration as the victim of another's action, and a defendant does not necessarily escape liability because the harm complained of was not caused by any of his actions. The causal nihilism of Coase's world,[2] which has its roots in utilitarian

thought extending back to Bentham,[3] thus subverts the misfeasance-nonfeasance distinction and changes the terms on which the rescue problem is discussed.

The most important critics of the economic approach to law have all in their various ways been concerned with rehabilitating causation as a central feature of law and morals.[4] It is the work of Professor Epstein,[5] among this group of scholars, that is of particular importance in connection with rescue. For Professor Epstein, causation is so pivotal a notion in a legal system that values liberty that it is not only *a* basis of liability in tort, but the *only* basis of liability in tort. This emphasis on causation has its roots in ethical thought leading back not to Bentham's utilitarianism but to Kant's injunction against treating other persons as means rather than as ends,[6] a principle that seems to presuppose an idea of acting upon others that does not encompass nonfeasance. Relying on this tradition for his critique of the economic approach, Epstein has argued that the absence of a general duty to rescue is not an unfortunate fossil of a more barbaric age but is a morally defensible thread in the overall fabric of the common law.

Critics of the common-law position have generally proposed that the courts ought to recognize a duty to effect what might be termed an easy rescue, that is, a duty that would arise whenever one person is caught in a dangerous situation that another can alleviate at no significant cost to himself. The requirements of emergency and lack of prejudice distinguish the proposed obligation to rescue from the usual tort duties connected with misfeasance: the latter duties can be present in routine situations and can impose considerable costs on those who are subject to them. The recent judicial and academic developments bear upon this proposal in diverse ways. The tort decisions that recognize the distinctive merit of the rescuer stand in easy harmony with the proposed duty. The academic writings, on the other hand, seem incompatible with a duty of easy rescue. The Coasian framework would reject the restrictions on the duty because these restrictions acknowledge the fundamental character of the distinction between misfeasance and nonfeasance. For Epstein, by contrast, the difference between nonfeasance and misfeasance is fundamental, but the chasm between these two concepts is so deep that only duties respecting misfeasance can be accommodated within the common law of torts. The proposed duty to rescue thus seems to be unacceptable both from an instrumentalist and from a Kantian point of view.

This article sets forth an argument in favor of a judicially created duty to effect an easy rescue. Because any special principle about rescue presupposes the distinction between misfeasance and nonfeasance, section I delineates this distinction and shows how it informs the policies behind the general common-law rule on rescue and some of the special-relationship exceptions. Section II sets forth and analyzes the arguments that have been offered, especially by Professor Epstein, against a generalized legal duty to rescue. This analysis, having highlighted the legal and ethical issues central to the argument against such a duty, clears the ground for the argument for the recognition by the common law of a duty of easy rescue. Section III argues that our moral intuitions are reflected in a coherent and growing pattern in the common law, a pattern indicating that the understanding of liberty in a market society does not preclude a legal obligation to rescue. Finally, section IV turns to the philosophic aspects of this pattern; it argues that a general duty of easy rescue can find support either on Benthamite-utilitarian or Kantian-deontological grounds. The article argues, in sum, that a duty of easy rescue would strengthen an already-broad pattern of common-law principles and that such a duty can plausibly be justified within both of the ethical traditions that inform the common-law system.

I. The Distinction Between Misfeasance and Nonfeasance

In his classic essay of 1908, Professor Francis H. Bohlen pointed out that "misfeasance differs from nonfeasance in two respects; in the character of the conduct complained of, and second, in the nature of the detriment suffered in consequence thereof."[7] With respect to the first difference, Bohlen asserted that the distinction between active and passive misconduct is, though in practice difficult to draw, in theory obvious. About the second difference Bohlen was more specific. In cases of misfeasance, the victim's position is changed for the worse through the creation of a negative quantity in the form of a positive loss or new harm. In cases of nonfeasance, on the other hand, there is merely a failure to benefit the victim, which is a loss only in the sense that a positive quantity is not added.

Bohlen stated these distinctions in skeletal form only, without providing the elaboration they require. For instance, the use of positive and negative quantities to explain the difference in the nature of the detriment presupposes not only a computational ledger but also a baseline with reference to which the computation is performed. Bohlen seems to have assumed that the baseline was the victim's position immediately prior to the incident that gives rise to the litigation, as when the victim of an automobile accident complains of the loss of a previously healthy limb. Since Bohlen's time, however, tort law has come to permit the imposition of liability for injuries that are not most naturally described as the loss of something actually possessed at an early time. A plaintiff, for example, can recover for economic injury not only when he has lost funds that he previously had, but also when the loss represents a potential profit that he had not yet realized. Similarly, when an infant sues for prenatal injuries, recovery does not depend on whether the injury was inflicted on a limb that was already formed or whether the injury prevented the formation of a limb.

Bohlen's other distinction, that concerned with the character of the misconduct, also needs elaboration. Bohlen himself acknowledged one of the problems when he pointed to the practical difficulties of characterizing behavior having elements of both active and passive misconduct. An illustration of this borderland situation is the old case of *Newton v. Ellis*,[8] in which the plaintiff sued for injuries received at night when passing his carriage by a hole in the highway that the defendant had excavated but had failed to light. The court viewed the digging of the hole and the failure to light it as one complex act rather than as two separate events, one an act, the other a failure to act. Bohlen would have agreed, but his distinction does not explain why one should prefer one characterization of the situation to the other. For principled use by courts, the unelaborated distinction between active and passive conduct is inadequate.[9]

To begin elucidating the distinction between misfeasance and nonfeasance, consider the following fairly clear and extreme paradigmatic situations:

A. An automobile driver (defendant) fails to apply his brakes in time, and a pedestrian (plaintiff) is thereby hurt.

B. One person (defendant) sees another (plaintiff) drowning in a pool of water and refuses to toss him an easily available rope.

In both cases there has been a failure to act: in A, a failure to press the brakes; in B, a failure to toss the rope. Yet A and B are not both instances of nonfeasance. On an intuitive understanding of causation, the defendant in A caused the injury, whereas the defendant in B did not. On one of tort law's prime understandings of causation, however, that conclusion is problematic. In both A and B, the defendants are but-for causes of injury: neither the injury in A nor the drowning in B would have happened had the defendants not failed to act in the specified ways.

The but-for test of factual causation first focuses on the time at which the defendant failed to act to prevent harm to the plaintiff, then compares the actual course of events after that time with a hypothetical course of events for the same subsequent period. Within that temporal framework, the structures of A and B are identical. What differentiates A from B is the course of events prior to the starting point. In B, there was no significant interaction between the plaintiff and the defendant in that earlier period: when encountered by the defendant, the plaintiff was already exposed to danger. In A, by contrast, the defendant, in the antecedent period, played a part in the creation of the very danger that he subsequently failed to abate. To treat A as identical to B is thus to start *in medias res*. Situations like A, in which misfeasance masquerades as nonfeasance, have aptly been categorized as "pseudo-nonfeasance."[10]

Action can be variously described, and pseudo-nonfeasance is one instance of the technique of distorting the description by focusing on only one of the phases of an action. This technique was presented in *Newton v. Ellis*, where the defendant argued that the gravamen of the suit was the failure to put up a light rather than the digging of the hole in the highway. This argument would have equated the excavator of the hole with the rest of the world by confining judicial attention to a phase subsequent to that in which the defendant established a unique relationship with the particular hole and thereby with all passing drivers. Although not all courts are sensitive to the dynamics of pseudo-nonfeasance, the court in this case was alert to the distorting technique and insisted upon looking at the excavator's behavior in its entirety.

The difference between real nonfeasance and pseudo-nonfeasance can be formulated by transforming the but-for test so that it attends not to the actual injury but to the risk of injury. In this view, situation B is a case of real nonfeasance because the risk of drowning existed independent of the defendant's presence or absence; the defendant's part in the materialization of the risk has no bearing on this fact. Situation A, by contrast, is a case of pseudo-nonfeasance because the defendant's driving of his car was a factual cause of the plaintiff's exposure to the risk of the injury that he suffered. In *Newton v. Ellis*, for example, the danger of falling into the excavator's hole would not have existed but for the defendant's having dug it.

Distinguishing misfeasance from nonfeasance on the basis of the defendant's participation in the creation of the risk is adequate not only for the extreme situations of A and B but also for more complicated situations. In particular, because this formulation of the distinction focuses on the defendant's having had some role in the creation of the risk, and not on the quality of that role, the defendant's fault in creating the risk is irrelevant to the decision whether a case is one of nonfeasance or not. Fault, of course, is relevant to the decision whether the defendant is liable, but the fault need not attach in the phase of risk creation; rather, it might be found in the subsequent phase, when the defendant failed to abate the risk. Consider the following situations, in which the faulty conduct at issue is intentional:

C. An automobile driver (defendant) intentionally drives onto another's (plaintiff's) foot and leaves the car there.

D. An automobile driver (defendant) without fault drives onto another's (plaintiff's) foot, but when he becomes aware of his action, he refuses to remove his car.

In D, the defendant might argue that the court should assess his conduct only from the time of his refusal to move the car, and that from that perspective, the car's position on the plaintiff's foot was an unfortunate happenstance for which he was not at fault. This argument, like the one put forward in situation A, equates the defendant with all bystanders by ignoring the distinctive role of the defendant in bringing about the tortious contact between car and foot. The defendants in both C and D participated in the creation of the plaintiff's peril and intended the consequent harm to the plaintiff. The only difference is one of sequence: in D the intent followed, whereas in C it preceded, the arrival of the automobile on the plaintiff's foot. The law recognizes this difference by refusing in D to impose liability on the defendant for harm caused during the period between the initial contact and the formation of his intention to continue it.

The same analysis can be applied to cases of negligence. In *Oke v. Weide Transport Ltd. and Carra*,[11] the defendant driver, without fault, knocked down a traffic sign, embedding the metal post in the ground. The next day, another driver drove over the post and was impaled. The plaintiff alleged that the defendant was negligent in failing to report the dangerous road condition to the police. On the analysis of nonfeasance under consideration, this case is essentially similar to *Newton v. Ellis*, which also concerned a failure by the defendant to abate a dangerous highway condition that he had created. The only difference is that in *Newton*, the defendant intentionally created the condition requiring abatement, whereas in *Oke* the defendant created the peril without fault. The defendant in *Oke* is exempt from liability for damage to the sign, of course, but with respect to liability to the injured driver, his position is identical to that of the defendant in *Newton*: each was negligent in failing to alleviate a danger that he himself had created. To ignore the defendant's role in creating the peril would be to equate the position of the defendant with that of any other motorist who happened to pass by and notice the danger. Those members of the court in *Oke* who considered the nonfeasance issue explicitly refused to make this equation.

Participation by the defendant in the creation of the risk, even if such participation is innocent, is thus the crucial factor in distinguishing misfeasance from nonfeasance. The law's acknowledgement of the importance of this factor is clear in some contexts, oblique in others. For instance, some statutes require a driver who is involved in an accident to offer assistance to its victims regardless of his fault in causing the accident. Courts also frequently hold occupiers of land liable for failure to abate the dangers to which their use of the land has innocently exposed others, at least where the injured party is an invitee. In addition, the common law now imposes a duty on the captain of a vessel to rescue a sailor or passenger who falls overboard. For many years, the law exonerated the captain who neglected to rescue as long as the need to rescue arose without his fault. Recently, however, courts have recognized that the very act of taking a person out in one's boat constitutes participation in the creation of the danger of drowning. The resulting duty to rescue is imposed only on the owner or operator of the boat because of this participation and because of the passenger's necessary dependence on him. The duty does not extend to other parties who might be in a position to rescue a person from a danger that arose independently of them: to impose such a duty would be to cross the line from misfeasance to nonfeasance.

The analysis of nonfeasance in terms of risk creation also explains why, even though a risk may have arisen independently of a defendant, he is responsible for aggravation of the danger, that is, for substantially increasing the likelihood that it will materialize in harm. By diminishing the ability of the victim or of others to abate the danger, the defendant, though innocent of the original danger, must account for the increased risk. Indeed, the defendant's action can occur before the original risk even begins to materialize, as when an insurance agent neglects to arrange for the negotiated coverage. Although the inducing of reliance is the most usual example of aggravating an independent risk, it does not exhaust the category. Cutting off the victim from the aid that third parties might naturally be inclined to give is as much misfeasance as lulling the victim into a false sense of security and decreasing his ability to remove himself from peril. Although it may be nonfeasance to refuse to rescue a drowning person whose predicament arose independently, it is misfeasance to hide the rope that others might toss out to him.

II. *Arguments Against a Duty to Rescue*

Both courts and commentators generally consider it morally outrageous that the defense of nonfeasance can deny endangered persons a legal right to easy rescue. Yet the defense is taken to be so basic to the law and so compelling that it overrides the moral perceptions of the judges and the shared attitudes of the community. This in itself is a tribute to the power of the idea of nonfeasance. Few legal concepts, however, are applied in an absolute or monolithic manner. The purpose of this section is to explore the justifications that can be offered in support of the common-law position, and thus to discover the limits of the nonfeasance idea.

The most explicit and elaborate justification of the absence of a duty to rescue—almost the only such attempt in the legal literature—appears in an important and ambitious article by Professor Richard Epstein.[12] Epstein's work challenges the conception of tort law as a body of law embodying utilitarian and economic assumptions and seeks to develop "a normative theory of torts that takes into account common sense notions of individual responsibility."[13] In his view, the idea that one is responsible for whatever harm one causes is the fundamental moral principle in the law of torts: unless one of a few specified excuses can be invoked, liability should follow from a finding of causation of harm. Thus strict liability should replace negligence as the dominant notion in tort law. More importantly for the rescue situation, absence of causation renders one immune from liability; in particular, there should be no duty to abate a danger one did not cause.

Epstein's conception of responsibility purports to reflect common morality in its attention both to the effects on other persons of an individual's conduct and to the motive with which actions are performed.

> [M]ost systems of conventional morality try to distinguish between those circumstances in which a person should be compelled to act for the benefit of his fellow man, and those cases where he should be allowed to do so only if prompted by the appropriate motives. To put the point in other terms, the distinction is taken between that conduct which is required and that which, so to speak, is beyond the call of duty. If that distinction is accepted as part of a common morality, then the argument in favor of the good Samaritan rule is that it, better than any possible alternatives, serves to mark off the first class of activities from the second. Compensation for harm caused can be demanded in accordance with the principles of strict liability. Failure to aid those in need can invoke at most moral censure on the ground that the person so accused did not voluntarily conform his conduct to some "universal" principle of justice. The

rules of causation, which create liability in the first case, deny it in the second. It may well be that the conduct of individuals who do not aid fellow men is under some circumstances outrageous, but it does not follow that a legal system that does not enforce a duty to aid is outrageous as well.[14]

This passage is problematic in a number of ways. First, the conclusion that there is no obligation to rescue under any circumstances seems to conflict with Epstein's general purpose to develop a normative theory corresponding to common-sense morality. Criticism of the common-law position on rescue, after all, rests on the perception that, as a matter of inarticulate common sense, it is wrong for one person to stand by as another suffers an injury that could easily be prevented. Moreover, Epstein concedes that the behavior of such defendants is "under some circumstances outrageous." There is a paradox in concluding, as Epstein does, that the legal doctrine in question, reprobated though it is, is actually in accord with common-sense notions of morality.

Second, as a defense of the common-law position on rescue, Epstein's single-minded concern with causation may prove too much. Although there is no general requirement of rescue at common law, rescue is required if any of several special relationships exists between the parties. Epstein's defense of the common-law position on rescue poses the dilemma of abandoning that part of the position requiring rescue in special circumstances or acknowledging that tort liability is not based solely on causation.

These criticisms of Epstein's argument point to a lack of coherence among the argument's premises, actual conclusions, and purported conclusion. The argument, however, is also somewhat obscure. Epstein's argument that the absence of a duty to rescue at common law is consistent with moral principles is open to any of several interpretations. It might be a denial that there is a moral obligation to rescue, even though failure to rescue arouses "moral censure" and outrage, because rescue falls in the class of conduct that is "beyond the call of duty." Alternatively, the argument might be conceding that there is a moral obligation to rescue but denying that the creation of a parallel legal duty is justified. Moreover, this second interpretation might suppose either that, as a matter of principle, a chasm exists between the ethical and the legal realms, or that the transformation of this particular ethical duty into a legal one is inappropriate. An assessment of Epstein's argument must begin by examining the far-reaching issues raised by these various interpretations.

Epstein seeks to justify the absence of a common-law duty to rescue by invoking the distinction in common morality between acts that are required and acts that are beyond the call of duty.[15] This distinction has been the subject of much attention in moral and legal philosophy—for example, in Lon Fuller's development of a contrast between the morality of duty and the morality of aspiration.[16] Acts that are beyond the call of duty demand of the agent extraordinary heroism or sacrifice, and "while we praise their performance, we do not condemn their non-performance."[17] The very fact that a failure to rescue may evoke moral censure, as Epstein concedes, is a strong indication that the rescue was obligatory and not supererogatory. The distinction that Epstein endorses therefore should not lead him to a simple denial of any duty to rescue; rather it should lead to efforts to structure the duty to avoid requiring of the rescuer the heroism or sacrifice that characterizes the morality of aspiration. In fact, all the proposals of the last two centuries for a legal duty to rescue have been structured in this way.

Epstein thus cannot sustain the position that failure to effect an easy rescue is not immoral. His remarks can alternatively be interpreted as conceding that rescue is a moral requirement but denying that it should be a legal one. That he probably intends this view is indicated by his comment that although failure to aid a person may be outrageous, "it does not follow that a legal system that does not enforce a duty to aid is outrageous as well." This attempt to separate morality and legality may in turn reflect any of the following three notions: that transforming this particular moral duty into a legal duty is administratively difficult, that legal duties are generally disjoint from moral ones, or that there is some reason of principle that disqualifies this particular moral duty from being a legal duty.

The first of these alternatives is frequently invoked. The adherents of this position point to the difficulty of determining who among the many potential rescuers should be held liable. This point can also be made in terms of fairness: singling out one from a group of equally culpable nonrescuers is unfairly to differentiate among like cases. Why

these difficulties should be of decisive weight, however, is hard to see. Even if there are many possible rescuers, the difficulties are no less surmountable than are those in cases of negligence involving many tortfeasors. Though potentially more complicated on average, the rules could be the same: the victim has a right to only one recovery, and all tortfeasors are liable to the victim, but they are entitled to contribution among themselves. The device of contribution, moreover, might be invoked by the defendant to prevent his being unfairly singled out: because the purpose of contribution is to prevent the unjust enrichment that would otherwise accrue when one party is forced by law to discharge an obligation to which others are also subject, a defendant would be able to claim contribution from other potential rescuers.

The second interpretation of Epstein's argument, that moral and legal duties are in principle separate, is the most comprehensive of the three. Under this approach, the immorality of not rescuing has no bearing on whether the omission should be legally condemned. Although this proposition seems to raise basic and long-standing jurisprudential questions, it does not raise the ancient dispute between natural-law theory and positive-law theory. An adherent of natural-law theory can more readily pass between the moral and the legal domains, but the positivist too, though perhaps more skeptical about the feasibility of discovering moral duties, can approve the creation of a legal duty to parallel a moral one. For the legal positivist, law may have any content, moral or immoral, and particular moral duties can be made into legal ones.

More affirmatively, the role of the common-law judge centrally involves making moral duties into legal ones. The disqualification or moral considerations from the judge's decision would leave him with very sparse resources. Formalist reasoning from preexisting rules is indeterminate in many cases. Moreover, if the system is consistent, no rules, including the premises for such formalist reasoning, could have moral dimensions. The first case in any new line of development could not be justified on legal grounds alone; yet it would be decisive for all posterity. Indeed, it is difficult to imagine how a judge in a case of first impression would proceed. Conversely, moral duties not only provide a basis for judicial justification; they also provide a minimal standard for legal legitimacy. If any legal obligations are legitimate, legal obligations that duplicate preexisting moral ones must be. The only grounds for opposing the imposition of such a legal duty would be the general one that law should not coerce.

The third interpretation of Epstein's position postulates a disjunction in principle not between moral and legal duties generally, but between the particular moral duty to effect an easy rescue and its proposed legal analogue. Such a position combines an admission that rescue is morally required, a recognition that legal duties may justifiably be created to parallel moral ones, and a principled argument that the moral duty to rescue is beyond the justifiable scope of state action. This position has a long history in both the utilitarian and non-utilitarian traditions, though Epstein, who does not explicitly take this position, makes no mention of its historic roots. Because the early statements form parts of comprehensive legal philosophies, and are not merely, as in Epstein's case, possible interpretations of murkily expressed reflections on the common law of torts, it is worth examining the eighteenth-century expositions and their relations to Epstein's position.

The principal utilitarian adherent to this position was the proto-anarchist William Godwin. Godwin's comprehensive view of morality required everyone to devote all of their resources, energies, and opportunities to the assistance of others in order to maximize the utility of all.[18] His position on rescue was that there was a moral duty to rescue even when it required extreme personal sacrifice.[19] This extreme view of individuals' moral duty, however, was matched by an equally narrow view of the role of law. In Godwin's ideal society, individuals would do their duties without any compulsion from the law, which would respect each person's right to private judgment, a right that was essential for the development of the person's moral capacities. Even in contemporary society, which was not ripe for the dissolution of government, this right to private judgment determined the scope of law. In this society, the government's function was to ensure that the exercise of each individual's private judgment did not intrude upon his neighbor's equal right to private judgment.[20] The government could legitimately prevent one person from harming another, because harm impaired the exercise of private judgment; but it could not legitimately force one person to benefit another, even though such benefaction might be morally required, because such coercion would violate the right to private judgment.

Godwin would evidently have agreed with Epstein that the moral outrageousness of a failure to act should not entail a legal duty to act. Yet Godwin's argument is not very secure. Particularly questionable is the place of the right to private judgment in Godwin's utilitarian framework. Rights are always problematic for utilitarians, and Godwin's right to private judgment is no exception. Godwin does not mean that this right is immune to the utilitarian calculus, but rather, that regard for it in the calculus will lead to the utilitarian goal of general happiness, and that it can therefore be suspended whenever utility requires.[21] The right is accordingly vulnerable to differing assessments of utility. Thus evaluated, Godwin's view that man's moral development requires the law's abstention from interference in private judgment is implausible. Both Plato and Aristotle disputed it;[22] and although the idea that legal action can effectively and legitimately promote virtue has not been as popular in the last two hundred years as it had been in the previous two thousand, it still has considerable force. Moreover, in the context of rescue, the immense gain in utility through the saving of life may plausibly be thought to outweigh the disadvantage of a small moral retardation inherent in legal compulsion; Bentham and Mill, at least, thought so.[23]

The most important non-utilitarian adherent to the view that the moral duty to aid another did not justify the creation of a parallel legal duty was Immanuel Kant. Morality, for Kant, was the internal phenomenon of a person freely fulfilling a duty that, using pure practical reason, he legislates for himself; and practical reason requires the duty to give assistance to others. Law, by contrast, coerces individuals by regulating external action. Although law and ethics may coincidentally legislate about the same conduct, law cannot make a person virtuous: virtue is by its nature indifferent to external compulsion.[24] Yet positive law can be just. To do so, it must reflect some formal and universal principle, and because positive law acts only upon the external freedom of the person, not on his internal freedom as a morally autonomous agent, justice, for Kant, was "the aggregate of those conditions under which the will of one person can be cojoined with the will of another in accordance with a universal law of freedom."[25]

For Kant, as for Godwin, freedom was central. But Kant reached a position similar to Godwin's without the utilitarian grounding that made Godwin's position vulnerable to differing predictive assessments. Acts of misfeasance may properly be prohibited by positive law because they cannot co-exist with the freedom of everyone as defined by a universal law; but beneficence, of which rescue is a part, was beyond the scope of justice. Either acts of beneficence were responses to specific needs and desires, or else they followed from a general policy of benevolence that had been adopted by the bene-factor. If the former, Kant thought, they were not a manifestation of morality because specific desires and needs cannot be the subjects of a universal law. If the latter, they were a manifestation of mo-rality because the adoption of such a policy was required by pure practical reason; but a policy of benevolence was an internal matter beyond the reach of the external constraints of positive law.

An objection to the artificiality of this distinc-tion between misfeasance and nonfeasance would point out that the liberty of an endangered person is equally limited by misfeasance and nonfeasance. For Kant, however, beneficence was special be-cause it is the subject of an imperfect duty—that is, a duty that varies according to specific circum-stances, so that "the law cannot specify precisely what and how much one's actions should do to-ward the obligatory end."[26] Kant viewed the moral duty to effect an easy rescue in an emergency and the moral duty to help the needy as indistinguish-able; both are merely instances of an ethically re-quired policy of beneficence not susceptible to a legal duty. Because no particular action can be re-quired in many circumstances—although there may be a duty to give charity, no particular person is required to give any particular amount to any particular charitable cause—the omission of any particular action cannot be considered a legal wrong.

At first glance, Kant's analysis does not seem to apply to the legal obligation to rescue that is usually put forward. A duty to effect an easy rescue in an emergency seems to have the specificity that Kant's imperfect duty of beneficence lacks. In fact, Kant's rejection of a legal duty can apply only if the apparent difference between the rescue proposal and the duty of beneficence can be proven illusory. Here Epstein provides the argument suggested by the Kantian analysis.

In his defense of the common-law position, Epstein argues that confining the duty to rescue to situations of emergency and lack of inconvenience would not be feasible. For Epstein, as for Kant and Godwin, freedom is a central value; indeed, he believes that "the first task of the law of torts is to define the boundaries of individual liberty."[27] If the proposed duty is admitted, he argues, no prin-cipled basis could be found to prevent unaccept-able infringements of individual liberty. Charitable contributions in amounts dependent on the do-nor's wealth would become compulsory if it were substantially certain that without them someone would die. Moreover, because the inconvenience to the reluctant rescuer could be eliminated by the victim's offer of objectively suitable reimburse-ment, the rescuer would find himself coerced to exchange the means of salvation for compensation. Once such forced exchanges are required, says Ep-stein, there will be no way to distinguish liberty from obligation or contract from tort.

This argument is the most powerful objection that can be made to the judicial creation and en-forcement of a duty to effect an easy rescue. The argument does not merely assert the priority of liberty: the rescue proposal's emergency and con-venience limitations, which are absent in misfea-sance situations, reflect that priority. Rather, Ep-stein's argument is that no principles that respect the priority of liberty can distinguish between res-cue and beneficence. The next two sections of this article explore and respond to this argument.

III. *Common-Law Foundations for a Duty of Easy Rescue*

To the extent that an issue of interpersonal action is not made the subject of a tort or criminal duty, it is remitted to the operation of the law of contract. If neither tort law nor criminal law imposes a duty to rescue, the relations between rescuer and victim are left entirely to the contractual arrangements between them. Absent any duty, a victim cannot conscript a rescuer's services; he must purchase them under the usual contractual mechanisms.

Contract law gives practical application to a market society's reliance on consensual private or-dering, and thus provides the principal embodi-ment in the law of the ideal of individual liberty. It both gives individuals the means to exercise their liberty and restricts liberty where, for either prac-tical or ideological reasons, the circumstances are not appropriate for its exercise. In particular, the law of contract presupposes a certain social equality of those who engage in the bargaining process. In thus giving shape to the ideal of liberty in its application to specific circumstances, contract law can be looked to for evidence of the extent to which, and the situations in which, the law prizes individual liberty.

To the extent that contract law reveals principles that distinguish a duty to rescue from a more thoroughgoing duty of beneficence, it provides a response to Professor Epstein's challenge to find a principled basis for imposing a duty to rescue that respects the law's ideal of liberty.

. . .

The relationship between tort obligation and contract values also provides a way of circumscribing the duty to rescue and thus of answering the formidable objections to recognizing such a duty. The responses depend in part on the fact that the duty is to be created and enforced by the judiciary, not by another branch of government. One of Professor Epstein's objections, it will be recalled, was that the imposition of a duty of easy rescue would be impossible to confine within acceptable limits: the wealthy, for example, would be compelled to make charitable contributions to alleviate hardships in emergencies. This result would be unacceptable in our legal system because it would make the wealth of the parties a consideration in the litigation and would thus confound corrective and distributive justice; it would transform the system of adjudicating private claims into an administrative agency of the welfare state. The duty of easy rescue, however, can be distinguished from the broader duty of beneficence. In the rescue context, the resource to be expended (time and effort directed at aiding the victim) cannot be traded on the market, and no administrative scheme could be established to ensure the socially desirable level of benefits. In the charity context, by contrast, the resource to be expended (money) can be traded on the market, and an administrative scheme could be established not only to ensure the socially desirable level of benefits but to do so at a lower social cost than could a judicially enforced duty in tort, or so the welfare state assumes. In other words, in Epstein's example of charitable contributions, but not in the rescue situation, there is a societal interest in preserving contractual liberty, and an administrative solution is preferable to a judicial one. There is

thus a principled reason why a duty of easy rescue need not lead to a general duty of charity or beneficence.

. . .

A legal duty to rescue would involve the recognition of an obligation to confer a benefit on a person whose plight is not the result of one's own actions. The traditional objection to the judicial enunciation of such a duty has been that coerced service for another interferes with personal liberty. The burden of this section has been to show that, to the extent that the notion of personal liberty is reflected in the values associated with liberty of contract, the imposition of a duty to effect an easy rescue in situations where such values are absent does not significantly violate personal liberty. Such a legal requirement of rescue would correspond to existing restrictions on the power to contract. It remains for the final section of this article to argue that the two principal philosophical traditions in our legal culture both provide affirmative arguments for the creation of the duty. Together with the observations that the special-relationship exceptions seem to be eroding the general rule and that even the defenders of the general rule admit the existence of a moral duty of easy rescue, this argument suggests that the refusal of the common law to impose a duty of easy rescue is an anomaly that can and should be corrected.

IV. *Philosophical Foundations for a Duty of Easy Rescue*

This article has been concerned with the interplay between our moral intuitions and various aspects of the legal structure. The distinction between misfeasance and nonfeasance was accepted as a suitable starting point that required elucidation rather than justification. Also accepted was the intuition that failure to effect an easy rescue was morally reprehensible. From these premises, the article criticized arguments supporting the legal order's refusal to reflect the moral intuition about rescue, and argued that a legal duty of easy rescue would fit into a coherent pattern formed by a miscellany of doctrines in the common law of contract and of tort.

Having eliminated objections to a legal duty of easy rescue, and shown its compatibility with existing doctrines, the final section of the article puts forth arguments for the adoption of such a duty. To this end, the section attempts to give philosophical specificity to the moral sentiment that condemns a failure to effect an easy rescue. Attention is devoted to the two traditions of moral philosophy represented by Kant and by Bentham, for those traditions have dominated efforts of the last two centuries to explicate and systematize our moral notions. If the law is to be "the witness and external deposit of our moral life,"[28] the demonstration that both traditions provide support for a duty of easy rescue implies that the absence of a duty to rescue at common law is an aberration that should be corrected.

Consideration of the utilitarian approach towards rescue must begin with Jeremy Bentham's thought on the problem. "[I]n cases where the person is in danger," he asked, "why should it not be made the duty of every man to save another from mischief, when it can be done without prejudicing himself . . . ?"[29] Bentham supported the implicit answer to this question with several illustrations: using water at hand to quench a fire in a woman's headdress; moving a sleeping drunk whose face is in a puddle; warning a person about to carry a lighted candle into a room strewn with gunpowder. Bentham clearly had in mind a legal duty that would be triggered by the combination of the victim's emergency and the absence of inconvenience to the rescuer—that is, by the features of most of the proposed reforms requiring rescue. Unfortunately, the rhetorical question was the whole of Bentham's argument for his position. With this question, Bentham appealed directly to his reader's moral intuition; he did not show how his proposed duty can be derived through his distinctive felicific calculus.

Can one supply the Benthamite justification that Bentham himself omitted? Because the avoidance of injury or death obviously contributes to the greatest happiness of the greatest number, the difficulties revolve not around the basic requirement of rescue but around the limitations placed upon that requirement by the notions of emergency and absence of inconvenience. Those limitations have no parallel with respect to participation in putting others at risk; they apply only in cases of nonfeasance. Indeed, Bentham's comments come in a section of his Introduction to the

Principles of Morals and Legislation that distinguishes beneficence (increasing another's happiness) from probity (forbearing to diminish another's happiness). Yet Bentham had earlier contended that the distinction between acts of omission and acts of commission was of no significance.[30] The utilitarian's only concern is that an individual bring about a situation that results in a higher surplus of pleasure over pain than would any of the alternative situations that his actions could produce. Consequences are important; how they are reached is not. The distinction between nonfeasance and misfeasance has no place in this theory, and neither would the rescue duty's emergency or convenience limitations, which apply only after that distinction is made.

One solution to the apparent inconsistency between the rescue limitations and Benthamite theory's regard only for consequences is to drop the conditions of emergency and convenience as limitations on the duty to rescue. The position could be taken that there is an obligation to rescue whenever rescuing would result in greater net happiness than not rescuing. This principle, it is important to observe, cannot really be a principle about rescuing as that concept is generally understood. As a matter of common usage, a rescue presupposes the existence of an emergency, of a predicament that poses danger of greater magnitude and imminence than one ordinarily encounters. The proposed principle, however, requires no emergency to trigger a duty to act. The principle, in fact, is one of beneficence, not rescue, and should be formulated more generally to require providing aid whenever it will yield greater net happiness than not providing aid.

Eliminating the limitations regarding emergency and convenience might transform a requirement of rescue conceived along utilitarian lines into a requirement of perfect and general altruism. This demand of perfect altruism would be undesirable for several reasons. First, it would encourage the obnoxious character known to the law as the officious intermeddler. Also, its imposition of a duty of continual saintliness and heroism is unrealistic. Moreover, it would overwhelm the relationships founded on friendship and love as well as the distinction between the praiseworthy and the required; it would thereby obscure some efficient ways, in the utilitarian's eyes, of organizing and stimulating beneficence. Finally, the most fundamentally, it would be self-defeating. The requirement of aid assumes that there is some other person who has at least a minimal core of personhood as well as projects of his own that the altruist can further. In a society of perfect and general altruism, however, any potential recipient of aid would himself be an altruist, who must, accordingly, subordinate the pursuit of his own projects to the rendering of aid to others. No one could claim for his own projects the priority that would provide others with a stable object of their altruistic ministrations. Each person would continually find himself obligated to attempt to embrace a phantom.

Although the utilitarian principle that requires the provision of aid whenever it will result in greater net happiness than failure to aid easily slips into the pure-altruism duty, it need not lead to so extreme a position. The obvious alternative interpretation of the principle is that aid is not obligatory whenever the costs to one's own projects outweigh the benefits to the recipient's. This interpretation avoids the embracing-of-phantoms objection to pure altruism, but it is subject to all the other criticisms of the purer theory. Because the cost-benefit calculus is so difficult to perform in particular instances, the duty would remain ill-defined. In many cases, therefore, it would encourage the officious intermeddler, seem unrealistically to require saintliness, overwhelm friendship and love, and obliterate the distinction between the praiseworthy and the required. Moreover, the vagueness of the duty would lead many individuals unhappily and inefficiently to drop their own projects in preference for those of others.

A different formulation of the rescue duty is needed to harness and temper the utilitarian impulses toward altruism and to direct them more precisely toward an intelligible goal. One important weakness of a too-generally beneficent utilitarianism is that it tempts one to consider only the immediate consequences of particular acts, and not the longer term consequences, the most important of which are the expectations generated that such acts will continue. If, as the classical utilitarians believed, the general happiness is advanced when people engage in productive activities that are of value to others, the harm done by a duty of general beneficence, in either version discussed above, would override its specific benefits. The deadening of industry resulting from both reliance on beneficence and devotion to beneficence would in the long run be an evil greater than the countenancing of individual instances of unfulfilled needs or

wants. "In all cases of helping," wrote John Stuart Mill, in a passage concerned only with the reliance costs,

> there are two sets of consequences to be considered: the consequences of the assistance and the consequences of relying on the assistance. The former are generally beneficial, but the latter, for the most part, injurious. . . . There are few things for which it is more mischievous that people should rely on the habitual aid of others than for the means of subsistence, and unhappily there is no lesson which they more easily learn.[31]

Utilitarianism can use the notion of reliance to restrict the requirement of beneficence. If an act of beneficence would tend to induce reliance on similar acts, it should be avoided. If the act of beneficence does not have this tendency, it should be performed as long as the benefit produced is greater than the cost of performance. In the latter case, there are no harmful effects on industry flowing from excessive reliance to outweigh the specific benefits. This rule can account for Bentham's restriction of the duty to rescue to situations of emergency. People do not regularly expose themselves to extraordinary dangers in reliance on the relief that may be available if the emergency materializes, and only a fool would deliberately court a peril because he or others had previously been rescued from a similar one. As Sidgwick put it, an emergency rescue "will have no bad effect on the receiver, from the exceptional nature of the emergency."[32] Furthermore, an emergency is not only a desperate situation; it is also a situation that deviates from society's usual pattern. The relief of an emergency is therefore unlikely to induce reliance on the assistance of others in normal conditions. The abnormality of emergencies also means that rescuers can confidently pursue their own projects under normal circumstances. The motive for industry that Bentham located in each person's needs is not undermined by extraordinary and isolated events.

The role of emergency in the utilitarian obligation to rescue corresponds to, and illuminates, the definition of a legal duty to rescue by reference to the absence of contract values, as set out in the previous section. Utilitarian philosophy and the concept of the market are closely related. Both regard individuals as maximizers of their own happiness, and both see the use of contracts to acquire and to exchange property as conducive to the public good. Contract law's refusal to enforce certain transactions sets them apart from the usual structure of relationships, in which the satisfaction of the parties' needs and desires can legitimately serve as a stimulus to exchange. The person who sees a member of his own family in difficulty and the police officer who notices a hazard on the highway may not act as ordinary members of the market with respect to those endangered. Those pockets of contractual nonenforcement are sufficiently isolated that they are unlikely to be generalized: they will not generate a widespread reliance on assistance or sense of obligation to assist in settings where market exchanges are permitted and common.

An emergency is similar. Contract values are absent in such a situation because the assistance required is of such a kind that it cannot be purchased on ordinary commercial terms. Suspension of contract values in an emergency will not result in a general deadening of individual industry; the utilitarian can therefore confine his calculus to the specific consequences of the rescue. The denial of relief to the Southwark squatters[33] is a case in point. The desperate situation there was a consequence of poverty and not an extraordinary condition that deviated from the ordinary pattern of contemporary existence. The utilitarian must be concerned in that situation that judicially coercing individual assistance to the poor will generate a reliance whose harmful effects will, in the long run and across society as a whole, outweigh the benefits of the specific assistance.

Bentham's intuitive restriction of beneficence to situations of emergency can thus be supported on utilitarian grounds. Is the same true of the inconvenience limitation? As with the emergency restriction, finding utilitarian support requires looking behind the specific action to its social and legal context. For the utilitarian, the enforcement of a duty through legal sanctions is always an evil, which can be justified only to avoid a greater evil. If the sanction is applied, the offender suffers the pain of punishment. If the prospect of the sanction is sufficient to deter conduct, those deterred suffer the detriment of frustrated preferences. Moreover, the apparatus of enforcement siphons off social resources from other projects promoting the general happiness.

Accordingly, a utilitarian will be restrained and circumspect in the elaboration of legal duties. In particular, he will not pitch a standard of behavior at too high a level: the higher the standard, the more onerous it will be to the person subjected to it, the greater the pleasure that he must forego in adhering to it, and the greater his resistance to its demands. A high standard entails both more severe punishment and a more elaborate apparatus of detection and enforcement. Applied to the rescue situation, this reasoning implies that some convenience restriction should be adopted as part of the duty. Compelling the rescuer to place himself in physical danger, for instance, would be inefficacious, to use Bentham's terminology, because such coercion cannot influence the will: "the evil, which he sees himself about to undergo . . . is so great that the evil denounced by the penal clause . . . cannot appear greater."[34] Limiting the duty of rescue to emergency situations where the rescue will not inconvenience the rescuer—as judicial decisions would elaborate that limitation and thus give direction to individuals—minimizes both the interference with the rescuer's own preferences and the difficulties of enforcement that would result from recalcitrance. Bentham's second limitation can thus also be supported on a utilitarian basis.

The utilitarian arguments for the duty to rescue and for the limitations on that duty rest primarily on administrative considerations. The arguments focus not so much on the parties and their duties as persons as on the difficulties that might be created throughout the whole range of societal interactions. The elements of the duty are evaluated in terms of their likely consequences, no matter how remote. In the convenience limitation, for instance, whether the rescuer *ought* to feel aggrieved at the requirements of a high standard is of no concern. The likelihood that he *will* feel aggrieved is all that matters: for the Benthamite utilitarian, general happiness is the criterion of evaluation and not itself an object of evaluation. Moreover, recalcitrance necessitates more costly enforcement, and that consequence must also enter the calculus. The same is true for the emergency limitation. The argument for that limitation focused on the possibility that a particular instance of assistance would, by example, induce socially detrimental general reliance or beneficence. This use of example does not explore either the fairness of singling out particular persons for particular treatment or the consistency and scope of certain principles. Rather, the argument examines the cumulative consequences of repetition, and decides whether a particular person should perform a particular act on the basis of the act's implications for the entire society's market arrangements.

At least one philosopher has argued that administrative considerations of this sort are not moral ones at all, or that they are moral only in a derivative sense.[35] In this view, the administrative and enforcement considerations on which the utilitarian account of rescue rests are irrelevant to the individual's obligations as a moral agent. The individual should ask what he ought to do, not how others can compel him to fulfill his duty. The merit of this view is its observation that any utilitarian version of a duty to rescue has nuances that do not ring true to the moral contours of the situation. The person in need of rescue stands in danger of serious physical injury or loss of life, harms not quite comparable by any quantitative measure to other losses of happiness. Health and life are not merely components of the aggregate of goods that an individual enjoys. Rather, they are constitutive of the individual, who partakes of them in a unique and intimate way; they are the preconditions for the enjoyment of other goods. Moreover, there is something false in viewing an act of rescue as a contribution to the greatest happiness of the greatest number. If there is an obligation to rescue, it is owed to particular persons rather than to the greatest number. Any such duty would require the rescuing not only of the eminent heart surgeon but also of the hermit bachelor; and even the duty to rescue the heart surgeon would be owed primarily to him, not to his present or prospective patients.

Because the utilitarian account of rescue thus appears to lack an important moral ingredient, and because utilitarianism is not the law's only important philosophical tradition, it is worth attempting to outline a non-utilitarian version of the obligation to rescue. Although the two approaches support the same conclusion, the arguments are different in texture. In particular, the non-utilitarian argument recognizes the distinctive importance of avoiding physical injury or death; it resists the assimilation of health and life to other goods. This attention to the centrality of the person avoids the utilitarian dilemma of either demanding excessive beneficence or having recourse to administrative considerations, which shifts the focus away from the rescuer's obligation to a particular endangered individual. In the non-utilitarian argument, of course, administrative considerations are not ignored; to do so would be impossible in elaborating an argument that attempts to provide an ethical foundation for a judicially enforced duty to rescue. Nonetheless, the non-utilitarian's use of administrative considerations differs from the utilitarian's. The utilitarian weaves the fabric of the duty to rescue out of administrative strands; the cost of administration and enforcement are relevant to the very existence of the duty. The non-utilitarian, by contrast, justifies a legal duty to rescue independently of the administrative costs; the mechanisms of enforcement are invoked only to structure and to coordinate the operation of the duty.

The deontological argument begins with the observation that the idea of an individual's being under a moral duty is intimately related to the notion that health and life are of distinctive importance. The concept of duty applies only to an individual endowed with the capacity to make choices and to set ends for himself. Further, the person, as a purposive and choosing entity, does not merely set physical integrity as one of his ends; he requires it as a precondition to the accomplishment of the purposes that his freedom gives him the power to set. As Kant put it, physical integrity is "the basic *stuff* (the matter) in man without which he could not realize his ends."[36]

A person contemplating the ethical exercise of his freedom of action must impose certain restrictions on that freedom. Because morality is something he shares with all humanity, he cannot claim a preferred moral position for himself. Any moral claim he makes must, by its very nature as a moral claim, be one to which he is subject when others can assert it. Acting on the basis of his own personhood therefore demands recognition of the personhood of others. This recognition, however, cannot be elaborated in the first instance in terms of the enjoyment of ordinary material goods. Because no conception of happiness is shared by everyone and is constant throughout any individual's life, the universal concept of personhood cannot be reflected in a system of moral duties directed at the satisfaction of unstable desires for such goods. Physical integrity, by contrast, is necessary for the accomplishment of any human aim, and so is an appropriate subject for a system of mutually restraining duties.

An individual contemplating his actions from a moral point of view must recognize that all others form their projects on a substratum of physical integrity. If he claims the freedom to pursue his projects as a moral right, he cannot as a rational and moral agent deny to others the same freedom. Because his claim to that freedom implies a right to the physical integrity that is necessary to its exercise, he must concede to others the right to physical integrity that he implicitly and inevitably claims for himself.

This conception of the right to life and health derives from the notion of personhood that is presupposed by the concept of moral action. So too do the right's natural limitations. The duty of beneficence exacted by this right need not collapse into a comprehensive and self-defeating altruism. Respect for another's physical security does not entail foregoing one's own.[37] The right to life and health, seen to give content to the universal concept of personhood, must be ascribed not only to others, but also to oneself. As Kant put it,

> since all *other* men with the exception of myself would not be *all* men, and the maxim would then not have the universality of a law, as it must have in order to be obligatory, the law prescribing the duty of benevolence will include myself, as the object of benevolence, in the command of practical reason.[38]

Moreover, the universalizing process radiates outward from the actor: it is only one's desire to act that makes necessary the exploration of the action's implicit claims and thus of the rights that he must rationally concede to others.[39] The priority of the actor is thus embedded in the structure of the argument and should be reflected in the concrete duties that the argument yields.

This outline of deontological analysis can be applied to examine the standard suggestion that the common law should recognize a duty to effect an easy rescue. Such a duty would be the judicial analogue of the moral obligation to respect the person of another and to safeguard his physical integrity, which is necessary for whatever aims he chooses to pursue. The emergency and convenience limitations also fit quite readily into the analysis. An emergency is a particularly imminent threat to physical security, and the convenience limitation reflects the rescuer's entitlement to the priority of his own physical security over that of the endangered person. Although the proposed legal duty fits comfortably within the deontological moral duty of beneficence, however, the two are

not co-extensive. Emergencies are not the only circumstances in which life and health are threatened; disease, starvation, and poverty can affect the physical substratum of personhood on a routine basis. If legal duties must reflect moral ones, should not a legal duty to rescue be supplemented by a legal duty to alleviate those less isolated abridgments of physical security?

The convenience limitation on the rescue duty might similarly be loosened in a deontological analysis. One tempting extension would be very far-reaching: if the physical substratum is the "basic *stuff* (the matter) in man without which he could not realize his ends," and if we are under a duty to safeguard that substratum in others as in ourselves, the priority that the rescuer can legitimately grant to himself can be only with respect to his physical integrity. Under this extension, a rescuer could—indeed would be obligated to—abstain from acting only if the act would place him in physical danger; if it would not put him in danger, he would be required to attempt a rescue, no matter what the disruption of his life. In Macaulay's famous example, the surgeon would have to travel from Calcutta to Meerut to perform an operation that only he could perform, because the journey, though inconvenient, would not be dangerous. Indeed, he would have to make the trip even if he were about to leave for Europe or to greet members of his family arriving on an incoming ship. The patient's right to physical security would rank ahead of the satisfaction of the surgeon's contingent desires.

The deontological approach to rescue does not compel such a drastic extension. Although every moral person must value physical integrity, its protection is not an end in itself. Rather, physical security is valued because it allows individuals to realize their own projects and purposes. Whatever the reach of the right to physical integrity, therefore, it must allow the rescuer to satisfy his purposes in a reasonably coherent way. Still, though the extension of the moral duty cannot be so drastic as to require the sacrifice of all of a person's projects, it can be substantial. It can require the rescuer to undergo considerable inconvenience short of fundamental changes in the fabric of his life. The deontological duty relaxes both the emergency and convenience limitations of the duty of easy rescue in emergencies: it applies not only in emergencies but whenever physical integrity is threatened, and it applies even when the rescuer might have to undergo considerable inconveniences. The duty might, after all, obligate Macaulay's surgeon to travel from Calcutta to Meerut. Would it also require the wealthy to use at least some of their resources to alleviate the plight of the starving and the afflicted? For those concerned about the possibility of setting principled limits to a duty of rescue, the question is critical.

The objection to an affirmative answer to the question rests on the premises that even the wealthy are under no obligation to be charitable and that the afflicted have no right to receive charity. Under the deontological theory, those premises are incorrect. The duty of beneficence derives from the concept of personhood; it is therefore not properly called charity, for the benefactor's performance of this duty is no reason for self-congratulation. Although the duty is an imperfect one—"since no determinate limits can be assigned to what should be done, the duty has in it a play-room for doing more or less,"[40] as Kant said—it is nonetheless a duty to the performance of which the recipient is entitled.

The extent of the duty of beneficence, of course, can still be troubling. It is the indeterminateness of the duty, the "play-room," that is particularly relevant to this problem. Kant meant by this expression that the form and the amount of the benefaction would vary, depending on the resources of the benefactor, the identity of the recipient, and the recipient's own conception of happiness. The indeterminateness, however, applies not only to the form of the benefaction but also to the linking of particular benefactors to particular beneficiaries. Why should any particular person be singled out of the whole group of potential benefactors, and why should the benefit be conferred on one rather than another person in need? If a duty "may be *exacted* from a person, as one exacts a debt,"[41] it is a debt that leaves unclear the precise terms of discharge as well as the identities of obligor and obligee.

The proper response to this indeterminacy is not to deny that there is a duty. What is required is to set up social institutions to perform the necessary tasks of coordination and determination. Those institutions would ensure that no person is singled out unfairly either for burdens or for benefits, and that the forms of benefaction correlate both with the resources of those who give and with the needs of those who receive. In fact, all Western

democracies undertake to perform this task through programs for social assistance. The institutions they establish, however, are primarily legislative and administrative; precisely because a general duty of beneficence is imperfect, it cannot be judicially enforced. The traditional claim-settling function of courts does not permit the transfer of a resource from one person to another solely because the former has it and the latter needs it. Such judicial action would unfairly prefer one needy person over others and unfairly burden one resourceful person over others. Because the duty of beneficence is general and indeterminate, it does not, in the absence of legislative action that specifies and coordinates, yield judicially enforceable moral claims by individuals against others.

The significant characteristic of the emergency and convenience limitations is that, in combination, they eliminate the "play-room" inherent in the duty of beneficence, thus providing a principled response to Kant and to Epstein and rendering the narrower duty to rescue appropriate for judicial enforcement. An emergency marks a particular person as physically endangered in a way that is not general or routine throughout the society. An imminent peril cannot await assistance from the appropriate social institutions. The provision of aid to an emergency victim does not deplete the social resources committed to the alleviation of more routine threats to physical integrity. Moreover, aid in such circumstances presents no unfairness problems in singling out a particular person to receive the aid. Similarly, emergency aid does not unfairly single out one of a class of routinely advantaged persons; the rescuer just happens to find himself for a short period in a position, which few if any others share, to render a service to some specific person. In addition, when a rescue can be accomplished without a significant disruption of his own projects, the rescuer's freedom to realize his own ends is not abridged by the duty to preserve the physical security of another. In sum, when there is an emergency that the rescuer can alleviate with no inconvenience to himself, the general duty of beneficence that is suspended over society like a floating charge is temporarily revealed to identify a particular obligor and obligee, and to define obligations that are specific enough for judicial enforcement.

Conclusion

The problem of rescue is a central issue in the controversies about the relationships between law and morality, between contract and tort, and between utilitarian and deontological ethics. The argument of this article has been that tort law's adoption of a duty of easy rescue in emergencies would fit a common-law pattern, found principally in contract law, that gives expression to the law's understanding of liberty. This pattern reveals that the common law is already instinct with the attitude of benevolence on which a duty to rescue is grounded. The attitude of benevolence is accepted by many legal commentators as a basic moral intuition, yet the particular duty proposed in this article can be systematically elaborated in both the utilitarian and deontological traditions. For those who believe that law should attempt to render concrete the notion of ethical dealing between persons, as well as for those concerned about the method of common-law evolution or about the social costs of legal rules, the article provides an argument for changing the common-law rule on rescue.

Endnotes

[1] *See* Coase, *The Problem of Social Cost*, 3 J. L. & Econ. 1, 2 (1960).

[2] *See* G. Fletcher, Rethinking Criminal Law 592 (1978).

[3] *See* J. Bentham, An Introduction to the Principles of Morals and Legislation 74–83 (J. Burns & H. Hart eds. 1970).

[4] *E.g.*, G. Fletcher, *supra* note 11; C. Fried, Right and Wrong (1978); Epstein, *Defences and Subsequent Pleas in a System of Strict Liability*, 3 J. Legal Stud. 165, 167 (1974); Epstein, *A Theory of Strict Liability*, 2 J. Legal Stud. 151, 160–89 (1973) [hereinafter cited as *Epstein Theory*]; Fletcher, *Fairness and Utility in Tort Theory*, 85 Harv. L. Rev. 537 (1972).

[5] *Epstein Theory*, *supra* note 4, at 189–204.

[6] I. Kant, Fundamental Principles of the Metaphysic of Ethics 62 (10th ed. T. Abbott trans. 1955).

[7] Bohlen, *The Moral Duty to Aid Others as a Basis of Tort Liability*, 56 U. Pa. L. Rev. 217, 220 (1908).

[8] 119 Eng. Rep. 424 (K. B. 1855).

[9] Nonfeasance is not equivalent to the nonperformance of an act in one recognized sense of the word "act." Tort theory defines an "act" as a voluntary muscular

contraction or as an external manifestation of the will. *See* O. Holmes, The Common Law 54 (1881); Restatement (Second) of Torts § 2 (1965). Though primitive, *see* G. Ryle, The Concept of Mind 62 (1949); Fitzgerald, *Voluntary and Involuntary Acts*, in Oxford Essays in Jurisprudence 1 (A. Guest ed. 1961), these definitions capture a basic feature of our notions of responsibility by setting as a minimal condition of liability the defendant's ability to avoid inflicting the harm that his behavior has caused. Thus, no liability attaches to a person who has been carried forcibly onto another's land, Smith v. Stone, 82 Eng. Rep. 533 (K. B. 1647), or has injured another while unconscious, Stokes v. Carlson, 362 Mo. 93, 240 S.W.2d 132 (1951); Slattery v. Haley, (1923) 3 D.L.R. 156 (Ont. App. Div.). A defendant who is pleading nonfeasance, however, has performed an act in this narrow sense. Indeed his act may have been quite callously deliberate, as when an employer vindictively refuses to make an elevator available to employees who wish to emerge from a mine. Herd v. Weardale Steel, Coal, & Coke Co., [1913] 3 K.B. 771 (C.A.), *aff'd*, [1915] A.C. 67 (H.L.). A defendant in a nonfeasance case, then, can concede that in one sense he has acted and yet argue that in a second sense he has not acted.

[10] McNeice & Thornton, *Affirmative Duties in Tort*, 58 Yale L.J. 1272, 1272–73 (1949).

[11] 41 D.L.R.2d 53 (Man. C.A. 1963). For comparable cases, see Simonsen v. Thorin, 120 Neb. 684, 234 N.W. 628 (1931); Montgomery v. National Convoy & Trucking Co., 186 S.C. 167, 195 S.E. 247 (1937).

[12] *Epstein Theory*, *supra* note 4, at 189–204.

[13] *Id*. at 151.

[14] *Id*. at 200–01.

[15] The Epstein paragraph quoted above says many things in a small compass, and interpretation is difficult. Epstein seems to regard cases in which conduct is beyond the call of duty as equivalent to cases in which a person should be "allowed" to benefit his fellow man only if prompted by the appropriate motives. I have no idea what Epstein means by this. The issue is whether rescue is obligatory, not whether it is permitted. John Stuart Mill mentioned the problem of whether it is right to rescue a person if one's motive is to preserve him for torture, J. S. Mill, Utilitarianism 26 n.* (1888), which may be the problem that Epstein had in mind, but such a tiny problem cannot be relevant to the issue of a general duty to rescue.

[16] L. Fuller, The Morality of Law 3, 30–32 (1964). In recent moral philosophy, the seminal essay is Urmson, *Saints and Heroes*, in Essays in Moral Philosophy 198–216 (A. Melden ed. 1958); *cf.* R. Flathman, Political Obligation 34–38 (1972) (distinguishing obligation from aspiration towards ideal).

[17] H. Sidgwick, The Methods of Ethics 219 (7th ed. 1907); *see* R. Flathman, *supra* note 16, at 155–56. Flathman points out that to think that obligation implies praise bespeaks either misapprehension or an unsettled moral environment. But there may be exceptional circumstances where praise is in order. If the jewelry in Guy de Maupassant's story, *La Parure*, had been real, would not the enormous sacrifices undergone by the borrowers have been praiseworthy, even though they were endured solely for the purpose of repaying a debt? Similarly, would not the soldier be praiseworthy who undertakes an exceptionally dangerous, though obligatory, mission in wartime?

[18] *See* . . . W. Godwin, Enquiry Concerning Political Justice and Its Influence on General Virtue and Happiness 165, 192, 219, 327 (I. Kramnick ed. 1976).

[19] *Id.* at 169.

[20] *Id.* at 198, 234.

[21] *See* W. Godwin, *supra* note 18, at 225.

[22] *See* Aristotle, Nicomachean Ethics 1179b (W. Ross trans. 1954); Plato, Gorgias 517 (W. Woodhead trans. 1953).

[23] *See* J. Bentham, *supra* note 3, at 292–93; J. S. Mill, *On Liberty*, in Essential Works of John Stuart Mill 255–56 (M. Lerner ed. 1961). The utilitarian position is explored in more detail below [*See* Section IV *infra*.]

[24] I. Kant, The Metaphysical Elements of Justice 19 (J. Ladd trans. 1965). Epstein apparently refers to this tradition of ethics when he says that the compulsion of positive law is destructive of the moral worth of the act. *See Epstein Theory, supra* note 4, at 200. Kant's point is different; it is that legal compulsion is irrelevant to the moral worth of the act.

[25] I. Kant, *supra* note 24, at 34.

[26] I. Kant, The Metaphysical Principles of Virtue 49 (M. Gregor trans. 1964).

[27] *Epstein Theory, supra* note 4, at 203.

[28] Holmes, *The Path of the Law*, 10 Harv. L. Rev. 457, 459 (1897).

[29] J. Bentham, *supra* note 3, at 293; *see* 1 J. Bentham, The Principles of Legislation 85–86 (R. Hildreth ed. 1840).

[30] *See* J. Bentham, *supra* note 3, at 74–83.

[31] J. S. Mill, The Principles of Political Economy 967 (W. Ashley ed. 1923).

[32] H. Sidgwick, *supra* note 17, at 437.

[33] London Borough of Southwark v. Williams, [1971] 2 All E.R. 175 (C.A.).

[34] J. Bentham, *supra* note 3, at 162 (footnote omitted).

[35] [*See* Fried, *Right and Wrong—Preliminary Considerations*, 5 J. Legal Studies 165, 181–82 (1976).]

[36] I. Kant, *supra* note 26, at 112.

[37] [*Id.*] at 53, 122.

[38] *Id.* at 118.

[39] [*Id.*] at 112.

[40] [*Id.*] at 121.

[41] J. S. Mill, *supra* note 15, 232–33.

Study Questions

1. It is a widely followed rule that once you *begin* a rescue, by taking steps upon which the victim or other potential rescuers might rely, you may not legally stop or abort the rescue, saying that you are merely leaving the situation unaltered; once you have acted, any subsequent abandonment is no longer, the law says, a mere failure to act. Why is it worse to begin treatment and then abandon the victim than never to have begun in the first place? Can you see how this rule might create perverse incentives for potential rescuers?

2. In *Depue v. Flateau* (111 N.W. 1 [1907]), a traveling cattle buyer called upon a customer and asked to stay for dinner. During the meal he was overcome by a "fainting spell" and fell seriously ill. He asked permission to stay the night (it being a cold winter evening in Minnesota) but this was refused. Flateau led Depue to his cart, set him in it, handed him the reins (which Depue was too weak to hold), and started the horses on their way. Depue was found in a ditch the following morning, nearly frozen to death. Depue alleged that Flateau was negligent in not allowing him to stay the night. The court, ruling in favor of Depue, articulated the following principle: "Whenever a person is placed in such a position with regard to another that it is obvious that, if he does not use due care in his own conduct, he will cause injury to that person, the duty at once arises to exercise care commensurate with the situation in which he thus finds himself . . . to avoid such danger." Should the law incorporate this language as stating a general duty of rescue? If applied across the board, what consequences would this principle have?

3. Why was the "intrusion" into David Shimp's body requested by McFall an impermissible one? The donation procedure required the insertion of a curved needle into the donor's hip bone and the removal of 5 cc of marrow. Since 500 cc

would have been required by McFall, roughly 100 such taps would have been performed on Shimp. Consider that the law not only permits but actually requires some forms of "bodily intrusion," vaccinations, for example. And a few courts have allowed blood transfusions to be performed upon patients who oppose them on religious grounds (*John F. Kennedy Memorial Hospital v. Heston* 58 N.J. 576 [1971]). Why are these cases different from Shimp's? What is an intrusion anyway? Is simply breaking the skin enough? If so, then how is a bone marrow transplant more an intrusion than a blood transfusion? Would it make a difference had a scalpel been necessary for the marrow donation procedure?

4. Why should so much weight be placed by the law upon the misfeasance/nonfeasance distinction? Imagine the following (this hypothetical is taken from John Harris, "The Survival Lottery," *Philosophy* Vol. 50 [1975]:81–87): Two patients, Y and Z, will each die soon unless they obtain, respectively, a new heart and a new lung. As no donor organs are available in the normal way, Y and Z make a proposal. If just one healthy person, A, were killed, his or her organs could be removed and transplanted into Y and Z, saving two lives at the cost of one. Using this approach, many lives could be saved. To allay the inevitable insecurity that would attend such a proposal (Will I be the next to go?) and to quell the legitimate fear of abuse, Y and Z suggest a "survival lottery": Everyone is given a number; if and when your number is called, you are secretly taken into custody and painlessly killed so that your organs might "give life" to others. To the doctors' objection that killing the innocent A is morally impermissible, Y and Z respond that, should the doctors fail to kill one to save two, then *they* (the doctors) will be responsible for the deaths of the two; and even if it is wrong to kill "innocent" persons, Y and Z are just as innocent as A. Is there some morally relevant difference

between bringing about the death of A through misfeasance and bringing about the deaths of Y and Z through nonfeasance? Given the assumption that a world in which Y and Z both live is better overall than one in which A lives, can it matter how that world comes about? Compare the reasoning of Y and Z to the case of Robert McFall. Can it be said that Judge Flaherty, by refusing to grant McFall's request, is responsible for McFall's death? Did McFall die as a result of the inaction by Judge Flaherty or by "natural causes"? Is there a difference?

5. Recent critics of negligence law argue that existing doctrine and its language of "standards of care" for the "safety of others" and "unreasonable" conduct focuses upon abstract categories and cost-benefit calculations in a way unresponsive to real human needs. Preoccupation with a reasoned and distanced analysis of such cases as *McFall v. Shimp* fails, they contend, to show respect for persons and to acknowledge their sufferings, forcing out the caring, compassionate human response that the plight of people like McFall tends to evoke. Rather than appeal to the duties of the "reasonable man," one critic has suggested that the law "measure the conduct of a tortfeasor [one who commits a tort] by the care that would be taken by a . . . responsible person with conscious care and concern for another's safety," the way one would act "out of care for a neighbor or friend" (Leslie Bender, "A Lawyer's Primer on Feminist Theory and Tort," *Journal of Legal Education*, Vol 38 [1988], p 25). The duty to act with the conscious care and concern of a responsible neighbor would require an affirmative duty to rescue "under appropriate circumstances," measured by one's "ability to aid and one's proximity to the need" (*ibid*, p. 36). Does this language state a workable standard? Does the proposed standard represent an improvement over the existing reasonable-man standard? Why or why not?

Cases for Further Reflection

United Novelty Co. v. Daniels
42 So. 2d 395 (1949)
Supreme Court of Mississippi

This brief tort case is included because of its bizarre albeit tragic facts. Should the defendant be liable? Evaluate the implications for a decision in this case of the "*sine qua non*" test; Hart and Honoré's analysis; and Cardozo's "foreseeability" approach, articulated in *Palsgraf*. Under which theories would the defendant be liable? Not liable? Was the action of the rat an "intervening" or "superseding" cause? Would it make a difference in any of these theories if the room in which the plaintiff had been set to work had been much larger? Suppose it had been a gymnasium with the gas heater at the opposite end from the machines on which the plaintiff had been working?

Action by Sandy Daniels and others against the United Novelty Company, Inc., to recover for the death of William Daniels, a minor, who was fatally burned while cleaning coin-operated machines as an employee of the defendant.

From a decision in favor of the plaintiffs in the Harrison Circuit Court, L. C. Corban, [Judge], the defendant appealed.

Alexander, Justice.

The decisive principles here involved are, while important, not novel. Appellees include the members of the family of William Daniels, a minor aged nineteen years, who was fatally burned while cleaning coin-operated machines as an employee of appellant.

. . . The work was being performed in a room eight by ten feet in area, in which there was a gas heater then lighted with an open flame. The cleaning was being done with gasolene. The testimony yields the unique circumstance that the immediate activating cause of a resultant explosion was the escape of a rat from the machine, and its disappointing attempt to seek sanctuary beneath the heater whereat it overexposed itself and its impregnated coat, and returned in haste and flames to its original hideout. Even though such be a fact, it is not a controlling fact, and serves chiefly to ratify the conclusion that the room was permeated with gasolene vapors. Negligence would be predicated of the juxtaposition of the gasolene and the open flame. Under similar circumstances, the particular detonating agency, whether, as here, an animate version of the classic lighted squib, or as in Johnson v. Kosmos Portland Cement Co., . . . 64 F.2d 193, a bolt of lightning, was incidental except as illustrating the range of foreseeability. . . .

. . . It is argued that the decreased disobeyed instructions in using gasolene. Without discussing the efficacy of such contention as a complete bar, the record fails to show that any such orders were ever given the deceased. The insistent and consistent testimony of defendants' witnesses that there were repeated admonitions to employees not to use gasolene is more relevant to the foreseeability, even expectancy, of defendant that resort would be made to this cleaning agency, than to the fact of disobedience, since there is no showing that deceased himself was warned.

. . . Negligence and disobedience of a servant are not excluded from the outreach of a master's duty to foresee probable conduct. The duty of the master is not met by the adoption of rules for safety, but includes a duty reasonably to enforce them. . . .

. . . We do not set out the instructions complained of as given or refused. Those refused the defendant either were peremptory in character or invoked the doctrine of assumption of risk. An instruction for plaintiff which postulates the issue of negligence vel non upon acts set forth in the declaration and supported by the testimony is proper. . . .

. . . It is not to be condemned as unduly emphasizing testimony nor as comment upon the weight of evidence, but is to be commended as "[informing] the jury what was necessary to make out the case stated in the declaration." Other instructions requested by defendant and refused excluded the concept of the master's duty as nondelegable.

We have examined the other assignments and found in them no reversible error.

Affirmed.

Summers v. Tice
199 P. 2d 1 (1948)
Supreme Court of California

A classic case in the annals of tort, *Summers* should be read in conjunction with a review of the essay by Judith Thomson. In this case, a sole reliance upon the idea of *sine qua non* or "factual" causation yields not only an indeterminate result but what seems to be precisely the wrong result: namely, that neither defendant caused the injury. Can you see why?

Actions by Charles A. Summers against Harold W. Tice and against Ernest Simonson for negligently shooting plaintiff while hunting. From judgments for plaintiff, defendants appeal. . . .

Carter, Justice.

Each of the two defendants appeals from a judgment against them in an action for personal injuries. Pursuant to stipulation the appeals have been consolidated.

Plaintiff's action was against both defendants for an injury to his right eye and face as the result of being struck by bird shot discharged from a shotgun. The case was tried by the court without a jury and the court found that on November 20, 1945, plaintiff and the two defendants were hunting quail on the open range. Each of the defendants was armed with a 12 gauge shotgun loaded with shells containing 7½ size shot. Prior to going hunting plaintiff discussed the hunting procedure with defendants, indicating that they were to exercise care when shooting and to "keep in line." In the course of hunting, plaintiff proceeded up a hill, thus placing the hunters at the points of a triangle. The view of defendants with reference to plaintiff was unobstructed and they knew his location. Defendant Tice flushed a quail which rose in flight to a ten foot elevation and flew between plaintiff and defendants. Both defendants shot at the quail, shooting in plaintiff's direction. At that time defendants were 75 yards from plaintiff. One shot struck plaintiff in his eye and another in his upper lip. Finally it was found by the court that as the

direct result of the shooting by defendants the shots struck plaintiff as above mentioned and that defendants were negligent in so shooting and plaintiff was not contributorily negligent.

. . . First, on the subject of negligence, defendant Simonson contends that the evidence is insufficient to sustain the finding on that score, but he does not point out wherein it is lacking. There is evidence that both defendants, at about the same time or one immediately after the other, shot at a quail and in so doing shot toward plaintiff who was uphill from them, and that they knew his location. That is sufficient from which the trial court could conclude that they acted with respect to plaintiff other than as persons of ordinary prudence. . . .

Defendant Tice states in his opening brief, "we have decided not to argue the insufficiency of negligence on the part of defendant Tice." It is true he states in his answer to plaintiff's petition for a hearing in this court that he did not concede this point but he does not argue it. Nothing more need be said on the subject.

. . . Defendant Simonson urges that plaintiff was guilty of contributory negligence and assumed the risk as a matter of law. He cites no authority for the proposition that by going on a hunting party the various hunters assume the risk of negligence on the part of their companions. Such a tenet is not reasonable. It is true that plaintiff suggested that they all "stay in line," presumably abreast, while hunting, and he went uphill at somewhat of a right angle to the hunting line, but he also cautioned that they use care, and defendants knew plaintiff's position. We hold, therefore, that the trial court was justified in finding that he did not assume the risk or act other than as a person of ordinary prudence under the circumstances. . . .

The problem presented in this case is whether the judgment against both defendants may stand. It is argued by defendants that they are not joint tort feasors, and thus jointly and severally liable, as they were not acting in concert, and that there is not sufficient evidence to show which defendant was guilty of the negligence which caused the injuries—the shooting by Tice or that by Simonson. Tice argues that there is evidence to show that the shot which struck plaintiff came from Simonson's gun because of admissions allegedly made by him to third persons and no evidence that they came from his gun. Further in connection with the latter contention, the court failed to find on plaintiff's allegation in his complaint that he did not know which one was at fault—did not find which defendant was guilty of the negligence which caused the injuries to plaintiff.

. . . Considering the last argument first, we believe it is clear that the court sufficiently found on the issue that defendants were jointly liable and that thus the negligence of both was the cause of the injury or to that legal effect. It found that both defendants were negligent and "That as a direct and proximate result of the shots fired by *defendants, and each of them,* a birdshot pellet was caused to and did lodge in plaintiff's right eye and that another birdshot pellet was caused to and did lodge in plaintiff's upper lip." In so doing the court evidently did not give credence to the admissions of Simonson to third persons that he fired the shots, which it was justified in doing. It thus determined that the negligence of both defendants was the legal cause of the injury—or that both were responsible. Implicit in such finding is the assumption that the court was unable to ascertain whether the shots were from the gun of one defendant or the other or one shot from each of them. The one shot that entered plaintiff's eye was the major factor in assessing damages and that shot could not have come from the gun of both defendants. It was from one or the other only.

It has been held that where a group of persons are on a hunting party, or otherwise engaged in the use of firearms, and two of them are negligent in firing in the direction of a third person who is injured thereby, both of those so firing are liable for the injury suffered by the third person, although the negligence of only one of them could have caused the injury. . . . Oliver v. Miles, Miss., 110 So. 666, 50 A.L.R. 357. . . . The same rule has been applied in criminal cases . . . and both drivers have been held liable for the negligence of one where they engaged in a racing contest causing an injury to a third person. . . . These cases speak of the action of defendants as being in concert as the ground of decision, yet it would seem they are straining that concept and the more reasonable basis appears in Oliver v. Miles, supra. There two persons were hunting together. Both shot at some partridges and in so doing shot across the highway injuring plaintiff who was traveling on it. The court stated that they were acting in concert and thus both were liable. The court then stated . . . : "We think that . . . each is liable for the resulting injury to the boy, although no one can say definitely who actually shot him. *To hold otherwise would be to exon-*

erate both from liability, although each was negligent, and the injury resulted from such negligence."

. . .

. . . When we consider the relative position of the parties and the results that would flow if plaintiff was required to pin the injury on one of the defendants only, a requirement that the burden of proof on that subject be shifted to defendants becomes manifest. They are both wrongdoers—both negligent toward plaintiff. They brought about a situation where the negligence of one of them injured the plaintiff, hence it should rest with them each to absolve himself if he can. The injured party has been placed by defendants in the unfair position of pointing to which defendant caused the harm. If one can escape the other may also and plaintiff is remediless. Ordinarily defendants are in a far better position to offer evidence to determine which one caused the injury. This reasoning has recently found favor in this Court. In a quite analogous situation this Court held that a patient injured while unconscious on an operating table in a hospital could hold all or any of the persons who had any connection with the operation even though he could not select the particular acts by the particular person which led to his disability. Ybarra v Spangard . . . 154 P.2d 687. . . . There the Court was considering whether the patient could avail himself of res ipsa loquitur, rather than where the burden of proof lay, yet the effect of the decision is that plaintiff has made out a case when he has produced evidence which gives rise to an inference of negligence which was the proximate cause of the injury. It is up to defendants to explain the cause of the injury. It was there said: "If the doctrine is to continue to serve a useful purpose, we should not forget that 'the particular force and justice of the rule, regarded as a presumption throwing upon the party charged the duty of producing evidence, consists in the circumstance that the chief evidence of the true cause, whether culpable or innocent, is practically accessible to him but inaccessible to the injured person.'" . . . Similarly in the instant case plaintiff is not able to establish which of defendants caused his injury.

The foregoing discussion disposes of the authorities cited by defendants . . . , stating the general rule that one defendant is not liable for the independent tort of the other defendant, or that ordinarily the plaintiff must show a causal connection between the negligence and the injury. There was an entire lack of such connection in the Hernandez case and there were not several negligent defendants, one of whom must have caused the injury.

Defendants rely upon Christensen v. Los Angeles Electrical Supply Co., 112 Cal.App. 629, 297 P. 614, holding that a defendant is not liable where he negligently knocked down with his car a pedestrian and a third person then ran over the prostrate person. That involves the question of intervening cause which we do not have here. Moreover it is out of harmony with the current rule on that subject and was properly questioned in Hill v. Peres, 136 Cal.App. 132, 28 P.2d 946 (hearing in this Court denied), and must be deemed disapproved.

Cases are cited for the proposition that where two or more tort feasors acting independently of each other cause an injury to plaintiff, they are not joint tort feasors and plaintiff must establish the portion of the damage caused by each, even though it is impossible to prove the portion of the injury caused by each. . . .

. . . In view of the foregoing discussion it is apparent that defendants in cases like the present one may be treated as liable on the same basis as joint tort feasors, and hence the last cited cases are distinguishable inasmuch as they involve independent tort feasors.

. . . In addition to that, however, it should be pointed out that the same reasons of policy and justice shift the burden to each of [the] defendants to absolve himself if he can—relieving the wronged person of the duty of apportioning the injury to a particular defendant, apply here where we are concerned with whether plaintiff is required to supply evidence for the apportionment of damages. If defendants are independent tort feasors and thus each liable for the damage caused by him alone, and, at least, where the matter of apportionment is incapable of proof, the innocent wronged party should not be deprived of his right to redress. The wrongdoers should be left to work out between themselves any apportionment. . . . Some of the cited cases refer to the difficulty of apportioning the burden of damages between the independent tort feasors, and say that where factually a correct division cannot be made, the trier of fact may make it the best it can, which would be more or less a guess, stressing the factor that the

wrongdoers are not in a position to complain of uncertainty. . . .

. . . It is urged that plaintiff now has changed the theory of his case in claiming a concert of action; that he did not plead or prove such concert. From what has been said it is clear that there has been no change in theory. The joint liability, as well as the lack of knowledge as to which defendant was liable, was pleaded and the proof developed the case under either theory. We have seen that for the reasons of policy discussed herein, the case is based upon the legal proposition that, under the circumstances here presented, each defendant is liable for the whole damage whether they are deemed to be acting in concert or independently.

The judgment is affirmed.

Walker v. Superior Court of Sacramento County
253 Cal. Rptr. 1 (1988)
Supreme Court of California

Though it involved a criminal proceeding, the *Walker* case is included here because it raises a central issue in the definition of negligence: Why shouldn't the "reasonableness" of conduct alleged to be negligent be defined solely by reference to the actual beliefs and abilities of the defendant? Illustrative of a wave of recent cases pressed against Christian Scientists, *Walker* involved charges of involuntary manslaughter (negligent homicide) and felony child endangerment brought against a woman whose young daughter died from an illness that the defendant had sought to treat with prayer, through the aid of a Christian Science practitioner. As a defense, the mother pointed to California's financial support law, which exempted from liability under its terms parents who substitute prayer for traditional medical care; and she argued that California law refused to consider children treated by prayer as "for that reason alone" abused or neglected. The California Supreme Court, in an opinion by Justice Stanley Mosk, rejected these defenses, arguing that the state's general criminal prohibitions still applied to the defendant's conduct: "When a child's health is seriously jeopardized, the right of a parent to rely exclusively on prayer must yield."[1] In the portion of the court's opinion excerpted below, Justice Mosk faces the central question: May a jury be permitted to find that the defendant acted negligently despite the

fact that she and those around her sincerely believed they were taking appropriate measures to
care for the child's health? Why does Mosk answer
in the affirmative? Could a jury find that Walker
was at fault in acting as she did? Why would a jury
be entitled to assume that only those who seek
relief through "traditional" medicine are "reasonable"? Suppose Walker had gone to a Chinese
herbalist or other practioner of "non-Western"
medicine? Same result? Also, consider in connection with the idea of religious freedom the additional defense raised by the defendant: that the
charges brought against her impermissibly interfered with the "free exercise" of her religion. Does
Justice Mosk respond appropriately to this argument when he writes that "parents have *no* right to
free exercise of religion at the price of a child's
life"?[2]

Mosk, Justice.

Defendant Laurie Grouard Walker is a member of the Church of Christ, Scientist (hereafter the
Church). Her four-year-old daughter, Shauntay,
fell ill with flu-like symptoms on February 21, 1984,
and four days later developed a stiff neck. Consistent with the tenets of her religion, defendant
chose to treat the child's illness with prayer rather
than medical care.[3] Defendant contacted an accred-
ited Christian Science prayer practitioner who
thereafter prayed for Shauntay and visited the
child on two occasions. Defendant also engaged a
Christian Science nurse who attended Shauntay on
February 27 and again on March 6 and 8.[4] Shauntay
nevertheless lost weight, grew disoriented and irri-
table during the last week of her illness, and died
on March 9 of acute purulent meningitis after a
period of heavy and irregular breathing. During
the 17 days she lay ill, the child received no medical
treatment.

The People charged defendant with involuntary manslaughter and felony child endangerment
based on allegations that her criminal negligence
proximately caused Shauntay's death. . . .

. . . [D]efendant . . . contends that she cannot be convicted under either the manslaughter or
felony child-endangerment statutes regardless of
the availability of a religious exemption. She rests
this contention on a claim that the People will be
unable to prove the degree of culpability necessary
to convict her under either provision, both of
which require criminal negligence in the commission of an offending act. . . .

. . . We have defined criminal negligence as
" 'aggravated, culpable, gross, or reckless, that is,
the conduct of the accused must be such a departure from what would be the conduct of an ordinarily prudent or careful man under the same
circumstances as to be incompatible with a proper
regard for human life, or, in other words, a disregard of human life or an indifference to consequences. . . . [Such negligence] is ordinarily to be
determined pursuant to the general principles of
negligence, the fundamental of which is knowledge, actual or imputed, that the act of the slayer
tended to endanger life.' " . . .

. . . Defendant contends that her actions are
legally insufficient to constitute criminal negligence under the definition of that conduct established in the decisions of this court. Emphasizing
her sincere concern and good faith in treating
Shauntay with prayer, she claims that her conduct
is incompatible with the required degree of culpability. Defendant does not dispute, however, that
criminal negligence must be evaluated objectively.

. . .

. . . The question is whether "a reasonable
person in defendant's position would have been
aware of the risk involved. . . ." (*People v. Wat-
son*, . . . 30 Cal.3d at p. 296. . . . If so, "defendant is presumed to have had such an awareness."
. . .

The significance of this principle was well illustrated in *People v. Burroughs* (1984) 35 Cal.3d
824, . . . a case involving a "self-styled 'healer' "
who provided " 'deep' abdominal messages" to a
leukemic who thereafter died of a massive abdominal hemorrhage. . . . We observed that "There is
no allegation made, nor was there any evidence
adduced at trial, that [the defendant] at any time
harbored any intent even to harm [the victim] in
the slightest fashion." . . . "Indeed, nowhere is it
claimed that defendant attempted to perform any
action with respect to [the victim] other than to heal
him. . . ." Nonetheless, we determined that the
defendant could be charged with criminally negligent involuntary manslaughter. . . . The relevant
inquiry, then, turns not on defendant's subjective
intent to heal her daughter but on the objective
reasonableness of her course of conduct.[5]

In view of this standard, we must reject defendant's assertion that no reasonable jury could characterize her conduct as criminally negligent for

purposes of sections 192(b) and 273a(1). As the court in *People v. Atkins* (1975) 53 Cal.App.3d 348 . . . observed in affirming the involuntary manslaughter and felony child-endangerment conviction of a parent whose child died for want of medical care, criminal negligence "could have been found to have consisted of the [mother's] failure to seek prompt medical attention for [her son], rather than waiting several days. There is evidence she knew, or should have known, that [her son] was seriously injured. . . . Viewing [the evidence] in the light most favorable to the prosecution, there is substantial evidence here of involuntary manslaughter based on the lack of due caution and circumspection in omitting to take the child to a doctor." . . . When divorced of her subjective intent, the alleged conduct of defendant here is essentially indistinguishable.

Defendant's arguments to the contrary are not persuasive. She first asserts that the various statutory exemptions enacted for Christian Scientists demonstrate a legislative acceptance of the reasonableness of their spiritual care that is incompatible with a finding of "gross, culpable, or reckless" negligence. As discussed at length above, however, California's statutory scheme reflects not an endorsement of the efficacy or reasonableness of prayer treatment for children battling life-threatening diseases but rather a willingness to accommodate religious practice when children do not face serious physical harm. Indeed, the relevant statutes suggest that prayer treatment for gravely ill children is sufficiently *unreasonable* to justify the state in taking the draconian step of depriving parents of their rights of custody. . . .

The two cases cited by defendant in support of her claim are clearly distinguishable. In *People v. Rodriguez* (1960) 186 Cal.App.2d 433, . . . the court reversed the involuntary manslaughter conviction of a mother who had left her children alone at home where one died in a fire. The court ruled that the mother's conduct did not reflect a course of conduct sufficiently reckless to justify a finding of criminal negligence. . . . In terms of unreasonableness, however, the failure of defendant to seek medical attention for a child who sickened and died over a 17-day period is plainly more egregious than the decision of Mrs. Rodriguez to leave her children alone at home for an afternoon. In *Somers v. Superior Court* (1973) 32 Cal.App.3d 961, . . . the court granted a writ of prohibition barring the manslaughter prosecution of a police officer who

had shot a fleeing youth whom the officer mistook for a felon. The court observed that the situation was "tense and menacing" because of earlier reports of robberies in the vicinity, that the victim matched the description of a suspect and appeared to be carrying a shotgun, and that the victim continued to flee after the officer had shouted "Stop, police." . . . Again, the objective unreasonableness of defendant's course of conduct, compared with the officer's actions in *Somers*, is of an evidently greater magnitude.

In sum, we reject the proposition that the provision of prayer alone to a seriously ill child cannot constitute criminal negligence as a matter of law. Whether this defendant's particular conduct was sufficiently culpable to justify conviction of involuntary manslaughter and felony child endangerment remains a question in the exclusive province of the jury.

. . .

Endnotes

[1] *Walker v. Superior Court* 253 Cal. Rptr. 1 (1988), p. 15.

[2] *Ibid*, p. 19.

[3] Members of the Church "believe that disease is a physical manifestation of errors of the mind." (Comment, *Religious Beliefs and the Criminal Justice System: Some Problems of the Faith Healer* (1975) 8 Loyola L.A. L.Rev. 396, 397, fn. 7.) The use of medicine is believed to perpetuate such error and is therefore discouraged. (Schneider, *Christian Science and the Law: Room for Compromise?* (1965) 1 Colum.J.L. & Soc.Probs. 81, 87–88.) Nonetheless, "the Church sets up no abstract criteria for determining what diseases or injuries should be treated by prayer or other methods but, rather, leaves such questions to individual decision in concrete instances. . . . If some turn in what they think is an urgent time of need to medical treatment for themselves or their children, they are *not*—contrary to some recent charges—stigmatized by their church." (Talbot, *The Position of the Christian Science Church* (1983) 26 N.E. Med.J. 1641, 1642, italics in original.)

[4] The Church descibes in an amicus curiae brief the role of Christian Science practitioners and nurses: "[Christian Science practitioners are] individuals who devote their full time to healing through prayer, or spiritual treatment. These individuals are approved for listing by the Church in *The Christian Science Journal*, after having given evidence of moral character and healing ability. Practitioners determine their own

charges, usually seven to fifteen dollars per day of treatment, and are paid by their patients. . . . The practitioner's work, however, is a religious vocation, a ministry of spiritual healing in its broadest sense. [¶] Christian Scientists may also call upon the services of a Christian Science nurse, who provides such practical care as dressing of wounds for those having spiritual treatment."

[5] Compare LaFave and Scott's comment that "an honest belief that prayer is a better cure than medicine, that Providence can heal better than doctors, might serve to negative the awareness of risk which is required for manslaughter in those states which use a *subjective* test of criminal negligence." (LaFave & Scott, Criminal Law (1972) p. 590, fn. 23, italics added.)

Yania v. Bigan
155 A. 2d 343 (1959)
Supreme Court of Pennsylvania

Frequently cited as among the more egregious examples of the "no-duty-to-rescue" rule, this case should be read with these questions in mind: Did Bigan cause Yania's death? How would Hart and Honoré's theory handle this case? Would it change the outcome of these theories if Bigan knew Yania to be especially susceptible to dares or to attacks upon his manliness and prowess? Why didn't Bigan have a legal duty to rescue Yania once the latter was in the water? Might the answer to this question turn on whether Bigan caused Yania to be in the water? Is Bigan's conduct misfeasance or nonfeasance, according to Weinrib's definitions?

Benjamin R. Jones, Justice.
A bizarre and most unusual circumstance provides the background of this appeal.

On September 25, 1957 John E. Bigan was engaged in a coal strip-mining operation in Shade Township, Somerset County. On the property being stripped were large cuts or trenches created by Bigan when he removed the earthen overburden for the purpose of removing the coal underneath. One cut contained water 8 to 10 feet in depth with side walls or embankments 16 to 18 feet in height; at this cut Bigan had installed a pump to remove the water.

At approximately 4 p. m. on that date, Joseph F. Yania, the operator of another coal strip-mining operation, and one Boyd M. Ross went upon Bigan's property for the purpose of discussing a business matter with Bigan, and, while there, were asked by Bigan to aid him in starting the pump. Ross and Bigan entered the cut and stood at the point where the pump was located. Yania stood at the top of one of the cut's side walls and then jumped from the side wall—a height of 16 to 18 feet—into the water and was drowned.

Yania's widow, in her own right and on behalf of her three children, instituted wrongful death and survival actions against Bigan contending Bigan was responsible for Yania's death. Preliminary objections, in the nature of demurrers, to the complaint were filed on behalf of Bigan. The court below sustained the preliminary objections; from the entry of that order this appeal was taken.

. . . Since Bigan has chosen to file preliminary objections, in the nature of demurrers, every material and relevent fact well pleaded in the complaint and every inference fairly deducible therefrom are to be taken as true. . . .

The complaint avers negligence in the following manner: (1) "The death by drowning of . . . [Yania] was caused entirely by the acts of [Bigan] . . . in *urging, enticing, taunting and inveigling* [Yania] to jump into the water, which [Bigan] knew or ought to have known was of a depth of 8 to 10 feet and dangerous to the life of anyone who would jump therein" (emphasis supplied); (2) ". . . [Bigan] violated his obligations to a business invitee in not having his premises reasonably safe, and not warning his business invitee of a dangerous condition and to the contrary urged, induced and inveigled [Yania] into a dangerous position and a dangerous act, whereby [Yania] came to his death"; (3) "After [Yania] was in the water, a highly dangerous position, having been induced and inveigled therein by [Bigan], [Bigan] failed and neglected to take reasonable steps and action to protect or assist [Yania], or [extricate Yania] from the dangerous position in which [Bigan] had placed him." Summarized, Bigan stands charged with three-fold negligence: (1) by urging, enticing, taunting and inveigling Yania to jump into the water; (2) by failing to warn Yania of a dangerous condition on the land, i. e., the cut wherein lay 8 to 10 feet of water; (3) by failing to go to Yania's rescue after he had jumped into the water.[1]

. . . The Wrongful Death Act . . . and the Survival Act . . . really confer no more than rights to recover damages growing out of a single cause of action, namely, *the negligence of the defendant* which caused the damages suffered." . . . While the law presumes that Yania was not negligent, such presumption affords no basis for an inference that Bigan was negligent. . . . Our inquiry must be to ascertain whether the well-pleaded facts in the complaint, assumedly true, would, if shown, suffice to prove negligent conduct on the part of Bigan.

. . . Appellant initially contends that Yania's descent from the high embankment into the water and the resulting death were caused "entirely" by the spoken words and blandishments of Bigan delivered at a distance from Yania. The complaint does not allege that Yania slipped or that he was pushed or that Bigan made any *physical* impact upon Yania. On the contrary, the only inference deducible from the facts alleged in the complaint is that Bigan, by the employment of cajolery and inveiglement, caused such a *mental* impact on Yania that the latter was deprived of his volition and freedom of choice and placed under a compulsion to jump into the water. Had Yania been a child of tender years or a person mentally deficient then it is conceivable that taunting and enticement could constitute actionable negligence if it resulted in harm. However, to contend that such conduct directed to an adult in full possession of all his mental faculties constitutes actionable negligence is not only without precedent but completely without merit. . . .

. . . Appellant next urges that Bigan, as the possessor of the land, violated a duty owed to Yania in that his land contained a dangerous condition, i.e., the water-filled cut or trench, and he failed to warn Yania of such condition. Yania was a business invitee in that he entered upon the land for a common business purpose for the mutual benefit of Bigan and himself. . . . As possessor of the land, Bigan would become subject to liability to Yania for any physical harm caused by any artificial or natural condition upon the land (1) if, and only if, Bigan knew or could have discovered the condition which, if known to him he should have realized involved an unreasonable risk of harm to Yania, (2) if Bigan had no reason to believe Yania would discover the condition or realize the risk of harm and (3) if he invited or permitted Yania to enter upon the land without exercising reasonable care to make the condition reasonably safe or give adequate warning to enable him to avoid the harm. . . . The inapplicability of this rule of liability to the instant facts is readily apparent.

The *only* condition on Bigan's land which could possibly have contributed in any manner to Yania's death was the water-filled cut with its high embankment. Of this condition there was neither concealment nor failure to warn, but, on the contrary, the complaint specifically avers that Bigan not only requested Yania and Boyd to assist him in starting the pump to remove the water from the cut but "led" them to the cut itself. If this cut possessed any potentiality of danger, such a condition was as obvious and apparent to Yania as to Bigan, both coal strip-mine operators. Under the circumstances herein depicted Bigan could not be held liable in this respect.

. . . Lastly, it is urged that Bigan failed to take the necessary steps to rescue Yania from the water. The mere fact that Bigan saw Yania in a position of peril in the water imposed upon him no legal, although a moral, obligation or duty to go to his rescue unless Bigan was legally responsible, in whole or in part, for placing Yania in the perilous position. Restatement, Torts, § 314. Cf. Restatement, Torts, § 322. The language of this Court in Brown v. French, 104 Pa. 604, 607, 608, is apt: "If it appeared that the deceased, by his own carelessness, contributed in any degree to the accident which caused the loss of his life, the defendants ought not to have been held to answer for the consequences resulting from that accident. . . . He voluntarily placed himself in the way of danger, and his death was the result of his own act. . . . That his undertaking was an exceedingly reckless and dangerous one, the event proves, but there was no one to blame for it but himself. He had the right to try the experiment, obviously dangerous as it was, but then also upon him rested the consequences of that experiment, and upon no one else; he may have been, and probably was, ignorant of the risk which he was taking upon himself, or knowing it, and trusting to his own skill, he may have regarded it as easily superable. But in either case, the result of his ignorance, or of his mistake, must rest with himself—and cannot be charged to the defendants." The complaint does not aver any facts which impose upon Bigan legal responsibility for placing Yania in the dangerous position in the water and, absent such legal responsibility, the law imposes on Bigan no duty of rescue.

Recognizing that the deceased Yania is entitled to the benefit of the presumption that he was exercising due care and extending to appellant the benefit of every well pleaded fact in this complaint and the fair inferences arising therefrom, yet we can reach but one conclusion: that Yania, a reasonable and prudent adult in full possession of all his mental faculties, undertook to perform an act which he knew or should have known was attended with more or less peril and it was the performance of that act and not any conduct upon Bigan's part which caused his unfortunate death.

Order affirmed.

Endnote

[1] So far as the record is concerned we must treat the 33 year old Yania as in full possession of his mental faculties at the time he jumped.

Farwell v. Keaton
240 N.W. 2d 217 (1976)
Supreme Court of Michigan

The court in this case makes a seemingly large exception to the no-duty-to-rescue rule: Siegrist and Farwell were "companions engaged in a common undertaking," and the court finds this to be a sufficiently "special" relationship to hold Siegrist liable for Farwell's death. How much of a "common undertaking" is having a few beers and chasing some girls? Is it because Siegrist knew Farwell that he acquired an affirmative duty to care for him? What wouldn't be a special relationship under this theory?

Levin, Justice.

On the evening of August 26, 1966, Siegrist and Farwell drove to a trailer rental lot to return an automobile which Siegrist had borrowed from a friend who worked there. While waiting for the friend to finish work, Siegrist and Farwell consumed some beer.

Two girls walked by the entrance to the lot. Siegrist and Farwell attempted to engage them in conversation; they left Farwell's car and followed the girls to a drive-in restaurant down the street.

The girls complained to their friends in the restaurant that they were being followed. Six boys chased Siegrist and Farwell back to the lot. Siegrist escaped unharmed, but Farwell was severely beaten. Siegrist found Farwell underneath his automobile in the lot. Ice was applied to Farwell's head. Siegrist then drove Farwell around for approximately two hours, stopping at a number of drive-in restaurants. Farwell went to sleep in the

back seat of his car. Around midnight Siegrist drove the car to the home of Farwell's grandparents, parked it in the driveway, unsuccessfully attempted to rouse Farwell and left. Farwell's grandparents discovered him in the car the next morning and took him to the hospital. He died three days later of an epidural hematoma.

At trial, plaintiff contended that had Siegrist taken Farwell to the hospital, or had he notified someone of Farwell's condition and whereabouts, Farwell would not have died. A neurosurgeon testified that if a person in Farwell's condition is taken to a doctor before, or within half an hour after, consciousness is lost, there is an 85 to 88 per cent chance of survival. Plaintiff testified that Siegrist told him that he knew Farwell was badly injured and that he should have done something.

The jury returned a verdict for plaintiff and awarded $15,000 in damages. The Court of Appeals reversed, finding that Siegrist had not assumed the duty of obtaining aid for Farwell and that he neither knew nor should have known of the need for medical treatment. . . .

Siegrist contends that he is not liable for failure to obtain medical assistance for Farwell because he had no duty to do so.

Courts have been slow to recognize a duty to render aid to a person in peril. Where such a duty has been found, it has been predicated upon the existence of a special relationship between the parties; in such a case, if defendant knew or should have known of the other person's peril, he is required to render reasonable care under all the circumstances. . . .

Farwell and Siegrist were companions on a social venture. Implicit in such a common undertaking is the understanding that one will render assistance to the other when he is in peril if he can do so without endangering himself. Siegrist knew or should have known when he left Farwell, who was badly beaten and unconscious, in the back seat of his car that no one would find him before morning. Under these circumstances, to say that Siegrist had no duty to obtain medical assistance or at least to notify someone of Farwell's condition and whereabouts would be "shocking to humanitarian considerations" and fly in the face of "the commonly accepted code of social conduct." "[C]ourts will find a duty where, in general, reasonable men would recognize it and agree that it exists."

Farwell and Siegrist were companions engaged in a common undertaking; there was a special relationship between the parties. Because Siegrist knew or should have known of the peril Farwell was in and could render assistance without endangering himself he had an affirmative duty to come to Farwell's aid.

Fitzgerald, Justice (dissenting).

The unfortunate death of Richard Farwell prompted this wrongful death action brought by his father against the defendant, David Siegrist, a friend who had accompanied Farwell during the evening in which the decedent received injuries which ultimately caused his death three days later. The question before us is whether the defendant, considering his relationship with the decedent and the activity they jointly experienced on the evening of August 26–27, 1966, by his conduct voluntarily or otherwise assumed, or should have assumed, the duty of rendering medical or other assistance to the deceased. We find that defendant had no obligation to assume, nor did he assume, such a duty. . . .

Defendant did not voluntarily assume the duty of caring for the decedent's safety. Nor did the circumstances which existed on the evening of August 26, 1966, impose such a duty. Testimony revealed that only a qualified physician would have reason to suspect that Farwell had suffered an injury which required immediate medical attention. The decedent never complained of pain and, in fact, had expressed a desire to retaliate against his attackers. Defendant's inability to arouse the decedent upon arriving at his grandparents' home does not permit us to infer, as does plaintiff, that defendant knew or should have known that the deceased was seriously injured. While it might have been more prudent for the defendant to insure that the decedent was safely in the house prior to leaving, we cannot say that defendant acted unreasonably in permitting Farwell to spend the night asleep in the back seat of his car.

The close relationship between defendant and the decedent is said to establish a legal duty upon defendant to obtain assistance for the decedent. No authority is cited for this proposition other than the public policy observation that the interest of society would be benefited if its members were required to assist one another. This is not the appropriate case to establish a standard of conduct requiring one to legally assume the duty of insuring the safety of another. Recognizing that legal commentaries have expressed moral outrage at those decisions which permit one to refuse aid to another whose life may be in peril, we cannot say that, considering the relationship between these two parties and the existing circumstances, defendant acted in an unreasonable manner.

Plaintiff believes that a legal duty to aid others should exist where such assistance greatly benefits society and only a reasonable burden is imposed upon those in a position to help. He contends further that the determination of the existence of a duty must rest with the jury where questions of foreseeability and the relationship of the parties are primary considerations.

It is clear that defendant's nonfeasance, or the "passive inaction or a failure to take steps to protect [the decedent] from harm" is urged as being the proximate cause of Farwell's death. We must reject plaintiff's proposition which elevates a moral obligation to the level of a legal duty where, as here, the facts within defendant's knowledge in no way indicated that immediate medical attention was necessary and the relationship between the parties imposes no affirmative duty to render assistance. . . . The posture of this case does not permit us to create a legal duty upon one to render assistance to another injured or imperiled party where the initial injury was not caused by the person upon whom the duty is sought to be imposed.

Suggestions for Further Reading

Aune, B., *Kant's Theory of Morals* (Princeton, N.J.: Princeton University Press, 1979).

Balkin, J. M., "The Rhetoric of Responsibility," *Virginia Law Review*, Vol. 76 (1990): 197–263.

Bender, L., "A Lawyer's Primer on Feminist Theory and Tort," *Journal of Legal Education*, Vol. 38 (1888): 3–37.

Calabresi, G., *The Costs of Accidents* (New Haven, Conn.: Yale University Press, 1971).

Coleman, J., "Moral Theories of Tort: Their Scope and Limits, Parts I & II," *Law and Philosophy*, Vol. 1 (1982): 371–390; Vol. 2 (1983): 5–36.

Epstein, R., "A Theory of Strict Liability," *Journal of Legal Studies*, Vol. 2 (1973): 151–204.

Kant, I., *Groundwork of the Metaphysic of Morals* (trans. H. J. Paton) (New York: Harper & Row, 1964).

Keeton, W. P., *et al.*, *Prosser and Keeton on Torts* (St. Paul, Minn.: West, 1984).

Kupperberg, M., and Beitz, C., *Law, Economics, and Philosophy* (Totowa, N.J.: Rowman & Allanheld, 1983).

Landes, W., and Posner, R., *The Economic Structure of Tort Law* (Cambridge, Mass.: Harvard University Press, 1987).

Posner, R., *The Economic Analysis of Law*, 3rd ed. (Boston: Little, Brown, 1986).

Rabin, R. (Ed.), *Perspectives on Tort Law*, 2nd ed. (Boston: Little, Brown, 1983).

Ratcliffe, J. M. (Ed.), *The Good Samaritan and the Law* (New York: Anchor Books, 1966).

Shavell, S., *Economic Analysis of Accident Law* (Cambridge, Mass.: Harvard University Press, 1987).

Symposium on Causation in the Law of Torts, *Chicago-Kent Law Review*, Vol. 63 (1987): 397–680.

Thomson, J. J., *Rights, Restitution, and Risk* (Cambridge, Mass.: Harvard University Press, 1986).

Weinrib, E., "The Special Morality of Tort Law," *McGill Law Journal*, Vol. 34 (1989): 403–413.

West, R., "Economic Man and Literary Woman," *Mercer Law Review*, Vol. 39 (1988): 867–878.

Appendix

Legal Citations and Law Reports

This appendix provides a brief explanation of the system currently in use for collecting, publishing, and citing judicial opinions and decisions. We'll begin with an example of a typical case citation, of the sort found throughout this text. Take the citation to the *Zabella* case in Chapter 1:

Zabella v. Pakel
242 F. 2d 452 (1957)
U.S. Court of Appeals, Seventh
Circuit

The first line of the citation lists the last names of the parties involved. If the case is a civil rather than a criminal case, the first name appearing in the citation normally is that of the *plaintiff* in the case, the individual filing the complaint. If there is more than one plaintiff, the name of the first plaintiff (listed in alphabetical order) is given. In a criminal case, the complaining party is the state; hence a criminal case citation typically reads *State v. Bradbury* or *People v. Burroughs*. The second name appearing in the first line is that of the person responding to a suit or charged with a crime: the *defendant*.

Occasionally, a citation will refer to a case that is being heard on *appeal*. This means that the party who lost at the lower or trial court level, where evidence is presented and a judgment rendered, is requesting that a higher or appellate court review the record of the trial court proceedings to determine if an error occurred in the definition or application of the rules of law applicable to the case. If the citation refers to a case being heard on appeal, the order of the names—plaintiff/defendant—is the same if the plaintiff is the party instituting the appeal (called the *appellant*); a few states, however, reverse the names when the defendant is the appellant or "plaintiff in error."

When a citation refers to a judicial proceeding that does not involve two adverse parties—for example, as in the case of General Yamashita in Chapter Five—the title appears as *In Re Yamashita* ("In the Matter of Yamashita").

The publication of court opinions is sanctioned by statute throughout the states and by the federal government. *United State Reports* (cited as *U.S.*), for example, is the official collection of opinions issued by the United States Supreme Court. Opinions and decisions are also collected and published by private firms: *The Supreme Court Reporter* (cited as *S. Ct.*) is the collection of the Supreme Court's decisions published by the West Publishing Company.

Court reports are organized in several ways: by jurisdiction of the court issuing the opinion (for example, *California Reports* contains the opinions of the Supreme Court of California); by geography (for example, West's *Pacific Reporter* includes opinions by appellate courts in a number of Western states); and by subject matter (for example, the *Military Justice Reporter* reports the decisions of the Court of Military Appeals).

The second line of the citation for *Zabella v. Pakel* reads:
242 F. 2d 452 (1957)
This refers to volume 242 of the *Federal Reporter, Second Series*. The *Zabella* case appears beginning on page 452. The case was decided in 1957. The *Federal Reporter*, published by West, collects opinions handed down by all the various "circuits" or divisions of the United States Courts of Appeals. West's *Federal Supplement* (cited as *F. Supp.*) does the same for United States district courts (the trial courts of the federal system). (A table outlining the federal system and a typical state court system appears in the figure.) The last line of the citation for *Zabella* indicates that the case was heard by the Seventh Circuit of the United States Court of Appeals.

Many judicial opinions are easily obtained through West's National Reporter System, consisting of a set of volumes reporting both state and federal cases. The United States has seven regional reporters: Atlantic, North Eastern, North Western, Pacific, South Eastern, Southern, and South Western. (Abbreviations for many of the regional and federal reporters are given below.)

In addition to the regional reporters, West publishes special reporters for two states: the *California Reporter* and the *New York Supplement*.

Abbreviations for Selected State, Regional, and Federal Reporters

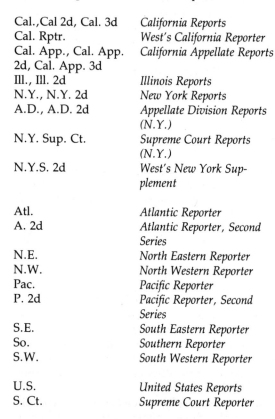

Cal.,Cal 2d, Cal. 3d	*California Reports*
Cal. Rptr.	*West's California Reporter*
Cal. App., Cal. App. 2d, Cal. App. 3d	*California Appellate Reports*
Ill., Ill. 2d	*Illinois Reports*
N.Y., N.Y. 2d	*New York Reports*
A.D., A.D. 2d	*Appellate Division Reports (N.Y.)*
N.Y. Sup. Ct.	*Supreme Court Reports (N.Y.)*
N.Y.S. 2d	*West's New York Supplement*
Atl.	*Atlantic Reporter*
A. 2d	*Atlantic Reporter, Second Series*
N.E.	*North Eastern Reporter*
N.W.	*North Western Reporter*
Pac.	*Pacific Reporter*
P. 2d	*Pacific Reporter, Second Series*
S.E.	*South Eastern Reporter*
So.	*Southern Reporter*
S.W.	*South Western Reporter*
U.S.	*United States Reports*
S. Ct.	*Supreme Court Reporter*

The U.S. Court System

California State System

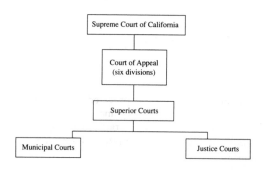

Glossary of Legal Terms

Acquittal: The verdict in a criminal trial in which the **defendant** is found not **guilty**.

Actus Reus: The "guilty act" or "deed of crime"; an act of wrongdoing that is forbidden by the law and that, when committed in conjunction with a specified state of mind (*mens rea*), constitutes a **crime**.

Amicus Curiae: "friend of the court"; a person or group who files a **brief** with the court, supplying relevant information bearing on the case or urging a particular result. While not parties in a case, *amici* typically are third parties who will be indirectly affected by the court's decision.

AMICI: *see **amicus curiae***

Answer: The legal document by which a **defendant** responds to the allegations contained in the **complaint** of the **plaintiff**.

Appeal: The resort to a superior or *appellate* court to review the decision of an inferior or *trial* court.

Appellant: The party or person who appeals a decision (usually, but not always, the loser in the lower court).

Appellee: The party or person against whom an **appeal** is taken (usually, but not always, the winner in the lower court).

Brief: A written statement prepared by an attorney arguing a case in court; a summary of the facts of the case, relevant laws, and an argument of how the law applies to the facts in support of the attorney's position.

Cause of Action: A claim in law based on facts sufficient to bring the case to court; the grounds of an action against another (e.g., a **suit** in **negligence**).

Certiorari: A writ issued by a superior court to an inferior court requiring the latter court to produce the records of a particular case heard before it. Most often used with regard to the U.S. Supreme Court, which uses "cert." as a means of deciding which cases it wishes to hear.

Citation: A reference to an authority used (e.g., a prior case, a statute) to substantiate the validity of one's argument or position.

Common Law: The origin of the Anglo-American legal systems; the system of law originally based on the customary and unwritten laws of England and developed by the doctrine of **precedent** as opposed to legislative enactments. In theory, law that is not created by the courts but rather discovered in the customs, habits, and basic principles of justice acknowledged by society.

Complaint: The legal document (also called a **petition**) that informs a **defendant** of the grounds on which he or she is being sued.

Crime: A wrongful act against society as defined by law; a wrong that is prosecuted by a public official and punishable by fine, imprisonment, or death.

Damages: Monetary compensation awarded by a court for an injury caused by the act of another. Damages may be *actual* or *compensatory* (equal to the amount of loss proven) or *exemplary* or *punitive* (in excess of the actual damages given as a form of punishment to the wrongdoer).

Decedent: One who has ceased to live; in criminal law, the victim of a **homicide**.

Defendant: The person against whom a lawsuit (**cause of action**) or criminal action is brought.

Dictum: A statement or remark, not necessary for the decision of a case, made by the judge in the judge's **opinion;** a statement not binding as **precedent**.

Discovery: That set of procedures through which the parties to a **suit** obtain information about matters relevant to the case.

Dissent: An **opinion** given by a judge in a case which differs from that given by the majority of the court. A dissent typically points out the deficiencies of the majority position and states reasons for arriving at a different conclusion.

Equity: Justice administered according to fairness as opposed to the strictly formulated rules of the common law; a system of principles that originated in England as an alternative to the perceived harshness of rigidly applying the rules of the common law in every case.

Ex Post Facto: "After the fact"; a law that makes illegal an action which was done before the law was passed. Such laws violate Article I, Sections 9 and 10 of the United States Constitution.

Felony: Any of a group of "high" or "serious" crimes (as distinguished from minor offenses called **misdemeanors**) generally punishable either by death or imprisonment.

Felony–Murder: An unlawful **homicide** occurring during the commission of (or attempt to commit) a **felony** and which (under this doctrine) is considered first-degree **murder.**

"Fighting Words":   Words that, given their nature and the context in which they are uttered, are very likely to provoke their hearer to an immediate breach of the peace. Such words have been held not protected by the First Amendment to the U.S. Constitution.

First Impression: A case that presents a question of law never before considered by any court within the relevant **jurisdiction** and that is therefore not controlled by the doctrine of **precedent.**

Guilty: The condition of having been found to have committed the crime charged.

Holding: A declaration or statement of the law as it applies to the facts of a specific case and given by the court in its **opinion.**

Homicide: Any killing of a human being by another human being. Homicide does not necessarily constitute a **crime;** to be a crime, homicide must be an *unlawful* killing (e.g., **murder**).

Ignoratia Legis Non Excusat: "Ignorance of the law is no excuse"; the fact that the defendant did not think her or his act was against the law does not prevent the law from punishing the prohibited act.

Infancy: The state of being a minor; not yet having attained the age of majority.

Injunction: A judge's order that a person do, or more commonly, refrain from doing a certain act. The court's power to issue an injunction is based in **equity.**

Instruction: Directions the judge gives to the jury, informing them of the law that they are to apply to the facts of the case in order to reach a **verdict.**

Judgment: The final decision of the court in a case, resolving the dispute and determining the rights and obligations of the parties involved.

Jurisdiction: The power of a court to make legally binding decisions over certain persons or property; the geographical area in which a court's decisions or a legislature's enactments are binding.

Liability: The condition of being responsible for **damages** resulting from an injurious act, for discharging an obligation or debt, or for paying a penalty for wrongdoing.

Malum In Se: "That which is wrong in itself"; refers to an act that would be thought evil or wrong even without a specific criminal prohibition (e.g., **murder**).

Malum Prohibitum: "That which is wrong because prohibited"; refers to an act that is wrong only because it is made so by statute (e.g., failure to file for income tax).

Miscegenation: "The mixing of the races"; older statutes (now invalid) typically defined miscegenation as marriage between a Caucasian (white) and a member of another race.

Misdemeanor: That class of criminal offenses less serious than **felonies** and punished with lesser severity.

Misfeasance: The doing of a wrongful or injurious act.

Moot Case: A case that no longer presents an actual controversy, either because the issues involved have ceased to exist or they have been rendered "academic" by the circumstances.

Motion: A formal request made to a judge pertaining to any issue arising during a lawsuit.

Movant: The party who requests a motion.

Murder: The unlawful killing of a human being. Modern law distinguishes between several degrees of murder. *First degree murder* is a deliberate and premeditated homicide; *second degree murder* is a homicide committed with malice but without premeditation.

Negligence: The failure to exercise due care for the safety and welfare of others; failure to exercise that degree of care which, under the circumstances, a **reasonable person** would take.

Nonfeasance: Nonperformance of an act that one has a duty to perform; neglect of a duty; failure to act so as to prevent harm.

Nuisance: An unreasonable or unwarranted use by a person of his or her own property that produces such annoyance, inconvenience, or discomfort as to interfere with the rights of others to use and enjoy their property.

Obiter Dictum: see **dictum.**

On the Merits: A decision or **judgment** based upon the essential facts of the case rather than upon a "technicality," such as improper **jurisdiction.**

Opinion: A statement of the reasons why a certain decision or **judgment** was reached in a case. A *majority opinion* is usually written by one judge and represents the principles of law that a majority of the members of a court regard as central to the **holding** in the case. A *concurring opinion* agrees with the ultimate judgment of the majority but disagrees with the reasons leading to that result. A *plurality opinion* is agreed to by less than a majority so far as reasoning is concerned but is agreed to by a majority as stating the correct result. A *per curiam opinion* is an opinion expressing the decision of the court but whose author is not identified. *See also* **dissent.**

Ordinance: The equivalent of a municipal **statute** passed by a city council and dealing with matters not already covered by federal or state law.

Overbreadth: A situation in which a law not only prohibits that which may constitutionally be prohibited but also prohibits conduct which is constitutionally protected (e.g., the freedom of speech under the First Amendment).

Overrule: To overturn or invalidate the **holding** of a prior case. A decision can be overruled only by the same court or by a higher court within the same **jurisdiction.**

Petition: A formal, written application to a court requesting judicial action on a particular matter.

Petitioner: The person presenting a petition to a court; one who starts an **equity** proceeding; one who takes an appeal from a judgment.

Plaintiff: The person who brings a lawsuit or **cause of action** against another.

Plea: In the law of procedure, an **answer** or response to a **complaint** or allegation of fact; in criminal procedure, the response of the **defendant** in answer to the charge made against him or her.

Pleadings: The **complaint** and the **answer** in a civil **suit.**

Precedent: The doctrine of Anglo-American law whereby once a court has formulated a principle of law as applied to a given set of facts, it will follow that principle and apply it in future cases where the facts are substantially similar. See *stare decisis.*

Preponderance of the Evidence: The general standard of proof in a civil case (i.e., one involving a lawsuit); to prevail, a party must show that the preponderance of the evidence (better than 50 percent) weighs in her or his favor.

Prima Facie **Case:** A case that, at first view or "on its face," is supported by enough evidence to entitle a party to have the case go to a jury.

Probation: A procedure whereby a **defendant** found guilty of a crime is released into society subject to conditions laid down by the court and under the supervision of a probation officer.

Proceeding: The form and manner of conducting legal business before a court or judicial officer; the series of events constituting the process through which judicial action takes place.

Prosecution: The act of pursuing a lawsuit or criminal trial; the party initiating a criminal suit, i.e., the state.

Proximate Cause: An event without which injury or damage would not have occurred and which is closely enough related to the occurrence of the injury to make it fair, reasonable, or just to hold the **defendant** liable for that injury.

Ratio Decidendi: The point in a case that determines the result or **judgment;** the basis or reason for the decision.

Reasonable Doubt: The degree of certainty required of a juror before the juror may find a **defendant guilty;** innocence is to be presumed unless the guilt of the defendant is so clearly proven that the jury can see that no reasonable doubt remains as to the guilt of the defendant.

Reasonable Person: A phrase used to refer to that hypothetical person who exercises those qualities of attention, knowledge, intelligence, and judgment which society requires of its members for the protection of their own interest and the interests of others.

Recidivist: A "habitual criminal," often subjected to extended terms of imprisonment under habitual offender statutes.

Relief: That assistance, redress, or benefit sought by a person filing a **complaint** before a court.

Remand: To send back for further proceedings, as when a higher court sends a case back to a lower court.

Remedy: The means by which a right is enforced or the violation of a right is redressed or compensated. The most common remedy at law consists of money **damages.**

Respondent: The party who contends against an appeal; the party who makes an answer to a **complaint** in an **equity** proceeding.

Reversal: The invalidating or setting aside of the contrary decision of a lower court.

Scienter: The **defendant's** "guilty knowledge"; refers to the defendant's alleged previous knowledge of the cause that led to the injury complained of.

Sentence: The punishment a court orders to be inflicted upon a person convicted of a crime.

Sine Qua Non: "That without which there is not"; in tort law, the act of the **defendant** without which there would not have been a **tortious** injury to the **plaintiff.**

Stare Decisis: "Let the decision stand"; refers to the doctrine that courts should follow **precedent,** the authority of earlier, analogous cases.

Statute: An act of a legislature, consistent with constitutional authority and in such proper form that it becomes the law governing the conduct to which it refers.

Statute of Wills: Those statutory provisions of a particular jurisdiction stating the requirement for a valid will.

Strict Liability: Liability without proof of fault. In civil law, one who engages in activity that carries an inherent risk of injury or is ultra-hazardous (e.g., blasting) is often liable for all injuries proximately caused by that activity; in criminal law, strict liability offenses are those that do not require proof of *mens rea* (criminal intent).

Subpoena: A court order compelling a witness to appear and testify in a **proceeding.**

Suit: Any **proceeding** before a court in which a person pursues that **remedy** which the law affords as redress for the injury that person has suffered.

Summary Judgment: A judgment in a civil **suit,** granted on the basis of the **pleadings** and prior to trial, holding that there is no genuine factual dispute between the parties regarding the legal issues involved and that the case need not therefore go before a jury.

Testator: One who is disposing of property by **will.**

Tort: A civil wrong, other than a breach of contract, for which a court will provide a **remedy.**

Tortfeasor: One who commits a **tort.**

Tortious: Used to describe conduct that subjects a person to **tort liability.**

Trial: A judicial examination and determination of issues between parties to action.

Ultra Vires: An act beyond the scope of one's powers or authority, as, for example, by a corporation.

Verdict: The decision of a jury following the **trial** of a civil or criminal case.

Vicarious Liability: The imputation of **liability** upon one person for the actions of another person.

Void: That which is entirely null, having no legal force.

Volenti Non Fit Injuria: "To one who consents, no harm is done"; in **tort,** the doctrine that one generally cannot claim **damages** when one has consented to the activity which caused an injury.

Will: A document executed with specific legal formalities containing a person's instructions about the disposition of his or her property upon death.